3995

THE DOCTRINE OF RECONCILIATION

CHURCH DOGMATICS

BY
KARL BARTH

VOLUME IV

THE DOCTRINE OF RECONCILIATION

PART TWO

EDITORS
Rev. G. W. BROMILEY, Ph.D., D.Litt.
Rev. Prof. T. F. TORRANCE, D.D., D.Theol.

EDINBURGH : T. & T. CLARK, 36 George Street

THE DOCTRINE OF RECONCILIATION

(Church Dogmatics, Volume IV, 2)

BY

KARL BARTH, D.Theol., D.D., LL.D.

TRANSLATOR
Rev. G. W. BROMILEY, Ph.D., D.Litt.

EDINBURGH : T. & T. CLARK, 36 George Street

Original German Edition
DIE KIRCHLICHE DOGMATIK, IV:
Die Lehre von der Versöhnung, 2

Published by
EVANGELISCHER VERLAG A.G.
ZOLLIKON—ZÜRICH

Authorised English Translation © 1958
T. & T. CLARK
EDINBURGH

PRINTED IN SCOTLAND BY
CLARK CONSTABLE
EDINBURGH, LONDON, MELBOURNE
BOUND BY HUNTER & FOULIS LIMITED, EDINBURGH

FOR

T. & T. CLARK LTD., EDINBURGH

0 567 09042 6

FIRST PRINTED 1958
LATEST IMPRESSION 1985

EDITORS' PREFACE

READERS of this second part-volume of Barth's *Doctrine of Reconciliation* are directed to the initial survey in the first (*C.D.*, IV, 1, pp. 79 ff.). The threefold content of the doctrine is there described as the knowledge of Jesus Christ (1) as very God humbling Himself to reconcile, (2) as very man exalted and reconciled, and (3) as God-man, guaranteeing and attesting reconciliation. What we now have is an outworking of the second of these themes in terms of the kingly work of Christ, as compared with His high-priestly work in the first and prophetic in the third. The exposition corresponds closely to that of the previous part. To the downward movement of Christ in contrast to our pride there now answers an upward movement in contrast to our sloth. Subjectively realised by the Holy Spirit as a divine direction, this carries with it the sanctification of man worked out in the upbuilding of the community and Christian love.

The schematic parallelism does not mean that Barth is dividing the reconciling work of Christ into different or successive actions. As he lays constant stress on the unity of the person and work of Christ, he makes it quite clear that the downward and upward movement of the Son, the divine verdict and the divine direction, justification and sanctification, gathering and upbuilding, faith and love, are only different aspects of one and the same thing. The one person of the incarnate and exalted Son is the basis of this unity of the whole reality of our reconciliation in Him.

The account of Christ's exaltation as the royal man leads us in this volume to a full consideration (1) of Chalcedonian Christology, and (2) of the historical figure of Jesus as presented in the Gospels. Concerning the first, it is to be noted that, although Barth tries to choose new phraseology, he keeps closely to the detailed formulations of Lutheran and Reformed orthodoxy, yet lifts them up into a new significance by the thoroughgoing integration of Christology and soteriology. In the second we are given a notable example of synoptic exposition controlled by the true subject of the narratives, and not by questions or assumptions alien to their proper purpose.

The transitional discussion in § 66 is perhaps the most complicated and elusive in the whole volume, wrestling as it does with the mystery and miracle of the Holy Spirit. Yet it is also in many ways the most rewarding. It establishes the link between the exaltation and sanctification already accomplished for us in virtue of Christ's union with and presence among us as the royal man, and our participation in this exaltation and sanctification as a community and as individual

vii

Christians. This link is particularly important in relation to the Church, for it means that ecclesiology is given a firm root in the one reconciling work of God as the humiliation of the Son of God and exaltation of the Son of Man. It is from this basis, and from its calling to be a provisional representation of the new humanity in the midst of the old, that the Church learns its true nature and order. Similarly, it is from this basis and calling that believers learn the meaning and manner of Christian love.

The present volume makes no concessions to those who are not ready to work at their theology, and thus take up the fashionable complaint at Barth's verbosity which, in indirect tribute to the translators, now seems to have ousted the earlier charge of obscurity. The reasons for Barth's expansiveness have already been given in the Preface to I, 2, and need not be repeated. But the following points should be remembered. First, Barth is virtually giving us a series of commentaries, a history of dogmatics and a full-scale ethical treatise as well as a theology. Second, his work is really more compact than that of some of his great patristic, mediæval and reformed predecessors. And third, he is studying an inexhaustible theme commanding an exhaustive attention which can finally exhaust itself only in prayer and praise. There are rhetorical passages, and these give force and colour to the whole. But what may seem to be tedious, laboured or repetitive will usually have rich rewards for those willing to give the time and effort demanded.

In the preparation of this volume we are again indebted to the vigilant eye and caustic pencil of our assistant, the Rev. T. H. L. Parker, and to the enthusiastic and competent co-operation of our publishers and printers.

EDINBURGH, *Easter* 1958.

PREFACE

I AM sorry to have disappointed those (perhaps not a few) who had counted on taking this continuation of the *Church Dogmatics* with them on their summer or autumn holidays. In view of the particularly outstanding size of this further part-volume, it would have provided very troublesome reading, but after all nothing has come of it. Well, I now have to accept without complaint or contradiction the fact that I am sometimes called "the old man in Basel," so I can only ask that I may have the indulgence of such if I fail to produce with the regularity of clockwork. I could not do this, indeed, even when I was younger. I can only say that I have the best will in the world to press on, but have been burdened with the responsibility of a task which this time was too much for me, and found it impossible to finish it earlier. To finish it? I doubt whether I have really finished with this part any more than I have with the whole. Those who have so kindly waited for the volume will surely find some other time for it, and if they read it as it was written they will appreciate how fine a thing it is to be occupied with this great matter, and not by a long way to have finished with it.

What I am now seen to represent may provoke—glad or angry—surprise in some circles, as has occasionally happened before on the long journey of the *Church Dogmatics*. Those who still find its essence (perhaps as a result of the confusion caused by my *Epistle to the Romans* of 1921) in the alternative: Either the ascent of man to God or the descent of God to man, or who imagine (to their satisfaction or annoyance) that even in the first part of this fourth volume they can see little or nothing of the renovating work of the Holy Spirit, of the raising of man, of his participation in the event of reconciliation, of sanctification and love, will now have to reckon with the fact that this aspect of the matter is treated in great detail and at great length. The content of this book might well be regarded as an attempted Evangelical answer to the Marian dogma of Romanism—both old and new. I have nowhere mentioned this, let alone attacked it directly. But I have in fact shown that it is made superfluous by the "Exaltation of the Son of Man" and its anthropological implications. I can hardly expect that my Roman Catholic readers—to whom I turn more and more in the *Church Dogmatics*—will accept this, but I am confident that they will at least see that there is a positive reason for my Evangelical rejection. The fact that the man Jesus is the whole basis and power and guarantee of our exaltation means that there can be no place for any other in this function, not even for the

mother of Jesus. I have not made this particular delimitation in the
text, but I hope that in relation to Roman Catholic theology some
contribution has been made to an understanding of what is there
called " sanctifying grace." It is another question whether on our
own side I have even remotely satisfied the concern of the Pietists and
"Evangelical groups." To the best of my knowledge and conscience I
have tried to do this, although I could not simply adopt their view.
If I am not mistaken, there is much more openness and thoughtful-
ness among them now than in the forms of doctrine and practice that
I knew when I was younger—or thought I knew, for I am not ashamed
to confess that I now understand them better than I did. But it
will be quite right if they are not entirely satisfied, for at the decisive
points they cannot fail to hear something of the rolling thunder of
the 1921 *Romans* even in the more accommodating tones in which I
now express the things which particularly affect them. But I seem
to hear from one and another of my former friends and fellows the
question whether in the aspect of the matter which is now to the
forefront I have not gone too far in what I ascribe to man, rather like
an old lion who has finally learned to eat straw. Is there not obviously
demanded of those who firmly take Luther as their starting-point
what is to them the intolerable position which they saw outlined some
twenty years ago when the inversion of the relationship of Law and
Gospel was first articulated ? Well, all this will appear in the book
itself. It has not been my wish to disturb or annoy anyone. But
again I have had no option. Perspicuous readers will surely notice
that there is no break with the basic view which I have adopted since
my parting from Liberalism, but only a more consistent turn in its
development. To make this clear, I had to give particularly careful
expression to the christological section which stands at the head and
contains the whole *in nuce*, speaking as it does of the humanity of
Jesus Christ. I cannot advise anyone to skip it either as a whole or
in part in order to rush on as quickly as possible to what is said about
sanctification, etc. For it is there—and this is true of every aspect—
that the decisions are made. There is no legitimate way to an understanding of the Christian life than that which we enter there. As I
see it, it is by the extent to which I have correctly described this
that the book is to be judged.

May I conclude with a more general observation—especially in
view of a sentence which I came across some time ago—that " for the
moment only the angels in heaven know where the way of this *Church
Dogmatics* will finally lead." The writer presumably meant that its
future way—on which there may well be some further surprises—
could easily end in the darkness of more or less serious heterodoxies
or even heresies. Well, we shall have to hope for the best. I can
certainly confirm his view to this extent. When I take up the theme
of each part-volume, or even embark upon each new section, although

I keep to a general direction, only the angels in heaven do actually know in detail what form the material will take. But to me it is very comforting that the angels in heaven do know, and as far as I am concerned it is enough if I am clear that at each point I listen as unreservedly as possible to the witness of Scripture and as impartially as possible to that of the Church, and then consider and formulate whatever may be the result. I am, therefore, a continual learner, and in consequence the aspect of this *Church Dogmatics* is always that of quiet but persistent movement. But is the same not true of the Church itself if it is not a dead Church but a Church which is engaged in a living consideration of its Lord ? Would it not be abnormal if I were in a position to show the eternal mysteries, and the truths of the Christian faith as they are revealed in time, like a film which has been taken and fixed, as though I were myself the master of them ? Of course it would. Am I then groping in the dark ? Is anything and everything possible ? Not at all. In the twenty-three years since I started this work I have found myself so held and directed that, as far as I can see, there have so far been no important breaks or contradictions in the presentation ; no retractations have been necessary (except in detail) ; and above all—for all the constant critical freedom which I have had to exercise in this respect—I have always found myself content with the broad lines of Christian tradition. That is how I myself see it, and it is my own view that my contemporaries (and even perhaps successors) ought to speak at least more circumspectly when at this point or that they think they have discovered a " new Barth," or, what is worse, a heresy which has seriously to be contested as such. Naturally, I do not regard myself as infallible. But there is perhaps more inward and outward continuity in the matter than some hasty observers and rash interjectors can at first sight credit.

I must draw express attention at this stage to a rearrangement which is not as I see it of essential import. In the Introduction to IV, 1, I had in mind that the doctrine of baptism and the Lord's Supper should be treated in the two first and constitutive parts of the doctrine of reconciliation (in each case in the sections on the Church). But on a nearer approach to the problems I have adopted a different course. And it will perhaps have been noted in Volumes II and III that I made less and less use—and finally none at all—of the general term " sacrament," which was so confidently bandied about in Volume I. I cannot now explain the reasons for this rearrangement, because a brief statement would inevitably give rise to misunderstanding. I can only indicate that here, if anywhere, I have learned to regard a cautious and respectful " demythologising " as expedient and practicable. Baptism and the Lord's Supper are given only incidental mention in the present volume. But they are not forgotten, and will be given what seems to be their appropriate and worthy place as the basis and

crown of the fourth and ethical section of the doctrine of reconciliation.
I know that this will expose me in advance to many suspicions. The
Evangelisch-Lutherische Kirchenzeitung as well as the angels has long
since known that this is how things would turn out. But I must
bear this cheerfully, and with a good courage.

In Geneva, Scotland, England and America, good heads and busy
hands are at work translating the *Church Dogmatics* as a whole into
French and English, and an obviously well-informed visitor from
Japan tells me that a similar project is under consideration there. I
give my greetings to all those who are selflessly prepared to devote so
much of their time and energies to this task—and the courageous
publishers whom they have found or will find—and I hope to know
something of how the work will fare in these wider spheres.

As I hurry to the end of this Preface, I must not forget to make
some necessary amends. I am not referring to the strange (but not
entirely novel) confusion which caused me (somewhere·in IV, 1) to
transport the land of Israel to the western shores of the Mediterranean.
I am thinking rather of the fierce attack which I made on Dutch
Neo-Calvinists *in globo* in the Preface to III, 4. The wrath of man
seldom does that which is right in the sight of God, and never when
it is *in globo*. I have to acknowledge this now that I have come to
know the great book on myself and the *Church Dogmatics* by a representative of that group, G. C. Berkouwer (*De Triomf de Genade in de
Theologie van Karl Barth*, 1954). For all its reservations and criticisms
this work is written with such care and goodwill and Christian *aequitas*
that—in the hope that there are others like its author—I should like
to withdraw entirely the generalised and therefore ill-founded words
which after many years of provocation I then suddenly unleashed.
There are obviously " Fundamentalists " with whom one can discuss.
Only butchers and cannibals are beyond the pale (e.g., the one who
summarily described my theology as the worst heresy of any age), and
even they only provisionally, for there is always hope that they will
attain to a better mind and attitude. Those who were wounded then
can take comfort in the fact that I myself have now come under the
charge of " Fundamentalism," and indeed of an " existentialist Fundamentalism " (whatever that may be). And if in the future they do
not say any more unseemly things about Mozart, they need have
nothing to fear from me.

When will the next volume appear ? and how many more are there
to be ?—are questions which I always hear soon after the publication
of a new one. And one student asked me, in a well-chosen phrase,
what is going to happen when " if I may be permitted to say so, you
are no longer there " ? He was quite right to remind me of this
possibility. " Fast falls the eventide " is only too true of me, but I
am still here and I will address myself at once to the next part, hoping
only that the present one will be " thick " enough to spare me these

questions for a little time yet. The wider issue does not rest in our human hands and will declare itself in good time.

I am much indebted to *stud. theol.* Hinrich Stoevesandt of Bremen for technical help in the preparation of this volume.

And as a final unusual, but practical note, may I mention that after October 1 of this year my address will no longer be Pilgerstrasse 25, but Bruderholzallee 26 in Basel.

GYRENBAD BEI TURBENTHAL (KT. ZÜRICH).
August, 1955.

CONTENTS

CHAPTER XV
JESUS CHRIST, THE SERVANT AS LORD

CHAPTER XV

JESUS CHRIST, THE SERVANT AS LORD

§ 64

THE EXALTATION OF THE SON OF MAN

Jesus Christ, the Son of God and Lord who humbled Himself to be a servant, is also the Son of Man exalted as this servant to be the Lord, the new and true and royal man who participates in the being and life and lordship and act of God and honours and attests Him, and as such the Head and Representative and Saviour of all other men, the origin and content and norm of the divine direction given us in the work of the Holy Spirit.

1. THE SECOND PROBLEM OF THE DOCTRINE OF RECONCILIATION

This chapter brings us to the beginning of a new book. The God who acts as Reconciler in Jesus Christ is one God, and so too is the man reconciled with Him in God. Similarly, the work of atonement which is His action is one. But the forms in which He and His act are revealed to us, the problems which have to be weighed and unfolded in dogmatics, cannot be treated at a single glance without violence, abbreviation and distortion. We cannot even know and confess the one God Himself except as the One who is Father, Son and Holy Spirit. Our present movement is to the second problem of the doctrine of reconciliation. But if we are to understand this further step, a short introduction and transition is necessary (expanding the general lines indicated in *C.D.*, IV, 1, § 57).

We begin with a retrospective glance. The first chapter of the doctrine of reconciliation now behind us had the title " Jesus Christ, the Lord as Servant." It treated of the atonement in its character as the free turning and condescension of God to the man who had turned away from Him and was therefore lost, of the grace of God in the fulfilment of His inconceivable self-offering to the cause of His unfaithful covenant-partner. We recognised the true Godhead of Jesus Christ in the humility of the obedience in which He, the eternal Son of the eternal Father, humbled Himself in the omnipotence of His mercy, and went into the far country, and was made flesh, and took our place as a servant in our cause, to fulfil the ineluctable judgment of God in our place and on our behalf, for the world and its salvation, by bowing Himself before it, and suffering on the cross the death to which we had fallen victim. We saw the verdict of God the Father pronounced in His resurrection from the dead—the revelation that the love of God for the world estranged from Himself attained its end in this His action and passion, that He, the humble servant of God, is our righteousness, i.e., that our wrong has been set aside in and with the judgment accomplished and suffered by Him, and our new right has been established in Him. As reflected in the existence and work of this servant of God, we understood the sin of man as the pride of man, and his justification as the way on which—in both cases with the same unconditional certainty—his wrong has been borne away in Jesus Christ and is behind him, and his new right has been established in Jesus Christ and is before him in the forgiveness of his sins, his institution as a child of God, and the hope of eternal salvation. We understood the Christian community as the gathering by the Holy Spirit of those who believe in Jesus Christ, and therefore as the place where the judgment of God accomplished in His death and the verdict of God revealed in His resurrection, the sin of man and his justification, are known and acknowledged. Finally, we understood Christian faith as the free human act of this acknowledgment, recognition and confession as established by the Holy Spirit. On this first aspect the whole work of reconciliation has shown itself to be a mighty movement from above to below, i.e., from God to man, the reconstitution and renewal of the covenant between God and man under the sign of the first element in the gracious saying of the Old Testament : " I will be your God." As the Christian community, and in it Christian faith, may receive and affirm this " I will be your God," its own existence belongs to this first, objective aspect of the atonement, as itself the final moment in that movement from God to man. But in the Christian community and Christian faith there exists—representatively for all men everywhere—the Christian, and therefore man with his work as a partner of God. He is the man who acknowledges, recognises and confesses his being in Jesus Christ. But he is also the man who in his being in Jesus Christ is different from God. In his spontaneity as such he is an object, but he is more than that. For as an object of the truly and effectively reconciling grace of God, in his own particular, subordinate and secondary place and manner and function he is also a subject of this whole occurrence. As, at the end of that first line of the doctrine of reconciliation, we were confronted in the Christian community and Christian faith with the man reconciled with God in Jesus Christ, intimation was already given of the turn which we have now to make.

It is the man reconciled with God in Jesus Christ who as such will occupy us along this new line : the covenant man who faces the covenant God in the reconstitution and renewal of the covenant ; the second element in that gracious saying of the Old Testament : " Ye shall be my people " ; the human answer to this divine pronouncement. This does not mean that we must now turn our attention away from the divine work of atonement to another actuality to be known outside this work. There can be no question of a second truth side by side with the first. There is only the one mighty truth of the reconciliation of the world with God as it has taken place in Jesus Christ. We do not cease, but continue, to be occupied with this truth, and this alone. In the strict sense, we are not even dealing with another part of the one truth. It is indivisible. It would not be the truth in any of its forms if it were not the whole truth in each of them. Even the two elements in the gracious saying of the Old Testament do not attest the one whole grace of God only as they are taken together, but each does so in and for itself. To express it in terms of the Trinity, the Father and the Son are not the one true God only as they are eternally united, but each is the one true God in and for Himself. There can be no question, then, of leaving one sphere of the one whole grace of God and turning to another. It is a matter of doing justice to this grace, and therefore to the truth of the atonement as it claims us, in all its fulness. It is rich and varied in its unity, and must be estimated accordingly. But we fail to do this if we try rigidly to see only one aspect of it—that which has so far occupied us. And if this is the case, however correct and true it may be in itself, even this aspect is all crooked and in the last resort false. The truth conceals itself from those who are not willing and ready to receive " grace for grace " (Jn. 1^{16}) from the fulness of the incarnate Word, who will not let themselves be led into " all truth " (Jn. 16^{13}) by the Holy Ghost. If we want to know only one aspect of it, we have already attempted to enclose it in the humanly made construction of definite systematisation and conceptual schematisation. But it evades this attempt. As the action and work of God it is divinely living truth. It is the friend only of those who respect its freedom and are therefore free to follow it, to know it afresh—the one truth which is rich in itself—in a new aspect. Therefore in the turn which we have now to execute there can be no question of seeing a new thing, but of seeing the old in a new way. We have not to consider a second thing, but the first one differently. There is not another doctrine of reconciliation, but a second problem of the doctrine (as there will later be a third).

The one divine work of atonement has also to be seen and understood—and not merely incidentally and marginally, but with the same, if distinctive, attention—in relation to the man to whom it applies and on whose behalf, for whom and to whom and with whom, it took place. For man does not stand on the margin or outside the margin, but in his own order he is there with God at the very centre of this event. The covenant God is not alone, but with Him there is also the covenant people, and therefore the covenant man. The centre of this event is indeed that God was not content merely to be God, but that *propter nos homines*, and without ceasing to be God, He Himself became man in His Son : an Israelite, this Israelite, the Son of Abraham, David and Mary, and therefore the Son of Man, for the conversion of all men to Himself. We have seen what God did when He did this, and what it means for Him and as it was done by Him. We must now turn our attention, and give particular emphasis in our investigation and presentation, to what was done for and to and with man when God did this, and what it means for man.

Now what was done to man, and the meaning for him of the divine work of atonement and therefore of the grace of God, is that, as God condescends and humbles Himself to man and becomes man, man himself is exalted, not as God or like God, but to God, being placed at His side, not in identity, but in true fellowship with Him, and becoming a new man in this exaltation and fellowship. It is true enough that the event of atonement is wholly and utterly a movement from above to below, of God to man. But it is also true that this truth encloses the further truth that the atonement is wholly and utterly a movement from below to above, the movement of reconciled man to God. It is true enough that it consists in the unity which God has established and maintains with sinful man in the sovereignty of His grace. But in and with this it is also true that there is this unity of man with God, the actual or virtual existence of the covenant people and covenant man, who (ordained to be this in the divine election, and made it by the work and Word of God) is the righteous partner of God. It is true enough that without the abasement which God elected for Himself when He became man, to make our cause His own and to prosecute it as ours, the judgment of man could have resulted only in his abandonment to the nothingness which he had chosen for himself, his eternal perdition. But it is also true that in and with His own abasement God has elected and achieved man's exaltation, that the *telos* of this judgment, in which God took it upon Himself, can be only the redemption of man—and more than that, the creation and existence of the new man who is well-pleasing to God. This is the second theme and problem which we must now discuss as radically as possible.

It is unavoidably posed by Holy Scripture as the witness of God's work and revelation of grace. If the Church hears the Word of God, it must also consider and answer this problem. If its proclamation is in order, it must also declare what is to be known and considered on this side. For the witness of Scripture very obviously refers us also to this aspect of the grace and truth of God.

It speaks of the great acts of God among men, in the midst of His enemies, for and to sinners, all of whom He consistently confronts as the One who alone is truly righteous and holy. But it also speaks of the difference made among and in these men, of what His acts really mean within the darkness which more or less thickly fills and surrounds them. In the Old Testament it gives us an account of the history of Israel, a people like all others, but as the Israel of God not just like all others. In the New Testament it tells of the developing community, a gathering of Jews and Gentiles who are not in any sense unworldly in their form and manner of life in the world, but who are not simply worldly. It is the record of particular men and women, the friends and servants and witnesses and emissaries of God, the prophets and apostles—all of them men, yet all of them in their humanity called by the Word of God and touched and filled and changed and impelled by His Spirit. In all this the free sovereign grace of God is all in all. Apart from it, there is nothing distinctive about Israel, or the community, or these particular men and women of the Bible. But the Bible cannot speak about the free sovereign grace of God without distinguishing those whom it encounters, without drawing attention to the fact that in its light and circumference there arises a kind of qualified humanity—deep in the shadow of sin and death, flesh like all flesh, not even remotely developed or comparable to the majesty in which God is good and wise and powerful, yet in all its relativity a new humanity, the witness that the grace of God was not in vain (οὐ κενὴ ἐγενήθη, 1 Cor. 15¹⁰) to these men. In the Bible the self-exaltation of man is always a sin : " And whosoever shall exalt himself shall be abased " (Mt. 23¹²)— and the question of his divinisation does not even arise. But there are men who are in different ways exalted by the grace of God. We cannot ignore this fact. Indeed, we are forced to take it very seriously. It is part of the revision and correction which the Church and its proclamation must always be ready to accept from Scripture, of its orientation to the total witness of the Bible, that it should be willing to face the question whether and how far it is willing and prepared to take this seriously and assert it both within itself and to the world. It does not know grace as a whole, which means that it does not know it at all, if it tries to escape this side of its biblical attestation.

Finally decisive for the necessity of putting this problem is the fact to which Old Testament history moves forward and from which New Testament history derives—the form of the incarnate Word of God in the man Jesus of Nazareth. In this first section at the head of the new chapter we shall have to speak particularly of Him, and of His exaltation which is incomparable in relation to that of all others, but for that very reason typical and basic. How can we be obedient to Scripture, which calls Him the Son of Man as well as the Son of God, and has in His form and person its centre, goal and origin, if we are not ready to take it seriously, even in detail, as a record of the new man ?

The necessity to do this obviously applies also and even primarily to dogmatics as the science in which the Church has to measure its proclamation by the Word of God attested in Scripture. The particular danger of dogmatics is to think schematically. And the specific danger of modern Evangelical dogmatics (unlike that of the two preceding centuries) is that it will overlook or fail to take seriously the side of the biblical witness which concerns reconciled man as such— constructing a doctrine of reconciliation in which the man reconciled with God is basically absent, or at any rate invisible. But because the truth is indivisible, this would mean that for all the art and eloquence with which it might turn to the reconciling God and His grace, it would not really speak of Him at all. And this must not happen at any cost. We have, therefore, to address ourselves to this second problem of reconciliation with no less attention than that which we devoted to the first.

The summons to do this is also sounded by the history of the exposition which the biblical witness has found in the doctrine and practice of the ecumenical Church. The *ecumenical* Church—for at this point it is incumbent that we should not try to orientate our doctrine merely by the normal forms of our Evangelical Christianity.

But are we not more likely to be frightened and held back as we consider the true history of the Church and theology ? It is almost customary to-day to approach great tracts of traditional Christian theology and piety with an attitude which is from the very first reserved and critical and even mistrustful. Man as a subject in the great event of reconciliation ? A line of thought from below to above, from man to God ? The exaltation of man to God ? The fellowship not only of God with man but man with God ? What kind of accents are these ? What associations do they conjure up ? What historical images, and with them what well-known and often mentioned dangers, are raised by them, and seem emphatically to warn us not to enter the way proposed ? Is not this the way of theological humanism, moralism, psychologism, synergism, and ultimately an anthropocentric monism—a way which in the last thirty years Evangelical theology has scarcely begun to learn again to see and avoid in all its aridity ? Is it not better to leave on the index—on which they had to be put for a while as the representatives of these errors (in order once and for all to exclude them)—the trends and aims and movements of the nearer and more distant past, with all their effects and continuations in the present, as they arise from a concern with this problem of the new and reconciled man ? Are we not forbidden to take up this question again when it is so obvious what dangers it has involved for so many and even the majority of those who have so far pursued it and who do so now, and what fatal result a concern with it seems always to have entailed ? Is not the supposed summons to take it up a temptation which we do well simply to avoid in view of all that happened in the 18th and 19th centuries, and further back in the Middle Ages and even in the Early Church, not to forget the constant warning of Roman Catholicism ? It is as well that we should devote some serious consideration to this question.

It is indeed the case that to-day we have emerged a little, but not decisively or finally, from the toils of the immanentist theology of the pious man which dominated the last two centuries and was secretly widespread even in the 17th century and that of the Reformation itself. In wide circles of the community and its preachers and even scientific theology the necessary movement of liberation has not yet been made, and the lesson has not yet been learned that in the first place we must think from God to man (as we ourselves have tried to do in the preceding chapter). And who is to boast that he has really learned this lesson and can make the movement with any certainty ? The invasion of theology by existentialism, the naivety with which optimistic youth especially has failed to recognise the old enemy in this new garb, has plainly shown us how basically adapted we are to prefer an approach which necessarily involves the denial of the primacy of God over man, if not of God altogether, as its presupposition no less than its consequence, so that the whole problem of our first chapter, to know the turning, the gracious condescension of God to man, and His decisive intervention for him, is made quite impossible. And Roman

Catholicism still warns or entices us as the classical compendium of all these errors—its constant temptation consisting in its unabashed preference for the problem which we are now about to take up. This being the case, the question inevitably arises whether it is not too soon and inopportune, or even basically mistaken, to take this course.

It is quite incontestable that the history and present state of the problem challenge us to the greatest vigilance and circumspection. There is indeed an element of risk in this diversion of attention to the question of the man reconciled with God. It is true enough that time and again this way has involved the most serious consequences, and that this is particularly true of the centuries from which we have just come, in which the problem that we call the " second " was treated as the first and only problem, the attempt being made to schematise theology according to a view and concept of reconciled man—an attempt which was bound to lead finally to the impasse in which Evangelical theology found itself about 1910. It is true enough that new sources of error of this type have continually broken out and spilled abroad, and that the man reconciled with God by God has often become a man reconciling himself with himself, the religious man, self-complacent and self-explained. It is true enough that even to-day this danger is not in any sense remote, least of all where it is thought that there are adequate safeguards against it. It is true enough that once we begin to look, let alone to think, in this way we shall immediately detect the sinister leaven—recognised perhaps, but even worse unrecognised—of Roman Catholicism, which seems to be most at home in this sphere.

We certainly cannot say that it is impossible, and excluded, that those who take this way will be tempted and finally fall. In the attempt to understand the grace of God as the grace which is addressed to man and exalts and changes and renews him, the perception of the sovereignty of grace, the whole side of the truth from which we have come, and especially the doctrine of justification by faith alone, but everything else both backwards and forwards from it, may easily be forgotten and concealed and subsequently denied. The *theologia crucis*, in which the true *theologia gloriae* has its roots, may easily be destroyed by a false *theologia gloriae*. This has happened time and again on the way which we are now entering, in the attempt to unfold the problem of the reconciled man. We have every reason to consider ourselves warned in this respect. *Vestigia terrent.*

But even in face of all the dangers that threaten, there can be no question of withdrawal, of rejecting this " second problem of the doctrine of reconciliation," of not taking it up. All the danger of the question of the reconciled man, all the anxieties to which the experiences of past and present give rise, cannot alter the fact that this is not a question which is arbitrarily and even malevolently invented and imported from without, but one which is inescapably posed by Holy Scripture, arising with an inward necessity from deliberation on the matter, and always putting itself in some form. Whatever the present-day situation may be, it does not allow us to suppress the question. We could not even draw our first line, that which runs from above to below, without touching this question, and even being deeply involved in it, in our final discussion of the Church and faith. No cautious expediency can be allowed to prevent us from taking it up again boldly and firmly. To be sure, the glory belongs to God alone at the heart of the Christian message of the atonement as it has taken place in Jesus Christ. Yet this does not alter the fact, but includes it, that the subject of this message is both God and man, the glory which God manifests by making Himself the righteousness and salvation of man. This is how the matter is stated in the Old and New Testament Scriptures. They do not put God abstractly at that heart of the message, but man with God. And it may well be a temptation and even dangerous to overlook this, to know better, to try to oppose to the continually threatening anthropomonism a no less abstract theomonism. A committed mistake is not put right by committing the opposite mistake. If, as history shows us, we are threatened at this point by the mistake of a theology of the man who is pious and righteous and holy in himself, and therefore of a doctrine of reconciliation which is hollow and empty and unreal on its objective side, it would only be the opposite error if in view of this possibility we decided for the theology of a man who is certainly envisaged and touched by the grace of God, but only touched outwardly and not changed, and therefore for the doctrine of a reconciliation which is unreal on this side. To close our eyes on one side because of possible distortions, but in this way to replace one distorted picture by what is in fact another, to move out of one *cul-de-sac* into the next, is a poor and in the true sense " reactionary " procedure. Even (and especially) in theology the fear of impending dangers is always a bad teacher. It is from this fear, in the flight from the distorted picture of an atonement which is unreal on the subjective side, that the fatal theology of the pious man has usually arisen. To harden its exponents, to strengthen them in their bias, to reintroduce their error, we have only to close our eyes to this side, to oppose to them the other distorted picture. But to overcome them, to prevent their resurgence, we must determine not to bristle excitedly at their error (only to fall ourselves into error) but to look calmly at the problem involved, not dropping and leaving it, but taking it up again in a new and better way, avoiding possible mistakes, but not avoiding the problem itself as it is posed by Scripture and the facts of the case. To be sure, this means a risk. But nothing venture, nothing win. There is no theology without risk. In face of all the transgressions of the past, both on the right hand and on the left, we may indeed sigh : *omnia vestigia terrent*. The enterprise is indeed a hazardous one on every side. For there have always been fears on every side, leading to the opposition of one distorted picture to another, the exchange of one *cul-de-sac* for a second. The necessary and incumbent risk is that we should break through this *circulus vitiosus* of reactions. This means concretely that we should not evade the problem of the man reconciled with God but in defiance of all the hazards pose it with due care and circumspection, adopting a genuinely active and not merely a passive attitude towards it.

In relation to history this also means that we have good reason to give to the Christian tendencies and movements which in this connexion are usually thought of in a predominantly or even exclusively critical way the cool and collected discussion which is their right. Can it really be that they have missed altogether the Evangelical message attested in Scripture, and represented a doctrine which is completely alien to the Word of God, so that we can only repudiate them ? Or may it not be that in their own way—involving perhaps very serious or even the most serious mistakes—they have been stirred up by a particular concern to give particular attention to a particular element in that message, that they too have been occupied legitimately (in intention at least) with the exposition of Scripture which is the duty of the Church ? We cannot and will not be compelled to make common cause with them or espouse their errors. But we owe it to them—or rather to Scripture and the matter itself—at least to give them a hearing ; at least to accept the question which they raise, whether we have sufficiently taken into account the particular element which they think they have represented, and (badly perhaps) have actually represented and still represent ; to learn from them, it may be, that it is fitting and even high time that we should do so.

I will try to make this clear with an example. We might take Christian mysticism, or the associated movement of Pietism in the sphere of the Reformed and Lutheran Churches, or the remarkable theology and piety of the so-called Enlightenment, which became so effective over so wide a front. Or why not the classical conception in which—in the fulness of time—Schleiermacher gathered up the development of post-Reformation Evangelical Christianity ? But because of its distinctively blatant character, I will choose a movement which is particularly significant and characteristic in this connexion. In a wealth and complexity of continually new forms, it has asserted itself almost from the very beginnings of the Christian Church, and not only is it still with us to-day, but we can say with tolerable certainty that either in its traditional forms or in new ones it will be so in the future. Yet it was one of the main strongholds attacked by the Reformation of the 16th century which is our own basis. I refer to the phenomenon which in Church history is known by what is in one respect, of course, the very misleading name of monasticism.

The shadow which lies over this movement and the institutions to which it has given rise is thick and heavy. The Reformers knew what they were about when they refused to accept it and overthrew the institutions. This was inevitable as matters stood in the 16th century. And where attempts are now made within the Evangelical Church of the present to revive monasticism in various forms, good care must be taken that in the antithesis then disclosed, and not yet legitimately overcome, there is not an imperceptible movement over to the wrong side and therefore into the shadow. This does not mean, however, that it is incumbent and legitimate to ignore *a limine* and as a whole the idea and enterprise involved, discrediting it as " monkery " and evading the question of its problem and significance even for our Evangelical life and thinking. On the contrary, in the light of the history and present reality of monasticism we have to make certain distinctions. We have to distinguish, first, between the motives and intentions which demonstrably underlie this enterprise in its various manifestations, and the institutions and other forms to which it has given rise. And we have to distinguish, second, between its first and great exponents and their lesser and sometimes very small successors, who often enough (as is the way in separatist developments and groups on our own side) are only imitators even in the second generation, and from whom we can gather only in a confused or distorted way what was originally at issue. We may have many serious objections to the ancient and modern theory and practice (and sometimes the *usus* and *abusus*) of Eastern and Western monasticism, and we may be constrained to voice them, yet without invalidating in any way the underlying will and intention—even if there is reason to think that this, too, is not altogether free from error. The serious repudiation of a Macarius the Great or Basil the Great, a Benedict of Nursia, a Francis of Assisi or Dominic, a Thomas à Kempis, even an Ignatius Loyola or Theresa of Avila, is not quite such a simple matter— either in their own time or to-day—as many good Protestants have supposed, not only because they seem to have been conscious of at least some of the things that we think we know better, but also because they have given us other things at least to think about. It is advisable to advance very cautiously at this point, not at all in a censorious spirit, but for all our firmness with a definite anxiety to learn.

The word "monk" (*monachus*) derives from μόνος, alone. And so we read in A. Bertholet's analysis of the general religio-historical phenomenon of monasticism (*R.G.G.*² IV, p. 130) that it "developed out of the need felt by those religiously inclined to isolate themselves, to withdraw from their worldly surroundings, in order to live the more freely their own particular lives." Its ideal is "understandable only on a pessimistic judgment of the world, inspired by the thought either of its natural transitoriness, its ethical inadequacy or its religious emptiness" (*op. cit.*, p. 131). It is, therefore, a flight from the world and man. And there can be no doubt that something of this is to be found in many of the attempts at Christian monasticism. In illustration of this motive reference has been made to the tragic political and social conditions in Egypt in the second half of the 3rd century. But the—lyrically or enthusiastically intended— solution: *O beata solitudo—sola beatitudo*, does not need to be caused by any particular or particularly unsatisfactory contemporary conditions. How a man can be inspired to become a monk in this literal sense of the term—*monachus*— has been classically described from his own experience by one who was very far from being a monk in the Catholic and technical sense, the English Baptist John Bunyan, at the beginning of his *Pilgrim's Progress* (1675), where Christian, in the *status nascendi* as such, rises up to flee from the City of Destruction to Mount Zion. He sees himself in a dream as he leaves his house and starts to run. And his wife and children come crying after him to return. But he sticks his fingers in his ears and runs on with the cry: Life, life, everlasting life, not looking behind him, but taking a straight course across the plain. And is it not exactly the same—at a more exalted level—in the life of Bunyan's older contemporary, Blaise Pascal? This then, or some similar way, is how we shall have to picture the apparently quite unfounded radical unrest and consequent attitude of hundreds and thousands who at that decisive point towards the end of the 3rd century fled into the Egyptian desert and became anchorites (those who withdrew, or drew back). This, or some similar way, is how it went with many others. The question that we have to put to this mode of conduct is the obvious one that one does not have to be a Christian to be sated with the world and man, to wish to have done with the turmoil of earth, to hurry away as fast as one's feet can carry one. And to become and be a Christian one does not need to be up and off into the desert. A flight from the world is not in any sense identical with the flight to God. And one thing is sure—that even in his hut or cave the hermit will never be free from the most dangerous representative of the world, i.e., himself. Nor can this flight claim to be an imitation of God. For neither in

Himself (as the Triune) nor outwards (as the Creator and Sustainer of the distinct being man and his cosmos) is God isolated or alone.

It is also to be noted that this meaning of *monachus* is not characteristic of the phenomena of the second and even the first century, and incipiently perhaps the apostolic age itself, in which the origins of what were later called monasticism are to be found. From the very first there were Christians who did not marry (1 Cor. 7²⁵ᶠ·), or hold possessions (Mt. 10⁹ᶠ·, Ac. 2⁴⁴ᶠ), or eat flesh or drink wine (Rom. 14¹ᶠ·)—who were therefore ready to accept some of the restraints, or even all three like the great Origen, of which at least the first two later became important marks of monasticism. It seems that these Christians enjoyed a place of particular estimation in the community and may even have made particular claims, but they did not live alone or together in cloisters, shunning their fellow-Christians and other men, and exchanging their residence in towns or villages for an abode in the wilderness. What we learn of these earliest Christian ascetics is that they sometimes travelled for the edification of the congregations and for the rest made themselves useful with sacrificial activity and concern for the destitute and sick. Even·Origen obviously did not withdraw from at least academic intercourse with his contemporaries.

Even if we find the beginning of monasticism proper in the appearance of hosts of Egyptian anchorites, it is not to be overlooked how quickly these came together in colonies and unions and fellowships to the commonly ordered and directed life of coenobitic monasticism—a form which is in the strict sense a contradiction in terms, but which established itself in both East and West as the normal form of the enterprise, true anchorites like the famous Coptic saint Antonius—a kind of Nicholas of Flüe—being the exception. Benedict lays down in his rule (*c.* 1) the historically paradoxical demand that we should become hermits by prior spiritual training in the cloister. And if Thomas Aquinas (*S. th.* II, 2, *qu.* 188, *art.* 8) rather grudgingly concedes that the *vita solitaria* is properly the most excellent form of the *vita religiosa*, he does not delay to add that it is *periculosissima* without the special assistance of grace, and he cannot recommend or allow it without the fulfilment of this condition. When we speak of " monks " to-day we think of members of an order and usually of inmates of a cloister and not of hermits. Even the monks who still live in the strictest seclusion on Mont Athos form a community of hermits, an anchoretic society.

The material question has also to be asked whether the need for isolation and therefore for a certain spatial withdrawal from the world—assuming that this is at least a partial explanation of monasticism—does not relate only to its negative side, and is not to be understood only as an indolent and ultimately self-seeking retreat into oneself, " an underestimation of the realities of the external world " (Bertholet). Was it in any sense meaningful or praiseworthy from the Christian standpoint that the 5th century North Syrian Simon Stylites —in a supreme gratification of his desire to be alone—spent the last thirty-six years of his life on the top of a high pillar ? It may well be doubted. Nor must we exclude the possibility that in the case of many who took it the way into the desert, for which there were notable precedents in the Bible, had little or nothing to do with what we describe and usually disparage as escapism, but was made as (in its own way) a highly responsible and effective protest and opposition to the world, and not least to a worldly Church, a new and specific way of combating it, and therefore a direct address to it—a retreat, in fact, for the purpose of more effective attack. The term " secularism," which is so important in the modern apologetics of the Evangelical Church, reaches back to the " secularisations " in which enlightened governments of the late 18th and early 19th centuries strangely thought that they had to protect themselves against these recluses by the suppression of monastic institutions. Do we not see in these movements of retreat a sign of the power and vitality of the Church ? It might well be the law of the Spirit to which regard was had in the form of these withdrawals and

the possibility of new and better Christian action which was sought and found
in them. The proof is to be seen in the concrete and influential movements of
reform which have always issued in fact from this individual and collective
ἀναχωρεῖν. The debt owed by European civilisation and culture to the Benedictine
claustrum is well-known. Did it really underestimate the realities of the external
world ? And even a typical hermit like Nicholas of Flüe did not regard himself
as prevented by his withdrawal from playing a well-informed and resolute part
in Federal politics when the moment came. A Trappist or a Carmelite may
seem very far from the world, but the monk in the form of the Jesuit can seem
uncomfortably close. A Benedict, or Francis, or the author of the *Imitatio
Christi*, or the other classical exponents of monasticism and their better disciples,
cannot be described as pessimists in the modern sense of the term. We may
rather ask whether in their own way and along their own lines they did not take
too optimistic a view of human possibilities. And the question has to be faced
whether there is any Christian existence which does not involve even a spatial,
not to speak of an inward, separation from the world and even from the
Church—a separation which is certainly for the sake of solidarity and impact
and thus a form of ministry, but which is in fact the dialectical withdrawal
which (wrongly, if we like) is made a principle, a system and an external law
in the theory and practice of monasticism. Can there be either for the Church
or for individuals any genuine approach to the world or men unless there is an
equally genuine retreat ? Has there not to be (not merely a healthy but a
spiritually necessary) rhythm in this matter, in which there will always be a
place for the ἀναχωρεῖν ?

In this connexion (but originally also outside it) asceticism, or a more or
less extended system of abstentions, obviously became the most prominent and
distasteful feature of monasticism as seen by the external observer. The later
spatial withdrawal from the world, the residence in the cell or cloister, was only
for the purpose of withdrawal from intercourse with the opposite sex, from the
cares of money and possessions, and therefore for the observing of the vows of
chastity and poverty. Basil the Great seems with good reason to have regarded
the demand for the utmost possible silence as almost as important as these two
main ascetic laws. And this plays a not inconsiderable role in the Benedictine
rule and is particularly emphasised in the Trappist order. Originally, however,
ἄσκησις simply means exercise or training for the successful attainment of a goal.
Even the fulfilment of these prohibitions is meant to serve the liberation from
those passions connected with a preoccupation with the other sex or the question
of money or possessions, from the " inordinate desires " which are obviously a
constant threat in these spheres. It may also be said that asceticism is meant
to serve the liberation of man from the downward drag of sin. And this liberation itself is to serve the redemptive and exclusively necessary freedom of man
for God and his fellows, for the Church and therefore for the world. Even the
negative principle of asceticism is only the reverse side of a positive. It is a
matter of the perfection to be attained by following the " evangelical counsels,"
i.e., of the perfect dedication to an end without which Christian existence is not
adapted to serve. If this perfection is not demanded of all Christians, it is
demanded of some, of those who are called to this service. And it is to be
attained by them, by means of these abstentions, representatively for the others,
who do not have the vocation to this service, or cannot produce the necessary
joy and power in this renunciation. The few who do, the ascetics, are the monks
and their female counterparts, the nuns, the *virgines velatae*.

But again, there are some crying questions which have to be put. Do not
these abstentions rest only on an arbitrary choice ? Are they not an attack,
not only on sin, but on the nature of man as created by God ? Are sex and
property (and speech) really the occasion of particular temptation, a particular
danger to Christian freedom and fitness to serve God and our neighbours ? And

even if they are this—as the Gospels seem to indicate, less in relation to sex, more clearly in relation to property, the unrighteous mammon—is the danger which is to be expected really met by the mechanical sealing off of these whole spheres ? Is not the ordering of these inordinate desires, and its goal of Christian freedom for Christian service, really a matter of the heart, which may still be lacking in spite of this sealing off, or may be there without it ? Is there no passion or inertia of the heart which is not stronger and more influential than all the passion or inertia of sex or property, for all their rigid exclusion ? Is there no trace of imperfection and unfitness for service in and in spite of the most radical asceticism, and no true fitness and perfection without it ? And is it tolerable that in the Christian community the establishment of these basically ascetic demands should mean a prior distinction between a perfect and an imperfect Christianity, between one which is seriously free and serves and one of which this cannot be said, so that we have to reckon systematically with a twofold participation of man in the grace of God, the one total and the other only partial ?

It is right and necessary that these questions should be put. But we have to remember that—even if the answers given by the theology of monasticism cannot be regarded as altogether satisfactory—certain points still remain open. With its principle of asceticism both Eastern and Western asceticism has in fact rendered one obvious service to the Church—that of bringing and keeping vividly and concretely before it (by way of analogy and example) the passing of this world and its lusts (1 Cor. 7³¹, 1 Jn. 2¹⁷) and the existence of a new man and the direction which he gives. This may not be so *de iure*, but even in what are sometimes far more repellent than illuminating and inviting forms, by the establishment and more or less fulfilment of these prohibitions, it is certainly true *de facto*. The question of Christian perfection as the perfect dedication to an aim (τελειότης), as the consistent orientation (unfailingly included in the grace of God) to minister to the man addressed by the same grace, cannot be suppressed, not even by a reference to the faith by which alone man can be just in the sight of God. Monastic asceticism was an unmistakeable repetition of this question—indeed, it was an impressive attempt to answer it—within a Christianity which even at an early, the very earliest, stage was always a little (and even very much) engaged in the de-eschatologising and secularising of its life and message. It lay in the very nature of the case that distinctions had to be drawn between the vigilant and active on the one side and the sleepy and indolent on the other. No *de iure* ought to have been made out of them. They ought not to have been interpreted as distinctions between perfect and imperfect, or gradations of calling. They ought not to have been equated with the fulfilment or non-fulfilment of prohibitions. But we have still to consider—even as concerns the substance of these prohibitions—whether in the spheres of sex and especially property (even if we do not grant them the central position which they often assumed in monastic phantasy) we do not really have to do, at any rate in relation to sin in its form as passion or inertia, with particularly outstanding problems, with centres of particular demonic energy and human temptation, with characteristic elements of the world that passes, to which man can particularly easily lose his heart, i.e., himself, and therefore become particularly easily unserviceable in the kingdom of God ? Monasticism was no doubt in error when it expected relief and a solution by the simple sealing off of these spheres. As the general principle of a particular state, this could hardly be reconciled with openness to the question of God's commandment. But was it really at fault in demanding a particular vigilance and strictness in these spheres ? And if in different ways the arbitrariness of the monastic rule and manner of life avenged itself severely enough in many known and not so well known cases, it is still patent that there always existed what we might call the normal monk whose life did not at all consist in an unceasing conflict with the different *libidines* of the flesh, but could and can be relatively quietly and continuously and richly and fruitfully occupied with spiritual and physical labour, with all kinds of arts and serious scholarship, with the exercise of hospitality and works of charity, even with preaching and pastoral work among the people, with social work and teaching, and above all with the supremely monastic *opus Dei*, the *officium*, the adoration of God in private and communal worship, and above and beyond all this—we have only to read and note the 72 *instrumenta artis spiritualis* of the Benedictine rule (*c.* 4)—with a whole range of other and very inward problems of individual and social morality. In his own way he could and can positively attest something of that freedom for God and his fellows which is supposed to be the *telos* of monastic asceticism.

And again, with particular reference to ourselves, we have finally to ask whether there can be any Christian existence at all in Christian freedom, in that direction to the goal set for man by the grace of God, whether there can be any worship of God in Spirit and in truth or genuine service to our fellows, whether there can be any fitness for it, without an acceptance of the conflict in these spheres, without definite renunciations and abstentions, and therefore without asceticism—not perhaps an asceticism in principle and subject to rule, but all the more serious on that account. This certainly seems to be an impossibility in the Gospels and according to the nature of the case, both individually and collectively. Only those who can and will sacrifice can and will serve and are free to do so. A question is also posed by monastic *taciturnitas*. Is it not, perhaps, a weakness of Protestantism that we speak too much, too quickly (without proper punctuation), and without due and proper reflection ? Might not a reasonable asceticism in this regard be a valuable asset even in our Christian and theological circles ? Is it not indispensable to a true speaking ? These are the kind of questions which we for our part must be prepared to face, without any desire or obligation to become Benedictines, Franciscans or Carmelites —and, incidentally, Roman Catholics.

But apart from these rules of abstinence the monastic life means a canonically ordered and disciplined life under a definite rule and guidance. This is where the third monastic vow comes in : the obligation of obedience to the superior or superiors of the order, and, of course, to the higher authorities of the Church up to and including the Pope himself. According to the Benedictine rule (*c.* 5) this is an obedience which in a given case is to be rendered *ac si divinitus imperetur*, and therefore without hesitation, *velocitate timoris Dei*, *non trepide*, *non tarde*, *non tepide aut cum murmure vel responsione nolentis*, and positively *cum bono animo*, freely and spontaneously : *quia obedientia quae maioribus praebetur, Deo exhibetur*. The younger brethren owe it also to the older (*c.* 71). After a modest expression of all possible questions it is to be rendered in love and confidence in God even where what seems to be impossible is demanded (*c.* 68). This third principle received its sharpest form and greatest importance in the Jesuit order, where the strongest accent was also laid on the existing Pope as summarising the authority which demands obedience. In his interesting interpretation of monasticism (*Die Antwort der Mönche*, 1952) Walter Dirks has placed this rule alongside those of chastity and poverty as one of abstention. Its concern is with the renunciation of the right to exercise power, and it is, therefore, a defence or attack against the third principal demon side by side with *eros* and mammon— the belief that might is right. This interpretation may be profitably considered, especially in Germany (and America), but it is artificial. It cannot be contested that the achievement of obedience does in practice acquire ascetic significance. But all the same, the idea of an asceticism to be achieved in monastic obedience does not appear to play any independent role even in the ideology of the Jesuit order which emphasises it most strongly. According to Thomas Aquinas (*S. th.* II, 2, *qu.* 186, *art.* 5 *c*) obedience is necessary to the *homo religiosus* because he needs direction in his efforts to attain monastic *perfectio*, and must therefore be subject to his superiors. As I see it, it can be more easily and effectively understood as a presupposition and regulative principle of the communal life in the cloister which is distinctive of classical monasticism. Characteristically, the Benedictine rule begins (*c.* 1) with a demarcation of the coenobitic monasticism which had long since established itself as normative in the 6th century from more ancient and certainly more or less degenerate neighbouring forms : from the anchorites ; the so-called Sarabaites, who (according to G. Grützmacher, *P.R.E.*[3] 17, 481) were nothing other than the rather dubious successors of the oldest of all ascetics, those who lived within the community and the world ; and the Gyrovagi, who went round begging, i.e., from one monastery to another, and whose manners and morals make it impossible to regard them as anything but pseudo-monks, or spiritual swindlers. At any rate, the reproach is made against the two latter forms : *quicquid putaverunt vel elegerunt, haec dicunt sanctum et quod noluerunt putant non licere.* They and the original anchorites obviously lack the principle of obedience which makes the monastic fellowship a fraternity in which the commonly elected abbot occupies the place of the father, representing both the heavenly Father and the holy father in Rome. That is why the word PAX stands over the inner door of the Benedictine cloister. Above and beyond what it means for individuals the monastic life aims to be a perfect representation of the *communio sanctorum* set there as an example to the Church and the world and therefore serving the Church and the world, and, above all, the glory of God. To achieve this, in concrete application of the obedience originally and properly owed to God, it needs the subjection which is to be made unconditionally and *bono animo* to the command of the superior as the one who proclaims the idea affirmed and accepted by all and interprets with ultimate decisiveness the particular rule of the order, the *regula*, as it is again accepted by all and recognised by the Church.

It involves, therefore, the institution of a thoroughgoing theonomy, the strictest heteronomy, and genuine autonomy—a bold and almost Promethean venture, which cannot be attacked, let alone overthrown, by the catchwords of modern Liberalism, but which is very dubious and very dangerous all the same. For is there any relationship of man with man whose structure may try to imitate that between God and man institutionally ? Is there any authority of man which can represent to other men the authority of God institutionally ? Is there a real obedience, not of works only but of the heart, which men can feel bound to render to other men institutionally ? In a relationship between sinful men, will not this necessarily mean that the majesty of God is obscured, that a burden is laid both upon those who have to command and those who have to obey which neither can bear ? Will not the attempt to actualise institutionally a representation of the *communio sanctorum* inevitably result in an illusion which does injury to God and falsely exalts one man and falsely abases another ? These are serious questions which can and must be asked. The only thing is that we must not think that we can dispose of monasticism on this side either. If what is impossible with men is possible with God, and the Spirit bloweth where He listeth, it cannot finally be disputed that a genuine fellowship of the saints could and can take place in the form of genuine commanding and genuine obeying even in the sphere of this kind of institution. The Benedictine rule, which is our best guide in this whole matter, is a document which not only displays an extraordinary knowledge of life and the soul and men, but is also characterised by a true fear of God, and it must not be overlooked—its first concrete regulation has to do, for example, with the responsibility and obligations of the abbot (*c.* 2)—that the danger which threatens in the sphere of authority and obedience was at least well known to its authors. A " good " monastery—and there were and are such—was never the den of arrogance and tyranny that the majority of average Protestants imagine. Rule and obedience could and can actually be exercised and rendered with great wisdom, humility and sincerity. And if it is incontestable that the *communio sanctorum* can be achieved only in the distinctive triangle of God, a man and a fellow-man—the two latter being united in a definitely ordered relationship—we cannot reject out of hand the recognisable purpose of the *vita monastica*, for all the questions and objections which we may have to level against its theoretical and practical execution. Were not the great leaders of monasticism right when they asked whether the task of this *communio* (not only in worldly society but also in the Church itself) has not been continually neglected within the limits of the attainable, and when they determined to apply themselves seriously to this task ? And again we cannot escape the counter-question whether this concern and purpose, this question of brotherhood and its presuppositions, is not perhaps a little alien to us, and what better we can propose or do along these lines.

To sum up, the desire and aim of monasticism was to achieve in its own distinctive way a form of that discipleship of the Lord which is not only commanded generally in the Gospels but partially at least, and by way of illustration, more specifically outlined. Its desire and aim was, therefore, a concrete individual and collective sanctification, a teleological concretion of the Christian status, a practical and regulated brotherhood, and all this in the service of concrete and total love. It is certainly good that we should definitely and inflexibly oppose to this desire and aim the truth that the sinner is justified only for Jesus Christ's sake, by faith and not by the works of any law, not even a law taken from the Gospels, not even the law of love. It is a pity that in the four books of the *Imitatio Christi*, and the rule of the Benedictine and other orders, although this truth is not denied, in practice it is almost completely obscured by the plenitude of directions and counsels given for the doing of these works in their outward and inward form. It is a pity that the final sentence in Benedict is as follows : *Facientibus haec regna patebunt superna*. This cannot be admitted for a moment. The statement must be resolutely reformulated. It is not because and as they do this that the *regna superna* will open up to them. It is because and as the *regna superna* are opened up to them in the death of Jesus Christ that they will do this in the power of His resurrection. It has to be remembered, however, that this sequence and basis seem to have been predominant in the historical form which we have perhaps to regard as the closest non-Christian model for Christian monasticism—the discipline of the Essenes recently discovered near the Dead Sea, a sect which strangely enough seems obviously to have known a basic truth in the Pauline doctrine of justification (Gal. 1^{17} ?). This sequence and basis was certainly suppressed in the history of monasticism, and even denied and contested in many of its forms, but once it is established we have always to learn from monasticism that it derives from faith and that necessarily in faith it has to do with discipleship, sanctification, concretion, brotherhood and love. Those who recognise what has been revealed for the world and for them in the resurrection of Jesus Christ will do this in the power of His resurrection. The monastic formulation of what has to be done may be open to question. The context in which monasticism has done it may be perverted. But this is no reason why we should suppress or neglect this action. And if we see clearly that this action, put in the right context, must not on any account be suppressed or neglected, but given its proper place, in justice and respect we can concede to the purposes and even the enterprises of monasticism that for all our reservations the particular standpoints from which it has described and demanded and attempted this action deserve our serious consideration in detail.

Monasticism has been introduced at this point only as one example of a movement which arose and still continues within Christianity and which compels our attention with its disputable but deliberate and energetic treatment of the problem of the reconciled man—our attention, that is, to this problem, and therefore a historical appraisal. A related example would be that of what the Roman and Eastern Churches claim to be the existence of special Christians distinguished from the rest by the fact that after their death they are officially declared to be "saints" and on account of their exemplary life are commended to the congregation for imitation, honour and invocation, the Roman cleric having them daily before him in the *Proprium de Sanctis* of the Breviary. Similar examples could also be mentioned. But *mutatis mutandis* what we have considered in relation to monasticism would apply to all of them. The result would not always be identically the same, but it would always be the corresponding one that there is in fact this second problem of the doctrine of reconciliation posed not only by Scripture but very seriously by the history of the Church.

We have only to add that within Protestantism the problem was seen from the very first, and given both theoretical and practical recognition, in the theology of Calvin in particular, and of the Reformed Church which followed him. It is not for nothing that both earlier and more recently this has been suspected of legalism and a certain kinship to the essence of monasticism. It would be historically interesting to compare with the theology of monasticism the doctrine of *sanctificatio* and the *vita hominis christiani* which in Calvin embraced and included what was substantially a Lutheran doctrine of justification, testing them carefully for agreements as well as contradictions. A mere reference ought to be enough to show that we are not leaving the ground of the Reformation, but following a powerful Reformation impulse, when we give to this matter rather greater and more insistent attention than is customary in the present theological situation, or generally expected, perhaps, in our own dogmatics.

The decisive certainty which we need on this way will necessarily consist in the point of departure which we have to choose and to which we must assign an absolutely controlling position and function. It is the same as that from which the first problem of the doctrine had to be developed. The problem of reconciled man, like that of the reconciling God, has to be based in Christology, and can be legitimately posed and developed and answered only on this basis. It has its roots in the identity of the Son of God with the Son of Man, Jesus of Nazareth, in what this man was and did as such, in what happened to Him as such. In and with His humiliation (as the Son of God) there took place also His exaltation (as the Son of Man). This exaltation is the type and dynamic basis for what will take place and is to be known as the exaltation of man in his reconciliation with God. In His fellowship with God, and therefore in our fellowship with Him, this One, there is achieved our fellowship with God, the movement of man from below to above, from himself to God. It is primarily and properly this human Subject, who, as the object of the free and liberating grace of God, cannot be only an object in the event of atonement, but also becomes an active Subject. In Him man is made the new man, reconciled with God. According to 1 Cor. 1[30] He is made unto us not only righteousness but also sanctification. First of all, then, in this chapter we must speak of Him specifically. But even later we must always speak of Him. It would be a strange Christology which did not give the same attention to the true humanity of Christ as to His true deity, or, according to the older view of His work, to His royal office as to His high-priestly office, to the exaltation of the Son of Man. It is from this point therefore, in the particular light of this, the human, side of the truth of the Mediator and Reconciler, that we have now to consider and present the whole event of reconciliation. It is from this point that we have to consider and present the specific form of sin as the sloth of man as it emerges in the mirror of the exaltation which has come to him in the man Jesus. It is from this point, as it has taken place in Him, that we have to consider and present the whole sanctification of man for the service of God and his fellows, the edification of the Christian community as it is gathered by and around this man, and finally Christian love as it knows and seeks God and this man, as it strains after this man—the work of the awakening power of the Holy Spirit. And we have to do all this in such a way that the line leads clearly and deeply into the sphere of human existence (both general and particular), and yet is never more than a repetition and confirmation of its christological starting-point. We have to do it, therefore, as an exposition, a series of variations on the words of Eph. 4[15] : that we "may grow up into him in all things, which is the head, even Christ, from whom the whole body fitly joined together and compacted by that which every joint supplieth, according to the effectual working in the measure of every part, maketh increase of the body unto the edifying of itself in love."

Reversing the title of the first chapter, we have called the whole of this second chapter " Jesus Christ, the Servant as Lord." If we are successful in doing what is indicated by this title, not only once but in every necessary turn and connexion the dangers which inevitably threaten in this sphere will be avoided, and above all we can hope to do some measure of justice to the problem as it is posed by Scripture, the exposition of Scripture in the ecumenical Church, and the matter itself.

2. THE HOMECOMING OF THE SON OF MAN

There are two elements in the event of the incarnation as it is attested in Jn. 1[14]. If we put the accent on " flesh," we make it a statement about God. We say—and in itself this constitutes the whole of what is said—that without ceasing to be true God, in the full possession and exercise of His true deity, God went into the far country by becoming man in His second person or mode of being as the Son— the far country not only of human creatureliness but also of human corruption and perdition. But if we put the accent on " Word," we make it a statement about man. We say—and again this constitutes the whole of what is said—that without ceasing to be man, but assumed and accepted in his creatureliness and corruption by the Son of God, man—this one Son of Man—returned home to where He belonged, to His place as true man, to fellowship with God, to relationship with His fellows, to the ordering of His inward and outward existence, to the fulness of His time for which He was made, to the presence and enjoyment of the salvation for which He was destined. The atonement as it took place in Jesus Christ is the one inclusive event of this going out of the Son of God and coming in of the Son of Man. In its literal and original sense the word ἀποκαταλλάσσειν (" to reconcile ") means " to exchange." The reconstitution and renewal of the covenant between God and man consists in this exchange—the *exinanitio*, the abasement, of God, and the *exaltatio*, the exaltation of man. It was God who went into the far country, and it is man who returns home. Both took place in the one Jesus Christ. It is not, therefore, a matter of two different and successive actions, but of a single action in which each of the two elements is related to the other and can be known and understood only in this relationship : the going out of God only as it aims at the coming in of man ; the coming in of man only as the reach and outworking of the going out of God ; and the whole in its original and proper form only as the being and history of the one Jesus Christ. As we read in Eph. 4⁹ᶠ· : " Now that he ascended, what is it but that he also descended first into the lower parts of the earth. He that descended is the same also that ascended up far above all heavens, that he might fill all things." It is to this ascension, the coming in, the return home of the Son of Man, as it took place in Him, that we have now to address ourselves. This is the root of the second problem of the doctrine of reconciliation.

When the whole of this subject is before us, we can hardly fail to think of the New Testament passage which in every age—and with a rather dubious preference in our own day—has always been valued in the Church (with all kinds of different interpretations) as central to the whole New Testament and especially the Synoptic tradition. I refer to the so-called parable of the Prodigal Son, the son who was lost and was found again (Lk. 15¹¹⁻³²).

It would be a strained interpretation to try to give to it a direct christological reference, as has been attempted. In what it says directly, i.e., with its parabolic reference according to the context (in concretion of the parables of the Lost Sheep and the Lost Coin) it speaks of the sin of man and the mortal threat which comes to him in consequence, of his repentance and return to God, and of the overwhelming grace with which this one who turned away and then turned back to God is received by Him. According to vv. 1–2 this is all with a view to the " publicans and sinners " who come to Jesus and hear Him, whom He receives (προσδέχεται), and with whom He eats—in contrast to the scribes and Pharisees, who seem to shun Him for this reason. In the parable the latter correspond to the elder son, who will not rejoice at the return of the younger, but (v. 28) is angry, and will not take part in the feast prepared by the father. But the elder son is only the—indispensable—contrast, just as the scribe or Pharisee, the righteous who needs no repentance, has only the significance of contrast in relation to the main statement of the passage. The real message is to be found in the story of the son who left his father but then returned and was received by him with joy and honour. And in this story it tells of the turning away and turning back of man in his relationship to God, in which there is not only no diminution but a supreme heightening and deepening of the fatherly mind and attitude of God towards him. We cannot say that more than this is said directly in the passage, nor can we extract more than this from it in direct exegesis.

But if there is the danger of a strained interpretation, it is also possible not to do full justice to the passage, to miss what is not expressly stated but implied in what is stated, and therefore necessary to what is stated, as that which is said indirectly. To this category there belongs that which was emphasised by Augustine (*Quaest. ev:*, 2, 23), very cautiously by C. Starke (in his *Syn. Bibl. exeg. in N.T.*, 1741) and on a more scientific basis by F. C. Baur and his school : the relationship between the lost and re-found younger son, the sinful but penitent *'am ha'aretz* of publicans and sinners, and the election, calling and redemption of the Gentile world as it turns to the Gospel—in contrast to the Israel as revealed in the elder brother, which (v. 29) has served God for so many years, and thinks and claims that it has never transgressed His commandment, and in so doing excludes itself from the Messianic feast. There is no explicit mention of this relationship to the Gentiles in the text. But is it not there, as everywhere where the New Testament deals with this *'am ha'aretz* ? Was it not definitely in the mind of the third Evangelist with his very pronounced universalistic interest ? Is it really read into the text ? Is it not the case that we cannot really expound the text without taking it into consideration—not in direct exegesis, because it is not there—but in and with and under what is said directly ? Do we not fail to do full justice to the passage if we ignore this relationship ?

But the question also arises whether we have not to take from the text, in the same indirect way, a christological content, because it does actually contain this—although not explicitly. It has often been maintained, and in recent years triumphantly emphasised, that in the act of penitence to which this parable refers (as in the parable of the Pharisee and the Publican in Lk. 18⁹ᶠ·, or the discourse on the Last Judgment by the Son of Man in Mt. 25³¹ᶠ·) there is no mention at all of the person and work of Jesus Christ. From this it is hastily concluded (as in Harnack's *Essence of Christianity*, Lect. 8) that not the Son and the atonement accomplished in Him but only the Father and His goodness belong to the Gospel preached by Jesus Himself, and that according to this Gospel of His nothing extraneous can interpose itself between God and the soul, the soul and its God. And, indeed, there is not a single word in the parable about Jesus Christ and the atonement accomplished in Him.

But does this mean that a discussion of what is not said but definitely implied along these lines like that of Helmut Gollwitzer in his *Die Freude Gottes* (1941, II, p. 91 f.), is illegitimate, or even avoidable ? As he sees it, the scribes and Pharisees did not understand that the Messianic work of salvation does not consist in the coronation of righteous Israel but the blessing of sinful Israel. Jesus' eating with the publicans and sinners is a fulfilment of this blessing. Not the theory of a Father-God who self-evidently and consistently pardons, but the miraculous actuality of this act of God, is the non-explicit but indispensable presupposition of the happening between God and man which is envisaged in the relations between father and son described in the parable. In the parable, then, Jesus is " the running out of the father to meet his son." Jesus is " hidden in the kiss which the father gives his son." Jesus is the power of the son's recollection of his father and home, and his father's fatherliness and readiness to forgive. This is the indirect exegesis. And it is not allegorical but legitimate if there is to be an exposition of the parable in the context of the whole of the Third Gospel, and the whole New Testament message. It does justice to what is there in the light of its background, i.e., it expounds it from its context. Yet although there can be no objection to it on grounds of method, it is not altogether satisfactory. For, throwing all the emphasis upon the action of the father, and deriving the reference to Jesus Christ from this, it destroys the essential balance of the parable, and cannot therefore offset more recent Protestant exegesis— which is guilty of exactly the same error—as effectively as is required. For this reason, although not opposing it in content, I prefer to replace or rather to complete it by a different exposition.

For after all the main figure in the story is the younger son who leaves his father and is lost, but returns and is found again. And what we have to demonstrate in face of more recent Protestant exegesis is the presence and action of the Son of God, and therefore of the atonement accomplished in Him, in what takes place between God and man as indicated in the parable. Directly, this cannot be demonstrated from the text. That would be a strained interpretation. There can be no simple equation of Jesus Christ with the lost son of the parable —and even less, of course, with the flesh of the fatted calf which was killed for his reception, as Ambrose once suggested. But again we do not do justice to the story if we do not see and say that in the going out and coming in of the lost son in his relationship with the father we have a most illuminating parallel to the way trodden by Jesus Christ in the work of atonement, to His humiliation and exaltation. Or better, the going out and coming in of the lost son, and therefore the fall and blessing of man, takes place on the horizon of the humiliation and exaltation of Jesus Christ and therefore of the atonement made in Him. It has in this its higher law. It is illuminated by it. In this, and therefore in itself, it is clear and significant and important.

In the parable the son comes with his greedy and arbitrary demand, takes his inheritance from the hands of his father, makes his way into a far country, wastes his substance in riotous living—with harlots, as we are later told (v. 30) —and then suffers want in the famine which comes on that land, being glad at last to feed on the husks which do not belong to him, but to the swine which he is charged to keep. This is the way of man in his breaking of the covenant with God—the way of lost Israel, of the lost " publicans and sinners," of the lost Gentile world. It is certainly not in any direct sense the way of the Son of God who is obedient to the Father, the way of Jesus Christ. And yet it cannot be denied that the way of the latter is in fact the way into the far country of a lost human existence—the way in which He accepts identity and solidarity with this lost son, unreservedly taking his place, taking to Himself his sin and shame, his transgression, as though He Himself had committed it, making his misery His own as though He Himself had deserved it, and all this in such a way that the frightfulness of this far country, the evil of the human situation, is revealed in its full depths only as it becomes His situation, that of the holy and righteous Son of God. What is the fatal journey of the lost son as seen from this stand-point ? Surely it is only a sorry caricature of the going out of the one Son of God into the world as it took place in Jesus Christ, of the humiliation in which, without ceasing to be who He is, but in the supreme exercise and expression of His Sonship and deity, He became poor for our sakes (2 Cor. 8⁹). But it is obviously its caricature. As away from the heights to the depths, from home to a far country, it is analogous to it. It is similar for all its dissimilarity, like the being of Adam in relation to that of Jesus Christ : τύπος τοῦ μέλλοντος (Rom. 5¹⁴).

But then in the parable the lost son comes to himself among the unclean beasts with whom he associates, remembering the well-being in his father's house which he has exchanged for this imminent death by hunger. He resolves, there-fore, to return to his father with a confession of his fault and a request to be received at least as a hired servant. In execution of this resolve, he sets off on his way. But the father sees him afar off, and has pity on him, and runs to meet him, and falls on his neck and kisses him—and all this before he has even uttered his confession and request, let alone proved them by corresponding actions of amendment. And beyond all this the father gives the order to clothe the one who has returned with the best robe and a ring and shoes, to bring and slay the fatted calf, and there is a great feast with music (lit. "symphonies," v. 25) and dancing, which annoys the elder son so terribly as he comes home from his conscientious labours. This is the " way back " of man, the way of man as he turns again to God in repentance and sorrow, sincerely and therefore without claim, eagerly and therefore resolutely, and as he is received and accepted again by Him without hesitation or reservation, simply because he belongs to Him, and with even greater joy than He had in him before he left. Again, there can be no simple equation of this way with that of the exaltation of Jesus Christ, of the Son of Man as He goes to His heavenly Father and is crowned by Him. Yet again—and this cannot be denied—the way of Jesus Christ is primarily and properly the way to that home of man which is not lost but remains, not closed but open ; the way to his fellowship with God ; the way on which He precedes all men as a King who draws them after Him to share His destiny ; the way to the end of which He Himself has already come, so that this home of theirs is already visible and palpable to the men who still tread it. What is the redemptive return of the lost son as seen from this standpoint ? Surely it is only a feeble reflection of the entry of the one Son of Man into fellowship with God as it took place in Jesus Christ, of the exaltation in which, without ceasing to be true man, without being divinised, but in our nature and flesh, He is at the side of the Father in heaven, participating as man in His power and glory, in the exercise of His grace and mercy. More than a copy, an analogy, a type of this entry, the way of the refound son in the parable, and therefore of the man reconciled with God, cannot possibly be. But, on the other hand, it cannot possibly be less. It cannot be more because what he himself is and does and experiences on this way back can only be a very little thing in relation to that of the one Son of Man, and even this very little does not lie within the range of his own possibilities, as though even temporarily he could set himself even in the most imperfect fellowship with God. But it is also not less because the little that he is and does and experiences is carried and therefore capacitated by the great and original and proper being and action and experience of the one Son of Man, being empowered by the fact that in Him it is a wonderfully complete reality. It is not the original. It is only a copy. But it is the copy of this original, and therefore to be understood only in its relationship to it.

But the elder brother, the scribe and Pharisee, who forms a contrast in the parable, failed to understand, not only the going out and coming in again of the younger, but also and primarily the love of their common father, as it was not diminished but increased by this twofold movement. He failed to understand, therefore, the fact that in His grace God is the God precisely and exclusively of the man who makes this twofold movement. Primarily, originally and properly, the scribe and Pharisee does not reject merely a distasteful doctrine of sin and forgiveness, but the God who is the God of this man, the man who is the man of this God, the actuality of the Son of God and His humiliation, and of the Son of Man and His exaltation, the atonement which takes place in this One. He rejects Jesus Christ. This elder brother will finally bring Him to the cross, not merely because He said about God and the sinner what is said in this parable, but because He is the man in whom what is said in this parable (beyond anything that is merely said) is actuality. What puts this figure in the parable so terrifyingly into the shadows is that it is a personification of the conflict against the actuality of the God-man. But it is better to keep before us the final saying of the father to this elder son which forms the conclusion of the parable. In v. 28 f. he had summoned his servants to prepare the feast with the words : " Let us eat, and be merry : For this my son was dead, and is alive again ; he was lost (had gone off, disappeared), and is found." And now he woos the disgruntled brother with the pressing words : " Son, thou art ever with me, and all that I have is thine. It was meet that we should make merry, and be glad : for this thy brother was dead, and is alive again ; and was lost, and is found." Yes, this is also in the text. And if there is any point where we can ask whether there is not finally a direct as well as an indirect christological reference, and therefore need of a christological exposition, it is in face of these two verses, of this " my son " and " thy brother," of this dead man who was alive again, of this lost man who was found, of the rejoicing which rings out in these words. For to whom does all this refer ? Are not the expressions almost too strong to be applied, or applicable, to the lost son of the parable and what is represented in him ? I will not press the point, but will say only that in these two verses we are invited by the text itself to the indirect, not allegorical but typological, or *in concreto* christological exposition here attempted. So much we may say, and it will have to be taken into account in even the most cautious exegesis of the parable.

To return to the main theme, the dogma and theology of the earlier Church of all the great confessions has always laid as much emphasis on the *vere homo* as on the *vere Deus* in relation to Jesus Christ— indeed, in the first two centuries it actually laid more in the conflict against docetic Gnosticism. The actuality of the atonement accomplished in Him stands or falls no less with the one than the other. If Jesus Christ is not also true man, how can the true God have condescended to us in Him ? How does He really take our place as the Son and in the power of God ? How does He do for us what only God can do for us in our place ? But what does *vere homo* mean ?

The older dogmatics answered that the Son of God really condescended to us and became like us, one of us, and took our place to do for us what only God could do for us, by assuming our " human nature," by existing in it and therefore as a man like ourselves, by dying and rising again, so that, placed as one of us at the right hand of God the Father, He became and is and will be to all eternity the Mediator between God and us men. By the " human nature " in which He who is very God is also very man we have to understand the same historical life as our own, the same creaturely mode of existence as an individually distinct unity of soul and body in a fixed time between birth and death, in the same orientation to God and fellowman. From this standpoint " human nature " means quite simply that which makes a man man as distinct from God, angel or animal, his specific creatureliness, his *humanitas*. By " human nature," however, we have also to understand the " flesh," human nature as it is determined and stamped by human sin, the corrupt and perverted human nature which stands in eternal jeopardy and has fallen a victim, not only to dying, but to death, to perishing. It is human nature as characterised in this way, adamic human nature, that the Son of God assumed when He became man, and it is as the bearer of this human nature that He was and is the Mediator and Reconciler between God and us. Jesus Christ was and is very man in this twofold sense.

The answer is both right and necessary. It is right as a description of the likeness between the humanity of Jesus Christ and that of other men. It is necessary as the delimitation which we have to make with this description against every kind of docetic Christology, in which His likeness with us is either crudely or cunningly denied, His humanity is made a mere appearance, and His deity is therefore dissolved into a mere idea, and the atonement made in Him into a philosophical theory or a myth. Every sound christological discussion will necessarily start not only with an explanation of the *vere Deus* which declares the equality of Jesus Christ with God, but with an explanation of the *vere homo* which declares His equality with us. And it will always have to keep this at the back of its mind, and take it into the strictest account in the later development of the doctrine.

But close attention must be given to the sense in which this explanation is worked out in detail. What is the *humanitas*, the true humanity, in which Jesus Christ is like us ? What is the source from which our knowledge and declaration of it must always derive ? How is it to be surely grasped 'and confidently expounded ? The same questions have to be asked concerning His deity, although we cannot pursue them now (cf. *C.D.*, IV, 1, § 59, and *passim*). After the conflicts and decisions of the 4th and 5th centuries, the older doctrine and theology of the Church came to speak predominantly of the two " natures " of Christ. But this conception was exposed to serious misunderstanding, and showed itself to be at least in serious need of interpretation. This does not mean that we have to abandon it. But we have to remember that it is fatally easy to read out of the word " nature " a reference to the generally known or at any rate conceivable disposition of a being, so that by the concept " divine nature " we are led to think of a generally known or knowable essence of deity, and by that of " human nature " of a known or knowable essence of man, the meaning of the humanity of Jesus Christ—for this is our present concern—being thus determined by a general anthropology, a doctrine of man in general and as such. Let us assume that there is an anthropology of this kind, i.e., one which is more than an attempted demonstration of certain phenomena of humanity from a particular standpoint (naturalistic, idealistic or, it may be, existentialist) ; one which can be claimed to represent in some sense authoritatively and normatively a view and concept of man as he really is, so that theology can, and indeed must, make use of its presentation at this most vital point, the description of the true humanity of Jesus Christ. It has already been shown, of course, in *C.D.*, III, 2, that there is no such anthropology. But even if there were, what embarrassment would be caused if it tried to do justice both to its own presentation and also to Jesus Christ Himself as it sought to apply it to Him : to its own presentation, which is in general categories, and claims to be generally known or knowable ; and to Jesus Christ, who claims conversely that in His true humanity no less than His true deity He may be known only in the particular way in which He gives Himself to be known. What human nature is as His, and also what " flesh " is as the human " un-nature " which He has assumed—both human nature and this perversion in which He has made it His own can be learned only with and from Him, just as it is only with and from Him, and not from a general concept of deity, that we can learn who and what God is, and therefore His divine nature. The attempt at a general anthropology, however complete and established, will always founder on the particularity in which He is man. Or it will do violence to Him with its attempt to comprehend Him in its categories. This is the *cul-de-sac* into which we must not be enticed by the concept " nature." Christology cannot and must not take as its starting-point a knowledge of man in general. On the contrary (cf. *C.D.*, III, 2, § 43, 2, and *passim*), a genuine knowledge of man in general, a theological anthropology, and therefore a theological doctrine of the sin and misery of man, can be based only on the particular knowledge of the man Jesus Christ, and therefore on Christology.

But if we keep to the particular humanity in which Jesus Christ gives Himself to be known, we must first make the formal differentiation that it is characterised by the fact that it is both completely like and yet also completely unlike that of all other men.

Jesus Christ is like us in our creaturely form, but also in its determination by sin and death ; in our human nature, but also in its concealment under the human " un-nature " which results from the opposition of man to God. He is not, then, an angel, a middle being, a demi-god. He is man. He is man totally and unreservedly as we are. He is our Brother in which each of us can and may recognise himself as His brother, but also recognise the form and aspect of every other man : the form and aspect in which God the Creator conceived and willed him and in spite of everything still knows and loves him ; yet also his form and aspect as the man who has fallen away from God and is accused by Him and perishes under His wrath, adamic man. It is the situation of man who is the good creature of God and also flesh that the Son of God made His own when He became man. He is with us in this twofold situation. And it is in this way that He is very man. He is man in this contradiction and half-light of all human existence. He would not be very man, one of us, and He could not be our Lord and Saviour and Head, if He were not like us in this totality. And we could not know Him as such if He were not visible and accessible to us in this total likeness with us. It is in this complete likeness that He gives Himself—and only He Himself gives Himself—to be known by us.

But the fact that He is not only *a* true man, but *the* true man, is not exhausted by His likeness with all other men. He is not only completely like us, but completely unlike us—and it is only when we add this complementary truth that we realise the full meaning of the *vere homo* as it applies to Him. But the unlikeness consists in what must necessarily become, and has become, of " human nature " when He assumed it in likeness with us, of flesh when it became His. It relates to the particularity of the history which took place when He became man, and still takes place as He, the Son of God, is man.

His unlikeness with us does not consist, of course, only in the fact that He is something that we are not—the Son of God, very God. Rather, because He is the Son of God, it consists in the unlikeness of

His humanity and ours. Because and as He is the Son of God, He is
exactly the same as we are, but quite differently. If we do not have
regard to the totality, we do not see what has to be seen. It is not
merely a question of His particularity as an individual, that He is
unrepeatedly and incomparably this man and not another. In this
sense, as an individual, every man is unlike all others. But the fact
that in this sense, as an individual, every man is unlike all others,
belongs finally to their common likeness. Again, it is not a question
of a quantitative unlikeness of degree between His particular humanity
and ours—the fact that in a like humanity and fleshliness He is a better
and wiser and greater and more strong and pious man than the rest.
It belongs to the common human essence in which He is like us that
there are these gradations and distinctions between individuals in both
good and evil, and they do not justify us in speaking of a total unlikeness between men. This kind of distinction has no relevance when it is
a matter of His unlikeness with us. As rationalism and relativism have
rightly perceived in every age, He cannot be called *the* true man merely
on these grounds. We cannot deny Him this kind of particularity, but
He is not completely different from us in this kind of particularity.

He is decisively and totally different from us in the fact that in
His human existence, in the history in which He became and is man,
and suffers and acts as man, there took place an exaltation of the
humanity which as His and ours is the same. In the sense in which
the word is applied to Jesus Christ in the New Testament, "exaltation" does not mean a destruction or alteration of His humanity.
It does not abolish His likeness with us, emptying it of its substance.
Nor does it mean only one of the possible changes and improvements
within the humanity common to Him and us. It means the history
of the placing of the humanity common to Him and us on a higher
level, on which it becomes and is completely unlike ours even in its
complete likeness—distinct from ours, not only in degree but in
principle, not only quantitatively but qualitatively. He confronts us
in this unlikeness because and as He is the Son of God and man as
such, like us as such. As this divine Subject which became a man—
humiliating Himself as such—He exists in a history which cannot be
that of any other man. What else can the Son of God who humbled
Himself as man become and be but the Son of Man who is not divinised
but exalted to the side of God? What else can the Lord who became
a servant become and be but the servant who became a Lord? This
is the secret of the humanity of Jesus Christ which has no parallel at
all in ours. This is the basis and power of the atonement made in
Him on this side—as it is seen from below, from man. All that will
occupy us in this chapter has its root in the exaltation of this servant
to be the Lord, of the man Jesus of Nazareth to the side of God the
Father; and this exaltation is itself based on the fact that He is the
humiliated Son of God, the Lord who became a servant.

But what does this exaltation involve ? What is this higher level on which He who is a man as we are and completely like us confronts us in this complete unlikeness ? With this question we turn from the discussion of form to that of content. Looking quietly in the direction in which we are pointed by this view and concept of "exaltation," this man, and in Him the essence of man as determined not only in its creatureliness but also its fleshliness, in its nature but also its " un-nature," is set in motion from its very centre by the act of the Subject who exists here—in a motion in which no man finds himself, or will or can find himself, in any other way. In His person, as the *humanitas* of this man, *humanitas* itself is in motion—from here to there, from the far country to which the Subject who acts here as man, the Son of God, gave Himself, back again to the home which is shown to be the home of man by the fact that the One who came from it willed to become and be the Son of Man, and to which every man may really return, and has already done so, in the person of this One. It is an " exaltation "—the movement of man from below to above, from the earth which is his own sphere, created good by God and darkened by himself, to heaven which is the most proper sphere of God, from man in his creaturely and fleshly essence, and therefore his being in opposition, to peace with God His Creator, Judge and Lord. It is the movement initiated by the fact that there took place first the opposite movement from God to man, from heaven to earth, and therefore from above to below, and that it still takes place and is an event in the person of this One. With reference always to the person of this One, exaltation means the whole of the movement initiated in this way : its commencement, fulfilment and completion. Exaltation means the history in which this movement takes place, in which this man is man. When we say " Jesus Christ," we can say only " the humiliation of the Son of God," but this is also to say " the exaltation of the Son of Man." We cannot stop at an abstract *theologia crucis*, for this is full already of a secret *theologia gloriae*. We cannot be content merely with a view and concept of the high-priestly office and work of Jesus Christ, for, as the Son of God becomes a servant and exercises this office and does this work, He enters also, as the Son of Man, upon the office and work of a Lord, the King, who is ours as He is completely like us and yet so completely unlike us in this likeness. When we say " Jesus Christ " we have no option but to look at this movement from below to above as it takes place in Him, at His exaltation—the exaltation of man as it has taken place and still takes place in Him. When we see Him we see the Father (Jn. 14[9]), but we also see the child, ourselves, man—in the full sense of the word, the true man, the man who exists in this history.

But the true, exalted man in the person of the one Jesus of Nazareth is the man whose history takes place and declares itself in its totality, in its free, spontaneous, inward agreement with the will and decree

and action of God, and therefore as a service of God, which includes
also a service of men. We must impress upon ourselves again that
this does not mean a destruction or even diminution of His likeness
with us, so that it does not take place in any situation but that which
is ours. But again, it is not merely a relative rearrangement or improvement within the possibilities open to us all. It is the exaltation
of our essence with all its possibilities and limits into the completely
different sphere of that totality, freedom, correspondence and service.
It is the human history which has this content—a content which is
so completely unlike the content of our history and world-history and
each individual history. Jesus is the man in whose human being and
thinking and willing and speaking and acting there takes place the
grateful affirmation of the grace of God addressed to the human race
and the whole created cosmos—an affirmation which we all owe but
none of us makes. He is the man who (like us in His creatureliness and
fleshliness, at all points our Brother) does not break but keeps the
covenant of God with His people in the action of His life. The opposition of human existence, the half-light in which we all find ourselves,
is not just behind Him. On the contrary, He suffers its curse and need
at a depth into which we can hardly look even by way of surmise.
But the action of His life as it begins with the commencement of His
being as man is one long invasion and conquest of this opposition and
tension. And as this invader and conqueror He is the man who is
faithful both to God and therefore also to Himself, the man who is
reconciled with God, the true man, and in relation to all the rest the
new man. In this action which is executed by God Himself, present
in the person of His own Son, He is—inevitably—the man who is
well-pleasing to God. He is the total recipient of the grace of God.
At peace with Him, He participates in His peace. Doing His will,
He is accompanied and borne by the marks of His power. As the
revealer of His mystery, He is Himself surrounded by His mystery,
but also by the light of its revelation. He is His servant, but He is
also acknowledged and attested and confirmed and proclaimed by Him
as the Lord. In humility He addresses the Word of God to men, but
in the glory of God He is Himself the answer to the otherwise insoluble
question of human existence and the human situation. " The third
day he rose again from the dead, He ascended into heaven, And sitteth
on the right hand of God the Father Almighty "—He, this man, who
is so like us in all that we are, and yet so completely unlike us in all
that He does and experiences with us in this history.

　　In general outline, this is both formally and materially the " homecoming of the Son of Man," the " exaltation " of human nature as it
took place in Jesus Christ, the history in which He is the " true "
man, and as such—this time as seen from below, from man—the basis
of the reconciliation of the world with God. Our consideration of
this happening, or of this particular aspect of the one whole happening

as it took place in Christ, obviously needs to be filled out in detail. We shall have to do this in the light of the basic outlines of the New Testament tradition concerning the human existence of Jesus Christ. But before we turn to this task, it is as well that we should consider the great theological contexts in which the specific christological concept which now concerns us has its place and meaning and power. Three aspects claim our attention : (1) its first and final basis in the divine election of grace ; (2) its historical fulfilment in the event of the incarnation ; and (3) its basis of revelation in the resurrection and ascension of the man Jesus.

I

Our first glance is to the eternal beginning of all the ways and works of God in the act of His election of grace. This aspect has already been developed earlier in our *Church Dogmatics* (II, 2, § 32) in the context of the doctrine of God. We may, therefore, summarise it with comparative brevity at this point.

We have to do with the eternal beginning of all the ways and works of God when we have to do with Jesus Christ—even in His true humanity. This is not a " contingent fact of history." It is the historical event in which there took place in time that which was the purpose and resolve and will of God from all eternity and therefore before the being of all creation, before all time and history, that which is, therefore, above all time and history, and will be after them, so that the being of all creatures and their whole history in time follow this one resolve and will, and were and are and will be referred and related to them. The true humanity of Jesus Christ, as the humanity of the Son, was and is and will be the primary content of God's eternal election of grace, i.e., of the divine decision and action which are not preceded by any higher apart from the trinitarian happening of the life of God, but which all other divine decisions and actions follow, and to which they are subordinated. As a history which took place in time, the true humanity of Jesus Christ is, therefore, the execution and revelation, not merely of *a* but of *the* purpose of the will of God, which is not limited or determined by any other, and therefore by any other happening in the creaturely sphere, but is itself the sum of all divine purposes, and therefore that which limits and determines all other occurrence.

For God's eternal election of grace is concretely the election of Jesus Christ. But this means that it is the decision and action in which God in His Son elected and determined Himself for man, and, as we have now to consider, man for Himself. It is the decision and action of God in which He took to Himself the rejection of sinful man with all its consequences and elected this man—our present theme—

to participation in His own holiness and glory—humiliation for Himself and exaltation for man. The secret, the very depth of the secret, of God's grace is that at the beginning of all His works and ways He acted in this way and not otherwise, that He elected this so strangely merciful exchange. It is the election of grace as the election of Jesus Christ. It is in the reconciliation of the world with God as it took place in time in this One that the depth of this secret, God's eternal election of grace, is manifested as the beginning of all His works and ways. It is in Him that we see this exchange. For He is both. As the Son of God He is the One who elects man and therefore His own humiliation. As the Son of Man He is the One who is elected by God and therefore to His own exaltation. He is God's eternal, twofold predestination, from which everything else, all God's other purposes and therefore all occurrence, proceed, and in which all things have their norm and end. For what God willed and did, and still wills and does, and is to will and do, is—directly in the history of His incarnate Word (and the further history to which it gives rise, and which is the meaning of this last time), and indirectly in God's fatherly rule as Creator, Sustainer and Ruler of the cosmos—the execution and revelation of this twofold predestination, and therefore of the election of Jesus Christ, the unfolding of that which is enfolded in this eternal divine decree. He, Jesus Christ, is the One who was and is and will be, of whom and by whom and to whom are all things, very God and very man.

Very man—this is what particularly interests us from the present standpoint. As we have seen, at the beginning of all the ways and works of God it is a matter of the election of grace as made in the election of Jesus Christ, of the one Son of God as electing and the one Son of Man as elected, and therefore of God's predestination as it is directed from and to this One. But this means that we have to do with the eternal resolve and will of God, with His one primal decision, not only in the fellowship of God with man as established by the free grace of God but also in the fellowship of man with God as established by the same free grace ; not only in the divine movement from above to below but also in the human movement from below to above ; not only in the act of God as such but also in the human history which it sets in train. God was not alone, nor did He work alone, at that beginning of all His works and ways. He was not without man. And that man should be there for God and in His presence, that he should be loved by Him and love Him in return, he did not need first to be created, let alone to become a sinner ; to fall a victim to death, let alone to attempt all kinds of counter-movements in this situation. The man who by the grace of God is directed to the grace of God, and therefore exalted and caught up in this homeward movement is not one who comes late on the scene and must later still make his exit and disappear. He does not exist only secondarily. He is there at the point from which all things and he himself (created last) derive in the temporal execution of the will of God. For in the eternal election of God he is with God's Son the first, i.e., the primary object and content of the primal and basic will of God. He is not, of course, a second God. He is not eternal as God is. He is only the creature of God—bound to time, limited in other ways too, unable in his own strength to escape the threat of nothingness. But as this creature—because this is what God sees and wills—he is before all things, even before the dawn of his own time. As the primary object and content of the creative will of God he is in his own way just as really before and with God as God is in His. He, too, has a basic reality in the counsel of God which is the basis of all reality. At no level or time can we have to do with God without having also to do with this man. We cannot conceive ourselves and the world without first conceiving this man with God as the witness of the gracious purpose with which God willed and created ourselves and the world and in which we may exist in it and with it. It is not the world and ourselves, ourselves and the world, who are first elected and willed by God and come into being—and then at a later stage and place this man. But He was and is there first, the One whom God has elected and willed, who is there in being. And we in the world, and our being and existence before Him, can only follow and be subject, as we are elected and willed by God in Him.

He " is the image of the invisible God, the firstborn of every creature : For by him were all things created, that are in heaven, and that are in earth, visible and invisible . . . all things were created by him and for him : And he is before all things, and by him all things consist " (Col. 1¹⁵ᶠ·). It is to be noted that the One of whom all this is said is called " the head of the body, the church " and " the first-born from the dead " in v. 18, and that according to v. 20 it can be said of Him, this αὐτός, that it pleased the Father in Him to reconcile all things to himself, " having made peace through the blood of his cross." But there could obviously be no sense in talking of the blood of the eternal Son of God as such, or of this Son as the firstborn from the dead. The declarations of predestination from v. 15 onwards cannot, therefore, relate only to the Son of God, to a λόγος ἄσαρκος.

But, again, the statement in Jn. 1² : " The same (οὗτος ἦν) was in the beginning with God," would be a meaningless repetition of the second statement in Jn. 1¹ if it were not an anticipation of the incarnate Logos attested and declared by John the Baptist in the words : " This was he (οὗτος ἦν) who coming after me is preferred before me, for he was before me " (πρῶτός μου ἦν). The result is that we cannot possibly refer abstractly to the eternal Logos either Jn. 1³ : " All things were made by him ; and without him (χωρὶς αὐτοῦ) was not anything made that was made," or Jn. 1¹⁰ : " The world was made by him." The event attested in Jn. 1¹⁴ is one to which the whole Prologue looks back. So, then, the whole Prologue (with the possible exception of the first phrase of v. 1)—although it certainly speaks of the eternal Logos—speaks also of the man Jesus. The saying in Jn. 8⁵⁸, which reaches back to the Prologue : " Before Abraham was, I am," must be understood in the same way. And nothing could be more explicit than the way in which, in Jn. 6⁵¹, " the living bread which came down from heaven " is equated with " my flesh, which I will give for the life of the world."

C.D. IV-2—2

But the same is true of Heb. 1²ᶠ·, where it is said of the Son that by Him God made the æons (the worlds), that He is " the brightness of his glory, and the express image of his person," and that He upholds " all things by the word of his power." For immediately after we are told that " when he had by himself purged our sins, he sat down on the right hand of the majesty in high," and (in v. 4) is " made so much better than the angels, as he hath by inheritance obtained a more excellent name than they." This and the many statements which follow concerning his superiority to the angels would be quite inexplicable if the reference were only abstractly to the eternal Son of God, and He were supposed to stand in need of this exaltation and the inheritance of this more excellent name. Indeed, how could the eternal Son as such be put (in v. 1) in the same series with the fathers by whom God spoke at sundry times and in divers manners ? How could it be said of Him as such that God " hath in these last days spoken unto us " by Him ? This is only explicable if, as is expressly emphasised in v. 6, the reference is to the One who is brought into the world of men, the οἰκουμένη, and therefore to the One who is both Son of God and Son of Man He as such is the One by whom God made the æons, and who upholds all things by the Word of His power.

And so the One who (in 1 Pet. 1²⁹) " verily was foreordained before the foundation of the world, but was manifest in these last times," is obviously the One of whom it is said to the readers in vv. 18–19 that they are redeemed with His blood " as of a lamb without blemish and without spot." Again, the One of whom it is said in Eph. 1⁴ that God " hath chosen us in him before the foundation of the world, that we should be holy and without blame before him " is the One of whom it is said again in v. 7 that we have redemption through His blood. Again, in Rev. 13⁸, the book of life written before the foundation of the world (which does not contain the names of those who worship the beast) is called the book of the Lamb slain. In all these predestinarian passages the emphasising of the blood, of the putting to death, of Jesus Christ is obviously inexplicable if they are referred to a λόγος ἄσαρκος, and not to the eternal Son of God and therefore also to the Son of Man existing in time.

In the divine election of grace we have to do with the Son of Man elected by the eternal Son of God and therefore with the election of the one, whole Jesus Christ. And in it, as the election of the Son of Man, we have to do with His election to a fellowship with God corresponding to God's fellowship with Him, and therefore to His wonderful exaltation to be the faithful covenant-partner of God, to an existence as the brightness of His glory, to participation in His own, eternal life, in the perfect service of His Word and work. This is what is ascribed and promised and attributed to man in this One according to the primal decision of the divine counsel. It is in this determination that man exists in this One at the beginning of all God's ways and works, and therefore at the beginning of all things with God Himself, in the primal basis of all reality, God's eternal election of grace.

What, then, are the fruits of this first discussion ? It certainly does not give us any ontological basis for the concept of the humanity of Jesus Christ which is so decisive in the development of this whole problem. It would be impossible to establish any such foundation, and the attempt to do it could only compromise a concept which does not in any case need it. The real result is to throw into prominence the theological necessity of this concept—its first and final basis in the root of all Christian knowledge and thinking. It disperses the last appearance of contingency, externality, incidentality and dispensability which can so easily seem to surround the historical aspect of the Christ-event in its narrower sense. It is essential and integral to this event that it is not only the act of God but that as such it includes a human history, the history of the true man, which means the existence of the man Jesus. This is what we learn from our glance back at God's eternal election of grace. It shows us that there can be no dissolving of the unity of this human history with the act of God with which we have, of course, to do in the Christ-event. This human history is not merely a mode or vehicle of revelation, as against which that which is revealed is something higher, non-worldly, purely divine and eternal and spiritual, so that the human history can and must be distinguished and even separated from it, withdrawing and finally disappearing as a mere economy of only provisional and practical significance.

This was how John Scotus Erigena thought and spoke in the 9th century, and he is typical of many others both ancient and modern. As he saw it, the historical aspect of revelation is present only for the sake of simple believers. It is for them the indispensable vehicle of suprasensual, transcendent ideas. But for the speculative thinker it is only an allegory which he can and must perceive and unravel. Even the earthly life of Jesus does not mark the presence of God. It only symbolises it. It does not underlie anything. It only indicates. It cannot be an original. It can only be a type. *Perit, quod videtur, quod sensibile est et temporale ; manet, quod non videtur, quia spirituale est et aeternale* (quoted from H. Reuter, *Gesch. d. rel. Aufklärung im Mittelalter*, Vol. I, p. 61, 279).

The truth is that this human history, " the earthly life of Jesus," belongs with the act of God to that which is revealed. It is manifest with it in time (" in these last days," as 1 Pet. 1[20] puts it), but it is also with it as the content of the eternal decree and will of God. It was foreordained with it before the foundation of the world. There is no divine, eternal, spiritual level at which the Christ-event is not also " worldly " and therefore this human history. The concept of the true humanity of Jesus Christ is therefore primarily and finally basic—an absolutely necessary concept—in exactly the same and not a lesser sense than that of His true deity. The humanity of Jesus Christ is not a secondary moment in the Christ-event. It is not something which happens later, and later again will pass and disappear. It is not merely for the purpose of mediation. Like His deity, it is integral to the whole event.

All that follows depends on this. Reconciled man is not merely a shadow of the reconciling God. The exaltation of God is not to be envisaged only optionally with the humiliation of God. Sanctification is not a mere appendix of justification. The edification of the Christian community is not a mere accompaniment of its gathering. Christian love is not just an incidental by-product of Christian faith. All these developments of the second problem of the doctrine of reconciliation are intimately bound up with the first, and for all the differences they are of equal dignity. Every kind of Docetism is impossible and forbidden. But everywhere this depends upon the fact that as God sees it the fellowship of man with Himself is just as basically serious as His own fellowship with man. And we can know that this is the case only if we know that in the humanity of Jesus Christ no less than His deity we have to do with the *prima veritas*, i.e., the kind of truth on which not the tiniest shadow of contingency or inferiority can be cast by any higher truth.

But if we have to do with an original and basic truth of this kind in the humanity of Jesus Christ, this means that this One is not merely one man side by side with many others. He is not just an outstanding individual by whose existence that of others is determined, but only as a possibility, contingently and not necessarily; by whose existence that of others is affected, but only outwardly and incidentally, not inwardly and from the standpoint of their being as men. If He exists as the object of the eternal election of grace at the beginning of all God's ways and works, this means that He, the true Man, is *the* One, whose existence necessarily touches that of all other men, as the decision which is made concerning them, as that which determines them inwardly and from the standpoint of their being as men, in whom and for whom they too are elect. Being made man among them, He comes to His own possession (Jn. 1¹¹). Whether they recognise it or not, He is their Head from all eternity. He can be more to them than an example. He can do that which He does actually do in the atonement, representing God to them and them to God. His history can be their own history of salvation. In this one man God can reconcile the world to Himself. And this is not only something which can happen. It is something which does happen. As the true man, the One who was the Head before the foundation of the world, He shows Himself in this happening to be the presupposition and condition of the being of all men, whose claim on their existence and promise for them are valid from the very first—even before they accept them and take up a position in relation to them—and are therefore strictly valid. It is in this strict validity that they also become temporal history. It is in this strict validity that they will to be recognised and acknowledged.

To emphasise all this, we had first to see the concept of the humanity of Jesus Christ in this predestinarian connexion. The New Testament authors whose witness we have adduced knew perfectly well what they were about when they brought out this connexion.

II

Our second glance—and this brings us to the decisive centre of this christological basis—is to the historical fulfilment of the concept of true man and therefore to the incarnation, to the being of Jesus Christ in time as grounded in God's eternal election of grace and actualised accordingly. How are we to understand the event in which this One became and was and is true man ? At this point it is relevant to lay the greatest emphasis on the act of divine majesty which is the meaning and basis and power of this event and therefore of the humanly temporal being of Jesus Christ. This alone is indeed the *ratio essendi* and *ratio cognoscendi*, the ground of being and the ground of knowledge.

It is the ground of being. This man does, of course, exist as a creature with others. In virtue of His descent from Abraham, Isaac and Jacob, from David and Mary, He belongs to the totality and shares the form of the created cosmos, participating in flesh and blood, according to the realistic phrase of Heb. 2^{14}. But that there is in the context of cosmic being the production and existence of this creature, the fact of this temporal history, is not a realisation of one of the possibilities immanent in the created cosmos. It is certainly the event which is the goal ascribed and ordained for the created cosmos in the primal divine decision in which it has its origin. It is certainly the fulfilment of the promise given to Israel in the fathers. It certainly takes place as an actualisation—the final and supreme one—in the series of cosmic actualisations grounded in God's reigning as Creator, Sustainer and Ruler over all the being distinct from Himself. But within this series—and this is what brings us to the actuality of this man— it is an absolutely new event. Within this series it takes place as this event, the existence of this man, which is not a consequence of the series, which cannot be deduced from it, but which is the work of a new act of God. This means—the work of a divine act which certainly takes place also in the series of His acts as Creator, Sustainer and Ruler of the world, and therefore in the context of all created being, but which transcends the series of His acts as Creator and therefore the context of creaturely being and occurrence, so that in it the divine action and world occurrence move into a completely new dimension as compared with everything that precedes. For the simple fact of the matter is that in this act God becomes man and the Creator creature.

God *man* and the Creator *creature* ! It is to this extent that what takes place here takes place in the sequence of His whole action, in the context of all His works, as one event among others in the history of Israel and therefore in world history. But *God* man, the *Creator* creature ! To this extent what takes place here initiates a new series in the sequence of His whole action ; and in the context of His works, in the history of Israel and therefore in world history, there takes place an event which is *sui generis*, and distinct from all others. This act of majesty is the *ratio essendi*, the ground of being of the true man, the man Jesus. He is the new man who owes His existence as such wholly and utterly to the mercy and power, the new secret of this act of majesty which at once confirms and transcends the secret of creation.

But only this divine act of majesty can be the *ratio cognoscendi*, the ground of knowledge, of this man.

He existed in time like all other men as a creature among creatures. He was a human figure in the history of Israel and world history, a concrete element in the context of all cosmic occurrence. And this means that He is also generally visible to His fellow-creatures, and may be generally located and interpreted, within the limits that this is possible to creatures. Within these limits He is not inaccessible, but accessible, to their seeing and locating and interpreting. No special eyes are needed to be aware of Him, nor is any special understanding needed to interpret Him, within the limits in which man can interpret what he sees.

All views and interpretations of the created cosmos and its history which are to any degree open and competent will always have to reckon in some sense with this figure, Jesus, and find a place and significance for Him among their subjects. Wherever He is—and He is also there as one of the elements or figures in the context and on the level of cosmic being and occurrence—He can be seen and interpreted in the manifoldness and limits of what is possible along these lines, so that there is hardly a historian who can simply ignore Him, or a philosopher who will fail to give Him appropriate consideration in a carefully subdued acknowledgment side by side with Buddha and Socrates. He can actually be known, and He is known.

But it is one thing to know, another to recognise. To recognise is to know Him as the One He—and He alone—is, as the One in whom, in virtue of His ground of being, God's act of majesty, there takes place and is that which is new and unique in the series of all other elements and figures in cosmic being and history—the fact that, without ceasing to be the Creator, the Creator Himself also becomes a creature, and therefore, without ceasing to be God, God also becomes man. To know Him as this—just this, no more and no less—is to recognise Him. But as this He obviously does not belong to the sphere of what we can see and interpret, the sphere which is identical with cosmic being and history, with cosmic elements and figures as such in their cosmic nature, and which is therefore limited by its cosmic nature. As a man, He is certainly an element or figure of cosmic being and its history, with a cosmic nature. But beyond this He is also—He alone—the Creator, God Himself, who has His ground of being in the fact that this new and absolutely unique thing takes place in Him. To the extent that He belongs to the cosmic sequence, He may well be seen and interpreted and therefore knowable and known. But no matter how sharp or deep may be the seeing and interpreting, how can the knowledge possible in this human sphere ever become recognition? Recognition of this man can obviously take place only as a new act of cognition, i.e., one which shares in the newness of His being. It must therefore be aware of the divine act of majesty which is the ground of His being in the cosmos. It must attach itself to this. It must follow and accompany it. It must repeat it. But this means that it must be motivated and derive and have its goal at the point where this man derives, where He has His particular being, and is this man within the being and history of the cosmos. This recognition will also be a human seeing and interpreting, but it will be at once sustained and motivated, limited and positively determined, at this point. It will not think that it can master this object, nor will it actually master it, but will find itself mastered by it, and accept this fact. And as such it will be true and relevant knowledge, because it will be created and controlled by its object. The presupposition of this knowledge of the man Jesus is the participation of the knowing subject in the new thing which makes this One this man within the cosmos. And the presupposition of this participation is that the ground of being of this One penetrates and transcends of itself the limits of the sphere of what we can see and interpret and know, that it discloses and declares and attests and reveals itself in this sphere. But this means that in the power and mercy of the same divine act of majesty which is the ground of His being the man Jesus speaks for Himself, expounds Himself and gives Himself to be known, so that He is no longer just confessed in a way, but known and recognised as the One He is. This means that in and with His self-disclosure He induces and initiates the human seeing and interpreting which attaches itself to the divine act of majesty in and by which He has His being, following and accompanying it, repeating the being which He has on this basis, and therefore becoming and being a relevant human seeing and interpreting (as that which is mastered by Him). The essence of the knowledge of this One is that the divine act of majesty in and by and from which the man Jesus has His being should be reflected and repeated in the human seeing and interpreting which is awakened and controlled by Him and therefore corresponds to Him. Where He is not merely confessed in some way, but known as the One He is, we always have this self-repetition and self-reflection of the divine act of sovereignty in the power and mercy of which He has His being, for this is not only His ground of being but also His ground of knowledge, and shows itself to be such, and therefore creates this regard and respect. He who is by the Holy Spirit is also known by the same Spirit. How else could He be known or expounded but in the event of His own self-exposition as it corresponds to the event of His existence ? We can only refer at this point to the fact that participation in this self-exposition, in the event of the *testimonium Spiritus sancti*, is not for everyone, but only for those to whom this *testimonium* is given as they ask for it

But we must now turn our full attention to the event of the existence of this man as such, the event of the incarnation. What does it mean that, without ceasing to be the Creator, the Creator Himself

also becomes a creature within the cosmos, that, without ceasing to
be God, God also becomes and is a man ? What kind of an historical
act is this which—as we repeat—allows and orders us to know the
man Jesus as the One He is, and therefore—which is our present
interest—as the true man ?

Our first question concerns the nature of the divine act which
takes place in this event, the divine act of majesty which we have
described as the ground of being and the ground of knowledge of this
man. We need not waste words on its character as a supreme secret.
We have said already that it both encloses and transcends the secret
of creation, that it is the great Christian mystery and sacrament
beside which there is, in the strict and proper sense, no other. We can
only try to describe it as such—or better, to interpret it—in an
attempted conceiving of the inconceivable. But the inconceivable
actually takes place in this man, and is declared and revealed and to
be conceived as such. The attempt to interpret it as a mystery cannot
on this account be omitted. If it is, the concept of the true humanity
of Jesus Christ which is grounded in this mystery will be incomplete.
We shall not really know what we are saying when we try to understand and explain the reconciliation of the world with God in relation
to reconciled man. Reconciled man is originally the man Jesus. And
the man Jesus is originally reconciled man because and as God Himself,
without ceasing to be God, willed to be and actually became man as well,
this man Jesus. The existence of this man is the work of God in which,
without ceasing to be God, He willed to be and became also this man.

Our first emphasis must fall on the words " without ceasing to be
God." This work of God, the incarnation, does not include any renunciation by God of His deity. In it He does not change Himself
into a man. Otherwise, where would be the majesty and power and
mercy of His action to this man, and, through Him, for and to us ?
Everything depends upon the fact that in the doing of this work He
is always the One He is, that He becomes and is man as God, and
without ceasing to be God. In any case, the one thing that God cannot
do is to cease to be God. He cannot change Himself into another.
But we are speaking now with reference only to Jesus Christ, to His
self-revelation and self-exposition as the true man. How could a
God who had changed Himself into a man be like us, our Brother and
Head, and therefore true man ? As such, He would not be like us at
all, but only unlike. Everything depends again upon the fact that in
His unity with God this man is in full likeness to us, and only in this
likeness unlike us, man in a very different way from ourselves. The
secret of His existence, and of the divine act which takes place in
Him, is violated and destroyed, and its relevance denied from the very
outset, if we try to see and state it in any other way, if we do not
describe the being together of G·d and man in Jesus Christ as on
both sides a real being together. It is not that in Him a changed

God who loses His deity becomes and is a changed man who loses his humanity, but the one unchangeably true God becomes and is unchangeably true man.

But we must add at once, by way of explanation, that He becomes and is *also* true man. This " also " or " as well " is safeguarded once and for all by the phrase " without ceasing to be God." But we have still to explain and expound it. Its primary importance is to describe an act of God which, as it is freely resolved from eternity, is also freely executed in time. God did not owe it to man. He did not owe it even to the man Jesus. He did not owe it either in His eternal counsel or in its execution. He did not owe it even to Himself to an inner dialectic of His Godhead. Both in eternity and in time it was the act of His divine power and mercy as it is founded only in His freedom, in His free love to the world. Only in virtue of His free decision did it take place that as true God He willed to be and became and is true man as well. This event cannot be known except from Himself, in a knowledge of His power and mercy as present and operative and revealed in this event. It has no basis or possibility, and certainly no necessity, apart from His gracious good-pleasure. Its occurrence cannot, therefore, be perceived or understood or deduced from any ontology which embraces Himself and the world, Himself and man, or from any higher standpoint whatever. It can be known only as the act which God Himself has performed and which has therefore taken place as the revelation of the will of His free grace. This knowledge is the knowledge of faith in Jesus Christ, the true man— the knowledge of the love which we owe to God who neither owed nor owes us anything, but who in His prior love for us has willed to do this and done it of Himself.

Quae erant disiuncta, hoc est Deus et homo, illo soluto vetere dissidio inter se convenerunt et rursus unita sunt mediatore Christo, qui summa cum infimis per seipsum colligavit (Polanus, *Synt. Theol. chr.*, 1609, VI, 16, *col.* 2450). Note the *per seipsum colligavit*. What God did in Jesus Christ, what the Son of God present and active in Him did, was to unite in Himself two who could not be brought together in any other way—God with man and man with God—not on any other ground or in any other power or caused and conditioned in any other way, but *per seipsum*. God in Jesus Christ founded and created this " also," His being as the One who is both very God and very man.

Relatively the most appropriate characterisation and description of this free act of God which took place in Jesus Christ is perhaps that God assumed a being as man into His being as God. He has therefore taken up a being as man into unity with His being as God—a unity which did not belong to any human being as such, to which no human being as such has any claim, into which it can enter only because and as it was the good-pleasure of God to take it up into it. It therefore owes it wholly and utterly to this assumption, and the free good-pleasure of God operative in it, that it finds itself in this unity with the being of God. But on the basis of this divine good-pleasure, and therefore of this assumption, it does actually find itself as a true human being—this is the actuality of the man Jesus—in this unity with the Son of God and His true divine being.

In this formulation we adduce and confirm the concept of the *assumptio carnis* as it was applied in all the older dogmatics to describe the incarnation. The allusion is to Phil. 2⁷ : μορφὴν δούλου λαβών and Heb. 2¹⁶ : σπέρματος Ἀβραὰμ ἐπιλαμβάνεται, where the *assumere* is obviously a parallel to the σάρξ ἐγένετο of Jn. 1¹⁴, the ἐν σαρκὶ ἐληλυθότα of 1 Jn. 4², and the μετέσχεν τῶν αὐτῶν of Heb. 2¹⁴, to which the preference was not incorrectly given in view of its relatively greater clarity in the main point at issue : *assumpsit carnem*.

This act of God—the assumption of human being to the divine, the taking up of human being into unity with His own—is exactly the same in substance (although now described positively with a reference to man) as that which in the first part of the doctrine of reconciliation we described as " the way of the Son of God into the far country," His entry into the state of humility which is proper to man, and therefore the divine humiliation as it took place in Jesus Christ. Already in that first part we laid great emphasis on the fact that God did this without ceasing to be God. He differentiates Himself from all false gods (among whom the god of Islam is especially characteristic in this respect) by the fact that He is not a prisoner of His own exalted status, but can also be lowly—not in the surrender but the affirmation of His divine majesty. It is undoubtedly a way into the far country, and includes an inconceivable humiliation and condescension and self-abasement of God, that in His Son He wills to become and does actually become also a man, and therefore enters this state which is proper to man. It is the secret of grace—God does this for our sake, in fulfilment of His turning to us—which here shows itself to be the true secret of the incarnation. But it is not the case that in this grace God does violence or is unfaithful to Himself because as God He properly cannot and ought not to do this. He exists even in Himself as God, not only in the majesty of the Father, but also and in the same reality and Godhead as the Son begotten of the Father and following Him and ordered in accordance with Him. In itself and as such, then, humility is not alien to the nature of the true God, but supremely proper to Him in His mode of being as the Son. What God does in this assumption of human being into unity with His own is of course, as an *opus ad extra*, as an act of grace of God to His creature, as His divine action in temporal history, an application and exercise and revelation of the divine humility, the newness and strangeness of which as the content of this free divine decree ought not to be put into the shade or weakened by this reference to its inter-trinitarian background. It must be considered what is implied by the *assumptio carnis*. It is not merely that God willed not to be alone, but to co-exist as the Creator with the creature. It is not merely that He willed to bind and pledge Himself to the human creature. For the reconciliation of the estranged world with Himself He, the Creator, willed to exist also as a creature Himself. He, the Lord of the covenant, willed to be also its human partner and therefore the keeper of the covenant on this side too. This is the depth to which He willed to descend from His throne, and the height to which He willed to exalt the creature man to the right hand of His throne. For what reason ? In the light of the result of this action we can and must say : Because He willed to have mercy on this creature, and did have mercy, as radically and totally as was actually the case in this acceptance, this assumption, this taking up into unity with Himself. Why ? In face of God Himself as the First and the Last we can only say : Because He is the God of this mercy, and of the power of a mercy which is so radical and total. There is no sense in trying to find or give any other reason for the fact that the Word became flesh, and therefore for this *assumptio*. We can only say that in its great inconceivability—always new and surprising when we try to conceive it—this reason is holy and righteous and worthy of God because it corresponds to the humility of the eternal Son as it takes place in supreme reality in the intra-trinitarian life of God Himself ; and although it cannot be deduced from this, in the light of it it can be recognised as a reason which is in itself both clear and well-founded.

But the reference is also not superfluous because it shows us why it is that the God who acts in the incarnation is God in His mode of being as the Son. It is He who accepts and assumes man—human being—into unity with His own divine being. It is He, the Son of God, who becomes the Son of Man. It is He who descends so deep down to man in order to lift him up so high. It is He who goes into the far country in order that man may return home. He does not do this without the Father, but, as the Gospel of John constantly reiterates, He does it as the One who is sent by the Father, with whom He is one. He takes this downward way in the omnipotence of the Father, which will be manifest even in the depths as His glory. He does it as the One who is eternally loved by the Father, and loves Him eternally in return. But all the same it is He and not the Father who becomes flesh—the one God in this second and not the first mode of being. Again, He does not do it without the Holy Spirit, but in fulfilment of the divine act of majesty which (as we are reminded by the birth-story and in another way by the story of His baptism in Jordan) is the characteristic work of the Holy Spirit. For as the eternal love between the Father and the Son, the Holy Spirit is also the eternal love in which God is the one God outwards as well as inwards, the divine principle of creation, reconciliation and redemption, the principle of the decree in which all these works of God were and are His eternal resolve. But it is the Son and not the Holy Spirit who becomes flesh. The older dogmatics was quite right when it described the incarnation as the work of the whole Holy Trinity. None of the three modes of being of God either is or works without the other two : *opera trinitatis ad extra sunt indivisa.* But if the essence of God existing in these three modes of being is one, it is that of the one personal God, and not of the three " persons " in our sense of the term. This God as such is the Subject of the incarnation, of the assumption of human being into unity with Himself and therefore with His essence. But He is this in His mode of being as the Son, and not as the Father or the Holy Spirit. For—as we had first to show— it is in His mode of being as the Son, as the eternally Begotten of the Father, and to that extent, although of the same essence, first loved by Him and then loving Him in return, as the One who is in order secondary and therefore obedient to Him, that He is the one God in His humility. It is to Him, therefore, to God in this mode of being, that the act of humility of the incarnation corresponds. It is in Him, in this eternal mode of existence of the one God, that it has its trinitarian original. It is in Him that God can be not merely the One who sends but the One who is sent, the One who practises that basic and total mercy ; that, because His free mercy wills that He should, He can break through the bounds of the divine being and descend into the depths, into the far country, the world, and there become and be a completely different being—man ; and that as man He can open the frontier, not to make man a second God, but as man, by Himself becoming and being man, to set him within this frontier, to bring him to His own home, to place him in and with Himself at the side of the Father (Jn. 1¹⁻²). This is the work of the eternal Son, determined in God's eternal decree and taking place in time, as the meaning and basis and power of the reconciliation of the world with God. It can be His work, and it must indeed be His, because He—the one God in the mode of being of the Son—in unity with the Father and the Holy Ghost, in the deepest harmony of the whole Holy Trinity of the one God—is the humble God, and therefore exalted with the Father and the Holy Ghost.

It is, then, the secret of the becoming and being of the existence of Jesus Christ that it took place and is : (1) that this One, God, the Son, became and is also man ; (2) that His existence became and is also the existence of a man ; (3) that divine and human essence [1] were and are united by Him and in Him ; and (4)—our present goal—that He raised up human essence to essence in Himself and therefore as true God became and was also true man. We have now to consider this secret of Jesus Christ from all these angles.

We will begin with what is at once the simplest and the most

---

[1] As already explained on pp. 26 ff., Barth deliberately adopts *Wesen* (essence) instead of the traditional *Natur* (nature). But " essence " is possibly an even more misleading word in English, and it must be understood strictly in the sense of intrinsic being or nature.—Trans.

difficult—the basic consideration : (1) that this One, God, the Son, became and is also man. He became and is—according to the will of God the Father, in the humility of His own freely rendered obedience as the Son, in the act of majesty of the Holy Spirit. What kind of a happening and being is this ? From the nature of the acting Subject our first lesson is that it is God's own act, the free disposing of the Creator over the creature, without cause or merit or co-operation on the part of the creature. Mankind itself has not produced Jesus Christ as the realisation of one of its possibilities. It has no cause to boast of Him with others whom it considers its best. It was not itself the active subject in His becoming. It is not the guarantor of His being. It was only there when He became—in the form of the people Israel, which was itself elected without its own co-operation or merit, and concretely in the form of Mary, who concludes the history of this people. It was not, however, Israel or Mary who acted, but God—acting towards Israel, and finally (in fulfilment of the promise given with its election) towards Mary. In all these forms man was and is only admitted and adopted into unity with the Son of God. The Pauline concept of a "new creation" (2 Cor. 5^{17}, Gal. 6^{15}) cannot be avoided as a description of this event. It is not, of course, a creation like the first one—an absolute beginning, a divine causing to be where there was nothing. Mankind, Israel and Mary were there already. It was from within the existent world—how else could He be one of us ?—that the Son assumed humanity. But is not this difference overshadowed by the fact that the world was sold to sin and death, that it was a lost world, the world of Adam ? The chosen people Israel, and Mary too, belonged to this world. What room does this leave for any co-operation of the creature in this work ? Even the *fiat mihi* of Mary is preceded by the resolve and promise of God. It confirmed His work, but it did not add anything at all to it. It confirmed the election of Israel and Mary, but it did not give it either its truth or power. In what could and can all the participation of man in this work of God, the becoming and being of the Son of God as the Son of Man, consist, but in the fact that in good or evil (and more in evil than in good) he is its object and is willing to be this ? As well for him if he is at least willing to be this ! But there can be no question whatever of man—adamic man—providing a point of contact. When we consider the freedom of the divine counsel, the uselessness of the object and above all the One who acts towards it and with it, in respect of this event we cannot possibly ascribe the least honour to anyone but Himself, but can only give and leave all the glory to Him.

In this way, then, the Son of God became and is man. It is important to look at the completed fact established in this divine act. " The Word became flesh." The eternal will of God has been done in time. It is a once-for-all perfect. We cannot go back on it, or abstract from it, or act as though it had not happened : *et homo factus est.* This is the beginning of all beginnings in Christian thinking and speaking, the presupposition of all presuppositions with which the Christian community approaches the world. When we say Jesus Christ, this is not a possibility which is somewhere ahead of us, but an actuality which is already behind us. With this name in our hearts and on our lips, we are not laboriously toiling uphill, but merrily coming down. This is where all Christian knowledge and life derive their emphasis, or they are not what they give themselves out to be. It is equally important to remember that this fact is an event. The act of God in which it is a fact, and without which it would not be, is completed; but it is completed in its occurrence as the act of God—a being which does not cease as such to be a becoming : *et homo factus est.* To celebrate Christmas is to think of the *perfectum* but with a remembrance, and indeed in the face and presence, of the *perficere* in which alone it is always actuality. To say Jesus Christ is to speak of the *perficere* which creates the fact. Jesus Christ is the name at whose remembrance the event arises as such, so that if Christian knowledge and the Christian life are worthy of the name they can never lose their astonishment at participation in the act of that becoming which—as the Son of God once became man in time—can never become past or cease to be His act. Incarnation is the actuality of this work of God. A recognition of the ultimate character of this actuality depends upon our avoidance of all abstractions.

But what is the character of this divine act, of the actuality created in this work, of this work which in its actuality does not cease to be a work ? We have already adopted a term of the older dogmatics and spoken of a unity (ἕνωσις, *unitio, unio*). We have here the becoming and being of God the Son in human essence. God the Son is the acting Subject in this event. He is this even in what has taken place and become fact. He takes human being into unity with His own. There can be no question of man himself being the ground of this unity as an autonomous principle alongside and in face of God, nor of a third principle which is superior to both God and man, to which both essentially belong in some ultimate ground, and which expresses and fulfils and realises itself in their historical unification. Even the decree in which God and man do belong together from all eternity is the decree of God, not a determination immanent to man, and not the determination of a higher integrating law superior to both God and man. And if what God willed and resolved from all eternity took place as an event between Himself and man in time, this is not partly conditioned by an act of man, nor is it the outworking of a necessity which binds Himself to man and man to Himself, but it is the work of His own free initiative and act, of His grace. The divine act of humility fulfilled in the Son is the only ground of this happening and being. On this ground the unity achieved in this history has to be described, not as two-sided, but as founded and consisting absolutely and exclusively in Him. He is the One who did not and does not will to be the One He is—the eternal Son—without also being the Son of Man ; to be exalted without being lowly ; to be at home without also being in the far country. " The Father's Son, by nature God, A guest this world of ours He trod." It is not that divine and human-creaturely essence are found and united in Him simply and directly, but that He who is " by nature God " with the Father and the Holy Ghost took human essence to Himself and united it with His divine nature. He assumed and adopted that which is so completely different from His divine nature, so alien to it. He is the One who founds and sustains this union, who makes this different and alien thing, His being as man, both possible and actual as His own. He, the eternal Word, became and is flesh. His unity with it became and is irreversible. And so the statement in Jn. 1^{14} is irreversible. As abstract declaration about flesh as the Word is quite impossible. Flesh became and is the Word only to the extent that the Word became and is flesh. The exaltation which came to man in this unity took place and is always grounded in God's humiliation. In it it *did* take place, and it *is* grounded—it is work and actuality—but only in it. Its character as work and actuality, the real divine sonship of the man Jesus, is a fact, therefore, in virtue of the initiative and act of the divine humility, and not in any other way. Hence the movement from below to above which takes place originally in this man does not compete with the movement of God from above to below. It takes place because and as the latter takes place. It takes place as the response of gratitude to the grace of God. According to Mt. $13^{31f.}$ it is the great and spreading tree which grows from the grain of mustard seed sowed in the earth.

But to the content of this divine act there also belongs its object— the different and alien and creaturely thing which in it is assumed into unity with the Son of God and His own being. This is the human being on which He had mercy and which He therefore adopted from all eternity and then in time—had mercy and therefore adopted it so radically and totally that He made it His own as the Son of the Father and also made Himself one with it. We will speak later of the unity of God and man in Jesus Christ which arose and exists in consequence. Our present question—with reference always to the act of God as such—concerns the nature of this object. We have again described it as human being. We might also use the term human nature, like the older dogmatics, so long as we are careful—when we apply the term to the humanity of Jesus Christ—to keep the expression free from any idea of a generally known *humanum*, and to fill it out only as it can be filled out in this connexion. But whether we speak of nature, or being, or essence, or kind, or simply of humanity, or like Jn. 1^{14} of " flesh," the important thing is that we should keep in the background for the moment the idea and concept of " a man." What became and is in the divine act of the incarnation is, of course, a man. It is the

man Jesus of Nazareth. But its object, that which God assumed into
unity with Himself and His being and essence and kind and nature,
is not " a man," i.e., one of many who existed and was actual with
all his fellow-men in a human being and essence and nature and kind
as opposed to other creatures, but who was and is also this one man
as opposed to all other men. For this would necessarily mean either
that the Son of God, surrendering His own existence as such, had
changed Himself into this man, and was therefore no longer the Son
of God and by nature God in the human nature assumed by Him, in
Jesus Christ, existing as man ; or that He did not exist as One, but
in a duality, as the Son of God maintaining His own existence, and
somewhere and somehow alongside as this individual man. And if,
as is not possible, we could and should accept one of these absurd
alternatives, what would happen to all other men side by side with
the one man who is the Son of God in one or other of these curious
senses ? What significance could His existence, with its special determination, have for theirs ? How far could God, in and with the adoption of this one man to unity with Himself, adopt them all ? How
far could the one Son of God be not merely *a* son of man but *the* Son
of Man, the man who could represent them all, who could plead with
God for them all and with them all for God ? The more cautious
statement : " The Word became flesh," i.e., adopted our human nature
and kind, our human being and essence, does not, of course, oblige us
to abandon the idea and concept of " a man "—we shall have to do
justice to it at the right place and time—but rather to postpone it
for the moment. This does not mean that it allows us to evade the
attack of those questions which otherwise are obviously unanswerable.
What God the Son assumed into unity with Himself and His divine
being was and is—in a specific individual form elected and prepared
for this purpose—not merely " a man " but the *humanum*, the being
and essence, the nature and kind, which is that of all men, which
characterises them all as men, and distinguishes them from other
creatures. It is not the idea of the *humanum*, in which *per definitionem*
this could exist in real men either never and nowhere or only always
and everywhere. It is the concrete possibility of the existence of one
man in a specific form—a man elected and prepared for this purpose,
not by himself, but by God (this is the point of the election and calling
of Israel and Mary). But in this form it is that which is human in all
men. It is the concrete possibility of the existence of a man which
will be like the concrete possibility of the existence of all men and in
the realisation of which this man will be our Brother like ourselves.
Because it is our being and essence, our nature and kind, which the
Son of God willed to realise and has in fact realised in this one concrete
possibility of human existence determined and elected and prepared
by Him, His existence as a human existence, as this one man, has a
direct relevance for all other men, and in all the uniqueness in which

it is an event in Jesus Christ His incarnation signifies the promise of the basic alteration and determination of what we all are as men. In Jesus Christ it is not merely one man, but the *humanum* of all men, which is posited and exalted as such to unity with God. And this is the case just because there has been no changing of God into a man ; just because there was and is no creation of a dual existence of God and a man ; just because there is only One here, " the Father's Son, by nature God," but this One in our human likeness, in the form of a servant (Phil. 2⁷), in the likeness of sinful flesh (Rom. 8³).

At this point we have reached what the older dogmatics—using the language of later Greek philosophy—described by the term *anhypostasis*, the *impersonalitas* of the human nature of Christ. Hollaz defines the term as follows (*Ex. theol. acroam.*, 1707, III, 1, 3, *qu.* 12) : *carentia propriae subsistentiae, divina Filii Dei hypostasi tanquam longe eminentiori compensata.* By ὑπόστασις, *persona*, was meant the independent existence (the *propria subsistentia*) of His humanity. Its ὑπόστασις is, *longe eminentior*, that of the Logos, no other. Jesus Christ exists as a man because and as this One exists, because and as He makes human essence His own, adopting and exalting it into unity with Himself. As a man, therefore, He exists directly in and with the one God in the mode of existence of His eternal Son and Logos—not otherwise or apart from this mode. He certainly does not exist only ἐν ἰδέᾳ, but ἐν ἀτόμῳ, *in uno certo individuo* (Polanus, *Synt. Theol. chr.*, 1609, VI, 15, *col.* 2406), in the one form of human nature and being elected and prepared and actualised by God, yet not autonomously, as would be the case if that with which God unites Himself were a *homo* and not *humanitas*. With a more emphatic regard for this *anhypostasis* of the human nature of Jesus Christ, H. Heidegger (*Corp. Theol. chr.*, 1700, XVII, 36, quoted from Heppe, 2nd edit., p. 325) defined the incarnation as the *assumptio humanae naturae in personam Filii Dei*, qua Λόγος, *Filius Dei* . . . *naturam humanam propriae* ὑποστάσεως *expertem in unitatem personae suae assumpsit, ut* Λόγου *assumentis et naturae humanae assumptae una eademque sit* ὑπόστασις, *extra quam ipsa nec subsistit unquam nec subsistere potest.*

The objection has often been raised against this theologoumenon that it seems perhaps, by what it questions, and with the *enhypostasis* indirectly maintained by it (the identity of the existence of the man Jesus with that of the Son of God), to involve at an important point a denial of His true humanity, a concealed or even blatant Docetism, since it must obviously belong to the true humanity of Jesus Christ that He should have an independent existence as a man like us. But to this objection we may reply with Hollaz (*loc. cit.*) : *Perfectio rei ex essentia, non ex subsistentia aestimanda est.* It is true enough that the *humanum* exists always in the form of actual men. This existence is not denied to the man Jesus, but ascribed to Him with the positive concept of *enhypostasis.* But it is hard to see how the full truth of the humanity of Jesus Christ is qualified or even destroyed by the fact that as distinct from us He is also a real man only as the Son of God, so that there can be no question of a peculiar and autonomous existence of His humanity.

It may also be objected, however, that the theologoumenon is superfluous. We have seen what depends on it : no less than the fact that in Jesus Christ we do not have to do with a man into whom God has changed Himself, but unchanged and directly with God Himself ; no less than the unity in which as man He is the Son of God, and as the Son of God man ; and finally no less than the universal relevance and significance of His existence for all other men. And, looking back to the beginning of our analysis of the event of incarnation, we can add that the real divine sonship of the man Jesus would obviously be true otherwise than in virtue of the initiative and act of divine humility (which is intrinsically impossible) if its object were actual otherwise than in its fulfilment and not exclusively in that fulfilment—in the fact that God the Son took to Himself a concrete possibility of human being and essence elected and prepared by Him for this purpose and clothed it with actuality by making Himself its actuality. Against the fact that God has done this in Jesus Christ, and that this can be so only in Him, as this One ἐφανερώθη ἐν σαρκί (1 Tim. 3¹⁶), protest and contradiction will always be made, and, because it is against the confessedly (ὁμολογουμένως) great mystery, *the* Christian *sacramentum*, it may claim to be relevant and even necessary from the standpoint of the unbelief which indwells us all. But the protest against the concept of *anhypostasis* or *enhypostasis* as such is without substance, since this concept is quite unavoidable at this point if we are properly to describe the mystery.

We resume the discussion with the second statement in our description of the incarnation : (2) that the existence of the Son of God became and is the existence of a man. There are not two existing side by side or even within one another. There is only the one God the Son, and no one and nothing either alongside or even in Him. But this One exists, not only in His divine, but also in human being and essence, in our nature and kind. He exists, not only like the Father and the Holy Ghost as God, but in fulfilment of that act of humility also as man, one man, this man. The Son of God becomes and is as men become and are. He exists, not only inconceivably as God, but also conceivably as a man ; not only above the world, but also in the world, and of the world ; not only in a heavenly and invisible, but in an earthly and visible form. He becomes and is, He exists—we cannot avoid this statement ; to do so would be the worst kind of Docetism —with objective actuality. Does this mean, then, that He exists as one thing amongst others, and that as such He can be perceived and may be known like other things ? Well, we cannot deny that He is a thing like this, and can be perceived and known as such, if He was and is a man in the world, with an earthly and visible form. But, of course, a man is not merely a thing or object. As a man among men he is a human Thou, and as such distinct from all mere things. Now as a Thou man is not merely an existential determination of the I, but the sum of all the objective reality of the world. And in Jesus Christ God becomes and is man, the fellow-man of all men. As God He is not merely one of many such fellow-men, nor is He merely the idea of fellow-humanity. We are speaking of " the Father's Son, by nature God." He became and is man, the fellow-man of all men ; and therefore Thou, not merely in a simple, but in a supremely objective reality, *the* human Thou, which as such is also directly the Thou of the one eternal God. It is not that a man has rightly or wrongly taken it upon himself to be the objective reality of this human Thou, and has been grasped and understood and interpreted by others as the objective reality of this Thou. The fact is rather that God Himself, in His deep mercy and its great power, has taken it upon Himself to exist also in human being and essence in His Son, and therefore to become and be a man, and therefore this incomparable Thou. God Himself is in the world, earthly, conceivable and visible, as He is this man. We have to do with God Himself as we have to do with this man. God Himself speaks when this man speaks in human speech. God Himself acts and suffers when this man acts and suffers as a man. God Himself triumphs when this One triumphs as a man. The human speaking and acting and suffering and triumphing of this one man directly concerns us all, and His history is our history of salvation which changes the whole human situation, just because God Himself is its human subject in His Son, just because God Himself has assumed and made His own our human nature and kind in His Son, just because God Himself came into this world in His Son, and as one of us " a guest this world of ours He trod."

We have again reached a point where we can see and understand a term in the older dogmatics—the particularly solemn and weighty one of the *unio hypostatica*, also called the *unio personalis* or *immediata*. This term has occupied a kind of key-position in the classical doctrine of the incarnation in all the great confessions. We shall later meet a *communio naturarum*, the communion of the divine and human essence in the one Jesus Christ without change and admixture, but also without cleavage and separation. And in this connexion we shall also come across the *communicatio idiomatum*, the doctrine which became a well-known *casus belli*, and in which an attempt was made to develop rather more precisely this communion of the two natures. But however we may understand and expound these points in detail, they all rest on the " hypostatic " union, i.e., the union made by God in the *hypostasis* (the mode of existence) of the Son. They all rest on the direct unity of existence of the Son of God with the man Jesus of Nazareth. And this is produced by the fact that in Himself this One raises up to actuality, and maintains in actuality, the possibility of a form of human being and existence present in the existence of the one elect Israel and the one elect Mary. He does this by causing His own divine existence to be the existence of the man Jesus. This hypostatic union is the basis and power of the *nativitas Jesu Christi*, of the secret of Christmas, which as such is accompanied by the sign of the miraculous conception and birth of Jesus Christ (*C.D.*, I, 2, § 15, 3), yet which is not grounded in this miracle, but in the fact that it is (ὁμολογουμένως μέγα) event. This *unio immediata*—which includes, of course, a *communio naturarum*, but does not remove or alter either the divine essence of the Logos or the human essence existing by Him and in Him—is properly and primarily and centrally the divine-human actuality as which Jesus Christ expounds Himself and wills to be expounded.

W. Bucan (*Instit. Theol.*, 1605, II, 15) has given us this definition : *Unio personalis in Christo est, qua persona Filii Dei, iam ab aeterno existens persona, assumpsit humanam naturam purissimam, propria personalitate destitutam, in unitatem suae personae et suam propriam fecit, salvis utriusque proprietatibus.* Polanus uses a rather different terminology (*Synt. Theol. chr.*, 1609, XVI, col. 2426) : *Unio personalis consistit in communicatione subsistentiae Verbi cum natura assumta, i.e. qua communicatione Verbum humanae naturae, per se ἀνυποστάτου, i.e. nullam per se subsistentiam habentis, factum est hypostasis.* That these two authors were both pronounced Calvinists is betrayed by the emphasis in their definitions on the union of the Logos with the human nature, the implied and, of course, accepted union of the divine and human natures (which is what is usually understood by the doctrine of the two natures) being hardly touched at all, or at any rate not given prominence. Polanus, who naturally had no wish to deny this truth, could even describe it (*l.c.*) very cautiously as a *figurata locutio* ; for it was not the divine nature, the *divinitas*, but the Word which became flesh. With the 16th and 17th century Lutherans, on the other hand, all the emphasis fell on this *effectus unionis*, the union of the two natures in Jesus Christ, so that we have in Hollaz, for example, the corresponding definition of the *unio* (*l.c.*, III, 1, 3, qu. 29) : *Unio personalis est duarum naturarum, divinae et humanae, in una Filii Dei hypostasi subsistentium, coniunctio, mutuam, eamque indissolubilem utriusque naturae communionem inferens.* It is evident that the centre of interest here is the *coniunctio naturarum.* Of course, it is also emphasised that this takes place in the one hypostasis of the Son of God, and that the statement about the *coniunctio* is preceded by that about the *unio personalis.* We can hardly deny this to the explanation given by Hollaz. For all their pressing interest in the *communio naturarum*, the Lutherans could as little dispute its presupposition in the *unio personalis* as could the Reformed, for all their reticence in this respect, the consequence of the *unio personalis* in the *communio naturarum.* The accents were obviously put in different places, but the two schools were agreed amongst themselves (and with the traditional Christology of the primitive and mediæval Church) that thinking must start at that proper and primary and central union and unity. In other words, they were agreed that it was miraculously and one-sidedly and self-gloriously the divine faithfulness operative in God the Son in His initiative and act of humility which was and is the basis of the actuality of Jesus Christ in His unity as very God and very man. In an estimate of the difference we can say only that the basic nature of the common perception was perhaps better expressed in the less profound but more unequivocal formulations of the Reformed.

Before proceeding further, it will perhaps be worth our while, and helpful to our own understanding of the matter, to take account of the distinctions with which the period of Protestant orthodoxy attempted to characterise the basic secret of the hypostatic union, and to bring out its uniqueness. What does *unio* mean in this context ? There are so many unifications and unions both within the sphere of the language of theology and outside it. Is what we call a *unio* as the basis of the actuality of Jesus Christ formerly equivalent to other things which bear this name ? Is there thus a *schema*, visible elsewhere, by which this *unio* is to be understood ? Are there perhaps several *schemata* of this kind ? Or is it unique even in the formal sense, and not to be understood by a *schema* acquired in other fields ? Our older dogmatics was at one in the fact that the *unio hypostatica* must be distinguished even in the formal sense from all other higher or lower unifications and unions ; that it is *sui generis*, and therefore to be understood only in terms of itself. (In what follows, I am greatly indebted to the material assembled in Heppe's well-known compendium of older Reformed dogmatics, although I am not slavishly bound to it in detail.)

(*a*) This unification is not to be understood in terms of the unity of Father, Son and Holy Ghost in the one essence of God. It does not arise and consist συνουσιωδῶς. It is not a *unio coessentialis.* It does not consist in a twofold existence of the same being and essence. It is the unity of the one existence of the Son of God with the human being and essence which does not exist without Him. Above all, although the Son is equal with God the Father and God the Holy Ghost, He is not of equal being and essence with the humanity assumed by Him. Already in the eternal counsel of God, and especially in its execution, the divine humanity of Jesus Christ is not a relationship between two equal or even similar partners, but the work of the mercy of God turning in inconceivable condescension to very dissimilar man.

(*b*) But again, the unity which arises and consists at this point cannot be regarded as a special instance of the unity in which God (including God the Son as the eternal Logos) is in any case immanently present in all things and all occurrence. It does not arise and consist οὐσιωδῶς. It is not a *unio essentialis.* In relation to the doctrine of the providence of God we may indeed ask whether the incarnation of God in Jesus Christ is not surpassed and superseded by the general maintaining and accompanying and ruling of all being and occurrence which He never relinquishes. Is it really anything more than one event within the general *concursus divinus* (*C.D.*, III, 3, § 49, 2) ? The answer to this question is that the *enhypostasis* of the human being of Jesus Christ, His existence in and with the Son of God, is sufficiently sharply differentiated from the *sustentatio generalis* in which God maintains and accompanies and rules the whole world by the fact that the existence of God is not in any sense identical with that of the world, or the existence of the world with that of God, in virtue of His creative action, but God has and maintains His own existence in relation to the world, and the world in relation to God. It is one thing that God is present in and with everything that is and occurs, that in Him we live and move and have our being (Ac. 17²⁸), but it is quite another that He Himself became and is man. Even this union and unity cannot therefore be compared or exchanged with the *unio personalis* in Jesus Christ.

(*c*) But even the becoming and being one of two men, like that between friend and friend, or the being one flesh of man and wife (Gen. 2²⁴), fall far short of constituting a *schema* by which to understand the becoming and being one of the Son of God with human being. For one thing, two self-existent persons are presupposed in those unions, which is not at all the case in respect of the latter, in the relationship between the divine Logos and human flesh (*anhypostasis*). But again, the unity between these two is very different from the oneness of mind between two friends, or of life between husband and wife, to the extent that it does not rest on a mutual agreement and power of attraction, but one-sidedly on the act of God, overcoming the distance between Creator and creature and the antithesis between Himself and man introduced by sin.

(*d*) Absolute caution is needed in respect of comparisons like the following— that the Word is in flesh like a man in his clothes, or a sailor in his boat, or glowing and heat and light in iron. The fathers occasionally used pictures like this, and they have a passing value by way of illustration. But it must not be overlooked how incongruent they really are. We have to realise that the being of the Son of God in human art and kind is not really like the external association of two realities like a man and his clothes or a sailor and his boat, nor like the relationship between a substance like iron and its properties of glowing and heat and light, so that it has no real analogies in the proportions of these relationships.

(*e*) Again, the hypostatic union cannot be understood according to the *schema* of form and material, or idea and phenomenon, or transcendental truth and empirical reality, or spirit and nature, or finally heaven and earth. All these antithetical concepts betray themselves by the fact that their members are mutually necessary, that they are complementary, that they can be thought of only in their mutual antithesis, and that they therefore denote and comprehend secondary antitheses within the world. But the union in question is not at all like this. In the union between the Logos and flesh in Jesus Christ we have a union of the primary antithesis between God the Creator and man as he is determined for existence within these secondary antitheses. The Son of God does not need His humanity as form needs matter, or idea phenomenon, or transcendental reason empirical being, or spirit nature or transcendence existence (if it is to be actual), or heaven the conceivable earth (if it is to be the inconceivable heaven). The Son of God does not need any completion, any concretion, any form which perhaps He lacks. He is not an abstraction which follows something real and is attained by the interpretation of it. Nor is He an empty *prius* which waits to be filled out by something actual. He does not need the action of another to be who He is in reaction to it, nor the reaction of another to be who He is in His own action. He is not like Hegel's absolute spirit who can develop to a synthesis only in thesis and antithesis. He is actual in Himself—

the One who is originally and properly actual. And as such He is true in Himself—the One who is originally and properly true. He is the origin of all truth and actuality. In Him is the fulness of all forms and contents, the unity of form and matter, reason and being, spirit and nature, transcendence and existence, or however else we may describe it. He is the Creator and Lord of heaven and earth. And it is as such that He makes His existence that of another, of the man who is bound by all these antitheses and concerned to bridge them. What can He expect of this other ? What can this other give Him ? Divine faithfulness and mercy alone are the ground and basis of His giving Himself to existence as this other, as a man, and therefore to be the Mediator between God and all men. It need hardly be said that the modern misuse of the word " incarnation " in both religious and secular speech—which is even worse than that of the word " creation "—cries out aloud to heaven. There is the constant substitution of apparent mysteries for the one true mystery. There is the constant cry " incarnation " or the assertion that it has taken place and is real at this point or that. And all the time it is perfectly obvious that what is meant is simply an attempted and supposedly achieved union in the sphere of these complementary and secondary antitheses within the world. Here if anywhere sober thinking must be quite resolute in its flat and unqualified rejection of a comparison of these unions with the *unio hypostatica* in Jesus Christ.

(*f*) But what about the comparison of this *unio* with that of the soul and body in man ? Apparently influenced by a dictum of Athanasius, no less a theologian than Calvin (*Instit.* II, 14, 1) thought that he had found in this relationship the *aptissima similitudo* of the mystery. For man exists in the unity of these two " substances," and in such a way that each maintains its own nature within the unity. The soul is not the body, nor is the body the soul. There are many things that can be said only of the body, many only of the soul. Yet properties of the soul can also be found in the body, and properties of the body in the soul. The whole man who consists of both soul and body is one man and not two. Later Reformed theology, however, did not follow Calvin in this respect, and rightly so. In the argument for the comparison as he states it, it is immediately apparent that he does something here which he least of all ought to have done. For he is obviously thinking only of the conjunction of the divine and human natures in Jesus Christ, leaving quite out of account the basis of this union in the *unio personalis*. From the latter point of view, however, the conjunction of the divine and human natures in Jesus Christ is very different from the unity of soul and body. If we do not think in the abstract way of which Calvin is strangely guilty in this case, we shall see at once that in the unity of soul and body (cf. *C.D.*, III, 2, § 46) there is lacking the one factor which is quite essential if there is to be any formal likeness to the unity of the divine and human in Jesus Christ—the soul does not assume the body into unity with itself and in this way give it existence, i.e., its own existence. It is true enough that man is the ruling soul of a subservient body, and that he is both, and therefore one whole man, only in this relationship. It is also true that there is no body without the soul. But in this case the reverse is also true—that there can be no soul without the body. Obviously, however, there is no place for this reversal in the unity of the divine and human in Jesus Christ. The divine nature in the existence of God the Son is indispensable to the human, but the human is not indispensable to God the Son and therefore to the divine nature, whereas in the case of soul and body the subservient body is just as indispensable to the ruling soul as is the ruling soul to the subservient body. It is advisable, therefore, not to press this comparison, or to try to understand the unity of God and man in Jesus Christ in the light of it.

(*g*) There was and is an obvious temptation to compare the *unio hypostatica* in Jesus Christ with what the older dogmatics called the *unio sacramentalis*, i.e., the concurrence, on the basis of the divine institution and a divine act, of a divine and human, an outward and inward, a visible and invisible operation and reception of grace in the " sacramental " actions of baptism and the Lord's Supper. Does not this twofold operation and reception—the unity achieved by the Holy Spirit of what takes place really as an inward operation and reception and outwardly in sign—correspond exactly to the one being and operation of Jesus Christ in His two natures, the divine and the human ? Do we not need formally the same affirmations, and the same qualifications, for an understanding in both cases ? Is it accidental that the christological controversy within Protestantism ran parallel with the sacramental, and had in it, indeed, its historical starting-point ? The comparison is obviously striking, and it may be accepted so long as we realise that there is no sacramental union and unity at all as distinct from the unity of God and man in their unity as it is grounded and achieved in Jesus Christ. Was it a wise action on the part of the Church when it ceased to recognise in the incarnation, in the *nativitas Jesu Christi*, in the mystery of Christmas, the one and only sacrament, fulfilled once and for all, by whose actuality it lives as the one form of the one body of its Head, as the earthly-historical form of the existence of Jesus Christ in the time between His ascension and return ? Has it really not enough to occupy it in the giving and receiving of this one sacrament, whose actuality it has to attest in its proclamation and therefore in baptism and the Lord's Supper, but whose actuality it cannot represent or repeat in any other way either in its preaching or in baptism and the Lord's Supper ? However we may understand these " sacraments " (and then, of course, the sacramental character of the Church and its action), what was it that really happened, that was hazarded and achieved, when particular sacraments, or a particular sacramental action and being, were placed alongside that which took place in Jesus Christ ? It was quite in order that in the 16th and 17th centuries appeal was made to Christology in explanation and confirmation of a sacramental concept already presupposed to be legitimate. The only thing was that no one took the opportunity to ask whether the presupposed concept taken over from the Roman Church was really legitimate. We cannot pursue the question at this point. It is obvious, however, that the comparison of the *unio personalis* (and the *communio naturarum* in Jesus Christ based upon it) with the *unio sacramentalis* was actually made, and can only be made, on the presupposition that the institutions of baptism and the Lord's Supper, and their administration in the Church, are regarded as the ordering and fulfilment of this representation and repetition, i.e., of the repeated actualisation of the incarnation, and therefore as a sacrament alongside and after it in this sense. In other words, it is presupposed that the Church itself is a kind of prolongation of the incarnation. If this presupposition is not legitimate, then we can only say that the true *unio sacramentalis* is the *unio personalis* in Jesus Christ, and that the comparison is therefore left hanging in the air.

(*h*) The older Protestant dogmatics was already asking whether the unity of God and man in Jesus Christ does not have its most appropriate formal counterpart in what was then called the *unio mystica*, i.e., the presence of grace in which God can give Himself to each individual, or assume the individual into unity of life with Himself, in the Christian experience and relationship. But it was not suspected at that time how fatally productive would be the theological possibility touched at this point. The line of thought is that the personal life of faith of the Christian, understood as the supreme and most perfect form of the religious life, is a repetition of the being of God in Jesus Christ—a correspondence to it. It is, therefore, from this repetition and correspondence in the being of man with and in God, as it is most purely represented in Christianity, that we may most naturally and accurately know the being of God in Jesus Christ. This is the way in which Donald Baillie (*God was in Christ*) has recently approached Christology, attempting a new interpretation of the famous Chalcedonian definition. As he sees it, a text like Gal. 2[20] : " Nevertheless I live ;

yet not I, but Christ liveth in me," is not merely a statement about the being of the apostle or the Christian, but it offers a *schema* for the knowledge of Jesus Christ Himself. And, of course, this is not a new discovery. On the contrary, we may say that this is the secret *via regia* of all Neo-Protestant Christology—except that it has not always pressed forward from this point to the Chalcedonian definition. And somewhere along this way the question can and will always arise whether the relationship between the *unio hypostatica* and the *unio mystica* may not be reversed ; whether it is not better reversed ; whether the *unio mystica* is not to be understood as the true and basic phenomenon, the *analogans*, and the *unio hypostatica* in Jesus Christ as the secondary, the *analogatum*, the representation or mythological copy of the *unio mystica*, of the religious happening as it takes place in us.

With great accuracy and resolution A. E. Biedermann, who was undoubtedly the greatest exponent of Neo-Protestantism after Schleiermacher, described the relationship between the two unions as follows (*Chr. Dogmatik*, Vol. II, 1885, § 788 ff.). The principle of divine sonship is the subject of the content of which Church Christology tried to explain in the form of determinations of the person of Jesus Christ. The latter is certainly to be understood as a source, but only as a source, at which this principle, this relationship between God and man, has entered humanity as an essentially new religious force (§ 792). Divine humanity, as ascribed by the Church only to Jesus Christ, means generally divine sonship : " The real unification of divine and human essence to the real unity of the personal spiritual life, in which the essence of God finds its full revelation for man, and the essence of man the fulfilment of its true determination in God " (§ 795). But why " divine sonship " ? Because in the absolute religious self-consciousness actualised and made historically effective in Jesus Christ, the absolute spirit is the creative ground of a life of the spirit actualising its absolute spiritual life outside itself, in creation. It is, therefore, the " Father." And in the same absolute religious self-consciousness man finds in the self-expression of God the ground of his own essence and life. He therefore sees himself to be the son of this Father (§ 800). All the determinations of the God-man Jesus Christ as developed by the Church are thus determinations of this relationship between the absolute and finite spirit which entered history for the first time in the religious personality of Jesus (§ 801). He is, therefore, the model, but only the model, achieved for all ages in world history, of the effectiveness of the principle of redemption. His Gospel is the vehicle, but only the vehicle, of the whole Christian proclamation of basic salvation (§ 816). It is in this light that we have to estimate the statements of Church Christology, and to fix what is really meant by them. What is the true deity of Jesus Christ ? It is a necessary expression of the truth that the absoluteness of the spirit which expresses itself in the consciousness of divine sonship is no less than the revelation of God, of the absolute spirit (§ 820). And what is His true humanity ? It is the expression of the truth that the absolute religious self-consciousness of divine sonship is also the true and full actualisation of human essence in which even its sensual presupposition in nature comes to the fulfilment of its destiny as a subservient means (§ 821). What, finally, is the unity of the two natures ? With a kind of reminiscence of Chalcedon, but formulated with a reference to the absolute religious self-consciousness instead of pictorially and mythologically, it is an expression of the truth that in this the absoluteness of the spirit and the creaturely finiteness of the Ego form the two elements, distinguishable in logic but inseparable in fact, in the one personal life-process of the self-consciousness of divine sonship (§ 822). This is how Biedermann states the matter, and we have selected him only as a spokesman for many others.

There can be no doubt that this is a very impressive account. But its appearance of smoothness is only deceptive. It derives this smoothness from the fact that, as in the case of the *unio sacramentalis*, the concept which in this account is balanced against that of the divine humanity of Jesus Christ so powerfully that this as such can be only the basic vehicle of the whole Christian proclamation of salvation—the concept of the *unio mystica*, or the absolute religious self-consciousness—has been quietly and secretly filled out in a way which we can only describe as highly questionable. Anything and everything can pass for what it calls divine sonship. A full revelation of the essence of God for man, and at the same time a true fulfilment of the determination of man in God ! An absolute life of the spirit which is actualised in the life of the creature and in which man also discovers the basis of his own essence and life ! A life-process in which the absoluteness of God and the finitude of the creaturely Ego are to be distinguished only in logic as two elements which are in fact inseparable ! We could hardly go further. Chalcedon itself has become the description of what is supposed to be the content of Christian experience and consciousness (and Chalcedon in what is unmistakeably an Alexandrian, a Cyrillian and—there in the bright daylight of 19th century Zurich—a Lutheran understanding). It need not surprise us that filled out, or blown up, in this form the concept could be brought into some kind of parallelism and proximity to that of the divine humanity of Jesus Christ, being not only compared to it, but even given the priority and precedence. And the execution of the whole operation is not in any sense artificial once this presupposition is accepted. But can we really accept this presupposition ? What kinship is there between this absolute religious self-consciousness and what is called divine sonship and sanctification in the New Testament, emerging as the faith and love and hope of Christians ? Do we not have here an exchanging of ultimate things for the penultimate to which even our little portion of Christian self-consciousness also belongs, of the act of God for its reflexion in the existence of man as determined by it ? It is remarkable that a cautious mind like Biedermann's does not seem to have noticed that what he allots and ascribes to the Christian in these sections—giving away as plainly as he could the whole secret of Neo-Protestantism right up to its modern culmination in Bultmann—is the one great illusion of religious arrogance and the most venturesome of all myths—a product that we can only really describe as the work of a rationalistic enthusiasm bordering on lunacy. It is only at this cost and in this enthusiasm that the actuality of Jesus Christ can be equated with what the better Christian can know and experience as his *unio mystica* with God. Even Donald Baillie ought to have considered this before he too—quite innocently, of course, and without being guilty of the flagrant extravagances of Biedermann—made it his business to try to interpret Christ in the light of the Christian rather than the Christian in the light of Christ. Paul himself did not say that God lives in me, but Christ. And this will always be the language of a mysticism—if we must use the term at all—which has a proper sense of proportion. The Christian does not claim the fulness of the union of God with man for his own experience and self-consciousness, but professes that other, the Mediator, in whom it has taken place for him. He can therefore differentiate the Giver and gift of grace from himself as the recipient and from its outworking in his own life. But if this differentiation stands, it means the end of that equation or identification. And, as at the former point, we may even reverse the statement and say that the *unio personalis* of Jesus Christ is itself alone the true *unio mystica*—which means again, of course, that any comparison between them is left hanging in the air.

If appearances do not deceive, this excursus has had the result and conclusion of directing us to a material insight of decisive importance. The fact that the existence of God became and is also in His Son the existence of a man—the *unio hypostatica* as the basic form of the Christ-event—seems to dispense with formal analogies altogether, according to the general drift of our discussion. Is this only an appearance ? Is it that we have not yet found the true analogy ? Or is it necessarily the case that there is no such analogy ? When the older dogmaticians had all these deliberations behind them, and their readers waited perhaps, as some of ours may do, for a final and positive thesis, they made a very surprising move by simply giving a fresh definition of the *unio hypostatica* itself, the assuming and assumption of human nature into unity with the Son of God, its existence in and with His existence. What was the point of this? It was obviously that in Jesus Christ we have to do with an event and being which, as the direct revelation of God, not only speaks for itself, but speaks also for its own uniqueness, i.e., for the fact that it is analogous only to itself and can be understood only in terms of itself. We may, of course, like Biedermann and many others before and after him, misunderstand Jesus Christ as the representation and vehicle of a general divine-human (or divine-worldly) principle, and therefore as an exemplary " religious personality." Where this is the case, the search for analogies to what took place and is actual in Him will, of course, meet with success. Principles and the personalities which represent them do have analogies, and can therefore be understood in other terms than their own. But we cannot really know Jesus Christ without realising from the very outset the futility of this search for analogies, and the inadequacy of all analogies to His own becoming and being.

To be sure, certain analogies to the relationship between God and man, God and the world, are established and made possible in His becoming and being. One such is the relationship between heaven and earth described in Gen. 1^1 and often mentioned later in both Old and New Testaments. Again, the being of man as husband and wife (Gen. 1^{27}) is expressly described as a picture of the living God of Israel in His action and co-existence with man and the world. The relationships of father and child, king and people, master and servant, frequently emerge in the Bible as correspondent to this relationship. Everywhere analogies have their proper place where it is a matter of a consideration and understanding of the covenant as it was willed in God's eternal counsel and fulfilled in time in the incarnation of His Word. Again, in the connexion with their earthly surroundings the fulfilment of the covenant, Jesus Christ and the kingdom of heaven are all open to comparison. In this connexion they are obviously made a subject of comparison in the New Testament. But in Jesus Christ Himself—and it is of Him that we now speak—we have to do with the eternal basis and temporal fulfilment of the covenant and therefore with the ground and basis of all the natural and historical relationships in which the covenant is reflected as the basic relationship between God and man, God and the world, and in which it has therefore its analogies. We have to do with the presupposition of the connexion in which it can also be a subject of comparisons. In Him we have the basic reality which underlies the possibility of the basic relationship of the covenant, and therefore all the natural and historical relationships, and in them the analogies, and therefore His own connexion with His earthly surroundings and the comparisons which it invites. In Him we have their beginning, their meaning and their goal, the centre which unites and carries the whole, both creation and the covenant. This centre is the divinely established unity of existence between Himself and man, the *unio hypostatica* in the one Jesus Christ. But as a wheel with its different spokes can have no spokes in the centre, so in this centre of creation and the covenant, the origin even of its own connexion with its earthly environment, there cannot be a relationship between God and man, God and the world, which is comparable to natural and historical relationships, having an analogy or likeness in relationships of this kind. That the Creator became a creature, the Lord a servant (and as a servant, and the Brother of all other servants, genuinely the Lord), the divine I a human Thou, God's existence the existence of an essentially different man—in other words, the becoming and being of Jesus Christ—cannot be understood and apprehended, either in advance or afterwards, by means of any reflexion which looks beyond Him or from any neutral place apart from Him. With a strange, one-sided, self-glorious spontaneity, we have to do here with the work and action of the faithfulness and omnipotence and mercy of God Himself, which has no ground of reality except in Himself, or ground of knowledge except in His self-revelation. We have seen that in His work and action God is primarily true to Himself; that He can do this work as the eternal Son of the eternal Father. But not even in the being of the triune God is there any analogy for the fact that He does actually do it. We cannot deduce and understand it even from that point, as though God were under a necessity to do it. In relation to God as to man it can be acknowledged and recognised and confessed only in the light of the fact that this event has actually taken place between God and man, that it is a real fact grounded in the free and eternal counsel of the divine will and accomplished in the divine omnipotence. The incarnation of the Word is this fact, without precedence, parallel or repetition either in the divine sphere or (much less) in the human, natural and historical creaturely sphere. The incarnation of the Word is the great " Thus saith the Lord " to which theology can give only the assent that it has heard it and understood it as such, from which all reflexion which seeks and discovers analogies can only derive, but to try to subject which to analogies either in earth or heaven is quite nonsensical. *Humana ratione doceri aut accipi non potest : quod nullum eius in tota natura perfectum et omnino respondens existet exemplum, quamvis recta ratione non pugnet : verum divinitus e scriptura doceri et probari, oculisque fidei accipi debet (Leiden. Synopsis,* 1624, 25, 3).

Yet—without relapsing into the way of thought which we have critically rejected, but in elucidation of the main statement thus characterised in its uniqueness—we can and must conclude on a positive note. When we say Jesus Christ, and therefore speak of the existence of the Son of God in human nature as it was actualised in Him, we certainly speak of the One who exists as this man and in this way, but we do not speak of One who is alone as such, who became this man and existed in this way for Himself. When we say Jesus Christ we say Jesus Christ and His own—those who are co-elected by Him as the Son of God and in Him as the Son of Man. We say Jesus Christ and His community, Jesus Christ as the Head of His body, Jesus Christ in both His heavenly and also His earthly-historical form of existence. His existence takes both the one form and the other. He has the one as the One, the Head, for Himself. And He has the other, again as the One, the Head, but in and with His body, His people, His community. The relationship between these two forms of His existence is not so much comparable as indirectly identical to the relationship between Himself as the eternal Son of God and His being as man. As we have seen already, the human nature elected by Him and assumed into unity with His existence is implicitly that of all men. In His being as man God has implicitly assumed the human being of all men. In Him not only we all as *homines,* but our *humanitas* as such—for it is both His and ours—exist in and with God Himself. And where this is known in faith by the awakening power of the Holy Spirit, there arises and is, not a second Jesus Christ, a second Head, but the second form of His one existence, His people as the second form of His body, the community of those who, as they look to Him, are united with Him by the Holy Spirit in faith and love and hope, finding their own humanity caught up in His, and therefore exalted as such into existence in and with God. This people, this community, is the form of His body in which Jesus Christ, its one heavenly Head, also exists and has therefore His earthly-historical form of existence. It is of human essence—for the Church is not of divine essence like its Head. But it does not exist in independence of Him. It is not itself the Head, nor does it become such. But it exists (ἀνυπόστατος and ἐνυπόστατος) in and in virtue of His existence. It lives because and as He lives, elected and awakened and called and gathered as a people by Him. It is His work, and it exists as His work takes place. Not for a single moment or in any respect can it be His body without Him, its Head. Indeed, it cannot be at all without Him. It does not exist apart from Him. It

exists only as the body which serves Him the Head. For this reason—for otherwise it would have a separate and autonomous existence—it cannot even be His
likeness or analogy. We cannot speak, then, of a repetition or extension of the
incarnation taking place in it. But He, the one Jesus Christ Himself, exists as
man. He exists not only in heavenly form, but also in earthly-historical form.
To His heavenly form of existence as Son of God and Son of Man He has assumed
this earthly-historical—the community as His one body which also has this
form. He carries and maintains it in this unity with Himself as the people
which not merely belongs to Him but is part of Himself. In God's eternal
counsel, in His epiphany, and finally in His revelation at the end of the age,
He was and is and will be this *totus Christus*—Christ and Christians. And these
two elements of His one being are not merely related to one another *as* He Himself as Son of God is related to His human nature. But, in this second form, His
relationship to His body, the community, *is* the relationship of God and man as
it takes place in this one being as Head and body. Thus the community of Jesus
Christ can be that which the human nature of its Lord and Head is. It cannot
and must not be more than this. There can, therefore, be no question of a
reversal in which either the community or the individual Christian equates himself with Jesus Christ, becoming the subject where He is only the predicate.
There can be no question of a divinisation of the Church or the individual Christian
which Jesus Christ has only to serve as a vehicle or redemptive agency. All this
is cut away at the root and made quite impossible by the fact that He Himself
is the Subject present and active and operative in His community. " Christ
liveth in me." He Himself lives in this His earthly-historical form of existence,
in the community as this form of His body. We shall return to this comprehensive character of the humanity of Jesus Christ as the *totus Christus* when
we have again to speak of the Church. For the moment this reminder of the
totus Christus has the significance only of bringing out the positive side of the
frontier at which the incarnation as a hypostatic union is to be known in its
uniqueness as compared with all other unions. The reminder of the unity of
Jesus Christ as the Head with the community as His body does not violate this
frontier, but confirms and strengthens it.

From the second statement, that the existence of the Son of God
became and is also that of a man, the man Jesus of Nazareth, there
follows the third, (3) that in the one Jesus Christ divine and human
essence were and are united. This statement brings us to the doctrine
of the two natures in the strict sense. It says something which cannot
be relinquished and therefore cannot be evaded. It is not the mere
shibboleth of a correct knowledge of Jesus Christ. It is a consequence
of the two preceding statements about the action of God the Son,
His existence in human essence, the real exaltation of our human
essence as it has taken place in Jesus Christ. It could be a shibboleth
only in opposition to an obsuring or denial of the insight which underlies it and from which it derives. In itself, however, it has the character
only of an unavoidable transition. The particular dislike for it in
modern Protestantism—as for a shibboleth of so-called orthodoxy—
speaks less against it than against those who have brought the
charge. Obviously it cannot be understood if there is neither
the ability nor the desire to know either its origin or its goal.

By divine and human essence (the equivalent of divine and human
" nature," or quite simply divinity and humanity) we mean on the

one hand that which Jesus Christ has in common with the Father and the Holy Spirit as the Son of God, that which distinguishes His being and its nature from the being and nature of man, and of all other reality distinct from God, with an absolute (and infinitely qualitative) distinction ; and on the other hand that which (even in His exaltation) He has in common with all other human creatures as the Son of Man, that which marks off His being and its nature from the being and nature of God in His eternal modes of existence as Father, Son and Holy Spirit, and in His position and function as Creator and Lord of all things, with what is again an absolute (and infinitely qualitative) distinction.

It is apparent at once that divine and human essence cannot be united as the essence of one and the same subject. Offence at the statement that Jesus Christ is the One who is of divine and human essence, in whom the two are united, is quite unavoidable. However we may define divine and human essence, unless we do violence either to the one or the other we can only define them (with all the regard we may have for the original divine reference of human essence) in a sharp distinction and even antithesis. The statement that Jesus Christ is the One who is of divine and human essence dares to unite that which by definition cannot be united.

But if it is true that in Jesus Christ the existence of the Son of God became and is also that of a man, the statement must be ventured —although not, of course, *in abstracto*, not in a vacuum, not as the assertion of a general truth that that which by nature cannot be united, divine and human essence, may perhaps be united in a particular subject, but *in concreto*, in the encounter with this one Subject, in the acknowledgment and recognition and confession of its particular truth. This Subject, the one Jesus Christ, demands this statement, not as a statement about the possibility of uniting that which cannot be united, but as a statement about the uniting of that which is otherwise quite distinct and antithetical as it has actually taken place and been achieved in Him. How could there be a Jesus Christ, the One who as the Son of God exists also as man, if this uniting had not taken place, and did not still take place, in Him ? In the encounter with Him, are we not forced to acknowledge and recognise and confess that this uniting has actually happened in Him, and that (cost what it may) this statement must therefore be ventured ? It would, of course, be a rash and illegitimate venture if it were made only as a general statement, a general truth, about the metaphysical union (and its possibility) of the divine and the human. As such, it could only be described as a product of that rationalistic enthusiasm bordering on lunacy. But it is not the classical doctrine of the Church, only its later speculative interpretation, which understands it in this way, generalising it, relating it to the inward experience of the individual Christian. The classical doctrine of the two natures speaks of the one

Jesus Christ, and only of Him. And it does this *a posteriori*, with a reference to Him, to the Son of God actually existing in the flesh. It does not derive from a known *a priori*, a superior possibility, but only from the given actuality, from Him Himself. In this genuine sense and understanding the statement about the two natures is only the childlike venture of faith. Indeed, it is better not understood as a " venture," but much less pretentiously as obedience. It is the expression of a realism determined by this object. And in face of this object this realism will not allow itself to be disturbed by any general considerations and their results, which are obviously impossible in this connexion. Instead of subjecting this object to an alien law, it will allow its law to be dictated by this object.

In our last quotation from the *Leidener Synopsis* about the nature of the incarnation as an event which has no analogies and can therefore be known only in its self-revelation, there occurred the quite incidental observation : *quamvis recta ratione non pugnet*. The *recta ratio* which is not denied here, and therefore does not need to pick a quarrel, is not the *ratio* which is bound by the authority of Church dogma and therefore unfree, but the *ratio* which is directed to this object, which is determined by it, and therefore free in relation to it, and not burdened by any general considerations and their results. Offence at the statement about the union of the two natures in Jesus Christ is unavoidable only for a thinking which is unconditionally bound by certain general presuppositions. This unconditional binding, whether by Church dogma or general logic and metaphysics, is not proper to *recta ratio*, to a thinking which is basically free. *Recta ratio* is reason as it is ready for the realism demanded of it in face of this object, and therefore free reason—free in relation to this object. The so-called " free " scholarship of the 19th century, which was the supreme and final norm, e.g., for Biedermann, was in fact a scholarship betrayed from one bondage to another, and therefore not free, and not the typical exercise of *recta ratio* which it was for so many years considered to be, both by itself and generally.

From the unity with His own existence into which the Son of God assumes human essence while maintaining His own divine essence, there follows, as we have said, the union of divine and human essence as it has taken place and been actualised in Him. Jesus Christ, then, does not exist as the Son of God without also participating as such in human essence. And He does not exist as the Son of Man without participating as such in the essence of the Son of God and therefore in divine essence. On both sides there is a true and genuine participation. It is true and genuine in virtue of the act of God the Son, which has its basis and power in His being, in His eternal unity with the Father and the Holy Spirit. He in His divine essence takes part in human essence—so radical and total a part that He causes His existence to become and be also the existence of the man Jesus of Nazareth. Again, He gives to the human essence of Jesus of Nazareth a part in His own divine essence as the eternal Son who is co-equal with the Father and the Holy Spirit. This two-sided participation, and therefore the union of the two natures in Him, arises and consists, therefore, from Him. Hence it is " from above to below," and only then (and as we have seen, in a way which is characteristically different) " from below to above." It is two-sided, but in this sequence, and in the differentiated two-sidedness which this and the difference of the two natures involves. The Son of God, and His divine essence, does not need to have a part also in human essence. But He gives Himself in this man to human essence, and makes it participant in His divine essence. And the man Jesus of Nazareth does not take it upon Himself, as in an act of robbery, to be the Son of God and therefore participant in divine essence. Both are given to Him by free divine grace, so that His being in this exaltation can consist only in an action of the most profound human thankfulness. The unification of divine and human essence in Him, the One, and therefore His being as very God and very man, rests absolutely on the unity achieved by the Son of God in the act of God.

But as it rests on this unity, and is its direct consequence, it is clear that it is not itself a unity, but a union in that two-sided participation, the *communio naturarum*. In the one Subject Jesus Christ divine and human essence is united, but it is not one and the same. This would presuppose one of three things : that God had ceased to be God and changed Himself into a man ; that man had ceased to be man and become God (if anything, an even more dreadful thought) ; or (worst of all) that there had been formed of divine and human essence a third and middle thing, neither God nor man. But none of these corresponds to His picture as it emerges clearly in the New Testament witness. In acknowledgment, recognition and confession of the actuality of Jesus Christ neither the first, the second nor the third could or can be thought or said of Him. He is both together, in a true and genuine union, but without destruction either of the one or the other, the Reconciler and Mediator between God and man, the One who restores and fulfils the divinely instituted covenant between God and man. He is of both divine and human essence : " Very God, born of the Father in eternity, and also very man, born of the Virgin Mary " (Luther). The unity in which He is both demands this " and also," and therefore the idea of union, with its presupposition of the genuine distinctiveness of divine and human essence, and therefore the rejection of the thought of any identification or identity of the two. In this context unity would not say any more than union. Not only would it say much less, but it would completely miss the actuality of Jesus Christ and speak only of a figment of the imagination.

The first part of the Chalcedonian definition is relevant in this connexion with its safeguarding against the excesses of Alexandrian theology. One and the same Christ, the only-begotten Son and Lord, is to be confessed in two natures ἀσυγχύτως (*inconfuse*) and ἀτρέπτως (*immutabiliter*), and therefore without any idea of a commixture of the two or a changing of the one into the other.

The positive meaning of the definition on this side was that both the divine and human essence neither were nor are changed and self-alienated in their union in Jesus Christ. The divine is neither changed nor self-alienated from below in the humiliation which it undergoes to participate in the human, nor is the human from above in the exaltation which it experiences to participate in the divine. In this union and mutual participation both the humiliation of the divine and the exaltation of the human are real enough, but the one does not cease to be divine in its humiliation nor the other human in its exaltation. The mystery of the incarnation consists in the fact that Jesus Christ is in a real simultaneity of genuinely divine and human essence, and that it is on this presupposition that the mutual participation is also genuine.

But we must now lay an equally strong emphasis on the other side of this event and being. As it proceeds from the union and unity of the Son of God with human essence, it is also clear that the union of his divine with human essence in that two-sided participation—although it does not become unity—is a real and strict and complete and indestructible union. There is no element of human essence which is unaffected by, or excluded from, its existence in and with the Son of God, and therefore from union with, and participation in, this divine essence. Similarly, there is no element of His divine essence which the Son of God, existing in human essence, withdraws from union with it and participation in it. We shall have to say what this union and two-sided participation can and cannot mean in face of the indissoluble distinction of divine and human essence. For the moment, however, we must make the radical affirmation that the divine and human essence are indivisibly united in the one Jesus Christ who is the Son of God. We do not have here a divine and eternal and heavenly Christ who is not wholly of human essence, nor a human and temporal and earthly Jesus who is not wholly of divine. We do not have here a dual, but the one Jesus Christ, who as such is of both divine and human essence, and therefore the one Reconciler, Saviour and Lord. He pre-existed as such in the divine counsel. He was born and lived and died as such. He appeared as such to His disciples in His resurrection. He lives and reigns as such at the right hand of God the Father, in the last time which commenced with His revelation. He will be manifested as such to His community and the world when even this last time comes to its end. All acknowledgment and recognition and confession of Jesus Christ can refer only to the indissolubly one Christ. Luther's " and also " is true not only in a disjunctive but a conjunctive sense. If the word union were not strictly understood, we should completely miss the actuality of Jesus Christ, and speak this time of two arbitrary figments of the imagination.

This is where the second part of the Chalcedonian definition comes in with its safeguards against the excesses of Antioch. Jesus Christ, the only-begotten Son of God and our Lord, is to be confessed in His two natures ἀδιαιρέτως (*indivise*) and ἀχωρίστως (*inseparabiliter*), and therefore without any idea of a divisibility of one or the other, or a separability of the one from the other.

The positive meaning of the definition on this side was that even in their distinctiveness the divine and human essence were and are united in Jesus Christ, not merely in appearance but in fact, not merely partially but totally, not merely temporarily but definitively. The humiliation which comes to the divine essence in its participation in the human, and the exaltation which comes to the human in its participation in the divine, cannot be separated for all their distinctiveness. They are a single event and being. If we believe in Jesus Christ, in this One, we do not decide for one element in this history to the obscuring or even exclusion of the other, but we accompany the whole course of the history in its unity and totality. The mystery of the incarnation consists in the fact that the simultaneity of divine and human essence in Jesus Christ is real, and therefore their mutual participation is also real.

But if we are to understand this third statement, and make the necessary deduction in the fourth, it is vital that its content, the union of divine and human essence in Jesus Christ, should be seen together with its presupposition in the first and second statements—the fact that the Subject of atonement and therefore of incarnation, Jesus Christ, is the Son of God. This is the reason and compelling power of this history. This is the meaning and force in which what happened in this history has and is eternal and temporal being. As we have seen already, there can be no question of the human essence assumed and adopted by Him being the subject here. There was and is only one individual possibility which has its existence and became and is actuality in and by Him, and even this does not exist and is not actual in and for itself. How, then, can it be the subject? Yet even the divine nature as such cannot be considered as the subject of atonement and incarnation—and, strangely enough, for the same reason. For Godhead, divine nature, divine essence does not exist and is not actual in and for itself. Even Godhead exists only in and with the existence of Father, Son and Holy Ghost, only as the common predicate of this triune Subject in its modes of existence. Only the One who is God has Godhead. It cannot be ascribed to any other. Godhead, with all the perfections proper to it, is only the *modus* of His being. And what it is can be known and expressed only in relation to Him, as a perception and description of the *modus* in which He is. He, the divine Subject, carries and determines the divine essence, and not conversely. It is not really an accident, then, that we are not told that the Godhead, the divine nature, the divine essence became flesh (Jn. 1¹⁴). The Godhead as such has no existence. It is not real. It has no being or activity. It cannot, therefore, unite with that which is existent and real and has being and activity (which is not the case, of course, with human essence either). This is done by the divine Subject in and with His divine essence, by the One who exists and is and is actual, God the Father, Son and Holy Ghost, and therefore *in specie* God the Son. That is why it says that He, the Son, the Word became flesh. It is only as this happens, in the act of this Subject, that there takes place this union of divine and human essence. And all that we have seen concerning this union—the two-sided participation of the divine and human essence, the genuineness of both even in their conjunction, but also the reality of the union as such—in short, the whole doctrine of the two natures in the strict sense depends on this primary and proper union and unity as it is described in Jn. 1¹⁴. To put it even more simply, it all depends on the simple fact of the existence and reality of Jesus Christ as it is attested in the New Testament. The doctrine of the two natures cannot try to stand on its own feet or to be true of itself. Its whole secret is the secret of Jn. 1¹⁴—the central saying by which it is described. Whatever we may have to say about the union of the two natures can only be a commentary on this central saying. Neither of the two natures counts as such, because neither exists and is actual as such. Only the Son of God counts, He who adds human essence to His divine essence, thus giving it existence and uniting both in Himself. In Him, and Him alone, they were and are united. We shall have to consider this later when we come to speak of the consequences of this union, and especially of that which concerns us here in relation to the human nature of Jesus Christ.

The emphasis which from the very first, and now again, we have laid on this concept of the divine Subject of the incarnation, thus giving priority and precedence to the doctrine of the *unio hypostatica* over that of the *communio naturarum*, means that we have sided in principle with the Christology of the Reformed tradition. Of course, the difference at this point, although it is now more clearly noticeable, is not properly an antithesis. But we can hardly understand why it is that the ways diverge more or less seriously at a later stage if we do not observe that they begin to part company here. We must give a brief sketch of the historical facts.

It was almost inevitable that the Christology of Lutheran orthodoxy should build on the doctrine of the hypostatic union. But from the very first its main interest was not so much in this concept as in the resultant *communio naturarum* and its consequences. It was not so much in the primary mystery of the God-man Jesus Christ as such as in the secondary mystery of the relationship between His divine and human essence and their mutual participation. Reformed Christology, of course, was not without interest in the latter problems, nor did it evade the pressing consequences of this central concept. No one can evade them. But for the Lutherans these secondary problems form the burning point of attention. Their concern in practice was with the mutual participation enclosed in the union of the two natures, and, as we shall see, in particular with the communication of the properties of the divine nature to the human, or the participation of the human in the properties of the divine. Their concern was that the divine triumph over the distinction and antithesis between God and man took place directly, and is a fact, in the humanity of Jesus Christ. They also realised and said and even emphasised that we cannot experience and know the Godhead as such directly. But the drift of their discussion was that the Godhead can be seen and grasped and experienced and known directly in the humanity of Jesus Christ. Their intention was a fine one, although rather shadowed by the toying with one of those doubtful analogies, as we see clearly from a passage in the *Formula of Concord* (*Sol. decl.* VIII, 66) : " Thus there is always in Christ a single divine omnipotence, power, majesty and glory which is proper only to the divine nature ; but this is illuminated and proved and demonstrated wholly (if freely) in, with and under the human nature assumed and exalted in Christ ; just as in glowing iron there are not two forces which shine and burn, but the power to shine and burn is a property of fire, and yet (because the fire is joined to the iron) this capacity is proved and demonstrated in, with and under the glowing iron in such a way that from this source and by this union the glowing iron itself has also the power to shine and burn, but with no change in the essence and natural properties of either the fire or the iron." For them, therefore, the *unio hypostatica* was only a preparatory stage or spring-board for the attainment of the true end—the *communio naturarum*, and the christological περιχώρησις in which this is possible and actual. That is why they did not hesitate on occasion (e.g., B. Hollaz, *Ex. theol.*, 1707, III, 1, 3, *qu.* 30) to call this *communio* a *unio*, and they blamed the Reformed school (e.g., Quenstedt, *Theol. did. pol.*, 1685, III, 3, *sect.* 2, *qu.* 6, *antith.* 3) for not speaking of a direct but only an indirect union of the two natures—in so far as this results only *consequenter et per concomitantiam propter identitatem cum personalitate, quae sola primo unita sit*. That is also why their definition was as follows (Hollaz, *l.c.*, *qu.* 31) : that the *communio naturarum* is the *mutua divinae et humanae Christi naturae participatio, per quam natura divina* τοῦ λόγου *particeps facta humanae naturae hanc permeat, perficit, inhabitat sibique appropriat, humana vero particeps facta divinae naturae ab hac permeatur, perficitur et inhabitatur.* That is why they can advance the almost intolerable statement (Quenstedt, *l.c.*, *sect.* 1, *th.* 36) that the two natures in Christ are so united *ut ex utraque sibi invicem communicante fiat unum incommunicabile, una sc. persona.* What is obviously meant is the person observable in the humanity conjoined with divinity, which is also the principle of the whole event and being in the hypostatic union. And obviously there was a desire to maintain the ἀσυγχύτως and ἀτρέπτως of Chalcedon, and therefore the genuineness and integrity of the two natures, just as in the Lutheran eucharistic doctrine the bread did not cease to be bread as it was identical with the body of Christ. Yet the emphasis in Lutheran theology does not fall on this differentiating proviso, on the ἀσυγχύτως and ἀτρέπτως, but on the ἀδιαιρέτως and ἀχωρίστως of Chalcedon, on the *arctissima et intima* περιχώρησις and ἐνδύασις of the two natures (Quenstedt), on the equations which result from it, as that the Son of God, and therefore God in His divine essence, is this man, the Son of Mary, and above all, conversely, that this man, the Son of Mary, is the Son of God, and therefore God in His divine essence. These equations, which were regarded as deductions from the *unio personalis*, were called *propositiones personales.* They were not thought to be *essentiales et univocae.* They were not understood analytically, as if the subject were in essence what the predicate states concerning it. On the other hand (and it is to be noted that the Reformed agreed with the Lutherans in this), they were not regarded as *mere verbales*, as if the predicate were only—in Nestorian fashion—a name or title added to the subject to which its true being did not correspond. Again (and here, too, there could be agreement), they were not thought to be only *propositiones impropriae, figuratae aut tropicae*, as if the essence of the added predicate were not ascribed to the subject. But again (and at this point there could obviously be no agreement), they were not interpreted as *propositiones identicae*, as if the statement made of the subject could be true only in the sense and to the extent that there is a correspondence to the nature of the subject. This meant in practice that statements may also be made of the humanity of Jesus Christ which in themselves denote and describe only the divine and not the human essence. It is in the fact that such statements can and may and must be made of the humanity of Jesus Christ that we see the concern of the older Lutheran theology with its particular doctrine of the *communio naturarum.* It is clear that, although it did not side in this with the Monophysite heresy of Eutyches rejected at Chalcedon, it opposed that of Nestorius with particular sharpness, or, moie positively, appropriated the concern of Alexandrian theology as purified at Chalcedon. And obviously, in spite of every safeguard and precaution, in the heat of the conflict it could sometimes be accused of Monophysitism by the opposing faction, as it was not slack—for its own part—to level against the Calvinists the charge of Nestorianism.

Within the same Chalcedonian definition, the older Reformed Christology represented the diametrically opposite concern. The first and simple fact which emerges is that, although it had no wish to deny or conceal what ought to be said in this connexion, it did not have the same emphatic interest in the presence of the divinity in the humanity of Jesus Christ, in the fact that it can be seen and experienced and known in it. It did, of course, teach the *communio naturarum*. It did venture to make those *propositiones personales*. It did underline the fact that the Word became *flesh* (according to Jn. 1[14]). But on this view everything depended upon the One of whom it is said that the Word became flesh ; upon the *unio hypostatica* as the meaning and basis (not, of course, ignored or forgotten by the Lutherans) of the *communio naturarum* ; upon the Son of God as the Subject of the incarnation who creates and bears and maintains the *communio naturarum* ; upon His act of equating divine and human essence, and not so much upon the consequent equation. In the corresponding definitions, at any rate of more consistent Reformed dogmatics, we shall look in vain for a statement like that of Quenstedt, that the divine-human person arises (*fiat*) in the union of the two natures. As the Reformed saw it, this would be an inversion of the truth. And it is obvious that, while they did not question but solemnly affirmed the Chalcedonian ἀδιαιρέτως and ἀχωρίστως, they necessarily took a greater interest in the ἀσυγχύτως and ἀτρέπτως, in the opposition to Eutyches and therefore the distinction of the two natures, in their distinctiveness even in union, and especially in the continuing distinctiveness of the divine essence of the Logos, but consequently in that of the human essence united with it as well. Thus they could not understand the *propositiones personales* in the sense that statements can and may and must be made about the humanity of Jesus Christ whose content corresponds only to the Logos existing in divine essence, and not to the human essence assumed by Him into unity with His existence.

But why not ? Why is it that the Reformed dogmaticians were unable and unwilling (except, perhaps, with the greatest caution) to follow what was in its own way the generous sweep of Lutheran thinking ? Why is it that the protest was made : *creator in aeternum vult manere distinctus ab omnibus creaturis, etiam ab illa massa quam assumpsit* (Olevian, quoted from Heppe[2], p. 326) ? It is a complete—if common—misunderstanding to attribute this protest to a barren intellectual zeal for the axiom : *finitum non capax infiniti*, and therefore for the impassibility of the divine essence. In older Reformed dogmatics this axiom did not play the outstanding role attributed to it in later presentations. According to the whole movement of older Reformed thinking as it emerges in the documents, it is clear that if there was a zeal at all on this side, as there undoubtedly was, it was a zeal for the sovereignty of the Subject acting in free grace in the incarnation, of the living God in the person and existence of His Son, who ought to be kept in view even in His taking flesh, and not allowed to be merged and dissolved in the humanity which He assumed, or the nature which He blessed. It is He, this One, in the flesh, and therefore participating in human essence even in His divine essence. But He, this One, is Jesus Christ, and not a neutral thing, a human essence illuminated and impregnated by divinity. The result was that the Chalcedonian distinction of the natures acquired a new urgency. The Reformed looked with suspicion on what seemed to them to be the threat, in Lutheranism, of a divinisation of the humanity of Jesus Christ and a parallel de-divinisation of His divinity. They took precautions against this. From the point of view of Chalcedon, they made their own the purified concern of the school of Antioch. And in so doing they naturally came under the suspicion of a Nestorian tendency. All this is perfectly true. But to understand this, we must see and emphasise that they did try to think it out in the light of Chalcedon. They had no desire to divide up Jesus Christ into a Son of God and Son of Man. They had no desire to seek or see or grasp the overcoming of the opposition between God and man, and therefore the reconciliation of the world with God, elsewhere but in the humanity assumed by God, and therefore in the man Jesus of Nazareth. But to see and grasp it in Him, they tried to direct their true attention to the One who overcame in this overcoming, and to the act of His overcoming—to Jesus of Nazareth as the Christ, the eternal Son of God, and to the act of God which took place and is a fact in Him.

We, too, have accepted a similar orientation, and therefore attached ourselves to the Reformed tradition. But in so doing we do not fail to appreciate the attraction of the particular Lutheran interest in the *communio naturarum*, nor do we wish to ignore the concern which underlies it. It is only that the preference ought to be given to the Reformed concern, and the Lutheran taken up afterwards in so far as it shows itself to be justified.

We may conclude with the historical note that this particular interest of Lutheranism, and especially the developments which resulted from it, represented a novelty and peculiarity, at any rate in the Western Church. From the point of view of historical dogmatics, it was a kind of remote effect of the theology of the Eastern Church. The Reformed, for their part, were more conservative and less original in this respect. In face of this innovation, they gave a new emphasis to the understanding of Chalcedon traditional in the West.

We now come to the conclusion (4) that, as the Son of God became and is man, as He caused His existence to become that of a man, as He united divine and human essence in Himself, He exalted human essence into Himself, and as very God became very man. This is the particular aspect under which we are trying to understand the Christ-event in the present context. It is the history in which God Himself became and was and is and will be very man in His Son Jesus of Nazareth, the Son of Man. And the force of this history is the raising, the exaltation of human essence by the fact that God Himself lent it His own existence in His Son thus uniting it with His own divine essence. We refer to the essence common to all men. It is not destroyed or altered as such by the fact that in His Son God Himself exists in it, and it in Him ; by the fact that in Him it is united with the divine essence. Jesus of Nazareth was and is a man as we are— our Brother. But He was and is our first-born Brother. As a man like all men, He was and is the Head of all men. As He became a servant for us, He has become our Lord. For in Him, in this man, we have to do with the exaltation of the essence common to all men. In virtue of the fact that He is the Son of God, and therefore of divine and human essence, He is the Son of Man, the true man. Completely like us as a man, He is completely unlike us as the true man. In the essence common to us all, as a man like ourselves, He is completely different. This is His exaltation. This is why He is raised up above us and therefore for us. For He is the Son of God, and in Him our human essence is conjoined with the divine essence. In this being as the Son of Man, the true man, He is the Reconciler of the world with God. For the reconciliation of the world with God as it has taken place in Him, the restitution and fulfilment of the covenant between God and man, consists in the fact that there took place in Him the existence of a new and true man, and that human essence, as God lent it His own existence and made it His own, was exalted, and is

once for all exalted, to Him, to His side, to fellowship with His Son
in His divine essence. Our task is to understand this exaltation of
human essence as it has taken place in Jesus Christ with the greatest
possible precision and with all the necessary delimitations.

In our presentation of the union of divine and human essence
accomplished by the Son of God in His incarnation, we touched more
than once on the thought of the mutual participation of divine and
human essence as it follows this union, or rather takes place in and
with it. According to this concept, they are not united in the Son of
God, who is of divine essence and assumed human, like two planks
lashed or glued together—to use an image which often occurs in older
polemics—as if each retained its separate identity in this union and
the two remained mutually alien in a neutral proximity. The truth
is rather that in the Son of God, and therefore by the divine Subject,
united in His act, each of the two natures, without being either destroyed or altered, acquires and has its own determination. By and
in Him the divine acquires a determination to the human, and the
human a determination from the divine. The Son of God takes and
has a part in the human essence assumed by Him by giving this a part
in His divine essence. And the human essence assumed by Him takes
and has a part in His divine by receiving this from Him.

The indispensable closer definition of this mutual participation
must be this. The Son of God is the acting Subject who takes the
initiative in this event, and not either His divine or His human
essence. Of both these it is true that they are real and can act only
as He exists in them : in Himself with the Father and the Holy Ghost
in His divine essence ; and *per assumptionem* in His human. He
Himself grasps and has and maintains the leadership in what His
divine essence is and means for His human, and His human for His
divine, in their mutual participation. He is the norm and limit and
criterion in this happening. He is, of course, the One who is of divine
essence and assumes human, the Son of God and also the Son of Man.
But it is He Himself and not an it, either divine or human. If we
keep this clearly before us, it is apparent that the mutual participation
of the divine and human essence as it takes place in and by Him does
so in a twofold differentiation.

The first emerged already in our first attempt to define it. The
participation of His divine in His human essence is not the same as
that of His human in His divine. As His divine essence is that which
is originally proper to Him, and His human is only adopted by Him
and assumed to it, it is clear that we must see their mutual determination in the distinction in which we have described it. The determination of His divine essence is *to* His human, and the determination
of His human essence *from* His divine. He gives the human essence
a part in His divine, and the human essence receives this part in
the divine from Him. This means that the word mutual cannot be

understood in the sense of interchangeable. The relationship between the two is not reversible. That which takes place between them is not cyclic. Each has its own role. In the description of this event we must be very careful what use we make of such phrases as " in the same way," " to the same degree," " equally well," or " just the same." What we have here is a real history. It takes place both from above to below and also from below to above. But it takes place from above to below first, and only then from below to above. In it it is the self-humiliated Son of God who is also exalted man. He Himself is always the Subject of this history. It is not merely because they are different by definition, but because they have a different relationship to this Subject, that the divine and human essence bear a different character in their mutual participation.

But in respect of the Subject acting in this matter we must also make a second differentiation. The Son of God becomes man. That is, He adopts and assumes human essence to His own divine essence. He becomes and is Jesus of Nazareth, the Son of Man. We have, therefore, to say quite unreservedly that Jesus, the Son of David and Mary, was and is of divine essence as the Son of God, very God, God by nature. The Son of God exists as Jesus exists, and Jesus exists as the Son of God exists. As very man Jesus Himself is the Son of God and therefore of divine essence, God by nature.

It was to safeguard this unity of the person of Jesus Christ as Son of God and Son of Man (as was necessary against Nestorius) that the title " Mother of God " (θεοτόκος) was ascribed to Mary—not to her own honour, but to that of Jesus Christ—at the Council of Ephesus in 431. In practice, the Reformers could not make much of this title, and it seemed blasphemous in view of the current adoration of Mary. But even so, there was no question of changing it, and none of the Lutheran or Reformed orthodox of the following period disputed the necessity of this description (which had, of course, a biblical basis in Lk. 1[43]) in elucidation of the unity of Christ's person).

This does not mean however—and this is the second differentiation that we must respect in relation to that mutual participation—that the human essence assumed by the Son of God and united therefore with His divine essence became and is divine essence. Jesus Christ became and is the Son of Man only because and as the Son of God took human essence and gave it existence and actuality in and by Himself. There was and is, therefore, no Son of Man who, conversely, has assumed divine essence to His human essence and thus become the Son of God. But this means that the two elements in the history, the humiliation of Jesus Christ as the Son of God and His exaltation as the Son of Man, are not in simple correspondence. The first, His humiliation as the Son of God, means that He became man. But the second, His exaltation as the Son of Man, does not mean that He became God. How could He just become that which He already was from all eternity as the Son of God, and which He did not cease to

be even as the Son of Man ? That He is one and the same as Son
of God and Son of Man does not mean that He did not become a man
like ourselves, or that He became it and then ceased to be it, exchanging His human for divine essence, or changing it into divine
essence. That would surely mean that He did not really accomplish
His humiliation as the Son of God (His incarnation), or that He had
hardly accomplished it before He reversed it, so that He either did
not carry through His brotherhood with us, or at once broke it off
again. But how, then, could He be the Reconciler and Mediator ?
Thus, whatever may be the nature of this second element in the history
(the exaltation of the Son of Man who was also the Son of God), it is
not to be found—as logical, but not factual, consistency would seem
to demand—in a divinisation of His human essence corresponding to
His becoming man. That which is imparted to human essence in
Jesus Christ in its union with the divine essence of the Son in that
mutual participation, and that which it receives as something imparted to it, is rather to be sought in a determination in which it is
always human essence. The human essence of the Son of God will
always be human essence, although united with His divine essence,
and therefore exalted in and by Him, set at the side of the Father,
brought into perfect fellowship with Him, filled and directed by the
Holy Spirit, and in full harmony with the divine essence common to
Father, Son and Holy Spirit. It will be the humanity of *God*. But
it will still be humanity and not deity—human and not divine essence.
The human essence of the first-born of His brethren will be the human
essence of the One who is their Head and Lord in His identity with the
Son of God. But it will not be another and alien essence. Even from
this standpoint it will be human and not divine essence. It is as human
essence that the Son gives it a part in His divine essence and that it
takes and has this part.

This is the twofold differentiation of the mutual participation of
divine and human essence in Jesus Christ. For all their reciprocity
the two elements in this happening have a different character. The
one, as the essence of the Son of God, is wholly that which gives. The
other, exalted to existence and actuality only in and by Him, is wholly
that which receives. Thus, even as the two elements in this happening, they maintain their own distinctiveness. The humiliation of the
Son by the assumption of human essence is His becoming man. But
His exaltation as the Son of Man is not the divinisation of His human
essence. It means that, unchanged as such, it is set in perfect fellowship with the divine essence. If we keep clearly before us the necessary closer definition of the mutual participation of divine and human
essence in Jesus Christ—that it is true and actual in the existence
and act of the Son of God—we cannot escape an understanding of
this twofold differentiation in which it takes place.

We will now attempt a more precise explanation along three lines.

We will speak (1) of the impartation of the human essence to the divine, and the divine to the human, as it takes place in the one Jesus Christ as Son of God and Son of Man. We will then speak more specifically (2) of what is addressed to the human essence of Jesus Christ in this impartation. And finally we will speak (3) of the common actualisation of divine and human essence as it takes place in Jesus Christ on the basis of this impartation.

The particular sphere which we now enter, and which we must examine closely, corresponds to what was usually called in older Christology the doctrine of the effects (*effecta*) of the hypostatic *unio* and the *communio* of the two natures of Jesus Christ implicit in it. At this point both Lutherans and Reformed spoke of a *communicatio*, and they meant exactly the same as what in the first instance we described in general terms as the mutual participation of divine and human essence in Jesus Christ. Even the three suggested lines of explanation are already to be found in detail, and more or less clearly distinguished, in all the older dogmatics ; and all the Lutherans, and quite a number of the Reformed, gather them under the one concept of *communicatio*. If we accept this comprehensive term, the so-called *communicatio idiomatum* (a general title for the Lutherans) corresponds to what we call (1) the impartation of the human essence to the divine, and the divine to the human, as it takes place in the one Jesus Christ as Son of God and Son of Man. The *communicatio gratiarum* of the older doctrine corresponds to what we call (2) the address to human essence in Jesus Christ in this impartation. And the so-called *communicatio operationum* is what we call (3) the common actualisation of divine and human essence as it takes place in Jesus Christ on the basis of this impartation. As concerns the sequence of the three lines, we follow that selected, e.g. by J. Wolleb (*Chr. Theol. comp.*, 1626, I, 16, 4, *can.* 4) as affording the best survey.

1. Our starting point is the impartation as such. If the Word became flesh, this means that the one Son of God also became Son of Man—a man, yet not any man, but *the* Son of Man, the bearer of human essence, who as such is also the bearer of divine essence. The one Jesus Christ is unlimitedly and unreservedly both God and man. All that characterises human essence in distinction from divine or any other—the height of freedom and depth of love actual in God the Father, Son and Holy Ghost ; each perfection of true Godhead, holiness or mercy or wisdom, omnipresence or omnipotence or eternity—all this is unlimitedly and unreservedly proper to the One who as Son of God became also Son of Man. The one Jesus Christ exists also in this essence. But again, all that characterises human essence in distinction from divine or any other—its littleness and greatness in creation, its distinctive qualities, its capacity and limitations, its historicity and therefore temporality, its humanity as fellow-humanity, its responsibility before God and determination for Him, its susceptibility to temptation and suffering, its mortality, and more than this, its qualification by the aberration of man and all men, its consequent eternal jeopardy, its abandonment to nothingness, its character as " flesh "—all this is unlimitedly and unreservedly proper to the One who as Son of God became also Son of Man. The one Jesus Christ exists

also in this essence. In Him divine essence imparts itself to human, and human essence receives the impartation of divine. There is a complete openness on both sides, and therefore from above to below. There is a true and full and definitive giving and receiving. To see and think and say Jesus Christ is to see and think and say this impartation—divine and human essence in this relationship of real giving and receiving, God and man in the fellowship of this history. When we see Him, we cannot look here and there as though there were two side by side—a Son of God who is not Son of Man, and a Son of Man who is not Son of God. When we think of Him, we cannot imagine two—a divinity which does not yet impart itself to the humanity, and a humanity which still looks forward to the impartation of the divinity, and therefore still lacks it. We cannot speak of Him in words which refer exclusively to His divine or exclusively to His human essence. We have to see concretely in the one Jesus Christ, and to think and say concretely of Him, everything that belongs to divine and everything that belongs to human essence. Again, whatever belongs to divine or human essence, whatever characterises or distinguishes the one or the other as such, is to be seen concretely in Jesus Christ, and to be thought and said concretely of Him.

He, Jesus Christ, as Son of God is also Son of Man, born at Bethlehem, participating in His essence in every human capacity and every human weakness. He is a child and contemporary of His age and environment. In His action and experience He is one of many in the great nexus of humanity. He is subject to the particular Law which governs the life of Israel. He also participates in the alienation from God, the curse and burden and mortality, the character as flesh, to which human essence has fallen victim, and from which it cannot escape of itself. The Son of God suffers—the final extreme is also and primarily true of Him—He was crucified, dead and buried. With concrete reference to Jesus Christ, this is all to be said, not of a man called Jesus who was different from God, but of the Son of God who is of one essence with the Father and the Holy Ghost. For all this is an event and true and actual in Jesus Christ as the real participation of the Son of God in human essence.

But again, He, Jesus Christ, as Son of Man is also the Son of God, and as such of one essence with the Father and the Holy Ghost, and therefore the Lord of all lords, the source of all good, the Almighty and All-merciful, the Word by which the world was created and is maintained, the Eternal before whom all His creatures can and must only disappear and perish like dust, and yet shall not simply perish and disappear but persist, the One who in great and little things alike is present to everything near or far in time or space and sustains and keeps and rules it, the gracious One, who knows the transgression and weakness of man, whose anger burns but as the fire of His love, who does not will the death of man but his life and salvation. He, the

Son of God, is the One who was and is and will be, existing in the pre-temporality, the co-temporality and the post-temporality of God Himself. With concrete reference to Jesus Christ all this is not to be said of a divinity alien to our human essence, although bearing the name of Christ, but of the man Jesus Christ, in whom every other man can and may see, not himself but his human essence, thus recognising Him as a Fellow-man. All this is to be said of Him because all this is an event and true and actual in Jesus Christ as a real participation of the Son of Man in divine essence.

This is the impartation as it takes place in Jesus Christ. And we are compelled to see and think and say that this is the real point at issue in relation to Jesus Christ. The event of this impartation is the history of Bethlehem, the history of His way from Jordan to Gethsemane, the history of His cross and passion, the history of His first and provisional and particular manifestation in His resurrection. It is as the Subject of this history that He is the heavenly Head of His earthly body, the community, and will be revealed to every eye at the end of all days. We do not really have to do with Him if we do not see and consider and confess this impartation as it takes place in Him. To believe in Him and love Him and hope in Him is to look at this impartation. The grace of God manifested and effective in Him is the grace of this impartation. As He is, it takes place that the divine essence in all its distinctiveness is gifted to the human, and the human in all its distinctiveness receives the divine. As He is, there takes place the humiliation of the divine for the exaltation of the human essence, and the exaltation of the human by the humiliation of the divine. As He is, nothing is kept back. In the height of God and in the depths of man, nothing is excluded from this movement from the height of God to our depths, and back again from our depths to the height of God. As He is, God attains His full glory in the exercise of His mercy, and man attains his in the coming of this mercy. And all this is because and as He, the Son of God, of one essence with the Father and the Holy Ghost, became and is also the Son of Man, of one essence with us and all men.

This corresponds to what the older Christology—both Lutheran and Reformed—considered and presented under the head of *communicatio idiomatum*. By *idiomata* were meant the distinctive features (*propria, proprietates*) of the two natures of Jesus Christ. Thus the *communicatio idiomatum* meant the impartation in Jesus Christ, and in this impartation the realised communion, in which the peculiarities of both natures are those of Jesus Christ. We must add at once, of course, that what we have said corresponds to that in which the older Lutheran and Reformed were agreed in their development of the concept. It is not at all true, as we read in some modern presentations (like that of H. Stephan, *Glaubenslehre*[2], 1928, p. 169), that Reformed theology found no place for the concept of the *communicatio idiomatum*, and even disputed it in its insistence on the *finitum non capax infiniti*. It did, of course, resist a particular development of the concept, but not the concept itself and as such. We may quote Polanus (*Synt. Theol. chr.*, 1609, VI, 16, *col.* 2440 f.) : *Proprietates utriusque naturae Christi personae ipsi communicantur. Quae enim naturis singulis sunt propria, ea personae Christi sunt communia.* They are to be stated *indistincte* of His one person because they are true in it *indistincte : idque non verbaliter tantum, seu inanibus titulis, sed realissime.* For because He exists really in both natures, everything distinctive to each of them is *realiter et verissime* proper to Him. He, the One, is God and man, not merely *verbaliter,* but *realiter,* and in this unity, as *totus Christus,* He is *mediator, redemptor, intercessor et servator,* our *rex, sacerdos et propheta,* the Shepherd, the Head and the Vine in which we are members and branches, the Lord and Judge of the world. None of the older Reformed dogmaticians contested this. They all gave it particular emphasis. The general definition of Hollaz (*Ex. theol.,* 1700, III, 1, 3, *qu.* 37) might easily be that of one of the Reformed school : *Communicatio idiomatum est vera et realis propriorum divinae et humanae naturae in Christo θεανθρώπῳ ab alterutra vel utraque natura denominata participatio, ex unione personali resultans.* There would, of course, be alarm at the later statement (*qu.* 40) that this is only the first of three different *genera* of the *communicatio idiomatum.* Rather confusingly, it was called the *genus idiomaticum.* But the measure of agreement is not passed even when (*qu.* 42) this first genus is given the more precise, threefold definition : Qualities of the human nature are also those of the Son of God and therefore of Jesus Christ in His divine nature (ἰδιοποίησις) ; in relation to Him they can therefore be described as divine qualities (κοινωνία τῶν θείων) ; and the one Jesus Christ, who unites both natures in Himself, has divine as well as human qualities. Where the Reformed were not willing to follow emerges supremely in the fact that they refrained from certain statements which were quite possible within this common framework but seemed to be rather arbitrary and without biblical foundation, as, for example, that " God died " (" O ill most dread, that God is dead "), or that " the man Jesus Christ is Almighty."

Can and should and must the concept of the mutual impartation of divine and human essence as it takes place in Jesus Christ be developed further than this point ? The decision which we have to make is not an easy one. Is it enough to refer to the fact that it does actually take place in the one person of Jesus Christ as the One who is Himself true salvation and saving truth ? Or may it be that this is not enough because, to be quite clear, this reference needs to be more precisely filled out, and is capable of this more precise filling ? Is it illegitimate to ask what it is that actually happens in this mutual impartation of divine and human essence in the one Jesus Christ ? Or is this not a question which we can and should and must ask, with every prospect of a meaningful answer ?

The decision is not an easy one because the way to a positive answer to this last question, and therefore to a concrete filling out of the reference, is to some extent blocked by the fact that, although a positive answer is both possible and has actually been given in a very powerful way, yet it has proved to be intolerable—so intolerable that we may find ourselves frightened away from the question which it purports to answer, accepting the reference as such and not making any attempt to fill it out.

This is what the older Reformed actually did at this point. They were staggered, not to say horrified, by the development of the mutual impartation of the divine and human essence in Jesus Christ which they found in the Lutheran doctrine of the *idiomäta*. They were quite unwilling and unable to follow this line of development. And so they gave up the whole problem. They were content to point as zealously as they could to the fact of this impartation, to the person of the Mediator, the true Son of God and Son of Man, in whom it took place. And faced with a choice between the existing Lutheran answer and the existing Reformed rejection of the problem, we can only decide that the Reformed chose the better part. But the question still remains whether the dilemma cannot be evaded. Do we really have to make a choice between these two possibilities ?

We must first consider the possible (and given) answer by which we might find ourselves blocked. It is to this effect. This impartation consists in the fact that in the hypostatic union, or the union which it encloses, there is such an appropriation, illumination and penetration, not of the divine nature by the human but of the human by the divine, that all the attributes of the divine nature of Jesus Christ may be ascribed also to His human nature. This does not, of course, involve a destruction or alteration of the human nature, but it means that this nature experiences the additional development (beyond its humanity) of acquiring and having as such all the marks of divinity, of participating directly in the majesty of God, of enjoying in its creatureliness every perfection of the uncreated essence of God. And Jesus Christ is true salvation and saving truth in so far as this takes place and is actual in Him ; in so far as in His human nature (as could and was actually said) the Godhead present could directly reveal itself as a new and divine element of life entering the world of men, directly accomplishing its reconciliation with God and directly imparting to it its new and eternal life.

What we have just sketched is the Lutheran doctrine of the so-called second genus of the *communicatio idiomatum*—the *genus majestaticum*—a name which it owes to the fact that the *Filius Dei majestatem suam divinam assumptae carni communicavit* (Hollaz, *l.c.*, III, 1, 3, *qu.* 45). In express adoption of the terminology of the early Greek fathers, the *communicatio idiomatum* as understood in this way, was described as the προσθήκη μεγάλη, as μετάληψις θείας ἀξίας, as μετοχὴ θείας δυνάμεως, even directly as θέωσις, ἀποθέωσις, θεοποίησις, as the *deificatio* of the human essence of Jesus Christ (*qu.* 47). As is noticed by F. H. R. Frank (*Theologie der Konkordienformel*, Vol. III, 1863, p. 193), the main interest now centres on the communion of the natures quite apart from the personal union—if on the basis of it. Appeal is constantly made to the *locus probans classicus*, Col. 2[9] (" In him dwelleth all the fulness of the Godhead—the πλήρωμα θεότητος—bodily ")—and in substance to the necessity of its deduction from the *unio hypostatica* and the *communio naturarum* (*qu.* 49). The gifts made to the human nature are described as *dona vere divina, increata, infinita et immensa* (*qu.* 51). *Communicatio* is supposed to mean that even the human nature of Jesus Christ (expressly described as *subjectum* in *qu.* 50) is in full possession, and capable of full use, and participant in the full glory of the divine (*qu.* 53). *Communicatio* is thus supposed to mean, as is stated and proved expressly and with particular insistence, the omnipotence, omniscience and omnipresence of the flesh, the human nature of Jesus Christ (*qu.* 56 f.). And so the last and solemn declaration of the doctrine is that we must worship and adore His humanity with and like His divinity : *ut caro Christi mediatoris eadem adoratione cum divina natura τοῦ λόγου sit colenda et adoranda* (*qu.* 59).

Rightly to understand and appreciate this special Lutheran theory we have to consider that according to its express intention (for it, too, is based finally on the doctrine of the *unio hypostatica*) the Subject of this communication of properties is not the divine nature as such but the Son of God who assumes human nature (Hollaz, *qu.* 48). The only thing is that it was thought that we should know and say this concerning what took place in that Subject.

Again, there is no doctrine of a *genus tapeinoticum* corresponding to that of the *genus majestaticum*, i.e., no humanisation of the divine nature by its conjunction with the human corresponding to the divinisation of the human by its conjunction with the divine. At this point (as distinct from the first, the *genus idiomaticum*) there is no *reciprocatio*, writes Quenstedt (*l.c.*, III, 3, *sect.* 2, *qu.* 10, *ekth.*). The divine nature cannot experience any ταπείνωσις, κένωσις, ἐλάττωσις, for as opposed to the human it is immutable and not capable of any addition or diminution, exaltation or abasement. It was only with the so-called " Kenoticists " of the 19th century (cf. *C.D.*, IV, 1, p. 182) that there came the light (or the very curious obscurity) of the doctrine of a partial de-divinisation of the Logos with His incarnation. The older Lutherans were most careful not to take any steps in this direction. Indeed, they were too careful, as we shall see later. But in view of their strong restraint in this respect we must concede that they tried to maintain and did not derive from a purely logical consistency in the sphere of metaphysical speculation (which might well have applied on this side too) but from an honest if misguided zeal for a material concern delimited by Scripture.

Finally, we have to take into account the various careful restrictions which they made in an attempt to safeguard their thesis—at the expense of its clarity and cogency, but with a greater interest in the substance of the matter than its presentation—against certain absurd, or harmful, deductions. If all the divine attributes were supposed to be those of the flesh of Christ, their direct actualisation (*usurpatio*) in His flesh was restricted to the so-called operative qualities, the divine omnipotence, omniscience, etc. Eternity and infinity could be ascribed to it only indirectly (Hollaz, *qu.* 52). And although in His earthly lifetime Jesus Christ *qua* man was certainly in full possession (κτῆσις) of divine omnipotence, He suspended its full use (χρῆσις), and took it again only with His ascension (*qu.* 56). Similarly, He did not make constant use of the omniscience imparted to His human nature, but only used it when and where He willed (*qu.* 57). The same distinction between possession and use was made in respect of His omnipresence. This was not understood at all as physical, local and corporal, but as the participation of the flesh of Christ too in the *dominium* over all space exercised by the Son of God in virtue of His divine nature (*qu.* 58). According to Frank (*op. cit.*, p. 308 f.), the particularly difficult and objectionable thesis of J. Brenz concerning a general omnipresence of the body of Christ does not correspond at all to the sense of the Lutheran confession, which refers only to his humanity as such—a rather strained distinction. Of course, all these restrictions can and will be found rather artificial and laboured. They are illogical and disturb the formal beauty. But we are forced to admit that they testify to the realism, and the resolve to be faithful to Scripture, which control the development of this Lutheran theologoumenon.

What is the real meaning and intention of this remarkable train of thought ? We have to realise that for all its curious and alien features the reality of the high grace of the reconciliation of the world with God, the perfection of the fellowship established between God and man, and the presence and efficacy of God in our human sphere, are all taken with a final and total seriousness. An attempt is made to think out to the very last the fact and extent that all this did and does take place in Jesus Christ the one Son of God and Son of Man. If we, too, take this seriously, if we, too, think it out to the end, and if we are clear that the decisive word must be spoken in Christology, and particularly in an understanding of the humanity of Jesus Christ, we cannot keep our distance from at least the intention of this theologoumenon, which is so closely akin to the distinctive Eastern Christology and soteriology of the Greek fathers. We certainly cannot do this merely to bolster the prestige of Reformed confessionalism.

But when all this has been said, it has also to be perceived and said that this intention cannot be executed as attempted along these lines. It is not that there was any lack of energy in the attempt. But does not a recognition of the reality of the atonement as it has taken place in Jesus Christ, of the perfection of the new fellowship established in Him between God and man, and of the presence and efficacy of God in the human sphere as guaranteed by Him, imply that the look which we direct at Him, and at the act of God which has taken place in Him, should be not merely openly but totally directed at Him and Him alone, as a look at the Victor and His victory, to use our earlier expression, or at His giving and our corresponding receiving, at the history as such which takes place between God and man in Jesus Christ ? And, of course, the representatives of that theologoumenon did always make the serious reservation that this must actually happen.

In their presentation the Lutherans made a sufficiently pressing reference to the *unio hypostatica* as its final basis. And it may even be maintained that the Reformed controversialists overlooked this—that they perhaps had to do so, that they could not take it seriously—and then used arguments which their opponents could escape by advancing this *caveat*, by pointing back to the common starting-point.

But the real point at issue is whether a mere *caveat* is enough. Did the representatives of this view really look openly and directly at Jesus Christ in their thinking ? Did they follow through this history ? Or did they look only at the given happening as such, the victory which took place in the history, looking away from the event of the divine giving and human receiving to what is given to the human essence of Jesus Christ in this event, to a status mediated to Him in this event ? What is really meant by the humanity of Jesus Christ as it is appropriated and illuminated and inter-penetrated by His deity—loaded, as it were, with His deity, because participant in all its attributes ? The objection can obviously be brought at once against this view that it is a strange deity which can suddenly become the predicate of human essence, and a strange humanity to which all the divine predicates can suddenly be ascribed as subject. Does not this compromise both the true deity and the true humanity of Jesus Christ ? Does it not involve either a deification of the creature, or humanisation of the Creator, or both ? The representatives of this view never succeeded in offering a convincing answer to these objections. But these objections acquire their full weight only when they are set in the context of the wider question whether the humanity of Jesus Christ as conceived in this way is not one long abstraction : abstracted, that is, from the history to which we cannot even for a moment cease to cling if we are to see and think and confess " Jesus Christ " ; abstracted from the one true Son of God and Son of Man in whom the divine and human are genuinely united, without admixture or separation. On this view are they not both admixed and separated : admixed, to the extent that the human is deified, as is expressly stated, in this union with Godhead ; and separated, to the extent that this deification can be ascribed to it only as it is considered statically in and for itself, isolated from the dynamic of the history in which it was and is one with the divine ? In this isolation, on the basis of which it appears as an apotheosised humanity, directly filled and furnished with all the majesty of the being of the triune God, is there not committed, in spite of every precaution, the very serious mistake of looking away from the Subject in whom God and man became and are one, from the history in which it took place, and therefore—contrary to the express intention—from the reality of the atonement, the perfection of the new fellowship between God and man, the real presence and efficacy of God among us, the new element of life which has actually come down into the world of men in Jesus Christ ? Jesus Christ is this element, for He is the one Son of God and Son of Man. But a status conferred upon His humanity cannot be—if what is conferred is divine majesty—because in this case it is hard to see how it can be genuine majesty which is conferred in this way or genuine humanity on which it is conferred. On this pre-supposition the real connexion between the world of God and that of man is most severely compromised. The recognition of Jesus Christ as true salvation and saving truth is not really strengthened, as intended, by the theory of a divinisation of His human essence, but weakened and even jeopardised completely. This is one reason why we have no option but to reject it.

There is no reason at this point to state explicitly the arguments of the older Reformed dogmaticians against the Lutheran *genus majestaticum*. They are put implicitly in our own independent presentation. If the Lutherans did not succeed in making the matter clear to them, they for their part did not succeed in showing them their error. Their reaction was much too negative. Thus the correct objections which they raised, partly against the absurdity of the consequences, and partly against the inconsistency of the thesis contested, could not really affect the Lutherans in substance, although they could, of course, cause them quite considerable embarrassment in detail.

But there is another aspect from which the conception against which we must now delimit ourselves makes an impression which is frankly shocking and necessarily strengthens the suspicions already aroused against it. This second aspect had not yet been perceived in the 16th and 17th centuries. But it is now obvious in the light of later and recent developments in Evangelical theology. It therefore demands our consideration.

As we have seen, in this conception—within the sphere of Christology, and on the presupposition of the divine sonship and therefore the true Godhead of Jesus Christ—all the emphasis is laid on His existence as the Son of Man. This is not the only way in which it can be considered and expounded, but it is certainly a legitimate one. As the Son of God, He is also the Son of Man, and wills to be known as such. To do this is also our own particular concern in the present context. This conception, again, considers the exaltation of human nature as that which has been imparted to it in Jesus Christ. And this, too, is legitimate, and the theme of our present discussion. But when it speaks of a divinisation of human essence in Jesus Christ, and when this divinisation of the flesh of Jesus Christ is understood as the supreme and final and proper meaning and purpose of the incarnation—even to the point of worshipping it—a highly equivocal situation is created. All this is still said, of course, within the sphere of Christology. And it is all said with a reference only to the humanity of Jesus Christ. But how are we to guard against a deduction which is very near the surface, which once it is seen is extremely tempting, and once accepted very easy to draw, but which can compromise at a single stroke nothing less than the whole of Christology? For after all, is not the humanity of Jesus Christ, by definition, that of all men? And even if it said only of Him, does not this mean that the essence of all men, human essence as such, is capable of divinisation? If it can be said in relation to Him, why not to all men? But this means that in Christology a door is left wide open, not this time by a secular philosophy which has entered in with subtlety, but in fulfilment of the strictest theological discussion and ostensibly from the very heart of the Christian faith. And through this door it is basically free for anyone to wander right away from Christology. Who is to prevent him? For, as we have seen, what is said is not said strictly and exclusively in relation to Jesus Christ Himself, but with a side glance at the abstraction of the "human nature" of Jesus Christ, at what the union with the divine nature in Jesus Christ means for it. The reservation with which its divinisation was asserted was, of course, that it is that of *His* human nature. But the reservation itself was and is quite unable to set aside the suspicions which necessarily arise against the concept of this divinised human nature as such. And quite obviously it cannot meet the question whether the christological bracket in which the divinisation is asserted may not be dissolved, and everyone be free to stride through the door opened by this concept, and away from the christological centre. But where does the way through this door lead? It obviously leads smoothly and directly to anthropology:

and not to a dull naturalistic and moralistic anthropology, but to a
" high-pitched " anthropology ; to the doctrine of a humanity which
is not only capable of deification, but already deified, or at any rate
on the point of apotheosis or deification.   If the supreme achievement of Christology, its final word, is the apotheosised flesh of
Jesus Christ, omnipotent, omnipresent and omniscient, deserving of
our worship, is it not merely a hard shell which conceals the sweet
kernel of the divinity of humanity as a whole and as such, a shell
which we can confidently discard and throw away once it has performed
this service ?

   Obviously, to open this door, and therefore to make this transition from
Christology to an imitative general anthropology, was not even envisaged, let
alone intended, by a Quenstedt or Hollaz, or by the even older Lutheran fathers
who represented what was the called the *genus majestaticum* against the Calvinists at the turn of the 16th and 17th centuries, or by the *Formula of Concord*
or Luther himself, who first broached the matter in the eucharistic controversy.
We may well ask whether the emphasis with which he did this was not an effect
of the fact that in his earlier years (up to 1519 ?) he had championed a theology
in which Christology had for the most part only an exemplary function in consolidation of what was essentially an anthropological or mystico-anthropological
tendency and *schema* (cf. Gerhard Ebeling, " Die Anfänge von Luthers Her-
meneutik," *ZThK*, 1951, p. 172 f.).   The young Melanchthon, as attested not
merely by the well-known derogatory reference to early Christology in the *Loci*
of 1521, but by the whole drift of this first attempt, seemed ready to follow
him along this way.   He later left it, like Luther himself.   But it is worth considering that Luther's distinctive insistence on the presence and efficacy of the
divinity in the humanity of Jesus Christ (as also in the identity of its glorified
corporality with the bread and wine of the Lord's Supper) was not without
connexion with this first phase of his theological thinking—in which case his
Christology was from the very first a Christology with this open door.   But
however that may be, there can be no doubt that when Luther first propounded
the doctrine, and for many generations Lutheranism thought it necessary resolutely to espouse it, the door was there, and open, in this sphere—whether it was
used or not, or its significance even perceived and appreciated or not.   And this
was not actually the case from the standpoint of serious theology so long and so
far as early Christology still retained its force in the Evangelical Church.
   But we have to grasp what it meant that for almost two hundred years this
was the Christology which controlled preaching, instruction, pastoral work and
public worship in the orbit of Lutheranism.   The time came when with many
other elements of Christian perception it was abandoned in its explicit theological
content, first by the world at large, and then in the Church itself, to the direct
and indirect, the declared or secret criticism of the so-called Enlightenment,
and then forgotten, or overlaid.   But did this mean that it was no longer there ?
Was it not still exercising an influence ?   Surely it was not an accident that on
the same soil of profound German thinking on which this Christology had once
grown and been defended for two hundred years against the Calvinistic correction, and become the current form of all instruction in the Gospel of Jesus Christ,
there could and did arise, in the fulness of time, the wonderful flower of German
Idealism, with its far more than local and Lutheran significance.   For does not
this correspond more or less exactly to the anthropology which is so easily reached
from this Christology once its open door is passed—the anthropology of a humanity which is destined and able to be deified, and already on the point of deification ?   Is not its characteristic inversion of above and below, heaven and earth,

God and man, a realisation, at bottom, of the possibility which as the apotheosis of human nature had long since been prefigured by the Lutheran form of the doctrine of the *idiomata*, although still enclosed in its christological shell? Was Hegel so wrong after all when he thought that he could profess to be a good Lutheran? Was it mere impudence that L. Feuerbach usually liked to appeal to Luther for his theory of the identity of divine with human essence, and therefore of God's becoming man which is really the manifestation of man become God? And it was only in refinement and adornment of this rather brutal thesis of Feuerbach that Biedermann as we have seen—expressly within the Lutheran conception of the doctrines of the *idiomata*, and the underlying Alexandrian Christology—attempted to find the profoundest possible expression for the unity between absolute and finite spirit as it takes place in the absolute religious self-consciousness. It is far from our purpose to suggest that Luther and Lutheranism ever intended all this. But it can hardly be denied that with their heaven-storming doctrine of the humanity of the Mediator they did actually prepare the way for the distinctive modern transition from theology to a speculative anthropology. It was only " incidentally " and " by way of implication," as Frank puts it (*op. cit.*, p. 232 f.), that there emerged in the Lutheran confession the speculative principle which has been rightly emphasised in more recent times, and according to which the finite and infinite do not absolutely exclude one another, but the former is capable of the latter. The boast is a cautious one, but it would be better not made at all. Luther and the older Lutherans did in fact compromise—at a most crucial point—the irreversibility of the relationship between God and man, long before the message of the Church was similarly affected by a secular human self-understanding which drew its nourishment from a very different quarter. Their successors necessarily find themselves embarrassed and defenceless in face of this secular humanism, and if modern Protestant theology could and has become essentially anthropology, this was not so much due to external pressure as to its own internal entanglement. It was also not an accident that the opposition to this tendency which arose about 1920 came from the Reformed side.

This, then, is the second thing which gives a suspicious character to any movement in our present direction, warning us against treading this way, and giving us every reason to drop a question which was, and obviously could be, answered with this very doubtful development. Even with the best intentions, and in satisfaction of the most legitimate interests, we cannot toy unpunished with inversions of this type.

But because we have to reject this answer, does it really mean that we can refuse and drop the problem itself : the question what it is that takes place in the Son of God and Son of Man, Jesus Christ, between the divine and human essence united in Him ; of a filling out of the reference to the One in whom this union takes place ? To this we can only say No, not allowing the way to a positive answer to be blocked. It is seldom a good thing simply to reject a problem which has once been seriously raised. We will not serve the cause of understanding within the theology of the Evangelical Church if we are merely content to criticise and reject the Lutheran solution. And, above all, our present goal is to know Jesus Christ as the Son of Man, true man. But we fall short of the goal if we will not try to rescue the question from the impasse into which it was led by the christological discussion of the older Protestants.

2. We have, therefore, to take the second step, and speak of the
address to human essence in Jesus Christ, to the Son of God and Son
of Man—corresponding to what was called the *communicatio gratiae*
in the older doctrine. It is in this address that there takes place the
mutual participation of divine and human essence which results from
the union of the two in the one Jesus Christ. It is here that we can
see that the basic concept of the one Son of God and Son of Man (of
the hypostatic union) is not an empty one ; that the reference to it
has a meaning in that it points to the fulness of the concretion in
which the union of the two natures takes place in Jesus Christ. The
event in the fulness of its concretion consists in a movement which is
made to human essence.

Remembering what we have already said, we maintain that this
address has a twofold character. On the one hand there is the acting
Subject, God Himself in His mode of existence as the Son, who is of
one divine essence with the Father and the Holy Spirit. And on the
other hand there is human essence, to which the Son of God gives
(His own) existence and actuality, no longer being only the Son of
God in this act, but becoming and being also the Son of Man. What
takes place in this address has thus a two-sided reference, as we have
seen, although a very different one on the two sides.

We must begin with the fact that what takes place in this address
is also and primarily a determination of divine essence : not an alteration, but a determination. God does not first elect and determine
man but Himself. In His eternal counsel, and then in its execution
in time, He determines to address Himself to man, and to do so in
such a way that He Himself becomes man. God elects and determines
Himself to be the God of man. And this undoubtedly means—and
we must not deny the fact—that He elects and determines Himself
for humiliation. In so doing He does not need to become alien to
Himself, to change Himself. The Godhead of the true God is not a
prison whose walls have first to be broken through if He is to elect and
do what He has elected and done in becoming man. In distinction
from that of false gods, and especially the god of Mohammed, His
Godhead embraces both height and depth, both sovereignty and
humility, both lordship and service. He is the Lord over life and death.
He does not become a stranger to Himself when in His Son He also
goes into a far country. He does not become another when in Jesus
Christ He also becomes and is man. Even—and why should we not
say precisely ?—in this He is God in supreme constancy, in supreme
affirmation of His faithfulness, not only to us, but primarily and
supremely to Himself.

It is only the pride of man, making a god in its own image, that will not
hear of a determination of divine essence in Jesus Christ. The presupposition
of all earlier Christology has suffered from this pride—from the fathers to both
Reformed and Lutheran orthodoxy. This presupposition was a Greek conception

of God, according to which God was far too exalted for His address to man, His incarnation, and therefore the reconciliation of the world and Himself, to mean anything at all for Himself, or in any way to affect His Godhead. In other words, He was the prisoner of His own Godhead. As if transfixed by this conception, the older theologians thought that they should close their eyes entirely to this aspect. They were only to speak of what happened to human essence in this address. We have already seen something of the anxiety of the Lutherans —who were at one with the Reformed in this—to dispel the thought of any *reciprocatio* in the union of natures in Jesus Christ, of any *genus tapeinoticum* corresponding to the *genus majestaticum*. The recollection of the *immutabilitas Dei* had for them the same effect as a Soviet veto, and completely stifled any further thinking. It was with this anxiety on the one side that they tried to take up the thesis of the divinisation of the human nature of Jesus Christ on the other. Was it any wonder that they were constantly exposed to the rather malicious question of the Reformed why they were so inconsistent on this first side, and whether they did not fall on the other side into the very danger which they were here trying to escape. But this question only betrayed the fact that the Reformed themselves regarded the presupposition as inviolable. Even Schleiermacher still thought that he was absolutely bound at this point. And when the " Kenoticists " of the 19th century—the problem was still an urgent one—attempted to think further in this direction, they could only oppose to this immutability of God a quite intolerable mutability. Even in the eyes of the Liberals (e.g., Biedermann) and the Ritschlians (e.g., Loofs) it appeared as if they were reducing all earlier Christology *ad absurdum*. What they were really reducing *ad absurdum* was the orientation of all earlier Christology by the profoundly unchristian conception of a God whose Godhead is supposed not to be affected at all by its union with humanity. It has often been pointed out that it was not the terminology of this Christology as such, but its false terminology at this decisive point—the static picture with which it worked of a God who is dead of sheer majesty—that gave to it the shadowy character of which it has been constantly accused.

If we shake off the spell, and try to think of the Godhead of God in biblical rather than pagan terms, we shall have to reckon, not with a mutability of God, but with the kind of immutability which does not prevent Him from humbling Himself and therefore doing what He willed to do and actually did do in Jesus Christ, i.e., electing and determining in Jesus Christ to exist in divine and human essence in the one Son of God and Son of Man, and therefore to address His divine essence to His human, to direct it to it. Even in the constancy (or, as we may calmly say, the immutability) of His divine essence He does this and can do it (new and surprising and alien though it may be to human eyes blinded only by their own pride) not only without violation but in supreme exercise and affirmation of His divine essence. It is not that it is part of His divine essence, and therefore necessary, to become and be the God of man, Himself man. That He wills to be and becomes and is this God, and as such man, takes place in His freedom. It is His own decree and act. Nor is there anything in the essence of man to make necessary this divine decree or act. On the other hand, it is indeed a part of the divine essence to be free for this decree and its execution, to be able to elect and determine itself in this form. No diminution comes to it by the fact that it is wholly directed and addressed to human essence in Jesus Christ, sharing its limitation and weakness and even its lostness in the most radical and consistent way. But again, in this address, direction and participation, it does not acquire the increase of any alien capacity or even incapacity. No difference at all is made. What is, then, the divine essence ? It is the free love, the omnipotent mercy, the holy patience of the Father, Son and Holy Spirit. And it is the God of *this* divine essence who has and maintains the initiative in this event. He is not, therefore, subject to any higher force when He gives Himself up to the lowliness of the human being of the Son of God. The Father, He Himself, gives Himself up. This offering is, therefore, elected and determined by His own majesty—the majesty of the divine Subject.

If all this is clear, there can and must be room for great and true and thankful astonishment at the fact that God did actually will and do this in unbroken faithfulness to Himself, electing and determining Himself for man, to be the God of man, Himself to be in human form. What does all this mean ? What does it mean that " God was in Christ " (2 Cor. 5[19]) ? It obviously means that all that God is, without either needing or being subject to any change or diminution or increase, is characterised by the fact that He is everything divine, not for Himself only, but also, in His Son, for the sake of man and for him. Col. 2[9] tells us : " In him dwelleth all the fulness of the godhead bodily." Therefore the sovereignty of God dwells in His creaturely dependence as the Son of Man, the eternity of God in His temporal uniqueness, the omnipresence of God in His spatial limitation, the omnipotence of God in His weakness, the glory of God in His passibility and mortality, the holiness and righteousness of God in His adamic bondage and fleshliness—in short, the unity and totality of the divine which is His own original essence in His humanity. The actuality of the incarnate Son of God, the union of the two natures in Him, is the direct confrontation of the totality of the divine with the human in the one Jesus Christ.

The totality of the divine—for there is no obvious necessity why we should cautiously make reservations and instead of speaking of the totality speak only of certain properties of God which are addressed to the human and confronted with it in Jesus Christ. Nor is it very obvious how such a division is even possible. Is not each perfection of God itself the perfection of His whole essence, and therefore in any modification the sum and substance of all others ? How can some of these perfections be separated off from others ? Would it be the divine essence of the Father, Son and Holy Spirit if such separations were to take place in it ?

But if they do not, if it is true that in the divinity of Jesus Christ we have to do with the unity and totality of the divine, if it is true that in Him all the fulness of the Godhead dwells bodily, and that it is therefore directly confronted with the human, then it is obvious that although it is not changed it is given concrete form in Him. It is concretely determined as the essence of the Son of God who also assumes and adopts human essence. For all its difference it is therefore addressed to this human essence. It condescends towards it with open-handed generosity. Even in Jesus Christ it is not itself human essence. But in Jesus Christ it is not without it, but absolutely with it. That God in Jesus Christ can be and is pleased to do this, that this is indeed His supreme good-pleasure, is that which deserves our worship in the incarnation, the mystery of Christmas. God is not only love, but He loves, and He loves man—so much that He gives up Himself to him. He is not only gracious, but He exercises grace, and He does this by becoming the Son of Man as the Son of God, and therefore in the strictest, total union of His nature with ours. This does not take place at the expense but in the power of His divine nature. It is, however, a determination which He gives it. It acquires in man its *telos*. Directed and addressed to human nature, it acquires a form, *this* form.

This is why we cannot possibly maintain that the participation of the two natures in Jesus Christ is only one-sided, that of the human in the divine. In the first instance, indeed, it is that of the divine in the human. And in the fact that it is this first it has its ultimate depth and unshakeable solidity as a participation of the human in the divine. We can now express it quite simply in this way. It is grounded in the fact that it was God first who took to His own heart the situation of man, binding Himself to Him, committing and compromising Himself with him. This is the one side of what takes place in this address. And we must speak of it first because it is the presupposition of the other and so easily overlooked.

But our present concern is, of course, with the other, with the involved determination of human essence by the divine. We ask concerning the *humanitas* of the Son of Man who was and is also the Son of God ; concerning what was imparted and given and received ; concerning what happens to the human essence of the One who (because God became man) was not only man but is also God. We ask concerning what it means for Him in the human sphere that all the fulness of the Godhead dwells in Him bodily. We ask concerning the human nature which has its basis in this fact.

As in the question of the determination of divine essence in Jesus Christ, the answer must move strictly within the framework of the mutual participation. It cannot, therefore, be that His human nature as such also receives the divine, i.e., that it is deified. We have already weighed and rejected this answer. In Jesus Christ there is no direct or indirect identification, but the effective confrontation, not only of the divine with the human, but also of the human with the divine essence, and therefore the determination of the relationship of the one to the other which, without altering its essence, takes place in this confrontation. Each of them is determined in a way peculiar and not arbitrarily ascribed to it : the divine in such a way, as we have seen, that it remains the divine ; and the human in such a way that it remains the human, but is as such confronted with the divine in the One who as the Son of Man is also and primarily the Son of God. What is this determination ?

We shall first attempt a general answer and say that it is human essence as determined wholly and utterly, from the very outset and in every part, by the electing grace of God. This confrontation with divine essence takes place in the fact that it pleased God in His grace to condescend to it, Himself to become man in His Son, to become this particular man, and therefore to unite His divine with human essence, to give this *telos* and form to His divine essence for the sake of man. This is the electing grace of God. It is this which is addressed to human essence in Jesus Christ, and by which human essence is determined and characterised in Him. And only and utterly by it— we must at once add. For there is no other subject apart from the Son of God which can give even partially a different determination or character to human essence. The Son of Man exists only in His identity with the Son of God, and His human essence only in its confrontation with His divine. Its determination by the electing grace of God is not only its first but also its last and total and exclusive determination. It is human essence, but effectively confronted with the divine, in the character with which it is invested by the fact that God willed to be and became man as well as God, so that without itself becoming divine it is an essence which exists in and with God, and is adopted and controlled and sanctified and ruled by Him. This is the exaltation which comes to human essence in the one Jesus Christ.

Expressed in the language of the older dogmatics this means that the concrete filling out of the concept of the *communicatio idiomatum*, and more deeply of the *communio naturarum*, and more deeply still of the *unio hypostatica*, is on this side the *communicatio gratiarum*, the total and exclusive determination of the human nature of Jesus Christ by the grace of God. It is, therefore, the exaltation of Jesus Christ the Son of Man which follows the humiliation of Jesus Christ the Son of God, and is indeed fulfilled in and with it. The older Lutherans did not think that this was enough. It did not sufficiently distinguish Jesus Christ the Son of Man from all other men, or safeguard the power of what He has done for us in His humanity. If justice is to be done to the *communicatio idiomatum*, the *unio naturarum* and the *unio hypostatica*, what the human nature has received must consist—beyond the grace and its gifts addressed to it—in the impartation and appropriation of the distinctive qualities of the divine nature to the human, and therefore in its divinisation. It is hard to see where this necessity arises. It is hard to see why its total and exclusive determination by the grace of God is not enough. It is hard to see why this should not be the absolute distinction and empowering which has come in it to the one Son of Man who is also and primarily the Son of God. It is true that the fulness of the Godhead dwells bodily in Jesus Christ (Col. 2⁹). But even in this *locus classicus* we must not overlook the κατοικεῖ. And can we really understand this in any other way than Calvin did (*Instit.* II, 14, 1) : *e virginis utero templum sibi delegit in quo habitaret* ? Is temple or dwelling—a dwelling which is certainly filled with Godhead and totally and exclusively claimed and sanctified, but still a dwelling —not really enough to describe what we have to say of human essence in relation to Jesus Christ and the history which took place in Him ? Do we have to deify this temple, this dwelling as such, in order that the dwelling of the Godhead in it may be a real one ? If it is deified, does it not cease to be His temple ? Or, to abandon the metaphor, does not a deified human essence cease to be our human essence, usable as such for the work of the Son of God for us and to us, and accessible and recognisable to us as such ? If the human essence of Jesus Christ is deified, can He really be the Mediator between God and us ? He is totally unlike even the most saintly among us in the fact that His human essence alone is fully, because from the very outset, determined by the grace of God. This is the qualitatively different determination of His human essence, and of His alone as that of the One who as the Son of Man is also and primarily the Son of God. But He is like us in the fact that His human essence determined in this way is in fact the same as ours. In this, even as the exalted Son of Man, He is still our Brother, and as such accessible and recognisable and able to be the first-born among many brethren, our Head. But it does not alter the human essence that it becomes the recipient, the only and exclusive recipient, of the electing grace of God. The likeness between the Son of Man, Jesus Christ, and us is not broken by the fact that He confronts us in this unlikeness. On the contrary, as the recipient of the electing grace of God, His human essence is proved by its exaltation to be the true essence of all men. It is genuinely human in the deepest sense to live by the electing grace of God addressed to man. This is how Jesus Christ lives as the Son of Man. In this He is the Mediator between God and us men in the power of His identity with the Son of God and therefore in the power of His divinity. How can it be otherwise ? How can this fail to be the supreme thing that may be said of His human essence, and therefore that which also distinguishes Him from all other men ?

It is, then, a matter of "the grace of our Lord Jesus Christ" (2 Cor. 13[13]) to the extent that the divine grace particularly addressed to Him as man, and therefore the particular determination of His human essence, is the determination on the basis of which, as very God and very man, He is gracious to us all ; the determination which in His person can be and is the divine grace addressed to all men. We will now try to describe it from this standpoint as the grace given to Him as man and received by Him as man—bringing out at least its most prominent features.

We must realise that this can be done only with reference to Him and to the particular history which took place in Him. We cannot do it in abstraction from this happening, or with side-glances at something which took place and arose and came into being in Him, at a kind of status of the human essence of Jesus Christ as such. We cannot do it apart from the act in which it was given and received its particular determination.

It was fatal that in this respect the older Reformed dogmaticians (e.g., B. Bucan, *Instit. theol.*, 1605, 2, 23) adopted in principle the same approach as the Lutherans. They could not avoid in substance the same side-glances. And in terminology they had suspicious affinities to later mediæval scholasticism. Thus they spoke of a *gratia habitualis*, or many such, imparted to the human nature of Jesus Christ by infusion. *Habitus* comes from *habere*, and therefore denotes possession. But grace is divine giving and human receiving. It can be " had " only in the course of this history. Our present consideration is of the way in which it was actually received by Jesus Christ the Son of Man who was also and primarily the Son of God, and therefore becomes the determination of His human essence. But we cannot look away from the event in which this receiving takes place. We can only look to the event in which it does also take place. There can be no question, then, of a *habitus* proper to the human essence of Jesus Christ. It is relatively understandable that it made a poor impression on the Lutherans when they heard the Reformed speak "only" of a habitual grace infused into the human nature of Jesus Christ at a point where they themselves —also and above all looking away at what had happened and arisen and come into being, and preoccupied with a status of this nature—thought that they could see and recognise a deification. Their own looking aside was more generous and fertile—it led them to that Promethean undertaking—and for this reason it was the more sinister. But the side-glance is sinister as such, even in the relatively sober form in which it was conducted on the other side. For it involves a refusal to be directed by the history in which " the grace of our Lord Jesus Christ " takes place as a grace addressed to Him as the Son of Man and received by Him as the Son of Man. We ourselves must be at great pains to guard against a similar aberration.

The particularity of Jesus Christ, and therefore of the history between God and man which took place in Him, and therefore of the determination of His human essence by the grace of God, emerges at once and comprehensively when we look first to the origin of His being as the Son of Man, of His human existence. It is not a matter of the Virgin Birth. This does not constitute, but only indicates, the grace of His particular origin. The grace of His particular origin consists in the fact that He exists as man as in the mode of existence of the Son God Himself exists. It is not only because God exists that this One exists as man. The same is true of every man and every creature, for all things need the existence of God as Creator for their own existence. But it is true in particular of the Son of Man Jesus Christ that although He, too, exists as a creature and therefore because God exists, He also exists as God exists. His existence as man is identical with the existence of God in His Son. God in His Son becomes man, existing not only as God, but also as man, as this One, as the Son of Man, Jesus of Nazareth. This existence of God as the man Jesus Christ is the particular grace of His origin addressed to human essence in Him. The existence of the man Jesus Christ is an event by and in the existence of the Son of God, i.e., by and in the event of the divine act of reconciliation, by and in the electing grace of God. He derives wholly from this ; or, concretely, from the will of the Father who sends Him, the Son who obeys, and the Holy Spirit of the Father and the Son ; from the act which executes this will. He derives exclusively from this will and this act. As man He is also the creature of God. But even His existence as a creature is from no other source. The grace of God is not addressed to Him in the sense that He is first without it and subject to other determinations but then receives it beyond these other determinations, in fulfilment, or perhaps alteration, or even partial or total replacement of them. The grace of God alone is His origin and determination. He is by it and in it, and only in this way—not abstracted or loosed from its demonstration or occurrence. He is not of Himself. He derives entirely from His divine origin. In all this we are again describing the *enhypostasis* or *anhypostasis* of the human nature of Jesus Christ. We may well say that this is the sum and root of all the grace addressed to Him. Whatever else has still to be said may be traced back to the fact, and depends upon it, that the One who in Jesus Christ is present in human nature is the Son of God, that the Son is present as this man is present, and that this man is none other than the Son.

We can and should state this as follows. It is only as the Son of God that Jesus Christ also exists as man, but He does actually exist in this way. As a man, of this human essence, He can be known even by those who do not know Him as the Son of God. They can see and know and in some way interpret Him like all other men. He stands before Caiaphas and Pilate, and can be judged and condemned and put to death by them. At a distance, He appears before Josephus, and at an even greater distance before Suetonius and Tacitus. He exists, and there are all kinds of traditions concerning Him, for later historians with their varying degrees and forms of partisanship or prejudice. As Jesus of Nazareth He is a figure of world-history and of different views of the world. But even for Caiaphas and Pilate, for Josephus, Suetonius and Tacitus, for so-called historical scholarship and the authors of different views, He does not exist apart from the grace of His origin, and therefore in virtue of the fact that He is the Son of God. They know Him and His existence, but they do not really know them. They do not know with whom they have to do. They call Him by His true name—Jesus of Nazareth. But they do not know to whom they give this name, or how it is that they come to see and know and in different ways interpret Him. They do not know what they are really doing, as their action itself shows. Conversely, where He is known as the Son of God who became man and exists in human essence, this does not mean that something is conferred on Him, or that His appearance as such is penetrated and interpreted. The question who men (the people) or the disciples say that He the Son of Man is, is critical and divisive (Mt. 16[13, 15]). To recognise Him is to see and know Him—without any penetration or interpretation—as the One who He, Jesus of Nazareth, really is. It is not a matter of interpreting an appearance but Himself, His existence, beside which He has no other. And it is a matter of interpreting it in the light of the origin from which He comes, without which He would not be, without which there would not be any appearance. It is a matter of interpreting Him as the One He is. It is to recognise Him as the Son of God, as identical with this Son—"Thou art . . .," in the traditional words of Peter in v. 16.

This grace of His origin does not involve or effect any alteration in His human essence as such. It does not result in any change, diminution or increase. His essence is that of a man like ourselves, the individual soul of an individual body, knowing and willing and feeling as a man, active and passive in the time allotted, responsible to God and tied to its fellows. What the grace of His origin does involve and effect, with supreme necessity and power, is the exaltation

of His human essence. Exaltation to what ? To that harmony with
the divine will, that service of the divine act, that correspondence to
the divine grace, that state of thankfulness, which is the only possibility in view of the fact that this man is determined by this divine
will and act and grace alone, and by them brought in His existence
into not merely indirect but direct and indestructible confrontation
with the divine essence. We may indeed say that the grace of the
origin of Jesus Christ means the basic exaltation of His human freedom
to its truth, i.e., to the obedience in whose exercise it is not superhuman but true human freedom.

From this point it can be understood as the grace of the sinlessness
of His human essence. This, too, is grace—a determination of the
human essence of the Son of God from the fact that it has existence
in Him alone, that it is actual only in the Son of Man. It is not, then,
self-evident. It does not follow analytically from a quality of His
being as man. This is not sinless in itself. The Word became flesh—
not just man, but the bearer of our human essence, which is marked
not only by its created and unlost goodness but (in self-contradiction)
by sin, so that it is a perverted essence and lost as such. If His human
essence were sinless as such, how could it be our essence ? How could
He really be our Brother at this decisive point ? How could there be
any solidarity with us in our lostness ? Would it not mean that the
Son of God had become the Son of Man but had not as such taken
to Himself our sin and guilt ? But if He had not done that, how
could He have taken them away, as He has done ? He did in fact
bear them. But He bore them without sin. " Without sin " means
that in our human and sinful existence as a man He did not sin. He
did not become guilty of the transgression which we in our human
essence commit. He bore an alien guilt, our guilt, the guilt of all
men, without any guilt of His own. He made our human essence
His own even in its corruption, but He did not repeat or affirm its
inward contradiction. He opposed to it a superior contradiction. He
overcame it in His own person when He became man. And we can
and must say that He overcame it at the deepest level by not refusing
to accomplish the humiliation of the Son of God to be not only a
creature but a sinful creature, to become and be the bearer of human
essence in its inward contradiction, to repent as such, to become the
friend of publicans and sinners, to suffer and die as a malefactor with
others. All the purity of His human action depends upon the purity
of this life-act of His. However we may interpret it, the sinlessness
of Jesus was not a condition of His being as man, but the human act
of His life working itself out in this way from its origin. And on this
aspect, too, the determination of His human essence by the grace of
God does not consist in the fact that there is added to Him the remarkable quality that He could not sin as a man, but in His effective determination from His origin for this act in which, participant in our

sinful essence, He did not will to sin and did not sin. As a determination for this act it is, of course, His absolutely effective determination. He accomplished it, He did not sin, because from this origin He lived as a man in this true human freedom—the freedom for obedience— not knowing or having any other freedom. The One who lived as a man in this harmony with the divine will, this service of the divine act, this correspondence with the divine grace, this thankfulness, had no place for sinful action. Necessarily, of course, He knew it well enough when He took our human essence. He knew it even as a tempting question addressed to Himself, as emerges clearly enough in the Gospels. But there could be no question of it ever becoming His act. Because and as He was man only as the Son of God, it was excluded from the choice of His acts. In virtue of this origin of His being, He was unable to choose it. Therefore He did not choose it. And He did not do it. This, then, is the exaltation of our human nature in Jesus Christ as seen from this standpoint. It is an exaltation to sinlessness, to freedom from sin. Note that from this standpoint too it is real exaltation, not change or replacement. From this standpoint again there is no addition or increase or change. It is not really of necessity, but only in fact, that human nature wills to sin, and does sin, and therefore can sin. We are in self-contradiction in this capacity, in our *posse peccare*. It is not our genuine freedom, our *liberum*, but our *servum arbitrium*, that we choose evil. It means an alienation not only from God and our neighbour but also from ourselves. We do not act freely, but as those " possessed," when we do wrong. And it is only as we actually do it that it shows itself to be a determination of our human essence which, although we cannot shake it off, is supremely inappropriate and improper. Thus the man Jesus does not transcend the limits of the humanity common to Him and us, or become alien to us, when in His acceptance of human essence even in its perversion He does not repeat the perversion or do wrong, when in virtue of His origin He cannot will or do it. He is just what we are and how we are. The only difference is that He is it in genuine human freedom. If He takes to Himself the contradiction of our essence, it is only to overcome and resolve it. It does not need deification, but it does need the exaltation of our nature by the unique grace of God's becoming man, to bring about this sanctification, to introduce this living Son of Man in genuine freedom. Yet we cannot say that in this freedom He is not like us, our Brother. On the contrary, it is in this *non peccare* and *non posse peccare* that He confirms His brotherhood with us, the fellowship with our true human essence which we for our part continually break with our *peccare* and *posse peccare* and *non posse non peccare*.

And again it is only another form of the one grace addressed to human essence in Jesus Christ that His humanity as that of the Son of God is determined by the fact that as the Son of Man He is fully and completely participant not only in the good-pleasure of God the Father but also in the presence and effective working of the Holy Spirit—fully and completely because in virtue of His origin, because as the Son of God He is also the Son of Man. If He exists only as He is the Son of God, this does not mean that He is isolated, that He exists " only " as the Son of God, and that He is therefore suspended, as it were, over the abyss of non-being. The three divine modes of existence are to be distinguished, but they cannot be separated. As the Son, therefore, He is sustained outwardly by the inflexible Yes of the Father and His inexhaustible blessing, and enlightened and impelled inwardly by the comfort and power and direction of the Holy Spirit. For where the Son is, of the same divine essence there is also the Father, and again of the same essence the Holy Ghost. The Son of Man is not deified by the fact that He is also and primarily the Son of God. He does not become a fourth in the Holy Trinity. But necessarily He acquires and takes as man the same full share in its being and work in creation as He has in its inward life as God. Godhead surrounds this man like a garment, and fills Him as the train of Yahweh filled the temple in Is. 6. This is the determination of His human essence. It is again apparent that there can be no question of a transferred condition, or an infused habit, in this grace addressed to Him. It is all a history against the background and in the light of this inward life of God : a history which in the living Jesus Christ is played out between His human being as the Son of Man and His divine being as the Son of God which He is also and primarily ; a history between the Father, and also between the Holy Ghost and the Son, who as such is also the Son of Man. How else, then, can this determination of His human essence take place and be seen and understood except as an event ? What *habitus* could either belong or be ascribed to Him in His relationship to the grace of God ? The grace of the Father's Yes and the Spirit's power a *habitus* ! Even the man Jesus of Nazareth exists in a concrete history as its recipient. He takes the road which leads from His birth to His death, from His secret preparation to the beginning and fulfilment and completion of His human work. He takes the road on which the good-pleasure of the Father, the gift of the Spirit and His own existence as the Son of God must always mean something new and specific at every step. He takes the road on which there can be no permanent state of blessing, but the continuity of which can be assured only (although, of course, definitively) by the fact that He is always the same elect man confronted and surrounded and filled by the same electing grace of God. But if we keep clearly before us this active character of the existence of Jesus Christ in His unity as Son of God and Son of Man, it is obvious that from this standpoint too there can be no question of an alteration of His humanity. As the Son of God He participates without measure in the unconditional affirmation of the Father and the Holy Ghost (Jn. 3[34]), and this distinguishes Him qualitatively as well as quantitatively from all other men. This is again the exaltation which comes to human essence in His person. But it does not invade or violate it. It does not make Him a superman in a middle essence who as such is dissimilar and alien. It is indeed unique that the existence of a man is this history and has this character. But it is not the case, and we must not state or complain, that it contradicts the concept of man which embraces us too. It only contradicts all other actualisations of this concept. But it is not on this account an ideal which transcends the concept. Is there any reason why a man who shares fully in the good-pleasure of the Father and the fulness of the Holy Spirit should be only an empty ideal and not a real man ? Why should not this unique thing, His contradiction of all other actualisations of the concept of man, be the real fulfilment of the concept, the exaltation of human essence to its truth ?

If we may mention it at this point, it is not the case then that the full grace of God addressed to human essence in Jesus Christ is either compromised by, or itself compromises, those passages in the Gospels in which we see clearly the limited and conditioned nature of the humanity of Jesus as such. There is the verse in the childhood narrative in St. Luke which is often quoted as difficult in this respect : " And Jesus increased in wisdom and stature, and in favour with God and man " (2[52]). There is also the frequently quoted statement from Mk. 13[32] that knowledge of the day and the hour is withheld from the Son. There are also, of course, the stories of the temptation and Gethsemane, and the prayer in Gethsemane, which if anything is described even more drastically in Heb. 5[7] than in the Gospels. There are also the passages which refer to all kinds of very human inward and outward deprivations and reactions. It has been asked whether the wrath of Jesus, hardly concealed if at all, in the cleansing of the temple, or the sharpness of His judgment of the Pharisees and scribes as recorded in Mt. 23[13f.], do not cause us serious perplexities in this connexion. And the greatest difficulty of all along this line is the decisive fact of His suffering and death. Now obviously it is only with great difficulty, and very artificially, that these facts can be harmonised with the thesis that the human nature of Jesus Christ was divinised, and it is hard to see how some kind of approximation to docetic conceptions can be avoided if we propound this view. But if we do not accept it, or that of an infused *habitus*, there is no apparent reason why it should not correspond to His existence as Son of God and Son of Man that His humanity and its limitations are not eliminated from the New Testament, but sometimes assiduously emphasised. It would be a great pity if these limitations were not visible and brought out in the New Testament. For then we should not be able to see Jesus Christ as the Brother of all men who as such, even in the weakness of His human essence, was the Son of God, the object of the good-pleasure of the Father and participant in the fulness of the divine Spirit. If the Word became flesh, if God became man, He necessarily existed as a man in a human history, and trod a human way, and on this way had human wants, was subject to human temptations and influences, shared only a relative knowledge and capacity, and learned and suffered and died as a man. It was as this man that Jesus of Nazareth was " the Father's Son, by nature God." It was as this man that He was sustained by the Father and filled by the Spirit. The only thing is that we must not measure Him by a preconception of what is divine, of what is worthy of the Son, of what is pleasing to God the Father, of what is meant by the presence of the Spirit in fulness. On the contrary, we must be content to recognise what is divine and worthy and well-pleasing and spiritual at the very point where it is human history—in the happening of this history, in the way of Jesus of Nazareth, and therefore in His human essence. This does not make everything clear at a stroke. It brings us to the beginning of a way on which we have to accompany this history, recognising the divine in the human. But we shall know that when it is a matter of knowing what is truly divine there can be no evading the child in the crib at Bethlehem, the Tempted in the wilderness of Jordan, the One who prayed in Gethsemane and the man on the cross of Golgotha. This is how it is when the Son of the Father becomes a guest in the world under His unqualified Yes and wholly participant in His Spirit. Here, in the flesh, there dwells the eternal Word, and His glory is seen—in the exaltation of human essence which takes place here and in this way—and nowhere else and in no other way.

To develop it further, the grace addressed to human essence in Jesus Christ is His qualification to be the organ of the action or work of the Son as the Mediator between God and men, the Reconciler of the world with God. This work is accomplished in a history which takes place in the world itself, on the earth, in time, among men. He, God the Son, in His divine essence is its active Subject. It is to discharge this office, to do this work, that the Father sends Him, and He is obedient to the Father, humbling Himself, becoming a man among men, assuming human essence. He commends Himself as the indispensable organ for this office and work. But it is not self-evident that He is adapted for it. This is not something which is in and of itself. His is a creaturely, human and even sinful essence. It is flesh with all the weakness of flesh. It is the electing grace of God—and this is its exaltation from this standpoint—which makes it adapted for this purpose. The older dogmatics called what is imparted to the human essence of the Son of God in this respect the *potestas officii*. This impartation could be understood as His sanctification. But this is fulfilled in the act of the Son of Man, who is also and primarily the Son of God, which is sinless, or, positively, affirmed by the Father and enlightened by the Holy Ghost. It is the decisive presupposition, but only the presupposition, of what we have now to consider. This is the empowering which this organ needed to be capable of the service which it was destined to render as the human essence of the Son of God. And this empowering has to be understood as the impartation of what is comprehended in the New Testament concept of the *exousia* given to Jesus and exercised by Him. The word speaks generally of freedom of action, and then more particularly either of power in the sense of capacity or force, or power in the sense of authority or control. Because and as He is the Son of God, the Son of Man has freedom of action in this twofold sense. In this twofold sense the human essence of the Son of God is empowered to render this service by the electing grace of God.

He receives power. Power for what ? We must remember that He, the Son of God, acts. He is obedient to the Father. He humbles Himself and goes into the far country. On earth He is born of Mary.

He is baptised in Jordan. He calls the disciples. He preaches to them and the people on the Sea of Galilee and on the mountain. He proclaims the kingdom, according to the Synoptists, and Himself, which is the same thing, according to John—Himself as sent by the Father and therefore come down from heaven. He forgives sins. He demands discipleship. He disputes with the scribes and Pharisees. He goes to Jerusalem and cleanses the temple. He is betrayed and denied and taken and judged and scourged and crucified. He dies and is buried. He is raised the third day and His glory is revealed. And after all these things, after accomplishing once for all and altogether the reconciliation of the world with God, He returns to His home, to the glory already revealed to His witnesses and concealed only from the world, the glory of the divine essence which He shares with the Father and the Holy Ghost. He returns to heaven, which is the dwelling of God in His creation. But in so doing He does not cease to exist here as well. For Himself He is in heaven with the Father. Here He is for us and the world in the work of the Holy Spirit : in the gathering and edifying and sending of His community ; in the kindling of the faith and love and hope of the Christian. He justifies and sanctifies and calls His own, and as He does so He is the hope of the whole world. For He will come again. That is, He will be revealed as the One who exists both there and here, who has accomplished once for all and altogether the reconciliation of the world with God. He will no longer be concealed but revealed (even to the world). And in Him there will be revealed the end of all God's ways. He, the Son of God, did and does and will do all these things. But He does not do them in the nakedness of His divine power, in which they could not have been done as the reconciliation of the world with God, but as the Son of Man, in His identity with the man Jesus of Nazareth. But this means that His divine power, all power in heaven and on earth, is given to this man in His identity with the Son of God. In His person there is given to human essence the human power fully to attest His divine power, to serve it in a way commensurate with it, effectively to execute its act and acts. All this is given to it as the human essence of the Son of God—not of itself, but as His organ, as the body of which He is the Head. But it is given to it as the human essence of the One who is Son of Man as well as Son of God. The fact that He is given the power for this attestation, this service, this execution of the mighty acts of God—the *potestas officii*—is the grace of God addressed and imparted to Him from this standpoint.

But it is a matter of authority as well as power, of *potestas* as well as *potentia*. What the Son of God does in divine power, He does not do arbitrarily, but in execution of the divine will and decree, sent by the Father and obedient to the Father. Nor does He do it for Himself, but for the world, in place of all men, who could not do it for themselves, and therefore to them, in radical alteration of a situation which they themselves were quite unable to alter. He does it as their Mediator. In Him, in His action, a decision is made for and concerning them all. As the Son of God He has power to act in the place of God and in our place—and to act decisively, with the authority of our Saviour. He exercises His power with this authority. It is the power of the legitimate Lord of all men and all things. His action is, therefore, legitimate. But we have to say again that in His authoritative action He is not merely the eternal Son of God. The authority exercised by Him in the name of God and the name of all men is not simply that of His naked Godhead. He has and exercises it—and otherwise He could not exercise it as the Reconciler of the world with God—as the Son of Man, in His identity with the man Jesus of Nazareth. It is, therefore, given to this man too in virtue of His identity with the Son of God. This man, too, is the Mediator, the Executor of the divine will and decree in the place of God, the One who acts in our place and for and to us all—this man who is both the servant of God and the Lord and King of all men and all things. In Him, therefore, this one man, it is given to human essence to attest the divine authority, to serve and execute it, to be its indispensable organ. It, too, may participate in the mediatorial action of the One who represents God to us all, to the world, and us all, the world, to God. Thus His divine authority has also the form of human authority. What this one man does within the limitations and conditions of His human essence is really done for God and really done for us—and not merely significantly and effectively, but with a holy legitimacy and therefore in eternal power. The grace addressed to human essence in Jesus Christ is thus the authority to attest and serve and accomplish the " for God and for us " of the eternal Son. And it is addressed to Him as and because it is in Him the human essence of this eternal One who causes it in its humanity to participate in the divine authority of His action.

There is no reason to mistake the pure humanity of Jesus Christ in relation to the empowering which comes to His human essence by the electing grace of God. We insist that its function is that of an organ of the Son of Man who is also and primarily the Son of God. It is to Him and not this organ, to His human essence as such, that there is given " all power in heaven and in earth " (Mt. 28^{18}). It does not possess, but it mediates and attests the divine power and authority. It bears and serves it. It is adapted in its function for what the incarnate Word, the Son of God and Son of Man, wills to do, and does actually do, for and to the world as He exists in it, in the human sphere. It is not, therefore, itself a divinely powerful and authoritative essence in which Jesus Christ, very God and very man, the divine Subject existing and acting in the world, makes use of His divine power and authority. But it is empowered as the necessary creaturely medium for His action. This work concerns man and the world. It therefore demands a human soul and a human body, human reason and human will, human obedience and human humility, human seriousness and anger, human anxiety and trust, human love for God and the neighbour. And it demands all this in an existence in our own human and created time. The speaking and acting, the suffering and striving, the praying and helping, the succumbing and conquering have all to be in human terms. That is why human essence is necessary to Him. And the empowering to serve Him in this way is the exaltation which comes to it in this one man. Surely this is a supreme exaltation. But what is supremely exalted in this way is none other than the human essence common to us all, and it does not change in this exaltation. The saving act of God takes place in the man Jesus of Nazareth. The power and authority of God are revealed by Him and to Him, in His words and in His actions. But while this is the case, He does not cease to be a man as we are, our Brother.

But if we are not to go astray at this point, we must remember always that this grace of office or service or work addressed in Him to human essence is a history and not an appropriated state. We have to consider the whole of the work which He has done and does and has still to finish and ask ourselves what place there is in it for any state of human essence. What was and is and will be effective and revealed in this man and therefore in and through human essence is not a supreme form of human and creaturely power and authority —although even the older Reformed, with their doctrine of *habitus*, had to use very artificial aids to escape this conclusion. It is nothing less than absolutely divine power and authority. And it does not follow from this—the Lutheran alternative was just as artificial—that omnipotence and therefore divinity accrue to the human essence of this man as such. It follows rather that in the existence of this man we have to reckon with the identity of His action as a true man with the action of the true God. The grace which comes to human essence is the event of this action. And what takes place in this event is that it acquires even in its pure creatureliness divine *exousia*, even in its human weakness divine power, even in its human meanness divine authority, even in its human particularity (for individuality with all its limitations belongs to its humanity) divine universality—and all this in the occurrence of this event, or, to put it more simply, as Jesus Christ (for we are speaking of His human essence) lived and lives and will live. Yes, we are speaking of the life of Jesus Christ, which He lives not only in divine but also in human essence, which therefore conquers death, even the apparent death ascribed to it in different forms (Lutheran as well as Reformed), which as His life is an event and not a state or *habitus*. In this event His human essence (while it is still totally and unequivocally our human essence) acquires divine power and authority. It acquires the quality which it lacked to bear and attest this power and authority. There thus takes place its inconceivable exaltation. It wills to be known and in some sense—this is the secret of the Holy Spirit in all true knowledge of Jesus Christ—accompanied or repeated with grateful understanding in its occurrence. Where this is the case, there need be no fear that the true and genuine humanity of the Son of man who is exalted in this way will be missed or mistaken.

And now we take a further step. In Jesus Christ, the Son of Man who is also and primarily the Son of God, our human essence is given a glory and exalted to a dignity and clothed with a majesty which the Son who assumed it and existed in it has in common with the Father and the Holy Ghost—the glory and dignity and majesty of the divine nature. As His human essence it shares the Creator's precedence over all His creatures. When the Word became flesh, when it willed to become and be also Jesus of Nazareth, when it became identical with this man, it associated its own divine essence with human. The humiliation in which it takes human essence is therefore the exaltation of human essence. As the Creator· condescended to be a creature, He did not make the creature Creator, but in its unity of existence with His Son He adopted it into fellowship with His being as God, Creator and Lord. He did not do this only in the resurrection and ascension of Jesus Christ. His resurrection and ascension were the first, particular, temporary revelation of this action, and therefore the revelation of the exaltation of the Son of Man in His human essence to the right hand of the Father. Nor, again, is this only a matter of His return in glory. His return will be the second, universal, definitive revelation of that which He has already done, and never ceased to do, in His existence as the Son of God and Son of Man. No, it is the act of the humiliation of the Son of God as such which is the exaltation of the Son of Man, and in Him of human essence. As the Son of God He goes into the far country. As the Son of Man He returns home. And what He brings with Him—we might ·almost say as the spoils of the divine mercy—from that far country, what He places in the closest proximity to God from the greatest distance, is the human essence assumed by Him. As He adopts it, making it His own existence in His divine nature, He does not deify it, but He exalts it into the *consortium divinitatis*, into an inward and indestructible fellowship with His Godhead, which He does not in any degree surrender or forfeit, but supremely maintains, when He becomes man. Already in the eternal will and decree of God He was not to be, nor did He will to be, God only, but Emmanuel, God with man, and, in fulfilment of this " with," according to the free choice of His grace, this man, Jesus of Nazareth. And in the act of God in time which corresponds to this eternal decree, when the Son of God became this man, He ceased to all eternity to be God only, receiving and having and maintaining to all eternity human essence as well. Thus the human essence of Jesus Christ, without becoming divine, in its very creatureliness, is placed at the side of the Creator, πρὸς τὸν θεόν (Jn. 1¹). It is a clothing which He does not put off. It is His temple which He does not leave. It is the form which He does not lose. It is an organ the use of which He does not renounce. He is God in the flesh—distinguished from all the idols imagined and fashioned by men by the fact that they are not God in the flesh, but products of human speculation on naked deity, λόγοι ἄσαρκοι. The glory and dignity and majesty of the true God exercised and revealed in His Son consist in the fact that He is God in the flesh, and therefore that He has also human essence as His clothing and temple and organ, because and as He is also called Jesus of Nazareth. But to the extent that according to this will and decree, and in this act, God is with us in this way, we too in the same way—in the human essence of this One from among us—are with God. For He is not God to us, nor can He be known or glorified or loved or worshipped by us as God, except in and with the human flesh assumed by His Son as the Mediator of the covenant. The electing grace of God addressed to this essence in the one Jesus Christ consists in the fact that there is established, and will never cease, a connexion between God and Him and therefore between Him (and in Him ourselves) and God. And the direct and practical significance of a knowledge of this grace is that we cannot have to do with God without at once, *eo ipso*, having to do also with His human essence (our own), with the flesh of His Son (and in Him our own flesh). There is, therefore, no knowledge of God, no calling upon Him, no worship, no trust or hope, no obedience to His will, no single movement towards Him, which on any pretext or in any way can escape His humanity (and therefore our own), or in which the Father and the Spirit can be sought except in and by Him.

There is, therefore, no natural religion, no natural theology, no natural law. In all these concepts " natural " means apart from Jesus Christ, apart from the Son of God who became also the Son of Man, who is called and is also Jesus of Nazareth, who in His unity with Jesus of Nazareth has also human essence. The antithesis to this " natural " is not in the first instance the concept of " revealed," but that of human nature once for all and definitively exalted in Jesus Christ, once for all and definitively placed at the side of the Father and in fellowship with Him. Without this—and without, of course, God's revelation in it—even the true God would be to us a hidden God, and therefore in practice no God at all.

God is God in His connexion with the human essence of Jesus Christ (and therefore our own) as it has taken place in Him and is indissoluble in His existence. And it is only in this divinely established connexion with human essence that we can know God, and magnify Him, and love Him and call upon His name.

What we have here is a union, and therefore in this respect as well a history, an act of God which is exclusively His alone, and from which as such we cannot abstract even in this respect with reference to His human essence. In relation to His human essence, it is always a matter of Himself and what He does in it and to it. It is, therefore, a matter of knowing and glorifying and loving and worshipping God in His humanity. From God, in His action, this humanity, too, acquires and has a glory and dignity and majesty which those who know and glorify and love and worship Him cannot possibly overlook, but the grateful acknowledgment of which is rather included in all the knowledge and honour and love and worship addressed to Him. But it does not have these things of itself. As God cannot be considered without His humanity, His humanity cannot be considered or known or magnified or worshipped without God. Any attempt to treat it *in abstracto*, in a vacuum, is from the very first a perverted and impossible undertaking. As Son of Man, and therefore in human form, Jesus Christ does not exist at all except in the act of God, as He is first the Son of God. Where He is not known as the latter, He cannot really be known in His humanity as abstracted from the divine Son as its Subject.

This was the difficulty which beset all the modern attempts—now, of course, more rare—to sketch a biography of Jesus, a picture of His life and character. It is no accident that the New Testament material for this purpose is so sparse and unsatisfactory. The scholars and men of letters who attempted it in their different ways were necessarily betrayed from one difficulty into another. A predicate cannot be properly seen and understood and portrayed without its subject. But in itself and as such the humanity of Jesus Christ is a predicate without a subject. And although the attempt was made—and very seriously sometimes—it was absolutely impossible to try to ascribe a religious significance, or to enter into a religious relationship, with this predicate suspended in empty space. It is only rhetorically that the empty predicate of His humanity could and can be counted as a subject which summons us in this way.

Even greater is the difficulty of representing Jesus Christ in the plastic arts. It is even greater because here there emerges unavoidably, and indeed purposively and exclusively, the particular and delicate question of the corporeality of Jesus. The prior demand of a picture of Christ is that its subject should be seen. And He must be seen as the artist thinks he sees Him according to the dictates of his own religious or irreligious, profound or superficial imagination, and as he then causes others to see Him (and sometimes in such a way that they cannot possibly fail to do so). As against this, the biographer of Jesus only speaks, or writes, on the basis of texts by which he can in some degree be checked by his readers or hearers, and in books which can be left unread or forgotten. The claim of the biographer is an impossible one. But that of the artist who portrays Christ is so pressing as to be quite intolerable. It must also be added that every picture in pencil, paint or stone is an attempt to catch the reality portrayed, which is as such in movement, at a definite moment in that movement, to fix it, to arrest or " freeze " its movement, to take it out of its movement. The biographer has at least the relative advantage over the artist that whether he does it well or badly he has to tell a story and therefore to see and understand and portray what he takes to be the life of Jesus on a horizontal plane, in a time-sequence, in movement. In addition to everything else, the picture of Christ is far too static as a supposed portrayal of the corporeality of Jesus Christ in a given moment. But what will always escape both the biographer and the artist, what their work will always lack, is the decisive thing—the vertical movement in which Jesus Christ is actual, the history in which the Son of God becomes the Son of Man and takes human essence and is man in this act. In this movement from above to below He presents Himself as the work and revelation of God by the Holy Spirit, as the Jesus Christ who is alive in the relationship of His divinity to His humanity. But He obviously cannot be represented in this movement, which is decisive for His being and knowledge, either in the form of narrative or (especially) in drawing, painting or sculpture. The attempt to represent Him can be undertaken and executed only in abstraction from this peculiarity of His being, and at bottom the result, either in literary or pictorial art, can only be a catastrophe. We say this with all due respect for the abilities of the great artists, and the good intentions of the not so great, who in all ages (incited rather than discouraged by the Church) have attempted this subject. But this cannot prevent us from saying that the history of the plastic representation of Christ is that of an attempt on the most intractable subject imaginable. We shall have to remember this when in the doctrine of the Church we come to the question of instruction by means of plastic art. It is already clear that from the point of view of Christology there can be no question of using the picture of Christ as a means of instruction.

When we abstain, as we ought, from all abstraction, we can see the concrete reality which is an event in Jesus Christ, an event which is both wonderful and simple, infinitely disturbing and infinitely comforting, the *communicatio gratiarum* which comes to all flesh in His flesh, the exaltation of human essence to fellowship with the θεία φύσις (2 Pet. 1⁴). It does actually take place in the homecoming of the Son of Man which, although it is seen and known and confessed from the opposite standpoint, is identical with the way of the Son of God into the far country. The spoil of the divine mercy, the result of the act of atonement, is exalted man : new in the power of the divine exaltation ; no longer far from God but near to Him, a man who even as such and precisely as such is a man as we are ; the first-born of a new humanity ; the second Adam who is still our elder Brother and in whose exaltation our own has already taken place.

His history is the Word of God addressed to us and to the whole world. It is the promise that we shall be like Him (1 Jn. 3²) ; that we are "predestinate to be conformed to the image of his Son" (Rom. 8²⁹) ; "that the life also of Jesus might be made manifest in our mortal flesh" (2 Cor. 4¹¹).

We have now encircled, and provisionally described, the point which is the point of departure for all that we shall have to think and say concerning man's sin and sanctification, the edification of the Christian community, and Christian love. All that we know of man's exaltation derives from what we know of the return of the Son of Man as the act which took place in and with the way of the Son of God into the far country, of the exaltation of our human essence as it is an event in Him. Our life is hidden—not yet revealed—with Him. It is not to be sought on earth, but above, in Him. But with Him it is *realiter* hidden and lifted up in God (Col. 3¹ᶠ·). It is exalted to His glory and dignity and majesty. We can develop this in the fourth part of this basic section when in a third we have realised more concretely than has so far been possible what is meant by the homecoming of the Son of Man and the exaltation of our human nature as

it has taken place in Him. But already at the goal of this first christological discussion we are directed to the fact that when we speak of
the one Jesus Christ we speak of that which in Him is an event for
us and to us. *Tua res agitur—in aliena forma*, but *tua res*.

4. But first—and still under the fourth main heading in our presentation of the incarnation—we must take the third step already
indicated and speak of the common actualisation of divine and human
essence as it takes place in Jesus Christ—what the older dogmatics
called the *communicatio operationum*.

It was also called the *communicatio apotelesmatum* (the co-operation of the
two natures to specific ends or results), and the definition of Petrus van Mastricht
(*Theor. pract. Theol.*, 1698, V, 4, 13) was to the effect that it is the *concursus
utriusque naturae ad operationes mediatorias, sic ut opera illa procedant a persona
θεανθρώπου per efficaciam distinctam utriusque naturae.* The older Lutherans
spoke of the same thing under the concept of a third genus of the doctrine of
the *idiomata*, called the *genus apotelesmaticum*, which called for consideration
in so far as (Hollaz, *l.c.*, qu. 61) *in actionibus officii utraque natura Christi agit,
quod suum est cum alterius communicatione in agenda.* These definitions and the
corresponding expositions clearly reveal again the common and yet different
interests and concerns by which the Christology of older Protestantism was
influenced, for there is no formal antithesis at this point, but, as in the general
doctrine of the *communio naturarum*, a series of characteristically different
emphases. What the Lutherans tried to underline and stress—and this is why
they treated it under the communication of attributes—was the oneness or
harmony of the two natures as found in the work of Jesus Christ. But if this
could not be contested by the Reformed dogmaticians, for them the whole
emphasis was on the reference to the basis of this concord in the unity of the
person of the Son of God and Son of Man as the subject of the two natures co-
operating even in their distinctiveness. The totally different pictures which
could and did result can be readily understood. If we try to stress the concord
of the two natures in the work of the Mediator, in this concord the divine is the
active and the human the passive, and so in relation to the action of Jesus Christ
we shall again speak of the direct interpenetration of the human nature by the
divine, of the human as the direct bearer of the attributes of the divine. Conversely, if we stress the unity which underlies this harmony of the two natures,
that of the person of the Mediator as Son of God and Son of Man, within His
working which is both divine and human we shall distinguish the divine element
as that which determines and controls the human, and the human as that which
is determined and controlled by it, as that which serves it. Both Lutherans
and Reformed said that the two natures of the Mediator do not work *separatim*
but *conjunctim*. But whereas the Lutherans made to the *conjunctim* the addition
et unite, the Reformed safeguarded it in the opposite way : *non confuse, sed
distincte*. Both Lutherans and Reformed said that the *principium quod* of this
activity consists in the divine-human person and its *principium quo* in the two
natures. But whereas the Lutherans were content to bring the two natures
into significant conjunction without any attempt at closer elucidation, the
Reformed said that in the one divine-human activity the divine nature is the
causa principalis and the human the *causa minus principalis* or *ministra*. Both
Lutherans and Reformed declared that the work of atonement is accomplished
neither by the divine nature alone nor by the human alone. Yet whereas the
Lutherans continued : But by the union of both fulfilled in Jesus Christ, the
Reformed continued : But by Jesus ~hrist, in whom both are united. Both
Lutherans and Reformed emphasised that in His work each nature does that
which is appropriate to its distinctive character : dying, for example, in the

case of the human ; and the establishment of the infinite and universal significance of His death in the case of the divine. Yet whereas the Lutherans concluded from this that the atonement is the *apotelesma* the Reformed did not
make this conclusion—in spite of its logical possibility—but said that neither
the divine nor the human nature as such, nor their union, is the active subject
in the atonement, but that their union is the *apotelesma* of the person of the
one Jesus Christ active in and through both natures, while what is done by the
two natures as predicates of this subject can only be called an action which is
not autonomous but serves and accomplishes its working. That is why the
Reformed were careful not to speak of a *communicatio idiomatum* in this connexion, but of a *communicatio operationum*. A mere battle of words ? A split-
ting of hairs ? That may be our reaction. But surely it is better to respect the
care with which the older theologians, instead of making wild assertions, marked
off their positions even to the final details.

From the very first we have understood and interpreted the doctrine
of the incarnation, which we have considered from all angles, in
historical terms, as an actuality, as an *operatio* between God and man,
fulfilled in Jesus Christ as a union of God with man. We have represented the existence of Jesus Christ as His being in His act. Relatively,
therefore, there is not a great deal more to say as we conclude our
fourth main point. It may be said, indeed, that all the time we have
been thinking and speaking within this concept of the *communicatio
operationum*. Our only remaining task is to make one or two things
more clear and precise.

The first concerns the important term *operatio* itself. In a basic
attachment to the Reformed tradition, but without following it in
detail, and transcending it at some points, we have given this a sense
and position which it did not have in all earlier Christology. We have
" actualised " the doctrine of the incarnation, i.e., we have used the
main traditional concepts, *unio, communio* and *communicatio*, as con-
centrically related terms to describe one and the same ongoing process.
We have stated it all (including the Chalcedonian definition, which is
so important in dogmatic history, and rightly became normative) in
the form of a denotation and description of a single event. We have
taken it that the reality of Jesus Christ, which is the theme of Christology, is identical with this event, and this event with the reality of
Jesus Christ. We must now consider what this involves.

It is true, of course, that the older Christology also spoke of an event at the
beginning of its presentation, and of events, of the *operationes* of the one Jesus
Christ, at the end—a necessary transition to the discussion of His mediatorial
office and work in a special second section. The event at the beginning, however, was found in the underlying basis of the *unio hypostatica* in the *unitio* of
the divine Logos with what He assumed as the possibility of His human being
in Mary and thus endowed with His own existence, i.e., in the event of the
incarnation in the narrowest sense, in the history as it then took place : *et homo
factus est*. What was seen between these two poles was a kind of great phenomenon with its own definite structure, and the ensuing doctrine of the person of
Christ a kind of great phenomenology of the relationship between the Logos
and its two natures, or between the two natures themselves, as created by that

unitio and presupposed in the work of Jesus Christ, but itself static, immobile and at rest. A dynamic movement was found both before and after, in the form of an event of divine-human existence and actuality, but here itself there ruled the great calm of a timeless and non-actual being and its truth. This calm was distinctively reproduced in the doctrine of the work of the Mediator in the form of His two successive " states " : the state (*status*) of humiliation in the time between His birth and burial ; and, sharply separated from it, the state of exaltation beginning with His resurrection.

The distinctive feature of this whole conception is the calm both in the description of the divine-human being of Jesus Christ and in the doctrine of the two states. And it was a conception common not only to the traditional Christology of the Middle Ages and the Early Church, but also to that of both Lutherans and Reformed. We have given a relative preference to the Reformed because of its persistent and certainly instructive and pregnant centring on the decisive concept of the *unio hypostatica*. But there can be no doubt that in our departure from this whole conception we have left even Reformed Christology far behind. We cannot expect to be praised for our " orthodoxy " from any quarter.

What is it, then, that we have done ? We, too, have considered and attempted to describe the being of Jesus Christ in its truth and reality. There can be no dissolving or weakening the hard reality, the genuine " objectivity," of this basic element in the divine action for us and to us which is as such the basic element in all Christian knowledge and confession. What has happened, however, is that we have left no place for anything static at the broad centre of the traditional doctrine of the person of Christ—its development of the concepts of *unio, communio* and *communicatio*—or in the traditional doctrine of the two states. We have, in a sense, kept company with the older dogmatics in each of the three concepts, as in those of *exinanitio* and *exaltatio*, to the extent, that is, that they are all terms which speak of actions, *operationes*, events. But—thinking and speaking in pure concepts of movement—we have re-translated that whole phenomenology into the sphere of a history. And we have done this because originally the theme of it, which here concerns us, is not a phenomenon, or a complex of phenomena, but a history. It is the history of God in His mode of existence as the Son, in whom He humbles Himself and becomes also the Son of Man Jesus of Nazareth, thus assuming human essence, uniting this with His divine essence, addressing the two one to the other, especially the divine to the human, and in this way accomplishing its exaltation. We have thus done justice to the doctrine of the humiliation and exaltation of Jesus Christ, not as a description of two different and successive states, but to denote two opposed but strictly related moments in that history which operate together and mutually interpret one another. God becomes man in order that man may—not become God, but come to God. It is in the actual occurrence of this history that we have seen that which particularly interests us in the present context—its movement from below to above, the exaltation of the Son of Man who in His identity with the Son of God comes to God as the bearer of our human essence. According to the translation which we have attempted, this history itself, and in its dynamic, is the reality, the *mysterium*, the sacrament of the being of Jesus Christ. In every theological context in which we must name the name of Jesus Christ—and there is none in which we do not have to name it at the decisive point—it is this history which is meant according to our assumption : the act of God in which the Son of God becomes identical with the man Jesus of Nazareth, and therefore unites human essence with His divine essence, and therefore exalts the human into fellowship with the divine ; the act of God in which He humbles Himself to exalt man. The Subject Jesus Christ is this history. This is the content of the eternal will and decree of God. As it takes place, there takes place the reconciliation of the world with God. It is the divinely spoken Word of truth and life and judgment and comfort and commandment and hope. It is the justification of man, his sanctification, and his calling to the kingdom of God. It is the being of the Church in the world. It has been manifested a first time, particularly and provisionally, in the resurrection and ascension of Jesus Christ. Ultimately it will be manifested universally and definitively—and this will be the return of Jesus Christ. God (the God who acts and reveals Himself in this history) will be all in all (1 Cor. 15[28]). But when we speak of this history, we mean the history which took place once and for all in the birth and life and death of Jesus Christ and was revealed for a first time in His resurrection. To that extent it unquestionably belongs to a definite time. It has happened. But in so far as it has happened as this history, the act of God, it has not ceased to be history and therefore to happen. As this history it is not enclosed or confined in that given time. " My words shall not pass away " (Mk. 13[31]). They have not passed away, they have not become merely historical fact. " Lo, I am with you alway " (Mt. 28[20]). Who ? Jesus Christ. But that means the history in which He, the Son of God, becomes and is the Son of Man, going into the far country as the Son of God to come home again as the Son of Man. " Jesus Christ lives " means that this history takes place to-day in the same way as did that yesterday— indeed, as the same history. Jesus Christ speaks and acts and rules— it all means that this history is present. Whether confessed and acknowledged or not, it is the great decisive event of to-day. It is the most up-to-date history of the moment. Is it only that ? Does it only take place to-day, in the present ? Does it take place only as a reflection of our own present history ? No, it has a backward reference. It took place then, at its own time, before we were, when our present was still future. And it has also a forward reference. It is still future and will still happen—" even unto the end of the world." In other words, when we say that Jesus Christ is in every age, we say that His history takes place in every age. He is in this *operatio*, this event. This is the new form which we have given to Christology in our present understanding and development of it. But is it really a legitimate and possible and necessary form ? Are we really presenting a true account of the matter ?

The questions of legitimacy and possibility are decided by that of necessity. That of legitimacy is a serious one, because the transposition of the static statements of older dogmatics into dynamic is undoubtedly an innovation which, although it does not really jettison or ignore any of the relatively more important elements in the older conception, may well arouse suspicion because of the radical alteration in form. But if there is a real necessity, the legitimacy cannot be questioned in spite of every suspicion. Necessity means respectful freedom in relation to tradition. Similarly, the question of possibility is a serious one. For the transposition undoubtedly means a disturbance of the relatively perspicuous pragmatics of the older conception. And it involves logical difficulties which, if they were not really overcome, were carefully concealed in the latter. How can a being be interpreted as an act, or an act as a being ? How can God, or man, or both in their unity in Jesus Christ, be understood as history ? How can humiliation also and at the same time be exaltation ? How can it be said of a history which took place once that it takes place to-day, and that, having taken place once and taking place to-day, it will take place again ? How much easier it seems at a first glance to speak of the given fact of this person and His structure, and then of His work, or, to use the language of more modern theology, of His " significance for all succeeding ages, or His influence and effects " ! How can the birth and life and death of Jesus Christ be an event to-day and to-morrow ? Are these thoughts and statements that can really be carried through ? But again, if there is a genuine necessity, even suspicions as to the possibility cannot be regarded as finally decisive. Difficulty or no difficulty, we must attempt to think and state the matter along these lines.

And, of course, in this matter there really is a necessity which the older Christology evaded in a way that we can neither approve nor imitate. Obviously it is not a powerful tradition as to the course to be taken, nor a general conception of practicability, but only the Subject itself which can be the law controlling what we think and say about a given matter. And this is a very categorical law. It demands that we think and state what is there. If it is really the point at issue, it does not ask concerning legitimacy or possibility. It simply requires that—whatever the cost—it should be done ; that we should do justice to the theme itself in what we think and say concerning it. But in Christology, as the name itself tells us, we are thinking and speaking about Jesus Christ. He, then, is the law controlling what we think and say. Justice must be done to Him. But who is He ? The older Christology gave us the right answer that He is the Son of God and Son of Man who as such is of divine and human essence. A Christology which does not give this answer does not speak about Him at all, but about a fantastic divine essence or an equally fantastic human essence. In the first instance, we can only return the answer given by the older Christology. To that extent we are in continuity with it. We accept its insight, even if we have to give it another form. But the whole point is that we do have to give it another form.

For what is the meaning, in this answer, of the little word " and " ? This " and " tells us who He is. But is there any standpoint from which we can see and expound it as the description of an immobile and rigid contiguity and fusion of two elements ? Certainly, the word speaks of a union. But it is a union in which there can be neither mixture nor change, division nor separation. The being of Jesus Christ consists in this union. " Union " ? To say this is already to suggest an act, or movement. Naturally, there has to be a oneness. But for this oneness a conjunction or unification is needed if it is to be a oneness of God and man, of Creator and creature, a oneness which is not at all self-evident, but inconceivable in itself. Was it an accident that at this point even the older Christology used terms which verbally at least suggest activity and movement : *unio, communio* and *communicatio* ? How, then, does it come about that in spite of these concepts there is that static conception, that calm, at the centre of the older doctrine of the person of Christ ? On what ground, *quo iure*, is the distinction made between *unitio* and *unio*, which necessarily results in *unio* acquiring the sense of *unitas* and denoting a static and non-actual twofold being, with inevitable consequences for the interpretation of *communio* and *communicatio* ? Can we say " Jesus Christ," and therefore " God and man," " Creator and creature," without making it clear that we are speaking of the One who exists in this way only in the act of God, and therefore the occurrence of this history ? Can we see what He became in this act, " God and man," but ignore— or leave behind as a mere presupposition—the act in which He became it, and therefore His becoming ? Can we say *Verbum caro* but conceal, or give no emphasis to, the *factum est* ? Is Jesus Christ, *Verbum caro*, actual in any other way than in the full actuality of the *factum est* ? Is it not essential that the latter should be expressed in the concept of His actuality ? Does not everything depend on our doing justice to the living Jesus Christ ? But, at root, what is the life of Jesus Christ but the act in which God becomes very God and very man, positing Himself in this being ? What is it but the work of this conjunction ? Presupposing that we are speaking of the living Jesus Christ, can the being of Jesus Christ be distinguished from what actually takes place, as the act of God, in His existence as the Son of God and Son of Man ?

We will look at the matter from another angle. When we say " Jesus Christ," and therefore " God and man," with reference to the One who is both we say the " humiliation of the Son of God and exaltation of the Son of Man." This is what the older Christology was trying to state in its doctrine of the " states " of Jesus Christ. But in relation to the One who is both can we really speak of two different and successive " states," or even of " states " at all ? The terms used— *exinanitio* and *exaltatio*—are again better than what they were supposed to denote, for they, too, obviously speak of a history. When they were used to describe particular " states," the being of Jesus Christ was not robbed at a stroke of its historicity as such, but it lost the material distinctiveness of its historicity, which is that of God humbling Himself in His grace and at the same time that of man exalted in the reception of God's grace. For where, now, was the " at the same time " ? Jesus Christ was first humiliated and not yet exalted, not yet set in the glory of God ; and then He was exalted and no longer humiliated, no longer the child born in the manger at Bethlehem and the man crucified on the cross of Golgotha. What a tearing apart of the unity of descending and ascending so plainly indicated in Jn. 3¹³ and Eph. 4⁹ᶠ· ! And how fortunate that it could never be carried out in practice ! For if it could be, would the One who was only humiliated, or only exalted, really be the one Son of God and Son of Man ? And if He was not this, and therefore the Reconciler of the world with God, in either of these " states," could He really be it at all ? Surely Jesus Christ does not exist only in this abstract succession of two " states." Does not everything depend on the inter-connexion : that the exaltation of the Son of Man begins and is completed already in and with the happening of the humiliation of the Son of God ; and conversely that the exaltation of the Son of Man includes in itself the humiliation of the Son of God, so that Jesus Christ is already exalted in His humiliation and humiliated in His exaltation ? Is it not the case, then, that His being in the unity of God and man is this history in its inter-connexion ? If we are speaking in any respect of this history, can we really abstract from the literal sense of the two concepts ? Do we really see and understand Him concretely if we do not see Him in this twofold movement, and at the same time in both the one movement and the other, so that there can be no question of a halt and therefore of a " state " ? We ask again : How could He be the living Jesus Christ if He were not the One He is in this movement ?

But a third question arises. What is the real nature and meaning of the existence of Jesus Christ in time, in past, present and future ? The older Christology did, of course, take into account the fact that He was and is and will be. But then it went on to understand by the " He was " His being in the real but past state of His humiliation, His birth and life and death as a man—to which it added the transition to a state of exaltation, His resurrection and ascension. On the other hand, by the " He is and will be " it understood His eternal being in a state of exaltation as it then began—a continuation (which we cannot

describe more narrowly because it is beyond the sphere of our per
ception) of His activity as our Advocate with God and as the Ruler,
Guardian and Sustainer of His community on earth until His second
coming in judgment, in which He will conduct the history of the world
and the Church to its goal and end. There in the past it saw Him in
the known and recognisable form of His history as it then took place.
But here, unfortunately, as the present and coming Jesus Christ, it
saw Him as basically formless, or in a form which can only be briefly
sketched, the details being left to pious phantasy. Again we have to
ask : Who is this One who was and is and will be ? We agree with
the older Christology that He is the Son of God and Son of Man,
humiliated and exalted. But if we begin with the " He was," and mean
by this His being in the history which then took place, how can the
" then " (the " then " of this history which is His history) be the
boundary of a " now " or " some day," a boundary by which He is
prevented, as the One who existed and acted and spoke and suffered
and conquered in that history, from present and future being in His
then known and recognisable form ? How can that which God did
in Jesus Christ yesterday not be His act to-day and to-morrow ?
How can it be present and future only as the significance or influence
of His then act ? For all its " then-ness," is it not once-for-all, and
therefore His act to-day, which cannot and need not be continued or
augmented or superseded ? And will it not be the same to-morrow ?
Again, if we continue : " He is and will be," how can this present
and future being—our question is now reversed—be anything other
than His present and future as the One who exists and acts and speaks
and suffers and conquers in that completed history, His being in the
outlines of His then form ? Is there any reason, then, to understand
His being after that " He was," after that completed history, the
continuation of His being beyond that given time, as a present and
future being in a second and different history which we obviously do
not know ? Was He not in the history of that time altogether and
once for all the Son of God and Son of Man, humiliated and exalted
as such, and therefore the Reconciler of the world with God ? Can
His being in that accomplished history—as though it were not His
perfect being in that " then," that yesterday—be dissolved or augmented or superseded by any other history ? Can it find its continuation in any other history ? Can it continue to-day and to-morrow
except as His then history, and therefore in such a way that His then
history takes place also to-day and will take place also to-morrow ?
How is He, as the Son of God with the Father and the Holy Ghost,
Himself the eternal God ? How is He, as the Son of Man, by and with
God ? How is He our Advocate before God ? How is He the Ruler,
Guardian and Sustainer of His community ? How can He and will
He come again to judgment ? Can He do any of these things except
as the One who was, and therefore is and will be, wholly and altogether

in that history the One He is ?   Who is Jesus Christ ?   Must we not
answer : The One who is to-day and will be to-morrow in the then
completed *operatio* of His being as God and man, His humiliation and
exaltation, in the reconciliation of the world with God then accomplished in His death and revealed in His resurrection ?

Is not this how His community, in its concrete relationship to
Him, has always basically seen and understood the matter when it
has not given free rein to its imagination ?   At bottom, has it not
always been in abstract theory, which analyses the unity of His being
instead of accepting it, that He has been seen and understood otherwise ?   In their own life of faith, have not even abstract theorists
always, in fact, seen and understood Him in this way ?

What is the meaning of our keeping Christmas, Good Friday and Easter ?
What is the meaning of our proclaiming and hearing Jesus Christ as the Word
of God spoken to the world and ourselves ?   What is the meaning of our believing
in Him, and loving Him, and hoping in Him ?   What is the meaning of the
Lord's Supper ?   Do these things really make sense if they are only acts of
remembrance and representation, analogous to the many memorials and festivals
and acts of commemoration that may be found in the secular sphere ?   Or is it
not the tacit presupposition of all these actions that, preceding our remembrance,
the One whom we remember is Himself in action now, to-day and here ?   In
what action ?   In the very action which as His then action we have not im-
perceptibly but perceptibly before us when we proclaim and hear Him as the
Word of God.   In the act of Christmas and Good Friday and Easter, in the
whole life and death and conquest of the Jesus Christ attested in the New Testament, which as it took place then takes place to-day and will again take place
to-morrow, in the course of which He is the living Jesus Christ, in which we
now, to-day and here are invited to participate with supreme realism, being
personally summoned as individual Christians and gathered as the community.
Why with such realism ?   Because and as He overcomes the barrier of His own
time and therefore historical distance.   Because and as He is present and future
in His then act.   Because and as He is among us to-day, and will be among us
to-morrow, in His then act.   Did any living Christian or living community ever
live except on this presupposition ?   Would He or they exist at all if this presupposition were not a reality ?

I must interpose at this point a small but sincerely grateful tribute.   It is
to a theologian who cannot be called great, but to whom I am greatly indebted.
I refer to Abel Burckhardt, who a hundred years ago—a contemporary of the
more famous Jacob Burckhardt—was the second pastor at the minster here in
Basel.   He composed and edited a collection of songs for children in the local
dialect.   This was the text-book in which, at the beginning of the last decade
of the last century, I received my first theological instruction in a form appropriate
to my then immaturity.   And what made an indelible impression on me was
the homely naturalness with which these very modest compositions spoke of
the events of Christmas, Palm Sunday, Good Friday, Easter, the Ascension and
Pentecost as things which might take place any day in Basel or its environs
like any other important happenings.   History ?   Doctrine ?   Dogma ?   Myth ?
No—but things actually taking place, so that we could see and hear and lay
up in our hearts.   For as these songs were sung in the everyday language we
were then beginning to hear and speak, and as we joined in singing, we took our
mother's hand, as it were, and went to the stall at Bethlehem, and to the streets
of Jerusalem where, greeted by children of a similar age, the Saviour made His
entry, and to the dark hill of Golgotha, and as the sun rose to the garden of

Joseph. Was this representation, like the unbloody repetition of the sacrifice of Christ in the Roman doctrine of the Mass ? Was it the kind of faith which in that rather convulsive doctrine is supposed to consist in a re-enactment of the crucifixion of Christ in our own existence ? Again, no. It was all present without needing to be made present. The yawning chasm of Lessing did not exist. The contemporaneity of Kierkegaard was not a problem. The Saviour Himself was obviously the same yesterday and to-day. All very naive, and not worth mentioning at all in academic circles ? Yes, it was very naive, but perhaps in the very naivety there lay the deepest wisdom and greatest power, so that once grasped it was calculated to carry one relatively unscathed—although not, of course, untempted or unassailed—through all the serried ranks of historicism and anti-historicism, mysticism and rationalism, orthodoxy, liberalism and existentialism, and to bring one back some day to the matter itself. As far as was still possible in the 19th century, and not without an obvious influence of Pietism, good Abel Burckhardt stood firmly on the older Christology, presumably of a moderate Reformed type. But, obviously, in all simplicity he had in fact overcome its deadness, and he gave us an impulse to overcome it again. For that reason—academic circles or not—he deserves to be mentioned in this connexion.

We have been concerned to underline and elucidate the concept *operatio*. But we must now turn to that of the *communicatio operationum* in the narrower sense of the older doctrine. When and as the one Jesus Christ, true Son of God and Son of Man, acts and speaks and suffers and dies and conquers, when and as He is who He is in His work for and to us and all men (our justification, our sanctification, our Saviour and Lord in His life-action, the ruling Head of His Church and the coming Judge), it is all in a common and co-ordinated work of His divine and human essence. This was the older thesis—with characteristic nuances in the two Evangelical confessions. And the fact that we cannot agree to the underlying distinction between being and act must not prevent us from a brief consideration of its distinctive and special meaning.

Our first point, in relation to the main concept, is that it is a matter of the existence of Jesus Christ in the common *actualisation* of divine and human essence.

In the inner life of God, as the eternal essence of Father, Son and Holy Ghost, the divine essence does not, of course, need any actualisation. On the contrary, it is the creative ground of all other, i.e., all creaturely actualisations. Even as the divine essence of the Son it did not need His incarnation, His existence as man and His action in unity with the man Jesus of Nazareth, to become actual. As the divine essence of the Son it is the predicate of the one God. And as the predicate of this Subject it is not in any sense merely potential but in every sense actual. But His divine essence—and this is the new thing in Jesus Christ from the divine standpoint—needed a special actualisation in the identity of the Son of God with the Son of Man, and therefore in its union with human essence. In this union it is not immediately actual. In this union it is addressed to what is of itself totally different human essence. It is directed to a specific goal

(*apotelesma*), the reconciliation of the world with God. It is made
parallel to divine essence, as it were, although with no inherent change.
It is the divine essence of the Son in the act of condescension. It is
the divine essence determined and characterised by His act, by His
existence not only in itself but also in human essence. And as such
it has to *become* actual. It needs an actualisation which is new even
from above, from the divine standpoint. It needs the *novum* of the
execution of the eternal will and decree in which God elected man for
Himself and Himself for man, giving this concrete determination to
His own divine being. The being and therefore the work—all that
Jesus Christ does and says as the one Son of God and Son of Man—
includes this new thing in itself, the new actualisation of divine essence,
which is, of course, actual in itself, in its address and direction to the
human essence of this one Son of Man.

Of human essence, on the other hand, we have to say that it, too,
is actualised in as many cases as there have been and are and will be
men. It is actualised, of course, as human essence : not of itself,
but by the creative will and power and act of God, as the One who
alone is actual originally and in Himself ; and as a creaturely essence,
absolutely conditioned and limited by His will and power and act.
It, too, does not await the incarnation of the Son of God for its actualisation. It is another matter that it is created with a view to this,
and has in it its meaning and *telos*, and is only true human essence by
it and in it. But, since the Son of Man Jesus Christ is only one of
countless other men who also bear this essence, we cannot say that it
is actualised only in Him. It needs, however, a special actualisation
in the identity of this One, the man Jesus of Nazareth, with the Son
of God, and therefore in its union with divine essence. In this union
it finds actualisation only in this one case. In this union, as that
which is so totally different from it, it for its part is addressed to human
essence, being directed to a new end (*apotelesma*), the reconciliation
of the world with God to be accomplished by the Son of God and
Son of Man, to whom it is subordinated. Thus it, too, is made parallel
to the divine essence, although not inherently changed, as in the
communicatio gratiarum of which we have already spoken. In the
person of Jesus Christ it becomes and is human essence exalted into
fellowship with God. It is not, therefore, actual of itself. Under this
determination it, too, is a new actualisation. It is again the *novum*
of the execution of that eternal will and decree in which God elected
Himself for man and man for Himself. On this side too, in accordance
with what we have said previously, we must say that the being and
therefore the work—all that Jesus Christ does and says as Son of God
and Son of Man—includes also this human *novum* in itself, a new and
special actualisation (among all the many actualisations of human
essence) in the address and direction of the human to the divine essence
of the one Son of God.

But now we must shift the emphasis and say that in the existence of Jesus Christ it is a matter of the *common* actualisation of divine and human essence—the *communicatio operationum*. It is not just a divine *novum*, nor just a human, which appears, and is effective and revealed, and is to be seen and recognised in Him. At one and the same time it is the great divine and the great human *novum*. He does His work in pure and total divinity, in the essence which was and is and will be that of Father, Son and Holy Ghost. But He does not do it only in this. He does it also in His human essence. And He does it in pure and total humanity, in the essence which is that of all other men. But, again, He does not do it only in this. He does it also in His divine essence. The One who acts and speaks is One. And as such He guarantees the common nature of His self-actualisation as this divine and human *novum*, the unity of the great *novum* in its twofold form.

That is why the older theology likes to describe Jesus Christ in one word as the God-man (θεάνθρωπος), and His essence as divine-human or divine-humanity. The term is possible and tempting. But, except in quotations, we ourselves have preferred to avoid it. It obliterates the historicity of the subject : the Son of God who as such became and is the Son of Man ; and especially (by conjuring up the image of a third and middle being) the historicity of the relationship of His two predicates. He acts as God when He acts as man, and as man when He acts as God, not in the state but the event of the co-ordination of the two predicates. The word God-man obscures again the event, the *novum* of the act of God, in which Jesus Christ actualises Himself and is actual.

Common actualisation means that what Jesus Christ does as the Son of God and in virtue of His divine essence, and what He does as the Son of Man and in exercise of His human essence, He not only does in the conjunction but in the strictest relationship of the one with the other. The divine expresses and reveals itself wholly in the sphere of the human, and the human serves and attests the divine. It is not merely that the goal is the same. The movement to it is also the same. It is determined by two different factors. But it is along the same road. At no point does the difference mean separation. Nor are abstractions possible to the one who knows Jesus Christ. There is no place for a dualistic thinking which divides the divine and the human, but only for a historical, which at every point, in and with the humiliation and exaltation of the one Son of God and Son of Man, in and with His being as servant and Lord, is ready to accompany the event of the union of His divine and human essence.

Common actualisation also means, however, that what Jesus Christ does as the Son of God and in virtue of His divine essence, and what He does as the Son of Man and in exercise of His human essence, He does (in this strictest relationship of the one to the other) in such a way that they always actualise themselves as the one and the other : *per efficaciam distinctam utriusque naturae*. Joined in the One who is

very God and very man, they are always as different as God and man
are different. And it is in this difference that they are co-ordinated—
commonly actualised—in His work. It is where the divine rules and
reveals and gives that the human serves and attests and mediates.
The one Word of Jesus Christ is His self-expression as God's eternal
Word, and it is also the corresponding, but not identical, word of the
proclamation of this man as humanly articulated and conditioned.
The one will of Jesus Christ is the eternal will of God and it is also—
absolutely conformable for all its dissimilarity—the motivated human
will which determines the way of this human life as such. The one
power of Jesus Christ is the omnipotent power of God and it is also
the distinct but fully attesting power, the great and yet limited
power, in which this man as such does signs and wonders. The one
death and passion of Jesus Christ is the final depth of the self-humiliation of God and it is also, following and completing it as a human
death and passion, the way which the man Jesus entered and traversed
secretly from the very outset, and publicly at the last, even to the
extremity of misery and need as prepared for Him, not by men, but
by God Himself. And the glory of Jesus Christ, the exaltation of
man to God in Him, is the triumph of God Himself, the end of all
His ways in His work of atonement, and also His human life in obedience, with the answer revealed to His human life in the public coronation of His resurrection from the dead. In the work of the one Jesus
Christ everything is at one and the same time, but distinctly, both
divine and human. It is this in such a way that it never becomes
indistinguishable. Where Jesus Christ is really known, there is no
place for a monistic thinking which confuses or reverses the divine
and the human. Again, there can be only a historical thinking, for
which each factor has its own distinctive character. The divine and
the human work together. But even in their common working they
are not interchangeable. The divine is still above and the human
below. Their relationship is one of genuine action.

III

We will pause for a moment and look back. The great central
tract of our first christological foundation under the title " The Homecoming of the Son of Man " is now behind us. We have understood
by this the history in which Jesus Christ is not only very God but
also (and this is our particular concern at the moment) very man,
whose existence, as seen from below, is the basis of the reconciliation
of the world with God. We began with a short discussion of the predestinarian aspect of the problem. We then went on to develop it in
relation to the doctrine of the incarnation—and it is this that has
formed the main part of our present exposition. Why did we do this ?

The answer is that it is in the incarnation of the eternal Word and Son of God that we have to do with the exaltation of our human essence in which the existence of this very man takes place. We have understood it, therefore, as the act of majesty in which the Son of God assumes human essence, and exists as the man Jesus of Nazareth, in which He unites in Himself His divine with our human and our human with His divine essence, in which He commits them to a mutual participation, in which especially He exalts our assumed human essence, i.e., to gracious fellowship with His divine nature, to the *consortium divinitatis*, and therefore, as we have just seen, to a common action with His divinity. This act of majesty, this divine act in its totality, is the incarnation as the historical fulfilment of the eternal will and decree of the covenant God of which we had to think at the outset. God humbles Himself to man, even to the final and most radical depth of becoming man, not to deify man, but to exalt him to perfect fellowship with Himself. We have tried to see and understand the event of the incarnation in the special light of this scope and *telos*. This exaltation comes to human essence in the person of Jesus of Nazareth who is the Son of God. It does so once, but once and for all, in this One. It does so in Him in a way which is valid and effective for all who are also of human essence, for all His brothers. It is to be seen only in this One. But in Him it is revealed as the divine decision which has been made and is declared concerning all men. In respect of all other men human essence can only be called an essence which in its creatureliness is sharply distinct from that of God, and in its perversion alien and opposed and hostile. But this is not the case in respect of this One. In Him it is certainly distinct from God as concerns its creatureliness. But it is also bound to Him. And its godlessness and opposition and hostility are not only denied but removed and replaced by His perfect fellowship with God. In Him the homecoming of the Son of Man has already taken place. The true man—and we have purposely used the term in a rather stronger sense than in the older theology—is already present. In spite of all that we are, and must be called, without Him, the divine promise that we shall be like Him has already been pronounced. In Him, in His being as man, the reconciliation of the world with God has already taken place, the kingdom of God has already come on earth, the new day has already dawned. And in a third main section of this chapter we shall have to confirm the truth of this exaltation of human essence in Him by a consideration of the evangelical record of His life—which was often neglected in older dogmatics. As it took place in His life, in virtue of the humiliation of the Son of God, this life, the life of the Lord who became a servant, is the life of the man who according to the records passes through the midst of all other men as the Lord. This is the decisive fact for this whole aspect of the doctrine of reconciliation. Because it is actual in Him, the existence of Jesus Christ is the great divine direction to all men, the commandment which unmasks and punishes their transgression, which sanctifies them, which edifies the community in the power of the Holy Spirit, which summons the Christian to love. We will have to refer back to it continually in all that follows. There is not only a way of God to man. Because there is a way of God downward to man, there is also a way of man upward to God. The one Jesus Christ is the way in both senses. He is also the way of man upward to God. And He is this because as very God He became and is also very man.

But first we must bring this second section to a conclusion. We considered first the basis of the divine election of grace of the exaltation of man as it took place in Jesus Christ. We then discussed rather more expansively its historical fulfilment in the incarnation. We now come to the ground of its revelation in the resurrection and ascension of Jesus Christ.

The question cannot be postponed any longer : How do we really know what we have declared and developed, and especially the decisive and central fact from which all the rest derives, that Jesus Christ was and is and will be the eternal Word of God in our flesh, the Son of God who becomes and is also the Son of Man, in whom, therefore, our human essence is exalted to fellowship with God ? How do we really know that there is anything at all corresponding to what we have described in these formulations, and if there is, that it is actuality in the one Jesus Christ ? How does it come about that dogmatics has to reckon with this fact as with a prescribed text which it has only to read and expound ?

For that is what we have done. Have we only been speculating about an arbitrarily presupposed or freely invented concept ? Have we created a myth ? That would be a sorry state of affairs. But are we really sure that it is not the case ? Or, to justify our action, can we only refer back to the Church, to its symbols and confessions in which that which is here presupposed is indeed solemnly and authoritatively handed down to us ? Or can we appeal only to the history of Christian theology, in the continuity of which we are now working, and which has always set out directly or indirectly from this presupposition, both in its classical and its less classical forms, and with a larger or smaller degree of agreement or divergence ? But is this really satisfactory ? Even the whole Church and all its dogmas and theologians might be mistaken when it counts on this presupposition. It might itself be resting on an enormous fiction. How does it come to make this presupposition ? We have to ask therefore, as Evangelical Christians, on what grounds we can recognise the authority of the Church, and appeal to it and accept its presupposition. There remains the appeal to Holy Scripture. The Church's symbols and confessions arose as summaries and repetitions and expositions of the scriptural witness to Jesus Christ. But perhaps the Church misunderstood Scripture when it took from it this presupposition. And, above all, even if we grant that the biblical authors really did bear this witness, how did they come to do it ? Can we trust them unconditionally in respect of their hearing and seeing of this factor, and their reproduction or interpretation of what they saw and heard. The answer that we hold to this fact, and start from it, because it is attested as such in the Bible, is not to be rejected. It can have a true sense. But it must have this true sense if we are to accept it with a good conscience. And this true sense is not the " fundamentalist " one, which would have it that the sacred text as such is the proper and final basis of knowledge.

But if the question how we know the decisive fact that we claim to know threatens our whole development of the doctrine of the incarnation, it is a particular challenge to the introduction in which we traced back the *Verbum caro factum est* to the eternal will and decree of God. It is clear that this prolegomenon is in truth a postlegomenon. None of us has sat in the divine counsels. We cannot, therefore, speak *a priori*, but only retrospectively, either of predestination in general, or in particular of the ground of the existence of Jesus Christ in God's eternal election of grace. We cannot do it in a vacuum, but only in relation to the fact of His existence as the true Son of God and Son of Man. In this central content, what is the doctrine of predestination but a necessary confession, in the light of this fact, that in Him we are not dealing with chance, nor with one history alongside many others, but with the fulfilment of the purpose which precedes all occurrence, that in this above all other history we can see and recognise the sovereign will which decides the purpose and way and goal of all occurrence ? But this means that the only source of the knowledge of the eternal will of God is the knowledge of His act fulfilled in time, and therefore the fact of the existence of Jesus Christ as the Son of God and Son of Man. And this means that from this standpoint, too, everything depends on the question of the knowledge of this fact.

We must first remember that in respect of the question of this normative ground of knowledge we proceed from a general decision which has been made already. When we took up the doctrine of the incarnation, we argued that the divine act of majesty which realises the existence of Jesus Christ in time, and therefore the exaltation of human essence in Him, and therefore the existence of the true man, is to be described both as the *ratio essendi* and the *ratio cognoscendi* of this fact. A new dimension of being and occurrence confronts all other possibilities of divine disposing and creaturely realisation. It discloses itself within the context of all God's other actions as Creator, and therefore within the cosmic nexus ruled by Him. And to this new dimension there corresponds a dimension of human seeing and understanding and thinking and knowing which is disclosed with and by the same act of majesty. Necessarily, this is new in relation to all other human perception, just as the act of God (the incarnation of the Word) with which it is confronted, the objective fact with which the subjective has to do, is also new as compared with all other actualities or possibilities—the *novum* which altogether and at the same time is both divine and human. To be sure, that act of majesty takes place within both the divine order and the cosmic order which corresponds to and is established by it. But it does not surrender to the latter. Taking place in the series of all other events, it is not controlled by that series, nor does it have its basis in their nexus. And in the same way, although the perception which it meets takes place within the order of all human perception, it is conditioned by the newness of the subject which confronts it, and it is not, therefore, limited by the limits imposed by other subjects. The actuality of this new being and occurrence, grounded in the divine act of majesty, creates the possibility of a special perception to meet it, a perception which is controlled and mastered by it, attaching itself to it, following and accompanying it, imitating and repeating it. Like all other objects, but as this particular one, it establishes itself in the knowing human subject. It does not allow itself to be halted by the normal and customary limitation and contingency of the latter's ability to know. Both *de facto* and *de iure* it makes a place for itself in human cognition, claiming respect and consideration. It accepts all responsibility for the fact that this cognition may not be equal to it in view of the fact that it is so new and strange. But it also deprives it of the pride of a self-complacent repetition and reflection of other objects, and therefore the insistence on its usual contingency and limitation. It gives it this capacity, and therefore summons it to see and think and interpret it as a reality, as this being and occurrence, repeating and reflecting it, both in thought and word, in all its singularity. In short, we have to reckon with the fact that the same divine act of majesty with which we have to do in the incarnation of the Word has not merely the character of objective being and occurrence, but also, as an event within the world and therefore in the sphere of human cognition, a subjective character as well—in a word, the character of revelation.

The reference of the biblical witness to this fact, especially in the New Testament, is to the divine act of majesty in its character as revelation. So, too, is that of the Church's dogma and confession, and of theology in all its anxiety to do justice to this fact. And it is to the act in this character that we ourselves refer as we are confident to participate in the work of Christian theology in the light of this fact.

The process is not at all then—to begin with a demarcation—that a doubtful presupposition is advanced by the apostles and fathers and doctors and finally ourselves, and there is then put to it a question which can be answered only with difficulty if at all—the question how we ever came to make it, how we are in a position to know this fact, how, then, we can really know Jesus Christ. For, of course, no one can. No one is in that unusual position. No one can make that presupposition. No one can say how it comes about that he thinks and speaks on the basis of it. The question of a demonstration of this capacity—which does not exist—is obviously a perverted one. And even more perverted is the attempt to satisfy it, and therefore to show how in some way the apostles and the Church and we ourselves have attained the position where we can make this presupposition, on what grounds we are justified in counting on it and using it, how right we are when we think we can know that fact and speak about it with definiteness. It is, unfortunately, in this way, as an attempted demonstration, that the question has often been answered, not by the apostles, but by the Church and theology. If we answer it in this way, however, we only prove that we are thinking of something very different from the incarnation of the Word, that although we know this fact from the outside, as it may be known by anyone in virtue of its outward aspect as an element in universal occurrence, we do not really know it in its particularity as this fact. If we do know it in this way, we will not speak like that. We will then know the divine act of majesty in virtue of which it is actual and may be known. We will then know its character as revelation, and therefore that the basis and *de iure* of its perception cannot lie or operate outside the fact itself, so that it cannot be demonstrated by anyone as though he himself could posit it, as though he himself could in some way come to recognise this fact, as though he himself could produce a *de iure* of his confession. Eye has not seen, nor ear heard, what God has prepared for them that love Him, nor has it entered into the heart of any man (1 Cor. 2[9])—that is, except by its self-impartation, except in such a way that the only basis, justification and explanation of his knowledge and confession is the actual fact of it. Those who have it in any other way, thinking that they can and should consider and analyse and penetrate this fact and themselves and other men in relation to it, or that they can and should find a basis for their acceptance of this presupposition—as though they did not have to do with a divine act of majesty in the character of God's revelation—need not be surprised if their answer to the question, whatever provisional satisfaction it may give to themselves and others, does not really clarify the situation. This is quite impossible even if their answer is a formally correct reference to tradition, the Church and the Bible. For if the reference is meant to be a demonstration, if they are trying to show by it how they came to know this fact and make this presupposition, or how they can know it, then even in respect of the true authority of tradition, the Church and the Bible, their answer is finally unintelligible. Answers which try to make these explanations or adduce this proof are quite irrelevant to the real process at work where there is a genuine knowledge of this fact, where it is genuinely the presupposition of theological thought and speech, where the latter genuinely derives from it. They may be advanced with great assurance, but they will always be ill-informed and confused, and cannot hope to convince either those who make them or others. At bottom, all answers which are not absolutely simple are completely false answers.

What is the true process? We have openly confessed that in our attempted thinking out and formulation of the doctrine of the incarnation we were reading and expounding a definitely given text. The texts of earlier theology ? Or those of the Church symbols ? Or those of the Bible ? Yes, all these—but in them the basic text which underlies them. It was this text which the apostles read and expounded directly. And it was the same text which the Church and its theology read and expounded indirectly and with greater or lesser faithfulness and fulness. Both attested the fact that it is actually given, and became authorities themselves in virtue of this attestation. We, too, stand or fall with this text and the fact that it is given. But this basic text is the fact created by the divine act of majesty to the extent that it has the character, not only of being and occurrence, but also, as this fact, of revelation. In this character it reveals and discloses itself. It gives itself to be known. It creates the possibility of a seeing and hearing and understanding of it. Or rather, it creates eyes to see it and ears to hear it and a mind to understand it. In this character it is light, and as such it can be seen and is actually seen—*in tuo lumine lumen videmus* (Ps. 36⁹). But this means that it makes itself a known fact. It opens, as it were, the barrier or door of its objectivity. It reaches out to a subject. It surrounds and encloses this subject. It becomes the known object of this subject. In the action of the object this subject becomes a knowing instead of an unknowing subject.

It is obvious that in the secondary character of this fact as revelation we have a perfect analogy to its primary character (as the being and occurrence as which it is revealed and known). In the one case we have its ontic, in the other its noetic character. In the one case we have the incarnation itself, in the other the revelation and knowledge of it. But it is a single and unitary action. To the humiliation of the Son of God on the one hand there corresponds the self-disclosure of that objective fact, in which it imparts itself to a knowing subject. And to the exaltation of the Son of Man there corresponds the endowment and equipment of the subject which is the operation and effect of that self-disclosure, i.e., its opening for the object, its openness for it, its seeing and hearing and understanding of the objective fact. The two are not identical. It is not self-evident that Jesus Christ should also give Himself to be known, and be known, as the One He is. It is not self-evident that His existence should also include that of the community which knows Him, that of Christians who know Him. But there can be no doubt that we have here the characters of one and the same fact, His ontic character being reflected in a noetic. There can be no doubt that in both cases we have to do with the life and action of the one Jesus Christ.

Jesus Christ in His self-revelation is, therefore, the basic text which was already read and expounded by the apostles, which they attested as its direct witness, and after them, on the basis of their witness, by the symbols and theology of the Church, and finally by ourselves as we venture to take up and continue the work of Christian theology in relation to this fact. With the New Testament therefore, and with the whole Church as it is orientated by it, we take our stand on the truth that the fact created by the divine act of majesty has also the character of revelation, that its ground of being is also its ground of cognition. It is for this reason that we know of this fact, and count on it, and take it as a presupposition.

For this reason—but only for this reason, we must add. There is no other ground of cognition. All other supposed grounds lead back to this one and are conditioned by it. We have to acknowledge again that in all our knowledge and confession of Jesus Christ, and therefore in all Christology, we cannot have any other starting-point than His self-revelation. If the fact that the Son of God became and is also the Son of Man may be known as such among all the other facts of world-occurrence, how else can it be but by His self-revelation ? Which of all the forms of contemplation and thought that we know and use for the perception of other subjects can be of any avail in this connexion ? What physics or metaphysics can even lead us to this subject, let alone enable us to know it—to know it, that is, in a way that permits us, as in theology, to see and handle it materially as a basis, and formally as an axiom, of all subsequent reflection ? What authority, even if it is that of an infallible Church or the apostles, can guarantee it if it does not guarantee itself in their witness ? If it is in fact guaranteed, it is by itself, because and as it is revealed in the sense described. Otherwise it is not guaranteed. Otherwise we will be forced to admit that we have only hazarded a hypothesis—a bold and profound hypothesis perhaps, but only a hypothesis. We have only *made* an assumption, and we will have to rely on the fact that we have made it consistently, and that it may be relevant and fruitful. But at bottom we will not really know. We will only suspect. And the whole Church will rest on this hypothesis. It will not really know, but only suspect, where and on what it really stands. If it does know, if we know, it is only on the ground that this fact is not merely a fact, but that as such it speaks for itself, that it makes that self-disclosure, that from its maintained objectivity there springs the fact that it makes itself known, that it therefore includes in itself a subject which knows it as such. It is better not to conceal the truth that there can be no sure knowledge of it at all except—in this sense— from itself.

We must now take a further step. Since the knowledge of this fact has its only ground in its self-revelation, in so far as we think we know it we can start from it only in fact and not in theory. That we take our stand on it, as we have said, is something which can only happen. We can only know it and confess it. We can only read and expound that basic text, as the apostles did primarily and basically. We can only act as those to whom it is given. We cannot try to go " behind " it, either behind the fact that it is given, or behind the way in which it is legitimate and possible for us to act in correspond-ence to this fact. It is a most dangerous distraction to try to peep " behind " instead of resolutely taking this corresponding action. The basic text does really consist in the self-revelation of this fact, or rather of the divine act of majesty which creates this fact. How could it be this self-revelation if we could explain its occurrence, or our own corresponding attitude, our knowing and confessing and thinking as it is based upon it and axiomatically determined by it ? How could it be this self-revelation if we could demonstrate its *quo jure* ? If we could do this, it would not be its revelation, but the speech of another subject. Our knowledge of this fact means that as the subjects who know it we are reached and seized and enclosed by it, that it makes itself known to us. It does not mean that we have made an assumption, and in some way come to make it. We ourselves are presupposed in the process of our knowing. We are presupposed as the subjects to whom it is given to see and hear and understand this fact. Our knowledge, therefore, encloses a renunciation of all prior knowledge of the disclosure of this fact or our openness for it. Our knowledge can only be an event. It can only take place. It, too, can only speak for itself to ourselves and others—not in its own power, but in that of its theme and content, the self-revelation of the fact reflected in it. If it is to be an authentic knowledge to ourselves and others, it can only be in the fact that—in the enlightening power of the fact itself—we do actually know what we know and then, of course, say what we know. What we know and say can have the value and power of witness only to the extent that we do in fact take up to it an attitude of the greatest childlikeness and promptness, as those to whom it has disclosed itself.

But we must now take a final step. We can never control our knowledge of this fact and therefore our authority to speak of it. It is not our own product, but the work of that fact in its character as revelation. It does not become our possession. We cannot put it in our pocket and carry it round with us. We can only use it at once as its work takes place in its character as revelation. We are not to hoard it, any more than the Israelites could hoard the manna in the wilderness. We can and may know that fact when it is revealed—and know it with the self-grounded certainty which corresponds to its self-grounded being and occurrence. But we should be fools—real fools in the biblical sense of the word—if either to ourselves or others we pretended to be the expert bearers of revelation, appealing for our authorisation (in our own eyes and those of others) to a knowledge of revelation which is either transmitted to us institutionally or infused personally, like the Roman Catholic to the authority of his Church, the " Fundamentalist " to the biblical texts, and the sectarian to his inner voice. We can and must act as those who know. But we must not claim to be those who know. For if our knowledge of this fact from its self-revelation is not new every morning, if it is not newly received from it, with empty hands, as a new gift, it is not this knowledge at all. And its flimsiness will be quickly and radically enough exposed. Its power consists in the divine act of majesty in face of which those who really know will always find and confess that they do not know. The attitude of those who know in this power can only be one of the greatest humility. It is the necessary converse of the resoluteness with which they make use of their knowledge. It distinguishes this resoluteness from the arrogance and timidity of mere opinion and hypothesis. It respects the freedom of God, and is therefore the root of the freedom in which they make actual use of their knowledge. It leads them to *pistis*, and therefore to *gnosis*, to unceasing prayer and therefore to knowledge. It is just because they can have no doubt as to the liberation which is quite outside their own control that those who are really free to know this matter can never lose a sense of humour in relation to themselves.

But what is the real reference in this attempt to show the basis of the knowledge, or rather the basis of the revelation of all our knowledge of the Christ-event ? In the first instance, we have merely tried to describe the place and function and operative conditions of this basis. And so far we have done this only in very general and formal considerations and concepts. We have stated that it is a matter of the divine act of majesty in its character as revelation, in which the incarnation and therefore the existence of the true man speaks for itself, making itself a known fact, breaking out of its objectivity to create a knowing subject. We have stated that this is the text which Christology must read and expound ; it is for this reason, and in the conditions which it involves, that there is a knowledge of the Son of God who also became and is the Son of Man. But what is it that is really described in this description ? What is really meant by these very abstract expressions ?

Already at an earlier point, when we touched on the problem of the ground of cognition in Christology, we gave the short concrete answer that it is by the Holy Spirit, by whom Jesus Christ is, that He is also known as the One He is. And now we can and must take up this answer again and say that the process in which all knowledge of Jesus Christ, and therefore of the history in which as very God He also became very man, is grounded, the process of cognition which underlies Christology and is executed in it, is identical with what we formerly described as the witness of the Holy Spirit. It is in His power that the will of the Father is fulfilled in the fact that the Son of God assumes human essence and therefore becomes the Son of Man, exalting human essence to fellowship with the Godhead. And it is in the power of the same Spirit that there takes place the self-revelation of Jesus Christ as the One He is.

It is to be noted that the well-known Latin formulation : *testimonium Spiritus sancti internum*, is incomplete and misleading. For primarily it is *testimonium externum* to the extent that in the first instance it is a matter of the unfolding of that which is objectively concealed from man. Only secondarily, and for this reason, is it also *testimonium internum*, to the extent that it is also a matter of the opening up of man for that which is objectively opened up to him. In relation to the witness of the Spirit we must always think of the totality of this event.

No human spirit can accomplish this revelation and disclosure of what Jesus Christ is and what takes place in His being. And no human spirit can open up itself or any other spirit to this being and occurrence. If this twofold disclosure takes place, the opening up of the fact and the opening up of the human subject to receive it, it does so in the event of the speaking of the Holy Spirit—the Spirit who is God Himself—to the human spirit. It then takes place on the basis of the fact, with all the authority of His witness and assurance and guarantee ; and towards man, in the power of his renewing and liberating and enlightening, in the power in which He causes the human spirit to participate in the light of this fact. It is His work when the fact speaks for itself, and when man hears it speaking for itself to him, and when he is empowered, but also summoned and constrained, to pass on what it says. What we have tried to describe can only be defined first as the secret of His witness.

There can be no doubt that, when it is rightly understood, this first definition of the ground of cognition, the basis of the revelation of the Christ-event, and especially of the new and true human essence exalted to fellowship with God in Jesus Christ, is in itself sufficient, exhaustive and all-embracing. Wherever there is knowledge of Jesus Christ, it takes place in the power of His witness, in the mystery and miracle, the outpouring and receiving, of the gift of the Holy Spirit. He is the lighting of the light in virtue of which it is seen as light. He is the *doctor veritatis*. He is the finger of God which opens blind eyes and deaf ears for the truth, which quickens dead hearts by and for the truth, which causes the reason of man, so concerned about its limitations and so proud within those limitations, to receive the truth notwithstanding its limitations. He creates the Christian community, and in it the faith and love and hope of Christians, and in and with their faith and love and hope the knowledge of Jesus Christ as the One He is : the true Son of God who became and is also the true Son of man. He causes the apostles to know Him. He was the convincing power of their witness as it was heard and given again in the Church. Wherever there is Christian *gnosis* it is His work. That is why it has no other sources or norms. That is why it can be had without any demonstration of its origin. That is why it is not a human product or possession. He is the basis of the humility and resoluteness of those who know by His gift. It is for Him that those who, even as they know, continually find and confess that they do not know, and must always sigh and pray : *Veni, Creator Spiritus.*

Again, there can be no doubt that this first definition of the basis of all knowledge in Jesus Christ is complete in that, rightly understood, it says the most concrete thing that can be said. A reference to the witness of the Holy Spirit means directly a reference to the situation which is peculiar to the knowledge of Jesus Christ, i.e., the event in which the objective is subjectively affirmed, the truth of God by man, finding human acceptance and obedience as His incarnate Word. A living community is that which is assembled and edified and sent by the witness of the Holy Spirit. A living Christian is a Christian who receives the witness of the Holy Spirit and conforms and is faithful to it. Living preaching is preaching which is awakened and activated by the witness of the Holy Spirit, challenging from within the community which has heard His witness, and summoning the community itself to a fresh hearing of His witness. The daily life of the Christian is a life which listens constantly to His witness, and is secretly or openly directed by it, among all the claims and whispers and provocations of the world outside, and especially of one's own heart. In all these forms in which it is a matter decisively of the witness of the Holy Spirit, the knowledge of Jesus Christ, which takes place in the power of this witness, also receives and has its concrete, indeed, its most concrete form. Even from this standpoint, practically, is not the description of this witness as the ground of the knowledge, the revelation of the Christ-event, both the first and also the final word concerning the basis of the knowledge of Jesus Christ as the true Son of God and true Son of Man ?

But we have always to make the proviso—rightly understood. For it is quite possible not to understand rightly this reference to the Holy Spirit and His witness. This is the case when it is taken to be a reference to something which is only formal. When we recall it, are we only adducing it as a kind of name or concept for what we earlier tried to state formally in our description of the basis of the knowledge of Jesus Christ ? Are we only trying to make clear to *what* it was that we were then referring ? Have we really taken a new step in our identification of what we have described with the witness of the Holy Spirit ? It may well be that the reference has only made the matter more obscure, that we have only exchanged a known quantity for an unknown or equivocal. But if so, the fault certainly does not lie with the Holy Spirit. Of itself, the reference to Him and His witness is quite in order at this point. When we refer to Him, we may do so in a way which is absolutely exhaustive and concrete. But it may well be that there is disorder in our own minds. It is so easy to think of a hovering or static, a present or absent something ; an indeterminate fluid ; an anonymous and formless and uncontrollable power which comes and goes ; perhaps even an empty concept of non-worldliness and transcendence and futurity. It is so easy to imagine His witness to be a kind of mysterious overtaking of man by this power, his confrontation with this non-given ; or to think only in terms of the dark feelings or impulses which are supposed to correspond to this overtaking or confrontation. In a word, it is so easy to think of a matter of which some boldly maintain that they know and experience such and such, while there are not a few others who say that in all honesty they have never had this experience, and, if they know themselves, are most unlikely to do so. But is this the divine act of majesty, the incarnation of the Word, in its character as revelation, as the basis of the knowledge of Jesus Christ ? What relationship is there between this anonymous power, or its possible effects on certain men, and a true basis of knowledge, especially in a matter which is so decisively important ? Can a reference to it really be of service when we are trying to understand the basis of the knowledge of Jesus Christ ? But then, of course, this is not really the Holy Spirit and His witness. It has probably more to do with the demonic which is so unhealthily important in so many religions. The numinous is not by a long way the holy. It is certainly quite inadequate as our present reference to the Holy Spirit because in practice it is a reference to the unknown, and the unknown may actually be, in part or in whole, the demonic. Even at best it is only a title or concept for what has to be said formally in elucidation of the process of revelation and the corresponding process of knowledge, and what is perhaps better said without this concept and title if in any case they do not lead us any nearer to that which is elucidated.

The reference to the Holy Spirit and His witness has, then, the force of a first and final word. But this is only when it is understood as a reference to the powerful and effective presence of Jesus Christ Himself—not to a second force beside Him, but to His force. When Jesus Christ encounters and approaches men who are far from Him, who cannot see and hear Him, but live somewhere and somehow in the world in isolation from Him ; when He is recognised by them not merely as an acquaintance but as their Neighbour, their elder Brother, the One who determines concerning them, their Lord—this means that He has given these men the Holy Spirit. When the remarkable thing takes place that He is known by men, simply known as in the exercise of their reason they receive other things, but known as the One He is, as the Word of God directed to all men and therefore to them, as the Word of God spoken in the flesh to men who are themselves flesh, as the obvious claim and promise of God, as the message which demands obedience because it declares to them the free grace of God, and therefore helps them radically, and sets them in the freedom of obedience—this means that these men receive the Holy Spirit. The Holy Spirit is the coming of the man Jesus, who is the Son of God, to other men who are not this but with whom He still associates. And the witness of the Holy Spirit is the disclosure to these men, and therefore their discovery, of the fact that because they are associated with Him they can be called what they are certainly not called of themselves, and be what they can certainly never become or be of themselves—children of God, children of light who in the midst of death are freed from the fear of death because as sinners they are freed from the curse of sin, and as such messengers to all those who, because they do not see the light, are still in darkness, but are not to remain in this darkness. And as and because the Holy Spirit is the coming of Jesus Christ Himself, and His witness this disclosure to men concerning themselves, He and His witness are in fact the self-revelation of Jesus Christ and as such the basis of the knowledge of Jesus Christ.

His work is, of course, the divine act of majesty in its character as revelation. He acts, therefore, with supreme power. There is a " leading "—to use the term with which Paul described His work in Gal. 5^{18} and Rom. 8^{14}. He takes captive (2 Cor. 10^5) all errant human reason and makes it obedient to Jesus Christ. But this power is not an obscure force to which man is subjected in an equally obscure way. It is a force which has form and contour, with far more affinities to the comfortable truth that two and two make four than to the most powerful conceivable, bitter-sweet irruptions from the sphere of the numinous. The Holy Ghost is light—the shining of Him who is the light of the world. And what He does is also light—the reflection of the glory of the Lord in the face of man, which is no longer covered, and not covered afresh, but uncovered. He is the Spirit of the Lord, and where He is there is liberty (2 Cor. 3$^{17f.}$)—not the old bondage, nor a new, but the genuine liberty for which the Son makes us free (Jn. 8^{36}), and genuine because its basic act consists in the fact that man may and can and actually does know Him as the One He is, and know himself in Him as His brother and therefore as the child of God.

Understood in this way, the reference to the Holy Spirit is undoubtedly the first and final word in answer to the question as to the basis of the knowledge of Jesus Christ.

What more do we want ? What more can we want ? It is in this way, as the Spirit of the Lord, and therefore His self-revelation, that the Holy Ghost was given to the apostles and received by them. It is as such that He created their faith and love and hope. It is as such that as He was given to them and received by them He created the Church. Grounded in the apostles, this became the community of those who could and did know the Son of God as the One who had come in the flesh to them, and for them into the world, and the Son of Man Jesus of Nazareth as this Son of God. It became the community of those who are freed by Jesus Christ for Jesus Christ and therefore genuinely freed. The witness of the Holy Spirit came to these men, and they accepted it, and therefore it was not just the witness of anyone, let alone of an anonymous, numinous, demonic or semi-demonic rustling and whispering, but of the Holy Spirit, because it was the witness to Jesus Christ and to His self-revelation.

On at least one occasion Paul could put this in the sharpest possible form : " The Lord—Jesus Christ Himself—is that Spirit " (2 Cor. 3^{17}). For them the Holy Spirit was simply and directly the existence of Jesus Christ as the divine act of majesty in its character as revelation. For them the act not only of Pentecost, but of all their walking and acting and speaking in the Holy Spirit, in His enlightenment· and power and under His lordship and direction—their own and that of all the others turned to them by the power of His witness—was basically, for all its new and extraordinary character, a very sober and literal fulfilment of the promise : " Lo, I am with you alway, even unto the end of the world " (Mt. 28^{20}). The Son of God and Son of Man Jesus Christ was present. He spoke and taught and called and acted and did things in their presence. He reached and seized and encompassed them and all other human subjects. For He gave Himself to be known by them, and then drew them into His own work as those who knew Him, made them fellow-workers and witnesses, sent them as such to Israel and the nations, and gave them authority to become and be the echo and reflection of His self-witness in the world.

The Holy Spirit is also at work in the Church grounded in the apostles, in its life and upbuilding and proclamation, in its inner life and being and attitude to the world around, in its confession and dogma and theology, to the extent that it is the Spirit of the Lord, the Lord Himself, by whom it is impelled to all these things ; and therefore to the extent that it hears His self-witness and is His echo and reflection, His body, His earthly-historical form of existence, His image, to which the men gathered and acting and thinking and speak-in it are conformed and integrated (Rom. 8^{29}) ; to the extent, then, that it recognises Him as His community. And conversely, when and to the extent that His community, the Church grounded in the apostles, reflects His glory and therefore recognises Him, to the extent that the life and therefore the thinking and speaking of the men assembled in it are conformed to His image and correspond to His being, to that extent its being and action, and therefore its confession and dogma and theology, attest that the Holy Spirit is at work in it. There can be no higher or deeper basis of knowledge, or revelation, than the witness of the Holy Spirit, who is the Spirit of Jesus Christ the Lord.

Why, then, can we not rest content with this bare reference to Him ? We obviously cannot do this if we have rightly understood and explained it as a reference to the Holy Spirit who as the Spirit of Jesus Christ renders witness to Him, His self-witness. For if we accept and follow this reference, if we listen to the witness of the Holy Spirit and give it its proper place, we find that we are not referred directly, but very indirectly, to the One who attests Himself in it. Indirectly ! But this means that those who accept the witness of the Holy Spirit cannot tarry with Him as such. There can be no abstract receiving and possessing of the Holy Spirit. There can be no self-moved and self-resting life in the Spirit, no self-sufficient spiritual status. The witness of the Holy Spirit does not have itself either as its origin or goal. It has no content of its own. It has no autonomous power. It does not shine or illuminate in virtue of its own inherent light. The Holy Spirit may be known, and distinguished from other spirits, by the fact that He does not bear witness to Himself. His witness is, of course, divine witness. No human witness can be put beside it, not even that of the prophets and apostles, let alone that of the Church or individuals within the Church. All human witness, if it is of God, comes from His witness, responding to it, living by its authority and power, having in it its norm and limit. But it is divine witness—the witness of the Holy Spirit—in the fact that Jesus Christ is its power and light, its content, its origin and goal. It is the fulfilment of His self-witness. It is the accomplishment of the divine act of majesty in its character as revelation. It is the transition or exit and entry in which the history and existence of Jesus Christ, which also have the character of revelation, which take place wholly in this character, are confirmed in the fact that they inaugurate and set and keep in motion the history of the community and of Christians in the community. The witness of the Holy Spirit, therefore, opens up the whole history which within the world flies like an arrow from its origin in the will and decree of God to the goal and end already set and declared for it in the history of Jesus Christ. The witness of the Holy Spirit brings about this transition—the transition of the self-witness of Jesus Christ into Church history, into the history of individual lives, into world history. And it is for this reason that we cannot make the bare reference to the witness of the Holy Spirit our last word. Or rather, it is for this reason that as our last word in the question of the basis of the knowledge of Jesus Christ it needs to be explained by a reference back to the self-witness of Jesus Christ as such. For the history and existence of Jesus Christ, which by the witness of the Holy Spirit are made the subject-matter of human knowledge, themselves take place in the character of revelation. In virtue of the witness of the Holy Spirit He Himself is the basis of revelation which this witness attests, and therefore its light and power, its origin and goal, its content. Jesus Christ in His self-revelation is the whence of that inauguration of the central history of all histories accomplished in the witness of the Holy Spirit. And He is also its whither—again in His self-revelation. Between His revelations, the first and the last, or rather in the interval included at the beginning and end of His one revelation, the witness of the Holy Spirit accomplishes the self-witness of Jesus Christ in the history of the community, and individual histories, and therefore world history. Thus the reference to the witness of the Holy Spirit as an answer to the question of the basis of the knowledge of Jesus Christ cannot actually be supplemented or transcended or replaced. It is both true and sufficient. But we must be clear why it is true and sufficient. And so we must go on to speak directly of what is meant by the self-witness of Jesus Christ as such—the witness which finds its accomplishment in that of the Holy Spirit.

It is the self-witness—we are now reaching the goal of this final discussion—of the Jesus Christ who has risen again from the dead and ascended into heaven. It is of Him as such that the witness of the Holy Spirit speaks. It is His Word and act of power which it accomplishes as it causes them to speak for themselves and to men. Jesus Christ Himself attests Himself in it. He as such is its origin and content. He as such is present in it, and speaks and acts and calls and does things before human subjects, reaching and seizing and encompassing them, giving Himself to be known by them as the One He is. He as such—but this means, He to whose history and existence there also belongs the integrating factor that He has risen again from the dead and ascended into heaven ; He in virtue of this special element in His history and existence, His being in this character.

The sequence Easter-Pentecost is, therefore, irreversible. If there is an open witness of the Holy Spirit heard by men, if this is given to men and received by them, if there is a Christian community in the world enlightened and led by it, it is on the presupposition, and derives from the fact, that Jesus Christ is risen and ascended. It is in this character that He sends the Spirit, and the Spirit is the Holy Spirit as sent by Him in this character. In this character Jesus Christ is the heavenly Head of the community in which He has His body, the earthly-historical form of His existence. For in this character He is present to it by the witness of the Holy Spirit, giving Himself to be known by it, and through its ministry by the world.

As is well-known, the Evangelists conclude their record of the history of Jesus Christ—the first part of which described His way from Jordan to Galilee and Jerusalem, and the second His passion—with a much shorter third part, almost an appendix, in which they give some account of His existence in this character, and His appearance as such to His disciples after His death. Their record would obviously have been incomplete—indeed, even with reference to the first two parts they could either have given no account at all or only a very different one—if the decisive factor had not been before them, and therefore called for presentation in this third part. Later, on the basis of what happened in this third part, the second main division of the Lucan account can go on to speak of the outpouring of the Holy Spirit and its fruits in the " Acts of the Apostles." And the Epistles and Apocalypse look back to what happened here, to Jesus Christ in this character, as the One who appeared as such according to the concluding section of the narrative. There is nothing in any of them which directly or indirectly is not thought and said, and meant to be heard and understood, on this basis. And it is apparent that even the first two parts of the Gospels are actually conceived and thought out in the light of the content of this third part, this short sequel. It is only with the help of very doubtful procedures that we can separate out from the Gospels a genuinely pre-Easter tradition. Everything points to the fact that there never was such a tradition, and that the well-known saying of Bengel is true not only of the Gospels but of their conjectured literary precursors : *spirant resurrectionem*. It is always noticeably the case that the community looks back to that sequel, to that interspersed history, and therefore to Easter and the ascension. It expects Jesus to come again in the character in which He then appeared to the apostles. It expects to see Him again as such. It recognises its own origin and goal in this Jesus Christ. The New Testament tradition is naturally concerned with Jesus Christ in His being and words and acts and especially His crucifixion on Golgotha, but its concern is with the Jesus Christ who even in His crucifixion existed in the character in which He encountered His disciples according to this sequel, this interposed history. We may confidently say that if He were not this One, and not known to the community as such, there would never have been any tradition about Him. And then there would have been no giving and receiving of the witness of the Holy Spirit in execution of His self-witness. He would obviously not have attested Himself as the One He was—or His self-witness would not have been worth speaking about, let alone worth executing by the witness of the Holy Spirit.

But " Jesus Christ in this character " means Jesus Christ as He reveals Himself in His resurrection and ascension. The significance of this event is to be found here. It is not to be found in a continuation of His being in a changed form which is its fulfilment. The being of Jesus Christ was and is perfect and complete in itself in His history as the true Son of God and Son of Man. It does not need to be transcended or augmented by new qualities or further developments. The humiliation of God and the exaltation of man as they took place in Him are the completed fulfilment of the covenant, the completed reconciliation of the world with God. His being as such (if we may be permitted this abstraction for a moment) was and is the end of the old and the beginning of the new form of this world even without His resurrection and ascension. He did not and does not lack anything in Himself. What was lacking was only the men to see and hear it as the work and Word of God—the praise and thanksgiving and obedience of their thoughts and words and works. What was lacking was only their service of witness and proclamation. How could men perform this service ? It was hidden from them. It was concealed, as by a thick and heavy cloud, by the appearance of ignominy and despicability and insignificance in which it was at first enveloped. It could only have been for them an event of passing impressiveness and importance like so many others. Who really knew Him in His origin and end, as the Son of God who became and was also the Son of Man ? Who knew what had happened in His history for Israel, the world and all men ? Who could possibly know it ? And the question has a permanent relevance. For who can ever know it ? Who can know Him ? Who can penetrate the secret of His history ? Who sees His glory ? Who is able to see it ? Who has ears and eyes and a mind to accept Him ? It is here that His resurrection and ascension came in, and still come in. For when the New Testament speaks of these events, or rather this one event, it speaks of the perfect being of Jesus Christ, and His accomplished reconciliation of the world with God, in its character as revelation. And that is how we must speak of it. The resurrection and ascension of Jesus Christ are the event of His self-declaration. As seen first by His disciples, and then by men generally, they are the event of Jn. 1¹⁴ : " We beheld his glory, the glory as of the only begotten of the Father, full of grace and truth." Thus the resurrection and ascension add to what He was and is and to what·took place in Him—they add to what was to be seen in Him—only the new fact that in this event He was to be seen and was actually seen as the One He was and is. He did not become different in this event. For how could He become anything different or better or higher ? In this event He was still the One He had been and is—the One who had been born and lived and spoken and acted and above all suffered and died on the cross. But as this One He could now be seen, and was actually seen, in His glory. To use the biblical term, He was manifested in His glory. As His self-revelation, His resurrection and ascension were simply a lifting of the veil. They were a step out of the hiddenness of His perfect being as Son of God and Son of Man, as Mediator and Reconciler, into the publicity of the world for the sake of those for whose reconciliation He was who He was and is who He is. His resurrection and ascension were simply the authentic communication and proclamation of the perfect act of redemption once for all accomplished in His previous existence and history, of the Word of salvation once for all spoken in Him. Now that He is risen and ascended, He is not only the One in whom there is life. Now that He is risen and ascended the life which there is in Him is the " light of men." It is the light of the world which is set on a candlestick. It now shines as such in the darkness. The darkness may not comprehend it, but it still shines in it (Jn. 1⁴ᶠ·). This is the decisive new thing which in His resurrection and ascension—although it is not added to His being—is actual and revealed as a character of His being. In this event His being is also revelation. It reveals and discloses itself. It also encloses, reaching out and encompassing. It has also the power to communicate and proclaim itself. It exercises this power. It has communicated and proclaimed itself, and it still does so. It has spoken for itself. It has declared itself as this being. It does not cease to do so. For as it still is, it still speaks for itself. It still declares itself to be this being. It is still what it is attested to be by the witness of the Holy Spirit—its own ground of knowledge.

It is surely evident why the whole of the New Testament thinks and speaks from this point, with a backward reference to the resurrection and ascension of Jesus Christ, and therefore with a forward reference to the most imminent and most distant and final future. If the men of the New Testament could think and speak at all of Jesus Christ, if they had any right to do so, it was only as He had given Himself to be known as the One He was in His resurrection and ascension, as His being was manifested to them in the revealing power of this event. In this event of His revelation He became for them what He had 'been in Himself, in the secret of His previous history, even without this event, but what He could be for them only in this event—the Son of God and Son of Man, and in His existence as such the event of salvation for them and for Israel and for the world. In His resurrection and ascension He gave Himself to be seen and heard and understood by them as the One He was and is. He became for them not only One who is but One who is also known. And what other ground could they possibly have for thinking and speaking of Him, for going out as His witnesses to Israel and the Gentiles ? As they did it on this ground, they did it as those who were authentically instructed, as those who genuinely knew Him, as witnesses of His history and existence whom He Himself had authorised.

But before we consider the detailed characteristics of this event, we must step back for a moment to gain a wider outlook. For if this event has to be seen and understood seriously for itself, it has also to be seen and understood in its relationship with the whole history and existence of Jesus Christ as the divine act of majesty in the incarnation of the Word. This act in its totality has the character of revelation. The resurrection and ascension of Jesus Christ, as the event of revelation which follows His death, are the definite and comprehensive and absolutely unequivocal exponents of the character of His being as revelation. That is why we have to give them the prominence we now do when it is a question of the basis of knowledge in Christology. But the whole being and history and existence of Jesus Christ have the character of revelation as whose decisive and in a sense typical exponents we have to see and understand His resurrection and ascension. Thus for all their novelty and peculiarity the latter stand side by side with the event or sequence of events of the preceding being of

2. *The Homecoming of the Son of Man*

the Word in the flesh, of the humiliation of the Son of God from the birth to the death and burial of Jesus Christ which as such was also the exaltation of the Son of Man. But as they stand side by side with this sequence, they illuminate and underline the new and peculiar features which already characterise this sequence. It is impossible to make the abstract distinction sometimes made between the sequence which precedes Easter and the event which follows the death of Jesus Christ, which means between the ground of the reality of His being and the ground of its knowledge. For the former sequence is not entirely devoid of the character of revelation. In it Jesus Christ is not absolutely concealed and unknowable and actually unknown as the One He was and is. The being of Jesus Christ in it is not abstractly that of the humiliated Son of God who was necessarily unknowable as the One He was. It was also the perfect being of the exalted Son of Man which could not be, and was not, surpassed in any other event. Therefore what has to be said about this exalted Son of Man, and our human essence as it is exalted in Him, can also be read from this sequence. This is only, of course, in the light of the event of Easter and the ascension, which means that this light is not entirely absent even in the pre-Easter sequence. On the contrary, this sequence is itself the completed act of God. If the event after the death of Christ confronts and accompanies it with all the singularity of another act of God—the divine act of the revelation of the first completed act— this does not exclude the fact, but includes it, that in anticipation the first act participated already in the second, i.e., that it had already the character of revelation, and was actually revelation.

It is no doubt the case that the desire for pragmatic clarity and doctrinaire simplicity militates against this conception. We can readily understand, therefore, how the different view could arise and gain credence that we have to distinguish two states in the being of Jesus Christ. The first (commencing with His birth as the Son of Mary) was that of His humiliation—the humiliation of the Son of God, to which there also corresponds the lowliness of the man Jesus. As such it was also a state of concealment—the concealment of His deity and of the humanity united with it. The second (commencing with His resurrection and ascension) was that of His majesty—the majesty of the Son of God and Son of Man. And in this state He revealed Himself as such in the Easter period.

The relative clarity and simplicity of this construction are admirable, but it has never been possible to work it out without confusing concessions and inconsistencies. For is the incarnation as such only an entry into the state of humiliation ? Did the being and action of Jesus Christ as Son of God and Son of Man in this supposed first state take place only in lowliness and not also in majesty ? And if they took place in majesty, did they really take place only in concealment, without being revealed at all ? Conversely, is the supposed second state which Jesus Christ attained in His resurrection and ascension really a state of abstract majesty, in which He is no longer the poor child in the manger and the man on the cross of Golgotha despised by His fellows and forsaken by His God ? Is it a state in which He is consistently revealed without also being concealed ? In actual fact, does not all proclamation of Jesus Christ worthy of the name speak very differently ? Can we really speak of His lowliness without also thinking of His majesty ? or of His majesty without also thinking of

His lowliness ? For those to whom He was revealed, and who saw and heard Him in virtue of His revelation, was He not always both the Humiliated and also, and on that account, the Exalted ? In His revelation was He ever the One who exists in those separate states, and not the Son of God in the history of humiliation and the Son of Man in that of exaltation ? Even in His humiliation as the Son of God—to come to our present question—did He not also exist as the exalted Son of Man in such a way that He was also manifest as both ?

All these questions are difficult if not impossible to answer on the basis of this construction. But the last question is obviously an urgent one, and fatal to the whole construction, if we remember how the New Testament tradition, and especially in the Gospels, represents the pre-Easter sequence of the history and existence of Jesus Christ. We have said already that there has never been a tradition about Jesus Christ which was not shaped by the reference back from His resurrection and ascension. But the bearing of this assertion is not merely literary. It is not that in the Gospels and their supposed sources we have the interpretative redaction of historical material which originally was very different. On the contrary, from the standpoint of the resurrection and ascension, in the light of this all-prominent event of revelation, the community found the anticipation of this event in the history and existence of Jesus Christ as such, i.e., the revelation which had already taken place objectively in the pre-Easter sequence. At that time, of course, although the disciples had lived through it and noticed it and remembered it, they had not actually perceived its true scope as a decision. They had only registered it. They had not appreciated it as a revelation of the divine act of majesty which had taken place in Jesus Christ. They were its witnesses, but it was not for them the conquering and liberating self-witness of Jesus Christ. It did not commit them irrevocably to Him. It did not confirm them inflexibly in a knowledge of His person. No witness of the Holy Spirit corresponded to it. In their receiving of it they did not offer themselves—and this is true especially of Peter—as a rock on which He could build His Church. For the time being He did not build it. And we must add at once that this was not merely because, in view of the disciples, He could not do it, but because He did not will to do it. According to the puzzling but quite unequivocal witness of the texts it was He Himself who gave this provisional and anticipatory form to His then revelation, fulfilling it, but with an evident restraint, making Himself fully known as the One He was, but not willing that He should as yet be confessed or proclaimed.

Of course, even then He did address Peter as the rock on which He would build, and did actually build, His Church : " Thou art Peter " (Mt. 16¹⁸). And He did this in answer to a saying in which Peter unequivocally stated His recognition of the man Jesus as the Christ, i.e., the Son of the living God—a saying for which Jesus called him blessed (v. 17), adding at once that flesh and blood had not revealed it to him, but His Father in heaven. There is a parallel for the saying in Jn. 6⁶⁹, which in the better manuscripts has the more restrained form : " We have believed and perceived that thou art the Holy One of God." But it is immediately apparent how isolated the saying is in the pre-Easter presentation given by the Gospels. The disciples are witnesses, but not genuinely alert, percipient and confessing witnesses of the revelation which then took place. There is a possible exception in the Lucan account of the entry into Jerusalem (19³⁷ᶠ·), in which it was the disciples who raised that song of praise to the Messiah. But according to Matthew and Mark the confession was that of an anonymous multitude. The disciples had asked : " What manner of man is this, that even the wind and the sea obey him ? " but in the majority of cases they do not attain to more than a kind of confused astonishment at the One they follow which is equally characteristic of the crowds who continually gathered around the prophet of Nazareth. And even when that penetration was made in the saying of Peter, they were sharply instructed by Jesus that " they should tell no man that he was Jesus the Christ " (Mt. 16²⁰). The only ones who address Him as the Holy One or Son of God are those possessed with demons (Mk. 1²⁴, 5⁷) and when they are healed these are told to hold their peace. In Mt. 21¹⁵ᶠ· it is the children in the temple who take up the " Hosanna to the Son of David." In Mt. 27⁵⁴ᶠ· it is the Gentile captain and his men who " feared greatly " after the death of Jesus on the cross, and said : " Truly this was the Son of God." Of a piece with this is the fact that in the Synoptic Gospels there is no explicit and direct self-witness of Jesus to this effect. But even in these Gospels, especially in the passages in which His own description of Himself as the Son of Man plays so great a part, the Messiah is not enveloped in an absolute mystery. The outstanding illustration is the " I am " of Mk. 14⁶², or the " Thou hast said " of Mt. 26⁶⁴, which He spoke before the high-priests. But (whether perceived and understood or not) the secret is continually broken also in the miracles which He performed in connexion with His proclamation of the kingdom. We do, of course, read that those who were healed were expressly forbidden to speak of it (Mk. 1⁴⁴, 3¹², 5⁴³, 7³⁶). But there are many other cases in which no such prohibition was given. And in Mk. 5¹⁹ the man who had been cured of demon-possession was commanded : " Go home to thy friends, and tell them how great things the Lord hath done for thee, and hath had compassion on thee." And he then went and published it in all Decapolis, " and all men did marvel " (v. 20). Again, we certainly read in Mk. 8¹² that when the Pharisees asked for a sign Jesus " sighed deeply " and said : " Why doth this generation seek after a sign ? verily I say unto you, There shall no sign be given unto this generation " —a saying which is expanded in Mt. 12³⁹ : " but the sign of the prophet Jonas." Yet this is balanced by the story of the healing of the paralytic in Mk. 2¹ᶠ· where the word of pardon which Jesus first proclaims is disputed by the question of the scribes : " Who can forgive sins but God only ? " and the reason for the second word of healing : " Arise, and take up thy bed, and go thy way into thine house," is expressly stated to be : " That ye may know that the Son of man hath power on earth to forgive sins." The fact that from the very first His fame (ἡ ἀκοὴ αὐτοῦ) spread throughout all regions (Mk. 1²⁸ and par.) is stated by all the Evangelists at the beginning of all their accounts, and it emerges again and again that He was always surrounded on His way by that joyful and startled θαυμάζειν. In its original sense the saying in Mk. 4²² : " For there is nothing hid, which shall not be manifested ; neither was anything kept secret, but that it should come abroad," may be taken as an exact description of what we have here called the character of revelation integral to the Messianic being and occurrence and therefore not to be suppressed. The fact that it is expressed and revealed in this first sequence only in a way which is muffled and restrained and provisional is obvious enough. But so, too, is the fact that it is actually expressed and revealed. Was it not seen and heard already by John the Baptist on the banks of the Jordan, according to Mk. 1⁹ᶠ· and par. ? Does not this theophany stand at the very beginning of the activity of Jesus ? And in the birth-stories of St. Luke is it not put right back to the beginning of the whole history and existence of Jesus Christ with the δόξα κυρίου which shone round about the shepherds of Bethlehem (Lk. 2⁹) ?

And, of course, we have not yet mentioned the account of the transfiguration of Jesus on the mount, which is obviously so very important for all the Synoptists (Mk. 9² and par.). However we may understand the event recorded, it is palpable that it is an anticipation of the resurrection occurrence. Its context is always the same. It follows Peter's confession, the first announcement of the passion (in which there is also the first reference to the resurrection), and the saying about what the following of Jesus means for the disciples—self-denial, the bearing of the cross, the saving of life which is possible only by the losing of it. It is always introduced directly by the saying that some of those present would not taste of death before they had seen the kingdom of God come ἐν δυνάμει

(Lk. 9²⁷), or the Son of Man coming in His kingdom (Mk. 9¹). And again in all three narratives the account of the transfiguration is followed by the story (particularly developed in Mark) of the healing of the epileptic boy which had been beyond the powers of the disciples. Again in all three versions there are three decisive elements in the account itself. The first is the change (Mk. 9² ; Mt. 17²) in the form (εἶδος, Lk. 9²⁹) of Jesus as it takes place before the eyes of Peter, John and James. His face shone as the sun (Mt. 17²). His clothes (obviously implying His whole human appearance) " became shining, exceeding white as snow ; so as no fuller on earth can white them " (Mk. 9³). (In the language of Apocalyptic white is the heavenly colour, or more precisely the eschatological.) There can be little doubt that the text means by this that in the case of these three disciples there has already taken place that seeing of the kingdom, or of the Son of Man coming in His kingdom, which was to be enjoyed by some of those present. It did not take place in the same way as during the Easter period or at His second and final coming when He will be seen by the whole world. But at any rate it did take place. Awakened from sleep, εἶδαν τὴν δόξαν αὐτοῦ, as Lk. 9³² has it in almost verbal anticipation of Jn. 1¹⁴. (For this reason there is no sense in adducing Mk. 9¹ and par. to support the unsubstantial thesis of a parousia manqué. We obviously have its first beginning in the event of the transfiguration.) The second element is of a piece with this. It is the simultaneous appearance of the two Old Testament witnesses of revelation, Moses and Elijah, who talk with Jesus—according to Lk. 9³¹ about the " exodus " (ἔξοδος) " which he should accomplish at Jerusalem." So, too, is the third. This is the cloud—the tabernacle of God which at once conceals and reveals the divine presence on earth among men. According to Mt. 17⁵ it is a νεφέλη φωτεινή. And from it a voice, which is obviously the same as that heard by John the Baptist by the river Jordan, declares : " This is my beloved Son," and then, as all the versions have it : " Hear him." The conclusion, too, is of an impressiveness which is surely not undesigned, for " they saw no man any more, save Jesus only with themselves " ('Ιησοῦν μόνον μεθ' ἑαυτῶν, Mk. 9⁸). In all the accounts, too, we have the injunction of Jesus that they should not speak of this ὅραμα, an injunction which fixes the provisional and limited nature both of what was seen and also of the seeing. To be sure, even in this injunction there is an express reference to His resurrection, for it was " in those days " (Lk. 9³⁶), i.e., " till the Son of man were risen from the dead," that they did not proclaim what they had seen. But the disciples questioned one with another " what the rising from the dead should mean " (Mk. 9¹⁰). And it is of a piece with this that immediately afterwards they were so impotent in face of the epileptic : οὐκ ἴσχυσαν (Mk. 9¹⁸), οὐκ ἠδυνήθησαν (Mt. 17¹⁶ ; Lk. 9⁴⁰). The cry of the father reported in Mk. 9²⁴ characterises the whole unclarified situation : " Lord, I believe ; help thou mine unbelief." But this is a note which is not altogether silenced even in the Easter narratives. It is basically overcome only when the disciples receive the Holy Spirit, i.e., when they for their part are definitely reached by the self-witness of Jesus definitively completed in His resurrection and ascension. There can be no doubt, then, as to the limitation with which the tradition speaks of this whole occurrence. Even so, however, it is plain that it does ascribe to it, and to the whole pre-Easter history and existence of the Kyrios, as explicitly as it possibly can, the same quality as it later gives to its definitive actualisation in the accounts of His resurrection and ascension.

Now obviously it is very difficult, not only in relation to the story of the transfiguration, but to every other element in the synoptic tradition, to distinguish with even approximate certainty between that which was contributed in retrospect and that which is direct recollection. We cannot sufficiently consider how indissolubly for the 1st-century community the earlier and later elements in the history of Jesus belonged together, how necessarily they lit up and interpreted each other. But is it not the case that the more highly we estimate the formative force of retrospection in the light of Easter the more remarkable the whole thing is ? For surely this last event must have had a strange force if in what was relatively so short a space of time after the life of the man Jesus of Nazareth it compelled the community to set this in the light of itself, and portray it in this light, and (against all the laws of dramatics) to describe it so blatantly, for all the restraint, as an anticipation of its true point and climax. And again, it must have been a strange story which, when the community pieced together the available literary or non-literary fragments of tradition to form the pictures we now have in the Gospels, represented itself as everywhere impregnated with what it could have only under the restrictive " not yet " because in the strict sense it belonged only to its end. How much simpler and more illuminating it would all have been if in the formation of these pictures a sober distinction could have been drawn between pure recollection and retrospective interpretation, and therefore between the being of the humiliated and that of the exalted Christ, between *theologia crucis* and *theologia gloriae*, as in later dogmatic theory ! But this seems to be possible neither of the concluding event nor of the preceding sequence.

In this connexion we must also think of the particular features of St. John. R. Bultmann has reduced its Christology to the concept of the " Revealer." It remains to be seen whether his view can be maintained and propagated in this narrow form. There can be no doubt, however, that in this Gospel the distinctive synoptic tension between the being and the revelation of Jesus, between the Messianic secret and its declaration, between the ζωή which is real in Jesus and its character as φῶς, if it has not disappeared altogether, has been reduced to a residual minimum. The two concepts πιστεύειν and γιγνώσκειν are now correlative and inseparable. The sequence of the pre-Easter history and existence of Jesus has become an almost unbroken series of self-declarations by the Son of God moving about the earth in the flesh. His sayings are a series of explanations of His mission and its significance for the world, of His relationship to the Father and the right relationship to Himself which this makes necessary. His miracles are from the very outset a series of manifestations of His glory. The word ἐγώ is almost twice as frequent in the Fourth Gospel as in all the other three put together. The passion-story is far more noticeably set in the light of the majesty of Jesus. What is the meaning of the term *exaltatio* as it was later taken pre-eminently from this Gospel ? Is there not always a twofold reference to His exaltation on the cross and His exaltation to the Father ? And how naturally the resurrection-stories follow on, impressing themselves on us as an almost necessary confirmation of the existence of the One who did not describe Himself only in general terms as the " light " of the world, but concretely in 11²⁵ as the " resurrection and the life." We might almost say that in the story of Jesus in the Fourth Gospel we have one long story of the transfiguration. θαρσεῖτε, ἐγὼ νενίκηκα τὸν κόσμον (Jn. 16³³). All the same, there is a specific Easter-story in this Gospel too, and prior to Easter the sending of the Holy Spirit is still a future event. There is no abolishing of the distinction between before and after. At this point as at so many others the account of Jesus in this Gospel was intentionally cast in a highly original form, but the Early Church was quite right when it did not hesitate to set it alongside the other three. Must we prefer its Christology to that of the others ? Or must we complain that it is a misunderstanding and misrepresentation ? Both courses have been adopted. But surely it is better not to see any real distinction, but confidently to maintain that in the Fourth Gospel the deductions are drawn which are necessarily forced upon the reader by the text of the other three. If we do not see it for ourselves, then perhaps this oldest comparative picture will show us that in respect of its character as revelation the story of Jesus before and after Easter is not merely a whole, but is one in substance. Conversely, it is not really possible to read the comparative representation in John intelligently unless we are reminded by the synoptic pictures what is the problem which it answers : the step from the relative concealment of the being of Jesus Christ to its absolute manifestation ; the historicity, even in this respect, in which His being is revealed before no less than after, but after differently from before.

We now turn to the particular elements in the event of revelation after the death of Jesus Christ—His resurrection and ascension as such. We have said that these take their place alongside the revelation of the being of Jesus Christ in His preceding history and existence. They are themselves a divine act of revelation which we have to distinguish from the first one. This means that the character of the being of Jesus Christ as revelation shares in the general historicity of that being to the extent that in its actualisation we have to do with a way on which for all their unity the before is not yet the after and the after is no longer the before. In contrast to everything which went before we have called the resurrection and ascension the definitive and comprehensive, the decisive and unequivocal event of revelation. But we must now ask what is the meaning and ground of this distinction.

To apply it to the evangelical tradition, what is the meaning and ground of the characteristic reservation and restraint of the self-revelation of Jesus Christ in the preceding sequence—of the Not yet which according to the texts coincides with the fact that even the disciples, like all others, cannot really see and hear, but which is shown by the demands for silence to have its decisive basis in the will of Jesus Christ Himself ? Why is it that before His death the Messiah is wrapped in that secret which is often penetrated but never really dispelled ? Why is it that this secret can be really dispelled only after His death ? Why is it that it is only in this obviously different after that He is so manifest as the One He was and is that the gift of the Holy Spirit is the necessary consequence for those who know Him in His revelation, and as a result of His witness the foundation of the community ? Why is it that even the Fourth Evangelist cannot and will not abolish this distinction ? Why is it that for him too the Easter-story is not merely a confirmation but a new thing, and as such the pre-condition of the witness of the Holy Spirit which is the basis of the community ?

The first thing that we have to say in reply to this question is so obvious that we may easily overlook it. What was to be revealed— the being of Jesus Christ as very God and very man, and therefore the humiliation of the Son of God and the involved exaltation of the Son of Man—was indeed virtual and potential from the very beginning of His history and existence, but it was only in His death on the cross that it was actually and effectively accomplished and completed.

According to Jn. 1[29], John the Baptist had already seen and proclaimed Him as the One who is in truth the Lamb of God which taketh away the sin of the world. But the One who has actually been and done this is only the One who according to Jn. 19[30], when He had received the vinegar, " said, It is finished : and bowed his head, and gave up the ghost."

His death on the cross was and is the fulfilment of the incarnation of the Word and therefore the humiliation of the Son of God and exaltation of the Son of Man. In the earlier sequence He was moving towards this fulfilment—but only moving towards it. How could that which had not yet been completed be revealed as completed ? How could it be revealed except in the form of anticipation, as that which has already taken place in truth, but not yet in definitive actuality ? It would be astonishing if this anticipatory revelation of truth did not figure at all in the tradition. But it would be even more astonishing if its anticipatory character were suppressed and it were not surrounded by that concealing Not yet. The Messianic secret is no more and no less than the secret of the Messianic work which has not yet been completed. The fulfilment comes in the passion. It is another question that this, too, begins with the commencement of the history and existence of Jesus, as we can see from clear anticipations. But it has not only to begin. It has to come to its bitter and glorious end. It is only at the end and goal of the passion—which showed itself to be such in the baptism in Jordan, and even in the infancy stories of Matthew and Luke—that the Messianic work was and is accomplished. It is only then—not before—that there did and does take place the realisation of the final depth of humiliation, the descent into hell of Jesus Christ the Son of God, but also His supreme exaltation, the triumphant coronation of Jesus Christ the Son of Man. And after this event the revelation of Jesus Christ could be and necessarily was the revelation of His completed Messianic work, distinguished from the preceding revelation not merely in degree but in principle. The Messianic secret was not just penetrated but removed altogether. The resurrection and ascension of Jesus Christ are the completed revelation of Jesus Christ which corresponds to His completed work.

But there is another and deeper answer to the question. The resurrection and ascension of Jesus Christ are the revelation which corresponds to *this* completion of His work, manifesting it as such, declaring its meaning and basis. There is disclosed in them that which took place definitively and decisively in His death on the cross, that which took place in His history and existence as they were to have this *telos*. What was revealed in His resurrection and ascension was the secret of His way—the way that was not just any way, but led from Bethlehem to Golgotha, the place where He was condemned for us but also acquitted, where in and with His life the life of all humanity represented in Him was judged, and justly rejected and condemned and destroyed, but also (because this took place in the loss of His life) justified and sanctified and saved in His life by the grace of God. It is in this way, in the divine No and Yes finally spoken on Golgotha, that His being was fulfilled as the humiliated Son of God and exalted Son of Man. It was in this way that the reconciliation of the world with God was accomplished in this unity of His being. And in this completion of His work His being is revealed in His resurrection and ascension. From the very outset and at all its individual points His whole history and existence aimed and aims at this end. It is in this that all His words and works have their meaning and basis. That is why the self-revelation which takes place from the very first is always His self-attestation as the Messiah and Servant who suffers and dies for the salvation of the world, as the Word which has come for this purpose in the flesh, as the coming of the kingdom in the fulfilment of this divine No and Yes. The real fulfilment of His self-revelation had necessarily to correspond to the fulfilment of this No and Yes and therefore to the coming of the kingdom of God. It could not take place, therefore, before His death, but only after it. He could and can be known as the One He was and is only on the far side of His completed being and work.

On this far side however, in correspondence to the revealed fulness of His being and work, He can be fully known, because He is fully revealed. For as His being and work, His history and existence, are completed in His death on the cross, and as there is made in it once for all a satisfactory offering before God for the men of all times and places—an offering which need not and cannot therefore be continued, augmented or superseded—the revelation of this event which follows His death on the cross is also perfect. It will not be replaced even in His coming as Judge and Redeemer, and therefore in the final revelation. It will still be the same revelation. And if this is the case, how much less can it be augmented or even superseded in the time which elapses before the end—the time of the community! For it is as the One who then came in glory, and was manifested to His disciples and known by them, that He will come again in the same glory (as three of the disciples had already seen Him on the mount of transfiguration) and be manifested to the whole world and known by it. And wherever He is revealed and known, by the witness of the Holy Spirit, in the time between, the time of the community, it is always in the glory in which He was then manifested to the disciples, and known by them. His completed being and work, and its completed revelation, were sufficient then, and they are sufficient to-day, and they will be sufficient for all times, and even when time shall be no more. The resurrection and ascension are this once for all and all-sufficient event of revelation—the event of His self-declaration, and therefore the event in which the basis of the knowledge of Jesus Christ which we seek was laid and is laid. This is the objective basis from which alone, by the witness of the Holy Spirit, all subjective knowledge of Jesus Christ can derive—the knowledge of the disciples, the first community and the later Church. It is the basis on which this knowledge is unconditional and completely trustworthy because it is grounded in its subject-matter. We may now make one or two formal observations.

A first is that in the resurrection and ascension of Jesus Christ we have to do with an inwardly coherent *event*. We shall have to say more about its coherence later. For the moment we must stress that it is an event. It takes place after the conclusion of the preceding sequence, and is obviously distinct from it externally, because this sequence ended with the death of Jesus Christ. But it has the same character as what had gone before to the extent that it, too, is an event within the world, in time and space. It, too, takes place in the body, although not only in the body. It, too, was experienced and attested, not only inwardly but outwardly, by certain men.

It begins outside the gates of Jerusalem on the third day after that of Golgotha, and according to Ac. 1³ it ends forty days later—again on a hill (although there seems to be some doubt whether it was the Mount of Olives or a mountain in Galilee). It is an event which involves a definite seeing with the eyes and hearing with the ears and handling with the hands, as the Easter-stories say so unmistakeably and emphatically, and as is again underlined in 1 Jn. 1. It involves real eating and drinking, speaking and answering, reasoning (διαλογισμοί, Lk. 24³⁸) and doubting and then believing. In spite of the extraordinary nature of what happens, the reaction of the disciples is a normal human reaction according to the unanimous testimony of the accounts. In its good points and not so good it is quite in keeping with all that we have been told concerning them. It is a striking feature of all the Gospels that they tell us that the first witnesses of what happened were the women—who had not so far played any very important role. This above all is a pointer to the fact that we are confronted by a highly unusual situation. Apart from the existing circle of disciples there are no witnesses at all of the event according to 1 Cor. 15⁵ᶠ. Ac. 10⁴¹ tells us expressly that the risen Christ did not appear to " all the people, but unto witnesses chosen before of God." Paul is the great exception as an unbeliever and even an enemy who was called to faith directly by an appearance of the risen Christ. But as he himself understood it in Gal. 1¹⁵ᶠ. he too was " separated " for this purpose. This means that there can be no demonstration of the event which has apologetic value, and no such demonstration is attempted in 1 Cor. 15. All the same, 1 Cor. 15 shows that within the circle of disciples there was a firm tradition in respect of this witness, and although much of the attestation may have been confused and contradictory in detail, this did not cause any particular concern, for it all related to the same specific event. The event is not perhaps " historical " in the modern sense, but it is fixed and characterised as something which actually happened among men like other events, and was experienced and later attested by them.

If this were not the case, if it were a supernatural or even supersensual event which as such would not be experienced or attested by men, it might be all kinds of things, but it would not be an event of revelation. The fact that it was an event of this kind, and had a decisive significance as such, emerges afterwards in the changed attitude of the disciples to their Lord, especially after Pentecost, but even in expectation of Pentecost. But if it was an event of this kind, it was a concrete element in their own history, and therefore a concrete element in human history at large.

A second formal observation is that the event consisted in a series of concrete encounters and short conversations between the risen Jesus and His disciples. In the tradition these encounters are always described as self-manifestations of Jesus in the strictest sense of the term. In this context self-manifestation means (1) that the execution and termination as well as the initiative lie entirely in His own hands and not in theirs. Their reaction is a normal one, but it is to an action in whose origination and accomplishment they have no part at all. They have really encountered their Lord. He controls them, but they do not control Him. Self-manifestation means (2) that the meaning and purpose of these encounters consists simply and exhaustively in the fact that the risen Christ declares Himself to them in His identity with the One whom they had previously followed and who had died on the cross and been buried.

On the first point, it is to be noted that we are nowhere told that the disciples sought or found or even expected Jesus. But " Jesus came " (Jn. 20²⁴). " Jesus himself drew near, and went with them " (Lk. 24¹⁵). He " met " the women (Mt. 28⁹). He stood in the midst of His disciples (Lk. 24³⁶ ; Jn. 20¹⁹, ²⁶). He stood on the shore of the sea of Tiberias (Jn. 21⁴). It is never explained where He came from, or how He came (a point which is underlined by the mention of the closed doors in Jn. 20¹⁹, ²⁶). He is always uninvited and unexpected. He really comes as a " thief in the night " (Mt. 24⁴³ ; 1Thess. 5²). He really comes suddenly as did the bridegroom (Mt. 25¹ᶠ·) to the sleeping virgins, ἐφανερώθη (Jn. 21¹⁴ ; 1 Jn. 1²), but Jn. 21¹ gives us what is surely the right interpretation, ἐφανέρωσεν ἑαυτόν. The word ὤφθη, which is used three times in 1 Cor. 15⁵ᶠ· (and also in Lk. 24³⁴), definitely means sensual perception. That is why we read in Jn. 20¹⁴ that Mary Magdalene " turned herself back, and saw Jesus standing " ; or in Mt. 28¹⁷ that " they saw him." But again, this perception is not as simple as all that. He can be perceived only as He comes. And whether or not they see Him effectively is not under their own control. The characteristic phrase of Ac. 10⁴⁰ is that " God raised him up the third day," καὶ ἔδωκεν αὐτὸν ἐμφανῆ γενέσθαι. Jesus was certainly seen and heard by those who went to Emmaus, but at first He was not recognised as Jesus. " Their eyes were holden " (Lk. 24¹⁶), and so too were their ears, although they agreed afterwards that their hearts had burned within them while He walked with them by the way and opened up the Scriptures (Lk. 24³²). Even Mary Magdalene saw and heard Him without realising that it was Jesus (Jn. 20¹⁴). And the disciples by the seashore " knew not that it was Jesus " (Jn. 21⁴). There is doubt even in the seeing and hearing (Mt. 28¹⁷). One alternative is that they see a spirit (Lk. 24³⁷). There is also an element of unbelief, not only at the report of others (Lk. 24¹¹ ; Jn. 20²⁵), but also at what is said to be their own joyful seeing and hearing (Lk. 24⁴¹). Thomas saw and heard Him and still did not believe (Jn. 20²⁶ᶠ·). When their eyes are opened, when there is the seeing and hearing of recognition —ἐπέγνωσαν αὐτόν (Lk. 24³¹) ; " We have seen the Lord " (Jn. 20²⁵) ; " It is the Lord " (Jn. 21⁷)—the possibility and freedom for this always seem to be given them by Jesus Himself. Everywhere, and especially in 1 Cor. 15⁵ᶠ·, it is finally presupposed that there is no longer any question of a continuous companionship of Jesus with His disciples, but always of individual encounters with them which He Himself both began and terminated. In Lk. 24³¹ we are told that immediately after the ἐπέγνωσαν αὐτόν " he vanished out of their sight," and the ascension itself has this character of a termination of one of these encounters, the final one, and therefore of the whole event : διέστη ἀπ᾽ αὐτῶν (Lk. 24⁵¹).

On the second point, the question how they came to recognise Him when they saw and heard Him is rather strangely answered—although not with equal definiteness—by the radical assertion that He was known as the One who had been among them before and was then crucified, dead and buried. It is a fault of the otherwise very fine and competent study of K. H. Rengstorf (Die Aufer-

stehung Jesu, 1952) that it lays rather too much emphasis on the importance of the new and glorified corporeality in which Jesus appeared to His disciples. Rengstorf finds in this the inauguration of the second creation, the new æon, and therefore the main theme and significance of the Easter-stories and the Easter *kerygma*. But is this really the case ? Is it not surprising that if we really wished we could find more along these lines in the story of the transfiguration than in the records of Easter, which mention the white (Mk. 16⁵) or even " shining" (Lk. 24⁴) raiment of the angels, but have no great interest in the new form of Jesus as such ? If we want information on the latter point we have to look for it, drawing deductions (as from the appearances through closed doors), and therefore answering questions which are not posed in this context by the Evangelists themselves. What the Evangelists really know and say is simply that the disciples saw and heard Jesus again after His death, and that as they saw and heard Him they recognised Him, and that they recognised Him on the basis of His identity with the One whom they had known before. And they say this because it seems to be their particular intention to say it. The disciples who went to Emmaus say that He was known by them ἐν τῇ κλάσει τοῦ ἄρτου (Lk. 24³⁵). And Luke tells us that " as he sat at meat with them, he took bread, and blessed it, and brake, and gave to them " (Lk. 24³⁰). But even to the very words and order this is exactly what had happened at the last supper and the earlier feeding of the five and the four thousand. In the ensuing appearance to the eleven, recognition comes when He allows them to see and touch His hands and His feet (Lk. 24³⁹). In Jn. 20²⁰, ²⁵, ²⁷, where there is also a reference to the touching of His side, this is rightly taken to mean that He gave Himself to be known by them as the Crucified. Mary Magdalene recognises Him simply by the fact that—obviously not for the first time—He calls her by her name (Jn. 20¹⁶). We may also ask how it came about, as the text so clearly implies, that in the scene by the lake the disciples were able and even compelled to leave off questioning : " Who art thou ? " because they knew " that it was the Lord " (Jn. 21¹²). The common meal in which Jesus took the place of host played again a very important, if subordinate, part in this incident. But surely the simplest explanation of their recognition is that the whole incident is an unmistakeable reflection, for all the variations in detail, of Peter's great draught of fishes as recorded in Lk. 5⁴⁻¹¹. It is true, of course, that the first to recognise Jesus as He stood on the shore waiting for the ship with its rich haul is " the disciple whom Jesus loved " (Jn. 21⁷). But it is Peter who plunges out of the ship to reach Him in the quickest possible way—the same Peter who had once done something like this before (Mt. 14²⁹), but who above all had been told in Lk. 5¹⁰ : " Fear not ; from henceforth thou shalt catch men." The closing section of John's Gospel, which comes immediately after, has as its theme the sending and future of Peter (21¹⁵⁻²³). Is Lk. 5⁴⁻¹¹ one of the many anticipations of the event of Easter ? Or is it not perhaps more natural to understand that part of the Easter occurrence described in Jn. 21¹⁻¹⁴ as the actualisation of this important element in the pre-Easter history ? If we can finally understand the missionary command in Mt. 28¹⁸ᶠ· as a forceful extension and yet also a confirmation of the commission of Mt. 10⁵⁻⁴², the question how the doubts of the disciples in Mt. 28¹⁷ were overcome is readily answered. The matter is not quite so clear, perhaps, in these latter passages, but this does not alter the fact that the relevance of the self-manifestation of the risen Christ is to be found always in the demonstration of His identity with the One who had lived and taught and acted and gone to His death. It is true that this One in His history and existence is the reconciliation of the world with God and therefore the new man, the dawning of the new creation, the beginning of the new world. But it is not only in His resurrection that He is this. He became and was and is it in His life and death. The point about His resurrection is that in it He reveals Himself as the One who was and is and will be·this in His life and death.

A third formal observation concerns the character of the Easter-event as revelation. This event is the concretely historical event of the self-manifestation of Jesus after His death. It is the event in which Jesus makes it possible for us to recognise in His history and existence as they terminated with His death the reconciliation of the world with God accomplished by Him as the Son of God who became and is also the Son of Man. It is the event in which He Himself makes it possible for us to see this even in its own space and time. It is the event in which the hidden being and work of Jesus Christ are exposed and exhibited. It is the event in which the incarnate Word is brought to light as the Word which God has spoken in His mercy and power, His faithfulness and righteousness. It is the event in which this Word becomes an effective Word as spoken to men. It is the event in which it can be, and actually is, known among men, in the sphere of human acceptance and experience and thought. What God willed and wills and will will as the Lord of the covenant, who from all eternity deter-mined Himself for man and man for Himself, is no longer hidden in His counsel, or true only in heaven, or only actualised objectively on earth, but as actualised truth it is now declared to the world, imparted by God Himself to the man for whom He willed and did it. This declaration and impartation of the will and act of God is the event of the resurrection and ascension of Jesus Christ. It is in the light of this event that there arises a knowledge of the will and act of God, which itself carries with it a love for Him as the One who first loved us, from all eternity and then also in time. The place where this knowledge and love arise is the community of Jesus Christ the Cruci-fied, who as such rose again from the dead and ascended into heaven. As such, in this event, He is known as the One He is, and in Him the will and act of God are also known.

But as the divine declaration and impartation which awaken and underlie this knowledge, the event of revelation participates in the majesty of the will and act of God revealed in it. It takes place in the world, on earth, among men. It awakens and underlies human knowledge. But in correspondence with the One who is revealed in it, and also with that which is revealed, it takes place with a sacred incomprehensibility. It awakens and underlies a human knowledge which is comprehension only to the extent that it consists in a compre-hending of this incomprehensible. By its sacred incomprehensibility we mean its necessary and essential and distinctive newness and differ-ence and strangeness as the event of the revelation of the hidden presence and action of God in the flesh, and therefore of the will and act of God within a world and humanity which are estranged from it. " It is the Lord " (Jn. 21⁷) who even in His hiddenness as a servant was already the Lord, and who now emerged as such from this conceal-ment—the Lord of the covenant who is also the Lord of the world and man. He *is* the Lord. And now He *reveals* Himself as the Lord.

As such He is now accessible to human acceptance and thought. Yet He remains always the Lord even of this human capacity to think and receive. He is not bound by its limits. He is free to give Himself to be known by man even within these limits. The fact that He reveals Himself means that He does this. He makes Himself accessible to the man who has no access to Him. He constitutes Himself this access. He appears, He comes to him. This is the light of this event (the resurrection and ascension) in which knowledge arises—the knowledge of Jesus Christ, the knowledge of the will and act of God. In any other light, in any other access than that which He makes by His own access, He would not be the Lord. The knowledge of the Lord is the knowledge which is created by Him as the Lord, in the act of His majesty.

There are clear traces of this in the texts. The short account in Mark (16⁸) speaks of the women fleeing from the empty tomb. Its abrupt conclusion is that " they trembled and were amazed : neither said they any thing to any man " : οὐδενὶ οὐδὲν εἶπαν, ἐφοβοῦντο γάρ. This is another of the inconsistencies in the tradition which no one thought it necessary to remove. We read of the same amazement and fear in Lk. 24³⁷ and Mt. 28¹⁷ : " When they saw him, they fell down before him." And in Jn. 20²⁸ Thomas makes a confession which we do not find anywhere else in the New Testament : ὁ κύριός μου καὶ ὁ θεός μου.

Because and as the event of revelation participates in the majesty of the will and act of God, because it is itself a divine act of majesty as the revelation of God in the flesh, it necessarily has the character of a miracle. Its occurrence involves an element which has no parallel in other events, which cannot be explained as an object of human acceptance, or repeated as an object of human thought, in face of which human acceptance and thought and therefore knowledge can consist only in the assertion of its factuality. We must realise, of course, that it is not because it is miraculous that it is majestic, but because it is majestic that it is miraculous. It is because it takes place in sacred incomprehensibility as the revelation of the Lord that it is also incomprehensible in the more usual sense. By its character as a miracle it declares itself in the world of flesh as the revelation of God in the flesh. How could this revelation take place in the world except in this most alien of forms ? How could there be any knowledge of it without an acknowledgment of this alien character ? But it is not this alien character, this negative aspect, the fact that it is a miracle, which makes it revelation and underlies the knowledge of Jesus Christ in this acknowledgment. It is the positive aspect and its acknowledgment—that it is the majesty of God, the Lord, who is at work in Him and gives Himself to be known in Him ; Himself and His will and the act of reconciliation accomplished in the crucifixion of the Son of God and Son of Man. The miracle is unequivocal in itself and as such. But it can sometimes be asserted only incidentally, or with a concern which is alien to the matter itself. Or it can be ignored, or even denied. It can also be explained away as a miracle. Even for those who have eyes to see, let alone those who know it only by hearsay, it can have quite a different significance from that of revelation. There are many things and events in the world which are to some extent or even totally unusual, which cannot be explained as the object of human acceptance, or repeated in human thought, and yet they are not God's revelation, and do not awaken and underlie the knowledge of Jesus Christ. The revelation of God in the flesh does imply miracle. It would not be the declaration and impartation of the genuinely new to human history if this were not the case. To try to sift away the miraculous element will always be a futile enterprise in which we can only deny the thing itself and harden ourselves against the knowledge to which it gives rise. But as miracle as such does not imply God's revelation, the acknowledgment of miracle does not imply the acknowledgment and therefore the recognition of the event of revelation in its majesty—the knowledge of the Lord.

The miraculous character of the event is brought out clearly enough in the Easter-narratives of the New Testament. This is inevitable. It was highly unusual, a miracle, that the One who had died and been buried should appear before them, and come among them, and speak and eat and drink with them, and then disappear again—not merely into the void, but into heaven as the hidden sphere of God in the world. But there is no reason (perhaps arbitrarily and tendentiously) to lay more emphasis than the accounts themselves do on the miraculous character of that which they record. If we read them carefully or compare them with apocryphal or other similar narratives, we shall find that they are relatively modest and restrained in this respect, and that it is not the miraculous character of the event as such which interests them and to which they desire to draw attention. They obviously give no description at all of the actual event of the resurrection, and strictly speaking there is only the one very brief statement on the ascension : " And when he had spoken these things, while they beheld, he was taken up ; and a cloud received him out of their sight " (Ac. 1⁹)—to which we might add the following verse which tells us that they looked steadfastly εἰς τὸν οὐρανὸν πορευομένον (v. 10). It is true, of course, that this statement controls the whole section from v. 4 to v. 14, and therefore the transition to the history of the apostles and its inauguration. Yet it does not do this as a mere miracle-story, but in relation to the whole miraculous happening of the outcome and end and goal of the event of revelation in the self-declaration of Jesus which had begun on the third day after His death, and to the new situation which this created for the disciples. In the same way the accounts of the beginning and progress of this event with which the Gospels conclude, are dominated by the attestation of the miraculous appearance and coming and entry and being, and the miraculous seeing and hearing and handling, of the Lord who was alive after death. Always, however, it is the Lord Himself who is in the centre of the picture, and not the miracle of His appearing (although this is emphasised too). They do not attest only a miracle of believing —their own recognition of the crucified Jesus as it dawns in some mysterious way, or is awakened by God. They attest Jesus Himself, who, having come back to them miraculously, creates and kindles this recognition. They attest the miraculous consequence of the divine act of His awakening from the dead as it took place for Him and therefore for them. They attest His living presence. If we put the accent in the wrong place—the place where it is not put in the texts themselves—we shall inevitably find ourselves in a position where we cannot see the wood for the trees, i.e., the real miracle of which the texts wish to speak, and do actually speak, for mere marvels which we either welcome with avid curiosity or superciliously criticise and reject. The statement that Christ is risen necessarily implies the assertion that a dead man is alive again and that his grave is empty. But it only implies it. If we abstract the latter assertions from the former, we may accept them or we may deny or demythologise them, but either way they are irrelevant for an understanding of the texts and their witness. They cannot be considered as a basis for the knowledge of Jesus Christ —not even if we affirm them "historically" in the sense of the remarkable investigation of H. F. von Campenhausen, *Der Ablauf der Ostervereignisse und das leere Grab*, 1952. The Easter-stories and the whole Easter message of the New Testament do not give us any reason to make this kind of abstraction. And, if not all, at least many of the questions that we have to put to them will lose their point if they are considered from this angle.

The singularity of the event of revelation conditions the singularity of the knowledge which it awakens and underlies. Because it takes place in the majesty of the will and act of God, the knowledge of it cannot derive from the knowing man, but only from the One who is revealed in it. It is bound always to Him and conditioned by Him. Because it has the character of miracle, the knowledge of it will include an acknowledgment of the inexplicable and inconceivable nature of its occurrence. Because the One who is revealed in it is the living Jesus Christ He will as such be an object and content which cannot be exhausted in any dimension. Because it is an event which took place for the apostles in their encounter with the living Christ, the knowledge of it will necessarily be ordered by their witness and continually orientated by it. And finally, because that which is revealed in it is God's good will and saving act for us, a genuine and fruitful knowledge of it will necessarily become and be the knowledge of our love for the One who has first loved us in Jesus Christ.

Is there really a "historical" knowledge of this event in the sense of one which can be maintained neutrally and with complete objectivity? This is certainly not the case if we are thinking in terms of our last definition—a genuine and fruitful knowledge of love for the God who reveals Himself in it. But it is necessarily the case as the introduction to knowledge in this decisive sense. Love does not know neutrally and with complete objectivity. But neutral and objective—"historical"—knowledge is its presupposition.

This will involve (1) the most impartial and painstaking investigation of the *texts* which speak of this event. Our knowledge of it will always begin with this, and must always return to it. If it is to be meaningful as an introduction, the "historical" element to which it addresses itself will have to be the attestation of this event as we have it in the New Testament texts in their character as historical documents. It will not be "the historical facts" which we have to find (or think we have already found) somewhere behind the texts, and which we then claim as objective reality. A conscientious affirmation and investigation of the true "historical element," i.e., the New Testament texts themselves and as such, is sufficiently difficult and important and rewarding to pose new tasks for each successive generation. It is in this that the necessary introduction consists. As against this, the investigation, and even the affirmation with varying degrees of assurance, of facts which lie in a vacuum outside the texts, can only mean the leading away into a Babylonian captivity in which there is no attestation of this event, and can have nothing to do with the knowledge of this event.

But (2) the "historical" knowledge required as an introduction in this first sense must really be *impartial*. It must be a consideration of what the texts say (and do not say) in their attestation of this event, without measuring them by an imported picture of the world and history, without reading them through these alien spectacles, without prejudice as to what is possible or impossible, good or less good, without prescribing what they have to say and what they cannot say, without imposing questions which they themselves do not ask, but entering into their own questions and remaining open to their own replies which, if our thinking is to be genuinely "historical," must have precedence over our own attitude (which we naturally reserve). And it will also belong to this impartiality that we allow the New Testament texts to say what they themselves wish to say and do actually say, and only lay down with the very greatest caution what they are supposed to be able to say according to the evidence of this or that contemporary literature. "Historical" knowledge in this impartiality is never a simple and self-evident matter, because none of us is really impartial. But we need not conclude that the fulfilment of this condition is impossible in advance. If its fulfilment is not taken seriously as a definite task, or even rejected altogether, "historical" knowledge will not be an introduction from this standpoint either. It will not lead up but lead away. And it will have nothing whatever to do with the knowledge of this event.

The resurrection and ascension of Jesus Christ are two distinct but inseparable moments in one and the same event. The resurrection is to be understood as its *terminus a quo*, its beginning, and the ascension as its *terminus ad quem*, its end. Between the two there take place the appearances of Jesus Christ which are the proper theme of the New Testament narratives. The distinction between the resurrection and the ascension of Jesus Christ reveals again the historicity of His self-revelation as it corresponds to, and repeats, the historicity of His being. We again have two definite points in space or time, and a movement from the one to the other which effects their unity. To the "He came" of the beginning of the evangelical narratives there belongs necessarily and inseparably the "He went" of their end, and *vice versa*. But at both points we have a revelation of the exaltation of Jesus Christ. We remember that it is the revelation of His exaltation as it had already taken place in the pre-Easter life, and found fulfilment in His death on the cross. We remember, too, that it is the revelation of the exaltation of the Son of Man. If it took place in the glory of the Son of God who became and was also the Son of Man, it was His exaltation in the human essence assumed by Him. As the Son of God He did not need to be exalted. In fact, He could not be exalted. In His majesty as the Son of God, which He did not forfeit but exercised, He became man. The Lord became a servant. He humbled Himself even to death, the death of the cross (Phil. 2⁸). But He was never greater as Lord than in this depth of His servanthood. And if He was and is revealed as the Son of God in His resurrection and ascension, it is in the power and glory of His unity with the man Jesus of Nazareth. In the pre-Easter history and existence of Jesus

Christ, fulfilled in His death on the cross, it was a matter of the exaltation and majesty of this man in His unity with the Son of God. And in the resurrection and ascension of Jesus Christ it was and is a matter of the revelation of exaltation and majesty of this man in His unity with the Son of God. What is revealed is that in His identity with the Son of God this man was the Lord. It is to Him, this man, that in this revelation there was given the name of the Lord, the name which is above every name (Phil. 2⁹). It is in the name of Jesus that (as the end and goal of the giving of this name) every knee shall bow, of things in heaven, and things in earth, and things under the earth ; and in praise of this man that every tongue shall confess that " Jesus Christ is *Kyrios*, to the glory of God the Father " (Phil. 2¹⁰). It is in the history and existence of this man that, as and because He was the Son of God, the eternal will of God was fulfilled in time, the covenant of grace broken by man was reconstituted, the reconciliation of the world with God took place, and took place perfectly and once and for all. As the Son of God humbled Himself and became a man, this man became the doer of the eternal will of God. He became the One who accomplished this work. And He was therefore adopted into supreme fellowship with God and in that way exalted. This took place in secret but it had to be proclaimed and accepted openly in the world. The name which belonged to this man had to be published in the cosmos and made known to the totality of its inhabitants, as described in Phil. 2⁹⁻¹¹. And it is this disclosure and revelation which took place as concrete history in the resurrection and ascension of Jesus Christ, between these two points.

The resurrection of Jesus Christ is the point of departure, the commencement of this history of revelation. " Jesus came "—but where did He come from ?

The first thing that we have to say is that He came from the earthly world, from the way of all flesh, from an existence which like that of all earthly creatures, and especially men, was limited and finite and transient, and even past. He came not only from dying but from death. He came from death in the most stringent sense of the term, in which dying means for man the reward of sin, destruction and perdition. And His specific death on the cross was in every sense the death of a judged and condemned criminal—an execution. As the Son of God took it on Himself to become man, the Judge to become the judged in our place, the man Jesus of Nazareth who was identical with Him had to die this death. And then, in unequivocal assertion and confirmation of what had happened, He was buried. There were some who mourned Him, of course, but for all that He was laid aside, removed from the sight of the living, delivered up to the long but accelerating process of being forgotten. He had gone to the place where all men must go and will finally be carried, but from which none can ever return. And it was from this place that He did in fact return.

He was brought back from death, from the grave, we might almost say from the earth, for it was in the earth that He had been put. He came from this. He now had behind Him that which can only be in front of all other men. This is what the Easter witness of the New Testament says and describes in the accounts of His appearances—assuming that we let it say what it does say.

There is something else, however, which the Easter records and the whole of tl e New Testament say but wisely do not describe. In the appearances He not only came from death, but from His awakening from the dead. The New Testament almost always puts it in this way : " from the dead." From the innumerable host of the dead this one man, who was the Son of God, was summoned and awakened and reconstituted as a living man, the same man as He had been before. This second thing which the New Testament declares but never attempts to describe is the decisive factor. What was there actually to describe ? God awakened Him and so He " rose again." If only Christian art had refrained from the attempt to depict it ! He comes from this event which cannot be described or represented—that God awakened Him. It is in consequence of this that He appears to His disciples. It is with this that there commences His revelation as the One He was before—the man who had been exalted, whom God Himself had placed at the side of God. He had already been present to His disciples and all the people as this man. He had already spoken to them as such, and called them and sent them and done signs and wonders. He had concealed Himself from them as such, but not totally concealed Himself. They had already recognised Him as such, but not properly recognised Him. As this man He had been the One who genuinely accomplished the work of God, as the Baptist had already seen and declared at the beginning of His way—the Lamb of God which taketh away the sin of the world. In this capacity, as the Lamb of God, in the true actualisation of His exaltation, in His suffering and dying and death and burial, He was wrapped in total concealment, and not at all known by them. " Be it far from thee, Lord " (Mt. 16²²) was the cry of Peter when this prospect came into view. How could He be seen and known by them as the King crowned with thorns ? But He was revealed as such, as the King who was crowned in this way, as the man who was exalted in this way in the power and glory of His divine Sonship, in His resurrection—or, rather, as the One who came from this event. To be sure, His divine Sonship was also revealed, but it was the divine Sonship of this man, this man as the Son of God. It was in the man who came visibly and audibly and perceptibly from this place, from His death, His execution, His tomb, but also from His resurrection from the dead, in His coming from the place from which none other has ever come, that they knew Him as the One He was and is, as the exalted Son of Man and in Him the humiliated Son of God in all His power and glory, and in this unity the Lord, the One who did the will of God and accomplished the act of God, the Reconciler of the world with God. And as they knew Him in this way, in His coming from this place, they fell down before Him (προσεκύνησαν, Mt. 28¹⁷)—the first of those who shall bow the knee at His name and confess that He is the Lord.

The ascension of Jesus Christ is the terminating point of this history of revelation. Jesus went—but where did He go to? We can and must give a twofold answer. It must first be to the effect that He went to the absolutely inaccessible place, to the cosmic reality by which man is always surrounded (for even on earth He exists under heaven) and from which to that extent he derives, but which he cannot attain or enter. The spheres which are accessible to him are earthly spheres, and only earthly spheres.

In biblical terminology heaven is in the first instance that side of the created cosmos which is absolutely different from earth and higher and as such in antithesis to it. It lies on the far side of the visible heaven, which as such does not belong to it but to earth. When we are told, with great reserve in Lk. 24⁵¹ and rather less in Ac. 1⁹⁻¹¹, that He went to this place (διέστη, πορευόμενος), this means that He went to the place where no man can go, to the sphere within the created world which is hidden from that which is earthly, to its ἄδυτον, to the cosmic holy of holies.

That is why the fact that He went there—it is again a miracle that can only be touched on lightly—is only stated and not described in the New Testament. How can the fact that He went there be described? Again it was only Christian art which unfortunately was not afraid to try to depict it. As far as concerns its goal this going obviously denotes that which is inexplicable and inconceivable in the history of revelation.

But here, too, there is another and decisive aspect. The *ascendit ad coelos* of the creed has its meaning and point in the *sedet ad dexteram Dei Patris omnipotentis*. When He went into this hidden sphere He went to God. In His identity with the Son of God, when He was lifted up into heaven, He was not deified, or assumed into the Godhead (for this was unnecessary for Him as the Son of God and impossible for Him as the Son of Man), but placed as man at the side of God, in direct fellowship with Him, in full participation in His glory.

In biblical terminology heaven is the dwelling place of God in the world which is not built with hands, the place of His throne, from which He exercises His almighty dominion, from which He rules and speaks and acts as Creator, Reconciler and Redeemer, from which He blesses and judges the earth and man, from which He causes His will to be done also on earth, His kingdom (the kingdom of heaven) to come on earth, from which He has sent His own Son to earth. And the "cloud" which parted Jesus from their eyes in Ac. 1⁹, like the cloud of the transfiguration, is nothing other than the aureole of the original sphere of the divine dominion, the dwelling of the Father as it becomes visibly present on earth, disclosing itself to the Son of God, and in and with Him to the Son of Man. The disciples saw the man Jesus received into this "cloud." That this is the decisive element in the conclusion of the Easter story emerges clearly from the New Testament statements in which the resurrection is brought into direct connexion with the *sessio ad dexteram* (Rom. 1[4], 8[34] ; Col. 3[1] ; 1 Pet. 3[22] ; Eph. 1[20], etc.).

It belongs to God to come from that place. We can also say that it belongs to man to be from that place—as the creature of the Creator who rules there, as the recipient of the grace of Father, Son and Holy Spirit which He sends from there, as the child of God that he is declared to be from there as the brother of His Son. But we cannot say that it belongs to man to go to that place. The one man Jesus goes, however. This is the conclusion of the history of His revelation. He goes to the place of origin of all the dominion of divine power and grace and love. It is not only God who is now there, but as God is there He, this man, is also there. That this is the case is the hidden thing which is revealed in the ascension of Jesus Christ. It is again a hidden thing which was true and actual before, in His whole history and existence as Son of God and Son of Man as it found fulfilment in His crucifixion. As the Gospel of John has it, His exaltation on the cross was also His exaltation to the Father. But how could it be revealed and known as such when to human eyes it seemed impenetrably to be the direct opposite ? It is revealed and knowable even to human eyes in the event which terminates with the ascension, so that from this side too it is the exaltation of this man, and positively to the side of God, and fellowship in His work. In this way there is revealed the eternal life of this One who was dead, the lordship of this servant, the election of this One who was rejected and delivered up—the Lamb of God which is before the throne of God as the Lamb slain (Rev. 5[6]). The risen Jesus declared Himself to His disciples as the One who went to this place, and He was known by them as such, and therefore as the One He was and is. In His going to this place He was known as the Lord, in the unlimited power of the concept. That is why Thomas could say : " My Lord and my God." That is why, in view of His going to this place, the disciples could look ahead to their own future and that of the world, awaiting the witness of the Holy Ghost from heaven, and awaiting finally the coming again of the same Lord from heaven. The Christian community arose in the attestation and recognition of the Jesus of Nazareth who went to this place, of the Son of Man who as He went to this place was revealed to them as the Son of God. At all times and in all places there is knowledge of Jesus Christ as there is knowledge of His revelation, of the homecoming of the Son of Man fulfilled on the way of the Son of God into the far country and revealed in the resurrection and ascension of Jesus Christ.

3. THE ROYAL MAN

The task to which we must address ourselves under this heading is that of developing the knowledge of Jesus Christ in so far as He was not only the Son of God but also the Son of Man, the man Jesus of Nazareth. It is as such that He is the substance of the christological foundation of this second part of the doctrine of reconciliation. We have now realised the fact and extent that in His self-humbling in Jesus Christ the true God became and was and is also true man, and therefore the exaltation of man to fellowship with God as it took place in Him. We have now to focus all our attention on Jesus Christ as the true and new man in virtue of this exaltation, the second Adam, in whom there has taken place, and is actualised, the sanctification of all men.

We call Him the " royal man " in recollection of the fact that we are now dealing with the *munus regium*, the " kingly office " of Jesus Christ : with the servant as Lord ; with the man who has not only declared and inaugurated, but in His own person was and is and will be the kingdom and lordship of the God who reconciles the world with Himself. It is true, of course, that the New Testament as well as the Old tells us that God is the Lord. But the specific feature of the New Testament as an interpretation of the Old is that it tells us that He is this in the form and person of this man. He rules His people and cosmos as this man is at His right hand, i.e., as He is the concretion and manifestation of His power and righteousness. He rules in the sense of what He willed and has done and will do in and with the incarnation of the Word, i.e., in and with the identification of His existence with that of this man. He has given the omnipotence of His grace and holiness once and for all the character and form of this man. His kingdom and lordship and dominion are concretely the kingdom and lordship and dominion of this man exalted by Him to fellowship with His being and work ; of the man in whom He, God, humbling Himself in His Son, became a servant. We gather together the New Testament witness to Jesus Christ as the " Son of Man " (in harmony with the meaning of the term in both Testaments) when we now call Him the " royal man." And in so doing we are thinking of the prophecy which the Gospel of John deliberately put in the mouth of Pontius Pilate: ἰδοὺ ὁ ἄνθρωπος (19[5]), and a few verses later : ἴδε ὁ βασιλεὺς ὑμῶν (19[14]).

We now stand before the *quaestio facti*—of the fact that we have tacitly accepted as such in all our previous questions and statements, as did also traditional Christology in its own fashion. For we have not been building in the air, nor was the Early Church with its doctrine of the incarnation of the Logos, its two natures, and their inter-relationship, but both we and it have taken as our starting-point the fact of the existence and history, attested in the New Testament, of the One who as the true Son of God was and is and will be also the Son of Man, the true and new and royal man. And we have always envisaged an explanation of this fact. But now the time has come when this fact, which has always been our starting-point and goal, must be emphasised and allowed to speak for itself. This is possible, however, only in concrete juxtaposition with its New Testament attestation. It is there that it is given us as a fact. It is there that the royal man Jesus Christ is to be found. To be sure, He does not exist only there. But He exists only there for our knowledge. For there we come up against His self-declaration. And there He has always been known and wills continually to be known again.

The older dogmatics was preoccupied with the general and fundamental question of the Godhead and manhood of Jesus Christ. And in this question it was more interested in the former than the latter. It did not, therefore, give any independent consideration to this fact. It was undoubtedly the presupposition and goal of its Christology, but no more. This lacuna in its presentation must be filled. The Son of Man, who is also the true Son of God, obviously wills to be considered and understood for Himself. He, the royal man, belongs to the very substance of Christology. Indeed, as seen from the angle now under discussion, He is *the* substance of the whole.

The royal man is the Jesus of the four Gospels—and especially the first three. He is particularly, although not exclusively, the Jesus of the Synoptics because in them the man Jesus of Nazareth occupies a central position as the subject of the declaration : " Truly this man was the Son of God " (Mk. 15^{39}), whereas the Johannine description points from above downwards to the human being of the eternal Son of God. We have to remember, of course, that either way the knowledge of Jesus Christ, and the presentation in the whole of the New Testament and therefore from the very outset in the Synoptics, rests on the self-declaration in which He revealed Himself to His disciples in the resurrection and ascension. The New Testament attestation would be valueless, and His history and He Himself as the royal man obscured, if we tried artificially to divert this light of His self-declaration and consider the pre-Easter prelude in abstraction from its Easter sequel. From the very first, and wherever it has been alive, the Church has lived by and with the Jesus Christ of the New Testament, i.e., of the New Testament as written and read in the light of His resurrection and ascension. We can and should put it this way—that in its relationship with Him and with reference to Him it has counted from the very first on the witness of the Holy Ghost, knowing that it was directed to this witness, and trusting in the power of this witness even in its relation to the world. We can confidently affirm that in so doing it gave the only relevant answer to the " historical " problem of the history and existence of Jesus. There can be no question of leaving this closed circle in our own attempt to consider the royal man Jesus and therefore the substance of our second christological foundation. It cannot be our intention to think and speak in a vacuum. We can think and speak only in and with the Church. But this means decisively that we can do so only in the school of the authors of the New Testament and those who taught them, " which from the beginning were eye-witnesses, and ministers of the word " (Lk. 1^2).

I

We shall now attempt a consideration of the evangelical tradition concerning Jesus (and especially, although not exclusively, the synoptic). We shall begin with a statement concerning the way in which Jesus was present as a man among the men of His time according to the presentation of the New Testament witnesses.

1. He was present—and at all its levels and in all its forms the tradition agrees in this—in a way which could not fail in some sense to be seen or heard. For those around Him His existence had the character of a qualified fact. He encountered men, and in the same way

they, too, had to encounter Him. They could yield before Him. They could turn from Him and even against Him. But they could not escape Him. He did not need to force Himself on any. In different ways He was present to all. In this respect He was—and He made— history.

" And they were all amazed, insomuch that they questioned among themselves, saying, What thing is this ? . . . and immediately his fame (ἡ ἀκοὴ αὐτοῦ) spread abroad throughout all the region (εὐθὺς πανταχοῦ) round about Galilee " (Mk. 1²⁷f.). He constantly took precautions to prevent this. The saying in Is. 42² was applied to Him (Mt. 12¹⁹) : " He shall not strive nor cry ; neither shall any man hear his voice in the streets." But He could not help being known. In the first instance He Himself was the hidden thing which could not but be manifested, the secret thing which could only come abroad (Mk. 4²²), the city on a hill which could not be hid (Mt. 5¹⁴), the light which gives light to all that are in the house (Mt. 5¹⁵), the leaven which a woman took and hid in three measures of meal until the whole was leavened (Mt. 13³³). The descriptions of His appearance resemble those of the effects of an earthquake or some other natural catastrophe. We continually find the words ἐθαύμαζον, ἐθαμβήθησαν, ἐξεπλήσσοντο ἐφοβήθησαν. " We have seen strange things to day " (Lk. 5²⁶). Blessed were the eyes and ears which were privileged to see and hear what was then seen and heard ! For this was something strange and unique. " Verily I say unto you, That many prophets and righteous men have desired to see those things which ye see, and have not seen them ; and to hear those things which ye hear, and have not heard them " (Mt. 13¹⁷). And to those who do see and hear Him it is said : " The days will come, when ye shall desire to see one of the days of the Son of man, and ye shall not see it " (Lk. 17²²). It was a matter of seeing and hearing the words and wonders of this man. But it is obvious that those who report it wish to point through and beyond these to the One who spoke and acted. He Himself was a source of amazement and even alarm to the people. He was an absolutely alien and exciting *novum*. This was how He was seen by His community. This was How He was present to them.

2. He was present in such a way—again according to their common testimony—that He not merely demanded decision from them, but introduced and made it. The exciting of that astonishment was not an end, let alone an end in itself. His existence was not in any sense neutral. There could be no neutrality, therefore, in face of it. It was a question which demanded either a Yes or a No. And if the answer was Yes, it meant a resolute redirection and conversion of the whole man. But we must put it even more strongly if we are to think and speak as the Gospels did. His existence, which derived from a prior decision, involved decision in those whom He encountered. It brought to light what was in them, who and what they were. It divided them both within themselves and among themselves. It brought about separations between man and man which had nothing whatever to do with other differences or antitheses, but ran right across them, and even across the closest of common ties. He was present and decided as the Judge, bringing about and bringing to light the final divisions in and among men. And yet, of course, in a final sense He was also present to unite them, His death being the judgment on the

sin of the whole world which He, the Judge, did not execute on the world but Himself. But even from the point of view of this goal and issue He was present as the Judge of all those in whose place He accepted judgment.

Our starting-point here is the first and final fact that the being of this royal man Jesus was not only identical with the glory of God in the highest, according to the praises of the multitude of the heavenly host in Lk. 2¹⁴, but also identical on earth with peace among men as the object of the divine good-pleasure. And as this peace, realised and fulfilled in the world of men, to which the divine good-pleasure can only be addressed in grace, realised and fulfilled in His death on the cross, this man demanded a choice and decision among all men, dividing men by His presence. Luke himself did not suppress the tradition (12⁵¹) which has it that Jesus said : " Suppose ye that I am come to give peace on earth ? I tell you, Nay ; but rather division " (διαμερισμόν). The word used in Matthew is " sword " (10³⁴), and it is obviously the same sword as was to pierce through the soul of Mary (Lk. 2³⁵) " that the thoughts of many hearts may be revealed." As Heb. 4¹²f. tells us, the Word of God is " quick and powerful, and sharper than any two-edged sword, piercing even to the dividing asunder of soul and spirit, and of the joints and marrow, and is a discerner of the thoughts and intents of the heart. Neither is there any creature that is not manifest in his sight : but all things are naked and opened unto the eyes of him with whom we have to do." The presence of the man Jesus meant the presence of this sword. He was the light of which we are told in Eph. 5¹³ that all things are reproved by it. From the very first, and radically, He was the *venturus judicare vivos et mortuos.* Already according to the reported witness of the Baptist in Mt. 3¹² : " His fan is in his hand, and he will throughly purge his floor, and gather his wheat into the garner ; but he will burn up the chaff with unquenchable fire." To use the words which preface the account of His activity in Mk. 1¹⁵, His presence meant that the time was fulfilled, and the kingdom of God was at hand, in threatening proximity to every sphere of human power and dominion. His presence meant that the axe was laid at the root of the trees (Mt. 3¹⁰). In face of Him there was only one real possibility for all men, that of μετάνοια, a radical re-thinking and conversion, equivalent to faith in the glad tidings proclaimed by His presence. He came as One who had already made His own decision. According to the story of His childhood in Lk. 2 He asks His parents : " Wist ye not that I must be about my Father's business ? " (v. 49). And in Jn. 9⁴ He says : " I must work the works of him that sent me, while it is day : the night cometh, when no man can work." It is because of His own clear-cut decision that in the encounter with Him others must choose between Himself and all the things that perhaps seem necessary and important to them, e.g., wealth or satisfaction or pleasure or reputation (Lk. 6²⁴, ²⁶), and even between Himself and that which is nearest to them. There is no alternative to either benediction or malediction. " He that loveth father or mother more than me is not worthy of me : and he that loveth son or daughter more than me is not worthy of me " (Mt. 10³⁷). It is to be noted that in Mt. 10³⁵ He takes a saying from Micah's denunciation of the social divisions of his time (7⁶) and uses it as a basis for the fact that He Himself has come " to set a man at variance against his father, and the daughter against her mother, and the daughter-in-law against her mother-in-law. And a man's foes shall be they of his own household." Whatever separates, or even restrains, a man from Jesus is σκάνδαλον. And no matter what it may be which constitutes this " offence," even if it is a hand or foot or eye, we must not hesitate to remove it and cast it from us (Mk. 9⁴³f.). In relation to Him there can be no serving of two masters : " for either he will hate the one, and love the other ; or else he will hold to the one, and despise the other " (Mt. 6²⁴). When He meets a man it is like the treasure hid in a field, or the pearl of great price, and if that man is not to lose what he has found, for good or ill he must be prepared to sell all that he has (Mt. 13⁴⁴ᶠ·). For His sake and the Gospel's we can only lose our lives, to find and keep and save them again (Mk. 8³⁵ and par.). The antithesis here is absolute. To hear and do His words, or not to hear or do them, is like building a house either on the rock or on the sand, with all that the one or the other course involves (Mt. 7²⁴ᶠ·). According to Mt. 7¹³ᶠ· we have to choose between the narrow gate and way which leads to life and the broad way which leads to destruction. According to Mt. 13²⁴ᶠ, ³⁶ᶠ· we are to be wholesome salt or salt that has lost its savour. According to Mt. 13⁴⁷ᶠ· we are to be good fish or bad fish—and it is only a matter of time before it will appear openly which is the case. There were some who, although they did not belong to the band of His disciples, cast out demons in His name, and of them He could say : " He that is not against us is on our part " (Mk. 9³⁸ᶠ·). On the other hand, when He encountered men, there were those who spoke all manner of evil against the Son of Man—although this could be forgiven, because it rested on a failure to see or understand His existence and words and acts. And there could also be a very different (and unforgivable) speaking against the Holy Ghost, the denial and calumniation of the revealed and recognised secret of His existence and words and acts. The Pharisees, who saw His work but explained it as a work of the devil, thus condemning as evil the good fruits of the good tree, had need to ask themselves whether they were not guilty of this blasphemy (Mt. 12³¹⁻³⁵). Either way, however, the saying is true and basic : " He that is not with me is against me ; and he that gathereth not with me scattereth abroad " (Mt. 12³⁰)—a saying which J. A. Bengel has rightly interpreted : *Non valet neutralitas in regno Dei.* And it is to be noted how strangely the last judgment described in Mt. 25³¹⁻⁴⁶, in which the Son of Man (now expressly called the " king ") separates men to the right and the left according to His own criterion, is anticipated and seems already to be present in the crucifixion of the two thieves (who were so very different according to Lk. 23³⁹ᶠ·) on Golgotha. It was in this way, with this critical function, that the man Jesus impressed Himself on the community and its tradition. It was in this way that they saw Him.

3. He was also there—and this, too, is a common assertion of the whole tradition—in a way which could not be forgotten. In this respect, of course, the emphasis and interpretation given by His resurrection and ascension exercise a particular influence. In His appearances His own had seen Him come from the place from which no other man had ever come, and go to the place where no other man had ever gone. What was revealed by these appearances ? They revealed that this man—a man in His time like all others—did not come and go again like all other men in their time. It is a tribute to the power of this self-revelation that it could shape the recollection of His life and death as it undoubtedly did, and to such an extent that we cannot separate in practice between a pre-Easter and a post-Easter picture of this man in the New Testament. Yet the Easter event had only disclosed the fact that in His life and death He had not been present like the prophet or the heroes of Greek and Roman antiquity before Him, or the many great and small after Him Necessarily, therefore, the recollection of Him was qualified. It was a recollection which, although it did not destroy that of others who were around Him, inevitably shaped it in such a way that it was

completely dominated by the recollection of Him, and could have significance only in this relationship.

The New Testament authors were all Jews, but this did not mean that for them Jesus was only one of the many figures in their Jewish history. On the contrary, He was the conclusion and fulfilment of this history, drawing into His powerful wake all those who recognised Him. Attention should be paid to the remarkable collection of Old Testament sayings (Gen. 46³⁰ ; Is. 25⁷, 40⁵, 42⁶, 46¹³, 49⁶) in the Song of Simeon in the temple (Lk. 2²⁹ᶠ·) : "Lord, now lettest thou thy servant depart in peace, according to thy word : For mine eyes have seen thy salvation, which thou hast prepared before the face of all peoples ; a light to lighten the Gentiles, and the glory of thy people Israel." "The law and the prophets were until John : since that time the kingdom of God is preached, and every man presseth into it" (Lk. 16¹⁶). Or, as Matthew puts it (11¹²) : "And from the days of John the Baptist until now the kingdom of heaven suffereth violence, and the violent take it by force." This was what happened when this man appeared. And so Moses and Elijah appear only in company with Jesus when He is transfigured in anticipation of His resurrection (Mt. 17³). The whole of the Old Testament could only be read and expounded as the promise of the coming of this man. The only point of mentioning the emperor Augustus (Lk. 2¹) or the emperor Tiberius and Pontius Pilate and other rulers of the period (Lk. 3¹) was to fix His time. It is not that He is contemporary with them, but that they are contemporary with Him.

The figure with which the four Gospels are most concerned apart from Jesus is that of John the Baptist. But the radical difference between the two is quite clear. "Among them that are born of women there hath not risen a greater than John the Baptist : notwithstanding he that is least in the kingdom of heaven is greater than he " (Mt. 11¹¹). We are told in Mt. 3¹⁴ that John tried to prevent Jesus from being baptised by him : "I have need to be baptized of thee, and comest thou to me ? " In Mt. 3¹¹ (cf. Jn. 1²⁷) we have his saying : "Whose shoes I am not worthy to bear," and also the sharp distinction which he makes (cf. Jn. 1³³) between His own baptism with water unto repentance and the baptism with the Holy Ghost and with fire which the One who is mightier than he will administer. In Jn. 1²⁰ᶠ· he explains quite definitely that he is not the Christ, or Elijah, or the prophet promised in Deut. 18¹⁸. If in the time of Jesus and after there was an independent movement associated with the Baptist, the New Testament clearly differentiated itself from it, not in the form of a polemic against John, but by subordinating him to Jesus: "For this is he of whom it is written, Behold, I send my messenger before thy face, which shall prepare thy way before thee " (Mt. 11¹⁰, cf. Lk. 1⁷⁶).

If it was really the case that the community in which the New Testament had its origin was conscious of being constituted by the Word as such (the so-called *kerygma*) handed down to it and accepted by it, this would surely be revealed in the fact that in the tradition a much more imposing place and function would be ascribed to its first bearers, the apostles—as those who discovered if they did not invent it—than is actually the case both in the Synoptics and also in the Fourth Gospel, which obviously looks back from a rather greater distance both in time and space. The apostles are, of course, indispensable. And they are more than marginal. As those who follow and accompany, they belong from the very first to the one man Jesus. But they do so only in this capacity. Their position and function are not in any sense autonomous, and therefore competitive with those of Jesus. It was He who called them to Him. It was He who made them what they were (ἐποίησεν, Mk. 3¹⁴, ¹⁶, cf. 1¹⁷). It was He who " gave " them δύναμιν καὶ ἐξουσίαν (Lk. 9¹). It was He who sent them out (Mt. 10⁵). "Without me ye can do nothing," just as the branches can do nothing of themselves but only as they abide in the vine (Jn. 15⁵). And

" except ye eat the flesh of the Son of man, and drink his blood, ye have no life in you " (Jn. 6⁵³). If appearances do not deceive, the interpretation of the figure of John the Baptist offered by the Fourth Gospel gives us by implication a positive and critical definition and interpretation of that of a very different John, and therefore of the apostle, and the bearer of the *kerygma* generally : " The same came for a witness, to bear witness of the Light, that all men through him might believe. He was not that Light, but was sent to bear witness of that Light " (Jn. 1⁷ᶠ·). The *kerygma* of the community refers back to the light of His *kerygma*. It is different from it, and dependent upon it. If it has in it its limit, its bearer also has his greatness in it. There is not the least sign of any shift of emphasis in a contrary direction—not even in the Acts of the Apostles. Stress is obviously laid on the importance of Peter, and later Paul, but these are in a completely different category, and it is only *per nefas* that there can be any comparison with what they witness concerning this one man. We remember the well-known passage on the divisions at Corinth. We cannot belong to Paul or Apollos or Cephas, as the Corinthians were saying. " Is Christ divided ? was Paul crucified for you ? or were ye baptized in the name of Paul ? " (1 Cor. 1¹³). " Who then is Paul, and who is Apollos, but ministers by whom ye believed, even as the Lord gave to every man ? " (1 Cor. 3⁵). In the case of Peter the tradition sees to it that his human limitations are presented with remarkable candour. And Paul takes good care—if anything this emerges even more clearly in Acts than the Epistles—that as he pictures himself there can be no possible confusion between the recollection of Paul and that of the man Jesus. And as far as concerns the majority of " the men which have companied with us all the time that the Lord Jesus went in and out among us " and who could therefore be " witnesses of his resurrection " (Ac. 1²¹ᶠ), sharing the same commission and the same promise as those who are more prominent, the tradition is content merely to record their names. At bottom, there was only the one man who could not be forgotten, but of Him this was true in a sense which is quite absolute.

Why was this the case, and in what respect ? The answer is that He was among His fellow-men as the Lord, the royal man. To be sure,.He was a man as they were. He did not enjoy or exercise divine sovereignty or authority or omnipotence. But all the same He was its full and direct witness. And as such He was unmistakeably marked off from other men. He was a free man. Neither on earth nor in heaven (apart from His Father) was there anyone or anything over Him. For He was wholly free to do the will of His Father. He was not bound by any man, by any power of nature or history, by any destiny, by any orders, by any inner limits or obstacles. He did not stand or fall with any of these things, nor did He need to fear them. For Him there was only one imperative. Subject to this one imperative, and therefore not arbitrarily if not under any outward compulsion or constraint, He came and went with absolute superiority, disposing and controlling, speaking or keeping silence, always exercising lordship. This was no less true when He entered and trod to the end the way of His death and passion. Indeed, to those who looked back, it was even more plainly true on this way. The presence of the man of Nazareth meant the presence of a kingdom—the kingdom of God or the kingdom of heaven the tradition calls it. This is what made Him absolutely unique and unforgettable.

We may recall a few concrete scenes described in the tradition. For instance, there is that of Mt. 4[1f.] and Lk. 4[1f.] in which He is led by the Spirit into the wilderness and resists the devil—and Mk. 1[13] has the majestic declaration that " he was with the wild beasts ; and the angels ministered unto him." Or again, there is the incident when He called the disciples with the categorical δεῦτε ὀπίσω μου of Mk. 1[17]. Or there is the perilous result of His visit to His own city of Nazareth : " But he passing through the midst of them went his way " (Lk. 4[30]). Or there is His θέλω, καθαρίσθητι at the healing of the leper (Mt. 8[3]). Or there are the words which express the impression made by Him on the centurion of Capernaum in Mt. 8[9f.] : " For I (also) am a man under authority, having soldiers under me : and I say to this man, Go, and he goeth ; and to another, Come, and he cometh ; and to my servant, Do this, and he doeth it." Or there is the way in which He drove out those who wept and wailed (and at first mocked) in the house of Jairus the ruler of the synagogue (Mk. 5[38f.]). Or there is His driving out of the traders and money-changers from the temple (at the end of His ministry according to the Synoptics—although with remarkable historical freedom, but not unintentionally, John places it at the beginning). Or there is the account of His hearing before the high-priests, or the description of His hearing before Pilate which is so particularly impressive in Jn. 18[28f.] and 19[1f.] The resurrection saying in Mt. 28[18] might well have stood at the beginning of the whole Gospel record : " All power is given unto me in heaven and in earth." We do actually read in the middle : " All things are delivered unto me of my Father " (Mt. 11[27]).

It is for this reason that this man is always called κύριος in the Gospels, and continually addressed as such. Even before the birth of Jesus, Mary was most respectfully greeted by her cousin Elisabeth as " the mother of my Lord " (Lk. 1[43]). There can be no doubt, of course, that at that time (as in our modern usage) the title could be applied to eminent personages as a mark of courtesy and respect. This conventional usage may also be found in the Gospels (especially the parables). But at that time it was also used in a more precise sense, amongst Greek-speaking Jews as a translation of the Old Testament name for God, and in the rest of the Hellenistic world as a designation of the divine emperor. And if in the New Testament Epistles, which for the most part precede the Gospels, the title κύριος is consistently applied to Jesus Christ in the strictest sense, we can gather from this that even when it is used of Him in the Gospels it has this precise and emphatic sense, expressing in a comprehensive way the sovereignty which made an ineffaceable impression on the community as the distinctive mark of the being of Jesus. Even at the beginning of Christianity there could, of course, be an empty and futile and even reprehensible use of the title by those who said " Lord, Lord " with their lips, and seemed to be active in His service as those who prophesied and cast out devils and did all kinds of wonderful works " in his name," but did not really do what He said, and therefore the will of His Father in heaven (Lk. 6[46]; Mt. 7[21f.]). But this criticism presupposes that the ordinary use of the title was not at all conventional, but important and significant. If those envisaged in it pronounced sentence on themselves (" I never knew you : depart from me, ye that work iniquity," Mt. 7[23]), this is because they, too, are really speaking the truth. He is in fact the Lord who demands obedience—and they themselves address Him as such even though they deny Him in practice. He Himself in His own person was that which He proclaimed in word and deed : the imminent kingdom of God impinging on all other kingdoms and therefore on every man. It was quite unnecessary to ask concerning the time and manner of the coming of this kingdom, " for, behold, the kingdom of God is among you." It is among them as Jesus Himself is among them (Lk. 17[21]). For " if I with the finger of God cast out devils, ἄρα ἔφθασεν ἐφ' ὑμᾶς ἡ βασιλεία τοῦ θεοῦ—no doubt the kingdom of God is come upon you " (Lk. 11[20]). The King and His kingdom, the Lord and His lordship, are one. As Origen puts it, He is the αὐτοβασιλεία. This was how His community saw Him, and it was for this reason that He could not be forgotten.

4. We may now gather together all that we have so far said and add that He was present in a way which was irrevocable. He *was* present ? Yes, He *was* present. The Gospels, and all the individual and collected documentations of oral tradition which may underlie them, are written in definite retrospect of the life of Jesus as something which was over and now lay behind. They are monuments to the memory of this man.

Luke in particular could introduce himself rather aptly in his Gospel, not as a modern " historicist," but as an alert and knowledgeable historian, who had made a closer investigation of everything from the earliest stages, and proposed to give an orderly account of the things which " had been delivered " to them. The aim of his work was to impart to Theophilus (a general name, perhaps, for the Christian of the second or third generation) the ἀσφάλεια, the sure foundation, of the instruction which he had received (Lk. 1¹⁻⁴). What was this foundation ? In his introduction to Acts, again addressing this Theophilus (Ac. 1¹ᶠ·), Luke gives the sum of his Gospel in the words : " all that Jesus began both to do and teach, until the day in which he was taken up (into heaven)." This was the ἀσφάλεια. The Gospels look back to the time and history of Jesus as they ended with this day of His ascension. The existence of the Gospels made it possible to follow the injunction in 2 Tim. 2⁸ : " Remember (μνημόνευε) that Jesus Christ of the seed of David was raised from the dead." Even within the evangelical records—and, rather surprisingly, not least in the Johannine—there are certain passages where this looking back is made explicit : in relation to the saying of Jesus concerning the temple in Jn. 2²² ; in relation to the entry into Jerusalem in Jn. 12¹⁶ ; in the description of the work of the Paraclete in Jn. 14²⁶ : " He shall teach you all things, and bring all things to your remembrance, whatsoever I have said unto you " ; in more than one demand of Jesus Himself in the Gospels that His words should be remembered (Lk. 24⁶ ; Jn. 15²⁰, 16⁴) ; in the account of the Last Supper in Luke (22¹⁹, cf. 1 Cor. 11²⁴ᶠ·), especially with the formula : " This do in remembrance of me " (εἰς τὴν ἐμὴν ἀνάμνησιν) ; and indirectly in the curious saying concerning the anointing in Bethany (Mk. 14⁹) : " Verily I say unto you, Wheresoever this gospel shall be preached throughout the whole world, this also that she hath done shall be spoken of for a memorial of her."

But we cannot speak of the Gospels as monuments to the memory of this man, and therefore of the fact that He was present, without a great question-mark and exclamation-mark. The " perfect " to which they look back is not a " preterite." It is not " past." The Lord whose memory they enshrine is not a dead Lord. He is not only unforgettable for the community, but it thinks of Him as the One who still is what He was. It is not the community, but He Himself who sees to it that He is not forgotten. He was present irrevocably— in a way in which His existence was not compromised or broken by His death. He was present to it. He lived in His community, and His community lived with Him. He was also future to it. It did not think of Him without expecting to see Him as the One of whom it thought. And all this, strangely enough, is in virtue of His death and passion, to the account of which all the evangelical records move with irresistible force. His crucifixion was not simply a catastrophe. For the whole evangelical tradition (and not merely for Paul) it was the *telos* of His whole existence. He was the man who met and defeated His mortality in His death. Here again, of course, His resurrection and ascension are particularly illuminating. But His appearance after His death did not crowd out His life as it hurried on to His death. It is the One that was finally crucified—this is what His resurrection and ascension reveal—who is the living Lord, present to-day, and coming again one day.

The community proclaimed the death of the Lord until He comes (1 Cor. 11²⁶). It obviously could not proclaim His death unless He was present to it in His existence as a man, unless His history was present to it. And it could not expect His coming unless it knew His existence as a man, His history. The Gospel record of His life in His time offered human ἀσφάλεια (Lk. 1⁴) concerning this presence and acquaintance with Him. It was not a Χριστὸς κατὰ σάρκα (a rather improbable construction which could only mean the Jesus of the Gospels) that Paul had once known but now knew no more (2 Cor. 5¹⁶)—and this saying ought never to have been used to depreciate the evangelical account of the life of Jesus. Surely what Paul is saying is that at one time the Crucified whom he now proclaims as the object of his knowledge, and in this way as the power of God and the wisdom of God (1 Cor. 1²⁴, 2²), had been known by him κατὰ σάρκα, i.e., that he had seen and judged Him in a way which was human and carnal, understanding His death as an obvious and shameful end, but that now this picture has been totally effaced and he can see Him in this way no more. The way in which he now knows Him is explained by what precedes and follows in 2 Cor. 5. That perverted picture has passed away with everything that belongs to the old life, and it has been replaced by a new one. He now sees that this one man died for all, that in Him God has reconciled the world with Himself. We have a similar explanation in Rom. 6⁹ᶠ· : " Knowing that Christ being raised from the dead dieth no more ; death hath no more dominion over him. For in that he died, he died unto sin once : but in that he liveth, he liveth unto God." Or again, in 2 Tim. 1¹⁰ : He " hath abolished death, and hath brought life and immortality to light through the gospel." The New Testament record speaks of One who was incorruptible, and therefore not only was present, but is and will be present. Thus the Gospels, while they document the recollection of Him, are not simply chronicles or registers. The Lucan description of their content is remarkable enough : " all that Jesus *began* both to do and teach," until the day of His ascension. Where the Gospel accounts reach their limit, we obviously do not have the limit of the being and speech and action of the One of whom they tell. Even before His birth the promise was given to Mary (Lk. 1³³) : " Of his kingdom there shall be no end." Hence the pregnant request of the disciples who went to Emmaus (Lk. 24²⁹) : " Abide with us : for it is toward evening, and the day is far spent." Hence the sayings in Jn. 6⁵⁶ and 15⁴ about His abiding with those who abide with Him. Hence Mt. 18²⁰ : " Where two or three are gathered together in my name, there am I in the midst of them." Hence Mt. 28²⁰ : " Lo, I am with you alway, even unto the end of the world." Hence the even more comprehensive Mk. 13³¹ : " Heaven and earth shall pass away : but my words shall not pass away." And it may well be that fundamentally we have to place in the same category, and need not try to explain in detail, the bewildering changes between past and present forms in narration which are so characteristic a feature of the style of the Fourth Gospel. When we read the Gospel records we cannot abstract from the fact that what is narrated on the basis and as the content of the knowledge of the community was the existence of a man who as they see it lives and speaks and acts to-day no less than yesterday (Heb. 13⁸). It was in this way that He *was* present for them.

Of course, they were really looking at this man and attesting the life of this man. Yet there did not, and could not, arise anything in the nature of a biographical portrait. What the New Testament offers and we can take from it, is only a fragmentary picture, and this in four different groupings of which it is difficult to grasp the continuity and inner coherence from a biographical standpoint, and each of which so clearly represents a whole that only artificially and without clear support from the texts can we construct an orderly progression from the beginning to the end. Does this mean that we are given a character-sketch, to use a favourite concept of the earlier 20th century? If so, it is singular that the attempts which have often been made to define this character have never succeeded. In point of fact they cannot succeed, because the texts do not give us, and do not even try to give us, the right kind of materials for this purpose. There is no doubt at all that a real human person is seen and described in them. But everything that characterises it as such is so singular, so out of scale in relation to other human persons, so unique and to that extent so alien, that there are no categories in which to grasp it. It is surely no accident that in the introduction to his Gospel already referred to Luke speaks anonymously, as it were, of the things most surely believed among us. The man in question existed in these events. And what took place in these events was always, finally, the existence of this man in the strange determinations of which we have learned to know a few—in His inescapability, in His critical function, in His unforget-table lordliness, in His irrevocability which bursts and transcends all the limits of His life and its time. The Gospels bear witness to Him as they bear witness to these events. The problem of these events and its solution is, as the New Testament knows and says, that of His divine Sonship which occupied us in the first part of the doctrine of reconciliation and can only be referred to now as the background of all that we have seen and have still to see. Our present theme is that the Son of God also was and is and will be the Son of Man, the royal man. But obviously, against that background, the tradition concerning the life of this man necessarily took a form in which it could not possibly give us materials for a biography or character study. It could attest Him as a man, and it has done this. But it could attest this man only as God and His revelation and Word and works can be attested by men; only in the pragmatics determined by His identity with the one Son of the heavenly Father.

All the same, it does see and attest this royal man—again, of course, in the light of His identity with the one Son of the heavenly Father—as an earthly reality of the first and supreme order.

When we say an earthly reality, we mean a reality of the same kind as that of everything which is made, and especially everything human. We do not mean an angel, much less an idea, but concretely a specimen—even if a very distinctive one—of human nature. We can only misunderstand the tradition from the very outset if we understand it docetically, closing our ears to the fact that it speaks concretely of a man who lived concretely in time and space—just as concretely as if it spoke of any other man. All that it has to say is said of this man and with reference to Him, and not on any plane of speculation. It saw and heard Him in the world of Israel, and therefore in the world of man, and it was at obvious pains to put Him expressly in this world in its presentation, and therefore to describe Him as the true fellow of all other men.

But what we have to see and consider, seeing and considering everything else in the light of it, is an earthly reality of the first and supreme order ; the concrete limit and measure and criterion of all other earthly reality ; the first and the last ; the creature, the man (He is called the firstborn of every creature in Col. 1[15]), from whom we have to learn what a creature, a man, really is ; that which is unconditionally sure in a whole world of that which is less sure and unsure. The New Testament tradition does not speak only about this royal man ; it speaks from Him. As its theme He was also its origin, as its theorem its axiom. And so it is one single demand, not merely to hear what it has to say about Him, but to obey the One of whom it speaks, i.e., to do the same as it does itself, to think from Him, to desire to follow Him. It has attested Him as the man who necessarily makes and demands this, who gives others the freedom for it. It is as this earthly reality (of the first and supreme order), as this royal man, that according to its witness He was and is and will again be present. We may refuse the knowledge it seeks to impart. But if we accept it, we are necessarily committed to instruction concerning the existence of *this* man.

II

We must now take a further step and attempt to add a material statement to the more formal deliberations with which we have had to begin. We can put it generally and comprehensively in the formula used to describe the " new man " in Eph. 4[24]. The royal man of the New Testament tradition is created " after God " (κατὰ θεόν). This means that as a man He exists analogously to the mode of existence of God. In what He thinks and wills and does, in His attitude, there is a correspondence, a parallel in the creaturely world, to the plan and purpose and work and attitude of God.

He reflects God. As a man He is His εἰκών (Col. 1[15]). In the human sphere He is τέλειος in the same sense, directed to the same goal, as His Father is in the heavenly (Mt. 5⁴⁸). In Him the will of God is done on earth as it is in heaven (Mt. 6¹⁰). In the act of His life the peace of creation triumphs and affirms and reveals itself. He is and reveals the Nevertheless of the Creator who is superior to chaos, the execution of His good creative will. But in Him, too, there triumphs and affirms and reveals itself the peace of the covenant, the solidarity of God with man, His perfect fellowship with His people and the perfect fellowship of this people with Him, the thanksgiving of human creation which corresponds to His grace, and therefore the teleology of the divine preservation and rule of the creaturely world. The covenant broken by Israel and the whole of humanity, but never repudiated or destroyed by God, is maintained in the life-act of this one man. He does that which is demanded and expected in the covenant as the act of human faithfulness corresponding to the faithfulness of God. As the Son of God He is obedient man, who is not only filled and impelled by the Spirit (Mk. 1¹⁰, ¹²), but exists in the activity of the Spirit, establishing His work, incorporating Him in Himself as the capacity to receive the grace of God and its influence in the creaturely world. He is πνεῦμα ζωοποιοῦν, as Paul calls Him (1 Cor. 15⁴⁵; 2 Cor. 3¹⁷), and as such the "man from heaven," the second and definitive, the ἔσχατος Ἀδάμ (1 Cor. 15⁴⁵·⁴⁷), the Elect, the Beloved, on whom there rests the divine good-pleasure in defiance of the sin of man (Mk. 1¹¹, 9⁷).

1. To see this concretely, it is best to begin with what seems to be a completely negative aspect. The royal man shares as such the strange destiny which falls on God in His people and the world—to be the One who is ignored and forgotten and despised and discounted by men. Among other men this One who is truly exalted is not as such a great man. He has nothing of what the world counts as recognition and authority and honour and success. His place is not one of the recognised peaks on the sunnier side of human life. His kingdom has neither the pomp nor the power, the extent nor the continuance, of even the smallest of the human kingdoms which all the same it overshadows and questions. His power is present to men in the form of weakness, His glory in that of lowliness, His victory in that of defeat. The final concealment is that of His suffering and death as a condemned criminal. He who alone is rich is present as the poorest of the poor. As the exalted Son of Man He did not deny the humiliation of the Son of God, but faithfully represented and reflected it even to the minutest details. This is often stated, but its inevitability is not always grasped. Does it not mean in the first instance that it pleased Him as man to exist in the same isolation and estrangement, in the same obscure and shameful corner, as was the lot of God in the world which had fallen away from Him?

As He Himself attested to Pilate in Jn. 18³⁶, His kingdom—although it is in—is not of this world. And because it is not ἐκ τοῦ κόσμου, in the cosmos it is an inconsiderable and from the human point of view an insignificant kingdom, a kingdom which is hidden like the leaven in three measures of meal (Mt. 13³³), like the treasure in the field (Mt. 13⁴⁴), like the grain of mustard-seed which is smaller than all other seeds (Mt. 13³²). It does not come μετὰ παρατηρήσεως, nor can it be proclaimed directly, or, as we should say, "historically," so that it may be said: "Lo here! or, lo there!" (Lk. 17²⁰ᶠ·). The saying in Mt. 11²⁹ in which Jesus described Himself as πραΰς and ταπεινὸς τῇ καρδίᾳ is surely not moralistic self-boasting, but His confession of the humiliation of the Son of

God put into effect by Him as the Son of Man, of the genuine incarnation of the Word as it took place in Him. And so, when He was born, His mother laid Him in a manger " because there was no room for them in the inn " (Lk. 2⁷). Foxes have holes, and the birds of the air have nests, " but the Son of man hath not where to lay his head " (Mt. 8²⁰). He was despised " in his own country, and among his own kin, and in his own house " (Mk. 6⁴). It could be, and actually was the case, that His appearance as a man, in the sharpest antithesis to what He was, became an " offence " to those around Him ; that He disguised Himself from them ; that He made Himself alien and incomprehensible and repugnant. It was not only the people of Nazareth who felt this (Mt. 13³⁷), but the Baptist as well (Mt. 11¹⁶), and even at the last His disciples (Mk. 14²⁹). His own family said of Him : " He is beside himself " (Mk. 3²¹). According to the judgment of the scribes He was in league with Satan (Mk. 3²²). As the Pharisees saw Him, He was " a man gluttonous, and a winebibber, a friend of publicans and sinners " (Mt. 11¹⁹), an insurrectionist (Lk. 23², ⁵, ¹⁴), and finally (in the judgment of the council) a blasphemer (Mt. 9³, 26⁶⁵). A strange reflection of the royal man ! The sport which the Roman soldiers made of Him before His crucifixion, decking Him with the royal purple and the crown of thorns (Mk. 15¹⁶ᶠ· and par.), is a drastic confirmation of this reflection, as is also the taunting cry at the cross : " He saved others ; himself he cannot save. If he be the King of Israel, let him now come down from the cross, and we will believe him. He trusted in God ; let him deliver him now, if he will have him : for he said, I am the Son of God " (Mt. 27⁴¹ᶠ·). The kingdom and the King were as deeply concealed as that. And this King had not entertained any earlier illusions : " Nevertheless when the Son of man cometh, shall he find faith on the earth ? " (Lk. 18⁸). Even His disciples forsook Him at the last and fled (Mt. 26⁵⁶). In the end He was absolutely alone in the world, even to the point of asking (Mk. 15³⁴) whether God Himself, and God especially, had not forsaken Him. He could not enter more radically than He did into the isolation of God in this world, or fulfil more basically His agreement with Him in this respect. We have first to realise (as the Gospels themselves do) that it was the servant of God who here—not in the form of a Lord, but in that of a servant (Phil. 2⁷)— entered the human scene as the Lord, as the κύριος at the heart of this Jewish and Gentile humanity. This hidden kingdom could not remain hidden. It pressed for revelation. And it was in fact revealed. For His lordship could not be compromised but only confirmed by all this. He was not least the κύριος in this agreement with God. But when and where He was revealed and known as such, it involved an exception from the general rule—" Blessed is he, whosoever shall *not* be offended in me " (Mt. 11⁶). This penetration could not be made by man, but only in man by God. " Children, how hard it is . . . to enter into the kingdom of God ! " For a rich man—and we are all rich as compared with Jesus Christ—it is no easier than it is for a camel to go through the eye of a needle (Mk. 10²³ᶠ·). It can take place only as there is a new birth of man from above (Jn. 3³). That is why Jesus says of the Messianic confession of Peter : " Flesh and blood hath not revealed it unto thee, but my Father which is in heaven " (Mt. 16¹⁷). Without His resurrection and ascension, and therefore without the witness of the Holy Spirit, Jesus would certainly have gone through world history, or rather gone under in world history, only as an obscure and unsuccessful Jewish eccentric and revolutionary like so many others. The parallel of His hiddenness to that of God was complete when it was removed by His self-declaration—as it could be removed only by His self-declaration.

2. It is of a piece with this that—almost to the point of prejudice —He ignored all those who are high and mighty and wealthy in the world in favour of the weak and meek and lowly. He did this even in the moral sphere, ignoring the just for sinners, and in the spiritual

sphere, finally ignoring Israel for the Gentiles. It was to the latter group and not the former that He found Himself called. It was among the latter and not the former that He expected to find the eyes and ears that God had opened, and therefore the men of good-pleasure of Lk. 2^{14}. It was in the latter and not the former that He saw His brethren. It was with the latter and not the former that His disciples were to range themselves according to His urgent counsel and command. Throughout the New Testament the kingdom of God, the Gospel and the man Jesus have a remarkable affinity, which is no mere egalitarianism, to all those who are in the shadows as far as concerns what men estimate to be fortune and possessions and success and even fellowship with God. Why is this the case ? We shall have to say more on this question later. But one reason is the distinctive solidarity of the man Jesus with the God who in the eyes of the world —and not merely the ordinary world, but the moral and spiritual as well—is also poor in this way, existing not only in fact and practice but even in theory, somewhere on the margin in its scale of values, at an unimportant level, as the mere content of a limiting concept. In fellowship and conformity with this God who is poor in the world the royal man Jesus is also poor, and fulfils this transvaluation of all values, acknowledging those who (without necessarily being better) are in different ways poor men as this world counts poverty.

It is common knowledge that in the New Testament it is especially the Evangelist Luke and the author of James who emphasise this aspect of the existence of Jesus. But it is also unmistakeable in the witness of Paul. We have only to think of the famous description of the elect in 1 Cor. $1^{25f.}$, of the importance of the concept ταπεινοφροσύνη in his ethics, of his saying about the grace of our Lord Jesus Christ in 2 Cor. 8^9-that, though He was rich, yet for our sakes He became poor, and of his saying about the power which attains its goal in weakness (2 Cor. 12^9). But the same is true of the whole Gospel tradition. The recognised sharpening of the beatitudes in Lk. 6^{20}, and the addition of the corresponding woes, underlines a declaration which is also contained in the Matthean account ($5^{3f.}$) and must not on any account be suppressed in our exposition of it—the declaration concerning Lazarus (Lk. $16^{19f.}$), who as a poor man is so devastatingly opposed to the rich man clothed in purple and fine linen and faring sumptuously every day. There should be no softening of the starkness with which wealth and poverty are there contrasted and estimated (as also in Jas. $5^{1f.}$) even in the economic sense.

But the Matthean version of the beatitudes guards us against another form of softening, i.e., the limitation of the concepts to a purely economic sense. For, after all, the publicans were not really poor in this way. They were poor in spirit (Mt. 5^3), "publicans and sinners," unrighteous. In relation to them Jesus compares Himself to the doctor who is not needed by the healthy but by the sick : " I am not come to call the righteous, but sinners to repentance " (Mt. $9^{11f.}$). We have here a supremely hostile decision of Jesus in relation to everything that counts as human greatness and littleness, strength and weakness. In the first instance the mammon which we cannot serve as a second master side by side with God (Mt. 6^{24}) is no doubt the sum of the material possessions which distinguish one man from another, but by implication it is no less certainly the sum of all such possessions. It self-evidently includes the enjoyment of the authority and power exercised so self-evidently—and even with the claim to be εὐεργέται (Lk. 22²⁵)—by the princes of the Gentiles, those that are great in the world. But above all it includes the possession of moral and religious righteousness (Mt. 5⁶) which undoubtedly differentiates the scribes and Pharisees from harlots (Mt. 21³¹ᶠ·), or the possession of insight and understanding which is an indisputable advantage of the wise over fools, the mature over the naive. The saying in Mt. 11²⁵ is relevant in this connexion : " I thank thee, O Father, Lord of heaven and earth, because thou hast hid these things from the wise and prudent, and hast revealed them unto babes." So, too, is the saying in Mt. 18¹ᶠ·, which tells us that unless we are converted and become as little children we cannot enter unto the kingdom of heaven, let alone be the greatest in it. So, too, is the verse about the little ones whose angels do always behold the face of Jesus' Father in heaven. It is true in every sense, irrespective of the concrete form taken by riches and poverty, that the hungry and thirsty and strangers and naked and sick and captives are the brothers of Jesus in whom He Himself is either recognised or not recognised (Mt. 25³⁵ᶠ· ⁴²ᶠ·). Those whom He calls to Himself are always the weary and heavy-laden (Mt. 11²⁸). His disciples can only be a " little flock " (Lk. 12³²), as sheep among ravening wolves (Mt. 10¹⁶), and therefore without gold or silver or brass in their purses, without scrips, without second coats, without shoes or staves (Mt. 10⁹ᶠ·), with no worldly security. It is worth noting that Matthew adds at this point the saying about the labourer being worthy of his hire—this insecurity seems to be the reward earned by those who work with and for Jesus. The disciples are also forbidden point-blank to allow themselves to be distinguished, like the scribes and Pharisees, by the title " Rabbi," " Master " or " Father " (Mt. 23⁸ᶠ·). The man who would be first in this circle must be the minister, and the chief among them can only be the servant of all (Mk. 10⁴³ᶠ·). And finally they will be delivered up to be afflicted, and put to death, and hated of all nations for His name's sake (Mt. 24⁹). It is this capacity, and as this happens, that they are blessed.

Along the same lines but on the far horizon, and more significant theologically, there is also the reversal of what seems this time to be the spiritually very necessary and legitimate precedence of elected and called and blessed and enlightened Israel in relation to the surrounding Gentile world. We do not forget the curt explanation in Mt. 15²⁴ : " I am not sent but unto the lost sheep of the house of Israel." And what he says directly to the Syro-phenician woman in Mk. 7²⁷ is even more uncompromising : " Let the children first be filled : for it is not meet to take the children's bread, and to cast it unto the dogs." Nor do we forget the firm injunction in Mt. 10⁵ : " Go not into the way of the Gentiles, and into any city of the Samaritans enter ye not." It is a valid rule that Jesus is the Son of Man who arose in Israel and for Israel (for the lost sheep of the house of Israel). But inevitably, as the One who is this, He breaks this valid rule. For as a fulfilment of the covenant-promise of the Old Testament " in Israel and for Israel " means " in the world and for the world." We have already mentioned how His fame spread beyond the confines of Galilee. Even at the beginning of the story of the Syro-phenician woman, when according to both Matthew and Mark (it is surprising that Luke did not take up the story too) Jesus was Himself visiting this neighbouring Gentile territory, we are told that " he could not be hid " (Mk. 7²⁴). And when the woman heard the Yes of Jesus concealed under the No (to follow Luther's inspired exegesis), and claimed the right of the house-dogs under the table to eat of the children's crumbs, her request did not fail to be heard, and she herself actually to be fed by the children's meat. It was exactly the same when Jesus found in the centurion of Capernaum a faith such as He had not found in Israel (Mt. 8¹⁰). And supposing those who are invited to the wedding refuse the invitation ? This necessarily gives rise to a situation in which the contrast between Israel and the Gentiles belongs to the whole relationship between the rich who are not blessed and the poor who are, as described in Lk. 14²¹ᶠ· : " Then the master of the house being angry said to his servant, Go out quickly into the streets and lanes of the city, and bring in hither the poor and the maimed, and the halt, and the blind," and again : " Go out into the highways and hedges, and compel them to come in, that my house may be filled. For I say unto you, That none of those men which were bidden shall taste of my supper." It gives rise to the situation described in Lk. 13²⁵ᶠ· in which those who properly and by right ought to be first and exclusively within are now without and knock in vain at the door, " saying, Lord, Lord, open unto us ; and he shall answer and say unto you, I know you not whence ye are ; Then shall ye begin to say, We have eaten and drunk in thy presence, and thou hast taught in our streets. But he shall say, I tell you, I know you not whence ye are ; depart from me, all ye workers of iniquity. There shall be weeping and gnashing of teeth, when ye shall see Abraham, and Isaac, and Jacob, and all the prophets, in the kingdom of God, and you yourselves thrust out. And they shall come from the east, and from the west, and from the north, and from the south, and shall sit down in the kingdom of God." And finally and comprehensively : " And, behold, there are last which shall be first, and there are first which shall be last." Or according to the commentary of Matthew on the parable of the wicked husbandmen (21⁴³) : " The kingdom of God shall be taken from you, and given to a nation bringing forth the fruits thereof." It may sound like a general truth of reason when Paul says in Rom. 3²⁹ : " Is he the God of the Jews only ? is he not also of the Gentiles ? Yes, of the Gentiles also : seeing it is one God." In fact, however, this is a description of the altered situation, the history and the way which are the theme of the second part of Luke's historical record and above all the decisive content of the apostolic action of Paul himself. " It was necessary that the word of God should first have been spoken to you : but seeing ye put it from you, and judge yourselves unworthy of everlasting life, lo, we turn to the Gentiles " (Ac. 13⁴⁶). But this action of Paul is only a reflection of the way which the man Jesus went and was led in obedience to the will of His heavenly Father. And the decisive turning-point in this way was His delivering up (παράδοσις, Mk. 15¹) to Pilate and the Gentiles by the leading representatives of Israel itself—the event which necessarily transformed the mission to Israel (Mt. 10¹ᶠ·) into a world-wide mission : " Go ye therefore, and make disciples of all nations " (Mt. 28¹⁹). But again, this way of the man Jesus is a reflection of the way which God Himself went from those who have all things to those who have nothing.

The saying of Mary in the *Magnificat* (Lk. 1⁵¹ᶠ·) might well be set over the whole of this inversion : " He hath shewed strength with his arm ; he hath scattered the proud in the imagination of their hearts. He hath put down the mighty from their seats, and exalted them of low degree. He hath filled the hungry with good things ; and the rich he hath sent empty away."

3. The conformity of the man Jesus with the mode of existence and attitude of God consists actively in what we can only call the pronouncedly revolutionary character of His relationship to the orders of life and value current in the world around Him. This was all the more sharply defined because it was not theoretical or systematic. Jesus was not in any sense a reformer championing new orders against the old ones, contesting the latter in order to replace them by the former. He did not range Himself and His disciples with any of the existing parties. One of these, and not the worst, was that of the Pharisees. But Jesus did not identify Himself with them. Nor did He set up against them an opposing party. He did not represent or defend or champion any programme—whether political, economic, moral or religious, whether conservative or progressive. He was

equally suspected and disliked by the representatives of all such programmes, although He did not particularly attack any of them. Why
His existence was so unsettling on every side was that He set all
programmes and principles in question. And He did this simply because
He enjoyed and displayed, in relation to all the orders positively or
negatively contested around Him, a remarkable freedom which again
we can only describe as royal. He had need of none of them in the
sense of an absolute authority which was vitally necessary for Him,
and which He could prescribe and defend as vitally necessary for others
because it was an absolute authority. On the other hand, He had no
need consistently to break any of them, to try to overthrow them
altogether, to work for their replacement or amendment. He could
live in these orders. He could seriously acknowledge in practice that
the temple of God was in Jerusalem, and that the doctors of the Law
were to be found in this temple, and that their disciples the scribes
were scattered throughout the land, with the Pharisees as their most
zealous rivals. He could also acknowledge that the Romans were in
the land with their native satellites, and that the emperor in Rome
bore supreme rule even over the land and people of the divine covenant.
He could grant that there were families, and rich and poor. He never
said that these things ought not to be. He did not oppose other
" systems " to these. He did not make common cause with the Essene
reforming movement. He simply revealed the limit and frontier of
all these things—the freedom of the kingdom of God. He simply
existed in this freedom and summoned to it. He simply made use of
this freedom to cut right across all these systems both in His own case
and in that of His disciples, interpreting and accepting them in His
own way and in His own sense, in the light shed upon them all from
that frontier. It was just that He Himself was the light which was
shed upon all these orders from that frontier. Inevitably, then, He
clashed with these orders in the interpretation commonly placed on
them in the world in which He lived. Inevitably their provisional
and relative character, the ways in which they were humanly conditioned, their secret fallibility, were all occasionally disclosed—not in
principle, only occasionally, but on these occasions quite unmistakeably
—in His attitude toward them and His assessment of their significance.
But it was not these incidental disclosures of the freedom of God
which made Him a revolutionary far more radical than any that came
either before or after Him. It was the freedom itself, which could not
even be classified from the standpoint of these orders. For where are
these orders when He expresses both in word and deed that abasement of all that is high and exaltation of all that is low ? Do they
not all presuppose that the high is high and the low low ? Was not
the axe really laid at the root of all these trees in and by His existence ?
In the last resort, it was again conformity with God Himself which
constituted the secret of the character of Jesus on this side too. This

is the relationship of God Himself to all the orders of life and value which, as long as there is history at all, enjoy a transitory validity in the history of every human place. This is how God gives them their times and spheres, but without being bound to any of them, without giving any of them His own divine authority, without allotting to any of them a binding validity for all men even beyond their own time and sphere, without granting that they are vitally necessary and absolutely authoritative even for their own time and sphere. In this way God Himself is their limit and frontier. An alien light is thus shed on them by God Himself as on that which He has limited. This is how He Himself deals with them, not in principle, not in the execution of a programme, but for this reason in a way which is all the more revolutionary, as the One who breaks all bonds asunder, in new historical developments and situations each of which is for those who can see and hear—only a sign, but an unmistakeable sign, of His freedom and kingdom and over-ruling of history.

Attention should first be paid to what we might call the passive conservatism of Jesus. Rather curiously, Jesus accepts and allows many things which we imagine He ought to have attacked and set aside both in principle and practice, and which the community in which the Gospels arose had to a very large extent outgrown. It did not—and obviously could not—find it a source of vexation to have to maintain this aspect of the traditional picture.

He accepted the temple as quite self-evidently the house of His Father (Lk. 2[49]). Even the astonishing act of cleansing it of the traders and moneychangers presupposes (Mk. 11[17]) that it is for Him the house of God. As we see from Mt. 23[16f.], He does not take it, or the altar in it, less seriously but more seriously than the scribes and Pharisees. He assumes that the pious Israelite will still go up to it to bring his sacrifices (Mt. 5[23f.]). When He Himself comes to Jerusalem, He does not teach in the streets and market-places, but daily in its forecourt (Mk. 12[35], 14[49]). It is there that the Pharisee and publican make their prayers in the parable which brings out so strongly the difference between Himself and those around Him (Lk. 18[9f.]). We may also note the description of the conduct of His disciples in the closing verse of St. Luke's Gospel : " And they were continually in the temple, praising and blessing God." We may also recall that after His crucifixion, resurrection and ascension they still continued " daily with one accord in the temple."

But respect may also be seen for the order of the family, for according to Lk. 2[51] Jesus was at first subject to His parents in Nazareth. And in Mk. 7[11f.] He insisted that the duty of caring for father and mother must take precedence of all cultic obligations. We may also remember, with reservations, the provision which He made for His mother even on the cross, according to the saying handed down in Jn. 19[26].

Again, at least at the beginning of His teaching activity, He did not separate Himself from the Galilean synagogues (Mk. 1[21], 3[1]). Indeed, in Lk. 4[17f.] we have an obvious description of the way in which He adapted Himself to current synagogue practice. As concerns the Law, He not only protests (Mt. 5[17f.]) that He has not come to destroy it and the prophets, but He maintains that He has come to fulfil it, that not one jot or tittle shall pass from it until heaven and earth pass away, and that only those can be great in the kingdom of heaven who practise and teach even its most minute regulations. In Mt. 23[1f.] He concedes (even if ironically) that the scribes and Pharisees who expound the Law sit in Moses' seat, so that if the people and His disciples have to be warned against their example, they are also enjoined : " All therefore whatsoever they bid you observe, that observe and do." And if in Mt. 23²³ᶠ· He accused them of hypocritically tithing mint and anise and cummin and omitting the weightier matters of the Law, judgment, mercy and faith, He added as something self-evident : " These ought ye to have done, and not to leave the other undone." In Mt. 13⁵² again, He recognised the possibility of the scribe " instructed unto the kingdom of heaven " who " is like unto a householder, which bringeth forth out of his treasure things new and old "—the old as well as the new. The antithesis in Mt. 5²¹ᶠ· (" Ye have heard that it was said by them of old time. . . . But I say unto you . . .") certainly implies a more radical understanding of the Ten Commandments, but this in turn involves a recognition. And the same is true of the more precise exposition of the three traditional exercises of almsgiving, prayer and fasting in Mt. 6¹ᶠ· Even to the sayings on the cross, the tradition likes to see Jesus speaking in direct or indirect quotations from the Old Testament, and it sets Him generally in the confines, not merely of the world of religion, but of the special religious promise given to His own people. In Jn. 4²² we even have the express saying that " salvation is of the Jews." The point is made so emphatically that it can be reported without any inhibitions that some of His more kindly-disposed contemporaries regarded Him merely as " a prophet, or as one of the prophets " (Mk. 6¹⁵), or perhaps a particularly " great " prophet (Lk. 7¹⁶). Similarly, in the later search for the so-called " historical Jesus " the suggestion could be made that He might be reduced to the figure of a (very outstanding) representative of a reformed and deepened Judaism.

It is also to be noted that we never see Him in direct conflict with the economic relationships and obligations of His time and background. We have only to think of the uncritical equanimity with which He accepted in the parables of the kingdom the existence of free employers of labour and employees dependent on their good will, of masters and servants and capital and interest, as though all these things were part of the legitimate *status quo*. In Lk. 16¹ᶠ· unqualified praise was given to the οἰκονόμος, not as a deceiver, but at least as one who knew how to act wisely within the current arrangement in relation to rents. To the man who asks Him to see that his brother divides the inheritance fairly He replies in Lk. 12¹³ᶠ· that it is not His office to judge and divide in such matters. In this request, at any rate in the context in which Luke reports it, He sees only the cry of covetousness and not at all a cry for justice. " Ye have the poor with you always " (Mk. 14⁷), is His answer to the disciples who would have preferred a corresponding almsgiving to the woman's lavish devotion. He thus takes it as almost axiomatic that there must always be poor people—a thought which has given an illusory comfort to many in subsequent periods. And then in Lk. 16⁹, ¹¹ we are told to make friends with mammon (even the unrighteous mammon), and that the true riches (τὸ ἀληθινόν) will not be entrusted to those who are not " faithful " in relation to it. This was certainly not an invitation to maintain and augment our financial possessions as cleverly as possible—a process which later came to be regarded almost as a specific Christian virtue in certain parts of the Calvinistic world—but it is obviously not a summons to socialism.

Traces of the same attitude may finally be discerned in respect of political relationships and orders and disorders. It is freely presupposed in Mt. 5²⁵ᶠ· and elsewhere that there are judges and officers and prisons. That there are those who " think to rule over the nations " (the qualifying δοκοῦντες is to be noted), and do in fact exercise dominion and authority over them, is certainly described in Mk. 10⁴²ᶠ· as a procedure which is not to have any place in the community, but there is no direct criticism of it as such. The God who does not allow His elect to cry to Him in vain (Lk. 18¹ᶠ·) can appear in the guise of a notoriously unjust judge who neither fears God nor has any respect for man. It is expressly recognised by Jesus in Jn. 19¹¹ that Pilate has an authority even in relation to

Himself, and that this is given him from above. In Mt. 26⁵² He did not allow Peter to offer any resistance to the Sanhedrin guard, but ordered him to put up his sword into its sheath. We do not find in the Gospels the slightest trace either of a radical repudiation of the dominion of Rome or Herod, or, for that matter, of any basic anti-imperialism or anti-militarism.

It is quite evident, however, and we must not ignore this aspect, that there is also no trace of any consistent recognition in principle. We can describe the attitude of Jesus as that of a passive conservatism in the further sense that it never amounted to more than a provisional and qualified respect (we might almost say toleration) in face of existing and accepted orders. Jesus acknowledged them and reckoned with them and subjected Himself to them and advised His disciples to do the same ; but He was always superior to them. And it was inevitable—we will now turn to this aspect—that this superiority, the freedom of the kingdom of God, should occasionally find concrete expression in His words and actions, that an occasional creaking should be unmistakeably heard in the timbers.

As regards the temple, He made it plain to the Pharisees in Mt. 12⁶ that there is something greater than the temple. When He paid the temple tax for Peter and Himself in Mt. 17²⁴ᶠ·, He did not do so on the basis of an unqualified recognition which the disciple was to regard as binding, but " lest we should offend them." For : " What thinkest thou, Simon ? of whom do the kings of the earth take custom or tribute ? of their own children, or of strangers ? " And when Peter answered : " Of strangers. Jesus saith unto him, Then are the children free."

Again, it was an unmistakeable assault on the order of the family, which is so firmly stabilised by nature and custom, when in Mk. 3³¹ᶠ He gave to His mother and brethren, who had " sent unto him, calling him," the following answer : " Who is my mother, or my brethren ? " and then, " looking round about on them that sat about him " : " Behold, my mother and my brethren." And we need hardly refer to the even harsher saying in the story of the wedding at Cana : τί ἐμοὶ καὶ σοί, " What have we in common ? " (Jn. 2⁴). It also has a most destructive sound in this respect when He replied to the man who wanted to be His disciple, but only after he had buried his father : " Let the dead bury their dead : but go thou and preach the kingdom of God " (Lk. 9⁵⁹ᶠ·), and to the other who asked if he might first make his farewells to those at home : " No man, having put his hand to the plough, and looking back, is fit for the kingdom of God " (Lk. 9⁶¹ᶠ·).

Again, there are breaches of the prevailing religious or cultic order. The accusation was made in Mk. 2¹⁸ᶠ· that His disciples did not fast like those of the Pharisees or even the Baptist. To those who raised this point He gave the puzzling answer : " Can the children of the bridechamber fast, while the bridegroom is with them ? " There was also the complaint in Mk. 7¹ᶠ· that His disciples neglected the purifications prescribed for meals : " Why walk not thy disciples according to the tradition of the elders ? " In reply, Jesus explains that it is not what is without but what is within that really defiles a man—the evil thoughts and acts which come from the heart (Mk. 7¹⁴ᶠ·). Above all, there is His attitude to the sabbath, which allowed His disciples to satisfy their hunger by plucking ears of corn (Mk. 2²³ᶠ·) and Himself to heal on the sabbath (Mk. 3¹ᶠ· ; Jn. 5¹ᶠ·, 9¹ᶠ·). The offence which He gave and the reproaches which He incurred at this point were particularly severe. His answers were as follows : " Is it lawful to do good on the sabbath days, or to do evil ? to save life, or to kill ? But they held their peace " (Mk. 3⁴). " If a man on the sabbath day receive circumcision, that the law of Moses should not be broken ; are ye angry at me, because I have made a man every whit whole on the sabbath day ? " (Jn. 7²³). And above all : " The sabbath was made for man, and not man for the sabbath : therefore the Son of man is Lord also of the sabbath " (Mk. 2²⁷ᶠ·).

As appears in Mk. 3⁶ and elsewhere, this breach was one of the most concrete things which made His destruction necessary in the eyes of His opponents.

Again, there are some striking breaches of the contemporary (and not only the contemporary) industrial and commercial and economic order. We may mention certain features in the parables which are definitely not taken from real life but are quite foreign to customary practice in these spheres. As Goethe pointed out, no sensible husbandman would ever sow as did the man in Mt. 13³ᶠ·, scattering his seed irrespectively over the path and stony ground and among thorns as well as on good ground. And what servants will ever be prepared to say that they are unprofitable when they have done all that they are required to do (Lk. 17¹⁰) ? What king will ever be so magnanimous as to pronounce unconditional freedom from punishment or guilt on the steward who has so obviously misappropriated that which was entrusted to him (Mt. 18²³ᶠ·) ? What owner of a vineyard will ever pay his workmen as did the owner in Mt. 20¹ᶠ·? And what sense does it make that the man whose land has been fruitful and who therefore plans (in good and sensible fashion) to pull down his barns and build greater, hoping to enjoy a future in which he can take his ease and eat and drink and be merry, is described by God as a fool—simply because he has the unavoidable misfortune to die before his enterprise can be completed, and he can no longer call all these goods his own (Lk. 12¹⁶ᶠ·) ? Nor does Jesus seem to have a proper understanding of trade and commerce when we consider the story, recorded in all four Gospels, of the expulsion from the temple of those who changed money and sold doves. " A den of thieves " (Mk. 11¹⁷) is rather a harsh description for the honest, small-scale financial and commercial activities which had established themselves there. These detailed signals only give warning of the real threat and revolution which the kingdom of God and the man Jesus signify and involve in relation to this sphere, but they are signals which we ought not to overlook.

There are similar signals in the political sphere as well. Can we adduce in this respect the not very respectful way in which Jesus describes His own particular ruler, Herod, as a " fox " (Lk. 13³²) ? However that may be, the question and answer in Mk. 12¹³ᶠ· are certainly relevant. Ought tribute to be paid to Cæsar or not ? Well, the coin bears the image of Cæsar, and there can be no doubt that authority rests in his hands, so : " Render to Cæsar the things that are Cæsar's—precisely those things and no more, is the obvious meaning—and to God the things that are God's." There is not a second kingdom of God outside and alongside the first. There is a human kingdom which is authoritative and can demand obedience only as such. And this kingdom is sharply delimited by the one kingdom of God. According to Jn. 19¹⁰ Pilate's power over Jesus is only the power to release Him or to crucify Him. When He asked : " Art thou the king of the Jews ? " Jesus did not owe him a defence which He never made— for although Pilate, like the high-priests, made a case against Him, Jesus did not conduct any case—but only the confession : " Thou sayest it." Even the more explicit statement recorded in Jn. 18³³ᶠ· is only a paraphrase of this confession, this καλὴ ὁμολογία as it is called in 1 Tim. 6¹³. With this confession as the one thing that He had to set against it He both honoured the imperial kingdom and yet at the same time drew unmistakeable attention to its limitations, setting it under a cloud and calling it in question. " Behold, I cast out devils, and I do cures to day and to morrow, and the third day I shall be perfected," was His answer when Herod threatened Him (Lk. 13³²). To the extent that it is another form of the same confession this saying is also relevant in this context.

But the crisis which broke on all human order in the man Jesus is more radical and comprehensive than may be gathered from all these individual indications. Our best starting-point for this deeper consideration is the comparison recorded by all the Synoptics in connexion with the question of fasting : " No man also seweth a piece of new cloth on an old garment : else the new piece that filled it up taketh away from the old, and the rent is made worse. And no man putteth new wine into old bottles : else the new wine doth burst the bottles, and the wine is spilled, and the bottles will be marred : but new wine must be put into new bottles " (Mk. 2²¹ᶠ·). For Jesus, and as seen in the light of Jesus, there can be no doubt that all human orders are this old garment or old bottles, which are in the last resort quite incompatible with the new cloth and the new wine of the kingdom of God. The new cloth can only destroy the old garment, and the old bottles can only burst when the new wine of the kingdom of God is poured into them. All true and serious conservatism, and all true and serious belief in progress, presupposes that there is a certain compatibility between the new and the old, and that they can stand in a certain neutrality the one to the other. But the new thing of Jesus is the invading kingdom of God revealed in its alienating antithesis to the world and all its orders. And in this respect, too, the dictum is true : *neutralitas non valet in regno Dei.* There is thus concealed and revealed, both in what we called the passive conservatism of Jesus and the individual signs and penetrations which question the world of human orders as such, the radical and indissoluble antithesis of the kingdom of God to all human kingdoms, the unanswerable question, the irremediable unsettlement introduced by the kingdom of God into all human kingdoms.

In Mk. 13¹ᶠ·, when His disciples were admiring the temple, Jesus answered them : " Seest thou these great buildings ? there shall not be left one stone upon another "—a saying that was brought against Him in Mk. 14⁵⁸ (and again on the cross in Mk. 15²⁹) as implying that He Himself would destroy the temple made with hands and replace it in three days by another not made with hands. Mark and Matthew ascribed this version of the saying to false witnesses. But according to the version preserved in Jn. 2¹⁹, although He did not speak of Himself destroying the temple, He certainly spoke of its rebuilding in three days. The comment of John is that He spoke of the temple of His body (Jn. 2²¹). Either way, while He honoured the temple as the house of God and was even jealous for its sanctity, He could not ascribe to it any permanent place or significance in the light of what He Himself brought and was. Unlike the Law in Mt. 5¹⁷ᶠ·, it was not to continue until heaven and earth passed away. The saying to the Samaritan woman is relevant in this connexion : " Woman, believe me, the hour cometh, when ye shall neither in this mountain, nor yet at Jerusalem, worship the Father " (Jn. 4²¹). And what is said about the heavenly Jerusalem in Rev. 21²² is like an echo of all these sayings : " And I saw no temple therein : for the Lord God Almighty and the Lamb are the temple thereof."

Everything else that we have to say concerning the radical antithesis of the new thing which was actualised and appeared in Jesus to the totality of the old order can be said only in relation to its complete ignoring and transcending of this order. We can merely attempt to see with what profundity He attacked it by this ignoring and transcending. He attacked it—in a way from which it can never recover—merely by the alien presence with which He confronted it in its own sphere. What was, in fact, this way in which He confronted it ?

In the first place, He Himself remained unmarried—no one has ever yet explained with what self-evident necessity. And in Mt. 19¹² He reckoned with the fact that there might be others who would remain unmarried for the sake of the kingdom of heaven. In this way He set against the whole sphere of the family (in addition to the sayings already adduced) the basic question of its right and permanence to which there could be given only a provisional and relative answer. " For when they shall rise from the dead, they neither marry, nor are given in marriage " (Mk. 12²⁵).

But above all we must take up again the question of His relationship to the economic order. It, too, was simply but radically called in question by the fact that neither He Himself nor His disciples accepted its basic presupposition by taking any part in the acquisition or holding of any possessions. It is as if the declaration and irruption of the kingdom of God had swept away the ground from under us in this respect. We have already mentioned the passage in the commissioning of the disciples in Mt. 10⁹ which refers to the total insecurity to which He abandons His disciples. Those who followed Him had left everything (Mt. 19²⁷), their nets and boats (Mk. 1¹⁸ᶠ·), their families and houses and lands (Mt. 19²⁹). "Lacked ye anything?" He asks them, and their answer is: "Nothing" (Lk. 22³⁵). But this is not due to acquisition or possession. Those who came to Him, those who went through the narrow gate, were told: "Sell whatsoever thou hast, and give to the poor, and thou shalt have treasure in heaven" (Mk. 10²¹). Those who were sad and went away grieved when they came to this narrow gate (v. 22) did not come to Him. A dangerous alternative for all the economic attitudes and practices conceivable or serviceable to man! As is well-known, in Ac. 2⁴⁴ we read of a bold attempt by the most primitive post-Pentecostal community to take up this basic challenge. " And all that believed were together, and had all things common ; and sold their possessions and goods, and parted them to all men, as every man had need." There is only one other direct mention of this attempt, in Ac. 5¹ᶠ· It has often been taken up since in different forms. But in whatever form can it ever have more than the significance of an attempt? It is worth pondering that the venture was at least made. And it will always be inevitable that there should be impulses in this direction wherever the Gospel of Jesus is proclaimed and heard. But it has never happened—least of all in the modern system called " Communism "—that even in smaller circles the way which leads in this direction has been trodden to the end. And the proclamation in Mt. 6¹⁹ is even more dangerous: " Lay not up for yourselves treasures upon earth, where moth and rust doth corrupt, and where thieves break through and steal," and especially in Mt. 6²⁵ᶠ· : " Take no thought for your life, what ye shall eat, or what ye shall drink ; not yet for your body, what ye shall put on. . . . Take therefore no thought for the morrow : for the morrow shall take thought for the things of itself." Surely there could be no sound or solid economy, either private or public, without this laying up and taking thought? But this is what Jesus says in words which are strangely illuminating and pregnant and penetrating—who can escape their truth and comfort and inspiration?—even though they obviously do not give to the community in which the Gospels arose any directions as to their practical realisation, and have a final validity even though they are exposed from the very outset to the accusation that they are incapable of practical realisation. And how dangerous it is when this laying up and taking thought are scorned as " Gentile " and there is opposed to them the freedom of the fowls of the air and the lilies of the field which neither worry nor work! How dangerous it is that the concept of mammon, which seems to denote only the idea of material possession, is used as a comprehensive term for the whole of that dominion which is opposed to the kingdom of God, the antithesis of the rich and the poor being adopted as a basic *schema* for all the blessedness or otherwise of man! Obviously this is to shake the basic pillars of all normal human activity in relation to the clearest necessities of life—and in the irritating form, not of the proclamation of a better social order, but of the free and simple call to freedom. This is indeed a new piece which cannot be sewn on the old garment, new wine which cannot be put into old bottles. Its relation to the old is that of something which is unmistakeably different and opposed, the strident proclamation of its end and of a new beginning beyond this end, a question and challenge and invitation and demand which cannot as such be silenced. It was the new thing—we must be content, for the moment, with the simple affirmation—of the royal man Jesus penetrating to the very foundations of economic life in defiance of every reasonable and to that extent honourable objection.

It is exactly the same in relation to the juridical and political sphere. Here, too, we have a questioning of the very presuppositions which is all the more powerful in its lack of any direct aggressiveness. What are all the attempts at reform or revelation in which Jesus might have taken part or which He might have instigated or directed compared with the revolution which He did actually accomplish in this sphere ? He did not oppose the evil which He came to root out. He was the Judge and He did not judge : except, perhaps, those who thought that they could be the judges ; except by causing Himself to be judged for these usurpers of judgment. His injunction to His followers, not as a law, but as a free call to freedom, is of a piece with this. They are not to resist evil (Mt. 5³⁸ᶠ·). They are to let themselves be smitten on the left cheek as well as the right. They are to give away their cloak if their coat is taken from them. They are to go two miles with those who compel them to go one. More than that, if they do not want to be judged, they are not to judge (Mt. 7¹ᶠ·). More still, they are to love their enemies (Mt. 5⁴³ᶠ·) and pray for their persecutors, as children of their Father in heaven who causes His sun to shine on the good and the bad and His rain to fall on the just and the unjust, and obviously as brothers of Jesus, who, when His enemies (really the enemies of God) did their worst against Him, prayed for them (Lk. 23³⁴) : " Father, forgive them ; for they know not what they do." It is again clear—for what political thinking can do justice or satisfaction to this injunction and to the One who gives it ?—that this involves a shaking of every human foundation ; that the right of God is in irreconcilable conflict with every human right ; that the divine state is quite incompatible not merely with the wicked totalitarian state but with every conceivable human regime ; that the new thing cannot be used to patch or fill the old. It is evident that human order is here betrayed into the proximity of a final and supreme menace. The community has again and again stifled and denied and even forgotten this, so that it could also be forgotten by the world around. But in this dimension too it has never been able to free itself completely from the unsettlement which it has within itself—whether it accepts the fact or not—as the community of this royal man. Nor has it been able completely to hide it from the world around. For in so far as it has been present as the community of this man, it has been present as such for the world, and the confrontation of the old order with the incommensurable factor of the new has been inescapable in this respect too. From the very outset and continually—cost what it may—the presence of this man has meant always that the world must wrestle with this incommensurable factor.

In all these dimensions the world is concretely violated by God Himself in the fact that the man Jesus came into it and is now within it.

But we have not yet mentioned the decisive point at which the man Jesus is the image and reflection of God Himself. In all the matters that we have emphasised so far we have been protecting this point against any attempt to render it innocuous or trivial. We have been forestalling the opinion that what we have to call the decisive point is something that can be attained and conceived and controlled by men, and incorporated into the scale of known relationships of magnitude and value. That is why we have first had to set Jesus against man and his cosmos as the poor man who if He blessed and befriended any blessed and befriended the poor and not the rich, the incomparable revolutionary who laid the axe at the root of the trees, who pitilessly exposed the darkness of human order in the cosmos, questioning it in a way which is quite beyond our capacity to answer. We do not know God at all if we do not know Him as the One who is absolutely opposed to our whole world which has fallen away from Him and is therefore self-estranged ; as the Judge of our world ; as the One whose will is that it should be totally changed and renewed. If we think we know Him in any other way, what we really know (in a mild or wild transcendence) is only the world itself, ourselves, the old Adam. In the man Jesus, God has separated Himself from this misinterpretation. And we have had to copy this divine separation in all that we have said so far. But again, we do not really know Jesus (the Jesus of the New Testament) if we do not know Him as this poor man, as this (if we may risk the dangerous word) partisan of the poor, and finally as this revolutionary. We have to be warned, therefore, against every attempt to interpret and use Him as a further and perhaps supreme self-manifestation and self-actualisation of the old Adam. But this certainly cannot be our last word. Indeed, it cannot really be our first word except didactically—a truth which is often overlooked in the justifiable reaction against every attempted softening and trivialisation of the Gospel.

4. The word which is really the first and the last word is undoubtedly that the man Jesus, like God Himself, is not against men but for men—even for men in all the impossibility of their perversion, in their form as the men of the old world of Adam. The decisive point to which we now turn is that the royal man Jesus is the image and reflection of the divine Yes to man and his cosmos. It is God's critical Yes, dividing and disclosing and punishing with all the power of the sword. And in this respect too, as we shall see, there corresponds to it the Yes spoken in the existence and act of the man Jesus. But, like the Yes of God, it is really a Yes and not a No, even though it includes and is accompanied by a powerful No. It is the image and reflection of the love in which God has loved, and loves, and will love the world ; of the faithfulness which He has sworn and will maintain ; of the solidarity with it into which He has entered and in which He persists ; of the hope of salvation and glory which He has given it by giving no less than Himself. The man Jesus is the royal man in the fact that He is not merely one man with others but *the* man for them (as God is for them), the man in whom the love and faithfulness and salvation and glory of God are addressed to man in the concrete form of a historical relationship of man to man : and this in spite of their own adamic form ; and therefore in spite of their own estrangement and fundamental error in respect of what they think to be good and true and beautiful and comforting and helpful and liberating and redemptive ; in spite of their attempted safeguards against Him ; and above all in spite of the misery to which they necessarily fall victim in this estrangement and error and the establishment of these safeguards. The divine Yes echoed by the royal man Jesus is the divine Word of comfort for this very misery, and only as such, and working back as it were from it, for the human corruption which is the basis of it. God grapples with sin as He has mercy on the men

who suffer in this way as sinners. His weapon against it is the Gospel, the good news of the end of their misery and the beginning of their redemption, the coming of His kingdom as the kingdom of peace on earth, the reconciliation of the world with Himself. The man Jesus is decisively created after God in the fact that He is as man the work and revelation of the mercy of God, of His Gospel, His kingdom of peace, His atonement, and that He is His creaturely and earthly and historical correspondence in this sense.

We were surely right to leave to the last what is in substance the first point that has to be made in this connexion. It is not at all obvious in the New Testament that Jesus does actually, let alone primarily and decisively, confront men in this character, just as it is not at all self-evident that in this character He represents the true and most inward will of God. He might well be seen—and necessarily (even from the standpoints which have so far concerned us)—as He was seen by Michelangelo : as the Judge of the world ; as the menacing and wrathful representative of divine wrath as the true attitude of God to man. We remember again the different ways in which His coming was surrounded with surprise and horror and dread. The New Testament is full of impressive accounts of the *mysterium tremendum* and the corresponding fear of man with which His appearance was enveloped—from what is recorded concerning the shepherds at Bethlehem (Lk. 2⁹) to the reported fear of the women at the empty tomb (Mk. 16⁸). And it is not at all self-evident that in spite of this the people should rejoice at the wonderful things done by Him (Lk. 13¹⁷), and that even out of great φόβος (Lk. 7¹⁶) God should be glorified because He had visited His people.

All the same, it is clearly the view of the whole tradition that this fear was an abnormal attitude which rested on ignorance and misunderstanding and which had to yield to a very different one. Zachariah (Lk. 1¹³), Mary (Lk. 1³⁰), the shepherds in the fields (Lk. 2¹⁰), Peter after the great draught of fishes (Lk. 5¹⁰), the disciples in the storm on the lake (Mk. 6⁵⁰) and when the risen Christ met them (Mt. 28¹⁰)—they were not to fear Him. The most impressive description of this reaction and its basis is not to be found in the Gospels, but in the vision at the beginning of the Apocalypse (1¹²f.), when the Divine turns and sees the Son of Man with all the attributes with which He is invested in Daniel : His eyes like flames of fire, His feet like burnished brass, His voice like the sound of many waters, stars in His hands, a sharp two-edged sword proceeding out of His mouth, and His countenance like the sun shining in its strength. " And when I saw him, I fell at his feet as dead. And he laid his right hand upon me, saying unto me, Fear not ; I am the first and the last. I am he that liveth, and was dead ; and, behold, I am alive for evermore, Amen, and have the keys of hell and of death." In and with the fear of Him all fear—fear as such—was to be taken away from men : the fear of death as the wages of sin (Rom. 6²³), through which they were all their lifetime subject to bondage (Heb. 2¹⁵). The blind (Mk. 10⁴⁹), the lame (Mt. 9²), the woman with a bloody flux (Mt. 9²²)—they were all to be comforted (θαρσεῖν). The disciples as a " little flock " were not to fear (Lk. 12³²). They were not to fear persecutors who can only kill the body (Mt. 10²⁶, ²⁸, ³¹). They were not to be afraid when they heard of wars and rumours of wars (Mk. 13⁷). Paul was not to be afraid of the opposition which He met with in Corinth, but to speak and not be silent (Ac. 18⁹). He was not to be afraid in the storm off Crete, because it was ordained that he should stand before the emperor. " Let not your heart be troubled (μὴ ταρασσέσθω), neither let it be afraid " (Jn. 14²⁷). " These things I have spoken unto you, that in me ye might have peace. In the world ye shall have tribulation (θλῖψιν) : but be of good cheer (θαρσεῖτε) ; I have overcome the world " (Jn. 16³³). This is the incursion of the Yes which in the man Jesus, in correspondence with the divine Yes, is spoken to other men.

But as and when this incursion took place, men were not only told not to fear but to find comfort. They were also told—much more strongly—that they should rejoice. This is denoted already in the infancy story (Lk. 1²⁸) by the angel's χαῖρε, and in the astonishing report (Lk. 1⁴¹) that the child in the womb of Elisabeth "leaped for joy" (ἐσκίρτησεν ἐν ἀγαλλιάσει) when the voice of Mary's salutation sounded in her ears. Then (in Lk. 2¹⁰) there is the angel's proclamation on the night of the nativity of the χαρὰ μεγάλη which displaced the φόβος μέγας of the shepherds and came to all Israel with the birth of the σωτήρ. Then there is the joy of the Baptist as the friend of the bridegroom who hears His voice (Jn. 3²⁹). Then there is the joy which the disciples are permitted and commanded because their names are written in heaven (Lk. 10²⁰)—permitted and commanded, not merely in spite of the fact that they will have to suffer persecution on earth, but just because of it : " Rejoice ye in that day, and leap for joy : for, behold, your reward is great in heaven " (Lk. 6²³, cf. Mt. 5¹²). And how striking it is that in the Easter story in Luke (24⁴¹) this joy is not merely that of faith, or connected with faith, but precedes faith and can even be a hindrance to it : " And while they yet believed not for joy, being ἀπιστεύοντες, he said unto them. . . ." According to Jn. 15¹¹ (cf. 17¹³) the whole meaning and purpose of the mission of Jesus is to bring joy : " These things have I spoken unto you, that my joy might remain in you, and that your joy might be full." According to Jn. 16²⁰ᶠ· this was also the purpose of the λύπη which would come first with His death : " A woman when she is in travail hath sorrow, because her hour is come : but as soon as she is delivered of the child, she remembereth no more the anguish, for joy that a man is born into the world." The same note rings out in Paul like an echo (Phil. 4⁴) : " Rejoice in the Lord alway : and again I say, Rejoice." But, as we are told in Jn. 8⁵⁶, Abraham had already rejoiced to see the day of Jesus, and he saw it and was glad. And we learn from Lk. 15⁷, ¹⁰ that there is joy in heaven among the angels of God at the Messianic event of the sinner repenting. In the first instance, however, both in the Johannine passages and in Lk. 10²¹, this joy is the joy of Jesus Himself : ἡ χαρὰ ἡ ἐμή, His ἀγαλλίασις in the Holy Ghost. Men neither appropriated it to themselves nor produced it of themselves, but it came to them in and with the man Jesus. It was given them in Him and by Him. In the first instance it was present for them objectively—and obviously identical with the kingdom of God, which is joy as well as righteousness and peace (Rom. 14¹⁷). It was this objective joy which could and should be reproduced in the joy which they too were permitted and commanded. In the presence of the man Jesus it was already actual for them and could not be resisted or destroyed by anything or anyone—" your joy no man taketh from you " (Jn. 16²²). They had a real and present joy : χαρά, ἀγαλλίασις.

What was the reason for this joy ? And what was its object ? When we ask these questions, the answer is to be found quite simply in the fact that what met them in this man was the clear, redemptive mercy of God speaking quite unequivocally and authoritatively. Certainly it was also His disapproval, His wrath. For there is no mercy without wrath. That is why this man could also fill them with fear. But it was not His wrath *in abstracto*. It was not, then, His wrath in a dark, dialectical antithesis to His mercy, as in the refrain " Law and Gospel." It was His wrath as the purifying fire of His mercy, of His free and unmerited but (for all its unexpectedness) real and active .grace, of His faithfulness to the world and His people and men. That is why there is great joy. That is what made the message given in the person of this man good news, the εὐαγγέλιον. For it is the best thing of all for man, the glad news which makes him glad if he may hear it and so hear it as to accept it and live by it, that God had not merely refused to abandon him but has turned to him as His God (the

God He always was and will be) and is the Saviour who has mercy on him. And this is what he learns, with a final clarity and authenticity, in the message which goes out in and with the existence of the man Jesus.

We are not by any means the first who at this juncture have been forced to use the word σωτήρ, deliverer, upholder, keeper, liberator, or, to use our common translation, saviour. In the older Greek-speaking world this was used as a title for the gods. In the later it was used to describe the deities of the mystery-religions, like Serapis and Isis. But it was also a title bestowed on outstanding human personalities. It may well be that it was from this Greek usage that it penetrated into the vocabulary of the New Testament. In the Gospels it is used only in Lk. 2¹¹ and Jn. 4⁴². In the Acts, again, we have it only twice, in 5³¹ and 13²³. In the undisputed Epistles of Paul it is applied directly to Jesus only in Phil. 3²⁰. Not until we come to the Pastoral Epistles and 2 Peter does it acquire any great importance as a description of Jesus. The case is very different, however, with the verb σώζειν. This is used on almost innumerable occasions in the Gospel tradition (especially in the Synoptics, rather less in John), in the Acts of the Apostles, and in the whole of the Pauline literature (with the curious exception of Galatians and Colossians). And the substantive σωτηρία, although it does not occur in the Gospels (except four times in Luke and once in John), is a frequent expression in the Epistles. In view of this well-established usage, perhaps we hardly need to appeal to non-Christian literature to explain the incursion of the word σωτήρ into the younger strata of the New Testament and its occasional use even in the Gospels themselves. Materially, it was the most obvious expression to gather up what the man Jesus was seen to be and to do as the basis of the " great joy " of Lk. 2¹⁰ and in correspondence with the being and action of the primary σωτήρ, as God Himself is called in Lk. 1⁴⁷ and a number of passages in the Pastoral Epistles. Jesus came and spoke and acted as the Deliverer, and therefore as the bringer of great joy, for He was the direct and omnicompetent witness of the redeeming grace of God Himself.

This aspect of the matter is given noteworthy literary form in the two hymns which Luke has incorporated into his infancy narratives—the *Magnificat* (Lk. 1⁴⁶⁻⁵⁵) and the *Benedictus* (Lk. 1⁶⁸⁻⁷⁹). The origin of these pieces is obscure. It seems likely that they come from a very early period of the Church, possibly from its early worship, or as private compositions of one or more of its members. For can we really explain v. 48 and v. 76 except against a Christian background ? On the other hand, it may well be that Christians have worked over hymns which originally came from the parallel movement of awakening and reform which we have learned to know much better through recent discoveries by the Dead Sea. We cannot say with any finality. But what we can cay is that Luke thought them sufficiently true and important to use them at this point as a kind of introduction to his account of the "things delivered unto us," ascribing them to such exalted personages as the mother of Jesus and the father of the Baptist. It will be rewarding, therefore, to try to grasp their content, and we will try to do this in a general consideration of what are obviously closely related texts.

The reference is to the Lord God of Israel (v. 68), as we learn from numerous Old Testament quotations and allusions. This God is to be praised, " magnified " (μεγαλύνειν, *magnificare*), by His own people, those who know Him, as the God who is their σωτήρ, and therefore the object of their ἀγαλλίασις (vv. 46–47). Why ? Because He is about to do a new work in faithfulness to His Word to the fathers and Abraham (v. 55), to what " he spake by the mouth of his holy prophets, which have been since the world began " (v. 70). He has not forgotten, but remembered, " his holy covenant ; the oath which he sware to our father Abraham " (vv. 72–73). " His mercy is on them that fear him from generation to generation " (v. 50). His aim in days past had been to deliver His people out of the hand of their enemies, to free them from fear, that they might serve in holiness and righteousness before Him all their days (vv. 74–75).

And this is still His purpose, and always will be. To that extent He has mercy directly on the fathers (v. 72) when He has mercy on us to-day. Remembering His former mercies " he hath holpen his servant Israel " (v. 54), i.e., taken up its cause again (ἀνελάβετο). And He has done this to-day, for " he hath regarded the low estate of his handmaiden " (v. 48). "he hath visited (ἐπεσκέψατο, as in Lk. 7¹⁶) his people " (v. 68). He Himself has done this, the dayspring from on high, " to give light to them that sit in darkness and in the shadow of death, to guide our feet into the way of peace " (v. 79). He, the Almighty, whose name is holy, "hath done great things " for them again (v. 49), bringing them redemption (λύτρωσις, v. 68), raising up " an horn of salvation " (σωτηρίας) in the house of his servant David (v. 69). It is again a salvation from their enemies, and from the hand of all them that hate them (v. 71). It is again His judgment in the putting down of the mighty and the exalting of them of low degree (vv. 51–53). His people are now to be given knowledge or experience (γνῶσις) of His salvation in the remission of their sins—and all this διὰ σπλάγχνα ἐλέους θεοῦ ἡμῶν (v. 78).

It is this merciful and redemptive visitation of Israel by God, in faithfulness to Himself and His people, which forms the subject-matter of these hymns. But in the mind of the authors, or at any rate in the mind of Luke, who incorporated them into his text, this visitation is indirectly identical with the life and words and works and passion and death and resurrection of Jesus of Nazareth, whose story he is concerned to tell. They are *indirectly* identical, we are forced to say, because their subject is always the merciful and redemptive God of Israel, and it is only once that we have a specific, but indirect, reference to Jesus, in a saying about John the Baptist that we have not so far considered (v. 76) : " And thou, child, shalt be called the prophet of the Highest : for thou shalt go before the face of the Lord to prepare his ways." But they are indirectly *identical* (at any rate in the mind of Luke), we are forced to say, because the introduction of these hymns could serve no literary purpose if they did not speak (at any rate in the mind of Luke) of the Son of Mary whose way was prepared by the son of Zacharias as the prophet of the Most High ; and of this One as the One in whom the new act of the faithful God of Israel to His people has found its human correspondence, in whom the divine visitation has become an earthly history.

We can now look rather farther afield. And for this purpose we will consider a single verse selected from the main Gospel records because it is so very instructive in the question which now occupies us. This is Mt. 9³⁶ : " But when he saw the multitudes, he was moved with compassion on them, because they fainted, and were scattered abroad, as sheep having no shepherd."

As we have already read in Lk. 1⁷⁸ about the σπλάγχνα of God, we now read about an ἐσπλαγχνίσθη expressly attributed to the man Jesus of Nazareth as He journeys through the towns and villages of Galilee, teaching and preaching and healing. The expression is a strong one which defies adequate translation. He was not only affected to the heart by the misery which surrounded Him— sympathy in our modern sense is far too feeble a word—but it went right into His heart, into Himself, so that it was now His misery. It was more His than that of those who suffered it. He took it from them and laid it on Himself. In the last analysis it was no longer theirs at all, but His. He Himself suffered it in their place. The cry of those who suffered was only an echo. Strictly speaking, it had already been superseded. It was superfluous. Jesus had made it His own. To the mercy of God which brings radical and total and definitive salvation there now corresponded the help which Jesus brought to men by His radical and total and definitive self-giving to and for their cause. In this self-giving, by the fact that His mercy, in this sense, led Him to see men in this way, He was on earth as God is in heaven. In this self-giving He was the kingdom of God come on earth.

According to this verse He had compassion because He saw the ὄχλοι, man in the mass, the multitude, the crowd, " the public," " everyman." The reference, then, is not merely to the lower classes, poor folk. Naturally these were included. But so, too, were men like the one who asked Jesus to take his side in the family dispute about an inheritance (Lk. 12¹³). In the strict sense, no one was not included. It is an unfortunate habit that we all like to think of others, but not ourselves, as belonging to the common herd, the mass, humanity. In so doing, we only show that we ourselves do belong. The crowd as it comes before us in the Gospel scenes, sometimes accompanying the disciples, sometimes the publicans and sinners, sometimes the scribes and Pharisees (and always including these, not excluding them)—the moving, pushing, jostling throng of those who all think of themselves as special cases, protesting their different individualities and wanting to be and have something for themselves, but who in so doing all merge into a sea of heads, a herd, in which names are indifferent and distinctive features are lost and this or that one emerges for a moment, only to disappear again in the common mass in which men are no longer men in any true sense—this is the multitude which when He saw it moved Jesus to compassion. This is the " people " which He called to Himself (Mk. 7¹⁴), which He gathered round Himself (Mk. 4¹). He saw their needs even in these mass-situations, as we see from the feeding of the multitudes twice recorded in all the Synoptics. And although He accused or upbraided the scribes and Pharisees and His disciples on many occasions, it is striking that this never happened in relation to the ὄχλοι—He did not flatter them either, of course. He stood with them in an almost imperceptible but strong unity and solidarity : strong because it was grounded in His compassion, in the fact that His only desire for them was to take from them their misery and to take it to Himself. Necessarily, of course, this also led Him into great isolation—the very greatest—from them. We already have a premonition of Gethsemane and Golgotha when we read in Mk. 6⁴⁶ and similar passages how He used to withdraw from them (and even from His disciples) to pray. But it was for them (to pray for them) that He went to solitary places, and finally to Gethsemane and Golgotha. It is true, of course, that only once do we read in the Gospels (Jn. 7³¹) that many of the people believed on Him, and even on that occasion these were offset by the many who did not. It is never said in any general way that the people believed on Him. There could be no question of that. The disciples who believed were people, but the people as such were not disciples. They were not the community. They do not normally believe. On the contrary, they are persuaded by the high-priests (Mk. 15¹¹f.) to ask for the release of Barabbas and to chant " Crucify him," so that Pilate thinks that he is falling in with their wishes by condemning Jesus to death. Yet we also read in Lk. 23⁴⁸ that the people smote their breasts when Jesus was dead, regretting that " Crucify him," that desire of theirs, as soon as it had been met. And even their evil action at the last does not altogether cancel what we are told about them earlier : how they always came together spontaneously where Jesus stood and went ; preceding and following Him ; waiting for Him and going to meet Him ; thronging Him in tens of thousands " insomuch that they trode one upon another " (Lk. 12¹) and once He could only speak to them from a boat (Mt. 13²) ; greeting Him (Mk. 9¹⁵) and hearing Him gladly (Mk. 12³⁷) ; rejoicing " for all the glorious things that were done by him " (Lk. 13¹⁷) ; being startled and glorifying God (Mt. 9⁸) when they saw that He spoke with authority and not as the scribes (Mt. 7²⁸f.) ; and causing alarm among the high-priests because of all these things (Mt. 21²⁶). There is no trace of irony in all these accounts. It has to be accepted as the serious view of the tradition that, although the ὄχλοι did not believe as such, although they did not become His disciples, they were themselves brought into a very real union with Jesus by the fact that He was moved with compassion when He saw them.

But what was the misery by reason of which the strength of the union between Himself and the people and the people and Himself could consist only in the compassion which gripped and filled Him when He saw them and was among them ? In the passage which concerns us we are told (in an obvious comment of the Evangelist) that He was moved with compassion when He saw them because they " fainted, and were scattered abroad, as sheep having no shepherd." This is an obvious allusion to Ezek. 34²⁻⁶, and must be understood in relation to it : " Woe be to the shepherds of Israel that do feed themselves ! should not the shepherds feed the flocks ? Ye eat the fat, and ye clothe you with the wool, ye kill them that are fed : but ye feed not the flock. The diseased have ye not strengthened, neither have ye healed that which was sick, neither have ye bound up that which was broken, neither have ye brought again that which was driven away, neither have ye sought that which was lost ; but with force and with cruelty have ye ruled them. And they were scattered, because there is no shepherd : and they became meat to all the beasts of the field, when they were scattered. My sheep wandered through the mountains, and upon every high hill ; yea, my flock was scattered upon all the face of the earth, and none did search or seek after them." This is how Jesus saw the multitudes around Him according to the witness of the Evangelists. He had compassion on them when He saw them because they had shepherds who were no shepherds —no true shepherds. This was the misery which Jesus saw, which moved Him to compassion, which He took away from them and took to Himself, and under the burden of which He had to die to the shouts of the very same multitude : " Crucify him, crucify him."

According to Ezekiel, the true Shepherd who was lacking was One who would know that He was responsible for them and would therefore act solely on their behalf. He would hear the general and foolish crying and bleating as each tried to assert his own individuality, and He would understand the basic reason for it better than the people themselves. He would not, therefore, reject or despise them. He would know what they need and how they can be genuinely helped. He would keep them together, bringing them both as a whole and as individuals to the place where what they need is to be found. Yes, as individuals too, for they would not be merely a nameless and inhuman mass for Him, but a company of men. He would know and call them each one by name, and feed them individually, each one having his or her place. This is how He would deal with them : Himself above them, but caring for them ; considering not only the whole but also the weak and sick and broken and lost and driven away ; and considering, too, the strong and healthy according to their own particular needs. In this way all would be safe in Him. Without encroaching on their freedom, He would be their Head. Without having anything to forgive Himself, He would be their servant. It was because it lacked this Shepherd that the multitude which Jesus saw fainted and was scattered, and Jesus was moved with compassion when He saw it.

There was no lack of other, so-called, but only ostensible shepherds according to that passage in Ezekiel. Someone had always to think and speak for the people. They had always to group themselves round an individual whom they could follow. A general assertion of individuality could only lead them to tread one another down, and bring them to an isolation in which they had to begin again in a state of bewilderment and confusion. In these circumstances ostensible shepherds continually offered themselves. It was always a fine and honourable and lucrative occupation to be shepherd and head of the people, to fill this gap, to be the man who could instruct and lead the people. Thus there have never been lacking those who seemed to have the desire and even for a time the equipment for it. There has never been lacking what was in the first instance a genuine calling to this task and commissioning for it. And so at all times the people have gathered with expectant confidence around particular individuals who regarded themselves as called and commissioned and were ready to attempt and did attempt to be heads over the others—shepherds, leaders and groups of leaders both great and small, and in all the different walks of life, political, economic, literary, even medical, and above all spiritual—and not least where the people was (and is) most convinced that it is its own master, a free people.

But the ostensible shepherds were not real shepherds, and the hopes put in them never materialised. They all had good heads, but there was no head. Their real concern was not for the people, but for themselves. They simply fed themselves. They acted as all the rest did. How, then, could they really help them ? They gladly accepted the confidence and respect and love and fear which were offered them, the gratitude and honour with which they were surrounded, and the material advantages which these also involved. But what about the rest ? Did it really make much difference to them which of these ostensible heads they had ? Did any of them lift off the tragic burden of that self-centred life and all that it involved ? " And they were scattered, because there is no shepherd." They were scattered the more terribly each time they thought that they had a shepherd and were again disappointed and " became meat to all the beasts of the field." The great gap which consisted in the fact that they had no shepherd was revealed the more clearly and painfully each time someone had thought that he should be the shepherd, and they themselves had imagined that he could.

Jesus saw their misery, and according to this passage His compassion for them stepped into this great gap. This was the very place where He Himself belonged. That is why He did not merely take their grief to heart, but took it right into His heart, into Himself. " I am the good shepherd : the good shepherd giveth his life for the sheep " (Jn. 10[11])—an exact fulfilment of Ps. 23 : " The Lord is my shepherd." This was the Shepherd who was needed, and it was as this Shepherd that the man Jesus came among and for all other men. The people of whom the tradition speaks did not see what it lacked. It merely suffered the lack. It was in misery without recognising the fact. And so it could not recognise the One who had come and was already there to take away this misery from it and to take it to Himself. It could be stirred by His presence and words and acts to that strange mixture of foreboding and lack of foreboding, of fearfulness and joy, and then sink back again into indifference. It could finally shout " Crucify him " as desired by its old shepherds who were no true shepherds. But it is striking that the Gospel records show very little interest in the palpable gracelessness of the ὄχλοι. Their failure to see did not alter their misery and their actual suffering of this misery. It did not affect the great gap in their existence. Even less did it make any difference to the fact that the One had come and was present who was to fill this gap, to be their head and therefore their σωτήρ, the true Shepherd who did not think that the flock was there for His benefit but He for theirs, the truly royal man whose compassion reflected the compassion of the God who had sworn fidelity to man and was now finally and conclusively to prove it. The people's failure to see did not alter in the very least the true and deep and strong union and solidarity of Jesus with this people, and of this people with Jesus. God's gracious visitation of His people had actually taken place in the existence of this one man. The " dayspring from on high " was earthly history in the form of the compassion which Jesus had for the multitude. The great joy which was to be for all people was already an objective event. And it is this fact as such which is the concern of the Gospel records. As they saw it, it is only by this fact as such that the question of faith was raised—the question which the community in which these records had their origin found to be answered by the work of the Holy Spirit.

We will conclude our discussion of this fourth point by a glance at the distinctive phenomenon of the evangelical *makarisms*, the beatitudes which in the Gospel narratives are always pronounced (with only a single exception) by Jesus

Himself. These are words or sayings in which a group of men—there are only two instances, and one of them is the exception already mentioned, in which the reference is to specific individuals—are told either in the second or the third person that they are blessed by reason of the outward or inward situation in which they find themselves, or in relation to the significance of this situation ; that—whether or not they themselves or others realise it or judge it to be the case—they are fortunate to be in this situation ; that their existence is to be honoured as one which is privileged in this sense. This form of address is not confined to the Gospels, and in the New Testament as a whole it is not regarded as peculiar to Jesus but used by the authors of the Epistles, and especially of the Apocalypse, to express their own evaluations. We can go further, for the form is not to be found only in the New Testament, but has its predecessors (and in this case we may definitely say its models) both in the Old Testament and in older and more recent Greek literature. Already in Jesus Sirach 25, 7–10, we have a collection of *makarisms* very like that in Mt. 5³ᶠ· or Lk. 6²⁰ᶠ·

Formally, there are two striking features in the Gospels. The first is that here, as elsewhere in the New Testament, only the word μακάριος is used, and not ὄλβιος or εὐδαίμων as in earlier parallels. The second is that so prominent a place is given to these small collections in the two sermons in Matthew and Luke. The latter point is the more significant. It means that these beatitudes pronounced by Jesus Himself had impressed themselves on the tradition as the basic Word in His proclamation of the kingdom of God. But the decisive origin-ality in the evangelical use of this form of address (and that of the New Testa-ment generally) is material. It consists in the fact that both the situation of those who are pronounced blessed and also that on account of which the beatitude is proclaimed, are in some way created and conditioned by the imminent kingdom of God: The beatitudes denote and describe the situation of these men, and its significance and promise for them, as grounded in the presence of Jesus. They are blessed because Jesus is there, and in relation to what He brings them. That is why they are put in the mouth of Jesus. In the sense in which the term is used in the Gospels, no one can pronounce himself blessed. And in the whole of the New Testament this is never done except rhetorically in Ac. 26². Even Mary does not call herself blessed (Lk. 1⁴⁸) but says that all generations will call her blessed. A man can only experience the fact that he *is* called blessed. The Gospel beatitudes are not analytical but synthetic statements. Unlike the *makarisms* of Greek literature, they do not refer to human endowments or the exercise of human virtues. They are the proclamation in human words of a divine judgment. Their content is a paradox—obviously so in many ways, and totally at bottom. It stands at an angle of 180 degrees to current ideas of happi-ness and good fortune. Strictly speaking, no one can ever come to the point of calling himself (or others) blessed in the way in which it is done here. The New Testament beatitudes speak of the blessedness of the kingdom of God. And so what they say to those to whom they apply is something quite novel. It can be said only by the royal man who Himself brings and is this new thing ; who is the Head, the σωτήρ, the true Shepherd, who is for them as the work of God's revelation ; who in their own name can give them the authoritative information about themselves which they could never give : " Blessed are ye." It is He alone who can pronounce this human Word, for He *is* this Word.

This, then, is the picture of Jesus which impressed itself on the community and tradition. He addressed men primarily in this synthetic statement, giving them this information about themselves. He called them blessed because the kingdom of God had drawn near with its promise. This is what His disciples were told by Him (Mt. 5¹ ; Lk. 6²⁰), and even the ὄχλοι, as we learn explicitly from Mt. 7²⁸. We cannot expound these sayings, or groups of sayings, in any detail in the present context. But we must touch on them in order to help us to a more concrete understanding.

Let us take the exception first. It is the saying of Elisabeth to Mary in Lk. 1⁴⁵ : " Blessed is she that believed : for (as the translation must be in analogy with Mt. 5³ᶠ· and Lk. 6²⁰ᶠ·) there shall be a performance (ὅτι ἔσται τελείωσις) of those things which were told her from the Lord." Now the only answer that Mary had given to the angel (Lk. 1³⁸) was this : " Behold, the handmaid of the Lord ; be it unto me according to thy word." This was her faith, in which she showed herself to be the one she already was after the saluta-tion of the angel in Lk. 1²⁸, the κεχαριτωμένη, with whom the Lord was, and who could and should therefore rejoice. It is obvious that she is blessed in the light of her faith, yet not because of her faith, but because of what was told her by the Lord and what she believed, and in relation to its accomplishment. It is in the same sense that we have to understand the sharp antithesis in Lk. 11²⁷ᶠ·, where we are told that while Jesus was speaking " a woman of the company lifted up her voice, and said unto him, Blessed is the womb that bare thee, and the paps which thou hast sucked. But he said, Yea rather, blessed are they that hear the word of God, and keep it." For those who are pronounced blessed it is indeed a matter of their own being, but primarily it is a matter either of the fact that their own being is lit up in a new way by the kingdom of God which has come near to them in Jesus or of the fact that it is ordered by this in a new and very definite manner. Either way, it is quite astounding. Jesus, the king-dom of God, indicates and explains and interprets their being and determines and directs and characterises it. And it is in this fact—this illumination or impression—that they are blessed in spite of all appearances to the contrary. This is what Jesus tells them about themselves. And they are to accept this and put it into practice. But this means that they can and should have the great joy which has come to all people. Either way it means that the kingdom of God is related to their own human being, the only difference in these two passages being one of aspect and emphasis.

It is evident that even where the emphasis falls on faith and the hearing and keeping of the Word of God it is primarily a question of the impress made on a man's action, its determination or characterisation. It is as κεχαριτωμένη that Mary believes. Those to whom the Word of God is spoken can and should hear and believe it. That is how those who believe and hear and keep are blessed. Mt. 13¹⁶ is relevant in this connexion : " Blessed are your eyes, for they see : and your ears, for they hear." So, too, is Jn. 20²⁹ : " Blessed are they that have not seen, and yet have believed." The case is exactly the same in the beatitudes in Mt. 5⁷⁻⁹ : Blessed are the merciful, the pure in heart, the peacemakers ; in Lk. 14¹⁴, where the blessed are those who do good which cannot be repaid ; and in Ac. 20³⁵, where an otherwise unrecorded saying of Jesus is introduced which tells us that it is more blessed to give than receive. And Mt. 24⁴⁶ (cf. Rev. 16¹⁵) has reference to a definite action : " Blessed is that servant, whom his lord when he cometh shall find so doing." So too, more generally, does Jn. 13¹⁷ : " If ye know these things, happy are ye if ye do them." And finally we may recall Mt. 11⁶ : " Blessed is he, whosoever shall not be offended in me." In these passages a man is always called blessed in face of the fact that he is minded and acts in this or that way. In exactly the same way James—quite in the manner of the *makarisms* of the Sermon on the Mount—can call the man blessed who " endureth temptation " (1¹², cf. 5¹¹), or who is not a forgetful hearer but a doer of the word (1²⁵). And again in the same way Rev. 1³ and 22⁷ tell us that the man is blessed who reads and hears the book and keeps and maintains its contents. But here too, and especially in the Gospel *makarisms*, we have to remember that the attitude and mode of action in the light of which certain men are addressed as μακάριοι are stimulated and moved and determined and ordered by the kingdom of God. It is not at all the case, then, that they have in themselves, in a vacuum, as it were, something which is excellent in itself (faith or mercy or purity or steadfastness), or that they exercise and practise something which is excellent in itself (a constant watchfulness, peacemaking, unselfseeking beneficence, reading and hearing and taking to heart the book of revelation), and that they are called μακάριοι because all these things are good and praiseworthy in themselves and bring self-satisfaction to the one who enjoys or exercises them. It is not just because they see and hear, but because they see and hear what they do see and hear, that the eyes and ears of the disciples are called blessed in Mt. 13¹⁶. The activity of these men with their eyes and ears, or hearts and hands, or faith and works, is not without a definite reference. It takes place in a particular context. Directly or indirectly, they are called and empowered and ordered and directed to do it by Jesus. And this is revealed in their action. And it is for this reason that blessedness is ascribed to them in view of their action, i.e., they are told that they are fortunate in it and have every cause to be merry and joyful. Showing by their mind and action that they are children of the kingdom of God, they can be of a good heart, not thinking, of course, of the particularly virtuous and meritorious character of their action, but of the root from which it proceeds. It is a rewarding action in virtue of this root, and therefore an action in which they should not be depressed and down-hearted, but happy and cheerful. The passage which forces us to this understanding of the way in which human action is declared to be blessed in the Gospels, and which is necessarily normative for an understanding of the others in view of its intrinsic importance, is Mt. 16¹⁷. Peter has just made his Messianic confession, which is surely the sum of human action in the sense of the Gospel tradition. And Jesus replies with the *makarism*, the second of the two addressed to particular individuals : " Blessed art thou, Simon Barjona "—blessed in that thou hast said this, yet not because thou hast said it, but because " flesh and blood hath not revealed it unto thee, but my Father which is in heaven," because it is from this source that it has found its way to thy lips. The one who confesses, then, is not blessed because of his confession, but because his confession has this origin. And it is obviously the same with the blessedness of those who believe, of the merciful, of the pure in heart, of the peacemakers, of those who watch, etc. That is why it is pronounced with such power and certainty to those who either are or do these things.

The same truth emerges even more clearly in the second series of passages in which the beatitude does not have reference to the action but to the situation and even the suffering of certain men. In this connexion we naturally think first of the four opening beatitudes in Mt. 5³ᶠ· : Blessed are the poor in spirit, they that mourn, the meek (πραεῖς) and they which hunger and thirst after righteousness ; or, to use the shorter and sharper Lukan version (6²⁰ᶠ·), the poor, the hungry and those that weep. It is obviously not the case that those who are called blessed here have sought or willed the situation in face of which they are described in this way. It is obviously not the case that they have put themselves in this situation. That they are poor and sad and meek and empty and in need of righteousness is only the situation which has come on them. And it is evident that what is described as the situation of these men is not a happy or desirable one in itself. Nor is there even the slightest hint of any secret or immanent value of any kind in that to which these beatitudes refer. The New Testament, like the Old, does not regard or magnify the happy and positive and vital as a secret quality of that which is unhappy and negative and dead. It does not call black white, or interpret the evil case of these men as their true well-being. It is not to men who are miserable only in appearance that the beatitudes refer, but to men who are genuinely miserable. Yet their misery is not seen abstractly and independently any more than their action. It is not seen in a vacuum. It is seen in a definite relationship. Not now in their action, but in their suffering, they are seen in confrontation with the kingdom of God. From this kingdom, or, as we must say, from Jesus, there falls a definite light on the situation which they have neither brought about nor desired and willed, on themselves in this unhappy and negative character which is already redolent of death. In their misery they find themselves on the outer edge of the cosmos as it is confronted with the kingdom of God and to be renewed by the man Jesus. Its vulnerability is revealed and can be seen in their misery. In the glory of the man who is wealthy and laughing and mighty and righteous and lucky as the world sees it, its mortal wound is concealed. But it is brought to light in the misery of those who suffer. It is not for nothing that the man Jesus comes and acts and is revealed as Himself a sufferer, the supreme sufferer and the partisan of all others. For it is in the existence, the situation, of the poor and sad and meek that the new thing of the kingdom of God shines in all the different spheres of the life of the old man. The fortunate of this world cannot help the fact that the cosmos is not revealed in them and the new thing of the kingdom of God does not shine in them. The malediction which is pronounced against them in Lk. 6[24f.] is not an accusation. Like the contrast of the rich man in hell with poor Lazarus on Abraham's bosom, it is simply a declaration that they are to be pitied because the nearness of the kingdom of God, the presence of Jesus, cannot be seen in their lives. Conversely, the sufferers of this world cannot pride themselves on the fact that their lives have this transparency, that the kingdom, Jesus, is in fact near to them. The declaration that they are blessed is a synthetic and not an analytic statement, referring to the objective thing that characterises their existence from above and not from below. To them, too, the new thing is said when they are called blessed in relation to their misery. Neither they nor their misery create the fact that they exist in that light of Jesus. It is simply the case, and they are called blessed simply because of that which is indicated by their misery : " The poor have the gospel preached to them " (Mt. 11[5]).

But there is a third group of beatitudes which we have not so far considered. They are few in number, but they are perhaps the most eloquent and emphatic. Those to whom they refer stand somewhere between, or should we say above, the doers and the sufferers to whom the first two groups are directed. And in them it is quite palpable that no other exposition is possible than that which we have so far pursued. Blessed are those (Mt. 5[10f.] ; Lk. 6[22] and also 1 Pet. 3[14] and 4[14]) who are persecuted and scorned and calumniated and hated and driven out for the sake of righteousness, or the name of Jesus, or Jesus Himself. The men envisaged here are obviously both active and passive, and they reveal the secret connexion between doers and sufferers. They are active in their confession of the righteousness of the kingdom of heaven, of Jesus. But they are passive because this action draws on them persecution, denigration and hatred. In some sense, therefore, they are both qualified doers and qualified sufferers. It is clear that this situation is not created by the men themselves, but has its direct basis in a supremely particular relationship between them and Jesus. It is also clear that in so far as it entails suffering it is not an enviable situation. In this connexion, too, suffering is not joy. Again the beatitude is a synthetic and not an analytic statement. They cannot deny Jesus, and so they cannot be spared and cannot refuse to be " partakers of Christ's sufferings " (1 Pet. 4[13]). They exist in the direct shadow of the cross. But this is what makes their situation so promising—a definite situation in the kingdom of heaven, in face of which Jesus does not pity them (for after all it is side by side with His own) but can only call them blessed, and much more forcibly this time (" Rejoice and be exceeding glad ") than in the case of any of the others. The blessedness of both doers and sufferers comes together, as it were, in that of these men who are persecuted for the sake of Jesus, who are sufferers because of their action, and particularly active even in their passion. There is no question of a lauding of martyrdom itself, or of a summons to enjoy it. What is praised is the situation of those who suffer martyrdom because they may be martyrs, i.e., witnesses of the kingdom, of Jesus Himself, and may prove themselves and genuinely act as such. They are blessed in the peculiar freedom which is obviously given them for this. And it is this peculiar freedom in which they are summoned to rejoice by the beatitude.

It remains only to add that to all these men, the active, the passive and those who are both, glad news is given—glad news to all those of whom it is said that the kingdom of God was among them. The New Testament beatitude is not an empty paradox. It points to the men whom it concerns, and not past them. It does not refer these men to a dark void, or a neutral sphere where the promise might just as well mean destruction as salvation or death as life, giving them just as much cause for sadness as joy. Always and unequivocally its message is one of salvation and life and joy. It is the beatitude which is spoken by Jesus the σωτήρ. It is the Word of His mercy, which is not an idle or ineffective but a powerful mercy. It is related to Himself, to the kingdom of God which has drawn near in Him. It is not for nothing that He is among them. It is not for nothing that the kingdom of God has drawn near them. That this is the case has for their existence the significance of salvation and life and joy. As a promise, and as a present fulfilment concealed in the promise, this is the most real and decisive determination of their existence. To be sure, it is their " eschatological " determination, still to be revealed in them. But above all it is their christological determination, their determination for the kingdom which as such does not remain future but has already become theirs, which is not merely a determination of the soul but the body too, the one whole man. The beatitude pronounced by Jesus tells us that He is the Lord of all these men, that their action too, since it is instigated and ordered by Him, and their suffering, since it is borne in His light, and above all their suffering action and active suffering for His sake, do not take place in vain. And in this context " not in vain " means " not without purpose," or, quite soberly, " not without reward," not without that which they do and suffer having its heavenly compensation and counterpart in salvation, life and joy—a recompense which does not stand in any real relationship to what is done or suffered, but which is true and concrete all the same. For the reward which He promises those who do and suffer, simply because they are in fact, directly or indirectly, His witnesses in their action or suffering, is nothing less than the kingdom of God as such, nothing less than Himself. We can only refer briefly to the wording of this promise. The sufferers are told that theirs is the kingdom of heaven ; that they shall be comforted (or laugh, Lk. 6²¹) ; that they shall inherit the earth ; that they shall be filled (Mt. 5³⁻⁶, ¹⁰). The doers are told that they shall obtain mercy ; that they shall see God ; and that they shall be called the children of God (Mt. 5⁷⁻⁹). Those who stand in temptation are told that they " shall receive the crown of life, which the Lord hath promised to them that love him " (Jas. 1¹²). When Jesus makes this promise in the beatitudes, it is not merely a promise and proclamation, but the present (if hidden) impartation of full salvation, total life and perfect joy. We cannot rate it any lower than this when it is a matter of the salvation and life and joy of the kingdom of God, the salvation and life and joy which have appeared and are resolved in Jesus. This man does not only speak. He accomplishes what He says. He makes actual what He declares to be true. He tells in and with the beatitudes that to-day, here and now, He is for those whom He addresses in this way ; that He is their σωτήρ, the One who shows them His powerful mercy, the One who gives them all that is His by giving them Himself. " I will give you rest " (κἀγὼ ἀναπαύσω ὑμᾶς, Mt. 11²⁸). He does do this. And in the fact that He does it He is the royal man, the supreme and most proper image of the invisible God.

III

We now come to a third aspect of our question concerning the royal man Jesus. The distinctiveness in which Jesus was present according to the tradition occupied us first. Then we considered the agreement of His existence with that of God, the parallelism of His work to the will and activity of God. We must now attempt, in a third and decisive discussion, to understand Jesus in the act accomplished by Him. It is in the act of His life that the distinctiveness of His existence and His likeness to God are actual and can therefore be seen and comprehended. His life *was* His act, and it has therefore the character of history. The community in which the New Testament originated looked back to this history, which was also its present and future. No distinction was then made, as later, between His person and work. It looked to His completed work, which was regarded as of absolute significance as the work of this person. And it looked to His person, which was regarded as of absolute significance as the Subject of this work. In His history, and therefore in His life as this act, Jesus was there for His community, not only as past, but also as present and future. The totality of His being in its scope for them and the whole world was identical with the totality of His activity.

It is of this, and in this sense of His history, that the living tradition within the community attempted to speak. The tradition itself was an undertaking which even in its original form (in view of the incommensurability of what had to be handed down) could never do adequate justice to the task, or make any claim to do so. And the Gospels which then arose were even more inadequate attempts to preserve the tradition of the life-act of Jesus. The community never went beyond certain of these attempts which we now have before us in what became the " canonical " Gospels. And it obviously thought that it ought not to do so. But it was surely evident—no one could fail to see their lack of external coherence—that none of these Gospels was more than one attempt among others. What finally counted was their internal coherence, which differentiated these Gospels from other unusable attempts of the same kind, proving that they were trustworthy and could therefore be used as a rule or canon for the true consideration—retrospective, concurrent and prospective—of the man Jesus. And this internal coherence, which was achieved in spite of all the external inconsistencies in presentation, consisted in the unmistakeable unity of the picture which they drew of the totality of the activity of Jesus. The basic features of this portrait proved to be the same in all these recognised Gospels—that is why they were recognised. And in the attested picture of His activity, which agreed in all its basic features, the self-constituting community saw Jesus Himself, and heard the witness of His own Spirit, the one Holy Spirit. It had to be content therefore, as it could be, with these attempts to preserve the tradition concerning Him. Although they are obviously not more than attempts (and could not be), they have approved themselves in the Church in every age and place. The life-act of the man Jesus, and Jesus Himself in it, have in fact been continually received in this witness to it. We must now ask concerning the basic features of this life-act as commonly attested by them.

There is no doubt where we must begin. For (1) His life-act was His Word in the concrete but comprehensive sense, the comprehensive but also the concrete. We are not to say that Jesus did not only speak, but also acted and healed and did good and instituted a community of Spirit, Word and act, and finally suffered: as though He did not also speak in all these things ; as though their totality was not the Word which He spoke ; as though His concrete speaking was not the culmination or light of this totality ; and above all, conversely, as though His concrete speaking was not also action or act, His decisive and effective act. If we are to think of the speaking of Jesus as understood in the Gospel tradition, we must abandon completely the current distinctions between *logos* and *ethos*, or speaking and action, behind which there usually lurk the differentiations of knowledge and life, theory and practice, truth and reality. Or, at any rate, we must abandon them to the extent that they involve either clear-cut division or the over-emphasising of the one at the expense of the other. Otherwise we shall completely misunderstand both His speaking and His action. In fact, a very concrete aspect of His life-act is to be found in the fact that He spoke concretely. And not only the Gospels, but the earlier tradition which underlies them, all agree that this was the primary and controlling aspect of His life-act : the most human form, basically, of all action ; impartation, His self-impartation by the Word which He spoke to His disciples, the people, the publicans and sinners, the scribes and Pharisees as His opponents, the high-priests and Pilate as His judges.

It was a *human* Word. The Evangelists and the original tradition did not attribute to Jesus any special language, or cause Him to use any distinctive terminology. His vocabulary as it emerges in their accounts, and the forms of address used by Him (the parable, the beatitude, the malediction, the admonition, the proverb and the polemic) are not as such original or proper to Him. The material originality of His teaching—what we might call His theology—stands or falls ultimately with the particular emphases, contrasts and connexions which well-known thoughts and chains of thought acquired by the very fact that it was He who spoke them. It is immediately apparent how free the community felt in relation to these human words. It had no thought of asking for His *ipsissima verba*. It did not scruple to receive the sayings attributed to Him in two or three different versions, or His theology (if there was such a thing) in the form of a doctrine which was obviously shaped by Matthew, Mark, Luke and John and their own personalities and historical and geographical backgrounds. How curious it seems to our ideas of historical seriousness that no one seems to have thought it worth while to make sure as to the Aramaic originals, which were surely still accessible, so that all that we have are a few sparsely scattered remains interposed into the Greek texts (Mk. 5[41], 7[34], 15[34]). It is also striking that no incongruity was seen in the fact that in the Greek texts Jesus used not only the terminology of later Judaism but also on occasion that of extra-Judaic Hellenism. Is it not worth pondering as a distinctive historical fact that the community in which the New Testament arose, far from being concerned at the problems which we to-day find so pressing, hardly seems to have noticed them at all? Ought we not, perhaps, to make this our starting-point and maintain that the human Word of Jesus was so constituted that objectively it was quite acceptable as a supremely particular and distinctive Word—His own Word—even in its formal and material similarity with so much of Rabbinism, even in the different versions given by the Evangelists, and even in its translation into Hellenistic thought forms and language? Perhaps it is only then that we really see concretely what power His human Word had to burst through all its limitations and to overcome all the involved obstacles, coming down to the 1st century community, which was responsible for the origin and recognition of the Gospel texts, in virtue of its content, i.e., as His own Word, as the Word of the Jesus who according to the tradition rose again from the dead and is alive for evermore. Through all these prisms His Word still reached and touched and enlightened and instructed and convinced the community as the royal Word of the royal man concerning the royal dominion of God. And it did so with an originality which could not be diminished by any Judaistic or Hellenistic covering, but was genuinely to be seen even in this covering and as it made use of it. That is why the originality could not be augmented by any approximation to the more primitive forms or texts that might have been discovered. His community heard Him speak. It heard Him say what only He had to say. And it heard Him say it as only He could say it. It was thus confronted with the primary and dominating aspect of His life-act, and therefore Himself. And in this way it was constituted and edified and directed and maintained as His community. But there is more to it than that. For as it heard Him speak, it saw the surrounding world, the nations and their orders, and disorders, the whole cosmos, confronted and addressed by Him. It heard His Word as the Word of reconciliation intended for the world and directed to it. And so, when it heard Him speak this Word, it knew at once to whom it was spoken and what it had itself to do when it heard it—to go and proclaim to the world what He had proclaimed to it. That is how matters stand with His Word as a human Word.

We can grasp this in detail by looking at the meaning and content of the most important of the active words used by the tradition to denote and characterise the speech of Jesus: εὐαγγελίζεσθαι, διδάσκειν, κηρύσσειν (cf. for what follows the articles in Kittel's *Wörterbuch*).

We will begin with some general considerations. First, all three terms—

and this is their primary use—are applied absolutely and not merely with a specific reference to what Jesus said and those to whom He said it. Even in this form, however, they are not abstract and empty. The reader knows what is meant. Indeed, he knows it with particular clarity. Second, although the terms are not synonymous, they converge so strongly in their application to the action of Jesus that in fact their sense cannot easily be distinguished. They meet at the decisive point. Third, although they are applied especially to the action of Jesus Himself, they are not restricted to this, but imply also the action of His disciples as commissioned and commanded by Him. They characterise, therefore, the action of the *totus Christus*, to which His community belongs as the earthly form of His body. Fourth, in the summaries of Jesus' work in the Gospels and Acts, and also in the charges to His disciples, one of these terms (either with or without the others) is always given the first place, and terms which denote the accompanying acts of Jesus (ἰᾶσθαι, θεραπεύειν, ἐκβάλλειν τὰ δαιμόνια)—for all their importance—can only be put second. The former can be used without the latter, but not the latter without the former. The prominent position of εὐαγγελίζεσθαι in the lists given in Lk. 4¹⁸ and Mt. 11⁴ᶠ·—in the one case at the beginning of the Messianic acts and in the other at the end—should be particularly noted : εἰς τοῦτο γὰρ ἐξῆλθον (Mk. 1³⁸). Even in the fine passage in Ac. 10³⁸ there is no exception to this rule, for when it is said of Jesus of Nazareth that God anointed Him " with the Holy Ghost and with power " and that He " went about doing good, and healing all that were oppressed of the devil ; for God was with him," this is prefaced by the saying in v. 36 that Jesus is " the word (λόγος) which God sent unto the children of Israel," that God Himself was εὐαγγελιζόμενος τὴν εἰρήνην διὰ ᾽Ιησοῦ Χριστοῦ. Similarly in Jn. 1¹⁴ Jesus is comprehensively described as the incarnate Word of God.

Turning to the words themselves, it is only right that we should begin with εὐαγγελίζεσθαι. In the Old Testament the term " gospel " (b'sorah) is used generally of good news, glad tidings. The one who brings it deserves to be rewarded because he gives peace to those to whom he brings it. The Greek word as such is originally a technical term for " news of victory," although here too there is at least a tendency for the three concepts, the event itself, the news of it and the one who brings the news (εὐαγγελιζόμενος), to merge into one another. In the Hellenistic world εὐαγγέλιον was a current term in the language of emperor worship. In the particular ideology of this cult the emperor was a saviour-deity and his appearance and presence and activity were *per se* the basis of all good fortune. All that concerned him was " glad tidings," including his mandates, but this was particularly true of the news of his birth, his coming of age and his coronation, for he was regarded as initiating a new age and instituting peace. Necessarily, something of the glory of this news falls again on the one who proclaims it, or on those who publish and execute his decrees. In the language of rabbinic Judaism there is a particularly noticeable impulse to transfer the element of joy from the thing itself to the news and the one who gives it. The content of this news—the nature and benefits of the Messianic age of salvation and peace—can be known from Old Testament prophecy. The new thing consists in the fact that someone comes with authority to declare that it has dawned, and that it does actually dawn with his declaration, the εὐαγγελίζεσθαι.

It is decisively in this sense that the man Jesus is called the εὐαγγελιζόμενος in the Gospels. The event of which He speaks, and His speaking of it, merge at bottom into the fact that as this One He is Himself the good thing, that which awakens joy, and that He speaks as its messenger and publisher (ἄγγελος). We again think primarily of Ac 10³⁶, where in the first instance God Himself is described as the εὐαγγελιζόμενος. εὐαγγέλιον τοῦ θεοῦ is what Jesus proclaimed even in Rom. 1¹ and Mk. 1¹⁴, and there is no point in disputing whether this means the good news that speaks of God (objective genitive) or the good news that God Himself has spoken in the world (subjective genitive), for it obviously means both. It naturally speaks of God, as the man Jesus speaks of Him. And conversely, it is God Himself who has spoken, awakening this man to speech. For what was it that God said as the εὐαγγελιζόμενος in Ac. 10³⁶ ? What was the Word that He sent unto the children of Israel ? It was peace. And peace (εἰρήνη) includes what we mean by the term, but basically it is the equivalent of shalom in the comprehensive sense of salvation " by Jesus Christ," this name being underlined as the sum of all real peace by the sharply defined insertion : οὗτός ἐστιν πάντων κύριος. Again, in Eph. 2¹⁷ we read : ἐλθὼν εὐαγγελίσατο εἰρήνην ; and just before in v. 14 : " He is our peace." The same coincidence between the content of the news brought by Him and Jesus Himself may be seen in Lk. 4¹⁷ᶠ·. Jesus reads in the synagogue from Is. 61¹ᶠ· : " The Spirit of the Lord is upon me, because he hath anointed me to preach the gospel to the poor ; he hath sent me to heal the broken-hearted, to preach deliverance to the captives, and re- covery of sight to the blind, to set at liberty them that are bruised, to preach the acceptable year of the Lord." And then, when the eyes of everyone in the synagogue are fixed on Him, He begins His own message : " This day is this scripture fulfilled in your ears." This day, then, the acceptable year of the Lord has dawned. This day the message of peace sounds in your ears. This day there takes place the liberation which it proclaims. For I am present as this One who is anointed and sent, who has the authority to declare liberty with His Word and accomplish it with this act of His Word, to bring in the new age in His person. We find exactly the same coincidence in Mt. 11³ᶠ· : " Art thou he that should come, or do we look for another ? " And Jesus tells them to go and give an account to the Baptist of the things that they now see and hear in His presence : " The blind receive their sight, and the lame walk, the lepers are cleansed, and the deaf hear, the dead are raised up, and the poor have the gospel preached to them. And blessed is he, whosoever shall not be offended in me." The content of this news of the events done by Him as it is entrusted to the disciples of the Baptist is decisively the One who dispatches it. According to the message con- firmed by what they see and hear it is He Himself who is the one that should come, and so they are not to look for another. Again, it is to be noted that in the sayings about the leaving of house and lands and family in Mk. 10²⁹, and self-sacrifice in Mk. 8³⁵, the reason given for this action lies in two factors which can both obviously be mentioned in one and the same breath : ἕνεκεν ἐμοῦ καὶ τοῦ εὐαγγελίου. Or again, the content of the εὐαγγελίζεσθαι of the Christmas angel (Lk. 2¹⁰ᶠ·), and therefore the subject of great joy, is the birth of Jesus and there- fore His whole human existence as such. Or again, that which the apostles preach as the Gospel in Acts and the Epistles is always He (αὐτός, Gal. 1¹⁶), or " Jesus " (Ac. 8³⁵), or " Christ Jesus " (Ac. 5⁴²), or " the Lord Jesus " (Ac. 11²⁰), or " the unsearchable riches of Christ " (Eph. 3⁸), or " the sufferings of Christ, and the glory that should follow " (1 Pet. 1¹¹ᶠ·), or " Jesus, and the (His) resur- rection " (Ac. 17¹⁸). There is no rivalry, however, between what we might have expected to see mentioned in all these passages instead of this name—the βασιλεία τοῦ θεοῦ preached by Jesus—and the mention of this name. For in the New Testament this kingdom, or better lordship, may just as well be called that of Jesus Christ as of God. " That ye may eat and drink at my table in my king- dom " (Lk. 22³⁰). " Remember me, when thou comest into thy kingdom " (Lk. 23⁴²). " My kingdom is not of this world " (Jn. 18³⁶), etc. Apart from all the other arguments against it, the idea that the kingdom of Christ is a special kingdom alongside that of God is proved to be an impossible thesis by the fact that Eph. 5⁵ can speak expressly of the βασιλεία τοῦ Χριστοῦ καὶ θεοῦ. Similarly, in the little hymn in the story of the entry into Jerusalem as reported in Mk. 11⁹ᶠ· the " Blessed is he that cometh in the name of the Lord " could be equated with the " Blessed be the kingdom of our father David, that cometh in the name of the Lord." And in Mt. 21⁹ and Lk. 19³⁸ the second part could drop out and only the reference to the ἐρχόμενος βασιλεύς remain. Again, " the kingdom of

God coming with power " of Mk. 9¹ could be calmly replaced by " the Son of man coming in his kingdom " of the parallel Mt. 16²⁸. " The Gospel " in the preaching of Philip in Ac. 8¹² is " the kingdom of God, and (the καί is surely to be understood epexegetically in all these passages) the name of Jesus Christ." According to the last verse of Acts (28³¹), Paul preached " the kingdom of God," and taught " those things which concern the Lord Jesus Christ, with all confidence, no man forbidding him." According to the great voice from heaven in Rev. 12¹⁰, the βασιλεία of God and ἐξουσία are given to His Christ. The references to the kingdom and to Christ are obviously to be understood in the light of each other in all these passages. We again think of the term coined by Origen (in relation to Mt. 18²³)—αὐτοβασιλεία—and of its fine exposition in an even older parallel in a statement of Marcion (quoted by Tertullian, *Adv. Marc.* IV, 33) : *In Evangelio est Dei regnum Christus ipse.* The totality, or rather the unity, of what is denoted is the content of the New Testament εὐαγγελίζεσθαι, and, seen in the light of this concept, the content of the active word of the man Jesus Himself. There can be no point in arguing, then, whether we have to understand by the ἀρχὴ τοῦ εὐαγγελίου Ἰησοῦ Χριστοῦ the beginning of the Gospel that Jesus proclaimed (subjective genitive) or the beginning of the Gospel that proclaimed Him (objective genitive). The point of the expression is to be found in the fact that both aspects converge in Him. All things considered, and with the necessary qualifications, we may add finally that the word of Jesus under the aspect denoted by the verb εὐαγγελίζεσθαι is to be understood particularly as the summons to peace which we have already considered in its essential features in our discussion of the beatitudes, which are the climax of this summons.

But the speech of Jesus is also described by the verb διδάσκειν, teaching. It would, of course, be an erroneous supposition that the use of this alternative description implies a differentiation between the sayings and addresses of Jesus, as though in any given instance we had to ask whether we were dealing with εὐαγγέλιον or διδαχή. In the strict sense everything is εὐαγγέλιον and everything is also διδαχή. But by the use of these alternative or parallel descriptions the readers or hearers are obviously pointed to the rich and manifold nature of the Word of Jesus itself, which *a parte potiori* we can and must hear and understand with a greater emphasis now on the one side, and now on the other.

To see Jesus' speech described as διδάσκειν is perhaps to find ourselves at first transported into a very different world, in which we have to find our bearings before we can see it again in its unity. In classical Greek διδάσκειν is speech which, based on the superior knowledge of the speaker, is directed to the theoretical and practical understanding of the hearer with the intention of leading him to independent knowledge and capacity. The διδάσκαλος (and it is interesting that the term is also used of the instructor of the chorus in Greek tragedy) is the original, authoritative in his freedom, of a copy which takes shape, again in freedom but this time the freedom of obedience, in the μαθητής. We must not suppress or forget this when we turn to the New Testament with its references to the διδάσκειν of Jesus. The only difference is that the word now corresponds to the Hebrew *limmed*, so that what is claimed or instructed is no longer the theoretical or practical understanding alone but the pupil as such and therefore, and decisively, his will. In the sphere of later Judaism a teacher is a man whom we can ask, as the publicans asked the Baptist in Lk. 3¹² : " What shall we do ? "—the very same question that Peter and the apostles were asked in Ac. 2³⁷ after the first sermon of Peter. But this also involved the fact that to the person of the teacher, the " rabbi " or " great one " in relation to his disciples, there was ascribed a significance which he could not have in the Greek world. And it is also a novelty in relation to the Greek idea of teaching that in this sphere instruction is always given with a definite backward reference to the Law and prophets of the Old Testament as already given for teacher and pupil alike. Teaching, διδαχή, takes place in the context of the *explicatio* and *applicatio* of these texts, the discovery and use of the Word of God attested in them. Nicodemus (Jn. 3¹⁰) is a διδάσκαλος because He is one of whom all Israel could expect that he had an outstanding knowledge of the Word of God laid down in the Law and the prophets, and could expound it and lead to obedience to it.

Now, if we are to understand this particular description and characterisation of the speech of Jesus, in the first instance we must see Him as a teacher in this sense of the διδάσκαλος of later Judaism. If He was more than this, He was also the " rabbi of Nazareth " to which He has been completely reduced by so much Liberal theology in our own time. This is particularly true in relation to the last of the points mentioned. For His speech, too, always has a backward reference to the Old Testament. It always takes the form of an exposition and application of the latter. He did not confine Himself to teaching in the synagogues, but He did also teach in the synagogues, and according to Lk. 4¹⁶ He did so κατὰ τὸ εἰωθὸς αὐτῷ, i.e., in pursuance of a rule which He accepted as self-evident. The same is said word for word of Paul in Ac. 17². It is worth noting that it is Luke who emphasises this point—obviously for the benefit of Gentile Christians. And what Jesus did (either in or outside the synagogue) was exactly what other rabbis did both in form and content. He read and commented on passages from the prophets (Lk. 4¹⁷) and the Torah (Mt. 5¹⁷). He called and gathered students (disciples), as was customary, and gave them more detailed instruction. From time to time, like other Jewish teachers before and since, He gave summaries of the Law or the whole of the Old Testament (Lk. 24²⁷), as in the well-known compression of the Law into the twofold law of love (Mt. 22³⁶ᶠ·), or the saying in Mt. 7¹² : " Therefore all things whatsoever ye would that men should do to you, do ye even so to them : for this is the law and the prophets." He also taught His disciples to pray (Lk. 11¹), " as John also taught his disciples." And with Him too—in this respect He is nearer to Pharisaic teaching than to what seems to be the more theoretical than practical scholarship of the scribes—the purpose of exposition is to teach a better righteousness than that of the scribes and Pharisees (Mt. 5²⁰) ; to serve the cause of application ; to call to obedience, to practical decision for the will of God revealed in the Law ; to a decision—here He resembles the Baptist—which is both comprehensive and radical, which claims the whole man ; to μετάνοια (Mk. 1¹⁵). It was to repentance that the apostles also called when asked concerning the practical bearing of their message. But it is at this point that we see the new and distinctive feature of the teaching of Jesus as compared with that of other rabbis— the feature which caused the astonishment of the ὄχλοι (Mt. 7²⁹) : ἦν γὰρ διδάσκων αὐτοὺς ὡς ἐξουσίαν ἔχων καὶ οὐχ ὡς οἱ γραμματεῖς αὐτῶν. The call to repentance as the existential climax of the message is grounded in the statement in which His διδάσκειν does, of course, pass over into εὐαγγελίζεσθαι or κηρύσσειν : " The time is fulfilled, and the kingdom of God is at hand " (Mk. 1¹⁵). It was in the light of this that Jesus expounded and applied the Old Testament. And it is for this reason that the cry " Repent " at the climax of His doctrine (again in Mk. 1¹⁵) means concretely what it could never mean even in the Baptist : " Believe the gospel." Like other rabbis, He looked back to the Old Testament and taught it. But for Him it was not merely the record of an honourable and distant if normative past. As that which was said by them of old time (Mt. 5²¹ᶠ·) it was also the book of the present and the future. And it was not this merely in the sense in which it might be said generally of any book that is still worth reading and instructive to-day, and presumably will be to-morrow. On the contrary, it was the book of the present and the future as the book whose account of what took place and was said once at that point has its true content and fulfilment in what takes place and is said now at this point. It is now at this point that there really takes place that which is declared in it—but declared only as an object is declared by its shadow. And this is the reality whose general and definitive revelation will also be the fulfilment and confirmation of the future.

For when Jesus taught in His here and now and to-day, as He saw it His presence was not one moment of time among and after and before many others, but fulfilled *kairos*—the moment of the event, the Word, to which every past word or event can only move, just as every future word or event can only move to the revelation of its actual scope. Jesus taught at the crucial point in this *kairos*. The new thing in His teaching was the fact that He was there, that He Himself was there. This could not replace or destroy the old thing which it had in common with the teaching of all the rabbis : the authority of the ancient records of the will and act of God ; the seriousness of concern for their exposition and application ; the necessity of obeying their voice. It was not at all the case that He came to destroy the Law and the prophets (Mt. 5¹⁷). He came to fulfil them. It was always a matter of their teaching and not a new and different teaching. But what was in fact their teaching, the old teaching beside which there was no place for any other ? Two sayings in John make this clear : " Search the scriptures ; for in them ye think ye have eternal life : and they are they which testify of me " (περὶ ἐμοῦ, Jn. 5³⁹) ; and : " There is one that accuseth you, even Moses, in whom ye trust. For had ye believed Moses, ye would have believed me : for he wrote of me (περὶ γὰρ ἐμοῦ). But if ye believe not his writings, how shall ye believe my words ? " (Jn. 5⁴⁵ᶠ·). In this context we may confidently interpret the περὶ ἐμοῦ as follows. The Scriptures bear witness and Moses writes of Me as the One who knows the will of God attested by them, who has the necessary superior knowledge to expound and apply them and therefore to teach, the freedom to be for others (when it is a matter of the knowledge of this matter) an authoritative model, and therefore the capacity and calling to bring them to independent knowledge and ability, but also (beyond this Greek sense) to call them to obedient volition, or, even more, to the total obedience of repentance. Moses, the Scriptures themselves, the ancient teaching —they all attest the truth and right and necessity of the teaching of Jesus, just as He Himself is not really a bold innovator with His ἐγὼ δὲ λέγω ὑμῖν, but expresses the will of God attested in Scripture. How does He actually come to be this teacher ? Again a saying in John can help us : " I am he (ἐγώ εἰμι), and I do nothing of myself ; but as my Father hath taught me, I speak these things " (Jn. 8²⁸). Of course, this ἐγώ εἰμι, the fact that He was taught directly by the Father as the One who speaks in Scripture, was not flaunted by Him as a kind of banner over His διδάσκειν. It is just that He did in fact teach as the One He was. It is just that He did in fact—and the fact is brought out in the speech ascribed to Him in John—proclaim Himself as the Son of the Father, the time fulfilled in Him, the kingdom of God drawn near in Him. He did actually do this in the absolute διδάσκειν attributed to Him in the Gospels. The conflict with other rabbis did not arise in relation to the teaching as such, but to this fact as it was irresistibly revealed in its (or His) ἐξουσία. It was revealed in the fact that, although He often debated with His opponents, He never debated on common ground, as was the custom and desire of all other teachers. There could never be any question of a mutual asking and seeking after the truth, but only of its defensive and (above all) offensive presentation. It betrayed itself in the fact that it was enough to tell the unknown man in Mt. 26¹⁸ : ὁ διδάσκαλος λέγει, to secure prompt obedience to His request. It is seen in the fact that He was understood and described as a prophet (a great prophet in Lk. 7¹⁶) both by the people and also at times His disciples (Lk. 24¹⁹). It emerges in the contrast of Mt. 23⁸ : " But be not ye called Rabbi, εἷς γάρ ἐστιν ὑμῶν ὁ διδάσκαλος ; and all ye are brethren." It is expressed supremely in the fact that after His death and resurrection His disciples did not actually claim the title διδάσκαλος, although it was not a true title of Jesus Himself, and could not be compared even remotely with κύριος, but only a description of status, and according to general practice nothing was more likely than that one of the leaders of His school would now have become the διδάσκαλος. Even Peter, the one on whom He would build His

Church, and James, the head of the Church in Jerusalem, did not allow themselves to be styled in this way. They obviously saw that the only possibility for them too was to be always μαθηταί of the one διδάσκαλος and to teach as such. It is only in the Gentile Churches that there arise Christian διδάσκαλοι (1 Cor. 12²⁸ᶠ·; Ac. 13¹; Jas. 3¹; Eph. 4¹¹), who bear a special (liturgical ?) office in the community, and are also called ποιμένες (Eph. 4¹¹), and ranked fourth after the ἀπόστολοι, the προφῆται, and the εὐαγγελισταί. It is only in this setting that Paul can call himself κῆρυξ καὶ ἀπόστολος καὶ διδάσκαλος in 2 Tim. 1¹¹, and more particularly, although in the same sequence, διδάσκαλος ἐθνῶν in 1 Tim. 2⁷. There could be no question now of competition with the one Teacher. For one thing, we see here a partial return to general Greek usage. But again, and decisively, the very idea of any such rivalry was ruled out by the true object and content of the apostolic διδάσκειν and that exercised in the community.

But what was it that the μαθητής of Jesus had to teach when he himself passed over to διδάσκειν? We are given the answer in Mt. 28²⁰: πάντα ὅσα ἐνετειλάμην ὑμῖν, i.e., the διδαχή which they have received from Jesus, which cannot possibly be the sum of abstract truths and demands in view of what we have just said. There could be no διδαχή in the sense of a dogmatics and ethics of Jesus, and there never has been. Christian διδαχή arose as it took place in the name of Jesus (Ac. 4¹⁸), as it became the act of the apostles and other Christians, or, concretely, in the διδάσκειν . . . τὸν Χριστὸν Ἰησοῦν (Ac. 5⁴²), in the διδάσκειν τὰ περὶ τοῦ Ἰησοῦ (Ac. 18²⁵, 28³¹). It was thus their διδάσκειν of the λόγος τοῦ θεοῦ (Ac. 18¹¹). There is an unmistakeable convergence of the term with that of εὐαγγελίζεσθαι, κηρύσσειν and even καταγγέλειν, etc. We can only say again that in its basic significance, which is very clear as applied to the Word of Jesus, the term refers back to that which is already given in the Old Testament, so that we may confidently presume that when it is used like the other terms to denote the preaching of Christ by the community its use is always with this particular reference to the Law and the prophets which is inalienable to it even in the Gentile Church. But this means that it aims always at a direct or indirect scriptural proof that the act and Word of Jesus are the fulfilment of the Word of God in the Old Testament. In the true sense διδαχή is the specifically exegetical substance of the apostolic preaching of Christ in the community and by the community to the world. But since, in its own way, the apostolic διδάσκειν is itself the preaching of Christ, it acquires the character of that call to repentance (Ac. 5³¹) which is already proper to it as the διδάσκειν of Jesus Himself.

Finally, the speech of Jesus, and therefore that of the apostles and the community, is very emphatically described as a κηρύσσειν. Luther usually translated this term as "preach." But the conceptual content that the latter term has for us is now so mixed that it is not advisable to follow his example.

It is worth noting, and pondering, that even the language of the Old Testament and later Judaism has nothing very significant to teach us concerning the meaning of the word κηρύσσειν. In the Old Testament it did not have either the prominent position or the pregnant meaning which it acquired in the New. This may well be due to the fact that the New Testament κηρύσσειν has its starting point in a fact which had not yet arisen as a fact in the Old Testament.

Formally, classical Greek is rather more instructive, although, in what seems to be a distinctive contrast to the New Testament, the substantive κῆρυξ is far more plentiful and important than the verb κηρύσσειν. A κῆρυξ was a public messenger specially commissioned by a king or city or sanctuary, and able also to act as an ambassador. The decisive prerequisite for the office was the ability and readiness to give the message exactly as commissioned. Beyond that all that was needed was a loud and resonant voice. The herald had simply to be an executive organ, a speaking-tube, a loudspeaker. But he had to be this perfectly. And as such he did not stand only in the service of man but also of the deity. He was a sacral personage. As the herald of a king or city or sanctuary he was *per se* inviolable. He had a divinely authorised freedom to speak. *Ex officio* he was also κῆρυξ τῶν θεῶν. He had to offer public prayers, and he took part in the preparation of sacrifices.

To be the herald of God (κῆρυξ τοῦ θεοῦ, without any official human commission) is something which in the New Testament world was also claimed by the Stoic philosopher (both Cynic and Epicurean), whether in attachment to one or other of the cults or in detachment from all cults, even that of the emperor, and with the bold intention of making them all superfluous and replacing them by something better. The Stoic had knowledge. He knew of the revelation of God, who had entrusted His secret to him. His task was publicly to declare what he knew to the ignorant. It was in this sense that he thought of himself as a κῆρυξ and called himself by this name. God was speaking through him, and would be heard and respected in his word. Having no possessions, without home or family (in an astonishing similarity to Mt. 10⁹ᶠ·, etc.), he preached a lack of care, criticised social and individual defects, comforted the weak, warned the prosperous, and issued a general summons to a concern for the soul's welfare. Thus he too was the declarer of a message entrusted to him, and almost indistinguishable in his whole conduct from the κηρύσσοντες of the New Testament. The opinion has been ventured that in 1 Thess. 2³ᶠ· we have a defence of Paul against the confusion of his activity with that of a Stoic preacher. The " God " of the Stoic was, of course, quite unmistakeably the sum of an anthropologico-ethical principle. His concern was for a kind of " moral rearmament," the freeing of the divine seed latent in every man, conversion in the sense of an impulse to the development of the whole man, and finally the deification of this man, the removal of all the obstacles in the way. He had nothing at all to say about the dawning of a new age, the presence of a kingdom of God, the grace and wrath of God, a radical conversion and renewal of man, the forgiveness of sins, or God becoming man. Hence, *duo cum faciunt idem non est idem.* Yet, *duo faciebant idem.* If we are to understand the κηρύσσειν of the New Testament we are forced to take into account the contemporary emergence of these people.

Ought we to mention in this connexion the literature of the so-called Hermes-mysticism ? Did it, too, know the expression κηρύσσειν prior to its use in the New Testament ? G. Friedrich (Kittel, III, 697) has certainly adduced some striking passages from a kind of sermon (in the first section of the *Corp. hermet.*) by the " shepherd of men " Poimandres (a personification of the spirit functioning as the mediator of revelation). It is not merely that the text expressly describes itself, like the expositions of the Stoics, as the κήρυγμα of someone divinely commissioned. But in its terminology it coincides—if not completely, at least at many interesting points—with that of the New Testament, for we find in it not only the terms φθορά, ἀθανασία and γνῶσις, but also ἁμαρτία, μετάνοια, πίστις, βαπτίζεσθαι and σώζεσθαι. But to what century does it belong ? Does it really belong to the 1st, or to the late 2nd, or even 3rd ? May it not be that this Gnostic *kerygma* is a copy of the Christian rather than a model ? And even if it does belong to the 1st century, we must still point out that the content of this *kerygma*, the common truth to which all these terms have reference, is the *gnosis* which leads to liberation from the material and therefore to deification, and which is to be attained in the fulfilment of a sacramental act. Here, too, it is a matter of rearmament, but this time it is sacramental rather than moral. There is nothing at all about the action of God in history, about a salvation which comes to man from without, and which is imparted to those addressed in the proclamation as an event which has taken place for them and therefore affects them. The " hermetic " κῆρυξ is essentially a mystagogue. It is true that even in the 2nd century, and then in different forms through the centuries which followed, the Church's *kerygma* had a constant tendency to become mystagogy, sacramental instruction, in approximation to this and other forms of pagan piety. One of these forms, in which from the 2nd century onwards New Testament Christianity was overpowered, was what we call "Catholicism." But we would need strange eyes not to see that in this process the Church moved right away from the New Testament *kerygma* both in form and content, so that it is quite out of place to interpret it in the light of this movement. The most that we can learn from the "parallel" does not amount to more than the (not insignificant) conclusion that in the world of New Testament κηρύσσειν there may well have been this further and very different κηρύσσειν in addition to that of the Stoics.

A positive result of this discussion is that we can make certain delimitations in our understanding of New Testament κηρύσσειν. For one thing, although the New Testament preacher was a divinely commissioned and committed announcer, he was not a recognised and (by right and custom) inviolable dignitary and official like the κῆρυξ of Greek antiquity. This had not been true of Jesus Himself, and it was not true of those who took up and continued His *kerygma*. Paul had no καύχημα in the fact that he preached the Gospel (1 Cor. 9¹⁶), and his whole existence is a commentary on this saying. On the contrary, " if they have called the master of the house Beelzebub, how much more shall they call them of his household " (Mt. 10²⁵, cf. Jn. 15²⁰). The glory of Jesus and His disciples was to be as sheep in the midst of wolves (Mt. 10¹⁶, cf. Rom. 8³⁶). They stood in the shadow of the cross. It may well be for this reason that the substantive κῆρυξ is so seldom used in the New Testament. The preacher has a true καύχημα which cannot be set aside by any shame, but it cannot accrue to him as a dignity of office. It can only take place in the act of his κηρύσσειν. To use the words of Paul, it consists in offering the Gospel without charge (ἀδάπανον, 1 Cor 9¹⁸).

Again, it is true that when Jesus and the apostles came to men with their *kerygma*, the Gospel, they claimed that they were sent, that they were sent and commissioned in a way which was absolutely binding and distinctive, so that in its delivery they were unshakeably upheld. " For therefore (i.e., for κηρύσσειν) came I forth," and as the One who came forth in this way " he preached (ἦλθην κηρύσσων) in their synagogues throughout all Galilee " (Mk. 1³⁸ᶠ·). Paul, too, spoke of an unconditional empowering that he had received (Gal. 1¹ᶠ·, ¹⁵ᶠ·) and an ἀνάγκη which was laid on him in consequence (1 Cor. 9¹⁶). The Stoic moralists and Gnostic mystagogues had made the same or a similar claim when they came with their κηρύσσειν. If we are to see the difference between what seem to be identical claims we must first note that there are two things lacking in the New Testament κηρύσσειν : the zeal of wanting to better things on the one side ; and the confidence of knowing better on the other. The guiding principle of both moralists and mystagogues was a programme for the education of the human race, a plan for its moral or sacramental elevation, for the development of its deepest (and hitherto unsuspected or neglected) potentialities, for their actualisation even to the point of what was conceived to be an attainable deification. And the constraining and, in its own way, obviously effective motive of their preaching was their certainty, not only of their power to see the human situation, but also of the form and goodness of the programme needed to deal with it. We can only affirm that both the motive of this better knowledge and the zeal of this desire to do better things are quite alien to the New Testament κηρύσσειν. Even in its form as διδάσκειν this is not a pedagogic action. Indeed, we may say that in this respect New Testament κηρύσσειν has more similarity to the action of the ancient Greek κῆρυξ, who was simply a mouthpiece for the one who gave him his commission, than to the κηρύσσειν of these contemporary moralists and mystagogues.

But there is also a distinction—and this brings us to the positive heart of the matter—from Old Testament speech, even in the form of prophetic proclamation. For although the New Testament still looks to the future, it does so in retrospect of a fact that has already taken place, and it looks to a very definite future which is concretely filled out by this fact. The New Testament κηρύσσειν is the point of conjunction of this concrete past and concrete future. It takes place between that which has already come and that which has still to come. Starting from the one and hastening to the other, it is something which takes place in a present which has, as it were, a twofold content. In this present it is an action in a way which the speech of the Old Testament could never be. The events to which the Old Testament always looks back—the exodus from Egypt, the crossing of the Red Sea, the entrance into Canaan, and the overarching events of the conclusion of the covenant with Abraham and on Sinai—cannot be equated with the event from which the New Testament derives. They had always to be presupposed and commemorated in the speech of the Old Testament, but they could not be " proclaimed " as the great act of salvation. They were the lasting promise of a fulfilment which had still to come, but they were not themselves the fulfilment. They are confronted by Israel's future in Old Testament prophecy as by an event or series of events of a very different character. They are that which is promised, not the revelation of a promise that is already fulfilled. The King has still to come. He is not the King who has already come and is coming again. At no point, therefore, in the sphere of the Old Testament, not even in the greatest prophets, do we have a speech which forms the point of conjunction of a concrete past and an equally concrete future, so that in its present, as a fulfilled *kairos*, it has the character of a definitive action. The speech of the New Testament has this character in its form as *kerygma*. It looks back to a conclusive event which has already happened, and forward from this to the revelation of the conclusion which has already taken place in this event. That is why it is itself a conclusive or definitive speech in all its forms. It means decision. Deriving from this event, and hastening towards its revelation, it shares its character as decision. It stands—and cannot fall—as it consists in the declaration or proclamation of this event. This is what the New Testament means by " preaching." The event proclaimed is the coming of the kingdom, the fulfilment of the lordship of God on earth, its concrete institution in direct contrast to all human lordships and kingdoms, the striking of the last hour for these dominions however long they may still persist, the once for all, complete and irrevocable seizure of power by God as a historical reality among men. The same cannot be said either of the exodus from Egypt or the conclusion of the covenant with Abraham or at Sinai. These—and the whole history of Israel, and the divine Word spoken in and with it and repeated by Moses and the prophets—were not depreciated but given their true and supreme value when this event took place, i.e., they were shown to be one great promise which had found in this event its fulfilment. It is obvious that it was only now, in the light of this event, that the fulfilment could be " proclaimed "—even if it was proclaimed as the fulfilment of this promise. " Many prophets and righteous men have desired to see those things which ye see, and have not seen them ; and to hear those things which ye hear, and have not heard them " (Mt. 13^{17}). This inability to see and hear is the limit of all Old Testament speech. And conversely, the new thing in the κηρύσσειν of the New Testament is that it starts from this seeing and hearing. Incidentally, of course, it is this that differentiates it positively from all other κηρύσσειν, whether moralistic or sacramentalistic.

We must now ask concerning the modern insistence on the coincidence and even identity of the New Testament *kerygma* with the event proclaimed in it. There is much to be said in favour of this, but we must be careful not to say too much, and to say the right things. In the strict sense there is only one example of what G. Friedrich (*op. cit.*, p. 702 f.) states as a general rule : that the action, the proclamation itself, is the new and decisive thing which brings about that which had been awaited by the prophets of the Old Testament ; that it is by the proclamation itself that God assumes power and His kingdom comes. This is true enough in so far as we have to do with the κηρύσσειν of Jesus Himself. For here we have more than participation. We have coincidence and identity. The saying in Ps. 33^9 is relevant in the case of Jesus : " For he spake, and it was done ; he commanded, and it stood fast." Jesus does not speak of someone or something that comes. He is Himself the One who comes, and with His coming there comes everything that is to come. It is as this ἐρχόμενος that He speaks. He does not speak, therefore, of an assumption of power which has still to take place, or does so in some other way, but of that which is accomplished as He Himself comes. It is He who accomplishes it as He speaks. What He proclaims becomes actuality the moment He does so. His proclamation is the blast of the trumpet which not only indicates but inaugurates the new year of the Lord (Lk. 4¹⁸ᶠ·), allowing every man to return unto his possession, and opening all prisons and remitting all debts, as in Lev. 25⁸ᶠ·. When He says to the lame man (Mk. 2⁵) : " Son, thy sins be forgiven thee," they *are* forgiven ; and when He says (Mk. 2¹¹) : " I say unto thee, Arise, and take up thy bed, and go thy way into thine house," this σοὶ λέγω is decisive : " He arose, took up the bed, and went forth before them all." Is there any speech of Jesus which is not also His act, this conclusive Messianic act ? And is there any act of Jesus which is not the definitive Word of His proclamation ? If no such separation is possible either in the Evangelists or the underlying tradition, it is surely gratuitous to try to establish a distinction between the Fourth Gospel, in which Jesus is the Word itself, and the Synoptics, in which He is the herald proclaiming the Word.

But it is only in this one case, in relation to the κηρύσσειν of Jesus Himself, that we can maintain the coincidence, or identity, in which the κηρύσσειν of the kingdom of God is itself the kingdom of God, and therefore unconditional, absolute κηρύσσειν, the Word which is also the content of the Word. All other genuine κηρύσσειν in the New Testament refers only to the κηρύσσειν of Jesus, which is as such a form of His life-act, and therefore of the redemptive act from which all proclamation derives. As it looks to Jesus, as it belongs to His own *kerygma* in all its autonomy and particularity, the apostolic *kerygma* and that of the community participates in that which is proper to it (and originally and strictly only to it)—the character of a definitive action in which the Word is identical with its content. This participation means that in so far as it proclaims the proclamation of Jesus it is something more than ordinary human speech, more even than the supreme Word of Old Testament proclamation, and self-evidently more—indeed, qualitatively other—than even the most beautiful κηρύσσειν of all ancient and modern moralists and mystagogues with their various calls to arms. As Christian faith can be obedient and therefore saving faith only as faith in Jesus Christ, so the Christian *kerygma* can be greater than any other human speech, and different from it, only to the extent that it is *kerygma* about Jesus Christ, and does not claim to be anything in and for itself, or even to be the true Jesus Christ, the powerful entity apart from which the man Jesus would have no further existence, or only a shadowy existence exposed to all the gusts and eddies of what is called historical scholarship. According to the New Testament, the κηρύσσειν of others alongside this One has its whole force in the fact that they avoid this presumption and are content to derive from the existence of Jesus Christ and therefore from His κηρύσσειν, looking steadfastly to Him and hearing His Word.

We must say a special word about John the Baptist. The question how the New Testament, or the different strata and trends of New Testament tradition, really understood his *kerygma* is a very difficult one to answer. In the Gospel of John, which prefers the term μαρτυρεῖν to κηρύσσειν, the Baptist is a kind of prototype of other preachers who are not identical with Jesus, the witnesses of Jesus. But to what extent is this the case ? Taken strictly, it would mean that with his water-baptism he would already have at least one foot in the Christian community, as a kind of apostle before the apostles. It can hardly be denied that in John's Gospel he is taken to be on this threshold. But how about the rest of the tradition ? It is only once said in the Synoptics that he declared that the kingdom of heaven was at hand and therefore called for repentance (Mt. 3²).

The impression given by the other accounts of his preaching is that they did not think of him primarily in this way, but tried to picture him as the last and greatest representative of the speech of the Old Testament, as the most effective bearer of a reference to the salvation which had still to come, and a proclamation of judgment and conversion shaped by the consideration of this future. We recall the saying in Mt. 11¹¹: "He that is least in the kingdom of heaven is greater than he." Like all the prophets, he stands before a closed door. He only looks forward to the event which is the turning-point. His κηρύσσειν still has the character of pure promise. It is a προκηρύσσειν (Ac. 13²⁴). For this reason the lordship of God is not a present event for those who are baptised by him. They have not yet received the Holy Spirit and the remission of sins. They merely look forward to these things from the nearest possible point. They compose and prepare themselves by their repentance, but they cannot do more than expectantly look for them. The distance of the Baptist from Jesus and the kingdom as it has already come in Him finds expression in the question : " Art thou the ἐρχόμενος, or do we look for another ? " (Mt. 11³). And it is only in answer to this question that the decisive instruction is given. Who else but the Baptist can Jesus have in mind when He says : " Blessed is he, whosoever shall not be offended in me " (Mt. 11⁶) ? We can neither forget nor erase this aspect of the matter. But there is, of course, the other side as well. For if John belongs to the series of Old Testament witnesses, as the last of these he is also set at the side of Jesus, or directly before Him, as the first in a new series. It is not for nothing that the account of his birth is so closely intertwined with that of Jesus. It is not for nothing that he is introduced as his cousin. It is not for nothing that the songs of Mary and Zacharias are so similar. And not only here, but even in Mt. 11²⁻¹⁵ where the distance is so great, the strange fact emerges that, as viewed by the synoptic tradition, the Baptist belongs to the history of the fulfilment of the Old Testament promise even in his Old Testament character, even as the last and greatest bearer of pure promise. Even as he promised, he was himself promised—not the promised One, but promised. " For all the prophets and the law prophesied until John. And if ye will receive it, this is Elias, which was for to come " (Mt. 11¹³ᶠ·). Thus, while he is still outside, he is already inside. And to the extent that he is also inside he can and must be called the first whose speech is described as κηρύσσειν in the Gospel story. And according to Matthew at least (Mark and Luke do not mention this) he too proclaimed that the kingdom was at hand (Mt. 3²). In view of Mt. 11²ᶠ· it is obvious that the First Evangelist did not think that this formula, which recurs in the first account of the *kerygma* of Jesus Himself in Mt. 4¹⁷, had exactly the same significance on the lips of John as it had on the lips of Jesus. But since he put it on the lips of both he obviously could not think that it meant two completely different things in the two cases. The only alternative is to adopt the explanation of the ἤγγικεν of the Baptist given by A. Schlatter (*Der Evangelist Matthäus*, 1929, p. 56)—that " what is promised is now brought into direct juxtaposition to the present." From what we have seen, and especially from Mt. 11²ᶠ·, the ἤγγικεν of Jesus definitely says more than this. It speaks of the present to which what is promised is not merely brought into juxtaposition but into which it is interposed—" the time is fulfilled " has now to be added by way of commentary (Mk. 1¹⁵). But, as all the Evangelists see it, the κηρύσσειν of Jesus Himself was directly preceded by this juxtaposition of the promise to the present, by this sum of the Old Testament word of promise, in which the latter passes over into proclamation (the κηρύσσειν of fulfilment), standing directly before the fulfilment (although still before it), so that it necessarily assumes in anticipation the character of a proclamation of the fulfilment. This προκηρύσσειν is the remarkable function of the Baptist—a function which is still of the Old Testament but already belongs to the New. No Evangelist took such radical pains to replace his person and function by that of Jesus as did the Fourth ;

and yet he was the very one who so radically linked him with Jesus as the witness of the light. The Baptist himself knows and says this in the Fourth Gospel : " There standeth one among you, whom ye know not " (Jn. 1²⁶) ; or again : " The next day John seeth Jesus coming unto him, and saith, Behold the Lamb of God, which taketh away the sin of the world " (Jn. 1²⁹) ; or again : " The next day after John stood, and two of his disciples ; and looking upon Jesus as he walked, he saith, Behold the Lamb of God " (Jn. 1³⁵ᶠ·). And note the complete self-effacement of the Baptist in this witness, which can hardly be surpassed for directness : " Whose shoe's latchet I am not worthy to unloose " (Jn. 1²⁷) ; and after the repetition of the saying about the Lamb of God : " And the two disciples heard him speak, and they followed Jesus " (Jn. 1³⁷) ; and then in the great contrast in 3²⁷ᶠ· : " Ye yourselves bear me witness, that I said, I am not the Christ, but that I am sent before him " (v. 28) ; and then the saying about the bridegroom and his friend (v. 29) ; and finally : " He must increase, but I must decrease " (v. 30). It cannot be contested that this Johannine presentation of the relationship between the witness of the Baptist and Jesus Himself involves a certain smoothing out or foreshortening of the problem. But it is certainly not avoided or obscured. On the contrary, the same differentiation and conjunction which were obviously the concern of the synoptic presentation with its more complicated strands are both clear and illuminating in this Gospel. If we reconsider the first Gospels along the lines suggested by the Fourth, we see on the one side that in the preaching of the Baptist the Word of the Old Testament transcends itself as such. In the moment when it stands directly before its promised fulfilment, and the proclamation of this fulfilment by the One who brings and is this fulfilment, it does not lose its Old Testament character, but it merges into this proclamation, and can even take the same verbal form according to Mt. 3². On the other side we also see that in the moment of the coming of the fulfilment the whole actuality of the Old Testament Word of promise emerges and impresses us for the first time. In its final form in the word of the Baptist it shows itself to be a true divine Word confirmed by the fulfilment which immediately follows. This enables us to understand the basic significance which according to the evidence of the synoptic texts, especially that of Matthew, the whole of the Old Testament had for the apostles and the community of Jesus in and with their own proclamation, and which it must continually acquire. In the κηρύσσειν of the Baptist it is unequivocally clear that the new thing in the *kerygma* of Jesus is also the old, the oldest of all—the incarnation of the eternal Word. To use the words of Jn. 1³⁰ : " After me cometh a man which is preferred before me : for he was before me."

But above all we have to consider the New Testament κηρύσσοντες who did not precede Jesus but followed Him. The primary and basic saying in this connexion is Rom. 10¹⁴ᶠ·. Paul considers the Jewish synagogues, which, although they have the Law of Moses and read it, do not confess Jesus as Lord, and are therefore in danger of perishing. He then asks : " How then shall they call on him in whom they have not believed ? and how shall they believe in him of whom they have not heard ? and how shall they hear without a preacher (χωρὶς κηρύσσοντος) ? and how shall they (the subject of the sentence has obviously changed) preach, except they be sent ? " When we quote this passage, we must not miss out the last link in the series. For it is on this that all the rest depends. The problem of the salvation of men, of their calling on the name of the Lord, of their faith in Him, of their hearing of His Word, is clearly the existence or non-existence of preachers. But the problem of these preachers themselves is that of their sending. At this point it is necessary, for the sake of a true understanding, to say what κηρύσσειν and κήρυγμα are and are not as the action and word of these others who follow Jesus in the New Testament. They can be preachers only as (in the narrower or wider sense of the term) they are " apostles," i.e., men who are sent. When they are commissioned to preach, they must start from the One (the man Jesus as He was raised again from the dead) of whom the Law of Moses speaks. They must be His witnesses. Summoned and empowered by Him to do this, they must proclaim His name and existence. This commissioning is the possibility and power of their κηρύσσειν, with all the consequences of this action for the hearing, faith, confession and salvation of them that are nigh and them that are afar off. But their sending does not rest on a direct encounter with God. It rests on an indirect. Like the Baptist (Jn. 3³¹ᶠ·), they did not come from above, from heaven. For them, as for the Baptist, it is a matter of proclaiming the particular and once for all event of the existence of the One of whom all this is to be said. That is why Paul can call himself a " servant (or slave) of Jesus Christ," " separated " by God to the Gospel, called by Him to be an apostle. " These twelve Jesus sent forth, and commanded them, saying. . . . And as ye go, preach (κηρύσσετε), saying, The kingdom of heaven is at hand " (Mt. 10⁵˒ ⁷). This is the third time this formula appears in Matthew. It was first anticipated by the Baptist, then put on the lips of Jesus, and now it is to be used by the disciples. Is it not at once apparent that their situation, like that of the Baptist (but from the other side), is concretely limited and in this way determined and characterised, not merely by the transcendent God as such, but immanently by His becoming man ? It is the κηρύσσειν of Jesus Himself, His self-proclamation, that is to form the content of their κηρύσσειν. How, then, can it turn in upon itself ? How can it be grounded in itself ? How can it crowd out the *kerygma* of Jesus ? How can it make this superfluous ? It is a call to hearing, faith and confession, news of an accomplished salvation, to the extent that it derives from His sending, consists in the execution of His commission, and therefore, dependent absolutely on His sending and commission, takes up and reproduces the *kerygma* of Jesus. The power of their action lies in this relationship. It is because of this relationship that there can be said of them and their work : " He that heareth you heareth me " (Lk. 10¹⁶). As they speak in this relationship, they are authorised, and, as is so impressively emphasised in the commissioning speech in Mt. 10²⁶ᶠ·, they do not need to fear anyone or anything. How is it that Paul, appealing to the faithfulness of God, can dare to say that his word to the Corinthians was not Yea and Nay, not the speech of a sentimental or existential or sacramental or any other human dialectic, not just the commending of a mere possibility, not something which merely called for decision, but that which exercised decision over them (2 Cor. 1¹⁸ᶠ·) ? It was because " the Son of God, Jesus Christ, who was preached among you by us, even by me and Silvanus and Timotheus, was not yea and nay, but in him was yea." The word of the apostle can be confident because it is spoken in this relationship. Without this relationship it would be nothing. It must say always, in supreme concretion : " We preach not ourselves, but Christ Jesus the Lord ; and ourselves (we regard as) your servants for Jesus' sake " (2 Cor. 4⁵). According to Rom. 16²⁵ " my gospel " is the *kerygma* of Jesus Christ—the Gospel which is proclaimed by Jesus Christ and therefore proclaims Him Himself. There is no place, therefore, for any appeal to the undoubted philosophy, scholarship, eloquence, moral impeccability and personal Christianity of the preacher, or for any notion that there is in his preaching any immanent power or value or salvation, or that the Christian *kerygma* is a self-sufficient and self-operative hypostasis which is as such the πρῶτον and the ἔσχατον. This notion is one of the most monstrous mythologoumena of all times. Christian preaching is the Word of the cross (1 Cor. 1¹⁸), the Word of reconciliation (2 Cor. 5¹⁹). As such it points beyond itself to the concrete history of Jesus Christ. To use the Johannine term, it is witness to Him. The preacher need not be ashamed, therefore, for as such it is the δύναμις of God to salvation to everyone that believes (Rom. 1¹⁶). Christ Himself is both its divine σοφία and its divine δύναμις (1 Cor. 1²⁴). It is not itself the kingdom of God, the divine seizure of power. It makes known the fact that this has happened. It is the proclamation of Jesus as Lord, the giving of factual information and the summons to an appropriate attitude of repentance and faith. And it is all this as the word of the ambassador who is not himself Christ, but speaks in His stead (ὑπὲρ Χριστοῦ). As it is wholly this and this alone, it shares in the truth and actuality of that which is proclaimed and imparted in it, in the power and authority of Christ. It can and must be spoken by His apostle, in the limits of his particular time and situation, in the sphere of his particular commission, as a definitive word in His community and from this to the world around. It takes place that " God beseeches you by us " (2 Cor. 5²⁰). " Therefore seeing we have this ministry, as we have received mercy, we faint not ; but have renounced the hidden things of dishonesty, not walking in craftiness, nor handling the word of God deceitfully ; but by manifestation of the truth commending ourselves to every man's conscience in the sight of God " (2 Cor. 4¹f.). But only because we have this ministry ! " We have this treasure in earthen vessels, that the excellency of the power may be of God, and not of us " (2 Cor. 4⁷). This is how matters stand with the preacher and his preaching *post Christum*, in succession to the preaching of Jesus Himself. And we may now look back and ask whether the description of the Baptist in the Fourth Gospel is not supremely appropriate. Was not this last bearer of the promise, in the final moment *ante Christum*, a reflection and prototype of all preachers of the fulfilment ? Although he was less than the least in the kingdom of heaven, did he not reveal the law by which the proclamation of even the greatest in the kingdom of heaven is inflexibly controlled ?

The second aspect of the life-act of Jesus as it impressed itself on the tradition is to be found (2) in the descriptions of His concrete activity which always accompany the accounts of His concrete speech. It is true, of course, that in the record of His preaching of the Gospel and teaching and proclamation we have to do with that aspect of His life-act which all the Evangelists regard as primary and predominant. Yet it is quite impossible to think of this second picture of His concrete work as accessory or subordinate ; as something which demands only incidental consideration and can at a pinch be overlooked. From our understanding of the different terms used to describe the concrete speech of Jesus we can see clearly that as His life-act was wholly His Word it was also wholly His activity, and that it was this, not alongside the fact that it was His Word, but *as* His Word. It is not merely in fact, but by an inner and basic necessity, that the accounts of His concrete activity are added to those of His concrete speech. It is quite impossible that they should not be there. His activity was as it were the kindling light of His speech—the light of the truth of His speech kindling into actuality. More pertinently, it is the demonstration of the coincidence, or identity, of His proclamation of the kingdom of God, the lordship of God, the divine *coup d'état*, with the event itself. It is not for nothing that in the first instance the activity itself usually consists in a Word which He speaks, but then in the Gospel record this Word tears aside the illusion that it might perhaps be " only " a Word, an event in the spiritual sphere, by immediately accomplishing the corresponding change in the material and physical sphere, in the visible and palpable circumstances of the world around. Not merely in part, but totally, His Word makes cosmic history. And it makes cosmic history on this earth, in space and time, by the lake and in the cities of Galilee, in Jerusalem and on the way to it, in the circumstances of specific individuals. There is a doing of the will of God on earth as it is done in heaven. The rule of God takes place in the sight of believers and unbelievers, of those who are wholly decided or only partly decided or not at all. As a Word, therefore, it is also an action—an individual, concrete action as an individual, concrete indication of the fact that as a Word it is spoken in power. As an action it points to the fact that it is a Word which is spoken in fulfilled time by the One who fulfils it, so that it is no longer a promise, but itself that which is promised; a definitive Word in the unequivocal form of a definitive action.

The activity of Jesus as preserved and described by the tradition has always (even where its commencement is not expressly indicated by the account of a Word spoken by Him) the characteristic that it is still His preaching of the Gospel and teaching and proclamation— but now in this total, cosmic form. It is always the revelation of the decision which has been made in the fact of His human existence among other man, and therefore in and with His speaking to and with them. It is always an activity in this distinctive sense.

The Gospels, and obviously the preceding tradition, did not think it worth while to give an account of any other activity of Jesus, of acts which did not have this specific character, which may have been interesting enough in themselves, but are quite irrelevant to this decision. That He visited different places, entered a ship here and a boat there, had a meal with this or that person—all these things form the framework of the account of His activity as a human activity, but they have no intrinsic importance. The well-meaning apocryphal record of His work as a carpenter in Nazareth belongs to a later period with different interests. We may deplore the fact that incidental details are lacking. We may think that they would have made Him a much more human figure. But the fact remains that the Gospels have no place for them. They do not even give ground for conjecture. It seems quite obvious that they had not the slightest desire either to know or to pass on information of this type. What interests them, and what we can find in them, is only an account of His activity as it was characterised in this specific way.

But this particular character of His activity in its relationship to His preaching of the Gospel and teaching and proclamation means that the great majority of the actions reported of Him have this negative difference from the actions of other men. They do not accord any more than His words with the normal course of human and earthly things. They represent a new thing in face of the usual order and form and development. That is why, even in relation to their nature, they have to be understood by those who have the necessary ears and eyes as signs of the kingdom of God drawn near. Let us put it first in this general way—they indicate the presence of an extraordinary reality.

We will mention some apparent exceptions to this rule. When Jesus was twelve years old He stayed behind in that striking way in Jerusalem (Lk. 2⁴³).

He took the children in His arms (Mk. 10¹⁶, cf. 9³⁶). He entered Jerusalem with all the claim of His unpretentiousness (Mk. 11¹ᶠ·). He washed the feet of His disciples (Jn. 13¹ᶠ·). He cleansed the temple—as He had, of course, no very obvious right to do. Now it is true that in the meaning and context of the Gospels these are significant and characteristic acts of revelation in the particular sense already mentioned. But all the same, they are acts which might well have been done by others. Their real meaning can be read only from what they are and tell us as His acts, elucidated by the circumstances in which they took place. That the Gospels know acts of this kind is important because it gives us a key to the proper understanding of all the rest. The significance of all His acts is finally and decisively to be sought in the fact that they are *His* acts.

Yet even in themselves and as such the great majority of His acts are, in a general sense, extraordinary in character. The astonishment, the amazement, the opposition and the fear, which according to the Gospels were provoked by His appearance, did not refer only to His acts, but this was obviously their primary reference. They had a " paradoxical " character, as Luke expressly tells us in one instance (5²⁶). In virtue of their particular, concrete form they had in themselves, in their very structure, a conclusive character, so that negatively at least they were signs of a new thing that He proclaimed in His Word and introduced in His existence. They were, in a general sense, miracles. In the acts of Jesus an alien will and unknown power invaded the general course of things in what the majority of men accepted as its self-evident and inflexible normality. The customary order was breached by an incursion the possibility of which they could not explain even though they did not understand the acts of Jesus, even though Jesus and the nature of the new thing which had dawned were concealed from them, even though they did not at all find themselves summoned to faith by them. Quite irrespective of these considerations, they were brought to the frontier of all that was known to them as the sum of human being and seeing and understanding.

It is to be noted and pondered that as the tradition sees it the same is true of the words of Jesus. Those who heard Him, whether they believed or not, were confronted with the same new thing, the same alien will and unknown power, at the very heart of man's known and customary possibilities and fulfilments. With the same actuality as those who were eye-witnesses of these particular acts of Jesus they stumbled against the kingdom of God drawn near. The Sermon on the Mount—we have only to recall the concluding words of the Evangelist (Mt. 7²⁹)—was no less a miraculous Word, the irruption and occurrence of something incomprehensible to man, than the raising of the young· man at Nain (Lk. 7¹¹ᶠ·) was a miraculous act. The same has to be said especially of the presentation in the Fourth Gospel, where in the works of Jesus we have " transparencies " of His words (to use an expression once suggested by W. Heitmüller) which among other things bring out the utter strangeness of His preaching. Those who try to throw doubt on the distinctive action of Jesus, as recorded in the Gospels, by referring it to the sphere of mythology must ask themselves whether in the first instance it is not His teaching, as recorded in the same Gospels, that must be referred to this sphere. For it leaves no less to be desired —and perhaps much more—in terms of normal apprehension.

It is inevitable that our further deliberations should now concentrate on the miraculous nature of the overwhelming majority of the distinctive acts of Jesus ; their extraordinary, alien and, let us not hesitate to say it, supernatural character.

We will begin by affirming that the degree of the incomprehensibility which characterises them does not seem to be the same in every instance. Indeed, there appears to be the possibility of explaining some of them, many of them, and perhaps even all of them, in a way which is at least approximately comprehensible, seeing and understanding them as one novelty in a series of others rather than the incursion and appearance of something completely new.

Among them there are those of which even the tradition knows and says that they are not without analogies, as that it seems to ascribe to them only a relatively miraculous character.

And rather curiously these are the very ones to which it accords, if not the highest, at least a very high significance—the exorcisms accomplished by Jesus. From Mt. 12²⁷ and Lk. 11¹⁹, in what is obviously a saying peculiar to the hypothetical source Q, we learn that these were also practised—and clearly not without success—by the disciples of the Pharisees.

Quite apart from any support for them in the text, such analogies might well have suggested themselves to those early hearers and readers of the Gospels who lived in the world of Hellenism, thus compromising and limiting, if not altogether destroying, the uniqueness and therefore the incomprehensibility of the records.

In a broad sense, at any rate, the healings of Jesus belong to the same category. To be sure, there do not seem to be any accounts of miraculous healings in the immediate environment of Jesus, in what we know of the activity of contemporary rabbis. But the role which they must have played in the life of the Hellenistic world seems all the greater in consequence. Whatever may be our attitude to their factuality, they were a well-known phenomenon in connexion with what was then the modern cult of the god Aesculapius, a strange mixture of highly developed medical technique and practice originally derived from Egypt and Greece and more recent religious methods, in which what was called incubation (healing in sleep, or by means revealed in sleep) played a very important part. The famous sanctuary of Aesculapius at Epidaurus seems to have been a kind of cross between a pagan Lourdes and an organised medical institution (in which there was also room for a theatre). The saying ascribed to Hippocrates : πάντα θεῖα καὶ πάντα ἀνθρώπινα, is particularly significant in this connexion. At a later period the conception of Aesculapius changed and he became an anthropomorphic mediator used by Julian the Apostate in all kinds of ways against Christianity. In this form he was (officially at least) the last of the old gods recognised in the Græco-Roman world. And quite apart from this whole complex, the earliest readers of the Gospels might feel that the current accounts of Appolonius of Tyana, the wandering preacher of the 1st century, reminded them of Jesus and His healings. As he emerges in the records, this man seems to vary between a vulgar magician and a god-man in the sense of the Mystery religions. But he was not the only one of his kind. And the divinity ascribed to the Roman Cæsars finds reflection in the fact that the emperors Vespasian and Hadrian were supposed to have cured the blind and the lame by their touch and spittle.

In this sphere at any rate no unusual happening was astonishing in the world of the Greek New Testament as we know it, except perhaps for the multiplicity with which phenomena of this kind seem to have occurred.

From the standpoint of the modern knowledge and assessment of these accounts and processes, there is more than one part of the traditional record of the acts of Jesus, if not all of it, which could and can finally entice us to an interpretation in what is either a wholly naturalistic sense, or a close approximation to it.

The achievements of 18th century exegesis in this direction have had to be abandoned as a little too crude and ingenuous. But is there not a place for something of this kind, at least in relation to the healings, so long as we go to work with rather more perspicacity than hitherto ? Modern medicine has long since accepted processes of this kind—denoted rather than explained by the term " suggestion "—and on this basis it has learned, where inclined, to treat with much greater circumspection the New Testament accounts (and those of Lourdes, and similar curiosities). In particular, there is to-day in many circles, even Christian and theological, a firm conviction that what the New Testament calls δαιμονίζεσθαι (" possession ") is identical with all kinds of mental disorder, and especially with certain forms of what we term " hysteria " ; and that what it describes as the ἐκβάλλειν of demons is the same as what modern psychiatrists, psycho-analysts and psychologists usually prescribe and practise for these evils. The accounts of Jesus' activity in this direction are quite credible when understood in this way. And what vistas have opened up for a rather broader " naturalistic " explanation of this and other miracles—perhaps all the miracles recorded of Jesus—in the case of those who have tried, as did H. de Balzac with such enthusiasm, to understand them from the standpoint of magnetism and the doctrine of Swedenborg, or more recently of occultism, spiritism, somnambulism and even anthroposophy !

It is to be noted, however, that the astonishing or, in a general sense, extraordinary aspects of the traditional activities could not and cannot be called in question either by contemporary or modern analogies and approximations and the light which these throw on them. Over a wide range they could and can be found supremely credible even in their extraordinary character. For what was done by the disciples of the Pharisees and the healings at Epidauros and the marvels reported of Apollonius were not in any sense everyday occurrences. Nor were the experiences of Swedenborg nor the results of mesmerism. Nor is the accredited news from Lourdes and its Protestant equivalents, nor the more credible accounts from the sphere of occultism, etc. Nor is it when a modern doctor of souls really meets with success and someone who suffers from genuine hysteria is brought back to reason, or even partly brought back. These things are all extremely strange. And the acts of Jesus would still have to be called " marvels " in this sense even if they belonged to the same order of phenomena and could to that extent be made approximately comprehensible. But in that case they would have become only relatively extraordinary actions.

The one thing that we must not imagine is that when we see and interpret the acts of Jesus in the sphere of these phenomena we are anywhere near the sense in which they were important to the New Testament tradition as extraordinary, supernatural actions, as miracles. And we have to realise that the credibility we may create for them by means of this interpretation has nothing whatever to do with the faith which the New Testament means to demand and waken when it re-counts them. Indeed, it might well be the last and strongest obstacle to this faith.

The dictum : *Duo cum faciunt idem, non est idem*, is relevant in this connexion too. And here too it is not affected by any emphasis we may lay on the presupposition in the first clause : *faciunt idem*. Attention should be paid to the complete lack of concern with which the Christian tradition set its accounts of the unusual acts of Jesus alongside current records of similar unusual occurrences. It is obvi-ously well aware of these—but it is confident all the same. We cannot ignore or contest the fact that it coincides with these records both in the general topic of its accounts and in some of the concrete details. Nor can we ignore or contest the fact that as it was passed on it may well have been subject as they were to all kinds of additions and embellishments. But as far as the tradition is concerned these records seem not to exist. With the exception of the reference to the action of the disciples of the Pharisees it makes no mention of them at all. And even in this case it does not make any polemical mention. It does not dispute their factuality, and it obviously does not feel any need to do so.

We remember what Paul says in 1 Cor. 8⁵ about the many gods and lords in heaven and earth which exist as λεγόμενοι, as so-called gods—and not only that, but do really exist in the fact that they are supposed to do so : ὥσπερ εἰσὶν θεοὶ πολλοὶ καὶ κύριοι πολλοί. On the analogy of this saying we may take it that the New Testament community reckoned with the genuine factuality of these widely reported miraculous occurrences.

But it has no interest at all in them—either positive or negative. It obviously does not seem to think that what it has to record of Jesus is in any way rivalled or levelled down or relativised by what was recounted in the world around about the god Aesculapius or the thaumaturge Apollonius or the wonder-working Cæsars. For all the unavoidable similarities, its movement in these accounts is obviously on a different level, on which it is neither attacked by these other records nor needs to attack them. And the same is true *mutatis mutandis* of the different ways in which attempts have been made to see and understand and estimate their accounts from a modern stand-point. We may quietly rank them with many other more or less credibly attested later and modern phenomena of a similar type. There is no sense in denying the connexions, or trying to discount these phenomena on their own particular level, as though even out-side the New Testament there were not many " more things in heaven and earth, Horatio, Than are dreamt of in your philosophy." But there is even less sense in trying to understand the acts of Jesus in the light of these connexions and therefore only as relatively extra-ordinary actions. As they are recounted and attested in the Gospels, they are absolutely new and different, in their unity with the good news, the teaching, the proclamation and therefore the existence of the man Jesus, from all other human or cosmic occurrence, usual or unusual, ordinary or relatively extraordinary. In relation to all other normal or abnormal events, they are absolute miracles (for which even the word supernatural or supranatural is not really adequate). It is only as such that they can be credible in the New Testament sense.

According to the proclamation in the Word of Jesus the alien and miraculous and inconceivable thing that takes place in His actions in the world, and in defiance of all human being and perception and understanding, is nothing other than the kingdom of God. But this means that in them there is disclosed an antithesis which makes quite insignificant all the antitheses in human thinking (the critical thinking of every age) between the ordinary and the extraordinary, the con-ceivable and the inconceivable, the natural and the supernatural, the earthly and the heavenly, the this-worldly and the other-worldly (in the ancient as well as the modern sense of these concepts). All these contrasts are ironed out and lose their ultimately improper seriousness in favour of the genuinely serious distinction necessarily made by the revelation of this very different antithesis.

The new thing of the kingdom of God is not the extraordinary, the inconceivable, the supernatural, the heavenly or the other-worldly of an epitome of formal transcendence, of an absolutely superior omnipotence which encounters man anonymously, and therefore of the empty secret of his existence. This would not really need a king-dom of God, nor would its manifestation the coming of that kingdom. For it is all present to man without God's seizure of power on earth. In one form or another, consciously or unconsciously, he knows it all very well. He knows it too well, for it is merely the sum of all the false gods imagined and fabricated by man. An ostensible or genuine miracle that merely consists in a manifestation of that formal trans-cendence, that anonymous omnipotence, that empty secret, is no miracle at all when it is compared with the miracles of Jesus. For it is not an absolute miracle.

In the same way the ordinary, the conceivable, the natural, the earthly, the this-worldly that confronts the kingdom of God as the old order, and is breached by its coming, is not just the epitome of the creatureliness of man, the definiteness and limitation of his capacity, experience and knowledge. It does not consist at all in the natural finitude and mortality of man. How can the kingdom of God, who is man's Creator, be merely the negation of his creatureliness? How can its coming be just the invasion of this creatureliness? There is this negation, and there are corresponding penetrations. But an ostensible or genuine miracle that answers only to man's dissatisfaction with his creatureliness, that consists only in the supposed and sometimes (why not ?) even the real extension of what were hitherto confessed to be the limits of his natural possibilities, is no miracle at all when compared with the miracles of Jesus. For it is not an absolute miracle.

The improper and merely relative miracle can always be known by the fact that it takes place within this relative—and ultimately artificial and false—antithesis. The new thing which it brings is only a revelation of the depth of the old—a depth which was always there and could even be discerned. Its repudiation of the old means only that the frontiers of the latter are pushed back a little at this or that point, but the thing itself remains impregnable. And in the New Testament tradition the miracles of Jesus, as the miracles of the kingdom of God, are placed quite unconcernedly and yet also defiantly among miracles of this type.

There are, of course, symptoms that they are not really miracles of this type. They are only symptoms, but we must not overlook them as such.

1. The majority of the miracle-stories do not give any indication that Jesus Himself took the initiative in their performance ; that He willed to do them of Himself ; that He acted according to a definite plan. On the contrary, they leave the impression that they were almost forced on Him, either in response to definite situations and needs and emergencies or frequently to meet the more or less urgent requests of those who needed His help. Sometimes, indeed, they seem to stand in the air. It is merely the case that He does them. He often does them merely by His presence among the thronging crowd. He is almost like His own spectator—" knowing in himself that virtue had gone out of him " (Mk. 5³⁰). " As many as touched him were made whole," is the very general statement of Mk. 6⁵⁶. Jesus does not " make " miracles. He does them. They take place by Him. Miracles which take place purposively are miracles of a very different type.

2. In His miracles of healing Jesus does not make use of any therapeutic technique. We are told that He spoke concrete words, but these never have the character of general incantations. On a few occasions (e.g., Mk. 6⁵ ; Lk. 4⁴⁰) we read of the laying on of hands. The extreme limit in this direction is the touching of the blind and deaf with His spittle, which occurs only three times in all (Mk. 7³³, 8²³ ; Jn. 9⁶). Even in these cases there can be no question of a definite practice. There is no such thing as a technique of healing in any serious sense. He did not control any art or craft which he applied in His acts. He did not practise at all in this field, whether as a doctor or magician or, for that matter, as a physician of the soul, for we never read of any spiritual or psychical preparation, or that He called those whom He healed to prayer, or prayed with them, or summoned or directed them to any kind of inward preparation. Miracles which are characterised by the application of any physical, magical or psychical technique are miracles of a very different type.

3. Jesus did not perform any miracles in His own interests, for the preservation of deliverance of His own person. The rejection of the first temptation (Mt. 4²ᶠ·) to make bread in the wilderness (as He later provided it for the ὄχλοι) is a general rule in this respect. He does not ask for the twelve legions of angels

to help Him (Mt. 26⁵³). " He saved others ; himself he cannot save " (Mt. 27⁴²). And indeed, He cannot try to save Himself. He does not come down from the cross. He also rejects the kind of miracle proposed in Mt. 4⁵ᶠ·—that He should jump from a pinnacle of the temple, demanding God's help in a venture of His own choosing,·and thus finding assurance of His relationship to Him. And He certainly does not expect or receive any reward on the part of men. " Freely ye have received, freely give," is His direction to the disciples who were commissioned to continue His work (Mt. 10⁸). What is expected of those who are helped by Him is simply that they should " give glory to God " (Lk. 17¹⁸)—and nothing more. Miracles which do not reveal this same absence of self-seeking are miracles of a very different type.

4. The miracles of Jesus do not take place in the sphere or as the content of even a partial attempt at the amelioration of world-conditions or an organised improvement of the human lot. Jesus was not in any sense an activist. As we shall see, His miracles followed a very definite line. But it was not the line of a welfare-programme executed with the assistance of supernatural powers. There must have been many other storms on the sea of Galilee after the calming of the tempest, and more than one boatload must have perished. The five thousand and four thousand fed in the wilderness knew what it was to be hungry again, and sooner or later those who were healed died either of the same or of a different disease. Even those who were raised from the dead had to die eventually. How gladly we would learn of a continuation, of definite and lasting results, of His beneficent activity. But the Gospels have nothing to tell us along these lines. His well-doing never became an institution. It did not found a Lourdes or a Möttlingen. And it does not seem to be of any concern to the Evangelists that they have no answer to the critical question addressed to all ordinary or extraordinary human activity : To what did it all lead ? They seem to find it quite in order, and accept the fact, that the actions of Jesus are beginnings with no corresponding continuations. Miracles which have continuations, which involve a programme or an institution, are miracles of a very different type.

5. The miracles of Jesus are the cosmic actualisations of His *kerygma*, and are performed in this context to summon men to faith. They are not independent, but render this twofold service to faith and the call to faith. There is an indissoluble connexion of proclamation, miracle and faith. The Gospel miracle cannot be isolated from this service. None of the miracles takes place in a vacuum. None of them takes place, or is recounted, or claims significance, in and for itself. Their significance is only as actualisations of His Word, as calls to repentance and faith. Apart from this context they are like the words of Jesus when these are either badly heard or not heard at all. They are the seed which falls by the wayside, or on stony ground, or among thorns (Mk. 4⁴ᶠ·). For Bethsaida, Chorazin and Capernaum, where many miracles are performed but there is no repentance, they become signs of judgment, the occasion of a particular denunciation (Mt. 11²⁰ᶠ·). It was because Jesus was not prepared to work miracles in a vacuum that He refused to satisfy the desire of the Pharisees for a sign from heaven (Mk. 8¹¹ᶠ·) : " There shall no sign be given unto it. . . . And he left them, and departed " (Mt. 16⁴). This is why He was so restrained in His performance of miracles in spite of the plenitude with which they took place. This is why He expressly commanded many who were healed not to speak of what had taken place. This is why we can even read (Mk. 6⁵) that apart from a few healings He could not (obviously, could not will to) work miracles in His own city—miracles which would only be gaped at as the revelation of a superior world or higher power or mystery, or be welcomed merely because of their pleasant consequences in human life. The Jesus of the Gospels could not and would not work miracles merely as a means of propaganda among those who would not accept His preaching and be converted and believe. Independent

miracles, which take place and are recounted and claim attention outside this context of preaching and faith, are miracles of a very different type.

6. What W. Heitmüller has called the transparent character of the miracles of Jesus is not true only of those which are narrated in St. John's Gospel. It belongs to the connexion between proclamation, miracle and faith that there is probably no account of any such action in the Gospels which (quite apart from its factuality and concrete content) does not also have what we may boldly describe as a symbolical quality. The Evangelists are not merely wanting to say that this or that happened in this or that concrete actualisation of the kingdom of God. They also say that as this or that happened in actualisation of the kingdom of God Jesus gave us a model or original of certain situations in the history of the development and being and formation and work of the community which in His discipleship is charged with the continued proclamation of the Gospel, the kingdom and His own name. In this respect, too, the miracles are not accidental but meaningful historical acts. When the community read and heard of the healing of the blind and the deaf and the lame, or the raising of Lazarus and the young man at Nain and Jairus' daughter, or other acts, it saw also, if not exclusively, what a total transformation had been needed for it, too, to come to faith in Jesus and therefore to a knowledge of salvation ; what a total transformation was continually needed for it to stand and walk in this faith ; and beyond that, what a wonderful hope it had in which it could go out into the surrounding world without fear. When it heard of Peter's miraculous draught of fishes (Lk. 5[4f.] ; Jn. 21[1f.]), it was summoned by the saying about " fishers of men " (Mk. 1[17]) to think also, if not exclusively, about the sending out of the apostles, and its own sending out into the world, and its presupposition in the divine act as it took place in Jesus, and the sure and certain promise which it had from this source. When it heard of feedings in the wilderness, the very wording of the description of these acts of Jesus made it inevitable that it should think also, if not exclusively, of the Lord's Supper which was so constitutive to it, and beyond that of the great feast to which it could itself invite thousands and thousands of those who hungered in the world, and whom it could already feed. When it heard of the disciples on the lake, and the calming of the storm, how could it avoid thinking also, if not exclusively, of the even greater peril of the frail bark of Peter in the world, and the salvation which comes to it in all the chaos and darkness and storms of world-history : " Lord Christ, come to us on the sea " ? And surely when it heard and read of the exorcisms it was bound to think also, if not exclusively, of the deepest and darkest problem of the alien cosmos with which it was confronted, and the solution of that problem. It would, of course, be quite wrong to reduce the exposition of the miracle stories to these considerations. Yet it is no *pudendum*, but a particular strength of these stories, that they do also have this dimension ; that while Jesus does actually make history in the actions reported they are also parables. The fathers were very conscious of this, and for that reason they were at this point far better exegetes than those who, in a panic-stricken fear of what is condemned root and branch as " allegorising," refuse to look in this direction at all. A miracle that does not have this direction, that is not a parable as well as history, is a miracle of a very different type.

When we take all these indications into account, we are at least warned that the miracles of Jesus cannot so easily be equated with the relative miracles which abound in ancient and more recent history and even in our own time. For, taken together, these symptoms do not characterise the latter miracles. The question has only to be put : Where, then, is the lack of purposiveness ? the absence of any technique ? the utter selflessness ? the difference from every kind of activism ? the dedication to the wider end of proclamation ? the transparency and parabolic character ? Yet when we take all this into account, we obviously do not indicate the positive reason why we are dealing with true and absolute miracle in the miracles of Jesus Christ. The realisation that this is the case depends wholly and exclusively on the insight that we have to do here with the kingdom of God as it has drawn near in Jesus. The actions of Jesus are the miracles of this kingdom, " the powers of the world to come " (Heb. 6[5]). And it is the fact that they are miracles of the kingdom which alone characterises them as true and absolute miracles as opposed to those which took place and still take place in our human antitheses. It is this fact alone which is the basis of the distinctive symptoms that warn us against any simple identification.

The Gospels make it quite clear that in these actions we have to do with the kingdom of God as it has drawn near in Jesus, with the event in which time is fulfilled, with the proclamation which as such is this fulfilment, God's conclusive action, the coming of the new æon. This emerges very distinctly in the fact that actions of this kind are not ascribed to John the Baptist, as might well have been the case in retrospect of Elijah and Elisha. This is made quite explicit in Jn. 10[41] : " John did no miracle : but all things that John spake of this man were true." The greatness of John is to be found in the latter part of the sentence ; his limitation in the former. The light which shines in the cosmos is the glory of Jesus manifesting itself in His acts (Jn. 2[11]). John is the faithful witness of this light. But he has no glory of his own to reveal, and therefore he does not do any such acts. This glory is the new thing at the end and goal of the history of Israel, to which the whole of this history (including, as the New Testament sees it, the miracles of Elijah and Elisha) could only point. In its astonishment at an exorcism the ὄχλοι know and say : " It was never so seen in Israel " (Mt. 9[33])—even though exorcisms were in fact practised among them by the disciples of the Pharisees (Mt. 12[27] and par.). The new thing which was now seen was that " the kingdom of God is now come unto you " (Mt. 12[28]). Whether it was recognised or not, this was the thing which was to be seen in the acts of Jesus.

But what is this kingdom of God, and what do we mean when we say that they were miracles of this kingdom ? We will try to answer this question by considering the general trend or nature of the miracles of Jesus.

A first thing which they obviously have in common is that they are all acts of power (δυνάμεις), and are often described as such. They are done, in fact, with a divine and unconditional freedom, and in this respect they are absolutely sovereign, alien, incomprehensible, and transcendent in relation to all the orders, forms and developments known to men. For this reason, if we may again refer to this in passing, they cannot be measured by the old idea of a fate which controls the affairs of men or by the modern notion of a mechanism which operates according to the norm of remorseless physical, chemical, biological or other natural laws. The dimension in which God is powerful has no place in these conceptions. But it is the power of God alone which is the power operative and revealed in the miracles of Jesus.

But we must be more precise. What we have here is the power of God. It is therefore more than a maximal freedom as such, which, abstractly considered, might well be maximal evil, the power of the devil. A power of this kind may play with man, but man can also play with it. It is mysterious, but it is also familiar. It is not alien or incomprehensible or transcendent in the strict sense of the terms. It does not confront him in genuine sovereignty. But this is the case with the power of God in the service of which the man Jesus does His miracles.

The saying which is appended to the cursing of the fig-tree has thus to be taken quite seriously, but, because quite seriously, as a figure of speech and therefore *cum grano salis*: " Have faith in God ($\check{\epsilon}\chi\epsilon\tau\epsilon$ $\pi\acute{\iota}\sigma\tau\iota\nu$ $\theta\epsilon o\hat{\upsilon}$). For verily I say unto you, That whosoever shall say unto this mountain, Be thou removed, and be thou cast into the sea ; and shall not doubt in his heart, but shall believe that those things which he saith shall come to pass ; he shall have whatsoever he saith " (Mk. 11²²ᶠ·). The unconditional nature of the act of power which takes place in the genuine miracle, and is achieved in faith, could not be more drastically indicated. But it is not its unconditional nature which makes it a genuine miracle accomplished in the $\pi\acute{\iota}\sigma\tau\iota\varsigma$ $\theta\epsilon o\hat{\upsilon}$. On the contrary, it is only when it is achieved as a true miracle that it is marked by this unconditional character. And the problem of the faith which accomplishes the miracle is whether it is $\pi\acute{\iota}\sigma\tau\iota\varsigma$ $\theta\epsilon o\hat{\upsilon}$. Is it really faith in God, or only in an anonymous omnipotence ? In the striking novel by Bruce Marshall, *Father Malachy's Miracle*, we are told the story of a man who in a powerful faith dared to do something very similar to what we are told in Mk. 11 and succeeded in removing a whole place of amusement from the centre of Edinburgh to a lonely rock on the edge of the sea, but was brought to the unequivocal realisation that the very evident success of his faith and prayer meant nothing at all as a revelation of God in the world, being viewed by the unconverted only as a passing sensation, and by the Church only as a disturbance to be hushed up by pious diplomacy, so that the second miracle which he believed and prayed for and succeeded in accomplishing could only be an inconspicuous reversal of the first. It is to be noted that Jesus Himself never commanded any mountain to be removed and cast into the sea, nor did His disciples make any ventures in this direction.

We have thus to ask concretely what it means that the miracles of Jesus are divine acts of power which took place in Him. We have to ask what it means that they took place unconditionally and are thus characterised as inconceivable. When we do this, we are led to the following description of the general character or trend discernible in all of them. What always takes place in them is that in and with them a completely new and astonishing light—and in all its different manifestations the same light—was cast on the human situation. And in the strict sense it was simply this light, and its shining, and the radiance which it shed, that encountered men as the unconditional power of God in the miracles of Jesus. This light was the genuinely incomprehensible, the genuinely miraculous, factor in these miracles. It was this that differentiated them from all other curious phenomena as absolute miracles, as signs of the kingdom of God drawn near and entering the human situation in the works of Jesus as the actualisation of His Word. The question whether or not we understand His miracles is the question whether or not we see this light running through all the records which now concern us and emerging more or less clearly in all of them. Set against this light, the antithesis of God and man in their mutual opposition and relationship, and the history which takes place between them, ceases to be something general and abstract and formal and anonymous. It acquires definiteness, content, character and contour. And this in its definiteness is the kingdom of God in its power and glory and its distinctive inconceivability, which cannot be confounded with any other, and also characterises its signs. We must now try to see something of what is to be seen at this point.

1. We must begin by saying something about the nature of the man who is in some sense illuminated by the light of the kingdom of God. What kind of a man is it to whom Jesus turns in this particular activity? The answer is obvious. It is the man with whom things are going badly; who is needy and frightened and harassed. He is one who is in every sense " unfortunate." His life may once have had (and still have) other neutral or more sunny aspects. But in the Gospel records he (and the whole human situation) is of interest only from this standpoint. The picture brought before us is that of suffering—the suffering of the blind and deaf and lame, the lepers and demon-possessed, the relatives of a sick friend who is dear to them, the bereaved and those who walk in the fear and shadow of death. We may turn away from this aspect of human existence. We may close our eyes to it. We may argue that human life as a whole is not really like a great hospital. But apart from this aspect the miracles of Jesus cannot be brought into proper focus and genuinely seen or understood. For human life as it emerges in this activity of Jesus is really like a great hospital whose many departments in some way enfold us all.

We are told in Mk. 2^{17} that Jesus is the physician who is needed by the sick and has come for their benefit. Appeals are constantly made to Him in the following terms : " If thou wilt, thou canst make me clean " (Mk. 1^{40}) ; " Jesus, thou Son of David, have mercy on me " (Mk. 10^{47} and *passim*) ; " If thou canst do anything, have compassion on us, and help us. . . . I believe, help thou mine unbelief " (Mk. $9^{22f.}$). In the storm even His own disciples cried : " Lord, save us : we perish " (Mt. 8^{25}). And we need hardly mention the particular cries of the possessed. Nor does He always wait for these appeals. He hears them before they can be uttered, and acts accordingly. But the point is that His action is always in response to human misery. There are a few instances which give us grounds to ask whether this is not too strong a statement to be generally applicable. Surely the inferred miracle of the coin in the fish's mouth (Mt. 17^{27}), and especially that at the marriage in Cana of Galilee (Jn. $2^{1f.}$), were not more than the relieving of a minor embarrassment. And in the miraculous draught of fishes (Lk. $5^{3f.}$) and the feedings of the multitudes in the wilderness there is no question of saving from actual starvation. But these are only petty considerations. All in all, we can say that here too the theme is that of human suffering, in which the distinctions between greater and smaller degrees of painfulness are of no decisive importance, the apparently slighter evil being often the greatest, and man being always a poor man for whom things go badly even when he is not actually *in extremis*. Even in the passages quoted it is to the help of this man that we see Jesus coming. The total impression made (and obviously meant to be made) by the majority of the records is plain : " They brought unto him all sick people that were taken with divers diseases and torments " (Mt. 4²⁴) ; " And great multitudes came unto him, having with them those that were lame, blind, dumb, maimed, and many others, and cast them down at Jesus' feet " (Mt. 15³⁰) ; " He healed all that were sick (πάντας τοὺς κακῶς ἔχοντας), that it might be fulfilled which was spoken by Esaias the prophet, saying, Himself took our infirmities, and bare our sicknesses " (Mt. 8¹⁷).

2. Again in relation to the man to whom He turns, but also to the purpose in which He does so, we cannot possibly conceal the fact that it is with their evil existence in itself and as such that He is concerned in His acts. It has often been said, and rightly, that He had to do with the whole man. But we must say, rather more exactly, that it is with the whole man in what is almost exclusively his " natural " existence in the narrower sense, his physical existence, his existence as it is determined by the external form and force of the cosmos to which he belongs. And it is as determined in this way that it means suffering. It is as he is subjected to this existence that man is a prisoner. That is the problem of the miracles of Jesus. He finds and sees man in the shadow of death. His miraculous action to man is to bring him out of this shadow, to free him from this prison, to remove the need and pain of his cosmic determination. He unburdens man ; He releases him. He calls and causes him to live as a creature. Man can again rise up and walk, again see and hear and speak. He can come from the heart of the storm to dry land. He can eat and be more than satisfied. He can drink and he is given wine—good wine. He is delivered from every torment and embarrassment and he can breathe again. He can be a man again—a whole man in this elemental sense. His existence as a creature in the natural cosmos is normalised. We must not ignore or expunge the phrase—as a creature in the natural cosmos. It is as such that he is radically blessed by the miracles of Jesus.

We are reminded of Ps. 124⁶ᶠ·: " Blessed be the Lord, who hath not given us as a prey to their teeth. Our soul is escaped as a bird out of the snare of the fowlers : the snare is broken, and we are escaped." But we must not forget that the " fowlers " in this Psalm were men (v. 2) who " rose up against us " and would have swallowed us up quick if the Lord had not been on our side. The New Testament, however, is not so much concerned with the suffering brought on man by his fellows—with historical and social evils—when it speaks of the actions of Jesus. It is more concerned with his physical suffering. The fowlers whose snares are broken by the acts of Jesus are obviously the powers of death which threaten him quite apart from anything that man himself does.

There is another remarkable and almost offensive feature of the miracle stories which has been continually obscured, i.e., painted over in ethical colours, in so much well-meaning exposition (especially in the Western Church). This is that in these stories it does not seem to be of any great account that the men who suffer as creatures are above all sinful men, men who are at fault in relation to God, their neighbours and themselves, who are therefore guilty and have betrayed themselves into all kinds of trouble. No, the important thing about them in these stories is not that they are sinners but that they are sufferers. Jesus does not first look at their past, and then at their tragic present in the light of it. But from their present He creates for them a new future. He does not ask, therefore, concerning their sin. He does not hold it against them. He does not denounce them because of it. The help and blessing that He brings are quite irrespective of their sin. He acts almost (indeed exactly) in the same way as His Father in heaven, who causes His sun to shine on the good and the evil, and His rain to fall on the just and the unjust (Mt. 5⁴⁵).

The truth is obvious, and it is brought out elsewhere, that the evil which afflicts mankind is in some sense a punishment ; that " the wages of sin is death " (Rom. 6²³). But there is no trace of this consideration in the miracle stories. It is, indeed, expressly excluded in Jn. 9²ᶠ· : " Master, who did sin, this man, or his parents, that he was born blind ? Jesus answered, Neither hath this man sinned, nor his parents : but that the works of God should be made manifest in him." We are reminded of the same truth in Lk. 13¹, where Jesus tells us that the Galileans who were put to death because of disturbances in the temple were no more sinful than other Galileans, and that the eighteen on whom the tower fell in Siloam were no more guilty than other inhabitants of Jerusalem. In the miracle stories σώζεσθαι has nothing whatever to do, directly, with the conversion of the " saved." It means that they are healed, made whole, normalised, brought back to life in the elemental sense. They are delivered from death. There is only one story, the healing of the paralytic in Mk. 2¹ᶠ· and par., in which there is a prior reference to the sin of the one who is healed, and even here there is no demand for repentance, but the sin is annulled unrequested and without examination, in view of the faith, not of the man himself, but of those who had brought him to Jesus : " Son, thy sins be forgiven thee " (v. 5). He says this, in fact, with just the same free initiative as He later says : " Arise, and take up thy bed, and go thy way into thine house " (v. 11). The obvious aim of the story is to bring out the connexion of Jesus' miracles with His proclamation. But instead of interposing a psychologico-moral dependence of the second saying on the first it is far better to see that in the immediate proximity of the second the first itself is pure, free proclamation and not a psychologico-moral encouragement. With the same free power with which the Son of Man later tells the paralytic to rise and walk He first forgives him his sins. And He does the second in order that " ye may know " that He has the power to do the first. And there is only one story again, the healing of the sick man at the pool of Bethesda, where we have a subsequent reference to the sin of the one who is healed : " Behold, thou art made whole : sin no more, lest a worse thing come unto thee " (Jn. 5¹⁴). It is to be noted, however, that Jesus' initial question to this man was simply : " Wilt thou be made whole ? " (v. 6), and that the only answer the man gave was to explain why it was that he had not so far found the healing that he desired in the pool of Bethesda : " Sir, I have no man, when the water is troubled, to put me into the pool : but while I am coming, another steppeth down before me " (v. 7). There is no question of any ethical purpose on the part of Jesus, or ethical insight on the part of the man. The warning tells us, of course, that there is something worse than thirty-eight years of infirmity, i.e., to treat the grace which has been given as though it had

made no difference and to continue in sin. But the point of the story is not to
be found in the warning. It is to be found in the sovereign removal of the
infirmity. And in any case—as we can see at once and have to take into account
—there is no mention of sin at all in the rest of the stories. It is tacitly presupposed that those who were healed were sinners and ought not to continue in
sin. But this has no thematic significance in the texts. In the true sense, their
transgressions are not imputed to them by Jesus (2 Cor. 5¹⁹). What is imputed
is only that they are poor and tragic and suffering creatures. In the strict sense,
it is only as such that they are taken seriously.

3. On this basis we can emphasise as a first positive element that
the God whose deity and power are active and revealed in the miracles
of Jesus is the God who is always directly interested in man as His
creature. Beyond or above or through his sin He is interested in man
himself in his being in the cosmos as limited and determined by Him.
He is interested in him as this specific cosmic being. He has not
forgotten him or left him to himself. In spite of his sin He has not
given him up. He maintains His covenant with him. He is always
faithful to him. He takes his sin seriously. But He takes even more
seriously, with a primary seriousness, the fact that he is His man even
as a sinner, and above all that He Himself is the God even of this
sinful man. The fact that God takes man seriously in this direct
divine way finds concrete realisation when Jesus' proclamation of His
kingdom, His *coup d'état* in the miracles, takes the form of this direct
comforting of the sad, this free liberation of the poor, these benefits
which come so unconditionally to man ; when in this form it consists
quite simply in the fact that oppressed and therefore anxious and
harassed men can breathe and live again, can again be men.

God's *coup d'état* on earth is that this actually takes place according
to the good news of the true Word of Jesus and in demonstration of it.
It is in this that God is glorious, making known His will, and in His
will His nature. And because this will, this nature and therefore this
God is new and inconceivable and miraculous to man, we can describe
and maintain it as at least one element of the new and inconceivable
and miraculous in the acts of Jesus that it is this God, the God who
is majestic in this way, who is at work in them, and may be known
as such as He makes history in this way. It is to be noted that a
God who lived His own divine life in some far height and distance
and transcendence would not be in any way strange to man. Nor
would a God who ruled no less impartially over man than over all
other creatures, having no particular interest in him. Nor would a
God who had a particular quarrel against man, signally accusing and
punishing and rectifying him because of his aberration. These are the
well-known conceptions of a deity which man himself has imagined
and which it does not need any miracle to reveal. The same applies
even to the conception of a friendly deity, arbitrarily filled out with
all kinds of notions of love and kindness. Where miracle is needed
is to reveal the living God who has elected and ordained to be the

God and Creator and Lord and Partner of man. And it is with this God and His work and revelation that we have to do in the acts of Jesus. This is what constitutes their strangeness. It is in this that they are miracles, and for this reason that they cannot be compared or equated with other curious things. That God is this God is something which never entered the heart of man either as experience or as an idea. It can only come on man as a new thing, in the occurrence of the miracle of the presence and action of this God. And it is with the occurrence of this miracle that we have to do in the acts of Jesus.

4. The second positive element that calls for emphasis is that the God who is operative and revealed in the acts of Jesus self-evidently places Himself at the side of man in this respect—that that which causes suffering to man as His creatures is also and above all painful and alien and antithetical to Himself. As Jesus acts in His commission and power, it is clear that God does not will that which troubles and torments and disturbs and destroys man. He does not will the entanglement and humiliation and distress and shame that the being of man in the cosmos and as a cosmic being means for man. He does not will the destruction of man, but his salvation. And He wills this in the basic and elemental sense that he should be whole. He does not will his death, but life. He does not negate but affirms the natural existence of man. And He does not affirm but negates that which attacks and frustrates it, the shadow of death and prison in which man is necessarily a stranger to himself. And as His affirmation is joyful to the very core, His negation is in every sense unwilling and vexed and wrathful. The sorrow which openly or secretly fills the heart of man is primarily in the heart of God. The shame which comes on man is primarily a violation of His own glory. The enemy who does not let man breathe and live, harassing him with fear and pain, is primarily His enemy. God Himself engages the nothingness which aims to destroy man. God Himself opposes and contradicts its onslaught on His creation and triumph over His creature. He also opposes and contradicts sin because it is sin which opens the door for the invasion of His creation by nothingness, because in sin the creature delivers itself up to it, itself becoming futile and chaotic. He is wrathful against His own true enemy, which is also the true enemy of man, when He is wrathful against sin. And the coming of His kingdom, His seizure of power on earth, is centrally and decisively the power and revelation of the contradiction and opposition in which, speaking and acting in His own cause, He takes the side of man and enters the field against this power of destruction in all its forms. That is why the activity of the Son of Man, as an actualisation of His Word and commentary on it, necessarily has the crucial and decisive form of liberation, redemption, restoration, normalisation : " Cast away, dear brothers free, All your woes, Wants and foes, All needs are met in Me." He goes right past sin, beyond it and through it, directly to

man himself ; for His purpose is always with man. And, forgiving his sins, He tackles the needs and fears which torment him, and lifts them from him : " Go in peace, and be whole of thy plague " (Mk. 5³⁴). He sets him on his feet again, giving him eyes to see and ears to hear and a mouth to speak, providing him with food and drink, and calling and causing him to live again as a man. His activity is first and foremost the Gospel in action. Only then is it the new Law which condemns the sins that he has committed and warns him not to commit fresh sin, thus closing the door by which chaos has invaded his life and being. It is a matter of saving his life and being, and of doing this for the sake of God's glory. For the glory of God is threatened by man's destruction. Hence God cannot tolerate that man should perish.

In John's Gospel there are frequent references to the " works " of Jesus, and primarily and concretely this term is used to denote His miracles. He, Jesus, has to do them (Jn. 10³⁷), or to " work " them (9⁴). But He does them in the name of His Father (10²⁵). The Father has given Him these works to " finish " (5³⁶). Strictly, it is the indwelling Father Himself who does them (14¹⁰). Strictly, then, they are the " works of God " (9³), given to Jesus to do, to work, to finish, in order to attest Him, and in His person the salvation and life granted by God to man (5³⁶), that life which is the light of men (1⁴).
In John's Gospel we are also told that Jesus healed on the sabbath day (5⁹, 9¹⁴f.), as is particularly emphasised at the beginning of Mark's presentation and in the stories peculiar to Luke (13¹⁰f·, 14¹f·). Is it really the concern of the tradition in these particular stories merely to draw attention to the formal freedom which Jesus displayed in relation to the law of the sabbath ? Can it really be the case that the cause in whose interests He made use of this freedom is a matter of indifference, the interesting thing in His attitude being simply transgression for the sake of transgression ? If this seems highly improbable, we can only assume that what the tradition wishes to emphasise is that, although He did not always heal on the sabbath, He did so deliberately and gladly because His own coming meant that the seventh and last day, the great day of Yahweh, had dawned, and healing was the specific Word of God that He had come to accomplish on this day (in the name of God and in fulfilment of His own work). Thus He not only did not break the sabbath with this work but genuinely sanctified and kept it. He was free also, and particularly, to do good and not evil on the sabbath, i.e., to save life and not to destroy it (Mk. 3⁴). And He looked (v. 5) " with anger, being grieved for the hardness of their hearts," on those who watched and criticised Him. We cannot understand this grief and anger, or the remarkable force with which He rejected the Pharisaic-rabbinic opposition to His attitude, if we do not see that it was a matter of defending His positive freedom on the sabbath, i.e., His freedom to do on this day of His, " while it is day " (Jn. 9⁴), the good and saving works of God ; to cause the " light of life " (Jn. 8¹²) to shine ; or, in synoptic language, to set up the signs of the kingdom of God as the kingdom of healing and salvation. He is not angry and grieved because they are so narrow in their exposition and application of the law of the sabbath, but because they fail to recognise and therefore reject these " signs of the times " (Mt. 16³).
And the sharpness of Jesus in defence of this positive freedom merely reflects the severity of the assault in which He is engaged as the One who does and works the works of God. And this again merely reflects the vexation with which God Himself, the indwelling Father, has gone to work against the rule of death in the cosmos created by Him, interposing Himself between its dominion

and that of the destruction which plunges men into fear and sorrow. We can gather something of what this means for Jesus, and of this vexation of God Himself, from the story of Jairus' daughter (Mk. 5³⁸ᶠ·). For when He entered the house, and saw " the tumult, and them that wept and wailed greatly," He summarily dismissed the mourners (as He did those that bought and sold in the temple). Why was He so severe ? He was face to face with the cult of death. Death was something which they all thought it a self-evident law of reason and custom to regard as an unassailable fact and therefore to treat with pious sentimentality as a supreme power. Jesus denied both the law and the power : " The damsel is not dead, but sleepeth." And then : " Talitha cumi. . . . Damsel, I say unto thee, arise." The reality of God, omnipotent in His mercy, is set against the obvious reality of death. Which will prove to be the greater, the true reality ? Jesus alone can see how the decision will go. He Himself stands in this decision and makes it. And His solitary No to death, in the power of His solitary Yes to the omnipotent mercy of God, is the reason for His severity in that house of death. When He enters this house, it can no longer be a house of death. It is exactly the same when He abruptly halts that funeral procession just outside the gate of Nain (Lk. 7¹⁴).

Above all we are reminded of the scene which precedes the raising of Lazarus in Jn. 11³³ᶠ· : " When Jesus therefore saw her (Mary) weeping, and the Jews also weeping which came with her, he groaned in the spirit, and was troubled." " What troubled Him in the first instance was this display of weeping, this tribute, as it were, to His opponent, death, this desire of men to grovel in their wounds, this tacit magnifying of the omnipotence of death which is really a murmuring against God. But His vexation extended beyond this to His opponent, the prince of this world, who had succeeded in reducing to such abject slavery the man who was called to bruise his head " (F. Zündel, *Jesus*, new ed., 1922, p. 236). The short statement follows very oddly in v. 35 : ἐδάκρυσεν ὁ Ἰησοῦς. He too ? Yes, He too. We may perhaps recall at this point the Pauline : " Weep with them that weep " (Rom. 12¹⁵). Jesus is not fighting sad and sorrowing men. He stands in solidarity with them, " sympathetically bearing the burden of the whole age." But His weeping with them means that He is fighting for them. It is therefore misunderstood by those who rather finely said : " Behold how he loved him," as well as by those who more maliciously suggested : " Could not this man, who opened the eyes of the blind, have caused that even this man should not have died ? " (v. 36 f.). For on the way to the grave of Lazarus, weeping with those who wept in face of the unequivocally revealed reality of death, the " participation " of Jesus is not a compromise. His weeping itself is a strict repudiation of the cause of their and His weeping. It is itself a resolute No to this reality. Looking this death and its terror more soberly in the face than anyone else, He is already on the way to banish it from the world. That is why it continues in v. 38 : " Jesus therefore again groaning in himself cometh to the grave. It was a cave, and a stone lay upon it." Just as David had faced Goliath, or anyone an enemy whom he himself as well as everyone else self-evidently recognised to be superior, but whom he is resolutely determined to destroy, and equipped to do so, and therefore confident ; so Jesus confronted the closed grave, the corruption which had already set in, the sealed finality of death. What is meant by His promise : " Thy brother shall rise again " (v. 23) ? Just the orthodox belief : " I know that he shall rise again in the resurrection at the last day " (v. 24) ? No, " I am "—not merely life, but because life, because its presence and power in a world given up to death, " the resurrection and the life," the life which asserts and maintains itself in face of death and overcomes it. " He that believeth in me, though he were dead, yet shall he live : and whosoever liveth and believeth in me shall never die " (v. 25 f.). This is the word which Jesus flings even into the sphere of death ; and the tense is both present and future, and the saying itself both an indicative and an imperative.

It is His Word as His act, for He speaks it right into the opened grave of Lazarus, crying " with a loud voice, Lazarus, come forth " (δεῦρο ἔξω, v. 43). This is the battle of Jesus for the cause of man as God's creature ordained by God for life and not for death. And when Lazarus hears it, and does as he is commanded, it is the victory of Jesus in this battle. And we have to remember, of course, that what is unfolded in this dramatic and almost breathtaking way in John 11 is the secret which the New Testament tradition thought it saw in all His acts and primarily in the Word which found concrete form in His acts.

Along these lines, finally, the passages are instructive which deal with the exorcisms of Jesus. We can hardly fail to recognise that they have a decisive importance for the tradition. In the summarised account in Ac. 10³⁶ᶠ· the whole action of Jesus is stated in the words : " Who went about doing good, and healing all that were oppressed of the devil ; for God was with him " (v. 38). We have a similar summary in the account of the return of the disciples in Lk. 10¹⁷, how they said with joy : " Even the devils are subject unto us through thy name." And the answer which Jesus Himself gave was this : " I beheld Satan as lightning fall from heaven " (v. 18). Elsewhere the exorcisms are ranged with healing as constituting the great sphere of the activity of Jesus, being put in the second place in Mk. 1³⁴ and the first place in Mt. 8¹⁶. And it is to be noted that in Mt. 12²²ᶠ· even the healing of the blind and deaf, and in Lk. 13¹⁰ᶠ· that of the woman with the bowed back, are described as exorcisms. It is certainly not an exhaustive description of what is envisaged in the passages which deal with exorcisms to explain that they deal only with what we now call mental or psychological ailments (clothed and decked out in terms of the current mythical understanding), and that their healing is simply by what we realise, or think we realise, to be the appropriate psychico-physical treatment.

Of course, we can neither overlook nor contest the fact—and we ought not to do so—that to the phenomena of the sphere of cosmic distress to which these passages refer when they speak of certain men suffering from demon " possession " there do also belong to what we call mental sickness. Although great caution is needed, we cannot altogether exclude the fact that in the activity of Jesus in relation to these men there may be an element of what we would now call (substantially if not technically) psychiatric treatment. Certainly, as far as the symptoms of the man himself are concerned, the outstanding example of the passages dealing with this disease and its cure, the story of the demoniac in Mk. 5¹ᶠ· and par., has many features which force us in this direction. Why should not the circle of Jesus' activity have touched and cut right across the sphere of cosmic suffering to which we now give this name ? And why should not Jesus' attack on this sphere have assumed sometimes a kind of psychiatric character ? For in what took place it was really a matter of human and therefore also psychical conditions and processes. The only thing is that we must not think that what the Gospel passages have in mind in relation to these sufferers, and especially to the action of Jesus, can be exhaustively described, let alone grasped in its decisive spiritual and theological meaning and character, in this explanation. Even at best, what we see in this explanation is only a subordinate and partial aspect of what the passages themselves envisage in their description of what took place. And it is so subordinate and so partial that we may well ask whether, even if the narrators had had our more enlightened knowledge of spiritual sickness and its treatment and eventual cure, they would have expressed themselves in essentially different terms from those actually used.

As far as concerns the so-called mythical understanding of the age, which is supposed to have given rise to the ideas of demons and demon possession, it has to be remembered that in what is recorded in the Gospel account we do not have to do with the dominant idea current in that age. It could not be the dominant idea because in the medical schools of antiquity there had already been those, like Hippocrates, who had refused to find any place for demons even in relation to sick mental states of every type, explaining the phenomena denoted by these terms very materialistically as due to abnormal movements of " juices " in the head. Even within the widely accepted consensus of opinion as to the existence and activity of beings of this kind the New Testament has certain distinctive features. It speaks of " demons" (no attempt is made to define them, and they are obviously regarded as incapable of definition) to whom it is proper (*a*) to take possession of man, to estrange him from himself, to control him, and to disturb and destroy him both in body and soul ; and (*b*) to do this in a very definite context, in the service of a whole kingdom of disturbance and destruction, summed up in the form (which is not defined) of the devil, or Satan, or Beelzebub. Now it is true that this view of demons and their operation and context is not original to the New Testament. Yet it does not belong to the general stock-in-trade of the so-called mythical understanding. It is a view which belongs specifically to later Judaism, and is therefore one of the marks of the last stage in the history of Israel. Whether and how far it was stimulated and conditioned by Old Testament reminiscences on the one hand and Persian or other foreign influences on the other is an interesting historical question, but theologically it is only of minor importance compared with the fact that at this point we find ourselves in a wholly distinctive sphere of actuality, in the time of a conclusion which is unique in its spiritual character, having all the marks of a no less unique transition into the void. We find ourselves in the historical sphere in which the Old Testament Canon was closed and its content became a magnitude belonging to the past, being studied and respected and honoured in the present, but having no present of its own, being handed down from one generation to another, and impressed by each generation upon its successor. It was the period when prophecy was silenced, being replaced by a non-historical apocalyptic. It was the period when the Law with its hundreds of possible and impossible demands became the one form of the revealed will of God. It was the period when Judaism finally developed out of the existence of Israel in covenant with Yahweh. Yahweh had spoken, but He was now silent. This terrible turn in affairs was the secret of this period, of this sphere, of what we call " later Judaism." And it was at this turning-point, in this spiritual and historical vacuum, that the idea which we are discussing arose and became predominant. Or perhaps we should say objectively that at this point there was a realistic perception and experience (as was inevitable, for was it not a real filling of the vacuum and not a mere figment of the imagination ?) of the replacement of what was no longer perceived and experienced by the fatal actuality of its opposite, of the abyss and darkness and horror of evil as the supremely present background of human existence, the invisible and yet supremely present background of human existence, the invisible and yet supremely visible and audible and palpable dominion of nothingness over man, which in its unity could be called the devil, or Satan, or Beelzebub, or any other name suggested by Persian or other influences, and in its multiplicity the host of his angels, the δαιμόνια or πνεύματα, in other words, the power and the powers of destruction. And it was perceived and experienced that the man who was specifically indwelt by these powers was " possessed," controlled, imprisoned, tormented both in body and soul, being haunted by them in various forms, so that he became self-estranged. And this self-estrangement was a very different matter from that which took place through the friendly and enlightening and inspiring, or at the very worst rather mysterious δαιμόνια and divinities whose visitations were assumed by Hellenism. For this time it was the Jew who was affected. And where else but in the Jewish world could there be the spiritual vacuum in which he existed ? Necessarily the Jew saw deeper than others. He saw that the δαιμόνια were πνεύματα ἀκάθαρτα or πονηρά, messengers of Satan, like that which troubled Paul according to 2 Cor 12[7]. They were not, of course, confined to the Jewish world, but it was only in the Jewish world that their true nature was perceived. And in the course of its general and detailed historical development the Christian community saw that the obstacles and opponents of the Gospel (Eph. 6[12] ; 1 Tim. 4[1]), and especially heathen worship (1 Cor. 10[20f.] ; Rev. 9[20]), were really the work of demonic spirits of this type.

In this matter, then, we have to free ourselves, particularly in relation to the Gospel records, from the basically subjectivistic habit of thinking and speaking which would have it *either* that Jesus accommodated Himself in the interests of pedagogy to the current Judaistic idea (the suggestion of earlier Rationalists), *or* that He was Himself a prisoner of this view (the modern alternative). It is, of course, also a matter of " ideas," but primarily and decisively it is a matter of objective facts, which cannot as such be jeopardised by a demonstration that the ideas in question are conditioned and limited. The truth was this. Jesus did in fact live in this Judaistic actuality with its presuppositions, which were not only subjective but also objective, not only anthropological but also theological and therefore cosmological. Like all other Jews therefore, but in a way which was incomparably more exact than all others, He saw and experienced what there was actually to be seen and experienced : an abyss of darkness which was not merely supposed or imagined or invented or projected into the sphere of being but was actual and concrete ; the presence and action of nothingness, of the evil in the background and foreground of human existence. He saw and experienced man as he was, invisibly, but also visibly, and in any case really, claimed and imprisoned by this actuality, terrified of his human environment and therefore chained, constantly breaking his chains and really suffering in the freedom won in this way, " possessed " by nothingness in one or other of its different forms, inescapably delivered up to it, corrupted even in the forefront of his being by this corruptive background of the human situation. All this was at issue in the exorcisms of Jesus. And that is why they have a representative as well as an intrinsic importance, characterising the trend or direction of His whole activity. Like His raisings from the dead, they reveal the total and absolutely victorious clash of the kingdom of God with nothingness, with the whole world of the chaos negated by God, with the opposing realm of darkness. Far beyond the sin and guilt of man, but also far beyond His need and tragedy, even beyond death itself, the activity of Jesus invaded at this point the sphere of that power which was introduced into the cosmos by the sin and guilt of man and works itself out in his need and tragedy, enslaving all creatures. It penetrated to the poisonous source whose effluents reach out to the whole cosmos and characterise its form as that of " this present evil æon " (Gal. 1[4]).

What was at issue for Jesus, as the tradition saw it, emerges in the terribly drastic and morally rather questionable image of Mk. 3[27] : " No man can enter into a strong man's house, and spoil his goods, except he will first bind the strong man ; and then he will spoil his house." Luke gives it a more martial turn : " When a strong man armed keepeth his palace, his goods are in peace : but when a stronger than he shall come upon him, and overcome him, he taketh from all his armour wherein he trusted, and divideth his spoils " (Lk. 11[21f.]). This is how Jesus acts in His exorcisms. He does not put new patches on old clothes. He goes to the root of the evil. Like the stronger man who comes upon the strong, He takes up the battle for man, the distinctive battle of the kingdom of God, at the point where a definite decision must be reached, where only one or the other can be the Lord, where one must yield to the other. " And Jesus rebuked him saying, Hold thy peace, and come out of him " (Mk. 1[25]). " Come out of the man, thou unclean spirit " (Mk. 5[8]). And the comment of the people : " What a word is this ! for with authority and power he commandeth the unclean spirits, and they come out " (Lk. 4[36]). And this total war and victory can be followed by the plundering of the house of the strong man, the dividing of the spoils, the forgiving of man's sins, the comforting of the sad and the healing of the sick. The peculiar feature in these passages is the absolute radical-ism of the attack of Jesus in reflection of that vexation of God Himself.

For here, and here alone, it is not only the sufferer with his cry for help who speaks, but on the tongue and lips of the sufferer that which imprisons and torments him, the demon or demons. Sickness does not speak. Nor does death. But the demons, the indefinable concretions of indefinable chaos as the true enemies of God and His kingdom—they speak and cry out. They do not do so in the name and on behalf of the sufferers. For they are enemies of the sufferers and not friends. If the latter are to be helped it will be in spite of them. On the other hand, they do not speak and shout out (as we might expect) blasphemies or protests or warcries. What we hear is that the darkness of which they are the concretion finds itself threatened and in supreme danger, and recognises that this is the case. It is more sharpsighted than all the men concerned. It sees with whom and what it has to do in this confrontation with Jesus. It knows that although it is accustomed to sheer victory and the assertion of its dominion, it has met its master. The inspirer of fear in others, it is now itself afraid. We see this in Mk. 1^{24} : " What have we to do with thee, thou Jesus of Nazareth ? art thou come to destroy us ? I know thee, who thou art, the Holy One of God." For here we have a confession in the form of the dreadful cry of a routed army. And this is what the demons say in all the passages. It is all that chaos can say in the presence of Jesus. What was manifested in the presence of Jesus is that chaos has no message of its own, nothing to say in its own cause. It cannot have in any case. But it needed Jesus to reveal that this is actually so.

There is a grotesque side to the matter. We have only to think of the story of the demoniac in Mk. 5^1 and par. Someone has described it as a burlesque. And why not ? For all its final seriousness what happens to evil in its confronta-tion with Jesus is grotesque and (if we like) farcical. In Lk. 10^{18}, for example, it tumbles down from heaven. And in this story it can only ask for permission to go, itself unclean, into the herd of unclean swine, to plunge with them over the cliff into the lake and to be drowned, thus perishing finally from the world. If only the community had let it rest at that, or learned again not merely to laugh, but genuinely to rejoice at this sign and what it so drastically signified !

Finally, it belongs to the grotesque side of the matter, although in a rather grim sense, that the accusation was made against John the Baptist (Mt. 11^{18}) and even against Jesus Himself according to the Johannine tradition (7^{20}, 8^{48}, 10^{20}) : " He has a devil," i.e., He is Himself a victim of the slavery from which He dares to try to free others, and He is this as and because He tries to accom-plish this inconceivably bold and comprehensive action. The accusation is even sharper in the Synoptics : " He hath Beelzebub, and by the prince of the devils casteth he out devils " (Mk. 3^{22} and par.). The reply of Jesus was given " in parables," and it was profoundly ironical : " How can Satan cast out Satan ? And if a kingdom be divided against itself, that kingdom cannot stand. And if a house be divided against itself, that house cannot stand. And if Satan rise up against himself, and be divided, he cannot stand, but hath an end." The meaning is obviously that he would have an end even if they were right in their wild supposition. But the supposition is a thoroughly bad one. That is why the darkest of all the sayings of Jesus occurs just after these " parables " (at any rate in Mark and Matthew)—the saying about blaspheming against the Holy Ghost which makes those who commit it guilty of an eternal sin for which there can be no forgiveness. " Because they said, He hath an unclean spirit " (v. 30). If they knew what they were saying, they had called the clean unclean, the holy unholy, the good bad, life death, the kingdom of God the kingdom of Satan, a self-exalting Satan. They had ranged themselves on the side of the demons. They had confessed that evil alone has actuality. And in so doing they had automatically excluded themselves from liberation, from the new æon, from the proclamation of forgiveness and salvation and the reception of both, from all hope. We do not read that Jesus is angry or indignant at this accusation. It is merely obvious that He has nothing more to say to those who think and speak in this way—not even that they have fallen into this sin. He simply draws their attention to this sin. If they have fallen into it, it is their own doing and not His. They have ranged themselves with the demons, and they must share their fate, the utter nothingness of that which is not.

Reviewing the whole of this fourth statement, we may say that the miracles of Jesus, especially in their most offensive forms, the raisings from the dead and the exorcisms, are quite clearly military actions, fulfilled by Jesus in the service of God, as accomplishments of His own work, and therefore as declarations of His will and essence, as manifestations of the nature and character of His kingdom. In this respect the words : " He rebuked the wind, and said unto the sea, Peace, be still " (Mk. 4³⁹), might be used as a text or heading for all these stories. The activity of Jesus, and revealed in it God Himself and His kingdom, are a defiance of the power of destruction which enslaves man, of φθορά in all its forms. They are not a neutral force or omnipotence, but the omnipotence of mercy—not quiet and passive mercy, but a mercy which is active, and therefore hostile to that power on behalf of poor man. It is with this that we have to do in the miracles of Jesus. And it is because we have to do with this that they are miracles. For what is miraculous and new and incomprehensible in them (from every standpoint, not merely from a scientific but from an ethical and religious and even an æsthetic) is that God is a God who for man's sake cannot stand aside in this matter, who cannot rest, whose sabbath—entered already by Himself, and with Him and under His lordship to be entered also by man—is a day of His worship, joy and peace.

5. As a final consideration in our discussion of the general nature of the concrete activity of Jesus we must again emphasise and underline a decisive element in what we have so far said—that it is gloriously free grace in which the man Jesus acts and which is active and revealed in His action as the truth and reality of God Himself. We have seen that the fact that man is a sinner and therefore the enemy of God is not taken into account or imputed to man in these merciful and warlike actions of Jesus. The whole perversion of the heart and attitude of man emerges here and there on the margin, but only on the extreme margin. From what we are told of Him, Jesus is not really concerned with what from the anthropological point of view is the cause of human misery, but only with the misery itself and as such. In these passages it is not at the side of the bad man but the suffering man that He, God Himself, sets Himself. It is to the help of the sufferer that He comes. And that He does so is quite undeserved by him, the creature, this cosmic being. It is ɔimply and exclusively because this is the good will of God for him.

3. *The Royal Man*

Looking back, we may well ask with amazement how it was that the Reformation, and (apart from a few exceptions) the whole of earlier and especially more recent Protestantism as it followed both Luther and Calvin, could overlook this dimension of the Gospel which is so clearly attested in the New Testament—its power as a message of mercifully omnipotent and unconditionally complete liberation from φθορά, death and wrong as the power of evil. How could Protestantism as a whole, only too faithful to Augustine, the " father of the West," orientate itself in a way which was so one-sidedly anthropological (by the problem of repentance instead of by its presupposition—the kingdom of God) ? In other words, how could it become such a moralistic affair—so dull, so indifferent to the question of man himself, and therefore so lacking in joy ? How could it possibly overlook the fact that it was depriving even its specific doctrine of justification and sanctification of so radiant a basis and confirmation by not looking very differently at the character of the self-revelation of God in the Son of Man as it emerges in the miracles of Jesus, in these works of God ; by not considering the freedom of the grace which appeared in Him ? And in spite of its many saints and their many miracles, there is nothing much to be learned in this respect from Western Catholicism, with its almost exclusive concentration on the work of man in canon law, mysticism and a correct social and perfect monastic morality. From the Reformers we can at least know what free grace might be, and therefore learn, perhaps, to recognise its radicalism as revealed in the miracles of Jesus. But where the Reformers were opposed and the doctrine of free grace completely rejected, it seems that an almost hopeless barrier was set up to any advance in this direction. It puts us to shame, however, that in its strange and contradictory fashion the Eastern Church has not ceased to see and to take seriously what has to be seen at this point—and seen in a way which is completely new for us troubled Westerners.

The time has now come finally to emphasise the connexion which emerges in the New Testament passages between the actions of Jesus and the faith of the men to whom and among whom they occur. This is sometimes so distinct that if we are really to understand the general nature or direction of the miracles of Jesus we cannot possibly ignore it.

In Mk. 11²³ the saying about the faith which can move mountains is introduced in relation to the cursing of the fig-tree. In Mt. 17²⁰, however, its connexion is with the failure of the disciples to cure the epileptic boy, and in Lk. 17⁶ (where it is a tree that is moved) it is Jesus' answer to the request : " Increase our faith." In the two latter versions a new feature as compared with Mark is the comparison with the grain of mustard seed, which obviously implies that what is needed is not a great or massive or heroic or striking faith, easily recognisable as such, but that even a minimum faith is enough for the performance of what is impossible (a miracle) to men. This faith as a grain of mustard seed, to which the promise is given, obviously has nothing whatever to do with the little faith which is so common in Matthew, which always has the form of direct speech (ὀλιγόπιστοι), and which is used always as a term of reproach, indicating a faith which is doubtful and vacillating, as in Mt. 14³¹. What is meant is clearly a faith which is minimal and insignificant from the quantitative standpoint (in respect of its physical intensity or power of external manifestation), but distinguished by a definite quality even in this supreme littleness. Those who have this faith are promised that their word will have the power to reduce even a mountain to this unaccustomed " obedience " (Lk. 17⁶). " And nothing shall be impossible unto you " (Mt. 17²⁰). In all three versions the saying has to do with the faith to which the disciples are called for the fulfilment of their commission in the world. They, too, are to preach the kingdom of God which has drawn near, not only in words but, as we are told with a startling definiteness in Mt. 10[8], by healing the sick, raising the dead, cleansing the lepers, driving out demons. We will return to this commission, and thus to the saying about this faith as a grain of mustard seed, at a much later stage, when we have to speak of the sending out of the community into the world. But the saying is important in our present context because, in general terms, it describes the faith which stands in a positive relationship to miracles as one which is definitely qualified— so qualified that even where it is present only in the minutest quantity it is the faith which has the promise of the performance of miracles.

This particular faith is obviously meant when Jesus reproves His disciples after the calming of the storm, asking : " Why are ye so fearful ? how is it that ye have no faith ? " (Mk. 4[40]) ; or when He encourages the ruler of the synagogue : " Be not afraid, only believe " (Mk. 5[36]) ; or when He asks the two blind men : " Believe ye that I am able to do this ? ", and when they reply that they do, says to them : " According to your faith be it unto you " (Mt. 9[28f.]) ; or when He says to the hesitating father of the epileptic boy : " All things are possible to him that believeth " (Mk. 9[23]) ; or when it is said that He saw the faith of those who uncovered the roof where He was and let down the bed on which the sick of the palsy lay (Mk. 2[4f.]) ; or when He says to the woman of Canaan : " O woman, great is thy faith : be it unto thee even as thou wilt " (Mt. 15[28]) ; or when He says of the centurion of Capernaum : " I have not found so great faith, no, not in Israel " (Mt. 8[10]) ; or when finally the short stereotyped formula occurs twice in Mark, once in Matthew and four times in Luke : " Thy faith hath saved thee " (ἡ πίστις σου σέσωκέ σε). With only one exception (Lk. 7[50]), this always stands in relation to the occurrence of a miracle, and in almost every instance it is clearly brought into direct connexion with the actual moment or event of its occurrence, which it seems to describe and explain ; whereas the other sayings that we have quoted (apart from the rebuke of the disciples) look forward to a moment of occurrence which has still to come. In every case it is obvious that in the twofold sense of that saying we have to do with the faith which it calls faith as a grain of mustard seed. That is to say, it is a faith which (a) is insignificant as regards its external appearance, and usually has to be the subject either of enquiry or even a definite demand. In many cases it is the faith of Gentiles, and never of those who habitually stand in faith or can point to it in any recognisable form. But it is also (b) a faith which for all its insignificance has a specific nature or quality in relation to which there is the prospect of a miracle, and in the light of which (according to that formula) it can, if it has it, be explained as that which brings about the miracle. And it is quite obvious from the Gospel records that Jesus definitely expected to find this faith as a grain of mustard seed in His actions, and that He did in fact meet with it.

What is this quality of the faith which has a share in the working of miracles and which Jesus expects or misses or sometimes welcomes in men ? What is it that makes it a faith which, even though it is no greater than a grain of mustard seed, can move mountains—a faith for which all things are possible ? What is this πίστις of which that formula can even say that it saves men ? This first question is decided by our explanation of the saying in Mt. 9[28], which is the only concrete indication in the Synoptics of the actual content of faith : " Believe ye that I am able to do this ? " (ὅτι δύναμαι τοῦτο ποιῆσαι). This might be taken to mean : Do you really accept the fact, are you convinced, that beyond and above the natural and human possibilities which you know there may be a higher possibility which you do not know, perhaps an absolute and unconditional possibility, which is so great and wonderful that it can, for example, make the blind to see ? Are you really persuaded that I control this higher possibility, and that if I will I can do this for you, giving you sight ? " Believe ye that I am able to do this ? " would then mean : " Do you believe in miracles, and that I can work miracles ? " But it is plain that a " faith " of this kind would be faith in Jesus only in so far as the two blind men accepted Him as a bearer and agent of this higher power who could of course be replaced by any other human person similarly gifted and equipped. It is plain that it would be faith in God, if at all, only in so far as they might (but did not necessarily) regard this power as the power of God or a God—a name which could easily be replaced by any other, e.g., by "higher nature" or even "super-nature." It is plain, finally, that it would as such be a strong philosophical conviction to this effect, fashioned as such convictions are usually fashioned and now finding this necessary and willing *ad hoc* expression. But was this really the faith for which Jesus asked, which they confessed with their : "Yea, Lord," and which He then had in mind when He answered (v. 29) : "According to your faith be it unto you"? Again, was this really the faith which He missed in His disciples during the storm, or which He found in the centurion and the woman of Canaan and those who bore the sick of the palsy ; the faith to which He summoned the ruler of the synagogue ; the faith which has the promise that all things are possible to it, even the moving of a mountain ; the faith of which He can say again and again that it hath saved thee ? It is surely evident that if this explanation of the question is correct, the way in which the word "faith" is here (and in other passages) used by Jesus according to the tradition is very different from the use of πίστις and πιστεύειν in the rest of the New Testament, and is at variance even with the literal sense of the terms. It is not with a philosophical possibility and its supposed realisation that faith is concerned in the New Testament, nor is it from anything of this sort that it receives its nature and form. Is there any reason, then, why the present instances should be an exception ?

It is to be noted, however, that the cry of the two blind men is actually : "Thou Son of David, have mercy on us." They do not turn to a wonderworker who, if he had not been Jesus of Nazareth, might well have been someone else. They turn to Jesus as the King of Israel, beside whom there can be no other. They do not ask concerning the operation of an anonymous higher power or omnipotence, nature or super-nature. They ask concerning the act of the God of Israel fulfilling His promise in the existence of the Son of David. Their cry is not inspired by any conviction (even a supernaturalistic), nor is it uttered with the corresponding expectation. It is a cry for mercy wrung out of their misery. Above all, it is a cry in which they recognise and confess the Son of David and therefore the God of Israel and His fulfilled promise, taking Him seriously and claiming Him for their own need. Therefore what they are asked is whether they did really believe this (τοῦτο) as their cry seemed to suggest. Did they really believe that the Son of David and therefore the God of Israel had come, and that He would have mercy on them, and could take their misery from them and dismiss it from the world ? Did they really believe that He, Jesus, had the power to do this ? And it is as they confessed this faith that Jesus touched their eyes and Himself confessed their faith : "According to (this) your faith be it unto you." And what took place was not at all unusual or strange—except that it had the strangeness, the newness, of the kingdom of God which had drawn near. "Their eyes were opened."

We may now consider the other passages to see if the faith demanded or missed or found by Jesus did not always have this nature and form in which it corresponds, although with a peculiar intensity, to the meaning of the term and its use in the rest of the New Testament. Generally speaking, is it not always the privileged and characteristic act of sufferers afflicted with a vital physical need in their relationship to the faithful God of Israel fulfilling His promise, which means, concretely, in their relationship to Jesus the Deliverer, in whom the hope of Israel has found its fulfilment ? When we are told in these passages that men believed, this means that they were in this relationship, which is only secondarily a matter of mind or will or disposition and primarily a matter of being. They belonged already to Jesus the Deliverer because they were already found by Him before they knew Him, because they were recognised by Him. They thus responded with their own recognition of Him as Lord. They had the freedom—this is the climax reached in these passages—to throw themselves and their vital physical need at His feet as it were, and in His person at the feet of the faithful God of Israel. They had the freedom to recognise and confess and claim Him as the One who could save them totally and therefore in this affliction, thus healing them physically, making them whole, restoring to them a normal life, rescuing them from the threatening power of death. He was under no compulsion to do this. But He could do it. For the fact that He had come from God as Israel's Saviour, that He was present with them as such and present in this way, that they belonged to Him as sufferers, and could count themselves His, and throw themselves at His feet and beseech Him—all this was God's free and absolutely unmerited grace, His sheer pity, to His people, to the world, to each individual, and therefore to them. They were thus confronted with the fact that, as an overflowing of this mercy, their Saviour saw also their particular physical need and could avert and remove and take it from them. There was no question, of course, of His having to do this, of their having a right to demand it, for in relation to Him they had no right to assert, no claim to anything. But they had the freedom to trust Him for this overflow of His mercy, to be absolutely certain that in the power of His free grace He could also do this. The freedom of this confidence was the faith to which He called some, which He missed in others, and sometimes found. The distinctive feature of the New Testament faith in miracles is that it was faith in Jesus and therefore in God as the faithful and merciful God of the covenant with Israel ; and that in this way and as such it was this confidence in His power.

Alongside Mt. $9^{27f.}$ we should set the story of the man born blind in Jn. $9^{1f.}$ As a commentary on the " Believe ye that I am able to do this " it is all the more instructive because the decisive question is now explicitly raised (v. 35) : " Dost thou believe on the Son of man ? "—and the whole story takes place in reverse as it were, thus reflecting as in a mirror the answer to our problem. This time the miracle takes place right at the beginning. We are given an active demonstration of the free grace of God in the specific form of the removal of the blindness of this man. In the first instance no question is raised either as to the sin of the man or his parents or as to the faith of the man, who has not even expressed a desire for healing. He is simply given his sight, almost, as it were, over his head, and quite irrespective of what he was or was not in relation to Jesus. " The works of God were to be made manifest in him " (v. 3). When Jesus had anointed his eyes, he had only to obey, to wash in the pool of Siloam, and he could see, and those around realised that he could see. In the long interrogation to which he was subjected he could only say that it was " a man that is called Jesus " (v. 11) who had done this, and given him this command, so that he could now see. When he was pressed, he admitted that he regarded Jesus as a prophet (v. 17). He gave no judgment whether or not He was a sinner (v. 25), but then argued, rather more loudly, that He could hardly have this power from God if He was a sinner. " But if any man be a worshipper of God (θεοσεβής), and doeth his will, him he heareth " (v. 31). And : " If this man were not of God, he could do nothing " (v. 33). When he said this he was cast out by the Pharisees with the explanation that he, too, was a sinner, and if anything even more so than Jesus (" altogether born in sins," v. 34). But this again obviously took place over his head as the text sees it, for he did not realise the true meaning and significance of what he said. His role is only that of object and not subject in the whole occurrence and the disturbance which it caused. But Jesus now meets him a second time (v. 35 f.), and He asks him directly, without any preparation or explanation : " Dost thou believe on the Son of man ? " He replies with a counter-question which clearly betrays his ignorance : " Who is he, Lord, that I might believe on him ? And Jesus said unto him, Thou hast both seen him, and it is he that talketh with thee. And he said, Lord, I believe. And he worshipped him " (προσεκύνησεν αὐτῷ).

In the first instance, therefore, we have simply the presence of Jesus in face of this little piece of human misery. In the first instance the sufferer experiences the mighty action of His pity and is enabled to see. For a long time there neither is nor can be any talk of his faith, but only of its object, only of the One in whom He was ultimately able and forced to confess that he believed, and before whom he then prostrated himself as before the presence and revelation of God Himself. And in the first instance it is only as through a veil that we even see this object of his faith. He does not reveal Himself as such to this blind man who could later see. The reference is only to the " man that is called Jesus," whom the Pharisees, unable to deny what had so obviously taken place, described as a sinner, and in respect of whom the healed man himself could only appeal again and again to what had happened, to the fact that he could now see. More under pressure than of himself, he is ready to go to the length of saying that he does not regard Jesus as a sinner, but as One who fears God. But that is all. Yet it is not quite all, for there is another side to the matter which emerges even under this veil. This is that the blind man obeyed Jesus and, in contrast to his more cautious parents (v. 18 f.), steadfastly confessed both the favour which he had received and the One who had conferred it—and whom he knew only by name. He finally allowed even the very dangerous saying to be wrested from him that He was necessarily from God. Are we not forced to see and say that he obviously belonged factually, objectively and ontologically to the Unknown who had done this. " Thou art his disciple " was the accusation of the Pharisees (v. 28), and they at once understood and condemned his final saying as a definite confession, casting him out as a sinner, making him as it were from the very first a witness who suffered with Him. This factual, objective, ontological reality—that Jesus was with Him and therefore, although he did not know it, he was with Jesus—was brought to light by Jesus' question concerning his faith. We are not speaking about a concealed faith of the man himself, but about its real presupposition—who and what Jesus was for him, and who and what he himself was for Jesus, even before he believed. For Jesus was for him the One who brought the free grace of God in its overflow as physical healing. And he was for Jesus the one who received this overflow, and was therefore confronted with Jesus as the One who brought this free grace. The two stood in this relationship the one to the other. They were genuinely bound together in this way. Without desiring it, without even understanding it, blind in this respect too, he had actually experienced what the Son of Man could do. This was the real presupposition of his faith. It had now only to be brought to light, as took place in the final conversation. The One whose capacity, whose power, the blind man had experienced, who had given him his sight, and could therefore bless him, was far more than a mere prophet or a man who feared God. He was the Son of Man whom all the prophets and those that feared God in Israel had hoped for and expected. He was the merciful God of Israel in the act of fulfilling His promises. It was only natural that as an Israelite he should be ready to believe in the God of Israel and therefore in the Son of Man. But what was the value of this readiness when he did not see the One in whom he was prepared to believe, when he did not recognise the One who fulfilled the divine promises ? " Who is he, Lord, that I might believe on him ? " He really did not see or know Him, although He was not merely able to be seen and known, but corporally present as the neighbour who had shown this mercy on him and was already believed in virtue of this demonstrated power. But this door could not be opened from outside. It could be opened only from inside, by Jesus Himself. As the Son of Man made Himself known to him—" it is he that talketh with thee "—He opened the eyes of faith as well as the physical eyes. With irresistible power, it took place that he was awakened and called to faith. He was hurled into that *proskynesis* as though he had been struck by lightning. All the different elements were necessary for this to happen : the factual, objective, ontological relationship between Jesus and Himself ; in this relationship the miracle of free grace in its overflow ; the physical encounter with Jesus as the actualisation of this relationship ; and again, and supremely, the decisive fact that Jesus Himself spoke of Himself, that of Himself He gave Himself to be known by him through His Word, that as the object of his faith, which He was already, He made Himself also the Creator of his faith.

The remarkable lesson of Jn. 9¹ᶠ· is that man starts at the very point (the miracle of Jesus and therefore Jesus Himself and therefore God) to which we see him moving in Mt. 9²⁷. Faith is not merely his entrance into the kingdom of God revealed in the miracle, but also his exit from it. It is not merely the root, but the fruit. To sum up, it is faith qualified in this twofold sense—man's turning to Jesus and His power upon the basis of the fact that Jesus has turned to man in His power. When all this is borne in mind, faith in miracles as the New Testament sees it cannot possibly be confused with the monstrosity of an acceptance of the possibility and actuality of all kinds of miracles of omnipotence.

And now we must address ourselves to another problem which forces itself upon us in this matter. This is the question of the connexion which links faith to miracle on the one hand, and miracle to faith on the other.

Let us take the second aspect of the question first. What is the way which leads from miracle to faith ? In the light of the story in Jn. 9¹ᶠ· it can hardly be contested that the connexion does also have this direction, that it does also include in itself this way. And this finds theoretical and rather harsh formulation in Jn. 10³⁷ᶠ· : " If I do not the works of my Father, believe me not. But if I do, though ye believe not me, believe the works : that ye may know, and believe, that the Father is in me, and I in him." It is likely enough that Jn. 4⁴⁸ is also to be understood in this positive sense : " Except ye see signs and wonders, ye will not believe." And in the first ending of the Fourth Gospel in 20³¹ we again have the categorical statement that the signs which Jesus did in the presence of His disciples are written in this book " that ye might believe that Jesus is the Christ, the Son of God ; and that believing ye might have life through his name." It is unmistakeable that in the context of the life-act of Jesus as it calls to faith and awakens faith miracles have an important and, rightly understood, indispensable function. He would not have been the One He was if He had not also done these acts. And since, as the One He was, He was one long summons to faith in the action of God as it took place in Him, the power of His summons was also the power of His acts. But some clarifications are needed at this point. It is a matter of His acts in their specific character as the omnipotent acts of the mercy of the God of Israel acting and revealing Himself in faithfulness to His promise ; in their character as signs, as manifestations of the kingdom of God drawn near. They led to faith where they were seen and understood in this character, i.e., where Jesus Himself revealed Himself in them as the Bringer of the free grace of God addressed to men, and where He Himself was recognised as such by men. Their occurrence in itself and as such did not lead anyone to faith : " Though he had done so many miracles before them, yet they believed not on him " (Jn. 12³⁷)—but only to that θαυμάζειν. The only practical result could be the *cul de sac* which is described in Mt. 11²⁰ᶠ· in relation to the unrepentant cities of Galilee. Indeed, there might even be a heightening and explosion of the offence already taken at Him, as we see from John's presentation. At the conclusion of the story of Lazarus (Jn. 11⁴⁷ᶠ·) it was the acts of Jesus which led the council to resolve on His destruction because of the fear that the people might be influenced. It was not at all the case that in themselves and as such the acts led to faith—merely as the unusual phenomena as which they immediately presented themselves to everyone's notice. They were not mechanically effective instruments to produce faith. They were not what they are presupposed to be in the question of Jn. 6³⁰ : " What sign shewest thou then, that we may see, and believe thee ? " If they were demanded from Jesus as necessary conditions of the faith which He expected, as " miraculous credentials," —" He sighed deeply in his spirit " (Mk. 8¹¹ᶠ· and par.) and refused to do them. His concrete aim in acting—and all His acts have a definite individual end—was to help, to do good, in His conflict for man against the power of chaos and death which oppresses him. And in this concrete form His action was that of the Bringer and Revealer of the kingdom. Those who did not ask for His mercy, and therefore for the Son of David, the Son of Man, for the faithfulness and omnipotence of the God of Israel, asked in vain for the acts of Jesus, and, even if they saw them, saw them in vain. They might well see an act of power, but they did not see the sign of the coming kingdom. They could not come to faith in this way. The Word of Jesus was needed to expound His acts, to light them up from within, as the acts of the mercy of God, the warlike acts of the Deliverer, the promised King of Israel who had now appeared, and therefore as the signs of the kingdom of God which had now drawn near. And it needed obedience to the Word of Jesus to accept this exposition, to receive the light which shone in His acts, and to awaken to faith in so doing. The mere fact that His acts took place was not then an infallible means to this result, any more than the mere fact that His words·were spoken. It was only Jesus Himself, acting in His words and works, who infallibly led men to faith. He did so as He was " mighty in deed and word before God and all the people " (Lk. 24¹⁹). But it was He Himself who did so in and through both His deeds and words. Thus the faith awakened by both, by the totality of His life-act, was faith in Himself, in the One who had sent Him and was in Him, in God's free grace. It was a faith in miracles, but it was a concrete and not an abstract faith in miracles, a faith which was directed by the miracles to the One who did them, to His purpose, to the revelation which took place in Him, to the mercy of God active in Him. Both in the Synoptics and in John, therefore, faith (even though it may be faith in miracles in the concrete sense that it has its origin in a miracle) is not at all faith in the miracles, or the inconceivability of their happening, or, generally, in their possibility or actuality. On the contrary, it is a recognition—in the light of the miracle which has happened, inspired and instructed and awakened and evoked by its happening, by its specific inconceivability—of the One who has acted in this inconceivable way, of the will and purpose and lordship of the One who has spoken through these acts of power and mercy, giving Himself to be known by them as the Son of David, the Son of Man, the King in the kingdom of free grace. It is to Him and not to the miracle that the believer gives his attention and interest. It is to Him and not to the miracle that he gives the glory. In all the majestic incomprehensibility of the miracle He Himself is the true and decisive factor which makes it incomprehensible. It is a miracle which He does, but what counts is He Himself and not the miracle. What is learned from the miracle is who and what He is—the Lord. It might just as well have been learned from His Word. Sometimes it has already been learned from His Word. That is why there is no strict pragmatics in the New Testament. There is no rule that must always derive in practice from the experience of miracle. Even the Word of Jesus is an incomprehensible act. It has the dimension of miracle. It has the character of an act of divine mercy and power. That is why the two blind men in Mt. 9²⁷ᶠ· (as distinct from the man born blind in Jn. 9¹ᶠ·), and many others in the New Testament, do not derive their faith from a miracle which they have already experienced, but go forward to the miracle which they are to experience with hands which seem to be empty. It is decisive, however, for the true hearing of the Word of Jesus that it, too, should belong to this dimension, that the faith which is based on a hearing of His Word should have this dimension, that it should therefore be faith in the One who in the mercy and power of God can also work miracles. To the extent that Jesus Himself is the One who is "mighty in deed and word," to the extent that He is not only light but as such life, there is no faith that does not have its origin also in miracle, that does not in some way rest on the miracles of Jesus, or, more precisely, on Jesus Himself as the great Wonderworker. If Jesus had not been this, how could He have been the Bringer of the kingdom of God, and therefore recognisable as the Saviour of man from the power of the devil and death ? How could His Word have been distinguished from purely moral teaching and religious instruction, such as could be and was actually given by the scribes ? How could it have proved itself to be a Word of power, the proclamation of the dawn of a new age ? Jn. 10³⁷ is relevant in this connexion : " If I do not the works of my Father, believe me not." And if in faith in Him it could have been overlooked and concealed that He was the great Wonderworker, how could faith really have as its theme and content Himself as the herald of the kingdom of God, and not just a deserving benefactor and individual and social reformer ? Jn. 4⁴⁸ may well have a lesson for us at this point : " Except ye see signs and wonders, ye will not believe." The necessity of the way from miracle to faith is ultimately grounded in the fact that a total faith, i.e., a faith which grasps the total liberation and renewal of man in Jesus, can derive only from the totality in which Jesus is really the Saviour of men and manifest as such.

But there is also a way which leads from faith to miracle. We will tackle the question at its most difficult point and ask point-blank what is really meant by the formula : " Thy faith hath saved thee " ? And our explanation will be decisive for an understanding of the function assigned to faith in other passages where sufferers are asked to believe in relation to acts of power for which they ask or which they simply need. It makes matters easier (in spite of appearances to the contrary) that the formula is not as Luther translated it : " Thy faith hath helped thee." The word " help " is weaker, but it so easily suggests something that Luther himself obviously did not intend—that there is a partial co-operation of man in the occurrence of the miracle which happens to him. But the original σέσωκέν σε (" hath saved thee ") does not refer merely to a part of the process. It refers to the whole. I maintain that this eases the exegetical situation because it does at least exclude the idea of a co-operation in the working of the miracle. " Saving " is an action in which there is a saviour and a saved, but not a co-operation of the two. The general reference of the formula is to man's salvation generally from the power of darkness, but also and concretely from the specific physical ailments which afflict him, the curing of his eyes or ears or limbs, his preservation from the lordship of φθορά which threatens and torments him. Of this salvation the formula seems to say that it is altogether the act and work of man, of his faith. The contradiction to which this gives rise seems unavoidable and intolerable. For is it not Jesus, and in what He says and does God, who saves man in both the general and the concrete sense ? " Jesus Christ maketh thee whole " (Ac. 9³⁴), says Peter to Aeneas. How is it, then, that in this formula man's faith can be called the saviour ? The obvious difficulty is sharply brought out by the puzzling relationship between two other sayings of Jesus. For in Mk. 10²⁷ we read : " With God all things are possible," but in Mk. 9²³ : " All things are possible to him that believeth." The problem would be vexatiously insoluble if we did not remember that in the miracle stories and throughout the New Testament faith is only secondarily described as a disposition or attitude or act of man. It is this, but the decisive thing is that it also reaches behind this whole sphere to a primary thing from which it proceeds as a human action when man is awakened and called to it. In the New Testament sense the word " faith " does not only describe the believing thought and knowledge and confession and activity of man. It also embraces the presupposition of all these things, which as such does not belong to the mental sphere, but the sphere of reality. We have called it the factual, objective, ontological standing of man—not all men, but certain men—in a concrete relationship with Jesus Christ and the God who is active and revealed in Him. Those who believe do so in this status—because, as Paul says, they are " in Christ," they belong to Him, they are set at His side. It is in virtue of this that they believe. The act or work of their faith derives from their being, just as a shoot does from a root. Who can say where the root ends and the shoot begins ? What is a shoot if it no longer grows from the root (as on a tree-trunk which has been cut down) ? Is not the only sure distinction between the two the fact that the one is visible and the other is not ? Those who believe in the New Testament sense do so, as their own free act, because they have the freedom to do so from the One in whom they believe. And in the exercise of this freedom they reach back to that which is before their faith and independent of it. They cling to Jesus, to the God active and revealed in Him. And they are sustained by this ontological reality both behind and before. Or rather, they are drawn and set in motion by it like an iron bar by a magnet, and in such a way, again, that it is futile to try to differentiate between the attraction and their own movement. The secret of faith is that as the work of man it has this origin and this goal. That is why Heb. 11¹ can call it the ὑπόστασις or actuality of that which is hoped for and the ἔλεγχος or demonstration of that which is not seen. That is why Paul can make the important statement in Rom. 3²¹ᶠ· that a man is not justified in the verdict of God, and therefore in truth, by any work that is demanded by the Law, but διὰ πίστεως, ἐκ πίστεως, πίστει, as πιστεύων. He is justified in truth because in faith he has both his origin and goal in this One who is in truth, in Jesus Christ. It is obviously in this sense that we can and may and must say that a man is saved, healthy, whole, preserved from death, by his faith ; that the experience of the divine act of mercy even in the physical sphere is not merely promised to his faith, but that faith itself is that which accomplishes it, the saviour ; that faith is that which redeems the believer from his own particular need, but also, as is presupposed in the charge to the disciples in Mt. 10⁸, that which by the ministry of the believer can and should redeem others from their specific needs. " All things are possible to him that believeth " (Mk. 9²³). " Said I not unto thee, that, if thou wouldest believe, thou shouldest see the glory of God ? " (Jn. 11⁴⁰). And again : " Verily, verily, I say unto you, He that believeth on me, the works that I do shall he do also ; and greater works than these shall he do " (Jn. 14¹²). Also : " He that believeth on me . . . out of his belly shall flow rivers of living water " (Jn. 7³⁸). We can accept these sayings because they are said to men about their faith by the One (Jesus Himself) whose sovereignty is not rivalled or diminished by what He ascribes to their faith (their πιστεύειν εἰς ἐμέ), but revealed in its full compass. When He says this about their faith He does not do despite to the glory of God, but gives it the greater praise. Everything would, of course, be obscured and falsified if we abstracted from the fact that in what is said about faith it is a matter of what He Himself ascribes to faith in Him, or if, in a further abstraction, we looked at the secondary means, at the human action of faith as such, at its mental fulfilment, thus regarding and admiring and broadcasting this aspect of faith, the believer himself, as the one who accomplishes the divine act, as his own saviour, and as the saviour of others in his ministry to them. The declaration of Heb. 11¹ and the Pauline doctrine of justification can only be obscured and falsified by these abstractions. If we are guilty of these abstractions, we need not be surprised if the way from faith to miracle seems both theoretically and practically to be one long absurdity which it is better to recognise and abandon as such, making a fresh start before the disillusionments and errors become too great. We understand all these sayings with the clarity and truth which they have as said by Jesus if we accept the fact that in the New Testament sense of the word the human action of faith can only represent the transition from this origin to this goal, from the free election of man to his free calling, or, to reduce it to its simplest and most concrete terms, from Jesus to Jesus : and if we then recognise that as this transition it has a real part in the being and power of this origin and goal, in Jesus Himself, from whom and to whom we can believe. When we look to the place from and to which faith goes we see in truth and clarity that it is indeed " the substance of things hoped for, the evidence of things not seen " ; that it does really justify the sinner ; that it does really save the sufferer and through him other sufferers ; that nothing is in fact impossible to it ; that the way from faith to miracle is indeed open and can be traversed. So great is the sovereignty of Jesus, and the glory of the God active and revealed in Him, that for faith in Him this way is actually open and can be traversed. These sayings do not claim too much if we let them say only what they do say, and let it be said by the One who said it. As faith in Him faith is actually that which saves man, and all things are actually possible for it. The inner delimitation of what is promised is self-evident. Because the reference is not to the human action of faith as such, but to it only in relation to its origin and goal, it does not ascribe to faith any possibilities or capacities that man might imagine or desire for himself or in the service of others, or that he might even try to assume in a burst (or better perhaps a spasm) of self-inspired credulity. It ascribes to it the true force in which Jesus Himself acted : the force of the kingdom of God drawn near ; of the faithfulness and mercy of the God of Israel ; of that spirit which is not a random spirit but the Holy Spirit. The way from faith to miracle would close at once—indeed, it would never be open—if the power of faith were desired and claimed as a power in which man had the capacity to do just as his desire or fancy led him. The promise is that as faith in Jesus and the God active and revealed in Him faith has the force which is proper to it under the discipline and in the concretion of this origin and goal, and in the exercise of which it is wholly and utterly this faith. But with this determination and limitation there is actually ascribed to it an unconditional force. We may well realise how very different is our own situation from that of the men of the New Testament at this point. But this need not prevent us from stating that the faith proclaimed in the New Testament and lived by men according to its witness was of such a kind that this unconditional force was ascribed and promised to it, and it could experience and exercise it. It had the freedom to do this.

To sum up, we may say that faith is a freedom. If we think and speak in New Testament terms we have also to say that it is not only the supreme but the true force of human freedom. For, as the freedom given to man (let us put it this way) by Jesus for Jesus, it is his freedom for intercourse with God, his freedom to be both from God and to God. Those who can have dealings with God as they are elected in Jesus and called by Jesus are free in the New Testament sense. And this does not have only the negative meaning that they are independent, but the positive that they are able and powerful. In the determination and limitation given them in their intercourse with God they are men of unconditional and unlimited capacity. They can think rightly and desire rightly, wait rightly and hasten rightly, obey rightly and defy rightly, begin rightly and end rightly, be with and for men rightly and by themselves rightly. They can do all these things and do them rightly—not as arbitrary or dilettante bunglers but diligently and efficiently—because in faith they have the freedom of God's partners ; not a freedom which they have chosen or sneaked or stolen or robbed, but the freedom for which God Himself has freed them. .It is because faith is the freedom granted to man by the grace of God that the believer can do all these things and do them rightly. In this origin which is also its goal, faith is contiguous with the free grace of God, and may be called its anthropological counterpart. And it is because in this fifth section of our explanation of the miracles which Jesus performed in fulfilment of the will and revelation of the kingdom of God we have called the free grace of God the meaning and power of these actions of Jesus that we have had to consider the term faith, which is brought clearly enough to our notice by the texts themselves, and forms this counterpart of grace. The faith which we have been investigating is that of those who had a part in the miracles of Jesus, and in all its contours and colours we see in it the one light of the mystery of all these miracles.

On the one hand there are men who move towards the action of Jesus as those who are absolutely needy and poor and suffering and in misery. The only thing is that they believe in Him, and that in this faith in Him they have the freedom to move towards Him, towards His action, as though the future were already present, as though the action had already been fulfilled. They have the freedom in a sense to anticipate its happening. This is what they do. And whence does their freedom derive except in the freedom of the grace of God, the grace which will work mightily in the occurrence of the miracle, but which is already mighty towards and in those who only move towards it, so that in their anticipatory faith they are themselves the anticipated, who have no option but to look forward with illimitable confidence to its occurrence ? The real truth is not that they themselves anticipate the miracle, but that they are anticipated by Jesus who performs the miracle, by the God active and revealed in Him. And He anticipates them by making them free for the faith in which they can move forward with irresistible steps to the miracle, or rather to the One who performs the miracle. He does it by causing it to shine as a light within them that He, Jesus, and God in Him, has remembered these poor sufferers, and is good and gracious to them in all their need and oppression, in all the darkness and corruption of their existence, without even asking who or what they are. The act of their faith is only their reaction to the shining of this light. As this reaction it is strong enough, not only to make them certain of the coming act of power in their deliverance, but to cause them to participate in it even before it happens, so that when it happens it is really their faith (as the free gift of the free grace of God, and its clear witness) which saves them, and in which they can also save others. Yet all this is not in their own name, but in the name of the One who has elected and called them.

On the other hand there are those who come already from the place to which the others are only moving ; those who have already received, who are already liberated and delivered, who see where they were blind, or walk where they were lame, or are no longer possessed, or have seen the liberation of their relatives, or have been witnesses of these acts of liberation without any direct participation on their own account. These acts have not taken place for them in vain if, quite apart from and contrary to their own expectation, without their demanding anything of this kind, they have been to them sudden signs (again like the shining of a light in a dark place) of the kingdom and its King, if they have revealed to them the Liberator, if by His action the Liberator has not merely restored to them the freedom of their eyes or ears or members or reason, but in and with this restoration has given them the completely new freedom to believe in Him and in the God active and revealed in Him. In the case of those who are made free to believe in retrospect of a miracle which has already occurred, what is it that really takes place in and with the miracle ? It means that they encounter a Lord who was previously unknown to them, but before whom they must prostrate themselves like the man born blind, because He has made Himself known as their Lord, the Lord who has control over them, but also as the Lord of the cosmos, who has power over all things. And yet He is not encountered by them just as a potentate, but as the King who has acted absolutely for them, who has fought for them, who has taken their side against all the enemies which afflict them, who has taken the side of the cosmos against all the forces which mar and disrupt it, who has made His own the cause both of the cosmos and of man. He is encountered by them as the Lord who has carried their cause, and that of the cosmos, to victory at a single point—it may be a cure in which only the sick themselves and perhaps their neighbours can possibly have any interest—but who has done this with supreme and illuminating force even at this tiny point. It is grace, free grace, grace which is powerful against the powers which bind all creatures, that has overtaken them. Or, conversely, it is freedom, absolute power, not just any power, but the power of grace, and therefore of the God who is the faithful Covenant-partner of man, who perseveres in His faithfulness even to man, who has contrived that even in man's unfaithfulness His own faithfulness should be maintained and demonstrated. Again, what is it that is given these men in this encounter—given them for their future way ? It is a new capacity, which, in whatever freedom they previously lived or thought they lived, they did not even remotely know. They will still live in this world and under its shadows. They can again become sick, and perhaps more seriously. They will necessarily die. To the very end they will have occasion to complain of their unfaithfulness to the faithful God. But in and through all these things they can now be quite free from any fear of the world or life or sin or hell. When they think of the grave, they can remember the grave which had to yield up Lazarus. When they think of Satan, they can picture him as the one who has been hurled down from the place which he had falsely usurped in heaven. When they think of demons, they can see them as those which have gone into the swine and perished in the waters. They can regard their own past and present and future sins as sins which are forgiven. They have no further need to study demonology, or to set up an independent doctrine *De peccato*, or to work out a theodicy. They have seen the signs of the kingdom and its King. They have seen Jesus as the Saviour of the whole man and the whole cosmos. They have seen Him after as the others saw Him before. And they can do all these things, not with a bravado and optimism which are not grounded in the facts, but with their gaze firmly fixed on Him ; in the freedom of the faith in Him which has been given them. And in this capacity of faith they merely reflect something which is much greater—the free grace of God disclosed in the miracles of Jesus, who at a specific point, in a way which is only localised and provisional, but for them unforgettable and indisputable, has overcome the world before their very eyes in a type of the very different triumph of His own resurrection and His return as the risen Christ.

We must now consider the distinctive element both in those who believe as they move towards the miracle of Jesus and those who believe as they come from them. What is it that the former desire in faith in Him, and the latter give thanks for in faith in Him ? We can only answer that it is something additional to what is usually connected with even a serious and profound and biblically determined conception of faith. On a normal view faith is to put our whole trust in God both for time and eternity, to expect all good things from Him and from Him all good things, and to do so in relation to Jesus Christ, in the confidence that for His sake God will be to us a Father, that in Him He will freely give us all things. On this normal view faith is the appropriation of the forgiveness of our sins as it took place in His death, the receiving of the Holy Spirit who gives us assurance of this and awakens us to a new life of obedience, the hope of the resurrection of the dead and everlasting life in which there can be no cessation of His onward movement. We may prefer some other formulation, but by and large this is a correct and complete statement of the norm or rule of Christian faith (and the expression *regula fidei* came into use quite early in the post-apostolic period). And there is nothing lacking in this rule except the additional element—the surplus, or, as we might almost say, the luxury—which constitutes the distinctive feature of the faith of those whom we see moving towards the miracles of Jesus, or coming from them, in the New Testament stories. The rule of faith may be understood quite generally as a description of the positive relationship of man to what is prospectively and retrospectively true for all in the light of the epiphany of Jesus Christ, to the divine truths of redemption which are to be proclaimed and heard in all ages and places. But the needy " Yes, Lord " of these men in their differing connexions with the miracles of Jesus cannot be understood only in this way. Their faith is apparently much less imposing than that of the general Christian *credo*, but it is a wholly concrete faith characterised by a remarkable particularity. Again, as distinct from this *credo*, it cannot possibly be understood merely as the affirmation of spiritual or religious truth. It may be disparaged because it is simply a faith in Jesus, or God, as the One from whom men expect, or have already received, the healing of their infirmities. But this transition to the concrete and physical is the distinctive feature in the faith of these men ; the additional element which it reveals. In their faith the epiphany of Jesus Christ is not like the sunrise illuminating a wide landscape from above, but like a single ray of light focussed on one point and piercing at this point what is otherwise an abyss of darkness. It is not our present task to defend the New Testament, or these men and the particular faith which is ascribed to them in the New Testament. We are merely noting the fact, and the remarkable way in which the free grace of God is reflected in this fact. If the faith of these men is in order—and we will assume that this is the case—it means that in the grace of God too (and this is the distinctive feature in the miracles of Jesus) there is a similar element of surplus and even luxury. Grace is also free in a way which usually escapes our notice even when we seriously describe it as grace, and free grace. It is not just applied to all men equally. It is applied specifically to these particular men. In this particularity it is not merely a divine promise and therefore divine truth for all men here and now. As a sign for all men, but a sign set up then and there, it is a promise which is divinely fulfilled and truth which is divinely actualised. Therefore at the very heart of time, in restoration of the glory and peace of creation, and anticipation of the glory and peace of the final revelation of the will and kingdom of God, it is free to accomplish real deliverances here and now. That is to say, it is free to accomplish deliverances which obviously and powerfully concern the whole man : man in his totality as the soul of his body and together with his body ; in the physical state in which he also exists, and is here and now subject to so many and varied afflictions and oppressions. " Where now with sickness, tears and woe, I shall with joy and gladness go. . . . All my weakness here on earth, Shall yield before my second birth." Is this only a future possibility ? No, says God in His free grace—if those men with their particular faith have rightly heard and understood His particular Word. No, the totality comes and takes place there and then, so that even the physical deliverance of man is already present here and now. The truth of the promise, the truth of what will be (and will be revealed) in the future, shines out already. It is thus distinct from all illusory hopes. Grace is so truly grace, and so truly free as grace, that it is capable of this (doubly undeserved) superfluity. And in the accounts of the miracles of Jesus the Gospels attest it in this superfluity. Those who are able to grasp it, let them do so ! It is quite understandable that not only the so-called world but even normal Christianity does not grasp it easily. The miracles may be denied, or rationalised, or accepted with a theoretical orthodoxy, but the Gospels do not give any real joy in this respect. They are found to be a stumbling-block. The miracle-stories are skipped over as a *pudendum*. Nothing can really be made of them. And this is all because the extraordinary character of the freedom of the grace of God as attested in the miracle-stories is far too extraordinary. At the beginning of this fifth point we mentioned the fact that we are confronted at this point by a particular rigidity on the part of Western Christendom, and especially of Protestantism. The normal Christian of the West is all for the norm and does not understand or trust the luxury, even if it is that of God Himself. There might be some hope if only he were not so proud of the fact. From the point of view of the Gospels and their attestation of the epiphany of the Son of Man it is quite right that he should be continually surprised by this super-fluity of the grace of God, and in this superfluity by grace itself in what he thinks to be its normal form. But it is not right that he should be rigid in relation to this superfluity. He must be careful that this does not mean that he is more rigid than he thinks in relation to what he regards as its normal form ; that he is still closed, at bottom, to its freedom. Can we really understand even the rule of faith if we refuse to know anything of this surplus ? Does not even the rule speak finally of the *resurrectio carnis* and the *vita venturi saeculi* ? Does it not all aim at this end, so that the luxury is not really a luxury ? But however that may be, and whatever may be the attitude of the world or Christians, if we are ready to keep to the only information we have (that which is given by the Gospels) about Jesus the Son of Man, we have to come to terms with the fact that what we are told about Him is that He was the man who put His proclamation into practice in these acts, thus characterising it as the proclamation of the kingdom, or—and it comes to the same thing—of the superabounding free grace of God.

V

We must pause for a moment and survey the sub-section which is now mainly behind us. We have been trying to see the Son of God as the One who as such was also the Son of Man ; the Humiliated as the One who as such was also exalted ; the Servant who as such was and is also the Lord of all men and the divinely created cosmos, the royal man Jesus of Nazareth. This is how He was seen by the community in which the New Testament arose. And this is how we have been trying to see Him, adopting, to the best of our knowledge and con-science, the same standpoint as that from which He was seen in the

New Testament. For this purpose we have presupposed as the " New Testament "—not naively, but deliberately and consciously—a fixed form of the tradition denoted by this term ; not a form which is hypothetical, but one which is as a whole well-known to us historically. We have thus refrained (again deliberately) from any critico-historical construction or reconstruction of this presupposition. In so doing we have consciously accepted what is surely obvious to any unprejudiced reader (not only of the Epistles but also of the Gospels), that the standpoint from which they saw Jesus and told us about Him lies beyond the temporal limits of His life ; that they saw and attested Him in the context of events which took place after His death and which they described as His resurrection and ascension and the impartation of His Holy Spirit to the community. From this standpoint they saw and represented the totality of His life as that of a royal man, not with the intention of adding something to the truth of His historical existence, or in any way glossing it over, but with the intention of causing the one and only truth of His historical existence, as it later disclosed itself to them, to shine out in the only way which is at all commensurate with it. We have simply followed it in this. Our position in relation to the New Testament, and therefore to Jesus Himself, is not one which is adopted in abstraction from His resurrection. We make no attempt to see and understand His life prior to His death as if it were not illuminated and interpreted, as if it were unsatisfactorily or mistakenly interpreted, by what happened after His death, as if we were free to see and represent it later either in this light, in one like it, or in a very different light. Neutrality of this kind is quite illegitimate when it is a matter of expounding the witness to Jesus in the New Testament as the witness to the kingdom of God drawn near in Him. This witness may be accepted or it may be rejected. But it must always be heard in the form in which it grew up and by which it stands or falls.

The following are particularly instructive on this point : B. Reicke : " Einheitlichkeit oder verschiedene ' Lehrbegriffe ' in der neutestamentlichen Theologie ? ", *Theol. Zeitschr.*, IX, 6 (Nov.–Dec. 1953), and O. Cullmann : *Die Tradition*, 1954, pp. 8–27.

We have tried to consider the totality of this witness by taking three great cross-sections. In a first part we considered the fact that the existence of the man Jesus as the Gospels saw it cannot be overlooked. We pointed to its character as a final decision which is not merely demanded but has already been taken objectively. We considered its sovereignty as the epiphany of the Lord, and its irrevocability as a fact. In the second part we noted the correspondence and parallelism of His existence with that of God as the Gospels see and represent it. We found that He resembles God in His unpretentiousness in what seems to be His world to human eyes ; in His corresponding partisanship of those who are lowly in this world ; in the revolutionary character of His relationship to the established orders ; in His positive turning to man as he exists and is oppressed in this world. Then in the third and most detailed part we understood His life-act as the self-representation of the new and redemptive actuality of the kingdom of God, His mighty activity in words and deeds which in their common reach indicate and fulfil in ever-extending circles the irruption of this kingdom. The man who was there in this way—in this unique distinctness of His historical appearance and His historical relationship to God Himself, in this historical activity—was and is the royal man Jesus of Nazareth. And it may be that the little that we have here taken from His fulness has been sufficient, when in the doctrine of reconciliation or dogmatics generally we come to this christological centre (as we always must), to protect us from having to look into the void, or at an unknown quantity, a mere symbol without content, when we speak of the Son of God who became the Son of Man. The name of Jesus Christ has on its human side the fulness which we have tried at least to envisage as a whole.

But in a consideration of this whole we must not lose sight of the final point which calls for brief discussion in this context in virtue of the insights which it can give us—insights which are quite indispensable for a true understanding of the whole. So far we have hardly touched on what is denoted by the word " cross " as a description of the whole existence and divine likeness and activity of the man Jesus. Yet it is the cross which controls and penetrates and determines this whole. The cross is the sign under which it must be seen both as a whole and in detail. As the Gospels put it, this man was not welcomed and accepted in the world and by the world in which He appeared in this superiority and in which He was the reflection of the fatherly heart of God and the self-representation of His kingdom. On the contrary, He was rejected and destroyed. One of His own disciples delivered Him into the hands of those among whom and for whom He had come. He was denied by the very one upon whom He was to build His Church. He was accused by the chosen representatives of divine authority and condemned by the chosen representatives of the highest human authority. He had to suffer and die, and to do so as a malefactor against divine and human law. And He consented to do this. He accepted it of His own free will. He took it upon Himself. The end of His way was that He was led away ; that He Himself went away into the darkness. This was the frontier from the far side of which the Gospels saw and understood and represented Him. And they did not delete this frontier. They did not gloss it over. They did not expunge it. On the contrary, they integrated the story of His passion with all that went before. They gave it a particular emphasis as its necessary outcome. Neither the Gospels nor the New Testament as a whole see and know and attest the risen and living and exalted man Jesus except as the man who had this end and outcome, whose story is finally the story of His passion. Indeed, even from beyond this frontier they see everything in the shadow—or rather, in the light which shines from the shadow—of this frontier. The risen and living and exalted Jesus is for them in His totality the man who was led away into this shadow, who Himself went away into it with uplifted head. There is for them no post-Easter Jesus who is not absolutely identical with the One to whose pre-Easter existence this limit belonged. In the whole of the New Testament He is the Crucified, enclosing in Himself the whole of His being within this limit. Faith in Him is faith in the Crucified. Love for Him is love for the Crucified. Hope in Him is hope in the Crucified. All the positive things included in the faith and love and hope of the community are confronted and characterised by, and related to this final negative. This final negative is the basis of the positivity of its faith and love and hope. The great light of Easter is for it the light of Good Friday penetrating the darkness. We have not seen the Jesus of the Gospels and the whole of the New Testament properly if we do not finally take account of the fact that the light in which we have tried to see Him is the light of His death as it shines forth in His resurrection, and that it is in this way that it is the light of His life, the light of the world.

There is obviously a glaring contrast between the beginning and content and meaning of the existence of Jesus and its outcome and end. The Gospels see this and draw attention to it, and to the question which it inevitably raises.

They tell us how blind the disciples were when Jesus spoke of His approaching death. An example of this is in Lk. 18³⁴ (cf. 9⁴⁵ ; Mk. 9³²) : " And they understood none of these things : and this saying was hid from them, neither knew they the things which were spoken." They also tell us of the impulsive reaction of Peter who only a few moments before had made his inspired confession, and who was later to betray Jesus at the decisive moment : " Then Peter took him, and began to rebuke him, saying, Be it far from thee, Lord : this shall not be unto thee " (Mt. 16²²). They tell us how at the last all the disciples forsook Him and fled (Mk. 14⁵⁰ᶠ·). They tell us with brutal frankness of the scornful taunts of His opponents when He was hanging on the cross (Mk. 15²⁹ᶠ·). And in Lk. 24²⁰ᶠ·, even in the Easter story, we seem to catch an echo of this scorn on the lips of the troubled disciples : " The chief priests and our rulers delivered him to be condemned to death, and have crucified him. But we trusted that it had been he which should have redeemed Israel : and beside all this, to day is the third day since these things were done." And Paul can still say (1 Cor. 1²³) how self-evident it was that the crucified Jesus whom he proclaimed should be a stumbling-block to the Jews and foolishness to the Greeks. Even more important is the fact that the Gospels, and the Epistle to the Hebrews (5⁷ᶠ·), are not afraid to represent Jesus Himself wrestling with the question—and they use the strongest possible terms, as in the Gethsemane passages—whether this end is really right or necessary, or whether there may not perhaps be some other possibility. Indeed, in Jn. 12²⁷ He could even pray : " Father, save me from this hour." And even more striking is the fact that in Mark (15³⁴) and Matthew (27⁴⁶) His only word on the cross, and therefore His final word, is the despairing question : " My God, my God, why hast thou forsaken me ? " The Gospels do not conceal the fact, but state it, that His death is a problem of the first magnitude. It is, in fact, the problem of all the problems of His existence and relationship to God and His life's work. The darkness of His end is a true and final darkness. It is a darkness which even He Himself could not see through directly, but which had to be traversed like a tunnel. If this were not emphasised by the Gospels, it is hard to see how any real weight could be attached to the further and decisive thing which they have also to say about it.

But there is one thing that the Gospels definitely do not do, and that is to invite their readers and hearers to prolong their consideration of this darkness and the problem it raises. As they represent it, even at the high points in the narrative, the passion of Jesus never assumes the character of a tragic entanglement which raises the possible and even necessary question of a partial error and therefore some element of guilt on the part of the hero. Nor does it have the character of a misfortune which breaks over Him either by chance or fate, so that the initiative is wrested from Him and He ceases to be the Lord. On the contrary, in His suffering and dying He is still the same as He always was, although in another form. The passion is not an alien element in His work as a whole. From the very first, and with decisive significance, all that He did was done under this sign. This emerged clearly in the death and passion, but it was there all the time. And the Gospels see this because they see the whole story in the light of Easter. We should have to adopt a different standpoint from that of the Gospels even to envisage—let alone investigate—it as an alien element. The Gospels do not allow the attentive reader to indulge in abstract considerations of that contrast or speculations on the problems to which it gives rise. There is no place for an approach of this kind. We should still have to say this even if we could forget for a moment the Easter story with which they all conclude. We should still have to say it if only in view of the remarkable coherence, the non-dramatic directness, with which they link together what took place in Galilee and what took place in Jerusalem (Luke uniting them by his account of the great journey, and all the Synoptists by the so-called predictions of the passion, which are common to all the accounts, in spite of the variations in detail, and especially in relation to the words actually used by Jesus). For all its glaring contrast, the story is seen by them as a single whole. And in spite of the change of setting, the approach and occurrence of the passion do not involve any basic change in the narrative, not even a change of narrative style. We have failed to understand them from the very outset if we are genuinely surprised or alienated by what we are told about the prediction and fulfilment of the passion, or if this challenges us to a reconsideration of all that goes before. We can interpret the passion as an unexpected climax, with all the considerations and discussions that this involves, only if we first subject the texts to certain critical operations which are far too obvious and facile to commend themselves. And if we do this, we unfortunately do not allow the Gospels to say what they are so clearly trying to say, so that from their standpoint we merely plunge into the void, with all the consequences that this involves. If we accept what they say, and clearly wish to say, we cannot fail to see that although the cross is the end and termination of the way of Jesus it is also its aim and goal. It is quite in order, and according to plan, that His way should lead to this point, ending in the darkness of a criminal execution.

It is best to anticipate the result in order to bring out the antithesis to the broken constructions in which we are forced to think. Jesus was not led to this place, nor did He go to this place, in contradiction of the fact that He was the royal man. On the contrary, it was in a sense His coronation as this man. The fact that His way issued in this darkness does not mean that what we have said about His existence and relationship to God and His life's work is in any way weakened or qualified, or has to be retracted. The very opposite is the case. What we have said finds its true climax and glory in the fact that—however hard this may sound—He finally hung on the gallows as a criminal between two other criminals, and died there, with that last despairing question on His lips, as One who was condemned and maltreated and scorned by men and abandoned by God. The story of His passion is all the more emphatically, although not very obviously, linked with what precedes, forming a single whole, because the latter is not at all denied or questioned by it, but finds in it its fulfilment. In His passion the name of the God active and revealed in Him is conclusively sanctified ; His will is done on earth as it is done in heaven ; His kingdom comes, in a form and with a power to which as a man He can only give a terrified but determined assent. And in the passion He exists conclusively as the One He is—the Son of God who is also the Son of Man. In the deepest darkness of Golgotha He enters supremely into the glory of the unity of the Son with the Father. In that abandonment by God He is the One who is directly loved by God. This is the secret that we have to see and understand. And it is not a new and specific secret. It is the secret of the whole. Nor is it a closed secret. It is a secret which has been revealed in the resurrection of Jesus.

What we have to say along these lines is incidentally in direct contradiction to the conception of the passion story which has found its classical exposition in the St. Matthew's Passion of Bach. We are not disputing the purely musical greatness of this work. But it also purports to be an exposition of Chapters 26–27 of Matthew's Gospel. And as such it can only confuse those who hear it. In an almost unbroken minor it is a wonderful cloud-pattern of sighs and lamentations and complaints, of cries of horror and sorrow and sympathy. It is a tragic ode culminating in a conventional funeral dirge (" Rest softly "). It is neither determined nor delimited by the Easter message, and Jesus never once speaks in it as the Victor. When is the Church going to realise, and to make it clear to the thousands and thousands who may have direct knowledge of the evangelical passion-story only in this form, that what we have here is only an abstraction and not the real passion of Jesus Christ ?

That the passion has to be integrated very differently into the totality of Jesus' existence is shown in the Synoptics by the three most comprehensive predictions of His suffering, to which Matthew adds a fourth in his introduction to the passion narrative proper (26¹ᶠ·), and a fifth and last immediately before the account of the arrest (Mt. 26⁴⁵ ; Mk. 14⁴¹). The second prediction in Luke (9⁴⁴) is almost identical with this last and very brief statement : " The Son of man shall be delivered into the hands of men " (they are called ἁμαρτωλοί in Matthew and Mark, where the tense is now present, παραδίδοται). Those who investigate the origin of these texts, and the actual words used by the " historical Jesus," will be naturally inclined to find their original setting and form in this final version given by Mark and Matthew, all the earlier occurrences, with the exception of Lk. 9⁴⁴, being regarded as later transpositions and expansions and therefore dismissed as of no consequence. But however illuminating this procedure may seem to be, it involves a destruction of the way in which the Gospels actually saw and wished to see the passion. The passion of Christ is not for them a catastrophe which burst unexpectedly into His life. It is the necessary result of it. It is thus essential that it should be announced in it.

It may be noted that the shortest of the earlier predictions (Lk. 9⁴³ᶠ·) is the very one which is most impressively introduced and in which the dumb astonishment of the disciples is most explicitly depicted. " But while they wondered every one at all things which Jesus did (πᾶσιν οἷς ἐποίει), he said unto his disciples, Let these sayings sink down into your ears (θέσθε ὑμεῖς εἰς τὰ ὦτα ὑμῶν τοὺς λόγους τούτους) : For the Son of man shall . . ." ; and it then goes on : " But they understood not this saying (this ῥῆμα), and it was hid from them, that they perceived it not : and they feared to ask him of that saying." This is in place only in the earlier setting, and not in the garden of Gethsemane. Yet the context of Mt. 26⁸ is also important. For as in Lk. 9⁴⁴ᶠ· there is a reference to all the works of Jesus and the astonishment to which they gave rise, so here there is a reference to all His sayings (ὅτε ἐτέλεσεν ὁ Ἰησοῦς πάντας τοὺς λόγους τούτους), which means, concretely, to the conclusion of His preaching in Mt. 24 and 25— the developed prediction of His coming again and the definitive end of the world. It may also be noted that the final saying (in the present tense) in Mk. 14⁴¹ and Mt. 26⁴⁵ arises from the background of the battle which has been victoriously fought out in Gethsemane. And in all the Synoptics the three earlier predictions are all introduced in connexion with climaxes in the preceding existence and activity and self-revelation of Jesus. All the accounts agree that the first follows immediately after the Messianic confession of Peter (Mk. 8³¹ and par.) ; the second immediately after the related accounts of the transfiguration and the healing of the epileptic boy (Mk. 9³⁰ᶠ· and par.) ; and the third immediately after the sayings of Jesus about the heavenly reward promised to His disciples (Mk. 10³²ᶠ· and par., Matthew interposing the parable about the labourers to show that even the disciple who comes last to the vineyard will receive the full recompense, Mt. 20¹ᶠ·). This agreement as to the order can hardly be accidental. And when in the case of the third prediction, instead of the usual emphasis on the astonishment of the disciples, Mark (10³⁵ᶠ·) and Matthew (Mt. 20²⁰ᶠ·) have the story of the curious request of the sons of Zebedee and its rejection, this only serves to bring out how completely the situation was misunderstood. Even here, then, the order is not in any sense accidental. It is integral to the passion story that it should be preceded by a particular demonstration of the Son of Man and the kingdom of God, and followed by the complete dumbfounding of the disciples.

In relation to all these passages, the question arises in face of this situation whether we do not have to do with an anticlimax in the relationship of the preceding demonstration of the Son of Man or kingdom of God to the ensuing

predictions of the passion. Do we have to do with a kind of " Yes, but "—a positive
Yes followed by a critical and negative, or at any rate qualifying and retarding,
No ? There can be no doubt that we do have an anticlimax in what the disciples
say, or do not say, when they hear these sayings which announce the passion.
Might it not be—although this makes the conception more difficult—that we
have here a twofold anticlimax, the first being within the proclamation and
self-revelation of Jesus Himself ? Might it not be that Jesus Himself is interrupted and temporarily, at least, contradicted by the prediction of His passion ?
Might it not be that a " but " is now put after the Yes that has been pronounced ?
But if this is the case, is it really of a piece with the Gospel record as a whole ?
Where else do we find Jesus making retractations of this kind ? Unless we are
to take it that the conjunction of these high points and the predictions of the
passion is quite haphazard, the only alternative is to accept the fact that in
this relationship we are dealing with a climax. It is not a " Yes, but " that is
spoken, but a " Yes, and therefore." What is said previously is not withdrawn
or limited, either as a whole or in part, but transcended. And it is because the
disciples do not see this that they so utterly fail to understand the predictions
of the passion, thus giving us a true anticlimax.

It is true, of course, that the content and theme of the predictions of the
passion is a movement in what is at any rate a completely new dimension. This
was not unknown to Jesus, nor unexpected by Him. Nor did He try to resist it.
But it was not self-evident. That is why the disciples found it so astonishing
and confusing. As they saw it—the tradition makes this very clear—these
sayings constituted a real anticlimax. The movement was in an intolerably
abnormal and crooked direction. It was a movement from the high points—
the revelation of Jesus as Israel's Messiah, the mount of transfiguration and
the triumphant miracle at its foot, the promise of a heavenly reward which they
themselves should share, all the words and acts of Jesus—to an absurd future
which meant the delivering up of the Son of Man, the Lord and King, into the
unclean and unworthy hands of men who ought to worship in the dust at His
feet ; the final triumph of the scribes and Pharisees and high priests and elders
in a Jerusalem which was disobedient to God as it had always been, and rejected
again, but this time finally, the salvation which it had always scorned ; the
condemnation and martyrdom and suffering and death as a criminal of the only
true and righteous benefactor. But what, according to their own statement,
the disciples did not see and hear then, they saw and heard, and the New Testament community also heard, later—that what was predicted and then took place
was not really a movement in an abnormal and crooked direction, but a movement from the high points, from the totality of the acts and words of Jesus, to
their true depth or height, to their hidden glory, to the perfection of the being
of the Son of Man, to the fulfilment of the kingdom of God inaugurated and
revealed with His appearance.

What the disciples originally saw at this point was either nothing
at all or only the frightful paradox of a radical contradiction and
destruction of the Son of Man, the overwhelming of the new actuality
which He had introduced by the old. But they now realised that it
was really His radical activation and affirmation. They now realised
that it was His coronation as the royal man He was, and therefore the
victory of the new actuality over the old. From the point where they
had once started back thinking that it meant defeat and retreat and
disaster, they now followed Him gladly and thankfully in the light of
the triumph which had been won there. His cross, which had then
been to them the symbol of hopelessness, became to them the solid

basis, as well as the sign, of the eternal and every temporal hope in which they could live and which they could proclaim to the world, of the forward reference in the power of which they not only came from Him as the One whom they had then encountered, but also went towards Him, from His past to His future epiphany.

Is it really possible to understand in any other way these predictions of the passion which the Synoptics have so singularly made the heart and limit of their presentation of the pre-Easter existence of Jesus ? Is not the forward reference of these passages indicated already by the fact that they almost all speak expressly of the rising again of Jesus on the third day ? The emphasis does not rest, of course, on this final statement. It merely indicates that even where the Gospels had to bring out unequivocally this dimension of death they still consider the totality of their presentation as a forward movement, and they invite and summon their readers to take this forward look. But the direction of this forward movement is primarily and decisively to the dimension of death. We cannot look past or beyond the death and passion of Jesus. We can only look to it—for the sake of the fulfilment which takes place in it. We can only look to the actuality of the event whose mere possibility caused the disciples such terror. We can only look to the end and conclusion of His existence—a triumphant conclusion as they later saw and heard, when they no longer thought τὰ τῶν ἀνθρώπων (Mt. 16²³) but τὰ τοῦ θεοῦ, when they had the freedom to consider from above and not from below the event of the death of Jesus which was then approaching but had now taken place. The little word δεῖ must not escape our notice. It dominates the first of the predictions in all three versions : " The Son of man *must* suffer many things." This " must " was and is decisive. " Must " He do this even though He is the Son of Man, the royal man ? Must He do it in spite of this fact and in opposition to it ? Or must He do it just because and as He is this man ? Must He do it in the service of an alien necessity, or in ineluctable fulfilment of His mission, the reconciliation of the world with God which it is His task to accomplish ? Must He do it as a great concession, even submission, to a cosmic law whose power He cannot escape, or is it an observance of the will of God, the fulfilling of all righteousness (Mt. 3¹⁵), and therefore the discharge of His royal office in an act of perfect obedience ? We surely cannot think that the Gospels used this δεῖ in the former sense, but only in the latter. If this is the case, however, it means that the predictions of the passion, and the passion itself, are not in any way an anticlimax, but the climax of their witness.

It also means that the witness of the Synoptics is in agreement with that of John. In John the situation is clear from the very outset. The puzzling nature of the passion is not concealed. On the contrary, it emerges very clearly. But as this Gospel presents it, it is drawn right into the proclamation of Jesus. It is integrated with the totality of His words and works. It is the dimension of death which as such is the dimension of life, the dimension of the forward reference and hope which necessarily characterise His existence. The fact that Jesus goes to His death means now that He goes to the One who sent Him, to the Father (Jn. 14¹², 16⁵, ²⁸, 17¹¹). " Father, the hour is come ; glorify thy Son, that thy Son also may glorify thee : as thou hast given him power over all flesh, that he should give eternal life to as many as thou hast given him " (17¹ᶠ·, cf. 13³²). That He should be " lifted up from the earth " (12³²) " as Moses lifted up the serpent in the wilderness " (3¹⁴) involves now, with a simultaneity which is both dreadful and illuminating, both His exaltation on the cross (He will be lifted up by the Jews, 8²⁸ and : " This said he, signifying what death he should die," 12³³) and yet also His triumphant exaltation as the Son of Man, which *must* take place (again δεῖ) " that whosoever believeth in him should not perish, but have eternal life " (3¹⁴) ; which must do so (δεῖ, 12³⁴) because in His exaltation

He " will draw all men " unto Him (12³²). If this Johannine view is right, and does not materially contradict that of Paul, the exaltation of the One who humiliated Himself in obedience (Phil. 2⁹) is not the divine act towards this man which takes place after His humiliation, but that which takes place in and with His humiliation. The Johannine insight is always : " Verily, verily, I say unto you, Except a corn of wheat fall into the ground and die, it abideth alone : but if it die, it bringeth forth much fruit " (12²⁴). " Because I have said these things unto you, sorrow hath filled your heart. Nevertheless I tell you the truth ; It is expedient for you that I go away : for if I go not away, the Comforter will not come unto you ; but if I depart I will send him unto you " (16⁶ᶠ·). " I go to prepare a place for you. And if I go and prepare a place for you, I will come again, and receive you unto myself ; that where I am, there ye may be also " (14²ᶠ·). He does not give His life casually or in vain, but with this definite and conscious aim in view. No one takes it from Him. He gives it of Himself. He has received this commandment from the Father (10¹⁷ᶠ·). He is the Good Shepherd who lays down His life for the sheep (10¹¹, ¹⁵). He is the true Friend who lays down His life for His friends (15¹³). In so doing, He sanctifies Himself for them, to use the striking expression of 17¹⁹. And the prince of this world is judged (16¹¹) and cast out (12³¹). This is the Johannine emphasis in the farewell discourses which replace the predictions of the passion, and not only in these particular chapters but throughout the Gospel. There is to be a true and serious parting, but it is not an occasion for sadness and lamentation. Only *per nefas* can it be understood in this way. On the contrary, it is one long promise of a saving present and future, of fulfilment, of the final benefit of eternal life, of a " Comforter " and a prepared place. Even at His first appearance by Jordan Jesus is attested by the Baptist to be the Lamb of God which taketh away the sin of the world—an almost unmistakeable allusion to Is. 53⁷. And it is obviously no accident that it is only in the passion story that emphasis is given to His description as a king, as is also the case in the Synoptics (Mk. 15², ⁹, ¹⁸, ²⁶ and par.). In John this title occurs not only in the dialogue with Pilate, in which the accused expressly acknowledges the title (18³³ᶠ·), but also in the saying with which Pilate presented Him to the Jews when He had been scourged and mocked : " Behold your king ! " (19¹⁴), and then again in the exchanges about the title on the cross : " Jesus of Nazareth the King of the Jews," when the Jews asked that it should be amended : " He said, I am King of the Jews," but Pilate bore unconscious witness to the truth with his famous dictum : " What I have written I have written " (19¹⁹ᶠ·). On this point it is worth noting that earlier in the story (6¹⁵) John introduced the strange report that after the feeding of the five thousand the people wanted to take Jesus by force and make Him a king, but that He evaded them. If He was to be present as a king, and to be proclaimed as such, it had to take place (and this was also His own will) as it did actually take place in the passion and not in any other way ; but with all due form and solemnity in this way. And again it is not an accident that His last word on the cross—a cry of despair in Mark and Matthew—is now τετέλεσται, because, as we are told earlier, He knew that everything was now completed. It was in this way, in this absolute fulfilment, that He now bowed His head, not before men, or death, but before the Father whose commission He had executed to the letter. It was in this way that He gave up the ghost (19²⁸ᶠ·).

This positive understanding of the passion even as it is presented in the Synoptics enables us to see its harmony with the Pauline theology of the cross. A detailed development of this theme is hardly necessary in the present context. Only the basic aspects need concern us. Formally, the whole significance of the historical existence of Jesus was concentrated for Paul in His death. Just because his thinking was all in the light of the resurrection, his gaze was fixed directly on this frontier, and therefore on the pre-Easter life of Jesus of which it was the limit. And materially, the supremely positive aspect of the significance of the historical existence of Jesus is disclosed, as he sees it, in the contemplation and apprehension of this limit as such. His aim was to proclaim (or " evidently set forth," Gal. 3¹, cf. 1 Cor. 1²³, 2²) Jesus to the world and the Churches as the Crucified. For he knows that He did not die in vain, but that He, the Son of God, " loved me, and gave himself for me " (Gal. 2²⁰). Without any attempt at systematisation, we will here recall only some of the most central of the Pauline statements. He " gave himself for our sins, that he might deliver us from this present evil world, according to the will of God and our Father " (Gal. 1⁴). He " hath redeemed us from the curse of the law, being made a curse for us " (Gal. 3¹³). Or, according to the strong expressions of 2 Cor. 5²¹, God " hath made him to be sin for us, who knew no sin ; that we might be made the righteousness of God in him." By His death, He has " condemned sin in the flesh "—the sin of the whole world (Rom. 8³). He has died to sin once, to our sin, by putting it to death in Himself (Rom. 6¹⁰). No more place is left for it. Those who live do not now " live unto themselves, but unto him which died for them, and rose again " (2 Cor. 5¹⁵). The righteousness demanded by the law (its δικαίωμα) may thus be fulfilled in us (Rom. 8⁴). In His blood, i.e., in the offering up of His life, God has set Him forth, like the ἱλαστήριον in the tabernacle, to be an effective and eloquent demonstration (ἔνδειξις) of His own just and justifying righteousness (Rom. 3²⁶). By the event of His death as this demonstration of the righteousness of God, He " blotted out the handwriting of ordinances that was against us, which was contrary to us, and took it out of the way, nailing it (and with it the old man of sin, Gal. 2¹⁹ ; Rom. 7⁴) to his cross ; and having spoiled princpalities and powers, he made a shew of them openly, triumphing over them in it " (Col. 2¹⁴ᶠ.). In His death as this demonstration He is in every sense our " peace " (Eph. 2¹⁴ᶠ.). In the death which He suffered on the cross He has broken down the middle wall of partition between Israel and the Gentiles, " having abolished in his flesh the enmity . . . for to make in himself of twain one new man . . . and that he might reconcile both unto God in one body." Col. 1¹⁹ᶠ. is even more comprehensive, for it tells us that " through the blood of his cross " He has created a cosmic peace which enfolds all things both in earth and heaven.

Whatever may be our interpretation of these statements both in detail and in their general context, there can be no doubt that, so far as the 1st century communities thought in Pauline terms, it was not in the resurrection but the death of the Lord that they found as it were *in nuce* the redemptive act and actuality of His existence, and heard the Yes which God pronounced in Him to man, and the corresponding Yes to sin and death and the devil. Something very remarkable must have happened if in this respect they had come to a different understanding of the Jesus tradition which found its concretion in the Gospels, i.e., if a different conception of the passion was really offered by the Gospels. And something even more remarkable must have happened if they did not understand the tradition correctly, or again, if the tradition as correctly understood in this way did not correspond to the objective historical data. For how can we explain the rise of a tradition whose content is so singular and contradictory—not the acts and achievements and works of a historical figure, but his shameful end, his destruction which so totally compromises everything that precedes it ? and this as an event of such dimensions, of a relevance which is so positive in every respect ? How does it help us to refer to the possibilities of myth, its invention, formation and elaboration ? How could a myth originate at this point or develop in these surroundings ? How could it come about that only 30–70 years after the death of a historical man, and in these different ways, all this could be narrated and said with such remarkable concentration about His death ? However that may be, there is no doubt that in the 1st century there were people—and they were the first members of the Christian community and Church—who did know and tell and say of His death, His death on the cross, that it had positive meaning as a decisive redemptive turning-point for them and for all men, His life being the way which led to this turning-point, and therefore to His death on the cross as the confirmation of His existence, His relationship to God, and all that He said and did. And if they were asked how they knew this, and could tell and say it, their answer (and they usually volunteered the information of themselves) was simply that He had encountered them as the One who had risen again from the dead, thus revealing the secret of His death, and therefore of His life, as the work of the saving and enlightening power of God, or, decisively and comprehensively, revealing Himself as the incomparable royal man. We cannot develop the theme in this context. But at some point and in some way the Christian Church did in fact begin to have this massive certainty. And we must beware of facile explanations of this beginning.

We must now return to our main path with some propositions concerning the pre-Easter life of Jesus.

1. What we have called generally the dimension of death is a more precise form of a readiness and willingness which characterised this life from the very outset as it is presented in the Gospels. In the words and acts recounted we cannot find a single trace of His expecting or envisaging or desiring or seeking any other outcome than that which was actually the case. It cannot, then, be said that when it had this outcome He was surprised or disillusioned or offended. On the contrary, there are clear signs that His whole existence was prepared and armed for this outcome, and directed towards it.

In this respect we must again recall His saying to the Baptist that " it becometh us to fulfil all righteousness " (Mt. 3¹⁵). His request was that He should be granted the baptism of repentance as one of the crowd which came to Jordan. He did not set Himself over others, but, in expectation of the imminent judgment of God, He set Himself in solidarity with them. In this way He not only entered on His office but took the first step on the path which would inevitably end with what took place at Calvary. In some sense His baptism was an anticipation of this event. And when He was baptised the Baptist saw the heavens opened, and the Spirit descending upon Him, with the " voice from heaven, saying, This is my beloved Son, in whom I am well pleased." It was in terms of baptism, again, that Jesus described His own part in the fire which He had come to kindle on earth. If only this fire were already burning ! If only the baptism, which is obviously the pre-condition of its burning, were already accomplished ! (Lk. 12⁴⁹ᶠ·). And it is not only legitimate, but obligatory, that we should think of the saying in Mk. 10⁴⁵ which tells us that the Son of Man has not come into the world to be ministered unto (like the supposed lords of this world), but to minister ; and not to minister partially or occasionally, like many of those whose real aim is to rule, but totally and exclusively, by giving His life for many, for the liberation of many, by becoming their λύτρον. This is the determination of His historical existence, His body and blood, as it is impressively repeated (however we may have to interpret the different texts in detail) in the thanksgiving and giving and receiving which took place at the Last Supper with the disciples (Mk. 14²²ᶠ· and par.). In order that others may receive from Him and appropriate what is active and revealed in Him, He will not and does not offer up anything less than Himself, His body and blood : This is my body ; And this is my blood. And He does this with thanksgiving, as the great act of His εὐλογία and εὐχαριστία. To the same context (understood either in relation to the Lord's Supper or apart from it) there belongs also the passage in Jn. 6⁵³ᶠ·—that if we are to have eternal life we must eat His flesh and drink His blood. We may also think of the very curious saying to the woman in Bethany about anointing His body for burial (Mk. 14⁸). But perhaps the most eloquent individual testimony is the quiet fact that when He called the twelve to be with Him, and to go out proclaiming Him with power to cast out demons, He also called Judas (who betrayed Him, as is noted in all the accounts, Mk. 3¹³ᶠ· and par.). Notice that it was He Himself who called him. And as the Gospels see it, He does not do this naively or in ignorance. He is not surprised by what Judas does later. He knows very well what he will do. He calls him with this in view. He makes (v. 14) even this man His apostle. He could hardly have integrated His self-offering more clearly into His life's work than by bringing His παραδούς into this orderly association with Himself.

2. What we have called His self-determination to this end and outcome is also the divine order which controls His life and its course. He fulfils voluntarily that which is resolved concerning Him. And the divinity of that which is resolved emerges in the fact that its execution is not suffered by Him as a burdensome constraint of destiny or a chance misfortune, but in this readiness and willingness, as the content of His own self-determination. There is a " must " for the Son of Man. He would not be the Son of Man otherwise, or if He had not accepted this " must." But the deity of the God who is and lives and rules in the One who is His Son is characterised by the fact that He, the Father of Jesus, has resolved this concerning Him, and claims His free obedience to it.

On this point we may first refer to a remarkable saying of Peter in his address at Pentecost (Ac. 2²²ᶠ·). As he puts it, it was the men of Israel who took Jesus, a man approved of God by miracles and wonders and signs, and by the hands of the Gentiles nailed Him to the cross and put Him to death. But all this took place as and because He was " delivered by the determinate counsel and foreknowledge of God." Christ " had " to suffer these things and in this way (not later) to enter into His glory (Lk. 24²⁶). God's providential rule was not contradicted by this event. God Himself had planned and willed it. It was not contrary to His promise, nor did it destroy it. It was according to the promise, and in fulfilment of it. The true God, the God of Moses and the prophets, is vindicated in the passion of Jesus. He sanctifies His name in this way. His kingdom comes, His will is done on earth as it is in heaven. That is why it is so necessary that in the infancy stories He should be threatened at once by Herod (Mt. 2¹⁻²³), and Mary should be warned of the sword which would pierce her own heart also (Lk. 2³⁵). That is why the disciples are told from the very outset that the days will come when the bridegroom is taken from them (Mk. 2²⁰). As men had done " whatsoever they listed " with Elijah, with John the Baptist, " likewise shall also the Son of man suffer of them " (Mt. 17¹²). As the first Herod had been restrained, so too, for the moment, was the second. But the work of Jesus was limited to the day, for " the night cometh, when no man can work " (Jn. 9⁴). And it did come : ἦν δὲ νύξ, to use the laconic and yet majestic statement with which Jn. 13³⁰ describes the departure of Judas. Of a piece with this is the statement which is almost a motto for the Lucan account of the great journey (Lk. 13³²ᶠ·) : " Behold, I cast out devils, and I do cures to day and to morrow, and the third day I shall be perfected (τελειοῦμαι). Nevertheless I must (δεῖ με) walk to day and to morrow, and the day following : for it cannot be that a prophet perish out of Jerusalem." The wicked husbandmen, who have previously beaten and maltreated and put to death the servants of their Lord (Mk. 12⁶ᶠ· and par.), will not be afraid of His beloved Son, but will destroy Him in order that the inheritance may be theirs. This is the order which prevails both in and over the existence of the Son of Man. It is a terrifying order, but it is a real order, and for all the unworthiness of the instruments an order set up and executed by God, and therefore a good order. In this world, and for its reconciliation with God, the way of the Son of Man can only be this way. We need not return to the accounts of the passion with their obvious δεῖ, although it is here primarily that this point is substantiated. In the basic positive meaning proper to them they are natural and necessary exponents of the determinate counsel and foreknowledge of God which in the passion of Jesus are executed with the perfection appropriate to a divine decree, but constitute already the determination of His whole way to this goal.

3. To the picture of the free but divinely ordained determination of the existence of Jesus to this outcome there must also be added everything that is said in the Gospels about the world around, in which the " wicked husbandmen " are given particular prominence as the decisive agents. We are not set at an indeterminate point in world history. The passion of the Son of Man is, of course, the work of the Gentiles, of Pilate and his race, but only secondarily and indirectly. Pilate has to be there. In more than one respect, especially as the responsible (although not really responsible) representative of government, he is one of the central figures in the Gospel story. Unwillingly and unwittingly he is the *executor Novi Testamenti* (Bengel). For by delivering Jesus to him, Israel unwittingly accomplishes— " they know not what they do " (Lk. 23³⁴)—His handing over to humanity outside Israel, and the Messiah of Israel becomes the Saviour of the world. Again, as Pilate delivers him to his men for execution, he is the man by whose will and work the divine act of redemption is accomplished. It is not the case however, as in some schematic presentations, that Israel and the Gentiles, Church and state, co-operated equally in accusing and condemning Jesus and destroying Him as a criminal. It is not for nothing that the one who initiates this action is the apostle Judas, and in his person the elect tribe of Judah to which Christ Himself also belonged, and in Judah (the Jews, as they are summarily described in John) the chosen and called people of Israel. It is in this sphere that we find ourselves in the passion story. We are not really in the main theatre of world history, but in the vineyard of the Lord. It is Israel, represented by its spiritual and ecclesiastical and theological leaders, but also by its *vox populi*, that refuses and rejects and condemns Jesus and finally delivers Him up as a blasphemer to the Gentiles, to be executed by them as a political criminal, although Pilate is quite unable and unwilling to pronounce Him guilty as such, and only causes Him to be put to death unjustly and against His better judgment. It was to this delivering up by this Israel which rejected and condemned Him, to death at the hands of this people, to this conclusion of His history that Jesus gave up Himself, and was given up by God. This is what we must always keep before us in our understanding of His passion.

" Ye would not " (Mt. 23³⁷). It can all be summed up in these words directed to the inhabitants of Jerusalem. This is the riddle of the existence of Israel in its relationship to Jesus. His will was to gather them " as a hen gathereth her chickens under her wings." For they were really His. " He came unto his own, and his own received him not " (Jn. 1¹¹). And He was theirs—the Son of David. The kingdom of God which had drawn near in Him was the fulfilment of their promise and hope. He would—but they would not. The whole history of Israel was repeated in concentrated form, in a single instant : the presence of Yahweh to the one elect people ; the divine offer which is also the active and powerful work of His faithfulness and goodness ; the prophetic man who could be claimed by no other people ; and the prophetic word as no other people could perceive it. On God's part it was all as it had been before—but in a supreme climax and concretion. And on Israel's part, too, it was all as it had been before : its murmuring against Moses ; its disobedience to Samuel ; its secret and open fury against Elijah and Jeremiah ; the obstinacy which answered faithfulness with unfaithfulness. This obstinacy later extended like a monstrous shadow to the Jewish colonies and synagogues of Syria and Asia Minor and Greece and Rome, constituting the problem to which Paul, who had met it in so many (even Christian !) forms, devoted Chapters 9–11 of his Epistle to the Romans. But now the shadow was only that of the event in which Jerusalem had opposed to the gathering of Jesus the oldest and thickest and most impregnable of all its walls—its own unwillingness : " Jerusalem, thou that killest the prophets, and stonest them which are sent unto thee." Now more than ever it was quite impossible that the elect people of God should be neutral in face of what God Himself said and did. Its existence before God, or rather the existence of God as the God of this people, allowed it only this either-or. And considering all that we have noted of the existence of Jesus and His relationship to God and His proclamation of the kingdom, it is not really surprising that where there could be no Yes there remained and was only the alternative of a No, the No of a most radical rejection, a most categorical repudiation and a most resolute resistance. Not on the part of the Gentiles, of Herod or Pilate, but on the part of the Jews, the scribes and Pharisees, the chief priests and elders, the people of Jerusalem ! They were not wicked. In many ways they were obviously much better than their heathen contemporaries. But in the Word and work of Jesus it was not a matter of disputable details. It was not a matter of developments and innovations which could be more or less accepted or rejected. It was not a matter of small revolutions, but the one great revolution. Everything was at stake. It was a matter of life and death. Israel could not fail to understand the question that Jesus put to it, and the situation to which this gave rise. It understood it only too well. And it could as little accept it as any people of that age or our own. It was inevitable that Jesus should be met by this typical repudiation and resistance on the part of Israel. Necessarily He had to suffer in Israel and be destroyed in Jerusalem.

What else is Mt. 23 but one long description of this wall, which was not merely there as an immovable barrier, but from which Jesus Himself would necessarily be subjected to severe and pitiless attack unless it could be shattered by Him, by the kingdom of God which had drawn ominously near in Him, as by an earthquake ? How primitive is world-empire in its Roman or Hellenistic forms as compared with the form in which it here confronts the kingdom of God, nourished and strengthened by the old divine election and calling, and therefore a supreme dominion, and maintaining itself as such ! What was all the paganism of Greece and Rome compared with this ! For here it took the form of the most exquisite and exclusive piety, and yet a piety which was only too ready to expand (v. 13 f.). Here it took the form of a historically grounded and most carefully constructed ritualism (v. 16 f.). Here it took the form of a supreme casuistry (v. 23 f.). Here it took the form of pride in a great past, of carefully keeping the tombs of prophets and other righteous men to whom it was worth while to appeal (v. 27 f.). All this—and therefore world-empire in what was inwardly its most glorious form—was at stake when Jesus came up against it. And it had either to be destroyed and abandoned, or defended at all costs. Against it Jesus Himself could only pronounce a woe if He was to say anything at all. It all belonged to the past, even if it was still maintained. What was at stake was man against God. This was true in Rome and Greece as well. But it could be recognised only in Jerusalem. And in Jerusalem—the Jerusalem which would not, which again, even in its final hour, preferred man to God—it had to be recognised. In an awful inversion of the sense in which Jesus Himself fought for man, the cause of man, his cause *against* God, had to be defended in all circumstances and at all costs. And therefore the battle had to be joined against the Son of Man. Here again there is a must, like that which the Son of Man freely chose for Himself, and that which was laid on Him by the divine determination of His life. Was it only a third form of one and the same must which controlled this whole event ? Was it only one of the threads which invisibly run together in the one eternal predestination with its interweaving of election and rejection and human freedom and its counterpart in human bondage ? However that may be, the unholy must of Israel also points to the end of Jesus at the cross. From this standpoint, too, His crucifixion is unavoidable.

It is only in accordance with the facts, therefore, if in the Gospels we see everything moving on this side with almost the precision of clockwork. The rejection and attack on Jesus in His own home town, as described in Lk. 4²²ᶠ·, is only a kind of prelude with no far-reaching consequences. But what happened, or did not happen, in the cities by the Sea of Galilee brings us to the very heart of the matter (Mt. 11²⁰ᶠ·). The real attack began with the rain of questions and objections about the sabbath and fasting and purifyings. At first the questions were polite and seemed to indicate almost a real desire for knowledge. But they soon assumed more serious proportions with the question of Jesus' own authority (Mk. 11²⁸) and that of the lawfulness or otherwise of paying tribute to Cæsar— a particularly difficult and dangerous question although couched in the most respectful terms (Mk. 12¹⁴ᶠ· and par.). Behind and in all this there lurks not only a position of determined hostility to Jesus but a desire to " catch him in his words " (Mk. 12¹³ᶠ· and par.) ; and sometimes the accusation (Mt. 12²²ᶠ·) that it may well be the power of the devil which He exercises to cast out demons, so that it is imperative that He should be resisted for the sake of God, and therefore with a righteous indignation and radicalism. Mark introduces even at an earlier point (3⁶) the account of a conference (συμβούλιον) between the Pharisees and the Herodians with a view to His future destruction : ὅπως αὐτὸν ἀπολέσωσιν. Similarly we are told by John's Gospel that comparatively early plots were hatched against His life (7¹, ²⁵), and even of some unsuccessful attempts to arrest Him for various reasons (7³², ⁴⁴ᶠ·, 10³⁹)—differing in this respect from Mk. 12¹², which speaks only of a plan which could not be put into effect for fear of the people. According to Jn. 11⁴⁷, it was after the raising of Lazarus, and in consequence of it, that the crucial debate of the council took place : " What do we ? for this man doeth many miracles. If we let him thus alone, all men will believe on him : and the Romans shall come, and take away both our place and nation." And it was on this occasion that Caiaphas spoke the pregnant words : " Ye know nothing at all, nor consider that it is expedient for us, that one man should die for the people, and that the whole nation perish not." Official plans for His elimination began to be made from this time. This is obviously the same discussion as that which is rather more casually recorded in Mk. 14¹ᶠ· According to this account it took place two days before the passover, and in view of the proximity of the feast, and for fear of popular disturbances, it was realised that the greatest secrecy and speed were demanded. What touched off the action in all four accounts seems to have been the proposal of Judas. There then followed the arrest in Gethsemane by the temple guard, the stormy hearing in the palace of the high-priest as depicted in Mk. 14⁵³ᶠ· and par., culminating in the demand that Jesus should confess His Messianic office and the sharply contrasted assertion of His blasphemy when He did so, with the denial of Peter significantly in the background. Early the next morning there was then held a solemn consultation (again a συμβούλιον) which issued in the agreement that Jesus should be delivered up to Pilate and executed (Mk. 15¹ᶠ· and par.). But even the events which followed were decisively determined by Jerusalem and not by Rome. Pilate could not see any guilt in Jesus. He hesitated and delayed. According to Mt. 27¹⁹ he was warned by his own wife. In Mk. 15⁶ᶠ· and par. he tried to evade the judgment demanded of him by bringing forward the murderer Barabbas, and in Lk. 23⁶ᶠ· by transferring the case to the court of Herod. To the very last he never pronounced any true verdict, but only a sentence, and it was not his own suggestion that this should be crucifixion. What he finally did was won from him in all due form by those who had delivered up Jesus and stirred up the people to bring pressure on him. And with their taunts at the foot of the cross the members of the council again confirmed that it was they who had willed and done what was willed and done. Pilate and his officers were only co-agents who had been forced to co-operate. The meaning of the Gospel story is clear. It was by the unwillingness of Israel that Jesus was brought to the cross. It was by Israel's own action that He was brought to the Gentiles as the Crucified, and His exodus became His entry into the world—the centurion at the foot of the cross being the first to greet and confess Him with his saying when He gave up the ghost (Mk. 15³⁹) : " Truly this man was the Son of God." To put it in epigrammatic form, the " handing over " of Jesus on the morning of Good Friday was the founding of the Church as a Church of both Jews and Gentiles, and therefore as a missionary Church.

4. There remains our final point, and we need only touch on this because we shall have to deal with it more fully in its own context. It may be stated as follows. The determination of the existence of Jesus for death, which is free and yet also controlled by God and necessary as the final action of the history of Israel, has in the existence of the disciples a counterpart which has an unmistakeable likeness for all its inferiority. We have referred to His disciples again and again in our depiction of the royal man, but only in passing. In relation to this final point, however, we must take an anticipatory glance at the first thing that is true of those who are His. They would not be His if in their own way they did not stand under the law which determined and delimited His existence. It is not that they stand in the shadow of His cross. His cross is for them light and power and glory and promise and fulfilment, present liberation and the hope of that which is still to come, the forgiveness of sins, and here and now eternal life. How could they be His if in His death they did not find and take to heart the positive element of the glad news of His existence ? But they do stand under the sign and direction of His cross. The " must " of His passion extends to them too. The fact that this alone was and could be the outcome of His life stamps and characterises their life too. It is in this form that they accept and believe the Gospel of His existence. It is in this form that they accept and believe Jesus Himself.

For the moment we must be content only to draw attention to the essentials as we have them in some of the most important sayings. The disciples, too, will be " delivered up " to men, and it is by this that they will be recognised as His apostles (Mt. 10[17f.]). They are to be blessed because they are reviled and persecuted and calumniated for righteousness' sake (Mt. 5[10f.]). Where He is, there shall also the servant be (Jn. 12[26]). It is not so much a matter of morals as ontology. " The disciple is not above his master, nor the servant above his lord. . . . If they have called the master of the house Beelzebub, how much more shall they call them of his household ? " (Mt. 10[24f.]). If they were ashamed of Him and His words in this evil and adulterous generation, He would be ashamed of them (Mk. 8[38]) when things turned out differently or they tried to escape the inevitable outcome. They, too, will drink the cup that He drinks, and be baptised with the baptism that He is baptised with (Mk. 10[39]). To follow Him (Mk. 8[34f.] and par.) involves for all those who are elected and called and willing and ready and really free to do this that they should deny themselves, i.e., that should not try to save their life for themselves, but yield it freely to this total service. And this means concretely that each of them should take up his own " cross," not fearing or hating or avoiding or evading or trying to escape by force or subtlety the affliction that falls on him, but freely accepting it and taking it up and carrying it. It is not the cross of Christ. This has been carried once and for all, and does not need to be carried again. There can be no question of identification with Him, of a repetition of His suffering and death. But it is a matter of each Christian carrying his own individual cross, suffering his own affliction, bearing the definite limitation of death which in one form or another falls on his own existence, and therefore going after Christ as the man he is, following " in his steps " (1 Pet. 2[21]). To try to save one's life from the claim of this discipleship is to lose it even though the whole world may be gained. And to lose it in obedience to the claim of this discipleship is to save it (Mk. 8[35]). Why ? Because this claim, this clear Law of God, is the form of the Gospel, of the promise of God's free grace, by which alone man can live, but by which he may live in the full sense of the term. It is as we go through this narrow gate that we are disciples of Jesus. If we do not go through it, we cannot be His disciples (Lk. 14[27]). This is not the primary *theologia crucis* of the Gospels, but it is certainly the secondary. And it has its exact parallels in Paul and the other Epistles. It must not be equated or confused with the primary *theologia crucis*, which is wholly and exclusively that of the cross of Jesus, but it cannot and must not be separated from it. It is not an expression of the one general law, of whose fulfilment the other is only the great example. But the word of the cross of Jesus is necessarily followed, in the case of those who hear it, by the necessary answer of the little cross which those who know Him and may follow Him as His own are willing and ready and free to take upon themselves and carry. In other words, they are content in their own place and their own way to exist only as those who are " delivered up." In view of what has taken place in His cross for them and for the world, they can greet their own cross as the welcome sign of their certain hope and confidence, of their only comfort both in life and death : " that I am not my own, but belong to my faithful Saviour Jesus Christ."

4. THE DIRECTION OF THE SON

In this sub-section we shall close our basic christological discussion by asking what is the meaning, or better the power, of the existence of the one man Jesus Christ for those among whom and for whom, as the Reconciler, He, the Son of God, became also the Son of Man and one of them, their Brother ; for us other men in our anthropological sphere which He also made His own when He became man. We have called the power of His existence " The Direction of the Son." By this we mean the direction which is given us in divine power and authority by the One who as the eternal Son of the eternal Father is also the Son of Man, the true and royal man, and as such the Lord, our Lord, *Dominus noster*, even in our own anthropological sphere. This power of His existence, His work in His royal office, as the One who became a servant for us to be as such our Lord, is the presupposition of everything that will follow in the course of this second part of the doctrine of reconciliation.

Here again a transitional discussion is required, corresponding to that which was necessary in the first part of the doctrine (under the title " The Verdict of the Father," *C.D.*, IV, 1, § 59, 3) before we could continue and conclude the presentation of the humiliation of the Son of God and the judgment which He fulfilled and suffered in His assumed humanity. Here, too, we must ask how we can proceed from our previous questions and answers to our further tasks. What is the power of the existence of the one man Jesus Christ for all other men ? To what extent is there a way from the one to the other, from Him to us ? To what extent is He our Lord ? How is it that what He was and is and will be can and must and will reach and affect us as the act of divine power ?

We assume at once that it does already reach and affect us. Jesus Christ is in fact our Lord, and power flows from Him. The way from the one to the other, from Him to us, is wide open, and He Himself already treads it. We are not speaking, then, of a power of His existence which is merely possible or hypothetical or contingent, but of the power which is operative and effective. His being as the Son of Man is *per definitionem* His being with us, and His action is as such His action for us. For it to be His being with us or action for us no addition or completion is needed. As the Son of Man Jesus is already within our anthropological sphere and already embraces and controls it. Whatever we may have to say later about the sloth and sanctification of man, and the edification of the Church, and love, is wholly included and enclosed already in the being and action of the Son of Man, and at bottom it can be understood and represented only as a development and explanation of it.

In the transitional discussion in which we must now engage there can be no question, therefore, of anything but a radical and comprehensive explication. We cannot even think of treating as an open question the operative and effective power of the existence of Jesus Christ. We take account of it as something which is absolutely given, so that what it demands is only development and explanation and not its establishment from an alien and neutral place. It has its basis in the resurrection of Jesus from the dead. We speak at once of something

else if we try to treat the power of His existence as an empty possibility
whose actuality has to be written and found on another page, not
accepting it as a fulfilled possibility, as actuality, and therefore as its
own basis and attestation.

But what is it that needs explication before we can pass on to
these further tasks ? What is there that is not wholly self-evident ?
The answer is simple. It is the fact that we are the ones who are
reached and affected by the existence of the Son of Man Jesus Christ.
It is the fact that we are the recipients of the direction of this Lord.
It is the fact that we are the ones to whom He is already on the way
as the Resurrected. How is it that in this context, in relation to the
power and lordship of the royal man Jesus, we go on to speak about
ourselves ? How is it that we put ourselves in this place instead of
man or men ? Does not this mean that to the knowledge of the being
of this royal man among us and His action for us there necessarily
corresponds a knowledge of ourselves—that, for better or for worse,
we are His ? But how can this possibly be said of us ? How can it
possibly be said in the anthropological sphere which is still the sphere
of the unreconciled world, of the man who contradicts and opposes
God ? Is it not a supreme novelty, and how can it possibly be, that
we are those who belong to this man, to Jesus, who have in Him their
Master ? How can the content of man's knowledge of himself, or, let
us say at once, our knowledge, my knowledge of myself, become and
be that *we* are His even if only as those who are really scanned and
known by Him as sinners, who in His light, and therefore in truth,
can and must see themselves as such, and therefore at least as such,
like Peter ? How can it then become and be that *we* are His as those
who by His power are set in contradiction and opposition to their sin,
who are called and sanctified to true and serious conflict with it and
to the fulfilment of the will of God, who constitute His community
of service and obedience, who as its members can love in sincerity and
truth ? Now all this is undoubtedly included and enclosed in the
knowledge of Jesus Christ. Not merely is it set in our head, but it
is written directly on our heart and laid on our lips, that *we* are indeed
His own. In the knowledge of Jesus Christ this is simply a fact which
cannot be escaped or contested. Where there is this knowledge, it
also includes man's knowledge of himself. This being the case, we
certainly must not indulge in abstractions as though it were a matter
of men or humanity in general and not of ourselves. We must avoid
all logical consequences and deductions from this given fact. We must
think only in practical terms, i.e., in relation to ourselves. And yet
we are still faced by the question how we come to a serious and transforming realisation of this enclosing and controlling of our anthropological sphere by the royal man Jesus, and therefore how we achieve
this knowledge of ourselves in which we know and confess that *we*
are Christians. When we examine it closely this self-evident truth

is not at all self-evident. What are the steps that have to be taken—in our thinking, if not only in our thinking—to make sure that this transformation is a reality ? All kinds of self-deceptions (or untruths from the objective standpoint) can arise if we take too short a leap, or come to too hasty and ill-considered a conclusion. A pious dogmatism can be the unholy source of a terrible futility of Christian proclamation in preaching and teaching and pastoral care—and even in dogmatics. In the supposed triumph of a supreme and happy but far too cheap Christian and ecclesiastical and theological logicality the forces of negation may win their supreme and darkest victory. What if this conversion and therefore this knowledge of ourselves are not really in order ? What if the simplicity in which we attain them is only the childish and at bottom arbitrary and arrogant simplicity of the skill of a very human dialectic, and not the true and divine simplicity in which they force themselves upon us and seek to be executed ?

On the one side we have to avoid any compromising or throwing doubt upon that which is given ; upon the power and lordship of the Son of Man, which as such reach and affect all men, the whole anthropological sphere, and therefore concretely ourselves as individuals, not merely as an offer and possibility, but as a reality, an event, which in its scope is actually determinative of all human existence. The significance of the existence of this man for ours is not just potential but actual ; a significance to which we and all men are to be referred at once and without reserve. *Vivit.* He, the royal man, lives as one of ourselves, our Brother. He does not have to become this. And the decision which this involves for us and all men cannot be altered or amended or completed. We may just as easily question the ground on which we walk or the air which we breathe as the perfection of the decision which has been taken concerning us in Him.

On the other side we have also to avoid any error as to the meaning or extent or depth of the change which—whether or not we can and will accept it ; and it is for us to do so—the perfect decision taken in the existence of the Son of Man means for our existence. We have not to overlook the sharp line which now separates the old that is made past in Him and the new that is already present in Him, a line which is drawn by the fact that He is with us and for us. We must not fail to realise the energy of the step with which we are led from the one to the other. The power and lordship of the Son of Man set us in a freedom which is quite interchangeable, which has to be exclusively used and lived out in its uniqueness. Do we know this freedom ? Do we use it ? Do we live in it ? Is it clear to us that it is a dreadful offence against the reality in which we stand not to distinguish it from every other freedom ?

It is natural that we should think at this point of the words used at the Last Supper (1 Cor. 11[26f.]) : " For as often as ye eat this bread, and drink this cup, ye do shew the Lord's death till he come. Wherefore whosoever shall eat this bread, and drink this cup of the Lord, unworthily, shall be guilty of the body and blood of the Lord. But let a man examine himself, and so let him eat of that bread, and drink of that cup. For he that eateth and drinketh unworthily, eateth and drinketh damnation to himself, not discerning the Lord's body. . . . For if we would judge ourselves, we would not be judged. But when we are judged, we are chastened of the Lord, that we should not be condemned with the world." In the eating of that bread and drinking of that cup we have to enter into judgment with ourselves (ἑαυτοὺς διακρίνειν) if we are not to fall victim to the divine κατάκριμα concerning this very eating and drinking.

The freedom which is granted us at once and without reservation and irrevocably in the existence of the royal man Jesus wills to be known and used and lived out as such. And the problem of the transitional discussion that must occupy us in this section is whether and in what circumstances this can and should and must take place. Can we really avoid offending against the reality in which we stand ? Can we really respect this reality ?

It is clear from the very outset that in our consideration of this aspect we must still keep our gaze fixed on Jesus Himself and not allow it to wander in any other direction. The given fact of His existence as the royal man, and His effective power and lordship, cannot be allowed to sink into the background, becoming the content only of a completed christological statement which we have now conveniently left behind to construct a second statement of which Christ is no longer the subject but we ourselves at a certain distance from Him— the Christian as a being which is certainly in relationship to Christ, but has also its own independent existence. We have to reckon quite seriously with the fact that the anthropological sphere is genuinely dominated by the Son of Man as its Lord, and therefore that our knowledge of ourselves is included and enclosed in the knowledge of Jesus. Our self-testing can only take place before Him. It is as those who are judged by the *Lord* (1 Cor. 11[32]) that we can go out from the judgment into which we must always enter with ourselves. He Himself is the answer even to the question of the discerning knowledge and use and living out of the freedom which we are granted in Him. He in whom the decision has been taken concerning us is not only the living, creative source of the change which it means for us, but also its measure and criterion. He determines its meaning and extent and depth. As the One who is with us and for us He decides what we can and should and must become and be in Him and through Him and with Him. He in whom the old is already past and the new has already come draws the sharp line between the two which we have now to know and observe. It is only as we look at Him, therefore, that we can know and observe this line.

It cannot be emphasised too strongly that as we are in Him He " of God is made unto us wisdom, and righteousness, and sanctification, and redemption " (1 Cor. 1[30]). Yes, He is made unto us sanctification. We shall have to return to this later. It might be taken as a title for all that we shall have to say both in general and in detail. But for the moment our concern is with the prior fact that He is made unto us wisdom, *ḥokmah*, the divine source, continually to be sought, of all practical knowledge, and therefore in the first instance of all man's knowledge of Himself. The same is said with an even sharper focus in Col. 2²ᶠ·, where Paul speaks of the battle he is fighting for the Church at Laodicaea and other Churches unknown to Him personally. His aim is " that their hearts might be comforted, being knit together in love, and unto all riches of the full assurance of understanding, to the acknowledgment of the mystery of God, and of the Father, and of Christ ; in whom are hid all the treasures of wisdom and knowledge." If it is true, and normative for us, that He is the mystery of God, the divine accessible fulness of all wisdom and knowledge, we shall refrain from trying to tap any other sources of knowledge even in this context.

In all our later developments and elucidations we shall never cease to derive all that we have to say concerning the man and men who stand under the power and lordship and direction of Jesus Christ from Jesus Christ Himself as the original of everything that in the relationships that will concern us can only be reflected as in mirrors. If this is true generally, it is particularly true in relation to the basic discussion which we must interpose at this point. The greater the concentration with which we look at Him, the better will be the knowledge that we have of ourselves.

We must begin, therefore, by emphasising a statement that we could only make implicitly, only announce, as it were, in the earlier stages of this christological basis when in the second sub-section we considered the incarnation of the Son of God, and its eternal foundation and revelation. For what was it that really took place in the event which we then recognised and described as the homecoming of the Son of Man, as His elevation and exaltation to fellowship with God, to the side of God, to participation in His lordship over all things, as the *communicatio idiomatum et gratiarum et operationum* ? Was it just the isolated history of this one man ? This is certainly the case, for what took place and has to be noted as this communication between divine and human being and activity in this One was and is only, as the reconciliation of man with God by God's own incarnation, His own history and not that of any other man. But for all its singularity, as His history it was not and is not a private history, but a representative and therefore a public. His history in the place of all other men and in accomplishment of their atonement ; the history of their Head, in which they all participate. Therefore, in the most concrete sense of the term, the history of this One is world history. When God was in Christ He reconciled the world to Himself (2 Cor. 5¹⁹), and therefore us, each one of us. In this One humanity itself, our human essence, was and is elevated and exalted. It is in perfect likeness with us, as our genuine Brother, that He was and is so unique, so unlike us as the true and royal man. To that in which a man is like all others, and therefore a man, there now belongs brotherhood with this one man, the One who is so utterly unlike him and all other men.

To human essence in all its nature and corruption there now belongs
the fact that in the one Jesus Christ, who as the true Son of God was
and is also the true Son of Man, it has now become and is participant
in this elevation and exaltation. There is no human life which is not
also (and primarily and finally) determined and characterised by the
fact that it can take place only in this brotherhood. And therefore
there is no self-knowledge which does not also include, which does not
necessarily have primarily and finally as its object, the fact that man
as such is the brother of this one man. Its true theme and origin can
only be a declaration of the Christmas message.

And what is this message ? It is not just the supernatural indicative
that there was then born an exceptional man who was God Himself,
a creature who was also the Creator who rules over all things, and that
this remote fact is our salvation if we to-day will accept it. Nor is
it the supernatural imperative that what took place then can and
should be repeated to-day, God Himself being born in us, or in our
soul. What it does tell us is that in the union of God with our human
existence which then took place uniquely in the existence of this man,
prior to our attitude to it, before we are in any position to accept or
reject it, with no need for repetition either in our soul or elsewhere,
we to-day, bearing the same human essence and living at a particular
point in time and space, *were* taken up (quite irrespective and even in
defiance of our own action and merits) into the fellowship with God
for which we were ordained but which we ourselves had broken ; and
that we *are* therefore taken up into this fellowship in Him, this One.
The Christmas message speaks of what is objectively real for all men,
and therefore for each of us, in this One. Primarily and finally we
ourselves *are* what we are in *Him*. But to be in Him is to be like Him,
to be His brothers, to have a share in that in which He is quite unlike
us, in His fellowship with God, in God's pleasure in Him, but also in
His obedience to God, in His movement towards Him. There can be
no question of our standing in any sense in this fellowship, or making
this obedient movement to God, apart from Him or without Him,
in an abstract and subjective selfhood. But there can also be no
question of our not being in Him as the elected, called, instituted and
revealed Lord and Head of all men, of our not being in His representative existence, as if our own obedience were not anticipated and
virtually accomplished in His.

In the self-knowledge whose object and origin is the declaration of
the message of the birth of the man Jesus we know ourselves—if we
seriously accept it in its direct and in both its primary and secondary
content—as those who are His, as Christians. But this means that
we know ourselves as men with whom God has fellowship and who
have fellowship with God ; to whom God has said Yes and who say
Yes to God ; as " men of goodwill," i.e., as men of the covenant as
it is maintained and fulfilled not only on the side of God but also on

that of man, so that the Vulgate rendering *hominibus bonae voluntatis*, although it is incorrect, is not absolutely impossible. For what took place in the history which is the content of the name of Jesus Christ is that the covenant between God and man was maintained and restored on both sides : on both sides perfectly, because in this history the Son of God became also the Son of Man ; and for the same reason representatively, i.e., in such a way that the case of all men is advocated and conducted by this One, all men being included in this One in the covenant as it is perfectly maintained and restored on both sides. There is no one, therefore, who does not participate in Him in this turning to God. There is no one who is not himself engaged in this turning. There is no one who is not raised and exalted with Him to true humanity. " Jesus lives, and I with Him."

It is this " and I " which is always the subject of the self-knowledge in which man may seek and find himself in this One. Except in Christ no one can know and confess that he is a Christian. No other self-knowledge, however deep or pious or believing, can lead to this " and I." Unless it begins with the " Jesus lives " it cannot possibly end with the " I." Apart from the one Son of Man whose existence is the act of the Son of God, there is no other man who keeps the covenant, who turns and is obedient to God, who shares the divine goodwill. The audacity of regarding ourselves as men who move and are obedient and are therefore pleasing to God, as Christians, except as we look to this One, and our being in Him as the One who takes our place and acts for us, is sheer foolhardiness—a flight of Icarus which, whether we realise it or not, will meet at once with its merited reward. In an abstract, subjective selfhood, apart from Jesus Christ, we none of us exist as those who move and are obedient to God, and therefore we cannot really know ourselves as such. It is only in this One that we genuinely exist ourselves as men like this, as Christians. A true knowledge of ourselves as such, and therefore of our Christian actuality, stands or falls for all of us with our knowledge of Jesus Christ. In Him we are hidden from ourselves. Only in Him can we be revealed. We cannot, therefore, be revealed to ourselves or know ourselves directly, but only indirectly, in relation to the One who for us too is the Mediator between God and men. We can boast of ourselves only as we do not boast of ourselves, but of the Lord.

Yet as we boast of the Lord we are undoubtedly invited to boast of ourselves ; of our being as those who keep the covenant, and are turned and obedient to God, in Jesus Christ ; of our true humanity ; of our elevation and exaltation. We, too, are directly elevated and exalted in the elevation and exaltation of the humiliated Servant of God to be the Lord and King. Apart from Him we are still below, but in Him we are already above. Without Him we are turned from God and disobedient, but with Him we are turned to God and obedient. Outside Christ, looking abstractly and subjectively at ourselves, we

are not Christians. But as we look at Him we are Christians indeed :
not presumptuous Christians but also not frigid ; not cocksure but
also not despairing or sceptical ; not Christians who either rend themselves in a dialectic or falsely deify themselves ; but genuinely happy
Christians who can and even should know and confess that they are
such. There is certainly a dialectic in all this, for we ourselves have
used the phrases : " apart from Him " and " in Him " ; " without
Him " and " with Him " ; " looking at ourselves " and " looking at
Him." But when we hear the Christmas message we are not spectators
of ourselves, so that we do not fall victim to the illusion that it indicates
and describes two scales, or the two sides of a see-saw, which alternately
rise and fall, thus inviting us to understand ourselves alternately or
simultaneously in abstract subjectivity and concrete objectivity, apart
from Christ and in Him, without Him and with Him, looking at ourselves and looking at Him. This dialectic of the scales or see-saw is
our own fatal contribution to the matter, and it is a contribution that
we must refrain from making, because it has nothing whatever to do
with the declaration of the Christmas message. This tells us unequivocally, unilaterally and positively that the " Jesus lives " also includes the " and I " ; that the latter cannot be separated from it ;
that there is, therefore, no place from which man can be his own
spectator and question the reality of the fact that he belongs to Jesus.
The dialectic of the Christmas message is that of a decision which is
being—and has already been—taken : the decision that we are not
apart from Christ but in Him ; that we are not without Him but
with Him ; that if we are to see ourselves we must not look at ourselves but look at Him. It tells us that we are those for whom He
stands surety as the Son of Man, whose turning from God is superseded by His turning to Him, whose disobedience is already overshadowed and outmoded by His ·obedience, whose abstract and subjective and therefore corrupt humanity is corrected and rectified by
His true humanity. It tells us that we are men whose selfhood He
has made His own affair, who can seek and find it, therefore, only in
Him. It does not tell us that we are Christians and something else,
but simply and unreservedly that we are Christians. Does this mean
that we are invited to a false assurance ? The only false assurance is
when we miss the Christmas message, and therefore think we can and
should seek and find and know ourselves otherwise than in the Son of
Man who stands surety for us, in Him as our sanctification. And the
falsest of all false assurances is when we imagine that in that " otherwise " we can order and please ourselves in a continual uncertainty.
As we shall see, the being of man in Jesus Christ, and the knowledge
of it, is a strict and bold and stimulating matter. We shall learn to
know its incisive consequences, and we shall then be amazed that
anyone could be afraid of a false assurance. But first and foremost
we have to realise that we are invited and commanded to understand

inclusively the message of the Son of God who became one with us, and therefore of the existence of the royal man Jesus. Our existence is enclosed by His, and therefore we ourselves are addressed and claimed as those who are already directed and obedient to God in Him, as those who are already born again and converted, as those who are already Christians. "We have peace with God through our Lord Jesus Christ" (Rom. 5¹). Many serious and penetrating things result from this peace, as emerges in Rom. 5–8. But they result from the fact that we *have* this peace. Only half-serious and superficially penetrating things can result from a lack of peace with God, or from a supposed peace that we have or think we have in some other way than "through our Lord Jesus Christ." The Christmas message is : "Peace on earth to men of (God's) goodwill." And what is meant is the peace with God which is included for all the children of men in the child who was born there and then.

We should note and remember at this point what Luther causes the Christmas angels to sing and say : that He is our flesh and blood, and we are now His people, and will live eternally with the angels themselves in heaven. The triumphant final verse of Nikolaus Herman's hymn is also relevant : "To-day He opens wide the door, To our fair paradise, The watchful cherub stands no more ; Our songs to God arise." So, too, is the final strophe of the song of Ambrosius Lobwasser : "Rejoice, eternal heavenly sphere, And thou rejoice O earth, For now your likeness doth appear, One kingdom comes to birth. 'Tis Thee, Lord Jesus Christ, we sing, Of this one realm th' eternal King, And Thou wilt take our cause, To save us from our foes." And not least the verses of Paul Gerhardt : "God is man, O man, for thee ; God's dear Son, Now all one, In blood with us we see " ; and conversely : "Of all my life the life Thou art ; So can I, Cheerfully, Have in Thee my part " ; or again : "Thou art my Head, and so again, I am Thy member and Thy gain ; And as Thy Spirit Thou dost give, For Thee, as Thou dost love, I live " ; and again, developing the predestinarian depth of these statements : "E'er I myself to life was born, Thou then wast born for me ; E'er I did know Thee I was known, For I belonged to Thee ; E'er I myself was fashioned man, Already in Thy thoughts I ran, As Thou wouldst have me be." We may also cite Max von Schenkendorf from the beginning of the 19th century : "Now one great King of all the world, His saving banner hath unfurled, A tender child is born. And all the ancient civil right, The devil had to man by might, He from his hand hath torn."

Because this is the case, Jesus Christ is our justification (1 Cor. 1³⁰). That is, as those who are of like humanity with Him, in Him as our Head and Representative we are righteous and acceptable and pleasing to God even as we are. In and with Him as our Brother, and therefore with the forgiveness of our sins for His sake, we are accepted and loved and blessed as God's dear children. But we must also continue that because this is the case He is also our sanctification. That is, as those who are of like humanity with Him, in Him as our Head and Lord, we are claimed as those who are regenerate and converted, as those who are already engaged in that turning to God, and therefore as Christians. It is only because this is the case, because we are what we are in Jesus Christ before God and therefore in truth, that it can be said of us that we are righteous before God and that we are also holy before God. If it were not so, both statements would be sheer madness. But because it is so, they are unavoidable and we have to risk them ; the second no less than the first. And it is the second which is important in the present context. We will not develop it for the moment. But we must look at its basis, which consists in the fact that the elevation and exaltation of the Son of Man, in the person of the One who was the Son of God and in this way and as such the Son of Man, includes in anticipation the elevation and exaltation —or shall we distinguish and say rather more cautiously the setting up—of all those who as men are brothers of this One. It is in the anticipation that takes place in this One that the sanctification of man has its root, and therefore the life of the Christian community, and Christian love.

In view of this objective basis of our sanctification, the *Heidelberg Catechism* dared to give to *Qu.* 43 : " What further benefit (over and above justification) do we receive from the death and sacrifice of Christ on the cross ? " the answer : " That by His power our old man is crucified, dead and buried with Him, in order that the lusts of the flesh should no longer reign in us, but that we should offer up ourselves to Him in thanksgiving." And then in answer to *Qu.* 45 : " What are the benefits of the resurrection of Christ ? " it listed as the second that " we are now awakened by His power to a new life." And then to *Qu.* 49 : " What are the benefits of the ascension of Christ ? " it gave as the second and even bolder reply : " That we should have our flesh in heaven as a sure pledge that He as the Head will also take to Himself us as His members." It is of a piece with this that in *Qu.* 52, which explains the consolation of the return of Christ, mention is made of the " uplifted head " with which we can look for the coming of the Judge. Also of a piece is the answer to *Qu.* 76 in the doctrine of the Lord's Supper : " What does it mean to eat the crucified body of Christ and to drink His shed blood ? It means not only to accept with a believing heart the whole death and passion of Christ, and thus to receive the remission of sins and eternal life, but also, by the Holy Ghost, who dwells both in Christ and us, to be more and more united with His blessed body, so that, although He is in heaven and we on earth, we are bone of His bone and flesh of His flesh, and live and are ruled eternally by His Spirit (as the members of our body are by a soul)." Above all, we remember the all-embracing answer to *Qu.* 1 : " What is thine only comfort in life and death ? That with body and soul, both in life and death, I am not my own, but belong to my faithful Saviour Jesus Christ."

These replies, and the quotations already adduced from the classical Christmas hymns of the Evangelical Church, are not arbitrary thoughts and statements. They belong to the broad stream of all the New Testament declarations in which it is evident that the first witnesses of the reconciliation and revelation in Jesus Christ, and therefore of the existence of the Son of God become the Son of Man, hardly ever pronounced His name except in an inclusive sense in which they themselves were comprehended and co-ordinated with Him, and in and with themselves other men and even the whole world. According to Phil. 2[9f.] He was for them the One who was supremely exalted by God, being given a name which is above every name (τὸ ὄνομα τὸ ὑπὲρ πᾶν ὄνομα), " that at the name of Jesus every knee should bow, of things in heaven, and things in earth, and things under the earth ; and that every tongue should confess that Jesus Christ is Lord, to the glory of God the Father." According to Ac. 4[12] they realised that the name of Jesus Christ of Nazareth was the only name given under heaven among men in which they found the history of their own salvation (ἐν ᾧ δεῖ σωθῆναι ἡμᾶς), this being the basis of the general declaration of Peter (to which it is linked by a γάρ), that there is no salvation in any other, but having the positive meaning in the context in which it occurs that in the One who bears this name there is salvation and that it has occurred for those to whom the confession is made and who are to be introduced to Him by it. The New Testament witnesses could not speak of the One whom they knew as He made Himself known to them without also speaking of themselves. And they could not speak of themselves without also speaking in anticipation of all those who did not know Him and therefore their own salvation as it had been accomplished in Him. Everything that they said about Him was a testimony to His sovereignty over themselves and over those to whom they addressed themselves with their word and witness. It was an ontological declaration about their own being under His sovereignty, as those who were righteous and holy before God in Him, as those who belonged to God's covenant which in Him was kept and fulfilled from the human side as well as the divine. And in anticipation, i.e., looking beyond the ignorance and unbelief of the men around them, it was also an ontological declaration about these men and every man as such. It belongs to the distinctive essence of the Jesus Christ of the New Testament that as the One He alone is He is not alone, but the royal Representative, the Lord and Head of many. And in the New Testament it belongs to the distinctive essence of the many for whom He is, and who to that extent are " in Him," that in so far as they realise that they are members of His body they distinguish themselves from the world in this knowledge, in this peculiarity of their being in Him, yet do not keep themselves aloof, but claim the world for the fact that the decision which has been taken in Jesus Christ, and which they see clearly as distinct from the world, has been taken objectively for the world as well, and for all those who live in it. For in the New Testament it belongs to the distinctive essence of all who live in the world that the decision which has been taken in Jesus Christ does actually affect them too and their being. Jesus Christ is their Lord and Head as well, and they too, whether they have known Him or not, are only provisionally and subjectively outside Him and without Him in their ignorance and unbelief ; for objectively they are His, they belong to Him, and they can be claimed as His *de iure*.

It is this ontological connexion between the man Jesus on the one side and all other men on the other, and between active Christians on the one side and merely virtual and prospective on the other, which is the basis of the fact that in the New Testament the gathering and upbuilding of the community, of those who know Him, is depicted as a necessity grounded in Himself, and that this community is sent out, again with a necessity grounded in Himself, and entrusted with the task of mission in the world. Jesus Christ would not be who He is if He had no community and if this community did not have or need not have a missionary character. We can sum it up in this way. This ontological connexion is the legal basis of the *kerygma* which forms the community and with which the community is charged. And this ontological connexion is also the basis of the fact that the *kerygma* does not indicate possibilities but declares actualities. These are matters to which we shall have to return at a much later point, i.e., in the third part of the doctrine of reconciliation, when we consider the prophetic office of Jesus Christ. We shall then explain them in greater detail. Our present concern is with the basic fact that when we say Jesus Christ in the New Testament sense we make a declaration, an ontological declaration, about all other men ; the kind of statement that we find in the passages quoted from the ▪*Heidelberg Catechism* and our Church's hymns.

It will be instructive at this point to turn to Heb. 6[17-20], which speaks of " two immutable things " (πράγματα ἀμετάθετα) in which Christians whose refuge is to lay hold of the hope set before them have a " strong consolation " (ἰσχυρὰ παράκλησις), for it is impossible that God, by whose promise they are called, should deceive them. The first of these two things is the solemn character of the promise itself, the fact that God has pledged Himself in His Word. The second consists in the fact that those who trust in His Word have in the hope which is set before them and for which they reach out " an anchor of the soul, both sure and steadfast, and which entereth into that within the veil," so that in it, although they are still here in this life, they are already in the life beyond, living, even in the hope itself, in the fulfilment which is before them. But the anchor of the soul is that " the forerunner is for us (πρόδρομος ὑπὲρ ἡμῶν) entered, even Jesus," so that He is there in their place, Himself being the second " immutable thing " which is before them, as the Word of God is the first from which they come. They hope, therefore, as they stand both behind and before in an ontological connexion. On both sides the declaration that Jesus is our confidence is sure and not unsure because it has an immutable foundation.

We turn next to an expression which occurs frequently in the Johannine writings. It is that of the " abiding " (μένειν) of the disciples in Jesus and of Jesus in them. " He that eateth my flesh, and drinketh my blood, dwelleth in me, and I in him " (Jn. 6⁵⁶). This is the verse referred to by the Heidelberg Catechism in its explanation of the Lord's Supper in Qu. 76. The same thought recurs in Jn. 15⁴ᶠ· : " Abide in me, and I in you," and the picture is given of the branch which must abide in the vine if it is to bear fruit. " He that abideth in me, and I in him, the same bringeth forth much fruit : for without me (χωρὶς ἐμοῦ) ye can do nothing " (v. 5). And again : " If ye abide in me, and my words in you, ye shall ask what ye will, and it shall be done unto you " (v. 7). The warning is also given in 1 Jn. 2⁶ : " He that saith he abideth in him ought himself also so to walk, even as he walked." The direct promise is also given to Christians in 1 Jn. 2²⁷ : " But the anointing (τὸ χρῖσμα) which ye have received of him abideth in you, and ye need not that any man teach you : but as the same anointing teacheth you of all things, and is truth, and is no lie, and even as it taught you, ye shall abide in him." And on any other presuppositions 1 Jn. 3⁶ is so unequivocal as to be quite startling : " Whosoever abideth in him sinneth not." Then the further admonition or warning is given in 1 Jn. 3²⁴ and 4¹³ : " And he that keepeth his commandments dwelleth in him, and he in him. And hereby we know that he dwelleth in us, by the Spirit which he hath given us." The presupposition of this abiding is obviously a being. It is not a dead being, but a living and vital being, which bears fruit in knowledge and conduct, and is active in the keeping of the commandments. Nor is it a being which is under the control of men or subject to their caprice or sloth, but a being which determines and commits them, a being in which they are exhorted and summoned to abide. Nor, finally, is it a being which is immanent to these men in their creatureliness, or inherent in their existence as such, but a being which they are promised and given by the Gospel. That is why we read in 1 Jn. 2²⁴ : " Let that therefore abide in you which ye have heard from the beginning. If that which ye have heard from the beginning shall remain in you, ye shall also continue in the Son and in the Father." But even when we define it more precisely in this way it is still a being : not just an experience that we have, nor a disposition, nor an attitude of the will or emotions, nor a possibility that is available but has still to be realised ; but our truest reality, in which we are to see and understand ourselves in truth, for which we are claimed, from which there automatically result certain consequences which we have necessarily to draw, which we can question neither in itself nor in its consequences, in which we are to remain (for this is our only possibility ; to choose any other is to choose the impossible) ; to remain both where we are and what we are. We are in Him of whom we have heard, who has been proclaimed to us. It is not for nothing that we are in Him. Nor is it by good fortune, or of ourselves. It is only of Him. But we really are in Him. And from this being there follows necessarily all that we have to will and do. From this being there follows the necessity of avoiding anything that would deny it. From this being there follows above all the necessity of remaining where and what we are.

And now we come to Paul with all the wealth of his statement about that which, while it is primarily the history of Jesus Christ, is secondarily and as an irresistible consequence his own history, and the obvious history of all those who have discovered or will discover Jesus Christ, and themselves in Him. The life which he now lives in the flesh, as he tells us in Gal. 2²⁰, he lives " by the faith of the Son of God, who loved me, and gave himself for me." The old has passed away in Him, and he is a new creature (2 Cor. 5¹⁷ ; Gal. 6¹⁵). " I live ; yet not I, but Christ liveth in me " (Gal. 2²⁰). These statements have a typical and not merely an individual significance. They are the necessary self-declaration of all Christians. To be a Christian is *per definitionem* to be ἐν Χριστῷ. The place of the community as such, the theatre of their history, the ground on which they stand, the air that they breathe, and therefore the standard of what they do and do not do, is indicated by this expression. The ἐν Χριστῷ εἶναι is the *a priori* of all the instruction that Paul gives his Churches, all the comfort and exhortation that he addresses to them. They, too, live in the flesh, in the world. But as Christ gave Himself up for them, it is not only for Himself but for them that He lives in them, enfolding them and ruling them. Each of them is His " body," and He is the clothing which is put on, or has already been put on, by all their members (Rom. 13¹⁴ ; Gal. 3²⁷). In Him both the community as a whole and all individual Christians " are builded together for an inhabitation of God through the Spirit " (Eph. 2²²). The community and its members live because they are ἐν Χριστῷ, or, to use the other important expression, σὺν Χριστῷ. And to be " with Christ " is to take part in His history, so that in His history that of the community and all its members has already happened, and has therefore to find in His history its model and pattern, to see itself again in it ; the result being that the community and its members necessarily cease to be what they are if they are guilty of any arbitrary deviation from His history. This " with Christ " determines their past and present and future ; their whole history. They are crucified with Him (Gal. 2¹⁹, 6¹⁴), dead with Him (Rom. 6⁸ ; Col. 2²⁰, 3³), buried with Him (Rom. 6⁴ ; Col. 2¹²), made alive with Him (in the bold anticipation of Col. 2¹³ and Eph. 2⁵), and even made to sit together with Him in heavenly places (in the even bolder anticipation of Eph. 2⁶, which is repeated in *Qu.* 49 of the *Heidelberg Catechism*). It is an understatement when Bengel finds in Eph. 2⁶ only the reference to a *sedes assignata, suo tempore possidenda* in heaven. What is really meant is that they are already with Him in heaven, that they have already taken this *sedes*, that they live already in the πολίτευμα ἐν οὐρανοῖς of Phil. 3²⁰. Living in the flesh, therefore, they are to have before them, and keep in mind, and consider, only that waking or sleeping they should live with Him (1 Thess. 5¹⁰) ; only that they should seek those things which are above where Christ is seated at the right hand of God—their life which is hid with Christ in God, but which is their true life because it is their life with Him (Col. 3¹ᶠ.). The interpretation of Calvin is the true one (*Sermon on Eph.* 2³⁻⁶, C.R., 51, 372) : " *Il est impossible que le chef soit séparé des membres, et nostre Seigneur Jesus Christ n'y est pas entré pour soy. Il nous faut tousiours revenir à ce principe. Quand nous confessons que Jesus Christ est ressuscité des morts et monté au ciel, ce n'est pas seulement pour le glorifier en sa personne. It est vray que cela viendra en premier lieu . . . Mais tant y a que ceste union . . . est accomplie : que Jesus Christ nous ayant recueillis en son corps, a voulu commencer en soy ce qu'il veut parfaire au nous, voire quand le temps opportun sera venu. Ainsi donc Jesus Christ est entré au ciel, à fin qu'aujourd'huy la porte nous soit ouverte, laquelle nous estoit close par le peché d'Adam : et voilà comme desia nous sommes colloquez avec luy.*" It is because and as and to the extent that Christians are already there in Christ and with Him, that they are already elevated and exalted in Him and with Him; that they are here and now the saints of God, as Paul usually addresses and claims them at the beginning of His Epistles; and that—in spite of the fact that their existence is still in the flesh and determined by their own nature and corruption and that of the world around, in spite of all that can be brought against them on this score—no sentence (κατάκριμα) of condemnation can affect them, to menace or even destroy their being as saints (Rom. 8¹ᶠ·). In so far as it is their being in Christ, and therefore their being where He is, with God, it is an indestructible being.

Paul develops this insight in the closing section of Rom. 8. There at God's right hand it is Christ that died and rose again and ascended who intercedes for them (ἐντυγχάνει ὑπὲρ ἡμῶν, v. 34). God foreknew them (προέγνω) even before they came into being, before the world was. He predestinated (προώρισεν) those whom He foreknew to be conformed (σύμμορφοι) to the image of His Son. And it is according to this foreknowledge and predestination that He has acted for them in time. He called them to the place where they belonged on the basis of His eternal election—to use the phrase of 1 Pet. 2⁹, " out of darkness into his marvellous light " (ἐκάλεσεν). And as those whom He called He justified them (ἐδικαίωσεν)—without any co-operation on their part, and therefore unconditionally. And as those who are genuinely justified by Him He glorified them with a heavenly glory (ἐδόξασεν). He gave them this being with Christ in heaven, with Himself. It is to be noted that at every point, even the last, this *catena aurea* (vv. 29–30) speaks of an event in which God acted for Christians and from which as Christians they can only come, as those who are already foreknown and predestinated and called and justified and even glorified. They are the people they are in virtue of this eternal and temporal will and action of God. They are this as Christ intercedes for them, as God Himself is not against them but for them (v. 31). This is the condition, but it is also the basis, of their being. It is this that makes it an indestructible being. They do not dispose of it themselves, any more than they dispose of Christ or God, for it is God's free grace that He is for them and not against them. But this does not alter the fact that disposition has been made concerning them and their being by Christ and therefore by God Himself. Everything else follows from this basis. " He that spared not his own Son, but delivered him up freely for us all, how shall he not with him also freely give us all things " (τὰ πάντα χαρίσεται, v. 32)? " Who can say anything to these things ? " (v. 31). Who can accuse or condemn the elect of God, or effectively question or contradict their being as His saints ? (v. 33). God is always there first as their δικαιῶν (v. 33), for Christ is there (v. 34). Their being as God's saints could only be imperilled or destroyed by a breaking or snapping (χωρίζειν) of the connexion between Christ and them and therefore between God and them. But how can this be possible ? Who or what has the right or power for this χωρίζειν ? " Who shall separate us from the love of Christ ? "—the love in which none has taken up himself into this ontological relationship but in which He has assumed them all into it. Paul considers all the things that men can do and do to Christians and records them—tribulation, distress, persecution, famine, nakedness, peril and sword. All these things might speak and work against their being as God's saints. They might mean accusation and condemnation. They might mark them out as God's enemies, rejected by Him. It is true enough : " We are killed all the day long ; we are accounted as sheep for the slaughter." This is the fate of the ungodly. Can it be that Christians too, and Christians especially, are ungodly. This is the charge of the Jews and Gentiles who threaten them. Why, then, are they treated in this way ? Ἕνεκεν σοῦ, for thy sake, as witnesses and confessors of the Christ who Himself was killed, and therefore as those who love Him, and therefore (for how else could this be the case ?) as those who are loved by Him, who are not separated from His love. As those who are persecuted for His sake, how can they be shaken or assailed in what they are by Him and in Him and with Him (vv.

35–36) ? " Nay, in all these things we are more than conquerors " (ὑπερνικῶμεν, v. 37). They emerge from all these things as victors. But they do so as those they are : not as those who are rejected by God but as those who are elected ; not as the ungodly but as the saints of God. They ? Yes, they—διὰ τοῦ ἀγαπή-σαντος ἡμᾶς, through Him that loved them, as this worked itself out in the fact that they could love Him in return, and therefore came to experience all these things at the hands of men as His witnesses and confessors, being placed in this repetition of His own passion. If they were not loved by Him, if they were not His own and therefore the elect and saints of God, they would not suffer these things. As they do suffer them, it is revealed that they are. And the love of Christ has the power to bring them out as victors from all these things because it is the love of God. As Christ intercedes for them, God is for them. And note that this time Paul does not ask the corresponding question : " Who shall separate us from the love of God ? " (vv. 38–39, cf. v. 35). He has already given the answer to this question. For the love of God is simply the love of Christ from which Christians cannot be separated. It is the ἀγάπη τοῦ θεοῦ ἡ ἐν Χριστῷ Ἰησοῦ τῷ κυρίῳ ἡμῶν (v. 39). Those who cannot be separated from the love of Christ cannot be separated from the love of God. Hence at once : πέπεισμαι. Verses 38–39 merely emphasise that there can be no breaking of the connexion between Christ and us because it is a connexion which is created and maintained by the love of God. But this new emphasis results in an important enlargement of vision in which there is the implicit answer to a latent question. Paul now looks away from the significance of the acts of other men for the being of Christians to the very structure of the cosmos, or its disruption ; to the aspect of hostility and mystery and demonism and peril which its scattered elements—all with a claim to total authority and power—present to man ; to sinful man, whose situation and appearance Christians know only too well as the men they still are here below in the flesh. What is meant by Paul's " in all these things we are more than conquerors " in face of this situation, in which the sun is continually obscured by an interposing cloud-sheet of ever-changing form and colour and direction and proximity, summed up by Paul himself in terms and concepts borrowed from his own age as death, and life, and angels, and principalities, and powers, and things present, and things to come,'and height, and depth ? What is its value in face of this situation in which the boundaries of the objectively and subjectively real, of the good creation of God and its disturbance and dis- solution, continually intersect, and for the understanding of which each age and nation has sought and found its own terminology : the " gods many and lords many " (1 Cor. 8⁵) ; the great factors of world-occurrence in the natural and historical, the material and spiritual, the visible and invisible world which ought to be the home of man as the creature of God but is now an alien land—factors which are so obscure to man in their origin, nature and functions, which can only dazzle and confuse him in his little perception and understanding, now working and disclosing themselves with what seems to be the height of constancy, and now with the height of contingency ? What is meant by being in Christ, the being of the saints here and now, when the human perception and understanding even of Christians continually stumbles against these dark factors ; when they too cannot conceal from themselves the alien character of this here and now, the mad interplay of so many things which cannot be co-ordinated, the chaotic, or near-chaotic, destructive and supremely dangerous nature of the human situation ; when they of all men are necessarily most keenly aware of it—what- ever terminology they use—and have to take it with a supreme and final serious- ness ? Might it not be the case that, living in this world, and threatened on all sides, Christians too are victims and subjects of this world ? Might it not be the case that it means for them too accusation and condemnation and curse and cosmic imprisonment and bondage and therefore indirectly rejection and divine judgment ? This is the latent question which Paul does actually answer if he does not pose. He does not contest the situation depicted. He does not minimise or rationalise it. Himself living in this situation, and taking it as he finds it, he simply proclaims his πέπεισμαι. Even all the factors of world occurrence, even the whole disruption of the structure of the cosmos, cannot separate us from the love of God. We may perhaps see a basis of this conviction in the incidental recollection in v. 39 that all these threats are in the sphere of the κτίσις, so that they are not superior or equal to God, but always subordinate ; just as we are incidentally reminded in 1 Cor. 8[5] that the gods many are only called gods. But we are nearer to the true sense if we take it that the πέπεισμαι of v. 38 is simply a repetition and application of the ὑπερνικῶμεν of v. 37. Paul displays, as it were, this ὑπερνικᾶν to the community. In this declaration of faith he gives a factual demonstration. He himself, the apostle, is one of those who see and know nothing of this separation, and who have, therefore, nothing to say about it. He lets the inviolable love of God in Jesus Christ speak for itself, attesting it both in the name of the community and for its comfort and admonition. Christians must hear his confession, and realise from the fact that he is able to make it that its content is normative for them too. Whatever that cloud-sheet may be, it cannot separate them from the love of God any more than it can Paul. Paul, who is in the cosmos as they are, is a witness to this fact. For it has not separated him. It has, therefore, no power to do so. They do not need to fear it. What seems to be his personal venture and defiance is in effect the common rule. As a being in Christ their being as Christians is one which cannot really be assailed by any human attack or cosmic situation. And from v. 35 f. as from v. 38 f. we must look back to the even bolder v. 28 : " We know that all things work together (πάντα συνεργεῖ) for good to them that love God." And this includes whatever man might do to them, or the cosmic situation in all its darkness and ferocity. These things are not a genuine violation, but a genuine confirmation and strengthening of their being in Christ. Since all these things must and will serve God, they must and will serve them too, helping them, prospering them, turning to their advantage, leading to that victory and conviction, causing them really to be the men they are, not in spite of the fact but because of the fact that they are attacked in this way by their fellows and threatened by the cosmos. All these things can only speak and work for them and not against them—for their peace with God as it is concluded in Jesus Christ. For all these things can only invite and lead and move them to rest in this peace with God as the surest of all things, and therefore to rest in Jesus Christ. This is how Paul viewed the being of Christians as grounded in that of Jesus Christ. And it was in this sense that he could boast of its impregnability.

But before we go further it is high time that we should halt for a moment and even take a temporary step back.

What is it that we have heard and said ? We have maintained that the necessary statement about the being of Jesus Christ no less necessarily includes in it a statement about all human being ; the statement which the Christian can and must venture in view of the fact that his confession " Jesus lives " involves also the confession " and I with Him." What the community recognises in faith in the the being of Jesus Christ its Lord is the divine decision which in this One as the Lord of all men has been taken for all men and concerning the being of all men. It is, therefore, their participation in His exaltation. The connexion between these two statements is quite unequivocal in the New Testament. The New Testament does not know of a Jesus Christ who is what He is exclusively for Himself. Nor does it know of a self-enclosed human being confronting this man Jesus. We might think of sinful man. But according to the New Testament it was to seek and save sinners that the man Jesus came. Even sinful man is seen together with the man Jesus, which means that in the man Jesus even sinful man is confronted by the One in whom the divine decision has been made concerning him, in whom there is already resolved and accomplished his deliverance from sin, his elevation, his restoration as a true covenant-partner of God. In other words, there is no Jesus existing exclusively for Himself, and there is no sinful man who is not affected and determined with and by His existence.

Christian proclamation orientated by the New Testament cannot possibly escape seeing the two together. It will magnify the antithesis between the being of Jesus and that of sinful man only to magnify even more the divine decision which has been made concerning sinful man in Jesus, and therefore the onto-logical connexion between the two. And if it fails to do this, if it wanders off into abstractions concerning either Jesus or other men, dogmatics is always there to point it to the unequivocal witness of the New Testament, to the message of Christmas, and therefore to remind it that abstractions of this kind are for-bidden, that if the full Gospel is to be proclaimed (and if it is not a full Gospel it is not the Gospel at all) it has necessarily to speak of this connexion. The Church's proclamation everywhere suffers to some extent from the fact that it does not speak of this connexion with sufficient emphasis. In our responsibility to the Church we cannot, therefore, say less concerning it, or speak with less distinctness, than we have tried to do in this first part of our discussion.

But we must not have any illusions as to the alien and unpre-cedented and even monstrous nature of the connexion between these two statements and therefore of a common survey of their contents. We regard this connexion as a light and easy matter only if we do not take seriously either one or other of the statements, and therefore both; only if we regard either the statement of faith about Jesus or that about the man who confronts Him, or both, as mere value-judgments, whose content is left open for more detailed proof, from whose " enthusiastic " implications tacit or even explicit deductions have to be made, and which can be safely expressed with all kinds of qualifications. But the matter itself, as well as the New Testament school in which we have to consider it, forces us to take these state-ments seriously, i.e., both the statements and also this connexion, as statements about a being of the man Jesus, and therefore a being of other men (our own being), as statements of an ontological character. To be sure, they are statements of faith. But we must not add, in the common feeble way, that they are " only " statements of faith : as if statements of faith in the New Testament sense were not meant to be taken seriously ; as if they were not also statements of knowledge, of the knowledge of being, and the power of this being ; as if they could be analysed, attention being drawn on the one side to their character as extravagant speech about a value which is enlightening for faith, about the reach and significance of an objective content, and on the other, distinguished from this and subject to historico-psychological demonstration, to their character as speech about the actual content as it is seen in faith ; as if there were two forms of speech, the one not being obligatory for the other, but the one limiting and compromising the other ; as if we could and should say in faith that this or that *is*, but leave open the question of its significance, or that this or that is what is *signified*, but leave open the question whether and in what sense there is anything to signify it ; as if a statement of faith did not include as inseparable elements both a statement of being and a state-ment of the power of this being as such. When the New Testament describes Jesus as Lord, it says and means that He really is the Lord, with all that this also implies both for us and for all men.

But where does it lead us when, taught by the matter itself and the New Testament school in which we must think in the Church, we cannot take a light and easy way, but are forced to understand what has to be said about the connexion between the man Jesus and all other men in ontological and for this very reason in dynamic terms ? We must try to take seriously, and to realise what it means, that He is on the one side as the royal man, in all His majesty and uniqueness, which are grounded in the fact that He is the eternal Son of the eternal Father, and therefore God, and as such man ; and that we are on the other as those who are not these things, who are only men, but who are under this Lord, who are His, who belong to Him, who are ordered in relation to Him, who are in Him (" abiding " in Him) and with Him, who are therefore exalted into His fellowship with God, who have been arrested and turned on our own evil way, who are obedient to God and saints of God and true covenant-partners with God in Him. And when we consider ourselves we have to remember that we on this side are all these things with the inviolability, impregnability and indestructibility described at the end of Rom. 8 ; and with the sub-jective assurance which corresponds to this objective being, so that we can repeat in the sense in which it was originally meant : " I am persuaded that . . . nothing (in earth or heaven) shall be able to separate us from the love of God, which is in Christ Jesus our Lord." The point is that we really are these things. We do not say this merely as religious rhetoric, or enthusiastic hyperbole, or liturgical song, or a value-judgment of our faith, or an interpretation of our historical situation and existence. But with no literary devices or exaggeration we say it as a plain and sober statement of fact : We really *are*. But what do we mean when we say " we " ? And what do we mean when we say " are " ?

These questions have to be raised even (and precisely) when we build on the presupposition that it is actually the case that we are. For it cannot be taken for granted that in the attempt to grasp this thought we are really dealing with the actuality. We may so easily be groping for it, wandering in a fog, thinking that which is only trivial or nonsensical, telling ourselves and others an attractive fairy-story, presenting an inspiring piece of poetry, proclaiming a myth or merely spinning pious sayings whose meaning we cannot declare either to ourselves or others, so that for all our sincerity they can only be ambiguous and confusing. At this point, and even on the presupposition that it has to do with a reality, the Church right up to our own times has thought and said and preached, or rather dreamed and babbled, many things which in spite of their pious sincerity have nothing whatever to do with the reality, and are therefore sterile buds which can bear no fruit. Here, too, *vestigia terrent*. We have every reason to take at this point steps which, if they are firm, are also very cautious.

One thing emerges clearly from what we have already said. In our assertion that we are these things, and knowing that this is the case, we cannot be too strict or consistent in looking away from ourselves. It is a matter of knowing ourselves but of knowing ourselves in Christ, and therefore not here in ourselves but there outside ourselves in this Other who is not identical with me, and with whom I am not, and do not become, identical, but in whose humanity God Himself becomes and is and always will be another, a concrete antithesis. The knowledge of ourselves as what we are in Him can have nothing to do, therefore, with self-investigation, the consideration and evaluation of ourselves, or introspection in all its known and conceivable forms. This knowledge occurs only where enterprises of this type are all abandoned. For however it may be with the one I know or think I know myself to be, whether I find pleasure or the reverse in contemplating the strange figure I call myself, whether I have a more or less keen awareness of myself, whether I am sympathetic or unsympathetic, satisfied or dissatisfied with myself, whether I count myself fortunate or unfortunate, if I am really to know myself in the sense which now concerns us I must look and turn right away from this self that I can and do consider. In certain respects there may be a relative justification for our interest in this figure, for the loving attention and anxiety with which we surround it, for the satisfaction we find in it or the grief or irony it causes us, for the pains we take to nurture it and the safeguards we try to erect for it. But at this point all these things reach their frontier, and we have to look and march over this frontier, and therefore leave this figure and all its concerns behind us. What we are in Jesus Christ certainly cannot be grounded in this figure and its existence and activity and experiences, in what it does and does not do. Our concern now must be with Jesus Christ, and with myself, ourselves, in Him.

This seems to be a purely critical clarification. It is critical, but it has a supremely positive significance. To achieve it involves an incisive renunciation. For it is not self-evident that we should turn away from this figure, that we should look away from the one whom we not unjustly describe as our closest neighbour. But if we really do it, is not this a liberation? The great anxiety which introspection inevitably involves is not perhaps ended when we look away, but it is at least relegated to its proper place. Its problem still arises. It still continues. But it is not now before and above us, but behind and below us. It is no longer the great thing to which we continually look and must always move. It is no longer the steep incline that we have always to climb. To know ourselves is to know ourselves at the place, and to come to ourselves is to come to it, where the desire and also the burden of this anxiety are taken from us. Thus our thinking about what we really are in Jesus Christ misses this reality, and is purely illusory, if it is not a thinking which promises liberation, but is pursued in a lower or higher form of introspection, and involves a continuance at a higher or lower level of this anxiety with all its desires and burdens. Conversely, it is a true and substantial thinking, directed to this reality, if it takes the form of this renunciation and abandonment ; if in it we look beyond ourselves and find that it is for us a liberating thinking.

But we must now be more precise. We really look away from ourselves, and therefore know ourselves genuinely and freely, only as we really look to Jesus Christ. We do not do so merely as we look formally away from ourselves and beyond ourselves, in a purely formal negation of that figure " the self," to an empty beyond.

It is not the case that we can tell ourselves that we are something that we are *not*. To do so is merely to think of our death, and to do this with the absurd notion that we can regard our death as our life. To lose one's life is not of itself to find it. Nor is it to our salvation to think in this way, let alone to try to practise it, to achieve our own negation and loss. In a purely formal sense no one, not even a Spanish mystic, has ever really looked away from himself and beyond himself, let alone transcended himself in a purely formal negation. If we try to do this, looking into an empty beyond, we are really looking quite cheerfully at ourselves again, however solemnly we may pretend that it is otherwise. What we see is only our own frontier, and we see this only from within. We do not see it as it is really drawn. Nor do we see ourselves in the freedom which is beyond our self-contemplation and the great anxiety which it necessarily involves. We cannot lose ourselves. But this means that we cannot find ourselves either when we try of ourselves to lose ourselves. We are still the old man within the frontier which we see from within. We can only imagine that we are able to transcend ourselves and have actually done : no matter how certain we may be of this empty beyond ; no matter what extraordinary measures we may take—even to the extreme of suicide —to take this step and therefore to find ourselves. The look away from and beyond ourselves can take place only when it has an object which irresistibly draws it ; when it is a look which has a definite content ; when this beyond is not nothing but something or Someone ; when this Someone is the frontier which is actually and positively drawn for us from without, to see which is not merely a question but the answer, and to cross which is not merely supposed but genuine loss, and not merely imagined but real gain in loss ; when in this Someone as our beyond we really and finally encounter ourselves. How else but from a superior, genuine position can we achieve genuine negation, let alone that which has the power of a position ? How else but from the place where there is genuine gain, and it is therefore to be sought and found, can we achieve genuine loss, let alone that which is gain ? The only No which has power as such, let alone the power of a secret Yes, is the No which is spoken in and with a superior, genuine Yes. We have to hear this superior, genuine Yes. But we hear this superior, genuine Yes, in which even the unavoidable No is valid and effective, only when we look away from and beyond ourselves because we see something confronting us, and this something as a Someone, and in this Someone ourselves, so that in Him, in this Other, we are summoned and irresistibly impelled to seek and find ourselves.

This Someone, this Other, is Jesus Christ. And the distinction between those who genuinely and forcefully look away from and beyond themselves and those who cannot do this but only try ostensibly and ineffectively to do so, is to be found in the fact that the former abandon even this attempt at self-transcendence, not looking into an empty but filled beyond, not trying to think the thought of their death (and not really thinking it) but really thinking the thought of their own life, looking to Jesus Christ and knowing Him and themselves in Him. It is only in this knowledge that there is fulfilled the critical clarification, the liberation, in which man is given and shown his true frontier, and (without being merely cut loose from himself) is really brought behind and below himself. We have the old man behind and below us when we have Jesus Christ before and above us, and in Him ourselves as the new man who is elevated and exalted to fellowship with God ; who is certain of his elevation and exaltation, inviolably, impregnably and indestructibly certain ; who cannot be separated from the love of God, and can only speak, therefore, in the language of the closing verses of Rom. 8.

But if, to know ourselves as the saints of God, we have to look away from and behind ourselves, and if this takes place as we look at Jesus Christ because we are this in Him and only in Him, this means that we can have this knowledge only as we look into that which is concealed. For the being of Jesus Christ as Lord, as King, as Son of Man, as true man, is a hidden being. If He is seen, and we in Him, it is not the kind of seeing of which we ourselves are or ever will be capable. We have no organ or ability for it, nor the corresponding will and resolution to use it. This seeing is not a possibility of our own. It can be a reality, not in the actualisation of a potentiality that we ourselves possess, but only as it is given us in pure actuality. It can only take place, in a way which is quite incomprehensible to ourselves, that we do actually know Him, and in Him ourselves. And when it does take place it is always a confirmation of the fact that He is hidden from us, and that in Him we too are hidden from ourselves. That the love of Jesus Christ penetrates His hiddenness, and therefore the hiddenness of our being in Him, when He causes Himself to be seen and ourselves in Him, His lordship and kingdom, and ourselves as His own, His possession, dwelling in His kingdom—all this confirms the fact that He, and we, are hidden. It is the exception which proves the rule. And if in His love and revelation we can see Him and ourselves in Him, and love Him in return, we are merely seeing and loving that which is concealed, and in so doing necessarily confirming both His and our own concealment. The exception proves the rule. We do not exist (yet) in such a way that space and time, nature and history and the human situation are one continuous demonstration of the being of Jesus Christ and our being in Him and therefore of His love. We do not exist, of course, without some proofs of this love. His love is indeed revealed to us, and therefore we are revealed to ourselves in Him as His own, His possession. But we can only pass from one such proof to another. Space and time, nature and history and the human situation are not this demonstration as such. There has to be a penetration of their form and aspect. And this penetration is not a state but an event. It is not yet a steady, all-embracing and all-pervasive light by which we are surrounded on all sides in accordance with the being of Jesus Christ, and our being in Him, and therefore His love. Thus we for our part do not yet exist in a complete and unbroken perception of His being and our being in Him, and therefore in a full and perennial response to His love, in a response of love which is even remotely consistent. From this standpoint too, and particularly, we are wanderers who pass from one small and provisional response, from one small and provisional perception and love, to another. From our side too the penetration is not yet a state, a steady and perfect clarity, but an event ; an infrequent, weak, uncertain and flickering glow which stands in a sorry relationship to the perfection of even the smallest beam of light.

But this is only one aspect of the concealment of Jesus Christ and our being in Him. Nor is it this aspect—the discontinuity with which He may be, and is seen, as the hidden One—which makes the problem of this concealment so incisive. There is an even deeper mystery. It is not at all the case that what conceals Jesus Christ and therefore ourselves is a kind of protective garment or cover which certainly hides what is concealed but also reveals it to the extent that it fits what is concealed, following its lines, and thus allowing it to be sensed or even on a closer inspection known, so that there is no real need to penetrate or remove it. If this were so, the concealment of Jesus Christ and our being in Him could easily be mastered because He, and we in Him, could really be known even in this concealment. But the truth is very different. For the terrible aspect of His and our concealment is that what conceals, the garment or cover, gives to what is concealed by it the shape of its opposite ; to the Yes the form of a No. In other words, that which conceals does not correspond in the very least to that which is concealed. It contradicts it. Not merely in a simple sense, but in a supreme sense, we cannot know Him as He is, or ourselves as we are in Him, in what we see. What is there, and is also to be seen, cannot be perceived even indirectly or analogically through what conceals it. We cannot know it at all of ourselves, using the possibilities of our own perception. What conceals is not an analogy or likeness of what is concealed. It is completely dissimilar. It does not witness to it, but protests against it. It does not prove, but denies, the being of Jesus Christ and our being in Him. What it proves and demonstrates is that Jesus Christ is not the Lord, that there is no such thing as His kingdom, that we are not therefore His, and that we are not elevated and exalted to be the saints of God in Him. What conceals denies both Him and us. It shows us both Him and ourselves under this negation. It prevents us from seeing His being and our being in Him. If we are to see what is hidden, and therefore to know Jesus Christ and ourselves in Him, it will not be by looking through that which hides. To see and know Jesus Christ and ourselves, there has to be a penetration and removal of that which hides. And this penetration is always an event ; an exception and not a state. And its removal has not yet taken place.

We are now speaking of what is, unfortunately, the usual situation for all of us when we aim to look away from and beyond ourselves to Jesus Christ and therefore to know and seek and find ourselves in Him. It may well be said that in preaching and pastoral work, and in a good deal of dogmatic discussion, and above all in individual reflection, we do aim to look at Jesus Christ. And we transcend ourselves and thus come to ourselves. We hear the No which is a wholehearted Yes. We know the loss which is supreme gain. We enjoy the liberation which we so much need in that frightful self-preoccupation and the paralysing anxiety it involves. But however wide open our spiritual eyes may be, this does not mean that Jesus Christ is now at our disposal. It does not mean that in His glory as the Lord and King and elevated and exalted Son of Man He is, He now shines on us and illuminates us directly. It is not that only a little openness and readiness are now required to know Him and ourselves in Him, and to find ourselves established in Him and by Him, and set in the right place, and brought into a true covenant-partnership with God. The matter has often enough been conceived and presented in this simple and enthusiastic way. He Himself, and His fellowship with us and ours with Him, are often enough received and valued in this cheap and easy fashion. It is often thought that His atonement and salvation can be known and enjoyed in this facile way : as though it were only like pushing one's finger through a piece of paper, as any child can do ; as though it were only a matter of persuading oneself and others to make this easy and tiny movement. But the case is in fact quite different with Jesus Christ and ourselves in Him. His high being, and ours in Him, the whole exalted reality of the reconciliation of the world with God as it has taken place in Him, our salvation as it was resolved from all eternity and accomplished in the fulness of time, our peace with God—none of these things is attested in this way in the Bible to which we are rightly referred, whether we turn to the Old Testament or indeed to the New. For in the Bible neither He Himself is accessible and at our disposal in this way, nor do we who are so much concerned in this matter find ourselves in this position. Even in the most sincere and effective prayer He is not accessible and at our disposal in this way, nor is that which He is for us. For we are speaking of the One who is high and lifted up, and of the majesty of our being in Him and with Him. And there can be no question of any such accessibility.

The perception of Jesus Christ, and of our being in Him, is a perception of what is concealed. It is, therefore, discontinuous. It consists in events, so that we constantly pass from the one to the other. It is a perception of the very opposite of what is expected. There is something which does genuinely conceal both Him and ourselves in Him. But this is a disturbing fact, and one which demands serious consideration. For it obviously means that we are none of us in a self-evident position to repeat the great statements of Rom. 8. How, then, are we to view this concealment, and the concealing factor which is clearly at work in it and which always gives this character of the extraordinary to our perception of Jesus Christ, and ourselves in Him ? This is the further question to which we must now turn.

We cannot give a satisfactory answer merely by indicating the many errors and defects which trip us up in our attempts to see Jesus Christ and ourselves in Him. They are undoubtedly there—errors upon errors, defects upon defects, great and small, corrigible and incorrigible. But to open this dark chapter would be to commence our indictment of human sin. There will be a place for this indictment, and we shall not suppress it. It is only too true that we cannot know Jesus Christ, and ourselves in Him, without also knowing that (even in this knowledge) we are sinners, and without being hampered and disturbed by the distortion of our perception and thinking which sin causes. But this concealment, and the existence of this concealing factor, cannot be explained merely by our errors and defects and therefore by human sin. For Jesus Christ represents us. Our being in Him is our justification, and therefore the forgiveness of our sins, even that of our cognition. More than that, it is our sanctification, and therefore the renewal of our life, and therefore of our cognition. We have to reckon with the fact that, if this concealment of Him and us were merely a question of our sin (and especially our great stupidity), provision has been made in Jesus Christ to counteract its effects and therefore to remove this concealment. It is true enough even in respect of our cognition that we receive and enjoy in Jesus Christ the forgiveness of our sins and a renewal of our life. Therefore our sanctification in Him does specifically include at least a powerful restriction and mitigation of our very great stupidity, a certain clarification of our perception and thinking. But even if we look to the whole power and efficacy of His grace as it is now revealed to us prior to His return in glory, we are neither commanded nor authorised to count on a removal of the concealment of Jesus Christ. Even when we have and know in Him our justification, He is always concealed from us. Prior to His return in glory, He is concealed even from the cognition that He Himself has clarified. Therefore, even though this concealment and the presence of this concealing factor, may have, in our perception, subjective components in the form of the errors and defects rooted in our stupidity, their decisive basis is necessarily objective.

Our answer will also be quite inadequate if we merely refer to a metaphysical mishap which has overtaken Jesus Christ and ourselves in Him, a misfortune which is either accidental, or arises from some dark depth, and which may perhaps be made theologically tolerable if it is expounded as a secret dispensation of God—so long, of course, as we do not say who or what we mean by this God! In this case, we have to regard the concealing factor as an obscure obstacle whose nature and origin and purpose and duration, whether temporary or definitive, are quite unknown, but which has in fact interposed itself between Jesus Christ (with our being in Him) and ourselves as we would like to know Him and ourselves in Him, so that He is revealed to us only in this extraordinary and discontinuous and contrary way, and we can know Him only in the same way, but burdened also with our own stupidity. This thought is not only hazardous but quite impossible. For it would mean that there is something which (even if only partially and relatively) does actually separate us very forcefully from the love of God in Jesus Christ. If we believe with Paul that no alien power is able to do this, if we seriously accept the fact that Jesus Christ is the Lord, so that if there may be other lords beside Him, there is none that is superior or even equal, none that can even partially obstruct the exercise of His lordship or the course and progress of His grace—then this explanation falls to the ground. Far from competing with His love and its revelation, or opposing our knowledge of His love and its revelation, this concealment of Christ and the existence of this concealing factor are themselves a necessary, and perhaps even a decisive, element in the work of His grace.

In relation to the first no less than to this second distorted answer we must refer to Col. 3³, where we are told that our life is not merely " hid with Christ," but " hid with Christ in God." It is not, therefore, hidden in our sin. Even less is it hidden in a metaphysical accident. As we learn from the verse which immediately precedes, " with Christ " means with the Christ who is exalted to the right hand of God. The God at whose right hand Christ Himself reigns is definitely not a God who would even allow an alien lord effectively to oppose the reconciliation of the world accomplished in the same Christ, let alone mysteriously decree that this should be the case. If there is a concealment of Jesus Christ and our life in this God, it must be solidly grounded in His own reconciling will, and form an element in His reconciling act. Neither subjectively nor objectively can it have a merely negative force and significance. However disturbing this may be, however sharply it may call in question our own perception and cognition, it can only have a force and significance which are positive.

C.D. IV—2—10

For a correct answer to our question we must refer back to the conclusion of the preceding sub-section on " The Royal Man." Our subject then was the story of the cross and passion of Jesus Christ, which, although it is so clearly emphasised in the Gospels, does not interrupt the depiction of the Son of Man as the Lord, but constitutes the climax to which it moves. We maintained, as the Evangelists themselves make clear from the very outset and at every point, that there was a readiness and willingness of Jesus Himself for this outcome of His life. The basis was a divine necessity and ordination revealed and active in His life along these lines. Its historical actualisation came through the firm resolution of those around Him, and especially Israel, to bring Him to this end. We found the historical counterpart of this outcome, the cross, in the existence of the disciples under the sign of the cross. Having tried to assemble the remaining material about Jesus as He is portrayed in the Gospels in three great groups, we simply affirmed that this was their final word concerning Him, apart from the account of His resurrection. It was here above all, in the fact that He finally suffered, and was crucified, dead and buried, that (in the light of His resurrection) they attested Him as the Lord. It was here that they found the coronation of the King. The One who in His resurrection attested Himself as the Victor over death was the One who had given Himself to death in fulfilment and completion of His human existence. The definitive form of the elevation and exaltation of this man, of His identity with God's eternal Son, was that in which He gave human proof of His humility and obedience to the Father, of His humiliation, in His human suffering and dying as a rejected and outcast criminal on the wood of curse and shame. It was for this that He was sent as the Son of God. And He was true to His mission as the Son of Man. In this He Himself recognised and accepted His determination. This was the divine decree fulfilled in His life. This had to be, therefore, the final action in the story of the elect covenant-partner, the people Israel, and the beginning of the story of the new covenant with the whole world, at which the former had aimed from the very first, which had always been its meaning and promise. It was here, then, that the community was also constituted, with its commission to proclaim this new covenant of God to the world. It was here that it received its permanent impress and character. Everything moved towards this cross. And everything took place in this crucifixion—the whole reconciliation, the whole restoration of peace, between man and God.

Thus the whole existence of the royal man Jesus as it is attested in the Gospels stood under this sign. We again remember the characteristics which emerge so emphatically in the Gospels. We remember the sovereignty which the first community found in the life of this man. We remember His parallelism to the being of God and God's attitude to the world—a parallelism which the first community rather

strangely found both in His unassuming nature but also in His revolutionary character, which was all the more radical because it was so
secret. We remember finally, and above all, the self-representation
of the new and redemptive actuality of the kingdom of God in the
midst as they found it in the active life of this man, in His words
and acts. But as His life moved finally to this outcome, all these
things stood ultimately and supremely under the sign of the fact, in
which they had also their *telos* and character, that He gave Himself
up to this death, that He was ordained by God for this death and led
by God to it, that He was delivered up by Israel to this death, and
that even His disciples were to be His witness as those who are marked
by this death. The whole New Testament witness to Jesus, and He
Himself as echoed or reflected in this witness, points to this death.
And they point to it as the goal which as such is the new beginning
that He has made : the new beginning of the world as it is reconciled
to God in Him ; of a man who is changed and restored and justified
in Him, but also sanctified, converted to God, and elevated and exalted
to be a true covenant-partner of God. In His death He has not only
reached His own goal, but made this new beginning for us, in our
place, and with us, with man. In His death there took place the
regeneration and conversion of man. They took place in Jesus Christ
as the Crucified because it is finally and supremely in His cross that
He acted as the Lord and King of all men, that He maintained and
exercised His sovereignty, that He proved His likeness to the God
who is so unassuming in the world but so revolutionary in relation to
it, that He inaugurated His kingdom as a historical actuality. This
is how the disciples saw Him in His resurrection. This is how they
proclaimed Him as the Resurrected. His life was that of the One
who had been put to death. And their own life was that which had
been delivered in His death and by it brought into His own fellowship
with God. They saw in the Resurrected His lordship over them and
all men as it was set up in His death. They therefore saw themselves
as those who had been made His own possession in His death, and
translated by it from a state of disobedience to one of obedience.
They saw in the Resurrected His royal power of command as proceeding
from His death. They therefore saw themselves as those who by His
death had been bound and subjected to Him. His resurrection revealed
Him as the One who reigns in virtue of His death, from the cross
(*regnantem in cruce*). And it revealed themselves as those who are
ruled by Him in virtue of His death, from His cross.

But we are anticipating a little. We omit an important part of
the discussion, for which this is the place, if we do not attempt an
explanation which we did not attempt at the end of the previous sub-
section from which these statements are taken. In that context we
simply affirmed without comment that this is the case. The cross or
death of the Son of Man, as it is portrayed in the New Testament,

does not in any sense compromise or disavow or cast a shadow over
Him. It is His coronation. We can only return to this fact. We
can only keep to it. In all our future deliberations we can only start
from the fact that, according to the witness of those to whom He first
declared Himself as the One He is, we can know the royal man Jesus,
who has taken our place and accomplished our sanctification, regeneration and conversion, only as the One who finally, gathering up the
whole of His human being and activity, acted as the divinely instituted
King and Lord of all men by going to His death, by being led by God
to His death, by being harried by Israel to His death, by impressing
Himself upon His own in His death, by making His death the basis
and therefore the character of their life. In the present context however, as we try to answer the question which occupies us, we cannot
proceed from this fact without considering what we mean by it and
therefore in what sense we proceed from it. What does it mean that
His death is the act of the Son of Man, His cross the dominating
characteristic of His royal office ? In what sense is His death the
goal of His existence and therefore the new beginning of ours, and
anticipated in ours of the world, of the existence of each and every
man ?

    1. We have already touched on the decisive answer. This is all
true of His death because it is the clear and complete and consistent
fulfilment of His human abasement, and therefore the human complement and repetition of the self-humiliation, the condescension, in
which God Himself became one with us in His Son. In virtue of this
humiliation of God, as He became mean and poor, as His eternal Word
was made flesh, and took human essence and existed as a man among
men, this man, Jesus of Nazareth, was and is elevated and exalted
man, true man. He was and is this unique man among all others,
this Sovereign. His human work runs parallel to the work of God.
In His speech and action, in His person, there is actualised the kingdom
of God drawn near. His majesty derives from the depth of the omnipotent mercy of God, in which God Himself in His Son really gives
Himself to man as His creature, accepting and effecting solidarity
with him even to the bitter end. This divine basis of the majesty of
the man Jesus became a palpable and visible and quite unequivocal
event in the fact that His majesty expressed itself in His clear and
complete and consistent lowliness ; that He was King and Lord in
His death and passion, rejected and cast out and executed on the cross.
What we have called the way of the Son of God into a far country
and the homecoming of the Son of Man, and what older dogmatics
called the *exinanitio* and *exaltatio* of Jesus Christ, are one and the
same event at the cross. The humility and obedience of the Son of
God, and the corresponding majesty of the Son of Man, coincide as
they are represented in the event of Gethsemane and Golgotha. The
Word was really made real flesh. It was really God who really reconciled

the world to Himself—in the One who was true God, omnipotent in the depth of His mercy, and also (in His death and passion) true man, allowing free rein to this omnipotent mercy of God. There is involved both the depth to which God gave Himself for us in His own Son, and the majesty to which He exalted us in the same Son who also became man as we are. On both sides the covenant between God and man was genuinely restored. It pleased God wholly to give Himself in this way, and this man was pleased wholly to actualise in human terms this divine self-giving. That is why the temporal death of the Son of Man was the act and sign of the eternal love of God, and therefore the goal of the human life of Jesus, and in Him the new beginning of our own life. The secret of the cross is simply the secret of the incarnation in all its fulness.

2. But we can now continue that the cross was and is the crown of the life of the man Jesus because it came about conclusively in His crucifixion that He genuinely took to Himself the situation of man as it is in the judgment of God and therefore in truth, making it God's in His person, and therefore radically altering and transforming it. He was and is our Brother, and fulfilled His brotherhood with us, by accepting and not rejecting this outcome of His life from the very outset. The saving intervention of God for us was accomplished by His setting His Son as the Son of Man on this way, and leading Him to its final depths. The final depths of this way showed themselves to be the place where all men actually are by the fact that it was the divinely elected people (representing all other people) which could only bring down the King that had appeared amongst it to these depths, and crown Him in this way. And this King ordained His new people to solidarity with all men by appointing from the very first that all His members should also bear the sign of the need and shame that He had borne for all. This is man in the situation in which God encountered him in mercy and omnipotence, in which He took him to Himself, in which He reconciled the world with Himself, converting it and altering it so radically. He is the man who is guilty before and in respect of God, and his fellows, and therefore himself. As such he is the man who can only perish and pass and die. As such he is lost. In His omnipotence and mercy the Son of God has made Himself the Brother of this man, and as his Brother his Representative, taking his place, accepting his guilt, perishing and passing and dying and being lost in his stead. It was in this way, as the Neighbour of this neighbour, that He came to the cross and suffered and died on the cross. We recognise the man who has God for His Judge, who has to drink the bitter cup of His wrath, to accept the sharpest human accusation and condemnation, and finally to perish in shame and contempt and supreme agony and isolation as the champion of a lost cause. For it is obviously our own human essence, our flesh, we ourselves, who are there extirpated as we deserve. It is not on Him but on us

that this visitation had to fall. And yet it does not fall on us, but on Him. It falls on us as it falls on Him. It falls on Him for us, in our place. It falls on us only as it falls on Him. But the fact that this humiliation fell on Him in our place, that He did not refuse to allow it to do so, that it did so according to the will and decree of God, and as the final action of the history of the elect people Israel, that His own have in their own place and manner to share with Him this humiliation —all this is His exaltation. In all these things He is the Son of Man, the Holy One of God, His obedient Servant who is loved by Him and loves Him in return. But if this is the case, this too is for us and in our place. There is nothing exalted about our lowliness in itself and as such, which He makes our own, and which we see reflected only too clearly in His humiliation. As ours it is only the lowliness of our sin and sloth and well-deserved misery. Of ourselves we are the very reverse of saints. But if in His humiliation to brotherhood with us, as the One who took to Himself our lowliness, the Holy One of God, He is elevated and exalted as the man of the divine good-pleasure, then obviously this exaltation of His is not only His, but also that of those for whom He humbled Himself. Our exaltation took place in Him. In Him, in virtue of His death, we who in ourselves are not holy are the saints of God. We whom God can only chide for what we are and do in ourselves are men of His good-pleasure. In Him, in His death. on the cross, we are done away and put to death as the old men we are in and of ourselves, and are set up again in Him, being born again and converted to the life of a new man. Since He made Himself our Brother, taking the form of our disobedience and bearing its consequences, He has made us His brothers in the form of the obedience achieved in Him and the promise of this obedience already fulfilled for Him. The cross is the crown of the life of Jesus because in His crucifixion He was our Brother and accomplished our liberation from our old man to a new man.

3. But we can and must make the same point from the opposite angle. The cross is not merely the controlling sign, and His death the dominating fact, in the life of Jesus because in this determination it is His life for and in the place of the man who is marked for death and has fallen victim to it. Its final and controlling function is also grounded in the fact that the life of Jesus has and reveals in this determination the character of an act of God. It is this determination which gives to His life the power to be a life which intercedes for us and all men, which is lived in their place, which includes and controls their life and being. By it this life is distinguished, quite unmistakeably, from the acts and achievements of all other men, and from all creaturely movements and accomplishments. All other human acts and achievements, all cosmic movements and accomplishments, do indeed move towards death. This is what so deeply compromises and relativises and overshadows them. But none of them actually comes from death.

Death is for all of them the limit from which there is no return—no new thing—for their subjects. They are no longer mighty and fruitful in death, however fruitful and mighty they may have been before. In death they can neither create nor work, positively or negatively. What is even the greatest of men in death? And what can he do? Death is the end of all human and creaturely life and creativity and work. It relativises and overshadows even the exaltations previously attained. It is not a new human height, but the abasement of everything that precedes. In the human and creaturely sphere as such, and in relation to its forms and events, it is absurd to think of the abasement of death as itself an exaltation, an empowering for action, its accomplishment, and a kind of kingdom and lordship. But when we come to the life of Jesus, we find that according to the witness of the New Testament it too moves towards death, but is not in any way compromised or relativised for this reason. It moves towards death to take its full form in death. Death is not now the end, but the goal or *telos*. It has power and significance as it moves towards this death and really derives from it. We are forced to say that it is life from death. This is how the risen Jesus appeared to His disciples. He was the One who was alive from the dead. He had exercised and confirmed and maintained His kingdom and lordship in His death. He comforted and claimed His people from the place where there can be no question of the possession and exercise of human help and authority. He was the confidence for their own life from the place where all the confidence reposed in man can only fall because it loses its object. He was their hope where every human hope fails. He was exalted as the One who was abased. The light of His resurrection was the light of His cross. And it was in this light that His witnesses later and ever afterwards saw and understood His whole life, and proclaimed it as the life which is given to the whole world and to all men. But this orientation to and from His death, this exaltation in and with His humiliation, clearly differentiates His life from all other human and creaturely life. And we must continue that in this differentiation this human life was and is as such the act of God. It had and has power over all men : the power to represent them ; the power to judge them in their old being, and to direct them to a new ; the power of an incomparable lordship and supreme royalty. As distinct from all other life it had and has power from death, from the frontier of all life. But this means that it is not just a limited power. It is the unlimited power of the merciful God, who alone can act in this world from that absolute beyond of all creaturely being and life, of whom it is characteristic to act from that beyond, who in so doing demonstrates and reveals that He is the merciful and omnipotent God. But it is in Jesus Christ that all this—this action from beyond, from death, and therefore this action of God—has taken place in this world, on earth, in history, in opposition to all other occurrence in the human and creaturely sphere, and as the great turning-point of the human situation, no, of man himself. This is what makes this man the One that He alone is, the Deliverer, the Saviour of all other men. In Jesus who intercedes for us with His life, in the negative and positive liberation which comes to us in Him, we certainly have to do with a man and His work as such. But what makes His intercession and liberation authoritative and indisputably valid and irresistibly effective is the fact that in it we have also to do with God Himself and His act. God Himself is the eternally living One who intervenes and is at work in and as this man. For defeated, rejected, condemned and crucified, this man is the One who is alive from the dead, the Victor.

These are the points which have to be made in elucidation of the conclusion of the previous sub-section. And they give us the answer to our present question concerning the concealment of the being of Jesus Christ and of our being in Him. This concealment rests on the truth and clarity with which He was the royal man and as such our Lord and Representative and Saviour. It rests on the mystery of His cross. It is itself the mystery of His and our exaltation in His and therefore our humiliation. It has a critical character. But it is positively critical, not negatively. It is the mystery of atonement, of the salvation which has taken place and is directed to us in this man. It belongs inalienably and even centrally to Him, and in Him to us. He would not be the One He is for us, nor we those that we are in Him, if not in this concealment.

The point at issue is how we can ever see and know our being in Jesus Christ, and therefore ourselves as those who are established in Him, as those who are no longer turned away from God but towards Him, as regenerate and converted, the saints of God, Christians. There can be no question as to the being of Jesus Christ, and therefore our being in Him. There can be no question as to the love with which God has loved us from all eternity and once for all in time. This does not need our assistance or completion or co-operation or even repetition. It does not even need to be seen by us. From this standpoint there is no question. What is needed, and therefore the point at issue, is its attestation in a corresponding way of thought, direction of will, type of attitude and orientation and determination of our existence which come to us in relation to it, and which we have to fulfil in relation to it, so that in response to the love with which God has loved us we love Him in return. We have to do this because the being of Jesus Christ, and our being in Him, is irrefutably, incontestably and unassailably grounded in itself. How can His being, and ours in Him, fail to lead to a corresponding (the " Christian ") orientation and determination of our existence ? But how is this possible except in relation to this being ? How is it possible except in an awareness of it, i.e., as its reality acquires for us the charact ʏ of truth, i.e., as we see and know and understand it. Reality which does not become truth for us obviously cannot affect us, however supreme may be its ontological dignity. It cannot lead to any corresponding (" Christian ") orientation and determination of our existence. It will necessarily remain unattested on our side—a word which has no answer, a light which has no reflection. Unrecognised, the love of God in Jesus Christ cannot awaken and summon us to its attestation and therefore to a response of love. Between this love, between Jesus Christ (and our being in Him) and ourselves, who have to correspond to His and our objective being, there arises for us the question of truth, the question of recognition.

In other words, how can the unknown become for us the known reality, reality in truth ? How can there be a perception of Jesus Christ and our being in Him ? How is it to come to pass that we see Him and ourselves in Him ? We have learned that the real Jesus Christ is the Crucified, and that it is as such that He is the King, our Lord and Head and Substitute. It is in Him as such that we have our peace with God—or we have no peace with God. So, then, to look at the real Jesus and what He is for us and what we are in Him can only be to look at the Crucified. How, then, can we look at the exalted Jesus, the King and Lord, and ourselves as His, as His possession, as those who in and with Him are established and set in a new life in peace with God, the saints of God ? This is the question of seeing that which is concealed. What does it really mean to see the Crucified : the Servant who was and is the Lord ; the Humiliated who was and is the Exalted ; the King of Gethsemane and Golgotha ? What is truth if the real Jesus is the One who was rejected and condemned and executed, and the whole reality of our being is enclosed in this One who was put to death ?

One thing is sure. If His cross is the mystery with which we have to do, we are at once arrested, and no penetration to the truth is in fact possible from our side. For this mystery is a matter of His will and power and act. It is the free decision of the One who dwells in this mystery, of the real Jesus whom we are to see and understand and know. He Himself has concealed Himself in it. He Himself has closed the door. And the freedom of the decision taken is sovereign in relation to all our efforts and enterprises. His decision cannot be influenced or directed or breached by any of our decisions, however profound or forceful either in design or execution. He and He alone is His own truth. This door cannot be opened from outside, but only from inside. It cannot be opened by us, but only by the One who closed it. We can only knock at it, knowing that if it is to be opened it must be from within, by the One who dwells here, and praying that He will open it. Whether it is opened is for Him to decide. It is a matter of His will and power and act. We cannot, therefore, continue to discuss our situation outside this door, considering the various things that are possible or impossible, and what we might do or not do. This

type of discussion cannot lead anywhere. For the decision is not made
outside but inside. If He who is enclosed in this secret will not open,
there is no use our willing. Or if perhaps He cannot open, we certainly
cannot. If He will not do what has to be done, how can we? The
New Testament certainly does not tell us that there can be any question here of an effective and victorious volition and ability and action
on our part. Without leaving us in any doubt as to the objective
reality and truth of what is revealed, it describes this perception, this
revelation, as an event which either comes from the other side or not
at all.

But we must now give closer attention to the witness of the New
Testament than we have so far done. It is not the case that it attests
the reality of Jesus in such a way that it is left in the air—high and
remote and alien—as far as we are concerned, so that we can consider
and treat its relationship to us merely as a possibility. Nor is it the
case that it presents the truth of this reality as resting in a kind of
objectivity in which it is quite content to be closed to us, having no
subjective form, and therefore not known and finding no response.
To be sure, the fact that there is no response would not mean that
either its reality or its truth were in any way compromised or shaken
or destroyed. But this does not mean that it is satisfied merely to
sound in our ears and not come before our eyes and enter into our
hearts. Nor is it enough to say that it is truth which ontologically
and essentially presses for subjectivisation. This is the case. This is
what we are told, and we must accept it. But we are told more than
this. We are told that this reality and its truth—the being of Jesus
Christ, and our being in Him, in the concealment of His crucifixion—
are power. They are not just static power, but active; not just latent,
but manifest. They have all the force of truth; of something that
has really occurred—not merely that will occur, but that has already
occurred as described in the New Testament. And this event wills
to make itself known, and can and does do so. We are told that the
One who dwells behind the closed door which He Himself has closed,
far from being unable or unwilling to open it, flings it wide open.
We have only half heard, and therefore not really heard at all, what
the New Testament says of Him, and what He wills to say of Himself,
and does say, through its ministry, if we try to see Him only as the
One who in face of our perception and understanding and knowledge
encloses Himself in the mystery of His cross, and therefore to see ourselves only as those who stand without and are therefore, in relation
to Him, left to their own very inadequate resources. The New Testament overcomes this abstraction by telling us that the crucified Jesus
Christ has risen from the dead. But in the present context this means
that He discloses Himself to us with the same will and power and in
the same act as He closes Himself off from us. We have to hear the
two sides of the message in their irreversible sequence, the first as the

first (which has always to be heard too), and the second as the second. He is the Crucified who as such closes Himself off from us, and He is the Resurrected who as such discloses Himself to us.

We keep the first before us, and shall have to return to it, but for the moment it is the second on which the emphasis falls. He does not close Himself off from us to keep us away. He also discloses Himself to us. He is not only silent, but also tells us who and what He is. He not only hides Himself, but also reveals Himself to us. That is to say, He sets Himself before us. We would not see Him if He did not do this. But He does do it. And because He does, as the New Testament tells us, the message concerning Him is the Gospel, glad tidings, and as such it comes to the men of all times and places with the claim and promise of being the proclamation of truth which binds and looses. He is risen, and reveals Himself. He Himself, Jesus Christ, declares His majesty. He declares Himself to be the royal man. He declares Himself in that distinctive sovereignty as a human person. He declares Himself in that ·divine proximity of His attitudes and decisions. He declares Himself as the Herald and Bearer, the actualisation, of the kingdom of God on earth. And supremely, and in confirmation of everything else, He declares Himself as the One who in His death fulfilled in human form the gracious self-humiliation of God, interceding in His death for us who had fallen victim to death, and, as distinct from all human enterprises, interceding in the name and authority and power of God. This exalted One is the One who is concealed in the lowliness of His death. He is, in fact, exalted in this concealment. And as He bursts open from within the closed door of His concealment, of His death, He reveals Himself as this exalted One. No one has found or discovered Him as such. No one has brought Him out of His concealment. It is He Himself who has shown and revealed and made Himself known as such. And in so doing He has been seen and understood and known as such ; as the Messiah of Israel and the Saviour of the world. This was the event of His resurrection. It is quite easy to understand, therefore, why earlier theology described His resurrection as in some sense the *datum* of His exaltation. If we have read the New Testament aright, the *datum* of both the humiliation and the exaltation of Jesus Christ is the whole of His human life including His death. But His resurrection is the event, and not merely the *datum*, of the revelation of the One who is exalted in His lowliness. In the light of it as His self-revelation in majesty the New Testament is the Gospel concerning Him. He is its content. It stands or falls with the proclamation of His name. With this derivation it cannot be interpreted as the doctrine of a human religion or morality, or even subsequently, secondarily and relatively as the explication of a human faith, and to that extent a human self-understanding. With this derivation the Christian community has, necessarily, dared to call on Jesus Christ and the salvation achieved in

Him, on His lordship over all men, on His presence and future, on Him as the One who lives and gives life yesterday, to-day and for ever, on Him as ontological reality, on Him as the truth which is both surely established in itself and reaches out eagerly to all men, on Him the Crucified, on Him as the majestic and royal man on the basis of His self-declaration. All Christian knowledge and confession, all Christian knowledge of God and man and the world, derives from this self-declaration of Jesus Christ, from His resurrection. At the very least we reckon this among the things that we have to accept from the origins of all Christian knowledge and therefore directly from the New Testament itself, whatever may be our own attitude to it, and whether or not we can repeat this second New Testament declaration. We have to realise that this declaration does contain this second element. It tells us that this man who was humbled to the very depths has manifested Himself as the majestic and royal man, and that He is seen and understood and known as such, as the One who is alive from the dead.

But with the same emphasis on this second element there is something corresponding that we have to say about ourselves. It is not only He who is closed off from us in the death of Jesus Christ. We are also closed off from ourselves. For in His death we do not see our life sealed and affirmed, but only our death. Again, as He discloses Himself to us, He also discloses us to ourselves. For He is not without us. As He is man, the first-born Brother of all men, He is the Head and Representative of man. He Himself *is* only as *we* also are elected and called in Him. But if it is the declaration of the New Testament witness that He Himself was not only dead, but also the One who is alive from the dead, He reveals that in and with Himself we also are alive—because we are elected and called in Him. The fact that we see our own humiliation in His is not the end of the story. The revelation of His majesty discloses also the relative and subordinate but genuine majesty to which we are elected and called in Him. In the revelation of His being as the new man He reveals us too in a new being. In and with His life from death He manifests our life as it is saved in Him, as it is graciously, and for that reason with supreme reality, posited afresh in the fellowship with God which had been forfeited. He reveals the fact that we are set up in Him. Nor is all this abstract. Not for a single moment is it isolated from Him. It is concrete and supremely real in and with His self-revelation, His resurrection, His life from the dead. It has its sure foundation in our union with Him (quite apart from our recognition and response).

Thus in and with the being of Jesus Christ as the new man our new being is not merely concealed but brought to light—not, of course, as we discover it in Him, but as He Himself reveals it to us in Him. But this being the case, it means that the situation is radically challenged in which we think we are shut out in relation to the truth of

Jesus Christ and left to our own very inadequate resources. We should be compelled to see ourselves as those who are shut out and stand outside in this way, but could only do so, if it were merely a question of seeing our own death sealed and confirmed in the death of Jesus Christ. But if He is the One who is alive from His death, if His reality as the exalted and true and new man is revealed truth, and if our own truth is disclosed in and with His truth, it is also disclosed that, although that first word is true of us and our exclusion, it is surpassed by a second ; and that it is true, and can be rightly heard, only with this second and transcending word. But according to this second word, although there is a real distinction between without and within, it is one which is overcome. It is not overcome by the fact that we have penetrated within from without, but by the fact that the One who is concealed from within has emerged from His concealment and manifested Himself. And in Him we too are manifested as those who live, as those who are united with Him, as those who cannot be separated from Him either in His lowliness or in His glory. But if we are manifested as such in Him, then—whatever attitude we may adopt—we cannot possibly persist in our distance and strangeness towards Him, in our exclusion. The words of Laban to Abraham's eldest servant are apposite in this respect (Gen. 24^{31}) : " Come in, thou blessed of the Lord ; wherefore standest thou without ? " A persistence in ignorance is characterised as a senseless contradiction by what is here made known to us even concerning ourselves. According to what we are told concerning ourselves in the New Testament, we are not distant but near ; not in darkness but light. We cannot, therefore, be ignorant, or try to make out that we are such.

Before we go further, we have to realise what power the New Testament counts on in this second declaration, in the confession that Jesus Christ has new life from the dead in which He reveals Himself to us as the Lord, and ourselves as His. We have not only to think of the distance between death and life—a distance which is quite unbridgeable in any other application of the two concepts in the creaturely sphere, but which is represented as overcome at a stroke in the declaration of the resurrection of Jesus Christ. This general distance, which we might almost describe as scientific, is also involved, so that there is a philosophical difficulty in the declaration. But this is comparatively unimportant. The real problem is that of the pitiless seriousness of the cross as the crown of the human life of Jesus ; the strict reality of the self-humiliation of God in His Son, which the Son of Man had to follow, and did follow, with the same strictness ; the completeness of the divine but also the human will, and the divine but also the human act, in what took place at Calvary, not in appearance only but in truth, even to the dereliction of the Crucified ; the perfection with which He suffered as our Representative the death which we had merited, dying in our place. This perfection, which is the content of the first

New Testament declaration, has to be kept in view if the second is to be rightly understood and accepted. The resurrection is the resurrection of this One who was crucified. His life is His life from this death. And our life in and with Him is from this death. We ourselves in our new being come from the death which we have really died in His death. Everything derives from the event which in all its seriousness was not the end but the goal of the human life and obedience and will and action of Jesus, and was therefore the will and act of God fulfilled and accomplished in Him. And beyond this goal we have the revelation of the majesty of the royal man and ours as it is enclosed in Him. This is not only life, but the life of the new and true man, and this new life as our life. What is the distance between life and death compared with that which is overcome at this watershed? What power is this, that the one and total fact should be true, and true for us, in this sequence, that Jesus Christ died and that He is also risen! In His death we too have attained our goal; and in His resurrection we have been set in a new beginning. He (and we in Him) is first concealed and closed off and unrecognisable; and then He (and we again in Him) is revealed and disclosed and recognisable—no, actually recognised. What is the fact and force and event indicated by these two statements concerning Him and us? We cannot be too careful in our discussion of the power of the transition assumed by the New Testament when it relates these two statements in this sequence.

But this demands a further and decisive turn in our treatment. So far, and in the last discussion which led to this question of power, in our consideration of the revelation of the Crucified as the Lord and of what this includes in itself in relation to ourselves as His, we have referred to the fact that we are told this in the New Testament. We have kept to the fact that both statements—the first in transition to the second and the second in transition from the first—are attested in the New Testament; that the objective reality of the being of Jesus Christ, and our being in Him, has also the character of objective truth; and that this truth is not satisfied with a purely objective form but demands also a subjective, pressing in upon us and our seeing and understanding and knowing with the aim of the orientation and determination of our existence in the light of it, of awakening and summoning us to love in return the One who has first loved us. We have tried to hear this witness with ever increasing accuracy. And in so doing we have continually come closer to answering our question. But we have always kept closely to what is actually told us in the New Testament concerning the relationship between the reality and the truth of Jesus Christ. We have carefully shut off the question of our own attitude to what is said to us, leaving open the final question of our own perception and understanding and knowledge of what is said, with all that this involves. Are we really able and ready to go this way? Do we actually go it? Or do we for some reason hold back and aloof? We had to adopt this course in order to be clear that on our side it can only be a question of accompanying or following, of a correspondence and not the repetition of an original, just as on the other side it can only be a question of the reality and truth which are not in any way conditioned or evoked by, but themselves condition and sovereignly evoke, our accompanying and following. We had to give the glory to the work and Word of God of which we speak when it is a matter of the being of Jesus Christ and His work, and therefore to give unconditional precedence to what we are told in the New Testament about the humiliated and exalted Jesus Christ and His revelation in His majesty, with all that this includes for us. In order that this precedence should be genuinely unconditional, it was necessary in the first instance that the question of our attitude, our accompanying and following, should be left open. For the point at issue in this question is that of the decision which, although it is ours, cannot precede but can only follow the decision already taken in Jesus Christ.

It is clear, however, that if we are still to keep to the New Testament we cannot leave open any longer this question of our decision. For it is not left open in the New Testament. We have stated that we are told such and such in the New Testament. We are, in fact, told these things. That is where we must begin. And, as we have put it, we for our part must let ourselves be told these things, whether or not they seem either illuminating or acceptable. It is quite indispensable that we should let ourselves be told these things, whatever may be the outcome. But these stiff and cold and non-committal expressions are not the end of the matter. For what the New Testament tells us, at the very heart and centre which is our present concern, it tells us in a specific and distinctive way which addresses and summons us, applying what it says to ourselves and claiming us for it. It tells it to us as witness : witness to a person, to Jesus Christ, to the whole nexus and history of reality and truth bound up in this name, as it is given by those who have the necessary information ; but also witness addressed to persons, to us, who can also acquire this information by receiving the witness, and who are already claimed in anticipation as those whom it concerns. What we have said about the objective content of truth of the reality of Jesus Christ, which includes our own reality, presses in upon us, from its objectivity to our subjectivity, in order that there should be in us a correspondence. We have already seen this from what we find in its human attestation as it concerns us in the New Testament. It has its historical form in the existence of the New Testament. It becomes a historical event in the encounter between this witness and us. In the name and commission of the reality and truth of Jesus Christ we are concretely seized, whether we like it or not, in the course of this address and summons and application and claim. It is not with aloof detachment, but seizing us in this way, that the New Testament tells us what it has to tell us and what we have to let ourselves be told : who and what is real and true, Jesus Christ as the Lord and we as His ; who and what is also active and effective and reaches and affects us. This is not told us merely as an imparting of information, but as that which lays claim on us for what is imparted. In relation to all generations, and therefore to us, the New Testament has always come with this demand. It has always dared to claim man in this way. It has always dared to lay hold of him, for the impartation of its content, in order that he should receive it and at once become a new witness of its message. Thus to allow ourselves to be told what it tells us means rather more than is at first suggested by this formula. It is to be exposed to this attack which takes place in the New Testament. It is to be involved in the wrestling with this demand. When the New Testament encounters us, we are not at all the " we " that we think (but only think) we know so well, and that so boldly try to control themselves, in all their neutrality and with all their reservations and question-marks and pretexts and caprices and individual activities. But when its witness reaches us, when we are confronted by its witnesses, we are already in the circle of the validity of what they say to us, and are no longer the same in the sense that we are now marked, like trees for cutting, for the fulfilment of our own actual acknowledgment of its validity. This is how the prophets saw and treated their contemporaries, as did also the apostles, both Jews and Gentiles. They confronted them, and the world, with the very sober and not at all enthusiastic presupposition that they belonged to Jesus Christ, and were therefore ordained to hear the news concerning Him. By their very existence these witnesses are never present in vain for the rest, for the world around, for us. To hear them is to hear Him, and to hear Him is to be placed directly before and in the altered world situation, before one's Lord who is the Lord over all. The only thing is that we must not imagine that we are still somewhere alongside or outside the Word that God has spoken through these witnesses. We stand already under the Word.

It is also clear, however, that if the New Testament is not only declaration and impartation but also witness to all those whom it encounters, if it is this demand and the venture of this claim and seizure, then it counts on a very definite power which is more extensive and effective than appears in the demand as such. That the New Testament places us under the Word is not the end of the matter. The power on which it counts is the power to set us, the recipients of its witness, in a very definite freedom : the freedom to appropriate as our own conversion the conversion of man to God as it has taken place in Jesus Christ, the translation of man from a state of disobedience to one of obedience ; the freedom to keep to the fact, and orientate ourselves by it, that the alteration of the human situation which has

taken place in Him is our own ; the freedom, therefore, to set ourselves in the alteration accomplished in Him. The power on which it
counts does not operate only in the fact that this freedom is as it were
proffered to us from without, or commended and laid on our hearts as
a freedom which is also possible for us, but rather that it is actually
made our own. It is the power in whose operation we are motivated
and impelled from within, of ourselves, to be in this freedom, and to
use it as our own. It is the power to call us effectively to positive
decision in relation to what is said to us, to the freedom of that accompanying and following, of conversion. It is the power to keep us in
this as a correspondence to our conversion as it is already accomplished
in Jesus Christ, so that we live daily in a free fulfilment of this correspondence. It is the power to make us vigilant and eager and willing
and ready to realise this correspondence in ever new projects and forms
and dimensions. It is the power, not to repeat the being of Jesus Christ
and our being in Him, for this is not needed, nor is it fitting or even
remotely possible, but rather (and here we may take up again the
terms we used earlier) to see and understand and recognise it, making
a response of love to the One who first loved us. It is the power in
which we acquire and have and use the freedom to do this. It is,
therefore, the power in which we acquire and have and use the freedom
to become and be Christians, not second Christs, but those to whom
it is given to see Him as the One He is, and themselves as they are in
Him ; to understand that He intercedes for them, and therefore that
their own life is determined by the One who intercedes for them ; to
know and recognise Him as their Lord, and therefore themselves as His
possession, which stands under His protection but also at His disposal.
They have not undertaken of themselves, but it is given to them, to
love Him. This love is simply an answer to the love of God as they
may see and understand and know that they are loved by God in
Him. It is simply the attitude which is quite unavoidable for them
as the saints of God who find that they are loved in Him. Christians
are those who have this freedom. The power to put a man in the
freedom in which this is given to Him is the power on which the
New Testament counts. It counts on this power which does not merely
indicate or offer, but acts and gives. It counts on this power which
does not merely hold out or describe or commend or command with
all kinds of indicatives or imperatives the freedom of conversion, the
freedom to be Christians, but itself makes us free. In its operation we
are free. When we are told in the New Testament of the true state
of affairs, who and what Jesus Christ is and who and what we are in
Him ; when what is said in the New Testament is addressed to us ;
when we are exposed to this attack in the encounter with the New
Testament—all this takes place on the presupposition of this power,
with reference to it and confidence in it, with the assured expectation
that it is at work and will achieve the goal of this witness and address,

creating in those whom it encounters the freedom of conversion, the freedom to see and understand and recognise, the freedom to love, the freedom to be Christians.

But when we say this we say already that it is a power which is greater and other than what may be described as the power of the New Testament witness itself and of those who bear it, the Evangelists and apostles. It is greater and other than the power in which they tell us what they do tell us and challenge us as they do. For although they are commissioned and commanded to speak to us and challenge us in this way, all this is merely their human address. No matter how clear or forceful it may be, it can come to us only from without. It can place us under the Word, but it cannot place us in obedience to it. It cannot set us in that freedom. Nor is this power that of their Christian personalities active in this address. For even as witnesses to Jesus Christ they are still men, and it has never yet happened that a man has been able to create this freedom in others. No man, not even an apostle, has ever yet made another man a Christian. To be sure, this power does make use of the witness of the New Testament and those who bear it. It avails itself of what they say. It is active in and with it. We have to hear them if we are to hear Jesus Christ. For they are commissioned and commanded to speak this message and empowered to impart it with that arresting force. It is also true that they do not undertake of themselves, but it is given to them to count on this power, to rely on the fact that it will accomplish what they intend when they direct their message and address to others. It is true that they themselves obviously live and speak and act in the freedom granted them in this power. But the power is not their own power any more than it is ours. They, too, stand in need of it. Their freedom, too, was and is a freedom created in them and granted to them by this power. They, too, were and are referred to its operation and therefore to the fact that their freedom is granted and maintained and continually renewed by it. Their service as witnesses, which they fulfilled and fulfil in this given freedom, is dependent on the fact that this power is not denied as their source, but is always operative. And their service as such cannot have this power in relation to others. It neither controls nor exercises this power. It does not do its work. On the contrary, there can only be these witnesses and their service as this power itself is present and operative. And it is the work of this power when this service is fulfilled and attains its goal, so that those to whom they turn as witnesses are enabled to see and understand and know and therefore love, thus becoming Christians. The witnesses can only trust and hope and pray that this will happen, as they themselves have only been able to receive the fact that they are witnesses and may render this service. It was not their own will or resolve which made them this. And so their own speaking and address, their own imparting and arresting, their own challenge cannot bring it about that others acquire this freedom—the freedom to repent, and to keep on repenting. The power on which the New Testament witnesses count is a power which is sovereign on both sides, in relation to themselves, and also in relation to those whom they address. It is this power alone which on both sides unlocks the heart so that there is living speech on the one part and living hearing on the other, the Word flying like a well-directed arrow to its target and striking and sticking in the right place, being received with the meaning and content with which it is given. The New Testament counts on it that there will be between man and man the work of this other and greater power. The joyfulness of its witnesses rests on the confidence and reliance and hope that they have in this power. And whenever their witness is given to others in such a way that it is received with joyfulness, this other and greater power has been at work. And the joyfulness of the recipients rests also on the confidence and reliance and hope that this sovereign power has awakened in them too.

It is the power in which Jesus Christ discloses and reveals and makes Himself known as the new and exalted man, together with what we also are in Him. It is the power of His resurrection as it demonstrates itself to us. And it is as such the power which affects us by opening our eyes and ears and heart and conscience and reason for His revelation, and therefore for the new and exalted man and for what we also are in Him, so that we are there, or rather we are awakened and summoned to draw our conclusions from the fact that we are there. When we begin to draw these conclusions we begin to be Christians. The power of which we speak is the power of this beginning. But these conclusions have to be continually drawn afresh as long as we have time, as long as our allotted span of life endures. In Jesus Christ a Christian has already come into being, but in himself and his time he is always in the process of becoming. There are so many conclusions to draw, either as conclusions from conclusions drawn already, or as new conclusions from the fact that we are there as revealed in and with the resurrection of Jesus Christ. The power of which we speak is not only the power of that beginning, but also of the conclusions that have to be drawn afresh each day. And as this power it is each day afresh the power of the revelation of Jesus Christ Himself, the power of His resurrection, on which it depends that our presence is also revealed, and therefore the presupposition given from which we have continually to draw these deductions and to become Christians. We can never be too vividly aware of the mystery of this power. To put it simply, it is the power of the inconceivably transcendent transition from what is true and actual in Jesus Christ to what is true for us, or even more simply from Christ to us as Christians.

It is the one transcendent power which is at work on both sides, from Him on the one side and to us on the other. Could anything be more astonishing? Could there be anything greater to rouse our admiration and praise at this power and its work? For if only we do not lack the necessary sincerity and the necessary demand for concrete imagination we have to agree that the fact that I am a Christian, and therefore opened to Jesus Christ, one who sees and hears, who is willing and ready for Him and can love Him, is to say the least of it no less strange a thing to say and hear than the corresponding presupposition that Jesus Christ has opened Himself for me and my like, entering our sphere of vision, revealing Himself by His resurrection, and therefore revealing the love of God, and ourselves as those who are loved by God. How ingenuous it is to find it difficult or even impossible to accept and apprehend the fact that Jesus is risen and lives as our Representative and Lord and Head, but to regard it as quite possible and relatively easy that we, these men, as we know ourselves or ought to do so, are affected by it, encountering the decision there taken concerning us and caught up in our own decision, in the working out of conclusions from it, making again to-day the beginning which we have already made, as we were and are awakened and summoned to do. For how can we ever arrive at this second statement concerning ourselves—that we are Christians—unless there is rolled away from a grave-entrance a stone which is no less great and heavy, and perhaps greater and heavier, than that which was rolled away from the tomb in the garden of Joseph of Arimathea ?

If we are not to go astray at this point, we have to see clearly the force of the opposition which is overcome and removed when a man is really awakened and summoned to live in the " here " which corresponds to that " there," to come—each day—from that beginning, to draw continually new conclusions and to draw them each day, to exist as these conclusions are drawn and therefore in the freedom to convert and be Christians. What has to take place if a man is really to be a Christian ? We may happily and confidently presuppose that he is this, with no attempt to criticise or find fault. But our present question is this : What has to take place for this presupposition to be true and valid in relation to a particular man (e.g., myself) ? How is it that in spite of everything there can be such a thing as a " Christian " subjectivity ? How is it that this can and may and should maintain itself against all the suspicions and objections which arise even from within if we honestly investigate the matter ?—and we will not even mention those that arise from without, but happily and confidently presuppose that it does actually maintain itself against them too. But if it really does this, what is it that has taken place in us ? By what miraculous happening do we live ? Does not the raising of Lazarus pale before that of which we are ourselves the witnesses and theatre ? Or the Virgin Birth of Jesus Christ ? Or His empty tomb ? Or all the marvels that force us to decide whether we must laboriously accept them as history or firmly explain them as myth ? For here we are really forced to decision. And it is wise and worth while, perhaps, to consider primarily and supremely the decision that we have to make here, where what has to be explained is the fact that we are Christians, the fact of our Christian freedom. Does it not defy all explanation ?

It certainly defies any explanation in the light of what we ourselves are. A man can be a Christian only when he cannot be it of himself ; when he is not authorised or empowered to be it from any of the caves in which we find ourselves at home. What we find in ourselves, what comes ringing mockingly back from these caves if we enquire, is the very opposite of the fact that we are Christians, the contradiction of our Christian freedom. We surrender this, and deny ourselves as Christians, if we try to seek the basis of our being as Christians in ourselves. The leap which is made when a man repents (daily) is from the very first (and daily) too great to be interpreted as a leap that we have made or even prepared or facilitated or made possible of ourselves. If we know ourselves, as the Christian does, we cannot think that we are capable of this leap. And the whole idea of a leap that we have made or are making is best abandoned. No one makes this leap. As Christians, we are all borne on eagles' wings. Our heart is immediately closed again, and perhaps irremediably, if we ascribe to our own capacity the fact that it is opened, that we hear the " To-day, to-day " and therefore that it is not closed. The Christian " I can no other " is sharply and radically differentiated from every other by the fact that in this case there is absolutely no question of any ability of our own. It denotes a human act without the corresponding human potency, a pure act which takes place because that other and greater power on which the New Testament counts shows itself in might to and in a man, not merely declaring but fulfilling for him a Nevertheless and Therefore which transcend and leave behind both himself and the contradiction which derives from himself, putting him continually in that new beginning and on the way to those new conclusions in spite of his contradiction, setting him in the freedom of conversion. When his action has its basis here, it is genuinely the case that he can do no other, whereas in all his other actions, however loudly he may protest that he can do no other, this is not really so. When a man is a Christian, and understands and confesses that he is such, he counts on the work of this power as the basis of this being. He believes and confesses that it is " not of his own reason or power that he can believe on Jesus Christ his Lord or come to him, but . . ." He achieves this faith and coming only as he is witness of this greater power, and is thankful for its work and for the fact that he is its direct witness. In anything other or greater that he may want to be than thankful he is not a Christian. In every self-understanding in which he tries to understand his being as a Christian otherwise than as the fulfilment of this thankfulness, he misunderstands himself as a Christian. This is the very thing which must not happen if the presupposition which we accept with the New Testament is really to be true and therefore to be made happily and confidently—that we are Christians.

But if we are to see plainly what is involved in the power of the transition from Christ to us Christians we have to say more than just that it is a greater and different power in relation to all human capacity, that it is a miraculous power, and therefore that its work—the opening of men for Jesus Christ and their own being in Him—is a miraculous work. Unless we define this more closely it might seem to be no more than a purely formal and to that extent empty and therefore equivocal description of this power and its mystery. And if it is to be of any help to us in this context even the word power, which we have so far left undefined, stands in need of explanation. We have to distinguish the sense in which we use it from the idea of a power which either mechanically pushes, propels, thrusts or draws, or organically produces ; from a higher force of nature whose remarkable work and outcome are the creation of Christian subjectivity, the existence of

Christians. If this is all that can be said of it, even though we may keep before us and take into account its miraculous character, we may ask whether it is not one of the many cosmic forces which can produce from different origins correspondingly different results. And this inevitably raises the further question whether Jesus Christ as its origin, and the existence of Jesus Christ as its result, with the whole transition from the one to the other, are not just factors and phenomena in world occurrence, striking perhaps, but to be estimated in what is basically the same sense as all others. On this view, there may perhaps be an appropriate place for the miraculous nature of this power, but it need not be more than one cosmic force with others. In the New Testament, however, neither the origin of this power in the existence of Jesus Christ nor the result of its operation in the existence of Christians are understood as factors and phenomena in ordinary world occurrence, and therefore the power itself is not understood as one cosmic force with others—although distinctive and miraculous in operation. The power of the transition on which the New Testament counts when it looks from the basis and origin of its witness in Jesus Christ to its goal in the existence of Christians is absolutely unique as the power of the resurrection of Jesus Christ. It is operative in the world, but not as one of its forces, either mechanical or organic. It is distinguished from them, and from human capacity, not only by the fact that it is miraculous and sovereign, but also by the definite character of its sovereignty and miraculous operation. It is not just in general, but in this distinctive character, that it is sovereign and miraculous and acts to and in men, when it makes them Christians, in this way which transcends so absolutely their own capacity. And the New Testament does not leave us in any doubt as to the definite character by which this power is differentiated from all other forces, even miraculous forces. Whether we look at the origin or the result of its operation, we can read this character almost as in a book.

We may begin by saying that its character is light : light which shines out of the darkness back into the darkness, out of the darkness of the crucifixion of Jesus Christ back into the darkness of our own lives ; but unmistakeably light and exclusively light, without darkness or shadow. It is the power of the reality, shining from the darkness of His crucifixion, of the exalted and new and true man who is now seated at the right hand of God. And as such it is the power which shines into the darkness of our life, by which we are made bright even in the midst of darkness because we are as it were revealed to ourselves as those who belong to this exalted and true man, and can and may and must cleave to Him as their Head. In all circumstances, even as it places us under its judgment, it is the power of the light in which it is true to us as our own reality that we do not belong to ourselves, but to this man, and that we have no security except in Him, but all our security in Him. The power of His resurrection—and it is of this that we are speaking—is the light which falls from His resurrection into the murky den of our existence. Where this light shines—and it is the work of this power that it should do so—it is not only possible but inevitable that man should become light in this sense even in the darkness of world occurrence and of what takes place in his own outer and inner life. When this power is at work, we are no longer dark in the darkness but light, for its light reveals that we are those that we are in this man, and in the protection and name of this man, thus awakening us to see what is revealed, ourselves as those who belong to this man, to hold to Him and therefore to be held. A light which merely left us in the darkness of our lives, or even increased this darkness, adding new darkness to the old, representing us all the more forcefully as children of darkness, and thus giving greater depth and sharpness to our sorrow instead of breaking through it and removing it root and branch, would be recognisable at once as quite different from the power of which we are speaking, even though its strength were ever so great or indeed miraculous, and it came on us and controlled us as *mysterium tremendum et stupendum,* as the numinous in person. We could not respect a power of this kind, let alone surrender to it. The power of which we speak, the power of this transition, is light. It is light from the darkness of the cross of Jesus Christ into the darkness of our existence. It brings about this definite illumination. And in so doing, even in all the sadness which may otherwise engulf us, it effects a clear and invincible joyfulness. For it is always joy to belong to this majestic and true man and to be able to cleave to Him. If it is our reality to be able to do this, and if it is the effect of this power to reveal us in this reality so that we may do what we ought to do, it always results in joy. To live in this light which falls from above is always to have joy. And it may be known as this power by the fact that in all circumstances, even in the midst of suffering, it always brings joy. This is the sign that we must not resist its operation, but yield to it.

Again—and we are simply snatching at the first things suggested by its origin and result—its character is that of a liberation. We have already said that it frees us for conversion and therefore to be Christians. But let us first consider its origin, and therefore the revelation of the crucified Jesus Christ in His resurrection. What is it that we see here? We see the freedom of Jesus Christ Himself to be in His humiliation as the Son of God the truly exalted and royal Son of Man; to be in the likeness and situation of the disobedient the one man who is obedient; to suffer death and yet to be the One who is alive from the dead, the Holy One of God, beloved of God. We see His freedom to be all this in our place, as our Lord and Head and Shepherd. The transitional power on which the New Testament counts is the power of our liberation accomplished already in the freedom of Jesus Christ: our liberation from the compulsion of continuing in our disobedience now that the Son of God has humbled Himself to be one of us and to be obedient in our place ; and our liberation for a life as the brother of that exalted and royal man, and therefore for a life which cannot be harmed even by our death but will prove itself to be life even in our death. The character of this power is, therefore, that it gives us knowledge of this liberation ; that it introduces it into our prison as the fresh air which we may already breathe ; that it gives us a taste for what we are in virtue of our liberation ; that it enables us to see our reality—the freedom which is also ours in Jesus Christ. Its character is to give us the courage and resolution to reach out here and now for this reality, to orientate ourselves by it, or, in the true sense of the words, to come to ourselves, which always mean in practice : " I will arise and go to my father." That we arise and go takes place in the freedom in which we are placed by this power. It is this particular power, distinct from all others, as it makes us free for this movement which corresponds to the liberation already accomplished in Jesus Christ. No power under whose operation we may stand or be brought, however great or glorious or miraculous or supernatural, will be confused with this power so long as it does not give proof of the fact by making us free for this conversion. There are many other forces whose effects are striking in other respects and yet they leave untouched our being as the prisoners of sin and death, being quite unable to give us this knowledge, this fresh air, this taste for our liberation as it is already accomplished, or to awaken or summon us to this movement of conversion. Indeed, they may even confirm our captivity, making the walls of our prison all the thicker, our chains all the heavier, our sin all the more self-evident and our death all the more sure, being able only to restrain us from the accomplishment of this movement. The transitional power of which the New Testament speaks is unambiguously recognisable by the fact that by its operation we are prisoners who are already freed, already acquitted, already freed from the influence of all other neutral or opposing forces, already set in a final but real independence in relation to them, already summoned to resistance and offensive conflict against them, and already eager and equipped for this conflict. If it shows itself to be a liberating power, we have another sign that we can trust it, and therefore that we must not resist its operation but yield to it.

Again, it has the character of knowledge—of a knowledge which overtakes us and in which we are known, and of a corresponding knowledge on our part in which we can and must know ourselves as those who are known. To this extent—we need not fear the expression —it has a rational character. In Jesus Christ we are elected by God from all eternity, and therefore we are in every respect examined and seen and understood and known : each as the human creature that he is ; each in his particular disobedience and apostasy, and therefore under his own particular sentence of death ; each as this particular member of the covenant which God has made with man and for which He has elected him in his particularity. And when Jesus Christ suffered and was crucified and died, in Him God had each one before Him in his own particular lowliness but also in the particular glory for which he was ordained, as the old man that he is and the new man that he is to be, his particular death and his particular life from the dead. It was each one in particular that He had in mind, and to each in particular that He spoke in the resurrection of Jesus Christ. The power of the transition is the power of this particular divine seeing and thinking and speaking. Its effect is, therefore, something that takes place to and in the reason of each one. It is a receiving in which the divine seeing and thinking and speaking in Jesus Christ finds its response in a human, Christian seeing and understanding and knowing, in an awakening and enlightenment of the reason. To bring about this response is the operation of the power of which we speak. In accordance with the nature of the particular attitude of God to each one, it will be the particular answer of each one. But it will be a logical answer corresponding to the logical attitude of God. In virtue of this power man will be one who sees and understands and knows. If it did not have this effect, it would not be this power. It is not, therefore, the power of a blind and formless and inarticulate and irrational stirring, nor is its effect that of a blind and formless incitement or even pacification, of an irrational and inarticulate excitement or even peace. There are other forces which have effects of this kind. All religions bear testimony to this fact. Their most solemn mysteries are celebrated in an encounter and fellowship of blind gods with men who are genuinely and with supreme solemnity blinded in this encounter. Powers which work in this way are not to be confused with the transitional power of which the New Testament speaks. The latter is not to be understood as if it were one of these forces. Where it is at work, it always means light for the mind too, so that the eyes and ears and understanding are used as they have never been used before. The man in whom it is at work becomes a scholar. He begins to learn and think. He acquires a conscience, i.e., he becomes a *consciens*, one who knows with God. He will not be silent, or stammer or babble, but speak. He will speak in new and foreign tongues, but he will really speak. His faith will not be "introverted" but "extroverted." He is ordained to speak what he knows, to be a witness. When the apostles had to do with this power, its work found expression as a *fides explicita*. They were not incited and summoned either to an enthusiasm or a sacred silence, but to *theo-logy*. It was for this that they were equipped. This power may be very great and wonderful, but it has a clear and unmistakeable affinity with sound reason. It puts this in its right limits. It stops its roving and raving. But it also sees that there is no laziness in its use. It binds it and sets it in an appropriate and redemptive movement. It brings it about that man can think and say with absolutely unshakeable confidence that two and two make four and will never make five. If it did not do this, or did the opposite, it would be a different force which we could encounter only with the deepest mistrust. But when it does this we can trust it and we have a sign that we can let it take its course. When it shows itself to be rational, it is rational to yield ourselves with all our heart and mind and strength to this one thing which alone is rational, and to its work.

Again, it has the character of peace. Its origin is the reconciliation of the world with God as it is resolved in God's eternal will and fulfilled in time at Calvary. This reconciliation and therefore this peace are revealed in the resurrection of Jesus Christ from the dead. Their power, therefore, is the power to spread peace ; to spread on earth the peace which is resolved in heaven, which has come down to earth from heaven, and which is now concluded on earth. Following the biblical usage, we might just as well call it the power of salvation. But salvation consists in the occurrence of reconciliation, and therefore in a healing ; in a healing of the rent, a closing of the mortal wound, from which humanity (and openly or secretly every man) suffers. It consists in the removal of antitheses ; the antithesis between God and man ; then the antithesis between man and man ; and finally the antithesis between man and himself. In this sense salvation means peace. And the power of the revelation of the salvation accomplished for each and all on Golgotha consists in the fact that they are brought, and brought into, the peace which was there concluded in their name, so that they can consider and respect and to that extent have it even in the midst of strife. When this power is at work, man can no more imagine that on the frontier of his life he is confronted by an enemy whom he can meet only in a pitiful submission to his merciless rule or with a defiant shout of freedom. When this power is at work the One with whom he has to do, as a brother of Jesus Christ, is God as his Father. Nor need he see in his fellows only those who constantly disturb the peace, so that his only course is either to avoid them, or resist them, or at very best tolerate them. On the contrary, he now finds that these men are unmistakeable and undeniable, if sometimes very doubtful and difficult, brothers of Jesus Christ and therefore his own brothers. Nor can he live in an irremediable and limitless inward conflict, for in Jesus Christ he is really reconciled with himself. When this power is at work, peace is established in all these dimensions. A fine skin begins to grow over all these wounds, open and painful though they still are. They are not yet healed. But it is the sign and beginning of their healing. The evil conflict will not be interminable. It can no longer be waged with a final seriousness, whether it is against God, our fellow-men, or ourselves. There is at least a place of refuge from which we can survey the battlefield. This power may be known by the fact that when it is at work man is not only called and brought into conflict with the forces of sin and death, but also called and brought out of this threefold conflict with God, his fellows and himself. It may be known by the fact that it makes the good fight natural and the miserable contention in which he may still be involved supremely unnatural. It may be known by the small but increasing trust which it gives us in God and our fellows and even ourselves. As against this, all the forces which do not have this effect or have a contrary effect, although they may be very forceful and even mysterious, may be known as different from this power, and therefore as forces which command neither our respect nor fear, by the fact that they do not create peace, and may even create discord. To be more precise, the power of the resurrection of Jesus Christ may be known by the fact that at one and the same time and in one and the same movement it impels us to peace with God and our fellows and ourselves. The peace which it spreads is indivisible. As against this, other and alien forces which obtrude themselves on our notice may be known by the fact that though they perhaps lead us to a supposed peace with God (and it can never be more than that), they do this without giving peace with men ; or, conversely, though they perhaps give a supposed peace with men, this can never be effective or fruitful because it is not rooted and grounded in peace with God ; or, though they perhaps give peace with ourselves, this does not include peace either with God or our fellows ; or, finally, though they perhaps give a supposed peace with God and our fellows, this does not carry with it peace with ourselves. Where there is no operation in even one of these dimensions, so that it is an open question whether and how it will work out in the others, another power is at work, the power of a peace which is a worthless peace, even though it may be very pleasant in some respects. We can only treat it, therefore, with supreme mistrust. Where peace is effected in all three dimensions at once, however, we have a sign that we have to do with the power for which we can never find too much space—the peacemaking power of the resurrection of Jesus Christ.

What more is there to say about its character ? A great deal. It is the power of humility, of hungering and thirsting after righteousness, of fellowship, of prayer and confession, of faith and hope and above all of love. There could be no end if we were to read off everything that could be read off from the book of its origin and result. Our present purpose, however, is simply to establish that it is not an empty or equivocal power (however miraculous), but that it has a specific character by which it can be recognised and differentiated from other forces. We will therefore select only one other description which in the New Testament often seems to be exclusive and all-comprehensive. Its character is that of life. It is power aimed at the establishment of genuine human life, i.e., a true life which is lived in harmony with the will of God and therefore unspotted, inviolable, incorruptible and indestructible. A divine predicate is boldly ascribed to this life in the New Testament. It is eternal life. The man Jesus smitten on the cross is revealed to us in His resurrection as the Lord who became a servant for us, and in consequence of the humiliation of the Son of God, and correspondence to it, the exalted and royal man who lives eternally in virtue of His unity with God, and who is as such our Head and Representative. If there is a power of His resurrection—and the New Testament counts on the fact that there is—it is the power which when it is at work produces seeds of this life in man, sowing them in human existence. We cannot say more than this of men who still live in time, under the dominion of sin and death. Where do we find more than seeds in this sphere ? Where can we see that the seed sown is really the incorruptible seed of eternal life ? Where is man seen to be the bearer of this seed ? The important thing is not what is seen, but what is there—the power of the Resurrected as the power of the sower who always sows this good seed. When this power is at work, man is always nourished with the body of the Son of Man broken for him and His blood outpoured, so that he is preserved for eternal life. The presence of this life is always declared, and it wills to express itself and bear fruit as such. It is a human life. We are not dealing, therefore, with an angelic or animal vitality. The power which effects this life has its origin in the Son of Man, Jesus. Other forces may produce other forms of life. We must not confuse them with this power. This power aims at human life. But in the light of its origin it aims at an exalted life which overcomes the falsity of a merely vegetative life apart from and against God ; which is given up to the purifying fire ; which is freed from self-centred greed and anxiety ; which is directed to its determination to be life with God.

We can gather together at this point all that we have said earlier. It aims at an enlightened, liberated and understanding life which is at peace in all dimensions. There are other forces which do not aim at this exaltation of human life, which try to maintain man in an abstractly vegetative form of existence, or even to reduce him further. The power of the resurrection of Jesus Christ may be known by the fact that it snatches man upwards. But again we must make a careful differentiation. The higher level to which it snatches him is not the dubious height of an abstractly spiritual life, of pure inwardness. It is a matter of man's life in its totality, of man as the soul of his body, and therefore of the outward life, with all its distinctive elements and functions, in which he is related to other cosmic creatures, and not merely of rational and spiritual life which seems to differentiate him from them. It is a matter of his life including, and not excluding, its vegetative components. The exalted man Jesus, from whom the power of this life derives, is the One who is exalted in the totality of His soul and body, just as He is also the One who is humiliated in the totality of His outer and inner life. He is flesh and blood in His being, and therefore in its revelation. It is inevitable, then, that the power which proceeds from His resurrection, and He Himself as the Resurrected, should sow a seed which is not only psychical but physical, and give nourishment which is not only spiritual but material—a whole preservation of the whole man. Eternal life as it is applied to man by this power is the declaration and pledge of his total life-exaltation, from which not a hair of his head or a breath that he draws can be excluded. There are all kinds of purely spiritual forces. But we must note carefully that their purity is a spurious purity which may well be a supreme impurity. And so the abstractly spiritual life-exaltation at which they aim, omitting the outward aspect of man, his flesh and blood, either in neutrality or in scorn, can result only in self-deception as to the totality of his imprisonment in and with his actual life. The power of the resurrection of Jesus Christ will be seen in the totality of the upward movement which is its work. And it may well be the case that a single attempted movement in the sphere of physical order and discipline and health is a clearer sign of the presence and action of this power than the most profound spiritual upheavals or the supreme spiritual flights which are not supposed to have any serious or noticeable significance from this standpoint. It will be worth our while to devote a little more space to the decisive definition that the seed of life whose sowing is the work of this power is the seed of *eternal* life. Human life without the operation of this power, and therefore without this seed, can be represented only in a continual discontinuity as a continued flight from the past, through the present, to the future. We live in the shadow of death. The life of God is eternal life : life in the unity and continuity of times ; in unbroken rest and movement. If human life is to be lived in fellowship with God, and therefore with His life, it has to defy the discontinuity from which it suffers, and be arrested in the flight to which it is condemned, participating in eternal life even in the shadow of death. The life of the man Jesus is revealed in His resurrection to be this human life which is exalted to participation in the eternal life of God. It is, therefore, the promise of eternal life dawning over all men. The power of the resurrection is proved by the fact that it reveals to man this life of Jesus, effectively bringing him, and into him, the promise of eternal life which is given in it, making it his own, and moving him for his part to make it his own, to grasp it, to allow it to be the comfort and confidence and hope of his life as he still lives it in the shadow of death, in this discontinuity, and therefore in this flight through the times. In the form of the promise—but the promised eternal life itself ! In the man Jesus revealed in His resurrection from the dead, in His participation in the eternal life of God, the eternal God Himself is to the man who is His brother comfort, confidence and hope. For He is the unity and continuity of his time too, and the unbroken rest and movement of his life. To see, in virtue of the revelation of this man, the light of the

promise given in Him, to live with and before it, and therefore to be a
bearer of that seed, is to live a life which, while it is still assailed by the
shadow of death and discontinuity, while it is still a fleeting life, is
already represented and demonstrated, in virtue of that promise, as
unity and continuity, as incorruptible and indestructible rest and
movement, defying death, arresting that discontinuity and persisting
even in its transitoriness. Where it is at work the power of the resurrection of Jesus Christ has the irresistible result that man begins to
see the light of the promise by and before which he may live, and that
he does actually begin to live by this promise which is the form of
eternal life itself. No other force can achieve this. Other forces may
plant other promises in the hearts of men, but not the promise which
is the form of eternal life, and therefore not the promise which enables
them, when they receive and possess it, to live a life which already
defies death, and arrests that discontinuity, and persists even in that
flight through the times. They may all be known by the fact that
directly or indirectly they contest this promise and therefore allow
men to sink into the abyss, or even push them in. The power on which
the New Testament counts is distinguished from all other forces by
the fact that it gives man an immutable foundation in all the movements of his life. And in the same breath we must also say that it
sets him in a movement which cannot be arrested by any of the pauses
in his life.

This, then, is our answer to the question how it is possible and
actual, and can be said in truth, that a man becomes and is a Christian.
If we are to think and speak in New Testament terms the answer can
only be that, deriving from Jesus Christ, i.e., His resurrection, there
is a sovereignly operative power of revelation, and therefore of the
transition from Him to us, of His communication with us ; a power
by whose working there is revealed and made known to us our own
election as it has taken place in Him, His humiliation as the Son of
God as it has occurred for us, but also His exaltation as the Son of
Man as it has also occurred for us, and therefore the deliverance and
establishment of our own being, so that our existence receives a new
determination. It is by the operation of this power that we become
and are Christians. We have sketched the character of this power—
that which distinguishes it from others. It could not appear to us,
all things considered, as an obscure *Deus ex machina*. For all the
strange majesty of its nature, its operation, and the new determination
which it brings, could not have the form of a magical transformation
in whose achievement we fail to recognise ourselves. Why should we
not be able to see and know and confess ourselves as those who exist
with this new determination, although still, of course, in all our earthliness, in the limits of our creaturely being, in our humanity as it is
constantly assailed and oppressed by the power of sin and death ?
The work of this power is not to destroy our earthliness, but to give

to it a new determination. It is to this that all the distinctive operations of this power have reference : not to an ideal man or super-man ; but to man as he is there in his earthliness before God and his fellows and himself. In describing this operation, therefore, we have been careful to avoid the grandiloquence which says too little because it says too much. The Christian is not a second Christ, but a man like others. The only difference is that he participates in the elevation of man as it has taken place in Christ in such a way that it is revealed to him in his own limited and assailed and oppressed existence, and has therefore become a factor in this existence which in spite of its problematic character cannot now be discounted or ignored. He believes and hopes in Christ. He loves Him. He follows Him. In this he is a Christian. That this is the case, that the elevation of man which has taken place for him in the death of Jesus Christ is present as the source of indestructible rest and unappeasable unrest, as genuine comfort and genuine admonition, is something which he owes to this power. For all the mystery which confronts him in it, it is something which is very simple and straightforward. It is the concrete alteration of his existence, to be fulfilled and expressed in all kinds of definite actions and abstentions. It is conceivable in all its inconceivability. For although its origin is not in himself, it is a matter of his own will and action. In the last resort it consists in the fact that in all the limitation of his assaulted and oppressed existence he is confronted by the fact that the beginning of his reconstitution has been made, and that he can live on from this beginning. The night has not yet passed, but he moves towards the morning.

The power whose operation is presupposed in the New Testament is the outgoing and receiving and presence and action of the Holy Spirit. It is He who brings it about that men like all others, existing in the same limitations, can also be, and are, witnesses of Jesus Christ. It is He who brings it about that others are awakened and moved by their witness with them and like them to see Jesus Christ, and with them and like them to see themselves in Jesus Christ, and in the light of this knowledge, and determined by it, to think and speak and will and act in a new and different way. It is He who creates the fellowship in which both the witness and those who are reached and affected and changed by their witness become and are brothers and sisters in Jesus Christ and therefore one—His people, His community. It is He who opens its mouth to confess Him. It is He who directs its *kerygma*. And it is He who gives to it and all its members, to the witnesses and those who hear them and themselves become witnesses, to Christians as He makes them such, the appropriate contour and impression and form and direction in which, for all their likeness with other men, they are and act differently from others. It is He who calls them to action and gives them His orders and commissions. It is He who directs and controls their activities. It is He who gives them the power to execute them. Without Him and His creating and giving and commissioning and controlling and empowering there can be no Christian, no community, no Christian word or act. All these things are from Him and by Him, and from Him and by Him alone.

It is at once apparent how defenceless we make out and confess ourselves to be when at this decisive point we dare to count on this presupposition, and only on this presupposition ; to look to the Holy Spirit alone as the Alpha and Omega, the beginning and continuance, the principle and power of the Christian life ; to see that we are referred only to Him ; to contend only with Him ; to know and seek no other security for the possibility and correctness of our being and action. The high place in which we set ourselves with this presupposition is a very exposed and hazardous place from the standpoint of all other presuppositions. It might well appear to be safer not to find ourselves so exclusively directed to the Holy Spirit as is the case with the community, and Christians as its members, according to the New Testament.

To grasp the truth of this, we have only to think of the meaning of πνεῦμα (and the underlying Old Testament *ruaḥ*). It seems to denote only " wind," or the " breath " of animal life, or the " soul " as the ruling principle of man. In all these senses it describes a reality and its operation which are invisible and incomprehensible even to a " master of Israel " like Nicodemus, as we learn from the well-known saying in Jn. 3[8]. But if this is its nature, how can we presuppose for πνεῦμα so royal a character and so decisive a function ? How can we count on its work as the only foundation for the life of the individual Christian and the Christian community ? It is even the case—and the New Testament does not conceal this fact in its use of the word—that there are many other πνεύματα. We see from Lk. 24[39], Heb. 12[23] and 1 Pet. 3[19] that the departed or their appearances can be described in this way, and the same is true of the angels of God according to Heb. 1[7, 14] and of demons (πνεύματα ἀκάθαρτα) according to Mk. 1[23f.], etc. According to 1 Cor. 14[32] there are prophetic spirits in the community. And sometimes " spirit " is used as an equivalent for soul, as in Lk. 23[46]. The Holy Spirit is in strange company in an important saying like that of Paul in Rom. 8[16], where we are told that He bears witness " with our spirit " that we are the children of God. How is He to be distinguished, how can He distinguish Himself, from our spirit (πνεῦμα ἡμῶν) and all these other spirits ? The New Testament community itself was aware of this problem, as we see from 1 Jn. 4[1], which demands that the spirits should be " tried," or 1 Cor. 12[10], where among the different gifts of the Holy Spirit there is one which is called the διακρίσεις πνευμάτων. But the latter passage shows that there was also an answer to the problem—in the power of the Holy Spirit Himself.

In the New Testament sphere there never seems to have been any uncertainty or disquietude or anxiety at this vital point. When we enter this sphere we know also the existence and activity of this Spirit. We know Him in fact as the power whose mystery and character we have discussed, as the exclusive and sovereign Creator, Founder, Ruler and Fashioner of all individual and collective Christian being and essence. In this sphere there is no one who finds any difficulty in the invisibility of this Spirit or His apparent relationship with other good or evil spirits. There is no one who hesitates to entrust himself wholly and exclusively to His guidance and impulsion. There is no one who fears the danger of spiritualism and fanaticism, or feels it incumbent to seek or demand safeguards against this danger. The Spirit is not a second thing side by side with a first, which is a Christian institution and order and doctrine and morality that are given elsewhere and stable in themselves. Even institution and order and doctrine and morality are His gifts, and under His control and direction. To be anxious about Him is to be anxious about the Christian sphere as such, for this sphere is grounded and maintained by Him, and under His exclusive power. In this sphere there is no anxiety concerning the Spirit. The " pneumatic " is not a kind of virtuoso among other Christians who do not share this capacity and art. There is no such thing as a Christian who is not a " pneumatic." The community as such is pneumatic. There may be too little of the pneumatic, but never too much. It is from this " too little," from an imperfect and unclear and arbitrary or it may be hesitant obedience to the Spirit that all offences and distortions and aberrations and entanglements derive in the community. The community is healthy in proportion as it gives free course to the Spirit. Its strength, and that of all Christians, is in the defencelessness in which it commits itself wholly to the Spirit and trusts exclusively in the authority and overriding power of His rule.

It is His particular work that there is a community—and Christians—in this or that place. It is He who has there separated men and taken them aside and set them under His power and order. What has taken place has been ἁγιασμὸς πνεύματος (2 Thess. 2¹³; 1 Pet. 1²), the building (οἰκοδομή) of an οἶκος πνευματικός (1 Pet. 2⁵). The gifts of the grace granted to this community (χαρίσματα) may be many and varied (1 Cor. 12⁴⁻¹¹), but they all have one thing in common which guarantees their co-operation and the unity of the Church. It is not that they are co-ordinated by a constitution or a confessional position or the existence of an office. Only from the 2nd century onwards, when there was no longer the same certainty of the Spirit, was it thought necessary to find this kind of assistance. The real point is that they are all gifts of the same Spirit, who divides to every man severally as He will—for He is not a spirit of the community who exercises a neutral rule, but One who has as such His particular will for each Christian. All differences (διαιρέσεις) in the community rest on the variety of His distribution (διαιρεῖν). According to Eph. 4³ᶠ· " one body " is identical with " one Spirit." It is He who guarantees the " bond of peace." It is He who brings it about that there is one hope, one Lord, one faith, one baptism, one God and Father of all, above all and through all and in all. There is only one unity that we are to keep and cherish in the community—the ἑνότης τοῦ πνεύματος. Therefore even for individuals to be a Christian is *per definitionem* to be in the Spirit (ἐν πνεύματι). " If any man have not the Spirit of Christ, he is none of his " (Rom. 8⁹). Christians are as such μέτοχοι πνεύματος ἁγίου (Heb. 6⁴), " temples of the Holy Ghost " (1 Cor. 6¹⁹) and therefore πνευματικοί (Gal. 6¹). It is to be noted that even the Galatians are freely addressed in this way, and that to be pneumatic includes the fact that we judge all things, but can be judged of none (1 Cor. 2¹⁵). It is something scandalous and abnormal that in 1 Cor. 3¹ Paul is forced to say that in a particular connexion he cannot describe

C.D. IV—2—11

them as πνευματικοί but only as σάρκικοι, as νήπιοι ἐν Χριστῷ, as those who still stand without. Christians are those who have behind them the " washing of regeneration " which consists in " the renewing of the Holy Ghost " (Tit. 3⁵). It is in the light of this that they live and are to be addressed. They bear the seed that remains (1 Jn. 3⁹). They are recipients of an unction from the Holy One (1 Jn. 2²⁰). They are led by the Spirit (Rom. 8¹⁴). They are to be counted happy because " the Spirit of glory and of God resteth upon them " (1 Pet. 4¹⁴). They have the Spirit as ἀπαρχή (Rom. 8²³), as ἀρραβών (2 Cor. 1²², 5⁵), as σφραγίς (2 Cor. 1²² ; Eph. 1¹⁴), and therefore as promise (Lk. 24⁴⁹). He is given to them as those who are still pilgrims in time and the world, who are still menaced by the power of sin and death, who do not yet see but only believe. But He is given to them, and they have Him, as this promise. It is important that they should not " quench " Him (1 Thess. 5¹⁹), or " grieve " Him (Eph. 4³⁰), or " do despite " to Him (Heb. 10²⁹), let alone blaspheme against Him (Mt. 12³¹ ; Lk. 12¹⁰). This is the final point of all Christian admonition. It is the goal of all Christian self-examination that this should not happen. For here we have the inviolable presupposition of everything that follows. If this holds good and is not violated, we can and must speak with the boldness which the New Testament shows in 1 Jn. 2²⁷ : " Ye need not that any man teach you : but as the same anointing teacheth you of all things, it is truth " ; or in Ac. 5³² : " And we are his witnesses of these things ; and so is also the Holy Ghost, whom God hath given to them that obey him " ; or in Ac. 15²⁸ : " For it seemed good to the Holy Ghost, and to us . . ." ; or in Rev. 22¹⁷, where " the Spirit and the bride " (the community) together call and invite those who hear with their united " Come " ; or in Rom. 8¹⁶, which speaks of that συμμαρτυρεῖν of the Spirit of God with our spirit. There is then no limit to the confidence, the axiomatic certainty and joy, with which the community, and in the community all Christians, may believe and love and hope and pray and think and speak and act. " The Holy Ghost is a witness to us " (Heb. 10¹⁵). Where He is, there is liberty (2 Cor. 3¹⁷). This is the secret of the confidence with which they exist as the community and as Christians.

We are speaking of the Holy Spirit, and therefore, if we are to do justice to the meaning of the term, of a Spirit who is separate, and who separates, in the supreme sense. No other spirit is separate, or separates, in the same way. The naivety with which the New Testament counts on the Holy Spirit as self-evident rests on the fact that for the New Testament community and Christians He does not constitute any problem in His holiness, and therefore in the separateness in which He is Spirit, and works as such, and therefore separates. He is known to them directly in His holiness. They are continually questioned as to their own sanctification by Him, as to the consequences that they themselves have to draw from His sanctifying work. But the fact that He Himself is holy, and sanctifies, is beyond question. How is this ? What is it that prevents the counter-question concerning His own holiness ? Why is it that He is the Holy Spirit per definitionem ? Why is it that they are continually summoned and enabled to count on His authority and power with this exclusiveness and unassailable confidence ?

The answer is staggering in its simplicity. He is the Holy Spirit in this supreme sense—holy with a holiness for which there are no analogies—because He is no other than the presence and action of

Jesus Christ Himself : His stretched out arm ; He Himself in the power of His resurrection, i.e., in the power of His revelation as it begins in and with the power of His resurrection and continues its work from this point. It is by His power that He enables men to see and hear and accept and recognise Him as the Son of Man who in obedience to God went to death for the reconciliation of the world and was exalted in His humiliation as the Son of God, and in Him their own exaltation to be the children of God. It is by His power that He enables them to live in His presence, in attentiveness to His action, in discipleship as those who belong to Him. He is the power in which Jesus Christ is alive among these men and makes them His witnesses. He is the power by whose operation He allows and commands and empowers them. He is the power in which they become and are free, even in the limitations of their humanity, to be His witnesses, and to think and speak and act as such. He is the power of the Son of God and Son of Man : the power in which He humbled Himself in order that in His humiliation as God He might be exalted and true man ; the power which He did not keep to Himself as just His own power, but which He willed to reveal, to impart to men, to His community, to Christians, in order that they should be His witnesses, in order that the world should know by their witness that God has reconciled it to Himself in Him, that its discord is healed, that its peace has been made with God. It was in the power of the Spirit that He went to His death ; and it was also in the power of the Spirit that He was raised again from the dead in order that what happened in His death should not be hidden but revealed. Thus the Spirit who makes Christians Christians is the power of this revelation of Jesus Christ Himself—His Spirit. And for this reason, and in this fact, He is the Holy Spirit. For this reason His holiness can never be a problem for Christians. For this reason His particularity, and the particularity of His operation, is clearly distinguished from the particularities of all other forces. Hence the unassailable confidence with which Christians entrust themselves to Him alone. He legitimates and proves Himself as the Spirit of Jesus Christ, the Spirit who is " sent " or " poured out " by Him, the Spirit who is given by Him to the community, to Christians. When we receive Him we receive Him from Jesus Christ, as His Spirit. And we enter into the sphere of His presence and action and lordship.

In what the New Testament thinks and says about the Spirit there is in this respect a clear and almost a direct line from Jesus Christ Himself to His community, to us Christians. We will begin with Jesus Christ, and here the simplest formula is that He is the Spirit of Jesus Christ (Phil. 1^{19} ; Rom. 8^9), or the Spirit of His Son whom the Father has sent forth into our hearts (Gal. 4^6). But this means primarily that He is *His* Spirit, the Spirit in whose power and operation He is who He is and does what He does. He is ἅγιον because He is κύριον, as He was later called in the *Nic. Constant.* He is the Spirit of the Lord Jesus, i.e., because by Him and in the power which He gave Him the man Jesus was a servant who was also Lord, and therefore became and is and will be wholly by Him. He does not, therefore, need to receive Him. He came into being as He became the One who receives and bears and brings Him. And He was this and continued to be and still is. As is said of Mary to Joseph (Mt. 1²⁰) : τὸ γὰρ ἐν αὐτῇ γεννηθὲν ἐκ πνεύματός ἐστιν ἁγίου. A good reason why the *conceptus de Spiritu Sancto, natus ex Maria virgine* should not be regarded as a theologically irrelevant legend is that if we do this we obscure the important basic connexion between Jesus Himself and the Spirit. Jesus is not a man who was subsequently gifted and impelled by the Spirit like others, like the prophets before Him by whom the Spirit also spoke (*qui loquutus est per prophetas, Nic. Constant.*), or His disciples after Him, or ourselves also as Christians. He has the Spirit at first hand and from the very first. The Word became flesh (Jn. 1¹⁴), and therefore a man like the prophets and apostles, like ourselves. But because as a man He was not conceived of the flesh, but of the Spirit (Jn. 3⁶), He at once became spirit in the flesh ; a man who in the lowliness of the flesh, as from the very first He was on the way to His abasement in death, lived also from the very first by the Spirit, Himself creating and giving life by the Spirit. It is in this sense that we have to understand both the pregnant saying about the last Adam who in contrast to the first was a πνεῦμά ζωοποιοῦν (1 Cor. 15⁴⁵), and also the pregnant equation in 2 Cor. 3¹⁷ : ὁ κύριος τὸ πνεῦμά ἐστιν. What John the Baptist " saw " by Jordan (and we have to remember that it is definitely a matter of vision according to the texts)—the heavens opened, and the descent of the Spirit like a dove upon Jesus as He came up from the waters of Jordan (Mt. 3¹⁶ and par.)—was not just the individual event of that particular moment, as though Jesus had only now come to participate in the Spirit whom He had hitherto lacked. The voice which the Baptist hears from heaven says that this " is " (not " has now become ") my beloved Son. In accordance with the function and position of the Baptist in all the Gospels it is a matter of the revelation and knowledge of the man Jesus by John as the man who stands at the threshold between the old covenant and the new and is therefore the first to receive it. What we have here, in anticipation of the Easter revelation, is the first proclamation of the reality of Jesus before the eyes and ears of this man. Jesus is the beloved Son of God, and as such He is from the very outset and throughout His existence the spiritual man, i.e., the true and exalted and royal man who lives by the descent of the Spirit of God and is therefore wholly filled and directed by Him. He is the man of the divine good-pleasure.. And as this man, in order that the righteousness of God should be fulfilled and achieve its goal, He has subjected Himself to the baptism of repentance in solidarity with the whole people, so that He is concealed and wrapped in an incognito as this man. And He is to actualise and fulfil this sign of baptism in the even greater concealment of His death on the cross. " I saw the Spirit . . . abide upon him " is the phrase used in Jn. 1³², and repeated in the following verse ; and according to the later witness of the Baptist (Jn. 3³⁴) God does not give the Spirit ἐκ μέτρου to the One whom He has sent (i.e., with the διαιρεῖν of 1 Cor. 12¹¹, as He gave and gives Him to the prophets and then to apostles and the community and Christians). He gives Him without reserve or limit—the fulness of the Spirit—so that His being as flesh is directly as such His being as Spirit also. It is as this man who is wholly sanctified, and therefore not in the form of an individual and sporadic inspiration but in accordance with the comprehensive necessity of His holy humanity, that the Spirit drives Him into the wilderness (Mk. 1¹²), i.e., to His victorious conflict against Satan, in fulfilment of the penitence which He has accepted. And it is again as this wholly sanctified man that " through the eternal Spirit he offered himself without spot to God " in His death (Heb. 9¹⁴). It is as this man that He was " put to death in the flesh " (σαρκί, according to the law to which He bowed when He became and was flesh), but was " quickened by the Spirit " (πνεύματι, according to the law of His being as life-giving and death-destroying Spirit, 1 Pet. 3¹⁸). For as this man He is the Lord who is Himself Spirit. Or again, in terms of Rom. 1³ᶠ·, where Paul describes His two-fold historical descent, He is the Son of God who κατὰ σάρκα, as a man, derived from David and his seed ; but who at the same time—and it is in this that He was powerfully marked off (ὁρισθεὶς ἐν δυνάμει) and distinguished from all other men, and opposed to them, as the Son of God—κατὰ πνεῦμα ἁγιωσύνης, by the Spirit who sanctified Him as the Son of David and therefore as man, came from the place from which no other man has ever come, ἐξ ἀναστάσεως νεκρῶν. Or again, according to the remarkable hymn in 1 Tim. 3¹⁶, He was revealed in the flesh (and therefore in concealment) and justified in the Spirit (as He who He was in the flesh). It is in this radical sense that the Holy Spirit is the Spirit of Jesus Himself. Because and as He is the Son of God, Jesus is the spiritual man. It is as such that He traverses the way which leads to the cross. But it is also as such that He is revealed and known when He is raised from the dead. The latter point is decisive in this context. The Spirit is holy as the power in which the man Jesus is present and alive even after death as the One who was crucified for the world's salvation, and in which He continually acts as the man He became and was and is, as the One who was crucified in the flesh.

The second point that now calls for emphasis is that He does this as the One who has suffered and conquered His death and therefore ours ; as the One who was humiliated and exalted in His humiliation ; as the One who was con-cealed in His majesty but who also reveals Himself in and from His concealment. He lives in this twofold and simple majesty of the Son of God, as the Subject of this twofold and simple occurrence. As the One who lives in this way He does not will to be alone, but to have fellow-participants and witnesses of this life : men in whom both His humiliation and exaltation, His death and resur-rection, are reflected (although not repeated) ; in whose existence there is a correspondence to His life. And He does actually create this correspondence to His life in the existence of other men (His disciples, Christians, and even the prophets as the New Testament understands them). This is the event, the decision, which is described in the New Testament as His gift and sending and impartation of the Holy Spirit, as the outpouring of the Holy Spirit as proceed-ing from Him. We have to note that He is Himself the free active Subject in this event. But we have also to note that He is this as the Subject of that twofold and simple occurrence. Without Him, without His free and sovereign address to specific men, there is no Holy Spirit as a factor in the existence of other men. Nor is there any Holy Spirit except as the One whom He sends to them as the Crucified and Risen, who cannot deny that as a factor in their exist-ence He comes from Him as the Crucified and Risen. The Spirit is holy in the New Testament because He is the Spirit of Jesus Christ. He shows Himself to be the Spirit of Jesus Christ by the fact that He is given to men by Him, i.e., by the Crucified and Risen, as the power of His death revealed in His resurrec-tion. Both these points are brought out very clearly in the New Testament. To quote the Baptist again (Jn. 1³⁰), the One who comes after him is the One who baptises ἐν πνεύματι ἁγίῳ, in the power of the Holy Spirit and with the Holy Spirit, as the giver of the Holy Spirit. Or as He Himself puts it when He goes towards that twofold occurrence, He will send the Spirit from the Father (Jn. 15²⁶, 16⁷). Or as He tells the disciples : " I send the promise of my Father upon you " (Lk. 24⁴⁹). Or as we are told in Peter's sermon at Pentecost (Ac. 2³³), it is He who, exalted at the right hand of God, and as such the recipient and bearer of the promise, of the Holy Ghost, " hath shed forth this, which ye now see and hear." Or according to the abbreviated account in Jn. 20²² He breathes on His disciples as the Resurrected and says : " Receive ye the Holy Ghost." It is He Himself who does this, but He Himself on the far side and not on this side of that frontier ; He Himself as the One who has crossed it, who in His death has fulfilled both His humiliation and His exaltation, and in

His resurrection proved Himself to be the "holy servant" (Ac. 4²⁷ᶠ·) and therefore the Lord. It is He, the One who is crowned in His death and revealed as
the King in His resurrection, who achieves His presence and action in the existence of other men. If they have the Spirit, they have the Spirit from Him,
from this One, and therefore as the Holy Spirit. Prior to this fulfilment, and
otherwise than from it, there is no Holy Spirit, no empowered witnesses, no
apostles, no Christians, no community. As we are told in Jn. 7³⁹, " the Holy
Ghost was not yet (for others) ; because that Jesus was not yet glorified." " If
I go not away, the παράκλητος will not come unto you " (Jn. 16⁷). The power
of the reconciliation of the world with God as already accomplished and revealed, and therefore the power of the occurrence of Good Friday and Easter
Day, is the presupposition which is made in the New Testament with reference
to these other men. That this occurrence is reflected in their existence is the
event of their reception and possession of the Holy Spirit, of their life by and
with Him, of their government by Him. That they partake of the Spirit means
that in distinction from all other men they are made witnesses to all other men.
By Him they are to declare His being and action, His completed being and
action. To live in the Holy Spirit is to live with and in and by and for this
message.

But this brings us to the third point to which we are directed by the New
Testament. The Spirit shows Himself to be holy, i.e., the Spirit of Jesus Christ
Himself, by the fact that He testifies of Him. The men to whom He is given
by Him are called to Him, reminded of Him, set in His presence and kept close
to Him. They are brought to the place to which they belong according to the
will of God revealed in Him. The Spirit reveals to them, not only Jesus Christ,
but also their own being as it is included in Him and belongs to Him. He does
this by causing them to see and hear Jesus Christ Himself, as the One who has
power over them, as the One to whom they are engaged and bound, as the One
whom they have to thank for everything and to whom they are indebted for
everything, as the Lord and salvation of the whole world whom they are called
to proclaim. The Gospel of John is particularly explicit and impressive on this
point. The Spirit is τὸ πνεῦμα τῆς ἀληθείας, " the Spirit of truth " (Jn. 14¹⁷), the
power which does not work arbitrarily or independently, but simply declares
Jesus, accomplishing again and again the disclosure and revelation of His reality.
ὁδηγήσει ὑμᾶς εἰς τὴν ἀλήθειαν πᾶσαν, He will lead them to the fulness of the revelation of this reality, and finally to its last and perfect form (Jn. 16¹³). " He shall
glorify me : for he shall receive of mine, and shall shew it unto you " (Jn. 16¹⁴).
" He shall teach you all things, and bring all things to your remembrance, whatsoever I have said unto you " (Jn. 14²⁶). " He shall testify of me " (Jn. 15²⁶).
Μαρτυρία in the New Testament is a supremely active and aggressive impartation
which makes neutrality quite impossible for its recipients. It consists in a
παρακαλεῖν, i.e., a calling and summoning and inviting and demanding and ad-
monishing and encouraging, an address which at one and the same time asks
and corrects and comforts. The Spirit will thus be for the community and the
individual Christian the great παράκλητος. As applied to the Spirit in the Fourth
Gospel (14¹⁶, ²⁶, 15²⁶, 16⁷) this term describes Him as the Mediator and Advocate
and Spokesman of Jesus Christ to His own. He speaks both of Him and for
Him, as the representative of His cause, and with the aim of bringing them to
see that it is their own cause, and leading them to make it their own. He sets
them before Him as the One who is Himself (the same word is actually used of
Him in 1 Jn. 2¹) their Mediator and Advocate and Spokesman with God. He
sees to it that He is not forgotten or misunderstood as such, but always recognised and confessed as the One He is. He sees to it that He does not meet with
disobedience but obedience ; that His truth, i.e., His revelation is not halted
among them ; that His light is not set under the bushel, but remains on the
candlestick on which it belongs, and gives light to all that are in the house (Mt.

5¹⁴f·). He will be the ἄλλος παράκλητος (Jn. 14¹⁶) to the extent that His work will begin on the far side of the dying and rising again of the man Jesus, consisting in, and deriving from, the self-revelation of this man in His fulfilment. That as this man the Son of God was once revealed, in His own time and place, in the world, flesh of our flesh, as the reconciliation of the world with God in His death and the Reconciler in His resurrection, is not a fact which is confined to that one time and place, nor should it ever be regarded as such by Christians. What was then, and took place then, is the living promise given to the world to the men of all times and places, that it was and took place, not just once but once for all, and for them all. But this promise is a living promise because He Himself, raised again from the dead, lives within it, making Himself present in it. This is where the Spirit comes in as His Mediator, Advocate and Representative. " I will not leave you comfortless : I will come to you " (Jn. 14¹⁸). That is to say, world history, having attained its goal in this man and the death of this man, cannot continue as though nothing had happened. His community, Christians, are now present in the world as His witnesses. But these cannot and must not be left to their own devices. They cannot be without Him in the world. He Himself will be with them, even to the συντέλεια of the world, i.e., to the time when it is generally revealed that they and all men did actually attain their goal then and there (Mt. 28²⁰). The fulfilment of the promise of His coming in time before His final revelation is the presence and action of the Holy Spirit. He proves Himself to be the Spirit of the Son of God who was and is among us men by the fact that He continually makes the life of Jesus fulfilled in His death and revealed in His resurrection an object of the knowledge of the community and Christians, impressing it upon them, revealing it even in their own bodies and persons (2 Cor. 4⁶), causing it to be the decisive factor in their own human existence. It is in this way that He shows Himself to be the Holy Spirit.

But when we say this, we say already the fourth and final thing which the New Testament tells us concerning the Spirit on this line from above downwards. His presence and action may be unequivocally known by the fact that the men in whom He works know Jesus Christ, the Son of God in the flesh, the man Jesus, as their living Lord, as the living Head of His community, as the living Saviour of the world, but that in so doing they also know themselves as His own, as those who are bound and committed to Him. They stand in the light of His life bursting forth from His death, of the revelation of the atonement achieved in His death. They see and hear Him. And as those who see and hear Him, they think of Him and also of themselves. And in accordance with this thinking of Him and of themselves they may now live, starting each day from this beginning. On this final point we have to state and develop once again all that we have said already, in outline and by way of illustration, concerning the power of the Holy Spirit in the effecting of that joyous light, that liberation, that knowledge, that peace, that life. We shall have to treat of this more explicitly when we come to speak of the sanctification of man as such. For the moment, we note only the basic and comprehensive truth that the work of the Spirit in those to whom He is given consists in the fact that the being and life and presence and action of Jesus Christ as Reconciler, Mediator, Lord, Head, and Saviour— and all in the form of the royal man Jesus—is to them the decisive and controlling factor in their own existence. In the light of the miracle of Pentecost, Acts is bold to end the address of Peter with the proclamation (2³⁶) : " Therefore let all the house of Israel know assuredly (ἀσφαλῶς), that God hath made that same Jesus, whom ye have crucified, both Lord and Christ." This ἀσφάλεια is *in nuce* the alteration of their existence as it is effected by the Holy Spirit. " All the house of Israel " is assembled in this sure knowledge of Jesus as it is to be received and fulfilled by the Holy Spirit. By this knowledge it is marked off from the nations and enters on its mission to them. By this knowledge men are divided, not into the good and bad, the elect and reprobate, the saved and lost, but into Christians and non-Christians. They are divided, we may add, in the relative and provisional way in which they can be divided in the relative and provisional state of human history, where sin and death are still powerful, this side of this æon. They are divided, we may add further, subject to the judgment of Jesus Christ on those who are divided in this way, on the relative and provisional genuineness of their division, and therefore on whether or not they are really Christians or non-Christians. And we must also add that this division has to be made continually. Each new day we are all asked whether we are Christians or non-Christians. Each new day we must cease to be non-Christians and begin to be Christians. Each new day we need the Holy Spirit for this purpose. Yet it is still the case that there is a division at this point. As we are told in 1 Cor. 12³ : " No man speaking by the Spirit of God says : ἀνάθεμα ᾽Ιησοῦς (which is only a sharpened form of the confession of those who think that they can be neutral in relation to Him) : and no man can say : κύριος ᾽Ιησοῦς but by the Holy Ghost." Or again in 1 Jn. 4²ᶠ· : " Hereby know ye the Spirit of God : Every spirit that confesseth that Jesus Christ is come in the flesh is of God : and every spirit that confesseth not that Jesus Christ is come in the flesh is not of God." And the right to assert this criterion is underlined in 1 Jn. 4⁶ with the statements : " He that knoweth God heareth us (i.e., will acknowledge this criterion) ; he that is not of God heareth not us (i.e., does not acknowledge it). Hereby know we the spirit of truth, and the spirit of error." It should be noted how brief and general are the formulæ used in these passages. Neither in the λέγειν of 1 Corinthians nor the ὁμολογεῖν of 1 John is there any question of the acceptance or rejection of theological propositions. The attitudes described can, of course, be given the sharper and summarised form of propositions. But both Paul and the author of 1 John recognise that it is not the assent to propositions of this kind which divides the Christian (who does not withhold his assent) from the non-Christian. They and their readers must have known well enough the dominical saying about those who say " Lord, Lord " (Mt. 7²¹) but do not do the will of their Father in heaven. The First Epistle of John speaks elsewhere against an incipient dead orthodoxy, and its language is quite unmistakeable, being much sharper than that of any other New Testament writings. In the attitudes indicated by these short formulæ we have to do with man himself, the whole man—1 Jn. 4²ᶠ· speaks of a πνεῦμα which confesses or does not confess. We have to do with an orientation of man's existence as such. But for all their brevity the formulæ are quite explicit that we have to do with his attitude to the man Jesus, with His κυριότης, with Jesus Christ as the One who has come in the flesh. It is the rejection of this which makes a non-Christian. And it is the acceptance of this—seriously possible only in the Holy Spirit, in a decision that effectively determines his existence—which makes a Christian.

Paul hazarded the strongest expressions about the unity with Christ into which Christians enter with their acceptance as evoked by the Holy Spirit. ῾Ημεῖς δὲ νοῦν Χριστοῦ ἔχομεν, he can say in 1 Cor. 2¹⁶, and in 1 Cor. 6¹⁷ (capping even the συμμαρτυρεῖν of the Holy Spirit with ours of Rom. 8¹⁶) : " But he that is joined unto the Lord is one Spirit (ἐν πνεῦμα) with him." The whole context of Rom. 8¹⁴⁻¹⁷ (cf. Gal. 4⁶⁻⁷) refers to the relationship of the Christian to Christ as created by the Holy Ghost, and here the Spirit is described as πνεῦμα υἱοθεσίας, and therefore as the power in which the Christian is granted a part in the filial being and authority of Christ. In virtue of this πνεῦμα they can be sons of God here and now, and therefore free from the servile fear for which they would have good reason of themselves. Here and now de profundis, but in the depths in which they still dwell, they can cry with the one Son of God : " Abba, Father." Here and now they can already say of themselves : ὅτι ἐσμὲν τέκνα θεοῦ, and, because sons, heirs of the inheritance which this Father alone, God Himself, controls—joint-heirs with Christ. They can bear their suffering as a subsequent suffering with Him, and with Him, following the One who has gone before them, they can move toward the glory, their own glorification in the light of God. In short, in and with their " Jesus is Lord," their confession of the majesty and kingdom of this man, Christians find their own εἶναι ἐν Χριστῷ, themselves as the brothers and fellows of the royal man Jesus, who in Him and with Him are elected and beloved by God. " The love of God (in itself and from our own standpoint as much hidden from us as from other men) is shed abroad in our hearts by the Holy Spirit which is given unto us " (Rom. 5⁵). What makes them Christians and divides them from non-Christians is that they can find themselves at the side of the One on whom there rests the good-pleasure of God, and that they can live by this discovery. It is impossible to say whether the first consequence of this outpouring is their free acceptance of Jesus as the Lord or their free acceptance of themselves as those who belong to Him and share His prerogatives. For how can the second be lacking if they accept the first ? Or how can the first not be included in the second ? The love of God is directed to them, but it is directed to them in Christ (Rom. 8³⁹). There can be no pragmatising at this point. The love of God which is in Christ and directed to them is one event as it is gathered together in the " by the Holy Ghost." The only thing is that it is marked and characterised in its totality by the " in Christ," being clearly distinguished from all other happenings, even of a spiritual type, by the fact that it is the work of the Holy Ghost shedding abroad the love of God in our hearts. But to understand this we have to take into account the three passages which succeed Rom. 8¹⁴⁻¹⁷.

In Rom. 8¹⁸⁻²² we look back from the glory to which Christians already move forward in Christ to the παθήματα τοῦ νῦν καιροῦ which they still bear with Him. We are first told that these are not worthy to be compared with the glory which is to be revealed in them. They are so immeasurably small in relation to it. But, in the light of the fact that they have actually to be borne here and now in the following of the sufferings of Christ, we are then reminded that their Christian existence as those who suffer and hope is not something isolated and particular—an end in itself. They are surrounded by the ἀποκαραδοκία, the earnest expectation, of all creation, of the whole non-Christian world which does not yet know of the atonement accomplished for it in Jesus Christ, a world which as Paul saw it seems to have included all creatures, even the non-human. What is the existence of men, and other creatures, who are not participant in the Holy Spirit, and therefore in the knowledge of Jesus Christ, and therefore in the knowledge of themselves, and therefore in the new determination of their being ? Seeing that they too have to bear the παθήματα τοῦ νῦν καιροῦ, is it not in fact (and Christians know this as those who partake of the Spirit of Christ and live with Him) one in which they also groan and travail together with Christians, because they are subjected with them to vanity (ματαιότης), contrary to what they intend and seek and desire as the creatures of God, but with no possibility of effective resistance ? And is it not in fact an existence ἐφ' ἐλπίδι, in the hope of another form of being which can only be for them, as for Christians, a hope, because it is not yet seen ? Is this hope in vain ? No, says Paul. It can be positively asserted of them : " The creature itself also shall be delivered (ἐλευθερωθήσεται) from the bondage of φθορά into the glorious liberty of the children of God." Thus, although Christians are genuinely divided from them by their " Jesus is Lord," they are not really divided from them, but bound up with them in the twofold solidarity of suffering with them, bearing the burdens of the whole fellowship of time (as those who in the light of Jesus know why), and of hoping with them (as those who in the light of Jesus know for whom and what). For all its peculiarity, therefore, their existence is not a particular one, but that of a universal mission. In all the singularity of their existence they are the advance-guard of the crucified and risen Jesus Christ in a world which does not yet know Him and its atonement as it has been achieved in Him.

In Rom. 8²³⁻²⁵ the form of Christian existence as established and fashioned by the Holy Ghost is expressly described as provisional, and the world of the Holy Ghost as that which now determines it as the gift of a beginning (ἀπαρχή). In the words of Lk. 24⁴⁹ and Ac. 2³³ He is the promise which is given them. His work is to put men in possession of a hope which is certain, because it is already fulfilled in Jesus Christ, but even in its fulfilment not yet revealed and visible to them, to these men, to Christians. The man who partakes of the Spirit of Christ and is united with Him knows this. " Ourselves also, which have the ἀπαρχή of the Spirit (whose existence is already determined by the knowledge of the κυριότης of the man Jesus and our membership in Him), even we ourselves groan within ourselves, waiting for the adoption (the direct experience of what is bound up with the fact that in Christ we also are the children of God), to wit, the redemption of our σῶμα (the completed form of our persons, removed from φθορά, in which God already sees us, which belongs to us, and is already prepared for us, as those who are elect in and with Christ, but in which we do not yet live)." We are saved (ἐσώθημεν), but we are saved as we continue to hope that, although we do not yet see it, we are on the way to seeing it, so that even in the night in which we do not see it we are summoned to wait (ἀπεκδέχεσθαι) and to be patient. The only thing is that Paul does not put this in the form of an imperative, but of an indicative. It is a statement of fact : As those who do not see, but hope, δι' ὑπομονῆς ἀπεκδεχόμεθα. This is the present situation. This is what we do.

Finally, Rom. 8²⁶⁻²⁷ tells us that the fact that Christians live in and with the ἀπαρχή τοῦ πνεύματος is proved by the fact that they are in a position to hope, and to hope without wavering, even though they do not see ; that they can actually wait with patience. They can do this because He, the Spirit, helps their infirmities, i.e., strengthens them in the weakness to which they are exposed by the fact that they do not yet see what they are. And He does this (and the man who partakes of the Spirit of Christ knows that everything depends on this and that this is where help is to be found) by making prayer both a possibility and a reality : a possibility because He puts them in a union and relationship with God in which they can really speak with Him as they could not do of themselves, so that by His mediation, in virtue of His ὑπερεντυγχάνειν, they do actually talk with Him ; and a reality because in virtue of His mediation their own stammering (the στεναγμοὶ ἀλάλητοι), their own attempts to speak with God, are heard and understood by Him. As they speak with God and are heard and understood by Him, they endure the long night through, looking for the morning. And all this as the Spirit is the power in which the love of God, electing and acting in Jesus Christ, is shed abroad in their hearts. He makes them Christians. He divides them from non-Christians. But He also unites them with non-Christians. He is the promise which is given them, and He sets them in the position of hope. He gives them the power to wait daily for the revelation of what they already are, of what they became on the day of Golgotha. He is the power of the prayer which makes this expectation their own powerful action. And as He does all this, showing Himself in all this to be the Spirit of Jesus Christ, He is the Holy Spirit.

We were enquiring concerning the holiness of the Holy Spirit, and therefore concerning the particular aspect and operation of the power with which we have to do when we are concerned with the transition from Jesus Christ to other men, with a fellowship and unity between Him and them, and therefore with Christians : men who know Him (and themselves in Him) as the One who has emerged from the concealment of His crucifixion, as the One who is alive, as the royal man and Lord ; and who in this knowledge are placed at a new beginning of their own existence. The question forced itself upon us in face of

the confidence with which the New Testament counted on the fact
that there is actually a Christian community and Christians, and therefore, obviously, on the operation of the power of the Holy Spirit which
makes this both a possibility and a reality. The fact that the New
Testament does count on this constitutes for the whole Church which
is grounded on its witness, and therefore for ourselves, an invitation
and summons to do the same, and to do so with the same confidence
as we find in it. But we now enquire concerning the basis and meaning
of this confidence. And we must make this enquiry if we are to know
what we are doing when we accept this invitation, when in the light
of Jesus Christ we at once presuppose that there is also His community
and Christians, His own people, and when we are confident to assume
that we ourselves are His community, Christians. What is it that
makes the power in which this is possible and real a holy power, or
(to adopt the terminology of the New Testament) the Holy Ghost, to
whom we are permitted and commanded to give our confidence and
obedience just because He is holy, with the result that this presupposition becomes quite self-evident ? We have seen that the New Testament does not fail to give us an answer to this question. It explains
the holiness of the Spirit by simply describing and characterising Him
as the Spirit of Jesus Christ, and therefore as the self-revelation of
the One whose disclosure to other men, and fellowship and unity with
them, we have investigated with a certain anxiety in view of the
mystery of His majesty in the lowliness of His death, and our own
incapacity to penetrate this mystery. It explains, therefore, that the
door which is closed from within to the being of Jesus Christ and our
being in and with Him has actually been opened from within, in the
power of His life as the royal man. It has been opened once and
decisively in His resurrection, and it is continually opened in the
presence and action of the Holy Spirit. Thus according to the New
Testament the Holy Spirit is holy in the fact that He is the self-
expression of the man Jesus, and that as such He is Himself His effective turning to us and our effective conversion to Him ; His disclosure
for us and our disclosure for Him ; and, as this comes to us in this
twofold sense, the new thing in earthly history, the alteration in human
life and nature which is meant when we talk of the existence of the
Christian community, the existence of Christians.

Is this the only answer that can be given ? It is indeed the only
answer. It is complete in itself. It cannot be augmented or superseded. Jesus Christ is the Holy One beside or above whom there can
be none holier. In His being we have the sum of particularity, and in
His work the sum of particular operation. We say the supreme and
all-embracing thing of the holiness of the Holy Spirit when we follow
this New Testament line from above to below and call Him the Spirit
of Jesus Christ. All discussion of what authorises and legitimates
Him as the power above all other powers, of what makes Him the

genuine power for whose operation we must always sigh and cry when it seems to be lacking, and to whose operation we can never give ourselves too joyously or confidently when it may be seen, must continually circle around the name and the man Jesus Christ if they are to be in any sense meaningful, and lead up to the fact that the Holy Spirit is holy in the fact that He is the Spirit of this One, and comes from Him, and conducts to Him, as the Spirit of His revealing and revelation. If He were not His Spirit, if He came from some other or conducted to some other, if another revealed himself or were revealed in Him, He would not be the Holy Spirit, the One whom the New Testament calls holy, and whom the Church founded on the New Testament has every reason to respect as the one Spirit who exclusively deserves and claims its trust and obedience, for whom it has unceasingly to pray and in whom it may unceasingly rejoice.

Yet this one complete and satisfying answer needs perhaps a certain elucidation. For the New Testament itself shows us that when this one answer is given with a right understanding it has a higher dimension which has so far received only tacit consideration in our exposition, with no explicit reference. The fact is that the New Testament does not describe the Holy Spirit as consistently as we might at first sight expect as the Spirit of Jesus Christ. On the contrary, in a considerable number of passages, although with no deviation in the description of His operation, it calls Him the Spirit of God, or of the Lord, or of the Father ; and it often links the origin of His coming, of His being given, not only with the name of Jesus Christ, but also exclusively with these other names.

In the well-known definition of Jn. 4²⁴ God Himself is called πνεῦμα, with the result that those who worship Him (who bow down before Him) must do so, not as in Jerusalem or on Mount Gerizim, but in Spirit and in truth. In Rom. 8⁹ the Spirit is called in one breath, first the πνεῦμα θεοῦ, and then the πνεῦμα Χριστοῦ. In Rom. 8¹¹ He is " the Spirit of him that raised up Jesus from the dead." In 2 Cor. 3⁴ He is " the Spirit of the living God." In 1 Cor. 2¹² He is the Spirit " which is of God." In Rom. 8¹⁴, 1 Cor. 2¹¹ and elsewhere He is simply the " Spirit of God." In Ac. 5⁹ and 8³⁹, in obvious reminiscence of the Old Testament, He is the " Spirit of the Lord." Again, it is God who according to 1 Thess. 4⁸ " hath also given unto us his holy Spirit," and who according to Gal. 4⁶ sends Him into our hearts (as the Spirit of His Son). And it is obviously God who is the subject of the " ministering " (ἐπιχορηγεῖν) of the Spirit in Gal. 3⁵. In Mt. 3¹⁶ the Spirit who descends on Jesus at His baptism in Jordan is called the πνεῦμα θεοῦ. And in the quotation from Joel with which Peter begins his address on the day of Pentecost we read that God will pour out of His Spirit on all flesh (Ac. 2¹⁷). In the Fourth Gospel the Father has the same function as the origin and giver of the Spirit. " And I will pray the Father, and he shall give you another παράκλητος " (Jn. 14¹⁶). And then again in Jn. 14²⁶ : " The Father will send him " (in my name). And then again, with a very complicated inter-relating of the two subjects : " But when the παράκλητος is come, whom I will send unto you from the Father, even the Spirit of truth, which proceedeth from the Father, he shall testify of me " (Jn. 15²⁶). In Tit. 3⁶ God is the giver of the Spirit and Jesus Christ the One through whom He is given : " . . . which he shed on us abundantly through Jesus Christ our Saviour." And finally there is the distinctive teaching of Ac. 2[33] that when the risen Christ ascended to the right hand of God He there received from the Father the ἐπαγγελία τοῦ πνεύματος ἁγίου and then Himself shed forth that which was seen and heard in the miracle of Pentecost.

As a whole, if not in detail, the result is outwardly and formally clear. There can be no question of any material contradiction between the two ways of speaking, because they are often combined. We can find no trace of any intention of saying different things with the two different forms, or of playing off the one against the other. The more narrowly christological description and derivation occur rather more frequently and with the greater emphasis. It is obvious, therefore, that they constitute the basic schema, within which even such important writers as Paul and John have the freedom, and exercise it with a certain necessity, to use the name of God or the Father as well as that of Jesus Christ in relation to the nature and origin of the Spirit.

We have to consider this result. We can say at once that it does not involve any material restriction or amendment or even overthrow of our previous conclusion. It is not a superior conclusion by which we have to correct it. Nor is it a parallel conclusion which has to be placed alongside it. Its function is to elucidate. There is obviously needed an inward movement and explanation if it is to be made and established in the sense of the New Testament.

Hitherto we have been considering the history which takes place between the existence of the man Jesus and that of other men when there is between Him and them a transition, a communication and a union, and when as a result of this communication we have to reckon with the reality of His community, of Christians, as well as with that of Jesus Christ Himself. In relation to this aspect we have had to speak of the Holy Spirit as the self-revelation of the man Jesus. We have had to speak of the way in which He opened up Himself to other men, and opened up other men to Himself, uniting Himself with them, and them with Him : Himself as the One that He was and is in Himself and for them in the mystery of His death ; and others as those who lack not only knowledge and understanding but also the will or any other organ for His being and their being in Him. The outpouring of the Spirit as the effect of His resurrection, of His life in His death and in the conquest of His death, and therefore the occurrence of His self-impartation (" Because I live, ye shall live also," Jn. 14[19]) is the answer that we have given to this historical problem under the guidance of the New Testament.

But when the New Testament also speaks in the same sense and context of the fact that God or the Father is and acts as Spirit, it shows us that this history which takes place on earth and in time, and the being and operation of the Spirit in it, have a background from which they come, and in the light of which they have a decisive reach and significance, not only for the being or non-being of the community and Christians, but also for the being or non-being, the life or death, of the world and all men. In the presence and action of the Holy Spirit it is not simply a matter of what makes Christians Christians. It is this. But in the awakening and calling, or (as we may confidently say) the creation, of the community and Christians among all other men and within the created cosmos it is a matter of the attestation and proclamation of the one necessary thing that has to be said to this cosmos, of the most urgent and pressing thing that all men must hear and know, or that can in any case be declared and accepted. It has to be declared and accepted in the world which God, in spite of its alienation from God and enmity against Him, setting a term to its discord and destruction and perdition, creating for it peace and salvation, has loved, and loves and will love in the sacrifice of Himself. The will of God in the existence of the community, of Christians, is that this gracious and selfless and powerfully redemptive Yes of God should be declared and accepted as it was spoken in the existence of the man Jesus among those for whom it was spoken. God wills the typical existence of a people which responds to this Yes on behalf of the world to which it refers. This will of God is done on earth as He makes possible and actual the existence of this people by the presence and action of the Holy Spirit. It is this will of God which is the background of that earthly history; the second and higher dimension of His being and operation which we have always to keep in mind when we think and speak of the Holy Spirit and His work.

The address of Peter found an outpouring of the Holy Spirit on all flesh (Ac. 2^{17}) in what came on only a few on the day of Pentecost. The insignificant and petty history of Christians, as capacitated and actualised by the Holy Spirit, is not merely one history among others—however much this may appear to be the case from the external and historical standpoint—but a kind of central history among all others. It is in order that it may occur that world history and time continue. To put it epigrammatically, it is itself the true world history, and everything else that bears this name is only the rather remarkable accompaniment. There can be no doubt that this is what is meant and said in the New Testament. And the Church must also mean and say this, not in order to advance an empty claim for itself, but in order to be conscious of the incomparable responsibility of its existence and mission and task. In the light of that background in the will of God it is this typical people in the world. It has to keep to this fact, and orientate itself by it, or else it has nothing to do with the Holy Ghost or the Holy Ghost with it, and it is not what it seems and pretends to be. *Tertium non datur*. It is to this that our attention is directed by that variation in New Testament terminology in respect of the Spirit. From God's standpoint, and therefore with final seriousness, we have to do with the totality when we are dealing with the unity between the man Jesus and other men, and therefore with the being and operation of the Holy Spirit.

God Himself is at work in this occurrence. To realise what this means, we must not look away from this occurrence but we have now to consider the heights (or, as we might equally well say, the depths) from which it occurs, in which it is grounded, and by which it is also determined and ordered ; the heights and depths of God Himself who is at work in it. We will take it that the history of the communication between Christ and Christians has been told as such ; that the Holy Spirit has been characterised as the power of this communication, and the holiness defined in which He is this power and works as such. We will take it that for the moment there is nothing more to consider and say on this level. But in the light of the distinctive character and reach of this history, as already indicated, we have to consider and say with the greatest seriousness—and this opens up a new dimension —that God Himself is present and active in it. That is why it is so important a history. That is why it is so necessary to know and present it so accurately. The specific importance which marks it off from all other histories is that God Himself is at work in it : in the same sense, and just as fully and unreservedly, in its origin, in the existence of the crucified and risen man Jesus, the royal man ; in its goal, in the existence of the Christian community and individual Christians ; and in the transition or mediation from the one to the other, in the power and operation of the Holy Ghost. In all these decisive moments or factors in this history God is at work. Nor is this the case merely in the way in which He is undoubtedly present and active in all creaturely occurrence and all human history. In this history God Himself is at work in His own most proper cause—the cause in which it is a matter of the purpose and meaning of all creation and the attainment of His will with it. God Himself is at work ruling in His holiness at the heart of all world occurrence as it is directed by Him. We have now to ask concerning God in the light of this holiness and this particular history. Why is this? Because it might well be the case that, for all the pains we have taken to understand it, we are not really taking it as seriously as it has to be taken, but allowing it only to soar away from us as a kind of (logically and æsthetically, perhaps, very impressive) myth, if we do not realise that its pragmatics are the pragmatics of God, that in it we have to do with Him, with the First and Last in every human life, with the One who cannot be mocked because He is source and sum of all power as well as pity, with the One whom none can escape because He encloses us on all sides, and we all, unasked and whether we know and like it or not, derive from Him and return to Him. It is our present task to emphasise that this One is the Lord of this history.

It is not a matter of bringing our discussions into the obscure sphere of a metaphysics. We must not lose sight of the history, but keep it all the more clearly before us and understand ourselves all the more strictly as those who have a supreme part in it. But to do this we now set it resolutely to the light of the thought of God ; not of a thought of God which we have freely chosen or discovered for ourselves ; but of the Christian thought of God. It is in this light that it must be seen and understood if it is to shine on us and enlighten us as it should, but as it will not do so long as we accept and consider its occurrence only on the level on which we have so far tried to see and understand it. This is what shows us the heights and depths which constitute its true secret : the secret of all the secrets which we have come up against at every point ; the beginning and end and centre in our consideration of it on this level. It is the Christian thought of God which, when it is rightly thought, is kindled from the very outset in the history whose origin is the man Jesus, whose goal is Christendom, and whose centre is the Holy Ghost as the living transition from the one to the other. When it is rightly thought, it does not leave this history behind it to embark on a journey into the void. On the contrary, it could not and cannot be anything other than the thought of this history executed with a powerful underlining of these three decisive factors. It is simply the giving of this emphasis by means of the assertion that in it God Himself is always and everywhere the decisive factor, the true acting Subject. Because and as this history gives itself to be understood in this way, and, at an even deeper level, because it is this history at whose beginning and end and centre God Himself acts and speaks, because it demands this emphasis, because we cannot know it at all without knowing that it is a matter of God in it, because we must follow its own movement and try to reproduce it in our thinking, the Christian thought of God is necessary for its understanding. It is not a matter of trying to know God from another source and then applying that knowledge to this history, interpreting the history as a symbol of what is supposed to be known of God already and elsewhere. We cannot do this. What we can and must do is to learn to know God from this history, and thus genuinely to understand and estimate it as this particular history in its mysteries and singularity and importance and distinction from all myths and all other histories. To this extent the Christian thought of God is the powerful lever whose movement makes possible this understanding and appraisal when it emerges from this history and then returns to it. This is what is meant when we say that it is a matter of setting this history in the light of the Christian thought of God. It is simply a matter of setting it in the light to which it belongs because it is its own light.

We will begin with a general and formal statement concerning what we have called the three decisive factors in this history.

The existence of the man Jesus is the first and basic and controlling factor to the extent that it supplies the initiative which makes the whole possible and actual, and determines and fashions it. It is the height which gives this history (which from first to last is the history of Jesus) its momentum and character. But it also anticipates its goal. In it everything has already taken place which will take place in its course and consequence. But this anticipation as the work of a man, in the sphere of His limited existence, is as such a divine work. Thus the height from which this history has its momentum, its teleological power, is a divine height, and the initiative which it supplies a divine initiative. Thus the existence of the man Jesus (as the beginning of this history, which includes already the fulness of the whole) coincides with the history of God Himself. As God does not will to exist, to be God, merely for Himself alone, but in the world, in the midst of men and for them, this man exists as the origin which includes the execution and the goal of all that God wills to do, and has done, and still does among men and for them.

The second factor which we now emphasise, and which is really the third in order, is the goal of this history, the existence of the community, of Christians. The man Jesus does not exist only for their sake, but He does exist in the first instance for their sake. As the Lord and Saviour of the world He is primarily their Head, the One who is known and loved by them. In the first instance it is they who, typically for the world, are in the depth to which that history moves with all its downward force. But what is and takes place at this end, although it is again a matter of men, has also a divine character. That God is God even in this depth, that He is with these men and they are with God, that in virtue of His presence and action they are His children, witnesses of His work in the world, and preachers of His Word to it—this is what happens when they are taken up into fellowship and union with the man Jesus. They are found by God when they find in this man their Head, and themselves in Him as their origin. In their existence God achieves His own end.

The third factor is the one which links the first and second. It is the power of the transition, the downward movement, from the one to the other, from Christ to Christendom. It is the power which overcomes the distance between that one man and these many, between His height and their depth. What takes place in this history is that this distance is overcome. The man Jesus is not alone, nor are these other men. There takes place His disclosure to them, and their disclosure to Him. But this is a divine disclosure. It is God who wills not only to be there but also here, not only to exalt that one man but in the power of the revelation of His exaltation to cause these many to share in His exaltation. It is God who is revealed as the One who has already exalted them in that One. The third and middle factor in this history is that God Himself is revealed by God Himself as the One who is with Jesus, and, because with Jesus, with Christendom.

We are still considering it only formally and in its general structure, but our emphasis is upon the fact that God is present and active in it, not only in its origin, but also in its goal and in the conjunction and unity of the two. We have to say a threefold " God " if we are to see and understand this history. At no point have we to say it any less, or in a weaker or less proper sense, than at any others. At every point we have really to say " God." It would not be this history if it permitted us not to say " God," or not to say " God " seriously, at any of these three points. When we see clearly and forcibly that in the history as a whole, and equally in these three moments, we have to do with God, we have understood and seen and grasped it, not merely intellectually, but (to use the expression for once) existentially, as our own history. For when we find God present and active in this history, because we none of us do not first belong to God and only then to ourselves, we also find ourselves, really ourselves, not *a priori* but *a posteriori*, our own whence and whither and how as our part in the general whence and whither and how, the whence and whither and how of all things ; our part, therefore, in God. To know God in this history is also—subsequently and incidentally, but also seriously, as is only right—to know ourselves in it. And to know ourselves—in the subsequent and incidental but serious way which is demanded— is to know God in this history, in its three moments or factors.

Whatever may be the literary and religious derivation of the well-known formula in Rom. 11[36] with which Paul concludes his great discussion of Christ, Israel and the Church, and whatever may be the particular sense in which he meant it to be understood in this context, there can be no doubt that it does actually describe most exactly the presence and action of God in the history which takes place by this means between that origin and goal. 'Εξ αὐτοῦ has obvious reference to a beginning which produces and controls and determines and already anticipates everything that follows. Δι' αὐτοῦ has reference to a power and its operation which strive from this beginning to the corresponding goal and mediate the transition from the one to the other. Εἰς αὐτόν has reference to a goal which shows itself to be a genuine goal, i.e., anticipated by this beginning and attained by this power and its operation, by the fact that from it it is possible only to look back to this beginning and to return to it—the looking back, the return, the εἰς αὐτόν, obviously taking place in the same power, the same δι' αὐτοῦ, by which it is attained as a goal. And then τὰ πάντα : the whole occurrence stands under the threefold sign that it is all of Him and through Him and to Him. And therefore He, αὐτός, the same, is the Lord of this occurrence in the threefold mode of His being. He, the same, as we may now say, is the one Lord in a portion of earthly history—for it is to this that the formula refers even in the context in which it is used by Paul—but in this history in a threefold manner and form, as its origin and means and goal. Thus even in the application which we are making of the formula the liturgical conclusion cannot be lightly dismissed, but must be understood as the worship in which the Christian thought of God can alone be thought in relation to this history.

It is a matter of the Christian thought of God. This is the light of this history. It is in the light of this thought that it must be seen and understood. But the Christian thought of God is trinitarian. That God, who is present and active in this history, is the triune God, Father, Son and Holy Spirit, has emerged only in outline. Indeed, strictly speaking, it has emerged only in the outline of one of its reflections, of a *vestigium trinitatis*. We are not speaking, of course, of the mere fact that there are three factors in this history, but of their character, function and mutual relationship. There can be no proper or direct *vestigium trinitatis*, no direct and complete correspondences to the triunity of God, apart from God's own being and life and therefore within the creaturely world (cf. *C.D.*, I, 1, § 8, 3). Even the history with which we are now concerned cannot be described in this way. Only one of its three factors coincides with one of the three modes of being (or " persons ") of God, although in this case the coincidence is quite unequivocal, the third and middle factor, the divine power of the transition from Christ to Christendom, being identical with God in the mode of being of the Holy Spirit. It is from this centre that we shall have to think if we are to recognise the light of the Christian thought of God, or, let us now say objectively, the light of the triune God, which shines in and over this history. We cannot say, however, that the existence of the man Jesus at the beginning of this history is directly, i.e. materially, identical with God the Father, nor the existence of Christendom at its end with God the Son. We can point only to the formal character of the first factor—that it is the origin of the whole history, and the origin which already anticipates and includes within itself the goal, just as God the Father has to be called the *fons et origo totius Deitatis* in the trinitarian being and life of God. And we can point only to the formal character of the second factor— that it is the goal of this history which corresponds and refers back to its origin, just as in God Himself the Son is the One who is eternally loved by the Father and who eternally loves Him in return, so that He is *Deus de Deo, lumen de lumine . . . consubstantialis Patri*. The fact that in the third and mediating factor of that history, as in the third and mediating mode of being of God, we have to do with the Holy Spirit, in the one case within the undivided *opus trinitatis ad extra* and in the other in His specific *opus ad intra*, is a provisional confirmation that even the formal comparison of the first and second factors of that history with the first and second modes of being of God (however formal it may be) is no mere speculative venture. We cannot say more than this, but this at least we can say. With this obvious material coincidence at the heart, the whole outline and structure and pragmatics of that history reminds us of the triune being of God even though it may not be a direct reflection of it and cannot be claimed as a direct *vestigium trinitatis*. We cannot think of it as a whole without being at least stimulated and invited by the character and function and mutual relationship of its three factors to think *ceteris imparibus* of the triune God, and therefore to think the Christian thought of God. But to execute this thought, and therefore to prove our statement that in that history God Himself, the triune God, is present and active and recognisable, this result of the formal consideration of the totality of this history does not suffice. We are enabled to do this only at the one place where, beyond the formal similarity between that history as a whole and the triune being of God, we can also assert a material coincidence, i.e., in respect of the Holy Spirit, who is not only the divine power mediating between Christ and Christendom but the mode of being of the one God which unites the Father and the Son. At this point we are enabled to prove our statement, and thus to prove its validity for the totality of that history. More and more the Holy Spirit has forced Himself upon us as the true theme of this section, and He must now be our constant theme as we try to penetrate the matter at this dimension of height and depth.

At this point we are continually directed to the mysterious and

miraculous character of the intervention of the Holy Spirit even in His
function in this history. The Holy Spirit indicates in fact, as the
New Testament does not disguise, something which cannot be seen or
grasped, a reality of which we for our part can have true knowledge
only as we pray that it may take place in spite of its invisibility and
inconceivability. And as we pray for this, startled always by the
great hiddenness of the royal man Jesus in His crucifixion and our
own lack of openness to Him because of the dullness of our spirits,
we testify already that even in all His invisibility and inconceivability
the Holy Spirit is not for us merely the great Unknown, that it is not
the case that we simply do not have Him, but that we know His
power and efficacy. *Credo in Spiritum sanctum.* If it were otherwise,
how could we even pray for Him ? And how could the whole problem
of this mediation be for us even a problem, how could we even ask
concerning this twofold disclosure, if it did not in fact take place, if
Jesus Christ were not risen, if there were no community and no
Christians with their perceptible witness, if therefore the Holy Spirit
did not come and were not at work as the power of the resurrection
of Jesus, as *Creator Spiritus*, if the problem, however we may understand it, were not at least posed by these things as a genuine problem ?
—quite apart from the fact that we have the New Testament with its
unceasing witness to the coming and operation of the Spirit, His intervention and mediation, His penetration of all walls, His quiet movement through doors not really closed but open, which even as a miracle
and mystery it can attest so confidently. And when does it ever cease
to ask us whether we can accept responsibility for not having a similar
confidence on our own part, and therefore attesting that to which it
bears witness ?

Why is it that the miracle and mystery of the Holy Spirit are so
great and oppressive and yet, as we may gather from the New Testament, so liberating ? How is it that we are always so confused in
relation to the Spirit and His work, so that we can only make tentative
beginnings which are not worth saying, and at bottom can only pray
that He will be given us and not taken away from us ? And yet
why is it again that even in our uneasy efforts, if only we make them,
we always have the intrinsically clear knowledge that Jesus lives and
that we may live with Him, so that for all our sighing we have a
cheerfulness which can never be suppressed, but always keeps breaking
in ? Why is it that He is always so invisible and inconceivable, so
new, accessible only as He makes Himself accessible in order that we
may witness that Jesus lives and that we may live in Him ? And yet
again—and this must be our final word of questioning—why is it that
He and His work, that transition, that communication, that mediation,
that mutual disclosure, in which the man Jesus and other men find
each other and are united, are always so real, as is discovered by all
who have even the remotest knowledge of them, however they can

and will and may experience and assess them—more real, in fact, than all the more obvious and visible and conceivable connexions of earthly and human history ? We might also ask : Why is it that His coming at Pentecost must be described as it is in Ac. 2^{2f}, as the rushing of a mighty wind straight down, as it seems, from heaven ? And why is it that His operation is then described as the endowment of those men, so that they became what they had not been before, witnesses of the great acts of God as they had taken place in Jesus Christ, and could do what they had not been able to do before, express their witness in such a way that it could be heard and understood in every secular tongue ? What kind of an intervention is this ? Why is it that even on this level this is how things are with the Holy Spirit ?

The answer which we now make is that it is because in this mystery of His being and work in our earthly history there is repeated and represented and expressed what God is in Himself. In His being and work as the mediator between Jesus and other men, in His creating and establishing and maintaining of fellowship between Him and us, God Himself is active and revealed among us men, i.e., the fellowship, the unity, the peace, the love, which there is in God, in which God was and is and will be from and to all eternity. We speak of the fellowship of the Father and the Son. It is not as a supreme being, which is accidentally the sum of all conceivable excellencies and therefore of the unity of peace and love, that God is God, but concretely as the Father and the Son, and this in the fellowship, the unity, the peace, the love of the Holy Spirit, who is Himself the Spirit of the Father and the Son ; as the One who is thrice one in Himself in these three modes of being. It is with the unity of God, and therefore with God Himself, that we have to do when we have to do with the Holy Spirit in the event of the transition, the communication, the mediation between Jesus and us. This is what makes the mystery so singular and great. This is why the transition is so invisible and inconceivable, and yet so real for all its invisibility and inconceivability. This is why it takes place with such sovereign freedom, and cannot in any sense be controlled by us. This is why it can properly be known only in an act of worship. But this is also why it is an event, to which we may adopt all kinds of different attitudes, of questioning and doubt or of the childlike confidence and thankfulness of the New Testament, but the reality of which we cannot in any way change. It takes place first in God Himself. It is an event in His essence and being and life. It falls straight down from above into the sphere of our essence and being and life, repeating and representing and expressing itself in the occurrence of that history, in the unknown and yet known event of that transition. The divine intervention which creates fellowship reveals itself and takes place, not as something which is alien to God, but as a mediation which is most proper to Him, which takes place first in Himself, in His divine life from eternity to eternity, in His fellowship and inward peace, in the love which is primarily and properly in Him. What is revealed and represented and active is the unity of the Father and the Son in the Holy Spirit, who like the Father and the Son, as the Spirit of the Father and the Son, is the one true God, *qui ex Patre Filioque procedit, qui cum Patre et Filio simul adoratur et conglorificatur.* Is it not inevitable that this should be a mystery ? How petty is all the confusion or joy that we may know in face of this event, all the questioning and answering with which we may surround it, when even to ask, let alone to answer rightly we for our part have to look right into the "deep things of God" (1 Cor. 2[10]) in which this event has its basis, in which it is primarily and properly an event, yet in which it does not remain concealed or withheld, but becomes an event among us and for us—the love of the Father and the Son in the Holy Spirit, the love which is in God Himself ! The important thing, however, is not whether our little astonishment is commensurate or not with this mystery. It is a lifelong task to learn astonishment at this point, and therefore to know what astonishment really is. The important thing is that we do stand objectively before this mystery. In what takes place between the man Jesus and us when we may become and be Christians, God Himself lives. Nor does He live an alien life. He lives His own most proper life. The Father lives with the Son, and the Son with the Father, in the Holy Spirit who is Himself God, the Spirit of the Father and the Son. It is as this God that God is the living God. And it is as this living God that He is among us and with us in this event. This is what makes the event so powerful, so distinctive, so different in its nature and power from all other events. This is why the gift that is made us in it is so total, and so total, too, the claim that is made upon us. At the heart of this event we have to do unequivocally and unreservedly with God Himself. And because this is the case at the centre, it is also the case on the periphery, in the origin and goal of this event. That is why we must now think of it in relation to its centre.

In the sphere of earthly and human history the problem of the history between the man Jesus and other men is the proper form of the problem of distance and confrontation, of encounter and partnership. It is a problem because Jesus is the royal man and we are not ; but because again Jesus is what He is, not for Himself, but for us ; because He wills to be with us ; because in anticipation His existence includes within itself our existence with Him. How can the one be true and the other become true ? If the solution to this problem is the intervention and presence and action of the Holy Spirit, if God Himself takes up this problem in the Holy Spirit, then this means that we are summoned to understand it as a problem spiritually, i.e., in the light of its solution in the Holy Spirit. But this is to see and understand that it is not primarily our own problem, a human problem of earthly history, but that primarily it is a divine problem—the problem of God's own being, and the answer and solution in and with which, by His own personal intervention in the Holy Spirit, He also answers and solves our problem. It is not the case, then, that we have here something which is not really applicable to God, but which is in a sense alien to Him. Nor is it the case for us that in this intervention we do not really have to do with God Himself, but only with His external and not His internal participation, He Himself being withheld from us. The Holy Spirit is not a magical third between Jesus and us. God Himself acts in His own most proper cause when in the Holy Spirit He mediates between the man Jesus and other men. For God is not the great immovable and immutable one and all which can confront us and our questions and answers only at an alien distance ; to which, if we are to count on its intervention to answer and solve our problem, we are forced to ascribe a self-alienation of its own being, a kind of magic ; which is hard to believe and does not readily inspire our confidence ; and the participation of which in our questioning and answering can only be external. This is how man imagines " God " without realising that what he is thinking or trying to think— for he cannot really succeed in doing it—is only the thought of his own limitation, or, to put it more sharply, the thought of his own death. God in the Holy Spirit, as He acts and reveals Himself between the man Jesus and other men, is the living God, and as such our God, who really turns to us as the One He is and not under a mask behind which He is really another, because in the first instance distance and confrontation, encounter and partnership, are to be found in Himself. In Himself, therefore, there is to be found the eternal form of the problem posed by them, and in Himself again the eternal form of the answer and solution. So great is the power in which He is present among us with His Spirit and gifts ! So deep and basic is the comfort given us in the presence and action of the Holy Spirit ! So firm is the direction which this gives ! What we regard as the purely human and earthly antitheses of here and there, before and after, above and below—antitheses which we ascribe only to this world and think we can and must overcome in our own strength—were and are already, in their original and proper form, quite apart from us and before the world was, the antitheses in God's own being and life— antitheses which are eternally fruitful, which cannot be overcome as such even though they do not involve any rigid abstract separation, but which stand always in a mutual relationship of self-opening and self-closure. God is in Himself—and here we have the distance and confrontation, the encounter and partnership, which are first in Him —Father and Son. He is both in equal Godhead, so that He is Father and Son without any abstraction or contradiction. But He is really both, and therefore not merely Father or merely Son. As Father and Son He is twice ineffaceably the one God, twice the same. This is His divine here and there, before and after, above and below. This is the problem which with its answer and solution is primarily His own, so that we are not alien to Him, nor He to us, when in the Holy Spirit He intervenes with the solution and answer for the problem of these antitheses before and in which we also stand. He knew this problem long before we did, before we ever were and before the world was. For He knew Himself from all eternity, the Father the Son, and the Son the Father. And we must not try to know it in any other way than as a spiritual problem, characterised as the problem of God Himself by its answering and solution in the presence and action of the Holy Spirit.

A problem of God Himself ? We can say this only if we underline at once that in God Himself, as the question of the relationship of the Father and the Son, it never could nor can be posed except in and with its answer and solution. What is primarily in God is the transition which takes place in that distance, the mediation in that confrontation, the communication in that encounter, the history in that partnership. God is twice one and the same, in two modes of being, as the Father and the Son, with a distinction which is not just separation but positively a supreme and most inward connexion. The Father and the Son are not merely alongside one another in a kind of neutrality or even hostility. They are with one another in love. And because· they are with one another in a love which is divine love the one does not merge into the other nor can the one or the other be alone or turn against the other.

We will emphasise the last of the expressions used because it is particularly important for our present purpose. What was and is and will be primarily in God Himself, and not primarily in the form in which we know or think we know it, is history in partnership. It is in partnership, and not therefore the history of an isolated individual. God was never solitary. Therefore the thought of a solitary man and his history can only be the aberration of a thinking which is either godless or occupied with that alien God which is properly death. God was always a Partner. The Father was the Partner of the Son, and the Son of the Father. And what was and is and will be primarily in God Himself is history in this partnership : the closed circle of the knowing of the Son by the Father and the Father by the Son which according to Mt. 11²⁷ can be penetrated only from within as the Son causes a man to participate in this knowledge by His revelation ; or, in the language of dogma, the Father's eternal begetting of the Son, and the Son's eternal being begotten of the Father, with the common work which confirms this relationship, in which it takes place eternally that the one God is not merely the Father and the Son but also, eternally proceeding from the Father and the Son, the Holy Ghost. Thus the partnership is not merely a first and static thing which is then succeeded by the history as a second and dynamic. The presence of the partnership means also the occurrence of the history. And the occurrence of the history means the eternal rise and renewal of the partnership. There is no rigid or static being which is not also act. There is only the being of God as the Father and the Son with the Holy Spirit who is the Spirit of both and in whose eternal procession they are both actively united. This history in partnership is the life of God before and above all creaturely life. Along the same lines we might also describe it by the other expressions. It is transition in distance, mediation in confrontation, and communication in encounter. And in each case it is obviously in the third moment of the divine life, in the Holy Spirit, that the history, the transition, the mediation and the communication between the Father and the Son take place and are revealed as such, as the mode of being of God in which His inner union is marked off from the circular course of a natural process as His own free act, an act of majesty. The history between the Father and the Son culminates in the fact that in it God is also *Spiritus Sanctus Dominus vivificans, qui ex Patre Filioque procedit.* Clearly, therefore, it is not subject to any necessity. The Father and the Son are not two prisoners. They are not two mutually conditioning factors in reciprocal operation. As the common source of the Spirit, who Himself is also God, they are the Lord of this occurrence. God is the free Lord of His inner union. Concretely, He is Spirit. But this means that before all earthly history, yet also in it, He is the One who is also for us (in His own history) transition, mediation and communication, and therefore the One who creates and gives life, the answer and solution to our problem. It is He Himself who does this, and He does it out of His own most proper being. He is always active in Himself in His action among us. In what He does on earth He reveals Himself as the One He is in heaven, so that not only on earth but in heaven we have no reason to expect anything higher or better or more sure. As He bridges the gulf which opens up before us between there and here, before and after, above and below, He is Himself the pledge that it is really bridged, so that there can be no sense in looking for anything stronger, since stronger pledges, if they are genuine, can only repeat and confirm the guarantee that He Himself has already given.

The triune life of God, which is free life in the fact that it is Spirit, is the basis of His whole will and action even *ad extra*, as the living act which He directs to us. It is the basis of His *decretum et opus ad extra*, of the relationship which He has determined and established with a reality which is distinct from Himself and endowed by Him with its own very different and creaturely being. It is the basis of the election of man to covenant with Himself ; of the determination of the Son to become man, and therefore to fulfil this covenant ; of creation ; and, in conquest of the opposition and contradiction of the creature and to save it from perdition, of the atonement with its final goal of redemption to eternal life with Himself. It is to be noted that

God is not under any obligation to will and do all this. He does not lack in Himself either difference or unity in difference, either movement or stillness, either antitheses or peace. In the triune God there is no stillness in which He desires and must seek movement, or movement in which He desires and must seek stillness. This God has no need of us. This God is self-sufficient. This God knows perfect beatitude in Himself. He is not under any need or constraint. It takes place in an inconceivably free overflowing of His goodness if He determines to co-exist with a reality distinct from Himself, with the world of creatures, ourselves ; and if He determines that we should co-exist with Him. It is the will and work of His free grace if He does us this honour, making it His own glory to be God with this other reality, with us and for us, as our Creator and Preserver and Lord and Shepherd and Saviour ; to accept us who do not in the least deserve it ; to pledge Himself to us ; to compromise Himself with us ; to keep faith with us in spite of our unfaithfulness ; not to withhold from us finally the supreme gift of eternal life, of being in the light of His glory, but to ascribe it to us, to promise it, and cause us to see and hear and taste it, in the incarnation of His Son. God does not have to will and do all this. But He does will and do it. And because He is the God of triune life, He does not will and do anything strange by so doing. In it He lives in the repetition and confirmation of what He is in Himself. What then, on the one side, is the distance, the confrontation, the encounter and the partnership between Himself and the world, Himself and man, but a representation, reflection and correspondence of the distinction with which He is in Himself the Father and the Son ? And what, on the other side, is the transition, the mediation, the communication and the history which He causes to take place in the covenant with man, in man's election, in the incarnation of the Son, but also in the rule of His fatherly providence over the existence of all His creatures, and in the execution of the reconciliation of the world with Himself, but again the representation, reflection and correspondence of the union of the Father and the Son in the Holy Spirit as His own eternal living act ? As He causes the world, and in His grace ourselves, to be His creatures, His men, and to exist before Him as is appropriate, and as in the same grace He does not allow us to go our own ways and to fall, as He does not withhold Himself from us but reveals Himself as our Partner and acts as such, from the provision of our daily bread to our deliverance from all evil—in all these things He is primarily true to Himself, revealing Himself as the One He is in Himself, as Father, Son and Spirit, in expression and application and exercise of the love in which He is God. Thus we for our part, as history in partnership is the portion which is allotted us in His free grace, genuinely exist in participation in Himself, in His triune life, and in the problem of this life, and its answer and solution. Receiving the Holy Spirit, giving Him our trust and obedience, we are taken under His protection. We do not need to walk uncertainly. We stand and walk on a rock. Neither in heaven nor on earth can we expect any deeper comfort or higher direction. We can only cling to the fact that by the Holy Spirit we may be and live with God Himself. We may do so only of grace. But we may do so without reserve, because in His Spirit God Himself is present.

In these considerations we have tried to take into account and understand the fact that in the New Testament the Holy Spirit can be called the Spirit of God or the Father or the Lord as well as the Spirit of Jesus Christ. As we have followed this hint, there has opened up to us the upward dimension which we have to remember when we speak of the holiness of the Spirit who is the Mediator between the existence of the man Jesus and our own, asking concerning the reality and truth in which it takes place that there is a Christian community among men, and men who may become and be Christians. But this upward dimension has also to be considered in relation to the fact that in the New Testament the Spirit is called the Spirit of Jesus Christ in the fourfold sense which we have already established : as the Spirit who is first the Spirit of the man Jesus Himself ; who proceeds from Him and only from Him ; who witnesses to Him and only to Him ; and in whom we know ourselves in this man and may therefore be with Him. As the Spirit of Jesus Christ He is no other Spirit in this totality of His presence and action than the Spirit of God or the Father or the Lord—the power of the transition, mediation, communication and history which take place first in the life of God Himself and then consequently in our life, in the relationship of the man Jesus to us. The Spirit of this man—His own Spirit, who proceeds from Him and attests Him and unites other men with Him—is the Spirit of God the Son, and as such He is not different from the Spirit of the Father, but the Spirit in whom the Father and Son, eternally distinct, are also eternally united ; the Spirit of the antithesis but also the peace which is in God and in which God is the Creator, Reconciler and Redeemer of His creation, in which He freely elects man and causes him to be free, thus associating Himself with him in a faithfulness which is no less free. The mystery of Jesus, the Son of Man, is that He is primarily the Son of God the Father, and as such Himself God, and then, and as such, also the Son of Man. This being the case, His Spirit—the Spirit who controls this man, and proceeds from Him, and attests Him, and unites other men with Him—is none other than the Spirit of God acting and revealing Himself in the created world among and to us men. And within all earthly and human history the history between Him and us is primarily and properly the representation, reflection and correspondence of the life of God Himself, God's own most proper self-activation and self-revelation, in which there does not take place anything that is alien to God or only improperly or indirectly divine, in which God is not unfaithful to Himself but faithful

to us as He is primarily faithful to Himself and in this way seals the
reality and truth of His faithfulness to us. To develop this theme is
the task which still remains.

We cannot disguise the fact that in all that we have so far said
concerning Jesus Christ, and the reconciliation of the world as it took
place in Him, but also concerning our relationship to Him, the knowledge in which men may live as Christians, as the witnesses of Jesus
Christ in the world, we have been speaking in riddles. We have
spoken of the servitude in which He is the Lord ; of His crucifixion
in which He is the loving One and the Lifegiver ; of His end in which
He is the beginning for all men ; of His concealment in which He is
revealed ; in short, of His lowliness in which He is the high and true
and royal man. We have not invented or constructed this riddle.
Its severity is that of the New Testament witness to Christ. If we are
to do justice to this witness, we cannot disguise or soften it. Nor can
we even subsequently dissolve or remove it. The understanding of
Jesus Christ, even in His royal humanity, depends upon the fact that
we face the severity of this antithesis and always keep it before us.
All Christian errors may finally be traced back to the fact that they
try to efface the antithesis either on the one side or the other. But we
cannot stop at this point. " Paradox " cannot be our final word in
relation to Jesus Christ. Even as it is presented in the New Testament
this paradox is not in any sense in conflict with the *doxa* of God.
Therefore, although we have not to seek its removal, we have certainly
to seek its basis in the *doxa* of God, which means again in the trinitarian
life of God. We have to ask how far in this antithesis we have to do
primarily with God Himself, and, because with God Himself, with a
necessary antithesis, but also with the overcoming of it. We have to
ask how far the Holy Spirit is here the witness not only of the distance
but also of the transition, not only of the confrontation but also of the
mediation, not only of the encounter but also of the communication,
not only of the partnership but also of the history in the partnership.

The question of the Holy Spirit, and concretely of the Spirit of
Jesus Christ, of the basis of the riddle of His existence, of the necessity
of the antithesis which is to be found in it, and its overcoming, is a
question which has to be posed from two different standpoints—from
that of the humiliation of the Exalted, the Son of God, and from that
of the exaltation of the Humiliated, the Son of Man, as these have
taken place in Him as our reconciliation with God, as the humiliation
and exaltation which have been accomplished in our favour. From
these two angles we have to see the fact and the extent that the
Spirit of Jesus Christ, by which the latter is self-attested both as
humiliated and exalted, is the Holy Spirit, who as such has power
and authority over us.

1. We return in some sense to the subject of our first part, although
adding what we have learned in the christological grounding of the

second. The exalted One who is lowly in Jesus Christ is the eternal Son of God. He became lowly and mean and despicable. He became a human creature, flesh, a man of the race of Adam, a bearer of the guilt and need and shame and punishment under which this race lives in all its members. He became one of the members of this race. As such, and in full participation in its situation, He lives this high and true and royal human life which corresponds to His divine Sonship ; in this sovereign uniqueness, in this correspondence to the attitude of God ; as this One who proclaims and brings the kingdom of God. And it was the crowning of His life, announced from the very first, that He let Himself be led to the cross, that He willingly took this way, and that He trod it to the bitter end—He, the Son of God, who was also the incomparable Son of Man. He, the Lord of all lords in heaven and earth, becomes and is the most despised and wretched of all servants. He, the divine and human Light, was wrapped in the deepest concealment. He, the divine and human Judge, was judged. He, the living God and the only truly living man, was executed and destroyed, disappearing into the night of death. This is the one antithesis in the existence of Jesus Christ. And it is only right that we should think of this first when we ask why the existence of Jesus Christ is so inaccessible to us. Is this the fulfilment of the covenant ? Is this the Reconciler and Mediator between God and us men, the Messiah of Israel, the Saviour of the world ? Is this His revelation ? What place is there in this lowliness for the true Son of God, and the true Son of Man ? Was He not there only for a moment, and then no longer there ; shown to us, but now—with all the appearance of finality—withdrawn ; a short and beautiful dream on which we can only look back with deep disillusionment in our long and bitter waking moments ? And what became, and becomes, of us if it is true that that exalted One was humiliated and shamed and put to death in our place, that the Son of God and Man asked finally in our name why God had forsaken Him ? Is it that the incarnation of the Word, and therefore the existence of the Son of God as one of us, only makes clear what apart from Him we cannot do more than suspect—that we are all rejected and lost ? Does it merely seal the impossibility of the human situation ? And if it does mean anything more, if in His lowliness He is still the exalted One, the Lord and Deliverer, if His name still encloses the salvation of the world and our salvation, how can this be true for us when His death on the cross was His final work and Word ? How can we know Him as the true Son of God and Man ? How can we know His being for us in this concealment ? How can we cleave to Him or even believe that He is this, when this was His end, and the door was slammed behind Him and bolted from within ?

The Christian community and the individual Christian believe that He was and is the Son of God and as such for us, and cling to this fact. If we assume that it is given to us to be Christians, we can and must say that we know Him even in this concealment. He is our Lord and Hero, the Shepherd of the whole world and our Deliverer, even in this lowliness. He has acted as the true Son of God even in His suffering of death on the cross. And we are made alive and justified and sanctified and exalted to the status of the children of God and made heirs of eternal life in His execution. For it was in His humiliation that there took place the fulfilment of the covenant, the reconciliation of the world with God. It is in Him that we have our peace, and from Him our confidence and hope for ourselves and all men. Let us assume that we can believe this in our hearts and confess it with our lips. Where the Holy Spirit intervenes and is at work between Him and us as the Spirit of Jesus Christ, as the self-activation and self-revelation of the living Jesus Christ, we can believe and confess it in face of that hard antithesis. Christ the Crucified is a stumbling-block to the Jews and foolishness to the Greeks (1 Cor. 1[23f.]), but to those who are called He is the power of God and the wisdom of God.

But we have to realise that this conversion, faith and confession are not in any sense a marvel, not even as a miraculous act of God. The Holy Spirit is not the great magician who makes this possible for men. That is why we ask concerning the basis of this puzzle, i.e., the necessity of this antithesis of the existence of Christ, the necessity of keeping to it and not trying to evade it, the necessity with which all Christian faith and confession must relate themselves to it. It is also why we ask concerning the conquest of it, and therefore the freedom in which the Christian community and Christians can and may and must recognise, and therefore believe and confess, in that One who was so supremely humiliated the exalted Son of God, in that rejected servant the Lord, in that impenetrable concealment the Light of the world, their deliverance and their peace. We ask, therefore, how far the Spirit of Jesus Christ who leads the community and Christians to this point is in this conversion, in which there is revelation even in concealment, the Holy Spirit, and not a conjurer who merely creates illusions and not reality. How far is He the Spirit of truth in His own most proper work ?

Our answer is that He is the Spirit of truth because in Him it is none other than the living God, i.e., the trinitarian God, who is present and revealed and active. He is the Spirit of the Father and the Son. If He instructs us concerning the necessity of that antithesis in the existence of Jesus Christ, and all that this means for our existence, He also instructs us concerning the overcoming of this antithesis, which means that He leads us to the basis of this matter and sets us on it. He discloses and entrusts to us the will of the Father and the Son, in which the humiliation and death and concealment of the Son of God are resolved, and in accordance with which they are accomplished and actualised : a will which encounters but does not contradict itself in God ; a single will informed by the same purpose and directed to the same goal. Its common purpose is that of the love in which God turned to the world and man, and did not cease to turn even in face of the sin of man and the perdition to which he fell victim as a sinner, but really turned in answer to this situation. And the common goal—so serious and total is the purpose—is the self-giving of God to the world as it takes place in this turning, His interceding for man and in the place of man. It is this that the Father orders the Son to do as the decisive work of divine love. And it is this that the Son is willing to do as the decisive work of divine love. It is for this that the Father sends the Son, and the Son is obedient to this sending. In this obedience He becomes man. Because in this obedience, He becomes that true and exalted and royal man. But again because in this obedience, He becomes man in the place and situation of sinful, fallen man, in that deepest humiliation. It is to this depth that the Father causes Him, and He Himself wills, to condescend in order genuinely to intercede for us men and in His obedience genuinely to conclude our peace with God. And it is to this depth that He does in fact condescend. The Father wills this, and the Son also wills it. In divine freedom He accepts and chooses and goes the way which in the same divine freedom the Father has appointed for Him. But the divine freedom of the Father who orders and the Son who obeys is the freedom of the love in which God willed to take to Himself the world and man, and has in fact taken them to Himself in this total way, by His own interposition. This is the twofold but single will of God as it has taken place in the existence of Jesus Christ in that antithesis of exaltation and abasement. For all that it is so puzzling, it is a representation, reflexion and correspondence of the life of God Himself. It is only a correspondence to the extent that it takes place in the human life of the Son of God, which as such can only attest the life of God. But it is a true and faithful and perfect correspondence to the extent that the human life of the Son of God, and therefore the man Jesus of Nazareth who as such goes this way of obedience, is the direct and perfect witness of the life of God Himself. His witness is that in the first instance there is height and depth, superiority and subordination, command and willingness, authority and obedience, in God Himself—not in identity, but in a real differentiation, because He attests the height and superiority and command and authority of the Father rather than Himself, and the depth and subordination and willingness and obedience which He attests are His own and not the Father's. Yet for all that neither the one nor the other is alien to God : neither the height from which the Father sends the Son, and which cannot be concealed in the human life of the Son as His act of obedience, but necessarily shines out in His existence as the royal man ; nor the depth to which the Father sends the Son, and in which the latter treads the way of His humiliation to the very

end as the lowliest of all men. His witness is that although the two
are different in God they do not confront one another in neutrality,
let alone exclusiveness or hostility, but in the peace of the one free
divine love, so that there is no contradiction, no gaping chasm, between
them. He attests that the height and the depth are both united, not
merely in the love in which God wills to take man to Himself, and
does take Him, but first in the eternal love in which the Father loves
the Son and the Son the Father. He attests that their one eternal
basis is in this eternal love. He attests a divine height and superiority
and ruling authority which are not self-will or pride or severity, which
do not cramp God, but in which He is free to stoop to the lowest
depth in His whole sovereignty. And He attests a depth and subordination and willing obedience in God in which there is nothing of
cringing servility and therefore of suppressed ill-will or potential revolt,
but which are achieved in freedom and therefore in honour rather
than need or shame or disgrace, in which God is not in any sense
smaller but all the greater. He attests that there is in God the free
choice—the choice of His grace—to be lowly as He is exalted and
exalted as He is lowly. This is what the Son of God has to witness,
and does actually witness, of the life of God Himself in His human
life, as He is the royal man, and the royal man who is crowned on
the cross of shame.

And the Holy Spirit as the Spirit of Jesus Christ is simply the
power of this witness of the Son of God in His human life as it is
declared and received in His resurrection from the dead. He is the
Holy Spirit, the Spirit of truth, because He reveals the life of the man
Jesus as the life of the Son with the Father and the Father with the
Son ; because He discloses the antithesis which dominates this life in
its necessity as the antithesis which is first in God because it is first
opened up, but also overcome and closed again, in the will of God.
He is the Spirit of truth, who also awakens the knowledge of the community, Christian knowledge, as true knowledge, and its faith as true
faith and confession as true confession, because He not only sets man
before the riddle of the existence of Jesus Christ as such, but also
before and on its eternal basis in the *doxa* of God, in the freedom in
which God, the Father and Son, is exalted and lowly. In this *doxa* and
freedom, as He makes use of them for our sake, He has turned towards
us in the existence of Jesus Christ as our God, the Fulfiller of the
covenant, the Reconciler of the world with Himself, the source and
Giver of eternal life. This is what we are taught by the Holy Spirit
as the Spirit of the Father and the Son. He convinces us of the love
of God for us which became an event in earthly history in the existence
of Jesus Christ, and which is genuine and effective and immutable
because it is an overflowing of the love which is in God Himself.
Because and as He does this, introducing none other than God Himself as the witness of His work—the God who is differentiated in His

height and depth, but one in Himself, the Father and the Son—He
has a power which is irresistible when He exercises it, creating right
and righteousness against which there can be no legitimate contradiction. For this reason He has the power and authority of the
Paraclete, who comforts and directs us by telling us, as the force of
the self-witness of the existence of Jesus Christ, what really is for us
because and as it first is in God Himself.

2. We will now try to pose and answer the same question from
the opposite angle. The riddle of the existence of Jesus Christ is not
only that of His humiliation but also of His exaltation. It is not
only that of His concealment as the royal man, but of His revelation
as such. It is not only that of His death, but also of His resurrection
and life. The second aspect of His existence is that the eternal Son
of God is self-demonstrated in the exaltation of the man Jesus of
Nazareth ; that He has revealed the secret of His identity with Him.
It was and is the case that in His lowliness and in spite of it, transcending it—we might almost say (yet this is not really true) leaving
it behind Him, casting it off like an old garment—He was and is the
man who is unequivocally exalted. How, then, did He traverse this
earth of ours ? How was He and is He among us ? As a man like
ourselves, with all our frailty and limitation ! In solidarity with us—
indeed bearing our guilt and shame and misery in our place ! Finally
betrayed and rejected and condemned, dying a criminal's death ! Yet
all this pales before the way in which He was man and lived and
acted and suffered as such. For in all this, not least but supremely
in His death and passion, He lived the superior life of a new man
completely different from us. What a Lord among a race of servants
was this one perfect servant in His very being as a servant ! What
a cause He espoused for us all against us all—for us who are so occupied
with wretched causes ! What words He spoke—in human language
and with human limitations—but what words ! And what acts He
performed—human acts and with human limitations—but what acts !
This man came, and in and with Him there came the kingdom. In
and with Him there took place the divine seizure of power on earth.
Nor was this arrested or reversed by His death, when He trod the
way of His humiliation to the bitter end. On the contrary, it was
completed, definitively completed, by His death. What is it that we
beheld ? Flesh of our flesh ? And therefore the judgment of God
fulfilled on all flesh in Him ? And therefore His own and our misery ?
No, we beheld His glory—" the glory as of the only begotten of the
Father, full of grace and truth " (Jn. 1^{14}). What is it that we heard ?
That no man has seen God at any time ? That we are so far from
God, so godless and god-forsaken ? No, for although we did hear this,
we heard also the declaration of God brought us by the One who is
in the bosom of the Father, and " of his fulness have all we received,
and grace for grace " (Jn. 1^{16}). This is paradoxical, not merely because

it is said of the man Jesus, of the eternal Word which became flesh, of the humiliated Son of God as the Son of Man, of the One who entered into the great concealment of His Godhead, but also because this man was so superior and exalted, so genuine and glorious a man. The riddle of the existence of Jesus Christ has also this quite other side. There is in it not only night but also day, not only confusing darkness but also—no less and perhaps even more strangely—blinding light ; the sharp light of contrast, but genuine light. Thus we have not only to ask where and how we are to see and have access to the reconciliation of the world with God as it has taken place in Him, its and our salvation, the kingdom of God drawn near and its peace. With the answer to this question we have also to ask how that which is really present and visible can be seen by human eyes ; how we can stand before this man ; where and how there is a place in our heart and reason for the glory of man as it is present in Him ; whether and how we are endowed and adapted to receive grace of His fulness, or even to realise the presence of the fulness of divine, and therefore of human, glory. Is it really the case that the riddle of the existence of Jesus Christ has only the aspect on which it appears to signify that on account of the lowliness in which God meets us in it we can make too little, or nothing at all, of this God ? Is it not perhaps the case that it has, especially, this other aspect on which it signifies that we are quite impotent in face of it because in this man too much, indeed everything, is made of us, because there has taken place in Him an exaltation, a new beginning of our human being, which is quite beyond us, because there encounters us in Him a life that we cannot even conceive, let alone think or live, either as the life of this man or as the life which we are also given in Him ?

It is again the case that the Christian community and the individual Christian, coming from the resurrection of Jesus Christ, find themselves on the far side of this question, actually saying Yes to this royal man, to the glory of the Son of God revealed in His human majesty, to His human life and therefore to the exaltation of our life as it has taken place in Him. If we assume that we are Christians, and that we come from Easter, we do not close our eyes to this light, or gape and stare at it as at an alien marvel. There is a place in our heart and reason for the reconciliation of the world with God as it has taken place in this true Son of God and Son of Man, for the covenant as it has been fulfilled even on man's side, for the kingdom, the peace, the salvation of God, concluded in the existence of this man. We hear the Word incarnate, this man, and we obey Him. We can and must be His witnesses. We believe in the Lord Jesus Christ, the Crucified, but the One who conquers as the Crucified, and the One who is raised again and manifested as the Conqueror. We confess His human name as the name which is above every name. Whether we fully understand this and give ourselves to it, or draw back half-way, the fact itself is indisputable. The Christian community is the Easter community. Our preaching is Easter preaching, our hymns are Easter hymns, our faith is an Easter faith. We not only have a *theologia crucis*, but a *theologia resurrectionis* and therefore a *theologia gloriae*, i.e., a theology of the glory of the new man actualised and introduced in the crucified Jesus Christ who triumphs as the Crucified; a theology of the promise of our eternal life which has its basis and origin in the death of this man. It would be a false seriousness to try to disguise the fact that the Christian answer to the one riddle of the existence of Jesus Christ has also this other aspect. To affirm it is not to deny or forget or conceal the first side. It is only in the light of the first that it can have this second aspect. It is great and wonderful and necessary enough that in face of the deep humiliation and concealment of the Son of God there should be a violently resisting and attacking Christian Notwithstanding and Nevertheless; that in face of the cross there should be an acceptance and repetition, piercing the threatened despair, of the Yes that is spoken in and under this powerful No; that there should be therefore a Good Friday faith, a *theologia crucis*. At all periods in its history the Christian community has ventured fearfully but boldly to proclaim this Notwithstanding and Nevertheless. And it will never cease fearfully but boldly to proclaim it. The Holy Spirit encourages and instructs and impels it to make this defiant penetration, and will never cease to kindle and therefore to characterise Christian faith and confession on this first side. But is it not more great and wonderful and necessary that the one riddle of the existence of Jesus Christ is disclosed to the same Christian community —at all periods in its history—by a very different aspect? that the same faith in Him is set in its heart, and the same confession on its lips, in a very different form, in the form in which the Nevertheless has become a Hence and the Notwithstanding a Therefore? This is in fact the case. The acceptance and repetition of that Yes are more than a desperate resistance and attack. They are more than the piercing of a threatened despair. They are this, but they are also more. They are a simple acceptance free from all the strain and stress of conflict. It is not merely that the Yes is spoken in and under the powerful No of the cross, and has to be received and repeated in defiance of it. The fact is that in and under the No of the cross a powerful Yes is also spoken: " Christ is risen," and that this powerful Yes may also be received and repeated. This being the case, faith and confession are characterised more by joy and thankfulness than by fearfulness and boldness. The liberation has given rise to liberty. The riddle of the existence of Jesus Christ, which is the point of reference for the Christian answer and Christian faith and confession, is thus the fact that in the humiliation of the Son of God there is actualised and revealed the exaltation of the Son of Man, and our own exaltation in Him as our Brother and Head. Is it not almost more urgent, at any rate in the Western Church, that we should affirm that faith and confession must always necessarily have this form, and therefore that we should proclaim not merely the legitimacy but the indispensability of a *theologia gloriae* in which the *theologia crucis* attains its goal ? There can be no doubt, at any rate, that the Holy Spirit never can or will cease to kindle Christian faith and confession on this side too, summoning the Christian community not only to that penetration but also to the joy and thankfulness which correspond to this other aspect of the Christ-occurrence.

It is, therefore, a matter of the acceptance and repetition of the great Yes spoken in the existence of Jesus Christ (even in the riddle of His existence). It is a matter of the exaltation of the Son of Man as it has taken place in and with the humiliation of the Son of God. It is a matter of the victory of Jesus Christ attained in His crucifixion and revealed in His resurrection. It is a matter of our own triumphing in Him. But this being the case we have every reason to know that the great conversion of which the " Christ is risen " speaks even more strangely as the expression of that simple acceptance has nothing whatever to do with a marvel, and that the Holy Spirit who leads us to this acceptance is not in any sense a great magician. This is why we now ask concerning the basis of this riddle, and therefore the necessity with which Jesus Christ is as the Son of God the Humiliated in our place and for us, and as the Son of Man the Exalted in our place and for us : the necessity with which He has to be seen and understood in this antithesis, and the dynamic and teleology of this antithesis, as the Humiliated for the sake of His own (and our) exaltation and with a view to it, and as the Exalted for the sake of His humiliation and in the light of it ; the necessity with which all Christian faith and confession must consider the dynamic and teleology of this antithesis. This is also why we now ask—with particular urgency in view of the *telos* of this antithesis—concerning the overcoming of it, and therefore the freedom with which the Christian community believes in Jesus Christ triumphant in His crucifixion, in the life of the Son of Man which is not destroyed but maintained in His real death, in the grounding of the life of all men in the dying of this One, in the fulfilment of their election in the fulfilment of His rejection, in their glory in His shame, their peace in His chastisement ; the freedom with which it may therefore confess that Jesus is Victor, believing that we also are victorious in Him. The community and the Christian are not impelled to this second, decisive step of faith and confession by their own imagination or caprice, nor do they take it in their own strength. They do so as they are stimulated and empowered by the Spirit, in His freedom. Therefore we must again ask—and with particular urgency in view of the fact that this second step is the goal of the first—concerning the holiness of the Spirit, i.e., how far, when He moves us to this faith and confession, He is the Spirit of truth, in whom we believe and confess that which really is, and not merely that which we think may be.

Our answer is again that He shows Himself to be the Spirit of truth by leading us to, and placing us on, the eternal basis of this matter in the life of God Himself. The Father who glorifies the Son, the Son who glorifies the Father, and therefore the living God Himself speaks and acts when the community and the Christian can believe and confess that Jesus is the Victor—the Victor in our place. We have to do with Him, and we live in harmony with His life, when we believe and confess this as stimulated and empowered by the Spirit. For what is denoted, represented and reflected in the riddle of the existence of Jesus Christ is the dynamic and teleology of the divine life, the way of the divine will and resolve and work. This is true first in the fact that God gave and humbled Himself in His Son to become flesh and to bear our rejection, to take it from us, as one of ourselves. But it is also true in the fact that this One, elected by God to bear and to do away our rejection, and therefore in His lowliness, shows Himself in the same divine power in which He is obedient to *His* election and therefore righteous, to be the Representative and Revealer of *our* election, the royal man who is alive in His death and exalted in His abasement, and in whom we are destined and called to life, to exaltation, to a royal humanity.

For what is represented and reflected in the humiliation of God is the mercy of the Father in which He too is not merely exalted but lowly with His Son, allowing Himself to be so affected by the misery of the creature, of man, that to save it, to endow it with eternal life, He does not count it too high a cost to give and send His Son, to elect Him to take our place as the Rejected, and therefore to abase Him. It is not at all the case that God has no part in the suffering of Jesus Christ even in His mode of being as the Father. No, there is a *particula veri* in the teaching of the early Patripassians. This is that primarily it is God the Father who suffers in the offering and sending of His Son, in His abasement. The suffering is not His own, but the alien suffering of the creature, of man, which He takes to Himself in Him. But He does suffer it in the humiliation of His Son with a depth with which it never was or will be suffered by any man—apart from the One who is His Son. And He does so in order that, having been borne by Him in the offering and sending of His Son, it should not have to be suffered in this way by man. This fatherly fellow-suffering of God is the mystery, the basis, of the humiliation of His Son ; the truth of that which takes place historically in His crucifixion.

On the other hand, what is represented and reflected in the exaltation of the man Jesus is the majesty of the Son in which He too, as the One in whom there is fulfilled the humiliation of God grounded in the mercy of the Father, is not just lowly but also exalted with the Father ; not just weak but also mighty. It works itself out in the

fact that He became man, and that, fulfilling as the elect man Jesus
the humiliation of God, He is the new and true and royal man, who
is triumphantly alive even, and especially, in His death. How could
it be otherwise ? It is not the case that when He became man, when
He humbled Himself as man, when He humbled Himself to be a
servant, and as a servant to be obedient, even to death, He ceased to
be the eternal Son of God, of one essence with God the Father, and
therefore of equal majesty. It is the case, rather, that in His humiliation He acted and revealed Himself as the true Son of the true Father.
And how could this have taken place in vain ? He became and was
and is man. But because He did so as the Son of God He is from the
very first, from all eternity in the election and decree of God, elect
man, exalted in all the lowliness of His humanity, and revealed in
His resurrection and ascension as man set in eternal fellowship with
God, at the right hand of the Father. How can it be otherwise when
He is the man who in all His humanity exists only as the Son of God,
who as man is identical with the Son of God ? It was not only in
appearance, or partially, that He, the Son of God, became man like
us, but genuinely and totally. In His exaltation He does not cease
to be man like us. Otherwise He would not be our Brother, nor could
He represent us, nor bear and bear away our rejection in accordance
with His election. But as He became and was and is a man as the
Son of God, He became and was and is the one real and true and
living and royal man ; and it is as such that He represents us. The
majesty of the Son of God is the mystery, the basis, of the exaltation
of the Son of Man ; of the fact that the man Jesus of Nazareth is
called and is the Lord. Therefore " Jesus is Victor " is simply a
confession of the majesty of the incarnate Son of God.

It remains only to add that the riddle of the existence of Jesus
Christ is lit up by the glory of God because at the basis and in the
mystery of His existence both these things are true and actual. Not
just one but for all their difference both are true and actual as united
in the one free love which is God Himself : in the mercy in which the
Father has known and anticipated and Himself suffered even the most
impotent sighing and most foolish weeping of the most useless creature
in His eternal decree and its execution on the cross of Golgotha in
the determination of His Son to humiliation for the sake of its exaltation, transcending it by the agony which He Himself feels at it, and
taking it wholly and unreservedly to Himself ; and in the majesty
in which the Son in His humiliation, Himself becoming a groaning
creature, has exalted and magnified the creature in Himself, investing
it with the reflection of His glory, which is also that of the Father.
The deepest divine mercy and the loftiest divine majesty coincide
exactly at the basis of the existence of Jesus Christ. For the merciful
act of the Father aims at the majestic act of the Son. And the majestic
act of the Son takes place in exact fulfilment of the merciful act of

the Father. As God the Father and the Son is one God, the two acts
are, in this sequence, the one incontestable living act of God, the act
of the one free love which is His essence and work both inwards and
outwards.

The existence of Jesus Christ attests this living divine act. It
does this in the very fact that it is so puzzling. But, deriving from the
dynamic and teleology of its basis in God, it does not attest any of
our own foolish paradoxes. It does not attest a No alongside a Yes.
It does not attest a Yes that may revert to a No. It attests a No which
is spoken for the sake of the ensuing Yes, and which is powerful and
necessary and unforgettable in this order. And it attests Yes which
is a valid and definitive Yes—a Yea and Amen (2 Cor. 1^{20})—as it
comes from this No. Its witness does not, therefore, destroy the fact
that it is so puzzling, but transcends it by causing the work and
wisdom of God to be known in it.

This witness is the Holy Spirit as the Spirit of Jesus. He is the
Spirit of the Son who is also the Spirit of the Father—the Spirit of
God. We can now repeat that He is the Spirit of truth because He
lights up the life of the man Jesus as the life of the Son with the
Father and the Father with the Son ; and He lights up the antithesis
which controls this life in its necessity but also in its unity, in the
dynamic and teleology which are first in the living act of God Himself.
He awakens true knowledge and faith and confession because, proceeding from the man Jesus exalted at the right hand of God, poured
out and given, He is not merely the gift of the Father and the Son
and therefore of God, but is Himself God with the Father and the Son,
and therefore the Giver and source of truth, *Creator Spiritus* : the
Creator also of all knowledge of the truth, of all walking and life in
it ; the Paraclete who really guides the community into all truth.
That is why the community, when it hears and obeys His witness,
cannot go astray, or give itself too willingly or wholehcartedly to His
illumination and direction. It receives in Him—we may repeat this
too—that which is ; which is for us because it is primarily in God
Himself.

In this final sub-section of our christological basis we have been
asking concerning the power and lordship of the man Jesus. In other
words, we have been investigating the transition from Him to other
men, the power of our participation in the exaltation in which He was
and is man as the Son of God, to the extent that this has also come
to us in Him. We began at once by asserting that the answer to this
question is already given and has not to be sought. Without this
power and lordship, without His power for us, i.e., on our behalf and
over us, the man Jesus would not be the royal man He is. But we
could not too hastily receive or appropriate this given answer, the
knowledge of the reality of the transition from Him to us, the power
of our participation in Him, and in the exaltation which has come to

us in Him. We saw that it is not self-evident, either from our own standpoint, or especially from that of Jesus Himself, whose exaltation (and with it our own) has indeed taken place, but is also concealed in His crucifixion and therefore in His humiliation. Yet what could we do, if we were to be true to the New Testament, but hear and receive the positive answer, not merely as the Yes which is concealed under a powerful No, but as the powerful Yes which is spoken in and pierces this No, the Yes of the love of God shed abroad in our hearts ? What option had we but to give our assent, not with a sighing Nevertheless, but with a joyful Therefore, to the answer that the power and lordship of the man Jesus are present amongst us, that there is this transition from Him to us, that that power of our participation in His exaltation is at work, that our exaltation in Him has already taken place ? We deny the whole of the third article of the creed, and blaspheme against the Holy Spirit, if we reject this answer. The Holy Spirit, who is the Spirit of God because He is the Spirit of the Father and the Son, who is therefore Himself God, is with His power and lordship the power and lordship of the man Jesus. We have seen how different He is from other dominions and powers. We have seen that He is really the Holy Spirit. We have seen that in His work we really have to do with that transition from Jesus to us, and therefore our participation in the exaltation in which the Son of God became and was and is and will be man—true man. We have seen how far this Spirit deserves our whole confidence, and claims our total obedience, and is our one and only hope.

There remains only the question of the manner of His working and therefore of the development of the power and lordship of Jesus. How does the Holy Spirit act ? How does He encounter us ? How does He touch and move us ? What does it mean to " receive " the Spirit, to " have " the Spirit, to " be " and to " walk " in the Spirit ?

Since we know that in Him we have to do directly with God Himself, there is a temptation either to avoid an answer to the question put in this way (for who can know or try to say how God works ?), or to be satisfied with the veiling, and to that extent evasive, answer which merely indicates the mystery, as, for example, that there is an indefinable whispering and impelling, a movement of the human heart or conscience or mind or of immediate self-awareness which is powerful in its very quietness and quiet in its power, the operation of the Holy Spirit being in the first instance on the inward consciousness, and then expressing and representing itself in definite forms of thought and will, in concrete attitudes and actions. But how does this avoidance, or obscure description, harmonise with the fact that in the Holy Spirit, although we do have to do with God, we do not have to do with Him in His direct being in Hims. if, which might well reduce us to silence or allow us only to stutter and stammer, but with God (directly) in the form of the power and lordship of the man Jesus ? And what does this obscure description, if we prefer it to silence, really have to do with the operation of the Holy Spirit ? Does it not have reference only to a possible reflection of His working, and therefore to a very equivocal phenomenon to the extent that we can know from the history of all religion and mysticism, and even from that of æsthetic experience, that, as far as concerns supposed or real spiritual experiences, there are plenty of authentic records from the sphere of other spirits as well as from that of the Holy Spirit ? If that whispering and impelling, that quiet or powerful happening in the very depths of the soul, really characterise His operation, does He not show Himself to be simply one of many spirits, which as such cannot be known and acknowledged as the Holy Spirit ? And is this not equally true if we believe that complete silence has necessarily to be regarded as the best answer to the question of the How of His working ?

From what we have learned, neither the refusal to give an answer and therefore pious silence, nor the kind of answer which consists in a reference to emotional experiences, is in any sense adequate. The man Jesus as the exalted and true and new man has definite features, and so too have His power and lordship, so too has the transition from Him to us, so too the power of our participation in His exaltation, and therefore so too the operation of the Holy Spirit. His operation is neither anonymous, amorphous, nor, as we have already maintained, irrational. It is an operation from man to man. It is divine because the man from whom it proceeds is the eternal Son of God. But it is also human, and can therefore be defined and more clearly described, because the eternal Son of God who is its origin is a man. Because, for all the divine height and depth which are proper only to the work of the Holy Spirit, and in its whole character as an act of God to us, we have to do with something that takes place in a relationship of man to man, it can be precisely and soberly denoted by a definite concept of what one man can be for, or give to, another man, or many others. One man can be for, and give to, others direction. In general terms, He can be for them the one who commissions or commands or directs, and He can give them a commission, command or directive. We are describing something which lies on the outer edge of human relationships. In our human relationships as such it is something which always stands out as a final and extreme possibility that someone should be for, and give to, other men direction ; that he should be the wise man who shows in what " wise " they should be and think and will and act ; that he should be himself their exemplary wisdom.[1] But in the relationship between the man Jesus and other men, in the exercise of His power and lordship, and therefore in the operation of

[1] The full point of this play on words depends on the derivation of *Weisung* (direction) from the same root as *weise* (wise) and *Weisheit* (wisdom), and is unavoidably lost in English.—Trans.

the Holy Spirit, this is not one possibility among many, nor is it merely the norm, but it is the only reality. As this man is the Son of God, He is for us, and gives to us, direction. He does not merely give us a glorious example, or lofty teaching which has still to be tested in practice, or a radiant ideal which is incapable of realisation. He gives us direction which actually takes place in the way foreseen in the Book of Proverbs, where it is not merely a wise man but wisdom itself that cries at the gates and in the streets, and decides in what wise those who hear it have to be and act. Because and as the Holy Spirit is the power and lordship of the man Jesus, and because and as the man Jesus was and is the Son of God, we can say soberly and precisely of the How of the operation of the Holy Spirit that it is and gives direction in this real and dynamic sense. To receive and have the Holy Spirit has nothing whatever to do with an obscure and romanticised being. It is simply to receive and have direction. To be or to walk in Him is to be under direction, and to stand or walk as determined by it. And however it may be with the related spiritual experiences of enthusiasm or tranquillity, whatever similarity or dissimilarity the operation of the Holy Spirit may have to that of other spirits in the sphere of these experiences, the work of the Holy Spirit is always distinguished by the fact that it is and gives direction : the concrete direction which proceeds from the man Jesus, which is given us by the fact that this man lives ; His direction as that of the eternal Son of God. The Christian community exists as the people which is built up under this direction. Whether a man is a Christian or not is continually decided by whether his existence, whatever may be his attitude to it, is determined by this direction, or whether, however much he may stand out in other ways, it is not determined by it.

Our final discussion, which is necessary if we are fully to understand the transition from Jesus to us, must consist therefore in a development of this concept of the Holy Spirit as the given direction of the Son of God. We will think of it in three ways. It is (1) a direction which is indication, pointing us to a very definite place of departure which we have continually to occupy, to our very real freedom. In this sense we might almost describe it as a geographical direction. Its character is to fix or establish. It is (2) a direction which is a warning or correction, marking off the one possibility given by this place of departure from all the others which are excluded by it and are not therefore real possibilities. It separates our freedom from that which can only be for us a lack of freedom. In this sense it has a critical character. It is (3) a direction which is instruction. It declares and commands the one possibility that we are to realise. It summons us to act as the men we are, in real freedom. Its character is positive. In this threefold scheme we are following the three main lines of New Testament exhortation (παράκλησις) in an attempt to learn from it what is concretely at issue in the operation of the Holy Spirit as the direction of the Son of God.

1. If we first describe the being and work of the Holy Spirit, and therefore the direction of the Son of God, as an indication, we are to understand by this that a definite place is fixed. The Holy Spirit does not operate with open possibilities in relation either to what is behind us, to what is before us, or, therefore, to our present. He makes the power and lordship of the man Jesus, the fact that He lives, and lives for us, so that we also live in Him, the presupposition which obtains here and now for us. He shows us where we always and unreservedly belong because we are already there and have no other location. He does not, therefore, make us an offer or give us a chance. Other spirits with their counsels and requirements offer themselves, commending and promising specific possibilities which we for our part may take or not take from our very different points of departure. They parley with us. The Holy Spirit does not do this. He places us at once at a very definite point of departure, in a very definite freedom. From it and in it all kinds of other things will necessarily result in our own free and spontaneous and active doing or non-doing, but it will always be our doing or non-doing from this point and in this freedom. Above all things we can and should and must be awake to the fact and see that we are in this position, that this freedom is granted to us. We live as Jesus lives. We are not somewhere alone. We are in Him. And in Him we are not what suits ourselves, or what we think necessary or desirable. In Him, in spite of all appearances to the contrary, we are the new and true and exalted man. In Him our conflict with God has been turned into the peace of fellowship. In Him we are no longer below but above ; no longer in the far country but home again ; no longer servants of God but sons ; or no longer lazy and unprofitable, because disobedient, but obedient and profitable servants. The Holy Spirit does not create the ghost of a man standing in decision, but the reality of the man concerning whom decision has already been made in the existence of the man Jesus. The fact that decision has been made is revealed to man as his *terminus a quo* : a new thing, the newest of all, in his own knowledge ; but *in re* the original and proper determination of his existence, in face of which his past apart from this knowledge, and the whole world of his autonomous decision, was one long innovation, a foolish and futile innovation because it could not be executed, because (in spite of himself) he belonged to Jesus, because the Son of God did not accept his estrangement from Himself but confirmed in his calling who and what he was, because He was still for him. This is the basic indicative of the divine direction to the extent that it is an indication ; to the extent that its imperative amounts to a simple : " Be what thou art."

But it is a matter of the operation of the Holy Spirit on men for

whom, even though they may be Christians, and are regarded as such,
it is not at all self-evident that they should come from this point of
departure, or live in this freedom, or have even a theoretical, let alone
a practical, assurance of what they already are in Jesus because they
were it from the very first, from all eternity, or do justice even in
their will, let alone in their achievements, to their being in Him.
Man is always questioning that which the Holy Spirit establishes
beyond all question. He continually loses his footing. He thinks and
speaks and behaves and acts in a way which ignores that which he
already was and is in virtue of the indicative of the Holy Spirit, which
ignores his only possibility, his peace with God, his divine sonship,
his obedience and usefulness as a good servant of God, in short his
true and actual and exalted humanity. He treats this as though it
had never been ; as though he were quite another than the man he
is, and has confessed himself to be. As long as time continues, the
Holy Spirit will always be dealing, even in the Christian community
and among Christians, with men who do not realise their conversion
as it has taken place in Jesus, who contradict it, who in their thoughts
and words and works behave like sleeping and dreaming Christians,
or frozen and fossilised Christians, or wild and wandering and truant
Christians. Are we ourselves any better ? Are we not poor witnesses
of what the Holy Spirit tells us is not only our own true being but
that of the world—which we are to attest to the world ? Is it not the
case that (even if the world could not see and hear us, even if it did
not judge the message of Jesus by what it finds in us, and perhaps
reject it) we, to whom it is revealed and who have known Jesus Christ,
bring shame on this true humanity as it has been manifested and
confirmed in Him, and therefore on the blood which He shed for us
and for the world, and on His life as the Resurrected ? Freedom is
given us, and we are always grasping after empty possibilities, acting
as though we were still prisoners. This is the situation of the Christian
communities of the New Testament as they are always addressed by
the apostles—gently in some cases, more sharply in others. The basic
indicative of the apostolic exhortation is always unmistakeable. So,
too, is the fact that on this assumption (and therefore with supreme
definiteness) it is an appeal, an alarm, a summons, an imperative :
" Be what thou art." And from the apostolic exhortation to the
earliest communities, to the first Christians, we can see what is involved in the work of the Holy Spirit when it is understood as an
indication. It is a work which fixes and confirms, but it is also a
work which for that very reason alarms and incites and unsettles. It
is so intensely startling and disturbing just because it is only a reminder, not holding out an alien law, but putting a man straight,
placing him under his own law. It is the law to which he has been
adjusted, which he cannot escape or refuse because it is the law of
the grace directed to him, and as such the basic law of his existence ;

the law of freedom, peace and joy which demands only that he should have the courage to stand where he does stand, to affirm himself and act as the one he is, to proceed from the place where he already finds himself. Thus the work of the Holy Spirit consists simply in the fact that it brings man back to his own beginning from which he lives and alone can live. It does not burden him with any other " ought " than that of its liberating " may."

To sum up, the work of the Holy Spirit is in both respects a realistic work. There is no place for illusions either in the Holy Spirit or in the one to and in whom He acts. His indicative action is that of the Spirit of truth. He knows and reveals and deals with man just as definitely in the light of what he is in Jesus as of what he tries to make of himself ; just as categorically in relation to his true reality as to his false and empty. He holds him fast there to draw him here. He settles and confirms him there to encounter and stir him to action here. This is His power as direction in its first and basic character as indication. And rightly understood there is here included and anticipated already what He is as the power of correction and instruction.

In relation to this basic aspect we may recall how the subjects of exhortation in the New Testament are addressed and described. They are elect and called and loved. They are saints and brothers. And this understanding of their being is the lever which gives a basis and power to the warnings and encouragements addressed to them. Above all we may remember the wealth of aorists and perfects and presents used in the description of their being and nature as the presupposition of all the later appeals and prohibitions and promises—the characteristic height which gives to this exhortation its momentum. οἱ τοῦ Χριστοῦ (this is self-evidently assumed even of the Galatian Christians) have crucified the flesh with its affections and lusts (Gal. 5²⁴). With it their old man is crucified to the destruction of the σῶμα (the subject) of sin (Rom. 6⁶). They are buried with Him (Rom. 6⁴ ; Col. 2¹²). According to Rom. 6¹¹ they are to regard themselves, in the light of the death of Jesus, as those who are dead, or who have died (Col. 3³), to sin. They have put off the old man (Col. 3⁹). They are ἄζυμοι purged of the old leaven (1 Cor. 5⁷). More positively, God has made them alive with Christ (Col. 2¹³ ; Eph. 2⁵). He has begotten them by the Word of truth (Jas. 1¹⁸). They are born again of incorruptible seed (1 Pet. 1²³), and therefore to a living hope (1 Pet. 1³). They are of God (1 Jn. 4⁴). They are washed and sanctified and justified (1 Cor. 6¹¹), for Jesus Christ is their justification and sanctification (1 Cor. 1³⁰). And God has caused it to shine in their hearts, " to give the light of the knowledge of the glory of God in the face of Jesus Christ " (2 Cor. 4⁶). They have turned to the shepherd and bishop of their souls (1 Pet. 2²⁵). They are espoused to one husband and presented as a chaste virgin to Christ (2 Cor. 11²). They are created in Him unto good works which God has before ordained that they should walk in them (Eph. 2¹⁰). They have put on the new man which is renewed in knowledge according to the image of Him that created it (Col. 3¹⁰). They are, therefore, an " epistle of Christ ministered by us, written not with ink, but with the Spirit of the living God, not in tables of stone, but in fleshy tables of the heart " (2 Cor. 3³). They are the temple of God (1 Cor. 3¹⁶ ; 2 Cor. 6¹⁶) ; the body of Christ ; and individually His members (1 Cor. 12²⁷) ; " a chosen generation, a royal priesthood, an holy nation, a people of possession ; that ye should shew forth the praises of him who hath called you out of darkness into his marvellous light " (1 Pet. 2⁹). God works in them to will and to do (Phil. 2¹³). Their life is already above, hid with Christ in God (Col. 3³). Paul can thus ask them (in 2 Cor. 13⁵) whether they know not their own selves, that Jesus Christ is among them. But he can also say quite simply (Rom. 15¹⁴) that " ye also are full of ἀγαθωσύνη, filled with all knowledge, able to admonish one another," or (Phil. 2¹⁵) that they shine as lights in the world in the midst of a crooked and perverse nation. Particularly outstanding in this respect is the saying in Phil. 2¹, where Paul describes the movement in which he turns to the community—παράκλησις ἐν Χριστῷ, παραμύθιον ἀγάπης, κοινωνία πνεύματος, σπλάγχνα καὶ οἰκτιρμοί—as something which is known to the community itself, so that he has only to appeal to it in his address (knowing all this, " fulfil ye my joy . . ."). All the warning and admonition addressed to Christians—and it may be both urgent and sharp—is based on this sure foundation, which is not compromised by its sharpness but gives it its sharpness. To be firm, to remain firm, and to become firm again on this sure foundation is the basic problem of apostolic ethics, which is only the dynamic of the indication given by the Holy Spirit. But this foundation is the place of departure which is given to Christians as such, from which they live, and from which they have continually to enter and tread a definite path.

It is not self-evident that this should be the case. The life and ways of Christians might well start unintentionally at some other point than at the being and having which they know so well and which is so definitely ascribed to them. But all the New Testament epistles more or less assume that both in the communities and their individual members it actually is the case. Note the incisive contrast in the closing words of 1 John (5²⁰f·) : " And we know that the Son of God is come, and hath given us an understanding, that we may know him that is true (τὸν ἀληθινόν), and we are in him that is true, even in his Son Jesus Christ. This is the true God, and eternal life. Little children, keep yourselves from idols." Hence the summons : στήκετε ἐν κυρίῳ (Phil. 4¹) ; abide in Him (1 Jn. 2²⁸) ; hold fast the λόγος ζωῆς (Phil. 2¹⁶). Hence, too, the frequent evangelical summons to watch. Is this necessary ? The Holy Spirit, who speaks so indicatively in all these passages, seems actually to regard it as necessary and good and salutary. What a demand for a new beginning quasi ab ovo in the hymn cited in Eph. 5¹⁴ : " Awake thou that sleepest, and arise from the dead, and Christ shall give thee light." And this is said to Christians. How alien and drastic, in relation to this assumption, is the passage 1 Thess. 5⁴f· : " But ye, brethren, are not in darkness, that that day should overtake you as a thief. Ye are all the children of light, and the children of the day : we are not of the night, nor of darkness. Therefore let us not sleep, as do-others ; but let us watch and be sober. For they that sleep sleep in the night ; and they that be drunken are drunken in the night. But let us, who are of the day, be sober." This, too, has still to be said to Christians. And what an apparent contradiction it is that those who are already ἄζυμοι are summoned in 1 Cor. 5⁷ to purge out the old leaven ; or that those who have already put off the old man and put on the new are called in Eph. 4²²f· to do this (and obviously not to do it again) ; or that those who are crucified and dead with Christ are exhorted in Col. 3⁵ to mortify their members which are upon the earth ; or that those who are and walk in the Spirit are enjoined in Gal. 6⁸ to sow to the Spirit and not to the flesh. But this is all in order. The contradiction is only logical, not theological. And it shows us what is really at issue in the great, basic direction of the Holy Spirit. It is a matter not only of the establishment of that sure foundation but of establishing those to whom it is proposed. It is a matter of their direction continually to set themselves on it ; continually to begin there with the beginning which they themselves have not made but which has been made of them, and from which they can proceed only in one direction. " Be strong in the Lord, and in the power of his might " (Eph. 6¹⁰), is a saying which perhaps expresses the heart and totality of what has to be said from this first standpoint of the direction of the Son of God and therefore of the operation of the Holy Spirit—the ontology and also the dynamic of what we have here called His indication.

2. We next come to the critical element in the concept. When we speak of the direction of the Holy Spirit it involves warning and correction. It has to do with the possibilities selected and grasped by man, and therefore with the use or non-use of the freedom which he is granted at that point of departure. It is to be noted that there is no question of misuse—only of use or non-use. This freedom cannot be misused. If it is used at all it is used rightly. It can only be used rightly. But it can be used or not used. The possibility which corresponds to it can be chosen and grasped, but so too, in a lack of freedom, can other possibilities. This distinction is the point at issue in the work of the Holy Spirit as correction. The possibility selected and grasped in the freedom of this point of departure is marked off from the possibilities which are selected and grasped in a lack of freedom. But the possibility which is selected and grasped in that freedom and from that point of departure is always only the one possibility—a very definite thinking and speaking and willing and acting and behaviour. Conversely, the possibilities selected and grasped in a lack of freedom are always characterised by the fact that they are many, the one being preferred to the other by accident or caprice, rationally or irrationally. They derive, as does also their selection, from the sphere to which the Son of God humbled Himself and thus became the exalted, true and royal man. They derive from the sphere of the flesh, of sin and sloth, which the man Jesus abolished and destroyed in His death for all men and in their name. They derive from the kingdom of the dead which He closed, from the nothingness which He reduced to nothingness in His life. To select and grasp them is to select and grasp that which is destroyed and done away. It is to select and grasp, in defiance of that closure and reduction, an element in the kingdom of death, a form of nothingness. It is to select and grasp the flesh. It is to select and grasp—as though we could still have another beginning—that which in the light of our beginning in the power and lordship of the man Jesus is quite impossible. We are already free in Jesus, but we think and speak and will and act and behave as if we were not free, as if we were still below, as if we could still seek and affirm and love and express ourselves below, as if we ourselves were not already exalted and renewed and sanctified in the man Jesus. We put ourselves back in the shadow from which we are already taken, and in the face of whose kingdom we are already set in the sun. We place ourselves under the judgment and rejection which Jesus has borne for us too, and from which we too are liberated in Him. The work of the Holy Spirit consists in the fact that both possibilities are revealed and known and distinguished. On the right

hand there is that which proceeds from the Spirit ; that which is
thought and said and willed and acted in consequence of His indication, of His appointment to a particular place ; the one possibility
which is selected and grasped in the freedom of the children of God ;
the good work, and the pursuit of good works, for which the man in
Jesus Christ is created, and in the doing of which he is engaged on
the way to eternal life. And on the left hand there is that which stems
from the contradiction of the being of man in Jesus Christ ; that
which is done in a relapse and apostasy into unfreedom, into the
nothingness which is already abolished and done away ; that which
involves a return to the closed kingdom of the dead ; that which is a
continuance in the flesh (and is possible only below where we are no
longer) ; which we can select and grasp only in a complete failure to
see and appraise the true situation ; one of the many impossibilities
of a mere appearance of life the fruit and reward of which can only
be death. The Holy Spirit knows and distinguishes and separates in
the man to and in whom He works the new man which he is created
and elected and determined and called to be, which he may be, and
is in truth, with all the thoughts and words and works of this man,
his way and course, from the old man who is already superseded in the
existence of the man Jesus, who continually stirs and moves in us as
if he still had a right and place there, with all the reason and unreason,
the cleverness and folly, of his enterprises and adventures, with the
whole range of his activity and indolence. And the Holy Spirit affirms
the one man and negates the other. He fights for the new man against
the old. He champions freedom against unfreedom, obedience against
disobedience, our life against our death, the one possible thing against
the many impossible. And His work may be known by the merciless
and uncompromising way in which, impervious to bribes or threats,
He wages this war and plunges man himself into the battle. Other
spirits may also affirm and negate, but they can always connive and
acquiesce. This is never true of the Holy Spirit. Other spirits may
also be contentious, but they can also offer and come to terms. The
Holy Spirit never does this. Other spirits always place man at one
of the points of departure from which he has many possibilities for
discussion. They have no decisive or exclusive or judicial power or
efficacy. They do not really guide or correct man : not in such a
way as to penetrate to the heart and marrow ; not in such a way as
to cause him weal or woe ; not in such a way that he finds himself
placed under a strict command and a correspondingly strict prohibition. But the Holy Spirit does cause both weal and woe, for He is
both wholly for man and wholly against him, and He summons him
for his part to be wholly for himself (and his own best interests) by
being wholly against himself, against his whole selecting and grasping
of unreal possibilities, against his whole returning to a vanished past,
against the whole outmoded and anachronistic being that continually

tries to stir and assert and express and extend itself in him, and above all against his cunning desire to try to arrange a compact of unity, to make a deal, between the old nature which is past in Jesus and the future nature which is given him in Jesus, i.e., to take up an attitude in which he holds the balance, partly accepting and partly rejecting the decision which has been made concerning him. As the agent of the peace and joy in which man may live, the Holy Spirit inflexibly destroys this balance in which there can never be either peace or joy. The Holy Spirit says afresh with each new day and hour that he should now seriously and at all costs select and grasp the one thing which corresponds to the freedom which he is granted : that he really may do so, because it is a matter of selecting and grasping in the freedom which he is granted ; but also that he ought to do so, because in this freedom he cannot choose between many things, but can select only the one. But He also tells him afresh with each new day and hour that he should at once unconditionally and at all costs turn aside from that which contradicts this decision. He is thus the fire and sword which Jesus came to bring on the earth.

All this may sound hard and intransigeant and intolerant. But it does so only so long as we obstinately refuse to notice that in the direction of the Holy Spirit it can only be a matter of accepting as our reconciliation and exaltation the reconciliation of the world with God and the exaltation of man as they have taken place in Jesus Christ for us. Is it not inevitable that as such this direction should take the form of this radical, unconditional and basic guidance and correction ? It is a matter of recognising and acknowledging the transition from Jesus to us, and human life in face and in consequence of this transition. This recognition and acknowledgment cannot possibly be a painless operation—" cheap grace." What it cost God the Father and the Son, and the man Jesus, to cause to rise and shine the light of the world which illuminates the people that walked in darkness, is really far more than it costs us to submit to be guided and corrected by the Holy Spirit, to accept that separation between the old man and the new, that decree which plunges us into conflict. It is really far more than the slight terror and sacrifice which we cannot be spared in this correction. The point at issue is not that we have still to achieve, or even repeat, our reconciliation with God and therefore our exaltation as true men. The truth is—and this is the love of God the Father and the grace of our Lord Jesus Christ—that these have taken place and are proffered to us in Him, and in Him once for all, so that there is no further need of Golgotha. In Him we have both our justification and sanctification, both our regeneration and conversion. All this has been done and is in force. It does not need to be repeated or augmented. It is true and actual. What is at issue in the fellowship and operation and direction of the Holy Spirit is that we should accept this, so that it is just as true and actual in our lives as it is in itself. But this is really at issue. Hence the Holy Spirit will not allow us to escape it on any pretext. He will not tolerate either sorrowful neglect or ebullient extravagance in our attitude to it. There can be no going back on its truth and actuality, as though it were not really, or only partially, true and actual. With each new day and hour He prevents us afresh from going back on it. And as and because we know that with each new day and hour we need to be prevented in this way we have to be ready for the tiny cost that His direction, as a categorical indication, has also the character of correction, and therefore this supremely critical character. We have only to bear this cost, to pay this price which is so infinitely modest in relation to that which was paid by God and the man Jesus, and we find at once that as He guides and corrects us the Holy Spirit also grants us peace and joy ; that we have every reason to say Yea and Amen to His direction even in this character ; that we can only pray God that He will not withhold but continually grant us His direction in this form. What would become of us, of the community of Jesus in the world, even of the best Christians (not to speak of us poor ones), if the Holy Spirit were ever to cease to make cause against us, and therefore for us, in this supremely critical and radically corrective way ? Yet we need not fear. God would cease to be God if the Holy Spirit ceased to be our Judge—our gracious Judge—and to deal with us as such.

" The word of God (opened up to us by the Holy Ghost) is quick, and powerful, and sharper than any two-edged sword, piercing even to the dividing asunder of soul and spirit, and of the joints and marrow, and it is a discerner of the thoughts and intents of the heart " (Heb. 4¹²). We see here all the antitheses in which the exhortations of the New Testament find their critical culmination. If we reject in practice that God has called us ἐν ἁγιασμῷ, in the act of our sanctification, and therefore not to ἀκαθαρσία, we do not reject merely a man who chides us, the apostle, but God Himself, who has accomplished this act by giving the Holy Spirit to the heart of the Christian, even of the Christian who lives in this uncleanness (1 Thess. 4⁸). And this is the one thing that must not happen on any account. " Walk in the Spirit, and ye shall not fulfil the lust of the flesh " (Gal. 5¹⁶). For there is a conflict against the flesh. There can be no question to which side the Christian belongs in this conflict, for if he who is called to freedom (v. 13) follows the lust of the flesh he necessarily does that which he does not will (v. 17), whereas when he follows the Spirit he demonstrates that he is not under the Law (v. 18). " Wherefore, my dearly beloved, flee from idolatry " (1 Cor. 10¹⁴). " Ye cannot drink the cup of the Lord, and the cup of devils : ye cannot be partakers of the Lord's table, and of the table of devils. Do we provoke the Lord to jealousy ? are we stronger than he ? " (1 Cor. 10²¹f.). It is made impossible for man to live to himself by the fact that Jesus has died and risen again for him (2 Cor. 5¹⁵). The grace of God cannot be received in vain (2 Cor. 6¹). Therefore there can be no unequal yoke with unbelievers. Between δικαιοσύνη and ἀνομία, light and darkness, Christ and Belial, believers and unbelievers, the acts of believers and those of unbelievers, the temple of God and idols, there is no μετοχή, no κοινωνία, no συμφώνησις, no συγκατάθεσις (2 Cor. 6¹⁴f.). The friend of the world can only be the enemy of God (Jas. 4⁴).

The *locus classicus* for this differentiation, demarcation, and separation of that which is radically impossible for the Christian (in view of His Lord) from the one thing which is alone possible is the sixth chapter of Romans with its answer to the vexed question : " Shall we continue in sin, that grace may abound ? " (v. 1). " Shall we sin, because we are not under the law, but under grace ? " (v. 15). The twofold and emphatic μὴ γένοιτο reflects the horror with which Paul starts aside from such questions. Those who are dead to sin cannot live any longer therein (v. 2). Christians baptised with a reference to the death of Christ are dead in Him and buried with Him. More positively, they are set in a movement which is opposed to sin, in the περιπατεῖν ἐν καινότητι ζωῆς (vv. 3–5). They recognise that the σῶμα (the subject) of sin, the old man, is done away (καταργηθῇ) in the death of Christ, so that they can no longer serve sin (v. 6). They can believe only in their life with this One who died once for all, but is also risen and lives to God. They can therefore regard themselves only as those who are dead to sin but live to God in Jesus Christ (vv. 7–11). And then there follows a kind of decree of deposition and expulsion directed at sin in person : It is not to reign in your mortal σῶμα. It no longer exists as the σῶμα τῆς ἁμαρτίας whose lusts have to be obeyed (v. 12). A categorical assurance is given in v. 14 that it shall not have dominion over you—just because we are not under the Law, but under grace. For God be thanked, Christians were the servants of sin, but they are now obedient ἐκ καρδίας. Being made free (ἐλευθερω-θέντες) from sin, they have become the servants of δικαοσύνη, the servants of God (vv. 17–18, 22). The warning and prohibition addressed to them as such is self-evidently that they should not yield their members as instruments in the service of unrighteousness, of sin (v. 13) ; that this service should only be the past for those who stand in the service of God ; that an alternation between the one and the other is completely excluded (vv. 16, 19) ; and that there is no further possibility of a being and situation which can only have death as their reward and end (vv. 21, 23). This is the frightful end which Jesus made His own in their place in His death. This is the evil reward which He accepted in their place in His death. They cannot, therefore, live any longer a life which has this end and carries with it this reward, and they should not desire to do so.

The formulations of the First Epistle of John sound like a very short and concise summary of this chapter of Paul. He who is born of God, who abides in the One who was manifested to take away sin, does not commit sin (3[5f. 9], 5[18]). Νενικήκατε τὸν πονηρόν (2[14]). And this leads with the same necessity as in Rom. 6 to the exhortation : " Love not the world, neither the things that are in the world. If any man love the world, the love of the Father is not in him. For all that is in the world, the lust of the flesh, and the lust of the eyes, and the pride of life (ἀλαζονεία τοῦ βίου), is not of the Father, but is of the world. And the world passeth away, and the lust thereof : but he that doeth the will of God abideth for ever " (2[15f.]). It is from this that there follows the great " saying " and " testifying in the Lord " of Eph. 4[17f.] : " That ye henceforth walk not as other Gentiles walk, in the vanity of their mind, having the understanding darkened, being alienated from the life of God through the ignorance that is in them, because of the blindness of their heart : who being past feeling have given themselves over unto lasciviousness, to work all uncleanness with greediness." ὑμεῖς δὲ οὐχ οὕτως ἐμάθετε τὸν Χριστόν—how could they have " learned " Him thus ?— but in conflict with their former conversation they are to put off " the old man, which is corrupt according to the deceitful lusts " ; to put him off as one can only discard an old coat that is obviously in rags, and to do so in a movement in which there can be no hesitation, no looking back, no halting half-way, but which can only be accomplished at once and totally because it is a matter of life and death, because everything is at stake, and would be lost if it were not accomplished at once and totally. This is what is demanded by the injunction of the apostle. If we compare the older and later parts of the New Testament we may say that the exhortation grows continually in intensity, and its accusations and threats in sharpness. And if we do well to understand it as a reflection of the operation of the Holy Spirit, this is only to say that this is the aspect of His operation to the extent that it is correction, that it is His critical and judging and purifying work. It is with this either-or that He contends for man and therefore against him. Christians are among others those who come to see this. Just because they know and proclaim the reconciliation of the world with God, they cannot come to terms with the world. Just because they hope for the resurrection of the flesh as it has been revealed already in the resurrection of the man Jesus, they cannot concede to its desires any authority or right. Just because they live by the forgiveness of sin, they cannot adopt it into their programme. And just because they are the house of God, it is expressly with them that judgment begins on the fleshly, sinful, worldly man (1 Pet. 4[17]).

3. We describe the positive element in the operation of the Holy Spirit when we characterise it finally as definite instruction. If we are to express what is intended we must give to this word—or to any others which we might use, such as teaching or orientation—the strongest possible sense. The Holy Spirit is the Spirit of the Lord, and Himself the Lord. Therefore His instruction does not consist merely in the fact that He advances considerations, or provides the material for them. It is certainly part of His instruction to cause or summon us to test ourselves and our situation, to consider most carefully our possibilities and choices. This is the task of theological ethics, which shows itself to be such by the fact that it leads us, in face of the many possibilities with which we are confronted, to ask what God wills of us, what is the command of God here and now by which we are to direct our life and conduct. But the Holy Spirit is rather more than a professor of theological ethics. He is the One—and this is His instruction—who actually reveals and makes known and imparts and writes on our heart and conscience the will of God as it applies to us concretely here and now, the command of God in the individual and specific form in which we have to respect it in our own situation. The Holy Spirit does, therefore, that concerning which we ourselves, even in the very best theological ethics, can only ask. His instruction, which we might also call teaching or orientation, is a concrete assignment which has an authority and stringency that we do not find in any other instruction. What we are given in it is not merely general principles and lines of action which leave plenty of room for selection in detailed interpretation—as if it were not the details that really matter! On the contrary, He shows us the only good possibility which there is for us here and now in the freedom of our point of departure and which we not only may but must select and grasp in all circumstances. In face of the instruction of the Holy Spirit there can be only the most concrete obedience, or, in cases which are not foreseen or taken systematically into account, the no less concrete disobedience. As concerns its precision, too, it cannot be compared with any other instruction. It cannot, therefore, be caught up by man into any general law, or subjected to any regulation, or

pin-pointed in a written code. Surely this is quite impossible when the Holy Spirit is Himself our law and rule (the most particularised rule which has to be fulfilled to the letter), and when His instruction is the commanding of the living God which has to be heard directly and continuously by the community and the individual Christian. His instruction bursts all the fetters with which man in his concern for safeguards, i.e., for security against its attack, attempts to control it and make it his own instrument. It comes with a sovereignty quite alien to any other instruction. Thus it is only natural that in face of it man should hesitate ; that he should be disposed to limit its authority or precision or sovereignty, or preferably all three. The threat of fanaticism is perhaps seen. It is regarded as incumbent to surround the divine demanding of the Spirit with institutional guarantees which will protect both its objectivity, validity and continuity on the one hand and human responsibility on the other. But we shall abandon all such concerns and renounce all such devices when we realise that we have to do with the power and lordship of the living man Jesus who is the true Son of God—a power and lordship which are concretely . sketched, which are genuinely universal and continuous, and which genuinely summon men to responsibility. He, the eternal Logos in the flesh, is the One who unconditionally demands, who does so always and everywhere precisely and concretely, who can never be controlled but always Himself controls. And He has the right to instruct us as such and therefore with that authority and stringency. As He does this in a wholly distinctive way at every time and in every place and situation of the community and individual Christians, He makes Himself known always and everywhere as one and the same. He Himself sees to it, therefore, that there is a continuity in His instruction, that it does not disrupt fellowship but grounds and maintains it. And He does so by giving it always in the context of His own person which cannot be confused with any other, and especially with ours. He always confronts us as this Other. His instruction may always be distinguished from the self-instruction in which we all try in different ways, independently, apart from and to the disruption of our relationship with others, to be our own lords and rulers. The Holy Spirit who instructs the community and the individual Christian is concretely the Spirit of Jesus. Therefore He never speaks from men, but always to them. And in spite of the fact that He speaks so specifically and concretely, He speaks to them in common, thus creating brotherhood. Hence His operation is never identical with theirs, nor can it ever be that of their caprice. On the contrary, it is always a new and strange and superior work confronting their caprice. It is always the power and lordship of this One, the royal man, who as He exercises them will not surrender them to any other. It is the work of the Head of which we are members, but cannot be more than members. In face of it what place is there for any concern except that we might perhaps have ascribed to it too little authority or precision or sovereignty, that we always give it too little weight and honour, that we have limited it too much, that we have hardly begun genuinely to respect it, to observe and regard it in our own thought and speech and action.

That we have to do with His instruction may always be known finally from the fact that it is given in exact correspondence to that critical correction, that as we receive it we not only proceed from this but must always be ready to submit to it afresh. As instruction the direction of the Holy Spirit says Yes and Forward at the very point where in its capacity as correction it says No and commands us to halt and retreat. From the point where it is indication it both slays and makes alive. It unmasks and rejects man's lack of freedom, but it also discloses and magnifies his freedom. It closes and bolts the door on the left hand, to pass through which is necessarily to fall into the abyss. And it opens the door on the right hand, to pass through which is to enter into a freedom of thought and speech and action and attitude in which we are little brothers of the Lord, the royal man Jesus, and therefore brothers of all those who know and confess Him as their big Brother, and prospectively and presumptively even of those who do not yet know and confess Him as such. The instruction of the Holy Spirit awakens and calls us, with that authority, precision and sovereignty, to use and exercise our freedom in Jesus, to the good work which we specifically are to do here and now in unqualified obedience to Him, which I must do because " I am not my own, but belong to my faithful Saviour Jesus Christ." This is the gloriously positive element in His instruction, which is distinguished from all fanatical self-instruction by the fact that it shows itself to be the instruction of the living Jesus Himself, obviously awakening and summoning us to participation in His exaltation.

If we again turn to the apostolic admonition, we have first to realise that, as we have it in New Testament writings, it is only in some sense imperfectly that it can reflect the positive instruction of the Holy Spirit. The Son of God does not Himself speak here directly in His instruction, but His primary and yet human witnesses. The authority of the Holy Spirit to which they appeal, and with which they undoubtedly speak and write, has thus to be attributed to their words as a penetrative force, but cannot be visibly demonstrated in them as such. It is only infrequently (except in the First Epistle to the Corinthians) that they speak relatively concretely and authoritatively of specific phenomena and problems of the life of the community. When they do so, it is mostly in the form of prohibitions, and not of the positive commands which are our present concern. Even their commands—the exhortations to love and humility and peace and chastity and patience—have in the main the form of general direction rather than the particular or highly particularised indication in which we may recognise directly the distinctive operation and commandment of the Holy Spirit. What is meant by the precision of the divine instruction may be gathered from certain passages in Acts (e.g., 8^{29}, 10^{19}, 16^7), but in the admonitions of the Epistles we have to think in what is not visible in the words themselves, viz., the fact and extent that in the most specific way they applied to, and affected, specific communities and specific individuals within them. Even the sovereignty of the divine instruction, its inviolability against all attempts to comprise it in laws and rules, may be seen in the texts only in the fact that the directions given are not issued in legal form, but in their multiplicity often inter-cross in points of detail, and have in fact successfully resisted all codification right up to our own time.

With these qualifications, and on the condition that we also hear that which the texts do not say, we can see with perfect clarity in the main lines of apostolic admonition what is at issue in the instruction of the Holy Spirit.

What the Holy Spirit positively wills and effects—that to which He awakens and calls—is always a human existence that deserves to be called a life to the extent that it is lived in the light of the royal man Jesus, in an attentiveness and movement to Him, because the Christian who receives and has the Holy Spirit recognises and acknowledges that this man died for him and has risen again for him, that He lives for him, that He is the Owner and Bearer, the Representative and Lord of his life, and that in His exaltation he too is exalted and set in a living fellowship with God, that in Him he is a new creature (2 Cor. 5[17]). The Spirit wills and effects that in accordance with his being in this One he should cleave to Him, that he should be His disciple, scholar, fellow, companion, follower and servant. He leads him to this One, and keeps him there, and calls and causes him to be with Him, to go after Him, to go forward with Him. Christians are those who are led by the Spirit to this One, and are kept there, and go forward with Him. This is the certain and decisive thing which has to be said positively of the relationship of the Spirit to them. " Come unto me " (Mt. 11[28]) ; " Come . . . and follow me " (Mk. 10[21]) ; " Abide in me " (Jn. 15[4]) : this is the dominating appeal even in the Gospels. The life demanded and created by the Holy Spirit is one which is " worthy " of Jesus as the κύριος (Col. 1[10]), of the Gospel concerning Him (Phil. 1[27]), of our calling by Him and to Him (1 Thess. 2[12]). That is to say, it is one which stands in an appropriate and responsible relation to the archetypal and exemplary life of this man. The aim of the apostolic admonition, and the instruction of the Holy Spirit which it attests, is the " bringing into captivity every thought (νόημα) " with a view to the ὑπακοὴ τοῦ Χριστοῦ (2 Cor. 10[5]). Its aim is a συζῆν αὐτῷ (Rom. 6[8]), an ἅμα σὺν αὐτῷ ζῆν, which endures whether we wake or sleep (1 Thess. 5[10]). But what can and must be meant by this " living with Him," seeing that between Him and Christians there is the great difference that He is the Head and they are only members in Him, that He is exalted at the right hand of God and they are not yet exalted and never will be as He is, that they are still on earth, that even their life with Him is not yet visible and palpable, that it transcends their existence, although it is their real life, hid with Him in God (Col. 3[3]) ? To live with Him obviously means to seek our life above, where it is real, in Him. This is the meaning of the imperative (Col. 3[1f.]) : " Seek those things which are above, where Christ sitteth. . . . Set your affection on things above, not on things on the earth." To seek that which is above means that we are to seek here and now, but not in this here and now, not on the earth, because, there and then exalted for him, the true life of the Christian is with Christ, his true and exalted life, his own proper life, which begins with the death of Christ as his own death, the death of the old man. Christ is above, and so too is the Christian in so far as he is in Christ. When he seeks τὰ ἄνω, when he sets his affection on τὰ ἄνω, he lives here and now the life which is worthy of the Lord, the Gospel and his calling. He achieves his ἀγαθὴ ἐν Χριστῷ ἀναστροφή (1 Pet. 3[16]). It is really a going, a walking, in hope. Corresponding to the definition of baptism (1 Pet. 3[21]), it is one long request to God for a good conscience by the resurrection of Jesus Christ. This movement of seeking, of setting our affection, of walking and praying, which is directed towards the last and universal revelation of Jesus Christ and all human life, is initiated by the resurrection of Jesus Christ ; by His first and transitory and particular revelation, which is so decisive for the existence of the community, as the One who was exalted in His humiliation, who is alive from the dead. In the interval between these two revelations of Jesus Christ, here and now, " on earth," the Christian life cannot be represented except in terms of this fearless movement, in which there is neither anxiety nor looking back. In this respect we can never give too much attention to the self-description of Paul in Phil. 3[12f.] Apprehended by Jesus Christ, he can never think that he has already apprehended Him, and in Him his own life ; that he has already attained the goal. " Forgetting those things which are behind, and reaching forth unto those things which are before," he presses " toward the mark, for the prize of the high (or upward) calling " which is given him by God in Jesus Christ. This is the only possible aspect of life with Him here and now. And it is this aspect that it ought to have. Phil. 3[12f.] is obviously a variation of the image already used in 1 Cor. 9[24f.], that of the athlete in the arena. The only difference is that in Corinthians the emphasis is on the effort and training that are demanded of those who win. As Paul says of himself, he does not run uncertainly, or fight as one that beats the air. The two passages ought to be compared and viewed as a whole. Together they bring out the fact that the Christian situation is so obviously a provisional one, in which we can only run but must run, and yet also—and this is what makes it a Christian situation—that there is a plain necessity to run to the very utmost of our resources. And this is the whole point of the instruction of the Holy Spirit. He does not put the Christian at a point or in a position. He sets him on the way, on the march. And it is a forced march, in a movement which never ceases and in which there can be no halting. He does not put anything in his hands. He does not make him either a great or little *beatus possidens*. He makes him a seeker : not, of course, an indecisive and planless seeker ; one who knows what he is seeking ; yet a real seeker whose hands are empty, who has not yet apprehended, but wants to apprehend because he is already apprehended. And He does not allow him to be merely an occasional and distracted seeker who divides his powers between this running and either resting or some other running ; between this seeking and a possessing ; or between the seeking of this one thing, his life in Christ, and that of other possibilities. The positive instruction of the Holy Spirit consist always in a gathering and mobilising and concentrating of the whole man who is instructed. His existence is worthy of the Lord, a free act, a good work, when it is a decided and resolute existence. This is brought out especially in the words at the beginning of the exhortatory section of Romans (12[1f.]), where Paul, reminding and engaging his readers by the mercy of God addressed to them, summons them to present (παραστῆσαι) their bodies, their whole existence (quite irrespective of its value before God and for others or themselves), and to offer it up as a living sacrifice, holy and acceptable to God. This is the λογικὴ λατρεία which they are both permitted and commanded ; the only true and reasonable and appropriate worship of God in contrast to the religious *Quid pro quo* of Jewish and heathen observance. And it is to be rendered with the decision and resoluteness of those who have no option because they are disposed to make this sacrifice, because they can dispose themselves only in accordance with this prior disposition, because they are freed from the schematism of the world in which there is no place for this παραστῆσαι, because they are caught up in the renewing of their mind and can will only this one thing. And this one thing simply consists in a δοκιμάζειν, in a constant and in every sense testing and critical examination of the possibilities that offer and their own choosing and willing by the question of the one thing which is willed by God as that which is good and acceptable and perfect, which they have to choose and will and do here and now as that which is commanded. All this, their own true life, is again obviously outside them, and before them, and above them. It is again presupposed that what will be brought in and by them will only be their own persons ; that they are directed to an appointed goal. But it is again clearly and unconditionally demanded that they should be all this, and that they should be it with undivided attention and readiness, without reserve, like a sacrifice which, whether it be small or great, costly or less costly, can only be given unreservedly, can only be presented, can only pass from their own determination to that of the One who demands and receives it, can only cease to belong to those who offer it. The sanctification of man, and the *vita christiana* as its result, is that the claim for this claimless self-sacrifice finds a place and authority and power in a human existence. We share in the exaltation of the royal man Jesus as we may and must yield to this claim. In this the name of our Lord Jesus Christ is glorified in Christians, and they themselves are glorified in Him (2 Thess. 1¹²). In this there is attained the end which corresponds to the προθυμία τοῦ θέλειν, the readiness of their own will, their real ἔχειν, their freedom (2 Cor. 8¹¹). In this there is also to be found their obedience (2 Cor. 10⁶). In this they work out their σωτηρία, doing that which corresponds to it, actualising it—as those who are left no choice by the God who works in them to will and to do (Phil. 2¹²). In this they prove themselves to be stablished and anointed εἰς Χριστόν (2 Cor. 1²¹).

It is to be noted that in the apostolic admonition the frontier is never removed or crossed between God, Jesus Christ and the Holy Spirit on the one side and man, even the Christian, on the other. That the Christian is wholly and utterly (ὁλόκληρος) sanctified by the God of peace (1 Thess. 5²³), that he may live to God in Jesus Christ (Rom. 6¹¹), has nothing whatever to do with deification, but everything with humble subjection to God. If Paul says of himself in Gal. 2²⁰ that he no longer lives, but Christ in him, he at once explains : " And the life which I now live in the flesh, I live by the faith of the Son of God, who loved me, and gave himself for me." That Christians are ἐν πνεύματι because the πνεῦμα τοῦ Χριστοῦ dwells in them, because they have Him (Rom. 8⁹), and that they are therefore πνευματικοί, and as such can judge all things, but are judged of none (1 Cor. 2¹⁵), means that they have received the Spirit, and not that they themselves are the holy πνεῦμα. Nothing is more alien to the spirit of apostolic admonition than the fusions and identifications so often permitted by religious arrogance in this connexion. We have only to think again of 1 Cor. 9²⁴f. and Phil. 3¹²f. to realise and continually to remember that as the " firstfruits of his creatures " (Jas. 1¹⁸) Christians are those who are called by God, reconciled and exalted to fellowship with Him in Jesus Christ, and instructed by the Holy Ghost. It is their portion as such to seek, to set their affection, to go, to run, to press on and to sacrifice. They are with the Lord and they follow and serve Him, but they are not themselves lords. He alone is the Lord. His grace is sufficient for them. His power attains its end in all their weakness. They cannot glory except in their infirmities (2 Cor. 12⁸f.). If they ever forget this, provision is made that they should be reminded of it by some thorn (σκόλοψ) in the flesh, some messenger of Satan to buffet them (2 Cor. 12⁷). But it is even more important to remember—and with this we must conclude—that since the instruction of the Holy Spirit is His and not ours, leading us to give all the glory to Him and therefore to God the Father and the incarnate Son, the royal man Jesus, it is powerful, effective, fruitful and victorious. Yes, even here and now it is fruitful and victorious. No one ever attends the school of this Teacher in vain.

THE SLOTH AND MISERY OF MAN

The direction of God, given in the resurrection of Jesus Christ who was crucified for us, discloses who is overcome in His death. It is the man who would not make use of his freedom, but was content with the low level of a self-enclosed being, thus being irremediably and radically and totally subject to his own stupidity, inhumanity, dissipation and anxiety, and delivered up to his own death.

1. THE MAN OF SIN IN THE LIGHT OF THE LORDSHIP OF THE SON OF MAN

So far we have been occupied with the existence of the Son of Man, who is none other than the humiliated Son of God. We have seen that as it is attested in the New Testament this existence is that of the true and exalted and royal man Jesus. And we have considered the problem of the connexion, the transition from Him to other men, the divine direction as it has been given, and is still given, by this man in the power and work of the Holy Spirit. But the alteration of the human situation as it is brought about by this man and His direction in the act of His lordship works itself out in the fact that there were and are and will be a Christian community and Christians in the world. It is of this alteration that we shall have to speak both in general and in detail in the sections which follow; of the sanctification and upbuilding of the Christian community and of Christian love.

To see it and understand it, however, we have first to consider the human situation in the form which precedes this alteration and is not yet affected by it. It is determined by human sin, or, more strictly, by the fact that the man with whom the royal man Jesus has to do in the act of His lordship is the man of sin : the man who wills and commits sin ; the man who is determined and burdened by it. It is this man as such who is sanctified by the existence of the man Jesus, by the direction which is given by Him. In the Christian community and the individual Christian it is still a matter—with an incisive modification—of this man and the overcoming of this man. The Son of God abased Himself to be the Brother of this man, the Bearer of his responsibility, when He was made flesh and put to death in the flesh. And when He overcame him in Himself, neither willing nor committing his sin, He set him aside, making him the old and superseded and outmoded man, becoming and being in his place the new and true and exalted and royal man, heading a new and reconciled world and humanity, sending out in His resurrection His mighty direction, and bringing about in the work of the Holy Spirit the act of His lordship, the great alteration, within the human situation as determined by sin. In order that we may know what this means in all its concreteness and significance, we have first to see and understand as such this situation as it was determined by sin, and the old man who was overcome in Jesus and set aside by Him.

The light in which this man is to be seen and understood is none other than the light of his overcoming. It is in view of the lordship of the Son of Man, in the power of His direction, and therefore in the knowledge of Jesus Christ by the Holy Spirit that we may know sin and the man of sin.

The general basis of this proposition (*C.D.*, IV, 1, § 60, 1) need not be developed again, but only sketched. As the opposition of man to God, his neighbour and himself, sin is more than a relative and limited conflict which works itself out only in himself and which can therefore be known in the self-consciousness and self-understanding which he can have of himself. As the one who commits sin man is himself totally and radically compromised. Where this is a true knowledge of sin, it can be only as an element in the knowledge of God, of revelation, and therefore of faith, for which he cannot in any way prepare himself. Man is corrupt even in his self-understanding, even in the knowledge of his corruption. He cannot see, therefore, beyond the inner conflict and its purely relative compass. He can never really see his sin, and himself as the man of sin. He cannot turn to a true knowledge of his corruption, but only evade it. God and His revelation and faith are all needed if He is to realise the accusation and judgment and condemnation under which he stands, and the transgression and ensuing need in which he exists. But faith in an idol and its revelation has no power to give him this realisation. It cannot be given by any further work of corrupt man ; by any normative concept that he himself may freely construct of majesty, goodness, righteousness and holiness ; by any law that he thinks he has discovered but has really invented and planned and built up of himself. A law of this kind can never have the power to bind and commit, and therefore really to accuse and judge and condemn, because in his encounter with it man is finally in encounter only with his own shadow, and in his discussion with it he is finally engaged only in discussion with himself. Any normative concept that he may construct is ultimately himself. By means of it he may well be conscious of that inward and relative and redemptive conflict with himself, but not of sin as his destructive opposition to God, his neighbour and himself.

He may perhaps achieve this so long and so far as the materials that he uses to construct this concept are taken from the statements of Holy Scripture and do actually give the necessary sharpness in virtue of their context. This was the case with the regulative concept of the Law as it was adopted and applied by the theology of the Reformation. But in this as in other respects it is a very doubtful and dangerous enterprise to take materials out of the Bible rather than allowing them to speak in their own context and substance and from their own centre. For the critical question then arises on the basis of what presupposition they will be read and according to what plan they will be—even in the most strictly biblicist manner—constructed. In other words, how is it to be decided what is meant by God and His majesty and will and Law ? May it not be that in the answering of this question some other source of revelation and knowledge is secretly or even openly tapped as well as the Bible : the book of rational law ; the consensus of all races as to what is generally and self-evidently right and fitting for man ; the decision of the innate individual conscience ; in short a *lex naturalis* which is merely rediscovered in the Bible as the true *lex aeterna* because it has found in what the Bible calls good and evil only its positive revelation, application and concretion ? (On the questions of the origins of this pregnant concept, and its incursion into Christian theology, we cannot be too emphatic in our recommendation of the important book by Felix Flückiger, *Geschichte des Naturrechts*, Vol. 1, 1954.) May it not be that it has its effect, and is brought to light, that the builder of this Law which is presumed to be superior to man, and to confront him, is really man himself—the law being only an ideal by which he measures himself but which he himself has established ? Is it not likely that the biblical elements used in its construction, having lost the distinctive power which they have in their own context and substance and from their own centre, will necessarily appear in the long run to be intrusive and dispensable ? Is it not inevitable that a synthetic outlook and thinking will triumph, for which there is only the tension of a relative and redemptive antithesis between good and evil, between what man should be and what he is, and in the sphere of which there is no real place for genuine sin and a man of sin (in the serious meaning of the term) ? Is it not possible that there is betrayed at this point the latent rationalism and immanentism of the biblicist enterprise ? These questions are not merely hypothetical. They are a description (cf. *C.D.*, IV, 1, pp. 369 ff., 374 ff.) of the development which, in repetition of the mistakes of the Early and Mediæval Church, actually took place, in respect of the concept of law and the corresponding concept of sin, in the history of Protestant theology from the closing stages of the Reformation to the apogee of Neo-Protestantism.

If man measures himself by a normative concept, a concept of God and His revelation, which is in some way—planned and constructed with or without biblical materials—his own work and therefore a reflection of himself, it is basically impossible that he should see his aberration as a destruction of his peace with God, his neighbour and himself, and therefore as his exposure to the threat of eternal perdition. Even in his aberration he will then see and think always of himself together with that norm. He will always be able to order and control his encounter with it, i.e., with himself. He will interpret his transgression as an incident, a point of transition, a stage in development. But he himself will not really be affected by even the sharpest judgment which he may find in it. He will never see himself so humiliated that he does not stand at some level and is not capable at least of climbing higher. *Quanti ponderis sit peccatum*, that as a sinner he is under sentence of death, and that he needs redemption and total renewal will always be truths which are quite alien to his thinking.

A genuine knowledge of sin is possible, and actual, as an element in the genuine knowledge of God, of revelation and of faith. But as an element in this knowledge it does not consist in the assertion of this or that general or specific accusation which man may make against himself but which he can always evade because it is he who makes it. Nor does it consist in the acknowledgment and acceptance of individual passages in the Bible which accuse and condemn man in the name of God but which are robbed of their true force because they are taken out of their context and given a purely arbitrary interpretation. It consists in the insight into the human situation which is given by the substance and centre of the biblical message ; by the direction which is given us by the existence of Jesus Christ, in and with His resurrection, in and with the witness and work of the Holy Spirit. Where the Word of God became and is flesh, there it is disclosed that man is flesh, and what it means and involves that this is the case. Where the grace of God encounters him, there his sin is revealed, and the fact that he is a sinner. Where his salvation is achieved, there the perdition from which he is snatched cannot be overlooked or contradicted. The Gospel alone, which no man has invented or planned or constructed, but which encounters man, if at all, only as God's free revelation, is the Law in the knowledge of which man finds himself accused and judged and condemned. But the Word made flesh, the grace of God encountering man, his salvation, the Gospel, is Jesus Christ. He and His existence as the Son of God and Son of Man are the light in which man as the man of sin is made known to himself, in which he must see and confess himself as such. Where there is a genuine knowledge of sin, it is a matter of the Christian knowledge of God, of revelation and of faith, and therefore of the knowledge of Jesus Christ. We will now attempt a more specific formulation and establishment of this statement in our present context.

We must first bring out the truth and significance of what has to be said concerning the *humanitas Christi*, the existence of the man Jesus. He is the Son of God humbled to be a servant. And as such He is the Son of Man exalted to be the Lord. Both His humiliation as God and His exaltation as man as fulfilled in His death, both the true deity and the true humanity of His existence, are revealed in His resurrection from the dead. It is the second aspect which now concerns us : His true humanity as fulfilled in His death and revealed in His resurrection ; His exaltation to be the royal man who in virtue of His identity with the Son of God lives and rules in full communion and conformity with God the Father. In this man God has elected humanity as such, and therefore all men, to the covenant with Himself. This man is the Representative and Head and Lord of all other men. But this being the case they are all established in Him and directed to an eternal life in the service of God. Therefore the revelation of His exaltation as it has taken place in His resurrection is the revelation of theirs too. There thus went forth, and still goes forth, in the work of His Holy Spirit the direction of Eph. 5^{14} to them and all of us : " Awake, thou that sleepest, and arise from the dead, and Christ shall give thee light." It is not always and everywhere effective, or equally effective. It is not yet, or no longer, received and genuinely taken to heart by all. Yet in the present context it is not these and similar questions that are important, but the reality which is presupposed in all these questions and which precedes all acceptance or non-acceptance on our part—the objective fact of the existence of Jesus Christ among all the other men of every time and place.

" The rays of dawn were still concealed, That flood the world with light ; But, look, the Light is now revealed, Which shines for ever bright. The sun itself its slumbers kept, But forth in all its power there leapt The uncreated sun " (P. Gerhardt). But the light which has arisen before any dawn is the reality of the exaltation and institution which have come to man in the death of Jesus ; of his establishment in a vital fellowship with God. It is the reality of the revelation, in His resurrection, of this decisive alteration of the whole human situation. It has happened once for all and radically for all men in the man Jesus. What is said of the final and conclusive revelation of Jesus (Lk. 17^{24}) is virtually true of His first revelation which initiated the closing epoch of human history : " For as the lightning, that lighteneth out of the one part of heaven, shineth unto the other part under heaven ; so shall also the Son of man be in his day." " The true Light, which lighteth every man, came into the world " (Jn. 1^9). It " shineth in darkness," although the darkness apprehended it not. The fire which Jesus came to kindle on earth (Lk. 12^{49}) burns and cannot be put out.

Since God humbled Himself and became man, thus exalting man to Himself, there is no more peace in the lowliness of human existence. In the power of the eternal divine election of grace and its execution in time, i.e., in the existence of the man Jesus, and by the fact of the direction which has been, and is, given by Him, all other men, whether they realise and accept it or not, are already estranged from the place which in itself would necessarily be, and continue to be, their place, if this man had not existed among them. They are already startled out of it. They are already alarmed. They are already summoned to make the movement within which they too are put in virtue of the exaltation of this One. Because and as this man lives, and God is lowly and man exalted in Him, man is no longer bound absolutely to his lowliness, nor is there now any absolute impossibility of his being in the height of a vital fellowship with God and in the service of God. He is no longer imprisoned, if secure, below. He is no longer unfree to let himself be exalted and to exalt himself. The existence of this One, and the fact of the direction of the Holy Spirit which He gives, is equivalent in practice to a *Sursum corda ! Sursum homines !* which is called out, and applies and comes, radically and objectively to all men, even though they may be at the very lowest point and have never so much as heard of Him. Because this man exists, there is no man who does not exist under the sign of this *Sursum !* For this man is not a private person. As this One, this Individual, this First-born, this Lord and Head, He has taken the place of all others, to die for them and to live for them, to live for them as the One who dies for them. No one can alter the fact that he, too, is a brother of this One, and that this One lives for him.

It is the knowledge of the man Jesus which forces us to, or rather frees us for, a knowledge of sin ; a knowledge of man as the man of sin. It does so, in short, because human existence as we taste and know it is set in the light of the exaltation of our humanity as it has taken place in Him. It is set under the sign of the great *Sursum!*, the Forward ! and Onward ! It is set under the command and the promise and the power of the " Follow me " that He addresses to every man. We shall speak of this positive aspect in our next section, which treats of the sanctification of man. But we cannot speak of it meaningfully unless we are aware of the negative aspect which on our side is also and primarily revealed in the same light of the exalta-tion of humanity as it has taken place in Jesus ; of the depth from which it is (validly and effectively and for every man) lifted in Him.

The alteration of the human situation as it has taken place in Him is differentiated from a prior state in which it is not yet altered. The movement in which He has set it is preceded by an earlier im-mobility. To the above of man actualised in Him there corresponds a very definite below, and to the fellowship with God in which he is placed a separation from God. In order to overcome this prior state, this immobility, this below, this separation of man from God, and therefore to draw man to Himself, God took them to Himself in His Son. At this point of departure He accepted solidarity with us ; He became our Brother. Willing to accept and suffer the conditions and consequences of this situation, He took our place and died on the cross. Hence He became and was and is, in this very act of His suffering and dying, the Conqueror, the Victor : exalted as man ; entering into that above ; passing from dereliction by God to perfect fellowship with Him ; being set as man at the right hand of the Father ; and therefore putting into effect in our place and for us that alteration of the human situation. The prior state, the immobility, the below, the separation from God which He made His own in order to overcome, is the sin of man. It is quite useless to try to see or state or know this except in relation to this gracious act of God toward man. This is the Law which reveals it where any other law imagined and invented by man, no matter how holy or pitiless he may think it to be, can only lead to illusions as to his own true nature. It is only where man has ground for thanksgiving that he has ground for the remorse which involves also repentance, conversion and sanctification.

To put the same thing in another way, the life of a new man lived by Jesus is preceded by the dying of an old man suffered by Him, the rising of the true man in His existence and death by the destruction of a false and perverted, His being as the royal man by the accepted and conquered being of the enslaved, His life in the spirit by the vegetating and passing flesh in which He willed to be like us, to be one of us. God has had mercy on the man who even in the form of that old, perverted man, even as that slave, even as flesh, is still the good creature which He elects and loves. He has received him so basically and radically that He was ready to make Himself his Brother in His own Son, to share his situation, to bear his shame, to be put to shame in his place and on his behalf, thus removing man from the situation which contradicts His election and love and creative will, divesting him of his shame and clothing him with His own glory: Himself being the new and true and royal and spiritual and worthy man in his place and on his behalf; the man in whose person the covenant was kept and fulfilled even on the part of man, and who in peace with God may also be at peace with himself and his neighbour. The first, perverted, fleshly man, whom God has so graciously pitied and accepted, is the man of sin. He is revealed in the light of the divine act of grace done to him in Jesus. In the light of this act, confronted with its law, this man is shown to be the man of sin. Where he has the most reason to praise God, no place whatever is left for any praise of self.

We will try to bring what we have to say concerning the knowledge of this man, and therefore the knowledge of sin and the man of sin as it is enclosed in the knowledge of God, of revelation and of faith, under a single common denominator, by saying that the existence of the man Jesus and the event of the direction of the Holy Spirit as issued by Him involve the shaming of all other men. Shaming is the disclosure of shame. Jesus is distinguished from all other men, and the knowledge of Jesus from that of all other men, from that of all other real or possible objects of knowledge, by the fact that they involve our incontestable shaming; the disclosure of our shame. When we say this we affirm in the first instance the purely factual element in the relationship between Him and us that He is the One who shames us and we are those who are shamed, quite irrespective of whether we are aware of the fact and are ashamed of ourselves, or still close our eyes or close them again to that which has happened and still does so. In this respect, too, the reality precedes the knowledge of it. But at any rate it is a decisive criterion of our knowledge of Jesus that, in accordance with the fact that He is the One who shames us and we are those who are shamed by Him, we should be ashamed of ourselves. If there is not this corresponding result, we are sadly mistaken if we imagine that we have even the remotest knowledge of Jesus.

The parable of the Pharisee and the Publican (Lk. 18⁹ᶠ·) speaks of two men who are both equally shamed before God but who are completely different because of their knowledge or ignorance of the fact. On the one hand we have here in the temple, proudly displayed before the face of God, the man who is ignorant and therefore quite unashamed. He thanks God so beautifully that he is as he is and therefore not as other men, extortioners, unjust, adulterers, or even as this publican. He can claim that he is free from carnal appetites : " I fast twice in the week " ; and he can also claim that he is free from the rule of Mammon : " I give tithes of all that I possess." On the other hand, also in the temple and before the face of God, we have the man who knows and is therefore ashamed. He can only stand afar off, and dare not lift up so much as his eyes unto heaven, but can only smite on his breast, his confession of faith being simply this : " God be merciful to me a sinner." The shame of both is already disclosed. But the one knows that this is the case and the other does not. The one can only humble himself whereas the other sees many things which encourage him to exalt himself. It is by this problem of shaming, whether it becomes acute or remains latent, that the decision is made and the ways divide.

But man is shamed (whether or not he is correspondingly ashamed) because he finds that he is compared with God. With God ? Yes, if he is radically and totally shamed it is because he is compared with God, and measured by His holiness he necessarily sees his own unholiness revealed. When we compare man with man there can and will be occasional and partial and superficial shamings. And because, in view of the difference in the relationships in which men may be compared with one another, these shamings are always at bottom reciprocal, it is always possible either on the one side or the other, or both, to find good reasons for evading them. The basic and total shaming which we cannot avoid is either from God or it does not take place at all. But we must add that it is from the true God who meets us concretely in a living encounter. A supposed direct confrontation of man with a God who is only a God at some height or depth in and for Himself is not an encounter with the Holy One, measured by whose holiness man finds that he is revealed to be unholy. In these circumstances he is dealing only with an idea or concept of God which, however lofty or profound it may be, cannot give rise to any shaming, any disclosure of his shame, so that he can never really be ashamed before it because he is not really shamed by it. A God who is God only in and for Himself is not the true God. The concept of this God is that of an idol. Between Him and man there can be no comparison, with the result that there can be no serious shaming of man. And it is tempting to ask whether man does not usually invent and deck out for himself this idol just because he knows that he cannot be compared with it and therefore that there is no risk of his being put to shame by it.

But he is compared already, and in this comparison seriously and basically and totally shamed, in his encounter with the God who is distinguished from all idols as the true God by the fact that He is not merely God in and for Himself but also Emmanuel : " God with us " ;

very man even as He is very God. Between us men it is not the case
that the one encounters God in the other. It may well be that we
mutually attest God, and therefore the fact that we are compared
with Him and shamed by Him. It may well be that we can and must
lead one another to shame before Him. But none of us is confronted
with God Himself, or shamed by Him, in the existence of another
man. This takes place only, but genuinely, in the existence of the
true man in Jesus, the Son of God. It is in relation to Him—and we
all stand in relation to Him—that there is the comparison with a man
which is also our comparison with the holy God. And in this comparison with His of our actions and achievements, our possibilities
and actualisations, the true expression of that which is within us, and
the inwardness of that which we express, our whole whence and
whither, the root and crown of our existence, we are genuinely shamed.
We are shamed because our own human essence meets us in Him in a
form in which it completely surpasses and transcends the form which
we give it. In Him we are not encountered by an angel, or a being
which is superior and alien to our own nature, so that it is easy to
excuse ourselves if we fail to measure up to it. We are confronted
by a man like ourselves, with whom we are quite comparable. But
we are confronted by a man in the clear exaltation of our nature to
its truth, in the fulfilment of its determination, in the correspondence
to the election and creation of man. We are confronted by the man
who is with and for God as God is with Him, at peace with God and
therefore with His fellows and Himself. But this means that we are
all asked by Him who and what we ought to be as His brothers.
What about human life as we live it ? What about our thinking and
willing and speaking and acting ? What about our heart and actions ?
What about the use we make of our existence, of the time which is
given us, of our own distinctive opportunity both as a whole and in
detail ? What about our coming and going ? What about our motives
and restraints, our plans and attainments ? What about the ordering
of our relationship to God and our neighbours and ourselves ? And
finally and comprehensively, what about our life-act as God's good
creatures within the cosmos of God's good creation ? If we had the
freedom to orientate and measure ourselves by other men, or by an
abstraction that we regard as God, or by a law invented and established by ourselves, it might well be possible to acquit ourselves
creditably, or not too discreditably, in face of these questions. But
we do not have this freedom. We can only imagine that we have it.
The measure by which we are measured is the true man in whom the
true God meets us concretely in a living encounter. Compared with
Him we stand there in all our corruption. The failure of all that we
have and do is revealed. The lost state of our humanity is exposed.
Our holiness, however great or small, drops away. Our brilliance is
extinguished, our boasting reduced to futility, our pride deprived of

its object. The untruth in which we are men is disclosed. The need in which God has accepted us in His Son, and which consists in the untruth of our humanity, is incontestable. This is our actual shaming, whether we see it or not, whether we are ashamed of ourselves or not. We stand there as those who are shamed in this way, in this shame, because and as the man Jesus is among us.

And if we are ashamed of ourselves, this means that we are aware of the way in which we are shamed by the man Jesus, of the shame in which we stand when we are measured by Him, and that we are grieved at it, but are quite unable, however ardently we may desire, to free ourselves from it. Even if the whole world takes our part, we cannot satisfy ourselves as those who are responsible for it. Even if no one else sees it, we see it. Even if no one else accuses us, we can only accuse ourselves. And if we try to conceal it from ourselves, it is always the more painfully present, for we cannot conceal ourselves from ourselves. We are forced to see and know ourselves in the loathsomeness in which we find ourselves exposed and known. We may perish and disappear, but we now know of no place in which we are no longer the terrible creature which we are known, and know ourselves, to be. We have to put up with ourselves as such. We need to be Christians, to know the man Jesus, if we are to be aware of the shaming which has come to all men in the existence of this One, and if we are to be affected by it, taking it to heart and accepting the fact of our shame. We can try to resist it, and to be without shame, only so long and so far as we have not yet seen Jesus, or still try, or again try, to ignore Him ; only so long and so far as we have not realised that as men we all stand in relation to Him, and are compared with Him and measured by Him, and are therefore shamed, like all other men, by this true man and therefore by the true God. The Christian cannot and will not refuse this knowledge. He does not do anything strange when, in the eloquent expression of the Bible, he " smites upon his breast." He would not be a Christian if he did not do this. He does only that which it is for every man without exception to do, and that which in the day of judgment every man will do. We will all be ashamed before Him then as those who are compared with Jesus and measured and therefore shamed by Him.

It is striking, and worth considering, that in the Gospels the shaming of man is expressly revealed in a figure which is given great prominence—that of Peter. Peter is obviously shamed already (although the word itself is not used) in Mk. 8[33] and par. when, because he does not conceive of the death and passion announced by Jesus in divine but human terms, he is rebuked or " threatened " by Him, and has to be told quite plainly : ὕπαγε ὀπίσω μου, σατανᾶ, i.e., that he must remove himself from the sight of Jesus. He is shamed already when according to Lk. 22[32], in a saying which stands between a supreme promise given to all the disciples (that they will eat and drink and sit on thrones and exercise a judicial office in the coming Messianic kingdom) and a supreme assurance of loyalty from this first disciple, Jesus tells him that He has prayed for him that his faith should not fail in the great trial which is at hand : " And when thou art converted strengthen thy brethren." He is ashamed already when in Mk. 14³⁰ᶠ· and par. his far too rash (ἐκπερισσῶς) assertion of his own trustworthiness receives at once the answer : " Even in this night, before the cock crow twice, thou shalt deny me thrice " ; when according to Mk. 14³⁷ he is asked : " Simon, sleepest thou ? couldest not thou watch one hour ? " ; and when in Mt. 26⁵² and Jn. 18¹¹ he is commanded to put up his sword. Again, his particular distinction and commission as they are described in Jn. 21¹⁵ᶠ· are preceded by the shaming question whether he really loves Jesus ; whether he loves Him more than the other disciples as he had previously boasted ; whether he really loves Him at all. It is not only in Mt. 14³¹ that the one who is caught by the saving and uplifting hand of Jesus is the Peter who sinks before Jesus because of his little faith, his doubt. And we find a remarkable echo of the Gospel picture in the fact that it is he whom Paul has to " withstand to the face " in Antioch because of his hypocrisy (Gal. 2¹¹ᶠ·). But again, it is said expressly of Peter that he knows that he is shamed, and that he is ashamed of himself accordingly. " Depart from me ; for I am a sinful man, O Lord " (Lk. 5⁸), is the first saying of this first disciple that has come down to us, and it is his first reaction in his encounter with the Lord. And then, more drastically, we have the description of the scene after his denial (Lk. 22⁶¹ᶠ·) : " And the Lord turned, and looked upon Peter. And Peter remembered the word of the Lord, how he had said unto him, Before the cock crow, thou shalt deny me thrice. And Peter went out, and wept bitterly." And finally in Jn. 21¹⁷ : " Peter was grieved because he said unto him the third time, Lovest thou me ? " It is obviously the intention of the New Testament tradition that everything else that it can say concerning him, or that is known concerning him in the primitive Church, should be seen and understood against this background. This was the appearance, in relation to Jesus, of the rock on which He willed to build His community, and did in fact do so. Again, it is obviously the intention of the tradition to characterise in the person of this first disciple *mutatis mutandis* the situation and shame of all others in their relation to their Lord ; the Christian situation in its typical significance for the human situation as such. As it sees it, neither in the community nor the world is there anyone who is not shamed by Him as Peter is when measured by Jesus.

But the statement that man is shamed in the light of the lordship of the Son of Man needs to be filled out and explained before we can pass from the question of knowledge to that of fact. That there is a serious and radical and total shaming of man must not seem to be only a statement made and accepted at random. It is a matter of the truth of man in this shaming, and of the knowledge of this truth, when a man, the Christian, has to be ashamed of himself in accordance with the shaming of all men as it proceeds from the existence of Jesus. If he sees himself forced, or rather freed, to do this by the direction of Jesus Christ and therefore by the Holy Spirit, this is not a dead and formless and irresponsible awareness. He finds himself set in the light of the lordship of the Son of Man. He comes to participate in a knowledge of Him, and of himself. He is demanded and set in a position to give an account of his situation, to reflect on its origin and nature and significance and difficulty, to be clear about his sin and himself as the man of sin, and to make it clear to others and the world. He does not speak in the void. He does not merely assert. He does not merely appeal to an uncontrollable experience.

He knows what he is saying when he confesses that he is one who is shamed by Jesus, and when he approaches other men with the presupposition that in them too, whether they know and accept it or not, he has to do with those who are in fact shamed by Jesus. What the Christian knows of himself and all other men must now be developed in more specific statements and deliberations.

1. We must begin with the factual question whether it is really the case that all men do undoubtedly confront the one exalted man Jesus in the depths of abasement. Does the phenomenon of the shamed and sinking Peter really have a basic and general significance ? Are there not those in whom humanity confronts us, at least in tendency, or in part, in a certain exaltation ? Are there not those who can be compared with this One and do not emerge as men who are absolutely and unreservedly shamed in this comparison ? Are there not those who are at least nobles or princes beside this one royal man ? Is there not even something noble to be found in every man, even in those whose aspect is dominated by their abasement ? May it not be that the statement that all men are shamed by Jesus is true only in a relative sense ? Are we perhaps guilty of an exaggeration when we oppose to Him as the one true man the corruption of all the rest ? How is it that as Christians we know concerning ourselves and all other men that, however lofty or lowly we may be in other spheres, in face of Him, measured by Him, we do not find ourselves half-exalted, but in the very depths of a perverted humanity ?

The answer to this factual question is given by the simple fact that Jesus lives for the Christian, who alone knows what he is saying when he utters this name ; that He lives as the man of the history handed down in the Gospels ; and that the Christian himself has a personal share in this history, so that he cannot avoid recognising himself and all other men in the figures and manner and situation of those by whom Jesus is surrounded in this history. They may be distant and strange in other respects. But in the relation to Jesus he sees his own—and not only his own, but the characteristic relation of all men. In this respect he regards himself and all other men as one with them—no worse, but certainly no better, no different, when measured by this standard. What would he have to do with the Jesus who lives in the Gospel history if he had no share in it ; if he were not in solidarity with those who surrounded Him : with the people of Galilee and· Jerusalem ; with the publicans and sinners ; with the sick and possessed ; with the scribes and Pharisees ; with Caiaphas and Pilate and their men ; with the disciples of Jesus from Peter the rock to Judas who betrayed Him ; and if he were not forced to see and understand all other men in the same solidarity with them in relation to Jesus ? It is on this ground that the Christian knows that he and all other men, however noble or princely they may be compared with men, are shamed by this One, and that no matter what may be attempted or done in other respects this shaming cannot be explained away or relativised or weakened either in his own case or that of others. He stands together with those who confront this One in the Gospel history. This does not mean that he finds himself in particularly bad company. This may be said of Barabbas and the two who were crucified with Jesus. But by and large there are no outstanding villains, no titans of iniquity, no palpably disturbed social relations, in face of this One. He is set in an environment in which He has no serious opponent. But it is also the case that He has no serious companion or helper or fellow-worker. In the positive sense, too, there is a dearth of figures who stand out in some way when they are measured by Him. The only possible candidate for this position is John the Baptist, but he belongs only to the beginning of the story, and the Gospels take good care to characterise him in such a way that there can be no place for any thought of an equality or even a similarity in the comparison between him and Jesus. For the rest, there are the sick who are healed, those whose sins are forgiven, those who seem to be, and are, affected and shaken by the preaching of Jesus; those to whom He turns in a way which completely surprises both themselves and others, and finally those who are called to follow Him, and do in some sense do so. There is not a single one among them who has any independent significance or weight in face of Him. They see Him, and hear Him, and are helped by Him, and believe in Him, or think they do so. And in all these relationships He is always the One who gives, the One to whom none of them has anything to give. He goes through the midst of them in splendid isolation as the Lord. The men around Him, measured by Him, have no particular distinction either in good or evil; and if they have this in other respects, it pales in comparison with Him. They fall away beside Him. Measured by Him, they exist on a different level. What is revealed in the encounter with Him, in His light, is only the usual run, whether in good or evil, of mediocre and trivial humanity. And that the distinction and antithesis in relation to Him are not relative or temporary is proved by the fact that this humanity which is trivial in both good and evil is finally united in the fact that it doubts Him, that it does not understand Him, that it forsakes Him, that it rejects and denies and betrays, or at the very best impotently bewails, Him, that it judges Him either on spiritual or secular grounds, that it brings Him to the cross and that it finally abandons Him on the cross. It is the average man who does this. It is he who is the rebel that will not have this man to reign over us. It is he that is the perverted man who is so sharply distinguished, who so flagrantly distinguishes himself, from the true man. It is he who is the man of sin. And his sin consists in the very fact that he is the average man. The Christian knows that he belongs to this group, and he confesses that—whether he is a little above or a little below the average—he is in this group, together with all other men, man as such. He knows the Jesus who lives in this history and therefore in this human environment. He thus knows who and what all other men are. He knows the lowliness and misery in which we confront Him, both as individuals and in the mass, both in our better impulses and desires and our worse. He knows the descent in which we are all implicated as compared with His ascent. He knows that the best possibility of man is only to be like sinking Peter, who without the hand of the Lord to save him and lift him up could only sink in his triviality. This is the first thing that has to be said concerning the factual question. It may not bring out the distinction and the antithesis between the one Son of Man and other men in all its clarity and strictness and danger. But its seriousness is already apparent. All our mediocrity is revealed, and it is revealed as the form in which we are unequivocally opposed to Him.

2. But the question arises, and demands an answer, whether and how far there is really any disqualification of others as sinners in and with this distinction between Him and them. Can the mediocrity, or triviality, with which they confront Him really be regarded as bad or evil ? Is it really the case that in this confrontation with the man Jesus there is revealed a triviality of others in which they are not merely different from, but finally opposed to, Him ? Is it really the shame of man which this discloses ? Is he really shamed by Him because of it ? Is triviality real corruption ? Ought not mediocrity to be at least permitted as an optimum which is accessible to all ? May it not even be commanded as that which is basically normal ? Explanations and excuses might be sought and found for all those men in the environment of Jesus who were not prepared to be wholly with Him or definitely against Him, and therefore for us to the extent that we are like them, and in solidarity with them. Indeed, it might even be asked whether they were not right. Was it not this One that was so different and strange and isolated among them—so one-sidedly orientated on God, so imprudently occupied with the cause of man, so singleminded and emphatic in the proclamation of Himself—who was really perverted ? Was it not a sound instinct for that which is possible and to that extent right for men that caused the others to keep Him at a distance, not to commit themselves to Him absolutely or without the freedom to withdraw at the last minute, even perhaps to shake their heads and turn away from Him at once, or nonchalantly to pass by on the other side, and let Him go His own way, or, if He could not be resisted in any other way, and obviously willed to have it so, to make an end of Him altogether, driving Him out as One who was not wanted, as a disturber of the peace ? As Goethe put it : " Let every fanatic be nailed to the cross in the thirtieth year." Was it not most likely that they were all in the right against the One rather than He against them ? And may not we, if we belong to this

company of those who are different from Him, regard ourselves, not as disqualified by Him, but as excused in face of Him, and basically and finally in the right against Him ?

The question is a serious one to the extent that it undoubtedly brings before us an important aspect of the critical point where Christians and non-Christians necessarily divide. Decided non-Christians, however lofty their spiritual and moral principles, are always characterised by the fact that (more or less consciously and explicitly, but always resolutely) they usually defend those who are ordinary in relation to Jesus against the charge that in their ordinariness they are sinners. Many things may be conceded to the man Jesus, but not the fact that in their difference from Him all others are disqualified and shamed and ought therefore to be ashamed. Assuming that we ourselves are Christians, what is it that we know if in practice we regard this obvious question as just as self-evidently unimportant as it seems important to them ? What was it that Peter began to know when, as the first and best of the many who then surrounded Jesus, he could not bear the look of Jesus after the denial, but " went out and wept bitterly " ?

The first point is obviously that, if we know Jesus at all, we can never completely (but only temporarily) forget, nor can we absolutely (but only superficially) abstract from the fact, that this One is not a private person beside and among many others so that we can escape Him and keep ourselves to ourselves, but that in all the omnipotence of the merciful will of God He is the One who in all His isolation took our place, and the place of all men, so that what He is necessarily includes in itself our true being as it is ascribed and given us by God. If, then, He is very different from us, if there is this distinction between Him on the one side and all other men on the other, if we all confront Him in our ordinariness, we cannot excuse and vindicate and justify ourselves against Him in this ordinariness, or try to accuse Him because He is so different. In and with the existence of this One the ground is cut away from under our feet as those who are ordinary men. In and with this One who has taken our place there has come to us grace and liberation. This ordinariness is behind us and under us. We have become new men who are lifted out of this ordinariness and separated from it. This is the first thing that the Christian knows as he knows about Jesus Christ and himself and man. He belongs to Him, to His side ; and not therefore to that of the trivial humanity in which he confronts Him.

From this first thing there follows necessarily the second, that it is not normal or excusable or justifiable, but evil and wicked, that he does not stand at His side. He contradicts himself as he contradicts Him. Even from his own standpoint, he does that which is impossible. He cannot be below, but has to be above with this One who is there for him. His mediocrity and triviality, the ordinariness of his manner and place, is actually sin, and as such it is intolerable and inexcusable. It is undeniable ingratitude to the grace which is shown him. In it he is like a prisoner who when the doors are opened will not leave his cell but wants to remain in it. It clearly disqualifies him. As the ordinary man he is like all others, he cannot be endured. His shaming is an event. This is the second thing that the Christian knows.

And from this there follows the third—he knows that every attempt to escape his shaming, to defend and justify and excuse himself, to regard the abnormal as normal and his wrong as right, to turn the tables, not only has no prospect of success and cannot alter his actual shame, but can only confirm his shame. Is it not enough that he stands where he does, in the impossible contradiction to himself where he does not really belong? When he is absolutely assailed in his being below, is he still going to espouse it? Is he going to pretend that that which is so harmful is really innocuous? Is he going to acquiesce in that which cannot be? Is he going to glorify that which is plainly infamous? Is he going to reject and contest that which is his own health and greatness and glory? Surely it is clear that every step in this direction, all the activity or inactivity in which he participates in the repudiation of the One by the many, even the impulse of superior indifference or rejection, merely recoils upon himself and threatens to make his shaming final and definitive. This is the basis of the Christian answer to the question. The Christian is no real Christian, i.e., he does not know Jesus and himself, if he cannot give this answer at once, shaking it off as no less self-evidently meaningless than the non-Christian regards it as meaningful and profound. He knows that man is quite defenceless in face of the accusation arising from his confrontation by the man Jesus. In their differentiation from this One all others are indeed disqualified as sinners. This statement, too, which is directed primarily against themselves, belongs to the witness which Christians cannot withhold from non-Christians—quite irrespective of whether or not they receive it.

3. It might also be asked, however, whether and how far it is directly the individual himself who is actually implicated in this disqualification as a sinner which arises in his relation with Jesus. How far is the sin disclosed in his confrontation with Jesus really to be understood as a determination of his being, of all that he does or refrains from doing? May it not be that the term " man of sin " is too strong? We have to agree that the evil act of a man is not something that takes place automatically from within himself, nor is it a function of his creaturely nature. It is a new and responsible work, and it is in contradiction to his nature, so that when he does it he is a stranger to himself. We have also to agree that even as the doer of this act he does not cease to be in the hand of God, and to be the man who was not created evil but good. From this it might be deduced

that although it is right that he is disqualified in so far as he sins, i.e., as he frequently and seriously denies what he ought to be and might be as a man, yet the disqualification is not so far-reaching that it affects himself, his being, and all that he does or refrains from doing. The sinful act is a regrettable but external, incidental and isolated failure and defect ; a misfortune, comparable to one of the passing sicknesses in which a healthy organism remains healthy and to which it shows itself to be more than equal. On this view, the individual— I myself—cannot really be affected by the evil action. I do not have any direct part in its loathsome and offensive character. In the last resort it has taken place in my absence. I myself am elsewhere and aloof from it. And from this neutral place which is my real home, I can survey and evaluate the evil that has happened in me in its involvement with other less evil and perhaps even good motives and elements ; in its not absolutely harmful but to some extent positive effects ; in its relationship to my other much less doubtful and perhaps even praiseworthy achievements ; and especially in my relationship to what I see other men do or not do (a comparison in which I may not come out too badly) ; in short, in a relativity in which I am not really affected at bottom. I may acknowledge and regret that I have sinned, but I do not need to confess that I am a sinner. The alien nature of my act has not alienated me from myself. I am not really shamed, and therefore I do not have to be ashamed of myself. That there have often enough been, and will be again, mean and trivial and even unworthy things in our relationship to God and our neighbours and ourselves need not be concealed or unacknowledged, but this does not mean that we ourselves are mean in the totality of our achievements, and that we have to reckon with this fact. It is an illegitimate hyperbole to say that I am a man of sin, that I myself am ordinary and trivial and mediocre. How and why am I to see that I am prevented from regarding myself as secured against my sin, when all is said and done, by a kind of protective covering, by an alibi of this kind ?

Our attitude to this question is a further test whether we are Christians or non-Christians. Do we realise that it is quite impossible to think and speak in this way, that it is not only difficult but out of the question to take even a first step in this direction ? To be sure, we can follow this kind of argument. To be sure, it is all uncannily familiar, as though we ourselves do sometimes argue this way in our dreams. But in our waking thoughts we cannot possibly make it our own. It is self-evident that nothing less than the whole of it is basically false ; that it is not at all the case that in virtue of the goodness of his creaturely nature as it is undoubtedly maintained by man even as the doer of sin he is protected from being the one who does it, and therefore a sinner who is alienated from himself in committing this alien act ; that there is no neutral place from which he can relativise his evil and therefore be, and claim to be, a free man in respect of it ; that he has no alibi and cannot find one ; that he himself is really mean as the doer of these mean actions ; and that he has every reason to be genuinely ashamed of himself.

What reason ? Simply that he knows that the place which he might occupy and maintain in face of his doing and non-doing in order to secure himself against its loathsome and offensive character, and the disqualification and shaming which are involved for himself, is a place which is already occupied, so that it gives rise to quite a different train of reasoning from that which he himself might pursue. For it is at this very place that there stands the man Jesus, the Other beside him and among all other men, but as this Other beside him and among all other men the Son of God in his and their stead, who is instituted and determined and empowered as man to conduct his and their case— really in their stead and on their behalf. His existence, therefore, is the decision who and what they are and are not with what they do and do not do ; the decision as to their whence and whither. Thus the decision is taken wholly and once for all out of their hands. It is no longer a matter of what they themselves think. For all of them it can be only a matter of knowing the decision which has been made in His existence concerning them all, and of accepting and confessing it. For none of them can there be any retreat into the fantasies of stricter or milder self-judgments. The omnipotent mercy of God has introduced this man among them. It stands behind the decision which has been made in His existence and makes it incontestable and irrevocable. This is the first thing that the Christian knows in this matter. He can confess as his own only the being in which he finds himself known by the existence of the man who has taken and occupies the place of himself and all men.

But in this man Jesus who has taken his place he can and should also find himself known as a new man exalted into peace and fellowship with God, as God's dear child and welcome saint. In Him he can and should also find the reconciliation of the world, and his own reconciliation, with God. This is the goal of the divine decision which has been made concerning all men in Him. This is the goal of the movement in which the whole human situation is set by His existence. If the decision was made in the man Jesus in the place of all, in his place ; if in his and their place, as his and their Brother and Fellow, He was and is the new man in whom all others, and he too, may discover that they are known and proclaimed as regenerate, it is also fixed what his and their place is which He has taken and whose Brother and Fellow He has become, to be for them this new and different man, and as such their reconciliation with God. This is the second thing that the Christian knows in this matter. If his own whence is revealed in the existence of this man, information is also given in this existence concerning his whither. He could not find comfort and joy in the reconciliation with God which has taken place in this man, in the divine sonship and sanctification which have been won in Him, if he were not prepared to be told, as this man has taken his place, who and what he himself is as the one for whom this Other has intervened, and whose hope and confidence are grounded wholly and utterly in Him.

And this Other, to be the new man and the hope and confidence of all men, is the Son of God who has become unequivocally lowly, the Bearer of human mediocrity and triviality, the Friend of publicans and sinners, the Brother of the ordinary man, in order to reconcile the world as it is to God, in order to take up man to himself as the elect and beloved creature of God in the state in which he actually finds himself. It is not at a height far above us, but in our depths, as one of us, that He was and is the new man. If we do not see Him in these depths we do not see Him at all, and therefore we do not see the exaltation that took place in Him. These depths are the place which He has taken for us. This is the third thing that the Christian knows. In the Son of God come down from heaven he recognises the exalted Son of Man who as such is the Reconciler of all other men with God, their hope and confidence.

And this brings him to the fourth and decisive point. He finds himself in these depths, and therefore he himself is mean and lowly in what he does and does not do. It is with him as such that the Son of God has associated Himself in becoming man. It is he as such, the publican and sinner, estranged from himself and therefore disqualified, who in Him as the new man is reconciled with God, the child and saint of God. If he is not prepared to be such, to be a man of sin, this can only mean that he does not want to be one of those whom God has taken to Himself in this one man, with whom He has made Himself equal, whose place this One has taken to their salvation. In the measure that he tries to contest his disqualification, or to hedge it around with reservations, or not to be one of those to whom it refers, he only compromises his real qualification as a child and saint of God. The only alibi that he can find is hell. If we are not ready to be in the far country, we are not ready to allow that the Son of God has come among us. We want to be in hell. In the very One in whom the Christian sees himself qualified and exalted, he has also to see that he is disqualified and abased. The joy in which he can boast in relation to Him is absolutely bound up with the humility in which he is necessarily ashamed in relation to Him—necessarily because otherwise he would dash away fellowship with Him and therefore his own exaltation as it has taken place in Him, thus condemning himself. This One confesses *in toto* those who are shamed by Him, but only those. Hence no one can confess Him, and therefore be a Christian, unless he confesses that he is totally shamed by Him. It is for this reason that there can be no escaping the recognition that we are sinners.

Only the Christian can see the force of this reason. But it is valid and momentous for all men. For it is for all men that the Son of God has become lowly, and takes their place in lowliness as the new man, and is their hope and confidence. What distinguishes Christians is that they know this reason, and therefore cannot conceal either from themselves or others that we cannot withdraw or protect ourselves from our sin, that in this matter there can be no question of an alibi.

4. We will assume that the first three questions have all been answered along the lines suggested, i.e., that they have been rejected as impossible questions. In comparison with the man Jesus (1) we are all shown to be opposed to Him ; this opposition (2) involves our disqualification ; and this disqualification (3) actually and inescapably applies to ourselves. Yet even if this is conceded, the three statements might still be over-arched or bracketed by the final question whether there is not a higher or deeper synthetic view on which the situation of man as one who is shamed is indeed necessary, but as a kind of metaphysical *datum*, so that in spite of its seriousness it does not prove to be finally or genuinely disturbing. Is it not perhaps the case that it is simply laid on man as an unavoidable destiny to be a man of sin, and to be revealed as such, and objectively shamed, and therefore necessarily to be ashamed of himself ? Might it not be conditioned, for example, by his different nature and essence as a creature ; by the limit which is set for him as such ; by the fact that he does not confront that which is not with the same sovereignty as God but is exposed to its temptations and threats ; by the fact that he cannot avoid the proximity and co-existence of darkness and its power but has to participate in them, and cannot ignore or deny this participation ? Might it not be that his shaming is the characteristic feature of his existence as a man in the rest of creation (which might have the same experiences without being either shamed or ashamed) ? Might it not be that simply to be a man is also to be disqualified by this opposition and to be directly and most intimately affected ? Or, finally and decisively, might it not belong to the perfection of God, to His inaccessible and incomparable majesty encompassing both man as His good creature and the nothingness which menaces him, to have in the man who sins against Him and is therefore shamed by Him a kind of shadow, and therefore a counterpart with its negative attestation ? Might it not be that man in his abasement, his sin, he himself as the man of sin, and his shame as such, are all integrated in the all-embracing nexus or system of a harmony of being in which he is affirmed as well as negated, and in this twofold determination is concealed, and knows that he is concealed, in a final and supreme and assured and reassuring compulsion : not lost but sustained and upheld even as the one he was and is, in all his shame ; a free man ultimately even in that which speaks against him, and in the resultant misery, and in the knowledge

of this situation ? Might it not be that in the existence of the man Jesus, and the majesty and lowliness of the surrounding humanity which He receives and adopts, we have a supreme attestation and confirmation of this harmony which spans even the discord of human sin and is therefore all the more glorious in its universality, so that a basic calm is legitimate in spite of all the unsettlement to which our situation may give rise ?

Is there a penetrating Christian answer to these questions too ? Can it be shown that even this attempt to throw light on the human situation, inviting though it may be by reason of its largeness, only obscures it—and perhaps more deeply than ever ? We must not be too ready with our answer. It will not do merely to protest, attaching perhaps the derogatory label " monism." The question is the more seductive and dangerous because it seems to have overcome the first three questions by exposing their superficiality, and to have approximated in some sense to Christian truth. Even in a Christian doctrine of sin, although there can be no question of an innate potentiality for evil in accordance with creation, we have to reckon with the fact that, unlike God, man is indeed exposed to the assault of chaos by reason of his creatureliness, that he confronts the nothingness which is intrinsically alien to him, not with the superiority of God, but—although no possibility in this direction can be ascribed to him—with a certain reversionary tendency. Nor can it be contested, but only asserted, that within the created order it is the place of man to be not only the field and prize of battle, but himself the contestant in the divine conflict with nothingness which began with creation. Finally, there has to be confessed as in no other teaching the absolute superiority with which God controls and conquers nothingness even in the form of human sin, not in any sense being arrested by it, but setting it to serve His own glory and the work of His free love. All these are assertions which we cannot avoid if we are determined to derive our thinking on God, the world, man and even evil from Jesus Christ. And the fourth question which now engages us seems to be co-extensive with these assertions, aiming at the same bracketing of sin as we necessarily find in Christian doctrine. We have to be all the more careful, therefore, in our consideration whether we can decide for the view represented in this question, or whether as Christians, and therefore from the centre of Christian knowledge, we must return a negative answer, i.e., reject it, because even if we put only one foot on the ground indicated by this last question, it means that at the last moment we again obscure and even destroy the knowledge of sin and the man of sin.

What is it that the Christian knows if he finds that he is in fact absolutely prevented from having any part or lot at all in this higher or deeper view of his own and human sin ? from understanding it, in the light of the relationship between the Creator and the creature, or in relation either to man or to God Himself, as a necessary *datum* co-ordinated into an embracing nexus of being, as an unavoidable but not finally or genuinely disruptive discord in a superior harmony ? from finally explaining the fact that man is shamed and has therefore to be ashamed ? from a calm acceptance of the fact because there can be no question of any real damage to God or fear of perishing, or of anything monstrous and terrible, any incurable wound, any absolutely fatal contradiction, in the being of man in the abasement of sin ? What is it that the Christian knows which forbids him to regard himself as finally secure even as the doer of sin, the man of sin, within the framework of a universal systematisation of this kind ? What is it that he knows when he knows that there can be no question of any universal systematisation ; that he cannot find any framework within which he may be finally secure as a sinner ; that he cannot avoid the fact that as the man of sin he has every reason seriously to fear ; and that he can find himself secure, and therefore free not to fear, only at the place where he has no option but seriously to fear ?

In answer to this question the decisive content of Christian knowledge is again the man Jesus, and therefore the actuality in which the Christian finds that his sin, and that of the world, is contained, that in all its frightfulness, it is cancelled and overcome, and that it already dispersed like a fleeting shadow. It is the actuality by which all respect for sin, or anxiety before it, is in fact forbidden because sin has lost its power, because it has been made contemptible, because he has been freed and set on his feet in face of it, because he had already been lifted up out of its abasement. It is true enough that it is only subsequently that the light of the lordship of the Son of Man, His direction as it is issued in the might of His resurrection and the power of the Holy Spirit, discloses who and what is already overcome in His death, and from what situation this one is already snatched. But this radical limitation of sin and man as its doer, as it is known by the Christian to have taken place already in the one man Jesus (for how could he be a Christian if he did not know this?), has nothing whatever to do with a harmony of being in which sin and its shame are systematically co-ordinated, and God and man and sin peacefully united. Indeed, if any idea is excluded, like sin itself, in this limitation, it is that of this peaceful co-existence of God, man and sin, and of the comfort which can be derived from it.

For who and what is overcome in the death of the Son of Man is revealed in His resurrection. The Son of God died in our place the death of the old man, the man of sin. And the One who undertook to suffer the death of this old man in our place was the new man who lives in our place again as the Holy One of God in whom we are all exalted to be saints of God. There is no continuity or harmony or peace between the death of that old man and the life of this new. The containment of sin as it has taken place on the cross of the Son of Man, the complete replacement there of the man of sin, took place in the conflict of an irreconcilable and unbridgeable opposition in which only the one or the other could remain and one or the other had necessarily to give place. The old man could not be co-ordinated with the new, nor the new with the old. The new could only live, and the old yield and die. The divisive No of the wrath of God, which is the consuming fire of His love, lay on the old man, destroying and extinguishing him. This is the first thing that the Christian knows in relation to this question as he knows what took place for him and all men in the man Jesus. No compromise was made, no armistice arranged, no pact of non-aggression concluded at the place where he and all men were helped, but an unequivocal and intolerable and definitive enemy of God was treated as he deserved and utterly destroyed. This enemy is the sin of man ; it is he himself as the man who wills this sin. He was not tolerated at that place. No pardon was given him. An end was made of him. This is how he stands as a sinner in the light of the resurrection of the Son of Man. This is what his sin looks like in that light. It is unambiguously defined as that which God did not and does not will, and will never do so ; as that in which He has no part ; as that which He did not create ; as that which has no possibility in Him and therefore in itself. It is that which is absurd before Him, and therefore that which He has rejected and forbidden. God can be thought together with it only in the act of opposition in which He masters and contests and overcomes it. This is what He did at Calvary. Any systematic co-ordination of God and sin is made quite impossible for the Christian by his knowledge of what took place there. But so, too, is any co-ordination of himself with sin ; any attempt to make himself comprehensible, to explain and understand himself, as the doer of sin ; any desire to find security in the peace of a higher view or synthesis. To be sure, he may know, as the creature of God, that he is preserved and blessed by Him, and in the man Jesus that he lives in and with Him. But this knowledge stands or falls with the recognition that as the man of sin he is cursed and slain by God, thrust out into the void, dark in the darkness, a lost soul. There cannot, then, be any talk of harmony. In sin man strikes a chord which cannot be taken up into any melody. The Christian can understand it only as something which is overlooked, covered and forgiven—not as a reality which is adapted to his human nature or co-ordinate with his human destiny, but only as that which cannot be co-ordinated. And he can understand himself only as one who is delivered from its kingdom as a brand is plucked from the burning, as one who can only avoid and withstand it. If he knows the radical decision that has been made in Jesus Christ for the world and himself and against evil, how can he still try to create a synthesis of God and evil, the world and evil and himself and evil ?

The first point gives rise to a second. The One who in this decision acted against sin, i.e., who suffered in our place the death of the old man, the man of sin, is none other than God Himself in the person of the Son of Man. It is not only from a distance that God has reacted against this enemy as against one who has disturbed the peace of the created reality distinct from Himself, but whose evil work did not in any way affect His own life and being. As He sees it, this evil work is obviously not merely an imperfection, but something quite intolerable. It is not merely a final and relative, but an infinite and absolute evil. It is not an evil that can be countered by a mere arrangement within the world, or averted through the instrumentality and mediation of a creature. It is not an evil which any creature is good enough, or competent, or adapted to contest and remove. God Himself had to come down, to give Himself, to sacrifice Himself, in order that a place should be found for a man freed from this evil, and a reconciled world introduced in this man. On the cross of Golgotha God Himself intervened to accomplish this liberation, paying the price Himself, giving Himself up to death. If this was not too much for Him, if this intervention was not too big a thing or this price too high, if this decision against sin and man as the doer of sin could be taken only in this way, this brings home to us how great is the absurdity of sin, and how serious it is. God Himself is affected and disturbed and harmed by it. His own cause, His purpose for man and the world, is disrupted and arrested ; His own glory is called in question. He Himself finds Himself assaulted by it in His being as God, and He hazards no less than His being as God to encounter it. This being the case, we have every reason to repudiate resolutely and once and for all any idea of a limitation, counter-balancing or relativisation of sin apart from that which is accomplished in this way. The seriousness of this disturbance can be measured only by the fact that it is met and overcome by God Himself. As He is for us and against it, it is in fact limited and counter-balanced and relativised, but only in this way, only by the occurrence of this history in which God is the active, militant and suffering Subject, and not in a co-ordination in which sin, and we ourselves as the doers of it, are tolerated alongside Him. What has taken place for us and against sin in this history proves that it is not in any sense tolerated, and that we ourselves are not tolerated as the doers of it. The Christian knows this, and does not cherish any illusions, even the most kindly and beautiful, in this respect.

But this leads us to a third point. The dying of the old man of sin, and the rising of the new man in whom we are liberated from sin for God, did not take place as our own act, but as the act of the true Son of God and Son of Man in our place. Neither the destruction nor the emergence, neither the death of the old nor the life of the new, is our own achievement. We can participate in it only in such a way, and our sanctification, our exit as sinners and our entry as disciples of God and Jesus Christ, can consist only in the fact, that we love in return the One who has first loved us in this act. It is God's free grace that the battle which He Himself and alone has fought for His own glory is also a battle for our salvation, and that the victory includes also our deliverance and liberation. It is again His free grace that we have a part in this battle, being called and empowered to fight and suffer and triumph with Him in this cause. We cannot presume to do this of ourselves. It can only be given to us. No Christian can stand before the decision made at Calvary in the person of the true Son of God and Son of Man except in the pure gratitude of the knowledge that it took place for him but quite apart from him and against all his merits and deservings. And no Christian will obey the divine direction of the Holy Spirit as it was and is issued in the power of the resurrection of Jesus Christ except in the pure gratitude of this knowledge ; not, therefore, in the sense of an original achievement, but in that of a secondary correspondence, which he cannot evade because he knows that, apart from and even against him, disposition was made concerning him in that decision. It is free grace, an unmerited gift, that what took place on Golgotha as the death of the old man and the life of the new is valid for him too, and takes shape in his existence, when he must not and may not fear, when he may become and be a man who is liberated from sin for God. But the one who may become and be a man liberated in this way, by the free grace addressed to him in the person of another, is obviously completely enslaved when regarded in and for himself and his own person. He is not in a position to see his own imprisonment as limited in a higher synthesis, and therefore to understand his situation as finally harmful. Free grace is not one element in the totality of a nexus in which even that which man is without and against it also has its secure meaning and place and if possible a positive significance. Free grace is the event of the shattering and destroying of what he is without it and against it. It means his total disqualification from which he cannot find refuge in any system in which it has a relative significance and range—but also a limit. His only way of escape is forward. He can escape only to the place from which this disqualification comes ; to the free grace which also judges him, which disqualifies him as it qualifies him, which humbles him as it exalts him. Except in the light of this grace, and therefore in the knowledge of the Son of Man in whom it comes to us in this twofold form, there can never be this mercilessly critical self-judgment of man. It is the self-judgment of the Christian man, and the Christian man alone. It is impossible, however, that love for the Son of Man, who is the Lord over all, should allow the Christian man any other judgment of the human situation ; that it should not exclude absolutely the worthless consolation of a harmonising view. The light of the liberating lordship of the Son of Man, in which he views himself and all men, is what impels him towards, or rather liberates him for, this uncompromisingly sober assessment of the human situation ; the knowledge that in its determination by the meanness and lowliness of man it is an untenable situation. " There is no peace, saith the Lord, unto the wicked " (Is. 48^{22}).

2. THE SLOTH OF MAN

We now turn to the material question : What is sin as seen from the standpoint of the new man introduced in Jesus Christ ? What is the action of the old man overcome in the death of Jesus Christ ? What is the character of this man as he is subsequently revealed in Christ's resurrection, in the light of the divine direction which falls on him from this source ? Our present answer is that the sin of man is the sloth of man. The christological aspect which now occupies us calls for this or a similar term. We might also describe it as sluggishness, indolence, slowness or inertia. What is meant is the evil inaction which is absolutely forbidden and reprehensible but which characterises human sin from the standpoint presupposed in the deliberations of our first sub-section.

There is a heroic, Promethean form of sin. This is brought to light—as the pride of man which not only derives from but is itself his fall—when we consider man in his confrontation with the Lord who humbled Himself and became a servant for him, with the Son of God made flesh. Sin was unmasked as this counter-movement to the divine condescension practised and revealed in Jesus Christ when we reached the corresponding point in the first part of the doctrine of reconciliation. In its unity and totality human sin always has this heroic form, just as, in its unity and totality, the free grace of God addressed to man always has the form of the justification which positively encounters this pride. But as reconciling grace is not merely justifying, but also wholly and utterly sanctifying and awakening and establishing grace, so sin has not merely the heroic form of pride but also, in complete antithesis yet profound correspondence, the quite unheroic and trivial form of sloth. In other words, it has the form, not only of evil action, but also of evil inaction ; not only of the rash arrogance which is forbidden and reprehensible, but also of the tardiness and failure which are equally forbidden and reprehensible. It is also the counter-movement to the elevation which has come to man from God Himself in Jesus Christ.

In Protestantism, and perhaps in Western Christianity generally, there is a temptation to overlook this aspect of the matter and to underestimate its importance. The figure who claims our attention is Prometheus who tries to steal the lightning from Zeus and turn it to his own use : the man who wants to be as God, not a servant but the Lord, his own judge and helper ; man in his hybris as a defiant insurrectionary. We do well to consider this figure, and constantly to realise how powerfully he is contradicted by the grace of God which justifies the sinner and exalts the abased and only the abased ; how decisively he is routed by Jesus Christ, the Son of God, the Lord who became for us a servant. But the man of sin is not simply this insurrectionary, and his sin has more than the heroic form in which (however terrible it may seem to be) we can hardly avoid finding traces of a sombre beauty—the beauty of the Luciferian man. We are missing the real man, not only in the mass but individually, not only in the common herd but in the finest and most outstanding of all times and places, and especially in ourselves, if we try to see and understand his sin consistently and one-sidedly as hybris, as this brilliant perversion of human pride. At a hidden depth it certainly is this brilliant perversion in all of us. But sober observation compels us to state that, as it may be seen and grasped in the overwhelming majority, it has little or nothing of this Luciferian or Promethean brilliance, this sombre beauty ; and that even among those who may be regarded as exceptions there is a hidden depth at which, although they are still sinners, they are not at all insurrectionaries, but something very different and much more primitive, in which sin is merely banal and ugly and loathsome. It gives evidence of a very deficient or, from the Christian standpoint, very unenlightened self-knowledge if we try to deny that, beyond all that we may see and bewail in ourselves as pride, we have also to confess this very different and much more primitive thing in which there is nothing at all even of that doubtful beauty. And is it really " beyond " what we call pride ? Sin may have different dimensions and aspects, but it is a single entity. Ought we not to say, therefore, that this different form is there at the very heart of our pride and forms its final basis ? And yet the connexion between the two forms cannot easily be reduced to a common denominator. We might equally well say that this other, more primitive form has its final basis in human pride. The important thing is that we have every reason closely to scrutinise this second form. If we consider sin only in its first and more impressive form it might easily acquire an unreal and fantastic quality in which we do not recognise the real man whose heart, according to Luther's rendering of Jer. 17⁹, is not merely desperate but also despairing. And the result would be to obscure the concrete point at issue in the sanctification or exaltation of sinful man. The sin of man is not merely heroic in its perversion. It is also—to use again the terms already introduced in the first sub-section—ordinary, trivial and mediocre. The sinner is not merely Prometheus or Lucifer. He is also—and for the sake of clarity, and to match the grossness of the matter, we will use rather popular expressions—a lazy-bones, a sluggard, a good-for-nothing, a slow-coach and a loafer. He does not exist only in an exalted world of evil ; he exists also in a very mean and petty world of evil (and there is a remarkable unity and reciprocity between the two in spite of their apparent antithesis) In the one case, he stands bitterly in need of humiliation ; in the other he stands no less bitterly in need of exaltation. And in both cases the need is in relation to the totality of his life and action. We will gather together what we have to say on this second aspect under the term or concept " sloth."

The forbidden or reprehensible tardiness and failure of man obviously fall under the general definition of sin as disobedience. In face of the divine direction calling him to perform a definite action, man refuses to follow the indication which he is given. Even in this refusal to act, however, and therefore in this inaction, he is involved in a certain action. The idler or loafer does something. For the most part, indeed, what he does is quite considerable and intensive. The only thing is that it does not correspond to the divine direction but is alien and opposed to it. He does not do what God wills, and so he does what God does not will. He is disobedient and he does that which is evil. In all that follows we must keep before us the fact that because sin in its form as sloth seems to have the nature of a vacuum, a mere failure to act, this does not mean that it is a milder or weaker or less potent type of sin than it is in its active form as pride. Even as sloth, sin is plainly disobedience.

Again, this form obviously falls under the even more penetrating definition of sin as unbelief. For the disobedience in which man refuses the divine direction and does positively that which God does not will has its basis in the fact that he does not grasp the promise given him with this direction, but refuses to trust in the One who demonstrates and maintains His faithfulness in this overwhelming way, not claiming his obedience with the severity and coldness of an alien tyrant but as the source of his life, in the majesty and freedom of the love with which He has loved him from all eternity. He hardens himself against the divine benevolence addressed to him in the divine demand. The sloth of man, too, is a form of unbelief.

But we must define the term rather more closely as we use it of human sloth. In its form as man's tardiness and failure, sloth expresses much more clearly than pride the positive and aggressive ingratitude which repays good with evil. It consists in the fact, not only that man does not trust God, but beyond this that he does not love Him, i.e., that he will not know and have Him, that he will not have dealings with Him, as the One who first loved him, from all eternity. In relation to God there is no middle term between love and hate. The man who does not love God resists and avoids the fact that God is the One He is, and that He is this for him. He turns his back on God, rolling himself into a ball like a hedgehog with prickly spikes. At every point, as we shall see, this is the strange inactive action of the slothful man. It may be that this action often assumes the disguise of a tolerant indifference in relation to God. But in fact it is the action of the hate which wants to be free of God, which would prefer that there were no God, or that God were not the One He is— at least for him, the slothful man. This hatred of God is the culminating point of human pride too. The overweening pride of man, which consists in the fact that he wants to be and act as God, may at a pinch be understood—and this is perhaps the reason for its sinister beauty—as a perverse love of God, whose frivolous encroachment and usurpation, whose illegitimate attempt to control its object, do of course culminate in a desire that the object should disappear as such, that there should be no God or that God should not be God, that man should be able to sit unhindered on his throne. But sin as man's subservient and obsequious sloth is from the very outset his desire not to be illuminated by the existence and nature of God, not to have to accept Him, to be without God in the world. The slothful man, who is of course identical with the proud, begins where the other leaves off, i.e., by saying in his heart : " There is no God." This is the characteristic feature of sin, of disobedience, of unbelief, in this second form. It is from this root that all the constitutive elements of human sloth grow.

Sin in the form of sloth crystallises in the rejection of the man Jesus. In relation to Him the rejection of God from which it derives finds virulent and concrete and forceful expression. For it is in Him that the divine direction and summons and claim come to man. It is in Him that the divine decision is made which he will not accept, which he tries to resist and escape. It is to be noted that in the main there is no radical opposition to the idea of God as a higher or supreme being to whom man regards himself as committed, nor to the thought of a beyond, of something which transcends his existence, nor to the demand that he should enter into a more or less conscious or unconscious, binding or non-binding connexion with it. He will never seriously or basically reject altogether religion or piety in one form or another, nor will he finally or totally cease to exercise or practise them in an open or disguised form. On the contrary, an escape to religion, to adoring faith in a congenial higher being, is the purest and ripest and most appropriate possibility at which he grasps in his sloth, and cannot finally cease from grasping as a slothful man. His rejection of God acquires weight and seriousness only when it is made with a final and concentrated piety. But that in this piety it is really a matter of rejecting God, of rendering Him innocuous, emerges clearly in the fact that man definitely will not accept in relation to himself the reality and presence and action of God in the existence of the man Jesus, and the claim of God which they involve. He definitely will not accept them as the reality and presence and action of God which refer absolutely and exclusively and totally and directly to him, and make on him an absolute, exclusive, total and direct demand. As one who worships a higher being, as a religious or pious man, he is able to resist this. It does not matter what name or form he gives to the higher being which he worships; he finds that he is tolerated by it, that far from being questioned and disturbed and seized he is strengthened and confirmed and maintained in equilibrium by it. And he for his part can always show equal toleration to this being— and in this form to " God." It does not cause him any offence, and so he has no need to be offended at it. But he is not tolerated, let alone confirmed, by the reality and presence and action of God in the existence of the man Jesus. He is basically illuminated and radically questioned and disturbed and therefore offended by the deity of God in the concrete phenomenon of the existence of this man. His own tolerance is thus strained to the limit when he has to do with God in this man. His rejection of God finds expression in his relation to this man. Tested in this way, he will unhesitatingly avoid God even as the religious or pious man. But this means that he will unhesitatingly resist God. In his relation to God he will show himself to be the slothful man, turned in upon himself and finding his satisfaction and comfort in his own ego.

Why is it that this is expressed in the rejection of the man Jesus ? The reason is that in this man, as opposed to all the higher beings and transcendencies which he knows to be congenial and to which he may therefore commit himself, he has to do with the true and living God who loved this man, and was His God, from all eternity, and who will love this man, and be His God, to all eternity ; the God whose outstretched hand of promise and preservation, of deliverance and command, has always been, and always will be, the existence of this man. The reason is that what God always gave to all men, what He was and is and will be for them, is simply a demonstration of the free grace which became a historical event in the appearance and work, the dying and rising again, of this man. The God of this man, and therefore concretely this man, offends us. Our sloth rejects Him. In relation to Him it is our great inaction, our hesitation, our withdrawal into ourselves. Man rejects Him because he wants to elect and will himself, and he does not want to be disturbed in this choice. For he is disturbed, and he finds that he is disturbed, by Him ; by the will of God which always has and will have the name of Jesus, which has in this name its unalterable goal and ineffaceable contour. When he comes face to face with the will of God in Him he comes to the frontier which he can cross only if he will give up himself and his congenial dcities and find God and himself in this Other.· At this point he can only protest, for he is not tolerated and therefore he cannot tolerate. He regards it as vitally necessary to be free of this man, i.e., of the God of this man. This is a pious act which he must execute in his reverence for the higher being which does tolerate him. " There is no God " means concretely that there is no God of this kind ; that a God of this kind cannot and may not be.

Why not ? Why is it that human disobedience, unbelief and ingratitude in sloth have this culmination ? Why is the sin of man revealed in this opposition ? Our first and general answer is that it is because in himself and as such man will not live in the distinctive freedom of the man Jesus and is therefore forced to regard this Fellow and Brother as a stranger and interloper, and his existence as an intolerable demand.

He wants to be left alone by the God who has made this man a neighbour with His distinctive freedom, and therefore by this neighbour with His summons to freedom. He regards the renewal of human nature declared in His existence as quite unnecessary. He sees and feels, perhaps, the limitation and imperfection of his present nature, but they do not touch him so deeply that he is not finally satisfied with this nature and the way in which he fulfils it. A serious need, a hunger or thirst for its renewal, is quite foreign to him. He therefore sees no relevance in the man Jesus with His freedom to be a new man.

Again, he thinks he has a sober idea of what is attainable, of what is possible and impossible, within the limits of his humanity. This leads him to question the real significance of this renewal, of man's exaltation. The limited sphere with which he is content seems to him to be his necessary sphere, so that its transcendence in the freedom of the man Jesus is an imaginary work in which he himself can have no part.

Behind the indifference and doubt there is a definite mistrust. In the freedom of the man Jesus it seems that we have a renewal and exaltation from servitude to lordship. But this is an exacting and dangerous business if it necessarily means that we acquire and have in Jesus a Lord, and if His lordship involves that we are demanded to leave our burdensome but comfortable and secure life as slaves and assume responsibility as lords.

Again, if the freedom of the man Jesus as the new and exalted and lordly man has its basis and meaning in the fact that he is the man who lives in fellowship with God, the indifference and doubt and mistrust in which we confront Him have their basis and meaning, or lack of meaning ; in the fact that we regard it as unpractical, difficult and undesirable to live in fellowship with God. A life which moves and circles around itself, which is self-orientated but also self-directed, seems to hold out far greater promise than one which is lived in this fellowship.

It is for this reason that our brother Jesus is a stranger, and His existence among us is an intolerable demand, and the God who is His God is unacceptable. This is, in very general terms, the deployment, or rather the rigid front which human sin presents to Him, and in which it is actual and visible in face of Him, in the form of human sloth.

Why and to what extent is it sin ? The reason is that, as the rejection of the outstretched hand of God, the refusal of His grace, all this means that man neglects his own calling, that he is untrue to his own cause, that with his true reality he goes out into the unreal, into the void, where he cannot stand and be what he wants to be, where he cannot be a man, himself, but only his own shadow. The One who confronts him in the freedom of the man Jesus is not merely this Fellow and Brother as such, nor is it merely the God of this man. It is the God of every man, without whom none either is or can be who he is. And in the person of this Fellow and Brother given him by his own God it is he himself, his own true reality, his own humanity as it is loved and elected and created and preserved by his God in the person of this One. The terrible paradox of his sin in this form is that if he refuses the man Jesus, he does not refuse only this man and His (and therefore his own God) but he also refuses to be himself, breaking free from his own reality, losing himself in his attempt to assert himself, and thus becoming his own pitiful shadow. It is no light thing that man can unthinkingly accomplish when he takes his stand as a denier on this front of human sloth. He becomes and is "man in contradiction" : the man who contradicts God and therefore contradicts and hopelessly jeopardises himself ; the man who would be lost if in this self-contradiction which he achieves he were not confronted, in the man Jesus on whom he stumbles and falls, by the superior contradiction of God, whose will it never was or is or will be that slothful man should perish. We must now develop four main aspects of his mortal refusal of the freedom which he is promised in the man Jesus.

We are confronted by man's refusal (1) in his relationship with God ; (2) in his relationship with his fellow-men ; (3) in his relationship with the created order ; and (4) in his relationship with his historical limitation in time. These are the same four groups in which, in the light of the true humanity of Jesus Christ, we developed the doctrine of man as the creature of God (*C.D.*, III, 2) and, in the first part of theological ethics, the doctrine of the command of God the Creator (*C.D.*, III, 4). Again in the light of the *humanitas Jesu Christi*, we are now considering the sin of man in the form of his sloth, and therefore his refusal of his own reality as it confronts him in Jesus Christ. For all its varied character, this refusal constitutes a single inter-related and connected whole. We will thus turn our attention specifically to each of the relationships in turn, but we shall always look either forwards or backwards, as the case may be, to see how far his refusal in one of these relationships necessarily includes, presupposes and involves it in the other three.

1. The Word—God's eternal Word—became flesh. In the existence of the man Jesus it was and is spoken in human form to us men. It is with this Word, which was and is this man Himself, that we have to do in Him : proclaimed in and with what He was and spoke and did and suffered in His history ; proclaimed as He died on the cross ; proclaimed as He lives and reigns as the Crucified. It was and is His royal freedom to be as man the perfect hearer of God ; the One who knows God perfectly, and therefore the perfect servant and witness and teacher of God ; the light of God shining in the world for us ; the revelation in which He disclosed and discloses Himself to us and us to Himself ; both ear and mouth for the wisdom and purpose and plan and meaning of His omnipotent mercy ; sagacious and therefore able and equipped to make us wise and sagacious. Among all other men, as one of us, but exalted above us, and therefore the divine direction to us, He was and is the One who fulfils and brings and establishes the knowledge of God and His existence and nature and work, His presence and action. Nor is this knowledge which He fulfils and brings and establishes a superfluous or idle or partial or uncertain knowledge. On the contrary, it is universally relevant and indispensable, vital and active, total and firm and sure. It is to be grateful participants in this knowledge of God which He has fulfilled and disclosed and established on our behalf among us, so that we ourselves should be wise in virtue of His wisdom, that we are elected and created and determined in Him.

But we on whose behalf, for whose enlightenment and information and instruction, He has this freedom, refrain from making use of this freedom which is also, and precisely, our own freedom. The clear light of day has come, but we close our eyes and persist in the darkness which has been penetrated and dispersed in Him. We harden ourselves in our unreason, our ignorance of God, our lack of wisdom, our folly and stupidity. And this refusal to move where we can and should bestir ourselves and follow Him is the unreason and ignorance which makes us the stupid fools we are. This is the folly in which we want to remain as we are instead of being those we are in Him and by Him.

It belongs to the vanity of this human refusal and failure to budge that it is finally and objectively futile. That is to say, it cannot alter in the least what the man Jesus is for us and for all men in the freedom of His knowledge of God. Our refusal cannot make the Word of God spoken in Him an unspoken Word, nor can it kill His life nor silence His proclamation. It cannot conceal, let alone quench, His light, nor arrest His revelation, nor destroy His direction, nor dam up the stream of the knowledge of God of which He is the source. It is paradoxical and absurd, but it cannot cancel the fact of the new man Jesus who has a vital and active and total and sure and certain knowledge of God. It cannot control the fire which He came to kindle on earth. In face of Him it can be only the sloth of man—his puerility, his senility, his mediocrity. It cannot alter the fact, therefore, that in this one man all other men—even the most untaught and unteachable amongst countless thousands who are yet untaught—are elected and determined to be taught about God. I may close my eyes, I may shut them as tight as I can, or I may turn away from the sun, but this does not alter the fact that the sun shines on me too, and that I have eyes to see it. I may try to cease or refuse to be the man I am in that one new man, but I cannot in fact cease to be this man. Evading the knowledge of God, I may contradict myself. It is my folly that I do this. But in my folly I can only contradict myself. I can no more destroy myself than I can the light of the man Jesus in which I exist. My self-contradiction cannot touch the fact that in Him I am known by God even in my evil ignorance of God. It cannot set aside the reality in which I live by this divine knowing. As my proud attempt to be like God is futile, because this is quite impossible, so too is the slothful refusal in which I am content to be without God in the world, because He who has revealed Himself and acted in Jesus as the God of man, of every man, and therefore as my God, will not be God without me, so that even in the most secret recesses of this world I for my part can never be without Him, outside His light, without the eyes with which I may and should see Him, with which I am elected and determined to see Him as the fellow and brother of this One. The outcome of my refusal can be only another refusal, or the revelation of a refusal—the demonstration of the futility of my remaining at a place which does not exist. I cannot in fact remain alone. I can try to do so. And in so doing I can, and do, create a reality. But this reality is from the very outset a limited reality. It is a reality of the second—and inwardly and materially an inferior—degree. It is a reality which is condemned as such to failure. My folly can only reveal and express my sin and shame.

We do have to do, however, with this reality of the second degree, with the sin and shame (however limited) of the folly in which we make no use of the freedom which we are given in Jesus. The inner futility of human sloth, like the impotence of human pride, does not alter the fact that it does actually take place as a form of human corruption. It is a fact. Its character is purely negative. It is not necessary or genuine or, in the strict sense, possible. It is only impossible. It has no true basis. It cannot be deduced or explained or excused or justified. But it is still a fact. It is a fact in the whole futility in which it is created and posited. It is not, therefore, nothing. It is something. It is the something of our persistence in turning to that which is not, to that which God has not willed but denied and rejected. It is the something of our ignorance of God and therefore our self-contradiction. Man does actually will the impossible. He does actually will not to know God as he might and should know Him thanks to the freedom in which the man Jesus does so for him, in the bright light of the existence of this Fellow and Brother. And his thoughts and attitudes and actions express this non-willing, this refusal. He sets himself in mortal self-contradiction. This does not mean that he can set aside his Fellow and Brother Jesus, and his own reality as established in Him. All that he can do is to make himself impossible. And even this " ability " is as baseless as the nothingness to which he wills to turn in this non-willing. Yet he does will it, and in this will which is opposed to the good will of God he creates a fact and lives in it. He does not live as a wise man, but as a stupid fool.

We are thus forced to the rather unusual and hazardous statement that sin is also stupidity, and stupidity is also sin. By stupidity we mean, of course, that which the Bible describes and condemns as human folly. Of this it cannot be said that man would at once leave it if he were better informed. It cannot be advanced as an excuse or mitigation of man's corresponding thoughts and words and attitudes and actions. It is not just an unfortunate weakness, a vexatious drawback, which can be partially or totally removed by education and enlightenment, and which has perhaps to be suffered with tolerance and equanimity, and compensated by other and better qualities. It is the evil act of man ; of the whole man. Or better—for we have here the basic dimension of his sloth—it is his inaction, his responsible and culpable refusal to act.

When the Bible speaks of the *nabal* or *kesil*, as, for example, of those who say in their hearts that there is no God (Ps. 14[1]), there can be no question of any lack of intellectual endowment, or of powers of thought and comprehension, or of the erudition which we both need and desire. The biblical dolt or fool may be just as carefully taught and instructed as the average man at any particular cultural level. He may be below the average, but he may also be above it, and even high above it. What makes him a fool has nothing whatever to do with a feebler mind or a less perfectly attained culture or scholarship. It is not in any sense a fate. Those who have only weak intellectual gifts and a rudimentary scholastic equipment—the " uneducated "—are not necessarily fools as the Bible uses the word. We have only to think of the *νήπιοι* of Mt. 11²⁵ to realise that they may very well be wise. In the biblical sense a man is a fool or simpleton when (whatever may be his talents or attainments) he thinks that he has no need of enlightenment by the revelation and Word of God ; that he ought, indeed, to oppose it ; and that he can live his life on the basis of the resultant vacuum, and therefore by the norm of maxims and motives which are perverted from the very outset—on a false presupposition and therefore by a false method.

Anselm of Canterbury was quite right when, introducing the denier of God's existence of Ps. 14¹ at the beginning of his proof of the existence of God (*Prosl.* 2), he did not describe him as *ignorans* but as *insipiens* (=*insapiens*). His objection, which Anselm discusses, is that God is not a real object, but only one which we think or can think ; that He is not a *res*, and therefore does not exist : *non est Deus*. He does not think and speak in this way because he is limited or uneducated. He does so because of a fundamental lack which consists in the fact that he is not an *intelligens id quod Deus est* (*Prosl.* 4). · He does so because of his lack of understanding, grounded in his unbelief, of the revealed name of God, in virtue of which God is *quo maius cogitari nequit*. Anselm opened his own argument with a confession of his faith in God as the One who bears this name (the name of the Creator above which no legitimate thinking can exalt itself, but from which it can only derive). His enquiry and demonstration have reference to the knowledge of this faith, which necessarily includes the knowledge of the existence of God. They are evoked and stimulated by the objection of the denier, but it is obvious that the latter can have no part in the ensuing discussion. For he thinks and speaks as *insipiens*, and therefore from the point where he does not know, and as an unbeliever cannot know, the One whose existence he questions. This is his folly in which he excludes himself from the outset from the knowledge of God's existence. And it is in answer to his folly that Anselm deliberately proves that, presupposing the understanding of His revealed name, God's existence *cannot* be questioned. What a misapprehension it was that the good Gaunilo found it necessary to rush to the help of the atheist with the defence, *Pro insipiente* : as though his denial, deriving as it does from his folly, and denying what he does not know and understand, could still be championed and discussed ; as though, proceeding from stupidity, it could be anything else but stupid.

We have to realise that as the basic dimension of human sloth stupidity is sin. It is disobedience, unbelief and ingratitude to God, who gives Himself to be known by man in order that he may be wise and live. It is thus a culpable relapse into self-contradiction ; into incoherent, confused and corrupt thought and speech and action. We have to realise this if we are to estimate its power ; the strange but mighty and tumultuous and dreadful force of the role—the leading role—which it plays in world history, in every sphere of human life, and either secretly or flagrantly in each individual life. Whether great or small, every confidence or trust or self-reliance on what we can, and think we should, say to ourselves when we reason apart from the Word of God is stupid. Every attitude in which we think we can authoritatively tell ourselves what is true and good and beautiful, what is right and necessary and salutary, is stupid. All thought and speech and action which we think we can and should base on this information is stupid. And this whole frame of mind is self-evidently, and even more acutely, stupid in the form in which we think we have so heard the Word of God, and so appropriated its direction and wisdom in the guise of a principle or system, that we have no need to hear or practise it afresh ; in the form, therefore, in which we regard ourselves as so enlightened by the Word of God that we think we can throw off our openness to further and continuous instruction. Where an uncontrolled truth or rule, however clear, possesses man or men in the way in which they ought to be governed only in the knowledge of God Himself and by His living Word, we certainly have to do with a revelation, and in principle with the whole economy, of stupidity. And where men think they have a goodness which is assured, not in the active fulfilment of their knowledge of God but in itself, and try to live and act and assert themselves as good in this sense, this is not merely the self-righteousness in which faith is denied but also the stupidity which is forbidden by the Word of God and which wastes and destroys all the goodness that is really given. When Adam and Eve were not content with the Word and commandment of God, but wanted to know for themselves what is good and evil, this was disobedience, but it was also a step into the stupidity which cannot and never will know what is good and evil, but will always exchange and confuse them. And there is a deeper meaning in the common expression that for all his devilish cleverness and cunning the devil is finally stupid. This is inevitable when he is obviously the *insipiens* in principle, the personification of ignorance of God and the corresponding independence and autonomy in face of Him.

The stupidity of man consists and expresses itself in the fact that when he is of the opinion that he achieves his true nature and essence apart from the knowledge of God, without hearing and obeying His Word, in this independence and autonomy, he always misses his true nature and essence. He is always either too soon or too late. He is asleep when he should be awake, and awake when he should be asleep. He is silent when he should speak, and he speaks when it is better to be silent. He laughs when he should weep, and he weeps when he should be comforted and laugh. He always makes an exception where the rule should be kept, and subjects himself to a law when he should choose in freedom. He always toils when he should pray, and prays when only work is of any avail. He always devotes himself to historical and psychological investigation when decisions are demanded, and rushes into decision when historical and psychological investigation is really required. He is always contentious where it is unnecessary and harmful, and he speaks of love and peace where he may confidently attack. He is always speaking of faith and the Gospel where what is needed is a little sound commonsense, and he reasons where he can and should commit himself and others quietly into the hands of God. In Eccl. 3 we are given a list of different things for which there is a proper time—in accordance with the fact that God Himself does everything in its own time. The genius of stupidity is to think everything at the wrong time, to say everything to the wrong people, to do everything in the wrong direction, to lose no opportunity of misunderstanding and being misunderstood, always to omit the one simple and necessary thing which is demanded, and to have a sure instinct for choosing and willing and doing the complicated and superfluous thing which can only disrupt and obstruct.

Again we have to realise that stupidity is sin if we are to estimate the dangerous nature of its power. Its very character betrays how dangerous it is to life and society, to state and Church. Like the demons, and as one of the most remarkable forms of the demonic, stupidity has an astonishingly autonomous life against whose expansions and evolutions there is no adequate safeguard. It has rightly been said that even the gods are powerless in face of it. And it is in vain that we appeal to many gods to counter it. We may meet it in righteous anger, or with ironical contempt. We may play the schoolmaster. We may try to overcome it by approximation or advances. We may try to use it, to harness it for better ends. But even when we are trying to overcome it in ourselves, to liberate ourselves from it, we must always be on the watch lest we merely augment stupidity with stupidity, either secretly or openly giving it place and nourishment, and being only the more completely overrun by it as we seek to encounter it.

It is particularly and supremely dangerous because it has an uncanny quality of being able to attract, to magnetise and thus to increase. The folly of one seems irresistibly to awaken that of another or others : whether in the form of mutual boasting or sinister collusion, of cold or hot warfare or the formation of massive collectives and majorities which trample down all opposition like a herd of elephants ; or even more dangerously by an inward process, in the form of winning others, of begetting children, and of acquiring fresh vitality in them. It is also dangerous in the fact that we do not usually recognise it (or only when it is too late) as the beam in our own eye, our own stupidity, so that in our unconcerned and self-conscious pandering to it we only help it to gain a greater hold on others. It is also dangerous because it is only very seldom, and probably never, that we see it unmasked and undisguised and unadorned. It normally takes, as we shall see later, the form of its opposite, of a superior cleverness and correctness, or even of an excess of noble feeling. For how sure and quick and persistent it is in finding and building up reasons for what it thinks and maintains and does and impels to do ! With what assurance it always presupposes that it is right, and has always known better (" What did I tell you ? ") ! How it loves to make itself out to be either the pillar of society or the sacred force of revolutionary renewal ! How powerfully (in contradiction or agreement with the form in which it encounters one in others) it can strengthen and deepen and advance itself by itself, continually preparing for, and embarking upon, fresh adventures of basic inactivity ! It is also dangerous because at a first glance it is so innocuous, so kindly disposed, so familiar, knowing how to awaken tolerance or a pardoning sympathy or even a certain recognition, but concealing somewhere, and probably behind its probity and gentleness (like the claws of the feline species behind their soft pads), the supreme malice and aggressiveness and violence which will pounce on a victim and tear it to pieces before it is even aware of them.

But what is the value of marking its symptoms and warning against their particular dangers ? It is not merely in its symptoms and fruits but in its root that stupidity is sin ; nor is it merely because the symptoms and fruits are dangerous, but by reason of its root that stupidity as sin means destruction. It is from its root that the stupid action of man is sin, and that it is dangerous as such. But it is only from its root. There is thus no point in seeing it in its stupidity, and being on our guard against it, if we do not know the root which makes it sin and therefore dangerous. At its root it is the perverted action of that great omission which Paul described in 1 Cor. 15³⁴ as the ἀγνωσία θεοῦ, man's evil and culpable and irresponsible failure to know God. Anselm was right when he regarded even the stupid confession in his heart of the fool of Ps. 14¹ (" There is no God ") as only one of the symptoms and fruits of his folly, and pointed beyond this confession to its root in his true atheism, which consists in this wicked ignorance of God. The really stupid element in his stupidity, the true atheism of the fool which comes to light in that stupid confession and all the other symptoms and fruits, is not his theoretical but his practical atheism. It is only seldom, and seldom explicitly or definitively, that he comes to the point of theoretical rejection. He may regard it as unnecessary and even be opposed to it without being any the less an atheist in practice. There is a whole ocean of religious and even Christian stupidity, and those who swim in it always do so as those who are religious and even Christians. But practical atheism, of which the wise man will know and confess that he is no less guilty than the fool, and therefore human stupidity at its root consists in the fact that God is revealed to man but that man will not accept the fact in practice ; that in the knowledge of God, in the clear light of His reality, presence and action, he is radically known by God but refuses and fails to know God in return and to exist in this knowledge ; that he lets himself fall as one who is already lifted up by God and to God. It is this letting oneself fall—a process in which we are all implicated—that is the really stupid element in our stupidity, whether or not it is accompanied by theoretical atheism on the one hand or religion or even Christianity on the other.

But it would not be what it is—the primal phenomenon of sin in one of its most remarkable aspects—if there were any reason and explanation for this process. The stupid and inopportune movements of the fool in which stupidity reveals itself are always relatively explicable. They always have their more or less demonstrable grounds and causes, their active and passive impulses both internal and external, by which they can in large measure be understood. But their root, the stupid element in a fool's stupidity, the sin revealed in what he does and seeks to do, baffles understanding or explanation. There is no reason for it. It derives directly from that which is not, and it consists in a movement towards it. It is simply a fact, *factum brutum*.

We can only say concerning it that he does it. He is free, but makes no use of the fact. He is lifted up, but he lets himself fall. He is in the light and has eyes to see, but he does not see and therefore remains in darkness. He hears, but he does not hear or obey. Why? For what reason? There is neither rhyme nor reason. It is simply a fact. To try to find a reason for it is simply to show that we do not realise that we are talking of the evil which is simply evil.

Of all the symptoms there is only one—a very striking one—which points with any clarity to the depths of primitive stupidity from which stupidity derives. This is the fact that it always appears and acts in disguise. Who has ever seen it gape, even in his own heart, as it would necessarily gape if it were seen and known openly and directly for what it is? What fool will ever confess his own folly, his ἀγνωσία θεοῦ, his practical atheism, the fact that he lets himself fall? The moment we admit our folly, have we not become truly wise? Even the theoretical atheist, who is only one species of the practical, will not and cannot openly declare his folly, because he does not and will not know whom and what he denies. How, then, can he ever confess his folly? What is the reason for this shyness? Why is it that no one will allow that he is stupid? Why is this impossible? Why does stupidity always appear in disguise, in an incognito, anonymously or pseudonymously? The obvious explanation is that in the depth where he is a fool man knows that his folly derives from that which is not and consists in his movement towards it. He cannot see what is wrong, but he has instinctive awareness like a blind man who is groping towards an abyss. He is frightened to confess, or to be told or accused, that he himself belongs to that which is not. He is on the point of realising it, but he will not accept it. Nor is it really true. He does not belong to nothingness. Even in and in spite of his folly he belongs to God and is the good creature of God. How, then, can he accept and confess that this is not the case? May it not even be that the God whom he does not know, but who knows and does not cease to know him, keeps him back from this and makes it impossible, that the fact that he has this awareness and is frightened is the work of His gracious hand? This will, of course, only turn to his judgment, to which, in his attempts at concealment, he will react in the most perverse and perverted way.

However that may be, the folly of the fool shuns the light. It does not want to be known as such. And it hides itself with a sure instinct and touch in its opposite. It pretends to be wisdom. Not, of course, the wisdom whose beginning is the fear of the Lord. Only the fool who is converted from his folly, from his ignorance of God, will be prepared in a profound horror at himself to accept this wisdom, to humble himself before it, to be clothed by it and to take refuge in it. When this happens, he will not pretend to be a wise man, but exercise and reveal his true wisdom by the fact that—in the fear of the Lord—

he confesses his folly and in his folly cleaves wholly to the wisdom of
God. We are now speaking of the unconverted fool who does not
know the Lord and the fear of the Lord and necessarily lacks the wisdom
which begins with this fear. How can he confess his folly? Is it not
inevitable that he should deny and conceal it? And how else conceal
it but with what he regards as wisdom—his own wisdom, what Paul
in 1 Cor. 1[20] calls the " wisdom of the world " or in 1 Cor. 2[5] the
" wisdom of men " ? We might define this theoretically and generally
as the fulness of all the knowledge of truth and reality and experience
accessible to man minus the knowledge of God in His revealed Word.
Practically and in detail it will never appear in its fulness, but only
in an excerpt, in a particular form, in the realisation of one of many
possibilities. Within the framework or brackets of this minus, it may
be either a rather limited or a very imposing matter. It may take
either the modest form of the self-assertion of sound commonsense or
the prouder guise of an inspired profundity of thought. It may affect
a childlike merriness or a deeper melancholy. It may have the appearance either of scepticism or of the ripe wisdom of old age. It may be
academic, or æsthetic, or definitely moral, or non-moral, or even
political. And because even in his folly man is always the good
creature of God it is inevitable that in all its forms, even the most
primitive and suspect, his own wisdom, or what he regards as such,
should exhibit positively significant and impressive elements and
aspects which enable it to commend itself both to him and to others.
The wisdom of the world or of men is not, therefore, something which
we must rate too low. In many cases it may have a very high value.
It is never simply and unequivocally devilish. Within its limits, it
is often worthy of the most serious respect.

In its own way it may even have exemplary significance for those who are
truly wise—for Christians. When he described it as he did, Paul clearly indicated
its limits. It was the wisdom of the (passing) æon (1 Cor. 2[6] and 3[18]). But the
same Paul had no hesitation (in Phil. 4[8]) in giving to his exhortation to Christians
a form which in terminology might well have been the worldly wisdom of a Stoic
teacher of his day. They were to consider and ponder (λογίζεσθαι) " whatsoever
things are true, whatsoever things are honest, whatsoever things are just, whatsoever things are pure, whatsoever things are lovely, whatsoever things are of
good report." And this comes immediately after the saying about the peace of
God which commands and encloses their understanding like a wall, keeping their
hearts and minds through Christ Jesus. Again, in Lk. 16[8] we read that the
Lord Himself praised the " unjust " steward, or his worldly skill, concluding
that the children of this æon are in their generation (on their own level or in
their own sphere) wiser than the children of light are in theirs.

The worldly wisdom which conceals human stupidity can hardly
ever be effectively attacked and unmasked and overcome in a direct
encounter. In virtue of the qualities or excellencies which cannot be
denied to it in its own sphere, it is in a real position to serve as a
covering, to provide an alibi, for stupidity. The fact is that (in this

as in all its forms) sin profits by the goodness of the divine creation
in which even the godless and foolish man does not cease to participate.
In this pseudo-wisdom it is not, therefore, necessarily or certainly or
exclusively a case of pure pretence. Bracketed by that minus, there
are probably in most cases many things that are in a higher or lower
degree beautiful and true and good, or at any rate incontestable,
behind which the fool can find solid cover, and in the development of
which he can have the satisfaction of a good conscience and even make
an impression on his fellow-creatures. If he is not unsettled by the
knowledge of God, how can he even be aware of the fact that his
witness is actually deployed within this bracket ? How can he fail
to find comfort and even joy in the fact that within this bracket he is
doing his relative best with more or less zeal and success ?—especially
when in so doing he finds himself in the helpful company not merely
of the overwhelming majority but at bottom of all his fellow-men, in
whom we find other forms of exactly the same process of concealment
as that in which he himself lives. It may well be that within this
company it is inevitable that there should be constant friction and
collision between the different forms of worldly wisdom ; that mutual
animosity and depreciation and even conflict should be the order of
the day in the most violent of subterranean and global hostilities.
This does not alter the fact that as a fool man finds that he has the
inestimable advantage of being able to march in rank and step with
countless thousands of his fellows. For at bottom all fools understand each other very well, because the norm or standard of the
different wisdoms of the world behind which they conceal their stupidity
is always the same within this bracket for all the differences in detail.
Thus, although they may and necessarily do fight amongst themselves
in the most devastating way, yet in some way and at some point they
can always come to terms, and they often do so with astonishing
suddenness if seldom with any permanence, as in the case of Pilate
and Herod in Lk. 23¹². In the fact that they all try to take into
their own hands control of the good creation of God and the affairs
of men as if they belonged to them, and negatively in the fact that the
wisdom deployed and exercised by them never begins with the knowledge and fear of the Lord, they are all united in spite of their differences in other respects, and at bottom there can and will be mutual
understanding and mutual confirmation. This is infallibly revealed
and operative when they suddenly come up against the question
whether, for all its advantages and excellencies, the wisdom which
they deploy in some form within this framework is or can be genuine
wisdom ; or against the protest that they are abusing the good creation
of God ; or against the demand that prior to anything else this framework should be broken, this bracket with the presupposed minus dissolved, the whole purpose and character which is the mark of the
evolution of worldly wisdom abandoned, and the knowledge and fear

of God given their contested right as the true basis and beginning of wisdom. The trouble is that this question, protest and demand are perhaps encountered only in the unauthentic form of the pride of an ill-advised and at bottom worldly-wise Christianity in face of which they find themselves justified in the human sense and therefore grow all the more obdurate.

Who can say whether it was not due to his encounter with an ill-advised Christianity that the great Goethe took such offence at the saying in 1 Cor. 3$^{18f.}$ (" Let no man deceive himself. If any man among you seemeth to be wise in this world, let him become a fool, that he may be wise. For the wisdom of this world is foolishness with God ")—even arguing that life would not be worth living if this were true. It may well be, of course, that he would not have accepted the saying from a better advised Christianity. We can only say that as far as he himself is concerned he now knows better.

There can be no doubt that in spite of their divergence all the unfolding wisdoms of the world—even those within an ill-informed or better informed Christianity—attain mutual recognition and practical unity in the fact that they cannot admit that question, protest and demand, preferring every kind of compromise or settlement amongst themselves to surrender on this point. And this agreement always involves a further enhancing and intensifying of their activity as concealments—the one great concealment—of what man wills to be and do, or rather not to be and do, not to admit and confess that he is and does, a fool who commits folly. Nothing is more tempting at this point than to turn the tables, to represent that ignored and rejected wisdom of God as folly, as stupid, ridiculous, contemptible and even dangerous from the point of view of what he regards as wisdom, so that it can only be hated and contested. Without realising what is really taking place, he will again find that he is not tolerated, and therefore cannot tolerate. He will see and feel the point of the sword which according to Mt. 10^{34} Jesus came to bring on earth, and he will try to protect himself against this threat with an energy which far surpasses the violence of all the internecine conflicts of different human wisdoms. What he does not really like and would rather ignore, what can only be the object of his unconcern and passive resistance—the knowledge of God—will always appear to be irrational and nonsensical when in some form it comes, as it may suddenly do to anyone, with its insistent summons. In face of it he can only defend to the death his own stupidity, the great minus within whose sign he thinks he can and should be wise, as that which is truly rational. The wisdom of God, the cross of Christ (1 Cor. 1^{18}), is foolishness as he sees it. So much the better if he can feel justified in this view by reason of the pride of an ill-advised Christianity which in face of him regards itself *per nefas* as the wisdom of God. But even if it were set before him in the greatest humility by an angel of God, he would be adept at finding it quite incredible, regarding and expounding and defaming it as irrational nonsense, and belligerently maintaining his own wisdom in face of it. He can only evade it in some way, and therefore he will never find himself at a loss for ways and means to do this, maintaining that he himself is wise. And because in so doing he makes use of the good gifts of God Himself, he will always be relatively successful in escaping the knowledge of God, in maintaining and securing the incognito of his stupidity, in causing it to illuminate himself and others as true wisdom. His success can be only relative because the good gifts of God are neither ordained nor adapted to authorise or empower man in an absolute opposition to their Giver, and therefore to be used as the means of this concealment. But there is undoubtedly a relative success, and it is strong enough to create a fact which can be removed only by God's own Word and Holy Spirit.

Yet even the most effective concealment cannot alter the fact that the fundamental stupidity of man, hidden behind his supposed wisdom, is revealed as such on every hand. He may pretend that he knows God well, and try to be wise under the sign of this minus. But he cannot do so without serious consequences.

In and with the knowledge of God he necessarily loses (1) the relationship which gives to his existence the character of humanity—his relationship to his fellow-men. It is God who guarantees this relationship. Its order has its basis in that of his relationship to God. Without this it cannot be maintained. The knowledge of the divine Other by whom he is confronted, and therefore the knowledge that this Other is the triune and not a lonely God, is the indispensable presupposition of the necessity, dignity, promise and claim of the other who also confronts him in the form of man. But the fool lacks this knowledge. He tries to evade it. It is foolishness to him. He thinks that he can replace it by his own better wisdom. How, then, can he have the further knowledge to which it gives rise ? If God is dispensable, so is his neighbour. If he prefers his own society to fellowship with God, he will also prefer it to the company of his fellows. If he tries to keep God at a distance, he will do so all the more emphatically in the case of his equals. Who is to prevent him ? And conversely, how can the problematic being of his equals, his fellow-men, cause him to seek himself only in the encounter, fellowship and partnership of I and Thou, if God does not do so ? How can man seek and find his brother in man if he will not allow God to be his Father ? The necessary consequence of vertical self-withdrawal is horizontal self-withdrawal and isolation. It is possible, and it will indeed take place, that he may need another man, and claim him, and try to exercise a far-reaching control over him. But this does not involve a genuine fellow-humanity. It does not mean that the one sees and understands the other as a man, or that he accepts him as his ordained companion and helper, and himself as his. On the contrary, it means a radical superiority over him, an emancipation from him which because it has the character of a needing, claiming and controlling in which the other may not readily acquiesce, necessarily has, and will sooner or later reveal, the character of opposition to and conflict with him. The solitary man is the potential, and in a more refined or blatant form the actual, enemy of all others. The outbreak of war between him and them is only a matter of time and occasion, and often enough it will be caused by a ludicrous accident. The stupidity of man, the false estimation of his own (in other respects very worthy and excellent) wisdom, wills that this should be the case, and inevitably calls for it. Without the knowledge of God, which the stupid man despises, there is no meaningful companionship between man and man, no genuine co-operation, no genuine sharing either of joy or sorrow, no true society. But work which is not co-operation is busy indolence. Joy which is not shared is empty amusement. Sorrow which is not shared is oppressive pain. The man who is not the fellow of others is no real man at all. And a society composed of men like this breaks up as soon as it is formed and even as the most zealous attempts are made to build and maintain it. But the stupidity of man calls for this. Even in its noblest forms humanity without the knowledge of God has in it always the seed of discord and inhumanity, and sooner or later this will emerge. From the vacuum where there is no " Glory to God in the highest " even the sincerest longing and loudest shouting for peace on earth will never lead to anything but new divisions. This is the first thing which all the concealment of human folly can never alter.

This vacuum also involves inevitably (2) a dualism between the psychical and physical elements in his being. It is God who guarantees his unity, the whole man as such, who is not just soul and not just body, who does not consist of body and soul as two separate parts, but who is the soul of his body. God has created man in this ordered unity. He pledges its maintenance, so that man's responsibility in relation to this unity and its order has its basis in his responsibility to God. Thus his knowledge of himself in this unity is an expression of his knowledge of the one God, the Lord of heaven and earth, of all invisible and visible reality. If he renounces his responsibility to God and lacks this knowledge, he will also lack that which he can know only as its expression. This does not mean that he will destroy the work of God or himself in this unity. Only God, who has created him in this unity, could do that. But everything that he does of himself (in his folly as it is concealed by his supposed wisdom) will result in a disturbance of this unity, a dualism of the two elements, and a confusion of their relationship. In one of the countless fatal variations which are possible he will then lead a life which is either more abstractly psychical or more abstractly physical. He will live alternately to the spirit and to matter. He will let himself be ruled alternately by his head and by his nerves and appetites. He can never wholly do either. On both sides he will always find himself hampered and contained. On neither side will he be able to escape tension. He will never know peace or satisfaction. He will never have a good conscience. He will always be pressing and pressed from the one to the other. He will never be able to destroy, and never wholly to forget, the order, the super- and sub-ordination, in the unity of his nature. Nor will he ever be able to maintain it. He will never rid himself of the unrest caused by the twofold character of his existence. Or he will do so only by means of strange compromises and hypocrisies between an abstracted higher part of his nature and an abstracted lower, and therefore only in appearance. He will take refuge in an inner world, trying to build up a world of the spirit, in which, to be happy, he must close his eyes to the forces of his physical nature. In face of these forces he will find himself forced to make concessions of which he is basically ashamed—in view of the fact that he is primarily a soul and only then and as such a body. When he seeks this higher level he will always have a desire for the lower, and when he is on the lower he will always be homesick for the higher. He will never be healthy on either. In the depths or on what seem to others remarkable heights he will always be a man of disorder. For he does not know the All-Highest, and therefore he has no true knowledge of the higher and lower levels of his own structure as a human being. He does not understand the norm of their relationship, and therefore he cannot direct himself by it and live as a whole man. His primary folly inexorably entails this secondary folly which cannot be radically amended by even the cleverest of psychical or physical diagnosis and therapy. The injuries which are continually caused can certainly be stated and described, and hints and advice can be given to mitigate them. But the problem of changing the man of disorder into a man of order is the problem of overcoming this vacuum, the primary folly, in which man will not and cannot understand God, and therefore, in spite of every concealment, cannot understand himself and be fit and healthy. This is the second point that has to be made.

Again as a result of the basic failure, and in spite of every concealment, man is inevitably involved (3) in a perverted relationship to the limited temporality of his being. God is the Lord who guarantees the time and times of all individual men. The Yes of God makes both the limited individual time and all time with its beginning and end a time which is filled—filled by His dealings with man, by His call and claim and promise and patience and blessing. This relationship of man to God is the meaning of all his coming and going both individually and *en masse*. It is the meaning of history, of every human past and present and future. Thus the knowledge of God is the presupposition of all man's knowledge of his historicity, i.e., of his being as a being in time and in the limits of time. The loss of the one necessarily carries with it the loss of the other, and therefore of any clarity or certainty in the practice of life in its temporality, in the acceptance of historical responsibility. Whence do we come, and whither do we go, if not from God and to God ? What are we, and what is it that we think and will and do, if this beginning and end of our existence have no interest or relevance for us, and are even quite unknown to us ? What, then, is the meaning of our present ? In what sense is it to be taken seriously by us—yet with a seriousness which is not incompatible with a happy freedom ? In what sense are we continually committed by it, passing courageously through it from yesterday to to-morrow ? What is the meaning of the unique opportunity of the long or short life that we are given ? God is the only answer. He Himself gives and reveals Himself to us as this answer. The folly of the fool may be seen in the fact that this answer has no significance for him because he does not know God. We may each know what great fools we all are by considering how often we are tempted, and how vulnerable we are to the temptation, to regard this answer as without significance. And yesterday becomes to-day, the morning evening, youth old age, and time and its unique opportunity pass, and all that man does is to dream : perhaps of a finer or even more wretched past ; perhaps of a finer or even more wretched future ; perhaps of the possibilities of general or individual progress which he thinks he can advance and experience ; perhaps of its impossibility ; perhaps of a lasting fame that he can secure for his own name, at any rate in the immediate circle of his acquaintances, by his virtues and achievements ; perhaps of supernatural developments beyond this life either of a personal or a cosmic nature. He may even dream as a child does of its games and its little anxieties at school and its dislike of instruction. He may not even dream at all, but sleep a wakeful sleep in which there are neither dreams nor thoughts nor ends,. forgetting himself in more or less ceaseless activity and the satisfactions which he can attain. The wisdom with which he hides the full wretchedness of his plight may consist in the opinion that this is what life is, and in the resigned determination to see it through as bravely as possible, to make the best of it, perhaps with a higher or baser frivolity or the corresponding depression, perhaps with an anxious concern at approaching death or an unthinking forgetfulness. But what is all this if there is nothing more ? Yet if we are fools there is nothing more than this— with accidental or necessary variations. This is the whole fulness of our being in the limits of our temporality. This is the fulness of our history. In the light of our basic folly we will always have too much and too little time. There will never be any content for our time. And for the foolish man world history with its greatness and misery, its marvels and horrors, will be much the same in its own appointed limits, except that everything is now on a greater scale and has therefore an even darker aspect. It is simply a riddle which he may more or less boldly attempt to solve, or more or less boldly despair of solving ; regarding himself either as responsible on the one hand or not responsible on the other. There is no lack of ways—optimistic and pessimistic, sceptical, idealistic and historical, moral and non-moral, highly æsthetic and starkly brutal—in which we may try to conceal this situation, the being in time of the man who cannot understand because he will not know the Lord of time, of his own and all history. But there can be no alteration of this situation by any such concealment. This is the third consequence of this vacuum, of the basic stupidity of man.

This, then, in a first form and aspect, was the man whom God reconciled and seized and exalted to Himself in the man Jesus. Seen and measured by that One, he is this slothful man ; the man who from the standpoint of his own action, or inaction, lets himself fall in this way, and is so stupid, such a fool. God has taken this man to Himself—not in ignorance but with a full awareness of this sin. What God willed and accomplished in the existence of that One was the healing of the sickness from which we all realise that we suffer in the light of that One ; the instruction of the fools that we must all confess ourselves to be. His light shines in the darkness. And if it is true that the darkness has not comprehended it, it is even more true, and a better translation of Jn. 1[5], that the darkness has not overcome it.

The fool or simpleton in his godlessness and thé resultant imprudence and insecurity gives us a very concrete picture, as he is portrayed especially in Proverbs and Ecclesiastes, of the folly which stands in such marked contrast to the divine and practical wisdom of which these two books speak and which is personified in the wise man, the man of prudence and understanding, the man who fears God. We may recall at this point some of the basic traits in the character of the fool. He is the man who trusts in his own understanding (Prov. 28[26]). He does not think it necessary to take advice but thinks that his own way is right (12[15]). He thus gives himself heedlessly to that which is wrong (14[16]). Folly is joy to him (15[21]). He wears it like a crown (14[24]). He proclaims it (12[23]). The awful thing about him is that the speech in which he shows himself to be a fool continually emphasises the fact. His own lips " will swallow up himself. The beginning of the words of his mouth is foolishness : and the end of his talk is mischievous madness " (Eccl. 10[12f.]). He might pass for a wise man if only he would be silent, and for a man of understanding if only he would keep his lips shut (Prov. 17[28]). But he does not do so, and this means that he has a mouth which is " near destruction " (10[14]), for it covers violence (10[11]). Foolishness pours out from it (15[2]). We need to beware of a fool, because he is always meddling (20[3]). His lips bring contention and his mouth provokes blows (18[6]). " If a wise man contendeth with a foolish man, whether he rage or laugh, there is no rest " (29[9]). " A companion of fools shall be broken " (13[20]). " Let a bear robbed of her whelps meet a man, rather than a fool in his folly " (17[12]). There is also an infectious quality in folly. The fool passes on folly as the wise man bequeaths wisdom (14[18]). " A stone is heavy, and the sand weighty ; but a fool's wrath is heavier than them both " (27[3]). It is even worse when he is clever. As " the legs of the lame are not equal "—or " as a thorn goeth up into the hand of a drunkard, so is a parable in the mouth of fools " (26[7, 9]). Even his prayer is an abomination (28[9]). Can we do nothing for him ? Can he not improve himself ? No, " as a dog returneth to his vomit, so a fool iterateth his folly " (26[11]). " Though thou shouldest bray a fool in a mortar among wheat with a pestle, yet will not his foolishness depart from him " (27²²). For his heart is corrupt (15⁷). He will die in his lack of understanding (10²¹). He will always be a fool, for he cannot and will not receive admonition (12¹).

Who is this fool of the wisdom literature ? There can be no doubt that its authors have in mind specific individuals or groups. They are thinking of certain signs of decadence in the society of later Judaism. The reference is to concrete situations. Not all those whom they addressed were guilty of all the individual follies indicated—disobedience to parents, sexual and economic dissipation, drunkenness, blatant hardness of heart, bloodthirstiness, raillery, etc. We also misunderstand these proverbs if we expound them with reference to a recognisable group, an unpleasant stratum or party, that of " fools," which can be differentiated from the opposing group or stratum or party of the wise, and accused and condemned. The sign of decadence to which the term " fool " has reference is basically a characteristic of the whole life of Israel in its later stages. It applies virtually and even actually to all its members. And in the last resort it is a characteristic of the life of all men. " Therefore the Lord will cut off from Israel head and tail, branch and rush, in one day . . . for everyone is an hypocrite and an evildoer, and every mouth speaketh folly," is what we are told concerning Northern Israel in Is. 9¹⁴, ¹⁷ ; and in a condemnation of idolatry in Jer. 10⁸, ¹⁴ the same is said concerning the Gentiles : " But they are altogether brutish and foolish : the stock is a doctrine of vanities. . . . Every man is brutish in his knowledge." It is also to be noted how in Rom. 3¹⁰ᶠ· Paul quotes from the context of the saying in Ps. 14¹ about the man who denies God : " They are corrupt, they have done abominable works, there is none that doeth good. The Lord looked down from heaven upon the children of men, to see if there were any that did understand, and seek God. They are all gone aside, they are all together become filthy : there is none that doeth good, no, not one " (Ps. 14¹⁻³, cf. Ps. 53²ᶠ·). This is why even the righteous man (not the godless) has to confess (Ps. 69⁵) : " O God, thou knowest my foolishness," and (Ps. 73²²) : " So foolish was I, and ignorant : I was as a beast before thee "—although he can then continue : " Nevertheless I am continually with thee : thou hast holden me by the right hand." Folly even extends to the heart of the child (Prov. 22¹⁵), and the rod of affliction which is to drive it from him has much wider and deeper reference than to corporal punishment and other pedagogic measures. In Eccl. 9³ we read that " the heart of the sons of men is full of evil, and madness is in their heart while they live, and after that they go to the dead." If this is the case, the folly envisaged in these writings does not refer—for all the concreteness of its manifestations—only to specific individuals as opposed to others who are superior and unaffected. It is not just the affair of a group. It is a determination under which the wise and clever who understand and seek after God, while they are certainly distinguished from the fools and simpletons who do not understand and do not seek after God, are also united with them, because the latter are at the very place from which they themselves have come and continually come, from which they have constantly to break away, at which they would spend their whole lives were it not given to them—and this is what makes them wise—by the omnipotent Word of God, which liberates them for knowledge, to break away from it, to turn their back on their folly ; so that they too have need always to be recalled, and to recall themselves, by these proverbs. Folly is something which concerns Israel—for when was Israel not addressed by the prophets as a foolish people in its relationship to God ? It is also something which concerns the nations who come under the light of the history of Israel, i.e., of the God who rules Israel. It is the concern of every man as he is revealed in the divine judgment. This picture of the fool is the mirror of the merited rejection held out to all men—a rejection from which there is no escape except by the gracious election of God, by the mighty Word of God which calls and chides. Thus the unfolding of this picture involves the call to decision as it has been heard, and must be continually heard, by the wise man, and as he loves to hear it. Who is the wise man but the fool of yesterday who will also be the fool of to-day and to-morrow without a fresh issue of this summons and fresh obedience ? And who is the fool but the man who is summoned by the Word of God to be the wise man of to-day and to-morrow ? Even the fool who is incorrigible as such is man before God—or, rather, man in the history in which God is about to fulfil and realise His covenant with him, the covenant which he himself has broken but God has kept. The picture of the fool shows with pitiless clarity where it is that man comes from, who and what he is there where he does not seek but is found by God, and who and what he would remain if he were not found by God. No wise man will obviously see fools except as they are seen in the wisdom literature. None will fail to take with absolute seriousness their godlessness and their consequent imprudence and insecurity. On the other hand, it is not a wise man, but only a fool, who will not remember that God is also the God of the fool, and only as such the God of the wise ; who will therefore only contrast himself with the fool, and not admit his solidarity with him, and speak about him and to him in this solidarity. The picture of the fool in the Book of Proverbs is not an invitation to this unwise wisdom. The Book of Ecclesiastes can and must also be regarded as a warning against this misunderstanding of Proverbs. Particular attention must be paid in this respect to the remarkable passage in Eccl. 7[16-18] : " Be not righteous over much ; neither make thyself over wise : why shouldest thou destroy thyself ? Be not over much wicked, neither be thou foolish : why shouldest thou die before thy time ? It is good that thou shouldest take hold of this ; yea, also from this withdraw not thine hand : for he that feareth God shall come forth of them all." But even in the Book of Proverbs itself we have to take note of the surprising words of Agur the son of Jakeh (30[2f.]) : " Surely I am more brutish than any man, and have not the understanding of a man. I neither learned wisdom, nor have the knowledge of the holy. Who hath ascended up into heaven, or descended ? who hath gathered the wind in his fists ? who hath bound the waters in his garment ? who hath established all the ends of the earth ? what is his name, and what is his son's name, if thou canst tell ? " There can be no doubt that it is a wise man who puts these questions. But there can also be no doubt that it is one who is wise in the fact that in and with these questions concerning God he ranges himself with the fool, acknowledging himself to be a fool. Is he wise all the same, and able and called to teach the fool wisdom ? This is undoubtedly the case, for in vv. 5 f. he is given and gives himself the answer : " Every word of God is pure : he is a shield unto them that put their trust in him. Add thou not unto his words, lest he reprove thee, and thou be found a liar."

It is of a piece with this—with the required modesty with which alone the wise man, if he is to be truly wise, can look upon (and not therefore look down upon) the fool—that in Mt. 5[22] the address μωρέ, thou fool, is forbidden on the severest penalties as a term of reproach directly and personally flung by one man at another. It is, indeed, the most terrible form of what Jesus describes as " murder " in exposition of the Old Testament commandment. It does, of course, occur several times in the New Testament in the context of teaching or prophecy. For example, we find it in Lk. 11[40] in the condemnation of the Pharisaic view of cleansing : ἄφρονες, " did not he that made that which is without make that which is within also ? " ; in Mt. 23[17] in the attack on the pharisaic practice as regards oaths : μωροὶ καὶ τυφλοί : " for whether is greater, the gift, or the altar that sanctifieth the gift " ; in Mt. 25[2f.], where in the parable five of the virgins are called μωραί ; in 1 Cor. 15[36] : ἄφρων, " that which thou sowest is not quickened, except it die " ; and in Lk. 12[20], to the rich man who planned to build greater barns : ἄφρων, " this night thy soul shall be required of thee : then whose shall those things be, which thou hast provided ? " It is to be noted that this is not said to him by a man, but by God. It is also to be noted that in all these passages the primary condemnation is not of the individual but of specific ways of thinking and acting. It is the former which is forbidden in Mt. 5^{22} as a qualified form of murder, as an absolute breach of communication with one's brother. In this respect there is again brought out the whole basic seriousness of the concept " fool." For all its lavish and drastic appearance in the Old Testament it is always used in the third person, never in the second. It is impossible not to speak of the fool. There are innumerable representatives of folly—its poor slaves, but also its priests and bold prophets and protagonists. And therefore there are innumerable fools. Yet no one has either place or right to see and treat another as such. It may well be that he confronts me as such in a terribly concrete way, so that I seem almost to get the touch and smell of the fool. But he does not confront me in such a way that I can really recognise him concretely as such. To say " fool " of another man is to curse him, and as such to murder him, to invade the divine prerogative as a qualified murderer, to act in ignorance of God, and therefore to show oneself a fool. The curse is one which recoils on the man who utters it. For it is only those who are themselves godless and stupid that will feel free to apply this murderous term of opprobrium and condemnation to their companions in stupidity.

There is, however, one notable example in the Old Testament (1 Sam. 25) of a man who is as his name is (v. 25)—Nabal, a fool. This man, sharply contrasted with his wife Abigail as the representative of wisdom and David as the exponent of the divine action and promise in and with Israel, plays in the form of folly a very important—if, as is only fitting, subsidiary—role. It will be worth our while briefly to consider the story. It certainly provides us with a " study in desert customs " (R. Kittel), but it is hardly for this reason that it has found a place in the collection of dynastic records of which the two Books of Samuel form the starting-point. Even the contracting of David's second or third marriage (with Abigail), which is the culmination of the story, is hardly a sufficient justification for so detailed an account of what precedes. It is evident that in the depiction of the strange happenings which took place between these three characters our attention is drawn to something of material significance. And the emphasis given to them, especially to Nabal and Abigail, shows unmistakeably that what we have here is an encounter of David, the bearer of the promise κατ 'ἐξοχήν, with two contrasting types, the expressly foolish and the expressly wise, and his rejection by the former who is called Nabal, and acknowledgment and humble acceptance by the latter, Abigail.

The event takes place in Carmel, south-east of Hebron, which is the abode of the prosperous Nabal, the owner of 3000 sheep and 1000 goats, who is just about to keep the feast of shearing (v. 2). The story belongs to the records of David's experiences and activities when, although he is already elected and called and anointed to be the future king, he is forced into exile by the attacks of Saul. David and his 600 men are in the western part of the wilderness of Judah on the borders of Carmel, where the shepherds of Nabal have taken his sheep to pasture. David hears of the sheep-shearing, and sends ten of his men to Nabal. They are to greet him as a brother, saying : " Peace be both to thee, and peace be to thine house, and peace be unto all that thou hast " (v. 6). The message which they are to give is that no injury has been done to the shepherds (as they themselves can and do testify, v. 15) by the roving band into whose sphere of influence they have come, nor have the flocks themselves suffered the loss that might have been expected (v. 7). On the contrary, David and his men have protected the flocks and shepherds against alien robbers. Far from constituting a threat, they have been " a wall unto them both by night and day " (v. 16). David is not reminding Nabal of the positive achievement, but of the integrity and loyalty which he and his men have proved. And he requests only the customary hospitality at festivals of this kind when he asks Nabal to be generous to his emissaries

and to give them " whatsoever cometh to thine hand " for David and his servants.
He even describes himself as " thy son David " (v. 8).

It is at this juncture, however, that Nabal lives up to his name and shows
himself to be " churlish and evil," a true son of Caleb (v. 3), " this man of Belial,"
as he is later called by his own wife (v. 25)—and so much so " that a man cannot
speak to him " (v. 17). " Who is David ? and who is the son of Jesse ? there
be many servants now a days that break away every man from his master.
Shall I then take my bread, and my water, and my flesh that I have killed for
my shearers, and give it unto men, whom I know not whence they be ? " What
is the folly of this foolish speech ? Is it that it is the speech of an unusually
self-opinionated and standoffish and intolerably priggish bourgeois ? This is
one aspect of it. He seems to be completely lacking in any feeling for a neighbour
in need, or even in ordinary civility in his dealings with his fellows. He is a quite
impossible neighbour. But there is more to it than this if we are not simply to
read the story in moralistic terms. Nabal was addressed " in the name of David "
(v. 9). The different reaction of Abigail as soon as she heard the name of David
shows where the decisive folly of the speech is to be found. Note the beginning
and end of his words. It is not just a bedouin sheikh but the elect of Yahweh
that he refuses to recognise, and thinks that he can scorn and despise, accusing
him of being a runaway servant and so inhospitably refusing him food and drink.
How could he possibly miss the threefold *shalom* with which David greeted
him ? But he did miss it. It was really an encounter with his own and Israel's
salvation that he neglected and so rudely rejected. It was Yahweh's own presence
and action in the person of this man that he despised, refusing his services, and
insisting so snobbishly upon his own right of possession and therefore control.
He had to do with Yahweh Himself, and he acted as one who was completely
ignorant of Him. That is why he was so impossible.

David, of course, was a man like others, who normally give a rough answer
to churlishness, replying with anger and vengeance to foolish words and actions,
and in this way, i.e., in the name of avenging righteousness, with folly to folly.
When he received news of Nabal's reception he took 400 of his 600 men, and
when they had girded on their swords they set out westward towards Carmel—
a thunder-cloud which according to the practice of the times threatened complete extermination to Nabal and all his house (v. 12). We can see later (v. 21 f.,
34) how David looked at the matter : " Surely in vain have I kept all this fellow
hath in the wilderness, so that nothing was missed of all that pertained unto
him : and he hath requited me evil for good. So and more also do God
unto David, if I leave any men of all that pertain to him by the morning
light."

It is at this point that Abigail takes a hand. According to v. 3 she is a woman
" of good understanding, and of a beautiful countenance." One of Nabal's
servants has come (v. 14) and told her what has taken place (according to v. 25
in her absence) : " Now therefore know and consider what thou wilt do ; for
evil is determined against our master, and against all his household " (v. 17).
But her wisdom has as little need of lengthy deliberation as the folly of her
husband. What is it that she knows and he does not know ? That this is not
the way to treat people ? Yes, she knows this too. But this is not the decisive
point. She hears the name of David and knows with whom they have to do
(with the same immediacy as her husband does not know). She takes in the
situation at a glance and acts accordingly (v. 18 f.). " Whatsoever cometh to
thine hand " is what David had asked of Nabal. But she now takes two hundred
loaves, and two bottles of wine, and five sheep ready dressed, and five measures
of parched corn, and an hundred clusters of raisins, and two hundred cakes of
figs, and loads them on asses. Some of the servants are to go on before, and
she herself follows—eastward towards David. And she does all this without
even consulting her husband. When the elect of God draws near, and with him

the judgment, wisdom does not dispute with folly, but ignores it and does that which is commanded.

There then follows her encounter with David and his band. According to v. 20 it takes place in the fold of a valley, and is a surprise meeting for both parties, Abigail coming down from the one side and David from the other. " And when Abigail saw David, she hasted, and lighted off the ass, and fell before David on her face, and bowed herself to the ground " (v. 23)—the full prostration of worship like that of Abraham before God (Gen. 17³) and Joshua before the angel (Josh. 5¹⁴) and before the ark (7⁶). A sign of anxiety ? No, but of something very different—an unconditional respect. Abigail has no anxiety. She knows very well what she wants and what she has to represent with a very definite superiority. What she now does is the demonstration of the fact that in this situation she knows with whom she has to do in the rather threatening person of this man. This is the core and guiding light of the long speech which is now put on her lips (vv. 24–31). This is the reason for her attitude and for the gifts that she has brought to David. It is also the basis of the requests that she makes. It is on this account that she must and will make good the evil of Nabal, and prevent the evil that David himself is on the point of committing. It is in this respect that she shows herself to be of a good understanding. The point is that the name David means something to her. She knows and solemnly declares who he is and will be. Since the wordless anointing of David by Samuel in 1 Sam. 16¹⁻¹³—and it is not for nothing that the death of Samuel is reported at the beginning of this chapter—it has not been reported that anyone has said anything to this effect either of or to David : " Yahweh shall do to my lord all the good that he hath spoken concerning thee, and appoint thee ruler over Israel " (v. 30) ; and even more emphatically : " For the Lord will certainly make my lord a sure house, because my lord fighteth the battles of the Lord, and evil hath not been found in thee all thy days. Yet a man is risen to pursue thee, and to seek thy soul : but the soul of my lord shall be bound in the bundle of life with the Lord thy God ; and the souls of thine enemies, them shall he sling out, as out of the middle of a sling " (vv. 28b–29). Everything else depends upon, and has its meaning and power in, the fact that Abigail knows and has to say this of David, and therefore of the will and promise, the secret of the covenant, of the God of Israel.

It is this knowledge which commits and constrains her fearlessly and whole-heartedly to take up the cause of Nabal with David. As the one who does not know in this decisive respect, Nabal and all that he says and does in consequence can only be found wanting in this situation. This will be proved later in what is for him a terrible sense. In the first instance, it means that he does not even come into consideration in the discussion and bargaining with David : " Let not my lord, I pray thee, regard this man of Belial, even Nabal : for as his name is, so is he ; Nabal is his name, and folly is with him " (v. 25a). Abigail can only ask David to listen to her and not to him : " Let thine handmaid, I pray thee, speak in thine audience, and hear the words of thine handmaid " (v. 24). But this means that she accepts responsibility for what Nabal has said and done ; that she takes his place in relation to David. She knows and says that she had no part in the event : " But I thine handmaid saw not the young men of my lord, whom thou didst send " (v. 25b). And yet : " Upon me, my lord, upon me let this iniquity be " (v. 24a). The first practical meaning of her prostration is that she gives herself into David's hands for good or evil if only he will hear her, and hear her in the place of Nabal.

What is it that she has to say to him ? In the first instance, she has to act : to make good the mistake that Nabal has made ; to fulfil the request that he had rejected ; to unload the asses and present the bread and wine and sheep and corn and raisins and figs to David. " And now this present which thine hand-maid hath brought unto my lord, let it be even given unto the young men that follow my lord " (v. 27). And then : " Forgive the trespass of thine hand-maid " (v. 28a). Why should David forgive ? Because she has made good the mistake and given the present ? No, but because David—there now follow the words of promise in vv. 28b–29—is already the anointed and future king of Israel. It is as the one who knows him as such that Abigail has interposed her-self between him and Nabal. And it is as the one who knows this, and in view of what she knows, that she asks for forgiveness. And the granting of this request carries with it the sparing of Nabal and his house from impending destruc-tion. Even to her personally there will not now occur (as we learn from v. 34) the worst evil that could come on any woman in Israel, the loss of her sons. But she is not concerned about this danger, as had been the servant who first told her what had happened and what it would necessarily entail. What moves Abigail is not that vengeance should be averted from Nabal and his house and indirectly herself, but that it should not be committed by David. In her inter-vention she is particularly unconcerned as to the fate of Nabal. Indeed, she counts on it as something which is as good as done that he will come to a bad end : " Let thine enemies, and they that seek evil to my lord, be as Nabal " (v. 26b). What she wills to prevent when she throws herself down before David, and accepts the guilt of Nabal, and asks that it should be forgiven, is that David should be the instrument of Nabal's destruction, and therefore incur guilt himself.

Does she only will to prevent this ? The remarkable thing in her speech to David is that she regards it as something which objectively is prevented already. With such superiority does she confront the wrathful David (before whom she prostrates herself), so little does she fear him or doubt the success of her inter-vention, that from the very first she speaks in terms of an accomplished fact : " Now therefore, my lord, as the Lord liveth, and as thy soul liveth, seeing the Lord hath withholden thee from coming to shed blood, and from avenging thy-self with thine own hand . . ." (v. 26a). We find the same daring anticipation in the words of promise in relation to David's future as the one whom Yahweh has raised up and protected to be a prince over Israel. When God has done this (and it is assumed that He will), " this shall be no grief unto thee, nor offence of heart unto my lord, either that thou hast shed blood causeless, or that my lord hath avenged himself " (v. 31). This is the wisdom of Abigail in her relationship with David, who in the act of vengeance which he purposes stands in the only too human danger of making himself a fool. She knows that as the one he is and will be he may not and cannot and therefore will not actually do what he plans to do. The elect of Yahweh may not and cannot and will not avenge himself, making himself guilty of the blood of Nabal and many others who were innocent, and thus violating the prerogative of Yahweh, which none can ever escape. She towers above David with this knowledge as she makes this pronouncement.

And what of David ? The practical consequence is as follows : " So David received of her hand that which she had brought him, and said unto her, Go up in peace to thine house ; see, I have hearkened to thy voice, and have accepted thy person " (and intervention, v. 35). But the reason why he forgives, and therefore foregoes his intended revenge, is not because he has received the present or changed his mind as to what Nabal deserves. He still fully acknowledges his purpose : " For in very deed, as the Lord God of Israel liveth, which hath kept me back from hurting thee, except thou hadst hasted and come to meet me, surely there had not been left a man unto Nabal by the morning light " (v. 34). The ground of his forgiveness is exactly the same as that of Abigail's request for forgiveness. And in his words as in hers it is one which has to be taken into consideration and therefore discussed, but one which is already realised and operative, excluding from the very outset the execution of his purpose. The beginning of his answer is decisive : " Blessed be the Lord God of Israel, which sent thee this day to meet me : and blessed be thy advice, and blessed be thou, which hast kept me this day from coming to shed blood, and from avenging myself with mine own hand " (v. 32 f.). The request of Abigail did not need to be fulfilled. It had been fulfilled already—even before it was made. It simply reminded David of the accomplished fact that he could not and would not do what he intended to do. For, indicated by the voice of Abigail, it is Yahweh the God of Israel who withstands him as an absolutely effective obstacle on the way which he has planned to follow, arresting and turning him back again. And in face of this obstacle David can only break out into praise of God and of the understanding Abigail. As the one he is on the basis of the election of Yahweh, and as the one he will be in the power of the calling of Yahweh, he is not in a position to execute his purpose. As the Lord liveth—Yahweh and he himself would have to be other than they are if he were to be in a position to execute it. The wisdom of Abigail consists in the fact that she knows Yahweh and therefore knows David. When David hears the voice of this wisdom, no particular decision is needed. The matter is decided already. He is restrained from doing what he had intended to do.

The story has two endings. The first is a sombre one. Nabal has escaped the wrath of David. But he runs none the less to his destruction. The death overtakes him to which he has fallen a victim in his own corruption. The second is brighter. It speaks of the marriage of David and Abigail as the result of their encounter and remarkable agreement.

Nabal is removed. When Abigail returns from her enterprise to Carmel she finds this rash and foolish fellow engaged in a fresh act of madness : " He held a feast in his house like the feast of a king ; and Nabal's heart was merry within him, for he was very drunken : wherefore she told him nothing, less or more, until the morning light " (v. 36). But he has to learn what danger he has incurred, under what threat he has actually stood, and above all how—while he himself feasted and amused himself so regally, and therefore so little deserved it—he was saved from destruction in the power of the redemptive will of Yahweh as it is focused on David and known and proclaimed by Abigail. Therefore " in the morning, when the wine was gone out of Nabal, . . . his wife told him these things " (v. 37a). But it is not the fact that he has been saved that makes an impression on this fool and causes him to think, although this might have been an excellent opportunity to learn to know the one whom hitherto he had not known. Even now that he is sober he is still the fool he was in and before his carousal. And it is the account of that from which he has been saved, and therefore of that by which (like the rider on Lake Constance) he was threatened, that suddenly comes home to him and obviously affects him like a stroke—his subsequent fear being all the greater than his previous sense of security. " His heart died within him, and he became as a stone. And it came to pass about ten days after, that the Lord smote Nabal, that he died " (vv. 37b–38). The message of salvation itself, not being recognised by him, turns to his own judgment and death. He can and does only disappear from the scene. And on learning of Nabal's end, and in the light of it, David can only praise Yahweh, that He has acted as his avenger, and that He has kept David himself from evil (v. 39a).

But the death of Nabal means that Abigail is now a widow. She does not remain so long. She becomes the wife of David. At first sight this is rather surprising, for there are no hints of any romantic developments in the earlier part of the story. The dealings between herself and David had been strictly matter of fact, and it would be wrong to allow artistic imagination to impart to them a different and preparatory character in the light of the outcome. There is, in fact, no trace of sentimentality even in the portrayal of the conclusion itself. It must be understood in the sober context of the main part of the narrative. " And David sent, and communed with Abigail, to take her to him to wife " (v. 39b). The proposal was made by the servants of David (v. 40) and it was accepted by Abigail with the same unquestioning resolution as had marked all her previous speech and action, and the same unconditional subjection as that which she had known when she had fearlessly and critically instructed this great and fearsome leader, and told him the truth concerning Yahweh and himself. She does not compromise herself, but simply carries through to the end the role allotted to her in her wisdom, when we read that " she arose, and bowed herself on her face to the earth, and said (as though addressing David himself and not merely his servants), Behold, let thine handmaid be a servant to wash the feet of the servants of my lord. And Abigail hasted, and arose, and rose upon an ass, with five damsels of hers that went after her ; and she went after the messengers of David, and became his wife " (vv. 41–42). We really ought not to be surprised by this development, for as by an inner necessity the main narrative hastens towards the death of Nabal and the new life of Abigail in union with David. The meaning is not to be sought in any special importance of Abigail in the future history of David. There is only one other mention of her, together with David's other wives, in 2 Sam. 3³, where we read that she was the mother of Chileab, who in the parallel in 1 Chron. 3¹ is called Daniel. Michal and later Bathsheba play a much more imposing role in the tradition. But we are forced to say of Abigail that of all the wives of David, or even of the Old Testament as a whole, she is outstanding as the only one to whom there is ascribed the function described in 1 Sam. 25 : that of the woman of good understanding who recognises and honours the Lord's anointed, and therefore the Lord's will for Israel, at a time when he is so severely assailed and so deeply concealed, and when her foolish husband is so blind and deaf and stupid in face of him ; but who also represents and declares to the elect himself the will and purpose of Yahweh and the logic of his election and calling, keeping him from putting his trust in his own arm and sword and therefore himself becoming a fool. In this function she belongs to David even before she does so in fact. She belongs to him as the wisdom which takes the place of folly and speaks for it, and without which he could not be the one he is as the elect of Yahweh, or be the king of Israel, as he will be in virtue of his calling. Ordained to be his help-meet (Gen. 2¹⁸ᶠ·) in this function, she belongs indispensably to him. This is what David actualises and confirms with his swift proposal—once the existence of the fool and the work of his folly have been removed—and which she herself also actualises and confirms with her swift and unquestioning acceptance. David would not be David without Abigail and without recognising Abigail ; just as Abigail would not be the wise Abigail without David and without recognising David. Therefore He has to take her to wife and she has to become his wife, so that they are one flesh. To no other marriage of David, or indeed of the Old Testament, does the biblical account give the distinctive mark of this inner necessity in the context of the history of salvation.

2. We again begin with a christological statement. The Word of God became and is flesh. It was and is spoken to us, and present in power, in the existence of the man Jesus. The royal freedom of this one man consisted and consists in the fact that He is wholly the Fellow-man of us His fellows ; wholly the Neighbour of us His neighbours ; wholly the Brother of us His brothers ; the Witness, Teacher, Doctor, Helper and Advocate given as a man to us men. In the actualisation which it has found in Him humanity means to be bound and committed to other men. In Him, therefore, man is turned not merely to God but to other men. In Him he is quite open and willing and ready and active for them. In Him he gives glory to God alone, but in so doing sees and affirms and exalts the dignity and right and claim

of the other man. In Him he does not live only in fellowship with God, but in so doing he also lives in fellowship with other men. In Him, in this man, God Himself is for all other men. This cannot be said of any other. In the fact that as He is with us He is also for us He remains exalted above all. In this exaltation above all He is also a direction for all ; a summons to participate, as thankful recipients of His grace, in the humanity actualised in Him, to share this humanity with a concrete orientation on the fellow-man, the neighbour, the brother. To receive His Holy Spirit is to receive this direction and accept this summons. It is to see oneself in Him as one who is elected and created and determined for existence in this humanity.

But we, on whose behalf and for whose orientation He was and is man in this freedom, fail to obey the call to this freedom. Among all the others for whom He is a Fellow and Neighbour and Brother as we are, and who are therefore our fellows and neighbours and brothers, we remain in our isolation and seclusion and self-will and unwillingness, and therefore in our latent or patent hostility, in relation to them ; in a word, in our inhumanity. We are again inactive where we can and should and must let ourselves be moved in the direction of these others. This is the second form of our sloth, in which we want to be alone instead of being those we already are in and by this One.

This human reluctance has again to be considered primarily in its futility. Nothing can alter the fact that the man Jesus is for all, not only the light of the knowledge of God, but also the power of humanity. He cannot be dismissed from the world, this One who is the Fellow and Neighbour and Brother of all men. The fire which He has kindled on earth in this sense too cannot be put out. His direction cannot be reversed. No absolute fact can be opposed to Him. Nor can anything alter the fact that in Him all men, even the most deformed and unnatural, are elected and created and determined for fellow-humanity, for neighbourly love, for brotherhood. It is as well not to keep this from even the worst of our fellows, but to tell it to him plainly, and above all to accept it ourselves. In this respect, too, I can refuse to be the new and neighbourly man that I am already in this One. In this respect, too, we can involve ourselves in self-contradiction. But in this respect, too, we cannot destroy ourselves. We cannot, therefore, destroy the fact that others are there as our fellows and neighbours and brothers. We may cause them to wait, and wait in vain, for our corresponding action and attitude. But they are there as such, and we cannot alter the fact that they do wait for our corresponding action and attitude. They are always there and they always wait for us even though our indifference, our aversion and even our more refined or blatant wickedness in face of them is uppermost—especially so when this is the case ! It is not for nothing that the Son of God has made Himself theirs and ours. It is our sloth rather than His direction which is futile—the sloth in which we cause others to wait

for us in vain. In it we remain at a place where there is no solid
ground under our feet, so that we cannot maintain ourselves. In face
of the fellowship already established between all men in the one man
Jesus, no man can withdraw into a final isolation. I can, and do,
sabotage this fellowship. But I cannot make it a reality of inferior
quality which is destined to perish. Even in my inhumanity I can
only practise my sin and reveal my shame.

But this is bad enough, and we must now speak of it. For all its
relativity and ultimate futility, our sloth even in this form is a fact.
It is not nothing, but, in a way which is very painful for others and
even more distressing for ourselves, it is the something of our persistence in the direction to that which is not. Man wills that which
according to His incarnation God does not will. He wills the impossible.
He wills to be man without and even in opposition to his fellow-man.
His action and attitude in relation to others have nothing of the
freedom in which the man Jesus causes him to participate in the power
of His direction. For no real reason he dissociates himself from the
movement to his fellows which proceeds from Jesus. Or perhaps he
never really has any part in it at all, although he is in the sphere of
it. He does not live a genuinely human, but an inhuman, life, because
he does not live as a fellow-man.

Between humanity and inhumanity, divided by the criterion of
fellow-humanity, there is no middle term ; just as there is no middle
term between wisdom and folly, between the knowledge of God and
ignorance of God. " Inhuman " means to be without one's fellow-
men. We can either be with them, i.e., orientated on them, and
therefore human, thinking and willing and speaking and acting as
men ; or we can be without them, and therefore not human, but
inhuman, in all our acts and attitudes. If we are without them we
are against them. And as the stupidity of man does not have its
origin in the theoretical denial of God, but is merely practised in a
particular and not indispensable way in this denial, so inhumanity
does not have its basis in individual actions and attitudes towards our
neighbours, but either in these or without them in the fact that we
think we can and should be without our neighbours and therefore
alone—a distorted attitude which will necessarily find powerful expression in corresponding actions or omissions. It is from this basic
attitude that our repressions and actions in relation to others acquire
the character of sin, of a culpable lapse into self-contradiction in the
fulfilment of which we deny and oppose and shame both God our
Creator and ourselves as His good creatures, and therefore, while we
do not cease to be men, become and are inhuman men. We are always
inhuman from the very outset, even before we perform the corresponding action and either trespass against our neighbours and therefore ourselves or in some way leave ourselves and our neighbours in
the lurch. The great rejection has already taken place even when

and as it finds specific expression. It is not, therefore, determined by our more or less lofty, sociable, altruistic or egotistic impulses or qualities or inclinations, by our environment, or by the opportunities which we have or do not have. On the contrary, it is itself that which determines what takes place in the sphere of all these presuppositions as the activity, or inactivity, of our more or less lofty, sociable, altruistic or egotistic nature as such. What takes place reflects man's inhumanity as the second basic dimension of his folly. The form and texture may vary, but it is always his sin of disobedience, unbelief and ingratitude which is manifested in this sphere. It is his sin, because in it he turns aside from the grace which is given him by God to order his relationship not only to God but also to his fellows, violating the law of this grace, and therefore letting himself fall where he is in fact exalted and may and can and should stand.

We have to realise this if we are to see from what source the notorious inhumanity of human life and society draws its perennial strength and irresistible efficacy. It is so easy to say how simple and pleasant everything would be if only we were a little more human in our dealings, a little more attentive to one another, a little more understanding and ready to help one another. We may even suspect that all the essential evil of human existence could be avoided, and all the incidental evil mitigated and made supportable, if only it were not for this great and constant lacuna of our inhuman dealings. And the corresponding admonitions, to ourselves and others, are easily made and spring self-evidently to hand; just as great or small measures have been devised and executed, and will continually be devised and executed, to fill or bridge the gap. The only trouble is that in great and little things alike the gap always reappears. What the one thinks about another, and says to him, and does in relation to him, is decisively determined by the fact that he maintains a continual reserve, that he constantly withdraws into himself, that he has to do with him only from this standpoint and in the form of his own interests, that he is not really for him and therefore his fellow. This reserve common to us all is not affected by any admonitions or counter-measures, by any psychology or individual or social pedagogics, by any social revolution or individual conversion, however radical. On the contrary, it is appalling to see how all the great and little things which can and continually do and will take place around this centre can only reveal afresh at some point that in his relation to his fellows too man is this slothful and sinful being who falls back upon himself and acts and reacts in this inhuman fashion. If we do not realise this, if we will not accept it primarily of ourselves, we shall never understand the intrinsically incomprehensible fact of the continual complication of that which is so simple ; of the human life which can be lived only as a life in fellowship, but which is not lived as a life in fellowship and is therefore lived in inhumanity—an inhumanity necessarily and indissolubly connected with its godlessness.

We have also to realise this if we are to see how dangerous is the effect of man's inhumanity. We will consider again its outward aspect. As it takes place first in the distorted attitude and then in the corresponding acts it has the character of power ; of a force which once unleashed, as in the activity or inactivity of our refusal, escapes our control, follows its own law and has its own dynamic, whose effects we can experience only as spectators, thus adding to our own guilt. By renouncing our true humanity we do, of course, achieve a kind of liberation, an independence, a superior capacity to act, in the exercise of which we gain a peculiar advantage over others and seem to be the stronger. But even as we enjoy and assert it this power is strange and alien in relation to ourselves. It is stronger than we are. Our inhumanity sets us under a rule according to which every man's hand is necessarily against his brother's, and we are all subjects. Again, there is a certain finality about this power. Its development is along a line which moves from its origin to a definite end, and on which the first step is virtually the last, even if it is not taken in fact. It begins with the omissions and actions of an indifferent association with one's neighbour to which there can be no juridical and hardly any moral objection. It then becomes the secret or blatant oppression and exploitation of one's fellow. His dignity, honour and right are actively or passively violated. The final upshot is what we call actual transgression : stealing and robbery ; murder in the legal sense ; and finally war, which allows and commands almost everything that God has forbidden. It is obviously one and the same thing at every point on this way ; just as everything that is done by one man to another is at every step the same in essence. Society may not see it in this light. Nor may a less well-instructed Church. But in the judgment of a conscience enlightened and sharpened by God, the hard and relentless citizen (perhaps a public prosecutor or judge) who keeps within the bounds of what is customary and decorous is in exactly the same boat as the flagrant criminal judged and condemned by him. He carries the latter within himself, just as the latter was perhaps for many years like him. The man has yet to be found who does not bear murder in himself, who might not become a murderer even though he never does so. How dangerous is this inhuman life, which is the life of us all, is seen at the end of the line in the outbreak of strife and global warfare. But this only gives it palpable expression. It consists decisively in the fact that it is life on the steep slope which leads in different ways to this end. And its real menace, like that of stupidity, lies particularly in the fact that it is so supremely infectious. It has such great powers of reproduction. Lived by one, it is a challenge to others to live it. One man imposes on another by the power won and exercised through great or little inhumanities because by its exercise he raises the question why the other is so simple as not to exercise it himself. Is he not just as capable of doing so as anyone else? Indeed, when he is the accidental or intentional victim of someone else, he is given a legitimate reason to exercise it. Why should he be the fool? Why not repay like for like : indifference for indifference ; threat for threat ; pressure for pressure? Why not find a place for inhumanity in answer to inhumanity? Even the most pious man cannot live at peace if a bad neighbour will not let him. Why, then, should he remain a pious man, or the most pious? And in this way an endless series of aggressions and reprisals is initiated, as happens no less in the small sphere of personal relationships than in the greater of world-politics. Yet we cannot understand how irremediable is what we all do to one another and ourselves, but can know only a superficial and ineffective horror at it, unless we are aware of the root in which we are inhuman, and necessarily do sacrifice to inhumanity, and ourselves become its victim. It is there in the root—in the fruits too, but not primarily—that as sin it is the wasting and destruction which impends and falls. It is there where it consists so insignificantly in the fact that man does not follow the movement initiated for him by God, but evades it and lets himself sink and fall into the isolation in which he deludes himself that it is grander to live without his neighbour (as well as without God) than in the fellowship with him in which he is bound and committed to live if he is himself to be a man.

But here, too, we must remember the concealment in which man is inhuman. In this form of sloth, too, it is not the case that anyone will openly admit. We are prepared to admit that in some respects we are superhuman, and in others (rather ashamedly) subhuman. But surely not that we are inhuman? Our reluctance to admit this has a sound positive reason in the fact that a man cannot cease to be a man. He cannot change himself into another creature altogether. He cannot become an animal or a devil. For all the movement toward that which is not, of which he is guilty in his relationship to his fellows, he cannot reverse the good creation of God and therefore destroy himself as a man. This may well be the objective basis of his reluctance to confess his inhumanity. But the terrible nature of inhumanity is this. Without ceasing to be man, and as such the good creature of God, man acts as though he were an animal or devil and not man. Inhumanity is the denial of our humanity. But we deny our humanity when we think that we can and should exercise it apart from our fellow-men. And when we try to conceal this, to deny this denial of our humanity, we are not justified, but accused and condemned, by this sound positive reason for our reluctance. In our denial and concealment of that which we are and do we can and will only make it worse and really be and do it. Hypocrisy is the supreme repetition of what we seek to deny with its help.

The aim of hypocrisy is to conceal the inhumanity which we will not confess. But the result is only to make it worse rather than better. The veil chosen is selected with the attention of giving the appearance of the very opposite of what is concealed. We take up a position and attitude in which we think we can persuade ourselves and others and even God that they are supremely human, not least in relation to our fellows. It can all be summed up in the quite respectable word phil-anthropy. Philanthropy carries with it the thought of a *causa* in its exalted sense, a specific form of the great or little ideas, systems, programmes, institutions, movements and enterprises in which, under one name or another and in one direction or another, it is a matter of satisfying a more or less necessary and profound and general human interest or need, and therefore a matter of man himself, of his physical and psychical preservation, of the order of his collective life, of his education and culture, of the increase and safeguarding and exploita-tion of his material and spiritual resources, of his individual, social, scientific and cultural progress. Of course, in all this man is always understood in general. He is humanity, or simply man, anonymous man. Philanthropy, then, is the focusing and concentrating of human will and action on the prosecution of one such anonymously human cause to a victorious and successful outcome. And there can be no doubt that the genuine humanity which is fellow-humanity does in-clude philanthropy of this kind. The fact that there are always in human society questions and causes which claim the attention and loyalty of individuals and groups is in itself, because the ultimate concern is always man, a sign of the great inter-relatedness in which alone we men can be men. This brings us back to the good creation of God. To be concretely with the other means always to be occupied with some such cause in relation to him. In relation to him? This is the critical point. For it is not at all self-evident that when I am actually occupied with a cause of this kind I have concretely in mind the other, the fellow-man, the neighbour and brother ; that I am com-mitted to him rather than free in relation to a purely abstract and anonymous man. I can so easily escape this being with him in the prosecution of a mere cause, and the more effectively the better and more important the cause by which I find myself claimed, and the greater the urgency with which it claims me. Even in the good creation of God, and as myself a good creature, I can still evade the knowledge of God and therefore be stupid. In just the same way, again in the good creation of God and as myself a good creature, I can apply myself to a human cause, and give myself wholeheartedly to the prosecution and success of the relevant programme and enterprise, yet always have my own activity and therefore myself in mind rather than the other man, thus thinking and speaking and acting with a complete disregard for his questions and needs and expectations, for his existence generally, and proving myself to be quite inhuman. The inhuman element in us all is skilled to see and use this possibility. It plunges itself into philanthropy of this kind as though it were genuinely human. In this way it conceals its true intentions and projects. And because it is not human in fellowship, it is really inhuman. But the concealment cannot be stripped off from inhumanity by frontal attack any more than it can from the stupidity which decks itself out as wisdom. In fact, we seldom encounter it in its naked form either in ourselves or in others. In the majority of cases we are most sure to find it where it is concealed in the service of a great or little cause, artfully clothing itself, in its application to this cause, as the friend and servant of anonymous man, and therefore the more energetically turning away from concrete, individual man, trampling over him as though he were a corpse, which indeed he is, since the living fellow-man is regarded as non-existent, and is treated accordingly.

The field which opens up before us at this point is so vast that we can only give the briefest sketch with the help of one or two examples. The inhumanity of man may sometimes clothe itself in the necessary establishment and defence of institutions, of law and order. On the other hand, it may equally well take the form of their no less necessary criticism and overthrow. It may work itself out in the conservation of old, or the introduction of new, political and social forms. It may be active in the functions of the sacrosanct compulsory organisation of the totalitarian, or the no less sacrosanct free play of the forces of the democratic state, thus pretending to espouse either the claim of society on the individual or the freedom of the individual in relation to society. It can sometimes, as in Europe and America, disguise itself as ceaseless activity. It can cloak itself behind pure scholarship or pure art, or behind the promotion of the common interests of a national or economic or intellectual group, or behind officialdom with its concern for the regular functioning of an official apparatus, or simply behind the refinement of a technique with its different applications. It can find an instrument in marriage to the extent that this has the character of an institution and therefore a cause. The family and its stability and possessions and honour are a cause in the emotional respectability of which it can find particularly effective concealment. Again, it may give itself with particular zeal to the stern task of the schooling and education of the younger generation, which provides the necessary " educable material" for this purpose. Not least, the Church itself, the proclamation and hearing of the Word of God, the confession and doctrine and liturgy and order of the Church, and even its theology, offer a vast opportunity for philanthropic activity which is devoid of true humanity. All these things are " causes " which in their context do not lack the appearance of human justification, necessity and value, which from some standpoint can and must also be the concern of the man who is directed to his fellow-man, which have therefore a real claim to attention and service, which therefore call for the appropriate devotion which we call philanthropy. But there is not one of them which does not leave open the question how their promotion is going to affect the concrete man envisaged and embraced by them. Is he really considered at all, and if so to what extent ? How far is he only an end or goal, or even a more or less useful means, so much material for the purpose, perhaps a disruptive obstacle ? There is not one of them which cannot be appropriated by the inhuman element in us, which is not in fact appropriated by it both in little things and great, so that, screened by their humanity, it can dismiss the concrete man, attaining sovereignty without him or over him, and therefore secretly or openly turning against him. It cannot easily be denied that somewhere at the back or in the depths of the promotion of even the best cause—simply because and as it is promoted by men—there may usually be seen the hard and evil face of the man who at bottom has no more time for his fellow than he has for God, who refuses to consider him, but who, in order not to have to confess this either to him, to himself or to God, takes refuge in an activity in which his true purpose, or lack of purpose, will necessarily be all the more active and powerful. The cause is carried through to success—and man is really brought under the wheel. Sometimes, rather perversely, one could almost wish that there were not all these human causes the ceaseless promotion of which only seems to make everything worse, postponing the peace on earth which they all seem to desire, and merely intensifying an internecine warfare. In their service the inhuman element in all of us not only finds particularly effective concealment, but finds itself particularly well supplied with offensive and defensive weapons. Yet of what avail would it be to abandon the causes ? It is not the different causes themselves that are evil, nor the philanthropic zeal dedicated to them, but the inhuman element in us which has such an uncanny power of mastering and using them on the pretext of serving humanity.

One such cause deserves particular mention. Could it be that the clearest antithesis to inhumanity—love itself, humanitarian and brotherly love—is calculated in its own way to create a cause, to give rise to philanthropic endeavour in the narrower sense, and therefore to offer particular concealment to inhumanity ? It is a frightful thing to say, but this is actually the case. There is indeed a love which is mere philanthropy, a sympathetic and benevolent concern and assistance which we can exercise with zeal and devotion without taking even a single step away from the safe stronghold of being without our fellow-man, but in a deeper withdrawal into our shell. There is a form of love—mere charity—in which we do not love at all ; in which we do not see or have in mind the other man to whom it is directed ; in which we do not and will not notice his weal or woe ; in which we merely imagine him as the object of the love which we have to exercise, and in this way master and use him. Our only desire is to practise and unfold our own love, to demonstrate it to him and to others and to God and above all to ourselves, to find for ourselves self-expression in this sublime form. There is thus a form of love in which, however sacrificially it is practised, the other is not seized by a human hand but by a cold instrument, or even by a paw with sheathed talons, and therefore genuinely isolated and frozen and estranged and oppressed and humiliated, so that he feels that he is trampled under the feet of the one who is supposed to love him, and cannot react with gratitude. The great tragedy is that it is perhaps in the sphere of the neighbourly love established and shaped by Christianity, in Christian families and houses and societies and institutions, that we seem to have more frequent and shattering examples of this than in that of the worldly love, courtesy, affability and fellowship which are so much more shallow and undiscriminating, and therefore so much the less exacting. Certainly we have no reason to think that as Christians we have easily escaped from this whole field of inhumanity and its concealment.

The effectiveness of the concealment of this inherent inhumanity by various forms of philanthropy is beyond question. As a rule it is broken only in relatively few individuals, and in the lives of the rest of us only occasionally in comparatively harmless and excusable forms. More widespread penetration can be expected at certain times of crisis. Then inhumanity may and can burst every barrier and emerge in all kinds of wild and savage forms—to the horror of those who are not directly implicated. The bottom of the steep incline may then be revealed in many people, even in individuals or circles where we would least expect to see it. Man collectively may take on a terrifying and monstrous appearance. But these critical periods usually pass, and they are followed by periods of relative calm in which civilised life is resumed and these dangerous manifestations are again regarded as exceptional. The inhuman element withdraws for the most part into the wings. We are again ashamed of it. We would rather not mention the names which it has assumed and the events which betray its savagery. The face of society is again dominated by more or less sacred causes and the more or less sacred devotion they inspire. And in the light or half-light which they shed the situation again becomes fairly normal and tolerable. It again appears to be an excited and pessimistic and unjustifiable and disruptive exaggeration to point to certain unsettling but isolated phenomena as a reason for maintaining that this inhuman element is always present ; that it is at work even in these various forms of philanthropy ; that every man is at bottom inhuman ; that according to the well-known and much contested formula of the *Heidelberg Catechism* he is inclined by nature to hate God and his neighbour. Those who say this are themselves open to accusation as troublers of Israel, enemies of the human race, and guilty of a genuine inhumanity. The inhuman nature within us laughs at prophets of this kind, lurking, until the next outbreak, where it best loves to lurk, in the concealment of a good and necessary and solemnly exercised activity. In the same way its outbreaks in the life of the individual are only the relatively few interruptions of its normal exist- ence in the concealment in which its words and acts and attitudes are remembered as though it had never been, its whole activity now taking the very human rather than inhuman form of devotion to a cause. Everything now seems to be intact and in order again, so that the charge that everything is really in disorder, and profoundly in- human, may easily be dismissed as irrelevant. The power and effec- tiveness of this concealment cannot be too highly assessed.

Yet the concealment cannot alter the fact that the inhumanity which disguises itself as philanthropy does actually emerge, not only in its occasional individual or collective outbursts, but also in all the other spheres of that which makes a man a man.

If the bond which joins us to our fellow-men is hazarded and mortally endangered, so too is (1) that which unites us with God. We have described the dissolution of our relationship with our fellows as the necessary consequence of the dissolution of our relationship with God. But the folly of man is caught in a vicious circle, and the converse is also true that stupidity is always a necessary consequence of inhumanity. The clear-cut statements of 1 Jn. 4[20] are apposite in this connexion : " If a man say, I love God, and hateth his brother, he is a liar : for he that loveth not his brother whom he hath seen, how can he love God whom he hath not seen ? " He cannot do so. The relationship of man with his visible fellow-man is not in itself and as such a relationship with God. But since God is the God of his fellow as well as his God, the latter inexorably includes the former. The former is the horizontal line to which the vertical is related and without which it would not be a vertical. In non-mathematical terms, I cannot know and honour and love God as my God if in the words of the Lord's Prayer I do not do so as *our* God, as the God of the race which He has created, and therefore if I do not also know and honour and love in the appropriate way those who are members of this race as I am. If I choose myself in my isolation from other men, *eo ipso* I enter the sphere of the even more terrible isolation in which God can no longer be my God. If they are indifferent to me, I am involved wittingly or unwittingly in indifference to Him. If I can despise men, the praise which I may bring ever so willingly and joyfully to God will stick in my throat. If I merely exploit my neighbour according to my own needs, I will certainly think that I can do the same with God, and it will be my painful experience to find that He will not permit this. I have in fact hated and despised and wounded and attacked God if I have done this—not perhaps in actions, but " merely " with my words or in my heart—in relation to my brother. And if I have not done to him what I ought to have done, *eo ipso* I have not done it in relation to God. In short, if I am inhuman, I am also stupid and foolish and godless. The great crisis in which all worship and piety and adoration and prayer and theology constantly finds itself derives of course from the question whether and how far in these things we really have to do with the true and living God who reveals Himself in His Word, and not with an idol. But this question is decided concretely in practice by another one which is inseparable from it—whether and how far in these things we come before God together and not apart from and against one another. True Christianity cannot be a private Christianity, i.e., a rapacious Christianity. Inhumanity at once makes it a counterfeit Christianity. It is not merely a superficial blemish. It cuts at the very root of the confidence and comfort and joy, of the whole *parresia*, in which we should live as Christians, and of the witness which Christianity owes to the world.

For all that the lack of faith, or plight of doubt, is so profound and tragic, it has also to be asked whether the doubter has not also to consider how many men he has evaded and rejected, how many he has wounded and tormented, how many he may even have murdered in the sense of the Gospel, and whether he seriously thinks that he can find joy or even solid confidence in his faith in the light of this fact. And if—not without justice—we usually complain from the Christian angle that the increasing disintegration of human society is connected with the great modern apostasy from faith, the counter-question has also to be put whether it may not be the great secularisation and de-humanisation of human life in society which, having been so successfully accomplished without any serious or timely protest on the part of the Church or Christianity, have necessarily involved the great apostasy from faith.

If man wills and chooses inhumanity, he can only imagine that he can believe and attain to a knowledge of God. After a time he is forced to admit that, however earnestly he may desire or seriously he may attempt it, he cannot actually do so. At the point where it is a matter of God and His words and acts, where there can and should and must be the *intellectus fidei*, he is dealing with pure illusions and myths. Without one's fellow-man, God is an illusion, a myth. He may be the God of Holy Scripture, and we may call upon Him as the Yahweh of Israel and the Father of Jesus Christ, but He is an idol in whom we certainly cannot believe. This is the first thing which no concealment of our inhumanity can alter.

Again, the way leads directly from man's inhumanity (2) to a collapse of the structure and order of his human nature as the soul of his body, of the order in which he is he himself. Without his fellow-man he cannot be that which he would obviously like to be when he withdraws into himself—he himself in this totality, as the soul of his body. And I cannot and will not be an I without a Thou. If he does not see and hear the Thou, the other I which lives in this Thou (in distinction from all other objects), the automatic result is that he for his part is not seriously accepted and posited as a Thou (and therefore as the living I that he would like to be). How can he accept and posit himself when by his very nature he can be accepted and posited as himself, as this man, only in his co-existence with the other, only in his confrontation with him ? If he will not give himself to this other, he himself withers and perishes. Nor can a preoccupation with causes afford any substitute for that which only his fellow-man can offer him—the acceptance and positing of himself. It can do this only when in it he has a concern for man, and not to be free from man. If it is merely an instrument of this concealment he will not find himself in it ; he will lose himself. He will lose both soul and finally body and become a mere vehicle of the cause, a wheel which drives and is itself driven. He is then submerged in it. It consumes him. But this need not happen. The fellow-man in whose company he might come to himself is always there. Indeed, he is waiting for him. For he, too, might come to himself with him. But the help must be reciprocal. It is no use if he is indifferent or hostile to him. In the measure that he is this, he brings about his own undoing. He can only achieve his own destruction. He can only live to his death. He can only be sick : sick of the relationship in which he stands but which he also lacks because he refuses to fulfil it ; sick of his fellow-man who is always there but to whom he will not be a fellow. The real truth is that we are all openly or secretly sick of one another, of our mutual refusals, of the isolation in which we each think that we can help ourselves better without the other, of the pricks or blows with which we all try to assert ourselves and only do ourselves more harm than others. In the process it is we primarily who are abused and abased. Who among us does not in some way get on the nerves of all others ? We should have to take one another to heart if it were to be otherwise. But that is the very thing which our inhuman nature will not have. And its lordship triumphs always in the fact that most of all we get on our own nerves. The order of our psychical and physical nature, to which the nerves also belong, is not attuned to the lordship of our inhuman nature. It can only break under it. The price of the self-contradiction in which we involve ourselves with our contradiction of others can only be suffering ; the suffering which we heap up to ourselves. And it is a mortal sickness which we give ourselves and from which we necessarily suffer. This is the second thing which the concealment of our inhumanity may conceal but cannot remove.

Our inhumanity extends (3) to human life as characterised by its limited temporal duration. " It moves quickly away, as if we fled from it " (Ps. 90^{10}). But how does it move away ? The fulness, if there is such, of the time allotted to each of us (our life-time), that which when we have lived our lives will be before God and in His judgment, is our history. *Our* history ? It is ours only as we have lived and experienced and actualised and suffered it together with others, in a stretch of time which is theirs too. It is our history as the history of our relations with our contemporaries in the narrower and wider and widest sense of the term, including the older generation which accompanied us yesterday and the younger which already accompanies us to-day. It is the consecutive series, constituted in our striding from the past, through the present and into the future, of our encounters and fellowship with concrete men, which may directly or indirectly include men of the preceding generation, and often does so, together with those who belong to the age which follows. It is our part, our responsible co-operation, in world history. But if we are guilty of withdrawal, i.e., from our fellow-men, in this history, what are we in our time ? What is the meaning of our life ? Why have we been given time to live and work ? How shall we stand before God and in His judgment ? Will this not be brought against us ? Will we not be accused ? You were no help to me in my history which was interwoven with yours. You ignored me. I was of no interest to you. You disappointed me when I waited for you. You had no time for me. You merely played with me. Or again, you only appeared to help, but in reality harmed me. You led me astray, so that it was only with the greatest difficulty, if at all, that I was able to get back to the right path. You confirmed me in that from which you ought to have kept me. And you kept me from that in which I needed confirmation. Or again, you would not yield to me. In your great righteousness, or simply because you were the stronger, you pushed me to the wall. You humiliated and wounded me. You trampled over me contemptuously and perhaps even derisively, pursuing your own ends. For some reason which I cannot understand you blocked my path. You surrendered and betrayed me. You took from me the dearest that I had. The encounter with you cost me my life. Yes, we shall certainly have to render our accounts in relation to others, and we must see to it that they are in good order. But who of us will have any real advantage over the rest ? Will we not all have our own burden of accusation ? And what will be the net result for us all if the only upshot is an awful conflict of mutual recriminations ? Will it have been worth while to have lived for this fulness, this harvest, of our time ? We have to consider that the inhuman element in us all wills that we should pass our time in this way. It aims at this fulness, this harvest, of our time. It makes this history. Of course, it conceals this. It hides from us the fact that we give to our time this content. It consoles both itself and us with the reference to all kinds of causes which we finely and usefully espouse in the course of our time. It covers over the fact that we espouse them apart from and even against the other man who waits for us. Openly and under this cover it makes our life a history of these lost and wasted opportunities. Nor will it save this history that it has also been a history in which we have actually been busy with various causes. This is the third consequence that we have to consider in this connexion.

Here, then, we have the second aspect of the man who is affirmed before God in the one Jesus and exalted with Him to fellowship with God. As seen in the light of this One, he is this slothful and wicked shirker, not only in relation to God, but also in relation to his fellow. God knows him as this sinner. In spite of his sin, He has had pity on him, and continues to do so. In his reconciliation it is a matter of raising him up out of his inhumanity. On the one hand, he will not know his fellow-man ; he will not be his keeper (Gen. 4⁹) ; he is his murderer. But on the other—and this is the greater and final truth—he is told, as the disciples were, by the One who was judged in the place of Barabbas (Lk. 23²⁵) : " All ye are brethren " (Mt. 23⁸).

We will again illustrate the situation from the Bible, and we will choose for this purpose the sin of Israel as it is exposed by the prophet Amos in his message of impending judgment. We call him the prophet, although he is not only the oldest of the so-called writing prophets of the Old Testament but also the one who in 7¹⁴ expressly refused to be called a prophet or a prophet's son. In Northern Israel, where he ministered, this could only mean concretely that he did not wish to be regarded or accepted as a successor in the tradition which had had its acknowledged representatives for good or evil in Elijah and Elisha. His own distinctive description of himself is as follows : " I was an herdman, and a gatherer of sycomore fruit," and in the title he is introduced as " the herdman of Tekoa" in the Southern state of Judah (1¹). He does not come from the peasant class, the agricultural proletariat, but, as his style seems to suggest, he is him-self a proprietor. Yet his message cannot be explained by his social origin and situation. " Yahweh took me as I followed the flock " (7¹⁵). Although he did not belong to the prophetic class but was engaged in farming, God gave him a function which seemed to be interchangeable with the speech and action of the prophets (as was recognised by Amaziah the priest of Bethel in 7¹⁰ᶠ·), but which he himself regarded as separate and distinct. He, too, speaks in the name of Yahweh and in proclamation of His will and purpose as the Lord of the history of Israel. He, too, comes forward with a public denunciation. He, too, appeals directly to visions which he has been granted. Even the fact that his addresses contain warnings is not regarded as anything intrinsically new, as we learn from the account of that interview with Amaziah.

What is it then that gives him this consciousness of being out of the ordinary ? It is the absolutely direct compulsion by which he is constrained to speak. He does not do so because it was foreseen and prepared in his earlier life. He does so because he is overtaken, as it were, by an impelling force which he cannot escape. " The lion hath roared, who will not fear ? the Lord God hath spoken, who can but prophesy," he says himself in 3⁸ at the end of a whole series of metaphors which all describe the same thing—that he is aware of himself only as the effect of an all-powerful cause which objectively is described in the first saying ascribed to him in 1² : " The Lord will roar from Zion, and utter his voice from Jerusalem." Because and as he must lend his human mouth to this voice, he has to go to Northern Israel and cause trouble in the national sanctuary of Bethel, being advised to leave the country as an undesirable alien (7¹⁰ᶠ·). His appearance is not just a continuation of the previous history of the country, but marks a critical turning-point which is no less surprising to himself than others.

But there is a second peculiarity closely bound up with the first. This is that his message is so unequivocally a message of judgment. The evil which he proclaims is definitive and total. It is the destruction of the whole kingdom and nation and people of Northern Israel. As we read in 2¹³ᶠ· at the beginning of the book : " Behold, I will press the ground under you, as a cart is pressed that is full of sheaves. Therefore the flight shall perish from the swift, and the strong shall not strengthen his force, neither shall the mighty deliver himself : neither shall he stand that handleth the bow ; and he that is swift of foot shall not deliver himself : neither shall he that rideth the horse deliver himself. And he that is courageous among the mighty shall flee away naked in that day, saith the Lord." And then again at the end in 9⁸ᵃ and 10 : " Behold, the eyes of the Lord God are upon the sinful kingdom, and I will destroy it from off the face of the earth. . . . All the sinners of the people shall die by the sword, which say, The evil shall not overtake nor prevent us." The evil has not yet come. Amos speaks two years before the earthquake, as we learn from words in the introduction which are surely not without significance (1¹). But it is ineluctably determined and it draws inexorably near. The warnings given by the previous judgments of Yahweh had all been in vain : " Yet hath ye not returned unto me, saith the Lord " (five times in 4⁶ᶠ·). Amos had even entreated God for the " small " people Jacob. And " the Lord repented for this : It shall not be, saith the Lord." This was the result of the first two visions in 7¹ᶠ· and 7⁴ᶠ· But then the result of the third is : " I will not again pass by them any more : and the high places of Isaac shall be desolate, and the sanctuaries of Israel shall be laid waste ; and I will rise against the house of Jeroboam with the sword " (7⁷ᶠ·). The result of the fourth is similar : " The end is come upon my people of Israel : I will not again pass by them any more. And the songs of the temple shall be howlings in that day, saith the Lord God : there shall be many dead bodies in every place ; they shall cast them forth with silence " (8¹ᶠ·). So, too, is that of the fifth : " I saw the Lord standing upon the altar : and he said, Smite the lintel of the door, that the posts may shake : and cut them in the head, all of them ; and I will slay the last of them with the sword ; he that fleeth of them shall not flee away, and he that escapeth of them shall not be delivered. Though they dig into hell, thence shall mine hand take them ; though they climb up to heaven, thence will I bring them down. And though they hide themselves in the top of Carmel, I will search and take them out thence ; and though they be hid from my sight in the bottom of the sea, thence will I command the serpent, and he shall bite them . . . and I will set mine eyes upon them for evil, and not

for good " (9$^{1f.}$). It is all summed up in anticipation in the lament of 5$^{2f.}$:
" The virgin of Israel is fallen ; she shall no more rise : she is forsaken upon
her land ; there is none to raise her up." The roaring of Yahweh from Zion,
and the voice of the herdinan of Tekoa, is that this is irrevocably resolved.
And none of the recognised prophets prior to Amos had ever said this, not even
Elijah.

But the third and decisive peculiarity of his message consists in the fact—
and this is what makes it particularly interesting and relevant in our present
context—that the accusation which he has to make against Northern Israel,
and which is the reason for his proclamation of judgment, is so one-sidedly concrete and specific. Only a century has passed since the bitter conflict between
Elijah and Ahab and Jezebel, but there is hardly a mention of the Baal-cult
which then triumphed on so wide a front. Had this problem ceased to have any
relevance ? At any rate, Amos is not in any way concerned with it. Nor is he
concerned, like his younger contemporary Isaiah, with actions in the field of
high politics which are contrary to the covenant. Was Jeroboam II not guilty
of similar actions ? It is not on this account, however, that Amos proclaims the
certain and imminent and total destruction of Israel. Nor is. his accusation
directed (except perhaps tacitly) against the person or internal policy of this
monarch. It is simply and solely the inhumanity of the social relationships
obtaining in this kingdom which so seriously and radically and blatantly challenges
Amos—and in the first instance Yahweh himself—that there can be proclaimed
to it only His wrath, and the outpouring of His wrath as it is irrevocably determined and menacingly impends, and the end of the nation as its final consequence. His accusation—the reason for this threat as it is laid on his lips with
that direct urgency and that by-passing of the prophetic tradition—is focused
with astonishing exclusiveness upon the one point that in this state one man
does not live and deal with others as he ought to do according to the will of
Yahweh ; that wrong is done on the horizontal level of human relationships,
and therefore on the vertical level of the relationship of the people of Yahweh
to Yahweh Himself as the Creator and Lord of its history. The earlier prophets
and their disciples had never spoken in this way. The prophecy of Amos acquires
a new character even for himself from the fact that he refuses the role of a prophet
and—apart from the commission of Yahweh—wants to appear and to be heard
only as a herdman and a gatherer of sycomore fruits. In other words, he proclaims
Yahweh as the God of the fellow-man who has been wronged and humiliated and
oppressed by man, and as the Avenger who has been challenged to direct and
implacable action by what has been done to him. It is to be noted that this is
shown to be the decisive matter in the complaints made in the first two chapters
against the neighbouring states—Damascus (1$^{3f.}$), the Philistines (1$^{6f.}$), the
Edomites (1$^{11f.}$), the Ammonites (1$^{13f.}$) and the Moabites (2$^{1f.}$). The three, yes
four transgressions of these other nations all consist in offences against humanity.
They are not in covenant with Yahweh, but they are judged no less by the
standard of His righteous will, and like Israel they fall victims to His judgment
because of their transgression in this respect. But the charge acquires sharp
and concentrated form only when it is made against Israel, and it is in this
form that it dominates the whole collection of pronouncements made by Amos.
As it is uttered with this one-sidedness and emphasis, the protest of Amos is
something entirely new. The presentation given in the Books of Kings does not
prepare us for the advancement of this as a reason for the wrath of Yahweh as
it has obviously accumulated over a long period but has now suddenly become
an imminent threat which cannot be averted. Certainly we find the same strand
in Isaiah, but in his case it is only one among many. It is not omitted by the
younger prophet of Northern Israel, Hosea, but the main attention of Hosea is
directed elsewhere. The note sounded by Amos occurs again and again in later
prophecy—and sometimes very loudly. But the remarkable feature of the

message of Amos as the first to sound it is that his accusation is confined to this strand. That is why we cannot fail to hear him. That is why his particular contribution to the biblical message is that the affair of God is the affair of man ; the affair of the fellow-man who is so severely and constantly hurt by man, and so inflexibly and relentlessly championed and defended by God. In the history of the active exposition of the Bible it is not for nothing that on the one hand Amos has been so frequently neglected and that on the other he has been the classical biblical witness for all the movements in which the conscience of the Church has been reawakened in this direction, and therefore to a repudiation of the base and dangerous overlooking of this basic element in Christian truth and the revealed Word of God Himself.

The middle of the 8th century, in which the accusation of Amos was made, was not a time of war or crisis. On the contrary, it was for both the Northern and Southern kingdoms (cf. M. Noth, *Geschichte Israels*, 1950, pp. 216 f.) a kind of golden age—the period of restoration after their long oppression by the Aramæans, who had succumbed to the Assyrians about 800 B.C. It is true that according to 2 K. 14²³ᶠ. Jeroboam II fell under the stereotyped judgment passed on all the Northern rulers. He had done that which was not pleasing to Yahweh, and had not separated himself from the sin of the first Jeroboam, which according to 1 K. 12²⁵ᶠ. had consisted in the institution of a separate cult of Yahweh before images of bulls erected in Bethel and Dan. Yet the same passage acknowledges his services in the recovery of Israel's former territory (from Hamath to the sea of the plain) and the military skill and valour which he had demonstrated in this achievement. Indeed, it is expressly said that Yahweh did not will to " blot out the name of Israel from under heaven : but he saved them by the hand of Jeroboam the son of Joash." This relatively happy state of political affairs must be considered together (M. Noth, p. 189) with a certain high-water-mark in a development which had begun already in the time of David and Solomon—that of a civic life modelled on the customs of the Canaanites, and the corresponding civilisation, the emergence of trade and commerce, the beginning of a monetary economy, and the consequent creation of distinctions between those who were economically, and then socially and politically, strong and those who were weak. This is the situation in which the Lord roars from Zion and the herdman of Tekoa speaks.

Is he merely voicing the resentment of the older farming community against this modern development as such ? As an educated countryman he might well have seen how mistaken it was far more clearly than those who had a direct part in it. But his accusation is far too basic and radical to be understood merely in terms of this kind of opposition. The prophet is not a statesman or sociologist. We must remember this if we are to understand his denunciation. For it means that, apart from a few flagrant instances, the evils of the situation as Amos censured them were not perhaps quite so palpable and blatant as his actual words might seem to suggest. To their own and our advantage and disadvantage, politicians and sociologists do not usually see visions. But a prophet does. And this means that in the historical reality around him he not only sees what is obvious and characterises it as any other critical and far-seeing observer might do. He is also given to see with the eyes of God, and he therefore sees to the bottom of things, and therefore gives them the name which they might not have, or generally have, in their external appearance, but which they have at root, in the light of the dominating factor in them, so that if they do not deserve the name according to human righteousness, they certainly do so according to the righteousness of God. It is for this reason that Amos stands under the compulsion, which is also as such his prophetic freedom, to foresee and proclaim their inevitable consequence—the judgment to which they irresistibly move. How could Amos have been a prophet (the prophet who did not wish to be a prophet) if his picture of the present and future had not stood in opposition to the more harmless or equivocal pictures which any acute contemporary might have painted of the same situation, or any pragmatic historian might still form of it. On the level of ordinary human perception and thought and speech (apart from the fact that he spoke the true Word of God), the truth of his vision was and is guaranteed only by the fulfilment of all that he had seen and said in the year 722. It is in this sense, therefore, that we have to ask what it was that he saw.

He saw first the prosperity and even luxury enjoyed by the circles which exploited that development and acquired power and authority and influence by means of it. He saw their accumulated possessions (3^{10}), their houses of hewn stone and pleasant vineyards (5^{11}), the convenience of separate residences for winter and summer (3^{15}), and the lavishness of their furnishings, especially the comfortable divans (3^{12} and 6^4) and the ivory-work (3^{15} and 6^4) that king Ahab had already so extravagantly affected (1 K. 22^{39}). He saw them luxuriously reclining at their meals. He saw and heard those " that chant to the sound of the viol, and invent to themselves songs, like David ; that drink wine in bowls, and anoint themselves with the chief ointments " (6$^{4f.}$). He saw the " kine of Basan " on the mountain of Samaria (4^1), namely, the ladies of this society, the fat and greasy wives of these pashas (to use the words of B. Duhm, *Israels Propheten*, 1916, p. 129), who say to their husbands : " Bring, and let us drink." Do we really hear in these descriptions " the champion of the old and simple customs . . . his opposition to new ways and foreign extravagance " (Duhm, p. 130) ? Is Amos to be hailed as a precursor of J. J. Rousseau ? Or when all these things are severely denounced and threatened with divine judgment, are they contested in the sense of modern reforming movements directed against luxury, gluttony and drunkenness (as interpreted by L. Ragaz in his biblical studies) ? This is certainly implied. But it is to be noted that in the text itself hardly one of these charges stands alone or has independent significance. If Amos saw that all this striving was condemned and rejected by God, it was because it constituted the folly of what in 6^6 he calls " the affliction of Joseph," for which this society has no concern but which directly or indirectly, consciously or unconsciously, it has helped to cause and to bring about ; the situation and fate of those for whom this golden age had no rewards, who were its victims, who were defrauded and oppressed by those who exploited it. Hence : " I abhor the excellency of Jacob, and hate his palaces " (6^8).

No picture is given of the situation of those who are oppressed and in darkness to offset the description of the life of the well-to-do. From the various attacks, however, we can see how they came to be pushed more and more into the darkness by those who enjoyed the light. This is the point which concerns Amos, and, according to his message, Yahweh Himself. It is because of this oppression of those who are less favoured, and therefore weaker, by those who further their own interest and in their greater glory constitute a higher society that God looks down in judgment and must bring this whole people under sentence of death. What is the reverse side of all this prosperity and success ? What is the foundation of this proud and ambitious structure ? A righteous man is sold as a slave because he cannot redeem a debt, and a poor man for the value of a pair of shoes (2^6). They drink the wine which they have purchased with fines on defaulting tenants and they stretch themselves upon pawned clothes (2^8). The innocent are harassed (5^{12}), the weak oppressed, and the needy crushed (for which the fine ladies of 4^1 are rather curiously blamed). The sick are pushed to the wall and their head is rolled in the dust (2^7). A particular occasion for this kind of conduct must have offered itself in the wheat market, which seemed to have been cornered by a few, and in which the consumers were burdened and cheated by all kinds of tricks masquerading as honest dealings (" making the ephah small, and the shekel great, and falsifying the balances by deceit," 8^5), and the small producers by all kinds of exactions (5^{11}). The inhabitants of Assyria and Egypt should come and see all these things, cries Amos : " Assemble yourselves upon the mountains of Samaria, and behold the great tumult in the midst thereof, and the oppression in the midst thereof. For they know not to do right, saith the Lord, who store up violence and robbery in their palaces " (3⁹ᶠ·).

And now there follows what is obviously the decisive characteristic of the situation as it is seen in the message of Amos. There is no actual law to restrain the great and protect the poor. There is, of course, a traditional, and perhaps even to some extent a written, code. There are also judges. In every town there is the " gate "—the open place within the city gate where markets were held and where on certain days there was the opportunity for complaints to be laid before leading citizens appointed to hear them. But of what value was this when the " gate " was the very place where the poor were oppressed (5¹²) ? when the justice which was sought was turned to wormwood (5⁷) and even poison (6¹²) ? when those who administered it took bribes (5¹²) ? when they were the very ones against whom justice was demanded ? or when there was no wish to lose their favour, and it was known only too well that " they hate him that rebuketh in the gate, and they abhor him that speaketh uprightly " (5¹⁰) ? Perhaps 5¹³ refers to a cautious man of this kind who is uneasy about the whole matter : " Therefore the prudent shall keep silent in that time ; for it is an evil time." At any rate, there can be no doubt that the voice of righteousness is not heard even, and especially, at the gate ; that might takes precedence of right. Who, then, is to help the poor ? Amos knows that even in his day there are obviously men of God in Samaria who might be considered in this connexion : " And I raised up of your sons for prophets, and of your young men for Nazarites. Is it not even thus, O ye children of Israel ? saith the Lord " (2¹¹). But even this voice has been silenced : " But ye gave the Nazarites wine to drink ; and commanded the prophets, saying, Prophesy not " (2¹²)—the very same order as was given to Amos himself. Thus Yahweh alone was left as the Friend and Champion and Helper and just Judge of the weak and poor who had suffered through this development—no, through the inhumanity of man to man. It was with His commission and in His name that Amos appeared in Samaria : " The Lord hath sworn by the excellency of Jacob (and therefore by Himself), Surely I will never forget any of their works " (8⁷).

Yahweh Himself ! But are there not centres of Yahweh worship in Israel— especially the monarchy and the national shrine at Bethel (7¹³) ? It is at this point that the accusation of Amos gains its full and final sharpness. It should be noted that his famous polemic against the cult in Northern Israel is hardly directed at all against its obvious syncretistic decadence. He certainly saw this. But it was not his present concern. It is recalled only in the tilt at temple prostitution in 2⁷ (for in 5²⁶ : " Siccuth your king, and Chiun the star of your god," we seem to have a later addition, since according to 2 K. 17²⁹ᶠ· these were the gods of the foreigners who settled in the country after the fall of Samaria). Even the bull-images of Yahweh set up by Jeroboam I do not figure in the attacks of Amos. He took the cult of Northern Israel as a serious cult of Yahweh even in the form in which he found it. And he attacked it as such ; as *usus* and not in the light of an *abusus*. The truth was that the whole in-humanity and injustice of Samarian society allied itself, not with a worship of gods or idols, but quite decorously with the worship of Yahweh ; that it was concealed and legitimated by this worship ; that it was from the shrine of Yahweh that the message of 7¹⁰ could be sent by the high-priest Amaziah to the king : " Amos hath conspired against thee in the midst of the house of Israel : the land is not able to bear all his words," and that Amos himself could be given the command which almost sound like an entreaty : " O thou seer, go, flee thee away into the land of Judah, and there eat bread, and there prophesy : but prophesy not again any more at Bethel " (7¹²ᶠ·). These were the communications of an ecclesiastic (not a heathen ecclesiastic, but a representative of the Church of Yahweh) who obviously regarded as self-evident the union not only of throne and altar (the altar of Yahweh) but also of mammon and altar. It is because of this alliance, because of the fact that the evil is masked by the good, the unholy by the holy, that Amos is even more severe in his condemnation of Samarian religion than in that of Samarian worldliness, proclaiming the pitiless judgment of God which will overtake this society not although, but just because, it is so religious a society. " Come to Bethel, and transgress ; at Gilgal multiply transgressions ; and bring your sacrifices every morning, and your tithes on the third day. And offer a sacrifice of thanksgiving with leaven, and proclaim and publish the free offerings : for this liketh you, O ye children of Israel " (4⁴ᶠ·). What is the verdict of the One in whose worship and to whose glory all this is done ? " I hate, I despise your feast days, and I will not smell in your solemn assemblies. Though ye offer me burnt offerings and your meat offerings, I will not accept them : neither will I regard the peace offerings of your fat beasts. Take away from me the noise of your songs ; for I will not hear the melody of your viols " (5²¹ᶠ·). Yahweh is not dependent on their Yahweh-worship ; He led Israel in the wilderness without Israel bringing any sacrifices (5²⁵). But their Yahweh-worship is dependent upon Yahweh. It can be offered only in fulfilment of His will and not to conceal its inversion. If it is offered only for the purpose of this concealment, it would be better not offered at all. This is what is meant when Amos says : " Seek ye me, and ye shall live : but seek not Bethel, nor enter into Gilgal, and pass not to Beersheba " (5⁴ᶠ·). Seek me, however, means " Seek good, and not evil, that ye may live : and so the Lord, the God of hosts, will be with you, as ye have spoken " (5¹⁴). " Hate the evil, and love the good, and establish judgment in the gate : it may be that the Lord God of hosts will be gracious unto the remnant of Joseph " (5¹⁵). " Let judgment run down as waters, and righteousness as a mighty stream " (5²⁴). This is what has to be done, and because it was not done Israel's worship of Yahweh, far from compensating the unrighteousness of its life, demanded His wrath and judgment. He did not need the stream of their gifts ; what was required was that they should exercise righteousness to their fellows. " Yahweh will not be worshipped, but will destroy, those who have no regard for justice " (Duhm, *op. cit.*, p. 133).

Finally, they hope for a " day of Yahweh " ; for the fulfilment of His promise as the Lord of the covenant which He has made with them, His people, in the inauguration of a glorious age which will surpass, with God's help, even the prosperity which they already enjoy. Well, God has not forgotten that He is the Lord of the covenant, and that as such His promise must be kept. On the contrary, is He not accusing and threatening " the whole family which I brought up from the land of Egypt " (3¹) ?—as He also brought the Philistines from Caphtor and the Syrians from Kir (9⁷). He can say indeed : " You only have I known of all the families of the earth," but it is for this very reason that He must also add : " Therefore I will punish you for all your iniquities " (3²). The very grace which has been addressed to them and which they have rejected will necessarily be their judgment. That day will come, but it will be a very different day from what they think. It will come as a day of the judgment of God which will necessarily fall on them with a final severity just because they are His people. Therefore, " woe unto you that desire the day of the Lord ! to what end is it for you ? the day of the Lord is darkness, and not light. As if a man did flee from a lion, and a bear met him ; or went into the house, and leaned his hand on the wall, and a serpent bit him. Shall not the day of the Lord be darkness, and not light ? even very dark, and no brightness in it ? " (5¹⁸ᶠ·).

According to Amos, God has no other answer to the inhumanity of man than that it can only be, and has already been, rejected like his stupidity. God would have to be unfaithful to Himself, and to the covenant with man which

He has made in His covenant with Israel, if He were to withdraw or even weaken this answer. He maintains the covenant by placing the inhumanity of man under His merciless denunciation and the judgment which remorselessly engulfs it.

3. Again we begin with the statement that in the existence of the man Jesus we have to do with the true and normal form of human nature, and therefore with authentically human life. He lives according to the Spirit even as He is flesh. This means concretely that He lives wholly to God and His fellow-man. He lives, therefore, in one long exaltation, purification, sanctification and dedication of the flesh, i.e., of the human nature which we know only as flesh, only in its' abnormal form, only in its decomposition. His life is its normalisation. It is thus the man who has come to himself who encounters us in Him ; the man who is at peace with himself as the soul of his body. He lives in the unity intended for the human creature, in the relationship of soul and body ordained in conformity with our nature. He Himself is wholly soul and wholly body. And both as soul and body He is wholly Himself, the soul of His body in its free control, the body of His soul in its free service. He is man as we are, but in this royal freedom : not, of course, in a freedom which He has attained, or which has been lent or given Him ; but originally, in His own freedom. He has His life in Himself. He fashions and normalises it. It is thus His own life which He both lives and can and does also offer as a free gift for us men in obedience to the will of God. He makes it a life for God and us, and therefore an incomparable life as His life in His time. He comes from the Spirit and lives according to the Spirit. The Spirit is not, therefore, an alien Spirit, but His own Spirit, in which He is flesh, and exalts and purifies and sanctifies and dedicates the flesh. Again we are forced to say that this is true only of Him, the Son of Man, who is also the Son of God ; and that in this respect He is exalted above all other men. But in this way it is God's valid and effective direction for us which we meet in Him. In a man like ourselves there confronts us the truth of our nature, the sanctity and dignity and right of man, the glory of human life. If, therefore, we receive His Spirit, we know ourselves in Him as those who are elected and created and determined for existence in the truth of His human nature, for an authentically human life.

But in this respect, too, we are those who, confronted by Him, refuse to be those we already are in Him, hesitating to make use of the freedom of the Spirit in the flesh which we are given in Him. Inactive where we ought to be stirred to action, we remain in a being as flesh without spirit, and therefore in a state of disorder, living our lives accordingly. We may describe this—in keeping with the force of the two terms " stupidity " and " inhumanity " which we have already used—as a life of dissipation. This is the third form of the sloth in which we withdraw into ourselves instead of existing as those we already are in and by that One.

Here again, we must first maintain the futility of this form of withdrawal. The normalisation of our nature, the event of the glory of human life, has taken place once and for all in Jesus. This man who in royal freedom is the soul of His body lives—and lives as our Lord and Head and Representative. His direction is issued and it comes to us all. It cannot be reversed. No dissipation of ours can form an absolute contradiction to it. His direction has reference to that to which we are elected and created and determined as men ; to ourselves as God irrevocably and from all eternity wills to have us. It summons us to be those we originally are. We cannot be destroyed or expunged as such. We can certainly interrupt God's purpose. But we can do so only as we involve ourselves in self-contradiction. Dissipation involves waste or neglect, and a resultant disorder, discord and degeneration. But we cannot degenerate to such an extent that we cease to be that which God has created us—men. We can live as though we were either mere spirits or mere animals or plants—dissipation involves both—but we cannot actually be spirits or animals or plants. Our souls and bodies constantly proclaim their rights and assert their power, and always in the direction of their original unity in which the soul controls the body and the body serves the soul. Their division, the conflict, the inversion of the order in which man is the soul of his body, is continually shown to be unnatural. As God and our fellow-men are there even though we may ignore and forget and oppose them, and as they show by their existence the falsity and error of our sloth, so we ourselves are there no matter how we may contradict ourselves. We protest, with superior right and greater power, against that which we do to ourselves. What we do is ultimately futile. In this respect, too, our choosing and willing of that which is not can create only a reality of the second order. In our dissipation, too, we cannot do more than practise our sin and reveal our shame. To say otherwise, to ascribe any greater power to the human sloth which has also this distinctive vileness, it would be necessary to call in question the existence of the true man Jesus as the Lord and Head and Representative of all men.

All the same, in all its vileness as man's dissipation it is an undeniable fact. In this form, too, it is not nothing, but something. It is a real disposition of the human will and its decisions and achievements. As man does not will to know God, and as he wills to be without and even against his fellow-men, so he wills himself in the disorder, discord and degeneration of his nature, declining to make use of the freedom to be a whole man which is addressed and given to him in the direction of Jesus, and contracting out of the purifying and sanctifying and reforming movement which derives from Jesus. Our general definition of the sin of man in the form of sloth—that he lets himself fall—is particularly applicable to this aspect of it. Man goes down to ruin when he slips from the place which he is allotted by the grace of

God. And he does this by his own choice. He lets himself go. He lets himself be pushed. Where he himself can and should be moving and pushing, he allows himself to be moved and pushed. This means that he falls. He suffers a mishap. But it does not come upon him as a fatality. He brings it about himself by letting himself fall. Sin as sloth, in this particular form of dissipation, is indiscipline. To live as an authentic man would mean to keep oneself disciplined, to remain at the height to which one belongs as a man, to be what one is as a man even at the cost of severity against oneself. But it is here that (from this point of view) the great refusal takes place. In every one of us—and we cannot seek him deep enough in ourselves—there is a vagabond who will not accept discipline, and therefore will not exercise it in relation to himself, however gladly he may do so in relation to others. He prefers to receive permissions rather than commands, and because he regards himself as the supreme court he lives—the basic vagabond—by giving himself permissions rather than commands. But this involves a disruption of the unity in which he is a man. He disintegrates. His soul and body begin to go their separate ways. His soul will no longer control his body, nor his body obey his soul. The two not only contradict one another in their mutual relationship, but also, refusing their distinct function in this relationship, contradict their own essence as the two integrated elements of human nature. If the dissipated man wills, as he does, to be without spirit, he has entered on the irresistible way on which he will finally be soulless and bodiless ; the way which can lead only to death.

Here again, we have to do with a decision from which we come in the details of what we do and do not do. It is a matter of the basic perversion of the human will which precedes all the great and little aberrations which are possible, necessary and actual in the light of it, and in which it takes concrete form. What takes place in man's detailed aberrations reflects the dissipation which in its original form, in its bitter root, is nothing other than the disobedience of man, his unbelief, his ingratitude, his enmity against the grace of God directed to him, the transgression of its law. This transgression as such is the law which all his thoughts and words and works will more or less obviously follow.

We do not underline this in order to see the practical dissipation of human life as a perhaps exculpating and atoning destiny. To do so would be particularly inappropriate at a point where it is a matter of our dealings with ourselves, and therefore of the neglect of our most direct responsibility. It has to be realised, however, that the dissipation of what we do and do not do has its efficacy from the fact that we want to be, although we are not, those who can exist only in a profoundly and diversely dissipated activity and inactivity. It was in the same light that we had to understand the ungodliness and inhumanity of man. Everything would be so fine and simple if

to set both ourselves and others on our feet we had only to indicate
the vileness and guilt of our carnal thought and speech and action,
the deep unnaturalness of our enterprises and achievements in that
dualism of soul and body, and the dignity of a life lived in the unity
and wholeness marked out for us ; if we had only to enlighten both
ourselves and others, and call us all to order. This enlightenment and
call to order is something that we can and should seek both for ourselves and others. But the power of sin in this form is greater than
that of any admonition of this kind. The whole history of morality
(including Christian morality) has always tried to be a history of this
particular appeal, of warfare in the name of the spirit against the
flesh (as was thought), of the conflict for man himself, for his exaltation and preservation and against his disintegration and decline. Yet
it is a fact that, superior to all morality, his sloth is continually re-
enacted in continually fresh manifestations in this form ; that the
vagabond in us can always merrily escape the discipline which is
brought to bear on him ; that even the reference to the ruinous nature
of his action never seems to make any serious or final impression on
him. The appeal is finely made, perhaps, but it does not stick or
penetrate. On the contrary, it seems to be defeated already by the
power of sin in this form, so that it cannot gain a foothold even with
the best of moral teaching. It is an unfortunate and supremely
irrational fact, but one which we have obviously to see and to try to
understand, that man himself, even as he makes this appeal to himself or others, even as he seriously participates in the history of morality,
in that conflict, is the lazy and dissipated creature who sinks back
into himself and hates and shuns discipline ; that in relation to himself no less than to God and his fellows he is sinful man. That is why
his dissipation is so powerful. That is why the appeal against it is
so feeble and ineffective. How can human dissipation be arrested
when in the first instance it is at work in the man who tries to make
the moral appeal to himself and others, when he himself is one who in
this respect wills what he ought not to will and does not will what he
ought ? If we do not realise this, especially in relation to ourselves,
then in face of that unfortunate and irrational fact we can only take
refuge in illusions or throw up our hands and finally give up in despair.
The power of human dissipation, like that of human stupidity and
inhumanity, is so great because man himself is no less dissipated than
stupid and inhuman. It is from this source, from within ourselves,
that our sloth draws its inexhaustible strength in this form too. That
which is born of the flesh, and thought and said and chosen and done
in the flesh, can only be flesh, and cannot overcome the flesh, even
though it may have the character of a most serious and sharp protest
against it.

It is to this as the source of evil that we must also look if we are
to realise from this standpoint the dangerous nature of sin. We are

again asking concerning the inner danger which is the basis of its awful effectiveness. From this standpoint, as we consider it in the form of man's dissipation, we have to say especially that it has a power which is released by man but itself enslaves him. We usually admit with some astonishment that the vagabond in ourselves and others is interesting to us ; that he captivates us ; that he fascinates and bewitches us ; in a word, that he has power over us. If we examine the matter more closely, we find that it is the power of an inclination which we allow ourselves to follow. This is a serious matter because it is actually the case that its power leads to a disarmament of man and therefore to a supreme disinclination. But we are not aware of this. We do not want to be aware of it. More will have to be said about this later. In the first instance it is a power which is at work ; the power of a definite inclination. It might be compared to the impulse of many children completely to take to pieces a toy which they are given, to divide it up into its constituent parts, and, of course, to make it quite useless. But do we not have an inclination—an irresistible inclination—to do this ? We are all children in this way. It is our pleasure—and this is the awful positive element in what we have called our indiscipline—to decompose our human nature. We promise ourselves a certain satisfaction in doing this. We think that we are particularly human in our desire to do it. It may be that we relieve our soul of its office as the ruler and guardian and preserver of our body so that, freed from the material concerns and problems of the body, it may wander and hover and fly away on its own. Inevitably it seems desirable to us to lead what we consider to be a purely spiritual or inward life ; to build a new and, as we think, eternal house in an academic world of thought or an æsthetic or religious world of dreams ; to look, if possible, wholly to the things which are invisible, and as little as possible to those which are visible. This possibility can appear very fine and tempting, and the desire to grasp it very noble. It is only if we do not know it that we do not realise its power. When we give way to it, we will not so easily accept the fact that it is the power of an evil desire ; that it too is only a particular form of the lust of this world ; that it is a form of our dissipation ; that it is sloth and therefore sin. Why should it not be holy ? On the other hand, it may be that we release our body from the service of our soul and give it free rein to pursue its own impulses and needs. Surely it is desirable that we should grant it its sovereignty and rights, that in a true honesty and realism and self-acknowledgement we should express ourselves confidently and uninhibitedly in this way ? This, too, can appear fine and tempting, and the desire to grasp this possibility justifiable, or at any rate strong. If we do not know it, or know it closely, we must not conclude too rashly that it has no power. We have only to acquaint ourselves with it to learn differently. Sensual desire, carnal lust, worldliness ? Evil lust ? The outworking of human dissipation, sloth and sin ? A protest may be lodged against defining it in this way. Why should it not be holy even in this form ? But, of course, these are only extreme possibilities which are seldom if ever realised in practice. The vagabond within us usually hovers some-where between the two. One moment he goes off as a liberated soul into the heights ; the next as a liberated body into the depths. Indeed, he does not just do one or the other. He does both at once. In what is perhaps the supreme and most refined form of desire, he darts from the one to the other, toying with both at once, denying himself here and confessing himself there, confessing himself here and denying him-self there, putting forth his attractions now in the one form and now in the other, and deploying his power to the full in this coquettish dance with its almost innumerable variations. When man has released this power, and is himself enslaved by it, how can he ever be free again ? It is dangerous because, in the one form or the other, it is the power of a genuine desire of the heart which exercises a distinctive control over man, but also proceeds from within him. We must also point finally to the fact that in this form too, as the desire of one awakens and inflames that of others, sin is infectious and propagates itself. Rather curiously, this is just because it is so expressly in this form the sin of weakness. To yield on the one side or the other, to let go the reins, and then to take them up again and let them go again, merely for the sake of change and because of a new attraction, is not for nothing the most " popular " form of sin ; the one in which it is known to all of us directly. In relation to this form we will all usually confess, if we must, that we too are sinners, and perhaps great sinners. But in relation to it, because it is so common, we think that we can readily find forgiveness, and even that it is assured to us in advance. We are all of us human. We do not realise what we are saying when we talk in this way. We are in the process of denying and destroying and dissipating ourselves as men. We are busily engaged in setting up our own caricature. We are sawing off the branch on which we sit. Yet it is true enough that we cannot re-proach one another in this respect. The one can take comfort in the fact that the other is at least not much better and probably much worse. We are all alike at this point. The only trouble is that when we realise this we think that we are justified in doing what we see others do. And so the one calls and draws the other after him.

At this point we are reminded of the host of the damned plunging down in one great clinging mass of flesh as portrayed by Michelangelo and Rubens in their pictures of the Last Judgment. But we may also wonder how they dared so self-evidently to oppose to them a host of saints who were obviously excepted from this attachment to the flesh and its lusts and corruption. Is there any real (and not merely painted) saint who can say that he is free from this attach-ment and therefore knows that he does not participate in this downward plunge of the mass of all flesh ? Is not the true saint distinguished from the false by the fact that—without taking comfort or finding forgiveness in consequence—

he too must confess that he is one with the rest, and that he as little, or even less, deserves anything but this plunge as any habitual sinner, however great or small ? Is it not the false saint who thinks that he can so easily separate himself from this mass ?

We live indeed in the solidarity before God and with one another in which, fused together by the power of weakness, we do actually live in dissipation, in negligence, in the more spiritual or material desire of the flesh, and therefore in the childish destruction of the dignity of our human nature, but in which we make the foolish boast, as though it made everything good, that we are all of us human. Yet we can see that this is futile, that it merely represents the mortal danger to which we expose ourselves, in which we are indeed already involved, only as we see the origin of our desire, only as we know the source at which it is evil ; the place at which it consists in the fact that we are too lazy to follow the movement of God which lifts us up, that instead we let ourselves sink and fall. Fall into what ? Into our graceless being for ourselves. It is there in our own heart that death is already enthroned. It is from this point that there necessarily follows our mortal dissipation, just as it is from this point that there necessarily and always follow our stupidity and inhumanity and their deeds.

We cannot properly discuss the problem of sin in this form without here too considering the matter of concealment. Sin in this form seems more open and acknowledged than in its other forms. The obvious reason for this is that we here find ourselves in the most direct and concrete dialectic of the self-contradiction in which we are all involved. It may be presupposed, however, that sin will know how to camouflage itself at this point even more effectively, if anything, than in its other forms. We do not confess it merely by admitting that in relation to it all men and therefore we ourselves are sinners. If we did, we should be involved in a denial and destruction of our dignity as men and therefore of ourselves. We are again prevented objectively from allowing that this is the sum and end of what we will by the good reason that we are in the hand of God, who according to Ez. 18[23] does not will our death but that we should be converted and live. But what do we really know of this reason ? It is not in God's hand that we wish to hide. This would mean to will what He wills ; to be converted and to live. What we want—and this is not a good reason for not admitting the self-destruction in which we are involved—is simply to live : to live but not to be converted ; to live on in the powerful weakness of our evil desire. Here, too, this minus is the very thing that we try to conceal from God, and others, and especially ourselves. The thing we will not accept is the corrupt tendency of the will in which we will not live of God, but only of ourselves. Here, too, hypocrisy arises as a repetition and confirmation and concentration of the sin itself.

And here, too, hypocrisy and therefore the concealment of the sin take place under the title and glory of their opposite. The only thing is that since their work consists in that cleavage of human nature it cannot be reduced to a single denominator. We protect that twofold desire of the flesh with the twofold pretext of freedom and naturalness. It is so easy on the one hand to pretend that the release of the soul from the link with the body and therefore from the obligation to be its lord and keeper, and the release of the body from the service and control of the soul, the two-sided self-abandonment and self-assertion, is the liberation from a twofold yoke of bondage. Is not the discipline which prevents these releases a kind of foreign rule which man does not need to accept, which—far from exercising—he can and must repudiate? Does he not begin to exist, achieving a genuine vitality, when he sees that this discipline is a superfluous and harmful compulsion; when he resolutely resists it as an attack upon himself; and when, therefore, for his own sake, in expression of his unity and totality as a man, he dares to take the step (from freedom) into freedom, thus undertaking those releases, and granting himself permission, or leave, for either that upward or downward flight, and if we are quite serious for both at once? Can this really be called dissipation, degradation, the work of a man who is without spirit and therefore soulless and bodiless? Surely it is the courageous work of the man who is free in spirit; the work in which he does justice to both soul and body, thus achieving maturity as a man and discovering and maintaining his dignity as such. Can it really be described as sloth? Surely what he thinks and does before this liberation is the true sloth. And sin? Surely sin is to oppose the rule of free spirit, and therefore not to carry through these releases? It is no less easy to regard and expound the results of these releases, the twofold Docetism of a way of existence which is spiritualised on the one side and materialised on the other, as a return to nature, to a being as genuine soul or genuine body in contrast to a supposed spirit which falsifies both. Does not man begin to be an authentic soul and body when he transcends the connexion in which only this so-called spirit can be claimed as human? Does not the discipline which this spirit demands of us, and requires that we should exercise, lead to a paralysis and self-deception in which we are not merely permitted but commanded in the name of reality to consider and seize and enjoy that release? Is this really an existence in antithesis and contradiction, and therefore dissipation, sloth and sin? May it not be that existence in the antithesis and contradiction of these two elements, the dialectic of this powerful weakness, is normal and natural? May it not be that true spirit triumphs in their dualism? May it not be that it is dishonest to try to escape this dualism, to try not to be in the flesh? May it not be that it is the proper thing to be two and not one, and therefore to be in the flesh? Is there not a whole anthropology, bearing the name of Christian, which expressly recognises this dualism, which finds it grounded in necessity, although it then goes on, quite inconsistently, to refuse any serious consideration to the body as the mere prison of the soul, to disqualify its impulses, and in a strange abstraction to describe the life of the soul as the act of its liberation from this prison? Why should we not take seriously this dualism which is confirmed by such ancient testimony? Why do we have to speak of sin when it is merely a matter of giving a proper place to both soul and body, and therefore of freedom in the satisfaction of their specific needs?

We cannot recognise what we have here called the dissipation of man until we have fully heard the ways in which it tries to conceal and vindicate and even glorify itself. We cannot know it until we have considered the show of holiness with which it knows how to invest itself, as we have just indicated. The vagabond in us is not prepared to be depicted as the rogue he really is. He prefers to portray himself as a nobleman, knight and hero. Although he is the very essence of the rule, of ordinary and trivial humanity, he flaunts the banner of freedom and naturalness and pretends to be the interesting exception to the rule. And, of course, we all want to be free and natural and the interesting exceptions. He needs this concealment. Without it, he would be frightened, just as the fool in us would be frightened if he did not pretend to be wise, our inhumanity if it did not espouse some very humane cause. Without this concealment we would stare death in the face. He thus pretends to be the man who is truly alive. And the concealment of our dissipation cannot fail to be effective. It allies itself with the effectiveness which the power of every destructive desire always has. It gives fresh potency to this power. It carries its work to a climax. It gives it radiance and beauty. So long as this concealment is not lacking, the dissipation of man will not merely continue but constantly receive fresh and highly qualified impulses. We can only say, indeed, that our carnal being lives decisively by the impulses which it receives from this concealment.

There is one thing which it cannot do. It cannot arrest or even conceal the destructive outworking of our dissipation. Like our stupidity and our inhumanity, the latter has certain ineluctable consequences. We shall now consider these in relation to the three aspects of our human life and essence.

It is inevitable that the jeopardising of ourselves which is necessarily involved when we abandon and assert ourselves instead of maintaining a disciplined life should mean directly (1) a jeopardising of our being before God and with God. Here, too, we are caught in a vicious circle. As we refuse the knowledge of God, we are involved in a decline into the disorder of our own being as man. And as we become and are men of disorder, God necessarily becomes a stranger and enemy. For He is a God of order and peace. He is the Creator and Guarantor of the peace designed for man in his own nature as the soul of his body.

To break this peace is to break with God as its Creator and Guarantor. In our unity and totality as it is constantly renewed by the Holy Spirit we belong to God, and we express the fact in the exercise of the discipline which is simply the obedience that we owe to God. But if we choose the flesh, i.e., one or other form of that dualism, we reject God. We are blind to His work and deaf to His voice. We are no longer able to pray in any true sense. We cannot do so even if our libertinism takes a more spiritual form : perhaps a very pronounced idealism ; or a bold inner enthusiasm ; or even an intensive religiosity, a very zealous concern for God and His cause. Born of the flesh, this will always be flesh. Far from binding us to God, it will separate us from Him—quite irrespective of the fact that we do not give free rein to the physical side but show it all possible severity. It is obvious, of course, that the more flagrant and customary form of libertinage, the so-called emancipation of the flesh in the narrower sense of the term, necessarily has the same result. Primarily, although not exclusively, it is in this sense that the lists of vices in the Epistles of the New Testament speak very emphatically of those who shall not inherit the kingdom of God. How can the debauched and dissipated slaves of their own rampant senses and impulses enter the kingdom of God ? Renouncing self-mastery, they have rejected the lordship of God. How, then, can they return to it ? But whatever form our debauchery takes, whether it is upward or downward, whether it is the libertinage of thoughts and feelings or that of the appetites, God is not there for the vagabond in us. He may pretend to be free, but he is not free for God. He can neither know Him nor serve Him. Again, he may pretend to be natural, but it can never be natural for Him to be before God and with Him. The habit of self-forgiveness spoils his taste for a life by free grace. Evil desire extinguishes the love of God, and therefore faith and hope in God, first in his heart, then in his thinking and action, and finally in the whole of his life. It may combine itself with the more crude or refined pretence of Christianity, but it can never go hand in hand with a true Christianity which keeps itself in temptation and is powerful in its witness to the world. It disturbs us when we seek God, and come before Him, and call upon Him, and try to do many things with Him and for Him. In the grip of its power, we are not really thinking of God at all, and we need not be surprised if we find that God for His part can make nothing of us and has no use for us. We can only repeat at this point what we said in our discussion of inhumanity as the true reason for the lack of faith, or plight of doubt, both in individuals and on a more general scale. The dissipation of man has to be reckoned as one of the basic reasons for these unfortunate phenomena. This is the first thing which cannot be obliterated by any concealment that it may use.

Again (2) it evokes inhumanity, as it is also its consequence. Here, too, there is a fatal action of cause and effect. How can a man

have openness and gladness of heart for others, and plan and achieve
the co-ordination of man with man, if he will not keep to the order
of human being in himself ? How can he respect the dignity of man
in others if it escapes him in his own person ? What can the dissipated
man be for his fellows, or offer to them, apart from the fatal power of
a bad example by which he confirms others to their hurt rather than
to their salvation, or perhaps, if the other is a little less depraved than
he is, the fatal impulse to exalt himself above him, and thus to enter
an even more dangerous path. We cannot take the point too seriously
that in the measure that we abandon and assert ourselves we are useless for society, refusing our responsibilities in relation to our fellows,
our neighbours, our brothers. The destruction of the I in which we
are involved necessarily means that there is a vacuum at the point
where the other seeks a Thou to whom he can be an I. The dissipated
man becomes a neutral, an It which is without personal activity and
with which the other cannot enter into a fruitful personal reciprocity.
But we have also to say that the vagabond in me not only causes me
to refuse my responsibilities in relation to others, but actually to be
a disruptive and harmful influence. My inward unrest necessarily
expresses itself outwards. Unable to satisfy myself, I am forced to
seek compensation in all kinds of attacks and outrages on that which
belongs to my fellows. My conflict with myself necessarily conceals
but also reveals itself in disputes with others. The man of disorder
is as such a dangerous man. He is potentially a menace to others.
As inward and outward peace are indivisible, so too, unfortunately,
are inward and outward dispeace. This is the second form in which
the dissipation of man always finds expression in spite of every
concealment.

It will also work itself out (3) in the fact that our allotted duration
of human life will become quite unendurable. The revolt against this
limitation, the attempt to escape it, is itself an original form of human
sloth. We shall return to this in our final discussion. For the moment,
we are concerned with a direct consequence of the destruction and
disintegration of human nature, of being in the flesh, as it now concerns
us in the form of man's dissipation. The dissipated man is full of
anxiety about himself and life and the world. He is not at all the
free spirit he pretends to be. He finds no pleasure in the merriness
he affects both to himself and others. " Be self-sufficient," he calls
to his proud heart. But if everything is going well, why does he need
to give this word of encouragement ? The truth is that his heart is
not at all self-sufficient. He is anxious. He is afraid. He may not
be afraid of dying as such. He can neutralise and even explain the
thought of dying. We can all do this. What we cannot do is to
reconcile ourselves to the fact that all things, and therefore man himself, have their time and are thus limited. It is not a matter of dying.
It is a matter of death as the determination of human existence in

virtue of which he is finite. And the dissipated man can never come to terms with this determination. He may pretend that he does, but his actions prove the contrary. He is the man who seeks either an upward or a downward flight, or both, from the unity and totality of human life. Either way he condemns himself to an endless and insatiable striving. The aim of every desire is infinity. It is renewed as soon as it finds satisfaction. Satisfaction can only lead it to seek it again. This is just as true of the desire of our thoughts and feelings as of that of our senses. Once unleashed, it can never be appeased. It drives us from desire to satisfaction, and in satisfaction it gives rise to desire. Its essence and beauty consist in the fact that both upwards and downwards it opens up magic casements with unlimited views which give us the thrill either of solemnity or of an arrogant rejoicing. But is not the heart of this thrill a terrible, irrepressible and irresistible longing in face of the infinity opened up on all sides by these casements ? Is it not a thrill of horror at the actuality which consists in the fact that we are limited and not unlimited, that our striving can never lead us anywhere in its infinity ? *Carpe diem* is the word of exhortation and comfort which the dissipated man addresses to himself. But this is simply an expression of the panic in which he lives as he is confronted by a closed door. Do we not always think that we are too late, sometimes even in youth, then in dangerous middle-age, and especially when we are old, and cannot conceal from ourselves the fact that in this or that respect we are indeed and finally too late, and we try to snatch the flowers that may be left, or surprisingly given, by the late autumn ? And then it is again too late. In youth or age, the hunt is pointless, because its object does not exist. There is no infinite to satisfy our infinite desires. But this is something which the dissipated man, who has broken loose from the unity and totality of soul and body in which God has created him for existence in the limit of his time, cannot grasp, but must endlessly repudiate in his own endless dissatisfaction. In what he takes to be his successful hunt, he is himself the one who is hunted with terrible success by anxiety. He may try to smother it, but he cannot do so. He may tell himself that he has it under control, but this is not the case. When we consider all the yearnings in what he plans and does, quite apart from his character and achievements, of what man can it not be said that his life-story is one of anxiety ? And the same is true of world history as a whole. The history of the nations, and their politics and cultures, their artistic and scientific and technical achievements, is a history of the great pursuit of man in which he grasps at the infinite and is continually brought up against his finitude, in which he is himself hunted by his anxiety, gripped and controlled by his panic at this closed door, and therefore incapable of any quiet or continuous progress. Is not man so great in all ages just because he is so little in this fear of his own limitation, and this attempt to escape it ? And is he not so little in this fear just because he lives in this attempted flight, the dissipated man who is essentially, of course, the slothful man? Engaged in this flight, he necessarily doubts and finally despairs of even the modest success which may come his way. For it is always far too modest. The infinite which is his true goal is still unattainably distant. There can be no modesty in the man who is involved in this upward or downward course of dissipation. For him it is not natural but unnatural to be modest. It is not his glory but his shame. And because he cannot be modest, he inevitably plunges himself (and, as we have seen, his fellows) into one disturbance after another—in utter antithesis to the life for which he is ordained by the divine election and creation, the life which is basically peaceful and inwardly assured, and which therefore radiates peace and creates assurance in others. This is the third thing which our hypocrisy may conceal but cannot alter.

We return to our starting-point. What we have here is a third aspect of the man whom God took to Himself in the man Jesus, exalting him in this One to fellowship with His own divine life. In the light of the existence of this Saviour he is the slothful man; the man who, from the standpoint of what he himself does and does not do, lets himself fall, thinking to attain on all sides this imposing profusion of wild growth. God knows us as men like this when He addresses His mercy to us in this One. He sees us as those who are in the flesh because we wish to be so. What is the plan and purpose of God when he wills and creates and sustains the existence of this One in the mass of men plunging headlong into the depths? Merely to show the law from which we have fallen? Merely to set in relief the fall itself? These are inevitable implicates of the divine work which it is our particular purpose to consider in this context. The sickness of our being as a sinful being in the flesh is undoubtedly revealed in the light of this One. But we must not forget something which is even more true—that " he hath borne our griefs, and carried our sorrows," and that " with his stripes we are healed " (Is. 53[4f.]). We must not forget that it was positively our salvation, our sanctification, that God willed and accomplished as the mighty direction to us all in the existence of the Son of Man, the free and royal man Jesus. Yet we for whom this was done are men like this.

We will again turn to the Old Testament for an illustration, and this time to the strange story of David and Bathsheba in 2 Sam. 11[1-12, 25]. It is a story which is strange even in relation to its context. It is set at the very heart of an account of the exploits of David after he was instituted king. It therefore forms an intrusive element, and the painful impression which it makes is not removed, although it is perhaps mitigated, by the tragic and yet conciliatory and even hopeful conclusion. If we note how the story of the Ammonite war which was begun in 2 Sam. 10 is taken up again at once in 12[26f.], we may indeed suspect that the incident was supplied by another source in the redaction of the Book of Samuel, especially as it is not to be found in the corresponding passage in

I Chron. 19¹–20³. Is it just a matter of introducing the person of Bathsheba, who according to 12²⁴ is the mother of Solomon, and therefore the ancestress of the whole later house of David, reappearing in the New Testament with three other curious women (Thamar, Rahab and Ruth) as one of the ancestresses of Jesus (Mt. 1³ᶠ·) ? If this is really one of the reasons why the story is inserted, it is only with the very different one of the demonstration of David's sin, in the shadow of which this personage is introduced who is so important for the establishment of the house of David. It is to be noted in this respect that the figure of Bathsheba remains rather a colourless one throughout the narrative. In supreme antithesis to Abigail, she seems to be only an object in the whole occurrence. She never has the initiative, and she does nothing to shape the progress of events. The transgression of David is the background which domin‑ ates the story of her introduction. And it is this that makes it so strange. In all the previous narratives of the Books of Samuel we have never been told that David sinned, but that he always refrained, or, as in the encounter with Nabal and Abigail, was restrained from doing so. But now, in remarkable contrast to that earlier story, he does not refrain in the very slightest, and there is no one to restrain him. He now does what he could not possibly do earlier as the bearer of the promise. And he does it without any shred of justification, but in a sudden act of wicked arrogance. He can only accept the accusation of the prophet Nathan (who is also introduced for the first time in this story) : " Thus saith the Lord God of Israel, I anointed thee king over Israel, and I delivered thee out of the hand of Saul ; and I gave thee thy master's house, and thy master's wives into thy bosom, and gave thee the house of Israel and of Judah ; and if that had been too little, I would moreover have given unto thee such and such things. Wherefore hast thou despised the commandment of the Lord, to do evil in his sight ? " (12⁷ᶠ·). Note the sharp contrast between the divine I and David, who now occupies the place which normally belongs to all Israel in the message of the prophets ; the place of the one who has received nothing but good at the hand of Yahweh and has repaid it with evil. To be sure, in and with this evil he has not ceased to be David, the one whom God has elected and called. He proves this at once by the fact that when he is accused by Nathan he freely admits : " I have sinned against the Lord " (12¹³). It is also proved by the fact that, unlike Saul (1 Sam. 15³⁰), he is given the answer : " The Lord also hath put away thy sin ; thou shalt not die." His sin is forgiven. But it has taken place with all its consequences. If the attitude of David on the death of the child of Bathsheba reveals a greatness which is wholly worthy of himself, this cannot alter the fact that the child conceived in the act of his sin had to die. And it is surely intentional that the whole story, embedded in the ultimately victorious war against the Ammonites, constitutes a sombre crisis in what had hitherto been the continually mounting way of David, beyond which he plunges at once into the great catastrophe of the revolt of Absalom. From this point onwards David no longer stands out in contrast to Saul as a figure of unambiguous light. We might almost say—although it would be a consideration which is quite foreign to the account itself—that he becomes a more human character. The whole point of the story, except in so far as it serves as an introduction of Bathsheba, is simply to prove that David too shares in the unfaithfulness of Israel to Yahweh, and thus stands with Israel (although not destroying His faithfulness) under the judgment of Yahweh.

The decisive content of the story is given with startling swiftness. In the affair in which David becomes a transgressor there is no element of human great‑ ness even in the tragic sense. It is primitive and undignified and brutal, espec‑ ially in the stratagem by which David tries to maintain his honour. How else can we describe it except as an act of dissipation ? When we turn to it from the first Book of Samuel, it surely strikes us that the same cannot be said of the sin of rejected Saul. The offence of Saul was to want to be a *melek* like the kings of other nations. In this perversion he ceased to be a charismatic and was possessed by an evil spirit. But Saul was a whole man even in his transgression (which was so slight from the moral standpoint). He was great even in his demon-possession and tragic end. On the other hand, the elect David who is called and set up in his place is painfully mean and undignified when he transgresses, despising the commandment of the Lord (12⁹). Indeed, he is contemptible even to himself. If only he had been caught up in an evil principle and programme ! If only he had gone astray and shown his fallibility in a significant entanglement ! But as far as he is concerned it is only a trivial intrigue, however savage and evil in its outcome. It amounts only to an almost casual departure from the order which he knows and basically recognises, although one for which he himself is fully responsible. It is a side-step, as it were, in which he takes on a character foreign to himself, and in consequence of which he does that which is equally foreign, almost mechanically involving the greater transgression which is obviously inevitable once he has departed from that order. At every point, both at the outset and in the sequel, it is all below his usual level and petty and repulsive.

The manhood of Israel (with the ark of Yahweh, 11¹¹) is encamped under Joab in the open fields. The king has remained behind in Jerusalem, and has just awakened from a siesta (11²). He is there on the flat roof of his palace. It is not an evil situation, but it is not a very promising one. He gazes indolently at the courtyards of the lower neighbouring houses. " Thou shalt not covet thy neighbour's wife " (Ex. 20¹⁷). The gaping David covets the woman—Bathsheba, the wife of Uriah the Hittite, as he is told—whom he there sees washing herself. " Thou shalt not commit adultery " (Ex. 20¹⁴). David wills to commit adultery with this woman. He has only to command her as the king, and he does so. Has he not already committed it in his heart (Mt. 5²⁸) as he looks on her and lusts after her—the wife of another ? But he does commit that which has already been committed. The woman becomes pregnant. Will he stand by what he has done, not only in her sight, but in that of her husband, of all Jerusalem, perhaps of the child who is yet unborn ? The king of Israel an adulterer ? The consequences are incalculable. He is afraid of them, not unreasonably, but unjustly. Already, however, he is his own prisoner. It is only by further wrong that he can avert the consequences of the wrong which he has already done. First, he tries to practise a clumsy deception. Uriah is recalled. The ostensible reason is that he should report to David on the progress of the campaign. The real purpose is to restore him to his own house and therefore to Bathsheba. He will therefore think, and even at worst cannot prove a contrary opinion, that the expected child is his own. But this plan is defeated by an unexpected obstacle : " And Uriah said unto David, The ark, and Israel, and Judah, abide in tents ; and my lord Joab, and the servants of my lord, are encamped in the open fields ; shall I then go into mine house, to eat and to drink, and to lie with my wife ? as thou livest, and as thy soul liveth, I will not do this thing " (11¹¹). He will not do it even when he is pressed to do so, and invited to the royal table and made drunk, but sleeps two nights at the entrance to the palace with David's bodyguard. He " went not down to his own house " (11¹³). David has come up against a man—and it is almost a final appeal to himself—who knows what is right, and who keeps to it even in his cups. His only option therefore—if he is not to retreat, as he is obviously unable to do— is to cause this man to disappear, to die, in order that he may marry Bathsheba and conceal the adultery which he has committed. As king, he has the power to do this. " Thou shalt not kill " (Ex. 20¹³). Well, he has the power to kill without having to admit it even to himself. And he does it by sending his famous directive to Joab, carried by the returning husband himself, to place him in the fiercest part of the battle against the besieged city of the Ammonites, and then to leave him in the lurch, so that he is killed by the enemies of Israel.

His orders were obeyed, involving an unnecessary, imprudent and costly attack which in itself David could only have censured. But he was quite unable to do so. For the report sent by Joab concluded with the news which he desired : " Thy servant, Uriah the Hittite, is dead also." This makes up for everything —even the death of the others who had lost their lives in this futile enterprise. " Then David said unto the messenger, Thus shalt thou say unto Joab, Let not this thing displease thee, for the sword devoureth one as well as another : make thy battle more strong against the city, and overthrow it : and encourage thou him " (11²⁵). He has no real interest now in Joab or the army or the city of Rabbah. The true encouragement is for himself. He can now enjoy the peace which he desires, and which is created by the death of Uriah that he has so skilfully arranged. Bathsheba mourns for her husband. " And when the mourning was past, David sent and fetched her to his house, and she became his wife, and bare him a son " (11²⁷). He could now be born without any scandal. It all belonged to the past. It had all been covered over.

" But the thing that David had done displeased the Lord." This was the message that the prophet Nathan had to give him. He had done what he should not and could not do as the elect of Yahweh. He had contradicted at every point himself, his election and calling, and therefore Yahweh. He had allowed himself to stray and fall into lust and adultery and intrigue and murderous treachery—the one following the other by an iron law—and therefore into the sphere of the wrath and judgment of God. " As the Lord liveth, the man that hath done this thing shall surely die," is his own confession when his act is held up before him in the mirror of Nathan's parable. And it invites the crushing retort : " Thou art the man " (12⁵ᶠ·). He is the one who has been involved in this incident. No, he is the one who has willed and done it even to its bitter end. He, the bearer of the promise, is also a man of this kind. This is what is revealed with such remarkable frankness in the story of 2 Sam. 11–12. David is now playing the role and aping the style and falling to the level of the petty *melek*, or sultan, or despot of other peoples. David is like all other men. He cannot be relieved of this charge. On the contrary, this is a charge and burden which rests on all Israel and every man. And this has to be brought home by David's very human, yet not on that account excusable, but supremely guilty slip ; by what is revealed to be at bottom the normal manner and action even of the heart and life of those who are elected and called.

4. The man Jesus, whose existence forms our starting-point for the fourth and last time, exercised and demonstrated His royal freedom finally and supremely and all-comprehensively in the fact that He gave up His life to God and man, that He allowed it to be taken from Him by men. To lose it ? Yes, but also in that way to win and keep it. To perish ? To be no more ? To belong only to the past ? Yes, but to reveal Himself as the One who is incorruptible in the very fact that He perishes and belongs to the past ; to live eternally and for all times as the One who was crucified at the conclusion and end of His time. It was in this way, as His life moved towards this coronation and found fulfilment in it, that it became and was and is His life for God and for us : the life of Jesus the Victor, the faithful servant of God, who as such is with the same faithfulness our Lord and Head and Representative ; the life of the new and holy and exalted man in whose person we who are still below are already above, we who are still sinners are already sanctified, we who are still God's enemies are lifted up into fellowship with His life ; and all this as the life of the

man who did not refuse death, and therefore the conclusion and end
of His time, but accepted it to find fulfilment in it. We are always
unlike Him in the fact that the issue of His life in this fulfilment, His
end in the character and significance of this goal, took place once and
for all for us, and cannot be repeated in the issue of our lives or our
end. But our end or issue is set in the light of His. It can and should
reflect it. His end and issue, His crucifixion, i.e., His life as it is fulfilled and triumphant in His crucifixion, because and as it is lived for
us, shines as a direction on the existence of us all as it is determined
by our finitude. We are not He, nor He we. But as and because He
is for us and therefore with us and not without us, we for our part
are with Him and not without Him. We are this finally and supremely
and all-comprehensively in the very fact that our existence is limited
and under sentence of death ; an existence in the short space of time
which we are pitilessly given. As the Crucified, He lives at the very
point where our frontier is reached and our time runs out. He is the
Victor there. He not only calls us, then, to look and move forward
confidentially and courageously. He gives us—and this is the power
of His direction—the freedom to rejoice as we arrive at our end and
limit. For He is there. He lives there the life which as eternal life
includes our own. He is our hope. And He bids and makes us hope.

But we—again this bitter turn has to be executed—start back at
the very place where we should not only be calm and confident but
also hope. We fret at the inevitable realisation that our existence is
limited. We would rather things were different. We try to arrest the
foot which brings us constantly nearer to this frontier. And because
we know that we cannot change things, that we cannot cease to move
remorselessly towards this place, we look frantically around for assurances on this side of the moment when they will all be stripped away,
anxiously busying ourselves to snatch at life before we die. This,
too, is a form of our sloth. In this, too, we set ourselves against God
and shun His grace ; the grace of participation in the movement and
exaltation which come from Jesus. In this, too, we fall back and are
behindhand. And this, too, is responsible transgression—sin. Our
term for this fourth aspect of it is human care. We have met it three
times already (under different names) as the fruit and consequence of
our stupidity, inhumanity and dissipation. It necessarily entered our
field of vision in relation to these aspects of human sloth. But it is
also an autonomous form of our sloth, and as such itself the basis and
cause of our stupidity, inhumanity and dissipation. All evil begins
with the fact that we will not thankfully accept the limitation of our
existence where we should hope in the light of it, and be certain,
joyously certain, of the fulfilment of our life in the expectation of its
end. The root of all evil is simply, and powerfully, our human care.

We must begin, as before, by asserting its emptiness. It is quite
futile. Why ? Because of the inexorable nature of the destiny, the

natural order, in virtue of which we and all things are corruptible and will perish ? This pedestrian thought cannot form a sure foundation for our statement. Always, and rightly, man will struggle against nature or destiny. It is not on this account that he will regard his care as futile. It is futile because our perishing, the terminating of our existence, which we think we should oppose without anxious striving, is the good order of God, one of the tokens of His gracious and merciful and invincible will as Creator. We do not choose something better but something worse, a definite evil, our own rejection and compact with chaos, if we oppose this order when we ought thankfully and joyfully to accept it. Chaos is what God did not will and will never do so. It is, therefore, that which is not. Hence our care is empty and futile. It is for this reason that we have to accept the fact that we cannot add to our lifetime (Mt. 6^{27}) and that it is senseless to try to do it. It is for this reason that we have also to accept the fact that our heavenly Father knows what things we have need of (Mt. 6^{32}). There is thus no ground for anxiety on our part. It is empty and futile because we have already been told that this is the case by the earthly Son of our heavenly Father—the One who became and was revealed as the Victor at the very frontier which causes us to start back and retreat and take anxious thought, at the end and issue of His own life. This invasion and destruction of the object of all care (even in its form as destiny and the natural order) has taken place and cannot be reversed. We may continue in care, but this cannot affect the force and validity of the veto which He has laid upon it, not only by His words, but by the act of His life as He sacrificed and fulfilled it on the cross. It cannot alter the fact that He is in fact the hope of the world and our hope. Against what, then, do we seek to assure ourselves ? We may be anxious, but we cannot provide for our anxiety the object which it must have if it is to have any final seriousness. We cannot give it an absolute character. We can only deceive ourselves and others if we think that there is good reason for it, and that we achieve anything by it. Our care is empty and futile. By it we can only realise and reveal our sin and shame.

But we do do this, and in this way (even from this standpoint) we create the evil fact of our self-contradiction. We act as though the work and Word of God were nothing; as though Jesus were not risen. We make no use of the freedom which we are granted in Him. The impossible—man's unrest as he tries to reject the ineluctable finitude of his existence—takes place. The negation which he permits himself becomes a " position." The evil of his fear of this frontier, which is the good order of God, acquires historical form and significance both individually and globally. The life of man becomes an unbroken chain of movements dictated by his anxious desire for assurances: either against possibilities which he fears and tries to avoid because he has to recognise in them the approaching shadow of the frontier which he approaches ; or in relation to possibilities which he desires because he expects from them fulfilments which for a time at least conceal his certain end, allowing him temporarily to forget that which is before him. Care is the remarkable alternation and mixture of this fear and desire against the background of what we think we must regard as a threat rather than our hope. From this angle, the disobedience and unbelief and ingratitude of man consist in his tragic persistence in this opinion, and the evil will which permits it. This opinion is the inexhaustible source of care, both as fear and desire, in all its great and little, all its more or less exciting or apparently only incidental and superficial, forms. On the basis of this opinion man is always one who is anxious in some way, although he is the one who ought to be without care, the one from whom all care is removed at the very point where he thinks that he is threatened, at his issue and end which is his appointed future. Because his care has its basis in this opinion, however, it cannot be overcome by a frontal attack. No other man, not even an angel from heaven, can successfully summon me—and I certainly cannot summon myself—to abandon these fears and desires and therefore not to be anxious.

If we ever take the risk (and it is a risk) of preaching on Mt. $6^{25\text{-}34}$, we at once meet with all kinds of sullen or dispirited or unwilling reprimands (expressed or unexpressed), and most of all, if we are honest, from our own hearts and minds. For how can we help taking care for our life ? How can we model ourselves on the fowls of the air and the lilies of the field ? How can we seek first the kingdom of God and His righteousness in the assurance that food and drink and clothes will be added to us ? How can we leave the morrow and its anxieties—the storm which may mount and break, or the sun which may shine through—and confine ourselves to the troubles (and perhaps the joys) of to-day ? How is all this possible ?

How can man let go his care when he is of this opinion ? We may remove all the things that he fears, or give him all that he desires, but new fears and desires will rise up at once from the inexhaustible source of this opinion and new cares will be his portion. For one day he will inevitably reach his end. If he has no positive joy and comfort, but only anxiety, in relation to this fatal point, if in his approach to this point, this far side of all his fears and desires, he does not see God but nothingness awaiting him, he can only be filled with care. He is a prisoner of the ceaseless movements of care which he himself has to make and has automatically made. We have to see this if we are to realise the power of man's sloth, his culpable negligence, even in this respect ; a power which is very real even though the opinion in which this negligence originally consists, and the whole tormented existence to which it gives rise, are quite pointless and therefore empty and futile. Just as inexplicably but in fact man is first a practical atheist, inhuman and a vagabond, and then can only think and speak and act accordingly, so first—how shall we describe him from this final standpoint ?—he is the dissatisfied man who necessarily becomes his own slave and lives in the bondage of his need of security. We have to grasp this if we are to be more than indolently surprised at the sea of individual and racial care in which we are all almost submerged. But when we do see it we recognise the danger. We may again describe this formally by saying that, although like man's dissipation, it seems to consist in a kind of human weakness in face of what is supposed to be an overwhelming opponent, it has power. The distinctive feature of care is that it derives its power from its opponent, from that which causes it and against which man tries to secure himself. It has all the power of the end, of death without God and without hope. This illusionary opponent, who has already been routed, this form of nothingness, is the force which inexplicably but in fact rules in human care and affects the life of man. The thought of it makes man dissatisfied. He thinks that he is menaced by it. Believing this, he can only be anxious. He can only look and move forward to his future with the deep unrest of one who is discontented with his finitude. And it is this illusory picture, the phantasy of a hopeless death, which with great definiteness and consistency dictates the law of his conduct. As he is anxious, he gives life to this phantasy, arming it with its illusory weapons and directing its illusory arm. Care is in fact existence from and to this death, because it is existence which is already smitten and maimed and unnerved and diseased by this death, and therefore a wasting and perishing existence. The care of man increases and deepens and becomes more acute in the measure that he allows it to find expression in that alternation or mixture of fears and desires. As man refuses to find joy and comfort in his end, it thrusts itself (in the form in which he sees it, and therefore without joy and comfort, but menacingly) into his present. He turns to his own grief, constituting it a graceless determination of his existence, that which is full of grace but which he fears as his distant end, the coming of which he tries to avoid, and from which he tries to conceal himself in all kinds of fulfilments. And he is now marked by this phantasy which he has conjured up. He falls victim to it in the present in which he is so concerned to secure his future. From this standpoint, too, he is engaged in that frantic hunt in which he himself is really the hunted. This is the curious power of care. It is only pseudo-creative. But all the same it is a real power even in its impotence. And there can be no escaping its effectiveness. For as man conceives and nourishes that view of his end, the end as he views and empowers it necessarily thrusts itself into his present. We must also mention the fact that it, too, has great powers of expansion and infection. We push one another into these anxious fears and desires and the corresponding joyless present. We mutually increase them, like the panic which spreads like wildfire from one, or a few, to whole masses of people. It may also be recalled in this connexion that many world-situations as a whole can be decisively represented only as states of epidemic anxiety, in which the call and compulsion of hopeless death in one of its forms, manifesting itself either in nervous defence or rapacious attack, and bringing inevitable suffering, constitute the main and universally menacing stream of historical occurrence. When we realise that this is not just something which overwhelms us like an avalanche or an earthquake, but that it derives from ourselves, and takes place in consequence of responsible human decisions, there is every reason to understand care as far more than a regrettable human weakness or an occasional mistake. As man's refusal and negligence it is from the standpoint of his temporality *the* human sin. In its unity and totality the sloth of man has also this form.

Of course, man never thinks of acknowledging what he is and does when he is anxious and therefore the prisoner of care. The self-contradiction in which he is involved is too striking and painful for him to admit that this is what he really intends and wills and does. Care has a merely ludicrous side on which it may be compared to the action of a man who in his desire for a bird in the bush (or for fear of a menacing bird of prey) lets go the bird in his hand. But who of us will admit that he acts foolishly in this way? And in reality this ludicrous folly is suicidal madness. In his anxiety man sets his own house on fire. He bursts the dyke which protects his land from flooding. He torments and crushes himself. In his attempt to find security, he loses it. But who of us will admit this? Behind our reluctance to do this there seriously stands somewhere the will of God in virtue of which what man intends and wills and does in his care is transcended and superseded and made impossible. He, the living God, is really the limit of man, in all His omnipotence and mercy. Is it not inevitable, then, that we should hesitate to confess our care? We are obviously prevented from doing so genuinely by the fact that there is no objective reality to cause us to do it. Objectively, there is only the bitter reality of our ludicrous but demented relationship to the shadow which we ourselves have projected on the wall. Unfortunately, however, it is not a knowledge of this fact which really restrains us from confessing our sin. If we knew this, if we lived with the objective truth that there is no reality in the enemy which threatens us or the abyss before us because we are in the hand and under the protection of God, we should not yield to care in the first place, and then we should not have to confess it and be ashamed of our confession. As we do yield to it, and can only be ashamed of our confession, the only alternative is to try to conceal from ourselves and others and even, as we think, God, the folly and madness of what we do. In a shame which is not authentic we must try to find a cover, a fine pseudonym which will declare the imposing opposite of what we do, an alibi.

The concealment of care will take many different forms because, although care is the same in all men (both as regards its origin in that false opinion and also as regards its outward expression), there are different views as to the imposing opposite by which it may best be covered.

There is the man who by force of circumstances, environment and history is essentially activist ; in general terms, the man of the western world to which we ourselves belong, although it is an open question how near or distant the time may be when the man of the east will bear the same activist stamp. The concealment which this man chooses is the high concept of conscientious work. He defends and justifies and magnifies his anxiety as the work which is laid on man by an inner as well as an outer necessity. He takes the side of that which he desires against that which he fears. He tries to use and exploit the time given and left to him, and in this time his abilities and power and opportunities and possibilities ; to pursue his own development within the natural and historical cosmos by which he is surrounded ; to make himself his own master both in great things and in small. He sets himself higher or more modest, nearer or more distant, but always binding ends. He can never be too serious or zealous in his efforts to attain them. He is out for success. He must have it. He must achieve something. He creates. And it is by this measure that he assesses himself and others. If he is not creating and achieving, he feels a want ; he is restless and fretful. He views with suspicion those who are not creating anything at all or anything worth while. He is happy when he finds himself compelled to work by definite obligations. He is refreshed and comforted by the thought that he is fulfilling his tasks to the best of his knowledge and ability ; that in his own place he is a cog which is pushed and pushes, or at any rate rotates, according to a specific plan. All his fears and desires against the background of the great overhanging threat, all his attempts to find security, flow into this canal with its solid banks. His care becomes his glory as it drives the mills and factories—his own or those which are collectively owned—erected by the waterside, so that something is actually achieved for himself and others by the fact that he is anxious. It may be that human care occasionally shines through at the heart of all his activity, but how gloriously transformed it is ! How its true character is hidden ! When it is translated into conscientious work, who can possibly recognise it as a form of human sloth ? The man who is hounded into activity by his care seems to be the very opposite of a slothful man. We need not waste words showing how effective is the concealment of man's denial (expressed as care) when it takes this attractive form.

But there is also the man who is essentially passive. Generally speaking, he is more at home in the tropical east and near the equator than in northern Europe or the United States. And he may not long survive even there—who knows ? Yet we must take him into account, for he appears even amongst ourselves. He, too, is a man of care. He, too, knows that human life is threatened by that limit, by death.

He, too, does not know that this limit or frontier means hope because it is the mercy of God which sets it for man. He, too, has to wrestle with what he knows and does not know. He, too, is concerned to hide his care. But he solves the problem in a different way. He conceals it behind the no less high concept and title of resignation, non-resistance and contemplation. He sees the illusions operative in the zeal and works and morality of the activist. He shakes his head over him no less than the latter does over him. And who is really in the right? He is not the slave of a clock constantly reminding him of what has to be done. He has plenty of time, and for him time is not money, or anything else particularly valuable. He does not find sanctity in work, but in leisure for deliberation and self-adjustment and expectation. His law is not the law of duty but of relaxation. Why should he wish to be a cog which is pushed and pushes? Is not this all empty—a mere snatching at the wind? If in these fortunate territories two days' work are enough to sustain oneself and one's family—why work six? Why create merely for the sake of creating? If the inscrutable will of Allah is done in any case, why not reduce to the very minimum the flame of fear and desire which we cannot altogether extinguish? If we cannot avoid the menacing of our existence by death, why act as though we could prevent it? Why not simply endure it as it declares itself at every moment and at the last definitively? We can only say that this, too, is in its own way a glorious transformation and therefore a concealment of care, and that in many, if not all, its forms it is far superior in dignity to the activity with which the activist usually tries to hide it. Is the passive man really anxious at all? Is it not superfluous, because irrelevant, to speak to him about the fowls of heaven and the lilies of the field? Is he not himself—perhaps too much so—a kind of fowl or lily? a sluggard? a lazybones? He may appear to be so to the activist. But he is also guilty of sloth in the stricter, theological sense. Even with the alternative which he has chosen, he too is the victim of a great illusion. The only thing is that as we say this we have also to recognise that in its own way his illusion too, is a fine one, and even heroic in a way which we do not readily understand, and certainly effective.

How strong the concealment of care is in both forms may best be gauged by the fact that on both sides it is easy not only to reject with a superior gesture the charge that we have here the evil concealment of an evil business but to go over to the counter-attack with the question whether an ethic of work or resignation is not a better antidote to what the Christian message condemns as care than this message itself. The positive content of this message is, of course, overlooked—the assertion of the being and life of God for man at the very point where man thinks he sees only his frontier and the threat this involves. In the light of this the assertion seems necessarily to be a mere postulate in the optative. That Jesus is risen and lives has to be heard and grasped if it is to be understood. And if the Christian message does not derive, or does so only uncertainly, from this point, how can the assertion be made with the radical emphasis appropriate to it ? How easy it then is either to minimise the seriousness of human care, divesting it of its character as sin and representing it as an unfortunate but natural deposit of human weakness, or to show how effectively it can be met with conscientious work or heroic resignation or even a not impossible mixture of the two ! How easy it then is to make out that the Christian assertion concerning that frontier is an illusion in face of which these two ways will always commend themselves as more sober and solid methods of bringing poor man release ! In line with what we had to say concerning the folly, inhumanity and dissipation of man, we can only say of his care that we have not yet recognised it if we have not paid close attention to what it has to say for itself in its concealment ; if we have not seen how powerful it is, not only in itself and as such, but also in its concealment ; if we have not realised how excellently it can defend and strengthen and confirm and express itself in the very act of concealment.

One thing, however, it cannot do. It cannot avert its inevitable consequences by any form of concealment. It cannot deny its character as sin, which means ruin, in these consequences. To make this clear, we will look back from this final point in our investigation to the first three. The disruption of the right relationship of man to his temporality, which we have now described as care, appeared already at each of the three earlier points as a consequence of the sin which we then considered from those different standpoints. Our present task is to see it as also a cause of the perversions with which we started.

In this form, as the false view of the threat which causes us anxiety in face of that frontier, it plays (1) a decisive and very special role in the development of what we first described as man's ignorance of God ; his unwillingness to honour and love Him as God. The specific operation of care in this respect consists in the fact that already at its root it means not only a general turning away from God but an incomprehensibly desired remoteness from God at the very point where God is nearest to man as God, where He encounters him most impressively and concretely as God : as God in His holy sovereignty as opposed to us and all His creatures ; as God in His power to take up our cause with His own distinctive efficacy ; as God in the mercy in which He is holy and makes use of His sovereignty. The point where God meets us like this is the limit which is set for us and which finds clear expression in the fact that it is appointed to us once to die. It is not self-evident, but needs the work of His Word and Holy Spirit, that we should know Him at this point where He is our hope in death. But if He is near to us anywhere it is here at this frontier. It is definitely at this frontier that His self-revelation is given, and it consists

specifically in the fact that at the very point where we meet our end
we are met by our Lord and Creator and Reconciler and Redeemer,
and that His being illumines us, in His character as the Lord of life
and death, where we think that we can see only the darkness of death.
In care, however, man obstinately insists that what he can expect at
this point is only darkness and not light, only destruction and not
salvation, only an eternal question and not the definitive answer—a
menacing opponent whom he must go out to meet, and with whom
he must in some way wrestle, prepared either for conflict on the one
hand or capitulation on the other. In care man makes his future his
own problem. He tries either to avert or to bring about that which
it might entail. He presumes to know it and in some way—by his
activity or passivity—to master it. His reading of the situation is
wrong from the very outset. The God who awaits him at that point,
and comes to him from it, is not the opponent of man. He is not
man's problem. Man cannot and should not try to strive with God.
Man cannot and should not presume to know and master God of himself. Yet it is with this perverted understanding that anxious man
looks to the point where God waits for him and wills to encounter him
in His self-revelation. In his anxious care man has secured and bolted
himself against God from the very outset. He thinks that he can and
should deal with God as if He were not God but a *schema* or shadow
which he has projected on the wall. Is it not inevitable, then, that
he should not have hearing ears or seeing eyes for His self-revelation?
How can he believe in Him and love Him and hope in Him and pray
to Him, however earnestly he may be told, or tell himself, that it is
good and right to do this, and however sincerely he may wish to do
so? In his care he blocks up what is for him too open access to the
fountain which flows for him. Care makes a man stupid. This is
the first thing which even the worst of its concealments cannot alter.

But when we turn to the horizontal plane care also (2) destroys
human fellowship. It does this in virtue of the unreality of its object.
The ghost of the threat of a death without hope has no power to unite
and gather. It is not for nothing that it is the product of the man
who isolates himself from God. As such it necessarily isolates him
from his fellow-men. It not only does not gather us but disperses
and scatters us. It represents itself to each one in an individual character corresponding to the burrow from which he looks to the future
and seeks to grasp its opportunities and ward off its dangers. Care
does not unite us. It tears us apart with centrifugal force. We can
and will make constant appeals to the solidarity of care, and constant
attempts to organise anxious men, reducing their fears and desires to
common denominators and co-ordinating their effects. But two or
three or even millions of grains of sand, however tightly they may be
momentarily compressed, can never make a rock. Anxious man is a
mere grain of sand. Each individual has his own cares which others

cannot share with him and which do not yield to any companionship or friendship or fellowship or union or brotherhood, however soundly established. By his very nature he is isolated and lonely at heart and therefore in all that he does or does not do. Even in society with others he secretly cherishes his own fears and desires. His decisive expectation from others is that they will help him against the threat under which he thinks he stands. And it is just the same with them too. Cares can never be organised and co-ordinated in such a way as to avoid mutual disappointment and distrust and final dissolution. And behind disappointment and distrust there lurks, ready to spring, the hostility and enmity and conflict of those who are anxious. It is a rare accident if different cares, although not really uniting, do at least run parallel and thus do not lead to strife. For the most part, however, they do not run parallel for long, but soon intersect. And, unfortunately, they do not do so in infinity, but in the very concrete encounters of those who are anxious. What is thought to be the greater anxiety of the one demands precedence over what is supposed to be the lesser anxiety of the other. The desires of the one can be fulfilled only at the expense of the desires of the other. Or the intersection is because they fear very different things, or—even worse—because the one desires what the other fears, or the one fears most of all what the other desires most of all. It is only a short step from a fatal neutrality to the even more fatal rivalry of different cares and those who are afflicted by them. If care itself remains—and it always does, constantly renewing itself from the source of the false opinion of human temporality—we find ourselves willy-nilly on this way in our mutual relationships, and we have no option but to tread it. There can be no genuine fellowship of man with man. There can only be friction and quarrelling and conflict and war. Care dissolves and destroys and atomises human society. In its shadow there can never arise a calm and stable and positive relationship to our fellow and neighbour and brother. It awakens the inhuman element within us. This is the second ineluctable consequence of care, no matter how fine or strong may be its concealment.

It leads no less necessarily (3) to the disorder which we have called the disintegration of the disciplined unity of man as the soul of his body. So strong is the self-contradiction into which the anxious man plunges himself in his discontent with his finitude that it is inevitable that this unity should be severely jeopardised. We remember the shadow and its power—the hopeless death—which the anxious man portrays on the wall as the picture of the future which supposedly menaces him, in this way summoning and introducing it into his present, and necessarily living with it, or rather dying of it. To do this is radically unhealthy. It pierces his heart and reins. In these circumstances he cannot be a whole man. He can no longer rule as a soul or serve as a body. He reacts against it as a soul by that roving flight into better regions which he himself has selected or invented. And his body reacts against it in the form of all kinds of self-assertion, or in the form of renunciation, or in the form of sickness in all its organs. In this respect, too, care involves the dissolution of humanity. We are describing the process only in its basic form. It will never express itself quite so crudely, or at any rate be revealed quite so abruptly. But there can be no question that care does bring man on to this steep incline. It constitutes a mortal danger. It consumes him. It has the character and effect of hopeless death. It is poison. It cannot serve to build him up, but only to pull him down in what we called dissipation. It introduces not only the atheist and the inhuman man but also the vagabond within us. The man who is dissatisfied with his finitude has all these three within him, as he himself is within all these three. This is the third thing which no concealment of our care can arrest or deny.

We pause and reflect that the man whose reconciliation with God and exaltation, sanctification and purification are at issue when the name of Jesus is proclaimed and believed is this man—the discontented man who in the hopeless attempt to deny his finitude necessarily destroys his peace with God and his fellows and does nothing but harm to himself. God has in mind this man who is slothful, and refuses to act, and rejects the grace addressed to him, in the form also of his care. God knows him, even though he will not and cannot know himself. And God does not love him in spite of the fact that He knows him. He loves him because of this fact. He loves him as His creature who does not cease to be such, and from whom God has not withdrawn His hand and will not do so, because He is true to Himself. It is to him, His creature and covenant-partner in all his corruption, that He has given Jesus to be his Saviour, and saving direction, and Redeemer in and out of his corruption—Jesus, the One who is for him the Victor and Liberator and Redeemer at the very point where in his relationship to the awful picture which he had projected he insults God and treads down his fellows and destroys himself. It is for this man that Jesus lives. The fulness of his eternal life is enclosed in this One. It is to him that this One is given as a promise. It is true that he is the unhappy man of care. But it is even more true that there is said to him with overriding definiteness and all the power of a once-for-all act of God : " The Lord is at hand. Be careful for nothing " (Phil. 4[5f.]).

Once again a biblical passage will give concretion to our analysis. And this time we turn to Num. 13–14—the history of the spies whom Moses sent to investigate the promised land.

We call it a " history," and this calls for a short hermeneutical observation which applies in retrospect to the three preceding *excursi* as well. The term " history " is to be understood in its older and naive significance in which— quite irrespective of the distinctions between that which can be historically proved, that which has the character of saga and that which has been consciously fashioned, or invented, in a later and synthetic review—it denotes a story which is received and maintained and handed down in a definite kerygmatic sense. In relation to the biblical histories we can, of course, ask concerning the distinctions and even make them hypothetically. But if we do we shall miss the kerygmatic sense in which they are told. Indeed, the more definitely we make them and the more normative we regard them for the purpose of exposition, the more surely we shall miss this sense. To do justice to this sense, we must either not have asked at all concerning these distinctions, or have ceased to do so. In other words, we must still, or again, read these histories in their unity and totality. It is only then that they cay say what they are trying to say. To be sure, the history of the spies does contain different elements. There is a " historical " element in the stricter sense (the persons and cities and localities mentioned). There is also an element of saga (the account of the branch of grapes carried by two men, and of the giants who inhabited the land). There is also the element which has its origin in the synthetic or composite view (fusing past and present almost into one) which is so distinctive a feature of historical writing in Old and New Testament alike. It is to the latter elements that we must pay particular attention in our reading of these stories if we are to understand them, for they usually give us an indication of the purpose which led to their adoption into the texts. But in relation to them, if we are discerning readers, we shall not overlook the historical elements or even jettison those which seem to have the character of saga. When the distinctions have been made they can be pushed again into the background and the whole can be read (with this tested and critical naivety) as the totality it professes to be.

The purpose of Num. 13–14 is to show how dreadful and dangerous is the retarding role played by evil anxiety in the transition of Israel from the wilderness to the promised land as an action in the history of salvation. It was perhaps in this way, in the shadow of this particular failing in relation to Yahweh, that at a later period—perhaps at the time of the Exile when it was confronted by a dangerous return to its own land—Israel saw its past. Yet this does not mean that at the earlier period of its existence in the wilderness its attitude was not exactly the same, or very much the same, as reported in the story. We shall now consider the picture which it gives.

The wilderness wandering seems to be reaching its end and goal. Israel is on the steppe of Paran (13[1]) on the very threshold of the land from which Jacob and his sons had once journeyed to Egypt—the country which their descendants had now left far behind them. The will of Yahweh in the great act by the Red Sea, which was their deliverance and liberation, and Yahweh's covenant with them, had had as their goal that they should dwell in the land which was now before them. Other nations lived there, but it was still, and already again, their land ; for Yahweh had promised it to them. In all their march through the wilderness the inhabitation of this land had been their absolutely sure and certain future, guaranteed by God Himself. And now it is to take place. Yet they are not to be brought in blindly and passively. Although led by Yahweh at the hand of Moses, they themselves are to act and dare, knowing where they are going, and knowing the land and its inhabitants and soil and cities (13[18f.]). This knowledge is to be given them by trustworthy witnesses who will summon them to joyous action. That is why the twelve spies are selected and sent out, all chosen from among them, one from each of the tribes, and in each case one of the princes or leaders. Caleb from the tribe of Judah and Oshea (whom Moses called Joshua) from the tribe of Ephraim are the representatives of what later become the leading tribes in the south and the north, and they will be particularly prominent later in the story. These spies are to be eyes for the rest of the holy people, and when they have seen they are to be the mouth of authentic witnesses to this people. With this commission they are to enter the land which God has promised Israel, which already belongs to it according to His will and

Word, and which has only to be appropriated ; and they are then to return and tell. This is all arranged by Moses at the commandment of Yahweh (13$^{1-21}$). There will, of course, be a certain element of risk in crossing the frontier, both for them and for the whole people after them. It will be a venture, as we can see from the exhortation of Moses : " Be ye of a good courage." Note that they are also told to bring back some of the fruits of the land : " The time was the time of the firstripe grapes " (13^{20})—not the true grapes, but those of the approaching harvest. The Israelites themselves will actually see these first-fruits. And Moses is confident that these will speak for themselves and kindle the gratitude and joy and courage of the people. In all this we have to remember that there is no question of establishing the glorious content of the promise or the certainty that Yahweh will fulfil it and bring them into this good land. On the contrary, the whole being of this people rests on the promise of Yahweh. The only purpose, then, is to confirm the promise and to remind the people of its content and certainty. The spies can only be witnesses of the promise, and the people is to hear it attested by them and see it attested by the proofs of fruitfulness which they bring.

But it is at this point that—quite unexpectedly and incomprehensibly from the standpoint of the story—there comes the invasion of anxious care. It arises first amongst the spies themselves. Ten of these prove to be fainthearts. They have faithfully and eagerly fulfilled the first part of their commission. They have gone through the whole of the south as far as Hebron. At Eshcol they have cut off the great branch of grapes " and they bare it between two upon a staff ; and they brought of the pomegranates, and of the figs " (13^{24}). And they return and tell Moses and Aaron and the whole congregation about the land, and show the fruits, and say : " We came unto the land whither thou sentest us, and surely it floweth with milk and honey ; and this is the fruit of it. Nevertheless . . ." (13$^{26f.}$). After all, there is a serious " But." It is not for nothing that they were told to be of a good courage. And without courage the promise given to the whole people cannot be fulfilled. There was a risk. A venture had to be made. All the spies had been aware of this. But ten of them had obviously not proved to be very courageous on the journey. It is these ten—the overwhelming majority—who, as is only right, act as the spokesmen. And the second part of their report is as follows : " Nevertheless the people be strong that dwell in the land, and the cities are walled, and very great : and moreover we saw the children of Anak there." There then follows a list of all the warlike people they found : the Amalekites, Hittites, Jebusites, Amorites, and Canaanites (13$^{29f.}$). The report is amplified later : " And they brought up an evil report of the land which they had searched unto the children of Israel, Saying, The land which we have gone to search it, is a land that eateth up the inhabitants thereof ; and all the people that we saw in it are men of a great stature. And there we saw the giants, the sons of Anak, which come of the giants : and we were in our own sight as grasshoppers, and so we were in their sight " (13$^{32f.}$). Even the milk and honey and great cluster of grapes did not compensate in their eyes for this drawback ; what they feared was incomparably greater than what they desired. The truth and power of the divine promise to attest which they had been chosen and now stood before the people could and should have been thrown in the scales against those hosts of people and their strong and secure cities and even the giants. But they themselves had not taken the truth and power of the promise into account, and so their report concluded : " We are not able to go up against the people ; for they are stronger than we " (13^{31}). They had not really seen as witnesses of Yahweh, and therefore they could not speak as His witnesses. They could not encourage His people, but only attest their own anxious care.

We remember that they are speaking to the people of Yahweh—the people to whom the promise and its content and certainty are not something new, for whom they are only to be confirmed, who are to be summoned by them to resolute action. Surely they will unanimously reject as false witness this report and its conclusion. Unfortunately not. Instead we read that when the people of God heard this report there arose a murmuring ; the murmuring of the care engendered in the people too. There were, of course, two witnesses who were not anxious and who were therefore true witnesses, Joshua and Caleb. And we are told (13³⁰) that Caleb " stilled the people before Moses " with the words : " Let us go up at once, and possess it ; for we are well able to overcome it." But the continuation of the report of the other ten swept aside this word of encouragement. When the people heard of giants, every restraint was cast aside : " And all the congregation lifted up their voice, and cried ; and the people wept that night " (14¹). The following day the murmuring was against Moses and Aaron, so that we have good reason to suspect that this was not an accidental but a supremely radical refusal which compromised everything. And indeed : " The whole congregation said unto them, Would God that we had died in the land of Egypt ! or would God we had died in this wilderness ! And wherefore hath the Lord brought us unto this land, to fall by the sword, that our wives and our children should be a prey ? " (14²ᶠ·). Thus from the future, in which they do not see Yahweh and His promise and its fulfilment and His faithfulness and power, but only these people and their strongholds, only these giants, before whom the spies saw themselves as grasshoppers, death reaches into their present in the form of this mad desire, and even into their past. They are afraid—their poor wives and children !—of what God promises and tells them to do. They would rather have been long since dead—what is the value of milk and honey and clusters of grapes and pomegranates and figs ?—in Egypt or in the wilderness. Better this than meet the obviously gigantic danger of their future. But even if they are terribly anxious they are still alive, and can do something to escape the danger. And so there comes the maddest thing of all—a conclusion which far surpasses the purely negative conclusion of the spies : " Were it not better for us to return into Egypt ? And they said one to another, Let us make a captain, and let us return into Egypt " (14³ᶠ·). Absolutely everything is called in question by the care which has now assumed gigantic proportions as a result of this report about giants : their deliverance and liberation ; the will and Word of Yahweh in this act ; His covenant with them ; and naturally the authority of Moses and Aaron. Their will is to choose another leader, to set off in the opposite direction, and to return to Pharaoh and slavery—the very thing which, in spite of the protest and warning of Jeremiah, is finally done by the Jewish remnant after the destruction of Jerusalem, " because of the Chaldeans : for they were afraid of them " (Jer. 41¹⁸). " No ; but we will go into the land of Egypt, where we shall see no war, nor hear the sound of the trumpet, nor have hunger of bread ; and there will we dwell " (Jer. 42¹⁴). The madness is complete. Panic knows no limits. This is how the people of Yahweh proves itself. This is the way in which it treats the divine promise and therefore its own history and election and calling.

What follows in face of this situation is quite majestic : " Then Moses and Aaron fell on their faces before all the assembly of the congregation of the children of Israel " (14⁵). They did not try to contradict. They did not speak any word of warning or exhortation. When the people of Yahweh holds back, the only hope for this people is Yahweh Himself : the absolute prostration of worship before Him ; the intercession of those who know Him for those who do not, of those who persist in His calling and the certainty of His promise for those who forget and deny and surrender it. Yet in the first instance we are not told of any intercession, nor is there any express reference to Yahweh. We are simply told that they fell on their faces before this crowd in all the madness of its anxiety.

But this is not all. For at a lower level, nearer to the people but resisting their anxious care, representing the true cause of the people because the cause of Yahweh, persisting in His calling and promise, there also stand the two faithful and reliable witnesses Joshua and Caleb (the two referred to, perhaps, in Rev. 11³ᶠ·). The first thing that we are told concerning them is that they rent their clothes (14⁶) as a sign of their supreme horror at what they recognised to be an act of supreme transgression. There then follows their entreaty in which in all the tumult of that raging anxiety they issue their call, their final appeal, for joy and courage and action : " The land, which we passed through to search it, is an exceeding good land. If the Lord delight in us, then he will bring us into this land, and give it us ; a land which floweth with milk and honey. Only rebel not ye against the Lord, neither fear ye the people of the land ; for they are bread for us : their defence is departed from them, and the Lord is with us : fear them not " (14⁷ᶠ·). Here again we have the clear line of the obedient human action corresponding to the goodness and certainty of the divine promise and sharing *a priori* its triumphant character. Yahweh is with us. Hence our enemies, even though they be giants, are impotent, and we shall overwhelm them. The only thing is that we must not fear, i.e., we must not be obstinate against Yahweh or question and therefore forfeit perhaps his benevolence. But this has already happened. The people is already deaf to this last appeal. It is in vain, therefore, that they recall once more the promise of Yahweh. " All the congregation bade stone them with stones " (14¹⁰). The two faithful witnesses ? Or Moses and Aaron as well ? Either way, there can be no doubt that raging anxiety now aims to destroy physically the protest made against it in the name of the divine promise, judging its divine Judge in the person of these men, and making this its final word.

It is to prevent this dreadful climax that at this moment the glory of the Lord appears before the tent of revelation in the sight of all Israel, averting the murder of the two witnesses and the irrevocable apostasy of the people, but also as an act of judgment on them. They have made an enemy of the God whose friendship they have despised and rejected. They have evoked death by fearing it. There is now interposed a long section (14¹¹⁻²⁰) which tells us how God threatens what they have deserved and how it is averted by the explicit intercession of Moses. We see here how extreme is the consequence of their extreme rebellion against Yahweh. It is nothing less than their destruction and therefore the annulment of the covenant and promise. But this does not take place. For Moses prays : " Pardon, I beseech thee, the iniquity of this people according unto the greatness of thy mercy, and as thou hast forgiven this people, from Egypt even until now " (14¹⁹). And Yahweh's answer is : " I have pardoned according to thy word " (14²⁰). This does not mean, however, that what has happened has not happened or has no consequences. The ten false witnesses must die a sudden death (14³⁷). And there can be no question of an entry into the land, and therefore of the fulfilment of the promise, for the whole generation which has been guilty of the anxious care, first in a childish, and then in a raging form. With the exception of Joshua and Caleb, who " had another spirit with him, and hath followed me fully " (14²⁴), " they shall not see the land " (14²³). " This evil congregation, that are gathered together against me, in this wilderness they shall be consumed, and there they shall die "—not in Egypt, for the will and act of God cannot be reversed, and the covenant and promise are not annulled, but in the wilderness as they have desired, without experiencing the fulfilment.

The story ends on a dark and unconciliatory note (14³⁹ᶠ·). " The people mourned greatly " when Moses reported what had happened. They suddenly realise that they have sinned. But it does not appear that they are so very concerned about their sin, their care, their obstinacy against Yahweh, and therefore their transgression of the covenant, or that their confession of sin goes so very deep, when early the following morning they come to Moses armed and ready to march northwards into the land : " Lo, we be here, and will go up unto the place which the Lord hath promised." Has their fear of the death which they desired in the wilderness, and which has been ordained for them, suddenly become greater than their fear of the giants ? At any rate, they are not ready to accept the destiny which now impends in consequence of their own guilt. They will march out and fight. But they can do this only in defiance of the command of Yahweh. The courage of those who are anxious is no more pleasing to Him than their cowardice. " It shall not prosper. Go not up, for the Lord is not among you ; that ye be not smitten before your enemies . . . because ye are turned away from the Lord, therefore the Lord will not be with you " ($14^{41f.}$). " But they presumed to go up unto the hill top. . . . Then the Amalekites came down, and the Canaanites which dwelt in that hill, and discomfited them, even unto Hormah " ($14^{44f.}$). *Ubi cessandum est, semper agilis, prompta et audax est incredulitas, ubi autem pergendi autor est Deus, timida est, pigra et mortua,* is Calvin's observation on this incident (*C.R.*, 25, 209). Their *incredulitas* met with the fate which it must always suffer whatever form it takes. The only note of comfort at the end of the story—apart from the existence of the little ones about whom they had been so anxious (14^{31})—is that in this careless enterprise the care-ridden Israelites did not take with them the ark of God, and therefore it was not involved in the catastrophe (14^{44}).

3. THE MISERY OF MAN

In this sub-section we shall be investigating man as the one who commits sin as we have learned to know it in the form of sloth. Who and what is he in the determination and character which he gives himself and has to bear as he commits it ? The starting-point for our answer to this question has already been decided in the first part of this whole section. In relation to the situation which sin creates, as to sin itself, we do not have to think and speak according to our own mind and judgment, but according to the act and revelation and Word of God. Our gaze must be directed on the Son of Man Jesus, on the royal freedom of His existence as exalted and sanctified man, which includes our own true and authentic existence. And it is in the light of this that we must consider our false and inauthentic existence as those who commit acts of sloth. The situation which we create (in our stupidity and inhumanity and vagabondage and discontent) is the misery of man in the sense of his exile as the sum of human woe. To this far country of ours the Son of God has come in order that He may return home as the Son of Man, not in isolation but as our Lord and Head and Representative, bringing us with Him. But instead of being those who are exalted in and with Him, as we are in truth, we are revealed in His light as those who lead a false existence, remaining in exile and therefore in misery as though the true God had come to us in vain, as though He had not taken us up with Him, as though we were not already at home in and with Him, sharing His royal freedom. This is what gives to the human situation the determination and character of human misery. It is the evil fruit of the evil sloth of man. It is the unavoidable fate of the slothful man. Remaining behind instead of going up with Him, he is necessarily the one who is left behind in misery. He prefers his own life below to the divine life above. He chooses to persist in it. He must have it as he himself wills to have it. He must be the one he himself wills to be. He is thus the man who remains below where he does not belong, and is not at home, but where he irrevocably has his place—so long as his corrupt will is not broken by the direction of Jesus. This is, from the standpoint of the sin of man as sloth, what we described as the fall of man from the standpoint of his sin as pride (*C.D.*, IV, 1, § 60, 3). It is what the older dogmatics called in its totality the *status corruptionis*. Our present term for it is the misery of man.

Even in this *status corruptionis* man is not outside the sphere of influence of divine grace. With all his acts of sloth he cannot leave this sphere. When he remains behind, the consequences of this dreadful act are severe, but he does not give God the slip. God does not cease to be the God and Lord and Creator and Covenant-partner even of the stupid and inhuman and vagabond and discontented man, or in the far country which is necessarily the place of this man. And man too, in all his slothful action and the misery which it involves, does not cease to be the creature and covenant-partner of God. As he has not created himself, he cannot disannul or transform himself. As he has not instituted the covenant, he cannot destroy it or even contract out of it as though it were a free compact. Let us say at once in concrete terms that the descent of the Son of God to our misery and the ascent of the Son of Man to God's glory, the existence of the man Jesus within our slothful humanity, His victory in the crucifixion as our Lord and Head and Representative, the revelation of this victory in His resurrection, the issue of His direction, the outpouring of the Holy Spirit on all flesh—all these are facts. As man has not brought them about, he cannot reverse them by anything that he does. They are facts even in face and at the very heart of his misery. Even in his turning to nothingness and under the overwhelming threat of it, he himself has not become nothing. Even in his misery he belongs, not to the devil or to himself, but to God. The Yes of divine grace is terribly concealed in the No of divine judgment, but it is spoken to him too : even to unhappy Nabal ; even to the people of Northern Israel ; even to David with his petty sin ; even to the murmurers in the wilderness. Jesus lives as very man, and therefore as the very God who humbled Himself to man, who came to him in his misery, who took his misery to Himself. Thus even in his misery man lives as the man for whom Jesus lives. To omit this qualification of man's misery is necessarily to deny Jesus Christ as the Lord who became a servant and the servant who became Lord, and therefore to blaspheme God.

We have to realise, however, that it is these very facts which make the misery of man so severe. The seriousness of the misery which results from the sin of sloth is distinguished from that of a fate by the very fact that the man who is overtaken by it is not in any sense released from the sphere of influence of God and His grace. We can draw the sting from even the worst of fates by not merely suffering but bearing it. It disturbs only so long as we are ourselves unsettled and resist it. In face of it there is a rest in which man can transcend, master and defeat it by surrendering to it. But this is not the case in relation to the hard hand of the living God which is the basis of the misery that results from sloth. Just because God does not let go the man who has plunged into this misery, just because His grace does not depart from him (Is. 54[10]), he cannot find in any opposing rest a way of avoiding unsettlement by it. No surrender can enable him to outmatch it. He cannot, then, transcend or defeat it. He cannot master it. There is no refuge, not even in hell itself, in which he can cease to be in misery. The work and Word of God's grace are still actual and valid for him. Even in this place he himself has not ceased to exist as the creature and covenant-partner of God. But he does so as one who is reluctant, in a perversion of his human creatureliness, as a covenant-breaker whom the Yes of God must strike as His No, who must suffer the grace of God as His disfavour and wrath and judgment. His misery consists in his ill-founded insufficiency, his inexcusable shame, his self-contradiction which cannot be smoothed over. The very thing which limits his misery—the fact that in it he belongs to God—is also the very thing which makes it so sharp. It is for this reason that we had first to think of its limitation.

But what is this misery which is the ineluctable consequence of his sloth ? In reply to this question we shall make three assertions, none of which is to be derived from, or proved by, a supposed empirical observation or conceptual abstraction, but all of which have reference to that which, as the reconciliation of man including his liberation from this misery, is a reality, our living hope, in the being and work of the man Jesus. In the light of this hope we acquire authentic information concerning our exiled present which is already our past in Him, i.e., in the Jesus who lives for us.

1. The liberation of man from the misery created by his sloth is a reality and therefore a living hope for all other men only in the crucified Jesus. To free us He took it to Himself. He made it His own misery. And as the bearer of it He could only die. It was only in His death that He could set this term to it ; that He could make an end of it. A sickness which can terminate only with the death of the patient, from which he can be liberated only by death, is an incurable sickness, or one which can be cured only as it reaches its goal and end with the destruction of the sick person, thus coming up against a frontier which even it cannot pass. If Jesus is the patient for us, in our place, burdened with our sickness, it is obvious that we have to say of our sickness that as the misery to which the stupid and inhuman

and dissipated and careworn man has fallen victim it is incurable—a fact which emerges with particular impressiveness in all the Old Testament passages to which we referred. Our first proposition is thus that it is a mortal sickness, i.e., that if we ourselves had to bear it, if Jesus had not carried it in our place, it could end only with our death and destruction.

It does in fact end with our death to the extent that Jesus, burdened with our sickness, suffered our death. It is true that in His death, triumphing for us even as He suffered for us, He accomplished our new and healthy birth. But this does not alter its character as a mortal sickness. On the contrary, it reveals its character. The misery of man is of such a kind that an end could be made of it (negatively) only by the death suffered by Jesus and (positively) only in a new life inaugurated by Jesus as He crossed this frontier. By what Jesus has done and is in order to free us from it it is distinguished as " my boundless misery " (Luther), i.e., the misery which has no measure or limit within my human being and thinking and willing and achievement, in the sphere of the whole act in which I exist as a man. There are no reservations, no islands on which and no pauses in which, in relation to myself and apart from what I am in Jesus, I am not in misery. I am wholly and utterly encompassed and penetrated by it. It is co-extensive with my existence. I can toss and turn on my sick-bed. I can transfer or be transferred from one sick-bed to another. When it is particularly severe, I can change hospitals, or, if I prefer, arrange for private treatment. But I am always sick, and my sickness is always the same. It is the incurable misery which dominates my life and always emerges in one form or another.

To what do we refer ? We refer simply to the fact that we have no option but to be those we are in the power or impotence of what we do. We refer to the destruction and decomposition of our being which takes place in the fact that we think we can accomplish the actions of our stupidity and inhumanity and dissipation and care. We have seen what is the source of these actions : our groundless and inexplicable but unfortunately real and dangerous turning to that which is not ; the perverse love of chaos in which we let ourselves fall where we ought to stand and lift up ourselves. We have also seen where this leads : to the net of our self-contradiction with all its inter-woven meshes ; to our own devastation ; to the perversion of our relationship to God and our fellows and ourselves and our temporality. Coming from the one we are necessarily on the way to the other, hastening towards it. Deriving from the one, our being necessarily bears all the marks of the other, of this whole perversion and devastation. This is the misery of man. It is indeed his being in exile, in the far country. For he is not really at home in his hurrying along this way. The marks of his being on this way do not really belong to him. But it is he who bears them. It is he who must bear them.

For it is he who hurries along this way on which he has no future but his own destruction and decomposition, nothingness and himself as its victim.

It is to be noted that we are not yet dealing with death. Man still exists. He still lives. The goal has not yet been reached. Or he himself has not yet been reached by the final thing that comes upon him from this source ; just as in the pictures of the headlong plunge of the damned the jaws of hell are only opened and eternal fire is only waiting for them. The misery of man is " only " his being in this plunge into them. It is " only " his being in the movement towards death. Only ! As though this were less serious ! As though being in death might not even seem to be better ! As though the irresistible plunge in this direction, which is the inevitable consequence of man's letting himself fall in his sloth, were not as such—in this qualitative sense—" my boundless misery " : the very fact that I cannot be free of it ; that I am still there ; that I have to accept this situation and can find no release from it. It is here that the sharpness of human misery as grounded in man's limitation works itself out. As God does not abandon him, he cannot abandon himself—not even if he wants to, or tries to realise his desire in what we call suicide. He himself does what he does—the work of sloth. And he himself inevitably is what he does. He can only follow the law of sloth under which he has placed himself. He can only hurry along this way. He cannot do so as his own spectator, as he would like. He can do so only as the active and therefore the suffering person ; the one who is not yet in death, but already, and hopelessly, on the way to it.

Note that we are referring to an objective reality which obtains irrespective of our own recognition of it. There is thus no substance in the objection raised by experience, i.e., by a deficient experience of this misery. No man but Jesus has ever known the true breadth and depth, the true essence and darkness, of human misery. What we see and note and know and more or less painfully experience of it is only the shadow of His cross touching us. In all its essence and darkness it is, of course, our misery. It is we who make that headlong plunge. But we can see this only before the passion of Christ, as we hear His cry : " My God, my God, why hast thou forsaken me ? " (Mk. 15³⁴). We cannot see it in the terror and doubt and despair which may come on us. Or we can see it in these only as a distant recollection of the misery of which He has made an end in His death ; only as a weak echo of His cry ; only as a sign that we are truly in Him, and therefore share His sufferings. We have no direct experience of it. We cannot speak of it as though it were an element in our own history. However severely we may be buffeted, there can be no question of repetitions of Golgotha. Not merely quantitatively, but qualitatively, all the content of our experience is completely transcended by Golgotha. But the fact that Golgotha never becomes the content of our own experience and consciousness does not alter the fact that the misery of man as it is there borne and revealed by Jesus and as it may also reflect itself in our experiences is objectively and truly our own misery. Whatever we ourselves may see or not see, God sees us as those who are on the way to death, and we are this in truth. And the fact that we are this is something that we have to let ourselves be told from the place where God has seen us all in the One ; from the cross and passion of Jesus. Those who think that they are particularly touched by that shadow in their own lives must not think that human misery is only theirs. And those who are able in their own lives to escape the shadow which reaches them with a certain gaiety and abandon must not think that the misery of man is any the less theirs. It is objectively the case that we are all away from home—exiles. In Jesus we are all back home again. Human misery is behind us. We have passed through the far country. We have died as those who lived there and are born again as new men. We already walk in the light. But it is in the light of Jesus in which we participate that we are accused as those who let themselves sink into their own past and therefore as those who sink in this our past ; as those who are still in the far country, still in misery.

We have thought of man's misery as an exile (a sense which used to be borne by the German word *Elend*). But if we take it in the customary sense (as *miseria*) the dreadful feature of this hurrying and plunging to death is that at every point man necessarily exists in a radical perversion. " Perversion " is the term that we must use—not transformation or destruction. Even in that which he is in virtue of his folly in all its forms, he is the good creature of God. Even in his sickness he does not lack any of his members or organs. All the features which make him a man still remain. He has not become a devil or an animal or a plant. Even in his misery he is not half a man, but a whole man. His misery consists in the corruption of this best. The perverted use which he makes of it is followed at once by his corrupt state—the worst. Things which are bright in themselves are all dark for him. Things that he desires all slip out of his grasp. His true glory becomes his shame. The pure becomes impure. The joyful is enwrapped by the deepest sadness. That which uplifts becomes a temptation ; every blessing a curse ; salvation perdition. We do not see deeply enough if we think and say that there is here *only* darkness, want, shame, impurity, sadness, temptation, curse and perdition. In the strict sense, the misery of man is not a *status*, a *continuum*, but his being in a history in which there can be no abstract " only." Thus the light is still there, but quenched ; the wealth as it slips away ; the glory as it turns to shame ; the purity to impurity ; the joy to sadness. They are all there in this movement from the right to the left, from above to below, in their perversion and corruption ; or, strictly, in the event of their corruption. The slothful man is and exists in the context of this event, in the sequence of such events, in this sinister history. It is the history of his impotent ignoring of the grace of God present to him. It is the history of the opportunities continually offered to him and continually let slip by him. It is his history under the judgments of God. His being in this history is his misery. As he is in this history, he is the *miser* who will inevitably be lost and in death without the *misericordia Dei*.

We emphasise the fact that he is this at every point. This means in the whole fulfilment of his existence and in all the features of his humanity. It does not mean that he is below and in darkness in everything that he is and does. On the contrary, in everything that he is and does he is above. But he is not merely above. He is also engaged in that slipping and sinking and falling on the one-way street from above to below. There is no firm point at which and from which he is involved in any other movement and therefore not in that corruption. He is wholly and utterly caught up in this history. There is no depth of his soul where he is not implicated in this perversion. It is quite futile to talk about a " relic of goodness " which remains to man even as a sinner and which is usually identified rather uneasily with the faculty of reason or a religious or moral *a priori* or the like. In answer to this kind of assertion we have to say (1) that the good which remains to man as a sinner is not merely a " relic " but the totality of His God-given nature and its determination, and (2) that in the same totality he exists in the history of the perversion of this good into evil, and is caught up in the movement from above to below. His total being in this movement is his *miseria* which has its limit only in the *misericordia Dei*.

What we call the misery of man corresponds fairly exactly to what the New Testament calls his being in the flesh. As is well-known, the term σάρξ is ambiguous. On the one side, like the Old Testament *basar*, it is a term which is simply used to describe man and his person as an existing temporal subject in the totality of his human nature, and especially in the determination in which he is a physical being in this totality. " Flesh and blood " is sometimes used to bring out this sense. To be or live ἐν σαρκί or even κατὰ σάρκα in this sense is simply to be, to exist, to live as a living human creature in time, with a special emphasis on the physical aspect, on the context of the physico-natural order to which we belong. The fact that this is the special reference is an indication that in it man is regarded, if neutrally, from the standpoint of the lower components of his being. On the other side σάρξ has a pejorative sense. It means man in the sphere which is dominated by the power of his own sin. It again means the whole man, but in the corruption which has entered and which works itself out as a result of his sin. It means man as he has turned away from God in his own lust, as he is hostile and opposed to God, as he lacks His Spirit, and as he has fallen a total victim to φθορά. To be and walk and act ἐν σαρκί or κατὰ σάρκα in this sense is to be a man—the lower side is no longer neutral but disqualified—in this sphere and therefore under this power, in this perversion, and with desires which are opposed to God and His Spirit, thus falling a victim to φθορά. In relation to this twofold meaning it is to be noted that the second is already indicated in the first. Even in the first sense σάρξ is not unequivocal

(like ψυχή, σῶμα or νοῦς). It is not a term used in a normal, but only in a patho-
logical, anthropology. It sees man already as the subject of the history in which
he will become σάρξ in the second sense. Conversely, however, we must not lose
sight of the first sense in the second. The man who lives in the flesh in the
pejorative sense is the same as the one who, as described by the same term,
simply lives in his humanity in time. We cannot dissolve with a word the tension
which there is in the term and which emerges in these changes of meaning. In
the various passages we may be pointed more to the one side or more to the
other, but the tension remains. In the relationship of the two meanings the
term describes the fatal history which confronted the New Testament authors
when they looked at man—not others but primarily themselves (Rom. 7)—as
he is apart from his being in the one man Jesus, opposing His Spirit and in total
need of liberation by Him. To denote his being in the history of the division of
his ego, his self-alienation and self-contradiction, they used the term σάρξ in its
twofold sense. The term describes the ταλαίπωρος ἄνθρωπος (Rom. 7²⁴) who can
only cry for redemption—man in his misery.

2. In our redemption from this misery, a new man, the saint of
God, has taken our place in the crucified man Jesus in whom our old
man died ; a new man as the subject of new and different acts which
are obedient and well-pleasing to God. We are freed from our misery
to the extent that in Him we too are new men and therefore the
subjects of new acts. Less than the new birth of man did not and
does not suffice to make him a doer of these new acts in which his
sloth is no longer operative and recognisable, in which instead of
continually sinking he may lift up himself and stand and be active
as a true man. Except as they proceed from the new beginning which
has been made in Jesus his acts—and this is our second proposition—
will always be the acts of his sloth and misery.

The misery of man as it may be seen in the light of his liberation
is a history and not a status or *continuum* in the further sense that it
has a life of its own in which it continually confirms and renews itself
in an endless circle. We have already stated that what man does he
is. But the converse is also true. What he is he does. And he will
do it continually to the extent that he does not become another man
in Jesus and his action does not become that of the other man who is
in Jesus. To use the language of older dogmatics, *peccatum originale*
necessarily gives rise to *peccata actualia*. *Peccata actualia* (acts of sin)
are *peccata in actione*. The misery of man is characterised by the fact
that man not only *is* a sinner. He certainly is, and makes himself,
this as he commits sin. But we might accustom ourselves to the fact
that he is this. We might learn to master it. We might explain it
as a kind of fate—merited, of course, but to be borne and endured by
the individual only in solidarity with all history and humanity, in
subjection to the sentence pronounced on Adam and on all men in
him. But this sentence is already misunderstood. For its reference
is to the culpability of the act, the basic act of evil, in which humanity,
which has its responsible subject in each individual, was and is implicated from the very first, in Adam. And what characterises the misery

of man is that he is evil, not only in his participation in this basic act, not only as a child of Adam, in his heart from his youth up, but also (as this) from moment to moment, " in evil thoughts and words and works from his youth up even to this present," in individual decisions which are wrong decisions in virtue of their source, each of them having its fatal aspect and consequence, each in its own way being an act of unfaithfulness, unbelief, disobedience and ingratitude, each in its own way a work of the sloth for which he is again and no less strictly responsible as for the basic act of his existence. It is true, but it does not release him (for he himself is the one who wills and does it), that as the child of Adam he proceeds continually from the great sloth of man. It is also true, but does not release him (for he himself is again a willing and acting subject), that in the form of concrete, the most concrete, achievements he continually returns to the sphere of that sloth. The liberation of man as it has taken place in Jesus is his true liberation from this circle. That he (he himself) moves in this circle is his misery.

And to the misery of his being in individual wicked acts there belongs the contradiction that there is no action which is evil in itself and as such, by disposition and constitution, but that the whole action of man is necessarily evil as it takes place in this circle. " For every creature of God is good, and nothing to be refused, if it be received with thanksgiving " (1 Tim. 4⁴). Yet that is the very thing which is lacking. The psychical and physical, spiritual and sensual functions in which the evil acts of men are done can be pure as the functions of the pure (Tit. 1¹⁵). They are this in themselves and as such. The good creation of God persists. We are forced to say this finally not only of the functions of those who are healthy but also of those who are sick in body or soul. The evil does not consist in a disposition of the *psyche* or *physis* but in the sloth of their physical and psychic action as it derives from the sloth of their heart. It is in this, and in its service, that that which is not evil in itself becomes evil—the psychic and physical occurrence in which the acts of men are done. Even to the smallest details the slothful man acts in contradiction and conflict with himself. Even to the smallest details he exists in the history of this perversion. In his actual sins it continually acquires new actuality in a whole inter-related sequence of open and secret detailed histories. Apart from his new beginning, apart from the new birth which has already taken place in Jesus, apart from his becoming a different man, and therefore the subject of new and different acts, in the power of His direction, there can be no question of an end of his misery in this respect too.

A dogmatico-historical observation is required at this point. It concerns the locus *De peccato actuali* which presents rather a curious picture in older Protestant dogmatics. It consists for the most part in a remarkable and very finely woven net of concepts which are intrinsically antithetical but which are paired off to show how from any particular standpoint the act of sin may take place between two very widely separated points and yet always have the essential character of sin. There are thus, it was taught, *peccata commissionis* and *peccata omissionis*, *peccata infirmitatis* or *ignorantiae* and *peccata malitiae*, *peccata voluntaria* and *peccata involuntaria*, *peccata regnantia*, i.e., sins which dominate a man, or which he allows to master him without a struggle, and *peccata non regnantia*, those which are not overcome by him, yet which he does not acquiesce in but contests. There is a *peccatum mortuum*, and in some sense latent or potential sin, of which we are not conscious, at least in its full range and extent, and a *peccatum vivens*, sin living and recognised in the sense of Rom. 7⁸⁻⁹. There are *peccata spiritualia*, of which the soul is particularly guilty (e.g., pride, envy and theological heresy), and *peccata carnalia*, like gluttony, drunkenness and lechery. There are *peccata clamantia*, those which cry to heaven, and *peccata tolerantiae*, those which for all their culpability are endured for a time by the long-suffering of God. The doubtful nature of the whole understanding emerges at once in the obvious difficulty and even impossibility of many of these distinctions. The general purpose was very largely perhaps to differentiate one sin from another as more or less dangerous and disruptive. It is tempting to try to do this, but it constitutes a threat to the presupposition which was sometimes maintained very strongly, that all sins are alike in this, *ut vel minima minimi peccati cogitatio, mortem aeternam millies mereamur* (Bucan, *Inst. theol.*, 1602, XVI, 9). Yet if we consider the results rather than the purpose of this whole theologoumen, we have to recognise, not merely that it has a certain practical value as a constituent element in a kind of penitential mirror, but that it helps us to realise that the whole action of man, caught in the cross-fire of the questions put by these distinctions, is unable to avoid the judgment that it is sin, and that it is brought under this judgment, not indiscriminately, but in its differentiation, in its own particular nature and character. If we keep before us the net of these opposing concepts in its totality, we realise that the judgment under which we stand is comprehensive and yet that it is also concrete and specific. If the Word of God pronounces us all guilty, it does not do so generally and amorphously, but with particular reference to each individual in his own place, and again with particular reference to this or that specific action, so that the misery of man is not a night which makes all cats grey, but in it each of us, in each specific action, has his own profile and his own shade of darkness.

One pair of concepts suggested in relation to *peccata actualia* was a subject of dispute between the Romanists and Lutherans on the one side and the Reformed dogmaticians on the other. This was the distinction between so-called mortal sins (*peccata mortalia*) and venial sins (*peccata venialia*). According to Roman doctrine there are some sins which are so slight that they do not leave behind any *macula in anima* (Thomas Aquinas, *S. th.*, II, 1, 89, 1). They are inevitably bound up with human life since the fall. But they are to be compared with what Paul in 1 Cor. 3¹² calls wood, hay and stubble. They do not prevent the attainment of salvation (89²) and they are reparable in themselves even apart from the counteraction of divine grace. In contrast, there are the seven deadly sins—according to Thomas (84, 4) *inanis gloria, gula, luxuria, avaritia, tristitia (quae tristatur de bono spirituali propter laborem corporalem adiunctum), invidia, ira.* These are not reparable in themselves. They can be made good only by grace, which means in practice the renewal of baptismal grace by the sacrament of penance. The older Lutheran dogmatics could also speak of a *peccatum mortale* as opposed to a *peccatum veniale.* " Venial " according to Hollaz (*Ex. theol. acroam.*, 1707, II, 4, qu. 20) is *omne peccatum involuntarium in renatis, quod neque gratiam inhabitantem Spiritus sancti excutit, neque fidem extinguit, sed eodem momento, quo committitur, veniam indivulso nexu coniunctam habet.* Mortal sin, on the other hand, is that which is committed in transgression of the divine commandment *contra dictamen conscientiae deliberato voluntatis proposito (qu.* 9). The older Reformed teachers rejected this whole distinction. As they saw it, they can be no resting-place even for the regenerate. On the one side every sin, however slight it may seem to be, is mortal sin. And on the other side every sin can be forgiven by the mercy of God.

In the light of our presuppositions there can be no doubt as to our own position in relation to this controversy. The Roman and Lutheran distinction between mortal and venial sin assumes a quantitative concept of sin which cannot be united with the decisive seriousness of the divine judgment and the human situation under this judgment. It can serve only to veil the depth of human misery and therefore the depth of the free grace of God. On the same ground we have to reject the distinction between voluntary and involuntary sin, and especially the notion that in respect of involuntary sins Christians are more advantageously placed than the unregenerate. Every sin, even the smallest, is mortal sin to the extent that it is worthy of death and involves our mortal sickness. How, then, can we restrict the term to the seven deadly sins, as though a venial sin not in this list could not be just as great as any of these, and even greater than all of them put together ? Which supposedly little sin, even the smallest, is not committed in an inner conflict of man and the will of man, so that it is not at one and the same time voluntary sin and involuntary ? And what is meant by the idea of a sin which is pardonable in itself, and therefore apart from the merciful God and independently of His pardoning grace ? Is there any other forgiveness but that of God ? Does not each one of us stand in absolute need of His forgiveness for every sin ? Is not His forgiveness promised equally to every sinner for every sin ?—excepting only those to whom He is revealed, and by whom He is known, as the merciful God, but who do not keep to His mercy, who try to evade forgiveness and the need of forgiveness in the case of some of their sins, and who thus make themselves guilty of what is indicated in Mk. 3[28] and par. as a limiting concept, the sin against the Holy Ghost. The distinction between lethal and venial sins cannot be sustained. It is quite irrelevant. And in the last resort it is to be rejected because it involves a dangerous tendency in the direction of this terrible limiting concept.

3. The liberation of man from his misery has taken place and is a fact only in the royal freedom in which the man Jesus has accomplished it by giving up Himself, His life as very God and very man, to death for us in obedience to God and as our Lord and Head and Representative. This is the act of free will, the decision of *liberum arbitrium*, in which the liberation of man from his misery has been once and for all accomplished. Jesus lives. He lives as the Doer of this act of the free and victorious human will breaking the circle of sinful human action and being ; the will of the new man, the holy man introduced by God in His person, the man who is free for Him and for us. As such, He lives for us. And in Him we also live as men of the same free will, as those who break through that circle, who overcome and conquer our misery, as free men. In Him the mercy of God which limits our misery is really present as the gift of freedom —our own freedom. But this means that in the misery from which we are liberated by Him, i.e., in our own tarrying in our past as caused by our sloth, we are not free apart from Him, nor do we participate in the free and victorious will which breaks through that circle of our sinning. Our third proposition is, therefore, as follows. Our misery,

as we have to learn continually from our liberation by Him, is the determination of our will as *servum arbitrium*.

It is always a mistake to try to establish or understand the assertion of the bondage of the will otherwise than christologically. It cannot be either proved or disproved by empirical findings or *a priori* reflections. As a corollary to the confession of the freedom which has been won for us and granted to us in the man Jesus it is a theological statement—a statement of faith. As such, it has nothing whatever to do with the battle between determinism and indeterminism. It is not a decision for determinism ; and the fact that this is not clear in Luther's *De servo arbitrio* is the objection that we are forced to raise against this well-known work and also against the ideas of Zwingli and Calvin. It can take up into itself both determinism and indeterminism to the extent that they are to be understood as the hypotheses of an empiricist or *a priori* philosophy. It necessarily excludes both to the extent that they set themselves up, on this or that foundation, as metaphysical dogmas. It describes the perversion of the human situation which results from the sloth of man in his relationship with God. It does not consist at all in the fact that man cannot any longer will and decide, i.e., that he is deprived of *arbitrium*, that he has no will at all. If this were the case, he would no longer be a man ; he would only be part of a mechanism moved from without. This would involve the transformation of man into another and non-human being—an idea which we have exerted ourselves to repudiate from the very outset in this whole context. But the freedom of man does not really consist —except in the imagination of the invincibly ignorant—in the fact that, like Hercules at the cross-roads, he can will and decide. Nor does the bondage of his will consist in the fact that he is not able to do this.

Freedom is not an empty and formal concept. It is one which is filled out with a positive meaning. It does not speak only of a capacity. It speaks concretely of the fact that man can be genuinely man as God who has given him this capacity can in His freedom be genuinely God. The free man is the man who can be genuinely man in fellowship with God. He exercises and has this freedom, therefore, not in an indefinite but in a definite choice in which he demonstrates this capacity. But since this capacity is grounded in His fellowship with God this means in the choice in which he confirms and practises his fellowship with God ; in the election, corresponding to his own election and creation and determination, of faith and obedience and gratitude and loyalty to God as the One who is the Creator and Giver not only of his human essence and existence but also of this capacity.

Again, we must not say that this great name is merited by the " freedom " so often described as *posse peccare* and *posse non peccare* : as though the possibility of *peccare* were a genuine possibility offered to man by God and not one which God has forbidden and excluded ;

as though he could have this possibility in genuine freedom, in his freedom to be genuinely man. The man who has, or can desire, this possibility is already the man who is not free and who must desire it. Of the free man it has to be said : *non potest peccare*. His freedom excludes this. It excludes the possibility of sinning. He " cannot " sin in the capacity granted to him by God. In this capacity he can only believe and obey and give thanks and give to the faithfulness of God the response of his own loyalty. He can sin only as he renounces this capacity and therefore, as we have repeatedly maintained, makes no use of his freedom. The sloth of man in all its forms (as stupidity, inhumanity, dissipation and care) and in all its individual acts or omissions consists in his failure to make use of his freedom. And all this is negative. It does not rest on anything that can seriously be called a *posse*. It has no basis either in God or in man himself by which it can be explained. It can be described only as a freedom not to be free—which is nonsense. Yet as man's turning to that which is not it does actually take place. It is the grasping of the possibility which is no possibility, but can be characterised only as an impossibility. It is the " choosing " which is not an alternative to the genuine choosing of faith and obedience and gratitude but only the dreadful negation of this genuine choosing. It is the irrational and incomprehensible decision of man. It is a fact only as *peccare*, ἁμαρτάνειν, transgression. Yet in this character it is a real fact. It is a sinister fact which is not illumined by any *posse*. It is the fact of sin in which man reveals and demonstrates that he is inexplicably the slothful man who does not make any use of his freedom. He can have his freedom only as he uses it, in the choice of the possibility which corresponds to it. If he does not use it, he goes out into the absolute void of a being in unbelief and disobedience and ingratitude, into a being which is no true being. And this means that he loses it. He does not have it. There is no freedom in this unreal being and for those who turn to it. It is *eo ipso* the sphere of bondage. As a sinner man has decided against his freedom to be genuinely man. And in this decision he will necessarily continue to decide against it. " Whosoever committeth sin is the servant of sin " (Jn. 8³⁴). In this briefest of biblical formulations we have the whole doctrine of the bondage of the will. *Non potest non peccare* is what we have to say of the sinful, slothful man. His sin excludes his freedom, just as his freedom excludes his sin. There is no middle position. For the slothful man there is only the first alternative. He has not ceased to be a man. He wills. He is a Hercules, the *arbiter* of what he does. But he does what he does in the corruption of his will. He does not, therefore, do it *libero* but *servo arbitrio*. In a deeper sense than the poet had in mind, it is the curse of an evil deed that it inevitably gives birth to fresh evil. To be sure, the slothful man chooses—in that dreadful negation of true choosing—as he always did. But he chooses only on the path that he has entered. And on this path, however he may choose, he cannot choose as a true man (for he has turned aside from this genuine possibility), but in all his choices, having yielded to corruption, he can only act corruptly. His starting-point is the repudiation of his freedom. He cannot, therefore, do that which corresponds to his freedom. He necessarily does that which he could not do in the exercise of it. This is the bondage of the human will which is the bitterest characteristic of human misery.

It has its limit in the mercy of God, or concretely in the liberation accomplished for man in Jesus. This limit is set for it in the sanctification of man of which we shall speak in the next section. But as a precaution we must already make the following statement. The concept of limitation (which we are forced to use in relation to the sanctification of man) includes that of a subject of limitation. The liberation of man in Jesus is his new birth and conversion as it has taken place in Him. The freedom which man has and exercises in Him is a new creation. In Him he is free from the committal of sin and for faith, obedience and gratitude. He is, therefore, genuinely free, ὄντως ἐλεύθερος (Jn. 8³⁶). This is the limit which is set to his bondage by his sanctification. But in this life even the sanctified man who partakes of this freedom, even the Christian, is not only in Jesus, not only what he is in Him, and therefore not only free. In solidarity with all other men he is also in himself, in the flesh, in the past which is continually present. He is the one who is limited by this limitation, and as such the one who needs sanctification, liberation. To the extent that he is this, he is not free, and everything that we have said about the bondage of the human will applies in all seriousness to him too. To the extent that he is in the flesh and not in the spirit he is " dead in sins " (Col. 2¹³ ; Eph. 2¹). He is not just half-dead, or apparently dead. He is a corpse awaiting the resurrection, and we have to speak in all seriousness of his past which unfortunately is always present. He is engaged in the conflict of the Spirit against the flesh, but also of the flesh against the Spirit (Gal. 5¹⁷), and in the last resort he will not refuse to confess with the apostle Paul " that in me (that is, in my flesh) dwelleth no good thing " (Rom. 7¹⁸). Conflict does not mean peaceful co-existence, let alone co-operation. Even in the Christian the old man is quite unambiguously the old man. In relation to the new he can be compared only to a rebel whose insurrection is so checked by the power of his sovereign that it cannot work itself out freely but as a limited operation will even serve to promote the general good. Yet even in this way he is a rebel ; he is not a servant of his king. The old man, even in the Christian, is not a herald and precursor and partner of the new. In the sense described, he is in bondage. He does not will *libero arbitrio*, but *servo arbitrio*. He does not believe or love or hope or pray—or he does so only in appearance, deceiving himself and others. He is useless, absolutely useless, as far as concerns the good. He is stupid, inhuman, dissipated and discontented. He chooses, but he never chooses the right, only the wrong. All this stands within the limitation, but within it it is just the same as in the case of the non-Christian who does not have a part in that limitation. Within the limitation, as the one who is limited by it, the Christian is himself a practical non-Christian. Freedom and bondage clash in one and the same man : his freedom as a new man in Jesus and in the Holy Spirit ; and his bondage as an old man, outside Jesus, in and for himself, in the flesh, in his past which is still present ; and both of them total ; no *tertium*, no bridge, no mediation or synthesis between them, but only the antithesis of that conflict, life in sanctification, the *militia Christi*. No co-operation, then, between the two ! For how can there be co-operation between total freedom and total bondage ? How can the Spirit give assistance to the flesh, or the flesh to the Spirit ?

The doctrine which makes this *caveat* necessary is the Romanist doctrine of man's co-operation in the accomplishment of his justification (which as Romanists use the term includes what we call sanctification) ; his *translatio ab eo statu, in quo homo nascitur filius primi Adae, in statum gratiae . . . per secundum Adam Jesum Christum* (*Trid.* VI, *c.* 4). Even on the Roman view this *translatio* cannot, of course, take place without regeneration in Christ, participation in the merits of His passion (*c.* 3) and therefore concretely the sacramental grace of baptism. It cannot take place without the *gratia praeveniens* which in the case of adults at least reaches and calls and supports them even before their baptism (*c.* 5). On the other hand, it cannot take place unless they themselves, moved by prevenient grace, are disposed *ad convertendum se ad suam ipsorum iustificationem*, to a free *assentire* and *cooperari* with this grace. Thus in relation to it man is neither inactive nor active apart from it (*c.* 5) when he comes to the point (we are still in a prior sphere to that of an acceptance of the true grace of justification) of assenting to revelation, of recognising that he is a sinner, of seeking refuge in the mercy of God, of believing in Christ and loving Him, and of beginning to hate his sin, with the ultimate result that he receives baptism and begins a new life and obeys the divine commandments (*c.* 6). All this can and must take place on the Romanist view because even in a state of original sin the *liberum arbitrium* of man is *minime exstinctum, viribus licet attenuatum et inclinatum* (*c.* 1). In other words, it is not so weakened or perverted that on the presupposition of *gratia praeveniens* man is not capable of that *assentire et cooperari*, of that *se disponere et praeparare* (*can.* 4). If this is the case with the man who has not yet participated in the true grace of justification, how much more is it the case with those who have received the grace of baptism (*c.* 7) or its renewal in penance (*c.* 14). This sacramental grace has cleansed away all sin in the strict sense (*totum id, quod veram et propriam peccati rationem habet*). What remains is a *concupiscentia vel fomes peccati*, a painful relic of earth which, although it derives from sin and inclines to it (V, *c.* 5), cannot harm those who do not give place to it, but manfully resist it *per gratiam Christi Jesu*. Indeed, those who do this are capable of an *incrementum iustificationis* in the form of good works (VI, *c.* 10). They still commit the little, everyday, venial sins in which they do not cease to be righteous. But they also do good works in which they are free even from venial offences (*c.* 11). Even if they fall into mortal sin, and must therefore begin again from the beginning by receiving the sacrament of penance, they will not lose faith (*c.* 15, *can.* 28). In addition, they can merit (*mereri, c.* 16, *can.* 24 and 33) an *augmentum gratiae* by good works, and, if they die in a state of grace, the actual reception of eternal life, and ultimately even an *augmentum gloriae*, a commensurate enhancement of their eternal blessedness.

These were the statements of Trent as they were drawn up in the year of Luther's death in opposition to Reformation teaching. They had been carefully worked out in a conscientious and critical scrutiny of the development of doctrine in Scholasticism and later Scholasticism, and they were formulated in such a way as to counter at every conceivable point the objection of the Reformers. At the heart of the exposition of the *meritum bonorum operum* (*c.* 16) we even come across the sincerely meant statement : *Absit tamen, ut christianus homo in se ipso vel confidet vel glorietur et non in Domino.* It is hard to see, however, what force this statement can have in conjunction with a doctrine the whole point of which is to maintain man in an unshaken self-consciousness balancing not only the grace of God but also and primarily his own sin. Both sin and grace are understood as quantities, and on this assumption they are compared and pragmatised and tamed and rendered quite innocuous. The meaning of the conflict between the Spirit and the flesh, of the new man in Jesus and the old in whose form we confront Jesus, of freedom and bondage as totalities which do not complement but mutually exclude one another, is not only unperceived but actually concealed in a whole sea of obliterating formulæ and objections and protests which are directed against every kind of quietism and fatalism, which have nothing whatever to do with what has to be said seriously concerning either the *liberum* or the *servum arbitrium*, and which can only secure us against having to see and say what really ought to be seen and said at this point. The teaching office the Roman Church neither willed nor could say this. It will not and cannot say it to-day. Instead it speaks on the one hand of that *assentire* and *cooperari* of the unregenerate man in his relationship to the obscure *gratia praeveniens* which is arbitrarily invented and cannot be defined with any precision but which results in his capacity for faith and penitence and a turning to grace. And on the other it speaks of the good works of the regenerate man, who is only a little sinner and commits only tiny sins, and who is in the happy position of being able to increase the grace of justification in co-operation with it, and even to augment the degree of his eternal bliss. The practical consequence of all this is that the misery of man is not regarded as in any way serious or dangerous either for Christians or non-Christians. The Reformation communions could not reunite with a Church which held this doctrine, and they cannot accept the call to reunion with it to-day. We ourselves have looked at the matter rather differently from the Evangelical theologians of the 16th century. We have considered the misery of man in the light of the liberation which has taken place and is actually present in Jesus. Our understanding of the enslaved will of sinful man has nothing whatever to do with determinism or pessimism. But for this very reason we cannot accept any more (indeed far less) than they could the mitigation of this misery offered by the Romanist doctrine. " Thanks be to God, which giveth us the victory through our Lord Jesus Christ " (1 Cor. 15[57]). It is a matter of the positive affirmation of this thanksgiving if in substantial agreement with the older Evangelical theology we are committed at this point to a decided negative.

§ 66

THE SANCTIFICATION OF MAN

The exaltation of man, which in defiance of his reluctance has been achieved in the death and declared in the resurrection of Jesus Christ, is as such the creation of his new form of existence as the faithful covenant-partner of God. It rests wholly and utterly on his justification before God, and like this it is achieved only in the one Jesus Christ, but effectively and authoritatively for all in Him. It is self-attested, by its operation among them as His direction, in the life of a people of men who in virtue of the call to discipleship which has come to them, of their awakening to conversion, of the praise of their works, of the mark of the cross which is laid upon them, have the freedom even as sinners to render obedience and to establish themselves as the saints of God in a provisional offering of the thankfulness for which the whole world is ordained by the act of the love of God.

1. JUSTIFICATION AND SANCTIFICATION

Under the title "sanctification" we take up the theme which constitutes the particular scope of this second part of the doctrine of reconciliation. The divine act of atonement accomplished and revealed in Jesus Christ does not consist only in the humiliation of God but in and with this in the exaltation of man. Thus it does not consist only in the fact that God offers Himself up for men ; that He, the Judge, allows Himself to be judged in their place, in this way establishing and proclaiming among sinners, and in defiance of their sin, His divine right which is as such the basis of a new right of man before Him. It does not consist, therefore, only in the justification of man. It consists also in the sanctification which is indissolubly bound up with his justification, i.e., in the fact that as He turns to man in defiance of his sin He also, in defiance of his sin, turns man to Himself. The reconciliation of man with God takes place also in the form that He introduces as a new man the one in relation to whom He has set Himself in the right and whom He has set in the right in relation to Himself. He has introduced him in the new form of existence of a faithful covenant-partner who is well-pleasing to Him and blessed by Him. "I will be your God" is the justification of man. "Ye shall be my people" is his sanctification. It is not the final

499

thing that has to be said concerning the alteration of the human situation which has taken place in the reconciliation achieved and revealed in Jesus Christ. In a third part of the doctrine of reconciliation we shall have to consider the whole in relation to the provisional goal of the covenant newly and definitively established in Jesus Christ and therefore in relation to the calling of man. But our present problem is that of his sanctification—his reconciliation with God from the standpoint of his conversion to Him as willed and accomplished by God.

What is meant by sanctification (*sanctificatio*) might just as well be described by the less common biblical term regeneration (*regeneratio*) or renewal (*renovatio*), or by that of conversion (*conversio*), or by that of penitence (*poenitentia*) which plays so important a role in both the Old and New Testaments, or comprehensively by that of discipleship which is so outstanding especially in the synoptic Gospels. The content of all these terms will have to be brought out under the title of sanctification. But there is good reason to keep the term sanctification itself in the foreground. It includes already, even verbally, the idea of the " saint," and therefore in contradistinction to the other descriptions of the same matter it shows us at once that we are dealing with the being and action of God, reminding us in a way which is normative for the understanding of the other terms as well of the basic and decisive fact that God is the active Subject not only in reconciliation generally but also in the conversion of man to Himself. Like His turning to man, and man's justification, this is His work, His *facere*. But it is now seen and understood, not as his *iustificare*, but as his *sanctificare*.

In the Bible God Himself is the One who is originally and properly holy, confronting man in his creatureliness and sinfulness, and the whole created cosmos, with absoluteness, distinctness and singularity, with inviolable majesty. " I am God, and not man " (Hos. 11⁹). The seraphim proclaim Him (Is. 6³) as the One who is thrice holy—" holy as it were to a threefold degree " (Proksch in Kittel, I, p. 93)—in this sense, in this uniqueness and superiority. But in this as in other respects the biblical teaching about God is not theoretical. It is given in the context of accounts of God's action in the history inaugurated by Him. Nowhere, then, does it look abstractly to this One who confronts us, in His own inner being. He is indeed holy in and for Himself. But he demonstrates and reveals Himself as such in His establishment and maintenance of fellowship with man and his world. The prophet Hosea was the first and, in the Old Testament, the only writer to understand and describe this Holy One as specifically the One who loves His people. But this equation is the implicit declaration of the whole of the Old Testament. In it we have to do with the Holy One who encounters the man who is so very different from Himself, and who does so in that unapproachable majesty, and therefore effectively, but who demonstrates and reveals Himself as the Holy One in the fact that He sanctifies the unholy by His action with and towards them, i.e., gives them a derivative and limited, but supremely real, share in His own holiness. The reference is to the Holy One of Israel, to use the term which dominates both parts of the Book of Isaiah. " God that is holy shall be sanctified in righteousness " (Is. 5¹⁶). It is by His acts of judgment and grace among and to this people that He sanctifies it as its Lord (Ez. 37²⁸) " before the heathen " (Ez. 20⁴¹), " before their eyes " (Ez. 36²³)—and in so doing sanctifies Himself in the world, i.e., activates and reveals Himself in His majesty in the forms and circumstances of human history. This people may and shall and must be " holy to me " (Lev. 10³), i.e., enabled to worship Me, the Holy One, and therefore to attest Me as the Holy One in the world. To use the classical definition of Lev. 19² (cf. 11⁴⁴, 20⁷) quoted in 1 Pet. 1¹⁶ : " Ye shall be holy : for I . . . am holy." The holiness of this God demands and enforces the holiness of His people. It requires that His own divine confrontation of the world and all men should find a human (and as such very inadequate, but for all its inadequacy very real) correspondence and copy in the mode of existence of this people. It requires this already in and with the election and calling of this people, in and with the fact that He has made Himself the God of this people and this people His people. The imperative : " Ye shall be holy," is simply the imperative indication of the irresistible dynamic of the indicative : " I am holy," i.e., I am holy, and act among you as such, and therefore I make you holy—this is your life and norm. It is not the glory of any man or creature, not even of Israel, but that of Yahweh Himself, which sanctifies the tent of meeting (Ex. 29⁴³). And at the central point in the New Testament —in spite of all the appeals and exhortations to holiness of life, or rather as their presupposition—there is set as the primary petition (Mt. 6⁹ ; Lk. 11²) : ἁγιασθήτω τὸ ὄνομά σου. The " name " of God is the holy God Himself, who is present as such in His holiness, present to His people as the Lord, to sanctify it, and in so doing to sanctify Himself. " The name of God is as little hallowed by men as His kingdom comes or His will is done by them " (Proksch, *op. cit.*, p. 113). " It is God Himself who proves His name holy " (p. 91). He proves it in and to men. He sanctifies men. His sanctifying involves a modification of their situation and constitution. They have to deduce the consequences of it. But the sanctifying by which He claims and makes them and their actions usable in His service and as His possession is " a manifestation of His own divine power " (E. Gaugler, *Die Heiligung im Zeugnis der Schrift*, 1948, p. 13), and as such it is wholly and exclusively His own act, and not theirs. " And the very God of peace sanctify you wholly " (1 Thess. 5²³). He it is who wills and accomplishes, not only His own turning to man, but man's conversion to Him, the claiming of man for His service. And He wills that we should call upon Him daily that this may happen. " I am the Lord which sanctify you " (Lev. 20⁸). In everything that we have to say further on this subject we must exert ourselves always to start from this point.

We must begin, and this is our task in the present sub-section, by glancing back at the first part of the doctrine of reconciliation and making some clarifications concerning the mutual relationship of justification and sanctification as roughly outlined.

For what follows, cf. Alfred Göhler, *Calvins Lehre von der Heiligung*, 1934, p. 81 f., 107 f., and G. C. Berkouwer, *Faith and Sanctification*, 1952, with which I am particularly happy to record my general agreement.

1. As we now turn to consider sanctification in and for itself, we are not dealing with a second divine action which either takes place simultaneously with it, or precedes or follows it in time. The action of God in His reconciliation of the world with Himself in Jesus Christ is unitary. It consists of different " moments " with a different bearing. It accomplishes both the justification and the sanctification of

man, for it is itself both the condescension of God and the exaltation of man in Jesus Christ. But it accomplishes the two together. The one is done wholly and immediately with the other. There are also different aspects corresponding to the different " moments." We cannot see it all at once, or comprehend it in a single word. Corresponding to the one historical being of Jesus Christ as true Son of God and true Son of Man, we can see it only as the movement from above to below, or the movement from below to above, as justification or sanctification. Yet whether we look at it from the one standpoint or the other our knowledge can and may and must be a knowledge of the one totality of the reconciling action of God, of the one whole and undivided Jesus Christ, and of His one grace.

In its later stages the older Protestant dogmatics tried to understand *iustificatio* and *sanctificatio* as steps in a so-called *ordo salutis*, preceded by a *vocatio* and *illuminatio*, and followed by the separate processes of *regeneratio* and *conversio*, and then (in the Lutherans) by a *unio mystica* and *glorificatio*. For the most part this *ordo salutis* was thought of as a temporal sequence, in which the Holy Spirit does His work here and now in men—the outworking of the reconciliation accomplished there and then on Golgotha. This temporal sequence corresponded only too readily to that of the temporal relationship between the humiliation and exaltation of Christ as it was viewed in the Christology of the older dogmatics. A psychologistic pragmatics in soteriology corresponded to the historicist pragmatics of Christology. Psychologistic ? This was not the primary intention, and it was indeed the fear of slipping into psychology, into a mere recording of the spiritual experience of the Christian, which for a long time restrained the older orthodoxy from constructing an *ordo salutis* in the sense of a temporal sequence. The original aim was to describe the order of the *gratia Spiritus sancti applicatrix*, of the appropriation to the needy human subject of the salvation objectively accomplished in Jesus Christ—that which is summed up in the title of the third book of Calvin's *Institutes : De modo percipiendae Christi gratiae et qui inde fructus nobis proveniant, et qui effectus consequantur* But if this *percipere* consists in a series of different steps, how can it better be made apprehensible than as a series of spiritual awakenings and movements and actions and states of a religious and moral type ? The greater and more explicit the emphasis on the *ordo salutis* understood in this way—and this was the tendency in the 17th century—the more clearly it was revealed by the uncertainties, contradictions and exegetical and conceptual arbitrariness and artificiality in which those who espoused it were entangled, that they were on the point of leaving the sphere of theology. And the nearer drew the time—the time of the Enlightenment which dawned already with Pietism—in which a religious and moral psychology would take over the leadership and suppress theology, first at this point, and then everywhere. Certainly there are rays of light, as when we suddenly read in Quenstedt (*Theol. did. pol.*, 1685, III, *c.* 10, *th.* 16) that all these ἀποστελέσματα of Jesus Christ and the Holy Spirit, and particularly justification and sanctification, take place *tempore simul, et quovis puncto mathematico arctiores adeo ut divelli et sequestrari nequeant, cohaerent*. This is inevitable if we are really thinking of the act of God as it comes to man in Jesus Christ by the Holy Spirit. If Quenstedt and that whole theology had taken this insight seriously, it would have meant that they could not have understood that *ordo* as a series of different divine actions, but only as the order of different " moments " of the one redemptive occurrence coming to man in the *simul* of the one event. This would perhaps have led to a collapse of the historicist pragmatic, and even perhaps to the dualism between an objective.

achievement of salvation there and then and a subjective appropriation of it here and now, in favour of a recognition of the simultaneity of the one act of salvation whose Subject is the one God by the one Christ through the one Spirit— " more closely united than in a mathematical point." The God who in His humiliation justifies us is also the man who in His exaltation sanctifies us. He is the same there and then as He is here and now. He is the one living Lord in whom all things have occurred, and do and will occur, for all. Unfortunately, however, the recognition of this *simul* did not lead even to a serious consideration of the relationship between justification and sanctification, let alone to any general advance in this direction. We cannot escape to-day the task of taking this recognition seriously.

2. When, however, we speak of justification and sanctification, we have to do with two different aspects of the one event of salvation. The distinction between them has its basis in the fact that we have in this event two genuinely different moments. That Jesus Christ is true God and true man in one person does not mean that His true deity and His true humanity are one and the same, or that the one is interchangeable with the other. Similarly, the reality of Jesus Christ as the Son of God who humbled Himself to be a man and the Son of Man who was exalted to fellowship with God is one, but the humiliation and exaltation are not identical. From the christological ἀσυγχύτως and ἀτρέπτως of Chalcedon we can deduce at once that the same is true of justification and sanctification. As the two moments in the one act of reconciliation accomplished in Jesus Christ they are not identical, nor are the concepts interchangeable. We are led to the same conclusion when we consider the content of the terms. In our estimation of their particular significance we must not confuse or confound them. Justification is not sanctification and does not merge into it. Sanctification is not justification and does not merge into it. Thus, although the two belong indissolubly together, the one cannot be explained by the other. It is one thing that God turns in free grace to sinful man, and quite another that in the same free grace He converts man to Himself. It is one thing that God as the Judge establishes that He is in the right against this man, thus creating a new right for this man before Him, and quite another that by His mighty direction He claims this man and makes him willing and ready for His service. Even within the true human response to this one divine act the faith in which the sinful man may grasp the righteousness promised him in Jesus Christ is one thing, and quite another his obedience, or love, as his correspondence to the holiness imparted to him in Jesus Christ. We shall speak later of the indestructible connexion between these. But it is a connexion, not identity. The one cannot take the place of the other. The one cannot, therefore, be interpreted by the other.

It is a *duplex gratia* that we receive in the *participatio Christi* (Calvin, *Instit.*, III, 11, 1). Similarly, its reception in faith and penitence is twofold: *etsi separari non possunt, distingui tamen debent. Quamquam perpetuo inter se vinculo cohaerent, magis tamen coniungi volunt quam confundi* (3, 5). For : *Si solis claritas non potest a calore separari, an ideo dicemus luce calefieri terram, calore vero illustrari* (11, 6) ?

Sanctification is not justification. If we do not take care not to confuse and confound, soteriology may suffer, allowing justification (as in the case of much of Roman Catholicism in its following of Augustine, but also of many varieties of Neo-Protestantism) to merge into the process of his sanctification initiated by the act of the forgiveness of sins, or by allowing faith in Jesus Christ as the Judge judged in our place (this is in my view the most serious objection to the theology of R. Bultmann) to merge into the obedience in which the Christian in his discipleship has to die to the world and himself. The " I am holy " is not merely a kind of preface or unaccented syllable introducing the really important statement : " Ye shall be holy." In all the thinking along these lines about the justifiable emphasis on the existential relevance of the atonement, where is the regard for the God who accomplishes it, the bowing before the freedom of His grace, the adoration of the mystery in which He really says an unmerited No to sinful man, the joy of pure gratitude for this benefit ? Where is the presupposition of a sanctification worthy of the name ? Is it not better to make justification, even in its significance for sanctification, genuinely justification, instead of trying to understand it from the very outset merely as the beginning of sanctification ?

On the other hand, justification is not sanctification. If we do not take care not to confuse and confound, soteriology may also suffer by allowing sanctification to be swallowed up in justification. It may be because of the overwhelming impression of the comfort of the grace which is effective and has to be understood as justification. It may be in view of the true consideration that justification is in any event the dominating presupposition of sanctification. It may be with the correct insight that even in his best works the sanctified man still stands in continual need of justification before God. It may be in a justifiable anxiety that under the name of sanctification a prior or subsequent self-justification may creep in to the detriment of the sovereignty of grace. These are all legitimate considerations which can be traced back to the younger Luther and Zinzendorf and H. F. Kohlbrügge ; and with the help of some of the more pointed statements of these writers, and an exaggeration (and therefore distortion) of their basic teaching, they can easily lead to a monism of the *theologia crucis* and the doctrine of justification. In this monism the necessity of good works may be maintained only lethargically and spasmodically, with little place for anything more than rather indefinite talk about a life of forgiveness, or comforted despair, or Christian freedom, or the love active in faith. If we do not give any independent significance to the problem of sanctification, do we not necessarily obscure in a very suspicious way the existential reach of the atonement, the simple fact that justification always has to do with man and his action, and that faith in it, even though it is a work of the Holy Spirit, is still a decision of man ? Can we ignore the fact that in the Bible the work of the sovereign grace of God as a work of Jesus Christ and the Holy Spirit includes the sanctification of man as distinct from his justification ? Is it not a serious matter to miss the sovereignty and authority of grace in this form ? If we do not understand it as sanctifying grace, we not only do despite to its richness, but far too easily, and indeed inevitably, we begin to look for the indispensable norm of the Christian way of life elsewhere than in the Gospel (in which we think we have only the consoling word of justifying grace), and are forced to seek and grasp a law formed either by considerations drawn from the Bible or natural law, or by historical convenience. But this means that we are involved in double book-keeping, and either tacitly or openly we are subjected to other lords in a kingdom on the left as well as to the Lord Jesus Christ whose competence extends only, as we think, to the forgiveness of sins. Is it not advisable to make sanctification, even in its connexion with justification, genuinely sanctification, instead of trying to understand it from the very outset merely as a paraphrase of justification ?

3. Yet it is even more important to remember, and the warning we have to give in this respect must be correspondingly sharper, that since justification and sanctification are only two moments and aspects of one and the same action, they do belong inseparably together. We have had to draw attention to the unavoidable dangers of confusion which threaten on both sides, and which have actually overwhelmed the Church and theology with very serious consequences. But we have to say that to ignore the mutual relationship of the two can only lead at once to false statements concerning them and to corresponding errors in practice : to the idea of a God who works in isolation, and His " cheap grace " (D. Bonhoeffer), and therefore an indolent quietism, where the relationship of justification to sanctification is neglected ; and to that of a favoured man who works in isolation, and therefore to an illusory activism, where the relationship of sanctification to justification is forgotten. A separation of justification and sanctification can have its basis only in a separation within the one actuality of Jesus Christ and the Holy Spirit ; in an isolation of the self-humiliating Son of God on the one side, and of the exalted Son of Man on the other. If we have also to accept the ἀχωρίστως and ἀδιαιρέτως of Chalcedonian Christology, justification and sanctification must be distinguished, but they cannot be divided or separated. We have only to ask ourselves : What is the forgiveness of sins (however we understand it) if it is not directly accompanied by an actual liberation from the committal of sin ? What is divine sonship if we are not set in the service of God and the brethren ? What is the hope of the universal and definitive revelation of the eternal God without striving for provisional and concrete lesser ends ? What is faith without obedience ? And conversely : What is a liberation for new action which does not rest from the very outset and continually on the forgiveness of sins ? Who can and will serve God but the child of God who lives by the promise of His unmerited adoption ? How can there be a confident expectation and movement in time without the basis of eternal hope ? How can there be any serious obedience which is not the obedience of faith ? As God turns to sinful man, the conversion of the latter to God cannot be lacking. And the conversion of man to God presupposes at every point and in every form that God turns to him in free grace. That the two are inseparable means that the doctrine of justification has to be described already as the way from sin to the right of God and man, and therefore as the way from death to life, which *God* goes with him. And it means for the doctrine of sanctification that it has to show that it is really with *man* that God is on this way as He reconciles the world with Himself in Jesus Christ.

It was Calvin who saw and expressed this point with particular clarity. There is hardly a passage in which we have any doubt whether the reference is to justifying or sanctifying grace, and yet he everywhere brings out the mutual relationship of the two moments and aspects. His primary statement and starting-point is as follows : *Sicut non potest discerpi Christus in partes, ita inseparabilia sunt haec duo, quae simul et coniunctim in ipso percipimus : iustitiam et sanctificationem. Quoscunque ergo in gratiam recipit Deus, simul Spiritu adoptionis donat, cuius virtute eos reformat ad suam imaginem (Inst.,* III, 11, 6).

There is thus no justification without sanctification. *Sola fide et mera venia iustificatur homo, neque tamen a gratuita iustitiae imputatione separatur realis (ut ita loquar) vitae sanctitas.* The proclamation of forgiveness has as its aim *ut a tyrannide satanae, peccati iugo et misera servitute vitiorum liberatus peccator in regnum Dei transeat.* Thus no one can apprehend the grace of the Gospel without *meditatio poenitentiae* (3, 1). It is certainly not in virtue of our holiness that we enter into fellowship with God. We have to stand in this already if, engulfed by His holiness (*eius sanctitate perfusi*), we are to follow where He calls. But it belongs to His glory that this should take place, for there can be no *consortium* between Him and our *iniquitas* and *immunditia* (6, 2). We cannot, therefore, glory in God without *eo ipso*—and this is for Calvin the basic act of penitence and the new life—renouncing all self-glorying and thus beginning to live to God's glory (13, 2). Thus the righteousness of God calls for a *symmetria,* a *consensus,* which must be actualised in the obedience of the believer. It calls for a confirmation of our adoption to divine sonship (6, 1). For this reason the one grace of God is necessarily sanctifying grace as well. *In Christi participatione, qua iustificamur, non minus sanctificatio continetur quam iustitia. . . . Inseparabiliter utrumque Christus in se continet. . . . Nullum ergo Christus iustificat, quem non simul sanctificet* (16, 1, and we find the same *simul* in 3, 19). *Fatemur dum nos. . . . Deus gratuita peccatorum remissione donatos pro iustis habet : cum euismodi misericordia coniunctam simul esse hanc eius beneficentiam, quod per Spiritum suum sanctum in nobis habitat, cuius virtute nos sanctificamur, hoc est consecramur Domino in veram vitae puritatem* (14, 9). There can thus be no doubt that, as Calvin saw it, the Reformation did not wish to give to the problem of the *vita hominis christiani,* of penitence and good works, any less but a much greater and more serious and penetrating attention than was done either by the Humanists (who followed Erasmus) on the one side or contemporary Romanists on the other. In the context in which it was set by him the *sola fide* obviously could not become a comfortable kiss of peace.

On the other hand, of course, there is no sanctification without justification. *An vera poenitentia citra fidem consistere potest ? Minime !* (3, 5). There is no *spatium temporis* between the two in which the man who is righteous before God in faith is not also holy and obedient to Him. But it is only this man who can and will be obedient and holy. How could he be seriously penitent if he did not know : *se Dei esse ? Dei autem se esse nemo vere persuasus est, nisi qui eius gratiam prius apprehenderit* (3, 2). How can there be a free and happy conscience towards God in penitence and therefore in the life of the Christian without the certainty of the righteousness before God which he is given, and has to be given continually, by God ? (13, 3). Even the obedient and holy and loving man who penitently lays hold of this righteousness still lives in the flesh and therefore as a sinner before God. Hence it follows : *Nullum unquam exstitisse pii hominis opus quod, si severo Dei iudicio examinaretur, non esset damnabile* (14, 11) and : *nec unum a sanctis exire opus, quod, si in se censeatur, non mereatur iustam opprobrii mercedem* (14, 9). Even the regenerate and converted stand in absolute need of forgiveness and justification in all their works of penitence and obedience, which of themselves cannot possibly justify them (14, 13). Good works, which God has promised to reward (18, 1 f.), in which we have to progress, and in the doing of which we may find confidence (14, 18 f.), can be present only as God of His free goodness justifies not only our persons but also our works (17, 5 f.), as *assidua peccatorum remissione* (14, 10 ; 12) He assesses and recognises and accepts as good, on the basis of the righteousness of Jesus Christ ascribed to us, that which we do in supreme imperfection and even guilt and corruption (14, 8 f.). There can be no doubt that Calvin—the reformer at the time of the reconstruction of the Evangelical Churches and the developing Counter-Reformation, and therefore with different interests from Luther—stands squarely on the basis of his predecessor. The notion of *duplex gratia* was not his own. Even the older Luther (cf. *C.D.*, IV, 1, p. 525 f.), in passages which are, of course, rather remote and obscure, had referred in the same sense as Calvin, and with the same conjunction and distinction, to justification and sanctification, healing, purification, etc. And Calvin for his part had not surrendered one jot of the decisive insight of Luther concerning justification. The only distinctive features—and they were not really un-Lutheran, or prejudicial to the content and function of the doctrine of justification—were the formal consistency with which he spoke of this *duplex gratia* and the material emphasis which he laid on the doctrine of the *novitas vitae* based on justification.

4. It remains only to ask whether there is perhaps an *ordo* (*salutis*) in the relationship of justification and sanctification and therefore a superiority and subordination, a *Prius* and *Posterius*, in the one event of grace and salvation. We presuppose that there is no such order in the temporal sense. The *simul* of the one redemptive act of God in Jesus Christ cannot be split up into a temporal sequence, and in this way psychologised. The justification and sanctification of man, manifest in the resurrection of Jesus Christ and effective in the Holy Spirit, are an event in this *simul*, and not therefore in such a way that his justification first takes place separately (as though it could be his justification by God if it did not also include his sanctification), and then his sanctification takes place separately (as though it could be his sanctification by God if at all its stages and in all its forms it were not based upon and borne by the event of his justification). No, they both take place simultaneously and together, just as the living Jesus Christ, in whom they both take place and are effective, is simultaneously and together true God and true man, the Humiliated and the Exalted. Yet this does not mean that we can lay aside the question of their order. It has to be raised and answered because it is necessary that we should dissipate the last remnants of the monistic and dualistic thinking which occupied us under (2) and (3). If there can be no question of a temporal order, the only order can be that of substance. And it is not quite so easy to answer the question of this order as might at first sight appear.

From our deliberations under (2) and (3) it is clear in what sense justification has to be understood as the first and basic and to that extent superior moment and aspect of the one event of salvation, and sanctification as the second and derivative and to that extent inferior. It is indeed in virtue of the condescension of God in which the eternal Word assumed our flesh that there takes place the exaltation of man in the existence of the royal man Jesus. It is in virtue of the forgiveness of his sins and his establishment as a child of God, both fulfilled in the gracious judgment and sentence of God, that man is called and given a readiness and willingness for discipleship, for conversion, for the doing of good works, for the bearing of his cross. It is in virtue of the fact that he is justified in the presence of God by God that he is sanctified by Him. Surely it is obvious that if we ask concerning the structure of this occurrence justification must be given the priority over sanctification.

Yet is this the end of the matter ? Do we not have to recognise that the existence of the royal man Jesus, and therefore the true answering of the question of obedience, the summoning and preparing of man for the service of God, have a radiance and importance in the Bible which are not in any way secondary to those of justifying grace ? Is the first the only possible answer ? In the question of the material order of this whole event do we not have to take into account—irrespective of the question of its inner movement—its meaning and purpose and goal ? And does it not seem that that which is second in execution (*executione posterius*), i.e., sanctification, is first in intention (*intentione prius*) ? What is it that God wills and effects in the reconciliation of man with Himself ? By the incarnation of His Word does He not will and effect the existence of the royal man Jesus and His lordship over all His brothers and the whole world ? By His humiliation to be the Judge judged for us, and therefore by the justification of man before Him, does He not will and effect the existence of a loyal and courageous people of this King in covenant with Himself, and therefore the sanctification of man ? And even this may not be the ultimate, or penultimate, word concerning the *telos* of the event of atonement. Yet in relation to the relationship between justification and sanctification are we not forced to say that teleologically sanctification is superior to justification and not the reverse ? It is obvious that we cannot help putting and answering the question in this form too.

Yet there are still good reasons for the first answer ; and it is not without its significance. This being the case, is it really necessary or wise to choose between them at all ? In so doing, might we not be encroaching on the actuality of the one grace of the one Jesus Christ ? And this is something which cannot be permitted merely out of a desire to systematise. In any case, are we not asking concerning the divine order of the divine will and action revealed and effective in Jesus Christ ? Might it not be that in this—in this particular function and respect—the *Prius* is also the *Posterius* and *vice versa* ? This would mean that both answers have to be given with the same seriousness in view of the distinctive truth in both—intersecting but not cancelling one another. In the *simul* of the one divine will and action justification is first as basis and second as presupposition, sanctification first as aim and second as consequence ; and therefore both are superior and both subordinate. Embracing the distinctness and unity of the two moments and aspects, the one grace of the one Jesus Christ is at work, and it is both justifying and sanctifying grace, and both to the glory of God and the salvation of man. Where else does God (the God known in Jesus Christ) seek and create His glory but in the salvation of man ? And yet who can say that the glory of God to the salvation of man is greater or smaller in man's justification or sanctification ? Again, where is the salvation of man (the man known in Jesus Christ) to be found but in the glory which God prepares for Himself in His action to and with man ? Yet who is to say that the salvation of man to the glory of God is greater or smaller in the fact that man is justified by God or sanctified by Him ? If we start at this point, and therefore at the grace of the covenant effective and revealed in Jesus Christ, we have the freedom, but we are also bound, to give to the question of the order of the relationship between justification and sanctification this twofold answer. There is no contradiction. As a twofold answer, it corresponds to the substance of the matter.

The question of the order of this relationship was one which claimed Calvin's attention, and it will help to elucidate what we have just said if we briefly recall his answer. We might almost say that this question poses *the* great problem of method in the third book of the *Institutio*. Is it on justification or sanctification that the emphasis must fall in what is to be said concerning the grace of Jesus Christ and its fruits and effects ? When we read Calvin we may still—although not necessarily—be baffled by this question.

There can be no doubt that in practice his decisive interest is primarily in the problem of sanctification. Those who come to him from Luther will be almost estranged when right at the beginning of the third book (1, 1), although not without justification in the linguistic usage of the Bible, he lays all the emphasis on the sanctifying power of the Holy Spirit, and it is not for a long time (only in chapter 11) that he comes to speak of justification at all. According to his own explanation (11, 1), he first wishes—and the whole sequence of chapters 3–10 is subservient to this aim—to show (1) that the faith by which alone, through the mercy of God, we attain the grace of righteousness before Him, is not a faith which is indolent in relation to good works, a *fides otiosa*, and (2), and more positively, *qualia sint sanctorum bona opera*. It is for this reason that he describes faith itself as regeneration, the regeneration which is realised in penitence (chapters 3–5), and then goes on to portray the Christian life in its character as self-denial, as the bearing of the cross, as *meditatio futurae vitae*, and as a right relationship to earthly and temporal possibilities and possessions (chapters 6–10). It is only at this point—we might almost say at a first glance as a great qualification and corrective—that he introduces the doctrine of justification (chapters 11–18). Then in what follows concerning Christian freedom (19) and prayer (20) we seem to have a continuation and completion of the interrupted theme. And since this can be abandoned only after a retrospective glance at its origin in God's election (21–24) and a prospective glance at its final goal in the resurrection of the dead (25), it obviously seems to constitute the true and proper substance of Calvin's teaching. *Ad colendam iustitiam renovat Deus quos pro iustis gratis censet* (11, 6). In the light of this sketch, and what constantly emerges as the admonitory tenor of the whole, we might regard it as established beyond any doubt that, as distinct from Luther, Calvin must be called the theologian of sanctification. He is this to the extent that the sharp underscoring of the new life and altered conversation of the believer in Jesus Christ, the reference to his essential inner and outer transformation was the particular concern which he took up in practice against the excesses which sometimes gained the upper hand in his own epoch (not without some support from the Reformation Gospel), and in answer to the humanistic and Romanist criticism of the *sola fide* of Reformation teaching. And quite apart from the contemporary background and occasion, his question was one which has also a true biblical foundation : What is it that God in His grace wills of man and achieves in his life ? In this—we might almost say, strategic—respect there is good reason for the primacy of sanctification in Calvin.

But the picture undergoes a curious transformation when we turn our attention from the practical intention to its execution. For we then have to say that it is on the doctrine of faith developed in the great second chapter of the book that he bases everything that follows as seen from the dominating standpoint of regeneration in conversion. But Calvin could not speak of faith (cf. especially sections 16, 23, 24, 29, 30 and 32 of chapter 2) without anticipating the decisive content of the doctrine of justification. Faith is a sure and certain knowledge grounded in the truth of the promise of grace given in Jesus Christ, and revealed in our understanding (*mentibus*) and sealed in our hearts by the Holy Spirit. The regeneration of man, and therefore his sanctification in all its stages and forms (2, 7), does not take place except in this faith ; in the faith whose *proprius scopus* is the *promissio misericordiae*, the evangelical Word concerning the free divine *benevolentia* to man (2, 29). Thus at the very beginning of the doctrine of justification (11, 1)—rather surprisingly, but not really so in view of this second chapter—we are told that this *iustificatio* which has hitherto been touched on only lightly is the *cardo praecipuus sustinendae religionis* to which we must give particular care and attention (*maior attentio curaque*) and in relation to which sanctification is only the *secunda gratia*. *Primum omnium* is necessarily to be found *quo sis apud Deum loco et quale de te sit illius iudicium*. Without this foundation there is neither assurance of salvation nor *pietas in Deum*. It should be noted with what extreme precision that which, in the light of so many Old Testament verses and passages, Calvin can say about the importance of the good works of the believer even in justification (especially chapters 13–14 and 17–18) is qualified by the most urgent recollections of the continuing freedom of justifying grace, and by a constant recall to the rest of faith in the promise which alone enables us to speak of the goodness and comfort and reward of the works of the believer. And it is to be noted finally that even in the description of the *novitas vitae* (chapters 3–10 and 19–20) which so strongly characterises the third book he not only does not lose sight of the totally unmerited establishment of man in a state of grace by the act of majesty of the divine mercy, but obviously sets that which he describes in the reflection of this act. His real subject is self-denial and the cross, the orientation to the life beyond, Christian freedom and prayer. And in the strict sense these are all critical and limiting determinations of the *vita hominis christiani*. Even in chapter 10, where the emphasis falls on the this-worldly qualification and responsibility of the Christian life, there is little real trace of the fabled activism of calvinistic ethics. This reserve in the portrayal of sanctification is connected with the fact that in Calvin this is not only related to the simultaneous justification of man but in this relationship and from justification it acquires the character of a submission to this act of majesty. When all this is taken into account we may well ask whether Calvin was not primarily a theologian of justification.

In fact we can and should learn from the classical example of his mode of treatment that we can give only a twofold answer to the question of priority in the relationship of these two moments and aspects. Calvin was quite in earnest when he gave sanctification a strategic precedence over justification. He was also quite in earnest when he gave the latter a tactical precedence. Why could he be so free, and yet so bound, in relation to the two ? Because he started at the place which is superior to both because it embraces both, so that in the light of it we can and must give the primacy, now to the one and now to the other, according to the different standpoints from which we look. The basic act in which they are a whole, in which they are united and yet different, and in which—without any contradiction—they have different functions according to which they must each be given the primacy, is as Calvin sees it (and as he describes it in the first chapter of the third book) the *participatio Christi* given to man by the Holy Spirit. What this involves calls for separate consideration.

2. THE HOLY ONE AND THE SAINTS

The reconciliation of the world with God in its form as sanctification takes place as God fashions a people of holy men, i.e., those who in spite of their sin have the freedom, which they have received from Him to live in it, to represent Him among all other men and to serve Him in what they are and do and suffer. " God so loved the world " is relevant in this connexion too. The sanctification of man, his conversion to God, is, like his justification, a transformation, a new determination, which has taken place *de jure* for the world and therefore for all men. *De facto*, however, it is not known by all men, just as justification has not *de facto* been grasped and acknowledged and known and confessed by all men, but only by those who are awakened to faith. It is the people of these men which has also known sanctification. Only God Himself knows the extent of this people, and its members. The invitation to belong to it is extended to all. Certainly it is not co-extensive with the human race as such. Certainly it is a special people of special men who are marked off from all others because they are set aside by God from among all others. Yet its special existence is not an end in itself. It is marked off from the race, from others, in order that it may make " a provisional offering of the thankfulness for which the whole world is ordained by the act of the love of God." It is the living promise of the positive meaning which in the act of atonement God has restored not only to its own existence but to that of all men. It is the witness of the love with which God has loved the world. What has come to it *de facto* has come to all men *de iure*. But in so far as it is only to it that it has come *de facto* (with the provisional task which this involves), it is concretely differentiated and separated from the world and all other men. To this extent it is a holy people of holy men. Among those who *de facto* are not holy it is the creaturely reflection of the holiness in which God confronts—not indolently but actively—both itself and the world, addressing it even as He is distinct from it. It is with this God who in His holiness acts to and with His people—the people of His saints—that we have to do in our present deliberations. His action is man's sanctification.

The phrase " holy people " is an obvious one, but it is used with astonishing infrequency in the canonical Old Testament. The most striking example is in

Ex. 19⁶ (quoted in 1 Pet. 2⁹), where Moses is charged by Yahweh to tell the Israelites that they of all peoples are to be His possession (" for all the earth is mine ") : " and ye shall be unto me a kingdom of priests, and a holy nation, *goy* (a word which is usually applied only to the Gentiles) *qadosh*. We find *am qadosh* in Deut. 7⁶ and 28⁹, Is. 62¹² and Dan 7²⁷. For the most part, however, it is only the worshipping congregation (or more exactly its convening) which is called " holy," and not the people as such. In many cases (as in the combination *qahal qᵉdoshim* in Ps. 89⁵ and in the Book of Daniel) the *qᵉdoshim* are the angels. The word *ḥasidim*, which Luther regularly translated as " saints " in the Psalter, denotes the pious in Israel. On one occasion Aaron is called " the saint of the Lord " (Ps. 106¹⁶), but the reference here is to his office rather than his person. In the history attested in the Old Testament many words and things are called " holy " in virtue of their meaning and function. It is in this sense that we have to understand the " holy princes " of Is. 43²⁸. When the remnant of destroyed Israel is called a " holy seed " in Is. 6¹³ the drift is obviously eschatological. The only other genuine references as far as I can see are Ex. 22³¹ : " Ye shall be holy men unto me," Ps. 16³ : " The saints that are in the earth," Ps. 34⁹ : " O fear the Lord, ye his saints," and Deut. 33³ : " All his saints are in his hand." There seems to be no doubt that the restrained use of the term is deliberate. The history attested in the Old Testament clearly has to do with the sanctification of this people and these men. But since the references to their sanctity are so few and incidental the main emphasis is obviously on the sanctification itself, or rather on the One who as the Holy One is the active subject who sovereignly confronts the holy people and the men who belong to it.

Even more surprising and complicated are the results of an investigation of the New Testament. We are forced to say at once that the number of texts from which we can deduce the important credal formula *sancta ecclesia* is even less than that of passages which describe Israel as the holy people. This does not mean that the formula is mistaken. But in our interpretation of it we must pay attention to the sense in which the New Testament does seem very occasionally to speak of a kind of *sancta ecclesia*. As far as I can see, there are only two passages which call for consideration. The first is the Old Testament quotation in 1 Pet. 2⁹ : " Ye are . . . an holy nation " (ἔθνος ἅγιον). But the ἔστε is lacking which would make this an analytical statement. The meaning obviously seems to be that those who are addressed (in contrast to the rejected of the preceding verse) are elected and called to execute as a holy people the commission which is described immediately afterwards. The other passage is Eph. 5²⁴f., and this, too, does not say directly that the Church is holy but that Christ has loved the ἐκκλησία and given Himself for it in order that, cleansing it with the washing of water by the word, He might sanctify it and " present it to himself a glorious church (ἔνδοξον), not having spot, or wrinkle, or any such thing ; but that it should be holy and without blemish." In this passage it is quite obvious that the holiness of the community is the goal and intended result of the sanctifying action of Jesus Christ, not as an inherent quality but as the character which He will give it in the fulfilment of this action. And it may well be asked in all seriousness whether the ἵνα παραστήσῃ does not refer to the form of the community as it will be in the future, when this action is completed, and the last time in which it lives now is over. At any rate we can speak only of considerable reserve in describing the Church as holy (as in the corresponding Old Testament references to Israel). As against this, however, the men who compose the Church (unlike the Israelites) are not only described with astonishing frequency as holy but are actually called " the saints." The term ἅγιοι or οἱ ἅγιοι does not figure in the Gospels, and only infrequently in Acts, but in the earlier and later strata of the Epistles and Revelation it has become almost a technical term for Christians, and in many passages (1 Cor. 16¹ ; 2 Cor. 8⁴, etc.) it is used specifically of the members of the original community at Jerusalem. Yet rather strangely no individual Christian is ever called a saint. John the Baptist is called "a just man and an holy " in Mk. 6²⁰, but this does not constitute a genuine exception. The saints of the New Testament exist only in plurality. Sanctity belongs to them, but only in their common life, not as individuals. In this plurality they are, of course, identical with the Christian community, so that the term " holy community," although it is only thinly attested, is not in any sense foreign to the New Testament. Indeed, in 1 Cor. 14³³ the congregations are generally referred to as " churches of the saints." Yet we must not imagine that their holiness derives from that of the individual members who constitute them, for as we have seen these are not called " saints " as individuals. The truth is that the holiness of the community, as of its individual constituents, is to be sought in that which happens to these men in common ; in that which comes to it and them in the course of this happening. We may hazard the provisional definition that the ἅγιοι are the men to whom ἁγιότης comes in a common history which constitutes them an ἔθνος ἅγιον. Thus the linguistic usage of the New Testament, for all its important differences from that of the Old, points us basically in the same direction. In other words, we are required to consider the history in which there takes place the sanctification, the ἁγιασμός, of these men and therefore their unification as a community. But this means automatically that we are required to consider the One who as the Holy One is the acting Subject in this history. The Holy One constitutes the saints.

In the original and proper sense of the term, the Holy One who is the active Subject of sanctification, and who constitutes the saints in this action, exists only in the singular as the saints do only in the plural. None of those who are outside Him is different as God is ; none is high and distant and alien and superior as He is. There is, of course, difference, gradation, and therefore holiness even within the visible and invisible, the material and spiritual world which is outside God. But with the exception of that which God Himself creates as He sanctifies this can always be transcended and the distance which it involves bridged. And if the final mark of the holiness of God is that, without destroying or even denying His own superiority, He can not only bridge but cross the distance which separates Him from that which He is not and which is therefore unholy, and that He does in fact do this in a genuine exercise and revelation of His superiority, this only means that no other holiness can be compared with His even in respect of this quality. For outside God there is indeed a superiority of one thing to another. And the distance may be bridged, the relationship reversed, the superiority of that which is superior destroyed. But there can be no crossing the gulf in such a way that that which is superior not only does not lose but exercises and reveals its superiority. To put it more simply, as the One who is always holy in His mercy, in virtue of His revelation as Creator, Reconciler and Redeemer, God the Father, Son and Holy Spirit is the only Holy One in the true sense. If there is any other holiness, it is the special work of His special act, the fruit of the action in which He, the Holy One, makes saints in reflection of His own holiness.

Saints ! We are not yet this by a long way. Sanctification, the action of the God who is always holy in His mercy, the activity in

which He crosses this gulf, does indeed involve the creation of a new
form of existence for man in which he can live as the loyal covenant-
partner of God who is well-pleasing to and blessed by Him. But
these are far-reaching and pregnant words if we take them literally.
They sound like " idle tales " (Lk. 24^{11})—no less strange (since they
refer to man and therefore to us all) than the report of the resurrection
of Jesus Christ. Where is man in this new form of existence, as the
loyal covenant-partner of God? Who of us is this man? Yet less
sweeping words (and even these words if we do not take them literally)
are quite insufficient to describe what is at issue in man's sanctification
by God. Even if it is only a matter of creating a copy of His own
holiness, its reflection in the world which is distant from Himself, the
reality of this reflection can be no less than that of a man who is
marked off from the rest of the world, not as a second God, but as a
man who can live the life of a true covenant-partner of God, i.e., not
disloyal but loyal, not displeasing but well-pleasing, not cursed but
blessed, and in this freedom able to exist in a form which is different
from that of all others. At any rate, this is not too strong an expression
for the content of sanctification as it is understood in the Bible. Later,
we shall have to find even stronger expressions. At the very least
we have to say of sanctification that its aim is the man who does not
break but keeps the covenant which God has made with him from all
eternity. The man who is awakened and empowered by the action
of the holy God does this. He is sanctified. He is a saint of God.
But who and where are the men of whom this can be said? We shall
certainly speak of them, but we are well-advised not to speak of them
too quickly or directly.

For if, as the Subject of the occurrence in the course of which
there arises the existence of saints, God alone is originally and properly
holy, this necessarily means that even human holiness, as the new
human form of existence of the covenant-partner of this God, cannot
originally and properly be that of many, but only of the one man
who on the human level is marked off from all others (even the holy
people and its members) as sanctified by God and therefore as the
Holy One. It is with a view to Him that the people Israel exists as
the people of God, and from Him that the community of the last time
derives as the community of God. The sanctification of man which
has taken place in this One is their sanctification. But originally and
properly it is the sanctification of Him and not of them. Their sanctification is originally and properly His and not theirs. For it was in
the existence of this One, in Jesus Christ, that it really came about,
and is and will be, that God Himself became man, that the Son of
God became also the Son of Man, in order to accomplish in His own
person the conversion of man to Himself, his exaltation from the depth
of His transgression and consequent misery, his liberation from his
unholy being for service in the covenant, and therefore his sanctification.

This is the divine act of sanctification in its original and proper, because direct, form ; in its once-for-all uniqueness. All its other forms, the sanctification of Israel and the community with the distant goal of that of the whole of the human race and the world, are included in this form, by which they are all conditioned. We look into the void if in respect of everything that takes place as sanctification on the circumference of Jesus Christ (whether in the Old Testament or the New), and in exposition of all its forms (discipleship, conversion, good works and the cross), we do not fix our gaze steadfastly on this centre as the place where alone it is a direct event, reaching out with the same reality (but only in virtue of the reality of this centre) to all the other places. How much false teaching, and how many practical mistakes, would have been avoided in this matter of sanctification if in direct analogy to the doctrine of justification by faith alone we had been bold or modest enough basically and totally and definitively to give precedence and all the glory to the Holy One and not to the saints ; to the only One who is God, but God in Jesus Christ ; and therefore to the royal man Jesus, as the only One who is holy, but in whom the sanctification of all the saints is reality!

According to 1 Cor. 1[30] Jesus Christ Himself is made unto us sanctification as well as justification. As E. Gaugler rightly observes (*op. cit.*, p. 76), this saying expresses in the shortest possible compass the truth that even sanctification has to be thought of in terms of the history of salvation. Sanctification takes place as history because and as this man who is directly sanctified by God is its acting Subject in the royal authority thereby given Him by God, God Himself being the One who acts through Him. In Jn. 10[36] He calls Himself the One " whom the Father hath sanctified." But being man as the Son of God He can equally well say : " I sanctify myself " (Jn. 17[19]). For according to Heb. 10[29] it is He Himself who in the first instance is sanctified by His blood as the blood of the covenant. He certainly addresses God : " Holy Father " (Jn. 17[11]). And He prays : " Sanctify (thou) them through thy truth " (Jn. 17[17]). But He Himself is the fulfilment of this request as the Son of the Father. In Ac. 4[27-30], as the One who is directly sanctified, He is called " the holy servant Jesus," and in Ac. 3[14] " the Holy One and the Just " whom the Jews denied. He was recognised as such by the demons who cried after Him (Mk. 1[24] ; Lk. 4[34]) : " I know thee who thou art, the Holy One of God." And according to Jn. 6[69] this was also the confession of Peter : " And we believe and are sure that thou art . . . the Holy One of God." As such He is the One of whom it is said (1 Pet. 1[15]) : " He which hath called you is holy." Heb. 2[11] is even stronger : He is the ἁγιάζων, the One who sanctifies, by whose existence and action there are also ἁγιαζόμενοι, saints. Everything that follows flows from this source and is nourished by this root. It is on this basis that the call goes out to others that they can and should and must " be holy in all manner of conversation " (1 Pet. 1[15]).

For this One is no more holy in isolation than the holy God. He is what He is in this unique and incomparable and inimitable fashion as the One who is elected by God and Himself elects as God, the One in whom the decision has been made concerning all men, in whom they have been set in covenant with God and therefore ordained for conversion to Him. He is thus the Lord and Head and Shepherd and Representative of all men, but primarily of His own particular people, of His community in the world. It has not always been taken with sufficient seriousness that He took our place and acted for us, not merely as the Son of God who established God's right and our own by allowing Himself, the Judge, to be judged for us, but also as the Son of Man who was sanctified, who sanctified Himself. Far too often the matter has been conceived and represented as though His humiliation to death for our justification by Him as our Representative were His own act, but our exaltation to fellowship with God as the corresponding counter-movement, and therefore our sanctification, were left to us, to be accomplished by us. "All this I did for thee ; What wilt thou do for me ? " The New Testament does not speak in this way. It knows nothing of a Jesus who lived and died for the forgiveness of our sins, to free us as it were retrospectively, but who now waits as though with tied arms for us to act in accordance with the freedom achieved for us. It is natural that He should be thought of in this way when it is overlooked and forgotten that He is not only the suffering Son of God but also the victorious and triumphant Son of Man. He is this, too, in our place and favour. This too, declared in His resurrection from the dead, is a moment and aspect of the mighty reconciling action of God which has taken place in Him. This, too, is the free and freely disposing grace of God addressed to us in Him. This means, however, that in and with His sanctification ours has been achieved as well. What remains for us is simply to recognise and respect it with gratitude in that provisional praise, the offering of which is the reason for the existence of His people, His community and all its individual members. We are not sanctified by this recognition and respect, by the poor praise that we offer. We are not saints because we make ourselves such. We are saints and sanctified because we are already sanctified, already saints, in this One. Already in Him we are summoned to this action. And the fact that this is so—not in ourselves but supremely in this One—is the reason for this action and the object of our recognition, respect and praise. The creation of man's new form of existence as God's covenant-partner is not, therefore, something which is merely before us, even as concerns ourselves. We have not to achieve it by imitation. Even if we could do this—and we cannot—we should be too late ; just as we should be far too late in any attempted creation of heaven and earth. All that we can do is to live under the heaven and on the earth which God has created good. Similarly, our only option is to see and accept as an accomplished fact man's new form of existence, our sanctification, and to direct ourselves accordingly. He Himself has accomplished it in a way which is effective and authoritative for all, for His whole people and all its individual members, and ultimately for the whole world. The fact that it is accomplished in Jesus as our Lord and Head means that we are asked for our obedience, or supremely our love ;

just as the fact that our justification is accomplished in Him means that we are asked for our faith. There is no prior or subsequent contribution that we can make to its accomplishment. As we are not asked to justify ourselves, we are not asked to sanctify ourselves. Our sanctification consists in our participation in His sanctification as grounded in the efficacy and revelation of the grace of Jesus Christ.

In this respect, too, the New Testament is quite unambiguous. " And for their sakes (ὑπὲρ αὐτῶν) I sanctify myself, that they also might be truly sanctified " (Jn. 17¹⁹). Curious saints, we might think, especially in view of the warning of 1 Cor. 6⁹ᶠ·: " Know ye not that the unrighteous shall not inherit the kingdom of God ? Be not deceived : neither fornicators, nor idolaters, nor adulterers, nor effeminate, nor abusers of themselves with mankind, nor thieves, nor covetous, nor drunkards, nor revilers, nor extortioners, shall inherit the kingdom of God. And such were some of you." How will Paul continue after this solemn statement ? With the demand that there should be no backsliding in this direction ? that there should be a destruction of every remnant of this type of conduct ? that there should be a concern for restitution and a corresponding new beginning in the opposite direction ? Is there not every occasion for this ? Is it not the natural drift of what he says ? Yet he himself develops his " Be not deceived " and his charge very differently. For in the immediate continuation in v. 11 he says : " But ye are washed, but ye are sanctified, but ye are justified in the name of the Lord Jesus, and by the Spirit of our God." To oppose to the raging flood of human vice a barrier by which it is set effectively in the past all that is needed is the ἀλλά of recollection of what has taken place in Jesus Christ, and in Him for them and to them. It is exactly the same in Col. 1²¹ᶠ·, where the readers are addressed as those who " were sometime alienated and enemies in your mind by wicked works," but whom Christ " hath reconciled in the body of his flesh through death, to present you (cf. Eph. 5²⁷) holy and unblameable and unreproveable in his sight." So, too, in Heb. 13¹² : " Wherefore Jesus also, that he might sanctify the people with his own blood, suffered without the gate." The meaning of all these ἵνα sentences is not that—by His own example maybe—He should offer them the possibility or chance or opportunity of sanctification, or that He should set them in a decision which they themselves have to make, but that in His death and passion He should make the decision and accomplish their sanctification in their place, laying the foundation on which they actually stand and are called and ordained to be ready to stand and go. This comes out most clearly in Heb. 10⁵ᶠ·, where Ps. 40⁷⁻⁹ is quoted and expounded as follows : The true High-priest Jesus has taken away the first, the gifts and offerings of men which God did not desire, in order to establish the second, the : " Lo, I come to do thy will, O God " (v. 9). Hence we can be told in v. 10 : " By the which will we are sanctified through the offering of the body of Jesus Christ once for all." Note the use of ἐφάπαξ in this context and with this reference. In substance, the statement is repeated in v. 14 : " By one offering he hath perfected for ever (εἰς τὸ διηνεκές) them that are sanctified (by it)." And note that according to v. 5 the replacement of the " first " (the gifts and offerings of men) by the " second " (His own doing of the will of God) was accomplished by Jesus already εἰσερχόμενος εἰς τὸν κόσμον, i.e., by His entry into the world as first concealed in the Old Testament promise. And we are taken even further back in 2 Thess. 2¹³, where Paul thanks God that he " hath from the beginning (ἀπ' ἀρχῆς) chosen you to salvation through sanctification of the Spirit and belief of the truth " ; and also in Eph. 1⁴, where the great opening hymn begins with the words : " According as he hath chosen us in him before the foundation of the world, that we should be holy and without blame before him in love." It is at this height that the decision concerning our sanctification was resolved—and since the resolve is God's already taken. It is at this depth that Jesus Christ is and acts for us as our Lord and Head even as concerns our own conversion to God. In so far as this is its meaning and content, the history of the royal man Jesus crowned in His death at Calvary had this dimension from the eternity of the will of God fulfilled by Him on earth and in time. That is why Paul can hazard a statement like that of 1 Cor. 3^{17} : " The temple of God is holy, which temple ye are." That is why those gathered into the community can and must be called " saints." They are sanctified and therefore " saints in Christ Jesus " (1 Cor. 1^2 ; Phil. 1^1) ; in and with the One who originally and properly is alone the Holy One. For He is their Head and Lord and King. They do not belong to themselves, but to Him. They are saints, not *propria*, but *aliena sanctitate ; sanctitate Jesu Christi*. They are holy in the truth and power of His holiness. It is not in defiance but in virtue of this fact that we can never take too literally the New Testament statement about the existence of sanctified men and therefore saints. Where has the New Testament to be taken more literally than in the passages where it speaks of the power and authoritativeness of the new form of human existence achieved in Jesus Christ and therefore created by God ? The realism with which it speaks about the existence of saints (in Jesus Christ) may be gathered from the fact that incidentally, but quite categorically, Paul hazards the statement in 1 Cor. 7^{14} that the existence of these men involves the sanctification of those around them who in themselves are not sanctified : " For the unbelieving husband is sanctified by the (believing) wife, and the unbelieving wife is sanctified by the (believing) husband : else were your children (also) unclean ; but now (in the New Testament this νῦν δέ recalls the christological reference with which all this is said) are they holy." That it is given to men to be saints (only, but with supreme reality) in their participation in the sanctity of the One who alone is holy means that there is created in the world a fact by which the world cannot be unaffected but is at once—wittingly or unwittingly—determined and altered. It is now the world to which there belongs also the existence of these men, this people. And it has to contend with this fact.

In the participation of the saints in the sanctity of Jesus Christ there is attested the sanctity of man as it is already achieved in this One who alone is holy. We shall have to ask later, in the specifically Christian ethics which will form the subject of the fourth and concluding part of the doctrine of reconciliation, what is the practical result of this self-attestation of man's accomplished sanctification in what he does and does not do. Our present concern is with this self-attestation as such. This consists in the participation of the saints in the sanctity of Jesus Christ ; in what Calvin called the *participatio Christi*.

We must first speak about its presupposition. It consists in the fact that the sanctification of man attested in it is actually accomplished in the one Jesus Christ in a way which is effective and authoritative for all, and therefore for each and every man, and not merely for the people of God, the saints. Not a little depends on our realising and considering this. In the participation of the saints in the sanctity of the one Jesus Christ, we are not dealing with the conclusion of a private arrangement between Him and them, but with His cause as the King, and the execution of His office as such. In their sanctification He attests that He is the Lord of all men. In all its particularity their sanctification speaks of the universal action of God, which has as its purpose and goal the reconciliation of the world, and therefore not merely of this group of individuals in the world. As it creates the fact of the existence of these men, this people, within the world, their sanctification attests the great decision of God which in Jesus Christ has been made not only concerning them but concerning all the men of every time and place. This takes away from the particular existence of these men any appearance of the accidental. It gives it the stamp of supreme necessity and obligation. It removes its declaration and expression from the atmosphere of the pride of religious self-seeking and self-sufficiency. It sets it in the larger sphere of the creation of God. It gives it a solidarity even with secular things with which it is contrasted. Even in its antithesis to these it is characterised as a humble rendering of service. This is the basis of both the dispeace and the peace of the saints in their relationship to others. They know that the sanctification of man, of all men, is already fulfilled (like their justification) in the one man Jesus, that it is effectively and authoritatively fulfilled in Him, and that it calls for their faith and love.

But this knowledge is the knowledge of the man Jesus as the " firstborn among many brethren," as He is called with magnificent breadth in Rom. 8[29], or " the firstborn of every creature " (Col. 1[15]). The one who in Him is elected by God and has elected Him is man ; man as such in this One. Thus the humanity of Jesus in the particularity in which He is this one man is, as the humanity of the Son of God, humanity as such, the humanity for which every man is ordained and in which every part already has a part in Him. What took place in Him—the exaltation of man, and therefore His sanctification for God —took place as the new impression of humanity as such. It was accomplished in the place of all others. In the exercise of His kingly office it took place for them too : with all the mercy of the love which seeks all ; with all the seriousness of the will which extends to all ; with all the power of the act which is done for all ; with all the authoritativeness of the decision which has been taken for all. In all His singularity Jesus Christ never was or is or will be isolated. For in this singularity He was and is and will be, and worked and will work, from and to all eternity for all. We do not see Him at all if we do not see Him in our place.; if we do not therefore see the direct relevance of His being and action for ours ; if we do not therefore see ourselves as determined by His being and action. But all this is not a private arrangement between Him and us. He is not merely our Lord and Representative. As He takes our own place He takes also that of our fellows and brothers. The relevance of His being and action is for ours, but also for that of others who are beside and around us in likeness with us. They no less than we are determined by Him. The knowledge of the man Jesus includes the knowledge and enclosure of

our own and every other human existence in His. There are, therefore, no saints (and saints are those who know the man Jesus) to whose
participation in the sanctity of this One there does not also belong a
knowledge of the all-embracing character of His existence in its comprehension not only of themselves but also of the children of the world.

Calvin's doctrine of the *participatio Christi* has one weakness which we can
never too greatly deplore and which we can never forget in all his thoughtful
and instructive presentation of justification and sanctification. This consists in
the fact that he found no place—and in view of his distinctive doctrine of predestination he could not do so—for a recognition of the universal relevance of
the existence of the man Jesus, of the sanctification of all men as it has been
achieved in Him. The eternal election which according to Eph. 1⁴ has been
made in Jesus Christ was referred by Calvin only to those who in God's eternal
counsel are foreordained to salvation and therefore to reconciliation, justification
and sanctification in Jesus Christ, while His existence has no positive significance
for those who are excluded from this foreordination, for the reprobate. The
consequence is that when Calvin describes the work of the Holy Spirit in which
Christ illuminates and calls men to faith (in the first chapter of the third book),
he restricts it from the very first to the circle of the elect. Thus the *participatio*
or *communicatio Christi*, and the justification and sanctification of man grounded
in it, is a divine action which has only particular significance. For the reprobate,
Jesus Christ did not die. For them He neither humbled Himself to be man as
the Son of God, nor has He been exalted to fellowship with God as the Son of
Man. Neither in the one way nor the other has He acted representatively for
them as their Lord and Head and Shepherd. We will not now develop either
the serious distortion of the biblical message which this involves (cf. *C.D.*, II,
2, §§ 32–35) or its inhumanity. We need only say that it carries with it (1) a
dissolution of the strict correlation between the glory of God and the salvation
of man. For Calvin the glory of God triumphs only in the salvation of specific
men, although it is also served by the perdition of the rest. It carries with it (2) the
fact that the final and proper ground of election even of the elect is not to
be sought in Jesus Christ, but in the inscrutable and immovable decision by
which it is decided whether or not they belong to the elect in Jesus Christ. It
carries with it (3) the fact that, although their election on the basis of this foreordination, and therefore their *participatio Christi*, and therefore their justification and sanctification, do serve the glory of God, they are also an end in themselves, and are thus pointless and unprofitable, since in their realisation they
have no positive function in relation to the rest of God's creation. It carries
with it (4) the fact that they can serve only to attest the holiness of a God whose
mercy is limited to them, and whose love is restricted by a limit which He Himself has arbitrarily and inscrutably set. But since this is not a total love it
cannot be accorded a total confidence. Even for those who are just and holy
in Jesus Christ this seriously compromises what appears to be their exalted
position. In Calvin's conception of the *participatio Christi* there is lacking that
which we have described as the objective presupposition of the participation of
the saints in the sanctity of Jesus Christ—the sanctification which has come to
man *a priori* in Him, which is absolutely sure to the saints, and which gives to
their existence teleological meaning among other men. In place of it there
yawns the abyss of the absolute decree of a God who is absolutely hidden and
anonymous, who does not act in Jesus Christ, who cannot be seen or known in
Him, who is God, not in His merciful omnipotence, but in a very different mystery.
This means that Calvin's doctrine of sanctification does not have the foundation
which is finally needed to carry it. At this point, therefore, we have to look
resolutely beyond his conception.

What has to be said about the sanctification which comes *de facto* on the saints in virtue of their participation in the sanctity of Jesus Christ acquires its weight from what has to be said concerning the sanctification which has already come on man—on the saint, but also on every other man—*de iure* in Jesus Christ. But now that we have referred to this presupposition we must turn to the question how the transition is made from this presupposition to the participation of the saints, of the particular people of God in the world, to the sanctification which has come on them *de facto*. How do they become witnesses of that which has come on the whole world and all men in the one Jesus Christ? What is the happening which constitutes it this particular people of God armed and commissioned with this witness? The development of the answer to this question is the task of this whole section. In this basic sub-section we must first indicate its general features and scope.

There can be only one point of departure. These saints, the people of God in the world, are men whom the Holy One, the royal man Jesus Christ exalted in His death to fellowship with God, does not confront only in a certain objectivity, as the " historical Jesus," as a problem set for them, as a possibility and chance offered them, or in such a way that they have still to actualise the relevance of His existence for themselves (and for all men). Do they not have to " wrestle " with Him? Later they do, and this in all seriousness. This is the problem of Christian ethics. But they have to do so only on the basis of the fact that there is no separation between Him and them, but only a companionship in which He Himself has set them as the One who has been raised again from the dead and lives, who was and is and will be in the power of the eternal will of God triumphing in His death, the crucified Lord of all men and therefore their Lord, and now their Lord in particular because it is not hidden from them, but revealed to them, that He is the Lord of all men and therefore their Lord. In the particularity of their existence it is not (or only subsequently) a matter of their understanding and interpreting His existence and its relevance. It is a matter of its self-interpretation as this is not now concealed from them but revealed to them. This is not without its effect on their existence. In it the basic decision is revealed which has been taken concerning them. It compels them at once to a re-interpretation of themselves in accordance with the truth concerning them which has hitherto been suppressed. If He lives, this royal man, and if He does so as the Lord, their Lord, this means even for their own self-understanding that they are His, the people of His possession. They for their part cannot, then, confront Him neutrally as those who are remote and alien—which would really mean hostile, for there is no such thing as neutrality at this point. They belong *to* Him, and in such a way that they belong to *Him*. They are not identical with Him, and never will be. He and He alone is the Holy

One of God, who originally and properly is the Holy One among them and at their head, for He alone is true God, and therefore the true and royal man. But He, the Holy One, being revealed to them as such and not hidden, present as their living Lord, has laid His hand on their creaturely and sinful being and thinking and action and inaction, claiming it for Himself as such, making them witnesses of His sanctity, and therefore and to that extent fellow-saints with Him, even as the sinful creatures they are. He has placed them and their whole being and thinking and action and inaction—we must now take up again the main statement of our christological basis (§ 64, 4)— under His direction. As the New Testament puts it, He has reached and touched them in the quickening power of His Holy Spirit. The Holy Spirit is He Himself in the action in which He reveals and makes Himself known to other men as the One He is, placing them under His direction, claiming them as His own, as the witnesses of His holiness. The Holy Spirit is the living Lord Jesus Christ Himself in the work of the sanctification of His particular people in the world, of His community and all its members.

At this point we rejoin Calvin. We cannot overlook the weakness introduced by his doctrine of predestination into his establishment of the *participatio Christi*. Much less, however, can we overlook the exemplary determination and power with which, in the first chapter of the third book (within this limit), he asserted the Christ-created participation of the saints in the sanctity of Jesus Christ, and therefore their membership in Him as their Lord, as the basis of all soteriology. It is because of this, as the result of his thinking from this centre, that he has the clear insight into the relation between justification and sanctification which we had cause to admire in our first sub-section.

It would not be Christ, we are told in 1, 1 if He existed *extra nos*, as a *Christus otiosus frigide extra nos, procul a nobis* (1, 3); as though He were the subject of the divine act of redemption in *privatum usum*; or as though He were One about whom, as those separated from Him, and believing that He exists outside us, we thought that we could "speculate." Our task is to be "graffed in" to Christ (*inseri*, Rom. 11¹⁷), to put Him on (Gal. 3²⁷), to form with Him a single whole (*in unum coalescere*). But it is He Himself who does this by the Holy Ghost. Without the Holy Ghost the promise of salvation would be quite empty. It would reach only our ears (1, 3), and all human teachers would cry in vain (1, 4). The Holy Spirit is the bond (*vinculum*) by which Christ binds us effectively to Himself (1, 1). His work consists in the fact that He enlightens us as *magister* or *doctor internus*, as *Spiritus intelligentiae*, as the Spirit of truth. That is, He brings us to the light of the Gospel, giving us eyes to see, causing us to grasp the heavenly wisdom, and thus giving us the faith in which the *communicatio Christi* with us as His own, and therefore our justification and sanctification, become a concrete event (1, 3 and 1, 4). Since the Holy Ghost is the Spirit of the Son as well as the Father, all this is, of course, the work and gift of Jesus Christ Himself. It is not for nothing that as the second Adam (1 Cor. 15⁴⁵) Jesus Christ Himself is called the *Spiritus vivificans* (1, 2).

We must now take some further steps from this starting-point in an attempt to gain an acquaintance with the most general features of the specific event in which the sanctification of man becomes an event *de facto*. From what we have seen, the "saints" are those whose existence is affected and radically altered and re-determined by the fact that they receive direction in a particular address of the One who alone is holy. He creates saints by giving them direction. This expression might seem to be too weak and external and therefore ineffective in relation to what it is meant to describe. But even in itself the word "direction" speaks meaningfully and dynamically enough of man's indication to a particular and new situation, of the correction which he must receive in it, and of the instruction which he is thereby given to adopt a particular attitude. Nor is this direction merely the type that one man may give to another. It is the direction of the royal man Jesus, who is the one true Son of God. And it is given by Him as the Lord as in the work of His Holy Spirit He is revealed and present to these men as the One who is risen and lives, as their Head and Shepherd. Thus, unlike any direction which one man may give to others, it falls, as it were, vertically into the lives of those to whom it is given. It is thus effective with divine power. It is the sowing and the developing seed of new life. It crushes and breaks and destroys that which resists it. It constitutes itself the ruling and determinative factor in the whole being of those to whom it is given. As is brought out by the German word *Weisung*—and it is in this sense that we are using it—it becomes their wisdom. We do not use the word in any restrictive sense. We use it merely for the sake of precision. It reminds us that the power or sowing which proceeds from the existence of the royal man Jesus, the critical and constructive force with which He invades the being of men and makes them His saints, is not a mechanical or organic or any other physical operation, nor is it in any sense a magical. It is the power of His Word spoken with divine authority and therefore in illuminating fruitfulness and power. The sanctification of the saints by *the* Holy One takes place in the mode appropriate to the being of the Son of the God who is the eternal Logos, and to the relationship of the Son of Man to other men. He speaks. He does so forcefully, not merely in words but in acts, in His whole existence, and all-comprehensively in His death. Yet He speaks. And others hear Him. They do not hear Him only with their ears, or as they hear other men, but effectively—as a call to obedience. Yet they hear Him. Hence the sanctification of man as the work of the Holy Spirit has to be described as the giving and receiving of direction. It is in this way that the Holy One creates the saints. It is in this way that He shares with them, in supreme reality, His own holiness ; man's new form of existence as the true covenant-partner of God.

Again in the most general terms we ask how this impartation is to be understood, and our best plan is to begin from the bottom upwards. These saints are indeed at the very bottom. They themselves are not royal men, nor are they exalted to fellowship and co-operation with God, as has to be said of this One. He indeed is enthroned at the right hand of God the Father. But this means that, as in virtue of His direction they recognise Him as theirs and themselves as His, He confronts them within the world as God confronts the whole world. They are not merely creatures. They are slothful, stupid, inhuman, dissipated and careworn sinners. And as His direction is given them, they have to see and confess that this is the case. They are still sinners—these saints, these recipients of the direction of the exalted man, of the Son of Man who is also the Son of God. They are still below. The direction given and received is one thing ; they themselves in comparison with it are quite another. What, then, differentiates them from the world, from other men, from those who are not saints ? There can be no doubt that they are differentiated from the world ; that as the Word is spoken to them and heard by them they are saints ; fellow-saints with the Holy One, His people. But in what sense is this true and can it be said concerning them ?

To describe their sanctity—in view of the fact that they are undoubtedly still sinners—we must first use a very modest and restrained, yet quite significant expression. They are disturbed sinners. Their sleep as such is broken. Their course as such is slow and lame and halting. Their activity as such is hemmed in by qualifications and doubts. They are no longer happy in the cause that they have espoused. Now it is not at all self-evident that man should be a disturbed sinner in this way. The unreconciled man, the man to whom the reconciliation of the world with God, which comprehends his own sanctification, is concealed, is an undisturbed sinner. Naturally, he too has his own restraints and periods of unrest. But he is able to surmount and master them. It is his conscious or unconscious, primitive or refined art of living to be able to master them, and thus in peace and harmony with himself to pursue his sleep and course and activity. These, and his whole activity below, are possible, necessary and natural in spite of all his unrest. And he cannot genuinely disturb himself. There is, therefore, no point in accusing him, or treating him ironically. He does not understand what we are talking about if we tell him that he ought to be seriously disquieted. The only disturbance that he knows is one which can be overcome, not one which cannot be overcome. The direction of the Son of Man, the work of the Holy Spirit, is needed if he is to be disturbed in a way which cannot be overcome. The saints are sinners who are disturbed in this way. As the sinners they still are they are confronted by the existence of *the* Holy One and therefore by the name and kingdom and will of God. It is not concealed from them that the kingdom has drawn near. It has approached others as well as themselves. But as distinct from others they are aware of the fact, and they have to live with the fact that it is the case. But the kingdom of God is the contradiction of all sloth, and therefore of their own. It is an active protest against what they do and do not do here below. They have

to accept this protest. As it is made and revealed to them, it applies
to their own being. They themselves are still sinners, and they have
to recognise and confess that this is so. But there is now no room for
complacency. They cannot happily pursue their course. They do
what they do. But they do it as those to whom it has been said, and
who have heard, that it is wrong. They have been deprived of all
authorisation to do it ; of every possibility of extenuating or excusing
it. They can no longer continue to do it with confidence. Why not ?
Because in the exalted Son of Man, the royal man Jesus, they have
perceived and have before them their Brother, and themselves as His
brothers. It is He who disturbs them in their activity here below. And
He continues effectively to disturb them. They are His saints as those
who are effectively disturbed. Sanctification is a real change even in
this restricted sense—the creation of a new form of existence in which
man becomes the true covenant-partner of God. As an undisturbed
sinner he is always a covenant-breaker, unreconciled with God and
unusable by Him. The better he succeeds in achieving inner harmony,
the less he can be reconciled with God and used by Him. But when,
although he is a sinner and here below like all others, he meets and has
to accept, in virtue of the direction of the incarnate Son of God, the
name and kingdom and will of God, and therefore that active protest,
even here below he is already placed where he belongs, at the side of
God, made a partisan of God even against himself and the world, and
radically and definitively separated from the unholy, who may not be
so great sinners as he, but who are still undisturbed sinners. It makes
a tremendous difference whether a man is on the one side or the
other ; whether in his person the sin of the world is arrested sin or
unarrested. The people of God in the world are those who still stand
in daily need of forgiveness but upon whose hearts and consciences
there has been written, not their own or a human, but the divine
contradiction of their sinning.

We will now choose another less restricted and rather more penetrating term to describe the men of this people. They are not merely
disturbed in their sinful will and action. A limit is set to their being
sinners by the direction which they are given. Within this limit
their being is still that of sinners. They still live in the flesh. In
relation to this " within " everything that has to be said about the
misery of man, and especially about his lack of freedom to do the
will of God, applies to them too. But this " within " is not infinite.
On the contrary, a definite limit has been set for it. And this is their
sanctification. It is from this limit that there comes on man that
which we have already described as the disturbance of his sinful action.
There can be no reducing the seriousness with which he has still to
recognise himself as a creature which is slothful towards God, and
which constantly reproduces its sloth. Nor can there be any reducing
the seriousness of the fact that he stands under the accusation and

condemnation of God. Yet we have also to recognise that this being is overwhelmingly limited (not merely *de iure* but *de facto*) by the direction which he is given. It is limited to this "within." It is, therefore, relativised. Its continuance is radically threatened. What limits it is again the revealed name of God, His imminent kingdom, His will which is done for man, claiming him as His creature, negating his being as a sinner, and destroying the force which binds him and reduces him to misery and bondage. The limitation which thus comes to him is his sanctification. Because it is God's act, it is an overwhelming limitation. It is not at all the case, then, that the being of saints is compromised by their being as sinners. On the contrary, their being as sinners, their life in the flesh, is overwhelmingly and totally compromised by their being as saints. As God enters their life actively and concretely in virtue of the direction which they are given, in the act of lordship of the Son of Man, in the truth of His Word and the actuality of the Holy Spirit, their being as sinners, however seriously it may still assert itself, is pushed into a corner. It may still intrude into the present, but it belongs to the past. The "within" is in this corner, and is itself the past. It no longer counts. What really counts is its limitation. For the reality of this limitation has its basis in the exaltation of Jesus Christ. It is, therefore, divine reality. The being of man as a sinner, on the other hand, has its reality only in virtue of that which is not. The people of God in the world are those to whom it is revealed, and who may live in and by the knowledge, that their being as sinners is one which is assailed by God, and therefore basically and definitively ; that the ground on which they are sinners has been taken away from them, even though they are still sinners. This is what distinguishes the recipients of the direction of the Son of God from the world which does not share this knowledge—although the ground has already been cut from under its sinful being as well.

The word "disturbance" which we used first to describe sanctification as *participatio Christi* refers to its critical character, although it is not on that account only a formal term. We must now take a further step. As sinners, the recipients of the direction of the One who alone is holy are disturbed in their sinful will and action by the fact that their existence is positively placed under a new determination. In other words, they are called. In their totality they are the ἐκκλησία, a gathering of those to whom the Son of Man has spoken and who have heard His voice. In this sense they are set aside by Him. Or better, here below, within the world which is not yet aware of its reconciliation with God accomplished by Him, its sanctification in Him, they are set at His side, in order that they may be there His witnesses, the witnesses of the Holy One. As such they are disturbed sinners ; sinners who are disturbed by the fact that He has made clear to them the divine No to their own sinful will and action, and that of all men. Because it is His No, it is effective. It thus involves for them an irresistible and invincible disturbance. But again, because it is His No it is not an empty or abstract No. It is concretely filled out with the Yes of His direction. This is not merely correction. It is also instruction. As those who are called by Him, they are not merely called out; they are also called in. They are called into the fellowship of their existence with His. It is to be noted that they are called as those they are, in their action here below, which still has all the marks of sinful action. They still exist here below. " Whilst we are at home in the body, we are absent from the Lord " (2 Cor. 5⁶). For we are not above where He, the royal man, exists. But there above He is our Lord and Head and Representative : the Son who is sanctified by the Father, and who sanctifies Himself, for us and for all men ; the true Covenant-partner of God in fellowship and co-operation with Him. He is all this, not for Himself, but for the saints, as theirs, as their Brother. It disturbs them below that they have this Brother above, bone of their bone and flesh of their flesh. For as the One who, exalted in this way, is theirs, their Brother, He is not concealed from them as He is from others of whom it may also be said that He is theirs, their Brother. He is not distant, a mere historical Jesus. He is revealed and near to them, their living Lord. As such He attests Himself to them, imparting Himself in the truth and power of His, the Holy Spirit. As such, and speaking to them as such, He disturbs them in their slothful sleep and course and activity. Awakening them as such, He startles them out of the peace in which they think that they can continually express their sinful being as others do. But calling them out in this way, He calls them to Himself. As those who still live below He calls them to fellowship with Him as the One who is exalted above. This does not mean only the critical disturbance but in and with it a positive alteration of their being below. They may and can and must lift up themselves as those who are summoned by Him. " Lift up your heads " (Lk. 21²⁸), is the call. What is meant is that they should look to Him, the exalted, royal man, who has come to them as their own, their Brother, and will come again, and is now present with them below even though He is above ; that they should look to Him, the Holy One, and in this looking to Him as their Lord and Representative be His saints. This looking to Him, not with bowed but uplifted head, is the setting up of these men. It is their positive sanctification—in contrast to others upon whom this has come *de iure* but not *de facto*. " Looking unto Jesus, the author and finisher of our faith " (Heb. 12²), they live. This looking is their sanctification *de facto*. As they are called by Him, and look to Him and therefore lift up themselves, they have a part here below in the holiness in which He is the One who alone is holy.

We speak of men who are always sinners like others ; who at every moment and in every respect need forgiveness, the justification before

God which is sheer mercy. Their sanctification takes place here below where there is no action that does not have the marks of sloth or can be anything but displeasing to God. This is true even of their lifting up of themselves, even of their looking to the Lord, which is their action as saints. Who is there who really lifts up his head, and looks directly and steadfastly at the One who is the Holy One for us, as we must do if our action is to be well-pleasing to God and to show that we are true covenant-partners of God ? How painfully we lift up ourselves ! How basically compromised is our attempt to do so by so much indolent and wilful slouching ! Is it really more than the eddy which may arise and be seen in a powerfully flowing stream but which cannot alter the course of the stream as a whole ? These men are saints as they lift up themselves in obedience to the call which comes to them. But they are not saints in virtue of the seriousness or consistency with which they make this movement, or look to the One who calls them. They are saints only in virtue of the sanctity of the One who calls them and on whom their gaze is not very well directed. He alone on whom they look takes from that which they do, their lifting up of themselves, the doubtful and questionable character from which it is never free in and for itself. He alone takes from it the powerlessness and insignificance, the inability to bear witness, which it inevitably shares with the action of all other men. He alone sanctifies it by accepting it as perfect, and therefore by continually justifying it. He alone gives to it here below in the world, where these men also exist, the power and significance of a right answer to His self-attestation and therefore of a witness to the sanctification of man as accomplished in Him.

More important for our present purpose, however, is the fact that He does actually do this. It is not just any call which comes to them and which they obey as they lift up themselves and look to Him. It is His call. If we accept the picture of the stream and the eddy, to make it true to the facts we shall have to say that the eddy does not arise through the inter-play of forces within the stream, but by the operation of an alien factor—perhaps a powerful wind which comes sweeping across it. The lifting up of man effected by his sanctification is his own act, and it is similar to all his other acts. Yet it is different from all his other acts to the extent that the initiative on which he does it, the spontaneity with which he expresses himself in it, does not arise from his own heart or emotions or understanding or conscience, but has its origin in the power of the direction which has come to him in these spheres. It is necessary and indispensable that he should rouse himself and pull himself together and find courage and confidence and take and execute decisions, but this is only the spiritual and physical form of a happening which does not originate in himself and is not his own work, but the gift of God. It is not as his own lord but as the recipient of this gift that he carries through the movement which we call his lifting up of himself. He executes it as the answer to a call which does not come from himself but from the One who encounters him, and is present and revealed to him, as the Lord and therefore as his Lord. No matter how similar this movement may be to those of all other men—for he has no other means to hand than those common to all men—it is absolutely dissimilar in the fact that it is his correspondence to the life-movement of his Lord as produced, not by his own caprice, but by the will and touch and address and creation and gift of this Lord. Those who receive Him, who are given the power to become the children of God, who believe in His name, are not born of blood, or of the will of the flesh, or of the will of man, but of God (Jn. 1$^{12f.}$). Their action is nourished by the mystery of the life-giving Spirit by whom the Lord has united these sinful human creatures to Himself. Their action attests this mystery, and therefore the One who has united them to Himself. This is what has to be said of them, and can be said only of them. This is their sanctification.

Because and as and to the extent that it comes to them from Him, and is His work, it is a real alteration of their being, They are still sinners. Their action is still burdened with all the marks of human sloth. It still stands in need of the forgiveness, the justification, which they cannot achieve of themselves, and which God does not owe them. All this is true. But even more true is the fact that as they lift up themselves they fulfil a movement in which their being —however questionably they may fulfil it—becomes and is conformable to His being, the being of their Lord. Yes, their being below is conformable to His above. Their painful lifting up of themselves in the flesh, in the world from which they are not yet taken, is conformable to his enthronement at the right hand of God the Father Almighty. " I, if I be lifted up from the earth, will draw all men unto me " (Jn. 12^{32}). The constitution of His people on earth takes place in the power of His drawing unto Himself. This drawing unto Himself is His kingly work fulfilled in divine power. It cannot, then, be called in question. But if this is the case, the same is true of the existence of His people, His saints, and the lifting up of themselves in which they are drawn to Him. As that which corresponds to His exaltation, as the attestation of the elevation of man accomplished in Him, it is a historical event. In what takes place to them as He calls them to lift up themselves, His exaltation has its concrete consequence in the world and its continuing and not yet arrested development. The eddy arises and is visible in the stream, first in the lives of these men, but then—seeing that they have their fellows—as a fact in the common life of all men. It is now not merely human sloth which rules here below. As it is given to these men to lift up themselves, in opposition to human sloth and defiance of it (in its sphere and not unhampered by it) we find also a willingness and readiness, a courage and joyfulness, to be the new man who is loyal to His covenant-partnership with God and therefore loyal to his human brothers. The stream flows on, and all men—even the saints, for they are still here below—flow with it. But the powerful wind is blowing from above. And stirred up by it there is obedience as well as disobedience. It is highly unsatisfactory obedience. It stands in constant need of forgiveness. But it is obedience. To that extent there is the sowing seed of new life in the field which is the world. It is only a sowing. It is only seed. And this seed must die if it is to bear fruit. But it is genuine seed—seed which while it is sown below does not come from below, but from above. This is sanctification, the actual sanctifying of the saints by the Holy One. Its dignity and reality are no less than those of justification, but the same. The human situation does not remain unchanged, as it would necessarily do in itself, and as it seems to do to those who do not have eyes to see. The change is only relative. For sanctification is not an ultimate, only a penultimate, word. Like justification, it is not redemption or glorification. Yet for all its relativity it is a real change. For there are now men who lift up themselves and raise their heads.

We must now return, however, to the second word which we used to describe the critical character of sanctification as *participatio Christi*. We called it the limit which is set for man in his being as a sinner. And in the case of this term, too, we must now step on to the positive significance. We have said that the name and kingdom and will of God limit the corrupt and miserable being of man, pushing it into a corner, making it his past, thoroughly relativising it. It is the act of lordship of the Son of Man, His direction, which in this way cuts as it were right across the existence of man and draws this frontier. Now obviously we do not exhaust the meaning of this event by saying that in it the being of man as a sinner is attacked and limited and made a thing of the past. As we learn from 2 Cor. 5^{17} there has also come into being something new. The space which the Holy Spirit makes outside the sinful being of man which He limits cannot be an empty space. He Himself fills it. For " where the Spirit of the Lord is, there is liberty " (2 Cor. 3^{17})—the liberty for being on behalf of God and one's brothers which the sinful man does not have as such, and the lack of which is the deepest woe in which he finds himself plunged as a sinner. In his sinful activity he should not merely find himself disturbed by the direction which comes to him but awakened to lift up himself, to look to Jesus, and in so doing to be sanctified and holy. But he needs the capacity, the ability, the freedom, to do this. It has to take place here below, in the flesh, in the world. But in this sphere there is no freedom for it. He exists *servo arbitrio*. He is a prisoner of sin who continually commits new sins. No true Christian has ever suffered seriously from the illusion that within the limit set by the divine direction he does not still live in this bondage in which he cannot even think of this lifting up of himself, of this looking to Jesus, let alone accomplish it. Yet as his sinful being is limited in the power of the divine direction he is given a total freedom in face of this total bondage. And in the New Testament sense of the term this freedom does not mean the possibility of either lifting up himself or not, of perhaps looking to Jesus and perhaps looking else-where to other lords. No, the One who has accomplished this powerful limitation could not be the Lord if He had merely opposed to the sinful being of man this paltry freedom of choice. What He imparts to man when He gives him His direction is not a possibility but the new actuality in which he is really free in face of that bondage : free in the only worthwhile sense ; free to lift up himself in the sense described. He can do this, not because he should, but because he may. The imparting of this capacity is the liberation of man—his sanctification. In this capacity he is set in sovereign antithesis to his being as a sinner. He is not compelled continually to commit new sins. He may refrain from doing so. He may do the opposite. In the capacity which is imparted to him, on the basis of the permission which he is given, he will—if he makes use of it—do the opposite. He cannot do anything else. Whether he makes use of it is, of course, another matter. Our present concern is with the permission which he is given ; the sovereignty in which he is set in opposition to his own being as a sinner. And to this as such there is no limit.

We say this even of the saints who are all very obviously and palpably sinners, in whose lives there is continually to be found much that is very different from this lifting up of themselves, who clearly continue to make use of very different freedoms and permissions from those given them by the divine direction ; of all kinds of supposed freedoms and permissions which they think they can and should give themselves, but which are in fact illusory. The total, unlimited, sovereign freedom of the Spirit is given them even though they are still in the world like all other men. Their being as sinners is radically assailed, but not destroyed. They still think and speak and act as those who are not free, but who, according to the classical formula of the *Heidelberg Catechism*, are " inclined by nature to hate God and my neighbours." What would become of the freedom of the saints if it had to be guaranteed by the use they make of it ; if its possession were dependent on the power with which they exercise it ? They do indeed have to use and exercise it. How can they receive it if they do not do this ? But the freedom of the saints is grounded and enclosed, not in the dignity and power of this reception, but in the dignity and power of the gift made, or rather of the Giver of this gift, in the freedom of the royal man Jesus to whom they are summoned to look. They do not look to Him very well. But they are made free, and are free, only in the fact that it is He to whom they look. They are saints only in the fact that He sanctified them. What Paul says in Gal. 4[25f.]

with reference to the Synagogue may rightly be applied to every form of the people of God on earth—that " the Jerusalem which is above is free, which is the mother of us all."

Here again, however, the emphasis must fall on the other aspect. The Holy One does actually give it to His saints to be free: free to lift up themselves and look to Him; and therefore freed from the compulsion to sin which results from their being as sinners. Even here below, as those who live in the flesh, they need never again bewail the fact that they have to sin: that they have therefore to make use of other ostensible freedoms and permissions; that they have therefore in certain respects to persist in the general sloth of man which characterises them too; that they cannot therefore lift up themselves. They have no time either for the arrogance of the indeterminists or the pusillanimity or melancholy or idle dissuasions of the determinists. In view of the One to whom they look—however well or badly—in their *participatio Christi*, everything is in good order as regards their freedom. Their sovereignty over their being in the flesh and in sin is unequivocally established and secured against every assault. There may often be good cause to bewail both new and old connexions with that which is below. They may often do things which apart from the forgiveness of sins would inevitably involve their ruin. But they cannot ascribe this to the incompleteness of impotence of the freedom which they are given. They lack it as they fail to make use of it. But it is still given, and in their fellowship with the Holy One they still have it. As they are called, so they are also equipped to be a brave people of their Lord. They make themselves equivalent to the children of this world, to whom they are supposed to be His witnesses, if they leave this in any doubt, accepting in relation to themselves the general deploring of human incapacity instead of resolutely doing what they are well able to do. The fact is that they *are* able to lift up themselves and look to Jesus and be what they are—His saints. For, as they well know, He has stooped down to them and looked on them. The positive element concealed in the limitation of their unholy being, the freedom which has become a factor in their life, has also to be thought of as real. Otherwise there would be no place for the apostolic admonition given in the New Testament to Christians. This is not given as a law or ideal proclaimed in the void. It is not given as though the question whether or not they can obey were still open and to be answered. It is obviously given on the assumption that they are free, and that they can make use of the freedom in which they have been made free in Christ (Gal. 5¹). Without this assumption there would be no such thing as Christian ethics even for us. All the things that we have to develop in ethics in relation to the command of the God who reconciles the world with Himself can only be concretions of the lifting up of themselves, the looking to Jesus, of which Christians are capable because they have been given the freedom for them. It is true that in its original and proper form they have this freedom, not in themselves, but in the One who is above. But called by Him to fellowship with Himself, placed in it, united with Him by His Holy Spirit, they are free here and now in correspondence to His kingly rule at the right hand of God the Father Almighty. To their salvation they are free only for this. But they are genuinely free for this. They can look to Him and be His saints in everything that they do in this look. 2 Cor. 5[17] is true of them : " If any man be in Christ, he is a new creature " ; and especially Heb. 12[10] : they are " partakers of his holiness " ; and above all Jn. 8[36] : " If the Son therefore shall make you free, ye shall be free indeed " —ὄντως ἐλευθέροι. It is all provisional, for the saints are still captives. But it is all very real, for they are already liberated. If it is true that they are still prisoners, it does not count. The captivity is behind them, freedom before them. And all this is in their fellowship with the Holy One. All this is in virtue of the fact that they are called by Him. " Now ye are clean through the word that I have spoken unto you " (Jn. 15[3]).

3. THE CALL TO DISCIPLESHIP

" Follow me " is the substance of the call in the power of which Jesus makes men His saints. It is to this concretion of His action that we must now turn. The lifting up of themselves for which He gives them freedom is not a movement which is formless, or to which they themselves have to give the necessary form. It takes place in a definite form and direction. Similarly, their looking to Jesus as their Lord is not an idle gaping. It is a vision which stimulates those to whom it is given to a definite action. The call issued by Jesus is a call to discipleship.

We must not waste time describing and criticising that which, in adoption of very earlier traditions, the later Middle Ages and certain Evangelical trends understood and attempted as an *imitatio Christi*. The matter is well enough known. It involves a programme in which we try to shape our lives by the example of the life of Jesus as sketched in the Gospels and the commandments which He gave to His own people and to all men generally. And the objections to it are obvious, and therefore facile. It will be more instructive for our present purpose if we turn at once to the problem which is unavoidably posed by these movements, and especially by the New Testament itself. The discussion of this problem will enable us to weigh both critically and positively the doctrine and exercise of the *imitatio Christi*.

Easily the best that has been written on this subject is to be found in *The Cost of Discipleship*, by Dietrich Bonhoeffer (abridged *E.T.*, 1948, of the German original *Nachfolge*, 1937). We do not refer to all the parts, which were obviously compiled from different sources, but to the opening sections, " The Call to Discipleship," " Simple Obedience " (omitted in the *E.T.*) and " Discipleship and the Individual." In these the matter is handled with such depth and precision that I am almost tempted simply to reproduce them in an extended quotation. For I cannot hope to say anything better on the subject than what is said here by a man who, having written on discipleship, was ready to achieve it in his own life, and did in his own way achieve it even to the point of death. In following my own course, I am happy that on this occasion I can lean as heavily as I do upon another.

Before we take up the problem as such, it may be as well to consider briefly what is to be learned linguistically from the biblical use of the decisive term ἀκολουθεῖν. In this respect I am indebted to G. Kittel's article in his *Wörterbuch*.

'Ἀκολουθεῖν means to go after or behind someone. Rather strangely, the Old Testament used the corresponding word mostly as a kind of technical term for the sinful pursuit of others gods. This gave to the word a pejorative sense, and Jer. 2² is perhaps the only occasion that we read of a following of Yahweh : " I remember thee, the kindness of thy youth, the love of thine espousals, when thou wentest after me in the wilderness, in a land that was not sown." The Rabbis doubted, indeed, whether there could be any following of God at all in the sense of a following of God Himself, of His *shekina*. For God is far too transcendent. As they saw it (in a striking parallel to the Greek idea of the similarity which man achieves with God by ἔπεσθαι as he acts like Him), it is a matter of following the qualities or acts of God : of planting the land as God did the Garden of Eden ; of clothing the naked as God clothed Adam ; of visiting the sick as God did Abraham ; of comforting the sad as God did Isaac ; of burying the dead as God did Moses. In this we have almost an early form of the later Christian idea of *imitatio*. For the rest, the Old Testament and Rabbis offer us only the " following " (which has no theological significance) of honoured leaders. The warrior follows his captain, the wife her husband, the bride her bridegroom, the son of the prophet his master, the scholar the rabbi who goes or rides before him on an ass. It is this that leads us to the New Testament with its thought of following Jesus. This occurs only in the Four Gospels (with the exception of Rev. 14⁴) ; and in the first instance it envisages an external going after him, the word being apparently limited to this sense in such passages as Mk. 3⁷, etc., where we are told that " a great multitude followed him." Following as they practised it had both an inward and an outward limit. Yet there were others—and it is here that the word acquires its pregnant meaning—who are called by Jesus and follow Him in the sense that they accompany Him wholeheartedly and constantly, sharing His life and destiny at the expense of all other engagements and commitments, attaching themselves to Him, placing themselves in His service, and thus showing that they are qualified to be His disciples ; not as though the Messianic salvation is ascribed only to them, or even to them in particular, but as those who particularly attest and proclaim it. Their qualification as disciples, and therefore for discipleship in this pregnant sense, is a gift, a εὔθετος εἶναι for the kingdom of God (Lk. 9⁶²), a capacity with which they are endowed. Normally the fact that they are endowed in this way means also that they accompany Him. Yet there are some qualified disciples who do not do so, and on the other hand there are others who accompany Him but are not qualified disciples in this sense. It is worth noting in conclusion that the New Testament never uses the substantive " discipleship " (ἀκολούθησις) but only the verb ἀκολουθεῖν or ὀπίσω μου ἔρχεσθαι. This is a warning that in our consideration of this question we must always remember that we are dealing with what is obviously on the New Testament view an event that cannot be enclosed in a general concept. The further implications of discipleship must be developed from concrete passages within this wider context.

1. We will again begin by stating that the call to discipleship is the particular form of the summons by which Jesus discloses and reveals Himself to a man in order to claim and sanctify him as His own, and as His witness in the world. It has the form of a command of Jesus directed to him. It means the coming of grace, for what is

disclosed and revealed in Jesus is the reconciliation of the world with God as his reconciliation and therefore the fulness of salvation. But as it encounters him in this summons, grace has the form of command, the Gospel the form of the Law. The grace which comes to him requires that he should do something, i.e., follow Jesus. It is thus a grace which commands. Jesus is seeking men to serve Him. He has already found them to the extent that He has elected them as ordained to this end. They are already His people even as He claims them. He thus establishes His particular relationship to them by commanding them. He does this in His authority as the Son of Man who is their Lord, who can thus dispose concerning them, who has already done so, and who addresses them accordingly. Both Jeremiah and Paul understood that even from the mother's womb they were ordained for the action commanded. Jesus is already the Lord of those whom He calls to follow. He calls them as such. He commands them as those who already belong to Him. This is what constitutes the overwhelming force of His command. This is why there can be no legitimate opposition to it. This is why there can be no question of any presuppositions on the part of those who are called : of any capacity or equipment for the performance of what is commanded ; of any latent faith ; of any inward or outward preparation. This is why there can be no question of self-selection on the part of those who follow. This is why those who are called cannot think of laying down conditions on which they are prepared to obey His command. Just because the command of Jesus is the form of the grace which concretely comes to man, it is issued with all the freedom and sovereignty of grace against which there can be no legitimate objections, of which no one is worthy, for which there can be no preparation, which none can elect, and in face of which there can be no qualifications.

Disobedience to the command of Jesus : " Follow me," as in the case of the rich young ruler in Mk. 10[17f.] and par., is a phenomenon which is absolutely terrifying in its impossibility. It provokes the question of the disciples : " Who then can be saved ?", for in it there is revealed the far too common rule of the natural, or unnatural, attitude of man to this command. In the light of the command of Jesus given to a man, disobedience is inconceivable, inexplicable and impossible. On the other hand, we might ask who is the man Levi that when Jesus sees him at the receipt of custom (Mk. 2[14f.]) He should at once issue the same command : " Follow me " ? How much we should have to read into the short account if we were to try to explain from Levi himself, and his moral and religious qualifications, why it is that he is given this command and proceeds at once to execute it. We can only abandon the attempt. The secret of Levi is that of the One who calls him. Again, we are told in Lk. 9[57-58] about a man who met Jesus in the way with the offer : " I will follow thee whithersoever thou goest." He is obviously one who has presumed to do this on his own initiative. And his answer is the terrible saying about the foxes which have holes, and the birds of the air nests, " but the Son of man—whom he is going to follow—hath not where to lay his head." He does not realise what it is that he thinks he can choose. He does not know how terrible is the venture to which he commits himself in the execution of this choice. No one of himself can or will imagine that this is his way, or take this way. What Jesus wills with His "Follow me" can be chosen only in obedience to His call. We can see this from the saying of Peter in Mt. 14[28] : "Lord, if it be thou, bid me come to thee on the water." Without being bidden by Christ, he could not do this. It has also been noted that there can be no conditions. The man mentioned in Lk. 9[61-62] lacked true discipleship, not merely because he offered it to Jesus as a matter for his own choice, but because he also made a condition : "But let me first go bid them farewell, which are at home at my house." Those who offer themselves to be disciples are obviously bound to be of the opinion that they can lay down the conditions on which they will do this. But a limited readiness is no readiness at all in our dealings with Jesus. It is clear that this man, too, does not really know what he thinks he has chosen. It is certainly not the following of Jesus. This is commanded unconditionally, and therefore it cannot be entered upon except unconditionally. The answer of Jesus makes it quite plain that this man cannot be considered as a disciple : "No man, having put his hand to the plough, and looking back, is fit for the kingdom of God."

2. The call to discipleship binds a man to the One who calls him. He is not called by an idea of Christ, or a Christology, or a christo-centric system of thought, let alone the supposedly Christian conception of a Father-God. How could these call him to discipleship ? They have neither words nor voice. They cannot bind anyone to themselves. We must be careful that we do not conceal the living Jesus behind such schemata, fearing that the One who can issue this call, who has the words and voice to do it, and above all the right and authority and power to bind, might actually do so. Again, discipleship is not the recognition and adoption of a programme, ideal or law, or the attempt to fulfil it. It is not the execution of a plan of individual or social construction imparted and commended by Jesus. If the word " discipleship " is in any way used to denote something general and not a concrete and therefore a concretely filled-out happening between Jesus and this particular man, the command "Follow me" can only be described as quite meaningless. For the only possible content of this command is that this or that specific man to whom it is given should come to, and follow, and be with, the One who gives it. In this One, and the relationship which it establishes between Him and the one He calls, a good deal more is involved. But there is nothing apart from Him and this relationship. That a man should come to Him is the one complete work which he is called to do. We may say, therefore, that in practice the command to follow Jesus is identical with the command to believe in Him. It demands that a man who as such brings no other presuppositions than that he is entangled like all other men in the general sloth of man, and has to suffer the consequences, should put his trust in God as the God who is faithful to him the unfaithful, who in spite of his own forgetfulness has not forgotten him, who without any co-operation or merit on his part wills that he should live and not die. In the call of Jesus he is met by the fulfilled promise of God as valid for him. In and with the command of Jesus, solid ground is placed under his feet when he is on the point

of falling into the abyss. What the command requires of him is simply, but comprehensively, that in practice as well as in theory he should regard it as able to bear him, and stand on it, and no longer leave it. This is what we do when we trust ; and in so doing we do all that is required of us. To do this is to believe. But in the faith here required we do not have a trust *in abstracto* or in general, nor do we have the rash confidence of a hazardous journey into space. It is demanded by Jesus—the Son of Man who as the Son of God speaks in the name and with the full authority of God. And what Jesus demands is trust in Himself and therefore, in the concrete form which this involves, trust in God. He demands faith in the form of obedience ; obedience to Himself. This is the commitment to Him which constitutes the content of the call to discipleship. We cannot separate any one moment of this happening from any of the others. That He, the Son of Man who is the Son of the Father, lives and rules as the Lord of all men ; that as the Saviour of all men He comes to a particular man, who is as little worthy of it as any others, to make Himself known to him as the One who is also his Saviour ; that in so doing He simply claims him for Himself as one of His, and for His service ; that He thus demands of him faith in God and trust in Himself ; that the faith demanded of this man includes the obedience which has to be rendered to Jesus : all these are inseparable moments of the one occurrence. There is no discipleship without the One who calls to it. There is no discipleship except as faith in God as determined by the One who calls to it and frees for it. There is no discipleship which does not consist in the act of the obedience of this faith in God and therefore in Him.

It is with these contours that the call to discipleship goes out as recorded and attested in the Gospels. Everything depends upon the fact that Jesus Himself is there and lives and calls men to Himself. We are never told what His will is for Levi or Simon Peter, or the others whom He calls. Nor is any attempt made to establish or explain His authority to call them. It is enough for the Evangelists in their description of the origin of the disciple-relationship, and it must obviously be enough for us too in our understanding of it, that Jesus does actually call them, and call them to Himself. He summons them. They are to give to Him the faith of which God is worthy and which is owed to Him ; the faith and therefore the confidence that they are helped by Him and therefore by God ; that within the world of human sloth and its consequences they are helped to overcome these and to be set up : " He that followeth me shall not walk in darkness, but shall have the light of life " (Jn. 8[12]). Or, as we are told of the 144,000 who " follow the Lamb whithersoever he goeth," they are the firstfruits of the redeemed from among men, and they bear His name and the name of His Father in their foreheads, and they sing a new song before the throne (Rev. 14[1f.]). His summons is, however, that they should give to Him and therefore to God a true and serious and total faith : not a mere acceptance of the fact that He is their Lord nor an idle confidence that they are helped by Him ; but this acceptance and confidence as a faith which is lived out and prac- tised by them ; a faith which is proved to be a true and serious faith by the fact that it includes at once their obedience—what Paul called the ὑπακοὴ πίστεως in Rom. 1⁵ and 16²⁶, and the ὑπακοὴ τοῦ Χριστοῦ in 2 Cor. 10⁵. " Why call ye me, Lord, Lord, and do not the things which I say ? " (Lk. 6⁴⁶). There can be no doubt that what moved those who were called to be disciples as they followed the call of Jesus was simply their faith in Him as the Lord, and therefore in God. But it was a faith which at once impelled them to obedience. There is nothing in the accounts of the call of the disciples to suggest a kind of interval, i.e., that they first believed in Him, and then decided to obey Him, and actually did so. It is never an open question whether, when and how obedience has to begin if faith is presupposed. Faith is not obedience, but as obedience is not obedience without faith, faith is not faith without obedience. They belong together, as do thunder and lightning in a thunderstorm. Levi would not have obeyed if he had not arisen and followed Jesus. The fishermen by the lake would not have believed if they had not immediately (εὐθύς) left their nets and followed Him. Peter on the lake (Mt. 14²⁹) would not have believed if he had not obeyed Jesus' call to come, and left the boat and gone to Him on the water. But Peter and all of them did believe, and therefore they did at once and self-evidently that which was commanded. It is true that in the continuation of the story Peter looked at the raging wind instead of Jesus, and was afraid, and doubted, and could go no farther, but could only sink, and would have sunk if he had not been gripped by the hand of the One in whom he had so little faith. But this only shows that the disciple cannot obey without believing, or conversely that when he believes he must and can obey, and actually does so.

3. The call to discipleship, no matter how or when it is issued to a man, or whether it comes to him for the first time or as a second or third or hundredth confirmation, is always the summons to take in faith, without which it is impossible, a definite first step. This step, as one which is taken in faith, i.e., faith in Jesus, as an act of obedience to Him, is distinguished from every other step that he may take by the fact that in relation to the whole of his previous life and thinking and judgment it involves a right-about turn and therefore a complete break and new beginning. To follow Jesus means to go beyond oneself in a specific action and attitude, and therefore to turn one's back upon oneself, to leave oneself behind. That this is the case may and will not always be equally perceptible from the particular step, the particular action or attitude, which is demanded as the act of faith. But—however imperceptible that which we do may be—it can never be a question of a routine continuation or repetition of what has hitherto been our customary practice. It always involves the decision of a new day ; the seizing of a new opportunity which was not present yesterday but is now given in and with the call of Jesus. Inevitably the man who is called by Jesus renounces and turns away from himself as he was yesterday. To use the important New Testament expression, he denies himself.

Where it is used in a pregnant sense, and not merely of a simple denial, ἀρνεῖσθαι always denotes in the New Testament the renunciation, withdrawal and annulment of an existing relationship of obedience and loyalty. Peter denies that he was ever with Jesus of Nazareth : " I know not, neither understand I what thou sayest " (Mk. 14⁶⁸ and par.). The Jews deny Jesus, their own Messiah, the Servant of God, in the presence of Pilate (Ac. 3¹³). There are also ostensible, but in reality anti-Christian, Christians who deny the Lord who bought them

(2 Pet. 2¹). In particular, they deny that Jesus is the Christ, thus making themselves guilty of a denial of the Father and the Son (1 Jn. 2²²). John the Baptist denies that he himself is the Messiah (Jn. 1²⁰), and in so doing he does not deny, but indirectly recognises, that Jesus is. Denial is the opposite of confession (ὁμολογεῖσθαι), in which a man stands both in word and deed to a relationship of obedience and loyalty in which he finds himself. The disciple who does not do this to others in respect of his relationship to Jesus—" whosoever therefore shall be ashamed of me and of my words in this adulterous and sinful generation " (Mk. 8³⁸)—denies Him as Peter did ; and this automatically means that so long and to the extent that he does this the relationship of Jesus to him, His advocacy for him before God, is dissolved : " Him will I also deny before my Father which is in heaven " (Mt. 10³³, cf. 2 Tim. 2¹²). This is the objective factor in the bitterness experienced by Peter in consequence of his denial. In the same sense, and with the menace of the same dreadful consequences, there is a denial of the name of Jesus (Rev. 3⁸) or of His πίστις (Rev. 2¹³). It is remarkable that the same verb which in this pregnant sense denotes the most dreadful thing of which the disciple can conceivably be guilty in his relationship to Jesus is also used (although this time with reference to himself) to describe the peak point in this relationship, the characteristic turning of obedience. In 2 Tim. 2¹³ the culminating reason for the impossibility of denying Christ as the Christian sees it is the fact that " he cannot deny himself "—for how can the Son of Man deny that He is the Son of God ? But at the decisive point in the Synoptists (Mk. 8³⁴) the very opposite is true of ourselves : " Whosoever will come after me, let him deny himself " (ἀπαρνησάσθω ἑαυτόν). The idea is exactly the same. The man who is called to follow Jesus has simply to renounce and withdraw and annul an existing relationship of obedience and loyalty. This relationship is to himself. When he is called to discipleship, he abandons himself resolutely and totally. He can and must say of himself instead of Jesus : " I know not the man " (Mt. 26⁷²). He cannot accept this man even as his most distant acquaintance. He once stood in a covenant with him which he loyally kept and tenderly nurtured. But he now renounces this covenant root and branch. He can confess only Jesus, and therefore he cannot confess himself. He can and will only deny himself.

But in the context of discipleship to Jesus, which is a definite happening, this is a very definite step. It is not merely a new and critical and negative mind and attitude in relation to himself. This will also be involved. But in and for itself, in the uncommitted sphere of inwardness, this might be present without the definite loosing of a man from himself, and therefore without a definite act of obedience. In this case discipleship would only be theoretical. It would not be an actual event. The call to discipleship would not have really reached and affected the man, or he would have imprisoned and tamed and rendered it innocuous in the sphere of emotion or reflection. An inner withdrawal from oneself is not by a long way a breach of the covenant or denial of acquaintance with oneself, and therefore self-denial in the sense of discipleship. In itself and as such, if this is the whole of the matter, it might be the most radical and obstinate denial of this breach or renunciation. Indeed, where this is the whole of the matter, it will certainly be such. Self-denial in the context of following Jesus involves a step into the open, into the freedom of a definite decision and act, in which it is with a real commitment that man takes leave of himself, of the man of yesterday, of the man he himself was ; in which he gives up the previous form of his existence, hazarding and totally compromising himself without looking back or considering what is to become of him, because what matters is not now himself but that he should do at all costs that which is proposed and demanded, having no option but to decide and act in accordance with it—cost what it may. " For God's sake do something brave," was once the cry of Zwingli to his contemporaries. Not feel, or think, or consider, or meditate ! Not turn it over in your heart and mind ! But *do* something brave. If it is to this that Jesus calls man in His discipleship, there can be no avoiding genuine self-denial.

To be sure, we have not merely to do anything that is brave, or that smacks of bravery. Even though we might find precedents for it in history, or Church history, or the Bible, a mere act of bravery might well be performed without self-denial. Indeed, it might even be an act of supreme self-assertion. For all his sloth, the old Adam whom we have to leave behind loves sometimes to emerge in great acts. It is a matter of doing that which is proposed to us by Jesus. It may be great or it may be small. It may be striking or it may be insignificant. But its performance is laid upon us, not by ourselves, but by the One who has called us to Himself, who has willed and chosen us as His own. And we are to perform it in the act of that obedience which cannot be separated from faith in Him. As a man renders this obedience, he will certainly not be able to assert himself. He can only deny himself. The call with which Jesus calls and binds him to Himself means that he should leave everything that yesterday, and even yet, might seem self-evident and right and good and useful and promising. It also means that he should leave a merely inward and mental movement in which he does not really do anything, but only speechifies in an idle dialectic, in mere deliberations and projects concerning what he might do but cannot and will not yet do, because he has not yet reached the point of action in his consideration of it and of the situation in which it is to be done. He takes leave of both, for in both the old Adam is enthroned—the self whom he has to deny in the discipleship of Jesus. This Adam is denied in the new act demanded by the call of Jesus, and the brave thing demanded of His disciples consists in what D. Bonhoeffer calls " simple obedience." Obedience is simple when we do just what we are told—nothing more, nothing less, and nothing different. In simple obedience we *do* it, and therefore we do not finally not do it. But what we do is literally and exactly that which we are commanded to do. The only possible obedience to Jesus' call to discipleship is simple obedience in these two senses. This alone is rendered in self-denial. This alone is the brave act of faith in Jesus.

Bonhoeffer is ten times right when at this point he inveighs sharply against a theological interpretation of the given command and the required obedience which is to the effect that the call of Jesus is to be heard but His command may be taken to mean that the obedience required will not necessarily take the form of the act which is obviously demanded but may in certain cases consist in the neglect of this act and the performance of others which are quite different.

This interpretation may be stated as follows. The command of Jesus is naturally to be heard and accepted and followed with joy. It is the commanding grace of God, and therefore the salvation of the whole world and of man, entering his life as a free offer. How can he resist it ? But what does it mean to follow ? What is commanded is obviously that he should come to Jesus ; that he should believe in Him as God ; that he should believe in God by believing in Him ; that he should trust Him wholly and utterly ; that he should be willing and ready, therefore, for every hazard or venture or sacrifice that in a given situation might prove to be necessary to confirm this trust. Yet as concerns the concrete form of the command of Jesus, in which we have to do with something definite that we are commanded to do or not do, this concrete thing is only designed more sharply to describe and emphasise the totality and depth with which the command requires faith, and with faith the willingness and readiness for what may in certain circumstances be the supreme and most perfect sacrifice. Obedience to it means an inward liberation from everything in which we might otherwise put our trust ; the loosening of all other ties to the point of being able to sever them at any moment. We need not do precisely what the command of Jesus explicitly demands. The point of the explicit command is the implicit—that we should believe, and that in our faith we should be alert to do either that which is explicitly commanded or something similar and along the same lines. When we have accepted that which is implied in the command, we have already obeyed in the true sense. We have " as though we had not." By what is meant in the command, and the willingness and readiness we bring to it, everything else that we have is radically called in question. We do everything only " as though we did it not." Inwardly, therefore, we are free. We are free even perhaps to do that which is explicitly commanded. But do we have to do it ? No, for that would be a legalistic interpretation of the command, which even in what seems to be its concrete demand that we should do this or that is really calling us only to the freedom in which we may do it but do not have to do so. On a true and proper interpretation the command of Jesus does not command us to do this specific thing. There is no question of having to do it. In obedience to the command we may just as well do something else and even the very opposite. For example, instead of giving all that we have to the poor, we may maintain and increase our possessions ; or instead of turning the other cheek, we may return the blow which we have received. All, of course, " as though we did it not " ! All in a willingness and readiness one day perhaps—when the opportunity and situation offer—to do that which is concretely demanded ! All on a true and spiritual understanding, and in a genuine exercise, of the obedience of faith ! All in a grateful appropriation of the salvation which comes with Jesus' call to discipleship ! But with the result that for the moment that which Jesus literally asks remains undone, and the outward state and course of affairs remains unchanged by His command and our obedience.

Bonhoeffer's commentary on this line of thought and its result is as follows (*Nachfolge*, p. 35) : " Where orders are given in other spheres, there can be no doubt how matters stand. A father says to his child : Go to bed, and the child knows what has to be done. But a child versed in this pseudo-theology might argue as follows. My father says : Go to bed. He means that I am tired. He does not want me to be tired. But I can dissipate my tiredness by going out to play. Therefore, when my father says : Go to bed, he really means : Go out to play. If this were the way in which children reasoned in relation to their fathers, or citizens in relation to the state, they would soon meet with a language that cannot be misunderstood—that of punishment. It is only in relation to the command of Jesus that things are supposed to be different."

The ghost of this interpretation cannot be too quickly laid. The commanding grace of God, and therefore salvation as Jesus' call to discipleship, never come into the life of a man in such a way that he is given leave to consider why and how he may best follow the command given. The command given is recognisable as the command of Jesus by the fact that it is quite unambiguous. It requires to be fulfilled by him only as it is given—and his reception or non-reception of salvation depends upon whether this is done or not. The faith which Jesus actually demands is not just a radical readiness and willingness for all contingencies—a kind of supply which is there to draw upon as required but is stored up for the time being. It is distinguished as trust in Jesus, and therefore as genuine trust in God, by the fact that as it is given to man and grasped by him it at once takes on the form of the definite resolve and act indicated by the call of Jesus. The command given to a man by Jesus is not given to the one who receives it in such a way that he may freely distinguish between what is meant and what is willed, between the implicit content and the explicit form, the former being accepted but the latter provisionally ignored. It has its content only in its specific form. Only as it turns to the latter can it keep seriously to the former. Again, it is not the case that in obedience to the call of Jesus we can and should and even (in all prudence) must postpone a full inward and outward rendering of it until we find a favourable opportunity and situation ; the psychological, historical, economic or political situation indispensable to its integral achievement. To be sure, we for our part have not to create a situation of this kind. But we have to realise that the command of Jesus given us itself creates the situation and all the conditions of the situation in which we have to obey, so that there is no place for any further waiting for a developing situation or suitable moment, nor for any further consideration, appraisal or selection of different possibilities, but only for instant obedience. In obedience we are not about to leap. We are already leaping.

The line of argument which we have been reconstructing has, of course, a ring of profundity. It seems to give a triumphant answer to monks and fanatics and other legalists. But this is an illusion. It is not simple obedience that is legalistic, but the arbitrarily discursive and dialectical obedience which evades the command. It is the disobedience, disguised as obedience, of a flight into inwardness at the point where the inward man can and should express himself outwardly. It is the disobedience of the flight into faith at the point where faith as the obedience of the heart relentlessly involves the obedience of action. It is not from the concrete command of Jesus that there comes the threat of the Law to whose dominion we must no longer subject ourselves ; it is from the forced conceptions in the light of which we think we can arbitrarily release ourselves from concrete obedience to the concrete command of Jesus. Those who acted legalistically were not the fishers by the lake who at the bidding of Jesus left the nets and followed Him, but men like the rich young ruler who when he heard what he had to do " was sad at that saying, and went away grieved : for he had great possessions " (Mk. 10²²). If we will not bear the yoke of Jesus, we have to bear the yoke which we ourselves have chosen, and it is a hundred times more heavy. The attitude corresponding to that line of argument has nothing whatever to do with the true flight to Jesus. On the contrary, it is a flight from Him. We refuse to take the first step towards Him, and therefore we cannot take any further steps. Where we undertake the flight to Him, it is inevitable that in and with the first step demanded not merely the outer but the inner state and course of our lives and therefore our surroundings will be affected and in some way basically altered. The call of Jesus makes history when it is heard and taken seriously. It is by this that we may know whether or not it is heard ; whether or not it is heard and taken seriously as a call to self-denial.

4. The call to discipleship makes a break. It is not the obedient man who does it, not even with his simple obedience. What he does in this obedience can only be an indication of this break. If he is not to be disobedient, what option has he but to do as he is told? But good care is taken—and he has to realise the fact—that in his action he can never accomplish more than an indication, demonstration and attestation of this break. It is the call of Jesus, going out into the world and accepted by him, which makes the break; which has already made it. The kingdom of God is revealed in this call; the kingdom which is among the kingdoms of this world, but which confronts and contradicts and opposes them; the *coup d'état* of God proclaimed and accomplished already in the existence of the man Jesus. The man whom Jesus calls to Himself has to stand firm by the revelation of it. Indeed, he has to correspond to it in what he himself does and does not do. His own action, if it is obedient, will always attest and indicate it. It will not do this in accordance with his own judgment or pleasure. It will do it in the way commanded. But because it is the man Jesus who causes him to do what he does it will attest and indicate only this revelation. It may do so to a smaller or lesser degree. It may do so in strength or in weakness. But always it will set forth the kingdom of God drawn near, and therefore the greatest, the only true and definitive break in the world and its history as it has already taken place in Jesus Christ and cannot now be healed.

It is with this that we have to do in the discipleship of Jesus exercised in self-denial. While it is a matter of the personal self of the individual called by Jesus, of the dissolution of the covenant with himself, the self-denial of the disciple is only a kind of culminating point in the great attack in which he is called to participate as His witness, and which he has to recognise and support as in the first instance an attack upon himself. If we are not ready to deny ourselves, of what use can we be as witnesses of the great assault which is directed against the world (for the sake of its reconciliation with God) in and with the coming of the kingdom? Our self-denial, and the first step which we are commanded to make by Him who calls us, are not ends in themselves. They stand in the service of this great onslaught.

But in this onslaught it is a matter of God's destruction, accomplished in the existence of the Son of Man, of all the so-called " given factors," all the supposed natural orders, all the historical forces, which with the claim of absolute validity and worth have obtruded themselves as authorities—mythologically but very realistically described as " gods "—between God and man, but also between man and his fellows; or rather which inventive man has himself obtruded between God and himself and himself and his fellows. The dominion of these forces characterises the world as the world of the slothful man. It continually makes it the world which strives against God, but which is for this very reason in a state of hopeless disintegration and in need of reconciliation with God and of His peace. When they are posited absolutely, possessions (which are significantly described as the "mammon of unrighteousness" in Lk. 16⁹) and worldly honour, the force which defends them, the family with its claims and even the law of a religion (and worst of all a religion of revelation) are all gods which are first set up by man, which are then worshipped in practice and which finally dominate him, interposing themselves between God and him, and himself and his fellows, and maintaining themselves in this mediatorial position. It is not men, or any one man, who can make the break with these given factors and orders and historical forces. What man does of himself may take the form of an attempted repudiation but it will always serve to confirm and strengthen them, continually evoking new forms of their rule. The little revolutions and attacks by which they seem to be more shaken than they really are can never succeed even in limiting, let alone destroying, their power. It is the kingdom, the revolution, of God which breaks, which has already broken them. Jesus is their Conqueror.

If we are His disciples, we are necessarily witnesses of this fact. We are awakened by Him from the dream that these forces are divine or divinely given actualities, eternal orders. We can no longer believe, and therefore we can no longer think or accept, that men, including ourselves, are indissolubly bound and unconditionally committed to them. In their place there stands for us the Conqueror Jesus, the one Mediator between God and man, and man and his fellows ; He who is the divine reality ; He who decides what can and cannot be, what is and is not, a divinely given reality for us. If we are His disciples we are freed by Him from their rule. This does not mean that we are made superior, or set in a position of practical neutrality. It means that we can and must exercise our freedom in relation to them. It must be attested in the world as a declaration of the victory of Jesus. The world which sighs under these powers must hear and receive and rejoice that their lordship is broken. But this declaration cannot be made by the existence of those who are merely free inwardly. If the message is to be given, the world must see and hear at least an indication, or sign, of what has taken place. The break made by God in Jesus must become history. This is why Jesus calls His disciples. And it is for this reason that His disciples cannot be content with a mere theory about the relativisation of those false absolutes ; a mere attitude of mind in which these gods no longer exist for them ; an inward freedom in relation to them. It is for this reason that in different ways they are called out in practice from these attachments, and it is a denial of the call to discipleship if they evade the achievement of acts and attitudes in which even externally and visibly they break free from these attachments. They can never do this, in any respect, on their own impulse or according to their own caprice. It is not a matter of our own revolt, either as individuals or in company with those likeminded. It is a matter of the kingdom of God and God's revolution. But the disciple of Jesus is always summoned to attest this in a specific way by his own act and attitude. He has no right, nor is he free, to avoid the concretely given command. This is where we see the relevance of what we said about simple obedience in 3. There can be no question in self-denial of a soaring and tranquillising mysticism of world-renunciation and freedom and conquest in which the obligation to the godless and hostile orders already broken in Christ is not only maintained but if anything validated and sanctified. If this is all that is involved, then no matter how profoundly or attractively it is present it is a highly irrelevant enterprise. No, it is important only as, in obedience to the One who demands it, it is an indication of His attack and victory, and therefore a concrete step out into the open country of decision and act ; of the decision and act in which, even though he can only indicate what is properly at issue, man can only seem to be strange and foolish and noxious to the world around him. Is it not inevitable that in the first instance he will have this appearance even to himself ? He must and will run the risk of being an offence to those around him—and in so far as he sees with their eyes, to himself. He will not seek or desire this. But he cannot avoid the risk that it will be so. In relation to the world he cannot, then, restrict himself to an attempted " inner emigration " in which he will not be offensive, or at least suspicious, or at the very least conspicuous, to those who still worship their gods. It is not merely a matter of saving his own soul in the attainment of a private beatitude. He loses his soul, and hazards his eternal salvation, if he will not accept the public responsibility which he assumes when he becomes a disciple of Jesus. It is more than doubtful whether he is doing this if his existence does not force those around him to take notice—with all the painful consequences this may involve for him. But they will not take notice, nor will they be disturbed or annoyed by his existence, if he does not come out into the open as the one he is, doing what they do not do, and not doing what they do ; if in his attitude to the given factors and orders and historical forces which they regard as absolute there is no difference between him and them, but only uniformity and conformity. This may have for him the advantage that he will not be disturbed or assailed by them, but can live by his faith, and find joy and even secret pride in what may perhaps be a very radical opposition in inward attitude. The only trouble is that he will be quite useless as a witness of the kingdom of God. As a quiet participant in the cause of this kingdom he will avoid giving offence to anyone, but he will also evade the obedience which he is required to render. For this obedience necessarily consists in the fact that publicly before those around him he takes what is in a specific form a new path which leads him out of conformity with them to a place to which he specifically is pointed, so that to those who still persist in conformity he involuntarily but irresistibly makes himself conspicuous and suspicious and offensive, and can expect to meet with serious or petty forms of unpleasantness from them. He will not provoke them. Like Daniel in the lions' den, he will be cautious not to pull the lions' tails. But he will encounter what he must encounter if God does not unexpectedly decree otherwise. He will have to endure it. It is better not to describe him as a warrior. If he is in his right senses, he will not think of himself as such. He does not go on his way out of conformity in opposition to any other men, but on behalf of all other men, as one who has to show them the liberation which has already taken place. The *militia Christi* will arise of itself, although there can, of course, be no question of Christian contentiousness against non-Christians, let alone of violence, crusades and the like. And even the *militia Christi* will not really consist in conflict against others, but decisively in conflict against oneself, and in the fact that one is assailed, and in some way has to suffer, and to accept suffering, at the hands of others. It is certainly not our commission to add to the sufferings of others, and therefore to fight against them. Even for the sake of the kingdom of God which we are ordained to serve we need fight only by indicating, in what we do and do not do, the fact that it has dawned, that it has broken into the old world, so that visibly—and not just invisibly—we refuse respect and obedience to all the generally recognised and cultivated authorities and deities, not lifting our hats to the different governors set over us. We know that the battle against them is already won ; that the victory over them is already an accomplished fact ; that their power is already broken. Our task is perhaps offensive to others, but intrinsically it is the friendly and happy one of giving a practical indication of this fact. In its discharge we are concerned with the release and liberation of these others too. And we cannot escape this task.

At this point we must think of the concrete form of the demand with which Jesus in the Gospels always approached those whom He called to discipleship. It is common to every instance that the goal is a form of action or abstention by which His disciples will reveal and therefore indicate to the world the break in the human situation, the end of the irresistible and uncontested dominion of given factors and orders and historical forces, as it has been brought about by the dawn and irruption of the kingdom. It is common to every instance that the obedience concretely demanded of, and to be achieved by, the disciple, always means that he must move out of conformity with what he hitherto regarded as the self-evident action and abstention of Lord Everyman and into the place allotted to him, so that he is inevitably isolated in relation to those around him, not being able or willing to do in this place that which is generally demanded by the gods who are still fully respected in the world around. At this particular place he is freed from the bonds of that which is generally done or not done, because and as he is bound now to Jesus.

We must emphasise the " because and as." Except as he is directly bound to Jesus, a man is never called out of conformity with those around, and therefore loosed from the bonds of that which is generally done or not done. And this binding to Jesus must be thought of as a very particular matter—something which comes to each individual in a highly particular way in his own particular time and situation. To *this* man He *now* gives—and this man now receives—*this* command as the concrete form of the call to discipleship now issued to him. It is not the case, then, that he is loosed from one general form of action, from the legalism of the world as determined by the dominion of those gods, only to be bound to the legalism of another generality, which simply consists in a radical, systematic and consistent penetration and destruction of the first. In face of the solid front of the action which is normative for the man of the world the commanding of Jesus does not establish what we might call the counter-front of an action which is normative for all His disciples in every age and situation. His bidding—and this is rather different—is that in accordance with the direction which He gives to each disciple in particular there should be different penetrations of this front and the establishment of signs of the kingdom in the world which is ruled by the gods and subject to their legalism. Thus, apart from Himself as the Lord, there is no new and revolutionary law to which His disciples are no less subject than others are to the old law of the cosmos dominated by these false absolutes. There is no such thing as a party which is rallied by this law and which has to contend for it as the parties of the divided world have to fight for their different conceptions of the laws which rule the world. There is only the new commanding of Jesus in its relationship to this particular man elected by Him and in this particular time and situation which He has fixed. This new commanding of His is the concrete form in which He calls these men, here and now, to discipleship, and therefore sanctifies them.

It is clear that in the directions to discipleship embodied in the Gospel tradition we have to do with collective accounts, even (and especially) where the call is generally addressed to a majority of His disciples or it may be to all of them. The fact that this was very quickly obscured led to the mistaken attempt to create out of these directions a *nova lex*, a general mode of Christian action in opposition to that of worldly action. The truth is, however, that what the Gospel sayings about the following of His disciples really preserve are certain prominent lines along which the concrete commanding of Jesus, with its demand for concrete obedience, always moved in relation to individuals, characterising it as His commanding in distinction from that of all other lords. And these sayings are read aright by individuals who accept their witness that they too are called to obedience to the Lord who may be known as this Lord by the fact that His commanding, while it does not require the same thing of everyone, or even of the same man in every time and situation, always moves along one or more of these prominent lines. And the lines recorded in the Gospel all agree that man is always called to make a particular penetration of the front of the general action and abstention of others ; to cut loose from a practical recognition of the legalism determined by the dominion of worldly authorities. Everything depends upon the fact that it is Jesus who demands that we make this penetration and cut loose in this way. If this is not demanded, we can be sure that it is not the command of Jesus. And if it is not effected, we can be sure that there is no obedience to Him. Even in action along the main lines of the concrete forms of His demands there can be no true action apart from a commitment to Him, i.e., except as it is done for His sake. Conversely, however, there can be no commitment to Him if the action of the disciple is not along one or more of the great lines and if the freedom of the kingdom of God is not attested—this is the common element in every case—to the imprisoned world in a visible concretion.

For us Westerners, at any rate, the most striking of these main lines is that on which Jesus, according to the Gospel tradition, obviously commanded many men, as the concrete form of their obedient discipleship, to renounce their general attachment to the authority, validity and confidence of possessions, not merely inwardly but outwardly, in the venture and commitment of a definite act. We do not have here the realisation of an ideal or principle of poverty as it was later assumed into the monastic rule. Nor do we have the basis of a new society freed from the principle of private property. It is simply, but far more incisively, a question of the specific summons to specific men, as in Mt. 5⁴² : " Give to him that asketh thee, and from him that would borrow of thee turn not thou away " (severely sharpened in Lk. 6³⁵ : " Lend, hoping for nothing again ") ; or in Mt. 5⁴⁰ : " And if any man will . . . take away thy coat, let him have thy cloke also " ; or 6³¹ : " Therefore take no thought, saying, What shall we eat ? or, What shall we drink ? or, Wherewithal shall we be clothed, For after all these things do the Gentiles seek " ; or 6¹⁹ : " Lay not up for yourselves treasures upon earth, where moth and rust doth corrupt, and where thieves break through and steal " ; or 6²⁴ : " No man can serve two masters. . . . Ye cannot serve God and mammon " ; or in the charge to the disciples in Mt. 10⁹ᶠ· : " Provide neither gold, nor silver, nor brass in your purses, nor scrip for your journey, neither two coats, neither shoes, nor yet staves " ; or the demand, illustrated in the parable of the unjust steward, that we should make friends with the mammon of unrighteousness as long as we have it (Lk. 16⁹), and in this sense be " faithful " to it ; or the radical command addressed to the rich young ruler whom Jesus loved : " One thing thou lackest : go thy way, sell whatsoever thou hast, and give to the poor " (Mk. 10²¹) ; and the echo in the words of Peter (Mk. 10²⁸) : " Lo, we have left all, and have followed thee." The line along which all this is said is obviously the same, although it cannot be reduced to a normative technical rule for dealing with possessions. On the contrary, it is palpable that these are specific directions given to specific men at specific times and to be specifically followed, not in a formalised or spiritualised, but a literal sense. The drift of them all is clearly that Jesus' call to discipleship challenges and indeed cuts right across the self-evident attachment to that which we possess. The man to whom the call of Jesus comes does not only think and feel but acts (here and now, in this particular encounter with his neighbour) as one who is freed from this attachment. He not only can but does let go that which is his. By doing exactly as he is commanded by Jesus he successfully makes this sortie, attesting that the kingdom of mammon is broken by the coming of the kingdom of God.

Along a second line the instructions given by Jesus have to do no less directly with the destruction by the coming of the kingdom of what is generally accepted as honour or fame among men : " Blessed are ye, when men shall revile you, and persecute you, and shall say all manner of evil against you falsely for my sake " (Mt. 5¹¹). For " if they have called the master of the house Beelzebub, how much more shall they call them of his household " (Mt. 10²⁵). And therefore " whosoever shall smite thee on thy right cheek, turn to him the other also " (Mt. 5³⁹). Or according to the parable of the wedding-guests (Lk. 14⁷ᶠ·) : " Sit not down in the highest room . . . but in the lowest room. . . . For whosoever exalteth himself shall be abased ; and he that humbleth himself shall be exalted." Or again : " Whosoever will be great among you, let him be your minister " (Mt. 20²⁶). Or again, in the presence of a real child whom Jesus called and set in the midst when His disciples were concerned about the question of the greatest in the kingdom of heaven : " Except ye be converted, and become as little children, ye shall not enter into the kingdom of heaven " (Mt. 18¹ᶠ·). Or again, in direct contrast to those who love and claim the uppermost rooms at feasts and the chief seats in the synagogue and greetings in the market, we are not to be called Rabbi or father or master (Mt. 23⁶ᶠ·). " How can ye believe, which receive honour one of another," is Jesus' charge against the Jews (Jn. 5⁴⁴), and by way of contrast He demands that the disciples should wash one another's feet : " For I have given you an example, that ye should do as I have done to you " (Jn. 13¹⁴ᶠ·). To come to Jesus is to take a yoke upon oneself like a gallant ox (Mt. 11²⁹). All this can hardly be formulated, let alone practised, as a general rule for improved social relationships. It is again clear that these sayings assume the existence of men who are freed by the concretely given command of Jesus from the universal dominion and constraint of ordinary conceptions of what constitutes social status and dignity and importance. It is not concealed from these men that all such conceptions are transcended and outmoded by the incursion of the kingdom of God ; that there is a transvaluation of all values where the grace of God rules. They can and should reveal this in their action and abstention, in which they are no longer concerned with what those around regard as honour or dishonour. The disciple of Jesus can descend from the throne— the little throne perhaps—which even he may be allotted in human society. He does not do this wilfully or of his own choice, but as he is commanded. Yet as he is commanded he *does* it.

Along a further line the command of Jesus, and the obedience which has to be shown to it, takes the concrete form of an attestation of the kingdom of God as the end of the fixed idea of the necessity and beneficial value of force. The direction of Jesus must have embedded itself particularly deeply in the disciples in this respect. They were neither to fear force nor to exercise it. They were not to fear it as brought to bear against themselves, for at the very worst their enemies could kill only the body and not the soul. Their true and inward selves would remain inviolate. Why should they not fear, and to what degree ? Because the very hairs of their head which might be hurt, and they themselves as they might be subjected to mortal attack, are all under the care of the fatherly assistance and protection of God, apart from which not even a sparrow can fall to the ground. And they are of more value than many sparrows. They may have to suffer force as it is used against them, but they are secure in face of it. Hence they are commanded : " Fear not " (Mt. 10²⁸ᶠ·). On the other hand, those who have no need to fear the exercise of force against them by others because it cannot finally harm them can hardly expect to apply force against others. Ought fire from heaven to be called down on the Samaritan village which would not receive Jesus (Lk. 9⁵²ᶠ·) ? According to one variant only a tacit answer was given in His turning and " threatening " them. According to the other He said explicitly : " Ye know not what manner of spirit ye are of. For the Son of man is not come to destroy men's lives, but to save them." And the story ends with the short statement that " they went to another village." To this there corresponds the direction given in Mt. 10¹³ᶠ· that where they are not received the disciples are to shake off the dust from their feet and move on. The peace which they aim to bring to those who for the moment are obviously unworthy of it will then return to themselves (whereas they would clearly lose it if they adopted any other attitude). Again, when the multitude came from the high-priests with swords and staves as against a robber (Mt. 26⁴⁷ᶠ·), and one of the disciples " stretched out his hand, and drew his sword, and struck a servant of the high-priest's, and smote off his ear," he was commanded by Jesus to put the sword back into its scabbard : " For all they that take to the sword shall perish with the sword. Jesus might have had twelve legions of angels from His Father. But He does not ask for them. For He does not need this protection and is not prepared to make use of it. Hence the disciple who draws his sword must be delivered from this vicious circle. Nor does the exercise of force begin with killing. It begins when we are angry with our brother, when we call him *raca* or fool, when there are judicial proceedings (Mt. 5²¹). The disciple of Jesus will have nothing to do with this kind of behaviour, let alone with retaliation for the sake of glory or possession (Mt. 5³⁸ᶠ·). It is to be noted that in all these sayings there is no reference to the greater or lesser atrocities usually involved inescapably where force is exercised. The decisive contradiction of the kingdom of God against all concealed or blatant kingdoms of force is to be seen quite simply in the fact that it invalidates the whole friend-foe relationship between man and man. Either way, force is the *ultima ratio* in this relationship. If we love only those who love us again, the publicans and sinners can do the same. If we show humanity only to our brethren, the heathen do likewise (Mt. 5⁴⁶ᶠ·). Of what avail is this? In spite of it, force is everywhere exercised because friend-foe relationships are not affected by it. What the disciples are enjoined is that they should love their enemies (Mt. 5⁴⁴). This destroys the whole friend-foe relationship, for when we love our enemy he ceases to be our enemy. It thus abolishes the whole exercise of force, which presupposes this relationship, and has no meaning apart from it. This is attested by the disciple in what he does or does not do. Quite seriously and concretely he himself now drops out of the reckoning in this twofold relationship. Once again, there can be no question of a general rule, a Christian system confronting that of the world, in competition with it, and in some way to be brought into harmony with it. But again, for the one whom Jesus, in His call to discipleship, places under this particular command and prohibition, there is a concrete and incontestable direction which has to be carried out exactly as it is given. According to the sense of the New Testament we cannot be pacifists in principle, only in practice. But we have to consider very closely whether, if we are called to discipleship, we can avoid being practical pacifists, or fail to be so.

If along the third main line of the texts in question we have to do with the overcoming, proclaimed with the incursion of the kingdom of God, of the false separation between man and man revealed in the friend-foe relationship and concretely expressing itself in the exercise of force, along a fourth line we have, conversely, the dissolution of self-evident attachments between man and man. It is a matter of what in popular usage, although not in that of the Bible, is usually described as the family. The relationships between husband and wife, parents and children, brothers and sisters, etc., are not questioned as such. Man would not be man if he did not stand in these relationships. What is questioned is the impulsive intensity with which he allows himself to be enfolded by, and thinks that he himself should enfold, those who stand to him in these relationships. What is questioned is his self-sufficiency in the warmth of these relationships, the resolving of their problems and the sphere of their joys and sorrows. What is questioned is his imprisonment in them, in which he is no less a captive than in other respects he may be to possessions or fame. The message of liberation comes to him in this captivity to the clan. Thus the excuse of the invited guest: " I have married a wife, and therefore I cannot come " (Lk. 14²⁰), is seen to be on exactly the same level as those of others who had bought land or oxen which claimed their prior interest. And in the same connexion Jesus gives the remarkable reply to the man who was ready to be a disciple but first wanted to bury his father : " Let the dead bury their dead : but go thou and preach the kingdom of God " (Lk. 9⁵⁹ᶠ·). To the same series belong all the provocative sayings of Jesus about the leaving (ἀφεῖναι), dividing (διχάζειν), disuniting (διαμερίζειν) and even hating (μισεῖν) which are involved in the discipleship of Jesus—not destroying the relationships as such, but certainly dissolving the connexions which continually arise and obtain in them. According to Mk. 10²⁹ we have not only to leave house and lands but even brother or sister, mother or father or children (the " or " shows us that we are dealing with individual cases), for His sake and for the sake of the Gospel. Jesus also warns us against the view that He has come to bring peace on earth (Mt. 10³⁴ᶠ·). He has not come to bring peace, but a sword. And if a man loves father or mother, son or daughter, more than Him, he is not worthy of Him. Or, according to the parallel passage in Lk. 12⁵² : " For from henceforth there shall be five in one house divided, three against two, and two against three." The strangest possible expression is used in Lk. 14²⁶ : " If any man come to me, and hate not his father, and mother, and wife, and children, and brethren, and sisters, yea, and his own life also, he cannot be my disciple." Hate ? It is not the persons that are to be hated, for why should they be excluded from the command to love our neighbours ? It is the hold which these persons have and by which they themselves are also gripped. It is the concentration of neighbourly love on these persons, which really means its denial. It is the indolent peace of a clannish warmth in relation to these persons, with its necessary implication of cold war against all others. The coming of the kingdom of God means an end of the absolute of family no less than that of possession and fame. Again, there is no general rule. No new law has been set up in competition with that of the world, which points so powerfully in the opposite direction. But there is proclaimed the freedom of the disciple from the general law as it is given to him, and has to be exercised by him, in a particular situation (by the particular direction which he receives). There can be no doubt that in its fear of the bogy of monasticism Protestantism has very radically ignored this proclamation of Jesus Christ, as also that of other freedoms. To a very large extent it has acted as though Jesus had done the very opposite and proclaimed this attachment—the absolute of family. Can we really imagine a single one of the prophets or apostles in the role of the happy father, or grandfather, or even uncle, as it has found self-evident sanctification in the famous Evangelical parsonage or manse ? They may well have occupied this role. But in the function in which they are seen by us they stand outside these connexions. In this respect, too, no one is asked to undertake arbitrary adventures. But again, no one who really regards himself as called by Jesus to discipleship can evade the question whether he might not be asked for inner and outer obedience along these lines. The life of the new creature is something rather different from a healthy and worthy continuation of the old. When the order is given to express this, we must not refuse it an obedience which is no less concrete than the command.

Along a fifth line, to which we can never devote too much attention, the required obedience consists finally in a penetration of the absolute *nomos* of religion, of the world of piety. It is worth reflecting that what Jesus has in mind was not the piety of heathen religion, but that of the Israelite religion of revelation. He has not, of course, come to deny or destroy or dissolve it (Mt. 5[17f.]). He Himself accepts it, and He does not require His disciples to abandon or replace it. But He does demand that they should go a new way in its exercise; that they should show a " better righteousness," i.e., not better than that of the people, the common herd, but better than that of its best and strictest and most zealous representatives, the scribes and Pharisees ; better than the official form which it had assumed at the hands of its most competent human champions. This better righteousness is not more refined or profound or strict. It is simply the piety which the disciple can alone exercise in face of the imminent kingdom of God. It has nothing whatever to do with religious aristocracy. On the contrary, the kingdom knocks at the door of the sanctuary of supreme human worship. The disciple must act accordingly. According to two groups of sayings (both contained in the Sermon on the Mount) Jesus summoned to this advance on two different fronts. It is a matter of morality on the one side and religion on the other. Morality is dealt with in Mt. 5[21-48]. The commandment : " Thou shalt not kill," is universally accepted. But what does it mean ? There is something worse than killing because it is the meaning and purpose in all killing. This is anger against one's brother ; a state of contentiousness and strife. And it is here that the obedience of the disciple must begin. Again, what is meant by adultery ? The real evil, from which the disciple refrains, is to be found much further back than the actual deed. It consists in the evil desire which is present prior to the act. And it is at the point of desire that we either refrain or do not refrain. Again, what is false swearing ? It is all swearing because this as such is an illegitimate questioning of God. The disciple renounces this because it is enough for him if according to the best of his knowledge and with a good conscience he says either Yes or No, and not secretly both at once. What is meant by just retribution ? The disciple does not exercise it in any form. What is neighbourly love ? There is enjoined upon the disciple a love which includes the enemy. But, of course, when we talk like this, what becomes of the whole structure of practicable morality ? And how will its representatives and adherents react to this interpretation ? Religion is dealt with in the sayings concerning almsgiving, prayer and fasting (Mt. 6^{1-18}), and the main drift in all of them is that these things are not to be done publicly but secretly. Where, then, is the witness ?—we might ask. The answer is that the witness of the disciple consists in the fact that he refrains from attesting his piety as such. If he is to display the kingdom of God, and proclaim it from the housetops (Mt. 10^{27}), he will not make a show of his own devoutness but keep it to himself, allowing God alone to be the One who judges and rewards him. This restraint will be a witness to the pious world with its continual need to publicise itself, and perhaps even to the secular world. It will speak for itself—or rather, it will speak for that which does seriously and truly cry out for publicity. No official religiosity will readily acquiesce in the silent witness of this restraint. But here too, of course, it is not a matter of formulating and practising principles. Nor does this twofold invasion of the sphere of common sanctity mean that a clear line of demarcation is drawn. How can we fail to see that here, too, His command refers to particular men in particular situations, demanding from them a no less particular obedience, the obedience of discipleship.

(There is another equally prominent line of concrete direction which we have not yet touched upon, and shall not do so in this context. In many of the New Testament records the call to discipleship closes with the demand that the disciple should take up his cross. This final order crowns, as it were, the whole call, just as the cross of Jesus crowns the life of the Son of Man. In view of its outstanding significance we shall reserve this aspect for independent treatment in the final sub-section.)

Looking back at what we have said about the concrete forms of discipleship, we may make the further general observation that the general lines of the call with which Jesus made men His disciples in the Gospels enable us in some sense to envisage the situations in which these men were reached by His call and how they had to obey it concretely. Indeed, the New Testament *kerygma* not only permits but commands us to do this. The picture of these men and the way in which they were concretely ordered and concretely obeyed is one which ought to impress itself upon us. In this respect it forms, with the call issued by Jesus, the content of the New Testament *kerygma*. The reason why we have to bring out these main lines along which it takes concrete shape is that the call to discipleship as it comes to us will always be shaped also by this correlated picture. Yet as it was for them, it will be a call which here to-day is addressed directly and particularly to each one of us, so that its specific content is not fixed by the specific content of His call there and then as we have learned it from the Gospels. To be sure, the call of Jesus will be along the lines of the encounter between the kingdom of God and the kingdoms of the world. And it will have to be accepted in this form. But this does not mean that the living Son of Man is confined as it were to the sequence of His previous encounters, or that His commanding moves only in the circle of His previous commanding and the obedience which it received. It is not for us simply to reproduce those pictures. That is to say, it is not for us to identify ourselves directly with those who were called then, and therefore to learn directly from what they were commanded what we are necessarily commanded, or from their obedience what our own obedience must be. We will always know that it is His voice which calls us from the fact that in what is demanded of us we shall alway s have to do with a break with the great self-evident factors of our environment, and therefore of the world as a whole, which will have to be made in fact, both outwardly and inwardly, along the lines indicated in the New Testament, corresponding to, and attesting, the irruption of the kingdom of God. In other words, we shall always have to do with a form of the free activity which Paul described in the imperative of Rom. 12² : μὴ συσχηματίζεσθε τῷ αἰῶνι τούτῳ. But from what the New Testament tells us of His commanding, and of the obedience demanded from these particular men and rendered by them, we have to hear His voice as He speaks to *us*, calling us in the particular situation of obedience determined by His Word. It is not enough, then, merely to copy in our activity the outlines of that in which these men had to obey His demands. This of itself is not an entry into discipleship. As we have to remember in relation to every "rule," we might try to copy everything that Jesus demanded and that these men did, and yet completely fail to be disciples, because we do not do it, as they did, at His particular call and command to us. There is, of course, no reason why He should not ask exactly the same of us as He did of them. But again—along the same lines— He may just as well command something different, possibly much more, or the same thing in a very different application and concretion. In these circumstances it might well be disobedience to be content to imitate them, for if we are to render simple obedience it must be to the One who, as He called them then, calls us to-day. It is now our affair to render obedience without discussion or reserve, quite literally, in the same unity of the inward and the outward, and in exact correspondence to the New Testament witness to His encounter with them. There can certainly be no question of a deviation from these main lines. What we find along these lines can never be a mere *consilium evangelicum*. It is always a binding *mandatum evangelicum* which demands the response of a corresponding decision and action. And there will always be reason for distrust against our selves if we think that what may be required of us along these lines will be something less, or easier, or more comfortable than what was required of them. Grace—and we again recall that in the call to discipleship it is a matter of grace, of the salvation of the world, and therefore of our own salvation—cannot have become more cheap to-day (to use another expression of Bonhoeffer's). It may well have become even more costly. Or, to put it another way, it may well be that the freedom given in and with obedience to the call to discipleship has not become less but greater. But however that may be, the freedom given in this way was then, and still is, our sanctification.

4. THE AWAKENING TO CONVERSION

Our starting-point is again the conclusion of our second sub-section—that the sanctification of man consists in fellowship with Jesus the Son of Man, in the power of His call, and in the freedom which we are given in the strength of His Holy Spirit to look to Him and thus to lift up ourselves in spite of the downward drag of our slothful nature. We are now dealing with this lifting up of ourselves in and for itself—or, let us say quite plainly from the very outset, with the divine mystery and miracle of this lifting up of ourselves. It characterises sanctification as a real happening which takes place to men here and now in time and on earth. It is real, of course, not because it takes place as human and earthly history, but because it takes place in fellowship with the life of the holy Son of Man. For all that it is so provisional and limited, the sanctification of man as his lifting up of himself is a work which is eternally resolved and seriously willed and effectively executed by God. In this divine reality, however, it takes place in time and on earth. It consists in the fact that as men may lift up themselves they acquire and have here and now, in all their lack of freedom, a freedom to do this of which they avail themselves. We must now turn our attention to this happening as such. How does it come about that men become Christians in fulfilment of this divinely real work.

The theme of our third sub-section was itself, of course, an answer to this question. It comes about as Jesus calls them to discipleship. We can never go beyond this answer. But we can and must put the counter-question : How does it come about that they are actually reached by this call in such a way that they render obedience, becoming the disciples of Jesus and doing what they are ordered to do as such ? We shall see at once—as already in our opening sentence we have taken up again and repeated from our earlier discussions— that it is a matter of the freedom which they are given by the One who calls them, by Jesus. How can it really take place except in freedom ? But we must now see how it takes place in the freedom which is given by Jesus to these particular men. Our present questions concerns the inward movement in which they are the men to whom this freedom is given and who may and must at once exercise it in the obedience of discipleship as we have described it. To put it metaphorically, we are investigating the source from which this living water has its direct and unimpeded flow.

The first thing that we have to say is that Christians (and therefore those who are sanctified by *the* Holy One) are those who waken up. This, too, is a picture. But it is a biblical one, and it tells us more clearly than any abstract term that we might substitute what is really at issue. As they awake they look up, and rise, thus making the counter-movement to the downward drag of their sinfully slothful being. They are those who waken up, however, because they are awakened. They do not waken of themselves and get up. They are roused, and are thus caused to get up and set in this counter-movement. Thus strictly and finally this awakening as such is in every sense the source in whose irresistible flow they are set in the obedience of discipleship. But we will leave this point for the moment.

Where someone is awakened and therefore wakes and rises, he has previously been asleep, and has been lying asleep. Christians have indeed been lying asleep like others. What distinguishes them from others is that this is now past ; that they have been awakened and are awake. Or is it not the case that they are still asleep, or fall asleep again ? Is there not still a Christianity which sleeps with the world and like it ?

" Therefore let us not sleep, as do others ; but let us watch and be sober " (1 Thess. 5⁶). " Now it is high time to awake out of sleep " (Rom. 13¹¹). " Awake thou that sleepest, and arise from the dead, and Christ shall give thee light " (Eph. 5¹⁴). This is not missionary preaching—or it is so only in the sense that the call is also and primarily to the Christian community. How the eyes of the disciples were overcome by sleep in Gethsemane (Mk. 14⁴⁰) ! And did not all the virgins become sleepy and sleep—the wise as well as the foolish—according to Mt. 25⁵ ? " Blessed are those servants, whom the lord when he cometh shall find watching " (Lk. 12³⁷). But is not this the highly exceptional case ? Do we not all need continually to be reawakened ?

We cannot, therefore, define Christians simply as those who are awake while the rest sleep, but more cautiously as those who waken up in the sense that they are awakened a first time and then again to their shame and good fortune. They are, in fact, those who constantly stand in need of reawakening and who depend upon the fact that they are continually reawakened. They are thus those who, it is to be hoped, continually waken up.

The sleep from which they awaken is the relentless downward movement consequent upon their sloth. Like all others, they participate in this movement, dreaming many beautiful or bad dreams but not really knowing what is happening to them. When they waken, or are wakened, they experience a jolt which both arrests them in this movement and sets them in the counter-movement. They realise where their way was leading, that they must not tread it any further, and that they now can and must take the opposite direction. In this event and realisation—which are both included in the shock that they receive—they wake up for the first time—which will certainly not be the last. In this awakening they become Christians—men who are now free, and who make use of their freedom, to look up and raise themselves. The verse 2 Cor. 5¹⁷ is true of them as this happens : " Old things are passed away ; behold, all things are become new." For in this awakening they are " in Christ " in the narrower sense of the term as it applies only to them.

But this awakening is also—and here the metaphor breaks down—an awakening and therefore a rising from the sleep of death ; the sleep from which there can be no awakening except in the power of the mystery and miracle of God. This is the real truth about the descent, the downward plunge, of sinful and slothful man, and the unawareness with which he makes and suffers it. We can waken ourselves from the sleep of all kinds of errors and phantasies and falsehoods. The very violence of the dream in which we surrender to them may rouse us. Or we may be wakened from these states of slumber or drowsiness by an accident, an external event or fate, or the intentional or unintentional intrusion of others. But from the sleep of covenant-breaking humanity, of the world in conflict with God, there can be no awakening, not even by the greatest catastrophes, by the crashing in ruins of whole cities, by the imminent threat of the worst personal evils, by the thunderous voices of the very greatest prophets. Certainly none of us can of himself supply the jolt which will awaken from this sleep. No salvation or perdition affecting man from without can reach him in this sleep, and startle and illuminate him, and fetch him to his feet. Nor are there any impulses, or emotional movements, or deep-burrowing reflections, in which he can reach and awaken himself in this sleep. The sleep which he sleeps is the sleep of death, and what is needed is that he should be wakened and waken from death. There is thus required a new and direct act of God Himself if there is to be the awakening in which a man becomes a disciple, a Christian.

At this point we may recall the saying at the conclusion of the story of the rich young ruler (Mk. 10²³ᶠ·), which is the same in all the parallel accounts. It tells us how hard it is—harder than for a camel to go through the eye of a needle—for a rich man to enter into the kingdom of God. And it causes the disciples the greatest astonishment (περισσῶς ἐξεπλήσσοντο), for they rightly perceive that it is not just a matter of the rich but of all men and even of themselves, the rich young ruler being the general rule rather than an unfortunate exception. " Who then (in these circumstances) can be saved (at all) ? " they say one to another. " And Jesus looking upon them saith, With men it is impossible, but not with God : for with God all things are possible." That a man should follow Jesus, and therefore enter into the kingdom and become a fellow and witness of the kingdom is quite possible with God, but only with Him. Hence the saying at the end of the story of the Prodigal Son : " This thy brother was dead, and is alive again ; and was lost, and is found " (Lk. 15³²). Hence the call of Eph. 5¹⁴ : " Arise from the dead." Hence the statement in Eph. 2¹ᶠ· : " And you hath he quickened, who were dead in trespasses and sins ; wherein in time past ye walked according to the course of this world, according to the prince of the power of the air, the spirit that now worketh in the children of disobedience. . . . But God, who is rich in mercy, for his great love wherewith he loved us, even when we were dead in sins, hath quickened us together with Christ (by grace are ye saved ;) . . . and that not of yourselves : it is the gift of God : not of works, lest any man should boast." We have really passed (μεταβέβηκεν) from death to life if we hear the Word of Jesus, and believe in Him that sent Him, and love the brethren (Jn. 5²⁴ ; 1 Jn. 3¹⁴). Nothing less than this transition, which cannot be initiated by ourselves or any experience of our own but has its analogy only in the resurrection of Jesus Christ from the dead, can even be considered when it is a matter of the awakening and rising up to the obedience of discipleship.

The awakening to which we refer belongs to the order and takes place according to the law of divine action. This does not exclude, but includes, the fact that it takes place in the context and under the conditions of human action. How could it be the real sanctification of real man if man himself were not present in his inner and outer activity, if it took place at some supernatural height or depth without him ? It certainly does not take place without him. It takes place to and in him. It involves the total and most intensive conscription and co-operation of all his inner and outer forces, of his whole heart and soul and mind, which in the biblical sense in which these terms are used includes his whole physical being. Otherwise it would not be his awakening. And his fellow-man, who is also indispensable if he is to be a man, is certainly not absent, or present only as a passive spectator, but also takes part in his awakening, perhaps as one who is himself waking, perhaps in some other way. As we have stated already, his awakening is an event on earth and in time. It has, therefore, a historical dimension. The narrower and wider social circles in which he lives are deeply implicated in it. It does not in any sense lack creaturely factors of every kind. Taking place wholly and utterly on the earthly and creaturely level, it does not merely have an aspect which is wholly and utterly creaturely, but it is itself wholly and utterly creaturely by nature. But, while all this is true, it has its origin and goal in God. It belongs to the order of that action which is specifically divine. It is a subordinate moment in the act of majesty in which the Word became flesh and Jesus Christ rose again from the dead. On this aspect—its true and proper aspect—it is a mystery and a miracle. That is to say, the jolt by which man is wakened and at which he wakens, his awakening itself as the act in which this takes place and he rises, is not the work of one of the creaturely factors, co-efficients and agencies which are there at work and can be seen, but of the will and act of God who uses these factors and Himself makes them co-efficients and agencies for this purpose, setting them in motion as such in the meaning and direction which He has appointed. We are thus forced to say that this awakening is both wholly creaturely and wholly divine. Yet the initial shock comes from God. Thus there can be no question of co-ordination between two comparable elements, but only of the absolute primacy of the divine over the creaturely. The creaturely is made serviceable to the divine and does actually serve it. It is used by God as His organ or instrument. Its creatureliness is not impaired, but it is given by God a special function or character. Being qualified and claimed by God for co-operation, it co-operates in such a way that the whole is still an action which is specifically divine.

For the moment we will postpone our investigation of the jolt or shock which initiates it, thus making it in its totality a divine action which seizes and dominates, while it does not exclude, all creaturely factors and their motions. Our first question must be simply concerning the awakening as such, and the meaning and content of this event. No matter what may be its origin and goal, which factor may be first and which second, or where the preponderance may lie, it does at any rate take place. And it takes place all at once. It does not take place in stages. It does not take place in such a way that first one thing happens with its own particular meaning and content, and then another with a different meaning and content ; the divine on the one side and the human on the other. Nor does it take place on two different levels, so that we are forced to look first at what happens on the top deck as it were, and then at what happens on the lower ; the gift and work of God in the one case, and the task and action and abstention of man in the other. This awakening and waking of man is one event with one meaning and content. In the first instance, therefore, it must concern us in its unity as such. We call it the awakening of man to conversion.

The Christian Church counts on the fact that there is such a thing as the awakening of man to conversion. If it did not do so, it would not believe in God the Father ; in the Son of God who became flesh and who in the flesh was the holy Son of Man, the royal man ; or in the Holy Spirit. In its supposed confession of God it would be thinking of a mere idea and staring at a dead idol. If we believe in God in the sense of the Church we believe in an awakening of man to conversion. We count on the fact that there is such a thing. No, we count on the fact that God Himself gives and creates and actualises it. We do not, therefore, count only on the chance or possibility of it. We do not count merely on the fact that there may be such a thing. To do this is itself quite impossible without faith in God. For we have to do here with the awakening which has the character of an awakening from the dead, with the conversion to which a man is awakened in this way, with his wakening and rising from the dead. How can we count on this apart from faith ? But in faith in God we do not count only on the fact that it may be so, or that God may give it. We count on the fact that God does actually give it. We count on the awakening of man to conversion as an actuality. As truly as God lives and is God, so truly this awakening takes place. To say God the Father, Son and Holy Ghost is to say also the awakening of man to conversion. This is the first nail that we have to drive in securely. The reality of this event depends wholly on the reality of God. And it depends on it so seriously and unconditionally and indissolubly that we can also say that the reality of God stands or falls with the reality of this event. Only for us ? It is perhaps better *not* to make this restriction. God would not be God if this awakening did not take place. For He would not be the God of the covenant ; of His free grace. He would not be the God who is true to this covenant as the Reconciler of the world which has fallen from Him, and therefore as the One who awakens man from the sleep of death and calls him to Himself. He would not, then, be God at all. As truly as He is God, so truly He does this. The basis of Christian existence lies as deep as this. It is not the Christian who guarantees it. It is God Himself. God Himself takes responsibility for its reality. We are thus given a simple test. Do we believe in God ? We do so only if we believe in the awakening of man to conversion. Conversely, do we believe in the awakening of man to conversion ? We do so only if we believe in God.

The Christian Church also counts on the awakening of man to conversion because it cannot conceal the fact that the Scriptures of the Old and New Testament count on it and call on the Church to do so. It is true that the Bible is one long account of the great acts of God which have their centre in Jesus Christ and which still have their hidden goal of which they are themselves the hidden beginning. But these acts of God take place, and the One in whom they have their centre and goal and beginning exists, among and in relation to many men. They are God's dealings with these men. They are God's revelation in the power of which these men become its witnesses. As we have already established incidentally at an earlier point, they also have their place in the biblical account to the extent that the divine speech and action has reference to them and constitute them its witnesses. As witnesses to it they form an integral part of the biblical witness to God's work and revelation. The totality of the biblical account thus includes the fact that, grounded in the acting and self-revealing God, in the promised and incarnate and expected Jesus Christ, the awakening to conversion is a reality among these men. It is just as real as God, or Jesus Christ, is real. For our present purpose it makes no odds with what degree of clarity or confusion, of perfection or imperfection, it impresses itself upon these men and finds expression in them. Either way, it is a reality. In and with the history of God and Jesus Christ there also takes place the history whose meaning and content is the awakening of men to conversion. There are men whose existence is positively or negatively or critically determined by this reality. It is determined by it because it is determined by the judicial and gracious speech and action of God, which is judicial as and because it is gracious. It is determined by it because it is determined by the existence of Jesus Christ. The whole weight of the witness about God and His Holy One carries in and with it, for those who let Scripture speak for itself, the witness which is less perhaps, but inseparably connected with the greater : the witness not only of the Holy One but also of the saints ; the witness concerning Abraham and Moses and David and the people Israel and its major and minor prophets and the community and the apostles as they are determined by the One to whom they themselves bear witness. In all its distinctness and indistinctness, *hominum confusione et Dei providentia*, this is the witness concerning this reality. When the Church allows Scripture to speak to it, even if it wished, it could not help counting on the reality of the awakening to conversion in view of these men. It could not prevent this reality from impinging upon it as a problem posed for itself—not merely the reality that there is such a thing, but that it is God who gives and creates and effects it. The witness of Holy Scripture is that God does this. We should have to reject its witness altogether if we were to deny that it is also the witness to this reality. What the Church makes of it is another question. It has made of it many things—some good and some bad. It has often seemed not to know how to make anything of it at all. But it can never, or never altogether, set it aside or ignore or forget it. The Church ? We are the Church. It is thus our turn to tackle it as we try to understand and explain the sanctification of man, and especially the way in which the men who lie asleep as slothful sinners look up and lift up themselves and become obedient instead of disobedient.

Let us go right to the heart of the matter at once and say that this rising up of man takes place in his conversion. The sleep from which man is awakened according to Scripture consists in treading a wrong path on which he is himself perverted, and can never be anything else. Thus awakening from this sleep, and the rising which follows, is far more than a vertical standing up. It makes no odds whether we go this false path erect or stooping. As Scripture sees it, waking and rising from sleep is turning round and going in the opposite direction. That God awakens us to this is the problem set for the Church, and therefore for us, by Holy Scripture. It cannot be exchanged for the (in themselves) very interesting problems of improvement or reformation or more noble effort in our further progress along the same path. It is not a question of improvement but alteration. It is not a question of a reformed or ennobled life, but a new one. And the alteration and renewal mean conversion—a term which we cannot avoid for all its doubtful associations. As it emerges in Holy Scripture, the human reality which is inseparably connected with, and determined by, the reality of God and Jesus Christ is the awakening of man to convert. The movement which we see made by the men of the Bible, or which is always aimed at, is *this* movement. We cannot say—for it simply would not be true—that we see in the Bible converted men. What we can and must say is that we see men caught up in the movement of conversion. If conversion is not behind them, it is also not in the mists before them. They are at the very heart of the movement. They had moved away from God. And it is saying too much to claim that they have moved right back to God. But what we must say is that they can no longer proceed without God. On the contrary, they are compelled to rise up and come to Him, and are now in the process of doing so. This is the movement of conversion. And the awakening to this movement which in some way comes to these men and characterises them is the reality which impinges upon us, and becomes our own problem, in and with the reality of God and of Jesus Christ.

Conversion, and therefore life in this movement, means renewal. In relation to a life which is not engaged in this movement, it is the new life of a new man. Conversion means the turning on an axis. The life of the old man, which is not engaged in this conversion, also involves movement. But it has no axis—and that is why it is not engaged in conversion. It moves straight ahead, and this means straight ahead to the descent—the plunge—to death. It is a life which is encircled by death. The difference between the life of the one who is engaged in conversion and that of others is not that the former moves itself, but that it has an axis on which to turn. It is properly this axis which makes this man a new man, giving him a part in its own movement. But the axis which makes his life a movement in conversion is the reality which is not concealed from him, but revealed as the truth, that God is for him and therefore that he is for God. God is for him as a proprietor is for his possessions, protecting and guarding and cherishing them but also controlling them, answering for them but also disposing them according to his own purposes. And he himself is for God as possessions stand under the protection and control, the responsibility and disposition, of their owner. This is the axis which, when it is established in his life, makes it a life in conversion. For with this twofold " for "—the second grounded in the first—he is told both to halt and to proceed. His former movement is halted ; and he is told to proceed in the opposite direction. And the two moments, which belong together in an indissoluble unity, constitute his conversion. Revealed to him as truth, the reality that God is for him and he for God sets him in this movement, in the *conversio* which is as such his *renovatio*. In the dynamic of this twofold principle—because God is for him and he for God— he can and may cease to proceed in the old direction and turn round and begin to move the other way.

Calvin summed up this principle of conversion and renewal with masterly brevity and comprehensiveness in the short statement : *Nostri non sumus, sed Domini (Instit.* III, 7, 1). In this way God's Yes to man and man's Yes to God, and the consequent turning from and to, are brought together in a single formula. We do not belong to ourselves. When we did belong to ourselves, when we knew only that we belonged to ourselves, we were old men involved in that descent and headlong plunge on the old way. But we now belong to God as our Lord. As we belong to Him we are free, and it is for us only to cease proceeding on the old way and to enter on the way appropriate to where we now belong. *Nostri non sumus, sed Domini.* As we follow the movement of this axis, we become new men.

The establishment of this axis in human life—or better, the establishment of human life on this axis—and the change of direction in human life which this inaugurates, is obviously the theme of the petition in Ps. 51[10f.] : " Create in me a clean heart, O God ; and renew a right spirit within me. Cast me not away from thy presence ; and take not thy holy spirit from me." The same principle of conversion and renewal is also the subject of Jer. 31[33] with its promise of the new covenant : " I will put my law in their inward parts, and write it in their hearts ; and will be their God, and they shall be my people." It is also at issue in Jer. 32[39] : " And I will give them one heart, and one way, that they may fear me for ever, for the good of them, and of their children after them " ; and of the parallel in Ezek. 36[26f.] (cf. 11[19f.]) : " A new heart also will I give you, and a new spirit will I put within you : and I will take away the stony heart out of your flesh, and I will give you an heart of flesh. And I will put my spirit within you, and cause you to walk in my statutes, and ye shall keep my judgments, and do them." These are the passages to which Paul referred in the much misunderstood words of Rom. 2[14f.] (cf. Felix Flückiger, *Die Werke des Gesetzes bei den Heiden nach Röm.* 2[14ff.], Th. at Basel, 1952, p. 17 f.), when he contrasted the disobedience of the Jews with those Gentiles—the Gentiles who are called to the God of Israel by the Gospel—who do not have the Law but who φύσει, of themselves, do what the Law demands and are thus a law to themselves, showing that " the work of the law is written in their hearts, their conscience also bearing witness, and their thoughts the meanwhile accusing or else excusing one another."

We can see what is meant by the passages in Jeremiah and Ezekiel if we note that they are developments of the promise and summons which we find so often and so urgently in the prophets Amos, Hosea, Isaiah and Jeremiah himself that Israel should and must return to Yahweh, i.e., to an unconditional and obedient trust in Him in contrast to any trust in man or in strange gods, and therefore to a no less unconditional renunciation of everything that is evil, i.e., that opposes the lordship of Yahweh. It is on the basis of the reality of the covenant, which includes the " I will be your God " as well as the " Ye shall be my people," that the imperative call is sounded to seek Yahweh and live (Am. 5⁴), to return to Yahweh instead of fleeing from Him (Jer. 4¹), to break up the fallow ground instead of sowing thorns, and to circumcise to the Lord, taking away the foreskin of the heart (Jer. 4³ᶠ·). But who does this ? In all the ancient prophecies the actual or even possible fulfilment of this demand is never really envisaged. They do not know of any people which actually converts to Yahweh. Even in the passionate Hosea we find the pointed saying (5⁴) : " They will not frame their doings to turn unto their God : for the spirit of whoredoms is in the midst of them, and they have not known the Lord." And in Isaiah (1³ᶠ·) : " The ox knoweth his owner, and the ass his master's crib : but Israel doth not know, my people doth not consider. Ah sinful nation, a people laden with iniquity, a seed of evildoers, children that are corrupters : they have forsaken the Lord, they have provoked the Holy One of Israel to anger, they are gone away backward. Why should ye be stricken any more ? ye will revolt more and more : the whole head is sick, and the heart faint. From the sole of the foot even unto the head there is no soundness in it." And again in Isaiah (30¹⁵ᶠ·) : " For thus saith the Lord God, the Holy One of Israel ; In returning and rest shall ye be saved ; in quietness and in confidence shall be your strength. But ye said, No ; for we will flee upon horses . . . we will ride upon the swift." And again in Jeremiah (13²³) : " Can the Ethiopian change his skin, or the leopard his spots ? then may ye also do good, that are accustomed to do evil." That a remnant will return in a not very closely delineated future (Is. 10²¹) is significantly emphasised by the name *sh'ar Yashub* which the prophet gave to his son (7³), but this is the most that can be said in this direction. For when we read in Is. 30²⁰ᶠ· about the teacher of Israel who will no longer be concealed, " but thine eyes shall see thy teacher, and thine ears shall hear a word behind thee, saying, This is the way, walk ye in it, when ye turn to the right hand, and when ye turn to the left," it may be suspected that what we have here is a voice from the later prophecy which dared to speak of the new spirit and heart and conversation given to Israel, and therefore of a fulfilment of the unfulfilled and unfulfillable demand of earlier prophecy which was not achieved by Israel itself but achieved on it, i.e., the actuality of the covenant as the truth revealed to man and forcefully changing his life ; the dynamic principle : *Nostri non sumus, sed Domini.*

We have to remember the dark folly attested in the older prophecy if we are to appreciate what is really meant by coming to conversion and renewal in the sense of the Old and New Testaments ; by the establishing of the life of man on that axis so that it is set in that movement. The order in which this takes place is defined once and for all in Is. 48⁶ᶠ· : " I have shewed thee new things from this time, even hidden things, and thou didst not know them. They are created now, and not from the beginning ; and previously thou heardest them not ; lest thou shouldest say, Behold, I knew them. Yea, thou heardest not ; yea, thou knewest not ; yea, thine ear was not previously opened." It is a matter of seeing the kingdom of God (Jn. 3³), of entering into it (Jn. 3⁵). But this is possible only for the man who is newly conceived and born of God (Jn. 1¹³ ; 1 Jn. 3⁹). It is " a new creation " (2 Cor. 5¹⁷), and " the wind bloweth where it listeth, and thou hearest the sound thereof, but canst not tell whence it cometh, and whither it goeth : so is every one that is born of the spirit." The question of Nicodemus is not really so stupid as it may sound : " How can a man be born, when he is old ? can he enter the second time into his mother's womb, and be born ? " (Jn. 3⁴). We may well ask : " How can these things be ? "

(Jn. 3⁹). There can be no question of any δύνασθαι, of any general possibility, of this γενέσθαι. The fact is that the reality of this twofold " for " is revealed as the truth ; that it takes place in its own possibility, as a " birth from above " (Jn. 3³). Thus, in relation to everything that man previously was or otherwise is, it is a beginning newly posited by God. The walking ἐν καινότητι ζωῆς (Rom. 6⁴) which corresponds to the resurrection of Jesus Christ is a transformation (" metamorphosis," Rom. 12) which comes over man in the form of a ἀνακαίνωσις τοῦ νοός. In Tit. 3⁵ it is described by the very word (παλιγγενεσία) which in Mt. 19²⁸ is used to describe the Messianic renewal of the cosmos which concludes the last age. We have to think in this order if we are to realise what is involved in man's conversion. *Conversio* and *renovatio*, applied to the actual sanctification of man, are nothing less than *regeneratio*. New birth ! The man involved in the act of conversion is no longer the old man. He is not even a corrected and revised edition of this man. He is a new man.

We continue at once that in conversion we have to do with a movement of the whole man. There are in his being no neutral zones which are unaffected by it and in which he can be another than the new man involved in this process. By the establishment of his life on this axis everything that he is and has is brought under its influence. If anything is not brought under its influence, and thus remains in the continuity of his previous being as the old man, he can be and have and do it only *per nefas*. This is the case because in the principle of his conversion and renewal, at the centre where his life is bound to this axis, we have to do with God. That God is for him, and he for God, is a total reality which asserts itself in his life in the power of total truth, setting him wholly and not merely partially in this movement, placing him wholly under the call to halt and proceed. We will try to see what is meant by the totality of this movement in some of its most important dimensions.

1. We cannot interpret the conversion and renewal of man merely in terms of a relationship between him and God, to the exclusion of any relationship with his brother. To be sure, we are dealing with the fact that God is for him, and he for God ; with this reality as a revealed truth which forcefully sets him in motion. But he is not a man without his fellow-men. How can this truth set him in motion if, as he makes this movement, it does not encroach at once upon his relationship with his fellows, necessarily involving the perishing of the old and the emergence of a new thing in this relationship ? It would not be the conversion of the whole man if it did not commence and work itself out at once in this relationship.

Calvin was on good biblical ground—that of the Old Testament prophets from Amos onwards—when in his detailed explanation of the main proposition, under the title *De abnegatione nostri*, he did not keep to the sphere of *Deus et anima* preferred by Augustine, but followed up his general development of the theme of self-denial, and his (rather cold) elucidation of the terms *sobrietas*, *iustitia* and *pietas* (which he took from Tit. 2¹¹ᶠ·), by showing (*Instit*. III, 7, 4–7) how *abnegatio nostri* expresses itself in the community and society generally as humility, gentleness, a readiness to serve, responsibility, and loyalty ; how this cannot be refused to any man, however mean his estate may be, however little he may mean to us, and however unworthy he may be of it ; and how finally and supremely it consists in the acts of an affectionate love which does not humiliate or bind others but exalts and liberates them—and all this just because it is a matter of the *gloria Dei* in the life of the new man, *ut sibi in tota vita negotium cum Deo esse reputet* (7, 2). It was in exactly the same way, and just because they understood it in the strictest sense, not merely in terms of ethics or reformation but as a return of Israel to its God, that at once and most emphatically the prophets interpreted it as a conversion and renewal in the practical, cultic, economic and political conduct of Israel, as a radical alteration of the ruling social relationships, so that Israel's great unwillingness for conversion was seen by them above all in its obstinacy in respect of human relationships.

2. Again, we cannot try to see and realise the conversion of man in a new movement and activity (whether purely inward or purely outward). Because God is for him, and he for God, it is a matter of his heart, his thinking, his will, his disposition and also of his consequent action and abstention on the same ultimate basis. It is a matter of his disposition and action together ; of the two as a totality. Conversion in a separate inner or religious sphere, or conversion in a purely cultic or moral, political or ecclesiastical sphere, is not the conversion of man as it is set in motion by God. The conversion in which he returns to this peace embraces in this sense too the whole man.

In explanation of the term μετάνοια we may take as our starting-point the fact that literally it speaks first of a change of mind, of a shift of judgment, of a new disposition and standpoint. But we must be careful not to leave it at that. For this would be to reduce the term from its biblical meaning to that of a mere change of mind, possibly linked with repentance, which it bore in the Greek world. As against this, the ἀνακαίνωσις τοῦ νοός of Rom. 12² takes place within the comprehensive movement which is described in Rom. 12¹ as a παραστῆσαι τὰ σώματα ὑμῶν θυσίαν ζῶσαν ἁγίαν τῷ θεῷ εὐάρεστον. τὰ σώματα ὑμῶν means your bodies, i.e., your whole persons. Even the μετανοεῖν proclaimed by John the Baptist is a tree which at once brings forth fruits (Lk. 3⁸). It extends (Lk. 3¹⁰ᶠ·) to the performance of very concrete acts in practical alteration of a prior human attitude. But again, it cannot exhaust itself merely in the performance of these or any other acts. It is here that the criticism of the prophets was brought to bear against an ostensible conversion supported by all kinds of practice. We have only to think of the well-known prophetic criticism of sacrifice, noting the context in which it appears, e.g., in Hos. 6¹ᶠ·. In this passage there is first quoted a pilgrim song of exemplary beauty, inviting to a penitential service : " Come, and let us return unto the Lord : for he hath torn, and he will heal us ; he hath smitten, and he will bind us up. After two days will he revive us : in the third day he will raise us up, and we shall live in his sight. Let us seek earnestly to know the Lord. As soon as we seek him, we shall find him ; and he shall come unto us as the rain, as the latter and former rain which refresheth the earth." How often this passage has served as a text even for Christian ministers on days of fasting and penitence ! The only thing is that we often overlook the continuation, the answer given by the prophet, which is as follows : " O Ephraim, what shall I do unto thee ? O Judah, what shall I do unto thee ? For your love is as a morning cloud, and as the dew it goeth away. Therefore have I hewed them by the prophets ; I have slain them by the words of my mouth ; and thy judgments are as the light that goeth forth. For I desired love, and not sacrifice ; and the knowledge of God more than burnt-offerings." What is lacking ?—we might ask. There is obviously no lack of deeds, nor of willingness, nor religious zeal, in the performance of them. But there is lacking in this case, not the outward but the inward thing which makes the movement in which they are engaged conversion—the true and radical and persistent love in which this willingness and its achievements must have their basis if they are to have any meaning. For a more radical and extended version of this passage we might well think of 1 Cor. 13³ : " And though I bestow all my goods to feed the poor, and though I give my body to be burned, and have not love, it profiteth me nothing "—it has nothing to do with conversion.

3. We cannot make the conversion of man into a purely private matter, as though it were only a concern of the individual, the ordering of his own relationship to God and his neighbour, of his inward and outward life, of his own achievement of pure and essential being. It is right to emphasise its personal character, its singularity, and the isolation in which this individual must perish as the man he was, and can and may become new. But we must remember at this point the basis on which alone, if it takes place, it is an affair of the individual. The biblical individual is not selfishly wrapped up in his own concerns. It is a matter of God—that God is for him and he for God. But to say God is to make mention of the name of God which is to be hallowed, the kingdom of God which is to come, the will of God which is to be done on earth as it is done in heaven. That God, the Subject of this universal mystery, and in this action, is for him, and that engaged in this action he for his part is for God—this is the axis on which the individual moves as he turns from his own way to God. His conversion and renewal is not, therefore, an end in itself, as it has often been interpreted and represented in a far too egocentric Christianity. The man who wants to be converted only for his own sake and for himself rather than to God the Lord and to entry into the service of His cause on earth and as His witness in the cosmos, is not the whole man. When we convert and are renewed in the totality of our being, we cross the threshold of our private existence and move out into the open. The inner problems may be most urgent and burning and exciting, but we are not engaged in conversion if we confine ourselves to them. We simply run (in a rather more subtle way) on our own path headlong to destruction. When we convert and are renewed in the totality of our being, in and with our private responsibility we also accept a public responsibility. For it is the great God of heaven and earth who is for us, and we are for this God.

The saying of Jesus to Peter : " When thou art converted . . ." (Lk. 22³²), is one of the few passages in the New Testament which brings out directly the personal character of this movement, although it is to be noted that it thus continues : " Strengthen thy brethren." Ac. 3²⁶ is also, of course, striking in this respect (cf. Jer. 25⁵ ; Jon. 3⁸) : " Unto you first God, having raised up his servant, sent him to bless you, in turning away every one of you (ἕκαστος) from his iniquities." In the Old Testament it is especially in Ezekiel (e.g., 3¹⁶ᶠ·, 18⁴ᶠ· ²⁰ᶠ·) that we find an " existential" application of the promise and call to the individual—that he should turn from his former way and live. Self-evidently, that which becomes explicit in Ezekiel is the meaning of both Testaments. The proclaimed conversion to God is an action and being ascribed and promised personally to each individual. It is a happening which applies particularly to him ; which reaches to the heart and veins, the bones and marrow, of this or that particular man. And there is biblical precedent in the Book of Proverbs for what becomes so important in the later Church as the individual cure of souls. In general, however, we cannot overlook the fact that in the Bible the call for conversion is usually addressed—even when it is in the singular— to a plurality of men, to the people Israel, to Jacob-Israel in its totality, to Jerusalem or Ephraim. We have to remember this especially in Deutero-Isaiah, where many statements are formulated in the second person singular and seem to call for an understanding in terms of an individual application. To be sure, they can and should be read in this way too. But in so doing, we must not lose sight of the original meaning in which they are addressed to a people. The preaching of the Baptist opens with a general μετανοεῖτε, as does also that of Jesus Himself. There is obviously no fear that the collective will weaken the seriousness of the decision demanded from the individual. Far from weakening it, it is the plural which constitutes it a genuine seriousness. Behind this plural there stands the seriousness of the great cause of God in the world, of His name and kingdom and will which the community and all its members have to serve ; the seriousness of His decision as in each individual it reaches and affects all men. The conversion of man is his conversion to God when in and with it he adds himself as *sanctus* to the *communio sanctorum*.

4. We cannot understand the conversion of man as a matter for only one period in his life, which others will follow in which he can look back on what has happened *quasi re bene gesta*, or in which he might have to repeat it at this or that specific point, the prior or intervening times being periods in which he does not live in conversion, either because he is already converted, or is in need, and capable, of conversion but is only moving towards it. If it is the revealed truth that God is for him and he for God which necessitates his conversion and sets him in this movement, the movement is one which cannot be interrupted but extends over the whole of his life. It is neither exhausted in a once-for-all act, nor is it accomplished in a series of such acts. Otherwise how could it be an affair of the whole man ? It becomes and is the content and character of the whole act of his life as such. Certain moments in the totality of the fulfilment of this act, certain impulses and illuminations, disturbances, changes and experiences which we undergo at particular times, may have the meaning and character of a particular recollection of its total content. But sanctification in conversion is not the affair of these individual moments ; it is the affair of the totality of the whole life-movement of man. To live a holy life is to be raised and driven with increasing definiteness from the centre of this revealed truth, and therefore to live in conversion with growing sincerity, depth and precision.

As seen by contemporaries the Reformation of the 16th century began on October 31, 1517, when Luther nailed his theses on indulgences to the door of the Castle Church, Wittenberg. The first two of these theses were as follows : (1) *Dominus et magister noster Jesus Christus dicendo " penitentiam agite, etc.," omnem vitam fidelium penitentiam esse voluit :* (2) *quod verbum de penitentia sacramentali (id est confessionis et satisfactionis, que sacerdotum ministerio celebratur) non potest intelligi.* We have substituted the word conversion for what

Luther called penitence because the latter term almost inevitably evokes associations which link the matter under discussion with a momentary event (whether once-for-all or repeated). Now momentary events of this kind—either in the Romanist form of the reception of the sacrament of penance, or in the Pietist and Methodist form of a simple or more complex experience of conversion—are not identical with conversion to God, because the latter is the totality of the movement of sanctification which dominates and characterises human life—a movement in which there can be no breaks or pauses when conversion is no longer needed or only needed afresh, but when he might also propose to fulfil it for the second or third, or hundredth time. No matter whether they are understood sacramentally, emotionally or ethically, individual moments of this kind, and all the specific liturgies and experiences and conflicts and confessions and achievements of penitence, can be understood only as particularly prominent moments in the whole life-movement from the old to the new man. If we can hardly lack such moments, none of them can be fixed, let alone estimated, with such precision that its specific content can be responsibly identified with the happening in which we become saints of God ; with our conversion as it is set in motion from this centre. If the latter takes place only in these moments, and not in the whole context of human life, it does not take place at all.

To convert, μετανοεῖν, in the sense of the Baptist and the synoptic Jesus does, of course, include the new beginning of human life at a particular time. It also includes all kinds of action commanded at a particular time. In this respect we have already recalled Lk. 3¹⁰ᶠ· in relation to John, and we may also refer to what we said on the subject of discipleship. But New Testament μετανοεῖν is differentiated from the well-known and highly estimated " penitential " (*t'shubah*) of current Jewish theology and piety, which consisted essentially in a once-for-all or repeated individual movement, by the fact that it is " a radical change in the relationship of God to man and man to God " (J. Behm, in Kittel, IV, 995), of which it is a distinctive feature that it is not in the background as something that has happened, nor is it present in isolation as something which has to be repeated from time to time, but it controls and characterises the whole life of man from this beginning. In New Testament μετάνοια man moves forward steadily to continually new things in the same movement. " Though our outward man perish, yet the inward man is renewed day by day " (2 Cor. 4¹⁶).

In this respect, we have to note the call to conversion as it is sounded in the letters of the Apocalypse to Christian communities which have behind them a " first love " (Rev. 2⁴), and " first works " (2⁵), and even sometimes later works which were more than the first (2¹⁹), but which seem to have come to a standstill, and therefore in practice to have given up, at one point or another. Μετανόησον is demanded of them almost with some degree of menace. And over against all of them—even the community of Philadelphia (3⁷ᶠ·) whose failure is least apparent—there is set ὁ νικῶν, he that overcometh, to whom Jesus gives to eat of that tree of life (2⁷), who shall not be hurt by the second death (2¹¹), who is given the white stone with the name which no one knows but he who receives it (2¹⁷), who is granted power over the nations (2²⁶), whom He will confess before the Father and His angels (3⁵), whom He will make a pillar in the temple of His God (3¹²), who is allowed to sit with Him on His throne as He Himself overcame and is set down with His Father in His throne (3²¹). " He that hath an ear, let him hear what the Spirit saith unto the churches," is what we read at the end of each of the letters. Who, then, is the contrasted " overcomer " in all the glory ascribed to him ? The content of the μετανόησον is clear in these passages. The first love must not be left behind, nor the first works left undone (2⁴ᶠ·). " Be thou faithful unto death, and I will give thee a crown of life " (2¹⁰). " Remember how thou hast received and heard, and hold fast " (3³). " Be watchful " (3²). " Behold, I come quickly : hold fast that which thou hast, that no man take it from thee " (3¹¹, cf. 2²⁵). Note the present tense in the well-known verse : " Behold, I stand at the door, and knock : if any man hear my voice, and open the door, I will comé in, and will sup with him, and he with me " (3²⁰). It is he who does this now, to-day, that is the " overcomer " who shares His glory. And the Spirit tells the communities that they are to do this, and to be overcomers, victors, in so doing. He tells them then—and in this consists their μετανοεῖν—that the content of the present day can only be that of the first day ; that it can consist only in a steadfast and responsible moving forward from this beginning.

It is a strangely eloquent fact that Paul uses the terms μετανοεῖν and μετάνοια with comparative infrequency, and John not at all. We may rightly suspect that the words were allowed to drop in view of their association with the Jewish theory and practice of penance. If Paul prefers to describe the same thing as ἀνακαίνωσις, or παλιγγενεσία, or the dying of the old and rising of the new man ; if in John πιστεύειν is defined from the very first in such a way that it includes conversion ; and if in the language and thought of 1 John especially there is a constant antithesis of light and darkness, truth and error, love and hate, life and death, God and the world, these are only expressions for the radical things which the Synoptics mean by μετανοεῖν as opposed to the Rabbinic call to penitence, and they serve to bring out its character as an act, and an act which is constantly renewed.

In this context we ought perhaps to consider what has always been regarded as a difficult passage, Heb. 6¹⁻¹⁰. It tells us plainly and sharply that there can be no repetition of conversion because, once it has taken place, it determines the whole life of man in a process which brooks of no interruption. It is instructive to consider how this is established and explained in the passage. The section opens in v. 1a with a summons that Christians should leave behind (ἀφέντες) the problem (λόγος) of the ἀρχὴ Χριστοῦ, of the beginning which Christ has made with us, as one which has already been solved and decided. We must not act as if we had still to make a beginning with Him. Instead, we should resolutely and decidedly allow ourselves to be carried by Him from this beginning made with us to the end which He has appointed. In other words, we should be constantly in movement, ἐπὶ τὴν τελειότητα φερώμεθα. We should thus refrain (vv. 1b–2) from trying to lay a fresh foundation with answers to questions which grope back beyond this beginning, as though it had not been made, as though we did not come from it, and as though we had still to posit it. Some of these questions are mentioned : How is it that I have turned away from dead works ? How can I believe in God ? What is the meaning of my baptism ? Is there a resurrection of the dead ? What is meant by eternal judgment ? In themselves these are all possible and justifiable questions—and it is not for nothing that that of μετάνοια is the first to be mentioned. But they can be raised only as questions which have been answered already. And they must be set aside as idle and unprofitable to the extent that they represent the attempt to lay a fresh foundation ; to the extent that they are posed in the void, where the ἀρχὴ Χριστοῦ, and therefore our own conversion, and faith, and baptism, and the resurrection and judgment are seen only as future possibilities. " This will we do " (καὶ τοῦτο ποιήσομεν) is the resolute continuation in v. 3. We will leave behind us the attempt to lay a fresh foundation, which is in any case a futile attempt, since we did not lay it and do not have to do so. We will set all this in the past and move constantly towards the goal, " if God permit." We will do it. But of ourselves we have no freedom to do it. If we have the freedom, we have it only as it is given us by God. But according to vv. 4–6 we can count on this freedom because the alternative of falling behind is quite impossible. For who are we ? In vv. 4–5 it is boldly assumed that we are among those who have been enlightened once and for all, who have tasted heavenly gifts, who have been made partakers of the Holy Ghost, who have tasted the good Word of God and the powers of the world to come. We may and must understand ourselves as such. For us a such it is quite impossible (v. 6) that as those who have fallen behind or away (παραπεσόντες) we should come afresh to conversion (ἀνακαινίζειν εἰς μετάνοιαν) as though nothing had happened. Would not this be to crucify afresh, and put to an open shame, the Son of God, the Victor, who has made this beginning with us, and set us in the movement from which we come so gloriously endowed ? Would it not mean that we go behind Him as well as ourselves, striking out not only the gifts but Himself the Giver ? We are not free to do this. We are free, therefore, to leave behind that which can only be behind as an enterprise foredoomed to failure. We are free to move forward. In vv. 7–8 the same lesson is enforced by a metaphor. The earth has drunk in the rain which frequently falls on it, and it brings forth useful vegetation for those for whom it is tilled (v. 7). If thorns and briers do also grow, of course, they quickly show themselves to be worthless, and the only option is to " curse " and burn them (v. 8). Christians, however, are to be compared to the good crop rather than the bad. The moral is drawn in vv. 9–10. The direction given in v. 1a is in force. It can and must be followed (v. 3). There can be no doubt that vv. 1–8 do include a good deal of anxiety and admonition and even warning. The readers do not seem to be readily identifiable with those who are freed for this action as described in vv. 4–6. May it be that *per nefas* they find themselves in the fatal sphere *ante Christum* ? May it be that they are not engaged in that movement to the goal ? May it be that they are occupied instead with those idle questions, and therefore with laying a fresh foundation ? May it be that they are denying Christ the Victor ? May it be that they are producing a crop of thorns and briers which can only be destroyed by the consuming fire ? It is evident that this question seriously engages the author : otherwise why should he have raised the issue ? He had already brought up the question in 3¹²ᶠ· : " Take heed, brethren, lest there be in any of you an evil heart of unbelief, in departing from the living God. But exhort one another daily, while it is called To day." And he will later (12¹⁷) recall the case of Esau who when he had sold his birthright found no τόπος μετανοίας, though he sought it carefully with tears. The whole tenor of the Epistle is that of a warning against this danger, of a most urgent " To-day, To-day." But in the particularly serious passage 6¹⁻¹⁰ the author does think of his readers as actually overwhelmed by the impending threat. On the contrary, he says : " We are persuaded better things of you, and things that accompany salvation—εἰ καὶ οὕτως λαλοῦμεν, though we thus speak " (v. 9). The basis of his certainty is that God is not unrighteous, but righteous ; that He does not forget but remembers that they are at work, and love His name, and have ministered to the saints, and do minister (v. 10). The danger may thus be discounted, for there is something far more certain than the danger in which the author obviously sees his readers stand and to which he earnestly draws their attention. They are in fact engaged in the movement described in v. 1a. And God knows and recognises that they are those who are engaged in it. In the passage which follows (v. 11 f.) there is required only the exhortation appropriate to the direction there given—that they should persevere, and not become slothful, in the movement initiated once and for all by their once and for all μετάνοια.

The post-apostolic and early catholic Church failed to take note of these warnings in the Gospels, Paul, John and Hebrews. Relapsing into the ways of thinking of later Judaism, it again made the conversion which rules the whole life of Christians into a matter of particular acts, and later of a special penitential discipline. This led finally to the special " sacrament of penance " which Luther contrasted so sharply with the μετανοεῖτε of Jesus. As Luther perceived, sacramental penitence is not the conversion demanded by Jesus. True conversion, or penitence, can take place only in the whole life of believers. Calvin's view was exactly the same. In opposition to the Anabaptists and their companions (*sodales*) the Jesuits, he found it necessary to state : *poenitentia in totam vitam proroganda est homini Christiano (Instit.* III, 3, 2). Believers know that this warfare (*militia*) will end only with their death (3, 9).

We may sum up as follows. By the revealed truth that God is for him and he for God, the whole man is set in the movement of conversion. It is for this that he is awakened in sanctification, and it is in this that his raising of himself consists. In every dimension we have to do with the whole man, as already explained in detail. In the light of this conclusion, we must now go on to make a second main proposition—that in this movement we have to do with a warfare, or, to put it a little more precisely and less dramatically, with a quarrel, or falling-out.

It is a pity that there is no English or French equivalent for the very useful German word *Auseinandersetzung*, which exactly sums up what we have in mind. Of course, it is a word that has to be used very cautiously and selectively in theology. We cannot wish to fall out with God, with Jesus Christ, with the Holy Spirit. We can only be glad and thankful that God is on our side. It is also better not to fall out with Holy Scripture or the Church as the communion of saints. And it is better that there should be no falling out in our relationship with our neighbours. But there is every cause—and it is with this that we are concerned in the present context—to fall out with oneself. It is just this that the man engaged in conversion can never cease to do. It can and must be said that his conversion consists in the fact that he is seriously at odds with himself.

We cannot overlook the fact that in the fulfilment of this movement a man finds himself under a twofold determination.

The first consists in the powerful summons to halt and advance which is issued, and by which he is set in this distinctive movement, in virtue of the fact that God is for him and he for God, and that this fact is clearly and powerfully revealed to him. In this determination he is the new man ; the man who is impelled by the Spirit of God, to use the phrase of Rom. 8[14]. In this determination he repents and renounces what he previously was and did, leaving his old way, abandoning himself as he was, boldly enterprising a completely new and different being and action, entering a new way, affirming and apprehending himself in the future which thereby opens up for him—and all this, commensurate with the powerful cause which sets him in this movement, in the unqualified totality of his existence and being as a man.

But the second determination under which he finds himself consists in the fact that it is still he himself who is wholly placed in this movement and constituted the one who makes it. It is he himself, i.e., the one for whom this call to halt and advance previously had no meaning or power. As he gives himself to enter this way, he comes from the old way. He repents, but he does so as the one who previously knew nothing of repentance. He boldly enterprises a new being, but he does so as one who previously had no boldness to do so. He affirms and apprehends himself in the future indicated by this cause which effectively moves him, but he does so as the one who has also his past. Even in the turn which he executes, at the very heart of the present of this happening he is never without his past. To-day, already impelled by the Spirit, he is still in the flesh of yesterday. He is already the new man, but he is still the old. Only in part ? Only to a limited extent ? Only in respect of certain relics ? The older theology was right when in relation to the sinful past of man as it still persists in the present of conversion it referred to the remains or relics of the old man, of the flesh and its sinful action. It is only as sorry remains that the being and action of man under this second determination can be seen and understood in the light of the first determination. But it was an unfortunate delusion if this remnant was regarded as fortunately smaller in relation to something other and better. On the contrary, if we are just a little honest with ourselves (as we will be in serious conversion), we cannot conceal the fact that it is again the whole man with whom we have to do in this residuum ; that it is still the whole man who under this second determination is in puzzling contrast with himself under the first. The man who to-day is confronted by that call to halt and advance, who to-day is set in that movement, in the totality of his existence and being, by the powerful truth that God is for him and he for God, is also to-day, and again in the totality of his existence and being, the sinful man of yesterday. Thus in the to-day of repentance we have not only to do with the presence of certain regrettable traces of his being and action of yesterday. No, the one who is under the determination and in the process of becoming a totally new man is in his totality the old man of yesterday.

The situation can be understood, therefore, only in the following terms. In the twofold determination of the man engaged in conversion we have to do with two total men who cannot be united but are necessarily in extreme contradiction. We are confronted with two mutually exclusive determinations.

It is worth pointing out that Calvin did not perceive this relationship between the new and the old in the 1539 edition of the *Institutes*, but had obviously come to do so by 1559. In the former case he spoke of a *pars nostri* which in regeneration remains subject to the yoke of sin. In it we cling to an *aliquod de vetustate*. The soul of the believer is thus divided into two parts which confront each other like two wrestlers (*duo athletae*), the one being stronger than the other, although attacked and hampered by him. *Praecipuo cordis voto et affectu* the believer strives after God, his *superiores partes* following the Spirit. He hates and condemns the evil which *per imbecillitatem* he still commits. He can sin consciously only in face of the opposition of his heart and conscience. And it is by this fact that the regenerate is differentiated from the unregenerate. At the corresponding point in 1559, however, this whole interpretation has been abandoned (III, 3, 9 f.). The old and the new, sin and grace, are no longer two parts in the being of the regenerate. The Romanist ideas of *fomen mali*, a mere *infirmitas*, still present and active in the believer have now disappeared. In opposition even to Augustine, and in strict agreement with Paul, Calvin now speaks of the *pravitas* peculiar even to the regenerate, of the sin which dwells in him too, and which can obviously be met, not by something higher (the *superiores partes*) in himself, but only by the new man as such, who is begotten of the Spirit. It is clear that on this basis—but only on this basis—what Calvin said about the justification and forgiveness needed by even the regenerate is possible and necessary and cogent in the strict sense intended. If, on the other hand, the saints are in some degree not sinners, we can hardly avoid the conclusion that to this degree, in respect of the stronger of the two wrestlers, they no longer stand in need of justification.

Luther's *simul* (*totus*) *iustus, simul* (*totus*) *peccator* has thus to be applied strictly to sanctification and therefore conversion if we are to see deeply into what is denoted by these terms, and to understand them with the necessary seriousness. It is certainly hard to grasp that the same man stands under two total determinations which are not merely opposed but mutually exclusive ; that the same man, in the *simul* of to-day, is both the old man of yesterday and the new man of to-morrow, the captive of yesterday and the free man of to-morrow, the slothful recumbent of yesterday and the erect man of to-morrow. But there is no easier way of seeing and understanding the matter. Static and quantitative terms may seem to help, but they are not adequate to describe the true situation. They involve a separation into constituent elements. It is true that the situation seems to cry out for this separation. It seems to be much more illuminating if, instead of saying that the whole man is still the old and yet already the new, in complete and utter antithesis, we say that he is still partially the old and already partially the new. But if we put it in this way we mistake the matter. For the new man is the whole man ; and so too is the old. And conversion is the transition, the movement, in which man is still, in fact, wholly the old and already wholly the new man. We are badly advised if we abandon this statement because we fear the severity of the antithesis. To do so, and thus to proceed to transform and divide the *simul* into a *partim-partim*, in which the old man of the past is sharply and a little triumphantly separated from the new man of the future, is to leave the sphere of the *vita christiana* as it is actually lived for a psychological myth which has no real substance. The *vita christiana* in conversion is the event, the act, the history, in which at one and the same time man is still wholly the old man and already wholly the new—so powerful is the sin by which he is determined from behind, and so powerful the grace by which he is determined from before. It is in this way that man knows himself when he is really engaged in conversion.

But now we must go on to emphasise no less sharply that the conversion in which he is simultaneously both, is an event, an act, a history. The coincidence of the " still " and " already " is the content of this *simul*. Because this " still " and " already " coincide in him, it is not the *simul* of a balancing or co-ordination of two similar factors. Nor are the positions of the two moments which are simultaneously present—the old and the new man—in any sense interchangeable. On the contrary, they are wholly and utterly dissimilar. There is an order and sequence in this *simul*. There is direction—the movement to a goal. The old and the new man are simultaneously present in the relationship of a *terminus a quo* and a *terminus ad quem*. Thus conversion, in which at one and the same time we are still the old man and already the new, and both wholly and altogether, is neither a juggling nor a movement in a circle. In accordance with the fact that it is initiated by the divine command to halt and advance, the man engaged in it finds that—with no possibility of interchange—he is wholly denied as the old man of yesterday and wholly affirmed as the new man of to-morrow ; that he is wholly taken out of identity with the former and wholly set in identity with the latter ; that he is in no sense taken seriously by God as the former but taken with unqualified seriousness by God as the latter ; that as the former he is wholly given up to eternal death and as the latter wholly taken up into eternal life. When he is simultaneously the old and the new man, and both in totality, he is not only forbidden to be this in neutrality, in a static equipoise of the two ; he finds that this is quite impossible in practice. He can be the two only in the whole turning from the one to the other. We speak of this turning when we speak of his conversion. And we emphasise the serious and radical nature of it when we speak of the twofold, total determination of the man engaged in it.

In these circumstances the thought of falling-out is perhaps the best to describe the situation. To begin with, it indicates that the coincidence of the " still " and the " already," of the old man and the new, of the *homo peccator* and the *homo sanctus*, cannot remain. It is true that there is no present in which we can look beyond this *simul*, in which the man engaged in conversion is not wholly under the power of sin and wholly under that of grace. Yet he is not merely not author-ised by the content of the two determinations coinciding in this *simul*, nor is he merely prohibited, but he is positively prevented from under-standing this *simul* as something lasting and definitive. To his own salvation, he has no continuing city. If it is true that we can never at any time see beyond this *simul*, it is equally true that this *simul*, in virtue of its dynamic as a moment in the history of God with man and man with God, points beyond itself, impelling to the only possible decision between the two total determinations which now coincide in man. He cannot remain what he still is *in toto*. He can no longer be this in face of what he already is *in toto*. And what he already is *in toto*, he may become and be in such a way that he is this alone (excluding what he still is *in toto*). What in this *simul* is still present in conjunction as a twofold determination of one and the same man cannot by its very nature remain in this conjunction. Its whole will and movement and impulse is to fall out or to fall apart, and to do so in the direction unequivocally characterised by the radically different content of this twofold determination; not dualistically in a division or re-stabilised co-existence of an old man and a new, a sinner and saint; but monistically in the passing and death and definitive end and destruction of the one in favour of the development and life and exclusive, uncompromised and inviolable existence of the other. In the quarrel in which a man finds himself engaged in conversion—as he who is still wholly the old and already wholly the new man—he has not fallen out with himself partially but totally, in the sense that the end and goal of the dispute is that he can no longer be the one he was and can be only the one he will be.

The great antinomies in John (light-darkness, etc.), and the alternative expressions of Paul (the putting off and death of the old and putting on and rising of the new, or the opposition and conflict between the Spirit and the flesh), may again be recalled in this connexion. We have to reflect that the New Testament speaks in this way of the present of the community and its members (the members of the body of Christ). The references are all to the life of believers, the regenerate. We are never given to understand that the one determination of the man engaged in conversion, the Christian man, is seen and regarded only as his heathen or Jewish past, and the other only as his future. On the contrary, it is the life of believers, the Christian present, which is here pitilessly but resolutely set in the light of this twofold determination, as illustrated by the concrete admonitions and promises of the Epistles. Again, however, we are nowhere given to understand that there will arise even momentarily a state of rest or equipoise as between two co-ordinated factors. Christians are forcefully ejected from any fancied equipoise or co-ordination by the fact that in this *simul* there are addressed to them very concrete warnings and promises concerning their present. They are not placed before or in a choice or decision, but under a choice which has been already made, a decision which has been resolved and executed, concerning them. They have been brought face to face with a powerful summons to halt and advance. And it is a divine summons which has a total reference in both cases to death on the one side and life on the other; in the power of which what they still are in their totality cannot continue but only cease and disappear; in which therefore the old thing, their being in the flesh, cannot be completed, but only replaced, by that which they already are in their totality, their being in the Spirit. They can now walk only as those they already are, not as those they still are; in the Spirit and not in the flesh. But this means that what they still are is now behind them, and it is only what they are already that is before them. We are not engaged in conversion, nor are we Christians in the New Testament sense, if we are not involved in this falling-out with ourselves in which it is not merely a matter of this or that on the one side or the other, but of death on the one side and life on the other— in this order and with this teleology.

Calvin was right, therefore, when he praised as scriptural the traditional description of repentance as *mortificatio* and *vivificatio* as Melanchthon and M. Bucer had introduced it into Reformation doctrine (III, 3, 3). But he added that it needs to be properly understood. He was obviously dissatisfied with the scholastic understanding of *mortificatio* as a mere *contritio cordis*; a *dolor* and even a *terror animae* on the ground of the knowledge of sin and ensuing judgment; a basic self-dissatisfaction in which man sees that he is lost and wants to be different; the inward shattering of man in self-despair. He was no less dissatisfied with the understanding of *vivificatio* as merely the comforting of man by faith in the light of the goodness and mercy and grace of God; his lifting up of himself, and coming to himself, in relation to the promised salvation in Christ. There is nothing wrong with these descriptions, in which the psychological aspect of conversion is considered and perspicaciously and on the whole accurately represented. But we may learn from Calvin himself (3, 8) why they are inadequate. This is obviously because they have to do only with the subjective and psychological side of the process, and therefore cannot do justice to the objective content of the weighty words *mortificatio* and *vivificatio*—no matter how strong may be the expressions used (*consternatio, humiliatio* and even *desperatio*), or how fine the description of the *consolatio*. By *mortificatio*, Calvin tells us in his own language, we have to understand *totius carnis, quae militia et perversitate referta est, interitus*. This involves the *res difficilis et ardua* of an action in which we have to put off ourselves like a garment, being forced to take leave of our *nativum ingenium*. If everything that we have of ourselves is not done away (*abolitum*), we can only suppose that *interitus carnis*, and therefore *mortificatio*, has not really taken place. Thus the first step to obedience is the *abnegatio naturae nostrae* ; the *abnegatio nostri* which later supplies a title for the decisive chapter in his doctrine of sanctification. This, he believes, is what the Old Testament prophets meant by conversion. And by *vivificatio*—again in the sense of the prophets—we have to understand the fruit of righteousness, justice and mercy which grows out of the heart and soul and mind of a man who has been filled by the Holy Spirit with what may rightly (*iure*) be called a new thinking and willing. But Calvin returns at once, almost anxiously and with striking emphasis, to the first point. Because by nature we are turned aside from God, we will never do the right *nisi praecedat abnegatio nostri*. There can be no awakening to the fear of God, no *initium pietatis, nisi ubi gladio Spiritus violenter mactati in nihilum redigimur*. There is needed the *interitus communis naturae* (the nature common to all men) in the above sense if God is to be able to reckon us His children.

Is not the impression left by this presentation strangely mixed ? There can be no doubt that Calvin brings out with great clarity the literal seriousness of the biblical terms, and therefore the radical sharpness, the objective and strictly antithetical character, of the dispute with himself in which the man engaged in conversion finds himself, of the resolute falling-out or falling-apart which is involved (as opposed to a mere tension of two opposing spiritual states, in respect of which terms like *mortificatio* and *vivificatio* might appear to be only rather exaggerated metaphors). Calvin was quite right when, renouncing all attempts at plastic representation, he spoke so inexorably of *interitus, abnegatio* and *reductio ad nihilum*, of the slaying sword of the Spirit, and then of the Spirit as the only principle of what may be seriously called a new life. There can be no objection to the radical nature of his presentation. Calvin points us most significantly to the height beyond all psychologising where the conversion of man is real and all the spiritual processes which attest it have their basis and superior truth. On the other hand, it cannot be denied (and the explanation is to be found in an even more deep-seated defect in his teaching) that the doctrine of Calvin obviously suffers (cf. A. Göhler, *op. cit.*, p. 41 f.) from a curious over-emphasising of *mortificatio* at the expense of *vivificatio* which might be justified to some extent from the older but not from the later prophets of the Old Testament, and certainly not from what is understood by μετάνοια in the New. What we have called the divine call to advance is in Calvin so overshadowed by the divine summons to halt that it can hardly be heard at all. The result is that his presentation is not merely stern, as is inevitable, but sombre and forbidding. And this is quite out of keeping with the themes presented. It does not enable us to see the decision operative in the *simul peccator et sanctus*, the teleology of man's falling-out with himself. Man seems almost to be left in the air. The truth is that in the New Testament the real dying and passing and perishing of the old man is matched by a no less real rising and coming and appearing of the new, and that it is in the power of this, the *vivificatio*, that there can be also the *mortificatio*. To take only one example, note the emphasis in statements like those of Col. 3¹ᶠ· and Eph. 2¹ᶠ· It is in view of the Yes pronounced to man in the omnipotence of the divine mercy that there arises this falling-out with ourselves and we hear the inexorable No to our being in the flesh. But this aspect is not given its proper place, and does not clearly emerge, in the presentation of Calvin. The impression is left that the *interitus* of the old man is what really matters in this happening, and in contrast to this the *vivificatio* is introduced only as a pale and feeble hope. It is not for nothing that in the description of the latter we miss the realism which is so impressive in the presentation of the *mortificatio*, and that—contrary to Calvin's true intention—the emphasis falls on the rise of new *cogitationes et affectus*. Why is it that Calvin could not speak of the life of the new man in terms no less radical and categorical—indeed, more so—than those which he used in relation to the death of the old ?

The same question has to be addressed (in an even sharper form) to the doctrine of conversion advanced by H. F. Kohlbrügge (cf. on this point W. Kreck, *Die Lehre von der Heiligung bei H. F. Kohlbrügge*, 1936, esp. p. 90 f.). It must never be forgotten that in the great pietistic, rationalistic and romantic twilight of the 19th century Kohlbrügge was one of the few who revealed a precise knowledge of the height where the conversion of man has its actuality and origin. In the light of this he gave powerful advocacy to the proposition (more than once explicitly stated in Calvin) that the renovation of man consists decisively in a growing and deepening knowledge of sin. In the light of the Law (Kreck, p. 98 f.) he becomes " more and more corrupt, and more and more sinful, until he finally realises that he is altogether man." " He is a great saint before God, and the best doctor and professor, who knows of himself only that he is a great transgressor." God dislocates the hips of His saints, so that they walk with a limp. " That which is of God acquires an attitude and gait like Jacob's, whereas Esau strides powerfully through the world." " The saints of God can do nothing in advance ; everything is taken out of their hands . . . they have no capacity of themselves, no wisdom, and even no faith when it is needed, but are full of fear and trembling and hesitation and anxiety." The pious are those who " do not hide the fact that they are not pious, and are prepared to live only by the pious God." " Even when you are a hundred years old in His service, you will be the same fool, and God will be the same merciful God " (p. 94). " All my own work and activity and faith is of such a kind that even if I were clothed with all the faith and works of all saints and patriarchs and prophets and apostles, and stood before you with an unvarnished faith, I should cast it all from me and shake it off like refuse in the presence of my God. For there is grace only for the naked " (p. 95). Can we read all this without assenting from the very depths of our hearts—and yet without also having to ask whether it is really true ? Are not these propositions different from those of Calvin (to their disadvantage) to the extent that the *mortificatio* of which they plainly speak is obviously conceived of again—for Kohlbrügge was a child of his age—on the psychological level, being understood and described as a process of awareness of an extremely negative type ? And the result is that Kohlbrügge can take up again a rather doubtful qualification that Calvin had abandoned : " You may indeed sin like a worldling ; you may sink below the level of cattle and demons " . . . but there is still the possibility of repentance and sorrow ; we cannot persist in it ; we cannot remain in it ; we have the means to deal with it ; we are to hate it and flee it (p. 99 f.). And this has the further result that conversely Kohlbrügge can describe the *vivificatio* which begins beyond this self-humiliation in terms which make it difficult for us (because they are still on the psychological level) not to catch suddenly the ring of perfectionism : " Yet I live, says the believer. I live in the sight of God. I live before His judgment throne in His grace. I live in His favour, light and love. I am perfectly redeemed from my sins. The ledger contains no debt against my name. The Law no longer demands, accuses, or condemns. I am holy as my Father in' heaven is perfect. The whole good-pleasure of God embraces me. It is the ground on which I stand, the rock by which I am sheltered. All the blessedness and rest of God lifts and bears me. I breathe in it, and am eternally whole. I have no more sin ; I commit no more sin. I know with a good conscience that I am in the ways of God and do His will, that I am wholly in accordance with His will—whether I go or stand, sit or lie, wake or sleep. Even what I think and say is according to His will. Wherever I may be, at home or abroad, it is according to His gracious will. Whether I work or rest, I am acceptable to Him. My guilt is eternally expunged, and I cannot incur new guilt which will not be eternally expunged. I am well kept in His grace, and cannot sin. No death can kill me. I live eternally like all the angels of God. God will no longer be incensed against me and chide me. I am redeemed for ever from future wrath. The world will no longer touch me, nor the world entangle me. Who will separate us from the love of God ? If God is for us, who can be against us ? " (quoted from Bonhoeffer, *Nachfolge*, p. 205 f.). Even though it is conceivable that *in extremis* a Christian may use the extravagant language of Kohlbrügge both negatively on the one side and positively on the other, the fact remains that with him as with Calvin the emphasis falls on the negative side, on the destruction of all our own holiness even as Christians, on the annihilating attack on all forms of self-righteousness, even the most refined, even those which appeal to the grace of God, to Christ, and to the Holy Spirit. Once we have read Kohlbrügge, we can never again forget this attack, and we shall be grateful that he has conducted it so radically. In some of his disciples the matter was pressed almost to the point of becoming a triumph for the publican and sinner, who almost jubilantly flaunts his self-consciousness as such and looks down on the poor pietists and others. This would never have happened, and the attack itself would have been more serious and lasting in its effects, if Kohlbrügge had been in a position to offset his exposition of *mortificatio* by a no less (and even more) powerful exposition of the corresponding *vivificatio*. Not, of course, in the form of " a depiction of Christian character " (Kreck, p. 102) and the like, which rather strangely he did attempt on one or two occasions, and rather pregnantly in the passage quoted above, but in the form of an exposition of the law of life under the rule of which a man finds himself when his own autonomy is irrevocably brought to an end. It is the power of this law which distinguished the attack from the mere assault of a half-depairing, half-complacent defeatism which it might easily seem to be as represented by Kohlbrügge. It is this power which makes it serious, effective and helpful, leading man to the humility of the genuine publican, not the arrogance of the false publican who is really in his own way a Pharisee. It is because and as God issues the command to proceed that He also issues the command to halt, and not conversely. He kills the old man by introducing the new, and not conversely. It is with His Yes to the man elected and loved and called by Him that He says No to his sinful existence, forcing him to recognise that we are always in the wrong before God.

This is what is obscured, or at any rate does not emerge clearly, in the discussions of both Calvin and Kohlbrügge, where the accent is placed on the other side. Both of them knew the superior place from which alone there can be conversion, and therefore a serious dispute with oneself. But both failed to allow its origin—in Jesus Christ—to speak for itself with sufficient force and clarity, and therefore to bring out the teleology of the dispute, i.e., the fact that *vivificatio* is the meaning and intention of *mortificatio*.

We must now speak more specifically of the basis and origin of conversion, of man's awakening to it, and of the power which sets and keeps it in motion as his falling-out with himself. At the beginning of this discussion we described it as an axis which establishes itself in the life of man, or on which his life is established, so that he has to follow its movement in his own life and being, its turning automatically making his life a life in conversion. We called this dynamic principle the power of the reality that God is for him, and he for God, as this reveals itself to him and shows itself to be the truth. Some elucidations are now needed in respect of this centre of the problem.

We must (1) abandon the figure of the axis with the magical or mechanical or automatic associations which it might conjure up, and call the thing intended by its proper name. When Paul speaks of a man led to conversion by the Spirit of God, it is not at all the case that he is betrayed into the sphere and influence of an overwhelming impulse with the alien movement of which he has to co-operate and by which he *nolens volens* sets himself in totality under that twofold determination as an old and new man, and therefore in that dispute with himself. It is true, of course, that it is by the omnipotence of God that he is awakened to conversion and set in this movement. But the omnipotence of God is not a force which works magically or mechanically and in relation to which man can be only an object, an alien body which is either carried or impelled, like a spar of wood carried relentlessly downstream by a great river. It is a matter of God's omnipotent mercy, of His Holy Spirit, and therefore of man's liberation, and therefore of his conversion to being and action in the freedom which he is given by God. To be sure, there is a compulsion. He *must* pass from a well-known past to a future which is only just opening up, " to a land that I shall shew thee " ; from himself to the old man to himself as a new man ; from his own death to his own true life. There is necessarily a compulsion. No question of a choice can enter in. He is not merely set in, i.e., before a decision. He makes the decision, looking neither to the right hand nor to the left, nor especially behind. But the compulsion is not a mere compulsion. It is not abstract. It is not blind or deaf. We have to realise that a mere compulsion is basically evil and demonic. The compulsion obeyed in conversion is not of this type. It is the compulsion of a permission and ability which have been granted. It is that of the free man who as such can only exercise his freedom. The omnipotence of God creates and effects in the man awakened to conversion a true ability. He who previously vegetated to death under a hellish compulsion, in a true comparison with the driftwood carried downstream, may now live wholly of himself and be a man. The coming, the opening up of this " may " is the revelation of the divine summons to halt and proceed ; the power which makes his life life in conversion. Because and as he is given this permission and ability, he necessarily stands at this point. He *must* leave those things which are behind, and reach forth unto those things which are before, pressing toward the mark (Phil. 3[13f.]). It is for this that he is freed, and free. In this freedom there has been taken from him once and for all any mere choosing or self-deciding. In the exercise of this freedom—still as the man he was, already as the man he will be—he fulfils his conversion.

Calvin was well aware of this (III, 3, 21) : *singulare esse Dei donum poeni-tentiam.* He rightly recalled that when the Christians in Jerusalem heard what Peter had to say in Ac. 11, " they glorified God, saying, Then hath God also to the Gentiles granted repentance unto life " (μετάνοιαν εἰς ζωήν, v. 18) ; and 2 Tim. 2²⁵ᶠ·, where Timothy is exhorted to instruct in meekness those that oppose themselves, hoping that God may give them " repentance to the acknow-ledging of the truth, and that they may recover themselves (lit. become sober) out of the snare of the devil, who are taken captive by him to do his will." He also observes with justice that it would be easier to create ourselves as men than *proprio marte* to assume a new nature. But this is what is at issue in Eph. 2¹⁰. We are created by God unto good works. *Quoscunque eripere vult Deus ab interitu, hos Spiritu regenerationis vivificat.* Penitence is inseparably connected with the faithfulness and mercy of God. According to Is. 59²⁰, He is the Re-deemer of Zion, who comes in and with conversion from transgression in Jacob. But if the case is as Calvin saw and stated it, it is hard to see why his penitential teaching as a whole could and should become that sombre picture in which the main features are the thunderings and lightnings of *mortificatio.* On his own presuppositions, ought he not to have described *vivificatio* as God's *opus proprium*, and *mortificatio* only as its reverse side, God's *opus alienum* ? Why did he not do this ? Who authorised him almost completely to conceal what is from its very basis and origin the clear and positive meaning and character of conversion as liberation by giving to *vivificatio* only a minor position as the reverse side of *mortificatio* (A. Göhler, *op. cit.*, p. 43) ? Or who forbade him to understand the relationship as it is truly established by the basis and origin of the whole ?

But as we enquire (2) concerning the specific character of the basis and origin of çonversion, and therefore the particular nature of the awakening of man to it, we must take a step backwards. The dynamic principle of this movement is the truth, revealing itself to man, that God is for him, and that—in virtue of the fact that God is for him—he is for God. It is this truth which frees him for God, and therefore for that dispute with himself. It is this truth which kills and makes alive. Thus in its origin and basis, at the superior place where it is set in motion, the conversion of man is a decision of God for him which not only makes possible a corresponding decision of man for God, the free act of his obedience, but makes this act and obedience real, directly causing it to take place. If in this basis and origin the order were different, and the truth revealed to man were that man is for God, and therefore God for man, the truth would not make us free. It would simply be a demand that man should be what he is not free to be. It would then have nothing to do with *vivificatio.* For how can the man who is against God become a new man merely by being asked to make a decision which is quite alien to him and to be for God ? But it could also have nothing to do with *mortificatio.* It might startle and frighten man, but it could not and would not in any way raise him out his existence as a sinner, or even affect this existence. It would simply be an abstract law—a law without any *locus* in a life fulfilling and embodying it, but merely advancing the arid claim that it is the law of God, and that as such it has the right to demand that man should be for God, and thus fulfil the condition under which God will also be for him. This abstract law has never yet led a man to conversion, even by killing him, let alone by making him alive. It has no power to do either. For it is not the living God, nor His quickening Spirit, who places man under this law. The revealed truth of the living God in His quickening Spirit has its content and force in the fact that it is He first who is for man, and then and for that reason man is for Him. God precedes therefore, and sets man in the movement in which he follows. He says Yes to him when man says No, and thus silences the No of man and lays a Yes in his heart and on his lips. He loves man even though he is an enemy (Rom. 5¹⁰), and thus makes him the friend who loves Him in return. As it is revealed to man that this is how matters stand between him and God—and this is what is revealed to him by the Holy Spirit— he comes to have dealings with the living God and the quickening Spirit. He is awakened to conversion. He is plunged into the dispute with himself in which he dies as an old man and rises again as a new. In short, it is unequivocally and exclusively by the Gospel, the revealed grace of God, that conversion is effectively commanded as a radical termination and a radical recommencement. But effectively means as a gift of freedom, and therefore as the law of his own free act apart from which he has no freedom to choose any other. The law which he obeys has its *locus* in his life as it is freed by the Gospel. As the " law of the Spirit of life " (Rom. 8²), it frees us, but in so doing it genuinely binds and engages us. It makes the divine summons to halt and advance quite unavoidable. It makes quite natural and self-evident the being in transition from what we still are to what we are already.

This brings us to the deep reason for the difficulty which we have in following Calvin's doctrine of penitence—for all our admiration for its many excellent features—and for the similar difficulty which we experience in relation to that of Kohlbrügge. Was it not Calvin himself who told us that conversion has its origin in faith (III, 3, 2), that no one can seriously repent unless he knows God, and no one can know God unless he has first laid hold of His grace, that the preaching of repentance by John as well as Jesus derives its weight from, and has to be understood in the light of, the approaching kingdom of God ? If only we could keep him to his statement about *mortificatio* and *vivificatio* (3, 9) : *utrumque ex Christi participatione nobis contingit*, or to the section (3, 19) where he returns to the same truth : *per evangelii doctrinam audiunt homines suas omnes cogitationes, suos affectus, sua studia corrupta et vitiosa esse !* But we cannot do this. He certainly does state unequivocally that it is the free and liberating grace, goodness and mercy of God revealed in the Gospel, His mighty Yes to man, which leads man to the Yes to God and to life according to His promise, and therefore to a No to self and to his previous life. But this line is continually crossed by another which tells us (3, 7) that the fear of God, the thought of impending judgment, the dread of sin, the obligation to give God the glory which is owed, is the true *principium*, the *exordium poenitentiae*, and therefore that which leads us to the knowledge of Christ (3, 20). Is not this the very opposite of the earlier view ? And unfortunately, in face of the striking over-emphasis on *mortificatio*, we can hardly maintain that in practice it was the first view which shaped his understanding of penitence. Why did he so morosely argue that *vivificatio* is not to be regarded as a joy (*laetitia*), but consists rather in the *studium sancte pieque vivendi* ?—as though there were any necessary antithesis between the two, or as though this *studium* could have any other origin than in a great joy, the joy of the one who has been made free for this zeal ! Why does the chapter which had begun so finely by relating faith and repentance end in sections 22–25 with a rather irrelevant discussion of the threatening sin against the Holy Ghost, and finally with a grim reminder of king Ahab and similar examples of a hypocritical and therefore useless repentance ? In so far as Calvin's teaching is shaped by these considerations, finding the *principium poenitentiae* in fear of God and its primary fulfilment in *mortificatio*, and thus acquiring a predominantly sombre character, we can only say that, contrary to his own initial statements, he develops his doctrine in the light of a concept of law which cannot be regarded as identical with the " law of the Spirit of life " of Rom. 8[2]. And it could easily be shown that the same is true of Kohlbrügge, who in this context (with similar results for his total view) made explicit use of the concept of the law which kills as that which initiates the movement of conversion. That conversion is really a liberation, and how this is the case, is something which does not emerge with adequate clarity either in Kohlbrügge or in Calvin. And how can it possibly do so if we do not see and say that it has its basis and origin in the Gospel, or if we do not take this fact with true seriousness ?

Finally (3), we have to ask concerning the superior place itself and as such where it is a real fact, and can thus emerge as potent truth in the work of the Holy Spirit, that God is for man and man for God. Everything that we have so far said depends ultimately upon whether we can say that this is not a mere suspicion, or hypothesis, or construct, or axiom of philosophical metaphysics, or dogma of theology, but that it is really the·case with unassailable objectivity. In other words, the event of revelation which has been our starting-point in all these discussions must be merely the manifestation of a real event which takes place with incontestable objectivity. It is in relation to this climax that—to look back for a moment from the point we have just reached—all our previous statements have been made : about the primacy of the Gospel in virtue of which the decisive work of that event of revelation is the new life, the *vivificatio*, of man ; about the liberation imparted to him in it ; about the force and depth and teleology of the dispute in which he fulfils this liberation ; about the totality with which, awakened to repentance, he finds himself claimed and impelled. How do we know all these things ? How is it that we can treat them as a reality, and interpret this reality only as has actually been the case ? On what basis have we thought and spoken about the totality of conversion, and reached our detailed decisions, partly for and partly without and even against Calvin, by whom we have especially tried to orientate ourselves in this field ?

The answer is quite simple. We have merely taken seriously what Calvin called the *participatio Christi*, making it the ultimate foundation of his whole doctrine of sanctification. The actual event which is an event of revelation in virtue of the enlightening work of the Holy Spirit, and as such sets in motion the conversion of man, is the Christ-event. Jesus Christ is the climax, the superior place, where it is properly and primarily and comprehensively real, where it originally takes place, that God (*vere Deus*) is for man, and man (*vere homo*) is for God. If the conversion of man is the movement which is initiated and maintained from the point where this is primarily and comprehensively real, this is only to say that it has its basis and origin in this climax, in Jesus Christ.

We ask how it may really come about that the divine summons to halt and advance breaks into the life of man, our life. And the answer is simply that when it comes about, then in the power of the Holy Spirit it is in virtue of the one man who is like us and near us as our Brother, but unlike and quite above us as our Lord, seeing that He has not merely received this summons to halt and advance primarily and properly and directly from God, but has properly and immediately and perfectly fulfilled it as a man, accomplishing it in the act of His own life and death. He, and in the strict sense He alone, is the One who hears and does what God summons us to do with His call to halt and advance.

We ask where and when there has taken place, takes place and will take place, as an actual event, this movement of man in the totality and with the radical dispute in which the old man dies and the new arises, this liberation by God's free grace. And the answer is simply that in the strict sense it is an actual event only in Him, in His life, in His obedience as the true Son of God and true Son of Man. In Him it is an event which is effective and valid for many in the power of the truth of the Holy Spirit. But properly it is an event only in Him.

We ask who is the man of whom we have spoken continually as one who is engaged in conversion. And the answer is simply that in the true sense it is He alone. It is not He without those to whom He is revealed as such in the power of the Holy Spirit. It is He as their Head. But it is He, and He alone, as the origin and basis of the conversion of the many.

Let us be honest. If we relate to ourselves, to you and me, to this or that Christian (even the best), that which is said about the conversion of man in the New Testament, and which we have to say with the New Testament, it will have the inevitable smack of hyperbole and even illusion—and the more so the more we try to introduce it, either by way of analysis or assertion, in the form of statements about the psychico-physical conditions or impulses or experiences of individual Christians or Christians generally, or in the form of general or specialised pictures of the Christian life. What are we with our little conversion, our little repentance and reviving, our little ending and new beginning, our changed lives, whether we experience them in the wilderness, or the cloister, or at the very least at Caux ? How feeble is the relationship, even in the best of cases, between the great categories in which the conversion of man is described in the New Testament and the corresponding event in our own inner and outer life ! How can we say, in relation to our own persons or those of others, that we or these others have come out of darkness into light, that we have passed from death to life, that the old man has died and the new is risen, that we are in a state of *mortificatio* and *vivificatio*, or merely that we are converted or in the process of being converted ? If all this is to be referred directly to ourselves, are we not condemned to vacillate between a heaven-soaring spiritual optimism and a mortally despairing spiritual pessimism (both perhaps in the astonishingly exaggerated form in which they meet us in the thought of Kohlbrügge), and therefore between legalism under the banner of the one and libertinism under that of the other ?

But everything is simple, true and clear when these statements are referred directly to Jesus Christ, and only indirectly, as fulfilled and effectively realised in Him for us, to ourselves. It is to be noted that they are indirectly, and therefore genuinely, to be referred to us : in virtue of the fact that He is the Head and we the members ; in virtue of our being in and with Him ; in virtue of the fact that by His Holy Spirit He has clothed us with that which properly He alone is and has ; in virtue of the fact that He allows us to have a share in that which belongs to Him. What more do we want ? We should have much less, indeed nothing at all, if we tried to demand and seize more. It is in His conversion that we are engaged. It is in His birth, from above, the mystery and miracle of Christmas, that we are born again. It is in His baptism in Jordan that we are baptised with the Holy Ghost and with fire. It is in His death on the cross that we are dead as old men, and in His resurrection in the garden of Joseph of Arimathea that we are risen as new men. Who of us then, in relation to our own conversion or that of others, can seriously know any other terminus for this event than the day of Golgotha, in which He accomplished in our place and for us all the turning and transforming of the human situation, and as He did so was crowned as the royal man He was, our Lord ? It is because this is the case, because everything is actual and true in the light of this climax, that the awakening to repentance is the power of the Gospel, a liberation, and that it has the force and depth and teleology which are proper to it, and claims man in his totality.

What remains, then, for us ? Jesus Christ remains, and in and with Him everything, in and with Him the whole reality and truth that God is for us and we for God, and therefore the whole power of our conversion. And the knowledge of faith remains, that He is the man in whose existence all this is true, and that the movement fulfilled in Him is therefore really ours. And there then remain the little movements of our own inner and outer life, our hearts and hands, which we have to make and judge modestly and soberly, of which we have not to boast, in which the great critical and positive movement which He has made for us and with us must and will be reflected, but in which we can only attest this (in the measure of seriousness and fidelity which we are given and which we have to exercise). It remains for us to know that in the whole capacity of our Christian existence we are borne by the great movement which He has fulfilled, and which far transcends all the measures of our movements ; and therefore as those who are His to love Him as the One who is ours— always and wholly and exclusively in response to the fact that He has first loved us.

5. THE PRAISE OF WORKS

Works are primarily the acts and fruits of human operation in contrast to the processes and products of organic nature. The term thus refers to history in the strict sense. As man exists as such, he works. His life is a sequence of conscious or unconscious, greater or smaller, important or less important, imposing or negligible works. And where can we define with any certainty or precision even the limits indicated by these distinctions, let alone say that the sequence of his works is ever broken ? " Oh may the soul do good e'en as we slumber ! " To our works there also belong, of course, the things we refrain from doing, with all the consequences involved. The sequence of works in which our lives consist can and will be broken only with our death. In the present context we are speaking of the life, and therefore of the works, of Christians according to our previous statements ; of those who are sanctified in the Holy One, called to His discipleship, and awakened by Him to conversion.

There is a praise of their works—and this will be the theme of our fifth and shorter sub-section. We use the term " praise " in the general sense of affirmation, acknowledgment, approval and applause. In relation to the works of Christians, the praise of these works necessarily refers in some sense to their particular relationship to God, or concretely to Jesus Christ, who as the true Son of God and Son of Man is their Lord and Head, to whom they belong, and by whom they and the works are measured. In this context the " praise " of works can have a twofold meaning. It can mean (1) that God praises them, affirming and acknowledging and approving them ; and it can mean (2) that their works praise God, affirming and acknowledging and approving Him.

For a New Testament illustration of the first sense of " praise " we may think of the conclusion of 1 Cor. 4⁵, where, in relation to the judgment which he also may personally expect at the hands of God, Paul says : τότε ὁ ἔπαινος γενήσεται ἑκάστῳ ἀπὸ τοῦ θεοῦ—" then shall every man have praise of God." An example of the second sense is to be found in Eph. 1¹², where it is said of Christians that they are elected and called and ordained of God εἰς τὸ εἶναι ἡμᾶς εἰς ἔπαινον δόξης αὐτοῦ, " that they should be to the praise of his glory." Both passages envisage only that the Christian with his action and its fruits will either receive praise from God, or be to God's praise. This is the more striking in 1 Cor. 4⁵ because in this verse the context is that of future judgment. It might have been expected that Paul would speak of receiving praise or blame. But it seems to be taken as axiomatic that we have all to expect only praise. And in Eph. 1¹² the possibility is never even considered that the works of Christians might serve the very opposite of the praise of God.

If we are to speak of the praise of works, we have to keep this twofold use of the term constantly before us. The two meanings converge in the fact that the works to which they refer are obviously good works. If they were not good—in a sense still to be fixed—they would not be praised by God, nor praise Him. If He praises them, this includes the fact that He finds pleasure in them as good works. And if they praise Him, this includes the fact that as good works they are adapted and able to do this. We might well have given to this subsection the more usual but hotly debated title " Good Works." We prefer " The Praise of Works " because (in this twofold sense) it at once tells us something definite and even decisive concerning what constitutes the goodness of works : that God can and will and actually does praise them ; and that they for their part can and may and actually do praise Him.

We may begin by saying in a very general way, and without detailed elucidation, that it is obligatory that Christians should do good works in this twofold sense. They cannot be Christians, and belong to Jesus Christ as their Lord and Head, to no purpose. If they are sanctified in Him, and called to His discipleship, and awakened to conversion, and engaged in conversion under His powerful rule, and if they are all these things in their lives and therefore in the sequence of their works, inevitably there will be in their works some element of the praise of God (in this twofold sense), and therefore of goodness. Otherwise the whole event of reconciliation, to the extent that it consists also in the conversion of man to God and therefore in his sanctification, would be quite futile. It would be in vain that the true Son of God became the true and royal man among all others, their living Lord. And we would have to add that the event of reconciliation would be futile even as God's gracious turning to man, even as the justification of man before Him ; and that it would be all for nothing that even as true God Jesus Christ had taken our place and given Himself up for our sins. If there are no human works which are praised by God, and praise Him in return, and are thus good, in what sense can we speak of a real alteration of the human situation effected in the death of Jesus Christ and revealed in the power of His resurrection by the Holy Spirit ? And how can our attestation of it fail to be pointless and empty ?

But we may dismiss this hypothesis. The scriptural testimony to the great acts of God includes the witness to what has come and comes and will come to men in and with these acts of God. And to this clearly attested work there undoubtedly belongs also the existence of men who do in fact do good works (whatever we mean by this) ; who do works in which God takes pleasure, which have therefore a share in His praise and which also serve to praise Him. It is the case according to the Old and New Testament that words are not only required of specific men but spoken by them, that acts are not only demanded but achieved, that attitudes are not only expected but adopted : words and acts and attitudes which God can affirm, which for their part indicate an affirmation of God, and in which the turning of man to God takes place no less than the turning of God to man ; good works which as such are clearly and sharply distinguished from other words and acts and attitudes as bad works.

It is also the case according to the Old and New Testaments that a reward is promised for these works. The concept is eschatological, and we cannot discuss it in this context. We mention it only to emphasise the definiteness with which Scripture counts on the occurrence of good works.

The divine judgment on all men is very sharply formulated in the Bible—that all are sinners (even and especially the saints). The absolute dependence of all on the free grace of God is unconditionally recalled. Yet while this is the case, what man does and does not do is never described, either in a recognition of the universal sinfulness of man or an acknowledgment of the sovereign mercy of God, as a night which makes all things dark. Just because God alone is righteous and holy, not remotely but in His acts among and to men, there are also righteous and unrighteous, holy and unholy men, goodness and evil, good works and bad, in the life of each individual man (including the holy and righteous). We have dealt with the evil works of men in the previous section. Our present concern is with their sanctification. We are thus concerned with the fact that there are also good works— good because they are praised by God and done to His praise. If we are to accept the witness of Scripture, we cannot ignore this, let alone deny it. Scripture not only trusts the God of the covenant, Jesus Christ and the Holy Spirit, that this will be the case. It attests it as a reality within its witness to God the Father, Son and Holy Spirit and His works. This must be our starting-point.

In all that we say (following the example of the Epistle of James) we presuppose the Pauline and Reformation doctrine of justification by faith alone without the works of the Law, as already understood and developed in *C.D.*, IV, 1, § 61. This gives rise to certain delimitations which we have consciously to bear in mind.

No works, however good (even the best), have the power to justify before God the man who does them ; to reinstate him in the right to exist before Him which he has forfeited, and continually forfeits, as a sinner ; to make him a child of God ; to earn for him the promise of eternal life. Works which we may try to do with this intention and claim are as such works of an unbroken pride, and are not therefore good works but bad. Man can be righteous before God, the child of God and heir of eternal life, only by the pardon which he can grasp in faith alone and not in any work, and which is that of the grace of the God active and revealed in Jesus Christ—a grace which consists in the unmerited forgiveness of sins.

It thus follows that there is no man—even the doer of good (or the best) works, even the most saintly—who does not stand in lifelong need of the forgiveness of sins and therefore of that pardon, and is not referred wholly and utterly to the faith which grasps that pardon. " The truth is that we are beggars " (Luther).

It follows further that because man exists in the sequence of his works, each of his works, as well as he himself, stands in need, as the work of a sinner, of justification, and therefore of forgiveness, and therefore of the unmerited recognition of God. His boast, as the man who does it, is grounded only in the free grace of God turned to Him—a grace which can be related only in faith to man and his works and acts and the fruits of his acts. Any other glory ascribed to himself or his works immediately disqualifies the latter as bad works, even though they may be the best.

Finally, since it is only in faith and not by direct perception or appropriation that we can seize our righteousness and that of our works (as the forgiveness of our sins, even of those which we commit in the best of our works), the final word concerning our right and wrong, and that of our works, is reserved for the universal and definitive revelation of the judgment of God—a revelation which we now await but in which we do not yet participate. " For we must all appear before the judgment seat of Christ ; that every one may receive the things done in his body, according to that he hath done, whether it be good or bad " (2 Cor. 5^{10}). Our only confidence and peace in face of this reservation is " that I expect the Judge who has exposed Himself for me to the judgment of God, and taken away all the curse from me " (*Heid. Cat. Qu.* 52). Yet we walk by faith, not by sight, even in respect of our certain knowledge of the pardoning sentence of this Judge.

All this is behind us as we now go on to speak of good works. This does not mean that it is forgotten or set aside. On the contrary, it is the frontier which we cannot cross again. It is the ground which we must always have beneath us if we are to read securely. Yet it is a frontier from which we may now move away, so that it need not cramp or confuse us. It is the ground on which we may securely advance. Our question does not relate to good works in general but to the good works of the Christian, and therefore to works which can be seriously called good on the presupposition of justification by faith alone. As a special form of the question of the sanctification of man, this question has to be recognised in its own right, and put and answered, in view of the fact that Scripture so blatantly counts on the existence of good works.

It is a step forward if we note that in the Bible the concept of work or works is applied in the first instance, and decisively for all that follows, to the acts of God and their consequences. Primarily it is God who is at work. And this shows us what is meant by the fact that man is also at work. But the works of God are good. It is said primarily and properly of God Himself that " He saw everything that He had made, and, behold, it was very good " (Gen. 1^{31}). And primarily and properly it is His works which praise their Master. If there are human works of which this can be said, we have to seek them in the context of the work or works of God.

That this is no mere surmise is proved by the fact that according to the witness of Scripture the work of God stands in a primary and basic relationship to man. It is, of course, a work which embraces all creation, heaven and earth and all that therein is. But it binds it together. It directs it to a specific goal—His covenant with man, His own glory in this covenant and the salvation of man. It is His work in the history of this covenant, in which the history of the whole cosmos participates, and which constitutes the meaning and true content of the history of the whole cosmos. As creation, according to Gen. 1, is the outward basis of this covenant, and this covenant the inward basis of creation, there begins at once in and with creation the history of this covenant, and therefore the proper work of God to which all His other works are subordinate. This history, and therefore the proper work of God, emerges with the election, calling, preservation and overruling of the people Israel, in which, according to the witness of the Old Testament, there is heralded the actualisation of the glory of God and the salvation of man. It attains its goal in the fact that God Himself becomes man and as such performs that which is promised, actualising His own glory and man's salvation. That this has taken place in Jesus Christ, that all human history and that of the whole cosmos can only hasten to the direct and universal and definitive revelation of this completed work of God, is what the community which has derived from Israel in its Lord and Head now has to proclaim, according to the witness of the New Testament, in the last time which is still left to itself and the world. This happening in its totality, beginning with creation, proceeding by way of the reconciliation resolved and accomplished in Jesus Christ, and culminating in the redemption awaited with its manifestation ; this history of the covenant is the work of God which all His other works serve and to which they are subordinate. It is the good work of God. He proves Himself to be good by nature, and therefore the source and norm of all goodness, by the fact that this is His work and therefore His will. It is the will of His goodness which is here at work. God ordains that in all His holiness, righteousness and wisdom, in all His omnipresence, omnipotence and glory, He Himself should be active in this work which has man as its aim and goal. He did not need to do so. He does not do it for Himself. He gives Himself up to it. In this work He is good in Himself only as He is good to man, actualising His own glory only with man's salvation. He has to do with man in this work. He has turned wholly to man. He has even given Himself up to him. In a relentless compromising of His own case, He has addressed Himself wholly to the cause of man.

We have first to consider again the work, the act and acts of God as the Lord of His covenant with man ; and Jesus Christ as the One who completes this work. " Come, behold the works of the Lord, what astounding things he hath done in the earth " (Ps. 46⁸). Or, as a summons to the whole earth : " Come and see the works of God : he is terrible in his doing toward the children of men " (Ps. 66⁵). The complaint lodged against the careless in Jerusalem (Is. 5¹²) is that " they regard not the work of the Lord, neither consider the operation of his hands." There can, of course, be no question, as we are told in Eccles. 8¹⁶⁻¹⁷, of fathoming and understanding and explaining this work in its totality, in relation to everything that takes place under the sun by day or by night. But it may be known—it makes itself known—at its heart and centre, as the history of the covenant of grace. " The works of his hand are verity and judgment ; all his commandments are sure. They stand fast for ever and ever, and are done in truth and uprightness. He sent redemption unto his people : he hath commanded his covenant for ever : holy and reverend is his name " (Ps. 111⁷ᶠ·). It is of this heart and centre of God's work, and therefore of the true and proper work of God, that Jesus speaks according to the Johannine saying (Jn. 5¹⁷) : " My Father worketh hitherto, and I work," doing the work of my Father (Jn. 10³⁷), and He Himself working as He dwells in me (Jn. 14¹⁰). The meat of Jesus—His very life—is to do the will of Him that sent Him, " and to finish his work " (Jn. 4³⁴). According to Jn. 17⁴ He had already finished it, thus glorifying on earth the One who sent Him. The divine work in question is the actualisation of the covenant between God and man, the achievement of reconciliation, as heralded in Israel and proclaimed by the community. We must start with this as the completed good work of God if we are to see what is the possibility and actuality of good works on the part of man.

If there are good works on the part of man—and the Bible says that there are—we can state (without defining the matter more closely) that it is only in relation to this good work of God. What man does and achieves is thus in some sense bright and powerful in the light and power of what God does and achieves. The distinction of a human work is to declare the occurrence of the good work of God. A human work can do this, because God in His work always has to do with men and what He does does not take place at a distance from men, but among them. From first to last it is God's history with men and among them. Why, then, should it not be declared and, as it were, reflected in a human work ? The works of the man Jesus show that human works are capable of doing this. The inner quality of man, not only by man's judgment but God's, is another question the answer to which is not decisive for the present question whether there can be a good human work which declares the good work of God. The man Jesus did the good works of His Father as He lived and died in our stead, in the place of sinners, in the flesh, in our character. We conclude that even a sinful man in his sinful work—and we are all sinners and all our works are sinful—may declare the good work of God, and therefore, even as a sinner and in the course of sinning, do a good work.

" I shall not die, but live, and declare the works of the Lord. The Lord hath chastened me sore : but he hath not given me over unto death " (Ps. 118¹⁷ᶠ·). The people are chastened—the reference seems to be to Israel chastened for its sins—but even as such they are rescued from the death they have deserved, and may live, in order that they may proclaim the works of the Lord. The Lord is their strength and song, and has become their salvation, they have been told (v. 14). And so they are those who according to Ps. 107³¹ " praise the Lord for his goodness, and for his wonderful works to the children of men " ; who have seen His wonders in the deep and whose soul melted because of trouble : " They reel to and fro, and stagger like a drunken man, and are at their wits' end " (v. 24 f.). And so we may but should not be surprised that after Paul has had to bring so many warnings and accusations against the Corinthians he can finally address to them the supremely natural summons : " Therefore, my beloved brethren, be ye stedfast, unmovable, always abounding in the work of the Lord " (1 Cor. 15⁵⁸) ; and then again : " Watch ye, stand fast in the faith, quit you like men, be strong " (16¹³). Even in relation to the Corinthians the ground of the work of the Lord and faith in it is obviously assumed to be strong enough to bear this curious people, so that Paul has only to summon them to stand fast on it and they will be a strong and manly people always abounding in God's work. There is absolutely no question of any work of their own, but only of what the ἔργον τοῦ κυρίου may do concerning them, and of their own capacity for it as granted by this work. We may appeal in elucidation to Tit. 2¹⁴, where it is said of Jesus Christ that He gave Himself for us to purify for Himself a people for His own possession, zealous of good works. Whatever else it may mean for a people, the completed work of the Lord can cleanse it, thus making it a people which in spite of its sin may be used in His service.

It is evident that there can be no question of any meritoriousness of works, or of any glory in their achievement which can either be claimed by or ascribed to the one who performs them. This is equally the case even when we are dealing with the less sinful and to that extent better works of someone who is not so notoriously a sinner. Works can be good only as they declare what God has done and accomplished—the goodness in which He has turned to man and given Himself for him. That works are capable of this declaration does not alter the fact that they are the sinful works of great or little sinners. It is with such men and their works that God has to do in His good work. If He is good to them, why should they not be able to declare His goodness as the men they are ?—not, of course, with a capacity that they have brought, but because there is something to declare, i.e., because the good work of God takes place, God being good to men (to these men who with their corresponding works are not good), turning to them and interposing and offering Himself up for them. It is only in this context and relationship that there can be, and are, good works on the part of men. All the works which are called good and described as good in the Bible take place in this context. Their goodness comes down from above into the human depths. It is imparted to them from above. And in the human depths it can only magnify the majesty of God to which it originally and properly belongs.

Only that which comes down from above, from the divine work of the fulfilled covenant, of completed reconciliation, into the human depths, is according to Jas. 1¹⁷ " a good and perfect gift." There can be no good human work unless it has this divine work as its basis and source. Bad works—those which Eph. 5¹¹ calls " unfruitful " and Heb. 6¹ and 9¹⁴ " dead " (which may include a dead faith, Jas. 2¹⁷f.)—are simply works which do not have this divine work as their basis and origin. They are blind mirrors which do not reflect or declare the work of God. They do not in fact take place, as they might, in this context and relationship. Conversely, the good action demanded by God in the Law—action on the way continually proposed to Israel especially in the Book of Deuteronomy

—is simply action which takes place in relationship to the work of Yahweh and corresponds to the grace of His covenant. Without this, and without recognising it, Israel could not even choose let alone perform this action. If it does choose and perform it, if it does works which are described as good and demanded by the Law, it does not do anything extraordinary but simply declares in its own works the work of the God who is gracious to it, confessing that it is His work and possession : " It is he that hath made us, and not we ourselves ; we are his people, and the sheep of his pasture" (Ps. 100³). Is there any trace here of a meritoriousness of its action ? What can this people earn that has not been given already as a work of the hands of God ? Is there any trace of glory in achievement ? How can they glory when they do only the good works which are expected and with which they can only declare that which they are by the goodness of God ? " When ye shall have done all those things which are commanded you, say, We are unprofitable servants : we have done that which was our duty to do " (Lk. 17¹⁰). Why is the Law of God so glorious as described in Ps. 119 ? Certainly not because it shows Israel, and sets in its hand, an instrument to make God gracious, and to assure itself by its own corresponding achievements of His faithfulness and assistance. The glory of the Law is that it gives Israel a direction which it gladly hears and obeys because, as it is continually given, it is continually aware that the power and mercy of God are already present, and that it knows already, and increasingly, His faithfulness and assistance. Where the will and command of God are not understood as a demonstration of His free goodness and favour to man, but as a demand the fulfilment of which is the condition on which God's goodness and favour will be addressed to Him, or on which he may direct them to himself ; where, then, man believes that he must earn merit and achieve self-glory in his relationship with God, there can be no question of true obedience or good works. He does not do that which he ought to do. Everything that he does is perverted from the very first. And according to the witness of the Old Testament it was the sin of Israel, as of all nations, not to recognise the grace of God, and therefore not to be capable of obedience, but only of bad, unfruitful and dead works. It is not insignificant that in these circumstances it continually turned to the gods of the surrounding nations. Only for very brief periods was Israel grateful to God, and therefore self-evidently faithful and promptly obedient. For the most part it was only in the life and words and works of individuals, of the prophetic men of the remnant, that the relationship between divine and human goodness was kept alive and maintained as a witness to the rest of the people as they continually fell into fresh transgression. In their protest against Israel's transgression they merely announced the fulfilment of the good work of God, and therefore the actualisation of good human works, which had been from the very first the goal of Yahweh's covenant with Israel. The witness of the New Testament proclaims the fulfilment of the good work of God and the actualisation of good human works as the message concerning Jesus Christ and the summons to faith in Him. It regards Himself, and faith in Him, as the right way which has already been chosen for us men ; the way on which we already find ourselves in Him : " For by grace are ye saved through faith ; and that not of yourselves ; it is the gift of God ; not of works lest any man should boast. For we are his workmanship (ποίημα), created (κτισθέντες) in Christ Jesus unto good works, which God hath before ordained that we should walk in them " (Eph. 2⁸ᶠ·).

We have now established that it is the good work of God which alone makes possible the good works of man. But the good work of God itself assumes always a special form as good works are done by man, and man's work declares the good work of God. What is meant by " declare " but to participate in the annunciation of the history of the covenant in the New Testament or its proclamation in the New, and, therefore, because this history is the work of God, in the attestation of this work? But even if our work has a part only in its attestation, in so far as this is possible for a human work it has a part in the divine work itself. It takes place in its service. And it is as it is done in its service that it is a good work. It is not self-evident that a man should really stand in the service of the good work of God, or that his own work should really be done in this service. It is not at all the case that all the works of all men are the work of God simply because it is done among them, and that they thus declare it and take place in its service and are therefore good works. Since all men are sinners and their works sinful, is it not more reasonable to suppose that there can never be any declaration of the work of God by human works, that it cannot be said of any human work that it takes place in the service of God's work and therefore as a good work? We do not need to be particularly pessimistic to come to this melancholy conclusion. We might say that it is shaped by the common rule which is broken when good works do in fact take place. But the rule is not broken from below by better sinners and their less sinful works. Even the best man cannot place himself and his work in the service of the work of God, or make his work a declaration of God's work and therefore a good work. When this takes place, it is obviously because God's own work assumes a special form. This work itself— and it is of this that the Old and New Testaments speak when·they speak of good human works—takes place in a very special way to particular men, declaring and indicating and attesting and making itself known to them, and in so doing impressing them into its service, empowering them for it, giving them a willingness and readiness to take part themselves in its declaration. We can put it in this way. The work of God which has taken place *for* them as for all men also takes place *in* them in the form of this illumination, with the result that as the men they are they have a share in it—only as its witnesses, but as such a real share. The history of the covenant, whose acting Subject is God, now takes place in its relationship to them in such a way that their personal history, whose subjects they themselves are, can no longer be alien or neutral in its relationship to it, but necessarily takes place in actual correspondence with it. To the extent that this is the case, they and their works are declarations of the work of God, having a part both in the annunciation of Jesus Christ in the Old Testament and His proclamation in the New, and thus being good works. It is to be noted that the men in relationship to whom the good work of God has this particular form are sinners like the rest— possibly to a less degree, possibly to a greater, but still sinners. They are not differentiated from others by the fact that they are not transgressors in the judgment of God, or that even their good works are not full of transgression. They are differentiated only (but genuinely) by the fact—and here we return to the controlling concepts of the previous sub-sections—that they are sanctified in and by the Holy One ; that they are called to His discipleship ; that they are awakened to conversion by His Holy Spirit ; and that they are engaged in conversion. To the extent that they are this, and exist as such, their works are taken into service by God and are good works, quite irrespective of what they might be apart from this relationship in the eyes of men and above all in the eyes of God, and quite irrespective of the fact that even as good works they are full of transgression. What these men do as those who are in Jesus Christ, and in love to Him, and correspondence with the work of God, is well done.

According to the Old and New Testaments it is an absolutely new and astounding fact that a man may be a co-worker (συνεργός) with God (1 Cor. 3⁹), and that his works, as an attestation of the work of God, may stand under the promise of being well done and therefore good works. Of none of us is this the case by nature. And none of us can take it upon himself. If it is true of us, it is true only on the basis of a special attitude of God within the covenant between Himself and man. It is true only as we are elected by God for His service, and called out to the side of God, quite apart from any fitness or value of our own. From us as such good works are expected. As such we can and should and may and will do them. We ourselves ! For our calling is to obedience, to our own free action as the men we are. Our good works can and should and may and will be our very own. Hence the saying of Jesus to His disciples in Mt. 5¹⁶ᶠ. : " Let your light so shine before men that they may see your good works, and glorify your Father which is in heaven." But the fact that they have or are this light—" ye are the light of the world," " a city that is set on a hill," the candle which is not " put under a bushel, but on a candlestick "—is not something that they have snatched or resolved of themselves, but something that they have become in virtue of His calling. It is in the power of this calling that their works are good works even as their own. It is as Yahweh stretches out His hand, and touches a man's lips, and puts His words in his mouth, and sets him here and now over the nations and kingdoms, that already in the Old Testament (Jer. 1⁹ᶠ.) the prophet becomes the man he is—the one whom Yahweh has chosen for this work even before he was fashioned in the womb (Jer. 1⁵). And it is in exactly the same way that the New Testament apostle (Gal. 1¹⁵) understands his existence and his freedom to speak and work. The people of God works out its salvation in a certain willing and doing, but it does so because God is the One who works (ὁ ἐνεργῶν) His own willing and doing (Phil. 2¹²ᶠ.). Paul speaks, but he "will not dare to speak of any of the things that Christ has not wrought by him to make the Gentiles obedient, by word and deed " (Rom. 15¹⁸). He hastens to apprehend (Phil. 3¹²), but he does so only as he is already apprehended by Christ. He works and fights according to His working (ἐνέργεια) which works in him mightily (Col. 1²⁹). It is true also of other believers that the word spoken to them " worketh effectually " in them (1 Thess. 2¹³). " What hast thou that thou didst not receive ? " (1 Cor. 4⁷). Where men are active in the community as awakened and endowed by the Spirit, it is God "which worketh all in all " (1 Cor. 12⁶). And not in spite of this fact, but because of it, they are all engaged in the full and manifold activity which can only praise Him, and which can be good only as it declares His work. In all this God is the δυνάμενος, the One who empowers (Eph. 3²⁰). He is this in His power which works in us (δύναμις ἐνεργουμένη ἐν ἡμῖν) impelling us to action. This power which works in us far exceeds anything that we can ask or think. How, then, can we fail to trust it, or trust it only to a limited degree, in our own action ?

When we do trust it we can only affirm : " Unto *him* be glory in the church and in Christ Jesus." A good work as Scripture understands it is one which is set in motion by Him, which finds itself in this motion, and which understands and demonstrates that this is the case.

We can now repeat with greater emphasis our previous statement that it is in the particular goodness of the work of God that a man may participate with his own good works. It is God's free gift if he finds that he and his life-history are set in this distinctive relationship with the history of the covenant, and impressed into the service of the work of God and used to declare it. And in each individual instance of working it is again God's free gift if His work is a real declaration of God's work, and in the performance of it he may genuinely share in the annunciation or proclamation of Jesus Christ. As he cannot make himself one of the particular men of whom this is true, he cannot assume that any specific work really takes place in this correspondence, in the light and power of the divine work, and therefore that it is well done. He can only believe in the grace of God encountering and and revealed to him. Even when he is supremely enlightened and filled and impelled by it, he can only be thankful that—as it is not hidden but revealed—it has come to him in this particular way. He can only pray that God will not hide His face or let him fall, as he must recognise each passing moment that he has deserved a hundred times. He can only dare to make use of the freedom given ; to keep before him, in all that he does, the fact that both in the totality and in specific works he may and must be thankful. He will then act calmly and resolutely and vigorously, but always knowing that he must lay himself and what he wills and does and achieves wholly in the hand of the God who has so graciously chosen and called him to participate in His work. He will constantly commend it to Him, that He may forgive that in which it is sinful, that He may receive it like himself, that He may sanctify it, that He may use it and order it, that He may give it the character of a service rendered and acceptable to Himself—which is something that can never be given by the man who performs it. None of the true saints of God can ever imagine that in his works he is really doing something outstanding in the sense of putting God under an obligation or earning His grace and favour. If he succeeds in restraining this foolish idea for a short time, or even inures himself to some extent against falling into it again, this is a sure criterion—though not a guarantee—that what he does is well done. He cannot create any such guarantee by his own humility of disposition in what he does. It can only be given by the God who elects and calls him, and grasped in faith. But in faith he can and may and will grasp it. And by the faith in which he does this, and the divine guarantee which he grasps in faith, there will be created the radical claimlessness, but also the calm and resolution and vigour, the free humour, which distinguish the work that is well done, the good work, fairly distinctly if not quite unequivocally from others. And he will do this work confidently. It will even be legitimate and possible for him to derive confidence, and the assurance of his freedom and therefore his holiness, from the fact that he lives cheerfully and gaily strides to work as one whom God has endowed with freedom.

He does it in the same way as a good tree (to use a favourite New Testament comparison) produces and bears good fruit. He does it as the work (Ac. 26[20]) or fruit (Mt. 3[8]) of his conversion, corresponding to its occurrence. He does it as the work of love (Heb. 6[10]) or faith (1 Thess. 1[3]; 2 Thess. 1[11]). In Jn. 6[28f.] we have the extremely succinct answer of Jesus to those who asked Him: " What shall we do, that we might work the works of God (ἐργαζώμεθα τὰ ἔργα τοῦ θεοῦ) ? " " This is the work of God, that ye believe on him whom he hath sent." Is there not included in this all human work in its relationship to the work of God ? Similarly, there has always rightly been derived from the well-known negative formula of Rom. 14[23] : " For whatsoever is not of faith is sin," the positive truth that what is of faith, and is the work of faith, is well done. But is it the work of faith ? The fact that in the doing of good works we have to do with works of conversion, love and faith makes it clear that even in detail the doing of good works is not something which is subject to the caprice or control of man (even of the man who stands in sanctification) ; that the freedom for it has to be continually given even in detail. It is not the case, then, that God has begun something in and with him which he himself has now the authority and power to continue and complete. " He which hath begun a good work in you will perform it (ἐπιτελέσει) until the day of Jesus Christ " (Phil. 1[16]). God is powerful enough (2 Cor. 9[8]) to pour out the fulness of His grace on His own " that ye, always having all sufficiency (lit. autarchy) in all things, may abound to every good work." It is God, and He alone, who has the power to give them the freedom to do such works of themselves. As it is given by Him, it will constantly be expected and hoped and asked of Him. Paul presupposes in 2 Thess. 1[11] that in the community we can count on the occurrence of the ἔργον πίστεως, and therefore, as we have seen, on an εὐδοκία ἀγαθωσύνης (on the divine good-pleasure in the good which takes place). Yet this does not prevent but seems to cause him to pray for the fulfilment of this ἀγαθωσύνη and ἔργον—as though it were a vessel which had still to be filled—and therefore for the glorifying of the name of Jesus Christ in the community. According to 2 Thess. 2[17], the community needs to be " stablished in every good word and work." Prayer is also made that it should " be fruitful in every good work " (Col. 1[10]) and " made perfect in every good work " (Heb. 13[21]). For the necessary perfecting of the saints Christ has instituted apostles, prophets, evangelists, pastors and teachers (Eph. 4[11f.]). And according to 2 Tim. 3[16f.] the saving power of the Scripture inspired by God is to be found in the fact that it sets the man of God in the right frame of mind (ἵνα ἄρτιος ᾖ) in which to be " throughly furnished unto all good works."

If in all good works it is a matter of their participation in the good work of God, to which certain men are selected and brought by God Himself, and for which they are empowered by Him in specific actions, it necessarily follows that they are distinguished from all other human works by the fact that they are done as ordered and commanded by God, or to put it in another way, in the freedom given by God. In conjunction with the work of God, and in the service of its declaration, their works have a particular function. In the exercise of this function this particular man can and must and may and will on this particular occasion say this or do that or take up this particular attitude. If he recognises and fulfils this function, his work is a good work. His speech and action and attitude are not according to his own inclination or desire or plan or caprice but according to the direction given to him and received by him. He hears this. And he obeys it, not mechanically impelled from without, but in the freedom which is given him ; yet in this freedom and not another. In any other freedom he would really be a captive. He serves, not to his humiliation and shame, but to his exaltation and honour ; yet only in the glory and dignity for which he is ordained as a participant in the work of God, and not therefore in any which he might fashion for himself (to his own true shame and humiliation) by serving himself or the opinion and plans of men or the dark forces of the cosmos and history. He is integrated into the communion of saints. With a particular place and commission he accompanies the people of God, the community. At his own place and time he is absolutely indispensable and responsible for the whole of its history. But he is this as a brother among brethren. And in this way he genuinely comes to himself and lives by his own faith. By this integration it may be recognised, and by integration in the doing of a particular work he himself may be assured, that all is well with his obedience and service and therefore his freedom ; that the direction which he hears is not secretly the voice of his own inclination or desire or plan or caprice. He will consider how the law and command and direction of God is received by others at other times and places. He will note the multiplicity which has characterised its declaration and reception in the history of the people of God as a whole. Thus, in order that he may hear the direction for himself here and now—the direction of God, and not that either of human tradition or his own heart or head—and to obey and serve this direction and not that of a collective or individual daemon, he will also listen to his brethren, and listen together with all or many of them, and then and on this basis exercise himself to obey. This is not because he does not trust the participation in the work of God granted to him, but because he knows that for all the particularity with which it applies to him it is granted to him only in his togetherness with them, as one of the fellowship of the saints. He will then go his own way all the more certain of his commission and all the more convinced of his freedom.

In this sense, and on all these presuppositions, we must say of man's sanctification that it already takes place here and now in works which are really good, i.e., which are praised by God and praise Him. We have had to consider rather more precisely, in the light of scriptural teaching, the way in which this happens (and does not happen). But the fact that it happens is something that we can deny only at the expense of questioning the whole divine act of atonement and revelation and concealing a main aspect of the biblical witness, with serious effects upon all other aspects.

A single illustration will be enough to prove this. We surely cannot evade what is stated in the great passage Heb. 11. We need not develop this as a whole. It is sufficient to note that the chapter is dealing with faith as the confidence of things hoped for, the certainty of things not seen. But in the depiction of this faith we have to do at every point with human acts and attitudes—those of Abel and Enoch and Noah and Abraham and Isaac and Jacob and Moses and Rahab the harlot and others. Of all these it is said (v. 13) that " they died in faith, not having received the promises, but having seen them afar off, and were persuaded of them, and embraced them, and confessed that they were strangers and pilgrims on the earth." But it is also stated of them that—each in his own particular relationship to the great acts of God, and united to a great people by this common relationship—they worked actively and passively in obedience. Their acts are of great consequence in the context of that history, and they are thus depicted in rather extravagant terms. They " subdued kingdoms, wrought righteousness, obtained promises, stopped the mouths of lions, quenched the violence of fire, escaped the edge of the sword, out of weakness were made strong, turned to flight the armies of the aliens," some being praised for exploits which belong very characteristically to the Old Testament (v. 33 f.), others for their suffering and constancy in the most violent persecution (v. 35 f.). It is said of them—with reference to their faith, but to the works of their faith —that the world was not worthy of them (v. 38). The purpose behind this depiction emerges clearly in 12[1f.] The New Testament community is as it were surrounded on all sides, and it is pledged and claimed—as by one mighty declaration and summons—by the existence and acts of these believers of God's former people. It cannot escape them. " Therefore, seeing we also are compassed about with so great a cloud of witnesses, let us lay aside every weight, and the sin that doth so easily beset us, and let us run with patience the race that is set before us, looking unto Jesus the author and finisher of our faith." It is Jesus who is obviously attested by this great cloud of witnesses. Being the end (τέλος) of the work of God, He is also the end of the Law of God (Rom. 10[4]). All these men with their works bore witness to Him ; and it is to Him that Christians can and should and may and will bear witness with their works— their good works.

We conclude by saying that in addition to many bad there are also good thoughts and words and works. God in the doing of His work sees to it that this is the case. None of those to whom the work of God is revealed—no Christian—will doubt or contest this. He has no excuse, therefore, if his own work is not a good work. He will not try to hide the fact that he too, and he particularly, is elected and called and empowered to do good works. In accordance with his election and calling and empowering, he will do them as works of faith, conversion and love. They will certainly not praise himself or the Christian as the one who does them. But they will have the praise of God, and will praise Him. God gives it to His own that in all their sloth and corruption and disintegration they may and will do such works.

He sees to it that among His people (known only to Himself) there are genuine good works performed by its members. We may mention a few examples drawn from our own observation (and well below the level of Heb. 11). There is the good assistance which one gives another. There is the good co-operation between few or many. There are good meetings and partings. There is the good attempting of big things and the good fulfilment of small. There is good conduct in difficult and testing conditions. There are good achievements in family and social life. There is the good upholding of the old and the good establishment of the new. There is good speaking and silence ; good laughter and weeping ; good work and repose ; good seeking and finding. There are also good political resolves and decisions. There is good Christian profession. There is also good prayer, good hearing and reading and study, and sometimes good preaching— and all the other concrete things we might mention. In all these things, of course, it is not of him that willeth and runneth, but of God that sheweth mercy (Rom. 9[16]). But there is no point in trying to avoid the fact—we can do so only in unbelief—that these things do exist because God gives them, and in His mercy will continually give them. There is no time when the Christian should not count seriously on the fact that God gives them with the superfluity to which there are so many allusions in the epistles. The sanctification of man decidedly consists also in the fact that God does give them, not merely in general but individually, and not magically or mechanically or when he is asleep, but for him to do. The saints of God receive and do them.

We will bring the discussion to a close by citing two questions and answers from the *Heidelberg Catechism* which are highly relevant in the present context.

Qu. 86. As we are redeemed from our plight by grace through Christ without any merits of our own, why should we do good works ? *Answer*—Because Christ, having bought us by His blood, has also renewed us by His Holy Spirit, that we should show ourselves grateful to God for His benefits with our whole lives, and that He should be magnified through us. Also in order that we may have assurance of our faith from its fruits, and win our neighbours to Christ by our godly conversation.

And *Qu.* 91. But what are good works ? *Answer*—Only those which of a true faith take place according to the Law of God and to His glory, and are not grounded in our own opinion or the evaluation of men.

6. THE DIGNITY OF THE CROSS

The cross—we have left to the last this indispensable element in any Christian doctrine of sanctification. It ought to be given this place (1) because it marks the limit of sanctification as the raising up of slothful man in the power of the resurrection of Jesus Christ—the point at which this event reaches out beyond itself to the second coming of Jesus Christ, the resurrection of the flesh and the last judgment, when the saints will be revealed as such, the contradiction will be ended between what they still are and what they are already, and they will enter into the eternal life, the light, to which as the people of God they are now moving with the whole cosmos. It ought also to be given this place (2) because under all the aspects so far considered—as *participatio Christi*, the call to discipleship, awakening to conversion and the praise of works—it is with reference to the cross that man's sanctification is seen to be his movement to that goal, and therefore set in the light of the great Christian hope.

It is at the corresponding place that the cross of the Christian is introduced in Calvin (*Instit*. III, 8) and A. de Quervain (*Die Heiligung*, I, 1942, pp. 151–221). D. Bonhoeffer has given it emphasis by speaking of it in the basic sections of *The Cost of Discipleship* already mentioned. On the other hand, it is striking that in Kohlbrügge's doctrine of sanctification (at any rate as presented by W. Kreck) the cross, while it is not ignored or uninfluential, is not given any very prominent position or role.

We refer to the cross which everyone who is sanctified in Jesus Christ, and therefore every Christian, has to bear as such, the people of God in the world being ordained to bear it. It is clear that this cross stands in the closest relationship to that of Jesus Christ Himself. The cross is the most concrete form of the fellowship between Christ and the Christian. As the bearing of the cross was and is for Jesus Christ His coronation as the one Son of Man, the royal man, so for the Christian the cross which he has to suffer is his investiture with the distinction, glory and dignity proper to him as a Christian. And this parallel has its basis in a material, historical connexion. Without the cross of Christ the Master there is no cross of the disciples, Christians. It is by the fact that He bore and suffered His cross that they are sanctified and called to discipleship and set in conversion and freed for the doing of good works. And it is by the same fact that they also come to bear and suffer their cross. It is on the basis of His exaltation in His death on the cross as the One who was rejected in our place that there takes place their elevation with its limit and goal in the fact that they too come to bear and suffer their cross.

According to all the synoptic accounts (Mk. 8[34f.] and par.) the declaration of Jesus that those who would be His disciples must deny themselves and take up the cross comes immediately after the Messianic confession of Peter and the first annunciation of the passion. Bonhoeffer is right when he lays his finger on the fact that in this annunciation as we have it in Mk. 8[31] and Lk. 9[22] express mention is made of His rejection by the elders and high-priests and scribes. In the crucifixion of Jesus Christ we have to do with the particular suffering of One who is rejected and destroyed and shamed by men—and not just by any men, but by the spiritual leaders of the people of God. It is quite obvious and understandable that the disciple who had just recognised and confessed Jesus to be the Messiah should take offence at this prophecy. But his confession naturally implied his willingness to follow Jesus. And it received the answer—his protest being brushed aside by the stern saying of Jesus—that he and all those who make this profession and share this willingness, if they are to be disciples of the Rejected and Crucified, must take up their own cross and therefore in their own place enter into the passion of Jesus, the shameful passion of One who is despised and rejected.

We must be clear at the very outset that the connexion between the cross of Jesus Christ and that of the Christian, for all its direct necessity, is not a direct but only an indirect connexion. Those who have to take up their cross only follow Him in this, although finally they do follow Him in this too. In the words of 1 Pet. 2[21], they follow in His steps. They do not accompany Him in an equality of their cross with His. And they certainly do not precede Him in the sense that His cross acquires reality and significance only as they take up their cross. Behind this view there stands the ancient mystical notion that it is Christ's own cross that Christians have to take up and carry. This notion is quite false.

Ἀράτω τὸν σταυρὸν αὐτοῦ is what is said in Mk. 8³⁴ and par., and the continuation is that the disciple must lose τὴν ψυχὴν αὐτοῦ (to save it). He is to do it ἕνεκεν ἐμοῦ, in the sense that he thus proves and confesses himself to be My disciple. But it is his own life, just as it is himself (ἑαυτόν) that he has to deny in the preceding verse. What Simon of Cyrene did (Mk. 15²¹ and par.), he did not do at the bidding of Jesus but under the compulsion of those who led Jesus away to be crucified. And it was Jesus Himself, not Simon, who was crucified. He gave up His own life (Mk. 10⁴⁵), not that of Simon.

The cross of Jesus is His own cross, carried and suffered *for* many, but *by* Him alone and not by many, let alone by all and sundry. He suffers this rejection not merely as a rejection by men but, fulfilled by men, as a rejection by God—the rejection which all others deserved and ought to have suffered, but which He bore in order that it should no more fall on them. Their cross does not mean that they have still to suffer God's rejection. This has been suffered already by Him (as their rejection). It can no longer be borne by them. Similarly the exaltation accomplished in His crucifixion and therefore in the suffering of that rejection is His and not that of His disciples or the world above which He was exalted as the Lord in His death. To His exaltation there corresponds that of His elect and called, the elevation which now comes to Christians and is promised to all men, their awakening from the mortal sleep of the slothfulness of sin. And we have seen already that this upraising of man has its basis and thrust in Him, in His exaltation to the right hand of the Father as effected in His death; that it becomes and is a fact wholly and utterly in virtue of this exaltation. Yet their elevation is not identical with His exaltation. It is only thanks to His exaltation, and in the strength of it, that it takes place at all. The relationship between the two is irreversible. And if their elevation consists ultimately in the fact that they have to take up and carry their cross, this is not a re-enactment of His crucifixion. It takes place in correspondence to it; with the similarity proper to a disciple following his Master; but not in any sense in likeness, let alone identity. His own crown and the dignity which comes to the disciple in discipleship are two distinct things. The crown of life, which the disciple is promised that he will receive at the hand of the King (Rev. 2¹⁰), is the goal of the way which he may go here and now as the bearer of this dignity.

When Paul says concerning himself in Gal. 2²⁰ that he no longer lives, but Christ lives in him, this does not mean that he identified himself with Christ, or gave himself out to be a second Christ. He at once interpreted the statement by that which followed : " And the life which I now live in the flesh I live by the faith of the Son of God, who loved me, and gave himself for me." Paul himself did not take part—except in so far as he received it in faith as done for him—in this self-offering of Christ, which took place for him as one who was loved by Christ. He did not mean this when he said in the preceding verse (Gal. 2¹⁹) that he was crucified with Christ (Χριστῷ συνεσταύρομαι), or in Gal. 6¹⁷ that he bore the marks (στίγματα) of the Lord Jesus, or in 2 Cor. 4¹⁰ that he bore about in the body the dying (νέκρωσις) of the Lord Jesus. Nor did he mean it in Gal. 6¹⁴ when he made his boast only in the cross of Christ " by whom the world is crucified unto me, and I unto the world," or in Rom. 6⁶ when he said of Christians generally that " our old man is crucified with him," or in Gal. 5²⁴ when he claimed that " they that are Christ's have crucified the flesh with the affections and lusts," or in Col. 3⁵ where Christians are summoned to mortify their members, or in other passages which refer to the dying of Christians. Both the text and the context of all these sayings completely exclude any idea of an interchangeability of Christ and the Christian, the Head and the member, the One who leads and the one who follows. They refer to a hard and painful and even mortal but redemptive attack which must and is and will be made on the Christian in fellowship with the suffering and crucified Christ, so that his whole life is determined and marked and characterised by its influence and effects. But the suffering which comes on Christians, the cross to which they are nailed, the death which they have to die, is always *their* suffering, *their* cross, *their* death, just as the salvation which accompanies it is *their* salvation, won for them and brought to them in the suffering and cross and death of Christ on their behalf (ἀντὶ πολλῶν). Their cross corresponds to the death of Christ. It does this with supreme realism. But it does not do more. It is not a repetition, or re-presentation, of the cross of Christ.

There is only one passage (Col. 1²⁴) which at a first glance seems rather obscure in this respect. Here Paul twice describes his suffering as an apostle as a suffering ὑπέρ, for others—an expression which elsewhere in the New Testament is used only in relation to the suffering of Christ. He rejoices in his παθήματα for his readers. He fills up, or completes, or repays (ἀνταναπληρῶ) by means of them that which is still lacking of the afflictions of Christ (τὰ ὑστερήματα τῶν θλίψεων τοῦ Χριστοῦ). He suffers in his flesh for (ὑπέρ) the body of Christ which is the community. The explanation is twofold. On the one hand, the community as the body of Christ, i.e., the earthly historical representation and form of the presence and action of Jesus Christ as its Head, has to exist in an earthly-historical correspondence to His afflictions, His passion (these are its ὑστερήματα). And, on the other hand, the apostle is appointed to be the messenger to the community in Christ's stead (ὑπὲρ Χριστοῦ, 2 Cor. 5²⁰), and therefore he has to see to it in his creatureliness (ἐν τῇ σαρκί μου), not as a second head, but as a special member of the body with a distinctive responsibility, that a witness is given to what must take place as the earthly-historical correspondence of Christ's passion. What Paul is saying in this passage is that as a bearer of his own cross he may do this, and rejoices to do it, in his apostolic παθήματα. In the verse which follows (v. 25) he tells us that he suffers as a minister to the community in accordance with the divine dispensation (οἰκονομία) which he knows that he is charged to fulfil. He rejoices in his apostolic suffering because he knows that he has this charge, and is invested with this dignity, in his suffering as a man. Even in this outstanding passage the connexion between the suffering of the Christian and that of Christ is only indirect.

We may now turn from this delimitation to the positive statement which must be made in this context. Because it takes place in Jesus Christ that man is set in this whole movement, it is integral to the event of sanctification—the *participatio Christi*, the call to discipleship, the awakening to conversion and the praise of good works—that as the life-movement of the Christian—as a human, earthly-historical life-movement—it is radically and relentlessly fixed and held and broken at a specific place. In the literal sense it is a happening which is crossed through, which is determined and characterised by a cross. The cross involves hardship, anguish, grief, pain and finally death. But those who are set in this movement willingly undertake to bear this because it is essential to this movement that it should finally, i.e., in its basis and goal, be crossed through in this way. We are necessarily outside the movement if we will not take up and bear our cross ; if we try to escape the *tolerantia crucis* (Calvin).

It is not a matter merely of hardship, pain and death in themselves and in general, just as it is not merely a matter of the human life-movement in itself and as such.

It is quite in order that this man should not wish to see himself arrested and disturbed and broken ; that he should try to ward off pain and death. Even the Christian does this. In themselves and as such, pain, suffering and death are a questioning, a destruction and finally a negation of human life. The Christian especially cannot try to transform and glorify them. He cannot find any pleasure in them. He cannot desire or seek them. For he sees and honours and loves in life a gift of God. And he is responsible for its preservation. He cannot be a lover of death, as the natural man may easily become in a strange reversal and unmasking of his pretended affirmation of life and avid desire for it. His Yes to life is not one which can surreptitiously change into a No. He knows better than others what life is, and what he is doing when he secures himself against its negation. He affirms it just because it is for him more than a matter of life. What is at stake is that the will of God should be done, which is his sanctification (1 Thess. 4³). Because he does not love his life in itself and as such, he cannot love its negation and therefore pain, anguish and death as such. He affirms his life in this context.

But in the same context he may and can and must also affirm its negation. " For whether we live, we live unto the Lord ; and whether we die, we die unto the Lord : whether we live, therefore, or die, we are the Lord's " (Rom. 14⁸). We are His possession " both in body and soul, in life and death." To be His possession, the doing of His will, sanctification, is thus that which is more than dying in the dying of the Christian. To be the Lord's includes this alternative of dying. The Christian knows better than others—than those who for different reasons have lost their zest for life and long for its end and dissolution—what he is doing when he says Yes to the negation of his life, to pain and suffering and death. He says Yes to these because his sanctification in fellowship with Jesus Christ, in His discipleship, in the conversion initiated by Him, in the doing of good works, ultimately includes the fact that he has to see and feel and experience the limit of his existence—even of his Christian existence engaged in sanctification—as the limit of his human and creaturely life, which necessarily leads to pain and suffering and death, leading to death, and proclaiming it, and finally involving it. To save his life he must surrender and lose it. He will not seek or induce this loss. It will come to him. But as a Christian, and because it is a matter of life, he will not negate but affirm it, just as elsewhere and right up to this frontier he will not negate but affirm life. He will not affirm either for their own sake. But he will definitely affirm both, even death, ἕνεκεν ἐμοῦ, for Jesus' sake. He will accept the fact that this limit or frontier is set, and that he has to note it. He will take up his cross.

"Whether we die, we die unto the Lord." It is Christ who sets this term to our life. It is not set accidentally, by fate or by an unknown God. It is not set merely with the limit of death itself, which belongs to our nature as a mark of our finitude. To be sure, natural death also belongs to the cross which the Christian has to take up. But this limit is not set according to a law of nature which the Christian has in common with all other men. It is set in his special fellowship with Jesus Christ, and therefore—because He is the King who controls this fellowship—according to the law of Him who is also Lord over nature and that which takes place according to its laws. Jesus Christ Himself has, of course, endured suffering and death as it is appointed for all men and in some form comes on all. But He endured it in obedience to His Father and the exercise of His office. He endured it in order supremely to glorify His Father and His love by taking on Himself the divine sentence of rejection on all men and thus opening the way for the actualisation of the election of all men. He endured it in the act of reconciling the world with God, as the man in whom God humbled Himself in order that man should be exalted. He endured that that limit should be set for Him in the negation of His life. And in so doing He tore down the wall of partition which separated man from God. Offering and losing His life, He was the living and true and royal man, as was revealed in His resurrection. This is the law of His crucifixion. It is in accordance with this law that a term is set for Christians and they have to bear their cross. In the sphere of this lordship they are wonderfully free from any other laws, divine, human or demonic, inward or outward, spiritual or natural, Or rather, they become free from any such laws as they come under this law. They do not have to fear any overwhelming force, but only the Lord who brings them under it because He is theirs and they are His. And they cannot really fear Him—only their own disloyalty— because His law which leads them to take up their cross is the law of the grace of God directed to the world and known by them ; because in the fact that He gives them to bear their cross they can see that God has given them this special light, and that they are honoured by this special fellowship with Jesus Christ.

At the end of the chapter already quoted (III, 8, 11) Calvin points out that the difference between philosophical (Stoic) and Christian patience is that the latter is quite free from any suggestion of necessity. The Christian does not take up his cross, and yield to God, because it is quite futile to resist One who is so superior in strength. If we obey God only because we must, our secret thoughts are all of disobedience and evasion, and we refrain from these only because they are impossible. The Christian yields in recognition of the righteousness and wisdom of the divine providence which rules his life. He obeys a living, not a dead, command. He knows that resistance or impatience is wrong. He understands that it is for his salvation that God lays his cross on him. He thus accepts it *grata placidaque anima*, not with his natural bitterness, but in thankful and cheerful praise of God. This is a true picture, and it is extremely surprising that to underline this distinction Calvin did not make use of the insight with which the chapter as a whole begins—that the God with whom the Christian has to do, and who meets him even in suffering, is God in Jesus Christ, so that he for his part can encounter Him only with this free and willing and joyous patience, and not with the gloomy resignation of the Stoic with his *necesse est*.

The special fellowship of the Christian with Christ involves participation in the passion of His cross. As Christians take up and bear their cross, they do not suffer, of course, with the direct and original and pure obedience which for all its bitterness it was natural and self-evident for the Son of God who was also the Son of Man to render to His Father. Their obedience will never be more than the work of the freedom which they are given. It will always be subsequent. It will always be so stained by all kinds of disobedience that if in the mercy of God it were not invested with the character of obedience it would hardly deserve to be called obedience. Nor is their suffering even the tiniest of contributions to the reconciliation of the world with God. On the contrary, it rests on the fact that this has been perfectly accomplished, not by them but by God Himself in Christ, so that it does not need to be augmented by their suffering or by any lesser Calvaries. Among other men, Christians are simply those to whom its truth and perfection are revealed (not hidden). They arise only as its witnesses. What they suffer is not what Jesus suffered— the judgment of God on the man of unrighteousness, the divine rejection without which the election of man cannot be accomplished. This was suffered by Jesus for the whole world and therefore for them. They exist only—and this is quite enough—in the echo of His sentence, the shadow of His judgment, the after-pains of His rejection. In their cross they have only a small subsequent taste of what the world and they themselves deserved at the hand of God, and Jesus endured in all its frightfulness as their Head and in their place. It is true—and we shall have to return to this—that they too have to suffer rejection at the hands of men. But they do not have to suffer rejection by God. On the contrary they have the sure knowledge that they are His elect. Again, they will not find, as Jesus did, that they are rejected by all men. At the very worst they will be rejected only by many, perhaps a majority. And in this as in other respects they will never be quite innocent in their suffering. They will never suffer merely through the corruption and wickedness of others, or through the undeserved decrees and buffetings of fate or the cosmic process. There is always a very definite (if sometimes disguised) connexion between the sufferings which befall them and their own participation in the transgression and guilt in which all men are continually implicated. And whereas Jesus was quite alone as the One who was rejected and suffered in their place, they can always know that even if they are rejected by ever so many they suffer as members of His community and therefore in company with at least a few others, and can count on the support and intercession, or at least the remembrance, of many more. Finally, whereas the suffering of Jesus is obviously on behalf of all other men, and for their salvation, liberation and exaltation, it is only with serious qualifications that we can say of the suffering of a Christian that it is significant and effective for others, and takes place in their favour. What it means to lay down one's life for one's friends (Jn. 15¹³) is only indicated from afar by any conceivable relationship of a human sufferer to others.

In short, the statement of the *Heidelberg Catechism* (*Qu.* 37) " that during the whole time of His life upon earth, and especially at the end, He bore both in body and soul the wrath of God against the sin of the whole human race, so that by His suffering as by a propitiatory offering He redeemed us in body and soul from eternal perdition and won for us God's grace and righteousness and eternal life," is one which cannot be referred to any Christian bearing his cross, not even to the greatest martyr. There applies to the Christian what is said in *Qu.* 44 : " That in the greatest trials I have the assurance that by His unutterable anguish, pain and terror which He suffered even in soul both on and before the cross, my Lord Christ has redeemed me from the fear and pain of hell."

Between Christ and the Christian, His cross and ours, it is a matter of similarity in great dissimilarity. There is, of course, a great and strong and obvious similarity. It is because of this that we can speak of the dignity of the cross. Christians are distinguished and honoured by the fact that the fellowship with Jesus into which He Himself has received them finds final expression in the fact that their human and Christian life is marked like a tree for felling. The sign of the cross is the sign of the provisional character of their Christian existence. It is not the whole or even the heart of the matter that these men find themselves on the way with their little looking to Jesus as the author and finisher of their faith, with their little obedience in His discipleship, in their noticeable transition (which has to be renewed day by day) from the old to the new, from death to life, and with their very problematical good works ; just as the life and speech and action of Jesus on His way from Jordan to Gethsemane was not the whole or the heart of the matter, the form in which He was truly Lord, apart from the fulfilment which came so terribly with the completely new development of the passion. In the life of Christians it is not just a matter of themselves and the fulfilment of their sanctification, but (since they have their activating cause in Jesus) of something far greater than themselves—of the glory and Word and work of God, compared with which they and all that they may become can never be more than dust and ashes. Or, from a different angle, it is a matter of themselves as God's witness, of their existence as individuals and as a community, but in the strict sense of the earth which is God's, of the whole world in all its blindness, need and care, which God so loved that He gave for it His only begotten Son. What are little Christians, with all the little things which may take place in the sphere of their existence in virtue of this Son of God, compared with this embracing plan and will of God ? And, from another angle again, it is a matter of these little Christians, but of them only in so far as, watching and waiting with all the great world for the revelation of the glory of its Creator and Lord (2 Pet. 3^{12}), they may look and move towards it. What is all that they can see and experience and grasp and attest here and now—even on their way in fellowship with Jesus— alongside the eternal future announced from God both to themselves and to the world ? What are they and have they compared with the glory of their Lord, who has risen again from death, and of whose fulness they have here and now received grace for grace, but whom they still confront as beggars, completely unworthy even in their fellow- ship with God by Him, sighing concerning themselves and the world which does not yet know Him, sighing for the true manifestation of that which has taken place for the world and themselves in this One ? This is the limit which is set for the Christian especially, and as a sign of which he comes to bear his cross, not in identity but in similarity with the cross of Jesus. His cross points to the fulness and truth of that which he expects, and to which he hastens, as one who is sanctified in Jesus Christ. It points to God Himself, to His will for the world, to the future revelation of His majesty, to the glory in which his Lord already lives and reigns. As he comes to bear his cross, he finds himself prevented from forgetting this truth and fulness, and encouraged to take comfort in it and stretch out towards it. His cross inter-crosses his Christian life. He will not desire, or will, or try to bring it about, that this should happen. It will come unasked and unsought. As he belongs to Jesus, it is inevitable that it should come. His sanctification is fulfilled in its coming.

Calvin was at his best in this context (III, 8, 1). In what has to be thought and said concerning the Christian's cross, it is not for him a question of manu- facturing a violent paradox, but of an *altius conscendere* ; of the recognition of the point where the sanctification of man points beyond itself from its root in the Holy One. *Quoscunque Dominus cooptavit ac suorum consortio dignatus est, ii se ad duram, laboriosam, inquietam plurimisque ac variis malorum generibus refertam vitam praeparare debent.* The heavenly Father did not make things easy but hard for His only begotten Son, the One whom He loved above all and in whom He was well-pleased (Mt. 3^{17}, 17^{5}), so long as He was upon earth.

We can say, indeed, and it is to this passage that reference is made in *Qu.* 37 of the *Heidelberg Catechism* : *totam eius vitam nihil aliud fuisse quam perpetuae crucis speciem.* He, too, had to learn obedience by the things which He suffered (Heb. 5⁸). And beginning with Him, the Father deals with all His children according to this rule. Christ having subjected Himself to it for our sakes, we cannot be emancipated from it as those who are destined to be conformed to His likeness (Rom. 8²⁹). It works itself out in the *res durae et asperae* which we regard as hostile and evil when we experience them. (And they are this, as Calvin emphasises in opposition to the teaching of the Stoics, III, 8, 8 : Poverty *is* hard, and sickness painful, and shame galling, and death terrible.) Yet in all these things it is a matter of *Christi passionibus communicare* ; of entering (like Him and with Him) " through much tribulation into the kingdom of God " (Ac. 14²²). The fiercer the affliction which assails us, the stronger the confirmation of our *societas cum Christo.*

Of the many New Testament references we will adduce only two. The first is Phil. 3¹⁰ (which is also quoted by Calvin). What does it mean for Paul to know Christ and the power of His resurrection ? The answer is that it means a knowledge of the κοινωνία τῶν παθημάτων αὐτοῦ in which he finds himself placed as an apostle. What does it mean to go forward to the resurrection of the dead ? The answer is that it means to be one who is made conformable to His death (συμμορφιζόμενος τῷ θανάτῳ αὐτοῦ). The second is 1 Pet. 4¹² : " Beloved, think it not strange (ξενίζεσθε) concerning the fiery trial which is to try you . . . but rejoice, inasmuch as ye are partakers of Christ's sufferings ; that, when his glory shall be revealed, ye may be glad also with exceeding joy."

In the light of this we can and must say a few words concerning the fact and extent that in the cross laid upon the Christian we really have to do with the fulfilment of his sanctification. The only decisive thing is, of course, the all-comprehensive fact which forms the point of departure—that as the cross of the Christian comes from Jesus it is in all its forms an awakening call and summons to look to Him, and therefore, as we have already seen, to arise. It is only in this context that we can say anything more concrete if we are not to be guilty of dubious moralising.

With this backward reference and proviso we may say (1) that it is necessary and good for the Christian, and serviceable to sanctification, to be kept in the humility which is not natural to any of us, or rather to be continually recalled to it, by the cross which he has to bear. If this limit were not set for him, and palpably before him, he might easily begin to hold up his head with a proud confidence, not in God, but in his own Christianity ; seeking, in the strength of the fact that he may be a Christian, to be strong in his own feelings and thought and acts, and thus jeopardising no less than everything. If he really takes up his cross, he will be prevented from doing this. Even if it consists only in an ordinary toothache, it will remind him of the limited nature of even his Christian existence, of his frailty and pettiness. It will restrain him from taking himself and his spirituality and his faith and its practical achievements with a seriousness which has no place for criticism or humour. It will summon him to seek and find his salvation and God's glory and the power of his own service only in the place *extra se* from which they come to him and in which alone they have an unshakeable foundation. They will teach him speedily to range himself again, as he ought, with other men ; not merely with Christians, but with the children of men generally. The cross breaks over Christians constantly to teach even officers of the highest rank to begin again at the beginning as privates.

We may say (2) that for the Christian it is also helpful to sanctification that he should accept the punishment which in some real if hidden sense somes in and with his cross. Jesus Himself has borne the great punishment for him and for the whole world. But it is inevitable that in the following of Jesus all sorts of lesser punishments should have to be borne by the one who belongs to Him, and that he will have good reason to see and accept that these are just. It will certainly not be the sword which smites him—the sword of the wrath of God. But it will be the rod of His fatherly love. And the Christian is yet to be found who has not deserved it, who in what befalls him may rightly see only the work of an alien evil or cosmic destiny and not the answer to his own corruption. It is the latter which is directly or indirectly brought before him in the suffering which overtakes him. And it may and will remind him of the great punishment which he is spared. It may and will renew his gratitude, and give to his movement of conversion the fresh impulse and seriousness which are always so badly needed.

We may also say (3) that the cross which is really taken and carried by the Christian is a powerful force to discipline and strengthen his faith and obedience and love. In this respect it makes common cause with his impulsion by the Holy Spirit. When this is translated into the impulsion of his own spirit, even in the man seriously engaged in sanctification it may easily happen that he falls into what he thinks to be a spiritual roving and wandering and marauding and even plundering, or perhaps into a higher or lower form of pious idling. He is not aware of this himself. But it is noted by others, especially by the sharp eyes of worldlings. And they have then good reason to shake their heads, to laugh or to be annoyed, and in any case to dismiss Christianity as valueless. When the cross comes, he is given the opportunity, and even forced, to see it himself. As it sets for him and shows him his own limit, it causes him to be startled at himself. It forcibly teaches him to think of the one necessary thing, to focus and concentrate all his attention upon it. It presents some form of an ultimatum, for it is really the last thing which is announced in his life and thinking and conscience. When the cross comes, man's own spirit is rightly directed by the Holy Spirit as it previously refused to be—although pretending to be full of the Spirit. The Christian is taken in hand. And this is obviously to the benefit of his sanctification, his faith and obedience and love. From this crisis—which will have to come more than once and in different forms—he will obviously emerge stronger than when he was engulfed by it.

We may finally say (4)—but with particular care and restraint—that in the bearing of his cross there may be for the Christian particular verifications. That is to say, there may be particular good works of faith and love, works which are particularly well-pleasing to God and which redound particularly to the praise of God. The Roman Church is quite right when in its legends and teaching concerning the saints it understands and portrays them all as great sufferers. What we are and have and think and do and attempt as Christians in good days, when the situation is calm and favourable and we are not exposed to any serious assaults from within or without, is always subject, for all its conscious zeal and sincerity, to the difficult question whether and how far it is tested, and hardened, and solid and enduring. Not every affliction or distress which comes on a man, even a Christian, has in itself and as such—however terrible it may be—the power to give this attestation, to make him the doer of an accredited work. But the fact that opportunities are often missed does not alter the fact that the cross is for the Christian the opportunity—and if he takes and bears it the power as well as the opportunity—to verify and therefore to purify and deepen his Christian existence and intensify his Christian work. When his own forces are reduced, when he is robbed of more than one of the aids which he values, when he is pushed into the corner and his back is against the wall, when he stands on unsafe and possibly crumbling ground and is thus thrown back with all the greater intensity on God and referred to the strength which comes from the covenant with Him, the Christian who takes up his cross and bears it will on this basis set his hand to the work with renewed willingness and energy, and although he may not do better or greater things, he will certainly do those which, since a limit has not yet been set, or is not yet felt or burdensome, will certainly be more tested and purified and substantial, and may indeed be better and greater, than ever before. There can be no doubt that every genuine good work of the Christian acquires finally the fiery glow mentioned in 1 Pet. 4[12].

But so far we have referred only incidentally to the question what we have to understand specifically by the cross which the Christian has to carry. We must now try to take our bearings in this respect, at any rate as far as the main outlines are concerned.

In the New Testament one aspect of the cross stands with absolute dominance in the foreground—and it is a serious question for much later Christianity, including that of our own day, whether all is well if this aspect has to a large extent lost its actuality except for a few isolated instances. In the New Testament the cross means primarily persecution ; the persecution of Christians by the world, by Jews and Gentiles, among whom Christians are sent " as sheep in the midst of wolves " (Mt. 10[16]). In the New Testament, and during the centuries which followed, the Christian existence and confession and life was always latently at least (if not uninterruptedly) an enterprise which stood under the threat of repression even to the point of physical violence. Later, and in our own time, the cross indicated in the New Testament has become rare, and for the most part exceptional, in this unequivocal form. At this point, therefore, we can speak only with great caution and in the light of certain analogies to persecution in the full sense. There can be no doubt that even to-day a Christian is a *rara avis*, under constant threat, even in an environment which is ostensibly, and perhaps consciously and zealously, Christian. However great may be the solidarity which Christians feel and practise in relation to the world, their way can never be that of the world—and least of all that of the supposedly Christianised world. From the point which inspires them, they have to go their own way in great and little things alike, and therefore in their thought and speech and attitude they are always at bottom, although in some cases more markedly than others, aliens and strangers who will give plenty of cause for offence in different directions. To some they will appear to be far too ascetic. To others they will seem to affirm life far too unconcernedly. Sometimes they will be regarded as individualists, sometimes as collectivists. On the one hand they will be accused as authoritarians, on the other as free-thinkers ; on the one hand as pessimists, on the other as optimists ; on the one hand as bourgeois, on the other as anarchists. They will seldom find themselves in a majority. Certainly, they will never swim with the stream. It is only occasionally and against their true character that they can ever tolerate the official and officious. Things generally accepted as self-evident will never claim their absolute allegiance, even though they take on a Christian guise. Nor will they command their complete negation, so they can hardly count on the applause of the revolutionaries of their day. Nor will their freedom, to which we referred in our discussion of discipleship, be exercised by them in secret, but revealed openly in free acts and attitudes which will never be right to the world. And the world will not like this. They do not even need to make an explicit confession, although this will sometimes sharpen the offence that they give. To-day, however, in an age of doctrinal tolerance, this may well be allowed. But there will be all the less tolerance for the free decision and act of Christians. To this the reaction will be sour and bitter. It will be met with mistrust and repudiation, with suspicion and scorn, and even sometimes open indignation. Its disruptive tendencies will be quietly or forcefully accused and condemned. Measures will be taken to silence or destroy it, or at least to render it innocuous. Sometimes matters may be pressed even further, and counteraction undertaken which brings Christians at least in sight of the situation of Mt. 10^{16-39}, if not quite so far. They do not need to go beyond this point to be marked by the cross of rejection. Surely it is disturbing and wounding and confusing and hampering enough always to be so isolated, and subject to attack, among our fellows. How much rather Christians would please than displease ! How much they would prefer honour than shame for an attitude that is to them so clear and simple and necessary ! But whether the shame be less or greater, they cannot cease to go the way which at the end will turn many, perhaps the majority, against them, and thus lead to their complete isolation. And even though they may not have to do with a Nero or a Diocletian, this will mean severe restriction by the limit which is so palpably and effectively set to their life-movement. Is it not surprising—when we think of the shame in which Jesus died, rejected not only by God but by men—that this particular cross seems to come upon relatively so few Christians ? Or is it the case that so many succeed in evading it by refusing to go the distinctively Christian way on which they will inevitably be threatened and assailed by their limitation in this form ?

Not by a long way, however, does the New Testament pretend that the sufferings of this present time are restricted to persecution. A passage like Rom. 8$^{19f.}$ is shot through by the conception that the cross of Christians also consists in their particular share in the tension, transience, suffering and obscurity by which every man is in some form constricted and disturbed and finally condemned to death, and in which man also seems to find himself in a painful connexion with creation as such and as a whole. The older Evangelical hymn depicted the cross of the Christian primarily in this light. In so doing, it departed to some extent from the New Testament. But it did it very impressively. If it is in its own way right, then in relation to the cross laid on the Christian we have also to think of the afflictions of creaturely life and being which come on him either suddenly or gradually, momentarily or continually, but in the long run with overwhelming force : misfortunes, accidents, sickness and age ; parting from those most dearly loved ; disruption and even hostility in respect of the most important human relations and communications ; anxiety concerning one's daily bread, or what is regarded as such ; intentional or unintentional humiliations and slights which have to be accepted from those immediately around ; the inability freely to develop one's life and talents ; the sense of a lack of worthwhileness in respect of particular tasks ; participation in the general adversities of the age which none can escape ; and finally the dying which awaits us all at the end. If Jesus Himself was a suffering creature, and as such the Lord of all creatures, we are not only permitted but commanded to regard all the human suffering which we have only briefly sketched as a suffering with Him, in His fellowship, and therefore to understand the irruption of this suffering into the life of the Christian as the sign of this fellowship, and thus the manifestation of the supreme dignity of the Christian.

Finally, we must think of the suffering which—perhaps quite apart from persecution, or the participation in other ills of human life, but perhaps also in connexion with them—arises in all its terror from the fact that the Christian too, in spite of what he already is, still stands under the law of sin, and is still afflicted with the burden of the flesh, and is therefore subject to temptation, and is in fact tempted, always latently and sometimes acutely, notwithstanding his age or maturity or serious Christian achievements ; tempted in his faith and love and hope, and therefore in the fulfilment of his relationship to God as it has been perfectly restored in the atoning death of Jesus. Temptation in the shape of intellectual or theoretical doubts is relatively the most harmless form of this cross. There too, of course, it is a question of truth. But in so far as it arises in a theoretical form it can be answered in an orderly induction by correct study and reflection. The trouble is that it then suddenly or gradually arises again in the new form whether the truth—that which is or can be known theoretically as true—is even for the Christian an authoritative and effective and illuminating truth—the truth of life. Here we have the practical doubt by which the real Christian especially is often attacked and perhaps steadily beleaguered as by an invincible enemy. He may accept and repeat the creed. But does he really believe, at bottom, in the presence and action of the Father, Son and Holy Spirit in his own life ? Has he really experienced His grace ? Does he know it ? Can he live in and by it ? Has it really been addressed to him ? Can this really be the case when in the innermost place where as a Christian he would be satisfied with even a little he is so empty and dry, so helpless in his attempt to seize and exploit the help which he knows is there, so unable to pray a prayer which is worthy of the One to whom he prays, and certain to be heard by Him ? Is he not always a fool before God, an unprofitable servant ? Has not God long since removed His face from him—if it ever lighted on him at all ? Would he not do better to be something other than a Christian ? In this form we may doubt even the truth which we know and sincerely confess. And God knows that—whether we are aware of it or not—we all stand constantly on the edge of this doubt. We must beware of transmuting and even glorifying it dialectically. Once we really know it, we will not do this. It is the sharpest form in which a limit is set to the Christian. It is the bitterest form of the cross. In this form it has been laid, with its hostile stimulation, even on what are humanly speaking the greatest of Christians. According to Mk. 15³⁴ Jesus Himself experienced the cross finally and supremely in this form. He, the only begotten Son of God, had to ask : " Why hast thou forsaken me ? " This is comforting. What are our doubts and despairs, disguised or acute, compared with His dereliction, which was also and especially suffered by Him in our place ? This means, however, that in fellowship with Him we have to reckon seriously with the fact that our cross will take, and may never lose, this character. In this character it cannot form part of an intellectual game. Unless we are to evade our sanctification at the decisive point, we have to bear it, to see it through, in this character. The only thing is that in so doing we are not forsaken by the One who raised and answered the question whether He was not forsaken by God. At this point, then, we find ourselves in the deepest fellowship with Him.

We may conclude the discussion with two observations.

First, we must emphasise again that those who know what the cross is will not desire or seek to bear it. Self-sought suffering has nothing whatever to do with participation in the passion of Jesus Christ, and therefore with man's sanctification. The cross which we have to bear in following Jesus comes of itself, quite apart from any wish or action of our own. No one need worry that there will be no cross for him. Our only concern is not to avoid it ; not defiantly or craftily to refuse to bear it ; or not to cast it away again when it is only half taken up. Our only concern, since we have to suffer in any case, is not to do so like the ungodly, which means without the comfort and promise of suffering with Jesus. It must be our constant prayer, not only when adversity comes but in the good days which precede it, that this should not happen, that the Holy Ghost should make us free to accept and therefore to bear the appointed cross, i.e., to make it our own.

Second, the *tolerantia crucis* is not an end in itself, and the direction to it, like every direction to sanctification, is not an ultimate but only a penultimate word. The dignity of the cross is provisional, indicating the provisional nature of the Christian existence and all sanctification. The crown of life is more than this. It is of the very essence of the cross carried by Christians that it has a goal, and therefore an end, and therefore its time. It signifies the setting of a term. That is why it is so bitter. But this limitation is not itself unlimited. Borne in participation in the suffering of Jesus, it will cease at the very point to which the suffering of Jesus points in the power of His resurrection, and therefore to which our suffering also points in company with His. It is not our cross which is eternal, but, when we have borne it, the future life revealed by the crucifixion of Jesus. Rev. 21[4] will then be a present reality : "And God shall wipe away all tears from their eyes ; and there shall be no more death, neither sorrow nor crying, neither shall there be any more pain : for the former things are passed away." P. Gerhardt is thus right when he says : " Our Christian cross is brief and bounded, One day 'twill have an ending. When hushed is snowy winter's voice, Beauteous summer comes again ; Thus 'twill be with human pain. Let those who have this hope rejoice." There cannot lack a foretaste of joy even in the intermediate time of waiting, in the time of sanctification, and therefore in the time of the cross.

THE HOLY SPIRIT AND THE UPBUILDING OF THE CHRISTIAN COMMUNITY

The Holy Spirit is the quickening power with which Jesus the Lord builds up Christianity in the world as His body, i.e., as the earthly-historical form of His own existence, causing it to grow, sustaining and ordering it as the communion of His saints, and thus fitting it to give a provisional representation of the sanctification of all humanity and human life as it has taken place in Him.

1. THE TRUE CHURCH

The upbuilding of the Christian community and then Christian love are the two themes which we have still to discuss at the conclusion of this second part of the doctrine of reconciliation. In these spheres, too, we have to do with the divine work of sanctification as a special form of the reconciliation of the world with God which was and is and will be an event in Jesus Christ. The difference in relation to our previous path can consist only in the fact that we are now looking especially at what is effected, and therefore actual, in this divine work. The powerful and living direction of the Resurrected, of the living Lord Jesus, and therefore the Holy Spirit, whom we have had to understand as the principle of sanctification, effects the upbuilding of the Christian community, and in and with it the eventuation of Christian love; the existence of Christendom, and in and with it the existence of individual Christians.

It seems as though we might (and perhaps should) reverse the order and say that the Holy Spirit effects the eventuation of Christian love and therefore the existence of individual Christians, and in and with this the upbuilding of the Christian community and therefore the existence of Christendom. But this is only in appearance. If it is true that Christian love is that which (with Christian faith and Christian hope) makes an individual man a Christian, we have to remember that the individual man does not become a Christian, and live as such, in a vacuum, but in a definite historical context, i.e., in and with the upbuilding of the Christian community. He does so on the basis and in the meaning and purpose of the existence of the community, in his specific participation in its upbuilding, and in the exercise of its faith and love and hope. Calvin is thus right when he takes up a comparison already used by Cyprian and Augustine and calls the Church (*Instit.* IV, 1, 1) the " mother " of all believers : *quando non alius est in vitam ingressus nisi nos ipsa concipiat in utero, nisi pariat, nisi*

nos alat suis uberibus, denique sub custodia et gubernatione sua nos tueatur (1, 4).
Did he perceive the full reach of the assertion expressed in this image ? If so,
why is it that it is only in the Fourth Book that he comes to speak of the Church,
and that he thinks of it as one (if the chief) of the *externa media vel adminicula*
by which God invites us to fellowship with Christ and maintains us in that
fellowship ? E. Brunner (*Das Missverständnis der Kirche*, 1951, *E.T.*, p. 9 f.)
is surely right in his conjecture that no apostle would ever have thought of the
community merely as an external means to serve a quite different end—the
sanctification of individual Christians. To be sure, we have not to speak too
exclusively in terms of ends and means. The existence of that mother, and
therefore of the community, is also a means, as is that of its children, individual
Christians. Another point not brought out by this comparison is that the community exists only in the common being and life and action, in the faith and
love and hope, of its members, and therefore of individual Christians. Again,
the existence of individual Christians is also an end, as is that of the community.
For individual Christians exist in the community, living by the special grace
addressed and for the special service allotted to it. Both are ends and both are
means. And if it is not merely externally that the sanctification of individual
Christians belongs to the fulfilment of reconciliation, the same is true of the
upbuilding of the community. By an inward necessity the one takes place in
and with the other. But because we cannot see and understand the individual
Christian except at the place where he is the one he is, and because this place is
the community, we have first to consider the community, although remembering
at every point that in it we have to do with the many individual Christians
assembled in it.

At the beginning of the previous section we stated that in the work
of sanctification God has to do with a people of men (consisting, of
course, of individuals) ; and that this corresponds to the fact that in
this work, as in that of reconciliation generally, His purpose is originally and ultimately for the whole world of men as such. As Jesus
Christ is the Reconciler of all men, and in this way (in His fellowship
with all) the Reconciler of each individual man, so as the Head of His
community He is the Lord of its many members, and in this way (in
His special fellowship with these many, with this particular people)
the Head of each of its constituents. At a later stage we shall have to
raise the question what makes a man a Christian, and speak of Christian
love. But we have first to see and understand the context to which
this question and the answer to it belong, and thus to consider that
what takes place in the work of the Holy Spirit is the upbuilding of
the community.

The fact that we are now considering what is effected in the work
of sanctification cannot mean—either when we speak of the Christian
community or of Christian love—that we have to turn our back on
the action of God in Jesus Christ by the Holy Spirit and to occupy
ourselves *in abstracto* with a being and work of men as its result.

We are, of course, dealing with a work done in common by a group
of men within the race and its history when we speak first of the upbuilding of the community. Sanctification generally is concerned with
the being and work of men ; with the wholly divine stimulation and
characterisation of the existence of those upon whom it comes as

something distinctive. So, too, the form of sanctification which we have now to discuss is concerned with the work of the quickening power of His spirit with which Jesus Christ builds up Christianity within the world ; with the divine inauguration, control and support of the human action which takes place among Christians.

For this reason I find it hard to see what Brunner means when (*op. cit.*, p. 106 f.) he says of the New Testament community that it was not " made " as the Churches of the Reformation were constituted by the acts of men, but that it " became " by a direct action of the Holy Spirit ; and when he argues that it is one of the advantages of the Orthodox and Roman Churches that the same can be said of them to the extent that they have become what they are to-day by a long and continuous and uninterrupted process of development (involving, of course, the fatal transformation of the original nature of the *ecclesia*). This is a curious alternative. The men responsible for the Reformation of the 16th century would hardly have recognised themselves in the statement that their Churches were ": fabricated by a human act." Did not these Churches expressly see and understand and say of themselves that they were reformed by the Word of God and that they therefore stood in continuity with the one Church of the first and every age as formed by God's Word ? Naturally there had to be all kinds of human decisions and acts, and therefore fabrication, corresponding to and serving this divine reformation. But these are also to be found—although of a very different kind—in the process by which the Orthodox and Roman Churches have evolved. They are also to be found even in the primitive community of the New Testament. It would be a strange historical development (even that of the Christian community as " the great miracle of history," *op. cit.*, p. 116), and a strange divine work of sanctification, which did not involve a human being and work, and therefore fabrication, inaugurated and controlled and supported by God.

It is clear, however, that to see and understand that which is effected by God, the Church, in its true reality, we have not to lose sight even momentarily or incidentally of the occurrence of the divine operation, and therefore concretely of the divine work of upbuilding the community by Jesus Christ. The Church is, of course, a human, earthly-historical construct, whose history involves from the very first, and always will involve, numan action. But it is *this* human construct, the Christian Church, because and as God is at work in it by His Holy Spirit. In virtue of this happening, which is of divine origin and takes place for men and to them as the determination of their human action, the true Church truly is and arises and continues and lives in the twofold sense that God is at work and that there is a human work which He occasions and fashions. Except in this history whose subject is God—but the God who acts for and to and with specific men—it is not the true Church. Nor is it visible as such except in relation to this history.

Thus, to see the true Church, we cannot look abstractly at what a human work seems to be in itself. This would not be a genuine phenomenon but a false. The real result of the divine operation, the human action which takes place in the true Church as occasioned and fashioned by God, will never try to be anything in itself, but only the divine operation, the divine work of sanctification, the upbuilding of Christianity by the Holy Spirit of Jesus the Lord, by which it is inaugurated and controlled and supported. To the extent that it is anything in itself, it is the phenomenon of the mere semblance of a Church, and it is only this semblance, and not the true Church, that we shall see when we consider this phenomenon.

The abstraction which this entails and of which we become guilty on this view is betrayed at once by the fact that all the biblical statements in praise of the ἐκκλησία can be applied only poetically or mythologically and not literally to what is here seen, or thought to be seen. How can that which tries to be something in itself be the people of God, or the city or house or planting of God, or the flock of Jesus Christ, or His bride, or even His body, or the communion of saints, or (according to 1 Tim. 3¹⁵) the pillar and ground of truth ? The Church which is a Church only in appearance may try to deck itself out with these predicates, but by its very nature (as a mere semblance) will it not make it quite impossible for these predicates to be taken seriously ? The same is true of the classical description of the Church (in the Nic.-Const. creed) as *una, sancta, catholica et apostolica* (on this point, cf. *C.D.*, IV, 1, pp. 668–725). None of these terms can be applied to anything but the divine operation which takes place in the Church. None of them can be sustained in respect of a phenomenon which is only the sum of what seems to be something in itself, pretending to be the Church, as a human work ostensibly occasioned and fashioned by God. When they are conducted with reference to this phenomenon, all discussions about the order and task of the Church, about its inner life and its commission in the world, are pointless and obscure. All kinds of theoretical and practical, enthusiastic and restrained, optimistic and pessimistic considerations and statements may, of course, be advanced, but they are none of them necessary. Where this is the case with thinking and speech about the Church, it is always an alarming sign that we are looking at a human work pretending to be something in itself, and thinking that we can formulate statements about this work as such. But the work of man which takes place in the true Church as occasioned and fashioned by God is revealed as such only as it points beyond itself and witnesses to the fact that it is occasioned and fashioned in this way, attesting the divine work of sanctification, the upbuilding of the community by the Holy Spirit, by which it is inaugurated and determined and characterised.

The Christian community, the true Church, arises and is only as the Holy Spirit works—the quickening power of the living Lord Jesus Christ. And it continues and is only as He sanctifies men and their human work, building up them and their work into the true Church. He does this, however, in the time between the resurrection and the return of Jesus Christ and therefore in the time of the community (cf. on this point *C.D.*, IV, 1, § 62, 3) in the world, i.e., in this context the human world which participates only in the particular and provisional revelation of Jesus Christ and to that extent is still a prisoner to the flesh and sin and death. Christianity, too, belongs to this world, and works and thinks and speaks and acts in it—even though its action is occasioned and fashioned by that of the Holy Spirit. Even at best, then, its action is an equivocal witness to the fact that it is occasioned and fashioned in this way. And there may be the less good cases, the bad and even the worst, when the witness that it ought to give is either omitted or obscured and falsified ; when the pride or sloth of man, or both together, is what is expressed and revealed as the work of the divine sanctifying and upbuilding. In short, it is to be feared—for this is where its determination by human pride and sloth ultimately leads—that it will express and reveal very little but itself ; itself as occasioned and fashioned by God, but with this high consciousness and pretentious claim ; itself and not the divine occasioning and fashioning which are its true meaning and power ; the semblance of a Church, therefore, and not the true Church. This is the particular sin which to some extent is always committed where the community arises and continues here and now.

Nor is it something self-evident, but always the omnipotent act of a special divine mercy, if the Church is not merely the semblance of a Church, but in spite of the sinfulness of the human action of Christians a true Church, and expressed and revealed as such. In its own strength this is quite impossible. Its institutions and traditions and even its reformations are no guarantee as such that it is the true Church, for in all these things we have to do with human and therefore sinful action, and therefore in some sense with a self-expression in which it can be only the semblance of a Church. If the divine occasioning and fashioning of this human action take place in spite of it, i.e., of its sinful tendency, this is not a quality of the Church in which it actualises its reality but the triumph of the power of Jesus Christ upbuilding it ; an omnipotent act of the special divine mercy addressed to it, which makes use of the human and sinful action of the community but does not proceed from it and cannot be understood in terms of it.

Let us accept for once the well-known definition of the *una sancta ecclesia perpetuo mansura* in the *Confession of Augsburg*, VII. It is the *congregatio sanctorum, in qua evangelium pure docetur et recte administrantur sacramenta.* Why is it then that in Art. VIII we read that " in this life there are many false Christians and hypocrites and even notorious sinners " amongst the pious, and that scribes and Pharisees sit in Moses' seat ? Obviously this does not indicate donatistic lack of faith in the superiority of the Holy Spirit to all Christian corruption. What it signifies is that the *pure docere* and *recte administrare* of VII are a matter of the human action of those gathered in the Church, and cannot therefore be presupposed as a self-evident quantity. They are a divine gift which is certainly promised to the Church, yet is not inherent to it as the content of the promise but has to be continually prayed for and received by it. With reference to the faith mediated and to be attained through preaching and the sacraments, it is said expressly in Art. V that it is the gift of the Holy Spirit awakening faith by preaching and the sacraments *tamquam per instrumenta— ubi et quando visum est Deo.* This is not meant by Melanchthon in any predestinarian sense, but with the *pure and recte* of Art. VII it is certainly meant to restrict the idea which is to be found in some forms and circles of a Church which is true and effective *ex opere operato*, having no need of the free grace of God and living by a very different grace.

We have also to consider the relevance of the matter to the question of the visibility of the Church. Are we not forced to put it as follows, namely, that the true Church (its upbuilding by God as the basis and determination of what men want and do and achieve) becomes visible as in the power of the Holy Spirit (the same Holy Spirit by whose victorious operation it is the true Church) it emerges and shines out from its concealment both in that which is established and traditional and customary and also in innovation and change ? This emergence and shining illustrate the freedom of grace ; the mighty act of the particular divine mercy which takes place when in spite of its sinful tendency the human action of Christians does not attest itself but its basis and meaning, depicting and expressing the divine sanctifying and upbuilding. This takes place only as we can see and read the dark letters of an electric sign when the current is passed through it. We can never see the true Church as we can see a state in its citizens and officials and organs and laws and institutions. We can, of course, see the members of the Church, and its officials and constitutions and orders, its dogmatics and cultus, its organisations and societies, its leaders with their politics, and its laity, its art and press—and all these in the context of its history. Where else is the Church visible if not in these ? If it is not visible in these, it is obviously not visible at all. But is it really visible in these ? Not immediately and directly. This something which claims to be the Church, and is before us all in these manifestations, may well be only the semblance of a Church, in which the will and work of man, although they allege that they are occasioned and fashioned by God, are striving to express only themselves. What is visible in all this may be only a religious society. And if we assume, not only that this is not the case, but that what we have here is really the true Church, it is not self-evident that this will be visible as such in all these things ; that its actuality will be eloquent truth. As it cannot create or confer its reality, the same is true of its visibility. It can only be endowed with it. If it is also visible as a true Church, this means that the victory of the divine operation, the mighty act of the Holy Spirit in face of the sinfulness of human action, finds further expression in a free emergence and outshining of the true Church from the concealment in which it is enveloped by the sinfulness of all human volition (and therefore of ecclesiastical), and in which it must continue to be enveloped apart from this continuation of the operation of the Holy Spirit. It will be always in the revelation of God that the true Church is visible. And it will be always in faith awakened by this revelation that it is actually seen by men—at the place where without revelation and faith there is to be seen (perhaps in a very confusing and deceptive way) only this many-sided ecclesiastical quantity in all its ambiguity.

It is in this sense that we count on the fact that the Church is a true Church, and visible as such, and in this confidence thus turn our attention to the history in which its being and visibility as the true Church have their living basis. We have called this the divine inauguration and control and support of the human action which takes place in the community and in which Christianity exists in the world. And we will gather up this whole happening under the concept of the upbuilding of the Christian community. In this first sub-section we shall take a comprehensive glance at the whole in explanation of this title.

This history has a direction and a goal. This is the first point to be noticed if we are to see and understand it. What is at issue has been stated in the concluding part of our introductory thesis. The Holy Spirit is the power by which Jesus Christ fits His community " to give a provisional representation of the sanctification of all humanity and human life as it has taken place in Him."

The existence of the true Church is not an end in itself. The divine operation by which it is vivified and constituted makes it quite impossible that its existence as the true Church should be understood as the goal of God's will for it. The divine operation in virtue of which it becomes and is a true Church makes it a movement in the direction of an end which is not reached with the fact that it exists as a true Church, but merely indicated and attested by this fact. On the way, moving in the direction of this goal, it can and should serve its Lord. For this reason it will not be the true Church at all to the extent that it tries to express itself rather than the divine operation by which it is constituted. As such it will reveal itself, or be revealed, in glory at this goal ; yet only as the Church which does not try to seek and express and glorify itself, but absolutely to subordinate itself and its witness, placing itself unreservedly in the service and under the control of that which God wills for it and works within it.

The goal in the direction of which the true Church proceeds and moves is the revelation of the sanctification of all humanity and human life as it has already taken place *de iure* in Jesus Christ. In the exaltation of the one Jesus, who as the Son of God became a servant in order as such to become the Lord of all men, there has been accomplished already in powerful archetype, not only the cancellation of the sins and therefore the justification, but also the elevation and establishment of all humanity and human life and therefore its sanctification. That this is the case is the theme and content of the witness with which His community is charged. It comes from the first revelation (in the resurrection of Jesus Christ) of the reconciliation of the world with God as it has taken place in this sense too. And it moves towards its final manifestation in the coming again of Jesus Christ. Christianity, or Christendom, is the holy community of the intervening period ; the congregation or people which knows this elevation and establishment, this sanctification, not merely *de iure* but already *de facto*, and which is therefore a witness to all others, representing the sanctification which has already come upon them too in Jesus Christ. This representation is provisional. It is provisional because it has not yet achieved it, nor will it do so. It can only attest it " in the puzzling form of a reflection " (1 Cor. 13^{12}). And it is provisional because, although it comes from the resurrection of Jesus Christ, it is only on the way with others to His return, and therefore to the direct and universal and definitive revelation of His work as it has been accomplished for them and for all men. The fact that it is provisional means that it is fragmentary and incomplete and insecure and questionable ; for even the community still participates in the darkness which cannot apprehend, if it also cannot overcome, the light (Jn. 1^5). But the fact that it is provisional means also—for in this provisional way it represents the sanctification of humanity as it has taken place in Jesus Christ—that divine work is done within it truly and effectively, genuinely and invincibly, and in all its totality, so that even though it is concealed in many different ways it continually emerges and shines out from this concealment in the form of God's people. It is with this provisional representation that we have to do on the way and in the movement of the true Church. It is to accomplish it that it is on its way and in this movement. It is in order that it may accomplish it that its time is given ; the time between the times, between the first and the final revelation of the work of God accomplished in Jesus Christ. The meaning and content of our time—the last time— is the fulfilment of this provisional representation as the task of the community of Jesus Christ.

We must assert already—and it is something that has significance for the whole of this section—that it is necessary that this provisional representation should take place. It is not merely possible. Nor is the necessity only external or technical or incidental. It is internal and material and decisive. It is a saving necessity. The true Church is no mere form of grace, of the salvation directed to men by God, of the reconciliation of the world with Him. It is not something which has a mere form we can take into account merely accidentally or relatively or perhaps even optionally. It is not just the means to an end which can be dispensed with, or treated with a certain aloofness, when other and perhaps better means are perceived. We may and can and should hold aloof from the semblance of a Church whose only aim is to seek and express and glorify itself. But the true Church —and where is the semblance which does not conceal the true Church, from which it may not emerge and shine out ?—is savingly necessary. We see and understand this when we understand this provisional representation as the meaning of the way on which—and the movement in which—it finds itself. The salvation addressed to man by God, and therefore in particular the elevation and establishment of man, of all men, as it has taken place in Jesus Christ, is not a self-enclosed saving fact either far behind us or high above us. It is a living redemptive happening which takes place. Or, more concretely, it is the saving operation of the living Lord Jesus which did not conclude but began in His revelation on Easter Day. In its totality, in its movement to His final manifestation, it has the power of that which was once for all accomplished by Him at Calvary. It is essential, and therefore necessary, to Him (Heb. 13⁸), to be not merely yester-day and for ever, but to-day—in the intervening time which is our time. And it is to-day in this provisional representation, in the form of the true Church. It would not be God's and therefore it would not be our salvation if it did not create and maintain and continually renew the provisional representation in which it is to-day. If we do not take it seriously in this, we do not take it seriously at all. If we hold ourselves aloof from this, we hold ourselves aloof from salvation and the Saviour. For the Jesus Christ who rules the world *ad dexteram Patris omnipotentis* is identical with the King of this people of His which on earth finds itself on this way and in this movement. He is revealed only and can be claimed only in the history ruled by Him. The Christian love and life of even the greatest saint cannot be more than a provisional representation, limited both in time and person, of the sanctification of all men as it has taken place in Jesus Christ. In its limitation it is referred to the fact that it must be surrounded and supported and nourished and critically limited by this representation in its totality, i.e., by the life and love of the community, if it is to make its own contribution to this representation in its totality. Even the greatest saint is only this one man—a saint with others in the com-munion of saints. And he is not *perpetuo mansurus*. He is a saint only in the *ecclesia perpetuo mansura*. He would not be a saint if he tried to be so in and for himself—apart from this provisional representation of the sanctification which has taken place in Jesus Christ. *Extra ecclesiam nulla salus*. We shall have good reason to remember this assertion.

The question arises, however, whether the Church is fitted to make this provisional representation. We have to remind ourselves that we are speaking of the representation which, although it is provisional, is a true and effective, genuine and invincible representation of the elevation and establishment of all men as it has been fulfilled in the exaltation of the man Jesus, and therefore of the divine work of sanctification in its totality. Is the people assembled in the com-munity—a race of men and not of angels—fitted for this necessary (this savingly necessary) event ? Can it fit itself for it ? We recall that it is a worldly people. If we can speak justly of its awakening and gathering to be the people of God, we can speak also of the sloth and pride which it is quick to perceive in other peoples but which are revealed all the more starkly in itself because it is the people of God (as we see from the history of Israel). Nor have we to forget what seems to be the characteristic sin by which the Church seems always to be threatened and into which it seems always to be on the point of falling : that of trying to represent itself rather than the sanctification which has taken place in Jesus Christ ; of trying to forget that its existence is provisional, and that it can exist only as it points beyond itself ; of defining itself in terms of a present status before God, in which it can believe and argue and proclaim that it is well-pleasing to men and therefore worthy to be represented. No, this people is never fitted of itself to make the representation which is the meaning and purpose of its existence. There can never be any question of this in the history of which we speak. It never takes place in virtue of the qualities of this people itself. Jesus the Lord, in the quickening power of His Holy Spirit, is the One who acts where this provisional representation takes place, and therefore where the true Church is an event. He does not act directly—without this people. He gives to this people the necessary qualities. He thus makes possible the impossible—that this race of men, just as it is, acquires and has the freedom to be able to serve Him. We are speaking, therefore, of the history of this race in the sequence of its human thoughts and efforts and achievements. But we are speaking of the history in which it is unfit, but continually fitted, in and with its human thought and word and will and work to make this provisional representation. More precisely, we are speaking of the history in which God continually sets this people on the way and in movement, continually indicating both the goal and the direction towards it. More precisely still, we are speaking of the history of the activity of Jesus, of the Lord who has come already, and will come again, but who is alive to-day ; of the activity of this Lord to and with His people. As He acts to and with His people, this people fills with His activity the time given to itself and the world. As a witness of that which has taken place in Him for all men, it looks and moves forward to the direct and universal and definitive revelation of this event.

There is a passage in Ephesians (4¹²⁻¹⁵)—we shall have to come back to it again in another connexion—which speaks with singular force and beauty and yet sobriety of this fitting of the Christian community for the provisional representation of the universal scope (concealed as yet) of the person and work of Jesus Christ.

In v. 12 we read of a preparation or equipment (καταρτισμός) of the saints (ἅγιοι). The charismatics given by Christ to the community, some apostles, some prophets, some evangelists, some pastors and teachers (v. 11), are all, within the limits and with the determination of their particular endowment (κατὰ τὸ μέτρον τῆς δωρεᾶς τοῦ Χριστοῦ, v. 7), the human instruments of this preparation in which Jesus Christ is at work to and with them. But it takes place—and this is our present concern—with a view to the service which they are to render by their human work (εἰς ἔργον διακονίας). And what is at issue in this service or ministry is the upbuilding of the body of Christ. We shall return later to the central concept of οἰκοδομή and we must postpone until the second sub-section a discussion of the σῶμα τοῦ Χριστοῦ. Both together denote the material point at issue in this provisional representation. For the moment, however, we must note what is to be learned from v. 13 especially about its provisional character, about the need to strive towards it, and therefore also about the equipment of the community. " Till we all come " (μέχρι καταντήσωμεν οἱ πάντες εἰς) . . . —these words describe the direction of the work for which the community is empowered by its Lord to serve the edifying of the body of Christ. It is a matter—and the οἱ πάντες seems to have a wider reference than the immediate circle indicated by the " we " of their reaching a certain place—of their attaining a goal which has not yet been attained but to which their existence, the work for which they are fitted, is directed as to an *eschaton*, so that they must allow themselves to be shaped accordingly. A threefold εἰς is used in v. 13 to describe this goal which is still future, but which in its futurity already determines and characterises their present, the work of their ministry, and their equipment to achieve it.

Εἰς τὴν ἑνότητα τῆς πίστεως καὶ τῆς ἐπιγνώσεως τοῦ υἱοῦ τοῦ θεοῦ. Their work, and their equipment for it, is directed to a unity which has still to be reached and attained and achieved, i.e., the unity of the faith and knowledge (the best translation would perhaps be " the knowledge of faith ") which have their original and proper subject (*gen. subj.*) and their one and all-embracing theme and content (*gen. obj.*) in the Son of God. The unitary achievement of this knowledge of faith is for the community still future, not merely in respect of the danger constituted by the conjunction of Jews and Gentiles (of which there is so keen an awareness in this Epistle, 2¹¹⁻²¹, 3¹⁻¹³) or other antithetical elements, but also in respect of those who are without, of the world. God has laid all things at the feet of Christ with His resurrection from the dead. He has given Him to be the Head over all things to the Church (1²², cf. Col. 1¹⁷ᶠ·). To all these, to every "fatherhood" (πατρία), to every race in heaven or earth which has its name from the one Father (3¹⁵), to the principalities and powers which control all men, there is now to be declared by the existence of the ἐκκλησία the manifold wisdom of God. But this has hardly happened yet, and it has hardly yet been accepted by those who are without. What exists and takes place without—as reflected in the disunity of the Church itself—does not by a long way take place and exist in the unity of the knowledge of faith for which the whole world is determined. With the whole world (this is the implication of the οἱ πάντες) the community itself is only looking and moving towards this ἑνότης. But as distinct from the world it is already fitted for this looking and moving.

Εἰς ἄνδρα τέλειον. In this context neither " mature " nor " perfect " seems to bring out the true meaning of τέλειος. If the εἰς is not suddenly to point to a different *eschaton* from the preceding, but to indicate the same goal, then in what is described we must have (1) a point which will be reached by the community, and (2) something which is still recognisable as what was previously described as unity. This makes it quite impossible to understand by the ἀνὴρ τέλειος the adult Christian, i.e., the individual Christian who has achieved maturity, or religious and ethical " perfection." The only alternative is to translate τέλειος as complete. But the only ἀνὴρ τέλειος is Christ : the *totus Christus* ; Christ including all those who are elected and justified and sanctified and called in Him ; Christ as the Head with His body and therefore with His community. It may well be that the Gnostic doctrine of a heavenly *anthropos* or *archanthropos* was the formal starting-point for this distinctive expression. But it is quite explicable purely in the context of the Epistle itself without seeking an external derivation of this kind. To Christ there belong all His own—the totality of those elect in Him before the foundation of the world (1⁴). To this Christ (with His πλήρωμα as the later phrase has it) there looks and moves His community to the extent that He is indeed proclaimed to it as such (as explained in chapters 2 and 3), but is not yet manifested, not yet given as the Head who is the Head over all things (1²²). The Christ in whom God in the dispensation of the fulness of times willed to gather together (ἀνακεφαλαιοῦν), and has actually gathered together, all things both in heaven and earth (1¹⁰) is Himself the complete man, the *totus Christus* to whom the community looks and moves as He is proclaimed to it and believed and known by it, but whom it has not yet attained because

He is not yet revealed to it any more than to the world, but concealed from it. It is for this looking and moving to Him that it is already fitted.

Εἰς μέτρον ἡλικίας τοῦ πληρώματος τοῦ Χριστοῦ. If it is again correct to assume that what is stated here is identical with what is described in the preceding phrases, so that (1) we are given fresh light on the one point not yet reached by the community and (2) there is a recognisable identity between what is denoted here and the earlier "unity" and "complete man," the result is that ἡλικία has to be translated "stature" rather than "age." Μέτρον ἡλικίας means the fullest possible measure, the maximum extent, to which a body can grow or stretch. This might refer, of course, to the ἀνὴρ τέλειος. But in this case the third phrase would not really add anything new. And it is not Christ Himself, but the πλήρωμα, to which reference is made. But according to 1²³ His πλήρωμα is the community, His body. It is called His πλήρωμα because, as He belongs to it and it to Him, He is the complete man, the Christ, the *totus Christus*, together with it. The present reference is thus to the community as this πλήρωμα τοῦ Χριστοῦ. It is of the community that it is said that it looks and moves towards the full measure of its stature, of which it still falls far short. This measure cannot be greater than that of the stature of its Head, but it cannot be smaller. For according to 1²³, as the community is His πλήρωμα, He is the One who for His part is τὰ πάντα ἐν πᾶσιν πληρούμενος (cf. Col. 3¹¹). It is to be noted that this is a thought peculiar to Ephesians and Colossians only in its christological form. In substance, exactly the same thing is said in 1 Cor. 15²⁸ in its description of the *eschaton* (θεὸς πάντα ἐν πᾶσιν), and here too it is Christ who introduces this *eschaton*, this complete presence and lordship of God in and over all things. The totality of created essence, in all its forms (ἐν πᾶσιν), cannot be and consist without Him who according to 1²² is its Head. And it must not be without Him. He has subjected it to God (1 Cor. 15²⁸), and God to Him (Eph. 1²²). He has "ascended up far above all heavens," ἵνα πληρώσῃ τὰ πάντα (Eph. 4¹⁰). The ἀνακεφαλαίωσις "of all things" (1¹⁰) has already taken place in Him. The fulfilling of the καιροί, which without Him would be empty, has already been brought about in Him. If the community for its part is the πλήρωμα of Him who is Himself the πλήρωμα of the cosmos, this means that in the full measure of its compass it will embrace no more, but no less, than the cosmos. In other words, the totality of the heavenly and earthly world now has no existence distinct from that of the community, which is the πλήρωμα τοῦ Χριστοῦ. It will still be the ἐκκλησία even when everything that is will be only in it. For it will be the body of Christ—Christ in and with this πλήρωμα. Obviously, in this form, in this measure of its extent or compass, the community itself is absolutely future, just as Christ is absolutely future to it as the ἀνὴρ τέλειος, the One in whom all this is comprehended, and just as that ἑνότης of the knowledge of faith is also absolutely future to it. But it now looks and moves towards itself in this future form. It exists as an "heir" (1¹¹), being predestinated according to the decision (πρόθεσις) of the One who works all things according to the counsel of His will, and therefore already in this status as an heir (1¹²), to magnify His glory as the community of those who already (as προηλπικότες) hope in Christ, the *totus Christus*, and therefore in their own hidden but realised future in the form of this full extent of their compass. And it is for this that the community is already fitted—to look and to move forward to Him in His future form, and therefore to itself in its future form, giving a provisional representation both of Him as the πλήρωμα of all things, and of itself as His πλήρωμα.

After this comprehensive glance at the *eschaton* to be attained by the community, and at its own absolute future, a surprisingly sober turn is given to the continuation in v. 14, which is linked with the preceding sentence by a ἵνα, but which returns us to the Christian present. We now see ourselves again in our present form, within the present world, and therefore as a collection of men who at the very least are in great danger, who are still νήπιοι, immature, "tossed to and fro, and carried about with every wind of doctrine, by the sleight of men, and cunning craftiness which they practise in the service of the μεθοδεία τῆς πλάνης (τοῦ διαβόλου, 6¹¹)." As it is determined and directed by this variegated "method" of the world, which always claims to be solemn διδασκαλία, the community will obviously be incapable of that movement of thought and life towards the *eschaton*. The world around does not know Christ, who is really its Head. Hence it does not know this *eschaton*. If the community, which is itself a race of men, listens to the world around, and thinks in its categories, and seriously (and not just occasionally) speaks its language and conforms its life to its standards, it makes itself incapable of its own hope, which also has reference to and embraces the world. Its view of that ἑνότης, of the ἀνὴρ τέλειος, of the measure of its own stature, is then obscured, and its way to this goal blocked. With its goal, it also loses its direction, as suggested by the picture of the wind and waves. This is what need not and must not happen any more (μηκέτι), for in respect of this danger arrangements have now been made by the Lord, through the ministry of the charismatics mentioned in v. 11 f., to fit it for this looking and moving. The preparation (καταρτισμός) of the saints consists in the recollection, first of what Christ already is, that as the Head of all things He is their Head, and second of what they already are in Him, that as the community they are His body, summoned to hasten towards this being of His and theirs, and therefore to that ἑνότης. This is the truth by which they are determined, and it is absolutely superior to every sleight of men or "method of error" (v. 15). The preparation of the saints consists in their equipment for ἀληθεύειν, i.e., for a life which here and now is lived by and for this truth ; in a love for their Head which will not fail to give inner unity to the Church. Ἀληθεύοντες ἐν ἀγάπῃ in virtue of this preparation, the saints will do the ἔργον τῆς διακονίας (v. 12) and therefore fulfil the meaning of their existence as saints. They will "grow" (a concept to which we shall have to return in the second sub-section), i.e., grow εἰς αὐτόν, into Christ who is their Head, in the direction which He thus gives, and towards the goal which He thus appoints. As the community makes this movement and is engaged in this growth, it exists εἰς ἔπαινον δόξης αὐτοῦ (1¹²). And it may at least be asked whether "in every respect or part" is not too weak a rendering for the τὰ πάντα of this statement ; whether in accordance with the common usage of Ephesians, and the whole tenor of the passage, we ought not to give to the phrase the inclusive sense that in and with the life by and for the truth which the community lives in love the totality of things, the whole world, grows into the One who as its Head is also its πλήρωμα. If this is so, the meaning corresponds to that of the οἱ πάντες of v. 13—that the cosmos, represented in the community which lives its separate life within it, participates in the provisional representation which is the special task of the community.

In v. 16 a description is given of this growing, which in the first instance and intrinsically is, of course, that of the community as such. But we will postpone until later our exposition of this statement.

It is, then, for this provisional representation, for its upbuilding, that the community is fitted. Other terms can, of course, be used to describe it, as, for instance, the growth or maintenance or ordering of the body of Christ. But "the upbuilding of the community" is the main heading which comprehends the others and enables us to see the main outlines of the whole. The important role which it has in the New Testament invites us to begin at this point.

Significant contributions to its understanding have been made by P. Vielhauer, *Oikodome*, 1939, K. L. Schmidt, "Die Erbauung der Kirche mit ihren Gliedern als den Fremdlingen und Beisassen auf Erden" (*Verhandl. des Schweiz. Ref.*

Pfarrvereins, 1946, published 1947), and O. Michel, Art. οἶκος, etc., in Kittel's *Wörterbuch*, V.

In the sense in which we are here using it on the model of the New Testament, the unequivocal reference of the term " upbuilding " is to the Christian community. It is not the Christian individual as such, but the community which, in its individual members and through their reciprocal ministry, is edified, and lets itself be edified, and edifies itself.

In modern times, under the influence of Pietism, we have come to think in terms of the edification of individual Christians—in the sense of their inward inspiration and strengthening and encouragement and assurance. The cognate idea has also arisen of that which is specifically edifying. Now all this is not denied. It is, indeed, included in a serious theological concept of upbuilding. But it is only included. In the abstract, it is quite impossible. Even in Jude 20, which as far as I know is the only verse to which appeal may be made, ἐποικοδομεῖν cannot possibly mean private edification. No such thing is ever envisaged in the New Testament. The New Testament speaks always of the upbuilding of the community. I can edify myself only as I edify the community.

It is a matter of the actual occurrence, the event, the fulfilment, the work of edification, and therefore of the construction of a building. The idea of some parts which have already been built, and are already present in rudimentary form, is no doubt unavoidable and included in the metaphor. But it is not intrinsic to it. Naturally the Christian community has in fact attained to certain states. But it is not the community in virtue of these states. It is so in virtue of the fact that they are the result of its previous development and history and upbuilding, and the starting-point for that which is to follow. It is in the process of passing through these lower or higher rudiments. But it is not actually in any of them.

Even more important is a further distinction that we have to make. The image of building naturally includes the idea—as a focal point for the human work of construction—of the completed edifice. We can and must say of this that it is essential to the whole metaphor. What would Christian edification be if it were not with a view to the future totality ? If the community did not look and move towards this, its building would be futile and it would not—in the course of building— be the Christian community. But in this instance the completed edifice—and the image breaks down at this point—is not identical with the result of the construction. As the community is edified and edifies itself, it looks and waits for the completed edifice which in face of the development and construction in which it is here and now the Christian community will, as its own *eschaton*, be something completely new : not the result of its own existence ; not the final word of its history ; but something which comes to it from God ; its genuine *eschaton*, and therefore that of the whole cosmos.

In the New Testament passages which speak of the οἰκοδομή we do find occasional reference to the outlines of the building as already present. Mention is also made of its completed form. But for good reason the latter is never identified with the result of the work of construction in which the community is engaged. Nor is it regarded as the supreme achievement of the community, even as made possible by the grace of God. The reference is always to another actuality in which the community is not merely future to itself, but transcendent. The holy city, new Jerusalem (Rev. 21²), does not grow up from earth to heaven, but "comes down from God out of heaven, prepared as a bride adorned for her husband." And according to the voice from the throne (v. 3), it is the tabernacle of God with men, in which He will dwell, and they shall be His people, and He shall be with them. The structure and plan and equipment of this city which comes down from heaven are expressly described in the vision of Rev. 21¹⁰⁻²³. But they are those of the building which is future and transcendent to the community. There is no corresponding passage in the New Testament to describe the οἰκοδομή which is the present actuality of the community. The community knows already that it is at home—but only in the there and one day, not in the here and now. " Our πολίτευμα (and therefore our πόλις) is in heaven ; from whence also we look for the Saviour, the Lord Jesus Christ " (Phil. 3²⁰). In our present οἰκοδομή—K. L. Schmidt has laid his finger on this point (*op. cit.*, p. 25)—we are in a foreign land (παροικία, lit. away from home, 1 Pet. 1¹⁷) like Israel in Egypt, so that, even though elect ἐπίδημοι (1 Pet. 1¹), we can be regarded only as πάροικοι καὶ ἐπίδημοι (those whose only right is that of squatters, of actual residence rather than established citizenship, 1 Pet. 2¹¹ and cf. P. 39¹²).

As I see it, we may also inquire at least whether it is really certain that the passage 2 Cor. 5¹⁻⁵ speaks only of the individual anthropological *eschaton* and does not belong rather to our present context, bearing also (although not exclusively) an ecclesiological and eschatological sense. Mention is made in v. 1 of our earthly house which is a tabernacle (ἐπίγειος ἡμῶν οἰκία τῆς σκηνῆς). This house is obviously temporary and will be pulled down. But as we move towards the pulling down of this house there is already prepared for us " a building of God (οἰκοδομὴ ἐκ θεοῦ), an house not made with hands, eternal in the heavens." In the first house we " groan " (vv. 2–4), i.e., with reference to the transition from the first to the second. As we desire to be clothed upon, or covered, by this house (οἰκητήριον) from heaven, we await fearfully the moment when the first house will have gone and we are not yet surrounded and protected by the second, when we are found naked, and find ourselves " on the street." It is no good removing out of the old if there is no assurance of the new. But correction and comfort are at hand. God Himself assures us of a certain entrance into the new, and therefore a calm evacuation of the old (v. 5), by giving us the pledge of the Spirit in our hearts (cf. 1 Cor. 1²²).

To what does all this refer ? According to the verses which precede and follow there can be no doubt that it has an individual and anthropological reference to the transition from our present abode (ἐνδημεῖν) in the σῶμα, the present physical existence of the apostle and Christians generally in which we are not really at home (ἐκδημεῖν) with the Lord (as may be seen from the fact that we now walk by faith and not by sight, vv. 6–7), to a corresponding abode with the Lord, which negatively includes the fact that we are no longer at home in the σῶμα but lose our present physical existence (v. 8). The old house—the earthen vessels in which we now have the treasure (vv. 4, 7), our ἔξω ἄνθρωπος which goes to destruction (4¹⁶)—is certainly (4¹¹) our mortal flesh in the individual anthropological sense of the term. Similarly, the new house prepared by God and awaiting us in heaven is certainly the incorruptible body, the new being, in which the apostle and Christians generally will be at home with the Lord.

On the other hand, the " we " of whom Paul says all this are not in the last resort a plurality of individuals who, taught by the Christian religion, engage in anxious and hopeful reflection concerning their individual death and that which lies beyond. What we have here is another instance of the well-known *pluralis apostolicus et ecclesiasticus*. It is also to be noted that the *eschaton* is expressly described as οἰκοδομή, which, when the ἐπίγειος οἰκία perishes, will come down ἐκ θεοῦ upon those who can longer live in the former. Here, too, their present state is described as only a transitory abode. Nor can we agree with P. Vielhauer (*op. cit.*, p. 108, although he is generally right in his exegesis) that " building " and " house " are anthropological terms in rabbinic Judaism. If they are to be understood as such (which is possible, but unnecessary), we shall have to appeal to Mandæan or Iranian sources. In the New Testament, however, these terms are used with a thoroughgoing ecclesiological connotation. In view of these various points it seems obvious to me that by " our earthly house, which is a tabernacle " and which is therefore doomed to perish, we have first and comprehensively to understand the community in its present form, and only then, and included in this, the present physical existence of the individual Christian as he lives in the σῶμα. Similarly, by " the house not made with hands, eternal in the heavens," we have first and comprehensively to understand the new form of the community (identical with the πολίτευμα of Phil. 3[20] and the heavenly Jerusalem of Rev. 21[2]), which here and now is future and transcendent, but which is perfect and comes down from heaven, from God, upon it, and only then the specific incorruptible οἰκητήριον, the eternal tabernacle (Lk. 16[9]), of the individual Christian which is included in it. In view of the context it cannot be contested that the second thought is in both cases comprised in the first. But in my view it cannot be maintained that the second thought exhausts what Paul has to say in this passage. On the contrary, it has to be recognised that the second is included in the first—the passage having primarily an ecclesiological and eschatological character.

At any rate, it is of this form of the community which here and now is absolutely future that we have to think in the closing words of the passage in Eph. 2[19-22], where in v. 20 (as in 1 Pet. 2[6]) Christ is described as the chief cornerstone (ἀκρογωνιαῖον) of the building erected on the foundation of the apostles and prophets, in v. 21 the whole οἰκοδομή is said to grow in Christ εἰς ναὸν ἅγιον ἐν κυρίῳ, and in v. 22 it is said that in Him " ye also are builded εἰς κατοικητήριον τοῦ θεοῦ ἐν πνεύματι." The antitheses of 2 Cor. 5[1-5] are lacking in this passage, nor is there any explicit indication of a subsidiary anthropological meaning. Here too, however, we have to do with an *eschaton* described first in christological, then in ecclesiological, terms. If the two εἰς of vv. 21 and 22 are to be understood on the analogy of the three εἰς of Eph. 4[13], and if the habitation of God to which the community is built up is to be thought of in terms of the city of Rev. 21[3], this κατοικητήριον and the ναός which is also mentioned are again the building which is built by God Himself and which comes down from heaven, being now constructed with a view to this coming and in the direction of it. In this respect the ναός of v. 21 reminds us of the passage 1 Cor. 3[16-17]. Here the community is no less than three times given the direct name of the temple of God, although immediately before, and with particular emphasis, there is express mention (in vv. 10-15) of the οἰκοδομή of the community on the basis of the θεμέλιος Christ. But perhaps we must assume with Vielhauer (*op. cit.*, p. 85) that the identification of the community with the sacral building of the temple has nothing whatever to do with the previous building ; or that it has to do with it only indirectly in the sense that the attitude of Christians in this building should correspond to the fact that as those they are in the world they are (like the temple in the state and country of Israel) the place where God's glory dwells (Ps. 26[8]). The *tertium comparationis* in this identification is not, then, the building of the temple, or the temple as a work of construction, but its holiness. That " the Spirit of God dwelleth in you " (v. 16) is what makes the community of God a temple which—at the risk of being destroyed by God—it must not defile. This does not mean that this temple is the work and result of the οἰκοδομή which is the problem of the existence of the community of Christ. It is not this, nor is its holiness. In this respect, too, it is helpful to use the term " provisional representation " as a description of what is proper to the community, and supremely obligatory for it. Paul was certainly not addressing either the Corinthian or any other Church as the temple of God already present or being constructed in their οἰκοδομή. He could hardly do this! The same considerations apply to the statements in 1 Cor. 6¹⁹ (" Your body is the temple of the Holy Ghost ") and 2 Cor. 6¹⁶ (" We are the temple of the living God "). Both these refer to the holiness of the place indwelt by the Holy Spirit (which is Christianity). Both have an exhortatory character. Neither makes against a strictly eschatological understanding of the holy temple of Eph. 2²¹. Again, this temple is identical with the temple not made with hands which according to Mk. 14⁵⁸ Jesus was to build in three days after the destruction of the old. Certainly this is the community, but it is the community in its eternal form which is still hidden and awaits a future manifestation.

After this necessary delimitation, we return to the concept of upbuilding understood as the actual work of construction. It is as this work takes place that the Church is the true Church.

What kind of a work is it? What is meant by this construction which is identical with the existence of the Christian community as a historical entity? We have called this concept a metaphor. In its relationship to the description of what we understand by the construction of a house or any other building, it is this. But this does not mean that we are speaking only improperly of a building, and in the strict sense of a very different process which for the sake of clarity we compare with the work of building. Compared with this building, what is the work of an architect and the masons and joiners and other craftsmen directed by him? Do we not have here the proper sense of the term building, and elsewhere only the improper and secondary sense, so that the metaphorical usage is in respect of ordinary construction, and the realistic reference is to this real and original upbuilding? But there is no need of Platonic conceptions. We have only to touch on the problems involved in this concept to be on our guard against any attempt to start from a general idea of what the upbuilding of the community means rather than from the thing itself.

Here too, of course, we do have different and diverse elements which in mutual dependence and support are so arranged and related and integrated with other elements prepared for the purpose as to form a solid structure. But in this case we are forced to use a term like " elements." We cannot possibly speak of " materials " as in ordinary building. For it is living men who are integrated in this way : each with his own original and spontaneous life ; each different from all the rest ; each having his own place and nature, so that he cannot be easily fused with or exchanged for others ; each in his freedom, with his own thoughts and speech and attitudes and acts ; each on his own life's journey and with his own life's work ; each with his own direct and unconditional responsibility. It is with these men and their works that this building is done.

Again, there is a purpose behind the building, and direction in the execution of this purpose. But whereas in ordinary construction we have an owner with his fixed and declared intention and a master-builder with his corresponding plans and directions, in the upbuilding of the community there is only the Lord whose purpose and plan are concealed, or are revealed and made known only in the orders which He continually gives, so that He cannot be nailed down to any intention or procedure supposedly known to those who take part.

Again, there is here a definite arranging and relating and integrating. But whereas in ordinary construction there are finished tasks which can be succeeded by others until the work is complete, in the up-building of the Christian community—although it takes place in a succession of events in time, and there is a progressive building upon that which is already built—it is remarkable that there is no such thing as a finished task. Every step forward includes a repetition of those already taken and those which have still to follow. All further building must be a fresh building from the very first, from the foundation upwards. And there can never be any question of a completion of the whole work.

Again, in the work of those who have a part in the building of the one Lord there is a definite order in which they and their work are graded, with different levels of responsibility and achievement. The only thing is that, as distinct from ordinary construction, there are no superior and inferior functions and tasks, nor can there be a rigid hierarchy of those taking part but only a very flexible hierarchy corresponding to the directness with which each receives orders from the Lord Himself. In this building new dispositions may be made at any time by which (without any question of degradation on the one side or decoration on the other) the last become first and the first last : a leading worker or overseer again dropping back into the ranks and having an important contribution to make as a labourer ; and a labourer or apprentice, without any long training or experience, having the opportunity to work at a higher or even the very highest job.

Finally, having considered various aspects at random, we must also make this point. The picture presented by this upbuilding is certainly one of well-directed effort and manifold activity on an excellent site. We are at the heart of human history in which man, even the Christian, must stir himself for good or evil. But whereas in ordinary building it is only this human activity that we see, we misunderstand the picture presented by this building if we do not see that there is here also a simple, quiet, natural development, an " automatic " yielding of the fruits of the good earth (Mk. 4[28]). It is not for nothing that in the New Testament the picture of building is often confusingly intermingled with that of the divine planting. We have here a growth which is as little the result of human industry as the completion of the building, and a human industry which is only the effect and symptom of this growth, so that whether man sets his hands to work or folds them or even lays them in his lap he can only be a spectator and affirm that it takes place " he knoweth not how " (Mk. 4²⁷)—in a process which continues both when he works and also when he does not, but is perhaps, in the words of Luther, " drinking Wittenberg beer with Philip and Amsdorf." An ordinary building does not grow in this way. And there are, of course, other ways in which we might bring out the difference. But what we have said should be enough to show that we should not allow the notions suggested by the image of building to prevent us from seeing the true nature of this building. It indicates that we must not expect a closely knit structure of thought in our attempt to do this, but only certain points which mark the movement which here (as so often, and at root always, in dogmatics) is the subject of our consideration.

The decisive question is simply this : Who is the true builder ? And there can be no doubt as to the answer. In the strict and primary and ultimate sense it is God Himself and He alone. This is the only correct answer. It is the only one which meets the comprehensive and imperious character of the action in question. It has to be tacitly implied as a self-evident addition even where other builders are seriously named. We are again referred back at this point to what we said at the beginning of the doctrine of sanctification. The upbuilding of the Christian community is a particular aspect and mode of operation of the sanctification in which, whatever may have to be said about the human subject and his work, it is God Himself who is primarily at work : not merely in the totality but in all the details ; not merely in the inauguration but in the completion ; not merely in the background but in the foreground. It is the same God who has created heaven and earth, and among whose earthly creatures are Christians with all that makes them even in the physical sense capable of this activity. It is the same God who in a completely new work of His hand sets and gives a goal for the upbuilding of the community : a goal which is only the further upbuilding of its earthly form in which even Christians are still strangers and pilgrims who seek a country (Heb. 11¹³ᶠ·) ; but which He sets and gives as the builder and maker of a city which hath foundations, although for the moment they have only the promise that they will see this city and dwell in it (Heb. 11¹⁰). The upbuilding of the community in the present time which is the time of its " sojourning " (1 Pet. 1¹⁷) is wholly and utterly the work of this God.

This is expressly stated in 1 Cor. 3⁹ : θεοῦ οἰκοδομή ἐστε (and just before in the same sense : θεοῦ γεώργιον, the field in which God is the husbandman). So, too, in Ac. 15¹⁶ with its quotation from Am. 9¹¹ : " After this I will return, and will build again the tabernacle of David, which is fallen down." As God creates a people for His name among the Gentiles, according to the context of this passage He accomplishes the rebuilding of the ruined house of David, confirming in a wonderful way His faithfulness to Judah-Israel as elected and called by Him, and fulfilling the promise given in and with this election and calling. Again, it is to God and the Word of His grace that Paul commends the Ephesian elders in Ac. 20³²; to God as the One who has the power to build them up and (as His second and new work) to give them an inheritance among all them which are sanctified. Finally, we may refer to 2 Tim. 2¹⁹ᶠ· in which the community is called a great house with all kinds of valuable and less valuable vessels, but God is both the sure foundation and also the master of the house who as such distinguishes between them : " The Lord knoweth them that are his."

This one God who builds is not, however, an anonymous God of power and activity. It is in and through the man Jesus in the power of His Spirit that the one God is at work in the upbuilding of His community. It is He concretely who is the Lord whose activity directs and determines all the activity of men in this work of construction, and who is Himself the One who is primarily and properly at work in every human work. The Christian community is what it is as He Himself is present and speaks and acts as the Author (in the fullest sense of the term) ; as it is therefore His community, and its history is basically His history. As we shall have to consider more particularly in the second sub-section, it is His body, the earthly-historical form of His existence. The more faithfully and distinctly His activity is—not, of course, completed, let alone replaced—but attested and reflected by its own activity, the more definitely there takes place its edification in and with that which is done in all humanity in its own sphere.

In Mt. 16¹⁸, where what is said about the particular function of Peter leaps at once to the eye, we must not overlook the main part of the sentence : οἰκοδομήσω μου τὴν ἐκκλησίαν, which even here and now, in all the temptations and threats of world history, will not be overcome by the powers of death and hell. It is not Peter who builds. Peter, proved to be a disciple by his confession, serves as the rock on which, according to Mt. 7²⁵, a wise man will build. But it is Jesus Himself who builds His Church. And it is because He builds that it is invincible. To the best of my knowledge, this is the only passage in the New Testament— Vielhauer calls it " an erratic block " (*op. cit.*, p. 76)—in which Jesus is explicitly described as the One who builds up the community. But how can He be anything else when He is called its Lord, and He is for the normative apostolic proclamation within it the first and final authority, the theme and unique content ? Who else can be the builder ? As He is a man among men, he builds up His community, integrating—not all men—but those who are called by Him into a common knowledge and faith and life and ministry. The idea of building is differently applied, but the meaning is obviously the same when in 1 Cor. 3¹¹ He is called the one θεμέλιος of the Corinthian Church beside which there can be no other. Why not ? Because this and this alone is laid by God through the ministry of Paul, and the existence and function of others who take part in the οἰκοδομή of the community, including Paul himself, cannot possibly compete with it. If we do not build on this foundation, or if, like those addressed in Heb. 6¹, we act as if the foundation had still to be found and laid, we do not build at all. There is yet another application, but the same meaning, in 1 Pet. 2⁴ᶠ· (and rather less clearly Mt. 21⁴², Lk. 20¹⁷ and Ac. 4¹¹), where a verse which the first community obviously regarded as very important, Ps. 118[22], is related to the idea of building, and Jesus is called the stone which was rejected by the human builders of the house of Israel but chosen and honoured by God and made the headstone of the corner. In 1 Pet. 2[4] He is called the " living stone," and Christians are themselves " living stones " which are built up into Him an οἶκος πνευματικός. In all these different applications it is perfectly clear that in this work of building He has a place and function which in their sovereignty are absolutely unique.

But the active Subject is the God who acts not only in the man Jesus but by Him to and with other men, electing and sanctifying them as well as Him. Thus, although the reference to Jesus is decisive, it cannot be our last word in respect of the subject of this building. Even if only in faith and not in sight, to say " Christ " is to say " Christ and His own "—Christ in and with His fulness, which is His community. As His community (His body), this cannot be merely a passive object or spectator of its upbuilding. It builds itself. And we are forced to say that as its upbuilding is wholly and utterly the work of God or Christ, so it is wholly and utterly its own work. As such, it is, of course, destructible. It constantly needs to be corrected and improved in accordance with the instruction and admonition of the apostles. Nor must we forget that it is subject to future judgment. Yet in all its weakness and need and dubious quality, as a provisional representation of the goal set and given by God it is its own work, a matter of its own activity and responsibility, and therefore its own glory.

There is thus no contradiction when Paul describes himself and Apollos, who had been particularly active in the development of the Corinthian Church, as God's συνεργοί (1 Cor. 3[9]), or when he calls himself the σοφὸς ἀρχιτέκτων who has laid in Corinth the only possible foundation, preaching Jesus Christ (v. 10). As he writes in 2 Cor. 10[8] and 13[10], cf. also 12[19], he has been given by the Lord ἐξουσία to build up—and not to destroy, as he twice adds in a clear allusion to Jer. 1[10] ; the clear and noteworthy distinction between the office of the New Testament apostle and that of the Old Testament prophet being that in the former it is unequivocally a matter of edification and not of destruction. If account has to be taken of a pulling down as well, this will be a matter for the coming Judge. He, Paul, has to build up. He is given ἐξουσία to do this. According to 1 Cor. 3[12f.] this cannot possibly mean that a similar authority is not given in different ways to others, e.g., to Apollos. And Paul realises, as we see from Rom. 15[20], that there have been and are others who have it in the same way as himself, as those who lay the foundation, so that, in a secondary sense, they themselves are a foundation (θεμέλιον) for the community gathered by their word. It is in this sense that in Mt. 16[18] Peter, as the first of all those to whom it is given to know and confess, is called the θεμέλιον on which Jesus will build His community, entrusting to him the keys of the kingdom of heaven. It is in this sense, too, that in Eph. 2[20] the apostles and prophets are called the foundation on which Gentile Christians " are no more strangers and foreigners " in relation to Israel, but " fellow-citizens with the saints, and of the household of God," being incorporated into the reconstruction of the ruined house of David. It is in this sense that Eph. 4[11f.] can call these first human builders, and other charismatics, the tools used for that preparation of the saints. It is specifically emphasised in 1 Cor. 14[3f.] that prophecy serves the edification of the community, the doubtful nature of speaking with tongues (which was so valued in Corinth) emerging in the fact that it is of use only for private edification (the possibility of this is here raised as it were on the margin, only to be rejected at once), but can edify the community only if there are interpreters. " Even so ye, forasmuch as ye are zealous of spiritual gifts, seek that ye may excel to the edifying of the church " (v. 12). " Ye "—note how the circle of those taking part has widened. In this building the apostles are workmen of the first rank, the charismatics of the second, but in 1 Thess. 5^{11} it can be said of Christians generally : οἰκοδομεῖτε εἰς τὸν ἕνα, and in 1 Cor. 10^{23} that which edifies is a criterion of the action which is not merely possible but also συμφέρει and therefore commanded. Edification takes place in love (Eph. 4^{16}) and therefore in that which specifically character-ises the action of all Christians. Love itself edifies (1 Cor. 8^1), whereas the *gnosis* practised in Corinth does not do this but puffs up. In short every Christian, the whole community, is the subject of edification. Within it there are, of course, degrees—the first and the last, the great and the small, those who begin and those who continue, teachers and pupils. But there are no delegated or dimin-ished responsibilities. No single member can evade the question whether and in what sense, in what he now is and does, he participates or not in the upbuilding of the community.

Building up means integration. This is what is done by God, by Jesus, by the apostles and charismatics too, and finally, if it is a true Church, by the whole community in all its members. We have a plurality of men, gathered by the proclamation of the Gospel for the purpose of proclaiming it in the world. These men need to be brought together, to be constituted, established and maintained as a common being—one people capable of unanimous action. For as men they are not in the first instance a common organism, but a heterogeneous collection of individuals who even if they do not conflict do not co-operate. By no natural or historical ties can they be what they have to be in the service of the one Father, as disciples of the one Lord Jesus Christ and in obedience to the one Holy Spirit. Men may some-times be united in other ways to achieve specific individual goals, but they cannot be united in any full or total sense. When they are gathered into the community, they are dedicated to the goal of all goals, and therefore their union must be total and complete and un-conditional. It must be a union in brotherhood. Not in a collective in whose existence and activity the individual is not required as such and his particularity is a *pudendum*. Union in brotherhood is a solid union, but it is a union in freedom, in which the individual does not cease to be this particular individual, united in his particularity with every other man in his. In this context, therefore, upbuilding and therefore integration does not mean the erection of a smooth structure with no distinctive features, but of one in which the corners and edges of the individual elements used all fit together in such a way that they are not merely æsthetically harmonious but also exercise their tech-nical function of mutual dependence and support. The establishment of a wholly positive relationship, in which the different pieces are fitted together, is thus the main problem in the construction of this building. It is love (for one's neighbour) which builds the community.

If this does not do it, the community will not be built. Thus the upbuilding of the community consists concretely in the fact that there is mutual love between the members of the community which is loved by God, by Jesus as its Lord. This leads us to the theme of our final section. For the moment, however, our concern is with the converse that love as the brotherly love of Christians (with no sentimental undertones) consists in the fact that, integrated by God, by Jesus, they mutually adapt themselves to be one organism which can be used in the world in His service. Without this integration and mutual adaptation, there can be no reciprocal dependence and support. And without this the community will inevitably fall apart and collapse. It cannot then be the provisional representation of the humanity sanctified in Jesus Christ. The temporal and historical judgments which overtake the Church in the form of aberrations and confusions, petrifactions and dissolutions, arrests and defeats, are all symptoms that there is no mutual integration. Its upbuilding by God, by Jesus, counteracts this failure, and its own task as it builds up itself is to counteract it. What it has to do in its life and teaching and especially its worship must be done in the mutual dependence and support which have this integration as a presupposition. As it integrates itself in this way, or rather allows the Holy Spirit to exercise it in self-integration, it is the true Church, prepared to look and move forward, to give this provisional representation, and thus to offer the witness which is the meaning of its existence in world-history.

We are using "integration" as an equivalent for the word συναρμολογεῖν as it is used in Eph. 2²¹ in replacement of the Attic συναρμόζειν. It need only be mentioned, and seems to have no exegetical implications, that συναρμόζειν could also be used of musical composition. In Eph. 4¹⁶ συναρμολογεῖν is also applied to the common functioning of the σῶμα Χριστοῦ or its different organs. But ἁρμός means a joint, and ἅρμοσμα is that which is joined together, so that the term belongs originally to the sphere of building and must be considered in this context.

In fact, the true form of this συναρμολογεῖν in the New Testament seems to consist always in an action as between man and man which necessarily has the character of ἀγάπη. And the simplest form of this action consists in a reciprocal relationship in which the one man is neighbour and brother to the other, and *vice versa*, and they meet and act accordingly. This is the "joint." If we ask what it is that takes place at this joint—or at the many joints which limit and bring together those who are built up—so that there is mutual edification (εἰς τὸν ἕνα, 1 Thess. 5¹¹), we do well to follow the hint given by O. Michel (*op. cit.*, p. 143, 28 f.) and note that in this passage the imperative οἰκοδομεῖτε is linked with παρακαλεῖτε ἀλλήλους, and that in 1 Cor. 14³ οἰκοδομή is brought into a similar conjunction with παράκλησις and παραμυθία (comfort). The answer, then, is that at this joint it takes place that "each one receives the consolation of the Gospel and passes it on to others." In some measure there is thus a repetition of the relationship in which the community as such lives in and with the world. But whereas in the latter case the relationship is irreversible, within the community it is reciprocal. We may recall all the passages in which ἀλλήλων occurs to describe the mutual attitude and action of Christians as they mind the things of others (Rom. 12¹⁶), have salt and keep peace among themselves (Mk. 9⁵⁰), receive one another (Rom. 15⁷), admonish one another (Rom. 15¹⁴), forgive one another (Col. 3¹³), subject themselves to one another (Eph. 5²¹), practise hospitality one toward another (1 Pet. 4⁹), bear one another's burdens (Gal. 6²), etc. We may also think of the passages in which the declensions of the pronoun ἑαυτῶν describe the same or similar reciprocal attitudes.

This brings us, of course, into the sphere of Christian ethics. But in its New Testament form Christian ethics is never concerned only with the requirement of an abstract private morality but always with instructions for the edifying of the community. As there is a mutual adoption of these attitudes, the community is built up. It is presupposed that in every detailed application this takes place on the one foundation beside which there can be no other (1 Cor. 3¹¹). But on this foundation there has to be building. There has to be this integration, or fitting together, of the different elements. Thus everything that Christians do is to be judged by the standard whether it serves this integration. Even the finest εὐχαριστεῖν is of no value if the other (and in him the community) is not edified (1 Cor. 14¹⁷). We have also to see to it—for it is men who are at work— that there is not built into this building that which has no value, which does not build up but is dangerous and destructive. If by my example, by the exercise of my freedom to eat flesh sacrificed to idols, I do not edify, i.e., encourage my weaker brother who is uncertain of this freedom, this triumph of my *gnosis* destroys the weaker brother for whom Christ died, so that the community is not built up. Far better not to eat flesh to all eternity than to build in this way (1 Cor. 8¹⁰⁻¹³)! Similarly, the community is not edified when Peter, having already associated with the Gentile Christians at Antioch, again separates himself as a Jew from table-fellowship with them, thus disavowing himself, acting as if, to be Christians, Gentiles must first become Jews, and building again (πάλιν οἰκοδομεῖ) that which he had rightly pulled down, and which in Christ has been pulled down once and for all (Gal. 2¹⁸).

There is, however, a "crisis" which overtakes even the best of Christian building. This is impressively stated in 1 Cor. 3¹²⁻¹⁵, which regards it as self-evident that, although the materials will include gold, silver and precious stones, they will also include wood, hay and stubble. And the day of the manifestation of the completed community (of the coming of the New Jerusalem from God, from heaven, Rev. 21², or the descent of the οἰκία ἀχειροποίητος αἰώνιος, 2 Cor. 5¹); the day of the final and universal revelation of Jesus Christ, will be a *dies irae*, not only for the world but also for the community in its present οἰκοδομή. It will be the day of judgment which begins first at the house of God (1 Pet. 4¹⁷). It will be a day of fire, when everything unserviceable and false that has been built in the community—the wood and hay and stubble with which so much building is actually done—will be burnt up. It is in the same sense that we must understand 2 Cor. 5¹⁰: "For we must all (those who now take part in building) appear before the judgment seat of Christ; that every one may receive the things done in his body, according to that he hath done, whether it be good or bad." Each will receive his reward, we are told in 1 Cor. 3⁸,¹⁴. This is true of those whose work stands, being tried by the fire (v. 13). But who shall stand? *Quid sum miser tunc dicturus?* Paul certainly does not think that those whose building is shown to be false and valueless, and will be burned as wood and hay and stubble, will themselves perish (1 Cor. 3¹⁵). Rom. 8¹ is pertinent in this connexion: "There is therefore now no condemnation to them which are in Christ Jesus." But bad workmen (and this surely includes us all) will suffer loss. This is inevitable, since their work is burned up and destroyed as if, for all the genuine but misplaced zeal they have brought to its performance, it had never been. Yet they themselves will be saved: not because there is anything good or worthy about them; but from the very brink of destruction (ὡς διὰ πυρός, like brands plucked from the burning), because their building has been upon the foundation of Christ, and on this foundation it is forgiven for all its uselessness. It is to be noted that this is the final standpoint from which Paul views, not merely polemically the οἰκοδομεῖν of others like Apollos, but his own work.

On the authority of Christ Himself it is not only necessary but permitted and commanded that all Christians without exception should set their hands to the upbuilding of the community. The integration of Christians, and therefore the edification of the community, must and shall take place. As each has a brother in his neighbour, to whom he must adapt himself and whom he must adapt to himself, the site of building is always present and clearly marked off. No one can excuse himself on the ground that this is a matter which is too high for him. No one can complain that he is unemployed. Each, with equal responsibility and honour, is required and able to be God's συνεργός, actively co-operating in this work which is decisively important for the whole cosmos and its history, for all men near and distant even outside the frontiers of Christendom. But the same Christ on whose authority all this is necessary and permitted and commanded will also be the Judge of his co-operation; of the understanding or lack of understanding that he brings to it; of his obedience or disobedience in its performance; of the zeal or sloth with which he works at the community as a provisional representation of the sanctification of all men as it has taken place in Jesus Christ. As this Jesus Christ will be definitively and universally manifested, he and his particular συνεργεῖν and the συνεργεῖν and οἰκοδομεῖν of all Christians will be revealed at their true worth, or worthlessness, i.e., their usefulness or otherwise in the service of this provisional work of God in a world hastening to its end. The divine glory and his own salvation demand that each should take his Christian being seriously from this standpoint, not regarding the certainty of his salvation ὡς διὰ πυρός as a feather-bed, or as a liberation for all kinds of capricious rovings (both pious and impious). He can have this certainty only as he takes seriously his obligation to this οἰκοδομεῖν, and the thought of the coming and perilous conflagration which will destroy all that which has been built in vain. If we do not take either the one or the other seriously, we cannot have the certainty of Rom. 8[1].

We conclude with a point which is quite indispensable if the picture is to take concrete shape. The work of construction in which the community is the true Church is at its centre, where it continually begins and is directly palpable and perceptible, the work in which, true to its name of ἐκκλησία, the community comes together as the congregation of the Lord and is at work and confesses and gives itself to be known as such before God and His angels and the world and not least itself and its individual members. This work is its common worship.

In connexion with what has to be said on this subject both here and in the fourth sub-section, I must not omit to make express reference to a work of Peter Brunner which is distinguished both for its breadth and profundity—" Zur Lehre vom Gottesdienst der im Namen Jesu versammelten Gemeinde " (in *Leiturgia. Handbuch des evangelischen Gottesdienstes*, Vol. I, 1951). If I cannot follow him at every point, I have been deeply impressed by the seriousness of his investigation and research, and I am pleased to record that we have many essential things in common.

It is not only in worship that the community is edified and edifies itself. But it is here first that this continually takes place. And if it does not take place here, it does not take place anywhere. This is the point where the building of God, and of the divine-human Lord, and of Christians as those who have a part in this building, is distinguished from the dominion and appearance of a mere idea. This is the point where in its totality it becomes a concrete event at a specific time and place. Here all Christians are present and not merely a few individuals. Here there is a general " integration." Here all are turned to all in a basic equality of receptivity and spontaneity, as hearers and doers of the Word of God (Jas. 1²²). And here, as they are summoned in the power of the Holy Spirit of their risen Lord to look forward together to His future manifestation and their own *eschaton*, they are commonly set in motion in the direction of the goal of their edification as given and set for the community at the end of the last time. In all its elements, not merely in the administration of the Supper but in its goal in communion, Christian worship is the action of God, of Jesus, and of the community itself for the community, and therefore the upbuilding of the community. From this centre it can and should spread out into the wider circle of the everyday life of Christians and their individual relationships. Their daily speech and acts and attitudes are ordained to be a wider and transformed worship. It is, however, at this centre that communion as the essence of Christian worship takes place in its primary form, affecting, engaging and claiming, but also supporting, all individual Christians in common. And it is again at this centre that the community—not a collective but the living community of living Christians—is unitedly at work and necessarily visible as such both by individual Christians and the outside world. It is here that it edifies itself, and it is here that it decides whether and in what sense it edifies itself elsewhere, outside, in the wider circle of everyday life ; whether and in what sense it will finally demonstrate to the world that it is a provisional representation of its reconciliation, justification and sanctification as they have taken place in Jesus Christ. If it does not edify itself here, it certainly will not do so in daily life, nor in the execution of its ministry of witness in the cosmos.

The hint given by Vielhauer (*op. cit.*, p. 115) is to be noted in this respect : " It is hardly a historical accident, or a result of the historical situation, that Paul uses the word (οἰκοδομή) most frequently where he speaks of the congregation gathered for worship, as in 1 Cor. 14. The cult is for the *ecclesia* the true mode of manifestation. . . . This is the true seat of edification." Rom. 12¹ may be quoted to this effect : " I beseech you therefore, brethren, by the mercies of God, that ye present your bodies a living sacrifice (θυσία), holy, acceptable unto God, and thus (render) your λογικὴ λατρεία." To be sure, the aim is the totality of Christian existence. But it is no accident that this is called " reasonable " (appropriate) worship, and that the " offering " of it is described in cultic terms as a " sacrifice." It is to divine service that all come in a common physical meeting, and therefore in worship that the Christian existence as a whole takes place and is revealed as it were *in nuce*. It is with a reference to this centre that we have also to understand Rom. 15¹⁶, where in his quality as an apostle to the Gentiles Paul styles himself a λειτουργὸς Χριστοῦ ᾿Ιησοῦ, charged in the

Gospel of God to fulfil a holy service (ἱερουργεῖν), offering the Gentiles as a sacrificial gift (προσφορά) pleasing to God because sanctified by the Holy Ghost. The same is true of Phil. 2¹⁷, where in reference to his awaiting martyrdom he says that he will be poured out (σπένδομαι like a drink-offering) with a view to the θυσία καὶ λειτουργία τῆς πίστεως ὑμῶν, i.e., the sacrifice, the priestly service, which the community for its part has to offer in and with its faith. Worship and the everyday life of Christians—a point which seems to be obscured at least in what seems to me to be the rather abstract presentation of E. Brunner (*op. cit.*, *E.T.*, p. 60 f. and 108)—are not two departments which are separate although they belong together, but two concentric circles of which worship is the inner which gives to the outer its content and character—an understanding which obviously enabled Paul (Rom. 13⁶) to speak of λειτουργοὶ θεοῦ even in relation to a wider circle still, that of the representatives of a heathen state. This does not mean that what takes place at this centre, in Christian worship, is a new sacrifice (as in the basic misunderstanding of the Eucharist from the 2nd century onwards). Paul and the first community could not possibly have said or intended this. For, as they saw so clearly, the sacrifice of Jesus Christ had been offered once for all and could not be repeated. The point of this terminology is to show that the action which was conjoined for Jews and Gentiles with the idea of sacrifice—that of the concrete assembling of the people of God—has to represent the fulfilment and termination of human sacrifice in the concrete συναρμολογεῖν of Christians: i.e., in their common speaking and hearing of the Word of God ; in their common calling upon God in thanksgiving, penitence, intercession and especially praise ; and finally and supremely in their common eating and drinking in remembrance of the death of the Lord, in joy at His resurrection, and in the expectation of His coming again. It is from this point that their whole life (in an extension and transformation of the term) has to be appropriate worship and thus to take the form of mutual edification—the upbuilding of the community.

It is true that although the occurrence and forms of divine service are continually touched on in the New Testament it is difficult for us to form a clear picture of it from the canonical texts. It is also clear that there are few explicit references to its central importance and necessity. To be sure, the warning of Heb. 10²³ᶠ· is most instructive in view of the context in which it occurs. But as far as I know this is the only place where Christians are expressly told to " hold fast the profession without wavering," to " consider one another to provoke unto love and to good works " (the concrete action of οἰκοδομεῖν), and not to forsake " the assembling of themselves together (τὴν ἐπισυναγωγὴν ἑαυτῶν), as the manner (ἔθος) of some is "—the less so as they " see the day approaching." We can be sure that this " manner " or custom, and therefore the possibility of a Christianity outside the Church and aloof from its common worship, could only be the object of supreme bewilderment to the New Testament community. To avoid ἐπισυναγωγή was on exactly the same level as to let go the profession, to fail to provoke to good works and therefore edify, or to ignore the approaching day. Assembling for divine worship is self-evidently the centre and presupposition of the whole Christian life, the atmosphere in which it is lived. It hardly needs to be specifically emphasised or described.

What we have to say concerning the New Testament writings as such is to the same effect. It is a matter for academic discussion whether the Fourth Gospel in particular is full of references to worship, especially to baptism and the Lord's Supper, as O. Cullman assumes (*Urchristentum und Gottesdienst*, 1944). There can be no doubt, however, that this Gospel, and the Synoptics and Epistles, are not written for private instruction but for mutual edification, and therefore with a view to, and partially perhaps directly for, public worship. At any rate, they give us the concrete form (or its deposit) of the *kerygma* preached in the assembled community. It is not for nothing, then, that interspersed among them we find numerous fragments of prayer and confession and hymns and greetings and blessings and doxologies and other liturgical elements. It is not for nothing that their language has to some extent a directly liturgical character. They are therefore misunderstood both as a whole and in detail if—not merely in general but also and primarily in this particularity—they are not understood as writings specifically designed to edify, i.e., to build up and integrate, the community.

2. THE GROWTH OF THE COMMUNITY

We have been considering how far that which is called the Church, and claims and seems to be the Church, is really the true Church. That is, how far does it correspond to its name ? How far does it exist in a practical expression of its essence ? How far is it in fact what it appears to be ? How far does it fulfil the claim which it makes and the expectation which it arouses ? We have given the general answer that it is the true Church in the event or occurrence or act of its upbuilding as a community. Our next task is to explain the concept of this event of upbuilding, unfolding it in its most important dimensions.

It will repay us if we first interpret it in terms of the credal concept of the *communio sanctorum*. The upbuilding of the community is the communion of saints.·

I may again refer to a book by Dietrich Bonhoeffer. This is the dissertation which he wrote and published—when he was only twenty-one years of age— under the title *Sanctorum communio, Eine dogmatische Untersuchung zur Soziologie der Kirche*, 1930. If there can be any possible vindication of Reinhold Seeberg, it is to be sought in the fact that his school could give rise to this man and this dissertation, which not only awakens respect for the breadth and depth of its insight as we look back to the existing situation, but makes far more instructive and stimulating and illuminating and genuinely edifying reading to-day than many of the more famous works which have since been written on the problem of the Church. As Ernst Wolf has justly remarked in his preface to the new edition of 1954, many things would not have been written if Bonhoeffer's exposition had been taken into account. I openly confess that I have misgivings whether I can even maintain the high level reached by Bonhoeffer, saying no less in my own words and context, and saying it no less forcefully, than did this young man so many years ago.

If we are to use it in interpretation of the concept of " upbuilding " the term communion must be given the strict sense of the Latin *communio* and the Greek κοινωνία. Communion is an action in which on the basis of an existing union (*unio*) many men are engaged in a common movement towards the same union. This takes place in the power and operation of the Holy Spirit, and the corresponding action of those who are assembled and quickened by Him. Communion takes place as this divine and human work is in train ; as it moves from its origin in which it is already complete to its goal in which it will be manifest as such. Communion takes place in the sphere of the incomplete between completion and completion, i.e., between union and union. At each stage of its fulfilment it is itself *per definitionem* incomplete. It takes place in the completion, the *unio*, from which it comes and to which it goes. In the measure that it takes place at this centre among many men, and their participation in this fulfilment, there also takes place the fact that these many are together and act in common, so that they are united among themselves—not because their unity has still to be established, but because it has taken place already, and they come from it together, and together move toward the revelation of its concealed reality. As they look backwards and forwards from this unity to the same unity, they are united, and are together, and act in common. In this communion there takes place the upbuilding of the community.

It is the saints who are and act in this communion. The saints are men who exist in the world, and after the fashion of the world, but who, in virtue of the fact that they come from the union presupposed in the event of their communion and move forward to its revelation, are integrated and engaged in self-integration. The saints are men who are gathered by the power and work of the Holy Spirit and appointed to do the corresponding work. They live and act in the occurrence of this communion, and therefore in mutual conjunction. As they now live and act on earth, in time, at the heart of world history (or as they have lived and acted, for those whose life is over have not dropped out of this fellowship), they are still the *communio peccatorum*, members of the race of Adam, participant in the transgression and fall and misery of all men. But in spite of this, and in triumph over it, they are already distinguished from all other men, constituting in face and on behalf of the world the *communio sanctorum* —a provisional representation of the new humanity in the midst of the old. These men—the saints—who live and act in the communion of the one Holy Spirit, and therefore in communion one with another, are Christians.

But what makes them Christians? In a final description of the basis of their particular being and action, we can and must reply that it is God's eternal election, His love directed towards them and embracing and activating them in this particular way, which makes them Christians, not only as individuals in their solitariness, but also in their common life, and therefore all together as a people of single descent. For the moment, however, we are concerned to know what it is that distinguishes their being and activity as men on earth and in time. What is the distinctive thing which becomes a historical event in their fellowship? To see this, we have to remember the twofold sense in which the Church is called the *communio sanctorum* in the creed. The genitive certainly indicates that it is the communion of the *sancti*, i.e., of those who are sanctified by the Holy Spirit, of all Christians of every age and place. But it also means—and apart from this we cannot see what it is that makes them *sancti* in their human being and activity—communion in the *sancta* : the holy relationships in which they stand as *sancti* ; the holy gifts of which they are partakers ; the holy tasks which they are called upon to perform ; the holy position which they adopt ; the holy function which they have to execute. From this standpoint the *communio sanctorum* is the event in which the *sancti* participate in these *sancta*. We may thus give the following material definition of the communion of saints. It takes place as the fellowship of Christians in the knowledge and confession of their faith. It undoubtedly takes place also and even basically— if we understand the terms in their comprehensive sense—as a theological and confessional fellowship. It takes place as the fellowship of their thankfulness and thanksgiving. It takes place as the fellowship of their penitence (leading to conversion), but also with the joy without which there cannot be this penitence in the conversion of the saints. It takes place as the fellowship of prayer, which, even when it is in the secret chamber, cannot be a private talk with God but only the prayer of the community. It takes place, in relationship to the world, as the fellowship of the need of those who are moved by the burdens of the world, and the promise given to it, as their own innermost concern ; yet also, in this relationship, as the fellowship in arms of those who are determined, in order to be true to the world and meaningfully to address themselves to it, not in any sense to be conformed to the world. It takes place as the fellowship of service in which the saints assist and support one another, and in which they have also actively to attest to those outside what is the will of the One who has taken them apart and sanctified them. It takes place as the fellowship of their hope and prophecy looking and reaching beyond the present, but also looking and reaching beyond every temporal future. Above all, of course, it takes place as the fellowship of their proclamation of the Gospel, of the Word by which they are gathered and impelled and maintained. For this reason, and because it takes place as the fellowship of prayer, it takes place as the fellowship of divine service—a liturgical fellowship. And in and above all these things it takes place as the fellowship of worship, of the silent or vocal adoration and praise of Almighty God. We do not claim that this is an exhaustive list, but these are the *sancta* with which we are concerned in the being and action of the *sancti*, of Christians, and therefore in the *communio sanctorum*. The *sancti* are those to whom these *sancta* are entrusted. They are not entrusted to any of us as private individuals. They are entrusted to us all only in conjunction with others. In this way, but only in this way, they are entrusted to each of us personally. Thus the *communio sanctorum*, as the upbuilding of the community, is the event in which, in the being and activity of ordinary sinful men, in a *communio* which is still and always a *communio peccatorum*, we have to do with the common reception and exercise of these *sancta*.

On the presupposition that the upbuilding of the community takes place in the communion of saints, we may now address ourselves to the proper task of this section. This is to see and understand the dimensions in which this event takes place.

In this sub-section we will take an inward look and try to understand the character immanent to this event as such. To describe this, we will venture the proposition that it takes place as a growth.

The term growth ($a\mathring{v}\xi\epsilon\iota\nu$, $a\mathring{v}\xi\acute{a}\nu\epsilon\iota\nu$) is one which in the New Testament is parallel to the main concept of $o\mathring{i}\kappa o\delta o\mu\acute{\eta}$. Sometimes, indeed, the two seem to cross and the idea of growth seems to confuse the sense in which the Bible speaks of building. In fact, however, it clarifies it. And we have already been forced to touch on it in our treatment of the thought of building, when we recalled the seed which grows of itself in Mk. 4²⁶⁻²⁹. The term denotes the distinctive character of this $o\mathring{i}\kappa o\delta o\mu\acute{\eta}$. It points to its secret. The community does not grow only because and as it is built by God and men. In this sense we can say of any other building that it grows. In this particular building the growth is primary. God and men build the community in consequence, confirmation, concretion and glorification of its growth. It grows, and its upbuilding manifests the fact that it does so. This is the secret of its construction.

Growth is an image taken from the organic world. Its use does not mean that the communion of saints is an organism, any more than the use of that of building denotes that it is an edifice. If we press them logically, the two images are mutually exclusive. In fact, however, the image of growth elucidates that of building. It shows us that the occurrence of the communion of saints, and therefore the upbuilding of the community, takes an analogous form to that of organic growth. The *tertium comparationis* is its augmentation, extension and increase from within itself; its development without any outward or alien assistance in the power of its own form and direction; the $a\mathring{v}\tau o\mu\acute{a}\tau\eta$ of Mk. 4²⁸. The secret of the communion of saints is that it is capable of this expansion and engaged in it. That human planning and speech and faith and love and decision and action are also involved according to the divine will and order is also true. This is not compromised by the reference to the secret of the growth of the community. But in itself this is no explanation of the secret, nor can it call in question the reference to it. That the community as the communion of saints grows like a seed to a plant, or a sapling to a tree, or a human embryo to a child and then to a man, is the presupposition of the divine as well as the human action by which it is built. It grows—we may venture to say—in its own sovereign power and manner, and it is only as it does this that it is built and builds itself. The fact that the saints become, that they are conceived and born and then live and act in the *communio* of all these *sancta* and therefore in mutual *communio*, is something which from first to last is primarily and properly a growth.

As I see it, not merely the parable of the seed which grows secretly but also that of the sower (Mk. 4³⁰⁻³² and par.) refers to the community existing in the last age of world history. Growth is a process which takes time. To what can the parables refer if not to the kingdom of God come in time and proclaimed in time ? It is in this form, and only in this form, that the kingdom can be compared to a seed which grows irresistibly larger until it reaches its full stature. As long as it has a history, the kingdom of God has its history in the community which exists in history. The two parables tell us that the history of the community, because and as it comes from the kingdom of God as the communion of saints, and moves towards this kingdom and proclaims it, is the history of a subject which grows of itself.

But before we probe the matter more deeply we must ask in what this growth consists.

The most obvious, although not necessarily the final answer, is not to be summarily rejected—that the communion of saints shows itself to be fruitful in the mere fact that as it exists it enlarges its own circle and constituency in the world. It produces new saints by whose entry it is enlarged and increased. Of course, we are not told, even by the parable of the seed, that it will become constantly greater in this way so that all living men may eventually become Christians. What we are told is that it has the supreme power to extend in this way, that it does not stand therefore under serious threat of diminution, and that as a subject which grows *per definitionem* it has an astonishing capacity even for numerical increase. It is not self-evident that this should be the case ; that it should have this capacity ; that there should always be Christians raised up like stones to be Abraham's children. The more clearly we see the human frailty of the saints and their fellowship as it is palpable both at the very outset and in every epoch, the more astonishing we shall find it that from the very first and right up to our own time it has continually renewed itself in the existence of men who have been reached by its feeble witness and have become Christians in consequence. It is no doubt true that its power in this respect has been largely denied through the fault of Christians, or its exercise confined to a limited sphere. But it is also true, and perhaps even more true, that it has always had and demonstrated this capacity. It has propagated itself even where everything seemed to suggest that this was quite impossible. It has continually, and often very suddenly, assumed new forms—sometimes for the better, sometimes not for the better, but without forfeiture of its essential and recognisable essence. For always, directly or indirectly awakened and gathered by its existence, there have been Christians, and therefore men who have come to this fellowship and then lived and acted in it. As these men—often in the strangest places, and the very last that one would expect—have arisen and come to it, i.e., have discovered, and confirmed the fact, that they belonged to it, the community has grown. It does not matter whether the growth has been big or little. The fact remains that it has continually grown. And it still grows. It has the power to do so.

The New Testament itself knows and emphasises this primitive, if we like, but not really non-essential aspect of the growth of the community, or its immanent power to grow in this sense. The Book of Acts is particularly relevant in this connexion. When Peter gave his witness on the day of Pentecost, some 3000 people were added to the Church, receiving the Word and accepting baptism (Ac. 2[41]). The joyful worship of the community had as its consequence that the Lord added daily to the Church those who are saved (2[47]). Very soon the number of those who had heard the Word and come to faith had jumped to about 5000 (4[4]). Further increase created the administrative problem solved by the commissioning of Stephen, and his fellows (6[1f.]), and this in turn resulted in a further increase in numbers (including a great company of priests), but also in the persecution which claimed Stephen as the first Christian " martyr." The remarkable expression used in 6[7] is that " the word of God increased ; and the number of the disciples multiplied greatly." The phrase occurs again in 12[24], and also in 19[20] where it is added that " it prevailed," i.e., for the winning of others. Similarly we are told in 16[5] that the faith of the Churches in Asia Minor was strengthened, and that they increased in number (in membership) daily. What Luke has in mind in these passages is the αὐξάνεσθαι καὶ πληθύνεσθαι over the whole earth promised to the first man in Gen. 1[28] (LXX), and also of the growth and increase of the people of Israel in Egypt (Ex. 1[7] and Ac. 7[17]), which for its part was the fulfilment of the corresponding promises already given to the patriarchs. It is clear that for Luke, with his universalistic outlook, this was an important matter. The community exists in universal history, and it undoubtedly has the power to multiply in this history and therefore extensively (or, as we may say with Luke, numerically), and thus to grow in this sense.

On the other hand, it would clearly be quite inappropriate to understand this distinctive power of the community only, or even predominantly, as a power for extensive growth. It is obviously vital to it, as a society existing in history, that it should continually increase and extend its numbers. It has constant need of more saints if it is to fulfil the purpose of its temporal existence. Its task is so varied and comprehensive that it can never have enough. But the process of numerical expansion is not as such unequivocal ; the less so when the increase is most imposing, but basically even when it is only slight. Where there is expansion, is it really to the saints that other saints are added, becoming disciples and witnesses with them ? Or is it merely a question, as in other human societies, of men drawing large crowds and thus enjoying success ? Is the growth in virtue of a power absolutely distinctive to the community of saints, or merely in terms of a dynamic which might also be, and is, that of the *communio peccatorum* as well ? A power which has only an abstractly extensive effect is certainly not the power which characterises the community ; and in the same way a growth which is merely abstractly extensive is not its growth as the *communio sanctorum*. Thus it can never be healthy if the Church seeks to grow only or predominantly in this horizontal sense, with a view to the greatest possible number of adherents ; if its mission to the world becomes propaganda on behalf of its own spatial expansion. It has to attest the Gospel. It has to seek a hearing and understanding for the Gospel's voice. It cannot do this without exerting itself to win new witnesses. But this cannot become an end in itself. It knows of only one end in itself—the proclamation of the kingdom of God. And it has to achieve this, not merely in its words, but in its whole existence. In the service of this end in itself it will necessarily also be an end to win new witnesses and by their addition to increase extensively. But it will not forget that it is a great and rare matter when a man comes to faith ; when he becomes a witness of the Gospel, a saint, a Christian. As it is out for the existence of as many Christians as possible, it will have to resist the temptation to win them by diluting the wine with a little water. It will certainly be disturbed and sad, but it will not be horrified, that the increase in the number of Christians is not so easy ; that it does not go forward indefinitely ; that a clearly defined limit always seems to be set to it. It will not imagine that, as itself only a race of men with others charged to give a provisional representation of the new humanity at the heart of the old, it will ever in its present historical form embrace the totality or even the majority of men. It will never equate itself in its present form with the *eschaton* which comes to it afresh from God. It will not, therefore, be of the opinion that it can and should actualise this *eschaton* here and now. It will be confident that the power of growth operative within it will not fail in this world, accomplishing no less, if no more, than that which is right and necessary here and now in accordance with its own law. It will thus allow this power to rule and give itself to serve it. But always it will be more concerned about the quality than the quantity of those who are already Christians, or who may become such. And it will be even more concerned about the realisation of its own communion ; the common reception and exercise of the *sancta* by the *sancti*.

It is no reproach to Luke, but it must be noted that he is the only one of the New Testament writers who is so obviously concerned about the numerical increase of the community. And the question may well be raised whether the few places in which he speaks of an increase of the Word of God, while they have this undeniable immediate reference, do not point also in a different direction. At any rate, it is worth noting that it is the same Luke who in the Gospel has recorded the saying about the little flock to which the kingdom is given (12^{32}), and also the saying which is quite unparalleled in the New Testament in respect of the implied restriction in the extensive increase of the community : " Nevertheless, when the Son of man cometh, shall he find faith on the earth ? " (18^8). In this bleak utterance it is shown to be questionable whether He will find and encounter the faith of anyone at all, even the faith of the community. How, then, can there be any question of the totality, or even the majority, of men standing in the Christian faith ? We can thus learn from Luke himself that the Lucan view has its limits—although we have also to learn from him that the personal and extensive and quantitative increase of the community is a serious and necessary problem. For the rest, on a right understanding there is no contradiction between increase in this sense and the fact that in relation to the world the community must always recognise and confess that it is a little flock, knowing only too well what it is to sigh with Ps. 12^1 (in the familiar Prayer Book version) : " Help me, O Lord, for there is not one godly man left : for the faithful are minished from among the children of men."

Of course, a rather different and wider conception may easily insinuate itself in the context of the legitimate concept of the extensive growth of the community, and of this we can only say that it has to be rejected out of hand. Can it really be characteristic of the communion of saints to increase in consequence and prestige and influence and outward pomp in the world around ; to command increasing authority and esteem for itself as a recognised force, both from the state and from all other human societies ; to win an assured and generally acknowledged place in the structure and activity of worldly politics and scholarship and literature and art ? We need hardly demonstrate or bemoan the fact that the Church has often acted as if a positive answer had to be given to this question. But the very opposite is the case. The Church has the promise that " the gates of hell shall not prevail against it " (Mt. 16¹⁸), but it has no promise to this effect. Its glory will be manifest when that of its Lord is manifest to the world. In the time between it is thankful for all the necessary space that it is granted in the world to fulfil its task. But the enlargement (or diminution) of this space has nothing whatever to do with its nature or commission. Its enlargement is not promised, nor its diminution demanded. It has its hands full with the task of filling it in the service of its cause according to measure in which it is given (whether great or small). It will not be surprised or annoyed if it is pushed into the corner ; or if sometimes it is forcefully deprived (*per fas* or *nefas*) of its outward majesty and pushed even more into the corner. It is always seriously mistaken if it tries to grow in this dimension. The Church of Jesus Christ can never—in any respect—be a pompous Church.

The true growth which is the secret of the upbuilding of the community is not extensive but intensive ; its vertical growth in height and depth. If things are well—and there is no reason why they should not be—this is the basis. The numerical increase of the community indicates that it is also engaged in this very different increase. But the relationship cannot be reversed. It is not the case that its intensive increase necessarily involves an extensive. We cannot, therefore, strive for vertical renewal merely to produce greater horizontal extension and a wider audience. At some point and in some way, where it is really engaged in vertical renewal, it will always experience the arising of new Christians and therefore an increase in its constituency, but perhaps at a very different point and in a very different manner and compass from that expected. If it is used only as a means for extensive renewal, the internal will at once lose its meaning and power. It can be fulfilled only for its own sake, and then—unplanned and unarranged—it will bear its own fruits. As the communion of saints takes place, the dominant and effective force is always primarily and properly that of intensive, vertical and spiritual growth.

This is the power in which the saints increase in the reception and exercise of the holy things entrusted to them ; in which as *sancti* they increase in relation to the *sancta* commonly addressed to them, and by them to others. In this relation there is enacted a history. For it is not just a step or two but a whole wide way from the lower to the higher, which in turns becomes a lower to that which is higher still, and so continually. Where do we not have to make this way from good to better faith and knowledge and confession, to better

thought and penitence and joy, to better prayer and hope and proclamation and worship or any other *sancta*, in short from good to
better communion of the saints in holy things ? The power immanent
in the community is the power of this history, and therefore the power
to go this way (or these many ways) as we should, not as individual
Christians but together as the community in which there is mutual
admonition and encouragement and warning and comfort and assistance and support. It is as the community goes this way, or these
ways, in its immanent power that it knows inward increase and extension and expansion—inward growth.

But we must not understand the matter too much in pedagogic
terms, as though there were a general curriculum of instruction which
must be followed point by point with a view to passing an examination, and which has actually been followed in the course of Church
history. For the *sancti* of the different times and places in which their
communio is achieved, what is lower and higher and higher still, what
is good and better in relation to the *sancta* may differ very widely in
detail. Old aims may drop away altogether, and new ones arise and
force themselves on our attention. There may be remarkable inversions in recognised and apparently immutable evaluations. Everything may take a very different course here and now from what it
did there and then. Nor can there ever be any question—we are
referring to the community in time and on earth, and therefore engaged
in pilgrimage as also a *communio peccatorum*—of achieving the highest
and best in any of these relationships ; of a point at which the community, or some Christians within it, think that they have already
brought their lambs to safety. We have always to reckon with the
fact that the community, and all the Christians living and acting in
it, are continually set on the way—and rather ungently sometimes if
they are disposed to slumber. We have also to accustom ourselves
to the thought that on all the ways on which Christendom journeys
we shall be constantly faced, not only by the limit of its creatureliness
and sinfulness, but also by the fact that, as in respect of its outward
extension, so also of its inward growth, there is a limit which it cannot
and should not pass because it is not ordained to give a. perfect but
only a provisional and therefore imperfect representation of the new
humanity, God having reserved the definitive and perfect representation for His kingdom which comes in the final manifestation. The
community of the *sancti* has to respect this limit of its relationship to
the *sancta*. Finally, we have also to accept the fact that even within
this limit the inward growth of the community may often have the
appearance of its opposite : of apparent pauses ; of narrow straits in
which it seems to be hemmed in inwardly by steep walls with no way
of escape or advance ; of apparent retrogressions in which even that
which has been believed and known and confessed or given seems to
be taken away again, but which have to be passed through and endured

and suffered in order that there may be real growth and increase and expansion. Nothing is more astonishing than the true, intensive, spiritual growth of the communion of saints on earth. In Church history—but who really knows how it really happened and does happen?—we are given a glimpse of the power which is continually at work in new and often contradictory and interrupted but ongoing processes of growth. To conclude, we may observe that this force effects even the spiritual increase of the communion of saints according to its own law. To be sure, it is the power of growth immanent in the community itself—and we have still to consider what this means. But its rule and efficacy are not according to the plans and efforts of Christians. It is a matter of their spiritual growth, and not therefore of a growth which they themselves can direct. It will continually have for them the greatest of surprises, sometimes glad and sometimes bitter. In moments when it is resolved to offer " reasonable service," the plans and efforts of Christians will have to be ruled by it, and not the reverse. To their own astonishment it will continually exalt the lowly, enrich the poor, give joy to the sad and make heroes of the feeble. The rule and efficacy of the power of this growth can never be measured, foreseen or assessed by the ordinary standards of history, even when Christians try to think of their own history in relation to that of the world. It leads the community on a new and distinctive path through world history. But it *leads* them, and as it does so the community grows, either with or without repercussions in world history. And as it grows spiritually, there is no compulsion but it may also grow in the first way, extensively and numerically.

It is hard to decide formally which of these two directions in the growth of the community is denoted by the parables in Mk. 4²⁶⁻²⁹ and ³⁰⁻³². It would be foolish, however, to argue that in their exposition there can be no other understanding than that illustrated in Acts, so that in view of these passages we can speak quite freely of the extension of the kingdom of God over the whole earth, or the evangelisation of the world in our own or the next or the next but one generation. The rest of the New Testament obviously points in the second of the two directions. Αὐξάνειν in 2 Cor. 10¹⁵ means growth in faith, as does also 2 Thess. 1³, which speaks of increase in love as well. In Col. 1¹⁰ᶠ· it is increase in the knowledge of God—with strengthening in endurance and joyful patience. In 2 Cor. 9¹⁰ it is the growth of the fruits of righteousness, and in 2 Pet. 3¹⁸ growth in grace. The πληθύνειν of 1 Pet. 1² and 2 Pet. 1² points in a similar direction. In 1 Cor. 15⁵⁸ περισσεύειν is increase in the work of the Lord, with a corresponding steadfastness and immovability. In 2 Cor. 1⁵ it is the increase of comfort, in 2 Cor. 4¹⁵ of thanksgiving, in 2 Cor. 8⁷ of faith, the word, knowledge and zeal, in 2 Cor. 9⁸ of grace for every good work, in Rom. 15¹³ of hope (by the power of the Holy Spirit). In Phil. 1⁹ it is the enrichment of love in knowledge and understanding, and in Col. 2⁷ it is again the deepening or enlarging of thanksgiving. Similarly, the expression προκοπὴ τοῦ εὐαγγελίου in Phil. 1¹²ᶠ· does not seem from the context to refer to numerical increase but to the strengthening of the attitude of the community which Paul expects from his presence within it. In short, the progress of the Church—to adopt a term which has gained a peculiar currency in the ecclesiastical politics of Basel—denotes in the New

Testament primarily and predominantly, although not exclusively, spiritual progress ; the progress of the *sancti* in their relationship to the *sancta*. Progress means that they go forward together on the appointed way from their origin to their goal. The New Testament sees that where there is the communion of saints this progress may be expected. And it finds in this progress the true form of the growth which the community has to owe to the power immanent within it. It is in this happening that there is actualised its true nature and essence ; its appointment to give a provisional representation within the old humanity of the new humanity sanctified already in Jesus Christ.

It is legitimate and even incumbent to gather together what has to be said about the occurrence of the communion of saints, in so far as it consists in its growth (both horizontal and vertical), in the simple statement that the community *lives* as the communion of saints. Growth is the expression, fulfilment and mark of life. The power by which the community grows is the immanent power of life. As we recognise the life of the community in its growth, and its power of life in its power to grow, we are brought face to face with the question which has not yet been answered in this discussion—that of the nature of this indwelling or immanent power of the community. We may give a preliminary answer in the second and very simple statement that the community lives as the communion of saints because and as Jesus lives. Jesus is the power of life immanent within it ; the power by which it grows and therefore lives. This is what we must now explain.

In the thesis at the head of the section we have spoken of the Holy Spirit as the quickening power by which Christianity is built up as the true Church in the world. But as we made it clear it is Jesus the Lord who is at .work in this quickening power of the Holy Spirit. And we must now take up again that which we have already said, and maintain that according to the normative view of the New Testament the Holy Spirit is the authentic and effective self-attestation of the risen and living Lord Jesus ; His self-attestation as the Resurrected, the living One, the Lord, the exalted Son of Man, in whom there has already been attained the sanctification of all men, but also the particular, factual sanctification of Christians—their union with Him and therefore with one another. In the Holy Spirit as His self-attestation we know Him ; which means again that we know Him as the Resurrected, the living One, the Lord, the exalted Son of Man, in whose exaltation all men are sanctified, and especially, factually and concretely Christians, who are distinguished in the first instance from all other men by His self-attestation and therefore by their knowledge. In the Holy Spirit as the self-attestation of Jesus they thus know themselves in and with Him ; themselves in their union with Him, and also with one another, in the fellowship of faith and love and hope in which they express themselves as His and find self-awareness as this people which has a common descent. It is in this sense that the Holy Spirit as the self-attestation of Jesus is the quickening power by which Christianity is awakened and gathered and built up to a true Church in the world. As the self-attestation of Jesus the Holy Spirit achieves the *communio sanctorum* and causes it to grow (intensively and extensively). It lives by His power—from the very first and on all its way and ways in the realisation of the relationship of the *sancti* to the *sancta* right up to its goal at the end of all history when it will meet the *eschaton* which will be the *eschaton* of the cosmos. But to understand this in all its fulness of meaning we must be clear that the Holy Spirit by which the community lives and becomes and was and is and will be is the self-attestation of Jesus.

The power with which He works is not, then, merely a remote operation of Jesus. It is this. Risen from the dead, ascended into heaven, seated at the right hand of God the Father, Jesus is remote from earthly history and the community which exists in it. He is unattainably superior to it. He is separated from it by an abyss which cannot be bridged. He is even hidden from it in God (Col. 3^3)— and with Him, of course, the true life of the community. He (and its true life) cannot be violated or controlled by it. If in spite of this He is still at work in earthly history, and in the community as it exists in it, by the quickening power of His Holy Spirit, we can certainly call this His operation at a distance. From the point to which there is no way, from heaven, from the throne, from the right hand of God, from His hiddenness in God, He overcomes that abyss in the Holy Spirit, operating here from that exalted status, working in time, in which the *communio sanctorum* is an event and has its history in many events, from the eternity of the life which He has in common with God. The man Jesus has also that form of existence, so that it is quite true that His action towards His community in the quickening power of the Holy Spirit is a remote operation.

But this is only the one aspect of His action, and if we are to under-stand it as the power of growth and life which does not only reach it from the majesty of God, touching and impelling it from without, but also as that which indwells and is immanent to it, it is the second aspect which we must now consider. It is to be noted that this does not replace the other. The first aspect remains. The man Jesus is above, superior even to His community and remote from it in absolute transcendence ; and with Him, so too is its own true life. He has and maintains also that heavenly form of existence characterised by His unique fellowship with God. He exists also at the right hand of God the Father where we men, even we Christians, are not ; where even the *communio sanctorum* is not. Thus the Holy Spirit, too, is the power which quickens from above, from a distance, from God ; from the God who dwells in light unapproachable. But the second aspect has also to be considered. For what does it mean to speak of there and here, height and depth, near and far, when we speak of the One who is not only the true Son of Man but also the true Son of God,

2. The Growth of the Community

the man who, exalted by the self-humiliation of the divine person to being as man, exists in living fellowship with God ? It certainly does not mean that these antitheses are removed and obliterated and equated in Him. But since God is not limited to be there, since He is not the prisoner of His own height and distance, it certainly means that in the man Jesus who is also the true Son of God, these antitheses, while they remain, are comprehended and controlled ; that He has power over them ; that He can be here as well as there, in the depth as well as in the height, near as well as remote, and therefore immanent in the *communio sanctorum* on earth as well as transcendent to it. He can have an earthly-historical form of existence as well as a heavenly-historical. He can create and sustain and rule the *communio sanctorum* on earth. He can exist in it in earthly-historical form. We speak of His heavenly form of existence, of the form in which He exists in the height and distance and hiddenness of God, when with the New Testament we speak of Him as the Head of His community. But we speak of His earthly-historical form of existence, of the form in which, in the sovereignty of the same God, He also exists here and now with sinners in this history which has not yet concluded, when again with the New Testament we speak of the community as His body (cf. on this concept *C.D.*, IV, 1, pp. 662–668). And in both cases, and either way, we speak of the one man Jesus Christ. It is He who is both there and here. It is He who is both the Head and the body. Similarly, the life of Christians as the life of those sanctified in Him is one. With Him as its Head it is hidden in God, but with Him it is also provisional manifest in the temporal being and activity of the community on earth. Similarly, His Holy Spirit is one. As the quickening power which accomplishes sanctification, He comes down with utter novelty and strangeness from above (as described in the story of Pentecost) and thus constitutes an absolute basis and starting-point. But as the same power He also rules and works in the events, in the sequence and multiplicity, of the temporal history of the *communio sanctorum* which is still the *communio peccatorum,* in all the relativities of that which is called Christian and ecclesiastical and even theological life. All this depends, however, upon the fact that first and supremely the one man Jesus Christ Himself exists both in the first form and also in the second : not in any contradiction of the one to the other and therefore to Himself ; but because in the one, therefore also in the other, and thus in the whole glory of His being as the true Son of God and Son of Man. Our present concern is with the second form : His earthly-historical form of existence ; His body ; the community in which, as the One who is with God, He is also with us as the true Son of God and therefore the true Son of Man, in whom we are already united and sanctified.

For a better understanding, let us return to the equation that the Holy Spirit, as the power which quickens the community, is the self-attestation of Jesus. Thus the only content of the Holy Spirit is Jesus ; His only work is His provisional revelation ; His only effect the human knowledge which has Him as its object (and in Him the knowing man himself). But as the self-attestation of Jesus the Holy Spirit is more than a mere indication of Jesus or record concerning Him. Where the man Jesus attests Himself in the power of the Spirit of God, He makes Himself present ; and those whom He approaches in His self-attestation are able also to approach Him and to be near Him. More than that, where He makes Himself present in this power, He imparts Himself ; and those to whom He wills to belong in virtue of this self-presentation are able also to belong to Him. In the Holy Ghost as His self-attestation He reveals and discloses Himself to certain men living on earth and in time as the Holy One who represents them before God and therefore in actuality, and also grants them the knowledge that He is theirs ; the Holy One in whom they also are holy, and are His—holy in His holy person. He reveals and discloses and grants to them the knowledge of His unity with them and their unity with Him. In this knowledge they find that even on earth and in time they are with Him, and therefore at unity with one another. It is in this way, by this self-attestation, self-presentation and self-impartation, that He founds and quickens the community, which is the mighty work of the Holy Spirit.

In virtue of and in the occurrence of this mighty work, the community lives and grows within the world—an anticipation, a provisional representation, of the sanctification of all men as it has taken place in Him, of the new humanity reconciled with God. Thus it can never be understood as a society which men join of themselves and in which they are active in the pursuit of their own ends, however religious. They are united only by and with Jesus, and only in this way with one another, and only for the fulfilment of His will and purpose. Nor can the community be understood as an organisation set up by Him, a machine for whose efficient functioning it has to provide, thus having its essential existence in its offices. It exists only as the mighty work of Jesus is done on earth, and as it allows it to take place in itself, and through itself in the world. It can be understood only with reference to Him, and only in Him can it recognise itself in its true actuality. It *is* only in Him. Even in its human being and action and operation it is from Him and by Him. It cannot recognise and take itself seriously in anything that is not from Him. What He is not, it is not, and in what He is not it is not His community, but can only be alien to itself, and withdraw in shame before Him and become small and as it were disappear. It does not live apart from the mighty work of His self-attestation. It lives as He Himself lives in it in the occurrence of this mighty work ; as it is the earthly-historical form of His existence, His body, standing at His disposal, and ruled and impelled by Him, in all its members and their various functions.

This brings us back to the statement which was a kind of axiomatic starting-point, anticipating all that was to follow, at the beginning of the prolegomena of our *Church Dogmatics* (I, 1, p. 3)—that the being of Jesus Christ is the being of the Church, and its self-understanding and proclamation and practice and enquiries and conclusions and internal and external politics and theology must all be directed accordingly.

We cannot avoid the statement that Jesus Christ is the community. Nor do we refer only to Jesus Christ in His form as its heavenly Head, in His hiddenness with God. In Jesus Christ as the Head it can only believe. Here and now it can only look up to Him from the depths as its Lord. It can only love Him as the One whom it has not seen (1 Pet. 1⁸). It can only wait for His revelation : " Amen. Even so, come, Lord Jesus " (Rev. 22²⁰). It can only move towards Him. Thus the statement cannot be reversed. It is a christological statement, and only as such an ecclesiological. The community is not Jesus Christ. It is not the eternal Son of God, the incarnate Word, the Reconciler of the world with God. The justification and sanctification of all men did not and does not take place in it, but only its provisional representation, its attestation by a handful of sinful men amongst others—saints who are holy only in the fact that He is, and has revealed and disclosed Himself to them as the Holy One, and that they have been recognised and confess Him as such. There does not belong to it the power of the sending and outpouring and operation of the Holy Spirit. It does not " possess " Him. It cannot create or control Him. He is promised to it. It can only receive Him and then be obedient to Him. There can be no thought of the being of Jesus Christ enclosed in that of His community, or exhausted by it, as though it were a kind of predicate of this being. The truth is the very opposite. The being of the community is exhausted and enclosed in His. It is a being which is taken up and hidden in His, and absolutely determined and governed by it. The being of the community is a predicate of His being. As it exists on earth and in time in virtue of the mighty work of the Holy Ghost, it is His body ; and He, its heavenly Head, the incarnate Word, the incomparable Holy One, has in it His own earthly-historical form of existence ; He Himself, who is not yet directly and universally and definitively revealed to the world and it, is already present and at work in it. The community is not Jesus Christ. But He—and in reality only He, but He in supreme reality—is the community. He does not live because and as it lives. But it lives, and may and can live, only because and as He lives. " Because I live, ye shall live also " (Jn. 14¹⁹). The sequence and order are all-important. But in this sequence and order it may and must be affirmed that Jesus Christ is the community.

We may say the same with reference to the central New Testament concept of the kingdom of God. The kingdom of God is the lordship of God established in the world in Jesus Christ. It is the rule of God as it takes place in Him. He Himself is the kingdom of God. Thus we cannot avoid a statement which Protestantism has far too hastily and heedlessly contested—that the kingdom of God is the community. We do not refer to the kingdom or dominion of God in its completed form in which it obtains for the whole world in the person of the one Son of Man, the one Holy Spirit, and in which it will be directly and universally and definitively revealed and known at the end and goal of all history. We refer to it in the guise of the new and obedient humanity, as in the historical time which moves towards this end it is provisionally and very imperfectly but genuinely actualised where in virtue of the mighty work of the Holy Ghost there is an awareness of its incursion and therefore the communion of saints. The community is not the kingdom of God. But—proclaimed and believed in its earthly-historical form of existence by sinners among sinners, as the unholy may become the saints of God in an awareness of its coming—the kingdom of God is the community. It is not for nothing that it comes from the resurrection of Jesus Christ as its first revelation, and goes towards its final revelation in the return of Jesus Christ. As the kingdom of God itself is on the way from the first to the last revelation, it is the community. As the kingdom or rule of God is engaged in this movement, it creates the sphere corresponding to it and is to be found on this way too. And this takes place in the mighty work of the Holy Spirit founding and quickening the community. The community is not the kingdom of God, nor will it ever be before the kingdom encounters it, and is revealed to it, in its glory at the end of all history. It prays for the coming of the kingdom, that encountering it in its true and perfect form it may be directly and universally and definitively revealed. But already on this side of the end, even in the form of the community which prays for its coming, the kingdom is really on earth and in time and history. The community would be nothing if it did not come from the kingdom and go towards it ; if the kingdom were not present in this transitional movement. The community can only follow it in this transition ; otherwise it surrenders its particularity and betrays its reality as the communion of saints. Its proclamation can only serve the self-proclamation of the kingdom of God which is present here and now because it has come and comes. If it does not stand in this service it is absolutely nothing. If it does, for all its unpretentiousness it is greater than all the greatnesses of world history, for it has to speak the final word among all the words spoken by men and to men.

In sum, there is a real identity, not present *in abstracto*, but given by God and enacted in the mighty work of the Holy Spirit, between the Holy One, the kingdom of God as perfectly established in Him, and the communion of saints on earth, which as such is also a communion of sinners. Thus the power of this Holy One, of Jesus Christ as the heavenly Head, in whom God's rule is perfectly established, is also the indwelling power of life and growth which is immanent in the community on earth. It is in the light of this identity that we have to understand everything that falls to be said concerning its life and growth (both in the extensive and the intensive sense). He, Jesus Christ, must increase (Jn. 3³⁰), and He does in fact increase. The kingdom of God grows like the seed. It is for this reason that the community also grows—the fellowship of men who with open eyes and ears and hearts come from Jesus Christ, from the kingdom of God, and move towards Him. It grows as it gives Him room to grow, and to the extent that it "decreases," as the Baptist said of himself. It lives because and as its Lord lives. It lives wholly and utterly as His people.

We will verify what we have said by the direct utterances of the New Testament—and first in relation to the concept which has been prominent in the later part of our deliberations, that of the kingdom of God. We have already proved from Mk. 4²⁶⁻²⁹ and ³⁰⁻³² that it is something which grows, so there can be no doubt that it is a temporal and historical subject. But apart from Jesus Christ what subject can be meant but His community in which the kingdom is proclaimed and believed and prayer is made for its coming? Again, we are told in Lk. 12³² that it is the good pleasure of the One whom the disciples may call Father to give (δοῦναι) the kingdom to them, the little flock. What can this mean except that it is already present in this little flock, so that it is not merely to be in the exalted Son of Man in heaven, but wonderfully yet genuinely on earth among men in the heavenly power of Jesus Christ? Again, what can entry into the kingdom of God mean in passages like Mk. 9⁴⁷ and 10²⁴ or Jn. 3⁵ except to become a disciple and therefore to enter the community? To do this, we have to be "fit" for it, according to Lk. 9⁶², and this is not the case if we set our hand to the plough and look back. Again, we are told in Lk. 17²⁰ᶠ· that the kingdom of God does not come μετὰ παρατηρήσεως, i.e., in such a way that we can establish its presence directly, indicating it with a Here or a There; nevertheless it is ἐντὸς ὑμῖν, "in the midst of you" (not with the invisibility of a mere idea, but in concrete if hidden form, so that the Pharisees see it and yet do not perceive it). The primary reference is to Jesus Himself, but according to the mind of the community which preserved the saying there is also a reference to itself in its wonderful but genuine existence as the provisional form of the kingdom in the world. The kingdom of God is used in the same sense in 1 Cor. 4¹⁹ᶠ·, where Paul says that the kingdom of God is not ἐν λόγῳ but ἐν δυνάμει and that it is by this standard that he will measure certain folk when he comes to Corinth. The same is true of Rom. 14¹⁷, where the kingdom of God is said not to be a matter of eating and drinking, but of righteousness, peace and joy in the Holy Ghost. We may also refer to what is said in Col. 4¹¹ about Paul's συνεργοὶ εἰς τὴν βασιλείαν τοῦ θεοῦ. Again, the reference can only be to the kingdom of God as provisionally actualised in history and therefore in the community when in 1 Cor. 15²⁴ it is said that Christ will finally deliver it up to God the Father. It is to be noted that the concept is not usually given this sense. Hence Augustine's general equation of the *civitas Dei* with the Church is quite impossible. But the reference in the passages mentioned (and we could easily strengthen them from the synoptic parables of the kingdom) is emphatic enough to warn us against a general and indiscriminate rejection of Augustine's identification. Apart from the absolute, christological and eschatological meaning of the term there is also an applied and relative and historical, and in this case the kingdom is in fact the Church. In this restricted sense the pietistic and Anglo-Saxon version of the kingdom of God may well have a place.

Yet, as Origen and Tertullian rightly perceived, on the New Testament view the kingdom or lordship of God is absolutely identical with Jesus Christ. *He* is the kingdom—the αὐτοβασιλεία. It is as His lordship that it is set up as the lordship of God in the world. The βασιλεία cannot be separated from Him any more than it can from God. This is true in the absolute sense. It is also true in the relative, to the extent that the kingdom is also the community. We read in Mt. 18²⁰: "Where two or three are gathered together in my name (συνηγμένοι εἰς τὸ ἐμὸν ὄνομα—probably a play on the confession which characterises the Christian συναγωγή), there am I in the midst." What does this mean? Does it mean only that He comes and is present as a third or fourth? Does it not mean rather that He is present and at work in the gathering together of the two or three, as the centre which constitutes this circle? Is not this also the sense of Mt. 28²⁰: "Lo, I am with you alway, even unto the end of the world" (ἕως τῆς συντελείας τοῦ αἰῶνος). What is meant by the μεθ' ὑμῶν? Does it mean that He is there as an interested spectator who occasionally gives friendly help? Does it not mean rather that when and as they act in accordance with His orders in the time which hastens to the end He is present every day to sustain and protect and save in His mercy, to accompany them in His omnipotent *concursus*, to rule them by His will which alone is holy—Himself the primary and proper Subject at work with and amongst them? That is why it can be said explicitly in Lk. 10¹⁶: "He that heareth you heareth me." That is also why the nations assembled for the Last Judgment in Mt. 25³¹⁻⁴⁶ are asked by the Son of Man concerning their attitude to His brethren and judged accordingly. What they have done, or not done, to the least of His brethren, they have done, or not done, to Him. It is not merely that there is a solidarity between Himself and His brethren. But He Himself is hungry and thirsty and a stranger and naked and sick and in prison as they are. That is why it is said to the persecutor of the community in Ac. 9⁴: "Saul, Saul, why persecutest thou me?" And that is why the eucharistic action as the crowning act of worship—τοῦτο, this, i.e., the common eating and drinking of the disciples according to His command —is no more and no less than His body and blood (the κοινωνία of His body and blood according to 1 Cor. 10¹⁶). This action then, accomplished εἰς τὴν ἐμὴν ἀνάμνησιν, is the direct proclamation of His death until He comes (1 Cor. 11²⁶). In this provisional form as the action of the community, it is His own action; the work of His real presence. Here and now He Himself is for them—His offered body and His shed blood—the communion of saints thanking and confessing Him in this action.

Similarly the formula ἐν ('Ιησοῦ) Χριστῷ, which is so common in the Pauline Epistles, indicates the place or sphere in which (determined absolutely by it) there takes place the divine working, creating and endowing which moves the apostle and his communities, and also the divine revealing, questioning, inviting and demanding, and the corresponding human thanking and thinking and speaking and believing and obeying. The ἐν Χριστῷ denotes the place where the *sancta* are proffered and the *sancti* are engaged in the realisation of their *communio* with them and therefore with one another. Jesus Christ *is*, and in His being the apostles and communities are. For this reason, directly or indirectly everything that is said about the being of Jesus Christ can be only an explication of the being of Jesus Christ, and everything that is said about the being of Jesus Christ applies directly or indirectly to the being of Christians. A single presupposition emerges, and for Paul and His communities this is not a hypothesis or theory (and therefore not a problem); in the light of Easter, and in a present because renewed confrontation with the revelation of Easter Day, it is as self-evident as the air which they breathe. For this presupposition is simply the fact that the crucified Jesus Christ lives. But He lives—and this is now the decisive point —as the *totus Christus*. And this means that, although He lives also and primarily as the exalted Son of Man, at the right hand of the Father, in the hiddenness of

God (with the life of Christians), at an inaccessible height above the world and the community, He does not live only there but lives too (in the power of His Holy Spirit poured out from there and working here) on earth and in world history, in the little communities at Thessalonica and Corinth and Philippi, in Galatia and at Rome. He does not live primarily in their knowledge and faith and prayer and confession, or in their Christian being, but as the place in which all this can and may and must and will happen, in which they are Christians ; as the air which they breathe, the ground on which they stand and walk. As we are told in Jn. 15⁴¹·, they have no being or life apart from Him, just as the branches are nothing apart from the vine but can only wither and be burned : " Without me ye can do nothing." But they need not try to do anything without Him. He *is* the vine, and they *are* the branches.

Thus we are brought back from every angle to the main statement that the community lives, not only because, but as Jesus lives, the kingdom of God in person. It is He who lives as it lives and grows as it grows. Thus the προκοπή τοῦ εὐαγγελίου (Phil. 1¹²) is His work. He is the προκόπτων, the One who strides forward, the inner man who renews Himself from day to day (2 Cor. 4¹⁶), the Subject of all progress in the Church. It is as He indwells the community and is immanent to it (as the Head to the body) that it grows : from Him as its Head, but also in and with Him as He has in it His body ; the earthly-historical form of His existence.

It remains only to conclude the discussion of Eph. 4¹¹⁻¹⁶ which we left unfinished in the previous sub-section. It is the final phrase (in v. 16) which particularly concerns us.

We saw in v. 15 that Christians are summoned, ἀληθεύοντες ἐν ἀγάπῃ (in a life by and for the truth which unites them in love with their Lord and with one another), to grow up into Him who is the Head —Christ. He is called the κεφαλὴ τῆς ἐκκλησίας in Eph. 5²³. And we have seen that according to 1²⁰⁻²³ He is primarily the Head of all things. God has raised Him from the dead, set Him at His own right hand in the heavenly world, and exalted Him over every ἀρχή and ἐξουσία and δύναμις and κυριότης, over every name that may be named, not only in this world, but also in that which is to come. He is the πληρούμενος τὰ πάντα ἐν πᾶσιν—the One who fills what would otherwise be the inevitable emptiness of all things in all their various forms. It is as such that God has given Him to be the Head of the community, and to Him as such that He has given the community as the body. He cannot and must not be without it as the *totus Christus*. It is His πλήρωμα (1²³) to the extent that it is only with it, only as He also lives and reigns in it, that He is the ἀνὴρ τέλειος (just as it is only with Him, as filled and ruled by Him, that all things can consist). But in this heavenly form, as the Head of the cosmos and also the Head of the community, He is absolutely future, because not yet revealed, both to the community and the cosmos. And its own form as the σῶμα and therefore the πλήρωμα of this Head is still future, because not yet revealed, to the community. It believes in Him as its Head. It looks and moves up towards Him from the depths and distance as to the One who exists in this heavenly form. And believing in Him it believes also in itself as His σῶμα and therefore His πλήρωμα. But it does not see this. It is still on the way to this future when it will be revealed that He is the πλήρωμα of all things and it is His πλήρωμα; that He is the One who rules the world and it is ruled by Him ; that He and itself with Him, as the *totus Christus*, is the ἀνὴρ τέλειος. Of course, all this—the *totus Christus*—has not still to evolve or to be made. In accordance with the predetermination of God, He has been instituted as such once and for all : not only in His relationship to the community but also in His relationship to the cosmos ; and both not merely in heaven but also on earth ; yet not visibly on earth even to Christians, and to that extent only in the sphere of the future. Thus, the community *is* His body, the πλήρωμα without which He would not be that which He has been appointed by God.

This is the point of the summons of 4^{15} : αὐξήσωμεν εἰς αὐτόν. How can the community be summoned to grow up into Him ? How can it do this ? According to v. 16 it can do it because its growth is already taking place quite apart from its own action, and it is to this, and the deduction to be drawn from it, that attention is directed in this summons. It is ἐξ οὗ that we are now told that this takes place. And this ἐξ οὗ refers back to Christ who is the Head of the community. It thus grows, we must reply, from the One to whom (εἰς αὐτόν) it is summoned to grow. What is it that grows ἐξ οὗ? It is the σῶμα itself. This is the subject of the statement that follows : τὸ σῶμα . . . τὴν αὔξησιν τοῦ σώματος ποιεῖται. The parallel in Col. 2^{19} agrees with this in substance, although in this case the verb is αὔξει, and it has the remarkable accusative τὴν αὔξησιν τοῦ θεοῦ, signifying that the body fulfils the increase which comes from God and is grounded in Him and given by Him. The only possible meaning even of this sharpened form of the paradox is that the body accomplishes its own growth. And it is more closely defined as its own growth in Eph. 4^{16} (and the parallel in Col. 2^{19}). The whole body accomplishes its αὔξησις as it is " fitly joined together and compacted by that which every joint supplieth, according to the effectual working in the measure of every part." It is clear that what is envisaged here is the unity and differentiation of the community as conditioned by the unity and differentiation of its gifts, according to the express account given in 1 Cor. 12^{4-31} and more briefly in Rom. 12^{3-8}. Thus the subject of the statement is not a mythological *soma* but the community as it exists historically in history. It is this which fulfils its own growth—the αὔξειν which is described in Col. 2^{19} as an αὔξειν τὴν αὔξησιν τοῦ θεοῦ. The conclusion shows that in this there is also envisaged the concrete action of Christians, the ἔργον διακονίας for which they are prepared according to v. 12. For the community grows εἰς οἰκοδομὴν ἑαυτοῦ ἐν ἀγάπῃ. Because and as it grows, it is edified as previously described—a term which also includes the fact that, working in human fashion in all its members and their mutual relationships, it has its own part to play and therefore edifies itself. The αὔξάνειν to which Christians are summoned in v. 15 is, of course, identical with this action. But what is the " increase " presupposed in this action ? How is it that the community has not first to accomplish its own growth in obedience to this summons, but is accomplishing it (ποιεῖται) already, so that it is on this basis that it can be summoned to growth, i.e., to its own edification in love ? There can be only one answer. Because and as Jesus Christ is its Head, it is already His body, although He is not yet revealed and therefore future to it in this quality, as it is also to itself. His being is its being. It has its being from Him (ἐξ οὗ) who is in heaven at the right hand of the Father. Because He as the Head is present to it as His body, in virtue of His life and growth it too grows infallibly, demanding the consequence of human action but not compromised by the problematic nature of this action. It is not thrown back on its own resources in this action. It grows ἐξ αὐτοῦ and therefore εἰς αὐτόν. It accomplishes its own growth—in virtue of His real presence.

3. THE UPHOLDING OF THE COMMUNITY

Communio sanctorum! We now turn to another and as it were outward aspect—that of its constitution and the possibility of its effective action in the world around. And we will try to understand its history as the history of its gracious preservation. As in the concept of " upbuilding " which dominates the whole discussion, and the particular concept of the " growth " of the community which we have just analysed, so in that of its " upholding " we have to consider both the divine and the human side of the happening under review. Here, too, both God and men (Christians) are at work : God in His omnipotent grace ; and Christians (if only they were it in this sense !) in the gratitude which corresponds to the grace of God. But in this case it is best from the very outset to see these two aspects together at the place where they are originally together, understanding the whole occurrence (in the light of what we have already learned from its character as growth) as a Christ-occurrence ; the work of the *totus Christus*. Our particular theme at this point must be the human weakness of the communion of saints on earth, but its preservation in defiance of this weakness. How could it be upheld were it not that it exists in Christ, and the Lord is its strength ?

It is surely relevant to quote in this connexion the magnificent definition of the *Heidelberg Catechism*, which might well have been used as the thesis for our whole section. *Qu.* 54 : " What dost thou believe concerning the holy, universal Christian Church ? *Answer :* That from the beginning of the world to its end the Son of God assembles out of the human race an elect community to eternal life by His Spirit and (His) Word in the unity of true faith, that He protects and upholds it, and that I am a living member of the same, and will continue to be so to all eternity." Note who is the acting subject in this definition. It is not a believing people which has to gather and protect and uphold itself as such. It is not a ministry controlling the Word and sacraments. It is not the Virgin Mary as a patroness who has already ascended into heaven and there represents it and acts for it. It is the Son of God. He it is who sees to it that in spite of everything the Church is. We may add to this first definition the explanation of the request : " Thy kingdom come," in the answer to *Qu.* 123 : " Rule us therefore by Thy Word and Spirit that we may be subject to Thee, maintain and increase Thy Church, and more and more destroy the works of the devil, and every power that vaunts itself against Thee, and all evil counsels that are devised against Thy holy Word, until the perfection of thy kingdom is attained in which Thou shalt be all in all."

The communion of saints needs defence, protection and preservation because it is in danger. It was always in danger. As long as time endures, it will always be in danger. For it is a human society among men. It belongs to the sphere of very different human societies —domestic, political, economic, social and academic—which have no thought of orientating from and to Jesus Christ and the kingdom of God which has come and comes, but the existence and activity of which is intersected in the most diverse ways by that of the community. And what is the community itself, from the standpoint of its human constitution and its own human action, but a part of the world ? It is given to exist as such in its own peculiar fashion, not as though its existence were an end in itself, but in order to be a witness and messenger pointing the world around to the truth of God which has relevance and validity for it too, to Jesus Christ and its own true reality which is unknown and ignored and even denied both in theory and practice ; in order to be a provisional representation of the new humanity, and therefore in the words of 2 Pet. 1[19] to be a light shining in a dark place, to the salvation of all those who dwell there. To be this light in the world is its task even as that which in its human constitution and action is only a part of the world. The danger in which it finds itself is obvious. In order to be what it is commissioned to be, in order merely to maintain itself in the world, let alone to do justice to its commission in the world, it must be the true Church, engaged in its upbuilding as such, and therefore as we have seen, living and growing. But its life and growth are continually menaced. They are threatened both outwardly by the world and inwardly by itself (in so far as it is a part of the world in its human status and activity). The question is whether it will be able to overcome this danger, to be upheld in it.

We will consider first the danger which threatens from without. In both the forms to be mentioned it is a matter of the restriction of what we have called its extensive growth and therefore the vital upholding, i.e., the constant renewal of its human position. In both forms the danger arises from the fact that it is not self-evident, or to be expected as a matter of course, that the world will accept at once the existence of this little fragment of it, or other human societies the existence of this particular society. For it claims both a very different origin and a very different goal. But how can the world and other human societies fail to be alienated if it does this seriously and effectively, if it exists within it as a living and growing community, and if it looks like making itself prominent both by the audible presentation of its universal message and if possible by the increase of its adherents ? Will they not feel that they are unsettled and questioned and disturbed and perhaps even menaced by it ? Its message is sufficiently revolutionary (as the community itself knows better than anyone) to make this a very understandable reaction. It proclaims Jesus Christ and therefore a new and different humanity ; the dominion of God over all other dominions ; the great freedom and necessity of conversion, of the *vivificatio* which inevitably involves *mortificatio* ; discipleship and the cross. To hear this willingly and not unwillingly, or even thoughtfully and not with scorn and anger ; to accept the Christian community if not seriously to receive its Word : this is not a human possibility, but (as the community itself knows better than anyone) that of the Holy Spirit who moves where He wills and whom no one can command. Where this possibility is not given, the community must be reconciled to the fact that in some form it will meet with the resistance and even the counter-attacks of the outside world ; that it will find that it is itself unsettled and questioned and disturbed and even menaced ; that its presence will be bewailed and deplored and unwanted, its activity ridiculed and misunderstood and suspected, and its propagation, i.e., the vital renewal of its constituency, represented as a danger and as far as possible hampered even to the point of definite attempts to prevent it. It will be accused of *odium humani generis* and it will be assailed by *odium humani generis*. Its only prospect may then be the ghetto and in the near or distant future its external repression and extinction : the less certainly in proportion as it is not perhaps the true Church ; but all the more surely in proportion as it is a living and (even externally) growing community. Though its external growth may not be all that striking, a living community will always have to reckon with the fact that it must be in some form a community under trial and perhaps even under the cross.

The first form in which this may happen consists in the fact that it comes under pressure from the world around which seeks either to do away with it altogether or at least to reduce it to a more innocuous form. It is not perhaps required to surrender to error or unbelief, or to suspend its activity, or to disband, or to deny its confession, etc., but only to practice greater reserve, to adopt a more positive attitude to the dominant spiritual and unspiritual powers of the world, to make a few concessions which may well appear at first sight to be non-essential, to accept certain restrictions and adjustments the extent of which may well be a subject' for discussion. In the first instance, the word " persecution " is probably far too dramatic for what takes place. The pressure is not exerted equally. It falls heavily only on a few, perhaps only on the more responsible and active of its members, and in such a way, in proportion as it is not really a living *communio*, that the majority of its members are hardly aware of it at all. More massive attempts may, of course, follow. There are means—and they will be used—to stop its mouth, or at least to make its voice more or less lifeless. Perhaps there will be the attempt to separate its most important spokesmen from it, and it from them. Perhaps it will be isolated from the rest of the world, its connexions with wider circles, especially with the younger generation, being restricted or broken, so that it is reduced to a cult, and as such pushed aside and made an object of ridicule and scorn and even hatred. Perhaps all the counter-measures it might take will be made difficult or even impossible. Perhaps in our own time the campaign will be conducted by the many-headed monster of the press, even by what are called its more responsible sections (themselves directed by the invisible forces which it has to serve). Or it may be the state, either in the background or the foreground, and perhaps in the form of an omnipotent state-party, that has a hand in it and even organises the whole affair, and is able to do it very energetically through its public and secret organs and the force which it can bring to bear indirectly on individuals and relationships. And it may well be that many Christians come to realise (for the first time) that it costs something to be a living member of the living community ; that it will mean decision and act and quiet but also open endurance ; and that the question has therefore to be faced whether it has been a good thing to confess oneself a Christian, or whether it is wise to continue to do so. Perhaps it is going to affect the most important relationships in life. Perhaps it is going to hinder advancement, or to involve the loss of profession or livelihood. Perhaps in the near future it may even mean one day the forfeiture of liberty, and in the more distant future—who knows?—of life itself. " And though they take our life, Goods, honour, children, wife, Yet is their profit small ; Let these things vanish all. . . ." Let these things vanish all ? It sounded very well when we sang it—so long as we had only to sing it. But now that it may be required in fact ? Will there not be many who allow that it is not to be taken literally ? Yet the community on earth, the *communio sanctorum*, lives in the persons of these many Christians who are so terribly assailed and harassed ; of the *sancti* who both as a whole and as individuals are also *peccatores*, and in whom the spirit may be willing enough but the flesh is weak. The *communio* itself is assailed as they are assailed. It can grow only as there takes place the *communio* of these members in relation both to the *sancta* and to one another. Will it take place and maintain itself even in these circumstances, in a situation in which each one is concretely faced by the question whether it is not better to yield to the pressure of the world around, to contract out of the common movement ? Will it be upheld in these circumstances and not come to a general standstill, so that the community as such is brought to dissolution, death and destruction ?

But the external attack may also take a very different form, and it is hard to say whether in the long run this second form is not more dangerous to the constitution of the community. Experience old and new shows that more brutal or refined persecution may well have the opposite effect from that intended. The community is strengthened under pressure. The separation of the chaff from the wheat means new and stronger growth. Even from the human standpoint there is consolidation in defiance of oppression by violent or subtle tyrants. In any case, it is not always or everywhere that the world around expresses its hostility or ill-will to the existence of the community in the form of this type of pressure. It is natural for Christians to dramatise unnecessarily figures like Nero and Diocletian and Louis XIV and Hitler and other modern dictators with their " anti-God " movements and new state-religions, but there have not really been so very many of them in the course of the Church's history. On the other hand, it may well be that the hostility and ill-will of the world express themselves differently. The world does not allow itself to take seriously the disturbance caused by the existence of the community. It quietly accepts it. It uses the most terrible weapon of intolerance —toleration. It meets it with sheer indifference. It may well be regarded by the world as the wiser- -or wisest—course to leave Christianity alone, to go its own ways as if it were not there, simply opposing to it the *factum brutum* of its own secular spirit and methods, of its

own sure and secular technics and economics and politics and art and
science and way of life. There can thus be presented to it in action
the fact that things work out very well after the fashion of what the
community describes and attacks as sin ; that we are here on solid
ground ; and that there is no need of the fantastic knowledge of our
beginning and end in God, of the grace of God and our reconciliation
with Him, of a renewal of humanity already accomplished and universally relevant, in short of Jesus Christ and the quickening power of
the Holy Spirit. This may well be, and often is, the reaction of the
world to the existence of the Christian community. And it is powerful
enough even though it never considers giving itself the superfluous
trouble of oppressing the community. For what is the result of this
type of attack upon it ?—now that there is no planned or purposeful
but only the factual opposition of a world preoccupied with its own
concerns, and completely uninterested in its message, and assuming
that its action is quite irrelevant to what the world regards as important
and opposes to it as such ; now that the world carries its toleration,
or scorn, to the point of laying occasional claim to the ministrations
of the community to give light and colour to its practical atheism—
as concerts and theatres and art galleries are used for its adornment—
in the forms of baptisms and confirmations and weddings and festivals
and national days of prayer and the like ; now that it has nothing
to fear in the world but also nothing to hope, or to fear only that it
is absolutely superfluous, like the fifth wheel which is obviously not
essential to the movement of a car ; now that it does not have the
consolidating and winning power of persecution because the world does
not persecute it, but quietly or hurtfully ignores it. How will it be
with Christians, and how will they maintain themselves, when, with
no particular malice and perhaps even with friendliness, the world
treats them in this way ? What will be the meaning for them, from
this standpoint, of their Old and New Testament, their worship, their
mission, their whole Christian thinking and willing and action ?
" Where is now thy God ? " (Ps. 42[10]). Will the saints continue to
believe and love and hope when they are harassed in this manner ?
Will they not be possessed by the desire to leave their own sphere
for that where the lord *Omnes* is at work ? How can the community
continue to grow ? How can it maintain itself ? Will not the occurrence of the *communio sanctorum* be arrested and cease for lack
of breath ? Will the community be upheld and not disintegrate
in face of this neutral but for that reason all the more weighty
attack ?

We will proceed at once to consider the danger which threatens
from within. It is not now a matter of its constitution but of the
effective action which corresponds to its nature. Here, too, we shall
have to speak of two forms of the danger. But first we must refer to
that which is common to it in both forms. In both forms it arises

out of the fact that the community in its human activity is a part of the world. The world, therefore, is not just around it but—in all its members—within it. But the world is the flesh of sin, the old man in all the variations of his pride and sloth, with all his possibilities and works. There is no single form of sin, of the rejection of God's grace, which cannot entice the *communio sanctorum*, and which in its history has not in fact enticed and overcome it. The enticement may come from without, caused by the pressure exerted or simply by the impression made upon it by the world around. But the men outside are no different from those inside—within the community. The saints are not, as it were, artless children unfortunately led astray by wicked rascals. They themselves are wicked rascals. They are only too ready to follow those outside. Indeed, they sometimes set those outside a bad example. Basically, the enticement which threatens the community is always the same. Stimulated from without and welcomed from within, it may suddenly or gradually feel that the requirement is too hard that its action should be wholly directed by what the *Heidelberg Catechism* calls that progressive subjection to the will of God ; that its own life and growth (in subtraction from it !) should be stimulated and determined by the fact that it is in the power of the Holy Spirit of Jesus Christ Himself who lives and grows in it. It may feel that it knows better and distrust the grace of God by and in which it lives. It may grow tired of it like a spoilt child. Coveting majesty and greatness for itself, it may repudiate the sovereignty in which it wills to rule in it. It may long for the solid bases, the clear principles, the success of promising methods, the sober or enthusiastic realism, which it sees in other human societies. There is no thought of treason or deviation, of heresy or apostasy. To give way to this desire, the community need not wish to become pagan or godless, let alone actually to become this—which is not so simple a matter. It is simply a matter of relaxing a little its friendlessness in the world, the incongruity of its existence as compared with that of other human societies. It is merely a matter of taking the tension out of the relationship ; of trying to find a suitable form in which to be a worldly community as well as a Christian. An inclination in this direction will always exist and show itself in the assembled *sancti* to the extent that they are also *peccatores*. We can only say that in proportion as this inclination gathers strength and achieves dominance in the community it will also relax its relationship to the Holy Spirit and His gifts, and the intensity of its growth will decline, its substance evaporate, and its existence become problematical both to itself and to the world around. In proportion as it will not live by the grace of God, it begins to die. At the end of this development it will still seem to be there as a Church both in its own eyes and in those of the world around. But in reality it will not be there. The more it is enticed in this direction, the less need it be the community under affliction and even the cross. But then (however imposing may be its outward aspect) it can be only the community in corruption, in a process of inner decomposition.

Again, there are two forms in which this may happen. It may fall victim either to alienation (secularisation) or self-glorification (sacralisation).

I was led to this distinction by a remarkable passage in the essay by Heinrich Vogel, " Wesen und Auftrag der Kirche " in *Bekennende Kirche* (for the sixtieth birthday of Martin Niemöller), 1952, pp. 49–50. Vogel rightly emphasises the fact that the one form usually involves the other, so that it is not difficult to see the face of the one in the other. All the same, it is as well to consider them apart.

The community is betrayed into alienation when instead of or side by side with the voice of the Good Shepherd to whom it belongs it hears the voice of a stranger to whom it does not belong but to whom it comes to belong as it hears his voice. This is something which does not have to happen, but which can happen in so far as it is in the world and forms a part of it. It does not have to happen, for it is not alienated by the mere fact that it belongs to the framework of the habits and customs and views of the men of this particular time and place and speaks their language and shares their general limitations and aspirations, rejoicing with them that do rejoice and weeping with them that weep (Rom. 12^{15}). Alienation takes place when it allows itself to be radically determined and established and engaged and committed and imprisoned in this 'respect : in its knowledge by the adoption of a particular philosophy or outlook as the norm of its understanding of the Word of God ; in its ethics by the commandment of a specific tradition or historical *kairos* ; in its attitude to existing world-relationships by a distinctive ideology or by the most respectable or novel or simply the strongest of current political and economic forces ; in its proclamation by allowing itself to be determined by what seems to be the most urgent and sacred need in its own particular environment. It is always alienated when it allows its environment, or spontaneous reference to it, to prescribe and impose a law which is not identical with the Law of the Gospel, with the control of the free grace of God and with the will of Jesus as the Lord and Head of His people. As and so far as it hears this law as a law, it does not hear the voice of the Good Shepherd but that of a stranger. It hears the voice of the world in one of its phenomena, accommodating itself to it, being " conformed " (Rom. 12^2) to its pattern, and therefore belonging to it. It is to be noted that this may often happen in weakness and therefore in the form of a movement of retreat or flight, or an attempt at self-preservation, in face of the all-powerful world. But it can also take the form of offensive action in which, by hearing the world and subjecting itself to its laws, the community seeks to live and grow and assert itself in it, conquering the world at the very points where it lets itself be conquered, subjecting it to its own law, or even to that of God and Jesus Christ, and thus acting *in maiorem gloriam Dei*. It will usually be argued that it is a question of mediation, of bridging the gap between those outside and those inside, of works of " sincerity " on the one side and serious and necessary attempts to win the world for Christ on the other ; or that it is a question of the translation of the Christian into the secular at the command of love ; or conversely of a translation of the secular into the Christian, of a kind of baptism of non-Christian ideas and customs and enterprises by new Christian interpretations and the giving of a new Christian content, or of a minting of Christian gold on behalf of poor non-Christians. And it is all very fine and good so long as there is no secret respect for the fashion of the world, no secret listening to its basic theme, no secret hankering after its glory ; and, conversely, no secret fear that the community cannot live solely by Jesus Christ and the free grace of God, no secret unwillingness to venture to allow itself to live and grow simply from its own and not a worldly root as the *communio sanctorum* in the world (not against the world but for it, not in conflict but in what is, rightly considered, the most profound peace with it). Where there is this respect, this listening, this hankering, this fear and unwillingness, it always means the secularisation of the community. Secularisation is the process at the end of which it will be only a part of the world among so much else of the world ; one of the religious corners which the world may regard as necessary to its fulness but which do not have the slightest practical significance for its manner and way. Secularisation is the process by which the salt loses its savour (Mt. 5[13]). It is not in any sense strange that the world is secular. This is simply to say that the world is the world. It was always secular. There is no greater error than to imagine that this was not the case in the much-vaunted Middle Ages. But when the Church becomes secular, it is the greatest conceivable misfortune both for the Church and the world. And this is what takes place when it wants to be a Church only for the world, the nation, culture, or the state—a world Church, a national Church, a cultural Church, or a state Church. It then loses its specific importance and meaning ; the justification for its existence. But its secularisation—the entry on the steep slope which leads to the abyss in which it is only the world—is its alienation. And it consists of mere men—Christians, of course—who are only flesh, and in whom there may be at any moment a triumphant insurgence of the inclination and desire for alienation. It certainly needs to be kept from corruption, from the declension by which it is threatened in this form.

The other form of this decay is its self-glorification. Its aim is still to develop and maintain itself in the world. But in this case it tries to do it, not by self-adaptation, but by self-assertion. It now has a highly developed consciousness of itself in the particularity of its being and action in the world. It now discovers that it has good reason to regard and represent itself as a world of its own within the world. In its own structure and dignity, grounded on the well-known secret of its existence, it is ultimately no less imposing than other factors. Indeed, in virtue of its secret, it is really the most imposing of all. It certainly knows the lordship and glory of Jesus Christ. And it discloses itself to be His body, the earthly-historical form of His existence, His ambassador to all other men, the representative of His right and claim to the world. It thus renounces any feelings of inferiority as compared with other societies and forms of life. It rejoices and boasts in its own vital and constructive power, in its own being as the incomparable *communio* : the *communio* of the *sancti* in their relationship to the *sancta* ; the *civitas Dei* on earth, which cannot be confused with any other society, but towers over them as once cathedrals did over the little towns clustering round about them. Is not this the case ? Is it not right ? The answer is that this is indeed the case, and that it is perfectly right, but that the terrible thing is that by trying to be right (in itself) it can set itself in the worst possible wrong. We have seen already that, although Christ is the community, there can be no reversing this important statement. The community is not Christ, nor is it the kingdom of God. It is the very last purpose of the lordship and glory of Jesus Christ (which it has to proclaim) to exalt these little men, Christendom, above all others ; to set them in the right against the world ; to invest them with authority and power ; to magnify them in the world. If the community nevertheless permits itself this reversal, it sets itself most terribly in the wrong. It makes itself like the world. And in so doing, by trying to be important and powerful within it instead of serving, by trying to be great instead of small, by trying to make pretentious claims for itself instead of soberly advocating the claim of God, it withdraws from the world. It is not inevitable that it will try to do this. But it may very well do so, thus setting itself in the wrong and supremely jeopardising its true life and growth. For if it does, its own common spirit replaces the Holy Spirit, and its own work the work of God—its offices and sacraments, its pure preaching of the Gospel, its liturgies and confessions, its acts of witness and love, its art and theology, its faithfulness to the Bible, its sovereign communities or collegiate governments or authoritarian heads with or without their vestments and golden crosses, its institutions and the specific events of its encounter with God's revelation, its whole *Kyrie eleison*, which is no longer a cry for the mercy of God and in which it does not even take itself literally, let alone allow the world to do so. And the result is the development in the world—for why should not Christians too enjoy some measure of worldly success ?—of ecclesiastical authorities which in some degree, greater or smaller or even very small, are self-exalting and self-established. In this respect we are not thinking only of the Pope and his Church, but of what can happen in even the tiniest of sects. We are thinking of what can and does always and everywhere happen in a hundred different forms ; of the slipping of the community into the sacralisation in which it not only cuts itself off from its own origin and goal and loses its secret by trying to reveal it in itself, but also separates itself for its own pleasure from poor, sinful, erring humanity bleeding from a thousand wounds, trying to impose itself where it owes its witness, and denying and suppressing its witness by witnessing only to itself. Sacralisation means the transmutation of the lordship of Jesus Christ into the vanity of a Christianity which vaunts itself in His name ,but in reality is enamoured only of itself and its traditions, confessions and institutions. Sacralisation means the suppression of the Gospel by a pseudo-sacred law erected and proclaimed on the supposed basis of the Gospel. Sacralisation means the setting up of an idol which is dead like all other images of human fabrication ; which cannot hear or speak or illuminate or help or heal ; in which the man who has discovered and created it cannot in the last resort admire or worship anyone or anything but himself. Sacralisation as well as secularisation (and the two are very closely related) means the end of the community. But the men—Christians—who constitute the community are flesh, and it is only too natural that they should have an inclination and desire in this direction. Indeed, the surprising thing is that the community has not perished long since in consequence of this particular inclination. In this respect too—and supremely—it stands in need of preservation.

This is the danger, or the complex of dangers, by which the Christian community and its constitution and action are threatened in the world. There is no lack of examples, both from history and our own day, to prove its reality. The world and man being what they are, both *extra et intra muros*, the dangers are unavoidable. And to some extent they threaten the Church from all four quarters. If for the time being one of them is, or seems to be, warded off and overcome, the only result is that the opposite one usually threatens all the more seriously. There are no final safeguards against any of them. Each has the tendency continually to present itself in new forms, and then to evoke a new form of the others by way of reaction. We may thus compare the Church both past and present to a boat betrayed into the very heart of a cyclone, so that there is every reason to fear that at any moment the very worst will overtake both the boat itself and its helpless and unskilled crew. How often outward pressure or the isolation of the community has been so bad, its alienation or self-glorification so blatant, that we could only think that it was all over—*finis christianismi* ! Nor is there any point in concealing the fact that each of the dangers which threatens the community, and especially all of them in their inter-action and co-operation, have the power to destroy it. Both outwardly and inwardly it is not merely a matter of human wickedness and sloth, severity and weakness, error and confusion, but in and behind all these the downward movement of a world on the point of perishing, the power of nothingness lashing out wildly in its final death-throes in this last time which is the time of the community, the violence of chaos which knows that its hour has come and, knowing that it cannot hurt the One who has trodden it underfoot, makes its last and supreme attack on His human attestation in an attempt to suppress and falsify and destroy it. If it has no power against the lordship of God established in Jesus Christ, the signs are all in favour of the fact that it will still enjoy a long and easy mastery over afflicted and anxious Christendom. All kinds of relative considerations and provisional consolations and partial defensive movements are no doubt possible and legitimate and demanded in face of this multiple threat. But we must not allow any illusions to blind us to the fact that finally and properly and incisively only one knowledge, and only one Subject of knowledge, can be of any avail against it. No one and nothing in the whole world is so menaced as Christianity and its constitution and action and future. No one and nothing is so totally referred for its upholding to a single and superior " hold " or support.

It is no accident that of all the books of the Old Testament the Psalter has always been found the most relevant. This is not in spite of the fact, but just because of it, that in so many passages it echoes the people of the covenant trembling for its preservation in final extremity before its all-powerful enemies. The Christian community always has good reason to see itself in this people, and to take on its own lips the words of its helpless sighing, the cries which it utters from the depths of its need. It turns to the Psalter, not in spite of the fact, but just because of it, that as the community of Jesus Christ it knows that it is established on the rock (as powerfully attested by the Psalms themselves), but on the rock which, although it is sure and impregnable in itself, is attacked on all sides, and seems to be of very doubtful security in the eyes of all men and therefore in its own.

That is why—to mention only a single passage—we catch the same notes in verses like Eph. 6$^{10-20}$. What is called for here is not merely patience and confidence and boldness but something very different—ἐνδυναμεῖσθαι in the Lord and in the power of His might (v. 10), and therefore (" to be able to stand against the μεθοδείαι of the devil ") the putting on of the πανοπλία τοῦ θεοῦ. No other equipment can be used, then, than that with which God Himself takes the field, and the whole of this equipment is needed (v. 11). For the conflict of the community is not just with flesh and blood, and definitely not just with the corruption of man both without and within, but (v. 12) with principalities and powers, with the great and generally accepted presuppositions which rule the world in the continuing darkness of this age, with the spirits of evil which seem to strive against it even from heaven itself. If it is to offer resistance in the evil day, if having done all it is to stand, it has no option but to take to itself the armour of God (v. 13). Listening to His truth, subjection to His righteousness, a readiness for His Gospel, faith in Him, the salvation which is in Him and comes from Him—this is how the equipment is described in vv. 14–17. And its last and supreme piece is " the sword of the Spirit, which is the word of God." Finally (vv. 18–19)—as a clear reminder that in all this we have to do with God's own equipment, so that there can be no question of self-evident triumph on the part of those of God's warriors who seize it—the passage closes with a simple call to prayer and watchfulness " with all perseverance and supplication for all saints," including himself, the apostle adds, that to him too (for it is not self-evident even in his case, or something peculiar to him) " utterance may be given," to open his mouth boldly and joyfully to make known the mystery of the Gospel. It is with this exclusive confidence that the community looks for its preservation from the danger which engulfs it. We remember that it is in Ephesians that the glory of the community is so finely described. But if we re-read the first two chapters and Eph. 4^{11-16} from this standpoint, we shall understand that the reference is to the glory of the community as it is genuinely threatened in the world.

If the radical jeopardy in which the community stands is not perceived, it will be difficult to understand the statement to which we must now proceed—that although it is destructible, it cannot and will not actually be destroyed. It is indeed destructible. It belongs to the creaturely world, which is the world of flesh, the world of the perishing man who is assailed by nothingness and all its demons, the world of death. With all that men think and imagine, will and do, plan and achieve along Christian lines, it is part of this world. Like so many other constructs and kingdoms and systems it might well have had its time and then disappeared. It might well have come to an end. It has no miraculous power to protect it against this fate, guaranteeing in advance its continuance in the world, the *perpetuo mansura est* of the *Conf. Aug.* VII. It might have been destroyed. But it cannot and will not actually be destroyed. It may be hounded into a corner, and reduced to the tiniest of minorities, but it cannot be exterminated. It may be destroyed at one point, but it will arise all the stronger at another. It may be ignored and humiliated and scorned by the world which rushes past it in triumphant hostility, but it cannot and will not break under this burden. On the contrary, it will reach a height which will put to shame the superiority of the superior. Its own sloth and dissipation may result in its secularisation, but this will never be so radical that even in its most serious alienation there does not remain an element which resists that which is secular—a remnant from which in some form a sudden or gradual counter-movement can and will always proceed. It may stage some form of the masquerade of sacralisation and suffer the consequences, but at some point, even in all the false glitter with which it is surrounded, the genuine light of the Gospel will again strangely shine out among the *sancti* united round the *sancta*, and the constitution of the *communio* will be maintained. In short, the community may often be almost overwhelmed by the danger which threatens from without and within ; but it will never be completely overwhelmed. It may become ill—and where and when was it not dangerously ill ? in what great or small society ? at what time of resurgence any less than in ages of decline ?—but it cannot die : *non omnis moriar*. There will always be a strange persistence : remarkable reformations and prophetic renewals ; notable discoveries followed by notable reversions to its origins and equally notable advances into the future. To be sure, this will all stand in the shadow of the destructibility of all human (even Christian) works both old and new, but it will also be an indication of the presence of the indestructible beyond all human works. Neither the wise and powerful of this world, nor the weak forms of Christianity itself, will succeed in setting a term to the community before its time is up and it has attained its goal. In spite of every opposing force it will always still be there, or be there again ; and in some hidden way it will always be as young as in the first days, mounting up with wings as eagles. The gates of the underworld (Mt. 16[18]) will open up powerfully against it, but will not in fact swallow it up.

But why not ? Do not all the indications suggest that it might do this, and that it ought to have done so long since ? All the individual Christians—great and small, good and bad—in whom the community has lived, and who have lived in the community, in all ages within the last time, seem not to have been immune against this power to the extent that they have come like all flesh and then departed, having played their various parts in the faith and error and superstition and unbelief of the community, in its action and passion. And we cannot too confidently say that any of the societies and dogmas and cults and traditions and institutions of the Church have enjoyed any obvious immunity against this power. How much artificial conservatism, and how many later interpretations and constructions, conceal the sober fact that even what seem to be the most solid forms in which the community has existed and still exists in time are no less radically subject to decay and destruction than all other forms of human historical life ! They may go back four or ten or fifteen centuries, but their continuity does not constitute a solid basis on which we may know the truth of the promise of Mt. 16[18] and dare to confess it in spite of all appearances to the contrary. At very best, it can only be a sign of its truth and therefore of the upholding of the community. And at worst it may even be a product of human anxiety, obstinacy and mendacity, and thus a very misleading indication of this truth. It is certainly not in and by the strength of continuity itself, any more than by that of the existence of individual Christians, that the communion of saints is upheld.

How, then, is it upheld, and how is the promise kept ? In reply to this question, our safest plan is to begin with the simple fact that right up to our own day the Old and New Testament Scriptures have never been reduced to a mere letter in Christian circles, but have continually become a living voice and word, and have had and exercised power as such. To be sure, they have sometimes been almost completely silenced in a thicket of added traditions, or proclaimed only in liturgical sing-song, or overlaid by bold speculation, or searched only for *dicta probantia* in favour of official or private doctrine, or treated merely as a source of pious or even natural and impious morality, or torn asunder into a thousand shreds (each more unimportant than the other) by unimaginative historico-critical omniscience. But they have always been the same Scriptures and the community has never been able to discard them. Scriptures? A mere book then? No, a chorus of very different and independent but harmonious voices. An organism which in its many and varied texts is full of vitality within the community. Something which can speak and make itself heard in spite of all its maltreatment at the hands of the half-blind and arbitrary and officious. There are many things—even things supposedly taken from Scripture—to which we cannot return once we have discovered and sufficiently admired them. But in some way there has always been a return to the Bible. There are many things which sooner or later become mere repetitions and therefore hollow and empty and silent. But the Bible has always spoken afresh, and the more impressively sometimes when it is surrounded by all kinds of misuse and misunderstanding. That Scripture upholds the community is not something that Christians can fabricate by their own Bible-lectures and Bible-study or even by the Scripture principle, but it is something that Scripture achieves of itself. It often does it by very strange and devious ways. It may not do it directly, to the shame of its most faithful and attentive readers, but in the form of an echo awakened in the outside world, so that its readers have to begin to study it in a new way. But at some point, as a fellowship of those who hear its voice, the threatened community begins to group and consolidate and constitute itself afresh around the Bible, and in so doing it again finds itself on solid ground when everything seems to totter. It is the Holy Spirit who upholds the community as it is He who causes it to grow and live. But according to the defiant saying in Eph. 6[17] the " sword of the Spirit " which protects and defends it is the Word of God. And according to what is often the reluctant recognition of the community of all times and places the Word of God has always been heard in its one, original and authentic form where Scripture has again made itself to be heard and created hearers for itself. Thus when the harassed community prays for its preservation its prayer must always take the concrete form : " Preserve us, Lord, by Thy Word," with the concrete meaning : By Thy Word attested in Scripture. The preservation of the community takes place as it is upheld by this prophetic and apostolic word, or as it is led back as a hearing community to this word. And so we can only say to Christians who are troubled about the preservation of the community or the maintaining of its cause that they should discard all general and philosophico-historical considerations (however unsettling or cheerful) and hear, and hear again, and continually hear this word, being confronted both as individual and united hearers by the fact that the community certainly cannot uphold itself, but that all the same it is in fact upheld, being placed in the communion of saints as this continually takes place in the hearing of this word. With the flowing of this stream, however low or sluggish its waters may sometimes be, the communion of saints takes place, and is therefore upheld.

But the reference to Scripture obviously cannot be our final and decisive answer to the question of the sure and reliable mode of its preservation. The word of all the prophets and apostles put together can only be a witness which requires—and does not lack—verification by the One whom it attests. It is in the power of this verification that Scripture is the instrument by which the Church is upheld. As the One whom it attests verifies its witness, it is He who primarily and properly upholds the Church. He verifies Scripture simply by the fact that He is its content ; that as it is read and heard He Himself is present to speak and act as the living Lord of the Church. There concretely, as the One who was and is and will be according to the word of the prophets and apostles, He exists for the world and community of our time—the last time. There concretely, i.e., in the form attested there, He is revealed and may be known. There concretely He encounters Christians and therefore the world. From there concretely His Holy Spirit comes and works and rules. It is thus true already that from there concretely the Church is upheld by the Holy Spirit. But it is upheld only as He who is attested in Scripture does this ; as He Himself is there not merely as letter but as Spirit and Life ; as He is not past and inactive and silent, but the Son of God and Man, and Saviour of the world, who is present to-day, and acts here and now, and speaks with His own. It is because He is within His community, conducting its cause (both for itself and therefore for the world) in face of the great impending danger, that the destructible Church cannot in fact be destroyed ; that the mortal Church cannot die ; that the gates of hell cannot swallow it up. It stands or falls with Him. But He does not fall, and so the Church cannot fall. It can only stand. It can and must and will rise again even though it falls. He cannot deny Himself, or be untrue to Himself. And as the One who cannot do this, He upholds the community, and it is always upheld—simply by the fact that He is who He is, and that in it we always have to do with Him, because it is His body, the earthly-historical form of His existence. The outward and inward threat which overhangs the community, the whole onslaught of the chaos which He has mortally wounded, is no match at all for Him. It cannot defeat Him, nor can it separate Him as the Head from the community as His body. He, as the *totus Christus*, cannot die. That is why the community of His harassed and anxious saints also cannot die.

Confidence in its cause and continuance and future and triumph depends absolutely upon the fact that it is always confidence in Him ; that renouncing all other helpers it keeps only to Him who is not only a Helper but already the Conqueror, the Victor, the death of death, and who as such is not apart from but with His saints. For the community everything depends upon its readiness not to try to be anything more or better or surer than His people, His body, and to live and grow as such on earth. In every deviation from confidence in Him, it can only be deceived as to its preservation, and know that it is doomed and lost. There is no objective need, or even possibility, of concern and anxiety or despair concerning its preservation. This can arise only when there is deviation ; when search is made for other helpers ; when there is a desertion of the Victor by whom the community—even though it may be threatened on all sides, even though it may be under assault or the cross, even though it may be secularised or sacralised—is objectively victorious, and thus able at all times to throw off every fear. There is objective need to rejoice in its actual preservation. As the community does this, it is in a position to take up its human responsibilities with new thankfulness, seriousness and soberness, not foldings its hands, but when it has prayed, and as it continues to do so, going boldly to work as if it were not threatened by any dangers. *Fluctuat nec mergitur.* The One who is attested and attests Himself in the Bible will never have any other message for His threatened community than that it should be confident, not because it has no reason for anxiety as it exists in the world, but because of the counter-reason which radically removes this reason—that He has overcome the world (Jn. 16[33]).

4. THE ORDER OF THE COMMUNITY

Conscious always that we have to do with the *communio sanctorum*, we will now look in a third direction and consider the form in which there is accomplished the upbuilding of the community (understood also as its growth and upholding). The form essential to it is that of order. We can put it in another way and say that it is essential to the upbuilding of the community and therefore to the *communio sanctorum* that its eventuation should not be without form, or in an indefinite or haphazard form, but that it should have a very definite form. Building is not something which is left to chance or caprice. It is not a wild or anarchical happening. It is controlled by a definite form and aims at the application, representation and vindication of this form. Building follows a law and is accomplished in its exercise and fulfilment. It is in this way—not in derived but original and typical fashion—that there also and primarily takes place the upbuilding of the community. In the sphere of human history the upbuilding of the community as the attestation of the reconciliation of the world with God accomplished in Jesus Christ is the great campaign against chaos and therefore against disorder. How, then, can it fail to have its own order ? Is it not vital to it that even in the form of its occurrence it should oppose law to lawlessness ? Even when we understand its upbuilding in the first instance as its growth and life, we have to say at once that its growth takes place in a definite form and according to a definite law peculiar to it. And when we understand it secondly as its preservation in the world, we have to say again that it is not a blind power but its distinctive form, its law, which is fulfilled and vindicated in the fact that it can find continuance and consistence in the world.

We speak of order where definite relationships and connexions prove to correspond and thus to be necessary to the matter in question ; where they call for recognition ; where they find confirmation and demand and receive acknowledgment and respect. The upbuilding of the community, the event of the communion of saints, is accomplished in definite relationships and connexions, and to that extent in. order. Let us again put it in another way. In the upbuilding of the community we have to do with that which is lawful and right. It is right particularly in the sense that it corresponds to the matter in question. If we are to speak of the order of the community we cannot help speaking in the same breath and with the same meaning of the right which is revealed and known and acknowledged and valid in it. Disorder is wrong, not merely as participation in chaos, but as the dissolution of the form essential to the community, as the destruction of the distinctness of its peculiar relationships and connexions. It is a wrong way of handling the matter in question. Order, on the other hand, is right, i.e., a right way of handling it, not merely as a protest against chaos, but as a confirmation of this form and distinctness.

The words " right " and " law " are an indication that we are about to enter a sphere which has been hotly contested in recent years. I may refer to some contemporary works which reveal not only the state of the discussion but also its historical presuppositions : Wilhelm Vischer, *Die evangelische Gemeindeordnung* (*nach Matth.* 16[13-20, 28]), 1946 ; Eduard Schweizer, *Das Leben des Herrn in der Gemeinde und ihren Diensten*, 1946, also *Gemeinde nach dem Neuen Testament*, 1949, and *Geist und Gemeinde im Neuen Testament und heute*, 1952 ; Emil Brunner, *Das Missverständnis der Kirche*, 1951 ; Erik Wolf, " Bekennendes Kirchenrecht " (in *Rechtsgedanke und biblische Weisung*, 1947, pp. 65 ff.), and " Zur Rechtsgestalt der Kirche " (in *Bekennende Kirche*, p. 254 f.), 1952 ; Max Schoch, *Evangelisches Kirchenrecht und biblische Weisung*, 1954 ; Max Geiger, *Wesen und Aufgabe kirchlicher Ordnung*, 1954. The contributions of Erik Wolf are particularly illuminating and deserve special mention.

To what do we refer ? What is it that must take place in order and therefore in a definite form, according to law and right ? The answer is that it is nothing more nor less than the whole human being and action of the Christian community as a provisional representation of the sanctification of man as it has taken place in Jesus Christ. For the sake of clarity we will mention some of the most important points at which the problem of order continually arises and demands an answer. It is a matter of the order of the particular event in which the existence of the community finds not merely its most concrete manifestation but also its central point, namely, public worship. It is also a matter of the determination and distribution of the various inter-related responsibilities, obligations and functions to be discharged by individual Christians within the general activity of the community. It is also a question how the community is to maintain its common cause, and the majesty of this cause, in relationship to its individual members ; how it is to exercise discipline and oversight and rule among its members in respect of the particular functions entrusted to them and their Christian life in general. It is also a matter of the relationship of individual Christian congregations to other congregations both near and distant ; of the preservation and exercise of the unity of all congregations ; of the achievement of reciprocity in action and therefore of mutual understanding ; of a comprehensive direction which will co-ordinate their existence and action. It is a matter of the regulation—so far as this is possible and necessary—of the relationships of the community to other social forms, and especially to the most outstanding and comprehensive ; of the order of its relationship to the existing and authoritative state and its laws, organs and measures.

We cannot undertake to develop and answer in detail these questions of order. This is a matter for canon law rather than dogmatics. But dogmatics cannot refrain from considering the standpoints normative for canon law. It has to take account of the place from which all the detailed questions of order have always to be answered and which must always be the starting-point of canon law if it is to be true *law*, but also the law of the *Church*.

If we have been on the right track in our previous deliberations concerning the upbuilding of the community, and if we have to follow the same track in the present question, the decisive point for everything that follows is that in this question of the order and therefore the right or law of the community there should be maintained the true relationship between the primary and the secondary subjects in the concept " community," and therefore that even in this question the relationship should not be reversed, or made dependent on any of its ramifications, or bracketed by them, or, for the sake of an answer, replaced by its opposite. In canon law there can be no question of a μετάβασις εἰς ἄλλο γένος. If it is the case that in the concept " community " Jesus Christ as the Head of His body is the primary acting Subject, compared with whom the acting human communion of saints can be regarded only as secondary, then in relation to the order of the community this fact must not only remain inviolate, i.e., it must not only be respected as theological truth, as a statement of Christian faith and its confession, but it must be given its proper place and expression in relation to the order of the community and in the solution

of all the problems of order involved. In the Church, law is that
which is right by the norm of this relationship. Everything else is
wrong. This is the axiom which dogmatics has to proclaim to all
existing or projected canon law, by which even its most detailed
provisions must be measured, and to the acknowledgment of which
it is invited or recalled.

It would be folly to try to derive canon law from any but a christologico-ecclesiological concept of the community. The community is
as Jesus Christ is—He who is the Lord of the human communion of
saints, the Head of His body, which is the earthly-historical form of
His own existence. Or, conversely, it is the human communion of
saints in which, as in His body, in the earthly-historical form of His
existence, He is the Head and the Lord. Only as we start with this
view of the community can two *desiderata* be fulfilled in the grounding
of canon law. For only on this view (1) can it be shown that we have
to inquire, and why we have to inquire, concerning order, and therefore concerning a definite form, concerning law and right in the life
of the Christian community ; that a distinction has to be made, and
how it has to be made, between an orderly and a disorderly community
(or, as we might also say in relation to our wider context, a sanctified
and an unsanctified). And it is only on this view (2) that it can be
shown what is the specific order and form, the particular law and right,
concerning which we have to inquire when it is with respect to the
Christian community, which as such cannot be equated with any other
human society.

The terms used by Rudolph Sohm, and by Emil Brunner after him, to describe
the essence of the Christian community, evade the christological question and
answer. As they see it, the community is the spiritual and voluntary Church,
the Church of love and faith (invisible according to Sohm). Or, according to
Brunner, it is a " pure fellowship of persons " (*op. cit.*, E.T., pp. 10, 17), a fellowship of brothers (p. 84), or a living fellowship (p. 110). I do not overlook the
fact that Brunner constantly uses the alternative term " fellowship of Christ,"
and that the phrase " Christian fellowship " occurs in no less than five of his
chapter headings. But I have not found a single passage where he improves
on Sohm by seriously thinking through and formulating the concept of the
community in terms of Christ. As he sees it, it is not the existence and lordship
of Jesus Christ which constitute the community, but the relationships which
those who belong to Him—Christians—have acquired in relation to Him and
especially to one another. What Brunner calls the fellowship of Christ does not
differ in substance from what Sohm calls the spiritual Church or the Church of
love. For him, too, Christ is a predicate of the Christian community, and not
vice versa. But however that may be, it is clear that on his view as on that of
Sohm there can be no fulfilment of the first *desideratum* ; no serious inquiry
concerning order and law in the life of the community. And self-evidently—
for the concepts are deliberately selected in order that the question itself (not
to speak of the answer) should be rejected as a " misunderstanding of the Church,"
and the true community, which is not burdened with problems of law and order,
polemically opposed to the organised Church. This being the case, it is pointless and ungenerous to ask whether these views are of any value from the standpoint of our second *desideratum* ; whether they can result in a useful investigation

of the specific order which characterises the Christian community. They can obviously have no value in this respect. Presupposing these views, it might of course be asked that evidence should be adduced to show that the distinctive rejection of the problem of order is in any sense peculiarly Christian. For there are other fellowships of persons and brothers, spiritual fellowships of love (e.g., private friendships and academic and artistic societies) which have no intrinsic interest in questions of order. The particular sense in which this is true of the Christian community is not shown by Sohm and Brunner, and it cannot possibly be shown on their view.

Our first proposition (1) is that the christologico-ecclesiological concept of the community is such that by its very nature it speaks of law and order, thus impelling and summoning us to take up this question. In the light of it, we cannot evade this particular problem, because it is itself a concept of law and order, and we cannot adopt it without being brought face to face at once with the whole question. If it is the case that the Christian community is the human fellowship in which Jesus Christ as the Head is the primary Subject, and the acting communion of saints as His body is the secondary, to say " community " is at once to say " law and order." The very term implies a definite form which is always peculiar to the event denoted by the *communio sanctorum*, a law to which it is always subject, a relationship and proportion which it must necessarily assume in correspondence with the point at issue. The point at issue is a provisional representation of humanity as it is sanctified in Jesus Christ. In correspondence with this centre it is always a question of the ordering and commanding and controlling of the Holy One in whom all are sanctified, and therefore of Jesus Christ, on the one side ; and on the other side side of the obedient attitude of the human communion of saints in subordination to Him. This relationship constitutes the Christian community. It is its principle of order, its basic law. As it is the Christian community, it has it within itself as the law of the Church, i.e., as the law established in the Church and valid for it. The many questions of what this means in the detailed life and action of the Church are not answered by this reference to its basic law. The community will have to answer these as it considers the legality of its life and action. But the fact that this is its basic law means that these detailed questions are continually raised. It cannot possibly be what it is unless it accepts them and makes some attempt to answer them. On this basis we cannot ignore the question of true Church law, or treat it as a matter of secondary importance.

The main definition of Erik Wolf hits the nail on the head. As he sees it, the Christian community is " the community of the Lord and of those who are elected by Him and thus made His brethren " (" Rechtsgestalt," p. 258 f.). It is a " brotherly Christocracy " (p. 261, note the relationship of subject and predicate). In a subsequent and subordina e sense, it can then be regarded and understood and described as a " christocratic brotherhood " (pp. 259, 261). Even so, the idea of Christocracy is dominant. And by it the brotherhood is characterised as a fellowship of law, i.e., a fellowship ordered by the superior law of Jesus Christ.

As against this, the definitions of Sohm and Brunner are quite impossible because, without any genuine support from the New Testament, they ignore that which is denoted by the term Christocracy, and therefore the basic law which prevails in and for the Church. Nor is it any help that it is in order to discriminate against all Church law as such the terms " spirit," " voluntariness," " love," etc. are used at the decisive point where there ought to be reference to Jesus Christ. The enslavement of the Church to law is, we are told, the great evil, or " misunderstanding," which has to be set right in this drastic fashion. As Brunner sees it, " the decisive act of Luther's reformation " was not the publication of the theses of 1517 but " the burning of the *Corpus juris canonici* " on Dec. 10, 1520 (p. 97). Church law as such is the work of those who are weak in faith (Sohm). It is a substitute for the missing fulness of the Holy Spirit (Brunner, p. 53). It is identical with a loss of Messianic existence or a weakening of Messianic consciousness (p. 59). " What we need is the Holy Ghost " (p. 115). Of course we do. But a community which does not ask concerning law and order, inevitably abandoning its life to chance and caprice and confusion, will be just as much in contradiction to the Holy Spirit of Jesus Christ as one which sets its answers to this question above or in place of the Holy Spirit. Enslavement to law is certainly one of the great dangers which threaten the Church (in the wider context of what we have described as sacralisation). But is it the only one ? And can we really meet it by disputing and anathematising the whole idea of Church law ? Is it not wiser to argue with Erik Wolf (p. 254 f.) that juridification and bureaucratisation, i.e., the reduction of Church life to a matter of forms and techniques, are symptoms of disorder which we can counter, not by a rejection of the problem of law or a dissolution of order, but only by a recognition and assertion of the true order of the community ; that they constitute a lawlessness of the Church in face of which we have to maintain the form of law which corresponds to the substance of the matter, and therefore a true Church law (which will also exclude every form of Chiliasm). But this true Church law is that which derives from the basic law valid in the Church, i.e., from the christologico-ecclesiological concept of the community. For all the problematical nature of his concrete answer (and of all answers) Calvin was fundamentally right when he stated : *Quant est de la vraye Eglise, nous croyons, qu'elle doit estre gouverne selon la police que nostre Seigneur Jesus Christ a establie* (*Conf. Gall.*, Art. 29). Note that he says : *nous croyons*. This is a statement of faith. It is thus a statement which has Jesus Christ as its theme and content. But because it has Jesus Christ, it also has the order established in Him, and therefore the consequent obligation to rule the Church in correspondence with this order. In face of this, the arguments of Sohm and Brunner are caught in a vicious circle. Because they ignore the basic christologico-ecclesiological law of the Church, they are forced to seek a definition of the Church which will make the question of Church law impossible. And because they try to eliminate the question of Church law, they are betrayed into this definition of the Church, and are necessarily blind to its basic christologico-ecclesiological law.

It is also the case however (2) that on a christologico-ecclesiological view of the community law and order are distinguished as Christian and ecclesiastical law and order from every other form, and are visible and effective in this distinctive form. The basic form which characterises the Christian community necessarily demands that the whole structure of its life whould be unique. There can be no question of its subjection to the rules which are valid, either generally or on certain historical assumptions, for the constitution and action of other human societies. When they ask concerning law and order in the life of the community, the men at work in it cannot start from the presupposition that they and their fellowship are the subject which has as its predicate their common faith and confession and prayer, their common message to the world, and finally and supremely the Lord Jesus Christ commonly recognised and acknowledged by them. They cannot start, then, from the presupposition that as this particular fellowship (like all other human societies) they themselves have to discover the law and order valid in their case. On the contrary, He, Jesus Christ, is here the Lord and Head, the primary acting Subject. It is He who gives them, not only their faith and confession and prayer and proclamation, but also the form of their life, the law and order of all that they do. .The community is not a law to itself, least of all in its relationship to Him. In its relationship to Him He is its living law. What the men who act in the community must do is to recognise, and continually recognise, that He is the regulative law of their relationship to Him, and therefore to be obedient to Him, and constantly to be better and more exactly and more perfectly obedient. A true inquiry concerning what is right in the Church will always be an inquiry concerning His ordering and commanding and controlling, and the corresponding obedience. From the very outset, and in all its ramifications, the law of the Church must be " spiritual " law in the strict sense of the term, i.e., a law which is to be sought and found and established and administered in the fellowship of the Holy Spirit of Jesus Christ. As such, all valid and projected Church law, if it is true Church law, will be clearly and sharply differentiated from every other kind of " law." In great things and small, in all things, true Church law arises from a hearing of the voice of Jesus Christ. Neither formally nor materially does it arise elsewhere. To seek and find and establish and administer this law is an integral part of the action with which the community is charged in and in relation to the world. For this reason, too, we cannot eliminate the question of true Church law, or treat it as a question of minor importance.

True Church law as it has to be continually sought is an integral part of the true confession of the community, which has also to be continually sought and safeguarded both inwardly and outwardly. Erik Wolf again hit the nail on the head when in his 1947 essay he described true Church law as " confessing law." It is astonishing that neither Sohm nor Brunner seems to have considered that beyond the curt alternatives of enslavement to law or lawlessness this third position is possible and indeed necessary ; for it is difficult to see what right the Church has not to confess, but to be inactive and to suppress its witness, on this level.

But we must be more precise and say that the voice which has to be heard is that of Jesus Christ as attested in Holy Scripture. It is in the form attested there that He is the Head, the living Lord, of the community. It is His Spirit as active in His attestation by the prophets and apostles that is the Holy Spirit, the power of His commanding and controlling with their requirement of obedience. It is concretely to Scripture that the community has to listen in the question of law and order, in the conflict against ecclesiastical lawlessness and disorder. It has to receive direction from the Bible. It is a matter of the Bible in which He is attested. Or, to put it in another way, it is a matter of Himself as attested and self-attesting in the Bible ; of His activity as *incarnandus* in the Old Testament and *incarnatus* in the New. His activity there and then is the law which the community must obey here and now. The direction given by the Bible is His direction. In the question of the form of its life as determined by Him the Church has not, then, merely to copy and adopt and imitate that which in response to His direction was achieved there and then, and may be seen in Scripture, as the form of life of Israel old and new. We can never handle the Bible in this way. On the other hand, it cannot listen to His direction here and now without paying close attention to the way in which He acted there and then as the Head of His body, and to the form, the laws and ordinances which corresponded there and then to His activity in the life of His body. As in its teaching and life generally, it must always orientate itself by the life of the Lord in the Old and New Testament community as the first and original form of " brotherly Christocracy " : not in order to reproduce it in the same form ; but in order to be induced by it to know Him there and then, yet also here and now, as the Lord Himself living and acting in His community. There can be no question of its obeying any given form of the body of Jesus Christ—not even the biblical—but only Jesus Christ Himself as the Head of His body. It is not a matter of adjusting itself either to the economy of the Old Testament or to that of the New, but of subjecting itself to the One who in both cases was the Director of the economy, the Head of the house, and who is still the same to-day, and rules as such here and now. How can it listen to Him if it will not listen to Scripture ? But it listens to Scripture—and in it to the witness of the Old and New Testament people of God and its laws and ordinances—in order to listen to Him, so that beyond that which must be law and order in its own life it will receive His own immediate direction. In this sense Scripture (itself *norma normata*) is the *norma normans* of its inquiry concerning true Church law, and confessing law must be in practice the confession of the law of Jesus Christ attested in Scripture.

A final note is demanded on the doctrine of a community without law (the invisible Church in the sense of faith, according to Sohm, and the visible *ecclesia*, according to Brunner). It is interesting that the representatives of this view still seem to be concerned about the question (as is indeed inevitable) how their purely spiritual fellowship of love is to exist in the world, and to co-exist with other human societies. Why is it that—whether they think of it as visible or invisible—they have not sufficient confidence in its pneumatic superiority and power boldly to oppose it as the one true Christian Church or community or fellowship to the world and all other Churches which on account of their apostasy are subject to canon law? Why is it that according to Brunner (p. 116) " it can never be a question of deriving from this distinction between the *ecclesia* and the Church a merely negative judgment upon or a hostile attitude towards the latter " ? Or why are not the erring Churches summoned to repent and become the *ecclesia* ? Why are we even assured that they cannot and should not do this (p. 107) ? It is hard to see why either the one or the other should not be the logical deduction from the assumptions of Sohm and Brunner. But the conclusion is not drawn. On the contrary, we are surprised to gather that apart from and alongside the *ecclesia*, which is so polemically exalted at the expense of Church law and the institutionalised Church, there may and must be ecclesiastical institutions, which can never as such be the true Church (for they have obviously fallen hopelessly victim to the misunderstanding of the Church), but which do at least have the task of constituting the " shell in which this precious kernel has been contained and preserved " (p. 116), so that not only are they indispensable " from the point of view of continuity of doctrine and preaching " (p. 111), but it is even required of them that they should serve, or at least not hinder, " the growth of the *ecclesia* " (p. 107). " In spite of everything the institutional Church has shown itself to be the most powerful *externum subsidium* of the Christian communion " (p. 116). The questions which I myself would find it impossible to answer if I were to adopt this view are as follows.

1. Who or what institutes and orders this Church in the sense of law, which is not really the true Church, and is to be sharply and definitively distinguished from the *ecclesia* (the Church in the sense of faith) ? By definition, the Holy Spirit cannot do so. According to the assumptions on which this view rests, He either will not or cannot have anything whatever to do with the discovery and establishment of this Church. But who then, or what ? A general, legal or historico-positivist conception of the nature of unions, and especially religious unions ? But who then is to interpret this conception ? The state with its own law ? Or members of the Christian communion, who are naturally interested in the existence of this shell, and who for the sake of its proper construction will occasionally defy the veto of the Holy Spirit and enter the sphere of this general, legal or historico-positivist conception ? Whatever may be the answer, there can be no doubt that the principle which is at work in the formation and preservation of this shell will have to be essentially different from that " precious kernel."

2. What will become of the precious kernel in this essentially different shell ? Will the life of this lawless spiritual construct of love maintain itself in face of the alien law of this legal construct, a law by which its own existence in the world is protected and governed ? Or will it be forced to adjust itself to it, so that sooner or later it will be conformed in practice to the course and life of the world ? It must be remembered that the task of proclamation and doctrine has been confidently entrusted to this construct. And even if the danger which threatens from this quarter is not acute in practice, in what sense can we imagine or expect that this shell will serve, or at least not hinder, this kernel, that the legal institution will serve, or at least not hinder, the growth of the pneumatic *ecclesia* ? Are we then to gather grapes of thorns, or figs of thistles ?

3. What will become of the pneumatic purity of the *ecclesia* if, as Brunner sees it, it is a historical quantity (p. 109), and even as a non-ecclesiastical construct it is characterised by ecclesiastical extension and activity (p. 108 f.), so that with reference to the past (quite apart from the primitive community) it is possible to point, e.g., to the Quakers as an approximate realisation of what is meant, or with reference to the present to the Home Mission of Wichern, the World Alliance of Y.M.C.A.s and Y.W.C.A.s, the Student Christian Movement, the Oxford Group Movement (now M.R.A.) and the Basle and China Inland Missions, or with reference to the future to expect the appearance of new and

hitherto unsuspected forms of the *ecclesia* ? Forms ! But that is the whole point. If the *ecclesia* exists visibly, this means that it exists in a form. But if it exists in a form, the question of the rightness of this form cannot be ignored and we are forced to attempt an answer. In all the spheres mentioned by Brunner there have been attempts of this kind. There has never been complete spontaneity (p. 58). There have always been unions and institutions on the basis of reflection and discussion. And we have to ask seriously whether this has not meant in every case a more or less evil enslavement to law. The same will always be the case in the future envisaged by Brunner. But this means that at no time or place has Brunner's *ecclesia* ever been a completely non-ecclesiastical construct. It is distinguished from the Churches—not always to its own advantage—only by the fact that it makes as light as possible of the problem of order, desiring to suppress it instead of tackling it openly, radically and seriously.

4. What will become of the witness to the world which is incumbent upon the Church in the sense of faith if according to Sohm this cannot be visible, but can only exist invisibly in the framework and shadow of the Church in the sense of law ? If it refuses to take on a distinctive form in the world, if it is content or even desires to be anonymous, or to be represented by the alien form of the Church in the sense of law, surely this can mean only that it relies for its Christian witness in the world on individual members and their word and life and work. Indeed, it will probably insist that this is the only possible and true form of its witness. But does not this mean that it withholds itself from the world in its essential being as the body of Jesus Christ ? And in so doing, does it not inevitably depreciate from the very outset the witness of individuals, exposing it to the suspicion that it is only a question of the expression of private opinions and piety which are not in any way obligatory for others ? Is it not also inevitable that the world will judge it, and with it the whole sphere of the Christian spirit and faith and life, by the alien screen through the chinks of which these individuals can be seen but behind which it is itself concealed, and with it the earthly-historical form of existence of Jesus Christ in its world-wide significance ?—and all because in misplaced self-will it regards itself as too superior in the fulfilment of its public mission to assert itself publicly for what it is, thus accepting and posing in all seriousness the question of its appropriate and distinctive form. Can Christendom really adopt this course ?

5. Our final question is the most incisive. How authoritative really is this controlling picture of the Church in the sense of faith, or the supposed New Testament *ecclesia* ? " The Christ community is the great miracle of history," says Brunner (p. 116). To portray the Church of the first centuries as such was the enterprise undertaken at the turn of the 17th century—a period which was particularly fateful for the history of Protestant theology—in the comprehensive and in its own way very scholarly work of Gottfried Arnold : *Die erste Liebe der Gemeinden Jesu Christi, das ist wahre Abbildung der ersten Christen und ihres lebendigen Glaubens und heiligen Lebens* (1696). The evaluation and purpose were much the same as those of Sohm and Brunner. But did these first Christians of Arnold, Sohm's spiritual Church of love and Brunner's *ecclesia* ever exist in such a way that they can even be conceived of as the source and norm of all subsequent reflection on the problem of the Church ? Does it not need a good deal of imagination to accept this portrayal as a genuine portrayal ? To put it bluntly, did this great miracle really happen ? Even according to what we find in the witness of the New Testament, not to speak of the first centuries, which Arnold adduces in evidence of this miracle ? Does not this picture belong to the sphere of that which never was on land or sea, to the world of ideas and ideals ? But even supposing that a kind of pneumatic community did actually exist in a recognisable form, the decisive question still remains how this community, or its portrayal, acquires the authority ascribed to it on this view. When we say : *credo ecclesiam*, does this mean that I believe in a model picture

of Christian community which I have discovered or adduced, or which has presented itself to me, and which I describe as a great miracle ? Basically, is not the attempt to discuss the problem of the Church in terms of this criterion a romantic undertaking which makes no serious attempt at theological deliberation ? What is the authority for this criterion ? Accepting the fact that in the New Testament and the Early Church we do have the witness to a particular form of the body of Christ, is this to be the law of the activity of the Christian community ? Neither in Arnold nor in the more recent attempts to exalt the first Christians do I find any answer to this question, nor, strangely enough, does it seem even to be taken into account. The decisive reason for this, as I see it, is that no answer can be given. The New Testament does not attest a model of Christian fellowship, but " the life of the Lord in the community " (E. Schweizer), and therefore the basic law which is valid and normative for the community in every age. It attests " brotherly Christocracy," " the living community of the living Lord Jesus Christ." As this witness was ignored, even in the first centuries both legalism and licence invaded the Church. But legalism is not warded off or evaded by contemplating or imagining or taking as a model a Christian fellowship in which it is permitted and commanded either to suppress altogether, or to discuss only occasionally and in application of alien standards, the question of the order of its life as posed by its basic law. It is avoided, as is also Chiliasm and disorder, only as this basic law is respected, and the question too of Church law to which it gives rise is neither suppressed nor treated lightly, but taken in all seriousness as a question of obedience ; as a question of the true form of *communio sanctorum* in the world ; as a question, therefore, of the true witness of the community in the world ; as a question which—whether we look upward or outward or inward—must always be regarded as of primary importance.

Before we try to press on to a recognition of the basic principles of true canon law, an intermediate explanation is demanded. It is inevitable that initially—and at the decisive point, so long as the present world lasts, finally—the world will have a very different understanding of the community from that which it has of itself. In other words, it will be guilty of a misunderstanding. For what does the world know—and what can it know prior to the return and manifestation of Jesus Christ on the clouds of heaven—of " brotherly Christocracy " as the basic law valid in the Christian community ? Lacking the categories necessary to understand it, the world regards it merely as one society with others, and it will necessarily classify and equate it with the other groups which have arisen and still arise within its own sphere. It will think of these as sociological constructs in which the men united within them are the acting subject and their particular convictions and efforts the predicate. No exception will be made in the case of so-called religious societies. The Christian community will be regarded and treated merely as one of these societies—a union or corporation of men united in Christian views and Christian action. With respect, or indifference, or sometimes rejection, their common confession of Jesus Christ as their Lord, and the Lord of the world, will be heard and noted. Some explanation will be advanced for the fact that large or small groups hold this belief (in one of its confessional forms). But it cannot possibly agree—otherwise it would not be the world—to treat with the Church on its own basis (taking seriously its faith and confession). In spite of its confession, it will still interpret it as a sociological construct. It will expect that at any rate in its relations with the world it will keep within the framework of that which is understood generally as the legal subject of a union, a corporation, a natural group, or one which has arisen or been formed historically, for the pursuance of a particular end. The community for its part cannot possibly accept this interpretation. The root of almost all the errors which have arisen in this question is to be found in the fact that it has more or less consistently done so; that it has understood itself in terms of the world's misunderstanding. It cannot forbid the world to interpret it in this way, and thus to misunderstand it. It has to realise that this is only to be expected from outside. It can and must clearly and firmly oppose to this interpretation its own confession and self-understanding. But it cannot force the world—and it must not try—to take this confession and self-interpretation seriously. It will always have to count on it in practice that it is surrounded by a whole ocean of world which is neither able nor willing to do this, and which it cannot therefore prevent from understanding it very differently from the way in which it must understand itself.

This is particularly true of the most important partner which stands in concrete juxtaposition to the Church in the world—the state. It is a separate question that of all human societies the Church has to understand the state, which comprehends and co-ordinates all the others, as a divinely appointed institution, as an element of the lordship of Jesus Christ, as the great human representative of His lordship over the world outside, so that in this wider sense its officials can be regarded as the " ministers of God " (Rom. 13⁶). It certainly can and must confess in relation to it that it understands its own spiritual centre to be the centre of the being and constitution of the state as well. But even when it might have the chance to do this in a particular historical situation, it cannot try to force it to understand itself in the same way as the Church understands it ; or to understand the Church in the same way as the latter understands itself. It will always find that even though the majority of citizens and many officials are good Christians the state confronts the Church as its worldly partner, and that in their mutual relationship it is always on its own presuppositions that it will think and reason and deal with it in its various laws and decrees. The most that it can ever expect from the state in practice is to be assigned a more or less exalted position and function within its own law in relation to corporations and societies.

The form in which the state regulates its connexion with the Church, i.e., the Church's assimilation into its own order within the framework of its understanding (or misunderstanding) of its nature and essence, is the law of Church and state, in which as the possessor of sovereignty in its own sphere, and the supreme guardian of all law and order established and valid within it, the state guarantees an appropriate place to the Church, but is also vigilant to see that it does not transgress the appointed limits.

It does this in virtue of the fact that with many other rights it also claims and exercises a *ius circa sacra* : not *in sacra*, in an attempt to shape its will and rule its inner life ; but *circa sacra*, as that which guarantees these limits on both sides. It may be the state itself which lays down the law of the Church, e.g., by definite articles of constitution and by the sanctioning of corresponding legislation in the Church. Or sometimes it is a matter for mutual arrangement in the form of concordats. The state may even grant certain privileges extending either to public recognition of the Church as a legal corporation, or even to its recognition (as everywhere in Europe once, and even yet in Spain) as the Church of the official state-religion.

Even at best, there can never be any question of the state adopting the Church's understanding of itself. This understanding will not, therefore, find expression in the legal status laid down by the state or arranged in conjunction with it. But this means that the law of Church and state can never be, or try to be, the law of the Church, nor can it be accepted and recognised as such. There can thus be no place for the provisions of this law in the constitution or order of the Church. For they presuppose, and directly or indirectly express, an understanding of the Church which the Church itself cannot adopt. The Church can only allow this legislation to come into being, and acquiesce in it. There is no reason why it should not do this. It cannot deny that it is one human society with others, and that as such it comes within the jurisdiction of the state, of which its own members, individual Christians, are citizens, and which it regards and recognises as of divine appointment. It will thus adapt itself loyally to the *ius circa sacra* claimed and exercised by the state. And if it is given the opportunity directly or indirectly to influence its form and exercise, it will do so with thankfulness, and with a consciousness of its responsibility for the existence and continuance of the state as well. But it will always realise that even in the best law of Church and state we have to do with a misunderstanding of the Church which ignores the basic law valid within it ; that the Church is always seen and understood as a union or corporation and therefore a sovereign subject of law (which it is not) ; that it is subjected to a tremendous optical distortion in which it can recognise itself only if it takes energetic measures to see things in their true proportion. It will thus adapt itself to all the legislation imposed or granted by the state, or agreed with it, only as it adapts itself to the world and its affairs generally. The phrase ὡς μή is applicable at this point—as though it did it not. Within the framework of the law of state it will not cease for a single moment to accept its original and true responsibility, which even the best state does not and cannot take from it. It can never be a question of its own power or prestige. But in all that it does and does not do within this framework it must keep clearly and constantly before it that which is entrusted to it in contrast to the state. As far as possible, it will understand all the provisions of the law of Church and state in accordance with the conception of law which it derives from its self-understanding. It will be vigilant to see that the state's *ius circa sacra* does not openly or surreptitiously—and there is always a tendency in this direction, even (and perhaps especially) in the most loyal state—develop into a *ius in sacra* ; the interference of the state in its own order, and ultimately an attempt to control its preaching, doctrine and theology, i.e., the practical fulfilment of its confession, if not the confession itself. It cannot allow itself to be secularised by the law of Church and state and its definitions. If necessary, it will not hesitate actively to withstand those responsible for its application (whether it is a matter of officials or political majorities). A frontier will always be perceived which it has to guard in virtue of its own self-understanding and beyond which it cannot accept either the commands or the prohibitions of the state. Above all, it will tirelessly give positive expression to its own understanding of itself. It will do this decisively in the contours of its life and activity within the sphere of the state. Ignoring the distorted picture presented in the law of Church and state, it will be present and speak and act in its own character, and the discharge of its commission, as a human society which does not belong to itself or govern itself, as the sphere which is ruled by Jesus Christ. It will demonstrate its faith in Him by serious and confident obedience. Even in the most critical of cases, it will not do this against the state, but with a true sense of responsibility for it ; in order that by its loyalty to itself, to its own basic law, it may remind the state of that which is the ultimate basis and commission and dignity of the state itself—the fact that it is from God, that it does not exercise an intrinsic but a transmitted authority, and that it too is a subject of law only in a restricted sense. What the state needs, within the framework of a particular law of Church and state, is a free Church, which as such can remind it of its own limits and calling, thus warning it against falling either into anarchy on the one hand or tyranny on the other. As a free Church, and only as such, the Christian community will always allow itself to be integrated, and willingly and gladly integrate itself, into the order instituted by the state.

After this preliminary clarification, we may now take up the task of stating the general presuppositions which on a christologico-ecclesiological view of the community as its basic law will always be normative for every true Church law, and operative and revealed within it. By Church law as distinct from the law of Church and state we mean the order which on its own basic law and in obedience to its Lord the community has to seek and establish and execute of itself, in complete independence of the law of Church and state, and without even the slightest interference on the part of national authority (in the form of constitutions or establishment).

In this connexion we can only indicate the general presuppositions which are theologically binding on all Churches and their law. We cannot develop the law itself. This is a matter for the different Churches in different places and times and situations, and it may often demand special legal knowledge and skill in addition to the necessary theological insight. There is, of course, this basic law, and its analysis will yield certain general presuppositions which underlie all Church law. But there is no such thing as universal Church law. On the basis of this law, and the presuppositions to which it gives rise, true Church law may develop in many different directions. Our present concern is with the presuppositions of all Church law as they arise out of the basic law and explain it. These presuppositions have a demonstrable theological validity for all Church law. To clarify and assert them as valid in this way, thus furthering their recognition and acknowledgment, is one of the tasks of dogmatics. It is to this task that we now address ourselves.

1. In the light of its basic law, the law to be sought and established and executed in the Christian community must always have the character and intention of a law of service. It must always be law within an order of ministry. The community of Jesus Christ, as the body of which He is the Head, exists as it serves Him. And its members, Christians, as members of this His body, exist as—united by the service which they render to their Lord—they serve one another. This first and decisive determination of all Church law has its basis in the fact that the Lord Himself, who rules the community as the Head of His body, " came not to be ministered unto, but to minister " (Mk. 10⁴⁵). Revealed as such in His resurrection, and ruling as such by His Holy Spirit, He is the King and Lord of the world and the community as the One who on the cross was defeated and in that way victorious, humbled and in that way exalted. He is the King and Lord as the One who serves His Father, and therefore His own and all men. It is as this One who serves that He rules and requires obedience. He is not, therefore, one of the lords who do not serve but only rule and leave the serving to others. He is the Lord as He is first the servant of God and all others. The two things cannot be separated or reversed. It is not the case that He rules and at the same time serves, or serves and at the same time rules. It is as He serves that He rules. It is as the humiliated Son of God that He is the exalted Son of Man. Thus the obedience of His community corresponding to His rule can only be service, and the law which obtains in it, in accordance with the basic law which consists in the lordship of Jesus Christ established within it, can only be the law of service. The community attains its true order as His body when its action is service. And its members, Christians, attain their true order when they serve. In the Christian community, unlike all other human societies, there is no distinction between privileges and duties, claims and obligations, or dignities and burdens. There can be privileges and claims and dignities only in

and with the duties and obligations and burdens of service. " And whosoever of you will be the chiefest, shall be the servant of all " (Mk. 10⁴⁴). From the point of view of the community and all its members, sanctification means exaltation, but because it is exaltation in fellowship with the One who came to serve it is exaltation to the lowliness in which He served and still serves, and rules as He serves. As in its Lord, and typically for all mankind, the community participates in this exaltation and rules with Him, both as a whole and in each of its members it can only serve, and in the law which obtains within it—Church law—the only real question is that of the correctness of its service.

This determination is (1) unequivocal, non-dialectical and irreversible. In the community it is not at all the case that the law of service carries with it an accompanying law of rule, as if the burden which has to be borne by and within it were bound up with all kinds of dignities, or the obligation laid on it and each of its members authorised all kinds of claims, or its active commitment to service were the basis of all kinds of privileges. This may well be the case, and quite in order, in other human societies. But it is far otherwise in the Christian community. Upon it, and each of its members, there is laid a demand —the demand that it should serve. Its whole law consists and is fulfilled in the fact that it stands under this demand. The question which arises is that of the right form in which both as a whole and in each of its members it must correspond to this demand. For and in the community a demanding which is abstracted from and even in some way conflicts with the fact that it is demanded is quite unlawful. There can be no autonomous demanding. For the community and each of its members legitimate demanding can be only the demanding of that which is necessary to fulfil the common requirement of service. The dignity can be only that of the burden, the claim that of the obligation and the privilege that of the fulfilment of duty. The rule can be only that which in itself and as such is service—and only service. Unequivocally, and unconfused by any speculative end, the freedom of the community and each of the Christians assembled within it is the freedom to serve.

No true Church law can hesitate to take into account the unequivocal nature of this determination. No true Church law can follow the example of the law of other societies and give place to a demanding which conflicts with the fact that it stands under a demand ; to a rule which is distinct from service. No true Church law can open the door, or leave it open, for this kind of rule. To be sure, there is rule in the community. There are also privileges and claims and dignities. There are demands which the community has to address to its members and its members to the community or to one another. There may even be demands which one community has to make on another, or which have to be made on many communities by a central authority, or which have to be made on the state or other worldly partners. But they must all be closely and strictly scrutinised—and this is where the true Church law that we seek must give guidance and direction—to ensure that it is not a question of the abstract demanding of dominion, or the abstract assertion of privileges and claims and dignities, but only the demanding of service, i.e., that which is made exclusively in the context and fulfilment of service, and expresses only the fact that a demand is laid on the community and all its members. This kind of demanding—and only this—can and should be recognised and regulated and protected in true canon law. On the other hand, the demanding which aims only to assert or secure the community or someone within it is not merely to be checked but eliminated. Neither for the community as such nor for any of its members can true Church law be anything but a law of service. The community knows and takes into account the fact that there are other laws in other spheres. But its own law is a law of service.

This determination is (2) total. That is to say, in the life of the Christian community it is not the case that there is one sphere which is ordered by the law of service but side by side with this there are others in which it does not have the character and intention of service but stands under another determination or is open to many different and even perhaps changing determinations. Service is not just one of the determinations of the being of the community. It is its being in all its functions. Nothing that is done or takes place can escape the question whether and how far within it the community serves its Lord and His work in the world, and its members serve one another by mutual liberation for participation in the service of the whole. That which does not stand the test of this question but is done merely because, even though it does not serve, it has always been done or is regarded as a possible line of action, is quite unlawful, and it must either be jettisoned as inessential and harmful ballast or made to serve (which is often easier said than done). Either way, there must be no dead corners where an alien lord pursues his doubtful or at any rate useless way. The community has neither time nor strength to waste on *allotria*. Nor must this question of service be put only by way of criticism. It can be a diviner's rod as well as a measuring rod. There are many old and disused and unjustifiably obsolete possibilities of service to be re-discovered and revitalised, and many new and un-justifiably disregarded possibilities to be discovered afresh and realised. When can the community ever be content with what it is doing, as though this were the totality of the service required, and that which is right and lawful for it and within it were either exhausted or on the point of exhaustion with present-day expansion? It is not the community itself which constitutes the limits of the totality in which it has to serve its Lord and its members must serve one another. It is its living Lord Himself, whose call to halt and advance it has to follow as His living community. Thus it may never imagine that it knows already and finally what is the totality in which it has to serve. It must know only that it has always to serve with the totality of its being and action.

We may recall in this connexion how futile have been the attempts to use the terms διακονία and *ministerium* to denote particular functions within the life of the community : diaconate to describe the loving assistance extended by the

Church to the sick and the poor, etc. ; and ministry the regular preaching office. Surely the freedom to serve granted to the community and practised by it cannot be narrowed down in this way. Surely its whole action can and must be a diaconate and the *ministerium verbi divini*. Surely there are no spheres in which this is not the case. Surely there can be no new activity, in spheres as yet undisclosed, which will not necessarily take the form of service. True Church law must guard against the emergence of these false distinctions ; and where they have been made already it must remove them. It must declare and maintain the radical openness of the whole life of the community for its determination to service. To take one or two examples, Church administration (which will largely be concerned with financial questions) is also a question of service, and it cannot therefore be regarded as self-evidently autonomous and suddenly bureaucratised or commercialised. Or again, the Church's scholarship (theology) is also a question of service, so that though it may and must claim the widest possible freedom in the choice and application of its methods there can be no question of any other freedom than that of serving—not the Church, let alone any authority within it, but in the Church. Again, there can be no question of an autonomy of philosophical or historical interests from this standpoint. The same is true of its discipline, in the order and exercise of which the motto : *fiat iustitia et pereat mundus*, is quite illegitimate because it is incompatible with the whole character of this activity as service. And because in the direction of the Church's affairs we are still in the sphere of service, it is better either to avoid altogether terms like monarchy, aristocracy or democracy, with their clear suggestion of the exercise of power, or at any rate to use them in such a way that in the understanding of the rule of the Church on a Christocratic basis " rule " is always firmly interpreted as outstanding service.

Finally (3) the determination of the law which obtains in the Church as the law of service is universal. That is to say, as there is no sphere of the Church's activity to which this determination does not apply, there are no individuals within the community who are exempt from service or committed and engaged to serve only to a less serious degree. To be a Christian, and therefore a saint in the communion of saints, is to serve in and with the Christian community. All Christians do not have to serve equally, i.e., in the same function. But they all have to serve, and to do so in one place with the same eminence and responsibility as others do at other places. As the community exists only as the body of its Head Jesus Christ, so it exists only in the totality of the members of this body, which as the *communio sanctorum* is not a collective where the individual is of no importance because if he dropped out he could at once be replaced by someone else. In the life of the Christian community each individual has his own necessary place, and the service of each individual is indispensable to that of the whole. This service is not the privilege or concern of a few whose selection stands in marked contrast with the exemption of the rest as a lowlier or better portion. Exalted into fellowship with Jesus Christ, each Christian as such is set in the lowliness of His service. How then can he be forced or how can he presume to think that he is set there, and therefore claimed, to a less extent than others ? At bottom, there is something wrong with the community itself if even one of its members has dropped out of its ministry or never had a share in it.

At bottom, all the members suffer if even one defaults in this way. This is something which must be avoided at all costs.

In fact, of course, it may well be the case that when some drop out either totally or partially there are others who will make good the service which is not rendered. But when this happens, it points to an emergency and not to the normal state of affairs in the community. Basically, there is neither discharge nor total or partial leave of absence from this service ; nor can there be any question of delegation or substitution. Each one is called, with equal seriousness, to play his part, and to do so as if everything depended on him. And the fact that each has his own particular and different part to play, or service to render, cannot mean that those who are particularly responsible at one point have no responsibility but can leave it to those responsible at another. The service of the community is a differentiated service. But it is a differentiated whole. Hence the concern of one, quite irrespective of the fact that it is his concern in particular, is also the concern of others. None can try to serve in his own small sphere without considering all the other spheres for which his own service will always have indirect significance, and may even acquire and have direct significance as in the pursuit of his concerns he is also involved in the problems of these other spheres as well. It will thus be an emergency and not the normal state if the differentiation and distribution of service leads in practice to disintegration ; if it means that the individual and different ministries flourish in mutual unconcern, robbing one another of soil and air and sun like the plants in an ill-tended garden, and generally competing with one another. All Christians equally will constantly need remission of their sins in their co-operation in service. But they must not calculate upon this in advance in the sense that it leads them to regard what is really an emergency as justifiable, and to proclaim it as the normal state. If we ask concerning law and order as we must, we cannot argue that we are even partially discharged from the obligation to serve because others can replace us, or that we have no responsibility for all other spheres because we are competent only in our own. Law and order in the community are never the particular priesthood of a few, but the universal priesthood of all believers.

It will be the task of true Church law to guard and constantly to rescue this truth from distortion and oblivion. Even linguistically, it must avoid the fatal word " office " and replace it by " service," which can be applied to all Christians. Or, if it does use it, it can do so only on the understanding that in the Christian community either all are office-bearers or none ; and if all, then only as servants. Even where this is recognised in theory, true canon law will have to be all the more vigilant against practical clericalism : against every distinction between the active and the inactive (or passive) Church ; against every separation into the ruling and the ruled, the teaching and the hearing, the confessing and the established, the taxable and the enfranchised community. Whatever may be the actual circumstances, in true Church law we cannot regard them as descended from heaven and therefore normative. The unity and universality of the Church's ministry will always be, not a beautiful ideal, but the absolute law of the community, and therefore that which must be maintained as the *conditio sine qua non* of its life. Distinctions of this kind cannot, therefore, be justified and sanctified. On the contrary, there is a constant summons and direction to overcome them : within the limits imposed by time and expedience, but clearly and progressively within these limits ; *suaviter in modo*, but *fortiter in re*, uncompromisingly as regards the thing itself. And if it is one of the duties of canon law to regulate the distribution of different functions to different members of the community, clearly declaring that they are qualified and instituted to serve in this or that sphere, in the unavoidable distinctions which this involves it must see to it that there is no possibility of a departmental isolation and autonomy or a struggle for power and prestige ; that with all the respect for particular gifts and tasks and their limits the responsibility of all for all and for the whole is maintained and asserted ; that the disorder which Paul reproved in 1 Cor. 14 in relation to the gift of speaking with tongues (which had achieved a false preeminence in Corinth) does not arise and gain the upper hand in very different forms which are perhaps more obvious and tempting in different circumstances. It is the task of canon law to guarantee to the community the freedom to obey, and therefore the peace and harmony of service.

2. We are looking from the same place and in the same direction, but more concretely, when in a rather bold expression we describe the law which has to be sought and established and executed in the community as liturgical law. Church law has an original connexion with the particular happening of Christian worship. It is here that it has its original seat. It is in the act of worship that it is originally found and known. It is to worship—as the order of divine service—that it is originally applied. It is from this point that it embraces and orders the whole life of the community. At an earlier point we have described and emphasised public worship as the centre of the whole life of the community ; as the true act of its upbuilding. The time has now come to give our reasons for this emphasis.

The necessity and central significance of this happening—or this particular service, as we may now call it in retrospect of our first point—have their immediate derivation in the basic law (the christologico-ecclesiological concept) of the community in virtue of which it is the body whose Head is Jesus Christ. According to Holy Scripture Jesus Christ is the One who exists in a history—His own particular history—within universal history. In virtue of His resurrection from the dead He will be this One, and therefore the Head of His community, in every age and to all eternity.

Our first emphasis must fall on the fact that He is the One who exists in His *history*. The One who is the Head of the community is the man who not only went but still goes and always will go the way from Bethlehem to Golgotha. The One who goes this way is manifested on Easter Day as the living Lord, and His Spirit, His quickening power, is the Holy Spirit, who has created and rules and upholds the Christian community. The being of the Head of the community is the event of the life of this man.

But we must also emphasise the fact that He is the One who exists in this *particular* history. The event of this life is indissolubly connected with His name. It is the event which exhausts itself in this name—concrete, limited in time and space, singular and unique. It is this event and not another ; a " contingent fact of history," to use the phrase of Lessing.

It is in this way, i.e., in Jesus Christ, in His particular history, that there was and is and comes true God and true man, the humiliated Son of God and the exalted Son of Man, the One who fulfils the covenant between God and man, the Reconciler of the world with God, the Word which was in the beginning with God and will also be His final Word, His eternal Word. In heaven, hidden in God, He whose being is this once for all act, this particular history, is the Head of His community.

If His community then, created and ruled and upheld by His Holy Spirit in the time between His resurrection and His return in glory, is His body, the earthly-historical form of His existence ; if this is its basic law, it is inevitable that His particular history, both as history and in its particularity, should be actively and recognisably reflected and represented in its life.

Hence it is not enough, but conflicts with its basic law, if it is merely present in the world as His legacy and endowment, as an establishment and institution founded and ordered by Him, and therefore as a mere phenomenon. It is true that it is His valid and living bequest to this intervening time. It is also true that it cannot be this living bequest unless in obedience to Him it takes all kinds of forms and establishes all kinds of institutions. But as His living bequest, as the body of which He is the Head, it is itself history. The Christian community is not a mere phenomenon, however distinguished. It is an event. Otherwise it is not the Christian community. It is another question that in this event it takes different forms and establishes different institutions. The fact remains that it is not itself a foundation or institution. In correspondence with the hidden being of Jesus Christ Himself, it is an earthly-historical event, and as such it is the earthly-historical form of His existence.

But it is also not enough, and conflicts with its basic law, if in its life there is no correspondence to the particularity of His history. By the event of the Christian community there certainly can and must be understood the more general truth that as the human fellowship of those who are elected and called and sent, who believe in Him and obey Him, it is comprehensively at work in time and space as its members belong together in virtue of their relationship with Him, and are inwardly and perhaps outwardly united, and meet occasionally on the basis of their common convictions and interests and hopes, and take certain steps together, and give various forms of assistance to one another and to those outside, in view of that which they have in common. In actual fact, there is no doubt that for the most part they live in dispersion, each one in his own place and occupied with his own needs and concerns as a Christian, although grouped in various ways with other Christians. And in this form, they will not be recognisable either to themselves or others as the concrete *communio sanctorum* in time and space. To be sure, the Christian community is an event even in this form. Its history does have this character and aspect. It has a real existence submerged in this way under the secularity of its environment. It wears also the working clothes of an anonymity which is broken only occasionally and haphazardly. It is a secret conspiracy whose members are largely unknown to one another, or meet only rarely, and cannot regard it as over-important —because its hour has not yet struck—to manifest it even to themselves, let alone to others, in its full dimension. The inward life of Christians will, it is to be hoped, shine out—decisively in the private or combined attitude and action and abstention of individuals—even though they may be "scorched by the sun outwardly." We refer to the everyday life of Christians, which must not be undervalued, although it has often been one-sidedly and thoughtlessly exalted. It is legitimate and necessary that the community should exist in this form. For one thing, it belongs to the everyday life and traffic of the world. But more than that, its Head is the One in whom God took the world to Himself, and therefore the everyday life of all men and of Christians. It is not enough, however, if the community exists only in this form. If this is all, if it does not correspond to the particularity of its Head Jesus Christ and of His history, it does not attest the concrete, unique and limited actuality of this history, nor does it attest Him as the One who exists individually as this man and not another. In its representation of His history there is lacking the offence and the glory of the fact that it is a "contingent fact of history."

This is where the particular happening of worship is supremely relevant. The event of the community takes place in other ways. And conversely, divine service in this particular sense of the term is not a continual but a particular event within the total event "community." As the total event "community" stands out from the world within the world, so divine service stands out from the total event "community" within this event. And it is only as the community has its distinct centre in its worship that it can and will stand out clearly from the world. But this is necessary as in its history there is to be a representation of the particular history of its Head, an attestation of Jesus Christ.

In divine service there takes place that which does not take place anywhere else in the community. In divine service the sabbath intervenes between six working days on the one side and six more on the other. In it it exchanges its working clothes for its festal attire. It is now an event as community. Unpretentiously but distinctly it stands out from the secularity of its environment in which it is for the most part submerged. It now casts off the anonymity of that which is distinctive and common to it ; the occasional and haphazard and private character elsewhere assumed by its manifestation. It now exists and acts in concrete actuality and visibility as the congregation to which many individuals—each from his own human and Christian place in dispersion—come together to one place at one time in order that together, occupying the same space and time, they may realise the *communio sanctorum* in a definite form. There can be no doubt that not merely their life in the world, but their own everyday life as Christians as it was lived yesterday and will be resumed to-morrow, is now left behind. There can be no doubt that the hour for which the conspirators otherwise wait in dispersion has now struck, even if only provisionally and not definitively. The dimension which embraces individual Christians and Christian groups is now visible to themselves, and in their common action to the world around. This is the distinctive feature of this action within the wider context of the life of the community ; the feature by which it is distinctly shown to be the centre of its life, not to be confused with the everyday either ot the world or of Christians. It is shown to be its centre because here— and in this way only here—the community exists and acts in direct correspondence to its basic law, in a particular and not merely a general historicity. In divine service it becomes and is itself a witness to its own being, to its determination in the world, to the factuality of its existence. And in divine service it exists and acts prophetically in relation to the world to the extent that in divine service—and here alone directly—there is a serious discharge of its commission to be a provisional representation of humanity as it is sanctified in Jesus Christ. We must not be too pretentious and say that divine service or any of its parts is an " eschatological event." It is quite sufficient, and startling enough, to say that on its journey between the resurrection and the return the community achieves in it this representation provisionally but in concrete reality, so that it is only here that it exists and acts in its true form. From this centre of its life there can and must and may and will be also true Christian being and action on the circumference, in the Christian everyday. From it there can and must and may and will be general law and order. Thus from its liturgical root Church law must be understood as a law which (1) is ordered by divine service ; (2) is continually to be found again in it ; and (3) has itself the task of ordering it. We shall now consider the problem from these three standpoints.

We must begin by asserting (1) that all law in the Church has its original seat in the event of divine worship, and that it is primarily established in this particular happening. Where two or three are gathered together in the name of Jesus, i.e., by the fact that the name of Jesus is revealed to them, He Himself is with them and among them (according to Mt. 18^{20}). The saying has unmistakeable reference to the gathering ("synagogue") of the community. If the saying is right, it means that in that which is done and takes place in the coming together of these men their King and Lord is present and at work ; the One who is as such the source and guarantee of the law which obtains for them. As they have not met by accident, or gathered together arbitrarily, but have been brought together by the revelation of His name, they are not left to their own devices in their common action, but their King and Lord Himself gives them direction and orders and commands, and consolation and promises. It is He who gives the freedom for what takes place. Because and as He, the righteous One, is present in their gathering, there takes place in it that which is lawful and right for these men, His own, in spite and even in defiance of the imperfection and corruption of their action, in which they set themselves wholly or very largely in the wrong. It is quite out of the question that the community assembled for public worship can exalt itself in this action, or even try to do so, to be itself the source and guarantee of the law which obtains within it. The men assembled, even if they act in His presence and under His direction and as those who are comforted by Him, are always sinners and therefore never righteous or in a position to establish a valid law or right by their action. They themselves are not and will never be the King and Lord. They are only His people ; worthy only as He makes them worthy to be witnesses in their activity to His presence, and therefore to the right established and made a law for them by Him. That He does this in their assembly, that He Himself is the right or law which underlies and shapes and orders this event of divine service, is the secret of this action which makes it the original seat of all their law. Essentially and decisively there are in this action four concrete elements in which, in spite and even in defiance of all the imperfection and corruption of the human action of Christians, Jesus Christ and therefore the law of the *communio sanctorum*, the right which obtains for it, is really present.

First, where two or three are gathered in His name, they speak with and to one another in human words. They do not do this merely because speech is the characteristic vehicle of human fellowship, but because from the very first this particular fellowship has its meaning and substance in the fact that there is something specific which calls for common utterance and must be declared by those who have been brought to this fellowship. In general terms, it is a matter of the common confession of the One who has brought them together by awakening them all to know Him and believe in Him and love Him and hope in Him. This knowledge and faith and love and hope, or rather the One who is known and believed and loved by them and the object of their hope, impels the two or three to make this common confession as He gathers them together. They hear Him together as the Word of God addressed to them, and they cannot do this without making their common human response. But they also owe this response to one another : for the mutual ratification and confirmation, consolation, correction and renewal of their knowledge and faith and love and hope ; for the *mutua consolatio fratrum*. And they cannot make this response merely in private, or in the accidental, local and optional encounters in which Christians may speak with and to one another. They can and may and should make it in this way too. But under the impulsion of the Word of God, the human response to this Word calls for something public. The unity of knowledge, faith, love and hope, and of the One who is known and believed and loved and the object of their hope, calls for the unity of their confession. Confession may well be the confession of individual Christians or groups of Christians. But it cannot be only this. Indeed, it cannot really be this unless it is first the confession of the community, and flows into the confession of the community, in which the human response to the Word of God is the common word of all, and the *mutua consolatio fratrum* does not take place in a corner between individuals but is the objective and obligatory work of all to all. This common response in the common hearing of the Word of God, the confession commonly spoken and received in the renewal of the common knowledge, is the first element in the public worship of Christians. It may include the common recitation of a creed. It will certainly involve singing. But it will take place decisively in free witness, bound only to its object, as the Word of God is proclaimed and published and taught and preached and heard by the community according to the commission of its Lord. As this is done, that which is lawful and right takes place in and for the community. It is constituted as a fellowship of confession : not in the power or weakness of the human words spoken and received but because these words are an answer to the Word of God ; because in these human words spoken in power or weakness it is a matter of witness to Jesus Christ ; because it is He who wills that they should be spoken ; because He Himself is present where they are spoken and heard by those whom He has gathered. Thus in the confession of the community that which is lawful and right takes place, and the community is constituted, even though— and when is this not the case ?—it sets itself in the wrong with its human speaking and hearing ; even in impotent witness and poor proclaiming and publishing and teaching and preaching. The right may be totally or partially concealed. Failing to see it, it may not be set to rights by it. But these are later questions. What is unquestionable is that in the liturgical act of confession as such we have to do with that which is lawful and right in the community and has to be perceived and practised as such. As the community gathers, and there is not merely speech but confession in this gathering, it is already constituted even though it may not be aware (or clearly aware) of the fact, and however it may constitute itself, and thus give expression to its law, on this foundation.

Second, where two or three are gathered together in the name of Jesus they will mutually recognise and acknowledge that they are those who are gathered by Him as their one Lord, and regard and receive one another as brothers because they are all brothers of this First-begotten. Who really belongs to them ? Who is awakened by the quickening power of the Holy Spirit, and therefore a saint, and as such a member of the communion of saints, a brother of those united with him in this fellowship ? They all see and judge one another with human eyes and not with those of God. They do not see into the heart. They can only trust one another. And which of them, looking even into his own heart, can give more than a human judgment that he himself is awakened by the Holy Spirit and a true member of the communion of saints, so that he belongs to this assembly ? This, too, and above all, is something that he can know only in trust. The Christian community is built on the fact that this trust is permitted and commanded : the mutual trust in which one recognises and acknowledges the other as a brother belonging to it ; and the trust that each must have concerning himself for glad and confident partici-pation. It is in this authorised and commanded trust that the com-munity gathers for divine service. How would its members stand in relation to one another and themselves if they did not have it, or if they arbitrarily assumed it on the basis of their own fancied knowledge of themselves and one another ? In these circumstances they could only assemble and at once disperse again. But they have this trust, which is not grounded in their own opinions of themselves and one another, even though they can see only that which is before their human eyes, and they know that appearances may deceive. What do they see ? They cannot see the Holy Spirit who has awakened and assembled them, nor can they see the knowledge and faith and love and hope to which He has awakened themselves and the others. They cannot see one another as brothers. But they see that these men, and they themselves, are baptised—in the one new name common to them all, in the name of Jesus, and therefore the name of the Father, the Son and the Holy Ghost. They see only that these men, and they themselves, are those who have obviously begun to know the salvation of the world enclosed in this name, and therefore their own salvation ; to know themselves as people who stand in absolute need of it—of the forgiveness of their sins, of justification and sanctification, of conver-sion. They see only that these men, and they themselves, have come to the community with the desire and request for this salvation ; that they have confessed this name with their lips ; that they have asked for baptism and therefore for recognition as members of the body of Jesus Christ, and acceptance into the body of Jesus Christ ; and that this recognition and acceptance have been granted in their baptism, not in the name of the community, but in the name of its Lord. They see these others and themselves accepted only as those who are bap- tised, and in the frame of mind in which they came to baptism, as beginners in this knowledge, with this desire and request, as those who make this confession with their lips. But in respect of others and themselves they hold to the fact that they all come from the fact that they are baptised in the name of the Lord. Because they all stand under this sign in the name of the Lord, they accept the sign. Hence they are permitted and commanded to do that which of them- selves they have no right or power to do—to take these others and themselves seriously as members of the body of Jesus Christ, and to be with them gladly and confidently in the congregation. As this takes place, there takes place that which is lawful and right in the community. It could not take place were it not for the presence in the midst of the One who has brought them together; were it not that baptism is His permission and command, and therefore the sign which not merely gives us good reasons for that trust but makes it an act of obedience undertaken in perfect confidence. And so our second point is that the Christian community is a fellowship of baptism. That is to say, when it comes together in the name of Jesus, in all its members it does so in virtue of baptism; and it is in the freedom given and received in baptism that it holds its public worship. What- ever else may be said either for or against itself or its members, coming and coming together from this point it is already constituted and is in the right, even though it may set itself a thousand times in the wrong against this right.

Third, where two or three are brought together in the name of Jesus, it is in order that they may be unitedly strengthened and pre- served to eternal life. Eternal life is their human life, but as their true life, hidden and glorified with God. They assemble as members of the Christian community, and celebrate divine service, to be pre- pared for the attainment of their life in this form. In going, or coming, to public worship they perform a movement which has a wider, typical significance. For all men are ordained to eternal life. The question of strengthening and preservation, of preparation to attain it, is thus necessarily a question which concerns them all. Christians are those who are awake to the question. Impelled by it, they hasten together; together because they know that the answer to this question can be received only unitedly in the Christian community as the provisional representation of the whole race for which it has already taken place and which needs to receive it. They know the truth about human life—their own life too, and especially their own. They know that it is the wonderful gift of God the Creator, to be enjoyed in thankfulness and lived out by man in daily prayer and labour in his allotted span. They know, too, that it is a life which is encumbered and radically jeopardised by the pride and sloth of man towards God and his fellows ; a forfeited life. But they also know that it is a life which is inflexibly ordained to be eternal life ; life in concealment and glory with God, and therefore true life. They know all this as they are brought together by the revelation of the name of Jesus, and united to the community where He is present in the midst. And so they go and come to Him as they go and come to the community, concretely participating in its assembly. They seek the answer to this question of the attainment of eternal life ; the answer which is given in Him, which is He Himself. They hunger and thirst to be prepared, to be strengthened and preserved, for the eternal life which in defiance of the frailty of the present form of their life is His work, and can be only His work. The promise with which they are brought together is that He will give them food and drink, that in the life in which they too are surrounded by death He will provide, and will Himself be, their wayside sustenance. And so they go and come to the gathering of the community to seat themselves, and to eat and drink, as brothers and sisters at the table where He Himself presides as Lord and Host, and they are His invited and welcome guests. They go and come to the Lord's Supper. In so doing, they do the very thing which they also do for the strengthening and preservation of creaturely life ; just as when they talk with and to one another they do something which is ordinarily done by men when they meet. They eat and drink. But as in their speaking in the community it is not a matter of the private and optional exchange of human convictions and opinions, but of the common utterance of the confession, so in the eating and drinking of the Lord's Supper it is not a question of the nourishment of one here and another there in company with neighbours, but of the eating of one bread and the drinking from one cup, of the common nourishment of them all, because it is He, Jesus Christ, who brings them to it, who invites them, who is the Lord and Host, who is Himself, indeed, their food and drink. It is thus a question of their nourishment by Him. It takes place in the fact that, as often as they here eat and drink together, He proffers and gives Himself to them as the One He is, as the One who is absolutely theirs ; and conversely, that He continually makes them what they are, absolutely His. He strengthens and upholds them in their existence as those whom He, the Crucified and Risen, accompanies in the valley of the shadow. More strongly, He strengthens and upholds them in their existence as His body and its members, and therefore to eternal life in the concealment and glory of God. He constitutes Himself their preparation to attain this. It is to be noted how the event of His own life is reflected and repeated in the event of the Supper (as in that of confession and baptism). In remembrance of Him there takes place here and now exactly the same as took place there and then between Himself and His first disciples, immediately prior to His death and resurrection. Provisionally

in the place of all men, the community in its reaching out in all
its members for eternal life necessarily lives by and in the fact that in
its life here and now there may be this reflection and imitation. And
the fact that this takes place is again the right or law established in
divine service. The community may set itself in the wrong against
it. It has continually done so, and will continually do so again. From
the standpoint of the community itself, of the company assembled
round the table of the Lord, what takes place will always be highly
problematical. Yet in spite of this it is a fellowship of the Lord's
Supper, united by Him both with Him and also, because with Him, in
itself ; *communio sanctorum* as a fellowship of the sure and certain
hope of eternal life. In its worship, which is also communion in this
concrete sense, this is made palpable and visible ; as is also, in the
event of this communion, the law or right which indwells it in spite
of all the wrong committed by it, and which in this special form
demands that it should be observed in every aspect of its life.

Fourth, where two or three are gathered together in the name of
Jesus, they are called by Him to pray with one another. Those
gathered by the revelation of His name are men who are wholly
referred and directed to God. That they are referred to God is something that they have in common with all men. But they are also
directed to Him. They know that in the last resort they are not in
their own hands and under their own control. They know that they
are only creatures and not the Creator. They know also that they
are God's sinful creatures ; that because of their own corruption their
activity is a corrupt activity. They thus know that they cannot avert
the sorrow and suffering of the world ; that they cannot avoid their
own misery ; that they cannot alter the human situation ; that they
cannot accomplish the reconciliation of the world with God as a genuine
transformation ; that they cannot hallow God's name as they should ;
that they cannot bring in the kingdom of peace and salvation ; that
they cannot do His will. Hence they know that they cannot and will
not of themselves receive their daily bread, know the forgiveness of
their debts, withstand temptation and overcome evil and the evil one.
They know that they can only pray that these things should happen.
They will do so in faith and love and hope, and therefore not indolently
but in practical act and activity to God's glory. Yet in principal and
as the climax of everything else they can only pray, seeking Him and
calling upon Him that He should begin and execute and complete all
the things for which they find themselves quite inadequate even in
their most zealous and eloquent action. The decisive work and the
driving force in their daily defensive and offensive action will consist
in their surrender ; the decisive work of their hands in the fact that
they lay all things, both great and small, in the hands of God. They
know that all that man can do can be helpful only in the renunciation
of all self-help, and the cry to God that He will be the helper and help

of man and all men. But they know that they may pray for this, and be certain that their prayer is heard. They have freedom and joy for this. And so they meet to pray with one another. They also pray, of course, individually and in small groups. But this is not enough, just as their private speech and their individual opinions of one another and their meals in one another's houses are not enough, but the confession and baptism and Supper, in short the action, of the community are also needed if everything is to be lawful and right. The prayer of Christians, too, demands that it should find its true and proper form in the prayer of the assembled community ; in the united calling upon God : " Our Father, which art in heaven. . . ." The reason why it must be united is not merely that it is easier and finer and more consoling to pray in company than individually—for this is an open question. It is because those gathered to the community may pray with the One by whom they are united and who is Himself present in the midst—their predecessor in prayer. The distinctive value and importance of the " Our Father " as the Lord's Prayer consist in the fact that in it Jesus ranges Himself alongside His disciples, or His disciples alongside Himself, taking them up with Him into His own prayer. The " We " of this prayer is the We to which the Lord attaches Himself with His people. The We in which He does this is the We of the community. And the We of the community has its concrete form in its coming together. That is why Christian prayer demands that it should be the prayer of the assembled community as well as the prayer of individuals and groups. That is why the prayer of individuals and groups can be true and serious calling upon God only as it derives from the prayer of the assembled community. To be true and serious, to be the prayer which is heard by God, it must first and last be the prayer of the One who as the true Son has the authority and power truly to address Him as Father. As His brothers and sisters, as the children of God in His name, Christians can and may call upon God as Father. As and because their prayer is that of His brothers and sisters, it does not need any particular art or power or intensity. Because it is prayed in fellowship with the First-begotten, it is a spreading out of the totality of man's true need, and a reaching out for the totality of what God will be for him and give him. Prayed in fellowship with Him, it is never in vain. It is always rightly addressed and prayed with the certainty of being heard and answered. In prayer prayed in the assembled congregation, there is done again that which is lawful and right. As it is prayed as the prayer of the Lord Himself, for all the poverty and thoughtlessness and uncertainty and distraction from which it will suffer on the lips of Christians, the right of God is set up on earth. For it is right before God that He should be called upon as He may be called upon by the assembled community in the prayer of its Lord. The community is constituted as it prays. And as it faces the many-sided question how it is to constitute itself, it will always hold and return to the fact that it is already constituted ; that the public worship in which it prays as the community, for all the weakness with which it may do so, is the place where that which is lawful and right for it both outwardly and inwardly already takes place, in its concrete life as a fellowship, not only of confession and baptism and the Lord's Supper, but also of prayer.

But in our explanation of the fact that Church law is liturgical we must now go on to state (2) that it is originally to be sought and found and known in the occurrence of Christian worship. Church law has this in common with all human law—and it is itself human law in the fact —that it must be found and known. The direction in which it is to be sought, in which we have to look when drawing it up, is already fixed ; for here as elsewhere we have to turn only to Jesus Christ, the Lord and Head of the community as He is attested in Holy Scripture. It is solely and exclusively in the light of His relationship to it, which is its basic and constitutive law, that we can consider what is lawful and right in the Church. But the concrete form of His relationship to it, and therefore the concrete form of its basic law, is His own presence and lordship in its assembling for divine service, in the occurrence of confession, baptism, the Lord's Supper and prayer. This being the case, we have to consider all questions of that which is lawful and right in the Church in the light of its assembling for public worship and therefore of this fourfold occurrence. In the formulation of all statements about Church law we have thus to look first in this direction. This does not mean, of course, that the community should orientate itself by its own action, making this a law and unfolding it as such. It cannot try to be its own Lord and King and Lawgiver : not even in its liturgy ; not even if this is ever so old ; and not even if it is sincerely thought to be in supreme agreement with this or that biblical precedent. In this respect we have to take into account at every point the human weakness and confusion of its own action ; the wrong of Christians contradicting the right of their Lord. But we have also and even more so to take into account Jesus Christ Himself present in their human action as the Lord of their confession, of their coming from baptism and going to the Lord's Supper, of their united calling upon God. He is their law ; He, the One who is attested in Holy Scripture. We do not therefore violate the Scripture principle when we say that the divine service of Christians is the concrete source of our knowledge of Church law. If the Lord present and active in divine service is its law (and therefore the law of the whole life of the community), it is clear that when we ask concerning Him as the Lord present and active in the divine service of Christians we are again referred wholly and utterly to Holy Scripture. But He who is attested in Scripture is the basic law, normative for that which is lawful and right in the Church, in the form in which He is present and active here at the heart of the Church's life.

The lordship of Jesus Christ in His community takes place as in divine service it makes to His summons the response of its confession. To this confession there must correspond even formally that which is regarded as law in its life. The propositions of canon law must follow the confession of the community, expounding and applying it with particular reference to the order of its human action. They themselves will not be liturgical (whether in the form of confessional statements, hymns, proclamation or preaching). Nor will they be theological. They will be juridical statements orientated by the liturgical event of confession and based on theological reflection. They have to fix the rules of the human shaping of the existence of the community as these are required by its message and commensurate with it. Whether they are right or not will be decided by the question whether and how far in their establishment and execution the community is committed and faithful to its message, or to the One who has entrusted its message to it ; whether and how far they are calculated to free and bind its members by keeping them to their faith as their response to the Word of their common Lord ; whether and how far they are adapted to reveal practically to those without the distinctive nature of the Christian community as grounded in its doctrine and preaching. Not directly but indirectly true Church law is necessarily " confessing," i.e., it is human law drawn up in view of the confession and therefore of the man who confesses it, and thus to be executed with this reference. The confessing community needs this confessing law, for its existence in the world is worked out and expressed in human and therefore in sociologico-juridical form, and as a community it is faced at this point by the question of obedience. If it does not ask concerning this law, this can only mean that it does not ask concerning the obedient fulfilment of its confession—at the very place where this is most directly commanded. In true Church law the community undertakes to fulfil its confession first in relation to itself. If the lordship of Jesus Christ is an event within it, this is something which has to be attempted.

The lordship of Jesus Christ in His community takes place as the community, assembled for public worship, comes in all its members from baptism in His name. We have seen that the confidence which each can and should have in respect of all others and himself rests on the permission and command received by the members in their baptism. But all the propositions of canon law rest on this confidence. In the community men trust that in spite of the dubious nature of all human seeking and finding they are summoned and able to seek and find these propositions. Their establishment and formulation take place, therefore, in this confidence. Without it they could not take place at all. Again, in the community there is trust that the propositions sought and found in this way will have sufficient authority for each and all to claim acceptance and respect. Even in their application the only appeal can and will be to this confidence. Negatively, this means that the competence of Church law (in contrast to all other) cannot at bottom be proved, because all possible determinations of its competence (e.g., of the authority of its assembly or representatives or other officers) can be reached only in the confidence that the few or the many are authorised in virtue of their baptism. Thus the definitions of canon law (in contrast to all other) are not at bottom enforceable, because even the greatest rigour with which they are asserted can consist only in their power to claim the confidence and obedience of those concerned. No true Church law can be established or executed apart from the common recollection of baptism and therefore apart from this mutual confidence. Conversely, the confidence which, having its basis in baptism, enables this law to be established and executed—far from being a hindrance—gives to it a spiritual power which no other, no worldly, law can ever have.

The lordship of Jesus Christ in His community takes place as the community, assembled for public worship, goes to the Lord's Supper and therefore to the common nourishment which the Lord provides on the way to eternal life. Drawn up and applied with reference to this happening, its lawful ordering necessarily acquires the character of a common ordering of the present life of the men assembled in it. We recall at this point the thought of the *communio* of the *sancti* in and in relation to the *sancta*. There are no *sancta*, no gifts and powers of knowledge and love, which any one of the *sancti* can and should have and use and enjoy alone and not with some of the others and even all the others. Even in the particular form in which they are his he can have them only in interchange with others. In the Lord's Supper, when it is rightly administered, there is no distinction of persons in the distribution of the bread and wine, but all eat the one bread and drink from the one cup and are strengthened and preserved to eternal life by the one Lord and Host. And this is something which has to be brought out in true Church law, and safeguarded against the disruption of its spiritual life into the private spheres of individuals, or of certain pious or more pious or wholly pious groups. Naturally, there can and should be all kinds of active fellowships for the promotion of specific ends and in the discharge of specific tasks which cannot be the particular concern of all but only of those specially called or endowed for the purpose. But the idea of an *ecclesiola in ecclesia*, of a special *communio* within the one, always involves either openly or tacitly an abandonment or relativisation of the one. No *ecclesiola*, however, can find any basis or authority in the Lord's Supper, to which all come with the same hunger and thirst, and at which all are equally nourished with food and drink. It may sometimes be the case that the living and true Church has to arise and is compelled and empowered to take new shape in a dead Church or a false. But in an order of fellowship derived from the Lord's Supper there can be no place for a true Church within the true Church. And we have to remember especially that in the Lord's Supper it is distinctively a question of outward and inward, visible and invisible, physical and spiritual nourishment at one and the same time. Where the human mind normally separates these two spheres, in the action of the Holy Spirit, and drastically in the action of the Lord's Supper, they are comprehended and united. And the eternal life to which the community is strengthened and preserved in the Lord's Supper is the glorification of the whole of human life. Thus the Church order to be derived from the eucharistic action will necessarily embrace, protect and claim the life of the community and its members as it is now lived in its totality and therefore at one and the same time in its physical and spiritual nature. It will aim at the living fellowship of Christians in both spheres. In each respect it will make the strong responsible for the weak, the healthy for the sick, the rich for the poor. It will make Christians answerable for one another and for the continuance of the community, outwardly no less than inwardly. It will claim the help of all in both spheres. And it will promise help to all in both spheres. It will remind the community that what is lawful and right in the Lord's Supper is lawful and right everywhere : fellowship in heavenly and therefore also in earthly things ; the *communio* of the *sancti* in and in respect of the *sancta*.

The lordship of Jesus Christ in His community takes place as the community assembles in public worship for prayer as the fellowship of those who are referred only to God, and therefore directed wholly to Jesus Christ. They address God as " Our Father " as they are freed to do so by the Son who has Himself the power to address Him in this way. From this standpoint the law which holds sway in the community must always be the law of men who have been freed to do this and have therefore become brothers. What has to be expressed in canon law is that they are united to one another both as a whole and individually by the fact that they all have equal need of God and all have equal access—with the same certainty, directness, fulness and worth. There will necessarily be stronger and weaker, older and younger, higher and lower brothers, and in their common life the law valid in the community will have to give them as such the necessary directions. But it will also have to make clear that the necessary differentiations not only cannot harm but can only strengthen the brotherly unity in which they are together in calling upon the Father in the name of the one true Son of God ; in which—with the exception of this One, the First-born—none can argue that he has any less need of God or claim any higher access ; in which none can try to be a mediator between God and others, or commend or impose himself upon them as one who is directly commissioned by God, or be accepted and proclaimed as such by others. In the community canon law cannot possibly establish a " hierarchy " because this term contains and evokes the idea of a ruling for which there is no place among brothers. Its task is to show in what way the one can be to the other a real brother : stronger, older and higher perhaps ; but a brother all the same, with the same need of God and the same access ; and therefore, without any essential precedence and claim but only in the name of the First-born and as His human witness, able to be a true helper and adviser, and therefore, with an actual and not an institutional authority, a leader and teacher and pastor. The man who most seriously and unreservedly ranges himself with others, even the most lowly ; who most sincerely gives himself to the depths where the sun of the Father shines on good and evil, the just and the unjust, the wise and fools ; who with them (and as one of them) can most humbly and joyfully call upon Him from these depths—he it is, and only he, who proves his call to be a true leader in the community. And he does this by the fact that he really is a leader and does not merely claim to be such, or receive investiture with the dignity of leadership. The freedom of the Holy Spirit, to order the christocratic brotherhood in this way, not preventing but guaranteeing the actual leadership of one brother in relation to another, poses the task and concern of true Church law.

Our final statement in defining Church law as liturgical law is that in divine service it not only has its original seat and its source of knowledge but also (3) its true and proper theme. It has to guard its peculiar basis and source. Even public worship as the centre of the life of the community is at every point a human action. It is men who confess, who baptise, who administer the Lord's Supper, who pray " Our Father." Hence this whole occurrence is not protected from misunderstanding and abuse. In this respect the community has its treasure in earthen vessels. It cannot escape the risk involved. Nor can it console itself with the reflection that everything human is imperfect, or the recollection that its sins are forgiven. The grace of sanctification, and therefore of Jesus Christ generally, is surely alien to it if it does not try to counteract the continual menace and process of a profanation of that which is holy by its own human and therefore unholy hands ; if it does not resist to the best of its ability and conscience. It is to do this that it asks concerning true Church law as the true ordering of its worship. It is well aware that only He who is present and active within it as its Lord has the authority and competence to order this and therefore to protect it against perversion. Its human ordering can thus consist and take place only in an obedient regard for His. It cannot refuse this. It cannot, therefore, regard its liturgy as inviolable because inerrant. It cannot shelter it (least of all for reasons of piety) from the critical question whether it is rightly done, or whether it might not be done differently and better. For this reason its concern for Church law as the ordering of divine service must be unceasing.

We can only indicate the questions involved. For example, who is to be responsible for the confession of the community, for its expression at the right time and place, and in the right form, as proclamation, teaching and preaching, for its purity and depth and ongoing interpretation and application, for giving it the appropriate form here and now in this or that specific historical situation ? Again, what are the conditions for the reception of baptism and therefore acceptance into the community, and what are the particular obligations of members of the community resulting (in this mutual confidence) from the fact that they are baptised ? Again, who is to be admitted to the Lord's Supper and who is not to be admitted, or not yet or no longer to be admitted ? What will be the shape of the living fellowship which is shown to be necessary by the Lord's Supper ? What activities are necessary for its achievement, and who is to discharge them ? Finally, how and by whom is Christian worship as a whole to be shaped and fashioned in accordance with its centre in a common calling upon God the Father ? What will be the relationship of the different elements ? Will there be place or not for subsidiary elements, e.g., æsthetic or social ? How far, if at all, can there be spheres, not of chance or caprice, but of free responsible judgment, of individual decision ? And what ought to be the relationship between spontaneity and receptivity in the frame of mind of those who take part in divine service ? All these questions can be gathered up in the one question how the community thinks that itself and its members are brought under discipline by its Lord at this centre of its life, and are thus to bring and keep themselves under discipline—Church discipline. Church law must give a decisive answer to this question, and in so doing it will implicitly give an answer in principle to all the questions which arise on the circumference of this centre. It will do so along the lines already indicated. Confession has not just to be spoken but fulfilled ; there is to be common action on the basis of confidence ; comprehensive and complete fellowship of life is to be attained ; and men are to deal with one another in brotherhood. Let us leave it all to the Holy Ghost, cry some impetuously. They are right enough, but the fact that we leave it to the Holy Ghost does not mean that we leave it to the rash and wilful, but that we ask ourselves unitedly and conscientiously, and in the light of Holy Scripture, what obedience means in this matter. The answer will lead us at once to Church order and therefore to canon law.

3. Church law is living law. This, too, derives directly from the basic law of the community by which it is the body whose Head, or the fellowship whose law, is the living Jesus Christ. Who He is emerges from the sketch of His person or history attested and made known in Holy Scripture. But His person as attested in Holy Scripture lives to-day and to-morrow in all its historical singularity. And as this living person He rules and upholds and orders His community ; He Himself at every moment in the quickening power of the Holy Spirit. It is He the Upright who decides what is now right and lawful for it and in it. Thus in the investigation, establishment and practice of what is right the community has to listen uninterruptedly and continually to Him, to have regard to His control and to respect His direction—yesterday, to-day and to-morrow. Its right or law will be all the more surely grounded and clear and firm and therefore valid and serviceable the more its development and application are rooted

in the fact that the community is engaged in this listening, regard and respect ; the less it loses in its discovery and administration a proper attentiveness, reverence and willingness in relation to its Head ; the less it evades the power of the Holy Spirit, thus inevitably falling victim to all kinds of arbitrariness old and new. As the living Lord Jesus is the law to which it is obedient in the discovery and administration of the law appropriate to it, its own law, Church law, necessarily acquires the character of a law which is living and dynamic. It cannot be moved by the spirit of the age, by political and social changes and revolutions in the world around, or by the whims and vacillations of Christians. But the Holy Spirit, by whom the Lord attested in Holy Scripture speaks to it, necessarily sets and keeps it in motion. No dynamic from below can or should have any influence on Church law. To the extent that this takes place, it ceases to be Church law. But it is certainly not Church law if it is not always wide open to the dynamic from above, both in its development and then in its continuance and application. We took this into account in our previous deliberations as we referred always at the decisive points to the investigation of valid law which the community that stands under obedience cannot possibly discontinue. It is actually the case that this law, as and because it is living law, demands constant re-investigation by a community which is open for new direction and instruction (not from below but from above), and is therefore willing and ready for new answers.

It is willing and ready for new answers. This is the first point that calls for emphasis. The recognition that canon law can arise and continue only as living law must not deprive it of the courage and pleasure of finding specific answers to its investigation of this law. They must not be arbitrary answers created from an alien or polluted source. They must be the answers of attention and obedience. But they must be definite answers. Concretely, they must be answers which mean the formation of legal propositions. Even more concretely, they must be answers which involve the establishment and execution of ecclesiastical and congregational ordinances in which one thing is commanded, another forbidden and a third permitted, or left to free and responsible judgment within certain limits in which explicit decisions are made according to the best of our knowledge and conscience. They must be answers which have legal form and precision, although without unnecessary refinement. If the inquiry is genuine, it will not seek to prolong itself *ad infinitum*. Those who ask will seek answers, definite insights and conclusions, on the basis of which they can then proceed to further inquiry. They will not be afraid of finding answers. They can and must venture these provisional insights and conclusions. Where there is the genuine dynamic from above, the power of the Holy Spirit (who is obviously no sceptic), the community cannot refuse this venture. Nor can the individual Christian tarry eternally in ethical reflection and deliberation, and because of the daunting profundity and difficulty of ethical tasks and problems fail to press on to *ethos*, i.e., to ethical decision and action. Living law does not mean law which is formless, which is unexpressed, which exists only in instincts and emotions, which finds utterance in uncontrollable inspirations and intuitions, which escapes juridical statement and codification. Like all human law, it will contain important unwritten elements. But it is not in any sense basically or exclusively unwritten. Nor is it characterised by the greatest possible vagueness, by a restriction to general lines, by a purposeful elasticity in its detailed provisions which allows the greatest possible latitude of interpretation. It is not distinguished and commended as Church law by the fact that its significance for the life of the community is reduced to a minimum. Like all the living expressions of the community (not excluding dogma, preaching and theology), it can have only the character of service. But this does not mean that it can have merely a subordinate and incidental and not a constitutive importance. As living Church law, it can offer no occasion but only resistance to the crude or· refined ecclesiological Docetism which threatens in all these forms. As the community constantly agrees and states what, with reference to the form of its existence as an earthly-historical and therefore a visible community, it regards as responsible and irresponsible, as right and wrong, in the sight of God and man, it takes itself with exactly the same seriousness as is demanded in divine service in the narrower and wider senses of the term. Here too—and in the closest possible connexion with divine service, as we have seen—it is a question of obedience. But when this question is raised, it is hard to see how it can be put and answered with a greater emphasis in the one case than the other. If Church dogmatics, for example, cannot achieve this differentiation (in an awareness of its own character as service and of the limits thereby imposed), it can hardly commend it to the community in respect of the necessary formation and practice of law. It has to investigate living law in the sense described, but its investigation must be serious. And if it is serious, this means that it must venture definite decisions in which it has to remain open for further decisions but which it takes courageously and does not seek to evade. If it is serious, this means that it is concerned to express itself as plainly and unequivocally and precisely as it can in accordance with its existing knowledge, giving a clear Yes or No even on points which it believes should be totally or partially exempted from a general ruling. If it is serious, this means that it must be willing to state and even codify what can be stated and codified according to the nature of the case and its own knowledge, and what must be stated and even codified to safeguard against the disorder which threatens or has already entered. If it is serious, this means that without affectation, because under compulsion, it must leave the sphere of a non-committal " It seems

to me " and use and even record obligatory expressions which in this
context will necessarily be legal. If it is serious, this means that the
community has to ask and has also in the true sense to answer : to
answer in order to ask again ; but genuinely to answer ; to say something and not to be silent—even with the silence of edifying eloquence.
Everything else that we have to say about the living quality of Church
law is based on the seriousness of the concrete venture in which it has
to be sought and established and practised. Apart from this, it can
be regarded only as unprofitable Liberalism.

But when we have said this we have also to say that all Church
law, however great the seriousness with which it is sought and found
and instituted, can only be human law and not divine (*ius humanum*
and not *ius divinum*). The same can and must be said of all law.
But the knowledge of God and man necessary to make this differentiation and to indicate its implications cannot be presupposed with the
necessary distinctness in all human societies, but only in the Christian
community. It is only this that can know unconditionally and plainly
what it is saying and what is meant when it calls its law human law
and not divine. All other law reveals an ultimate vulnerability to the
danger of a confusion of these two determinations and therefore to its
own absolutisation. In Church law, however, this danger is averted
by the very root and essence of this law, by the basic law of the community, by the lordship of Jesus Christ over His body. Church law
will respect absolutely this basic law of the community as the authority
with reference to which it has to order the community and to which
it has to subject it, and above all itself, in all its determinations. It
cannot try to be ·this basic law, to replace it, to give its authentic
interpretation, to invest itself with its authority. Like Church dogmatics, it cannot choose and decide and determine and state and
declare and enforce from heaven, but only on earth. It must always
remember that the *ius divinum* of Christocracy is not only its origin
but also its limit, and thus understand itself in all strictness as *ius
humanum*. And as it does this, it is living law in a sense in which
this can never be true of earthly law because the latter usually arises
and is executed without any direct or necessary knowledge of this
fruitful distinction and antithesis. This distinction and antithesis are
fruitful because they prevent canon law from becoming sterile, which
is the constant danger besetting all other law. They continually drive
it on. This is the secret of its living quality. As it respects this limit,
it places itself in the context of the life of the community which under
the lordship of its living Head is engaged in its upbuilding, growing
both outwardly and inwardly ; of the community which necessarily
surrenders or does not take itself seriously if it tries to be only an
ecclesia formata or *reformata* and not as such an *ecclesia semper reformanda*. How can it exist and know itself as such if it regards itself as
its own lord and therefore the sovereign subject of its law instead of

being strictly and exclusively the attorney of Jesus Christ, aware that at every step it is directly and freshly responsible and committed to Him ? It is when it acts as His attorney, especially in this matter of its law, and therefore when its law participates in its life as the body of which Jesus Christ is Head, that Church law is living and growing law ; a law which calls continually for reformation whatever its existing formation or reformation, and which is therefore unlike any other law, a *ius sui generis*.

But this has the following implication. Let us assume that in the Christian community there has been serious inquiry at this particular point, and in this particular situation in its inner and outer history, concerning that which deserves to be regarded and practised in its life as law. Let us suppose that this inquiry has been serious and therefore undertaken in the venture to receive and give, even in the form of statement and codification, definite answers to the best of belief and conscience ; and yet also with respect for its basic divine law, and therefore with a full realisation that what is now found and enforced as law is human law and no more. What, then, is to be the community's attitude to-day to the law which it saw and acknow-ledged and enforced yesterday ? It may be afflicted with a bad con-science which it had already in its earlier decision and action. But it must not doubt that the will in which it decided and acted yesterday, as its will to be obedient, was necessary—we may even say, necessary to faith and salvation—and therefore holy, just and good. It will thus adhere to-day to the conclusions and determinations of yesterday, to the canonical statements which were then formulated and wholly or partially committed to writing ; as must also be the case *mutatis mutandis* in Church dogmatics. It will declare and accept to-day the confessing law of yesterday, both following it in practice and giving it the necessary emphasis. It will live on to-day as the community which yesterday was ordered in this or that fashion. For it was not dreaming or playing yesterday, but genuinely praying and working. And it was not obedient to its own or an alien spirit, but to the Holy Spirit, so that along the lines of yesterday it may still think that it will be obedient to-day. In its freedom it has and exercises the freedom to accept and practise as true law the law which it then found and established. To-day—until to-morrow, until it takes further order ! As it accepts and practises it in the freedom of the Holy Spirit it rates it as high as this, but no higher : To-day—until to-morrow, until it takes further order ! It will not regard it as an eternal work or law, or even as one which is created and valid for all ages. The basic law from which it proceeded in the discovery and establishment of its law was and is necessary to salvation—an authority for all ages and to all eternity. No less necessary to salvation was the required will to think and resolve on this basis ; the will to be obedient to Jesus Christ as its Head. But it will be no less necessary to salvation to-morrow to be newly obedient to Jesus Christ regarding the form of its law ; to think and decide afresh in the light of that basic law. Hence the community will refuse to regard as necessary to salvation, or to invest with divine authority, the work of its obedience, and therefore the ecclesiastical propositions which it discovered and enforced yesterday. It may have prayed and worked very seriously yesterday when it discovered them. It may be quite convinced that in them it discovered that which is important and right. It may have observed them excellently in its life. But surely, to be valid and serviceable, they do not have to be necessary to salvation, or enjoy divine authority ! Surely their force is not weakened if they are not protected by the idea that they are valid for all ages and even for eternity ! As *ius humanum* no Church law can or should advance this claim. As it derives, in concrete obedience, from Jesus Christ present and active to-day and here, it necessarily relates to specific times and circumstances, to the life of the community in a particular stage of its history. Its necessity is thus relative. It is the particular necessity which it cannot have for the community in other times and places. Above all, the obedience in which the Church here and to-day confesses this or that form of law to be right is never unadulterated. Even at best it is only a partial obedience diluted by all kinds of misunderstandings and corrupt desires. On this ground, therefore, we cannot possibly ascribe perfection and therefore permanent validity and divine authority to the result of its inquiry and concern. Its law is always basically conditioned, and in practice as well as theory it is a fallible work which must always be improved and reformed. The fact that it takes it seriously includes rather than excludes an awareness from its inception and first enforcement that it is not definitive. The lordship of Jesus Christ is not exhausted by its emergence and continuance. It has not limited itself by the fact that the community is here and now granted this insight and led to this conclusion. If the community is conscious with ultimate fidelity of its faith in its Lord and obedience to Him, it must remain open for new direction and guidance from the point which it has now reached. And it cannot think that it has really been so faithful and successful a pupil in His school that no further instruction and better learning are required. We have already described the establishment and execution of Church law as a venture. What we mean is the necessary venture of obedience. But we can be genuinely bold for this venture only when we are bold for that which is provisional ; for an order of Church life which will obtain until it is replaced by a better. The community can find and have this boldness only where there is the conscious and explicit (and best of all fully explicit) proviso : the proviso of humility, i.e., that it has still to receive better instruction, that it will achieve a fuller obedience in the future, and that it will have to revise, not just to-morrow, but even to-day the work which it did yesterday ; but also the proviso of freedom, i.e., that it has the power to do this. Only in the form of this free humility can it be the true courage needed to answer the question of order. As courage in this free humility it is courage for the wholly living law, and its living exercise, which are alone appropriate to it as the community of Jesus Christ. As it takes this courage for living law, it will be protected against fatal indifference and negligence in respect of the question of order, and therefore against disorder. But it will also be protected against the fatal overestimation of any particular answer to this question ; against petrifaction in a particular tradition and against the legalism of sacrosanct institutions. As the free community—free in humility towards its Head—inquires concerning the living law normative for it, and as it is protected by this law both on the right hand and on the left, it steers between these two dangers like the horseman between death and the devil. It honours its past because it lived in its past with and therefore under Jesus Christ. And as it honours it, it looks to the future in which it longs and hopes and is sure that it will again live with and under Jesus Christ. In respect of its order, as generally, it lives in the transition from the one to the other. And it is as a transitional order that it will prove to be helpful and redemptive, and above all worthy of the law which it has adopted, under which it is placed, and under the lordship of which it is the Christian community, the *communio sanctorum*, the earthly body of its heavenly Head.

From this standpoint, it is obvious that there can be better and worse canon law. There can be that which at one point or another is strong or weak, serviceable or less serviceable, sober or turgid, in short, right or less right or even wrong—and all measured by the question of obedience which has to be answered in it. In practice, therefore, the Christian community both as a whole and individually will always be somewhere on the way in the movement from yesterday to to-morrow, and therefore *Deo bene volente* from the worse to the better. If Church law is living law this means that it will always have to move on this way. It will always have to tread this way—in the right direction, it is to be hoped. It will always have to move away from the worse and move forward to the better. If it were not somewhere engaged in this movement, it would be a sure sign that the Holy Spirit had left it and it had lost the attitude of obedience to its Lord. We recall again how much is involved in this—that it has to understand and fashion its whole life as service. We remember again the whole mass of problems raised at the centre of its life by and in relation to its divine service. Where and when will the Church not find itself in a situation in which a host of questions—some more pressing at one point and others at another—are awaiting a new and better answer ? We also remember the actual tension which there will always be in some sense between the possibilities of the necessary openness and yet definiteness of its order on the one side and the impossibilities of the evil inefficiency or rigidity of ecclesiastical jurisprudence on the other. Where and when does not the community need to judge itself seriously either on the one side or the other (and perhaps both), and thus to look and boldly work for an improvement of its law ?

And as it takes part in this work, at different times and places it can and will find itself at very different points in this transition, so that its law can and will assume very different forms. It is not important or necessary to salvation that at this particular time or place it should be at this particular point, but that this point should always be a point of obedience and therefore of transition and not a final point ; and that it should really be passing from one point to another in the constant movement from the worse to the better. It is not, therefore, important or necessary to salvation that at this particular time or place its law should assume and for the time being maintain this particular form, but that in this or that form it should be known and grasped and applied as living law—in obedience as the law which is here and now commanded, but which both in its origin and provisional constitution is only a *ius humanum* pointing beyond itself, and not therefore a *ius divinum* the establishment and execution of which it cannot control since it is subjected to it as its own law, and is not therefore its master. Presupposing that it is done in obedience, the community can and should give itself here and now, until it takes further order, this or that particular form of law. And it can and should also keep to it with a good conscience and in all seriousness, presupposing that in so doing it does not fall out of obedience, but is always open—as *ecclesia semper reformanda*—for the new ordering of its Lord, and is therefore ready for fresh obedience and prepared for the discovery and establishment of a new and better order on the basis of new and better instruction.

If it is always and everywhere a matter of living Church law, there can and should be a tolerable and meaningful and fruitful relationship between differently constituted and ordered Churches in different historical situations and at different points on the way : a calm appraisal of the positions which they themselves have adopted and maintain ; and an equally calm—and attentive and curious—appraisal of the positions which others are seen to adopt and maintain.

Where it is a matter of living Church law, and we live consciously and willingly in this transition, we will not regard even the law which in obedience to the Lord of the Church we believe we must now choose and apply and provisionally respect as a perfect form of law which is therefore universally valid for the Christian community at all times and in all places. Similarly, even in respect of the different forms of other Churches, which in obedience we cannot approve or accept or allow to be imposed on us, we can at least ask ourselves whether in their own place they have not been found good and chosen and enforced in obedience—in the obedience there demanded—and do not therefore constitute a true Church order : always assuming, of course, that they are not perfect but supremely in need of amendment ; and that even in their own place they are not seriously regarded and treated as *ius divinum*, but honestly and soberly as *ius humanum*. Indeed, the same judgment is demanded even where we think we see this confusion in an opposing system. When we have a right understanding of ourselves as the Christian community, we are at liberty to understand *in meliorem partem*—better than it understands itself—even that which seems to be, and is, an obstinately antithetical order ; so that in this judgment, and our contact with it, we will be guided by this better understanding.

This has nothing whatever to do with " relativism." In this encounter between Churches of very different order and constitution the only possibility is the open question whether the Lord has not spoken and been heard on the other side too. And this question cannot alter the loyalty of obedience on our own side. In matters of Church law, as of dogma and dogmatics and everything else, what is demanded *semper et ubique et ab omnibus* is that thought and decision should always have their source, not in principles, but in the manifest lordship of Jesus Christ, and therefore that they should always be in obedience. If we accept this demand—and we are all aware how imperfectly we do so—we are at liberty, and under an obligation, to count on it that others may also do so in their own way, and to count on it even though they may not return the compliment. Indeed, when the latter is the case, it ought to be a more intense provocation to do it more seriously. The suspicion of relativism is removed by some words of Paul in relation to different attitudes in the community at Rome. " Hast thou faith ? Have it to thyself before God. Happy is he that condemneth not himself in that thing which he alloweth " (Rom. 14²²). And : " Who art thou that judgest another man's servant ? to his own master he standeth or falleth. Yea, he shall be holden up : for God is able to make him stand " (Rom. 14⁴). No Church order is perfect, for none has fallen directly from heaven and none is identical with the basic law of the Christian community. Even the orders of the primitive New Testament community (whatever form they took) were not perfect, nor are those of the Western Papacy, the Eastern Patriarchate, the Synodal Presbyterianism which derives from Calvin's system, Anglican, Methodist, Neo-Lutheran and other forms of Episcopacy, or Congregationalism with its sovereignty of the individual community. Nor are the orders of all different systems which are derivative variations of these basic types. There is no reason to look down proudly and distastefully from one to the others. At one time they may all have been living law sought and in a certain exaggeration found in obedience, and therefore legitimate forms of the body of Jesus Christ. Indeed, they may be this still. Thus for all the problems to which they give rise they must be respected by the others. Indeed, as we have reason to leave this question open, we have equally good ground to put the counter-question how we ourselves are fixed in relation to living law ; whether the removal of the beam in our own eye (Mt. 7⁴) is not a more urgent task than concern about the mote in our brother's eye ; and whether in the last analysis we do not need to learn from this brother something for our own reformation. It is always perfectionism which makes Church law sterile, as it does also the life of the individual Christian, and theology. What is needed is openness and readiness to learn in the comparison of different forms. What is needed is a sincere ecumenical encounter—which will lead to integration as well as debate. Where there is this, the law of the community, like its theology and preaching, will always be fruitful in its particular forms. For these forms will not act as a restraint on any Church, but stir them, at the transitional point which they have

reached, to seek and find afresh, and with fresh seriousness, their living and
therefore their true law.

4. True Church law is exemplary law. For all its particularity, it
is a pattern for the formation and administration of human law generally, and therefore of the law of other political, economic, cultural
and other human societies.

I can best introduce this theme by quoting a passage from Erik Wolf (*Rechtsgedanke und biblische Weisung*, 1948, p. 93) : " What might it not mean for the
world if Church order and law were not merely spiritual adaptations of worldly
constitutions and codes, but genuine and original witnesses to the brotherly
fellowship of Jesus Christ ! What might it not mean if Church law were no
longer a positivistic-juristic order on the basis of a historical form of state, or a
positivistic-theological order on the basis of a historical confession, but a confessing Church law, a living order of fellowship, constituting for all other men
a witness to the centre and Head of this fellowship—Christ ! "

What is at issue ? Primarily, it is a matter of the insight that in
the formation and administration of its law the Christian community,
while it is first and decisively responsible to its Lord, assumes also a
two-sided responsibility—both inward and outward—on the human
level. This is not a divided or twofold responsibility. It is two-sided.
The inward responsibility to itself involves an outward to the world.
It orders itself—its own life which is distinct from that of the world.
It does this from its centre in public worship. It does it above all in
its ordering of public worship. But it does not do it for the sake of
itself. It does not do it in self-seeking, however holy. If it did, it
would come into collision with its basic law—the law that in its totality
and all its members it is pledged to service in the discipleship of the
One who came, not to be ministered unto, but to minister. We return
to our definition that the Christian Church, as the body of Jesus Christ
and therefore the earthly-historical form of His existence, is the provisional representation of the humanity sanctified in Him. Jesus
Christ did not sanctify Himself for His own sake, but for the sake of
humanity. That He did this, and that humanity is therefore sanctified
already in Him, is what the Christian Church has to represent to it ;
to the world which is not yet aware of it because it does not perceive
it. It has to represent it provisionally, for the full and definitive
representation of this alteration of the human situation is not its
affair but can only be that of its Lord in His manifestation to which
here and now it moves with the world. Provisionally to represent this
alteration, the humanity sanctified in Him, is, however, the task, the
determination, the clear commission, which the community cannot
evade in the time between His resurrection and return which is its
time. It exists in the service of the witness which in its existence as
the community it owes to the world, and cannot therefore withhold
from it. And its legal order is the form in which it represents itself

outwardly to the world ; in which it stands out visibly and conspicuously as one human society with others, and first and foremost in contrast to the state. But this has the following implication. It is right enough that Church law is a *ius sui generis* ; a law which in its basis and formation is different *toto coelo* from that of the state and all other human societies. It is right enough that it must be sharply distinguished, as *ius in sacra*, from the law of Church and state, which can be only the expression of a *ius circa sacra*. It is right enough, therefore, that it should be understood strictly as an expression of the majesty of the community itself, or rather as a reflection of the majesty of its Lord. But it would be quite wrong for the community to think that in its formation and administration it has to do only with itself, with its own affair, with its divine service as the centre of its life. For its own affair, that with which it is concerned in its divine service and in its whole life understood as service, is the witness that it owes to those who are without. In relation to those who are without it cannot, therefore, be indifferent or silent or preoccupied with itself. It can be genuinely preoccupied with itself only when it is also concerned with them and is aware of its responsibility towards them. It has to converse with them, and one way in which it has to do so is by showing them the law valid within it.

To what end ? Certainly not in order to claim that the law valid in the Church must also be the law of the state and other human societies. Certainly not to demand or invite these to appropriate the provisions of ecclesiastical law and therefore to replace their own law by canon law. Certainly not to ecclesiasticise the world and especially the state as the all-embracing form of human society. There will, of course, be only one law in the redemption which comes with the future manifestation of Jesus Christ, in the heavenly Jerusalem, in the glory of eternal life. But this will be the law of Jesus Christ over every sphere of life. It will be the law of the kingdom of God. It will not be a human law at all, and therefore it will not be Church law. What law of what Church at what stage of its transition from yesterday to to-morrow, from the worse to the better, can ever be held up to the world as a norm, or commended as an example to follow ? And, above all, how can it be expected that the world will even understand and recognise as useful for its own purposes, let alone practise in any meaningful sense, a Church law which may perhaps be approximately perfect ? To do this it would have to recognise what it does not recognise and acknowledge what it does not acknowledge : the lordship of Jesus Christ as the authority of the One in whom the reconciliation of the world with God has been accomplished ; the majesty of His Word and the power of His Holy Spirit. The law of the state and all other human societies is worldly law in the sense that, even though its members and representatives may themselves be Christians and belong to the community, it does not reckon with the basic law which is decisive for the community but is based upon, and shaped by, very different (historical and speculative) principles. Directly to take over the law of the community even at a single point the world would have to abandon its own assumptions and become the community. And if the Church makes this demand, if it tries to play the part of a school-master, where is the required respect for the independent divine commission revealed and operative especially in the existence of the state ? The exemplary nature of Church law cannot, then, be understood in this way, in the sense of a law which has to be imposed upon the world and observed by it.

But why not in the sense that it has to express the Gospel to the world in the form of its particular law ? What the Christian community owes to the world is not a law or ideal, not an exactment or demand, but the Gospel : the good news about the actuality of Jesus Christ in which it is helped, its sins are overcome and its misery ended ; the word of hope in the great coming light in which its reconciliation with God will be manifested. This is not the place to develop even in outline the whole question of the prophetic mission of the community in the world and especially of its responsibility to the divine order operative and visible in the existence of the state. It is not the place to discuss the whole complex of the Christian and the civil community. There can be no doubt however—and we may say this in anticipation —that the decisive contribution which the Christian community can make to the upbuilding and work and maintenance of the civil consists in the witness which it has to give to it and to all human societies in the form of the order of its own upbuilding and constitution. It cannot give in the world a direct portrayal of Jesus Christ, who is also the world's Lord and Saviour, or of the peace and freedom and joy of the kingdom of God. For it is itself only a human society moving like all others to His manifestation. But in the form in which it exists among them it can and must be to the world of men around it a reminder of the law of the kingdom of God already set up on earth in Jesus Christ, and a promise of its future manifestation. *De facto*, whether they realise it or not, it can and should show them that there is already on earth an order which is based on that great alteration of the human situation and directed towards its manifestation. In relation to those who are without it can and should demonstrate, as well as say, that worldly law, in the form in which they regard it as binding, and outside which they believe that they cannot know any other or regard any other as practicable, has already ceased to be the last word and cannot enjoy unlimited authority and force ; that there are other possibilities, not merely in heaven but on earth, not merely one day but already, than those to which it thinks that it must confine itself in the formation and administration of its law. It cannot produce any perfect or definitive thinking or action on this question of law. It can produce only a thinking and action which are defective because provisional. But for all the fact that they are defective and provisional, they can and should be different, corrected, pointing beyond themselves, and to that extent higher and better. The limits, the severity and weakness, the impossibility and inadequacy, the vulnerability and peril of a *ius humanum* drawn up in ignorance of the lordship of Jesus Christ will not be concealed from it. It knows that if there is to be right and order and peace and freedom on earth even in the defective and provisional forms of the present time, there is needed a recognition and acknowledgment of the law of the One who has reconciled them with God and in whom the sanctification of humanity has already taken place. The law of the Church is the result of its attempt to think and act in recognition and acknowledgment of the law of Jesus Christ—this human attempt which is so defective and provisional. On this basis and in this respect it has a relative—although not an absolute—advantage over all human law. On this basis and in this respect it attests the Gospel of the kingdom of God to all human law, whether it be common or statute law, civil or criminal, the law of property or the law of contract. The community knows perfectly well that it is itself in greatest need of hearing, and continually hearing, this Gospel. But this must not hinder it from causing it to be heard in the world, even in the form of its canonical order. In fact, it makes this all the more obligatory. Again, the community knows perfectly well that it cannot exemplify the law of God directly, but only in the broken form of its human law in which it can only point to the law of God. But it cannot and must not refuse to point to it in this way. Even though the world may not recognise the origin and basis of this indication, in the form of its relatively higher and better law it may be helpful and salutary to it, and therefore good news in this concealed form : the proffering of possibilities which it had never even considered ; the invitation to revise or correct its own legal thought and action at least in the direction of the possibilities suggested, clarifying here and deepening there, simplifying in one case and differentiating in another, loosening at one point and strengthening at another. The community cannot withhold this indication from the world, but must realise its responsibility towards it as it forms and administers its own law, because it recognises that Jesus Christ has and exercises not merely the claim, but also, *sedens ad dexteram Patris omnipotentis*, the power to rule in the world, so that it is no accident that even in the world which does not know and acknowledge Him as the One He is the question of law always arises, and some form of law is sought and found, in an attempted movement from the worse to the better. The community does not see in this a mere chaos of endlessly self-renewing human error and wrong. In a way which is opaque but very real, it sees the same Lord at work who is revealed to it in contrast to the world, and to whom it is consciously responsible and committed, again in contrast to the world. Thus, although it can see the limitations and weakness of this whole process, it cannot be scornful or hostile or even indifferent. It knows that it is itself involved in it. It accepts the fact that there too—from the centre which is its own centre— there is a real perception of law and a real way from worse law to better. And it knows that it is itself responsible for the fact that this way should be sought and found and traversed : not the way to the kingdom of God, for it is from this that even the world comes, and its manifestation comes without any human aid ; but the way to better law, more serious order, more certain peace, more genuine freedom, and a more solid maintenance and fashioning of human life, and human life in society. If the community were to imagine that the reach of the sanctification of humanity accomplished in Jesus Christ were restricted to itself and the ingathering of believers, that it did not have corresponding effects *extra muros ecclesiae*, it would be in flat contradiction to its own confession of its Lord. But if it accepts the fact that there are corresponding effects outside, it cannot escape but will confidently if modestly undertake the task of contributing to the improvement of human law, especially by its own order as this is founded on the recognition and acknowledgment of the Lord Jesus Christ.

The exemplary quality of Church law, and therefore the contribution of the community to the improvement of worldly law, may consist simply in the fact that it displays to those around the fact of an order which as an order of service has completely transcended the dialectic of fulfilment and claim, of dignity and responsibility, of taking and giving. Even in the best state, worldly law never transcends this hampering dialectic. It is always confronted by it as its true problem. And it suffers in consequence. How valuable it might be for the over-coming of this problem, even in an imperfect way, to have exemplified in Church law a pure order of service, or at least an indication in this direction !

Or it may be that Church law is a model because it is a concrete expression to humanity in its search for law of the order of a society which knows, strangely enough, that it is not qualified to be the subject of law, which is not therefore referred to any historical authority or speculation of natural law but to an authority which it cannot make clear to the world—that of Jesus Christ. Is it not salutary for the legal thinking and action of the world to find itself con-fronted by a human society which has no need to join this merry-go-round ? Does it not contribute to its own improvement to have to encounter in Church law the riddle of this freedom, the mystery of a subject of law which transcends human society ?

It may be model law because neither in its establishment nor its execution is it supported by any alien power, but can arise and be practised, as is actually the case, in mutual trust. No worldly law can be satisfied with this presupposi-tion. But might it not serve its own amendment to be reminded by the existence of Church law of the basis apart from which no order can ultimately be set up or administered even in state and society ? Of what value is the force which compels observance if it cannot also appeal to the mutual trust which is the law within law ?

Again, Church law may be a model in the sense that the men united in the Christian fellowship are not merely bound by it from certain aspects, but are totally bound together, so that they are placed under the protection and control of the fellowship at the very point where worldly law reaches its limit in the personal life of the individual. Church law is not content with anything less than a total common and reciprocal responsibility. No worldly law can imitate it in this respect. But is it not as well, and even perhaps necessary, for the development and continuance of good human law, that those responsible for it should be concretely reminded that this fellowship in the true sense of the term aims to be a true life-fellowship or communion, and in the last resort cannot be achieved even in part without the total self-giving of each to all ? The existence of canon law can demonstrate this truth in paradigmatic form.

Again, it may be a model to the extent that in it every member of the community—irrespective of his estate, endowment, background or nature—is in the first instance treated absolutely as a brother. Worldly law sees a man in purely material relationships. It regulates his integration into society and the state, and the duties which this entails. It protects and limits his living-space, his activity, his possessions and his honour. It determines the liberties which he is allowed or denied. But it does not touch the man himself, although in all these relationships it is first and last he who is concerned. In this respect, too, true Church law begins at the very point where all worldly law breaks off. Is it not salutary that the latter—even though and as it remains true to its own field—should be concretely reminded that man is its true theme and subject-matter ?

Finally, Church law may be a model in its character as wholly living law : human as opposed to divine ; but as such serious and fluid and open ; with an equal responsibility both to the past and to the future. Do those who are responsible for worldly law realise that even the law which they have to find and guard and apply can be true law only as living law ? How many of the severities and weaknesses of this law are caused by the fact that this is only too easily ignored or forgotten or disregarded in state and society ? By the established fact of its own law the Church can warn and encourage the world that even in the defective and provisional form of the present age true righteousness cannot be a frozen or static pond, but must be a living stream continuously flowing from the worse to the better.

We must not misunderstand the relationship between ecclesiastical and temporal law. The world and its law are evil. But even apart from their confrontation with the Church and its law they are not wholly evil. They are also in the hand of God and have not escaped His judgment and grace. For it is under the direction and guidance of God that even outside the Church the question of law is raised in the world, and law is proclaimed and respected and practised. Jesus Christ is the King over all men and all things, and as such He is not idle even *extra muros ecclesiae*. It is not the case, then, that the relatively higher and better and to that extent exemplary law of the Church is indispensable or always and everywhere new and strange to the world and its law. If it were the case that ecclesiastical and temporal law confronted one another in absolute antithesis and mutual exclusion, the witness which the former has to bear to the latter would be impossible and pointless. But the two have one thing in common. They are both human law, and in their humanity they can be established, and enjoy validity and force, only in the sphere of divine law. There is thus no reason in principle why there should not be reciprocity between them, for an absolute superiority of ecclesiastical law to temporal is quite out of the question. In the last resort it is genuinely superior—and it is so *toto coelo*—only by reason of its cognitive basis. In its forms however, as the recognised and established law of this particular Church at this particular time, it has no small share in the limitations and weaknesses of worldly law. And its cognitive basis, the lordship of Jesus Christ *ad dexteram Patris omnipotentis*, is the actual basis of all temporal law as well. Is it not to be expected, therefore, that in its forms—however defective these may be as they do not proceed from a knowledge of the basis of all law—there will be at least some analogies or correspondences to ecclesiastical law ? By reason of its actual basis, which it has in common with Church law, even worldly law both needs a parallel and can itself be a parallel. It needs a parallel because it is true right and not wrong only to the extent that the lordship of Jesus Christ is actually at work in its formation and administration. And it can be a parallel because the lordship of Jesus Christ can actually work itself out in its formation and administration. In principle, therefore, we have to reckon no less definitely with its share in the true basis of law than with the share of Church law in the limitations, severities and weaknesses of worldly law. And in practice we have to reckon with at least the occasional emergence of analogies, λόγοι σπερματικοί, of temporal law to ecclesiastical. For the very fact and reason that the Church has to keep so strictly to the revealed lordship of Jesus Christ when it asks concerning its law, it cannot refuse to be reminded of this, and perhaps recalled to it, by actual outworkings outwith its own sphere. In its encounter with the world it may sometimes happen that in this particular field the children of the world prove to be wiser than the children of light, so that in the question concerning its law the Church has reason to learn from the world (which does not know what it knows), receiving from it the witness which it ought to give. For all its awareness of the independence of its task, it cannot exclude this possibility.

But if it becomes a reality, it will gather from it only that it is itself the more seriously required to give as it should do, and better than ever before, the witness enjoined upon it. Nor will it do this in morose pessimism, as though it could not be received and accepted by those outside, but in confident expectation that so long as it faithfully makes its contribution to the improvement which by God's appointment can and should be achieved in spite of the defective and provisional nature of all present occurrence, this contribution will definitely not be made in vain but will bear fruit within the limits which are set for all human action. It is not a question of setting up the law and therefore the kingdom of God on earth. For this has been set up already, and its manifestation is the work neither of the world nor of the Church. More modestly, it is a question of clarifying and deepening, of simplifying and differentiating, of loosening and strengthening, in short of correcting the law which obtains in the world. This is genuinely necessary at every point. Is it not incumbent upon the

Church to hear how men cry for it, for righteousness, peace and freedom in a form and measure unknown in what was previously regarded as " law " ? Already the law of the world has been improved, and not without some assistance on the part of the Church. In many ways and by-ways is not the witness of the Church much stronger perhaps than Christian dispiritedness, and the sloth concealed behind it, will often allow ? The community must not be vexed that the model which it has to give to the world cannot have more than a corrective influence. How much it would mean for the world and its law if only in the formation and administration of this law it always stood under the modest but salutary corrective influence of the existence of the community and its law ! Men live in the world (even Christians) by the fact that, although there can be no question of perfection, this law is in process of correction. Does not even the community itself and as such live by the fact that it must continually let itself be corrected by the Word and Spirit of its Lord ? With the world and for the world, it waits and hopes for the eventide at which it will be light. In the meantime, it cannot and must not be too small a thing for it to give a provisional but real representation of the law of God in its concern for its own law, and in this way to be in the world of provisional but real assistance to the world and its children. In this way it will show that its law is true law ; a law which on the basis of the Gospel proclaims the Gospel.

§ 68

THE HOLY SPIRIT AND CHRISTIAN LOVE

The Holy Spirit is the quickening power in which Jesus Christ places a sinful man in His community and thus gives him the freedom, in active self-giving to God and his fellows as God's witness, to correspond to the love in which God has drawn him to Himself and raised him up, overcoming his sloth and misery.

1. THE PROBLEM OF CHRISTIAN LOVE

As we come to the end of this second part of the doctrine of reconciliation, we turn to the problem of the individual Christian. The same question occupied us at the end of the first part, and will do so again at the end of the third. The individual Christian is the individual member of the Christian community and therefore of the body of Jesus Christ as His earthly-historical form of existence. When it is a matter of the name and kingdom and will of God, of the grace and election of the covenant, and the fulfilment of the covenant and therefore of reconciliation, the individual Christian is not the centre of all things. He is only on the circumference of the true centre. In this matter he is the basis neither of reality nor knowledge. He merely has a part in that which is and is to be known; an important and supremely real part, but no more than a part. He belongs to the reconciliation of the world with God. He does so because he is in the world, and therefore the reconciliation is his and has reference to him. But he does so decisively as and because he belongs to the man Jesus in whom the reconciliation of the world with God has taken place. There is no man who does not belong to this man, who is not His brother. But this is true of the Christian in a very special way because his human existence has been altered and re-determined by the fact that what is true of all men is no longer concealed from him but revealed to him; because he, a man like all others, may live in the knowledge that he belongs to Jesus, and live in a very different way from those who do not have this knowledge. That God has reconciled the world with Himself in Jesus Christ is not merely true for each individual Christian personally, as it is for all men, but it acquires shape and form in his existence. It is given to him actually to live in communion with Jesus Christ, in and with Him. In this way and to this extent he receives and has his own specific part in the reconciliation which has taken place in Him. When, therefore, we speak of this reconciliation, we can and must speak also of him. And at the end we must do so explicitly. It does not take place in him, let alone through him. But it does so in such sort that it applies to him in this special way ; that it is to his advantage in this particular way which is exemplary for the grace of God addressed to all men ; *de facto* and not merely *de iure*. The reconciliation of the world with God takes place with its own peculiar force, which is that of God. But the existence of the Christian community, and in and with this that of the Christian, is the exponent of this happening. And when this reveals and attests itself, when it makes itself known, each individual Christian is involved as a secondary witness in and with the Christian community. Hence, if we are fully and precisely to understand the reconciliation, we must finally try to understand the individual Christian too—this remarkable and even astonishing phenomenon of men who stand in this special relationship to its occurrence and revelation.

At the corresponding point in the first part of the doctrine we thought of him from the standpoint of faith. Jesus Christ the Lord, who as the Son of God became a servant for us in obedience to His Father; this gracious condescension of God as the basis and power of the justification of sinful man, was the reality which determined this first form of the doctrine of reconciliation. In relation to the man confronted by this reality—the Christian—what other question could be put and answered but that of the Advent hymn : " How shall I then receive thee ? " What can and should and must be done by the man to whom the Creator and Lord of heaven and earth has stooped down from His eternal and inaccessible majesty in inconceivable goodness and overflowing mercy to take man to Himself by taking his place and bearing his curse and burden? What can and should and must be done by the man to whom it is given in the quickening power of the Holy Spirit to accept the fact that God is for him in this way ? What remains for the Christian to do ? What is his part ? Or rather, what is he allowed and commissioned and commanded to do ? Since this is the case, and he knows it, in what consists his Christian freedom ? There can obviously be only one answer to this question. This is the simple and unequivocal answer that he must accept and receive the One who comes to him and that which is given in and by Him ; that he must be content in unconditional and childlike confidence to hold to the fact that God is for him ; that he must acknowledge and recognise and confess this ; that he must place himself on this ground and walk on it without hesitation or vacillation ; that he must be satisfied and rejoice and constantly return to the fact that he may undeservedly but quite indisputably be the child of God. This living, active reception is faith ; the faith of the Christian community, and in and with it the faith of the individual Christian. Christianity consists wholly in this reception and therefore in the act of faith.

We say wholly—and this is quite right. But we must not say exclusively. Christianity consists wholly but not exclusively in this reception, and therefore wholly but not exclusively in the act of faith.

The Advent hymn of P. Gerhardt to which we referred is everywhere concerned with justification by faith alone. And it does not contain a single superfluous word. Yet the first verse goes on at once to speak of meeting Jesus as well as receiving Him. And there is then the prayer that He will Himself provide the torch to show us what delights Him. And the closing verse also speaks of " the one who loves and seeks Him " and will be found as such in the judgment of the world by Jesus. In the 17th and 18th centuries Protestantism (even Lutheran Protestantism) tried to bring out this aspect in many different ways, not all of them wholly legitimate. We ourselves must now take up the question how we are to meet Him. It is on (and from) this point that we must proceed to deliberate.

The occurrence of the reconciliation of the world with God has also the aspect which has occupied us from the very outset in this second part of the doctrine of reconciliation—the aspect not merely of the high-priestly but also with undiminished clarity of the kingly office of Jesus Christ, in the exercise of which He the servant, as a man like ourselves and among us, is exalted to be the Lord who as such draws to and after Himself and raises up in the power of God sinful man, the man who is slothful and miserable in His sin. And so it has not merely the form of the justification of this man, of the promised forgiveness of his sins, of his free acceptance to divine sonship, but also of his sanctification, of his no less gracious claiming and endowment and institution for obedience, work and service. Accordingly, we have now to say that in the vital action of the Christian it is not merely a question wholly and purely of this reception, but no less wholly and purely of the decision for a definite direction in the lifemovement of man, and therefore of his breaking out in this direction. In Jesus Christ a new man, the true man, has dynamically entered the human sphere, not merely demanding conversion and discipleship, but in the quickening power of His Holy Spirit calling and transposing into conversion and discipleship. Christians, then, are the men to whom Jesus Christ, and in Him their own completed sanctification, is revealed and present as this new, true man, and who know that they are co-ordinated with Him as their first-born Brother and subordinated to Him as their King instituted from all eternity. But this being the case, as they exist totally in the existence of this reception and therefore of faith, they do so no less totally in the act in which they can and must confirm their co-ordination and subordination in relation to the man Jesus exalted by God, not on their own impulse or in their own strength, but in the quickening power of the Holy Spirit in the unity of this second act with the first. The second act is the pure and total confirmation of what Christians are as those who purely and totally receive in the act of their faith. It is the act of a pure and total giving, offering and surrender corresponding to this receiving. When we ask how we are to meet Him the answer is that it is in the great self-giving which corresponds to the great reception and in which there takes place that which is pleasing to Him.

Before we proceed, it is essential that we should recall the context in which we have to speak of this matter. In the preceding section we were concerned with the upbuilding of the Christian community. The counterpart of Jesus Christ, which as the provisional representation of the world of men reconciled with God in Him is His body, His earthly-historical form of existence, is not in any respect the individual Christian as such, i.e., as an individual, but His community. In it, it is also the individual Christian, as its living member, in the freedom which he is given as such. His determination for faith, and therefore for the reception of that which is given the world by the condescension of the Son of God to our flesh, is his determination for faith in and with the community. He does not have it for himself, but as one who gives in the communion of saints, participating by the quickening power of the Holy Spirit in its gathering, in its acknowledgment, recognition and confession of Jesus Christ. In exactly the same way the freedom for this surrender on the basis of the exaltation of man in Jesus Christ is not given him privately but only with the fact that by the quickening power of the same Holy Spirit he is set in the community of Jesus Christ and made its living member. Conversely, it has, of course, to be said of the Christian community—whether from the standpoint of the condescension of the Son of God or of the exaltation of the Son of man, as in the preceding section—that it is not an amorphous collective but exists only as the differentiated communion of saints and therefore in the saints, in individual Christians, in that which distinguishes them both as a whole and personally, in the act of their reception and therefore of their surrender. In the existence of the community and in that of individual Christians we have to do materially with one and the same happening brought about by the Holy Spirit and having Jesus Christ as its primary Subject. We might almost say that the one is the macrocosmic form of this happening and the other the microcosmic. When we apply to this the determination with which we are now particularly concerned, this means that in and with the upbuilding of the Christian community there takes place as the act of the individual Christian—an act which is different but cannot be separated from it—that which we have provisionally called self-giving. And conversely, in and with this act of the individual Christian in his unity with all others there takes place the upbuilding of the Christian community.

We must now give to this act of self-giving its biblical name. We are speaking of Christian love. Love as self-giving stands contrasted with faith as reception. Yet on the divine side we do not have in the humiliatiòn and exaltation of Jesus Christ, and therefore in justification and sanctification and the work of the Holy Spirit which reveals them, two separate divine actions, but two undivided and simultaneous, although distinguishable, moments or forms of the one divine action. Similarly, on the human side faith and love, reception and surrender are two indivisible but distinguishable moments of the one vital movement and act which constitutes Christian existence. The contrast, then, is only relative, and we can hardly speak of love without (in other terms) making use of the views and concepts with which faith has also to be described, or of faith without attributing to it certain features which in the strict sense are those of love.

In this relative sense faith and love are often compared and linked together in the New Testament, from which we have of course taken the terms. Sometimes they stand alone, as in 1 Thess. 3⁶, 1 Tim. 1¹⁴ and 4¹², and 2 Tim. 1¹³. Sometimes they are grouped with hope, as in 1 Thess 1³ and 5⁸, and 1 Cor. 13¹³. Sometimes they are linked with patience, as in 1 Tim. 6¹¹ and Tit. 2² ; or peace, as in 2 Tim. 2²². In the general characterisation of Christian action attempted in these and similar passages, we obviously have two or more concepts which stand in a particular relationship with one another. Our present concern is with the particular relationship between faith and love. Most instructive for the meaning of this relationship is the famous passage in Gal. 5⁶, where the πίστις δι' ἀγάπης ἐνεργουμένη is opposed to the circumcision of the Jews and the uncircumcision of the Gentiles as that which avails in Jesus Christ. Paul never even dreamed of the kind of πίστις envisaged and criticised in Jas. 2¹⁴⁻²⁶—the faith which has no ἔργα, which is inactive, which does not amount to anything more than a mere knowledge, and which is rightly described by James in v. 26 as without spirit and therefore dead. Indeed, he did not even consider this kind of faith as an alternative. There is no other faith than that " which worketh by love." The πίστις to which he and the rest of the New Testament refer in their positive statements is as such ἐνεργουμένη. It is, in fact, a definite act. And generally speaking, it is the whole life-act of the Christian as seen from a particular standpoint. As such it is meaningfully opposed to the mere states of Jewish περιτομή and Gentile ἀκροβυστία. Nor is it ἐνεργουμένη merely in an ἀγάπη which is added as a second thing, making it a *fides formata* as the later expression had it. On the contrary, it proves itself to be such by the fact that one and the same Christian act has as δι' ἀγάπης ἐνεργουμένη the character of ἀγάπη. In other words, as it is pure and total reception, it is also pure and total self-giving. To avoid any misunderstanding, ought it not to be noted that whereas Christians are described actively as πιστεύοντες or πιστοί, they are passively (and sometimes almost technically) called ἀγαπητοί rather than ἀγαπῶντες ? The passive term is used of the very side of their existence where its active character, if it does not begin, at least finds concrete expression.

That this has to be said especially of ἀγάπη is the explanation of 1 Cor. 13¹³, to which we will make anticipatory reference. As the present reality which will continue even in the final future revelation, in which so many Christian and Spirit-impelled activities will find no continuation because they attain their goal and in that sense cease and perish, there now remains (note the singular) as that which is here and now essential and will outlast the end of all things, " faith, hope, charity, these three." And to this there is added the remarkable statement : μείζων δὲ τούτων, greater than " these" (obviously faith and hope), and surpassing them, is ἀγάπη. In what sense does it surpass them ? Certainly not as that which in the last analysis is alone essential and therefore lasting. In this respect faith and hope have already been linked with love in contrast to the spiritual gifts and activities mentioned in v. 8 (prophecy, tongues and knowledge). No, it surpasses them within the triadic concept by which the Christian existence is described in its essential and enduring character and differentiated from its transitory marks and expression. And it does so because in it there is expressed in visible and conspicuous form its active character (which is the character of faith and hope as well). The whole of 1 Cor. 13 is an answer to the question of the Christian " way." The Corinthian community thinks that it sees this in the possession of these spiritual gifts and the corresponding activities. Paul does not blame them for this. He encourages them to go farther along these lines. But at the same time (in view of the disunities and disorders involved) he draws their attention to *the* way, *the* act, which in and beyond all these activities is the καθ' ὑπερβολὴν ὁδός (1 Cor. 12³¹) and is to be understood as such. Our chapter then describes ἀγάπη as this true way. Why does it not take πίστις, like Heb. 11, where faith too is unmistakeably active ? Why does it not take ἐλπίς, of which the same might easily be said ? These are not forgotten, as we see from v. 13. The " more costly way " to which Paul directs the Corinthians is indeed the way of faith and of hope and of love. The three together, in contrast to all these activities, are the essential and enduring element in the life-act of the Christian. But love had to be named and described here because in this context the main need was to mark off the essential and enduring Christian act as such from non-essential and transitory activities. It was by love that there had to be made clear, as it was only by love that there could be made clear, what is the true nature of the " more costly way " which the Corinthians Christians, as they went the way of these activities and might still proceed along this way, seemed to have forgotten but ought not to have forgotten as *the* way and *the* act. The true Christian existence which is living and will outlast the fire of the last judgment is in its totality way and act. But it shows itself to be this, and may be recognised as such, by the fact that it is love.

We may also anticipate our consideration of a third saying of Paul—the terse statement in Rom. 13¹⁰ : πλήρωμα οὖν νόμου ἡ ἀγάπη. For this statement again shows how the life-act of the Christian finds its climax and visible expression in love. The preceding sentence in v. 8 makes it incontestably plain that the reference is to the Christian act : ὁ γὰρ ἀγαπῶν τὸν ἕτερον νόμον πεπλήρωκεν. In this context the meaning is as follows. Those who do what the Law requires in relation to their neighbours, and therefore those who love them, confirm and prove in this way that they are those who fulfil the law and therefore love God. A love of God which does not involve also the required love of the neighbour is not the required love of God. We will return to this later. Our present concern is only with the basic fact that the Law requires a definite action. This action is love. This love is the fulfilment of the Law. The man who loves has done what the Law demands ; he has fulfilled the Law. The same could not be said of faith (abstractly taken and considered), nor could it be said of hope or patience. Faith, too, is an act—a moment and aspect of the life-act of the Christian. But as faith it is the act of a pure and total reception. As this act it does not have to fulfil the Law, or try to fulfil it, but it comes thankfully from the fulfilment which has already taken place for us in Jesus Christ. But Paul (and the rest of the New Testament in its positive statements) knows nothing of a faith abstractly taken and considered, but only the faith which has love as a complement within the one vital act of the Christian (and not only love, but also hope and patience and peace). And in love (not an abstract love, but the love by which faith works), and therefore in the self-giving which corresponds to this reception, the Christian fulfils the Law, doing that which God requires and which is right in His sight. That love covers a multitude of sins (1 Pet. 4⁸) is said in the first instance of the sins committed by the neighbour who is to be loved, but it applies also to the sins of those who exercise love towards him. As he does this—and the Christian does—he acts as one who is justified before God, and, in and with what he himself does, he passes into a place which is sheltered from storm and sin. He is empowered and free to do this, and passes into this place, as one who receives purely and totally in faith. *Ama et fac quod vis.* If you love as a Christian, you cannot and will not sin. You can and will sin only if you do not love as a Christian. The man who loves as a Christian cannot blame the Law or be backward in respect of its demands. He fulfils it. For the pure and total reception of justification by faith alone cannot be separated from his pure and total self-giving in love. The two are one and the same. And conversely, the fact that against all his deserts but in genuine earnest God shows benevolence and beneficence to him as a sinner, and that he may know this, is confirmed by the Christian in the act of this surrender : " Her sins, which are many, are forgiven ; for she loved much " (Lk. 7⁴⁷). When a man performs this act, the will of God does not remain undone in his life, nor the Law of God unfulfilled. But the will of God is done, and His Law fulfilled.

We have first equated the concept of love in a general way with that of self-giving. Or rather, we have explained it by this term. What we have here—in Christian love—is a movement in which a man turns away from himself (in what amounts at first to much the same thing as the self-denial of which we spoke earlier). But this is only the critical beginning. In the continuation love turns wholly to another, to one who is wholly different from the loving subject. Yet the critical beginning is not left behind, but is still at work in the continuation. For it does not turn to this other, the object of love, in the interests of the loving subject, either in the sense that it desires the object for itself because of its value or in pursuance of some purpose, or in the sense that it attempts to perpetuate itself in its desire. Christian love turns to the other purely for the sake of the other. It does not desire it for itself. It loves it simply because it is there as this other, with all its value or lack of value. It loves it freely. But it is more than this turning. In Christian love the loving subject gives to the other, the object of love, that which it has, which is its own, which belongs to it. It does so irrespective of the right or claim that it may have to it, or the further use that it might make of it. It does so in confirmation of the freedom in respect of itself which it has in its critical beginning. It does so with a radically unlimited liberality. Nor is this liberality confined to that which the loving subject " has." For in Christian love the loving subject reaches back, as it were, behind itself to that which at the first it denies and from which it turns away, namely, itself : to give itself (for everything would lack if this final thing were lacking) ; to give itself away ; to give up itself to the one to whom it turns for the sake of this object. To do this the loving man has given up control of himself to place himself under the control of the other, the object of his love. He is free to do this. It is in this freedom that the one who loves as a Christian loves. Where this movement is fulfilled in all its aspects, and reaches its goal in this self-giving of the loving subject, there is Christian love. And this movement, together with faith (and hope, etc.) and inseparably and simultaneously fulfilled with them, is the life-act of the Christian both in detail and finally as a whole. Its fulfilment is the particular problem of Christian love.

As is apparent from this preliminary analysis, it is very different from any other movement which may have the name of " love " and in its own way is love, but which from first to last takes a very different form and direction. To sharpen the picture of the movement with which we are now concerned, we will attempt a brief analysis of this other kind of love. It does not have its origin in self-denial, but in a distinctively uncritical intensification and strengthening of natural self-assertion. It is in this that the loving subject finds itself summoned and stirred to turn to another. It is hungry, and demands the food that the other seems to hold out. This is the reason for its interest in the other. It needs it because of its intrinsic value and in pursuance of an end. As this other promises something—itself in one of its properties—there is the desire to possess and control and enjoy it. Man wants it for himself : for the upholding, magnifying, deepening, broadening, illuminating or enriching of his own existence ; or perhaps simply in a need to express himself ; or perhaps even more simply in the desire to find satisfaction in all his unrest. And so it takes place that, however much he may seem to give what is his, lavishing and dissipating it on the object of his love, he does not really give it up, but uses it as a means to win or keep or enjoy this object of his love (as the peacock displays its tail before its mate, or the woman exerts, as her own, all her inner and outer, natural and artificial advantages that the man may be hers also). And so it also takes place that the one who loves, however much he may apparently forget himself or however much he may transcend himself (in very high and noble and spiritual transports) in the direction of the object of his love, merely asserts himself the more strongly in face of it as he wins and keeps and enjoys it, since all the time it is himself that he has in view, and his own affirmation and development that he seeks. For all the self-emptying on the part of the one who loves, union with the beloved as the supreme goal of this love consists in the fact that this object of love is taken to himself, if not expressly swallowed up and consumed, so that in the event he alone remains, like the wolf when it has devoured, as it hopes, both Red Riding Hood and her grandmother. The movement of this love takes the form of a circle. It seeks the infinite in a transcendence of everything finite, but from the very first it is disposed in such a way that (even by way of the infinite) it must always return to its beginning. Its objects do not need to be sensual. It may be directed to the good, the true and the beautiful. Even in its sexual form, it may have reference (perhaps wholly and utterly) to the soul and not merely the body. Beyond all other goods and values, it may even reach out to the Godhead in its purest form and thus be a most wonderful love of God. But in all its forms it will always be a grasping, taking, possessive love—self-love—and in some way and at some point it will always betray itself as such.

But as such it is the direct opposite of Christian love—the love which seeks and attains its end as the self-giving of the one who loves to the object of his love. It is no light thing, of course, to dare to criticise and disqualify it from the standpoint of Christian love. For one thing, although Christian love is both permitted and commanded in the case of Christians, in a crude or subtle form (and perhaps both) they all love in this way too, according to the standards of this very different love. Thus they are all the first to be convicted by whatever may be said for the one love and against the other. And they have so much to do to wipe clean their own slate that it will be a long time before they can be too loud in their exaltation of Christian love and condemnation of the theoretical and practical forms of the other (whether Greek or otherwise). But above all reserve is enjoined by the fact that this other love can claim some of the greatest figures in the history of the human spirit, whom it would be a highly questionable enterprise to reject and repudiate in a curt and dogmatic Christianity, especially on the part of those who do not really know them and cannot therefore estimate them at their true worth. It has also to be taken into account that all of us (even we Christians) exist in a world which in its best and finest as well as its most basic phenomena is for the most part built upon this other rather than Christian love, and that we live by the works and fruits and achievements of this love, so that when the Christian calls it in question in the light of Christian love he always takes on a highly ambiguous appearance. What is clearly brought out by this distinction between Christian and every other love as it may be seen—we stress this point—even in the life of the Christian himself, is the wholly alien character of Christianity in relation to the world around.

Yet these considerations must not prevent a sober affirmation of this distinction. Christian love cannot in fact be equated with any other, or with any of the forms (even the highest and purest) of this other, just as this other love has obviously no desire to be confused with Christian. Nor can Christian love be fused with this other to form a higher synthesis. We cannot say of any other love that it is a kind of preparatory stage for Christian love. Nor can we commend Christian love by representing and portraying it as the purified form, the supreme climax, of this other love. There is an element common to both types of love—we shall have to speak of this later. But remarkably enough it is precisely in view of this common element that there must and will always be decision and decisions between them : not only in the history of the Christian community in its relations with the world ; but also in the history of the Christian community itself, which is also of the world, and consists of men who both as a whole and as individuals can be moved by both types, but cannot possibly

be moved by both at the same time or in the same way ; and finally
and above all in the individual histories of these men themselves.

Even a superficial glance at the two phenomena and concepts, or
rather at the realities of the two types of love, necessarily discloses
that we have to do here with two movements in opposite directions,
so that there can be no harmony but only conflict between them. The
first type cannot pass over and be transformed into the second, nor
the second into the first. Man loves either in one way or the other,
and he has to choose whether it is to be in the one way or the other.
If in fact he loves in both ways at the same time, as is often the case
even with the Christian, this can only be with the disruption, the
" falling out," which we had occasion to discuss in relation to " conversion." Where Christian love enters, there always begins at once
the unceasing controversy between itself and every other love. The
Christian life is existence in the history of the distinction between these
opposing types of love. It has not yet begun, or has been extinguished
again, where there is the desire or ability to be superior, or neutral,
or tolerant in relation to the two ; where Christian love (perishing
as such) can be brought to terms with this other love. Not the moment
of this other love as such, but the moment of tolerance, of the agreement of Christian love with this other, of truce in the controversy,
constitutes a hiatus, a cessation, a vacuum in the Christian life—a
definitely non-Christian moment. There can be only conflict and not
compromise between Christian love and this other. And there can be
only conflict and not compromise between this other love and Christian.

The biblical basis for this distinction and opposition will emerge, like the
material, only as we take up the various themes of the section. Our present
task is simply to show that there is always this distinction and opposition.
Nevertheless we are given a prior indication of the biblical basis when we
remember the linguistic usage of the Bible. It is immediately apparent that
the New Testament consistently avoids the use of the verb ἐρᾶν and the substantive ἔρως—the terms which in classical Greek plainly describe this other
grasping, taking, possessing and enjoying love. Even in the apostolic fathers
we find only a single occurrence of ἔρως (Ignatius, *ad Rom.* 7, 2), and here it is
used only to denote the love which the author declares that he has left behind
him as crucified. In the New Testament, however, it is not used at all, even
in a depreciatory sense. The reader who meets the concept of love in these
pages is obviously not even to be reminded of this other love. Apart from an
occasional use of φιλεῖν with its emphasis on feeling, the normal term for love
in the New Testament is ἀγαπᾶν, with the substantive ἀγάπη, which is unknown
in classical Greek and only sparingly used in hellenistic. It is only in New
Testament usage that this word has acquired the well-known meaning and content of a love opposed to ἔρως. In itself it is rather colourless. It has something
of the sense of the English " like." It speaks of the acceptance or approval of
something or someone. Perhaps this lack of distinctive significance was the
very reason why it was adopted in the New Testament. It lent itself readily
to the receiving of a new impress. But the New Testament was only following
the Septuagint, which had had to find a supportable rendering for the verb *aheb*
(and substantive *ahabah*), and its synonyms. *Aheb* can describe, with a positive
emphasis, all kinds of familiar and friendly relationships. Indeed, in the first

instance it is also used for that between a man and his wife, there being a material but no linguistic distinction in Hebrew between the love which is theologically significant and that which was later called " erotic." To avoid the latter, the Septuagint seized on the colourless terms ἀγαπᾶν and ἀγάπη, using them, strangely enough, even in the picture of the marriage between Yahweh and Israel in the Book of Hosea, and even more strangely in the Song of Songs. We can give as a reason for the choice of ἀγάπη only the intention to avoid at all costs the use of ἔρως to describe the love found in these passages. This intention was shared by hellenistic Judaism in its interpretation of the Old Testament and early Christianity in its attestation of Jesus Christ. Whatever we may say concerning ἀγάπη must be determined by the meaning and content which it was desired to give, and which were actually given, to this term (the other being completely eliminated) in the light of the origin, action and manner of this love which has to be so very differently described.

We must not form too impoverished a conception of the love which was linguistically eliminated by the Septuagint and the New Testament because it was the opposite of the kind of love that they were seeking to attest. That is to say, we must not seek it only in sexual love, or in degenerate and excessive forms of this love. The image of life and power and thought which is summed up under the catchword *eros*, and which dominated to a large extent the world of Greek antiquity and even the environment of the New Testament, is a magnitude which does of course include sexual love even in its more curious forms, and which no doubt has in this a striking symbol, but which cannot in any sense be understood in its depth and richness, and its dangerous opposition to Christian love, if it is considered exclusively or even preferentially with reference to its actuality in this sphere. Nor is it a magnitude which was potent and effective only in that particular period. On the contrary, although it did of course find particularly forceful expression in the Mystery religions and in thinking influenced by outstanding philosophers like Plato and Aristotle and later Plotinus, it is a general and very real human phenomenon which reaches back to the very beginnings of history and forward into every subsequent age, including our own. We are forced to say, indeed, that the warning given already by the biblical usage was largely in vain, and that the positive proclamation of Christian love has been a largely if not wholly futile swimming against the overwhelming flood of *eros*-love. As a proof of its power, *eros* invaded even Christian thought and life from the end of the 2nd century, and has been able to effect very radical and definite penetrations (sometimes with the conscious help or connivance of Christians, but the more effectively where there has been no awareness of its influence). The *caritas* which the Middle Ages had learned decisively from Augustine was a synthesis of biblical *agape* and antique or hellenistic *eros* in which the antithesis between the two can still be perceived, but not in any sense unequivocally, the tension having been largely destroyed with all its beneficial results. This was inevitable. As long as men love, even though they are Christians they will always live within the framework of *eros*, and be disposed to effect a synthesis between *eros* and *agape*, exercising all their powers both great and small to bring this about.

Heinrich Scholz (*Eros und Caritas*, 1929) has succeeded in bringing out the difference between platonic love and love in the Christian sense with the necessary plasticity and clarity (almost indeed in the form of a wood-cut), and in a way which compels to decision. The only trouble is that he confuses the reader historically by gathering Christian love under the dazzling concept of *caritas*, and by bringing together as its exponents the Gospels, Paul, Augustine, Dante and Pascal. I also find it rather difficult to follow him when at the climax of his presentation the platonic love practised exclusively by men is opposed by Christian love in various women like Dante's Beatrice.

Shortly afterwards Anders Nygren wrote his book *Eros und Agape*, 1930 and

1937, and with eyes sharpened (perhaps over-sharpened) by the controversial theology of Sweden, and especially of Lund, he certainly saw the historical contours more exactly, and was able critically to grasp and bring out the process of amalgamation between the two loves, and the inner contradiction in mediæval *caritas*. There is thus no real need to go back behind the work which he has done on this history. But it is another, and rather singular, matter that he has portrayed it as a history which reached its conclusion with Luther's destruction of the *caritas*-synthesis and reconstruction of *agape*-love. Is it not of the very essence of this history that the opposition can never be fully overcome ? For this reason I prefer Scholz's book, in spite of its doubtful features. In Scholz, too, the material antithesis is clear enough. And he does not offer any triumphant ending in favour of *agape*, being obviously oblivious to the fact that all the ways of God can and must end with Luther. Hence the question raised by the disclosure of the antithesis is finally left to the reader, no attempt being made to satisfy and dismiss him with a strongly reasoned answer and solution. I might also whisper that I am finally more at home with Scholz because in him I think I see better practised that which in Nygren is (from the historical standpoint) more consistently and polemically set forth in words—the Christian love which does not assert itself but gives itself even in the person of the historical investigator and critic. That even the representatives of *eros*-love and the *caritas*-synthesis are objects of Christian love is something which in my view is more forcefully brought out by Scholz than Nygren, and with it the ecumenical and missionary power of Christian love.

We will now attempt to give some indication, in a few light strokes, of the form in which *eros* confronted and was perceived by the New Testament and later Septuagint-Judaism with their view of love. Who and what was this *eros* ? What was the experience, and action, of the one who loved in this erotic fashion ? This is the form which our question must first assume. We are asking concerning a definite experience and practice. In its origin in Orphism and its myth and mysticism *eros* was something far more than the philosophical concept which was first and unforgettably introduced into Western thought by Plato. *Eros* was a doctrine of redemption and salvation claiming to be revealed, and believed and proclaimed as such. Indeed, it was an experienced actuality of redemption and salvation which found expression both in solemn rites and everyday practice. As such, and hence not unlike Christian *agape*, it could and inevitably did stand in direct opposition to the latter, rousing in its advocates the critical concern so strikingly illustrated by the consistent elimination of the term *eros*. As such it could also provoke the question, which was often to be given a positive answer, whether *eros* and *agape* were not intrinsically comparable and combinable realities, and even at bottom one and the same reality—a view which was first explicitly held by Origen. In the actuality of *eros*, and its varied literature, edifying, poetic or dialectical, mythological or rational, it is always a matter of man, his limitation and its meaning and removal, his existence and transcendence, his need and hope. More precisely, it is always a matter of man hovering but in some sense moving upwards between a lower world and a higher, a world of darkness and a world of light. It is a matter of the experience and practice of this twofold reality. As it is seen and portrayed, this reality consists in his inalienable want and the desire which it kindles, or in his inalienable desire and the want to which it gives rise, as the very essence of this central position. This position is necessarily that of want and desire because it is the centre between his below and above, between his proper and improper being, between his fulness and emptiness, between his being in disintegration and in reintegration with himself. *Eros* is the experienced and self-attained turning from his being down below in darkness and return to his being up above in light. *Eros* is the power and act in which he must lose himself on the one hand to find himself again on the other. And so *eros* is a hypostatised form of man himself in this central position and the movement—the turning from and to—which is commensurate with it. As this hypostasis of man himself, the dæmon of man, powerful and manifest in him and known and expressed by him, *eros* is understood as a, and finally *the*, metaphysical link (μεταξύ) between the world of appearance and the world of reality, as the sum of the movement from the one to the other. It was explained along these lines by Aristotle, who in this respect was more consistent than Plato. As he saw it, it is not merely an anthropological but a cosmological principle. It is the impulse in the power of which—at this point the concept of *eros* verges on that of entelechy—not merely psychic individuals but all cosmic elements, even the lower and higher physical bodies, strive after form in their materiality, actuality in their potentiality and the unmoved One in their movement and plurality, thus seeking their normal state, and being engaged in a universal dissolution and ascent. Plato was more restrained in his depiction of this great turning away and return, confining his gaze to the seizure and exercise of power by *eros* in man. On his view, in the visible *eidola* of transitory things and their relative values, there encounters man, not in visible form but perceptible to the enlightened eye, the *eidos*, the absolute value of that which immutably is, the beautiful, by which he is both attracted and impelled and therefore set in movement. How can he tarry with the *eidola* without being forced to flee them at once in the direction of the *eidos*? It is only for the sake of the *eidos* that he can love the *eidola*. But again, how can he flee them for the sake of the *eidos* without being forced to tarry with the *eidola* which have a distinct part in the beauty of the *eidos*? For its sake he may and must love them too. Plotinus brought out very strongly the religious significance of the *eros*-actuality, although here again we see affinities with originally platonic notions. His main contribution was to expand the theory to the point of maintaining that there is a departure of the soul from the higher world prior to its ascent from the lower, or an emanation of the soul from the deity prior to its return from the world, so that the want and desire, the turning from and to, the being in vacillation between world-denial and world-affirmation, can be described as a homecoming, as a return of the soul to its origin and therefore to itself—an innovation which merely serves to reveal the circular movement to which the practice and theory of the *eros*-actuality were exposed from the very outset. It is the actuality of the man who in his relationship to being both visible and invisible, and finally in his relationship to the Godhead, is engaged in realising his own entelechy, i.e., in needing and therefore in seeking, desiring and successfully finding and enjoying himself in his particularity. As he knows and approves and takes himself seriously in this actuality, as he presupposes himself in this form, he orders and understands the process of his life, and therefore loves.

This was the ἐρᾶν and ἔρως with which the authors of the New Testament and the translators of the Old before them refused to equate their own understanding of "love." In the foregoing sketch we have not touched on the concrete difficulties, the intellectual, moral and religious dangers and the corruptive effects which seemed to be involved in practice when the two types of love came face to face. The contrast between *agape* and *eros* arises even when we have to do with the latter in its essential nature and not in its degenerate form, in the vulgarisations to which that which Plato, Aristotle and Plotinus saw and understood as love was submitted on the streets and in the temples and dwelling-places of the antique and hellenistic world. If we are not merely to conceive but to grasp what Christianity and its " love " so resolutely rejected, nothing less than the best of what is held out to us by the plastic works of the time will suffice. If we do not take this into account, but capriciously restrict ourselves to the particular and very obvious antithesis between *agape* and the sinful forms of sexual love or even its most degenerate manifestations, then we shall not understand the consistency (so incisive in its very silence) with which *eros* is completely ignored in the language of the Bible, nor the fact that this could become so

important a matter in the sphere of Christian, nor finally the necessity of thinking and speaking of Christian love in a restrained and sober manner, i.e., on the
basis of its own presuppositions, and therefore not in the *schema* of the actuality
and doctrine of *eros*, and therefore not along orphic, platonic, aristotelian or
neo-platonic lines. We have to do here with an opponent whom we must estimate
at his true stature, and whom we can fully appraise as an opponent only if we
do so.

We cannot be content, however, merely to state that there is a
difference and antithesis between Christian and every other love. As
we bring this introduction to a close we will thus turn to the question
at what point and in what sense the two loves diverge. Unless we
do this we cannot understand their relationship and antithesis, nor
can we understand either *eros* on the one side or *agape* on the other.
But to ask concerning this critical point is to ask concerning a common
place from which they both come. We cannot ask concerning a place
where they can be seen together and understood as components, as
partial forms and aspects, of one and the same reality, and therefore
in the last resort as one. The question of an original point of identity
necessarily involves that of a synthesis, compelling to a new identification which *eros* as well as *agape* (being what they are both in actuality
and conception) must very definitely resist. Yet we can and must
ask concerning the point from which they both come in their true
nature, and can therefore be seen in full antithesis. We can and must
ask concerning the point from which they cannot possibly co-exist in
compromise or mutual tolerance, but only in the history of their
controversy. We cannot fathom this matter unless we put this question
and make some attempt to answer it.

" We can compare two forms only when they have at least one quality in
common. If this does not exist, there can be no comparison " (H. Scholz, *op.
cit.*, p. 47). This statement seems to be incontestable. The only point is that
when we are speaking of the quality which *eros* and *agape* have in common I
prefer not to speak, as Scholz does, of the point of coincidence of these two
movements, but of their point of departure. A. Nygren, on the other hand,
assumes from the very outset, when he first takes up and describes the problem,
that we have to do with two things which cannot be compared at all. *Eros*
and *agape* (*op. cit.*, Vol. I, p. 14 f.) are two phenomena which " originally have
nothing whatever to do with one another," but between which there can be
only " the chasm of an original lack of relationship." U. von Wilamowitz-
Moellendorf is cited as the leading witness for this basic assertion—his evidence
being to the effect that Paul knew nothing of *eros* and Plato nothing of *agape*.
When this is decided *a priori*, Nygren himself can ask what reason there is for
a comparison. " Is there not something arbitrary and therefore meaningless in
a comparison of two phenomena which rest on so very different presuppositions ?
We may justly ask whether the correct answer to the question of the relationship
between *eros* and *agape* in this sense (Nygren means as historical forms) is not
necessarily that there is absolutely no relationship between them at all." This
is perfectly true if his prior decision is true. It is a matter for surprise, however,
that he seems to think he can give another answer when he works back from the
historical forms to the " basic ethico-religious forms which underlie the two,"
finding here a relationship in the very antithesis between them. This is true in

substance. But it is no real answer to the question. For what is meant by "relationship," and how can it be thought of in terms of antithesis, when the two partners in this mutual relationship and antithesis are absolutely unrelated and cannot therefore be compared—which is the consistent assertion of Nygren on the presuppositions of the theology of Lund with its strangely manichean tendencies ? Is it enough merely to wrinkle our brows and dismiss it as an unfortunate circumstance that in English as in German (and presumably in Swedish) we suffer from the same poverty as Hebrew and have only the one word " love " to denote both *eros* and *agape* ? Does this mean only that we are required to make the most speedy and energetic distinction possible between *eros* and *agape* ? Is it not also an indication that we are perhaps required to consider what is possibly the one quality that the two have in common, and thus to inquire at what point and in what sense they divide ? Unless we answer this question, will it not be quite impossible to make clear historically how it comes about that *eros* and *agape* can and do continually replace and efface one another, or how *agape* can prevent itself from being hemmed in by *eros* as it managed to do in New Testament Christianity and again (as Nygren believes) in Luther after the long regime of the *caritas*-synthesis ? What was and is really at issue in this antithesis ? Can we take it seriously even in substance if we are so afraid that an answer to the question will result in a levelling down that we refuse to consider either the point at which or the manner in which the antithesis arises, being unwilling to do more than assert the existence of the cleft or chasm between them ? If it is really God who rules the world and not the devil, does not every abyss—without ceasing to be such, and as such to be dangerous—have a bottom somewhere ?

An obvious answer, and one which is not without real content, is that on both sides—whether we are thinking of *eros* or *agape*—we have to do with man, and with one and the selfsame man in the case of the Christian. It is man who loves either in the one way or the other, or in both ways in the Christian conflict between the two. However sharply we may see and define the difference, there is no question of the love of two different beings, or even of different individuals when we are dealing with Christians. In this very different and even antithetical determination, direction and form we have to do with the same human being. It is always man who encounters us in the two forms.

This does not mean, in the case of either determination, that the two are peculiar to or inherent and grounded in the nature of man. We can say this neither of *eros* nor *agape*. Neither the one nor the other rests on a possibility of human nature as such. Neither the one nor the other is a perfection of human nature achieved or to be achieved in the actualisation of such a possibility. We can only say and must say—and we now take a second step—that they are both historical determinations of human nature. It is the same human nature which, as man loves in one way or the other, shows itself to be capable of this or that form of love, not with a capacity which is proper to it, but with one which is (shall we say) generally contingent to it, i.e., which comes upon it, in the history and existence of man. It is merely the case that man does actually express himself in the form of *eros* or *agape* or (in the case of the Christian) the two in contradiction ; and that to this extent (in view of the fact that he actually does so) he can express himself in this way. It is merely the case that man does always encounter us in these two forms of love, and to this extent in the corresponding forms of his nature.

He does so in a definite expression of his nature—this is the third step that we have to take. What actually comes upon him as the one who loves in the one way or the other is a distinct and even antithetical determination and direction of the act in which he himself, existing as the man he is, gives expression to his nature in its totality.

H. Scholz (*op. cit.*, p. 46) speaks at this point of an attitude of mind. I myself would rather avoid the idea of a purely inward and abstractly spiritual affection and disposition which possibly, if not necessarily, lurks behind this expression ; and the danger that it might perhaps obscure the fact that in the case of either love we have to do with an action on the part of man. In both cases, therefore, I prefer to speak of the act in which man expresses himself, in which he exists in his essence ; and in both cases as the whole man, expressing himself in the totality of his nature.

Neither in *eros* nor *agape* therefore—this is the fourth step—can there be any question of an alteration of human nature. Whether he loves in the one way or the other he is the same man engaged in the expression of the same human nature. What comes upon him in his history, in the fulfilment of his self-expression, is the fact that in the two cases he is the same man in very different ways. As in neither case God ceases to be the Creator, in neither case does man cease to be the creature that God willed and posited when He made him a man, with the structure of human nature. Whatever form the history of man may take, there is broken neither the continuity of the divine will for man nor that of the nature which man is given by God. And although this may be seen in very different ways in the two forms of his loving, it can be seen in both of them. The only thing is that the human act is very different in the two cases. The only thing is that, as man loves in one way or the other, it comes upon him that the one unchangeable, perennial human nature is put by him to a very different use and given a very different character. The basis of the difference is not to be found in itself (so that it cannot be explained in terms of itself or deduced from itself), but in its historical determination.

Concerning this difference in the use and character of human nature in *eros*-love on the one hand and *agape*-love on the other, we have first to make—the fifth step—a formal statement. We can and must speak of the difference of the new thing (in relation to human nature) which, as a matter of historical fact, overtakes or comes on man as he loves in the one form or the other. Without being grounded in his nature, this act of love takes place in a distinctive relationship to it, to that which makes him a man. This is not by a long way the whole of what has to be said about this love. Our present inquiry concerns only the common point of departure where comparison is possible, and at once becomes impossible, between the two ways of loving. The common point of departure consists in the fact that they both take place in relationship to the human nature chosen and willed and posited and ordered by God. They are both new in relation to this human nature, but they both take place in connexion with it. They are together in this relationship, and therefore comparison is possible. But they diverge in it, and therefore comparison becomes utterly impossible. The decisive statement must be ventured—decisive for the distinction—that *agape*-love takes place in correspondence and *eros*-love in contradiction to this nature ; the one as its "analogue" and the other as its "catalogue"; the one as man does that which is right in relation to it, and the other as he does that which is not right in relation to it. *Agape*-love takes place in affinity, *eros*-love in opposition, to human nature. As we see, they both take place in relationship to it (and in this they can be compared). But in the one case the relationship is positive, in the other negative (so that they cannot be compared). In this antithetical use and character, in which the one unchanging human nature takes on form but which differ as Yes and No, being related only in respect of their object, *eros* and *agape* go their divergent ways.

This formal statement requires material clarification and substantiation in two directions which demand attention in this question. Our starting-point for a sixth step is that it is essential, natural and original to man, that it belongs to his very structure as this particular creature of God, to be with God, who is His Creator and Lord, as with his eternal Counterpart : deriving wholly from this God, participating from the very first and in all circumstances (as His elect) in His preservation and effective help, and being sheltered absolutely by Him and in Him ; and moving wholly towards Him, thanking Him (as the one who is called by Him), in responsibility before Him and obedience to Him, calling uppn His name. From this vertical standpoint, as it were, the very nature and essence of man is to be freed by and for this God ; to be engaged in the act of this twofold freedom (cf. *C.D.*, III, 2, § 44, 3). Man cannot escape or destroy or lose or alter the fact that it is only in this that he is truly and naturally and essentially a man. But in the life-act of every man (both as a whole and in detail) it is decided whether and to what extent, in relationship to that which he really is in his togetherness with God, he is true or untrue, in correspondence or contradiction, to himself (from this standpoint his being from God and to God). It is in this decision that there arises the new thing either of his *agape*-love in which he corresponds to his being from and to God or of his *eros*-love in which he contradicts it. In this respect *agape*-love consists in the fact that he accepts God as his eternal Counterpart, and therefore his own being as that of one who is elected by this God, being absolutely sheltered by His preservation and help, but who is also called by Him to thanksgiving, responsibility, obedience and prayer. It consists in the fact that he is determined and ready to live from and to God to the best of his knowledge and capacity : not raising any claim ; not trying to control God ; not with the ulterior motive of winning God for himself or demanding anything from Him ; but simply because He is God, and as such worthy to be loved. *Agape* consists in the orientation of human nature on God in a movement which does not merely express it but means that it is transcended, since in it man gives himself up to be genuinely freed by and for God, and therefore to be free from self-concern and free for the service of God. *Eros*-love consists in this respect in the new thing (which is absurd in relation to human nature) that man shuts off himself against this freedom. In it he prefers a being from and by and in and for himself to togetherness with God as his eternal Counterpart, and makes God the origin of this self-inflated and self-enclosed being. In it he thus fabricates his God out of the compulsion and impulsion to this being, and therefore his own caprice. In the name of this reflection he chooses himself as the basis from which he comes, and therefore accepts the whole burden and responsibility for his help and preservation, for the securing and sheltering of his being. He also makes himself his goal, and therefore finds no place for thanksgiving, responsibility, obedience and calling upon God, but transposes them into a desire and longing and striving and transcending in which he spreads himself with some degree of coarse or refined appetite and more or less skill and consistency in the sensual and spiritual world, using it and making it serviceable to himself, as his environment, as that which satisfies his needs, as a place to sow and reap, as his sphere of work, or it may be only as his gymnasium and playground. *Eros* is love which is wholly claim, wholly the desire to control, wholly the actual attempt to control, in relation to God. This is inevitable, seeing it is the love in which the one who loves and the object of love are one and the same, so that from first to last it is self-love. In both cases we are dealing with love, even with the love of God, although in very different senses. In both cases it is love in relation to that which is essential to man, to that which is peculiar to him in his nature as it is formed and fashioned by God. The difference is that *agape* (irrespective of its strength or weakness) corresponds to this nature, and *eros* (irrespective of its form or intensity) contradicts it. The one transcends it ; the other falls short of it. It will always be the case in practice that human nature orientated on God, and therefore *agape* as its correspondence, will be recognisable even in the negative of the most radical form of the contradiction and therefore of *eros* ; and on the other hand that the most perfect form of the correspondence, and therefore *agape*, will reflect to some extent the contradiction, and therefore *eros*, in and with human nat᾿re. Yet the distinction, and the necessity of deciding, between them is perfectly clear from that which they have conceptually in common, and in the way in which they accompany one another in practice.

The starting-point for a seventh and final step is that it is essential and natural to man not only to be with God but also, on the horizontal level and in analogy with this togetherness with God, to be with his fellow-man : not in isolation ; not in opposition or neutrality to this other ; not united with him in a subsequent relationship ; but bound to him basically and from the very first ; directed, that is, to the I-Thou encounter, in which there can be no I without the Thou, no man without the fellow-man, any more than there can be any man without God. He is a man as he sees the other man and is seen by him ; as he hears him and speaks with him ; as he assists him and receives his assistance. He is a man as he is free to do this ; as he can be a comrade and companion and fellow to the other, not under constraint, but voluntarily (cf. *C.D.*, III, 2, § 45, 2). In this respect too the nature of man is immutable, quite independently of his history. But in this respect too, in indissoluble relationship with his decision in the connexion with God, it is decided in the history and life-act of man whether and how far he is true or untrue, in correspondence or contradiction, to his nature, to his humanity in this special sense, and therefore to himself. And in this connexion too *agape* means correspondence and *eros* contradiction. In *agape*-love the essential fellow-humanity of man is respected. For the one who loves in this way there can be no opposition or neutrality in relation to the other. In his love there takes place the encounter of I and Thou, the open perception of the other and self-disclosure to him, conversation with him, the offering and receiving of assistance, and all this with joy. In this respect too the real man is at work in *agape*, not merely expressing but transcending his nature. In this respect too *agape* means self-giving : not the losing of oneself in the other, which would bring us back into the sphere of *eros* ; but identification with his interests in utter independence of the question of his attractiveness, of what he has to offer, of the reciprocity of the relationship, or repayment in the form of a similar self-giving. In *agape*-love a man gives himself to the other with no expectation of a return, in a pure venture, even at the risk of ingratitude, of his refusal to make a response of love, which would be a denial of his humanity. He loves the other because he is this other, his brother. But as the one who loves in this way sees a brother in his fellow, and treats him as such, he also honours him as a man. While *agape* transcends humanity, the man who loves in this way is genuinely human ; he gives a true expression to human nature ; he is a real man. The same cannot be said of *eros*-love. In most cases this does, of course, consist in an address to one's fellow, and perhaps with considerable warmth and intensity. But as in relation to God, so also to his fellow, the man who loves erotically is not really thinking of the other but of himself. His fellow is envisaged only as an expected

increase and gain for his own existence, as an acquisition, a booty, a
prey, to be used by him in the pursuance of some purpose. In these
circumstances how can he really be a comrade, companion and fellow ?
How can he see him openly, or disclose himself to him ? How can he
enter into honest conversation with him ? How can he assist him
and receive his assistance ? It is only in semblance and not in truth
that the one who loves erotically is well-disposed to him. As he grasps
at him, he has already let him fall and rejected him. And it is inevitable that sooner or later he will do this openly. In the duality apparently sought and found by the one who loves erotically there lurks
the isolation which he has never really left and in which he will finally
remain. Erotic love is a denial of humanity. To be sure, it is love ;
love for man ; an action in relationship, in this relationship, to humanity. Hence humanity and to that extent *agape* may be negatively
seen in it, and it may be confessed in this perverted form ; just as
agape-love as the act of man in his human nature is never so pure as
not to betray in some way the proximity of the *eros*-love which is its
opposite. Yet the two loves are still different—basically different in
their relationship to humanity. And since they have this common
point of departure from which they both come, it will always be the
case that man can only choose between *eros* and *agape*.

The problem of Christian love had to be developed with this
attempted clarification of its relationship to that very different love.
This was essential, and its antithesis to that different love had to be
clearly stated. Occasionally we shall have to touch on it again in
what we have to say further concerning Christian love. But it can
have thematic significance only in this introduction. Christian love
lives in this antithesis, but not by it. And a presentation of Christian
love cannot live by this antithesis, or be confined to a development
of this problem. " Love envieth not ; love vaunteth not itself, is not
puffed up " (1 Cor. 13⁴)—even in its relationship with erotic love.
How it disavows itself if it regards it as its only greatness to be different
from this love, not to be " as this publican," to nourish itself constantly on this opposition ! It is a strangely loveless love which is
content with that. Above all, it does not need to insist rigidly on this
antithesis. As we have seen, it comes from human nature, like that
other love. But it does not have its basis in it. It does not derive
from it—any more than that other love. Hence *eros*-love is not a
kind of twin sister whom it would have rejected, if possible, in the
nature of man as their common womb, and with whom it must necessarily be in conflict to maintain itself as Christian. On the contrary,
it is a new thing in face of human nature. It is not posited in it. It
is a contingent occurrence in relation to it. It merely happens to
man as he loves in this sense. Even of that other love we have to
say that it is not posited in human nature, but takes place contingently
and in relation to it. But how different the two loves are in the way

in which they come to man ! The difference is not merely that the one, as we have seen, corresponds to human nature and the other contradicts it. The primary and decisive difference—and here we must anticipate—is that it is in the quickening power of the Holy Spirit, and therefore in a new act of God who is man's Creator and Lord, that in his life-act and individual actions a man can actually love in the Christian sense and thus be a true man in this positive way ; whereas the new thing about *eros*-love can consist only in the inconceivable and absurd and materially impossible fact that man arbitrarily entangles himself in a contradiction of his own creaturely nature, of himself, and therefore of God and his neighbour. This means that Christian love—and the seriousness of the antithesis and severity of the conflict between it and *eros*-love must not conceal or cause us to overlook the fact—does not have in the latter a kind of equal partner, but stands to it, in spite of all its pretence and posturing of dignity and power, in a relationship of absolute and radical superiority. How can there be any equality between the *agape*-love which is grounded in God's Yes and the *eros*-love which is grounded in man's No ? Where Christian love arises, the other can only sink to the ground. When the sun arises, the shadows and mists in the valleys can only yield and disperse. Hence Christian love does not need to measure itself by *eros*-love, or to find strength and satisfaction in its difference from it. It lives its own life as the love which is true because it is grounded in God's love for man and not in man's self-love. It does so in antithesis to that other. But it does so as the love which is superior and triumphant in this antithesis. It is not, therefore, forced to insist on this antithesis.

I say this in face of the rigidity with which A. Nygren constantly underlines the antithesis between *eros* and *agape*. But I say it also in face of S. Kierkegaard's stimulating exposition of the " life and rule of love." If only the final impression left by this book were not that of the detective skill with which non-Christian love is tracked down to its last hiding-place, examined, shown to be worthless and haled before the judge ! If only it were not so rarely that in its preaching of the Law and judgment we come across profound and beautiful reflections on the Christian love which is so relentlessly marked off from its opposite ! We must be grateful for the precision with which this distinction is made, for we ourselves have just been trying to make clear the merciless severity of the antithesis. But it is disturbing to see from the example of Kierkegaard how easily reflection on this antithesis can be deflected from Christian love and find itself rivetted even by way of opposition (and the more firmly because inimically) to erotic love. It is even more disturbing to see how easily in reflection and discussion of this aspect pure zeal can result in a disregard or obscuration of the fact that Christian and this other love do not finally confront each other in equal dignity and power (or unequal in favour of the latter), but that in *agape* we have to do with a superior and triumphant human action, and in *eros* with one which is inferior and already routed—and this for the simple reason that the former has its basis in the good being and action of God, and the latter in the corruption of man. For all our acuteness of definition, are we not perhaps speaking of something other than Christian love (perhaps of the *eros* with which we think we can lay hold of *agape* !), so long as we oppose the love which lives by God's grace to human and sinful love only in the final form of Law, of the sum of a demand, and not primarily and ultimately and decisively as the Gospel of the kingdom and lordship of God ?

We will establish and explain this in what follows. But is not this a primary insight upon which we can and must and should agree ? Since *agape* is from God—as we shall see in the next sub-section—and *eros* from self-contradictory man, is it not one of the things which make comparison impossible that the former is absolutely superior to the latter, not only in dignity, but also in power ? *Eros* can only flee and perish and cease, and with it the whole world which is dominated and impelled and built up and characterised by it. But love, *agape*, never fails (1 Cor. 13[8]). With that which issues from it (as it does from God), it is imperishable even in the midst of a world which perishes.

For this reason, our final word can and must be conciliatory as we look back on our development of the problem of Christian love and therefore of its antithesis to *eros*. There can be no question of mediation, or of a weakening of the antithesis. But we can speak a word of reconciliation, not in respect of *eros*, but in respect of erotic man contradicting himself and shunning and opposing God and his neighbour. *Agape* cannot change into *eros*, or *eros* into *agape*. The one love cannot, then, be interpreted as the other. But if this is impossible, it is even more impossible that God should change into, or be interpreted as, another God who is no longer the God of man, even of the man who loves erotically ; and that this man should cease to be man, and therefore the creature elected and willed and fashioned by God, and therefore in the hands of God even in his corruption. But if he is in the hands of God, even erotic man must and will be affirmed in and with the love which is from God—Christian love. His erotic love will not be affirmed. But he himself will be affirmed as the man which he does not cease to be even as he loves erotically—God's man. And this affirmation proclaims his reconciliation ; the fact that God has loved, and loves, and will love even him. How can we love as Christians if we forget this, if we do not hold out this affirmation, this proclamation, even to the one who loves erotically ? How we judge ourselves —for we, too, love erotically—if we withhold this affirmation from the heathen who in contrast know no other love ! But if we love as Christians, and therefore with the love which is from God, and therefore in self-giving to God and our fellows, then in respect of the man who loves erotically our love must consist wholly and utterly in this affirmation : in the declaration that he, too, is loved by God and therefore in His hands ; that overlooking his erotic love God in His genuine, non-self-seeking love is the One who in His self-giving wills to be God only as his God, God for him, and to be majestic, all-powerful and glorious as such. If Christian love does not make this declaration to the non-Christian, it is not Christian love. It stops where the love of God, from which it derives, does not stop. And in so doing it parts company with the love of God. If a Christian believes, as he can and should, that he himself is not separated from the love of God by the fact that he loves erotically, he cannot refuse this declaration to the fellow-man whom he thinks he sees wholly entangled in the bands of *eros*-love.

The concrete content of this declaration, and therefore of the conciliatory word with which we must close our consideration of the antithesis between *agape* and *eros*, is to the effect that God simply espouses the cause of man, and therefore even the man who loves erotically. But this means that he understands him—far better than he understands himself. He cares for him—far better than he cares, or can care, for himself. This is how it is when he calls him out of the kingdom of *eros* and into the kingdom of His love, which consists in the act of self-giving and not in a campaign of aggression. And this is how it must be between the Christian and the non-Christian ; the man who loves erotically. It is not a question of subjecting man to an alien, cold and gloomy law, in the following of which he will be afraid of falling short, and can expect only to be invaded and disarmed and oppressed and destroyed, so that he has every reason to try to evade it. There is no reason for this. For it is a matter of his liberation when God loves him—even him—in spite of his corruption, and calls him to decision in favour of *agape* against *eros*. This call is a message of light and not darkness, of promise and not threat, of joy and not sorrow. What is it, then, that the man who loves erotically wills and desires and seeks and strives after ? What is it that he would achieve and maintain ? We have seen that in the circle in which he turns to the natural and spiritual world, to God and his fellow-man, it is first and last himself. May he not, then, be himself ? Will God refuse him this ? Can the God who has created him as he is refuse it ? Most certainly not. The truth is that he can never in all eternity find himself, his being as this self in the world before God and among his fellows, but, chasing his own shadow, can and will only lose it in all eternity, so long as he tries to will and desire and seek and strive after and achieve and maintain himself as the erotic man thinks it necessary to do. The love which is from God, the Christian love in which man can respond to the love of God, is his liberation from this supposed necessity, his dispensation from this forward-seeking in need and desire, his release from the obligation of this chase in which he is both the hunter and the hunted and which for this reason can only be utterly futile. Man can cease from this self-willing, and therefore from all the frenzied activity in which he can seek, yet never find, but only lose himself. For if the only meaning of life is that man must seek himself to find himself, he can only lose himself in this seeking, and life is meaningless. Christian love is

his deliverance because the one who loves as a Christian gives up
trying to save himself, to be his own deliverer. In Christian love a
man can finally leave that circle of destruction, which is in the true
sense a vicious circle. And not become himself? Quite the contrary!
It is only in this way that he can and will become himself. To renounce
that seeking, to leave that circle, is indeed a *conditio sine qua non* of
Christian love. But positively this love is man's self-giving to God
(not for what He can give, nor for the sake of some purpose that can
be achieved with His help, but for God Himself), and his self-giving
to his fellow (again, not for what he can give, nor for the sake of some
purpose, but for the man himself). As this self-giving, the Christian
love which is from God is man's response to God's own love. It is in
this way that God loves man. He does not seek Himself, let alone
anything for Himself, but simply man, man as he is and as such, man
himself. And God does not in any sense fall short of Himself when
He loves in this way. In this self-giving to man He is God in all His
freedom and glory. If the love of man, as his response to the fact
that God loves him in this way, itself consists in his self-giving, this
certainly means that there can be no more self-love, no more desiring
and seeking the freedom and glory of the self. But why, and how far,
is this really the case? Simply because he has already found himself
in great freedom and glory. What he cannot win by desiring and
seeking, he has already attained, not in the power of his renunciation,
but in the power of the self-giving in which he may respond to the
love of God. He *himself* is the one who is loved by God. He *himself*
is the one to whom God has given Himself in His Son, and gives
Himself as He gives him His Holy Spirit. He is cut off from *eros*-love,
and taken out of that circle, by the fact that, loving as a Christian,
he is already at the place which he was vainly trying to reach in the
Icarus-flight and self-assertion of *eros*-love. There is no further point
in erotic love. *Eros* is made superfluous by the *agape* in which man
may find himself and therefore has no more need to seek himself. He
himself discovers himself to be secure in his response to the love of
God.

It is obvious that at this point a second and theoretically more dangerous
aberration would be worse than the first. I cannot try to love as a Christian
in order to attain the goal and end which escapes me as one who loves erotically.
An *ut finale* necessarily means a relapse into *eros*-love. The only valid *ut* is the
radiant *ut consecutivum*. But this is indeed valid, and it makes any such relapse
quite impossible. For in Christian love I am already at the goal. I have found
myself, and cannot therefore lose myself by trying to love as a Christian in
order to come to myself.

I have only to love continually as a Christian, and therefore without
regard or purpose for myself, in self-giving to God and my fellows, and
I will come to myself and be myself. This is what we are told in the
saying in Mk. 8[35], which speaks about the saving and losing and the

losing and saving of life ; and also in the saying in Mt. 6³³, which tells us that if we seek first the kingdom of God and His righteousness all other things are added to us. These sayings are not Law but Gospel. They describe the *agape* which conquers *eros* by making it pointless and superfluous. They describe the man who loves as a Christian as already at the goal which the man who loves erotically—poor dupe— wants to reach but never can or will reach in erotic love. They make no demand. They take nothing away. They do not blame or judge. They merely show him that he is understood and accepted and received by God—not his erotic love, but he himself. He may save himself and find himself and be himself. But this is something which is given, which comes, as he loses his life, as he renounces his whole self-seeking —" for my sake and the Gospel's "—so that he is saved and has found himself already.

This is the concrete content of the declaration which the man who loves as a Christian owes to the other who does not seem to do so. It is with this declaration that the Christian encounters the heathen. It is this that he may—and only this that he can—say to himself, seeing that he too loves with erotic as well as Christian love and is to that extent a heathen. He encounters others as one who holds to this truth and lives joyfully in this conquest of *eros* by *agape*. In his very existence, then, he speaks the reconciling word in this antithesis. He does not merely discuss the problem of Christian love. He also lives it. And he lives it as it is meant to be lived, and in the last resort can only be lived.

2. THE BASIS OF LOVE

We could not expound the problem of Christian love without touch-ing finally on the theme to which we must now give specific attention —that of its basis. In the explanation of love the question of its basis has the same function as that of the object in the explanation of faith. The Christian believes *in*, and it is from this *in*, from the description of that which encounters him as a believer, of that which he is given and receives and apprehends in faith, that there proceeds (cf. *C.D.*, IV, 1, § 63) everything that has to be thought and said in the definition of the act of the Christian life as the act of faith. But the Christian loves *because*, and it is as he is confronted and impelled by this definite basis that there takes place his self-giving.

We might substitute the word " origin " for " basis." But " origin " can easily give rise to the idea of an identity between what takes place where the Christian act derives and is set in motion and what takes place in and with the act itself ; the idea of a stream in which the same self-giving takes place at two different points. But this understanding is very wide of the mark. There is a strict and conditioning connexion and similarity between what takes place at the two points, and the Bible uses the same word " love " to describe both of them. But the fact that there is similarity does not mean that there is identity. The first and evocative love is not the same as the love which is evoked. The relationship between them is that of a word and answer, of permission and the use made of it, of command and obedience ; not of the beginning and continuation of one and the same movement. In order not to obscure this difference, it is better to use the term " basis," which preserves the distance between the two.

At the climax of his book *Eros und Agape* (Vol. II, p. 555 f.), A. Nygren has the following train of thought under the heading : " The Christian as the Channel of God's Downstreaming Love." Not man, but God Himself, is the subject of Christian love. But He is so in such a way that divine love uses the Christian as its tool and instrument. The Christian receives the love of God in faith, and in love he passes it on to his neighbour. Christian love is " as it were a continuation and prolongation of the love of God." It is thus " through and through a divine work." It is the view of Luther (*W.A.*, 10¹, 1, 100, 9) that the Christian is set between God and his neighbour as an " instrument " " which receives from above and gives out below, like a vessel or pipe through which the stream of divine bounty should flow unceasingly to others." Now, with due respect to Luther, this is the view which I must set aside at the very outset and carefully avoid in all my future deliberations. Have we been released from *eros* only to say the more pietistically about *agape* that which effaces all clear contours and destroys all healthy distances ? It seems to me that if we are to say anything really worth while at this point we must say much less than this.

Love is a free action : the self-giving of one to another without interest, intention or goal ; the spontaneous self-giving of the one to the other just because the other is there and confronts him. It is not an action which has no ground or basis. The man engaged in it, the Christian, exists as and because God is his basis, and has disclosed Himself to him, and is known by him, as such. He loves on this basis in God, as one who is called and impelled by God to do so by the fact that He has disclosed Himself and is known as the One who first loves, and first loves *him*, in the glory and majesty of His divine essence. It is for this reason, in response to the Word in which God loves him and tells him that He loves him, in correspondence to it, that the Christian may and must and will also love. He does not do so as if he were himself God, or a second God. But he loves because God loves, and loves him ; because he belongs to God ; because he would not be a man without God and without being related to Him ; and because this is not concealed from him, but revealed in the love in which God has turned to him. He is called to follow as a man the movement in which God Himself is engaged ; to do as a man, and therefore in the form of a reflection or analogy, that which God does originally and properly. He does this as he loves—freely, and yet not without reason, but with good reason. This good ground for his love in the love of God thus precedes his love, quite irrespective of whether or not he follows, or of the perfection or imperfection with which he does so. It is there as an active summons. It is not a silent and static basis, but an eloquent and dynamic. And it is so in all the glory and majesty of the divine essence. It is so at all times and in all circumstances, without waiting for response and correspondence on the part of man, or being referred to them. Even the greatest refusal of human love does not mean that this good reason will be withheld. There can be no cessation of its summons and impulsion. Man must and may always receive it. And he may always come back to the fact that God loves, and loves him, to find that he for his part is set in motion by this first and divine love, following it with his human love. Hence love (and we are thinking now of the act of Christian love) has a basis —a good and powerful basis—which determines and evokes and impels it, from which it derives and may and will always derive as a human action. This basis is the love of God whose omnipotently enlightening and impelling action it may follow, as a secondary love following the primary.

But the more precise delimitation is inescapable that it never can or will precede the divine love. It never can or will begin of and with itself, or continue of itself. In both its inception and progress it stands in absolute need of this basis. In no element or form can it be a primary love, but only a secondary following the primary. It could not take place, or be maintained, apart from the summons and impulsion of the latter. For it is only the action of man confronted by God, whereas the latter is the action of God. Its dependence on this action does not violate its character as a spontaneous and responsible human action ; its character as decision. God and man, the one as Creator and the other as His creature, do not exist on the same level. There is no rivalry between the divine freedom and the human. Thus the dependence of man's action on God's does not involve any weakening, alteration or finally destruction of its freedom and its character as decision. That human love is dependent on divine love means that in its very freedom it can take place only on the basis of the latter, as a human response to the Word spoken in the love of God. If God did not love originally and properly, and if He did not love man, how could there be any reflection or analogy of His love in the love of man ? Man never can or will take the initiative in love. He can and will love only because God has first loved, and loves, him. And if he loves for this reason, and therefore secondarily, this does not mean—the relationship is irreversible—that there arises any dependence of the divine love on his love, or determination of the divine action by his action. The love of God is the basis for that of man, but the love of man is never a basis for that of God. The love of God always takes precedence. It always has the character of grace, and that of man the character of gratitude. There always remains a great difference in the order, nature and significance of divine and human love. The latter cannot repeat or represent the former. It cannot attain equality with it. It can only follow it and therefore be analogous to it. It can only correspond to it as a likeness and copy. Even in its highest forms human love always and in every respect needs to be called and impelled by the love of God. As love takes place from above, it can and may and must do so below, on the creaturely level which is the sphere of human sloth and the ensuing misery. But it is only as it takes place from above that this can and may and must be the case. The great saying of 1 Jn. 4⁷—that " love is of God "—is true in this sense.

To control the positive and limiting assertion with which we have begun, it will be helpful to consider some of the statements made in the context of this saying. In the same verse it serves as a basis for the exhortation : " Let us love one another." How can the Christians addressed come to do this ? In this passage we cannot explain the fact that they are called ἀγαπητοί merely as a convention of rhetoric. Those who are exhorted to love are already loved (above all by God), and in respect of what they are to do they are urged and claimed on this basis. The fact that they are loved (and therefore the possibility and necessity of the exhortation to mutual love) is established by the saying ὅτι ἡ ἀγάπη ἐκ θεοῦ ἐστιν. In the context this means quite concretely that the love to which I exhort you is " of God." Nothing strange is demanded by this exhortation, nor attained if it is fulfilled. The man who loves does so merely, but necessarily, because it comes to him " of God " to do so. As he loves, he testifies that this is the case ; that he is " born of God," to use the later phrase ; that he is a child who receives and takes of the fulness of his Father as he knows God to be his Father and himself to be His child, to whom there naturally belongs, and must therefore accrue, that which belongs to his Father. As against this, he who does not love (v. 8) bears witness to the terrible fact that he has not known God, and therefore does not know and understand that God is love, and that what comes to him from God is again love. We will not introduce at this point the equation ὁ θεὸς ἀγάπη ἐστίν, or its most important expansion in v. 9. But v. 10 is worth noting in the general explanation of the ἐκ θεοῦ which is our present purpose : " Herein is love (ἐν τούτῳ ἐστὶν ἡ ἀγάπη), not that we loved God, but that he loved us." So, too, are v. 11 : " Beloved, if God so loved us, we ought also to love one another," and v. 19 : " We love him (ἡμεῖς ἀγαπῶμεν), because αὐτὸς πρῶτος ἠγάπησεν ἡμᾶς, he first loved us." (There is a clear parallel in 1 Cor. 8³, where we are told that " if any man love God, the same is known of him.") All these statements speak of divine and human love ; of the priority of divine love ; of the determination of human love by divine ; of the irreversibility of the relationship ; but also of the necessity with which it comes about " of God," in virtue of the precedence of His love, that there follows a corresponding human love. No one can love except " of God," in virtue of the preceding love of God, as one who is already loved by Him. But " of God," in virtue of the preceding love of God, as one who is already loved by Him, man too can and may and must and will love.

In order that the basis of love (our love) may be established conceptually, as is only proper in dogmatics, we must begin our description of it in the transcendent sphere where it has its primary and ultimate foundation, namely, in the being and nature of God Himself. The authority with which God calls us to love, and the power with which He impels us to do so, have a specific force. This consists in the fact that they are the authority and power of the One who does not begin to love only when He loves us, but who loves in the very fact that He is and is in the very fact that He loves. This is what gives weight to the love with which He loves us and the Word and act by which He impels us to love in return (cf. *C.D.*, II, 1, § 28, 2). Even in Himself God is God only as One who loves. In this respect there is a real element of truth in the popular German designation recently suspected and decried by stricter theologians. God is *per se " der liebe Gott."* We say of Him, of His divine being and essence, of God Himself, that which it is possible and right and necessary and true to say—and we say it without making the reservation that our knowledge is limited, and thus toying with the question whether deep down, in a secret basis of His Godhead, He may not be very different—when we say that He is the One who loves in the freedom of His divine being, or that He loves and in this way exercises the freedom of His divine being. The statements " God is " and " God loves " are synonymous. They explain and confirm one another. It is in this way, in this identity of being and love, that God reveals Himself to us as He loves us. He reveals Himself as the One who, even though He did not love us and were not revealed to us, even though we did not exist at all, still loves in and for Himself as surely as He is and is God ; who loves us by reason and in consequence of the fact that He is the One who loves in His freedom in and for Himself, and is God as such. It is only of God that it can be said that He is in the fact that He loves and loves in the fact that He is. The same cannot be said of the Christian— even the perfect Christian—who is only a creature summoned and impelled to love by the love of God. But it must be said of God. And it means that God loves, and that in the fact that He does so He is the origin and sum of all true being and therefore of all true good ; the *summum esse* as the *summum bonum.* God loves, and in the fact that He does so He is worthy to be loved, and is actually loved prior to and in independence of any response of love on the part of the creature. He is both the One who loves and the One who is loved even though there were no creature for Him to love and to love Him in return. God loves, and the purpose of His being is to do this. As He loves, He fulfils His purpose, in accordance with which all His intentions regarding a being distinct from His own can be actualised only as purposes of His love. God loves, and to do so He does not need any being distinct from His own as the object of His love. If He loves the world and us, this is a free overflowing of the love in which He is and is God and with which He is not content, although He might be, since neither the world nor ourselves are indispensable to His love and therefore to His being. Thus the love of God is free, majestic, eternal love. And self-grounding and self-grounded, as it is addressed and revealed to us as eternal love, as it precedes our love in this majesty, it is the firm basis of our love. It is the eternal love in whose free and non-obligatory overflowing we are loved. With the authority and power of this love it is revealed to us that we are loved. It is God Himself in all the depths of His deity who summons and impels us to love. On this basis there can be no question of parity between our love and His.   We are loved with eternal love, but it can come to us only to love in time.   Yet our temporal love, as it must take place in time on this eternal basis, will take place in similarity to what God is in Himself as He proves to us.   For all the distance there will thus be supremely real fellowship with God : not merely with an event inaugurated by God ; but first and last with God Himself.   More will have to be said about the basis of love.   But everything that characterises and distinguishes this basis derives from the transcendent height that it is the basis which consists in the being and nature of God.

What we have been discussing is the equation of 1 Jn. 4⁸ and ¹⁶ : ὁ θεὸς ἀγάπη ἐστίν.   It is an ill-considered judgment that in this statement we do not have a genuine equation but only a predication of the first term by the second. For what is meant by this " only " ?   If we are dealing with God—the One whom the Bible calls God—every quality predicated of God, as the description of a specific self-exposition of the predicated Subject, can only denote God Himself.   And in each instance it can only denote God Himself in the perfection of His being : in scholastic parlance, not a mere *accidens*, but the *substantia* or *essentia* of God ; this substance or essence in a specific self-exposition, but in its totality.   If for the author of 1 John ἀγάπη is a predicate of ὁ θεός, the two are equated in such a way that—presupposing that the content of the terms remains the same—we can reverse the statement and say that love is God. The context shows that this was the mind of the author.   In v. 8 he calls the man who does not love one who does not know God, whereas in v. 7 he says of the man who loves that he does know God.   Love presupposes knowledge of God, and knowledge of God results in love.   The reason why this is the case is given in v. 8b : " God is love."   To know Him is to know His love as that in which He is and is God.   Hence it is love again (this time the corresponding love of God) which according to v. 7b comes to man " of God."   The continuation in v. 9, which speaks of the revelation of God's love in the sending of the Son, explains how this love is known, and therefore how God is known, and therefore how man may and should love in the realisation of this knowledge.   But what is revealed in this revelation and known in this knowledge is that which is formulated in v. 8b, namely, the being of God which is that of the One who first and as such is love, and by which the being of the man who knows God in this revelation must be directed.   The more immediate context in which the formula recurs in v. 16 is as follows.   As in v. 7 there is no beginning, so (in v. 12 f.) there is no continuation, permanence (μένειν) or finally completion (τελειοῦσθαι) of the Christian existence in fellowship with God where the love of God which is the basis of this continuance and completion does not find expression in our love for the brethren.   This permanence comes from the love of God (v. 12 f.), as does also, in the completion of its work, the fearless confidence (v. 17 f.) with which the Christian may stand in the day of judgment.   According to v. 16 this continuance and completion are guaranteed absolutely by the fact that the love which comes in God's act rests in and derives from the being of God as the One who loves eternally, and is thus an enduring love.   But in this majesty (v. 19 f.) it always summons the Christian to love both the invisible God and, in concrete demonstration of the genuineness of his love, the visible brother.

We are not guilty of arbitrary speculation when we begin our description of the basis of Christian love in the being and nature of God Himself.   The equation of the statements " God is " and " God loves " (the Johannine " God is love ") is merely the most succinct formula

to describe the reality in and as which God declares Himself according
to the implicit witness of the Old Testament and the explicit witness
of the New. The One who there spoke to man and still speaks to us,
and in so doing discloses His own being and nature, is not an isolated
monad which as such cannot love, or can love only itself, so that
love is fundamentally alien to it, and it is only casually (not internally
but externally) that it does also love. On the contrary, He is revealed
to us as first existing in Himself as the One who loves. For He does
not exist only in one mode. He exists in the mode of the Father and
the Son. And He exists—this is the decisive point in the present
context—in the mode of the Spirit who proceeds from the Father and
the Son, who is common to the Father and the Son, and who unites
the Father and the Son. In this triunity of His essence God loves
both as and before He loves us ; both as and before He calls us to
love. In this triunity of His essence God is eternal love. In Himself
He is both the One and the Other. And He is this, not in any reciprocal
self-seeking, indifference, neutrality or even enmity, but in the self-
giving of the Father to the Son and the Son to the Father which is
accomplished in the fact that He is not merely the Father and the
Son but also the Holy Spirit, and therefore as the Father is wholly
for the Son, and as the Son wholly for the Father. In virtue of His
trinitarian essence God is free and sovereign and competent and powerful to love us. He can and may and must and will love us. He does
in fact love us. And He makes Himself the basis of our love. In so
doing, He does not place us merely in an external and casual fellowship with Himself, but in an internal and essential fellowship in which
our existence cannot continue to be alien to His but may become and
be analogous. In virtue of His trinitarian essence the life and rule of
love is the most inward and proper life and rule of God. It is on this
ground that He loves us. And it is on this ground that, as He declares
His love to us, it is decided that to His glory and our salvation the
life and rule of love is also our determination—a determination which
on this ground is truly eternal.

The equation of 1 Jn. 4⁸, ¹⁶ : " God is love," is a peculiarity of the Johannine
witness. So, too, is that of Jn. 4²⁴ : " God is Spirit." The two explain one
another. To say " love " in the Johannine sense is to say " Spirit "—the Spirit
in whom God is wholly the Father of the Son and wholly the Son of the Father
and as such the One who first loves us. And to say " Spirit " in the Johannine
sense is to say " love "—the love which as and even before God loves us is the
love in which as the Father He loves the Son and as the Son the Father. It is
again in John's Gospel that this eternity of the basis of Christian love in the
Trinity is expressly indicated : " The Father loveth the Son, and hath given
(this is His eternal love, His fatherly and divine self-giving) all things (no less
than His whole divine worth, His whole divine sovereignty and power over all
things) into his hand " (Jn. 3³⁵, cf. 5²⁰). He has given Him His glory (Jn. 17²⁴)
as and because He loved Him from the foundation of the world. But this love
of the Father for the Son is described (Jn. 10¹⁷) as an answer to the fact that the
Son (this is His eternal love, His self-giving) staked Himself, His life, in obedience

to the Father, to receive it again in so doing. And it is to be revealed to the world (Jn. 14³¹) that He loves the Father according to whose commission He acts. He abides in the love of the Father (15¹⁰—the genitive is to be taken both subjectively and objectively) so that He is to be obedient to the Father His own are required only to abide in His love. For He loves them as the One who is loved by the Father and loves Him in return (Jn. 15⁹). But the same is true of the Father (and is also to be declared to the world). He loves them with the same eternal love with which He loves the Son (Jn. 17²³). It is from the fact that the Son loves them as the One who loves the Father and loves Him in return ; that the Father loves them with the same love with which He loves the Son ; and that they are free to love the Son (Jn. 14¹⁵· ²¹ᶠ·, 16²⁷) ; that the new commandment given them by the Son, i.e., to love one another (Jn. 13³⁴), derives its seriousness and force.

The basis of love in God Himself is nowhere else so explicitly denoted and explained as in John. But there is an indication of it, naturally without the trinitarian development, in Hos. 11⁸ᶠ· : " How shall I give thee up, Ephraim ? how shall I deliver thee, Israel ? how shall I make thee as Admah ? how shall I set thee as Zeboim ? mine heart is turned within me, my pityings are kindled together. I will not execute the fierceness of mine anger, I will not return to destroy Ephraim : for I am God, and not man ; the Holy One in the midst of thee, and not a destroyer." What is the meaning of this inability of God, of his pityings, of the holiness in which He will not forsake His mercy to an ungrateful people, because He is God and not man ? Does it not signify that the love with which He loved this people in its youth and called His son out of Egypt (11¹) was a love which according to the witness of this prophet belonged integrally to His essence, so that He could deny it only as He denied His very nature as God ? Again, in Jer. 31³ we are told expressly that Yahweh loved Israel with an everlasting love, and that " therefore with lovingkindness have I drawn thee," reminding us of the " cords of grace " and " bands of love " of Hos. 11⁴. And quite apart from these isolated sayings we have to ask whether it was mere accident, a casual choice with no inner ground or basis, that the God of the Old Testament elected to be the God of the covenant—a pure and free covenant of grace—with Israel, compromising Himself with this people in a history which begins so inconspicuously and continues and ends so ingloriously. But if this was not a casual or capricious choice, who and what was this God ? The eternally unmoved deity of Plato and Aristotle would never have compromised itself with this history or drawn this people to it. How could it ? And how could it have loved it with an everlasting love and been the Godhead in this love ? This would involve a flagrant self-contradiction. There is no self-giving in this deity. It cannot, then, summon or impel to self-giving. It can be loved only with that demanding love, with self-love, erotically. The God of the Old Testament, however, can obviously be loved only because He is not merely the first to exercise love but the One who loves primarily and eternally, and as such the self-moved and therefore the living God, who as such calls for an analogous and therefore a pure and free self-giving.

When we come to the New Testament, we cannot say that even the trinitarian development of the basis is absent except in the Johannine writings. For what does it mean when we are told in Col. 1¹²ᶠ· that the Father has set us in the kingdom of " the Son of his love " ; the same Son who is described in v. 15 f. as " the firstborn of all creation," in whom, by whom and to whom all things in heaven and earth were created, who was before all things and in whom all things consist ? That He became the Son of the Father's love *a posteriori*, for the sake of our deliverance from the power of darkness, is excluded by this description. No, it is in the One who was already the Beloved (ἐν τῷ ἠγαπημένῳ) that God showed us this grace (Eph. 1⁶). But if He is this already, love—the love between the Father and the Son—is here too ascribed to the eternal God as such as an essential determination. References are made to the same basis, to the same inner movement in which it is the basis of love, in the accounts of His baptism (Mk. 1[11] and par.) and transfiguration (Mk. 9[7] and par.) in which Jesus is addressed or designated by the voice from heaven as " my beloved Son (or " elect Son " in Lk. 9[35]) in whom I am well pleased "—a variation of the saying about the παῖς θεοῦ (quoted in Mt. 12[18] from Is. 42[1]) which is considerably heightened in its effect by the introduction of the term υἱός, the words " Hear him " being also added in the transfiguration story. The One baptised on this occasion is confirmed, proclaimed and revealed by God to be the Beloved of the Father : " Thou art," or " This is." He is it already, and therefore as the One He is He is already the object of the divine εὐδοκία. A prophet or apostle is elected in time (even if in his mother's womb), but the servant of God who is His own Son is already elected, His Beloved, the object of His good-pleasure, and enters time as such. And it is as such that He is to be heard by others. With reference to His epiphany others too can be described as ἄνθρωποι εὐδοκίας (Lk. 2[14]), and in Jn. 3[16] it can even be said that God loved the world—in the giving of His only-begotten Son, but with the same eternal love with which He loved the Son. Finally (in relation to the close connexion between the terms " love " and " knowledge ") we may refer to the saying in Mt. 11[27] and Lk. 10[22], which tells us that all things have been delivered to the Son by the Father, that no one knows the Son but the Father, and that no one knows the Father but the Son, and those to whom the Son will reveal Him. Within the structure of the thought and language of the Synoptists this element of pre-Johannine tradition is rather like a foreign body. But whatever may be its origin and age, according to this saying the revelation imparted to the νήπιοι (Mt. 11[25] and Lk. 10[21]) is grounded in a preceding movement in God Himself between the Father and the Son ; in the fact that the Father has already delivered all things to the Son. The saying tells us with what authority and power the Son calls the νήπιοι and enables them to know Him, and (within the appointed limits) to know the Father as the Son knows Him. The very least that we can say is that this saying is a close, exact and illuminating parallel to the Johannine statement about the love of the Father and the Son and those called by the Son. The New Testament as a whole forces us even more than the Old to the question whether it is only casually and externally that the One whom it calls God fulfils the fellowship with man foreshadowed in the Old Testament covenant by humbling Himself so deeply, and exalting man so highly, that He was ready to take the being and nature of man to Himself and to be concealed and revealed as the Lord in the man Jesus of Nazareth. If this act was not casual, if in it He did not estrange Himself from His divine essence, if on the contrary He was supremely true and just towards it, in this act and in His essence He was again the God who cannot in any sense be equated with the unmoved deity of Plato and Aristotle and therefore with a God who is to be loved erotically. In His very essence He was the Father who loves the Son and the Son who loves the Father, and as such, in the communion and reciprocity of this love, as God the Father, Son and Holy Ghost, the God who is self-moved, the living God, the One who loves eternally and as such moves to love.

We will now turn to the question of the basis of love in so far as this is identical with the *opus Dei ad extra*, the act of God's love in His relationship with the world and us men. We can see the force of this act. God Himself loves us. He loves us as He turns to us directly, as the One He is. He does not keep to Himself His being and nature as Father, Son and Holy Spirit—the eternal love which He Himself is. He is not the prisoner of His own Godhead. He has and exercises the freedom to be our God. As the One He is, and without ceasing to be this, but in a supreme revelation and expression of Himself, He goes beyond Himself into the sphere of that which He is not, which is only by Him, which is only His creature. In the love which is only His, and which, one might suppose, can be only in Him, He loves His creature, ourselves, triumphing over every supposition concerning Himself and His deity. When He loves us, what comes on us to our benefit is an inconceivable overflowing of His eternal love which we can only acknowledge, recognise and confess in its actual occurrence. It is no more and no less than that. And as God causes this to come on us to our benefit, He makes Himself the basis of our love. Called and impelled on the basis of His action to us, our Christian love arises and takes place as the human act which answers and corresponds to His act. Only His act can be the basis of ours. And only as it is determined by His can and will ours be the act of Christian love, of the love which gives itself purely and freely. We have thus to gain a full and clear picture of the act of His love before we can speak meaningfully of the act of ours.

What is involved in the act of God's love to us we learn decisively, centrally and comprehensively—in a first survey of the total substance of this act—from the Old Testament witness to the covenant of Yahweh with Israel and the New Testament proclamation of the kingdom, of the lordship of God on earth, which has been inaugurated in the existence of the one man Jesus of Nazareth. God loves us as He establishes and maintains the covenant with us and as He causes His kingdom to come to us. In both cases we have to do with the same reality of the act of God's love. The covenant is the promise of the kingdom. The kingdom is the fulfilment of the covenant. The covenant is God's encounter with man with a view to being man's salvation in His own person. The kingdom is God as man's salvation and therefore the meaning and goal of His encounter with man. The covenant is the divinely inaugurated and directed history of a nation in which His will is at work to unite with all nations and all men, and to unite all nations and all men with Himself. The kingdom is the divinely inaugurated and directed history of a man of this one nation as the representative of all others in which God has united with this One in the accomplishment of His will, and in this One has united all nations and all men with Himself. The single and continuous factor which links these two forms of His act is His self-giving to man, and therefore His love for him, as it is actualised in this willed and completed union. In this act it took place that He made Himself our God and therefore very small, and us His men and therefore very great ; that He humbled Himself to us and exalted us to Himself. This is God's self-giving ; His love. The revelation of God in the work of His Holy Spirit means the revelation of the covenant and the kingdom, the promise and the fulfilment, the will and the accomplishment of God, in their necessary and indissoluble connexion. It means the revelation of the one eternal act in which He has loved, and loves, and will love us in the power of His eternal love. It means the revelation of ourselves as those to whom God has turned in this act, and therefore as those who were and are and will be loved by Him as the One who performs this act. In this act in which He willed to be and became ours, and we were to be and became His, God is the authoritative and powerful basis of the love which is the subject of our present inquiry— love as the human act corresponding to the act of God.

According to the witness of the Old Testament the love of God is wholly an act and therefore not a feeling, disposition, attitude or fixation on the part of Yahweh. He remembers the people of Abraham, Isaac and Jacob captive in a strange land when He makes it His own. He sends Moses to be its leader. He brings it with a strong hand out of Egypt. He delivers it at the Red Sea. He gives it His Law at Horeb as a direction to remain under the lordship of His gracious will. He leads it across Jordan into the land promised to its forefathers. It is not in the revelation of any theory, or the form of any ceremony, but in this action as the God of Israel, in His treatment of Israel as His people, that He establishes the covenant between Himself and Israel, and establishes it as the positive and critical order within which, determined by His action, its history will develop. It is as He does this first and basic thing, and then that which corresponds to it, to and with Israel, that He loves it.

So far as the written records go, Hosea was the first to declare expressly that the action of Yahweh in His covenant with Israel is in every respect and form the action of His love. He did so very graphically by using the picture of a marriage between Yahweh and His people ; and his presentation is all the more impressive because it is set in contrast and connexion with the severest proclamation of judgment. God's action is that of love at the beginning of this relationship : " When Israel was a child, then I loved him, and called my son out of Egypt " (11¹). But it is also that of love in the present which is so seriously jeopardised by its disobedience : " And I will betroth thee unto me for ever ; yea, I will betroth thee unto me in righteousness, and in judgment, and in lovingkindness, and in mercies. I will even betroth thee unto me in faithfulness : and thou shalt know the Lord " (2¹⁹f.). It is also that of love in relation to the future : " I will heal their backsliding, I will love them freely : for mine anger is turned away from him " (14⁴) ; and " Therefore, behold, I will allure her, and bring her into the wilderness, and speak to her heart. And I will give her her vineyards from thence, and the valley of Achor (woe) for a door of hope : and she shall sing there, as in the days of her youth, and as in the day when she came up out of the land of Egypt. And it shall be at that day, saith the Lord, that thou shalt call me " My husband " ; and thou shalt call me no more " My Baal " (2¹⁴f.). The proclamation of the love which Yahweh exercises as a Husband in the covenant with Israel is also a characteristic of the prophecy of Jeremiah. More preponderantly even than Hosea, he describes it as a love which encounters only the ingratitude and infidelity of Israel, and is therefore threatened with extinction. Here, too, it emerges clearly that the loving action of Yahweh can take the form of the most terrible judgment. But we cannot fail to note the positive undertone which rings through a passage like the remarkable soliloquy of Yahweh in Jer. 31²⁰ : " Is Ephraim my dear son ? is he a pleasant child ? for since I spake against him, I do earnestly remember him still ; therefore my bowels are troubled for him ; I will surely have mercy upon him." In Deutero-Isaiah there is again a recollection of God's judgments, but this time the positive note is predominant, and nowhere in the Old Testament do we have more eloquent mention of God's love. It sounds almost like a polemic against the more extreme prophetic utterances of an opposing character when Yahweh flings out the question : " Where is the bill of your mother's divorcement, whom

I have put away ? or which of my creditors is it to whom I have sold you ? " (50[1]). No : " Fear not ; for thou shalt not be ashamed ; neither shalt thou be confounded ; for thou shalt not be put to shame : for thou shalt forget the shame of thy youth, and shalt not remember the reproach of thy widowhood any more. For thy Maker is thine husband ; the Lord of hosts is his name ; and thy Redeemer the Holy One of Israel ; The God of the whole earth shall he be called. For the Lord hath called thee as a woman forsaken and grieved in spirit, and a wife of youth, when thou wast refused, saith thy God. For a small moment have I forsaken thee ; but with great mercies will I gather thee. In a little wrath I hid my face from thee for a moment ; but with everlasting kindness will I have mercy on thee, saith the Lord thy Redeemer " (54[4f.]). And hence the positive pledge : " Thou shalt no more be termed Forsaken ; neither shall thy land any more be termed Desolate : but thou shalt be called My delight, and thy land Married : for the Lord delighteth in thee, and thy land shall be married. For as a young man marrieth a virgin, so shall thy sons marry thee : and as the bridegroom rejoiceth over the bride, so shall thy God rejoice over thee " (62[4f.]). And in a different but no less eloquent image : " Can a woman forget her sucking child, that she should not have compassion on the son of her womb ? yea, they may forget, yet will I not forget thee. Behold, I have graven thee upon the palms of my hands " (49[15f.]). Or again : " Since thou wast precious in my sight, thou hast been honourable, and I have loved thee : therefore will I give men for thee, and people for thy life. Fear not : for I am with thee " (43[4f.]). In the same connexion we might also quote Zech. 2[8] : " For he that toucheth you toucheth the apple of his eye " ; or Hagg. 2[23], where it is said of Zerubbabel that he will be made as the Lord's signet. The other book where there are frequent references to the love of God—not now in relation to the future, as in Deutero-Isaiah, but in relation to the past—is the Book of Deuteronomy. Why it is that Yahweh has inclined His heart to Israel, the smallest of all peoples, and elected it ? There is only one reason. It is " because the Lord loved you, and because he would keep the oath which he had sworn unto your fathers " that He " hath brought you out with a mighty hand . . ." (Deut. 7[8]). Again and again we read that it is only " because he loved thy fathers " (4[37], 10[15], 23[5]).

It may be seen that from the literary standpoint the concept and term " love " are introduced only at a relatively later period to describe what God has done, and does, and will do in covenant with Israel. But there can be no doubt that it is not a kind of later explanation or interpretation—the embellishment of something which was originally very different. The covenant relationship was not in the first instance one of pure law, or the will and action of God recognisable within it only the jealous assertion and validation of the claim to Israel's respect and obedience which resulted from His election. To be sure, the action of Yahweh as the Lord of this covenant does also establish and develop a relationship of Law (as is particularly well brought out in Deuteronomy). But behind the whole form of the covenant as Law and holiness there always stands the great context of the act of liberation (and the corresponding acts that followed) which was constitutive for the existence of Israel and quite unforgettable to it. But this is an act in which the will and achievement of Yahweh cannot be balanced by anything that Israel does, so that no demand can be made on Israel. It is on the basis of this act that the question of obedience will be put in its strict and supremely decisive character. But in the first instance the response of Israel will have only the character of a protective measure. By keeping the revealed commands of Yahweh the people will be kept from leaving the safe sphere in which He is present and known to it as its Liberator (and therefore in grace, in an evangelical character—if we may venture the expression —and only latently in His majesty as Judge). And what was it that underlay this act of liberation, or took place in and with it, but the free, unmotivated choice in which Yahweh elected and posited Himself as Israel's God and Israel as His people, binding Himself in holiness and righteousness, and therefore Israel to respect for His holiness and righteousness, but, because in the free choice of this concrete, contingent relationship, decisively—and in a way which characterises even His holiness and righteousness—in love ? What else is this free choice which takes place in this act, in His unmotivated reality, but love ? This is what Hosea and those who followed him in the introduction of this term and the picture of marriage, far from inventing or importing into the matter, drew from the actual relationship, discovering and affirming and proclaiming it as in some sense the nerve of the whole being and action of Yahweh as the Lord of the covenant.

Why is it they who do this ? Why does older Israel seem not to have used the word *aheb* and its synonyms in relation to God's action in this relationship ? To try to explain this, reference has been made to the sobriety with which the older period tried to maintain the distance between God and man, avoiding the application to God of " terms which derive from the sphere of the free emotional life " and the consequent approximation to the eroticism of Canaanite religion (cf. W. Eichrodt, *Theol. d.A.T.*, Vol. I, 1933, p. 127). I cannot accept this explanation because I fail to see why, if these considerations are relevant, a laxer view should have obtained a foothold in prophecy, which was engaged in so vital a conflict for the holiness of Yahweh and against any equation, confusion or exchange of the worship of Yahweh with the Canaanite fertility-cults. Is it not more natural to suppose that the thing itself, the mystery of the reality of the free and unmotivated act of Yahweh in which Israel's election was fulfilled as history, was present to the men of this people with such directness and impressiveness that to say: " God ' loves ' Israel " was not necessary because it was superfluous, because it could only be an analysis of the actuality in which Israel breathed and lived ? Naturally, however, this analysis could and had to be made, and the self-evident nature of the actuality in which Israel lived— " the power of love as the ultimate basis of the covenant-relationship " (Eichrodt) —could and had to be made explicit, in all the later situations in which that which was most self-evident was no longer so, and that which was most primitive had to be recalled ; situations in which Yahweh the Liberator had to prove and reveal Himself to an ungrateful and unfaithful people as also Yahweh the Judge. He derived His majesty as Judge from the very fact that He was still—precisely —the One who had acted and revealed Himself as the Liberator, as the One who had elected without external motivation, and dealt for and with Israel as such. It was with the authority and power of the Liberator of Israel that He now revealed and proved Himself to be its Judge. And in face of the apostasy of Israel, underlining the terrible senselessness of its ingratitude and disloyalty, lighting up the impenetrable darkness of the necessary consequences of its disobedience, reference had now to be made to the love of Yahweh, not as an arbitrary innovation, but to emphasise that which always was and always will be according to the origin of Israel in that act of its God, and with an assurance and warmth, yet also the sharp antitheses, which we find in Hosea and Jeremiah as they faced the infidelity of which Israel was guilty, and sought to convict Israel of its guilt and recall it to fidelity, by speaking of the fidelity of the divine Husband which had constituted and maintained this marriage. It is not that the prophets in faith break through the *opus alienum* of the wrath of God to His love, but that the wrath of God evinces itself by way of revelation to the prophets as *rebus humanis sic stantibus* the necessary form of His *opus proprium* which is His love. This declaration could not be weakened but, as we have seen (and again in all its antitheses), it could only become stronger and more explicit at a later date when the situation had developed and the people of the exile seemed to have become finally unworthy of the fulfilment of the promise and to have perished, so that, in sharpest contrast to the situation of its election and deliverance from Egypt, it could only think that it now had to do exclusively with Yahweh the Judge, with His No and not with His Yes. This was the situation of Deutero-Isaiah, in which prophecy could and had to become consolation—the consolation of the people of Yahweh. Not a light or empty consolation—for there is plainly implied an affirmation of the judicial majesty of God under which the people found itself bowed and had still to bow—but real consolation ; an affirmation of its election, and therefore of the love and loving promise of this God as evinced and revealed in His judgment and maintained even in its fulfilment. " For the mountains shall depart, and the hills be removed ; but my kindness shall not depart from thee, neither shall the covenant of my peace be removed, saith the Lord that hath mercy on thee " (Is. 54[10]). According to the tradition, neither Moses, the prophet of the Exodus, nor Samuel, the prophet of the incipient crisis, ever spoke like this. It was only now that the crisis had broken, and in its outworking, that this kind of language could be used. And it was only now that a book like Deuteronomy, not by way of interpretation but to indicate and emphasise the actuality, could look back to the act of liberation from Egypt and the act of the election of Israel as acts of the love of Yahweh for the fathers, speaking of them as the secret of the covenant which is to be perceived in all its relevance for the present.

When we consider the love of God as attested in the New Testament, we cannot possibly say that it has the character of an emotion or attitude ascribed to God. As we have seen, in the New Testament no less than the Old, it is the determination of God's own inner nature on the one hand, and on the other, and as such, His quite unsentimental action. But according to the witness of the New Testament the act of God is the goal of the covenant whose history is recounted in the Old ; the fulfilment of the promise actively given in the love of God to Israel. As such it is the establishment of the lordship or the kingdom of God on earth. But the establishment of the kingdom of God is identical with His own existence among His people and all peoples, all men. It is identical with the existence and history of the Son of Abraham, Isaac and Jacob, the Son of David, the man Jesus of Nazareth. God acts as, giving Himself up to humility in His Son, He introduces this man of Israel. He acts in the Word and work of His life and death in time, in the revelation of this man by His resurrection from the dead, in the life and rule of His Spirit. And this man acts as, sent by God and obedient to Him, He interposes His Word and work in human history, in His person justifying and sanctifying man as such before God, and exalting him to fellowship with Him. This action of the true God and true man is in its unity the love of God attested in the New Testament. No abstract term can describe it. It can be adequately denoted only by the name of Jesus Christ. But it is adequately, exhaustively, comprehensively and definitely denoted by this name—as the divine act to Israel, the world and all men which belongs to the very essence of God, beginning in His history with the poople Israel, and completed in His history with this man of Israel. Everything that we have to say about the love of God can only be an exposition of this name, of the actuality of the history of Jesus Christ. To cease to expound this name is to miss the actuality of God's love.

It is an interesting parallel to the problem which concerned us in relation to the love of God as attested in the Old Testament that there is no express reference in the Synoptics either to the love of God in general or to this love as particularly incorporated and revealed in the life of Jesus. At a pinch we might appeal to Mt. 5[45], where those who heard the Sermon on the Mount were warned, as children of their Father in heaven, not to love only those who loved them in return, since this Father causes " the sun to rise on the evil and on the good, and sendeth rain on the just and on the unjust." This is perhaps a very indirect reference to the love of God. And as far as the love of Jesus Himself is concerned we have only the isolated observation in Mk. 10[21] that when he looked on the rich young ruler He loved him. Apart from this, it is only in John (11³, ⁵, ³⁶) that we are told that He also loved Lazarus and Mary of Bethany, and that we read (13²³ and *passim*) of " the disciple whom Jesus loved." May we again suspect that the reality itself—the act of God's love, the life-act of Jesus Himself, the kingdom drawn near and concretely established in human history in His Word and work, His death as the crowning of His action in obedience to the Father and on man's behalf, His manifestation as Lord and Saviour in His resurrection from the dead—was all so directly present in its relevance and significance to the bearers of the most primitive tradition that they did not regard it as necessary to give this explicit name to the event which they sought to record ? Or, when it was a matter of the simple evangelical recording of this event, did they think it appropriate and incumbent not to make this reference, but to allow the event to speak for itself, to attest itself in all its sovereignty ? At any rate, the Gospels say of the man Jesus that He is present among other men with the authority and power of the Son of God ; that in what He says and does and proclaims and reveals the kingdom of God is a concealed but also manifested, or at any rate present, reality on earth ; that He sits at table with the Pharisees but also with the publicans ; that He is the friend of sinners but the enemy of those who are evil-disposed in spirit ; that He forgives sins against God and against Himself ; that He heals the sick ; and that finally and comprehensively, instead of asserting Himself, He sacrifices Himself, and is not concealed as the Lord and Helper active in His death and passion, but revealed to His disciples, and through them to the world, as the One who represents them to God, and God to them. They portray Him as this One who works in the name of God for us men. But what was this action but that of His love, and therefore of the love of God, which was the final Word of the history of Israel, and as such the first Word of the history of a new people and a new humanity ? It was spoken in His life and death and recounted by the Gospels, and heard and understood in the power of the Holy Spirit of the Resurrected, as whom He is attested in the closing section of the Gospels.

With this hearing and understanding, in recognition of the act of God as it had taken place in Him, it was both possible and necessary to begin to use the appropriate term. It is part of the distinctiveness of the Fourth Gospel that in this respect too it makes no difference between before and after, between the Word spoken in His life and death and its hearing and understanding, but already describes the pre-Easter love of Jesus as manifested, and causes Jesus to reveal Himself from the very first. This is why we find so many sayings in this Gospel which speak expressly of the reciprocal love of the Father and the Son—a love which is turned to men in the person of the disciples. In fact, it is not addressed only to the disciples, but to them first. Quite early in the Gospel—and adduced, be it noted, as a saying of Jesus Himself—we read of God's love for the world expressed in the giving of His only-begotten Son. It is of this divine love that we read in the Epistles, expressed in terms of proclamation and instruction. The basic note, or rather the basic chord in which no one note can be separated from the others, is that it is (1) the love of God in Jesus Christ, i.e., in His sacrifice for us ; (2) the love of Jesus Christ in His self-sacrifice as the embodiment and revelation of the love of God ; and (3)—for this aspect is not omitted—the love of God revealed to us, and operative in and towards us, by the Holy Spirit of Jesus Christ.

As regards the first point, we may consider 2 Thess. 2¹⁶, where in an order which has no parallel elsewhere we read : αὐτὸς δὲ ὁ κύριος ἡμῶν Ἰησοῦς Χριστὸς καὶ ὁ θεὸς ὁ πατὴρ ἡμῶν, " which hath loved us, and hath given us everlasting consolation and good hope through grace." When these two are mentioned together the order is usually the reverse : No creature can " separate us from the love of God, which is in Christ Jesus our Lord " (Rom. 8³⁹) ; or : " God, who is rich in mercy, for his great love wherewith he loved us . . . hath quickened us together with Christ " (Eph. 2⁴ᶠ·) ; or when we confess that Jesus is the Son of God " we have known and believed the love that God hath to us " (1 Jn. 4¹⁶). In meaning and context, however, 1 Jn. 3¹ is also relevant in this connexion : " Behold, what manner of love the Father hath bestowed upon us, that we should be called the sons of God." Other passages which explain this " God in Christ " are Rom. 8³¹ᶠ· : " If God be for us, who can be against us ? He that spared not his own Son, but delivered him up for us all, how shall he not with him also freely give us all things ? " ; Rom. 5⁸ : " But God commendeth his love toward us, in that, while we were yet sinners, Christ died for us " ; and 1 Jn. 4¹⁰ : " Herein is love . . . that God loved us, and sent his Son to be the propitiation for our sins." In short, " God was in Christ, reconciling the world unto himself " (2 Cor. 5¹⁹).

In relation to the second point it is the love of Jesus Christ Himself which in the power of the love of God impels or constrains us (συνέχει, 2 Cor. 5¹⁴). It is a matter of knowing this love which passes knowledge (Eph. 3¹⁹). It is from this that no one and nothing can or will separate us (Rom. 8³⁵). This is the declaration of Gal. 2²⁰ : " I live by the faith of the Son of God, who loved me, and gave himself for me " ; or Eph. 5² : " Walk in love, as Christ also hath loved us " ; or Eph. 5²⁵ : " Christ also loved the church, and gave himself for it " ; or Rev. 1⁵ : " Unto him that loved us, and washed us from our sins in his own blood, and hath made us a kingdom of priests unto God and his Father."

With reference to the third point we may consider Rom. 5⁵ : " And hope maketh not ashamed ; because the love of God is shed abroad in our hearts by the Holy Ghost which is given unto us." It is in the power " of our Lord Jesus Christ, and of the love of the Spirit " that Paul admonishes the Roman Christians to strive together with him in their prayers (Rom. 15³⁰).

It is all summed up in the famous concluding formula of 2 Cor. 13¹³ with its twofold epexegetical καί : ἡ χάρις τοῦ κυρίου Ἰησοῦ Χριστοῦ καὶ ἡ ἀγάπη τοῦ θεοῦ καὶ ἡ κοινωνία τοῦ ἁγίου πνεύματος μετὰ πάντων ὑμῶν. Our translation ought really to be : " The grace of our Lord Jesus Christ, in which the love of God is exercised, and the communion of the Spirit disclosed and imparted, be with you all." The trinitarian background of this whole witness cannot be mistaken in any case, but at this point it is directly revealed. It is in this way that the Word spoken in and with the kingdom of God drawn near in the life and death of the man Jesus is heard and understood and accordingly proclaimed in the New Testament community.

We will now consider the three decisive definitions of divine love as the basis of our own human love.

1. It is electing love. This is merely another way of saying that it is the free act of God. It is not a process within a given state and situation to the nature of which it belongs that God loves. In no relationship to another is God committed and bound to love. It is He who of Himself decides to do this. He determines and makes this other the object of His love. He differentiates him as such. It is true even and primarily of the essential love of the Father for the Son and the Son for the Father that it is free ; that it is not necessary in the form of a natural process ; that it is necessary only in virtue of the freedom in which God loves eternally and is God in the freedom of this action. But how much more is this true of His love in the *opus ad extra*. This is quite unmotivated ; or rather, it is its own motive. There can be no claim to be loved by God, because there is no quality or potentiality on the basis of which anyone or anything must be loved by Him, being a natural object of His love. To be loved

by God is not an immanent attribute of any of His creatures. For there is no value indwelling the one loved by God as the basis of God's love. The one loved by God acquires his worth from the fact that God loves him, and it stands or falls with the continuance or cessation of this love. The truth about God's love in His *opus ad extra* is that He loves the man whom He has made worthy of His love by electing and willing and determining him as His creature, but who for his part has made himself unworthy, proving himself undeserving of this love, adopting an attitude of hostility, so that in defiance of God's good will he can actually be only worthy of the divine hatred. God loves man as this enemy. He does not fail to hate that which is worthy of His hatred. He does not relax His wrath (of which we shall have to speak later). But so sovereign is He in His electing love that He loves this hostile man who is unworthy of His love. He loves him notwithstanding his unworthiness and hostility. Indeed, He loves him just because of it. He loves him in his pride and fall. He loves him in his sloth and misery. He loves him as He takes pity on him as this sinful man. He loves him not merely apart from his deservings —which is also true of His love as Creator—but in spite of, overlooking and overcoming, his deservings. He does not elect and love him because of what he has to offer. This could lead only to the divine rejection and hatred. He elects and loves him for His own sake ; for what He is for and to him as He gives Himself for and to him ; for what He awakens in him and gives to him ; for his new humanity which is exclusively the gift of His love. As this freely electing love the love of God for us is unconditional, strong and victorious. It is a burning fire which cannot be quenched. It is wholly trustworthy. It is a rock to which we can cling without fear of its crumbling. It is a refuge to which we can flee without doubting whether it will stand. It is nourishment which is always prepared for those who hunger and thirst for love, and never withheld from them. We have only to see that we are not worthy of it, that we have forfeited it, that we cannot secure it of and for ourselves, that we can only receive and accept it. We can only long and trust that God is the freely electing God for us, and that we ourselves are freely elected by Him. We then participate already in the unconditional nature and strength and victory of the love of God, in its sovereignty which consists in the fact that God is absolutely free to love man first irrespective of what he deserves or does not deserve. We then find that we are loved by Him, and therefore genuinely, basically and effectively. And in spite of every objection our understanding of God kindles directly a self-understanding : *amabar, amor, amabor*. Everything depends upon the fact that God's love is not a general function of His being in relation to the world and therefore ourselves, the particular reference of which to ourselves may well be questioned, but from the very outset a differentiation based on the free decision of God and having a particular reference to us which is originally and conclusively assured, not because it is appropriate to us, but because it is God's differentiation in our favour. Everything depends upon the fact that God's *diligere* is His own free *eligere*, and that the man who needs Him, who hungers and thirsts for Him, is content to be elected by Him, and as such to be loved by Him in all his intrinsic unworthiness to be loved. As that which elects him in particular the divine love is the eloquent and compelling basis of his own human love.

It is with this freely electing love that according to the witness of the Old Testament Yahweh concluded His covenant with Israel. The gods of the ancient world surrounding Israel also had their own peoples, and these peoples had their gods. But the relationships between these other gods and peoples were in some sort natural relationships, this particular god being originally and essentially and inescapably bound to this people as its genius or ideal or dæmon, and this people to this god, in a reciprocal relationship of solidarity and control. On every hand there was the temptation to construe the covenant with Yahweh along these lines, Yahweh being the bull in which Israel thought to see a reflection of its own power. It was against this temptation that, according to the tradition, Moses warned the people after the great apostasy at Sinai (Ex. 32 f.), as did all the prophets with greater or lesser concreteness. As is clearly emphasised by the traditional accounts of the call of Abraham (Gen. 12 f.) and that of Moses (Ex. 3 f.), Yahweh is not just the national God of Israel, but the sovereign Lord of all peoples and their history, as even the older prophets realised and declared. What, then, is the advantage of Israel ? Absolutely nothing. " Are ye not as children of the Ethiopians unto me, O children of Israel ? saith the Lord. Have not I brought up Israel out of the land of Egypt ? and the Philistines from Caphtor, and the Syrians from Kir ? " (Am. 9⁷). The one—and only—advantage is : " You only have I elected of all the families of the earth " (Am. 3²). " For the Lord hath chosen Jacob unto himself, and Israel for his peculiar treasure " (Ps. 135⁴). It is not that Israel has chosen Him, but He Israel. Nor is there any natural or historical claim that it should be Israel whom Yahweh chose and who should be chosen by Him. It is as Yahweh decides that Israel is separated from other peoples. It is as He elects Himself to be its God that it becomes His elected people. Yahweh has created and formed Israel—and we have to give to this statement the strict sense that He has caused it to be made new. It is for this reason, in the free grace in which He is its Creator, that He addresses it : " Fear not : for I have redeemed thee, I have called thee by thy name ; thou art mine. When thou passest through the waters, I will be with thee ; and through the rivers, they shall not overflow thee : when thou walkest through the fire, thou shalt not be burned ; neither shall the flame kindle upon thee. For I am the Lord thy God, the Holy One of Israel, thy Saviour " (Is. 43¹ᶠ·). This " I " must be taken in all its sovereignty. It is He, Yahweh, who guarantees this promise, and the fact that Israel is the people which may receive it and live with it comes from Him, from above, and not from below, from Israel, which is only the creation and construct of His free good will. It simply happened : " The Lord thy God hath chosen thee to be a special people unto himself, above all people that are upon the face of the earth . . . because the Lord loved you " (Deut. 7⁶ᶠ·, 14²). " Behold, the heaven and the heaven of heavens is the Lord's thy God, the earth also, with all that therein is." And it simply happened : " Only the Lord had a delight in thy fathers to love them, and he chose their seed after them, even you above all people, as it is this day " (Deut. 10¹⁴ᶠ·). The contingence of this event, the elective character of the covenant with Yahweh, is the basis of everything else. The faithfulness with which in self-decision Yahweh will maintain this inconceivably actual differentiation, this covenant, underlies the impregnable validity which it has for Him, and therefore the confidence with which Israel may cling to it but also the seriousness with which it is required to keep that which it has not instituted of itself, but the institution of which has come to it as the free act of the love of Yahweh. It also explains, of course, the frightfulness, pitilessly indicated by the prophets, of the abyss into which it causes itself to fall by breaking it.

There is an obvious continuity between the witness of the New Testament to the love of God and that of the Old Testament. In the New Testament this love has not ceased to be the love which elects Israel. If it is now said that God loved the world (Jn. 3¹⁶), this means positively that the purpose of the election of Israel, as emphatically declared in the Old Testament (especially in Deutero-Isaiah), is now revealed as its determination to be God's witness to all nations. It does not mean negatively—which would be a foolish thought in this context—that God is no longer the God who elects Israel, or Israel His elect people. It is " not as though the word of God hath taken none effect " (Rom. 9⁶). No unfaithfulness of man can overthrow the faithfulness of God (Rom. 3³). " The gifts and calling of God are without repentance " (Rom. 11²⁹). He has " not cast away his people " (Rom. 11¹). On the basis of the election, even though they are hardened, they are still His branches, " beloved for the fathers' sake " (Rom. 11²⁸). And Paul's final word in relation to his people—it is not for nothing that in Rom. 9³ he made that awe-inspiring declaration of solidarity with them—is quite unmistakeably that " all Israel shall be saved " (Rom. 11²⁶) —something which is not at all self-evident now that the election and love of God have transcended the sphere of this one people. That the election is primarily of Israel and not of other nations is sharply expressed in two synoptic sayings of Jesus which we must not overlook. The first is in His charge to the disciples in Mt. 10⁵ : " Go not into the way of the Gentiles, and into any city of the Samaritans enter ye not." The second is the answer to the request of the woman of Canaan in Mt. 15²⁴ : " I am not sent but unto the lost sheep of the house of Israel "—the parallel in Mk. 7²⁷ being even more emphatic : " Let the children first be filled : for it is not meet to take the children's bread, and to cast it unto the dogs." How can Samaritans and Gentiles possibly have any claim to be the fellow-elect of the children of Abraham ? How can God owe it to them to make them such ? If they are this, it is in a new and no less inconceivable revelation of His free good-will than that in which the children of Abraham are first elected. It is simply a fulfilment of the passages from Hosea (2²³ and 1¹⁰) quoted in Rom. 9²⁵ᶠ· : " I will call them my people, which were not my people ; and her beloved, which was not beloved. And it shall come to pass, that in the place where it was said unto them, Ye are not my people ; there shall they be called the children of the living God." The Gentiles will then be " cut out of the olive tree which is wild by nature, and graffed contrary to nature (against every rule of horticulture !) into a good olive tree " (Rom. 11²⁴). The one—and only—thing which helps the Gentiles is that there has now actually taken place a new and inconceivable revelation of the free goodwill of God. The crumbs do fall from the table of the Lord, and the request of the Syro-phenician woman is fulfilled (Mt. 15²⁸). There has actually taken place an engrafting of the branches of the wild olive into the fruitful branches of the good (Rom. 11¹⁷). Gentiles who followed not after righteousness have attained to righteousness (Rom. 9³⁰). The dividing wall between Jews and Gentiles is broken down (Eph. 2¹⁴), and Gentiles " are no more strangers and foreigners, but fellow-citizens with the saints, and of the household of God " (Eph. 2¹⁹). Hence the Galatian communities can and may and must be addressed as " the Israel of God " irrespective of their composition (Gal. 6¹⁶), and the Churches of Asia Minor as a whole are unreservedly described in 1 Pet. 2⁹ as " the chosen generation, the royal priesthood, the holy nation, the people of possession." " And they shall come from the east, and from the west, and from the north, and from the south, and shall sit down in the kingdom of God " (Lk. 13²⁹). The critical converse of this election of the Gentiles is a confirmation of something that the prophets of the Old Testament had long since and very clearly revealed, namely, that the constant election of Israel in virtue of the divine faithfulness is not placed under the control of the men of this people. It has to be known and apprehended and obediently believed as a grace which is and remains free. Where this is not the case, it is concealed under the terrible garb of rejection. We see this already in the saying of the Baptist in Mt. 3⁹ᶠ· when against the false confidence of the Pharisees and Saducees : " We have Abraham to our father," the sharp warning is given : " I tell you, that God is able of these stones to raise up children unto Abraham. And now also the axe is laid unto the root of the trees : therefore every tree which bringeth not forth good fruit is hewn down, and cast into the fire." The confidence which Paul maintained in relation to Israel's election even in the present and future was not then a cheap or facile confidence. He faced the terrible fact that " they are not all Israel, which are of Israel " (Rom. 9⁶), and that it is not merely one or two branches of the good olive which have been broken off (Rom. 11¹⁷), but that things have again come to such a pass as in the days of Elijah, that only a " remnant " of Israel, and this only on the basis of the ἐκλογὴ χάριτος, has escaped the hardness brought about by the spirit of blindness and deafness with which God has afflicted them (Rom. 11²⁻¹⁰). There is no reason for the engrafted Gentiles to think that they for their part have escaped and found shelter. " Ye have not chosen me, but I have chosen you " (Jn. 15¹⁶), is true of them too—and especially. They too—and especially—cannot and will not stand except in faith. They, too, must be warned : " Be not highminded, but fear : for if God spared not the natural branches, take heed lest he also spare not thee " (Rom. 11²⁰ᶠ·). Nor is there any reason to think that the election of Israel has been negated. God still has, and will exercise, the power to graft in again the branches which have been broken off (Rom. 11²³ᶠ·). The mercy now imparted to the Gentiles is the pledge that they too will find mercy (Rom. 11³⁰ᶠ·). Ex. 33¹⁹, which merits serious consideration as an explication of the divine name of Ex. 3¹⁴, has come to be regarded as axiomatic in the New Testament : " I will have mercy on whom I will have mercy " (Rom. 9¹⁵). Always and in all cases, as in the decision concerning Jacob and Esau (Rom. 9¹³), the love of God is God's free election of grace. In love He has foreordained us (προορίσας) for the adoption of sonship to Himself (Eph. 1⁵). Those who are elected by Him are those who are loved by Him (Col. 3¹²). They and they alone are those who also love God and for whom as such all things work together for good (Rom. 8²⁸). The parable of the labourers in the vineyard is relevant in this connexion. According to this parable (Mt. 20¹⁻¹⁶) the Lord selects the earlier or later hours at which He personally goes out to call the various men, some to longer and more arduous and others to shorter and less difficult work. And when it comes to payment, it is again the free good-will of the Lord to make the last first and the first last, so that the latecomers do not receive less than those who had started earlier, nor the former more. The protest of the former is quite irrelevant : " Friend, I do thee no wrong : didst not thou agree with me for a penny ? Take that thine is, and go thy way : I will give unto this last, even as unto thee. Is it not lawful for me to do what I will with mine own ? Is thine eye evil, because I am good ? " According to Rom. 9¹⁶ this is the freedom the divine election of grace which is not conditioned by any autonomous willing and running of man and which overthrows all human boasting. It is in this freedom that the love of God lives and rules according to the teaching of the New Testament. To love God in return is to love Him in the exercise of this freedom, i.e., for the very reason that in its exercise He leaves no room for human boasting but only for gratitude.

We can only indicate very briefly why this is necessarily the case in the witness of the New Testament (in profoundest unity with that of the Old). When they speak explicitly or implicitly of the love of God, the New Testament authors look always to Jesus Christ. They thus look to the manifestation of the promised Son of David and therefore to the fulfilment of the promise of God in His faithfulness evinced to Israel. They thus look to the indestructibility of Israel's election and its status as the first-born of all nations : " Salvation is of the Jews " (Jn. 4²²). But they also look to the act by which at the goal of its history Israel itself handed over its Messiah Jesus to the Gentiles. On the one side, therefore, they look to the fulfilment of the counsel of God concerning all nations, the whole world, as it is declared in God's covenant with Israel. And on the other side they look to the supreme obscuring of the covenant of God with an Israel which could and would serve the counsel of God only in this way, with the rejection of its Messiah. They look to the one beloved Son of God as the remnant of the remnant to which Israel has now been melted down, but also as the One in whom the true Israel had finally been introduced and who was therefore still the sure and certain hope of all Israel. They look to this one Beloved in whose crucifixion salvation for Jews and Gentiles, and therefore for the world, has been achieved and manifested. They look to the act of the electing God in the act of this elect man. Looking to this One, they are forced to describe the love of God with a distinctness no less, and if anything even greater, than that of the Old Testament witnesses, as an electing love.

2. The love of God is a purifying love. This term sums up all that has to be said concerning the character of the divine act of love in its relation to the perversion and corruption of man, to human sin. Man is not worthy, and does not deserve, to be loved by God. Yet, as we have said, God loves him in spite and even because of this fact. He loves him as He has mercy on the man who is lost by reason of his transgression. His love is addressed to man in all his weakness and godlessness and hostility (Rom. 5⁶ᶠ·). It can never be sufficiently underlined that God loves man in spite and even because of his worthlessness, for this helps to bring out the fact that as His self-giving to this man the love of God is grounded only in God and not at all in man, or relatively only in the sense that man is seen to need God's mercy.

But we have still to define rather more precisely what is meant by the fact that God loves in spite and because of man's worthlessness. If it is the case that we have to understand God's love as His act, there can be no place for the notion of a static paradox—sinful man on the one hand and the God who loves him in spite and because of his sin on the other. The true God, the God who has mercy on man, cannot be content, in face of the fact that man is a sinner against Him, with an empty and passive Nevertheless in which there does not take place something very radical in His relationship to man in this respect. If this were the case, the definition of His love as His self-giving to and for man would be absurd. What can self-giving mean if God is only a kind of strangely benevolent spectator of sinful man who can and does acquiesce in his sin ? In such circumstances love is not self-giving, but only a kind of capricious and irrational divine disposition concerning man the contemplation of which—if such is possible—gives man good reason to believe that, since the love of God is not disturbed by his sin, he may quietly acquiesce in the fact that he is a sinner.

No, in the relationship of God to man determined by His love there takes place something—something very radical. For God's love is not a divine state. It is an act. Indeed, it is *the* life-act of God. It is the act of His self-giving, of His self-giving to sinful man as such. If He loves this man in spite of the fact that he is sinful, this carries with it the fact that He opposes to man's sin His divine defiance and therefore His contradiction and resistance. If He loves him because he is sinful, being moved to compassion by the fact that He finds him in this weakness, godlessness and hostility, this carries with it the fact that He wills to free him from the necessity of being a sinner. He thus loves him in opposition to his sin. He says Yes to him, but in so doing He says No to his sin. As He gives Himself to and for man, there takes place in the one loved by Him the victorious encounter between Him and his sin. The sin of the one loved by Him is a stain which cannot stand against the fact that God loves him and gives Himself for him, but must yield and perish. It is the work of the love of God to cause this stain to yield. This is why we call it the purifying love of God. And we cannot afford to neglect this aspect of God's love. Without it it would be idle to talk of the God of love. God's love is total grace for sinful man, but also total judgment over him. It is total grace because it is God's perfect turning and goodness and friendliness : not in the impotence of a distant and inactive benevolence but in the power of His own presence in the inner and outer life of man ; in the fact that He proves Himself a benefactor and deliverer by concrete assistance and vivifying action, thus turning man away from his sin and to Himself, and summoning him to obedience to His will. But it is also total judgment because it is the holy severity of God : again not in the impotence of a distant and inactive disapproval but in the power of His whole presence and action in the psychic and physical occurrence of human life ; in the fact that God forcefully withstands man on his evil way, concretely revealing Himself as the pitiless avenger of his mistakes and follies, commanding him to halt : Thus far and no farther. The grace in which God loves man is distinguished from the other favours which he receives by the fact that he has not at all deserved it, that as this thing which he has not at all deserved it represents that which is God's aim and end for man, that in some degree of distance or proximity it always includes a painful, humiliating, hurtful and destructive judgment, that it may indeed be altogether hidden in the form of judgment, and yet that it always remains grace, and is not wholly unrecognisable as such. But the judgment which cannot be avoided if God loves man is also distinguished from the other ills which befall man by the fact that it represents what he has deserved as a transgressor but not God's final will for him, so that it has no independent significance or definitive character, but can only serve the grace of God, being a form of grace, and recognisable as such, even in its most frightful manifestations.

Thus grace and judgment do not take place in an accidental or arbitrary parallelism or sequence, but in the context of the purifying love of God, so that as the grace and judgment of God they work together in their coming and going according to the order and purpose which He Himself gives. Their binding order consists in the fact that God's will is to keep man in grace, or to lead him to it, by means of judgment. And their common purpose is to separate and liberate man from His sin. This purpose is served both by the enticement of His grace and the threat of His judgment, both by His chiding and His blessing. Man can and should, therefore, rise up and rejoice thankfully in the incomprehensible comfort and forgiveness of God, in all the assistance which he is given, in all the great and little lights which shine on his way, in all the strengthenings and encouragements, in short in all the unmerited favours addressed to him by the love of God. Yet he should also be prepared sooner or later to be recalled in some way to his limits by this love, to find himself forcefully redirected to the humility which he so easily forgets and loses when he basks in the divine sunshine. For it is God Himself, and not just a lucky fate, which is favourable to him. And so, when that which he has deserved overtakes him, the same man can and should bow before it, humbling himself to the dust, finding himself absolutely directed to accept the awful things which he does not like, allowing himself to be led where he does not want to go, yet clinging to the fact—for it is in the same love of God that these things come to him—that he will not fall into the abyss but will still be upheld. Even in these circumstances, there are always lights in the darkness, forgiveness in guilt, new life in death, breaks in the engulfing clouds, encouragements in despair. There is always reason for thankfulness even in the anguish in which he thinks to perish. For it is God Himself and not a sinister and hostile force who judges him. In both respects we have to do with the presence and action of God in its dynamic opposition to his perversion and corruption. In both cases the aim is his purification. God utters a Nevertheless, a merciful Therefore, both when He gives what is undeserved with goodness and what is deserved with severity. It is always His fatherly hand which is active both morning and evening, by day and by night, to his purification and therefore his liberation. In both cases God really gives Himself to him and for him. In both cases He comes into his life. In both cases He has a part in him as he is, and gives him a part in His Yes (which precisely in virtue of the No which it encloses is a strong and helpful Yes), and also in His No (which is wholly enclosed in His strong and helpful Yes). In both cases it takes place that he may find himself received and adopted by God—as the man who is loved by Him.

In this matter we may distinguish and integrate the witness of the Old and New Testament by finding in the one the initiation and in the other the completion of the divine love understood as purifying love. Since the relationship between God and man derives from God's election of sinful man, in both cases it is, from the divine standpoint, an unconditionally positive and yet also an unconditionally critical relationship. Even in the history of Israel, and especially in that of Jesus Christ, there can be no question of a breach of this relationship, and therefore of a withdrawal and cessation of the love of God in consequence of human sin. On the other hand, there can be no question of a toleration of human sin, and therefore of an armistice, or termination, in the movement of God in opposition to it. The divine Yes to man stands, as attested in both the Old Testament and the New. But in this Yes, just because and as it is unshakeable as the divine Yes to man, the merciless No of God is also pronounced against man's transgression. His love and election and grace necessarily have also the shadow-side of His hatred and rejection and judgment. According to the witness of both Testaments it is a question of the purification of the man affirmed and loved and elected and blessed by God.

To be sure, it often seems likely in the Old Testament that the One who has established and guaranteed the covenant between Yahweh and Israel will terminate and destroy it. It was broken by Israel, not only before its institution, but in a flagrant manner immediately afterwards, and then continually. According to the explicit testimony of earlier and later tradition alike, the history of Israel consisted in an almost unbroken series of breaches of the covenant. The first of these, as we learn from Moses' conversation with God in Ex. 32, might well have been answered by a complete repudiation of the covenant on the part of Yahweh. And among the later prophetic utterances in later situations there are some which come very near to declaring that Yahweh has grown tired of His partner and therefore ended it. But He never actually did this. " He hath remembered his covenant for ever, the word which he commanded to a thousand generations " (Ps. 105⁸). The history of Israel continues to be a history of the faithfulness which Yahweh maintains in relation to Israel in spite of Israel's failure and unfaithfulness. And so there constantly takes place in it the unmerited but real deliverance, preservation, assistance, blessing and triumphing of Israel, the hearing of its cries for help in all kinds of emergencies (as described in Ps. 107), the remission of all its guilt, the healing of all its transgressions, its redemption from destruction and crowning with glory and honour as extolled in Ps. 103²ᶠ⁻ Obviously in answer to tangible grace, there is continual thanksgiving and praise and rejoicing and solemn festivity and singing and playing and even dancing before Yahweh. All as if nothing had happened ? As if God overlooked and dismissed the fact that He had to do with a nation of transgressors ? On the contrary, it is obvious that according to the understanding of the relevant texts it is just when Yahweh saves and helps and blesses and gladdens that we have to do with His contradiction and active resistance against Israel's transgression and apostasy. He does not put Himself in the wrong but maintains His right in face of His people when He is so kind, when according to the depiction in the Book of Judges (with a notable parallel in Ps. 106) He responds to the constant defection and need of His people with the continual raising up and sending of new saviours. But the fact that in and with His favours, in a strict execution of His covenant, He maintains His right against His people, and in opposition to its unfaithfulness and transgression He does so on its behalf, emerges also in something which is particularly emphasised in the Old Testament witness to the history of Israel. As a sequence of breaches of the covenant it is an almost interminable sequence of the judgments which God causes to fall on its sins of commission and omission. To be sure, Yahweh does not break the covenant. But in the covenant which is not broken but kept by Yahweh, Israel necessarily learns—already in the wilderness according to the traditional account, and then in a terrible crescendo up to the destruction of Samaria and Jerusalem and its leading away to exile—what it means and involves to sin against so gracious a God. His grace does not yield but smites its enemies and despisers.

The election is not set aside but it is concealed and turns to the rejection of the disobedient. Love never fails—the saying might well have stood in the Old Testament—but it burns and shrivels and destroys where it is ignored and meets with no response, where it is spurned and trodden under foot. It was just as and because the prophets held fast to the promise and covenant of Yahweh, or rather proclaimed the fact that Yahweh Himself held fast to it,.that the accusation against His people, the threat of the judgment which necessarily accompanied its transgression, and lamentation when it burst upon it, became a terrifyingly strong—if not the strongest—note in the witness of the Old Testament. But we must not miss the basic note which not only holds together the antithesis of Yahweh's grace and judgment but gives to its strange conjunction the character, if not of a clear manifestation, at least of an indication whether grace or judgment is to be the final Word in the history of Israel. In spite of everything it is indisputably clear that the God of the fathers, whether He blesses or curses, does not cease to speak with Israel ; that in grace or judgment it is He and not an alien lord who rules its history. Hence it is also clear that the faithful love of Yahweh, whether it brings salvation or perdition, is not in vain ; that by the Word and work of its God the history of Israel is the history of a promise, or rather of a purification from sin which has not been completed but has genuinely begun in the twofold conflict of God for Israel and against its sin. This history does not lead, therefore, to a contradiction and a riddle. It is not a history which can proceed only as that of Israel dashing itself to pieces on God. There is no decision, no definite result, but in its issue it does point in a very definite direction ; and to the completion of that which has been begun in it.

When we turn from the Old Testament to the New, the dominant impression that we receive at once from the very outset, and can never lose again, is that the eventuality of a breach of the positive relationship of God to the race of men, which in the Old Testament had always been at last a marginal threat, has now become quite impossible. That which in the history of Israel, as the final and decisive Word in the antithesis of grace and judgment, is still awaited as an unfulfilled promise, is now the first Word of the history of Jesus Christ and His community which is now attested. That which was only future is now the basis and beginning behind which we cannot go but from which we can only proceed. It is still a question of God's grace and judgment, of His love which strives against human sin. But this conflict which was taken up according to the witness of the Old Testament is now carried through and victoriously ended according to the witness of the New. This is revealed in the fact that in the event from which the New Testament witness derives and which it declares grace and judgment are no longer two related but different and distinguishable sides or aspects of the love of God. But it is in His grace that God has exercised judgment, and in His judgment that His grace has triumphed. In the history of Jesus Christ—quite otherwise than in that of Israel—it is one and the same thing (not two) that God chides and blesses ; that He humbles and exalts ; that He smites and heals ; that He kills and makes alive. That which is deserved is itself that which is undeserved. And that in this history God has triumphed in the twofold conflict against human sin is shown in the fact that there is now—quite otherwise than in the history of Israel—no reversal of the two elements of His action ; that after His blessing there is no return of His wrath and curse ; that after His exalting and healing and making alive there is no renewal of His humbling and smiting and killing. This history therefore—again quite otherwise than that of Israel—does not need any continuation and completion. It needs only the proclamation that it has taken place, and the final revelation of its meaning and significance for all creation in all the developments and dimensions of its temporal existence. It is the completion of the history of the purifying love of God. For in it God has accomplished His judgment on sinful man in such a way that He has taken it upon Himself in the person of His Son, suffering it as the judgment of death, and thus removing it once and for all.   And in it God has evinced His grace to sinful man in such a way that again in the person of His Son He has brought in once and for all the man who is pure and free from sin.   It is in this, and in this way, that God loved the world, interposing and giving Himself for it.

This history of Jesus Christ—in which He gives a share to His disciples, and through them to the community founded by their ministry, and through this to the world—is the act of God in which His movement for man and against His sin is in its fulfilment an event for all times.   As this began in the history of Israel, we cannot say of the latter that it ended merely in an *aporia* or riddle. On the contrary, we have to say that for all its provisional and contradictory character it belongs to the history of Jesus Christ as a real promise of a real fulfilment, a real beginning to a real completion.   And together with it the history of Jesus Christ, the conflict completed in it, is *the* act of the love of God in which He has definitively ordered and revealed His relationship to sinful man. It is of this act of God that we speak when as sinful men we may speak of the love with which God has loved and does and will love us.   When we speak of the love of God, we can do so only with reference to the fact that it is God's love for sinful man.   We can speak only of the love of the One who is faithful to His covenant with Israel, and therefore of the love of Jesus Christ.   And this is the basis on which and in the strength of which we too may love, loving in return the God who has first loved us.

The love of God is (3) creative, i.e., a love which causes those who are loved by Him to love.   At this point we touch on the theme of the next sub-section in which we shall have to speak of the act of Christian love.   The connexion between the love of God and this effect is not accidental or external.   It is not the case that it might or might not follow.   It is a terrible thing—impossible and inexplicable— if it does not follow.   The fact that this terrible thing does continually happen is our condemnation to the extent that as those who are loved by God we ourselves do not love.   But it does not contradict God's love.   It does not alter its essential character.   As it is essential to it to be elective and purifying love, it is also essential to it to be the basis of human love :   the creative basis ;   not merely a rational basis, as though man had to draw from it the practical conclusion that he for his part can and may and should love ;   nor a purely moral basis, as though the love of God were a rule or example that he ought to follow ;   nor a quasi-physical basis, as though the impact of the love of God caused man to love like a ball which is set in motion.   Of themselves these explanations are quite inadequate.   To be sure, we certainly have to do with God's Word when God loves, but it is a creative Word.   We certainly have to do with His command, but as in Gen. 1 it is a creative command.   We certainly have to do with His power, but it is His power as Creator.   Loving is not a human possibility which we may and must actualise in certain prescribed conditions.   We have learned already that it is " of God " (1 Jn. 4⁷). But this means precisely that (as He made heaven and earth *ex nihilo*, or formed Adam from the dust of the earth according to Gen. 2⁷, or can raise up from the stones children to Abraham) He can make of those who cannot and will not love (for they are sinners) men who do actually love, proving the inconceivable fact that they are free to do so by the fact that they actually do. New and different men are needed in order that love may take place as a human act. And God creates these new and loving men. It is in this way that He is the basis of human love.

His love is His self-giving to and for man. He does not love, therefore, merely to be loved in return. He does not long for this, or court it, or bargain for it. He does not make this response a condition of His own love. His wrath where it is lacking has nothing whatever to do with the fury of scorned and unrequited love. And His grace where it is made has nothing whatever to do with the pleasure of a triumphant love which attains its desire. We must be careful not to make the love of God a kind of original or model for our own well-enough known self-love in which we all seek our own. What is it that God wills when He loves us ? He certainly does not will anything for Himself—for what have we to give Him ? But He does not will Himself without us. In all the fulness of His Godhead, in which He might well have been satisfied with Himself, He wills Himself together with us. He wills Himself in fellowship with us. He wills Himself as our Lord and therefore as our *summum bonum*, or rather as the one and perfect *bonum* of our existence, our being under His lordship. He wills Himself, not as the object of our wishes and desires, of our imagination and aspiration, of our willing and running, but as His gift freely imparted to us. It is in this way that God loves, that He is eternal love. It is in this way that He loves us—man.

And in this sense His love is creative love ; love which does not ask or seek or demand or awaken and set in motion our love as though it were already present in us, but which creates it as something completely new, making us free for love as for an action which differs wholly and utterly from all that we have done hitherto. We have to be liberated for an action of this kind, in which there can be love and therefore self-giving on the part of man. Of himself man is not free for this action. The action for which he is free of himself—in the fool's freedom of the one who is really captive—is that of *eros*, i.e., of the self-love which desires that which is another's, and the other himself, so that although it may also take the form, in a fulfilment of duty and exercise of virtue, of an ostensible self-giving and therefore an apparent suppression of *eros*, there is no freedom for genuine love. The presupposition of genuine love is the existence of a man who is free for it, and therefore—since he is not and cannot be this of himself—freed for it. The love of God is this liberation of man for genuine love. When it comes about that God loves a man, that He gives Himself to him and for him, that He gives Himself into his life, by this act of God that man becomes a different man ; not a second God, but a man whom God takes into fellowship with Himself just as he is and in spite of what he is, so that his existence is given a determination which is not only new, but so radically and totally new that the change can be described only as a new creation or a new birth. The newness of his existence consists in the fact that as God gives Himself to him he is stamped by God. In the words of Mt. 5^{45}, he becomes a " child of God " and as such free to model his action on what God does, shaping it in correspondence with the action of his Father. But if love is the action of his Father, its reflection and correspondence in the action of man can consist only in the fact that he also may love and therefore give himself. He is not God, of course, but only a child of God—and this by grace and not by nature. When he loves, therefore, he cannot give what God gives. Even that which he can give he gives only on the basis and according to the model of the divine self-giving. Hence it follows that the divine love and the human are always two different things and cannot be confused. Yet it is more important to assert positively that when the love of God establishes fellowship between God and man it makes man free to imitate His divine action in the sphere and within the limits of human action, and thus to love in human fashion as God does in divine. The one who is loved by God acquires and has this freedom. It is not that he *should* love—but that he *may* and *will*.

Now that we have introduced the ideas of new creation, liberation and therefore the radical alteration of man by the establishment of fellowship between God and himself, we have reached the point where we must take up expressly the theme indicated by the heading of the section : " The Holy Spirit and Christian Love." In their fulfilment in which they become the basis of Christian love the act and work of God are the act and work of the Holy Spirit in whom man is called and drawn by the Father to the Son and the Son to the Father. This is the new creation of man, his liberation, his radical alteration by the established fellowship between God and himself. In this calling and drawing of the Father to the Son and the Son to the Father there takes place the divine love by which man too is made one who loves. But the power of this calling and drawing is the power of the Holy Spirit. We can say only in retrospect that it is also in His power, of course, that there takes place the free election and the great purification of divine love fulfilled in grace and judgment. What we described in the first two characterisations of love was the sovereignty of the Holy Spirit and His mercy and righteousness maintained in face of human sin. We now speak of the creative character of love in which it is the basis of human love. At this point we must be bold to make the direct equation—that the love of God is the creative work of the Holy Spirit. As God is Spirit, the Spirit of the Father and the Son, as He gives Himself into human life as Spirit, and as He bears witness as Spirit to our spirit that we are His children (Rom. 8^{16}), God gives us to participate in the love in which as Father He loves the Son and as Son the Father, making our action a reflection of His eternal love, and ourselves those who may and will love. The fact that human action becomes the reflection, the creaturely similitude, of the divine can and must be described both as the work of God's love and also as the work of His Spirit. It is, in fact, both. As God loves man, giving Himself to him and for him, it comes about that the latter in his action can imitate the love of God, responding and corresponding to it. And it is the power of the Spirit, in which God gives Himself to man, to free him for this imitation, response and correspondence, and therefore to make his action the reflection of His own.

In the light of this equation we must close our deliberations with the statement that in its concrete form the love of God is identical with the action in which Jesus Christ builds His community, calling men to Himself, gathering them in it, giving them a part in its faith and mission, sanctifying them, and therefore treating them as His own, as members of His body. The power of the Holy Spirit works concretely in Church history and the many individual histories included in it, or in the many individual histories which together constitute Church history. And it is in the same sphere, we may now continue, that there operates and lives and rules the love of God as the creative basis of the liberation in which men become those who love ; in which they become Christians and therefore those who love, those who love and therefore Christians. We may distinguish but we cannot separate the upbuilding of the community from the sanctification of its members, or *vice versa*. We may distinguish therefore but we cannot separate the Holy Spirit who edifies and sanctifies the community from the love with which God creates a people of those who love Him. We may distinguish but we cannot separate being a Christian from loving (as though the fact that the one includes the other constituted a problem). We may distinguish but we cannot separate the love with which God by the Holy Spirit loves the community first and then Christians and the love with which, attested by the community and its members, He has turned to all men, to the whole world. By the love of God we have to understand the totality of this happening not only in its inner inter-relationship and movement but also in its unity. In the totality of this happening it is the creative and also the electing and purifying basis of human, genuine, Christian love.

To understand the biblical attestation of this third and final characterisation of the love of God we must start from the simple fact that in both the Old Testament and the New divine and human love are denoted by the same word.

In the first instance this means that we are challenged to consider what gives precedence to divine love over human. And in distinguishing between the two, there can be no question that we have first to ascribe a creative character to God's love in its relationship with that of man. *Duo faciunt idem* when God loves His people Israel, or in Jesus Christ the community, Christians, and typically in them the world, and when love seems also to be expected from Israel, from the community and its members and from men in the world. But *duo cum faciunt idem, non est idem.* And to understand the difference and the connexion between divine love and human we have to take into account the fact that the second can take place only as it is absolutely conditioned by the first, by the fact that the first takes place, so that in the first love we have to do in fact with the creative basis of the second. How does it come about that the Israelites do what is very definitely expected of them in Deut. 6[5], loving Yahweh their God "with all their heart, and with all their mind, and with all their strength"? As their whole history with God demonstrates, it is not that they can produce and achieve this love of themselves. The very idea is unthinkable in view of the radical and total nature of what is expected. But according to Ezek. 11[19] and 36[26] (cf. Jer. 32[39]) it is possible only as the God who has begun and does not cease to love them will finally give them another heart, putting a new spirit within them, taking away the stony heart out of their flesh and giving them a heart of flesh. Or, according to Deut. 30[6]: "Yahweh thy God will circumcise thine heart, and the heart of thy seed, to love Yahweh thy God with all thine heart, and with all thy soul, that thou mayest live." And how can there be any fulfilment when in Mt. 12[29] and par. Jesus takes up expressly the "Hear, O Israel"? In His community too, even in the person of His disciples and apostles, the only possibility is that of Rom. 5[5], that "the love of God is shed abroad in our hearts by the Holy Ghost which is given unto us"; or of Jn. 17[26], that the love with which the Father loves the Son is also in them— not self-evidently, but on the basis and in fulfilment of the petition of the Son— when in the words of Jn. 15[9f.] they abide in His love. According to 1 Cor. 2[9], in that which God has prepared for those who love Him, we have something which the eye of man has not seen nor his ear heard, and which has not entered into his heart. Thus the imitation of the divine action by a human rests on the presupposition that by this preparation certain men are made free and able to accomplish this imitation.

The use of the same term to describe the divine and human action draws our attention to the fact that in the action for which man is freed by the action of God we really have to do with imitation. In this connexion we may first refer to a very explicit New Testament saying in Eph. 5[1]: "Be ye therefore followers (or imitators, μιμηταί) of God as (His) dear children, and walk in love, according as (καθώς) Christ also hath loved you, and hath given himself for you an offering and a sacrifice to God." Paul often described his own apostolic existence as an imitation of this kind—a new "magnifying" (μεγαλύνεσθαι, Phil. 1[20]) of the sacrifice of Jesus Christ. He obviously has this in mind when he opens the concluding exhortation of Romans by summoning his readers to present their bodies (themselves) a living sacrifice, holy, acceptable unto God. But we can hardly understand the radical and total nature of what was expected from the people of Yahweh according to the "Hear, O Israel," if we do not see in the "all thine heart, and all thy soul, and all thy might" a reflection of the radical and total intervention of God Himself on behalf of His people. Indeed, in Deut. 30[11f.] we read the remarkable words (quoted by Paul in Rom. 10[6f.]): "For this commandment which I command thee this day, it is not hidden from thee, neither is it far off. It is not in heaven, that thou shouldest say, Who shall go up for us to heaven, and bring it unto us, that we may hear it, and do it? Neither is it beyond the sea, that thou shouldest say, Who shall go over the sea for us, and bring it unto us, that we may hear it, and do it? But the word is very nigh unto thee, in thy mouth, and in thy heart, that thou mayest do it." What Word and Law is this, which is near and not far off, known and not unknown, practicable and not impracticable, because it has already been set in the mouth and even in the heart of Israel? It is obviously that which is revealed and declared by the very fact that Yahweh Himself has turned to His people, thus taking up its action into fellowship with His own, determining and qualifying it from the very first as an action which responds or corresponds to His own, being the "analogue" of His own "Logos." According to the distinctive outlook and terminology of Deuteronomy, Israel must choose in exact correspondence with the choice or election of Yahweh. It must choose, that is to say, between life and death, between blessing and cursing (Deut. 30[19f.]), or according to Josh. 24[15] between the service of the God of its fathers and that of the gods of other peoples. It must make a right choice, i.e., one which in analogy to that of Yahweh means life and not death, blessing and not cursing, the service of its own God and not that of alien deities. In this right choice it will love Yahweh its God, hearing His Word, cleaving to Him, obeying the Word which has been spoken to it and which is nigh and known and practicable. According to Deut. 30[1f.] the Israelites will also do this when, as both blessing and cursing actually come upon them, they return, and thus give place, in their response of penitence and thankfulness, to the love of God in its character as purifying love. It is surely obvious that in the Old Testament as in the New obedience (to the decision and act and revelation, to the voice and Word and commandment of God) involves a correspondence ; that the whole Law (especially at its heart as a sacrificial order, but also in its legal and other ceremonial provisions) is the comprehensive direction to an attitude on the part of the people which will reflect that of Yahweh ; that the evangelical and apostolic exhortation as a whole is an invitation to discipleship of Jesus Christ and therefore to the imitation of God in what is done and not done by the community and its individual members ; that the prophetic denunciation of Israel has decisive reference to, and acquires its awful severity from, the fact that Israel's declension from its God and His commandments consists concretely in the breach of fellowship between its own being and Himself, which means in practice the breaking of the analogy between its action and that of its God ; and that, conversely, all the joy and thankfulness with which Paul thinks that he can affirm the faith and love and zeal and steadfastness of His communities has its substance in the fact that he sees, or hopes to see, Christ in them (Gal. 4[19]).

The ambivalence of the biblical terminology forces us, finally, to understand the positive connexion between God and man which is obviously envisaged as a liberation which comes to man from God, and not therefore as a demand which God addresses to him. Since the love of God is a creative love which introduces true human love as a new reality, the idea that this has to be demanded from man is rendered quite superfluous. Indeed, do we not have to say that the idea that love demands love is one which is intrinsically impossible, at least when we take the term in its biblical sense as in both cases self-giving ? Giving is a very different thing from demanding. If God's love as His free self-giving to and for man is the basis of man's love, it can have the character only of a liberation which man is given for an action which in correspondence to that of God can only be free and not one which is required or imposed from without, which he is constrained to fulfil. It would be a strange love which demanded love. And it would be a strange love which was merely a response to this demand. It is the nerve of the whole relationship between the love of God and that of man that by the love of God man is put in a position to love, that he may do so, that he is not bullied or prodded to do so by any compelling authority from without, that he is really free—made free—to do so of himself in imitation of the self-giving of God. If this is not the case, what does it mean that in this connexion the Old Testament speaks so emphatically of the heart as the place where this whole movement is initiated ? Surely it is not love from the heart, or with the whole heart, if there is any question of compulsion, if we have to love in the required fulfilment of duty or exercise of virtue ?

It was, of course, upon the constraint of a " Thou shalt love " that Kierkegaard thought it necessary to construct his whole book : *The Life and Rule of Love.* As he saw it, love is a duty, and it is as such that it is the revelation which with divine originality enters the lists against human self-love, the " eternal change " which not only astonishes man but stirs and provokes him (ed. Diederich, 1924, p. 27). It is only the duty to love which eternally protects love against every change, making it eternally free in happy independence, eternally assuring it against all despair (p. 31 f.). The " Thou shalt " of eternity is that which saves and purifies and ennobles. " Where that which is only human seeks to press forward, the commandment restrains ; where that which is only human loses heart, the commandment strengthens ; where that which is purely human becomes lifeless and prudent, the commandment gives fire and wisdom. The commandment consumes and burns up that which is unhealthy in thy love. By the commandment thou canst inflame it again when it bids fair to die down. Where thou thinkest thou canst easily counsel thyself, the commandment intrudes upon thy counsels. Where thou turnest to thine own counsel in despair, thou shouldest turn to it for counsel. Where thou canst think of no counsel, it will create it for thee, and all will be well." It may be sensed what Kierkegaard has in mind. But as he states it here, it is quite false. It is hardly surprising, then, that for all its individual beauties his book assumes on this presupposition the unlovely, inquisitorial and terribly judicial character which is so distinctive of Kierkegaard in general. It is not at all the case that we can be silent, as Kierkegaard is, about the creative, generous, liberating love of God, and speak instead only of the naked commandment : " Thou shalt," as the basis of Christian love. There are certainly no biblical grounds for doing so. It is not at all the case that eternity (at least in the biblical sense) must be described as the overhanging wall of this : " Thou shalt," which impresses because it provokes, and then suddenly becomes as such a saving power and the source of all good counsel. It may be so according to a particular understanding of Kantian ethics, but it is definitely not the case according to the Bible that a rigid " Thou shalt " confronts that which is human with the power to change self-love into love. And it is not the case that a love which is imposed and enforced as a duty—however it may be understood—can ever be more than an *eros* with its back to the wall as it were. It certainly is not the love in which man really gives himself.

The doubtful translation of *ahabta* (ἀγαπήσεις, *diliges*) by " Thou *shalt* love " (Deut. 6⁵) is responsible in part for the fateful misunderstanding of others as well as Kierkegaard at this point. In the pre-Kantian period the English " Thou shalt " may well have approximated to what is intended by the Bible both here and in the formulation of the commandments generally. But the ἀγαπήσεις of the LXX is better, as is also the *Tu aimeras* of the French version, which is based on the Vulgate *diliges*. What we have is not an abstract demand but a direction which points to an inescapable conclusion in the form of a future. From the being of Yahweh as the one God of Israel there follows for the latter (" Hear, O Israel ") : " Thou wilt love." Because God is bound to thee, and thou to Him, no other action can result but that which is envisaged and posited in this relationship ; the action in which this thy God (and thy neighbour, as Mk. 12³¹ adds from another passage) is to be loved by thee, His self-giving finding a response and reflection in thine. We may paraphrase as follows. By thy liberation from Egypt, which is the work of the electing, purifying and creative love of thy God, thou are made free for this action, being set on the way and in motion. It is in the power of this divine action, which according to the New Testament is the power of the reconciling act which fulfils the covenant of Yahweh in the person of Jesus Christ, that there consists, as the Bible sees it, all the authority and power of the divine commandment, of all the divine commandments, and the superiority (this is the place for Kierkegaard's favourite concept of eternity) with which man is directed to the way of love as the way of life, and therefore to enter this way and this way alone. By this authority and power human love is truly and solidly grounded as a genuine, spontaneous, natural and therefore sincere action which is necessary in its freedom and free in its necessity. " I will put my law in their inward parts, and write it in their hearts "

(Jer. 31[33]). This and this alone is the basis of the love which is the fulfilment of the whole Law. And as God does this His Law, in virtue of which love is expected of man, is the Law of the Gospel.

3. THE ACT OF LOVE

We are not forgetting, or leaving behind, what we have said about the basic love of God if now, in a turn of 180 degrees, we direct our attention to the human, Christian love based on it. Our specific concern in this section is to unfold the action of the Christian subject as such.

What does the Christian do ? He does what he may do, what he has the freedom to do, as one who is loved by God. He loves. He is a man, indeed a sinful man. He has a part in the pride and fall, the sloth and misery, of all men. He is a sinner more intensively than all others because he knows that he is. And so he does many things— far too many—which have nothing whatever to do with, but are in fact opposed to, the love for which he is liberated as one who is loved by God. But in so far as he is a Christian he also loves, just as he believes and hopes as such, in spite of all the other things that he is and does. We will have to come back to the limitation which results from the fact that we cannot truthfully say that he loves wholly and utterly and therefore exclusively, but only that he also loves. For the moment, however, we will keep to the positive fact that this action also consists in the fact that he loves. With its own limitation and in its own way, this too does take place in his life. And the fact that on the basis of the love of God this too does take place in his life has to be taken into account. It cannot be without significance for his other activity, however different or opposed. His love will secretly or openly counteract his other activity (not in the strength which he himself gives it, but in the strength of its divine basis). It will leave its mark upon the character of his life-act as a whole. To be sure, this will not be unequivocally evident. And he himself, we may hope, will be the last to imagine that his love is co-extensive with the rest of his activity. For to the extent that he reflects concerning it, and tries to cling to the results of this reflection, he will not love, and will thus destroy the very thing to which he clings. We cannot love in order to achieve something—not even the peace of a relatively good, or not too bad, conscience. Love is betrayed if we try to make it the object of this type of calculation. And in any case, the calculation itself is futile from the very outset, since there can be no question of a justification of man before God by his action, not even by that of a most powerful love in his life. This does not mean, however, that it is without significance if in his life it may also happen, with many other things, that he loves. For if this were the case, it would mean that it is without significance that God loves him, and that there may be an imitation of the love of God in his life. No, that which, surrounded and covered and compromised by a very different activity, takes place in the life of a man as the act of love, does so on the basis of the divine creation and is therefore a reality which counts in the sight of God, not to the praise or defence or justification of this man, but in the context of what He wills for him, of the service for which He has determined and uses him. In relation to the other things which the man is and does, it may be only like a spark under a heap of ashes. But apart from and side by side with everything else that he does, he does also love—because he may do so, because he has from God the freedom also to do so—and this makes his whole life different from what it would be if he did not love. As this too takes place in it, it is a Christian life. It would be unchristian only if the act of love did not take place in it at all. And this would mean that God cannot use him at all in His service.

But we must now be more precise and ask : What takes place in this act ? What takes place when a man and therefore the Christian —a sinful man, to be sure, and therefore one who does very different things as well—may love ? It is obvious that to understand the content of this act, we must consider its object, and therefore the fact that in it we have to do with the love of God and one's neighbour. But certain considerations concerning its general form will not be irrelevant or superfluous.

It is evident that the New Testament words ἀγάπη and φιλία, and the corresponding verbs, are not infrequently used absolutely, i.e., without any express mention of that to which they refer. Instances may be found in the passage 1 Jn. 4⁷ᶠ· to which we have already referred, in the various combinations of love (already quoted) with faith and hope and patience and other leading concepts which characterise Christian existence, and especially in 1 Cor. 13—a chapter which is central to our whole subject. As Christ dwells in their hearts by faith, Christians are ἐν ἀγάπῃ ἐρριζωμένοι καὶ τεθεμελιωμένοι (Eph. 3¹⁷), and their life is a περιπατεῖν κατὰ ἀγάπην (Rom. 14¹⁵). According to Col. 3¹²ᶠ· love is the sum of all the mercy, goodness, humility, long-suffering and mutual forbearance and forgiveness that those who are chosen and sanctified and loved by God are to " put on " as a garment which is prepared for them and suits them. It is the σύνδεσμος τῆς τελειότητος, the bond which unites all the individual elements, which embraces their activity, and from which they move unitedly to their goal. Love is the fulfilling of the Law (Rom. 13¹⁰). Now obviously in all these passages we have to think at once both of the living basis and also of the object of ἀγάπη, an object which is decisive for the content of the term. But as these are self-evidently implied, the term describes basically and comprehensively the form of life which characterises the existence of the community and its members, and which is indispensable if they are what they are.

We must first put the general question what kind of a form this is. And (1) there can be no doubt that in the life of the one who may perform it the act of love will have the character of something new and unusual and (from the human standpoint) unexpected. For in it

there is realised the deepest and true being of man—his determination
for God and for fellow-humanity. It is that which is expected on the
part of God. In view of the corruption of human existence it is not
self-evident that it should take place. *Eros*, self-love (in its higher
and lower manifestations), is the supremely natural, the old and accustomed thing, the repetition and outworking of which are to be expected
with the necessity of a law. The same cannot be said of Christian love.
That it takes place because and as a man like all the rest is free for it
and made capable of it, can never be deduced from some existing factor,
and therefore foreseen and expected, since it can be based only on
the event of new creation and new birth. If it takes place at all, it
does so in a mighty act of the Holy Ghost for whom we can only pray,
whose presence and action can only cause grateful astonishment even
to those who are active in love, let alone to others. That a man loves
will always be a source of wonder and surprise. It will always be the
great exception in his life. For a proper estimation of the greatly
devalued term " love " it is as well to be clear that where love takes
place we have to do with nothing more nor less than a revelation of
the real presence of God in Jesus Christ.

We cannot rightly interpret any of the New Testament passages which point
to this human act if we do not realise that the use of the term " love " is tacitly
enwrapped in thankful adoration, in sheer joy at the presence of the unexpected,
of what we can only pray for. This is brought out very clearly by the introduc-
tions to the Pauline Epistles, which deserve our closest attention.

But (2) we have also to underline no less definitely that we have to
describe love quite unequivocally as a free act of man. Already we
have found it necessary to think of it as a human response, correspondence, imitation, or analogy to the love of God as we spoke of the latter
as its basis. Two delimitations are essential in this regard.

Christian love, as we have had to indicate already, is not a kind of
prolongation of the divine love itself, its overflowing into human life
which man with his activity has to serve as a kind of channel, being
merely present and not at bottom an acting subject. It is not the
work of the Holy Spirit to take from man his own proper activity, or
to make it simply a function of His own overpowering control. Where
He is present, there is no servitude but freedom. This false conception
is contradicted by the great frailty of that which emerges as love in
the life of even the best Christians. If it were merely identical with the
flowing of the stream of divine love into human life, if our little love
were a manifestation or particle of the love of God, it could not and
would not be so weak and puny. But the work of the Holy Spirit
consists in the liberation of man for his own act and therefore for the
spontaneous human love whose littleness and frailty are his own responsibility and not that of the Holy Spirit. Christian love as a human
act corresponds indeed to the love of God but is also to be distinguished

from it. It is an act in which man is at work, not as God's puppet, but with his own heart and soul and strength, as an independent subject who encounters and replies to God and is responsible to Him as His partner.

The second idea that we have to reject is that in the human response to God's love we have only a correspondence in disposition or in thought and emotion. This is false because in the love of God we do not have to do primarily with a disposition or with thought and emotion but with an act which God has willed and executed with all the energy of the crucifixion. It is this act which is the basis, the creative model, of true human love. If the latter is its imitation, it too is an act, and not merely an internal but an external act, the act of the whole man. A man may have many thoughts and emotions of love and yet not love or give himself by a long way. If he does love, he does not do so partially, and therefore he does not do so just inwardly or just outwardly. It is another question how much or little of his whole being is lacking when he loves. There will always be a good deal. But no unfortunate deficiency in this regard can be justified theoretically by reducing the love for which he was liberated to something merely inward. He is freed by the love of God to love " in deed and in truth " (1 Jn. 3[18]). Where there is love, there takes place something from God, but in space and time, " with hearts and hands and voices." Where there is no human act in the full sense of the term, there is no love. For there is no imitation of God.

The new thing that man does as he may love has (3) the form and character of an impartation. To love is to do that which is " better than to receive " (Ac. 20[35]), namely, to give. It is because it is a matter of giving that we must insist so strongly that love cannot be a merely inward action. Dispositions and thoughts and emotions may be very lofty and profound, but their movement is inward ; they are not giving. A merely inward action is not a genuine action at all. It is not one in which something happens. But according to the example of God Himself love is the action of giving, and it is therefore one in which man moves out from himself. " God loveth a cheerful giver " (2 Cor. 9[7]). Giving is very different from keeping and taking. *Eros* takes and it then has to keep and take again. Love breaks this circle. The one who loves gives. He is marvellously freed to do this. In the power of the Holy Spirit he does this new and unexpected thing. It is not that he has not received and does not have—for how else could he give ? He is most generously endowed—the wealthiest man on earth—and he is correspondingly grateful. But he does not think about this. He simply is it. And he is it, and enjoys it, only as he gives. We recall that it is only side by side with and among many other and very different things—and not exclusively—that it also takes place in his life that he gives. But it is as he does this also that, while he is not justified, yet, as the great and miserable sinner that he is as well, he is useful to God, and set in His service—a Christian. Where there is love and therefore giving, there is always this happening ; and a house, if not a temple, of God is established in the midst of sinners. But giving, as we know, means self-giving—sacrifice. And in practice this includes many kinds of giving.

It is not sacrifice if—to speak with brutal frankness—it does not involve the offering of money, from which not even the Christian is parted too easily. The sacrifice of time will also be required, even at the risk of becoming victims of the terrible race of " Chronophagi."

But what is the value of all our giving of money and time and other good things if they are not given sacrificially—in self-giving ? The one who loves gives himself instead of trying to keep and maintain himself. It is in so doing and to this extent that he also gives the other things which are his. He gives nothing, and he does not love at all, if he does not give himself. Self-giving has a most impressive sound. It smacks of heroism and sacrifice. But in reality it is nothing out of the ordinary. For to love and therefore to give ourselves is simply to affirm in practice that we do not belong to ourselves, and never have done, or will or even can do. We give from that which is not ours, which we have seized unlawfully if we make it our own, which can be ours only as we give it. The love of God frees us for this action which is basically so self-evident. It is possible as we are newly created and enlightened and called and taught and impelled by the Holy Spirit. We may be rather startled at our own temerity as we do it, or concerned as to the possible outcome, but when we love we do it. It is as though a cave-dweller were brought out into the open, blinking a little because the sun shines so brightly, and concerned a little because there is also wind and rain, but at any rate emerging. And since love consists in the fact that man gives himself and therefore emerges from himself, it has the form and character of what is, in the most profound and comprehensive sense of the term, an impartation. The one who loves does not divide up himself, but without thought for what may become of him he imparts himself, so that he does not have his " part " (himself) only for himself, but together with the other, the one whom he loves, to whom he gives himself. This does not mean, as the matter is often represented, that there is an extinction or annihilation of the one who loves in favour of the one whom he loves. How can this be love ? On this unhealthy view how can there be anything but a withdrawal from the loved one —by a departure in death ? It is a matter of giving ourselves to the loved one, and therefore, as we continue to be ourselves, of renouncing the false idea that we belong to ourselves and being ourselves together with the loved one, in relationship with him. This relationship is the open into which the cave-dweller emerges when he is made one who loves by the love of God, by the work of the Holy Spirit. When he does not keep and maintain but gives himself, he does not exclude himself in relation to the loved one, but at all costs and whatever else betide he includes himself in the being of the loved one. He does not include the loved one in his own being (which would be *eros*), but his own being in that of the loved one, so that it is his own on behalf of the loved one. The one who loves gives to the one whom he loves no more and no less than his " heart." So seriously is love self-giving that his life is an " eccentric " life, i.e., one which has its centre outside itself. This is what God does when He loves us, and therefore gives Himself to us and for us. He does not cease to be the One He is, the eternal God, who is love in Himself. But as such He comes alongside us. In His life and work He does not exclude our life and work, but includes them. He imparts Himself to us, entering into relationship and fellowship with us. He gives us His heart, and in this way He not merely procures but Himself is our salvation. This divine action is what the man who loves, the Christian, may imitate in his action.

A most important feature would be lacking in this formal description of love if we did not emphasise expressly (4) that it necessarily means exaltation, gain and joy for the one who may perform this action, for the Christian. He does not perform it for this reason. We cannot insist too sharply that we do not love for any external reason, with any ulterior motive, or in the execution of any design or purpose. The one who loves does not want anything except to love, except more fully and seriously and perfectly to give himself, to enter into relationship with the loved one. If he has any other plan or project—however noble—it means that his love is betrayed and ended.

It is perhaps because this is continually forgotten that with all the talk of love—even among Christians—there is so little of the love which gladdens those who are supposed to love and therefore those who are supposed to be loved, and so much of the love which seems to be to them a burden rather than the joy it can and ought to be. In baroque fashion, this is just because the idea is prevalent that we can and should love for the sake of our own enjoyment, or more seriously our own elevation, imagining that (in the best sense) it will be to our advantage to do so.

But this warning must not be allowed to hide the fact that love not only brings with it, but definitely is, that which we cannot (without betraying it) seek to attain with its help : exaltation, gain and joy for the one who may love. It is only with the most stringent reservations, and in the last resort not at all, that we can say the same of *eros*. At bottom the well-known cycle of *eros*, with its alternation of possession and loss, intoxication and soberness, enthusiasm and disillusionment, is a tragic and therefore a melancholy business. But of love we have to say unconditionally that the man who loves is as such —and we may confidently use the captious term—a happy man, a man who is to be counted blessed. We may even add that the man does not love at all who does so with a tragic countenance, who does not find in so doing a well-being which far surpasses any other. If his action as one who loves is a burden to him, this merely betrays the fact that his real concern is elsewhere. God certainly does not like an uncheerful giver. The one who may love and therefore give, offering and imparting himself, entering into relationship with the loved one, may have joy—great joy—in doing so, no matter how high may be the cost or how little the success in the form of a response of love on the part of the one whom he loves. Nor is this merely because his liberation for love, whenever he avails himself of it, means his release from a whole mountain of unnecessary worry and anxiety created merely by the fact that his previous concern was so much with taking and keeping instead of giving. This is certainly one of the reasons. For no one can adequately describe the liberation which actually takes place when a man is finally prepared to give his heart instead of cherishing and pampering and nursing it as though this would in some way help. When love brings about even a momentary change, the quickening of the whole man beggars description. Yet the true and positive and genuinely indescribable joy of the one who loves consists simply in the fact that he may love as one who is loved by God, as the child of God ; that as he imitates the divine action he may exist in fellowship with Him, obedient to His Holy Spirit. This is exaltation and gain ; this is peace and joy. This is a reason for laughing even when our eyes swim with tears. For in face of this what is the significance of all the cares and failures which even those who love as Christians are certainly not spared ? This is the blessedness of him who loves—unsought, unplanned and undesired—even when his love beats against a stone wall, receiving no answer, or only a more or less hostile answer, from the one whom he loves. He does not love him for the sake of his answer, but because he is made free to do so by God. The peace and joy of the one who is liberated and who therefore loves in this way can never suffer disillusionment. The praise laid in his heart and on his lips of the God who has freed him for this action, and who orders it as the One who has freed him for it, is neverending, as drastically revealed in the seemingly never-ending magnifying of the Law in Ps. 119, and attested in the shorter but all the more intensive magnifying of *agape* in 1 Cor. 13. Love and joy have it in common—and therein reveal their profoundly necessary interconnexion—that neither of them is ordered or can be produced or practised to order. Both grow of themselves from God the Liberator, and from the occurrence of His act of liberation. And the one is the infallible criterion of the other. The man who genuinely loves is also a cheerful man—if he is not he does not genuinely love. And the genuinely cheerful man is also one who loves—if he is not he has good reason to ask how genuine is his cheerfulness.

We now turn to the main theme of this sub-section and the whole of this concluding section—the question of the meaning and content of this act. We will now have to speak of the object of Christian love. What self-giving is and means can be known only in the relationship in which the act takes place. But it takes place in the relationship of the one who loves to the one whom he loves. If this is the case, however, it is obvious that its meaning and content are not to be sought in the action of the one who loves in itself and as such, but where he gives himself, where his heart is—in the loved one from whom he does not exclude but in whom he includes himself, entering into a relationship of love. It is the loved one who decides what is done when he loves, and it is with reference to this one that we must understand it.

In the first instance this question does not present any difficulty. Christian love is the response of love based on the electing, purifying and creative love of God. It is thus love for God as the One by whom the Christian is first loved. In the act of love of which we have to speak in the concluding section of the second part of the doctrine of reconciliation it takes place—and this is its unfathomable meaning and content—that the relationship of the covenant, the covenant of grace, becomes two-sided instead of one-sided. The space which confronts the Word and work of God's grace does not remain empty. On the contrary, the monstrous hostility of man to God which invaded and dominated this space disappears. The word and work of human gratitude encounter and respond and correspond to the Word and work of God's grace. No more and no less than this takes place when man—the Christian—may love. " Being justified by faith, let us have peace with God through our Lord Jesus Christ " (Rom. 5[1]), is realised by man too in the act of love, for this is an irresistible consequence of the fact that Jesus Christ is very God and very man. The Christian attests this in the fact that he may love God. This is the meaning and content of the act of his love. And this explains all that we have had to say concerning its formal character. It is because it is no more and no less than an integral element in the divinely inaugurated and controlled history of the kingdom and salvation that it is so new and strange, that it must and may be the free act of man in the liberating power of the Holy Spirit, that it is that step into the open, into fellowship, and that it is necessarily the act of the cheerful man. No more and no less than the reconciliation of man with God attains in it its provisional goal and end.

It is worth pausing a moment to consider how inconceivable is this clear and simple fact—that to the eternal love which is in God, and with which He has turned to man, there corresponds the fact that man may love God. Is not the mystery of reconciliation almost greater on this human side, from below, than it is on the divine ? It is at least as great. For how can it be true, possible and actual, that a man loves God as God loves him ? We will leave aside for the time being the frailty and imperfection and doubtfulness with which even the greatest saint does this. In spite of all that may rightly and necessarily be said against his love, in face of the whole heap of mud and dross and rubble and ashes under which his little love is hidden, in face of the fact that there is nothing praiseworthy or meritorious in this action, it takes place by the quickening power of the Holy Spirit that small and sinful man may love the great and holy God, responding to the divine self-offering with his own. This is the will of God, and it takes place in fulfilment of His will—which is done on earth as it is in heaven. God wills that this should take place, and He sees to it that He acquires that which He does not need, which adds nothing to Him, which does not make Him richer, which He might just as well do without, but which He does not will to be without—the self-giving of man, and therefore man as the one who imitates and copies him, and the action of man as the echo of His own. " What is man, that thou art mindful of him ? and the son of man, that thou visitest him ? " (Ps. 8⁴)—that Thou art mindful of him and visitest him in such a way that Thou wilt and dost have pleasure in the praise of his love which he himself offers in his own free act ? Is it not enough that God is good to man ? Does He really will and bring it about that man should be good to Him ? Is it really the case that He has caused His Word to become flesh not merely in order that He may be and act for us in His own person, but in order that we also may be and act for Him ? Does He really will and need us to serve Him ? There is no end to the questions that we might put in face of that which God has actually willed and done, and does actually will and do, in this respect. But we must not ignore the fact that even the most serious and critical questions in this regard can arise only from the answer which is already given with the fact that the Christian may love God, and that in so far as he is a Christian he does actually do so. There is no sense in involving ourselves in these questions and childishly omitting to do what we may do. As truly as God loves us we may love Him in return. It is quite incomprehensible, but we may do it. Let us therefore do it : " Thou shalt love the Lord thy God with all thine heart, and with all thy soul, and with all thy strength." The tiniest movement in the freedom which we are given is better than the most elaborate deliberations whether or not it is permitted or practicable. But the fact that we have the freedom for this movement is a miracle which we can rightly value only as we grasp it. It is no less a miracle than the Virgin Birth of Jesus Christ or His bodily resurrection from the dead. Only if we measure it by the miracle of Epiphany, which is its basis and original, can we comprehend the mystery by which the act of love is surrounded as the love of man for God.

The Old Testament concept of love for God is older than Deuteronomy. " Those that love thee are as the sun when he goeth forth in his might," is the concluding verse of the Song of Deborah (Jud. 5³¹). Hosea, too, seems to presuppose it when he brings against Ephraim and Judah the accusation (6⁴) : " Your love (and the context makes it plain that what is meant is your response of love to Yahweh) is as a morning cloud, and as the early dew it goeth away " ; or when he states (4¹) that as there is no faithfulness nor knowledge of God, so there is no love in the land ; or when he says (6⁶) that Yahweh delights in love and not in burnt-offerings. The latter antithesis is instructive. In the burnt-offering the Israelitish peasant offers a part of his most valuable possession. With the shedding of the blood of the animal he yields up its " soul " to God, i.e., its life as a substitute for his own. And with the sacrifice of the animal, or part of it, to be burnt on the altar he offers himself to the fire of the might and holiness of the holy God. In the burnt-offering there thus takes place figuratively that which takes place literally and strictly in love for God. The offering can be brought either with or without that which it represents—love for God. The prophetic antithesis : Love, not sacrifice, is made in face of the offering which is brought without it. It points to the centre of the cultic event and the whole covenant with Yahweh ; to that which ought to take place as the human complement on the part of the people, but which is omitted and does not take place, being represented but only represented in the cultus. The positive point at issue emerges clearly in Ps. 18¹, where the thanksgiving ascribed to the victorious David (cf. also 2 Sam. 22), and especially the description of Yahweh as " my rock, and my fortress, and my deliverer ; my God, my strength, in whom I will trust ; my buckler, and the horn of my salvation, and my high tower," is prefaced by the statement : " I will love thee, O Lord, my strength." In the Old Testament to love God means not to have any strength of one's own in face of Him ; to give oneself wholly to Him ; to act as one who is enclosed and upheld by Him and sheltered in Him ; and thus to call upon Him with assurance as the One who delivers from death (Ps. 116¹ᶠ·). According to the usage of the Old Testament, exactly the same is meant, and not something weaker, by the more usual indirect references, i.e., to the acts of God in revelation. The pious Israelites love the name of Yahweh (Ps. 5¹¹), or the salvation which comes from Him (Ps. 40¹⁶), or His Word (Ps. 119¹⁴⁰), or His Law (Ps. 119⁹⁷), or the habitation of His house (Ps. 26⁸). There is obviously a sense of saying something extraordinary in these statements. There is obviously an awareness of touching on the inner secret of the existence of Israel on the side on which it is continually and most severely compromised by the Israelite. It is not surprising, therefore, if it is relatively seldom and only by individuals—like King Solomon (with his eschatological traits) in 1 K. 3³—that there is express mention made of love for Yahweh.

When we turn to the New Testament, we can only say that the situation is the same in this respect—that while the references are definite enough they are not particularly numerous. Mention has already been made of such well-known verses as Rom. 8²⁸, 1 Cor. 2⁹ and 1 Cor. 8³. We may also add 2 Thess. 3⁵ : " And the Lord direct your hearts into the love of God," and Jas. 1¹², which speaks of " the crown of life, which the Lord hath promised to them that love him." The accusation against the Pharisees in Lk. 11⁴² is that they neglected (παρέρχεσθε) judgment and the love of God, and against the " Jews " generally in Jn. 5⁴² that they did not have the love of God in them. This is about all—apart from the " first " commandment in Mk. 12²⁹ᶠ· and par., which claims our attention from the very outset. But, of course, we have to add the more numerous passages —corresponding formally to the love of God's name or salvation or Word in the Old Testament—which speak of love for Jesus. In the older Pauline writings this expression occurs only once, and it is used in a way which is almost terrifyingly categorical : " If any man love not (φιλεῖ) the Lord Jesus Christ, let him be ἀνάθεμα " (1 Cor. 16²²). We may add to this the concluding greeting of Ephesians : " Grace be with all them that love our Lord Jesus Christ " (6²⁴).

We may also refer to 2 Tim. 4⁸, where there is mention again of the crown which according to Jas. 1¹² is to be given to them that love God, but this time—and it obviously amounts to the same thing as the New Testament understands it— it is promised to those who love the *ἐπιφάνεια* of the *Kyrios*. In 1 Pet. 1⁸, too, Christians as such are addressed as those who love Jesus Christ although they have not seen Him, and believe in Him although they do not now see Him. For the most part, however, we have to turn to the Johannine writings. Here again we see that love for Jesus is identical with love for God : " And every one that loveth him that begat loveth him also that is begotten of him " (1 Jn. 5¹) ; or in the saying of Jesus to the Jews : " If God were your Father, ye would love me " (Jn. 8⁴²). Hence in Jn. 14¹⁵, ²¹, ²³ᶠ·, ²⁸ and 16²⁷ love for Jesus is expressly presupposed as the self-evident attitude and mark of the disciple. And that this is the case is something which finally we cannot overlook in the conversation between the risen Christ and Peter in the second concluding chapter of the Gospel (21¹⁵⁻¹⁷), where Peter is asked three times : " Lovest thou me ? " and three times, and the last time " grieved," he answers : " Lord, thou knowest it— thou knowest all things ; thou knowest that I love thee " (v. 17). According to the whole context love for Jesus and therefore love for God is obviously the presupposition of the discipleship laid upon and expected from Peter—hence the twofold " Follow me " (vv. 19 and 20)—which implies both his mission (" Feed my sheep," v. 15 f.) and also what will become of him, namely, that instead of being one who girds himself and goes where he wants, he will now be one who is girded by another and taken where he does not want. Love for Jesus and therefore love for God is the disciple's determination for both these things, and its nature is reflected unmistakeably in this twofold determination.

The Christian's love for God, identical in the New Testament with his love for Jesus, consists in the fact (if we may be permitted an expression which sounds banal but in the strict sense is full of content) that he is a man who is *interested* in God, i.e., in " God in Christ." God has him, and therefore for good or evil he must have God. God is for him, and so he has no option but to be for God. He is this not merely peripherally but centrally ; not merely momentarily but—no matter how often he may forget or deny it—in the continuity of his existence, of his life-act. He does not cease to confess that he is a great sinner. But like Jeremiah (1⁵) and Paul (Gal. 1¹⁵) he will think of himself as predestinated to love, and therefore, although his love may and will grow cold (Mt. 24¹²), there can be no question of its complete extinction. Otherwise, he would not love God. If he loves Him, he knows in advance and counts on the fact that he may and must and can love Him again, and will actually do so. There may be other notes—good and bad, beautiful and ugly. There may be periods of integration and dissolution, of clarification and confusion, of vivification and lassitude, of advance and retreat, of certainty and doubt, of enlightenment and folly. But once it has been sounded, the basic note continues. And the basic note in the life of the Christian as the man who loves God is that the One above, the Crucified and Risen, is—how shall we put it ?—important to him ; that everywhere and constantly and repeatedly, with a definiteness which cannot be excelled, in a way which cannot be said of the other things and factors which interest and claim and gladden and trouble him, or of other

men or the whole world or even himself, He has significance as the
axiom of all axioms. He loves God in that he makes use of the freedom
to give himself to Him. He has himself, and everything else, only as
God has him. His heart, and all that he may desire and need, and
not only his heart but also his reason and conscience and instinct for
life, are really above with God. He is God's prisoner, and therefore
stands strongly on this rock and is solidly at home in this fortress.
Worldly things and relationships affect and move him, and worldly
problems burden and excite him. He lives in the hope and despair
which are his lot in face of them. But he also lives under the distinctive
constraint (which is his distinctive freedom) to give the precedence
over these things to Him that is above ; so that if it is beyond his
capacity simply to see them in the light of God, he will constantly
reconsider them with the question how they appear in this light, what
corresponds to the will of God in his own relationship to them, what is
His secret in and behind all the mysteries of being, and therefore what
is the task which He has laid upon him. The Christian and therefore
the man who loves God is no heaven-storming idealist. But his
interest is in the *ens realissimum* : the cause of God on earth ; His
cause for and against and with the world and men and himself ; His
cause which is not a cause but His work, His kingdom, and in His
work and kingdom He Himself, the living God, the living Jesus. He
hears Him speak through every other noise. He sees Him at work
through all the clouds and mists. While he knows all the obstruction
and sabotage with which various individuals and above all he himself
oppose Him, he may and must continually discover and realise that
he is not at his own disposal but at God's disposal, and that he must
serve Him. He accepts this as right and good. And he thus learns
by experience that "all things work together for good " (Rom. 8[28]).
He tastes and sees "that the Lord is good " (Ps. 34[8]). And he therefore trusts Him. He is not afraid to cast himself on Him. He fears
neither the solitude to which he condemns himself by this curious
action, the strangeness by which he too seems to be enveloped, the
divine invisibility which conceals him too—not only from the eyes of
others but also from his own eyes—as he loves Him, nor the divine
sovereignty which he learns to know all the more tangibly the more
he submits to it. He has only one thing to fear : that God, Jesus,
will no longer love him—which would mean the end of his own love.
But this is the last thing he really has to fear or can fear. He is,
therefore, strong and ready. He is salted with salt and garrisoned with
peace. His love for God can and may and must be his joy in Him,
his rejoicing even in the deepest depth in which he may find himself
of his own guilt and need and lostness or that of others. What is the
meaning of love for God, for Jesus ? It means that God, Jesus, is so
urgent and pressing that he may and must yield to this constraint of
love in the experience of its glory, giving place to it, and taking it

into account, in concrete thoughts and words and works. And in this yielding he really gives himself to Him. And as he does so he acquires good cause and reason continually to do so again.

A short excursus may be inserted at this point in answer to possible criticism. In the course of the modern theological renewal, and under the influence of the ethics of Kant and the theology of A. Ritschl, a pronounced Puritanism has become the fashion in relation to love for God or for Jesus. The proviso of the Old and New Testament, that it is possible only in obedience to the will of God or Jesus, and in unity with love for one's neighbour, has not only been observed as it ought, but has been expounded in such a way as to eliminate any direct love for God or Jesus, identifying the Christian act of love in practice only with obedience in love for one's neighbour. And to prove that anything beyond this is a debased religious eroticism, terrifying examples are adduced from mediæval Mysticism, from older and more recent forms of Pietism, from Zinzendorf, and from the Romanticism of the early 19th century. Hymns like " How beauteous shines the morning star," " I will love Thee, Thou my strength," and others which point in a similar direction, are either omitted or sung only with inner misgivings. A kind of holy sobriety has mounted guard against all sentimentalisation, and with a strong insistence on justification by faith alone, and the practical demonstration of faith in deeds and works, it has been zealous to have the last word, sometimes expressing itself in strict prohibitions and condemnations. In his bitter fight for *agape* against *eros* A. Nygren (*op. cit.*, I, p. 104 f.) has even decreed that there can be no question of a spontaneous love of man for God, and that in the first part of the twofold command there is in the Synoptics a lack of clarity in this respect which is happily overcome in Paul. Since in my earlier period I myself made some direct and indirect contribution to this attitude, I think it only right briefly to state my present views on the matter.

There can be no contesting the relative justification of reactions of this kind (and this one in particular). Christian love, especially in its form as love for God and for Jesus, is continually exposed to transformation into its erotico-religious opposite. There have been and are manifestations of it in which this inversion is not merely a danger but, unless appearances deceive, has actually become and is a fatal event ; incursions of paganism which may well be compared to those of Canaanite religion into the worship of Yahweh. It was this that we had in view some forty years ago. The only thing is that we were a little late with our protest, since the final and true epogee of the type of love rejected was long since past. It lived on only in the form of reminiscences and repristinations. There was no obvious superfluity of living mystics and pietists of the first rank, and therefore no acute danger from this angle. All the same, it was a time when we had to deal with Neo-Protestantism, and since in the investigation of its origins we rightly came on Mysticism and Pietism it was natural that we should be sharp-sighted and rather severe in this respect. In the process, as often happens, we were only too wise and superior, and instead of arguing and speaking in Reformation categories, as we thought, we sometimes slipped back unconsciously in our zeal into the other basic aspect of Neo-Protestantism, that of rationalistic moralism, thus giving vital and earnest Christians of various types every reason to ask whether anything useful had been achieved with this kind of temple-cleansing. We imagined that we had freed ourselves from Mysticism, Pietism and Romanticism and their dangerous off-shoots. But were we not on the point of subscribing to a no less dubious antithesis (that of A. Ritschl and his disciples and successors), according to which the work of the Holy Spirit must be reduced to the management of an eternal working-day, and with the abolition of a true and direct love for God and Jesus there is basically no place for prayer ? There was scope for better instruction at this point. Perhaps we may put it this way. Since this had never been our intention, there was need for a better understanding of ourselves than had been possible, or communicable to others, in that revolutionary time.

The first point to be made is the simple one that the biblical witness to love for God and for Jesus is much too strong and explicit to permit us conscientiously to regard the concept merely as an alternative for " obedience " or " love for one's neighbour," thus evading its true meaning. To be sure, its content does call immediately and inexorably for that of these other concepts—we shall have to turn to this aspect later. But the biblical authors were surely introducing unnecessary complications if when they spoke so emphatically of love for God and for Jesus they had in mind only what in other places they called obedience and love for one's neighbour. We cannot overlook the fact that in the passages in which it occurs this concept has its own distinctive ring, and that this points to the fact that in relation to these other concepts it has also its own distinctive content, which cannot be separated from, but cannot be identified with, that of the other concepts. The restraint with which Scripture speaks of the matter, but also the unmistakeable solemnity with which it does so when the occasion arises, make it plain that in this respect we are not dealing with deductions (however necessary) but with the original, the presupposition, which gives rise to deductions ; not with the periphery which inalienably belongs to this centre, but with the centre itself. Without love for God there is no obedience to God or love for one's neighbour. Without love for Jesus there is no discipleship. Obedience, love for one's neighbour and discipleship arise automatically from this centre. But at this centre there takes place that which is their presupposition : the fact that man is comforted, and allows himself to be comforted, and comforts himself, with the one and only comfort ; that with body and soul, in life and death, he is not his own, but belongs to his faithful Saviour Jesus Christ ; that as one who is saved by God he is sheltered in God ; and that as such, but only as such, he is at once ordained and pledged and moved to obedience, love for his neighbour and discipleship. At this centre, where he has to do directly with God in Christ, he begins to make use of the freedom in which he is necessarily free for these things too. If he does not use his freedom for love for God, he is not free for these things. It is neither accidental nor without significance that the command to love God in Mk. 12²⁹ᶠ· and par. is called the *first* commandment.

.Nor is there any evading the Gospel account of the anointing of Jesus ; the story of the woman who according to Mk. 14³, as Jesus " sat at meat," brought " an alabaster box of ointment of spikenard very precious ; and she brake the box, and poured it on his head." According to Lk. 7³⁸ she did more, for she " stood at his feet behind him weeping, and began to wash his feet with tears, and did wipe them with the hairs of her head, and kissed his feet, and anointed them with the ointment." And in Jn. 12³ we read that " the house was filled with the odour of the ointment." The tradition is uncertain concerning the time and place and leading character in the incident. Indeed, even in relation to the point of the story it is unequivocal only in the decisive matter. According to Lk. 7³⁶ᶠ· the incident took place in the Galilæan period in the house of Simon the Pharisee. According to Mk. 14³ and Mt. 26⁶ it took place in Bethany in the house of Simon the leper shortly before the treachery of Judas and the Last Supper. Jn. 12¹ agrees that it took place in Bethany, but places it in the house of Lazarus and his sisters, prior to the entry into Jerusalem. And while Lk. 7³⁷ speaks of a γυνὴ ἁμαρτωλός, Mk. 14³ and Mt. 26⁷ refer to her indefinitely as a " woman," and Jn. 12³ identifies her as Mary the sister of Lazarus. It is to be noted that what finally made the incident significant for all four Evangelists is that it gave drastic and unexpected concretion to the anointing of the One who in the New Testament is called " the Anointed." This woman accomplished it ; and she did it, as we read not only in Mk. 14⁸ and Mt. 26¹² but also in Jn. 12⁷, " against the day of my burying," in direct preparation for the coronation of the royal man completed in His death. This is what took place, and it did so on the lavish scale indicated by the narratives. The same truth emerges in the Lucan account, except that here what gives offence to those present is that it is a sinful woman (7³⁹) who is at work, and whose work is accepted by Jesus (surely a poor judge of men !). In the other three accounts it is the lavishness which arouses indignation : " But when his disciples saw it, they had indignation, saying, To what purpose is this waste " (or " rubbish," according to the unrevised translation of Luther used in the text of Bach's St. Matthew's Passion). The reason why they were so critical is plainly given in Mk. 14⁵ (cf. Mt. 26⁹) : " It might have been sold for three hundred pence, and have been given to the poor." According to Jn. 12⁴ᶠ· it was Judas Iscariot who advanced this worthy argument, although the Evangelist notes that he said this, " not that he cared for the poor, but because he was a thief, and had the bag, and bare what was put therein." However that may be, it is practical love for one's neighbour which is played off against an act which can be made explicable only as an act of love for Jesus. Ethico-religious (or " religio-social " ?) Puritanism protests against a very doubtful pietistic undertaking. But Jesus ignores these ethical considerations in His answer : " Let her alone ; why trouble ye her ? she hath wrought a good work (καλὸν ἔργον) on me. For ye have the poor with you always, and whensoever ye will ye may do them good : but me ye have not always. She hath done what she could " (Mk. 14⁶ᶠ·, cf. Mt. 26¹¹ and Jn. 12⁸). And then, after the reference to His burial, to which the woman has anointed Him, He continues : " Verily, I say unto you, Wheresoever this gospel shall be preached throughout the whole world, this also that she hath done shall be spoken of for a memorial of her " (Mk. 14⁹, Mt. 26¹³). The point of the story, and of the saying of Jesus, is rather different but no less significant according to the Lucan account (7⁴⁷ᶠ·). The woman is a great sinner and Jesus knows this. But in her great love for Him she recognises that her sins are forgiven her, and (although, it is to be noted, she does not " confess " them or ask for absolution) He tells her this quite categorically : " Thy sins are forgiven. . . . Thy faith hath saved thee ; go in peace." The question is left open whether the Pharisee Simon, who has not shown Him this love, is forgiven to this extent or can receive such absolution. Appearances are to the contrary. What emerges clearly in all four accounts is that Jesus not only defends unconditionally the act of the woman but in all solemnity acknowledges that it is a good act which belongs necessarily to the history of salvation, even though it seems to be wholly superfluous, an act of sheer extravagance, which can serve " only " the purpose of representing direct and perfect self-giving to Him.

Even in the light of this story it would be unwise to maintain that love is real only in its form as obedience and love for one's neighbour, and thus to deny that, even to be real as such, it must have basically, and with reference to its basis primarily, the true and distinctive form of love for God. The fact that the source must and does become a river does not mean that the source is not something true and distinctive as opposed to the river. Indeed, without this true and distinctive thing which we call the source there could be no river. We must be clear what we are about if we attempt to deny this, and thus contribute to the concealment or damming of this source just because it has self-evidently no widespread or vital movement of its own. If we do, the result will be very quickly to dry up the river-bed. It was because they were once confronted by dried-up river-beds of this kind—the concealment or damming of the source being due sometimes to orthodox or internal, sometimes to rationalistic or external causes—that the older Mystics, Pietists and Romantics revolted, defying the instruction given by a domesticated Christianity, raising again the question of the source, finding (or thinking to find) it again, and thus, as it was given to them and as they were enabled and constrained, bringing and breaking and pouring out their alabaster boxes of ointment, and raising their corresponding hymns of devotion. Thus P. Nicolai : " Pour into my heart deep down, Thou glistering jewel, precious stone, The flame and fire of love ; That I, O Lord, for ever may, In Thine elected body stay, And in Thee live and move. Let me, in Thee unceasingly, Be caught in love's increasing tide, That death itself may not divide " ; or P. Gerhardt : " O Lord, my Shepherd, fount of joy, Thou art mine, I am Thine, Our love can none destroy. I am Thine for Thou didst give, Thine own blood, For my good, Thy life that I might live. Thou art mine, to Thee I cleave, In the night, Thee, my Light, From my heart I do not leave. O let me, let me, find a place, Where Thou me, and I Thee, For ever may embrace." To be sure, a good deal of this smacks of religious eroticism, and it would be easy to adduce passages in which this aspect is even more pronounced. But how arid would be our hymn-books if we were to purge out all elements of this kind ! And how deficient would be our preaching and teaching and pastoral work if there were no conscious utterance along these lines ! For, as far as the substance is concerned, what reason is there to carp and cavil ? In substance, is there not much more reason circumspectly but energetically to advance along these lines ? Is it very remarkable or meritorious that we do not fall into the temptation into which we may, of course, fall in this matter merely because we do not know from our own experience what is at issue and what has to find expression in some way ? If a choice has to be made, is it not better to say a little too much and occasionally to slip up with Nicolai and even with Zinzendorf and Novalis than to be rigidly correct with Kant and Ritschl and my 1921 *Römerbrief* and Bultmann, but in so doing to create a zone of silence in relation to the central matter of which the former rightly or wrongly tried to speak, and thus perhaps to do what the Pharisees did when, according to Lk. 11^{42}, they " passed over " the love of God, joining the company of the horrified disciples, if not of the treasurer Judas, but either way coming under the anathema of Paul in 1 Cor. 16^{22} ?

But we do not need to choose. It may well be that the older " friends of God " did sometimes slip into the sphere of religious eroticism, and that in so doing they ceased to think and speak as true " friends of God." If this is the case, it cannot be condoned and must not be imitated. But it does not mean that what they had in mind and tried to attest can be ignored or juggled away, namely, that which takes place at the centre where Christian love is originally direct love for God and for Jesus. Did Mary in Lk. 10$^{38f.}$ really choose the good part, or did she not ? Here, then, we must think and speak with the measure of sober passion or passionate soberness which corresponds on the one hand to the fire which burns at this centre and on the other to its holiness and purity. In no case must we evade or suppress that which cannot be evaded or suppressed. If we do, we do not guard against the paganism of religious sentimentalism and religious *eros*. On the contrary, we open up the way for it. For this paganism finds its excuse in the vacuum created by such evasion and suppression. It flourishes all the more vehemently in this vacuum. We must not help it in this way. The only thing which has power against it is positive : that at this critical point we should think and say the right thing and not the wrong ; and that we should think and say the right thing in all earnest.

The Puritanism in relation to which this excursus is required was an unavoidable but a dangerous contraction. The warning which it had to deliver is still valid. But as a contraction it has played its part and is no longer necessary.

If love for God in its distinctiveness and particularity is recognised and acknowledged as the content of the first commandment, we can and must emphasise by way of closer definition that the liberation of man for the love of God carries with it from the very first the liberation for obedience to God, so that it is ineluctably followed by man's obedience. To love God is to give oneself to Him, to put oneself at His disposal. And when man does this, his freedom for love becomes and is his freedom for obedience.

Already in the Old Testament we find that while they are separate these two things are also inseparable, being brought together into what amounts almost to a definite formula : To love God and to keep His commandments (Ex. 20⁶ ; Deut. 5¹⁰, 7⁹, 10¹²ᶠ·, 11¹ ; Dan. 9⁴ ; Neh. 1⁵), or : To love God and to walk in His ways and cleave to Him (Deut. 11²², 19⁹, 30¹⁶ ; Josh 22⁵), or : To love God and to fear Him (Deut. 10¹²). In the same connexion we may recall the striking connexion in Hosea (2²⁰, 4⁶, 6³, ⁶) between love for God and the knowledge of God, in which there is an obvious relationship—and a very important one in the present context—between knowledge and obedience. Along the same lines Paul in Phil. 1⁹ᶠ· prays that the love of the Philippian community may increase in knowledge and full understanding " that ye may test what is good and bad ; that ye may be sincere and without offence till the day of Christ." Love, according to Eph. 4¹⁵, is the action in which it is a matter of ἀληθεύειν ; which has to show itself " unfeigned " (2 Cor. 6⁶, Rom. 12⁹, 1 Pet. 1²²). It is the decisive action in which the community is to be edified (1 Cor. 8¹, Eph. 4¹⁶). It has to be " pursued "—obviously as regards its consequences (1 Cor. 14¹). And it is worth noting how explicit the Johannine writings are in this respect, for all that they give such prominence to love for Jesus. They certainly do not allow us to sink back into an idle contemplative enjoyment. The warning of Lk. 6⁴⁶ is sounded again : " And why call ye me, Lord, Lord, and do not the things which I say ? " Even verbally there is a recurrence of the Deuteronomic formula : " For this is the love of God, that we keep his commandments : and his commandments are not grievous " (1 Jn. 5³, 2 Jn. 6). " If ye love me, keep my commandments " (Jn. 14¹⁵). " He that hath my commandments, and keepeth them, he it is that loveth me " (Jn. 14²¹). " If ye keep my commandments, ye shall abide in my love " (Jn. 15¹⁰). We should have to be deaf to miss the indications of this connexion. How can it be said of love in Gal. 5⁶ that faith " worketh " by it if love is inactive, or if the order in which it expresses itself can be different from that of the obedience of act ?

For the man who really loves *God*, and really *loves* Him, there can be no question of any other order of his relationship to Him. How can he love *God* if he may even think that the relationship to Him can be fashioned either as one between two equal partners with claims to be asserted and respected on both sides, so that the only obligation is that of the easiest possible fulfilment of his own share in the contract, or tacitly or blatantly as one in which God is there to satisfy his needs, to carry out his wishes, to answer his questions, to fill the vacuum of his life, so that at root he himself is the lord and God is only his servant, mysterious perhaps, but pledged to obey him ? And how can he *love* God if he can ever imagine that he may control Him in this way ? This is how the heathen love their demons and genii and protective spirits or whatever else they regard as their gods, not knowing who God is or what it means to love Him. The Christian loves God and therefore the Lord, in relation to whom he has neither a total nor a partial claim, nor indeed any claim at all. He loves the God who is his Creator to whom he belongs ; the Holy One in face of whom he knows that he is guilty and hopelessly in arrears ; his merciful Father who does not rebuff him as he deserves but forgives his transgression and addresses and treats him as a son ; the Saviour who takes up his cause and draws him by His Spirit and makes him living and free ; the eternal love by which he finds himself first loved as God gives Himself to him in all his unworthiness. When the Christian loves this One and therefore God—not a figment of his own dreams and desires, but God—he cannot choose or will or even imagine any other order of this relationship but that of obedience. Love for God can express itself only in this order. Obedience is the act, willingly and readily and therefore freely accomplished, in which man subordinates himself to, and orientates himself by, that which God wills of him and commands him to do in His commandment. He does not love God because God commands him to do so, but on the basis of the electing, purifying and creative love with which God has first loved him, and in the quickening power of the Holy Spirit. But as he has—or rather receives from God—the freedom to do this, he inescapably discovers that in this freedom, which is the freedom to give himself to God in return, he has no option but to place himself under the will and Word and command and order of God as he hears it, and therefore to be obedient. Obedience is the required action of love, i.e., the action of love which is demanded by love itself, resulting directly from the fact that as man loves God he places himself at His disposal.

Since it is only the consequence of his love, this action is required, but as such it is also free. It is the action for which he is made free and willing and ready as he may love God. If it were not his free action, but took place naturally or inevitably or automatically that he had to love what God wills, under constraint and not voluntarily, how could it be real obedience ? A puppet does not obey. It does not move itself. It dances and gesticulates as it is moved. But to be quickened by the Holy Spirit is to move oneself, and to do so in obedience, listening to the order and command of God. It is now clear why in our general consideration of the act of love we had to insist so strongly that it cannot be understood as a prolongation or effluence of the divine action, of the love of God. The apparent grandeur of this theomonistic conception must not blind us to the fact that if it is true there can be no question of a free act of human love for God, and therefore of an act of obedience enclosed in it and following from it. Nor can we describe as a covenant relationship the kind of relationship in which God alone is really at work and man is only the instrument or channel of the divine action, so that the antithesis of Creator and creature, of Saviour and saved, of the One who loves and the one who is loved, has no significance. In the covenant relationship—the true relationship between God and man according to the witness of Scripture—the initiative is wholly and exclusively on the side of God. But this initiative aims at a correspondingly free act, at genuine obedience as opposed to that of a puppet, on the part of the man with whom the covenant is made. And this is the fulfilment of the covenant in the reconciliation of man with God accomplished in Jesus Christ, in so far as this has a human side and may now be considered from this lower, human aspect. As certainly as Jesus Christ is very God and also very man, it includes also the fact that there may be genuine obedience on the part of man ; the obedience of man as his free act.

We must lay express emphasis on the thought of act. We again look back to what we stated in our general consideration—that love for God acts. It does not merely think. It does not merely feel. It does not merely will. Naturally, it does think and feel and will. How else could it be the love of a real man, which means a man who thinks and feels and wills ? But it bursts through the limitations of an inwardness which reposes and moves only within itself. It acts. In the act of obedience it demonstrates the fact that love is giving, self-giving, in contrast to a human—an only too human—reserve and self-assertion. For the act of love man needs and fills time and space. In it he compromises and entangles himself by representing himself to the world as one who loves, entering (even with the smallest movements) into its relationships, responding with definite actions towards God and his fellows, participating in his own place in the history of the world with God. The one who loves God does not stand aside as one who is obedient to God. In weakness or strength, in wisdom or folly, he takes definite steps in the forms of words and works and attitudes ; steps which lead him into the complexities of his time and situation, which he cannot altogether escape in any case. It is there, and as one who is obedient there, that he loves. If he does not do it there, he does it only in semblance, and his love has nothing whatever to do with love for God.

We have still to make the final point that in the obedience of love it is a matter of obedience to the living God, or—and this is the same thing—to the living Jesus Christ. It is Him as such that he loves. It is to Him as such that he gives himself. Thus in the action of love as an answer and correspondence, an imitation of the love of God, there can be no question of the setting up of a static counterpart, perhaps in the form of a way of life which is fixed once and for all according to certain standpoints and regulations. The obedience of Christian love has often been understood in this way, and corresponding attempts have been made to practise it. But understood in this way it loses its character as a free action. It necessarily acquires the nature of a custom or routine which can be applied without concrete motivation by the love of God but follows its own laws and is thus performed mechanically in a given case, in actions which are soulless and loveless, which even the heathen can perform, and for which they will indeed be willing and ready in certain circumstances. Above all, when obedient action consists in the establishment of the rigid counterpart of a compact Christianity, it loses its significance as an imitation of

God's own love. For God, and therefore its original, is not a fixed and static and rigidly determined figure which is dead for all the majesty ascribed to it. He is a living and acting person, who for all His faithfulness to Himself is continually electing and willing and creatively producing new things, and thus speaking and commanding and ordering new things. Obedience to Him can consist only in a continual readiness and willingness to follow His action, to do justice in a continual subjection to His electing and willing and producing, and therefore to His speaking and commanding and ordering, and thus to correspond with the greatest possible loosening of one's own rigidity. Obedience to Him can take place only in the history of man with God in which love for Him can never be dispensed with but must be continually renewed, and in which man is constantly referred to God's own presence and encounter with him, to the eternal love which is the basis of his love, to the work and gift of the Holy Spirit. It is in this history with God that he loves Him and gives himself to Him. Its continuity is guaranteed by the faithfulness and immutability of the God who is not an idol that man can easily copy and therefore master, but his living Lord and Saviour. The Christian, the man who loves God, must demonstrate his love, and therefore render his obedience, in face of the continuity of His living action and commanding—a continuity which cannot be denied and may in fact be easily recognised.

The act of love stands in need, however, of a second and no less indispensable and decisive definition. From its basis in the love of God addressed to man, it follows naturally that in it we do not have to do only or exclusively with love for God, but that the human love which responds to God's love, even as love for God, has also another object side by side with and apart from God, and different from Him. According to the clear assertion and direction of the biblical testimonies this other ,who is loved by the Christian is his fellow-man, who stands to him in a definite historical relationship or context.

We must first be clear what this description involves, namely, that the one who apart from God is loved in the act of Christian love, being necessarily loved together with God, is the fellow-man who stands in a definite historical relationship to the Christian who loves.

It may sound harsh at first, but we have to note that neither the Old Testament nor the New speaks of a love for man as such and therefore for all men ; of a universal love of humanity. As the Bible understands it, love both for God and for man has the character of an action. The universal love of humanity can be thought of, if at all, only as an idea which dominates man or an attitude of mind which fills him. But Christian love, as we have seen, is an act of obedience which as such, even if we think of a sequence of such acts, takes place somewhere in time and space, which does not, therefore, take place always and everywhere, but in which there is always a demarcation and limitation of its object or objects. It is the concrete and not the abstract loving of someone who is concrete and not abstract. In correspondence to the love of God, it is a loving which chooses and differentiates. That this is the case in its form as love for the one God (this God and not another) is self-evident. But it is also the case in its form as love for men, and this emerges in the fact that the latter belongs to love for God, standing in an indissoluble connexion with it.

Love for one or more men, or a category of men, presupposes that the one or many who are loved stand in a certain proximity to the one who loves—a proximity in which others do not find themselves. This does not mean that the connexion with others is necessarily negative or neutral. There are other positive relations between men than that of the love which is bound up with the love for God—relations to which there are emphatic references in Scripture. Our present concern, however, is with what is called love in Scripture. This love between men takes place on the assumption that there is between them, not an indefinite, but a very definite and specific proximity ; a proximity between the one who loves and the one or many who are loved which is not general or accidental and which could not apply to all men, or indeed to any except on a particular basis. It is in this proximity that there takes place the act of Christian love. It may, but need not, be a geographical proximity. The proximity between the one who is loved and the one who loves can be supremely real even at a geographical distance. It may, but need not, be a temporal proximity. The one who loves and the one who is loved may be contemporaries, but this is not essential, for a man alive to-day may love someone long since dead. The proximity in which the act of Christian love takes place between man and man is that of a historical relationship in which the one who loves and the one who is loved both exist. Their relationship is not one which exists in any case, but it takes place that they are brought together and directed to one another in fact, either in the form of an event or in consequence of an event. And within the framework of this relationship, which is not between all men as such but between these specific men, there takes place the act either of the love of the one for the other or of their reciprocal love—an act which does not customarily take place between all men, and is not therefore to be expected of all or in relationship to all, but only of, and in relationship to, specific men.

What we have been attempting is a general and formal description of the important biblical concept of the " neighbour." The " neighbour " (*rea*, πλησίον) is the one who is loved apart from and side by side with God, but for the sake of love for God.

In the original and not the derivative sense the *rea* is, of course, the fellow-Israelite. The Greek word πλησίον is essentially much weaker, but in its biblical usage it has to be understood in the light of the much fuller Hebrew word, and it signifies the one who in fact, as may happen, becomes and is a neighbour. In fact, this one is a " fellow-man." But this term is foreign to the Bible. And if we have to love our fellow-man, it is not because he is such, but because as such he is the neighbour of the one who loves. The Israelite is expressly commanded to love his neighbour in Lev. 19¹⁸. The saying concludes and transcends a whole list of things that he is not to do to his neighbour : he is not to defraud or rob him ; he is not to keep back the wages of him that is hired until the morning ; he is not to curse the deaf or be a stumbling-block to the blind ; he is not to do unrighteousness in judgment ; he is not to despise the poor or favour the powerful ; he is not to slander or threaten his neighbour, to hate him, to take vengeance on him, or to bear any grudge against him (vv. 13–18). On the contrary (and the final saying obviously gathers up the opposite of all these things, and therefore fills the vacuum declared by these warnings), he is to love him as himself (v. 18). " I am Yahweh "—this, and this alone, is clearly the basis of this commandment. The reference is to fellow-Israelites as fellow-members of the covenant with Yahweh, although v. 34 expressly includes the " stranger " in this circle, and with the same direction : " But the stranger that dwelleth with you shall be unto you as one born among you, and thou shalt love him as thyself ; for ye were strangers in the land of Egypt : I am Yahweh, your God." For all this extension, however, the circle to which the direction applies is a closed circle. To be sure, it is commanded in Ex. 23⁴ᶠ· that if the ox or ass of an enemy is found straying it is to be restored to him, and his over-burdened ass is to be helped—exactly the same treatment as Deut. 22¹ᶠ· prescribes for the animals of fellow-Israelites. And in Prov. 25²¹ᶠ· we have a saying quoted by Paul in Rom. 12²⁰ which refers to the enemy himself : " If thine enemy be hungry, give him bread to eat ; and if he be thirsty, give him water to drink : for thou shalt heap coals of fire upon his head, and the Lord shall reward thee." But in both Old and New Testaments the " enemy " here is not a personal opponent ; he is the enemy of one's people who threatens them with persecution. And in neither case is there mention of love for this enemy. The most that can be said in relation to the members of other nations is found in Deut. 23⁷ : " Thou shalt not abhor an Edomite ; for he is thy brother : thou shalt not abhor an Egyptian ; because thou wast a stranger in his land." It is to be noted that even here we have to do with foreigners who stood in a specific and close relationship to Israel and its history. As we see from Deut. 23³, even this could not be said of an Ammonite or Moabite.

Similarly, in the New Testament the man who is loved is not the fellow-man as such. The closed circle to whose members the command to love refers is no longer that of the people of Israel and strangers casually associated with it. But—however irksome this may be to those who regard Christian love as a human virtue—it is still a closed circle : the circle of disciples, brothers, the saints, members of the body of Christ ; the circle of the community of Jesus Christ gathered by the Holy Spirit from Jews and Gentiles, and ruled and quickened by Him. All men may, of course, belong to this community. Every man is called to enter it. To quote only one passage, God offers faith to all (Ac. 17³⁰). But this side the end of all things with the coming again of Christ, faith is not a matter for everyone (οὐ γὰρ πάντων ἡ πίστις, 2 Thess. 3²), and all men do not belong to it. Thus the fellow-man can be loved only in the form of the other Christian who is brought into a definite relationship to the Christian by the love of God and of Jesus Christ. In this form he can be loved with all the necessity of love for God and for Jesus, but it is in this form alone that he can be loved. As the recurrent expression has it, Christians love one another.

There are, of course, important and positive active relationships to others and to all men which demand unconditional realisation by Christians. Above all, they must be ready to give an answer (ἀπολογία) to all those who ask concerning the hope which lives within them (1 Pet. 3¹⁵). Their light is to shine before men, that they may see their good works and glorify their Father which is in heaven (Mt. 5¹⁶). They are to be the witnesses to all men of God and of Jesus Christ and of His lordship. And this includes the fact that while they have to

3. *The Act of Love* 805

do τὸ ἀγαθόν especially (μάλιστα) to the οἰκεῖοι τῆς πίστεως, at bottom they have to do it to all men (Gal. 6¹⁰). They are to " follow that which is good, both among yourselves, and to all men " (1 Thess. 5¹⁵). They are to exercise themselves in the doing of καλά "in the sight of all men " (Rom. 12¹⁷). Their ἐπιεικές is to be " known unto all men " (Phil. 4⁵), which means : " Whatsoever things are true, whatsoever things are honest, whatsoever things are just, whatsoever things are pure, whatsoever things are lovely, whatsoever things are of good report ; if there be any virtue, and if there be any praise, think on these things " (Phil. 4⁸). Their patience (μακροθυμία) is to be for the benefit of all around them (1 Thess. 5¹⁴). They are to give due honour to all (1 Pet. 2¹⁷). They are to be friendly (ἤπιοι) to all and to seek to live at peace with everyone (Heb. 12¹⁴). In short, they are to be engaged in the exercise of humanity, in the demonstration of the fellow-humanity which is inalienably distinctive of the essence of man as such, not being surpassed by others but knowing how to show humanity better than others. And humanity is a good attitude always very definitely demanded and practised by the Christian who knows what love is. Humanity as demanded in the New Testament is as it were latent love ; the readiness of the Christian to love everyone.

As an act, however, what the New Testament calls love takes place between Christians. The one exception which confirms this rule is 1 Thess. 3¹² : " The Lord make you to increase and abound in love one toward another, and toward all men " (εἰς πάντας). This is a salutary reminder of the readiness of Christians for all men ; of the fact that the existence of the community (as formerly that of Israel) is not an end in itself ; and that the same is true of the mutual love of its members. As the community exists for the sake of the world loved by God, so the mutual love practised within it is practised for all, for the world, in a provisional and representative manifestation of the action for which all are determined. Yet it is practised here, between these men. It is based on the love of God and of Jesus, and as the fulfilment of the second commandment ordered in relation to the first commandment of love for God and for Jesus. It can flourish only on this soil. As it cannot be practised by all, it cannot be meaningfully addressed to all.

Only at one point is the closed circle of the community always pierced, and while this is the most unexpected point it does not destroy the internal and esoteric character of love. It is in respect of the love demanded in Mt. 5⁴³⁻⁴⁸— not also but specifically—for the enemy, for the persecutor of the community, to be addressed to him in the form of intercession, with its model and original in the prayer of the Crucified in Lk. 23³⁴. As the most interesting and relevant form of the non-Christian the enemy is proleptically received into the community when he is loved and not hated. According to Rom. 12²¹, it is a matter of not being overcome by evil, but of overcoming evil by good. Or, according to Mt. 5⁴⁸, it is a matter of the human analogy, represented by the Christian as the child of God, of the purpose and activity of the heavenly Father as reflected in the fact that He causes His sun to shine on the good and the evil, and His rain to fall on the just and the unjust. Even here, however, there can be no question of any extension in principle of Christian love to a universal love of humanity.

To sum up, the neighbour as the one who in Christian love is loved apart from and side by side and together with God is the fellow-man who stands to the one who loves in the historical context of the existence of Israel or the existence of the community of Jesus Christ. He is not the fellow-man as such, but this particular fellow-man.

But what is this historical relationship in which a fellow-man stands to another in this definite and specific way as a neighbour in the concrete sense of the term, so that it is decided from the very outset

that in all circumstances the latter must love him, and will in fact
love him as, and as surely as, he loves God ?

The relationship or context is simply that of the history of salvation, which does of course apply to all men and take place for all
men, although not with the active participation of all. The history
of salvation is the nexus of the particular speech and action of God
for the reconciliation of the world with Himself which at its centre
and climax is the history of Jesus Christ. On the part of the world—
in a way which is typical for all but which therefore entails differentiation—the people of God, namely, Israel, and arising out of Israel the
community awakened, assembled, built up, maintained and ruled by
the Holy Spirit of the risen Jesus Christ, has an active part in this
history. Indirectly the same is true of others, in the form of the
stranger who dwells among this people, or the enemy who persecutes
it. But it is true only with reference to this people and not another,
to the men of this people and not others. It is here in this people
that Jesus Christ has His body, the earthly-historical form of His
existence. It is here that God speaks with man and is heard by him.
It is here that He acts with him in the judgment of His grace and the
grace of His judgment. It is here that according to 1 Pet. 2⁹ He seeks
and finds witnesses of His glory, elected and called out of darkness
to His wonderful light and the proclamation of His great acts. His
purpose is for all men, and He addresses Himself to the whole world.
But—without prejudice to His fatherly providence over all creaturely
happening—He does so here and only here. For it is here that His
love is active as an electing, renewing and creative basis of the response
of human love. That it may be this response is the new and wonderful
thing in the act of love as a free human act. But it is a free human act
in the relationship or context of the history of salvation, of the history
of God with His people. The one who loves God cannot then be
solitary. He cannot be a religious individual with his individual concerns and joys and wishes and achievements. As one who has an
active part in the history of salvation he is accompanied from the very
outset not merely by fellows but by brothers, by those who belong
with him to the people of God, by fellow-partners in the covenant,
by the " household of faith " (Gal. 6¹⁰). He does not love God on the
basis of a revelation directly vouchsafed to him or in a private relationship. He began to love Him as there was in the world—even before
he himself was, or loved God—the community which, called and
gathered by the Holy Spirit, attested the love of God to him, and
summoned him by its ministry to love God in return. And if he does
love God in return, this simply means that he for his part is called to
the same ministry and will live in and with the community. But the
life of the community, by whose ministry he is summoned to love God
and in whose ministry he may participate as one who does, is not the
functioning of a mechanism but a nexus of human relationships between

those who have become and are members of the one body, having their common Lord and Head in the one person. To love God is, then, to live at a specific point in this nexus, and at this point to be together with the men who are also called to the service concerned and participate in life in this service. To love God, since it is always a question of definite action, is to stand at this point in one of the many human relationships which exist here, being united to this man or that by the fact that he too is awakened by the love of God to love God in return. And the content of the relationship and union which has this basis, and the saving character of human activity in this relationship and union, consist in the fact that one loves the other. We must now try to see why it is that this activity—the life-act of man in relationship to his fellow—has the character of love in this context of the history of salvation ; why Christian love, apart from and side by side with the fact that it is love for God, has also the form and dimension of love for the neighbour ; and what is meant by the command : " Thou shalt love thy neighbour as thyself."

But before we take up these questions a parenthetical statement is required. There can be no question of an extension in principle of the concept of Christian love for the neighbour into a universal love of humanity, unless we are radically to weaken and confuse it. On the other hand, there can be no question of a restriction in principle of this concept to love for those whom we know or think we know as those with whom we find ourselves in this context of the history of salvation. The sign of baptism under which we are united with our fellows has to be taken with positive seriousness. In any case, therefore, we must love those whom we know or think we know as our neighbours in the concrete sense. In any case we must regard as our brothers those who give outward testimony of love for God and tangibly confess Jesus as Lord. In any case we must accept the relationship and union between them and us in the history of salvation, and draw the resultant consequences. But this positive fact does not involve the negative one that we must in no case love the fellow-men whom we do not know or think we know as our neighbours in this specific concrete sense. Baptism and visible fellowship in confession are for us an inclusive sign, but they are not for this reason *a limine* an exclusive sign. *Tertium datur*. The other man may not have made himself known, i.e., visibly and tangibly, as one who stands to us in this relationship, and therefore as a neighbour. Yet he may well have been a neighbour—or on the way to being a neighbour—for a long time, the only thing being that we have not noticed the fact. In the last instance it is not we who have to decide whether or not this other man loves God. God may well have loved him as He has loved us, and his love for God (greater perhaps than our own) may have been a fact even though he has not so far been recognised by baptism as a member of the people and community of God. If we cannot count on this possibility it is difficult to see what is meant by the death of Jesus Christ for the sins of the whole world and therefore of all men, or by His lordship over all men as revealed in His resurrection.

Notable figures may be recalled even from the Old Testament in this connexion : the Moabite prophet Balaam and his fellow-countrywoman Ruth ; the Canaanite harlot Rahab ; Hiram, king of Tyre, and the queen of Sheba ; the Syrian Naaman, and Cyrus with his outstanding role in Deutero-Isaiah and the Book of Ezra. In the New Testament we can think of the wise men from the East, and rather strangely of a whole series of Gentile soldiers—the centurion of Capernaum, the centurion at the cross and the centurion Cornelius of Cæsarea. Above all, and typical in his significance, there is king Melchizedek of Gen. 14$^{18f.}$, who in Hebrews is set even against Abraham as a type of Jesus Christ. And it is not for nothing that in the parable of Lk. 10$^{29f.}$ it was a Samaritan who by showing mercy to the man who fell among thieves provided the classic instance and definition of a neighbour in answer to the question of the scribe. If it is the case that God can and actually does raise up children to Abraham from " these stones " (Mt. 3^9), in what relationship do these stand to the children of the household, and the latter to them ? They bring both comfort and warning, reminding them that they are not in their own house but in that of the Father of Jesus Christ, and that in this house (Jn. 14^2) there are many mansions, including some which they themselves do not yet know.

The statement that the neighbour is always the fellow-man who encounters and is united with me in the context of the history of salvation is not suspended by the recollection that we have to reckon with the hidden presence, and emergence, of these " foreign " children. But in the light of this recollection it certainly requires modification in the following direction—that in respect of the question who encounters and is united with me in this context, and who is therefore my neighbour, I have to be prepared and continually ready to receive new light beyond what I now think I know, always making new discoveries, and thus finding it possible and necessary to love to-morrow where to-day it seems out of the question to do so because I do not yet perceive the relationship in which the other stands to me. Hence the restriction of Christian love to the circle of brothers known to me cannot be theoretical and definitive, but only practical and provisional. In any case I have to exercise love at this point, and yet all the time I have not to be closed but open to the possibility that the circle of the brothers whom I must love may prove to-morrow, or even within the next hour, to be wider than I now realise. I thus address my love to the brother whom I know to-day, and am continually prepared to address it to-morrow to the brother whom I do not know to-day. I anticipate in my love to the brother of to-day what I shall be bound to do in relation to the brother of to-morrow. In the narrower love I am always reaching out to the wider. And since I cannot know of any man that he will not prove to be my brother to-morrow, I cannot withhold from any of my fellows an attitude of openness, of expectation, of good hope and therefore of readii.ess for love. I love neither God nor my brothers if I do not show openly to every man without distinction the friendliness emphatically recommended and even commanded in so many New Testament passages. The New Testament does not call this " love." And what the New Testament calls " love " is in fact other and more than this friendliness. But the latter is a kind of anticipation of it, as may well be indicated by the unique saying in 1 Thess. 3¹². It is the position of readiness of the Christian as he looks and moves to the neighbour or brother of to-morrow in each of his fellows, even including the " enemy " of the people and the community. Those who themselves exist in this context of the history of salvation, and may therefore love God and their neighbours, have no option in this respect. They must be ready and on the way to love for all, even in relationships in which its realisation is at the moment impossible. If—unlike the Bible—we want to say more than this, we must be careful that we do not say less. But it certainly must be said that, while the circle of vital Christian love for the neighbour is not the sphere of all men indiscriminately, it is not a hermetically sealed circle within this sphere, but one which continually broadens out into it.

Our present theme, however, is the act of Christian love as such ; the love which the Christian addresses in any case to the neighbour and brother known to him to-day, and is ready in given cases gladly to address in the same way to-morrow to the brother and neighbour not known to him to-day.

We must now turn to the question why Christian love is also love for the neighbour. How and in what sense does the neighbour come to stand side by side with the God whom we must love with all our heart and soul and strength ? How and in what sense does the second commandment come to have a place alongside the first ? To what extent does love for God necessarily entail love for the neighbour ?

Before we attempt any explanation, it is as well to state plainly and simply that this is the case. Christian love has these two dimensions and is thus love for the neighbour. The history of salvation is both a history between God and man and also a history between man and man. It is the second as and because it is the first. That is to say, as and because it is first a history between God and a people (Yahweh and Israel in the Old Testament and Jesus Christ and His community in the New) and only then a history between God and the world, between God and all men, the life of this people, the common life of its members, becomes part of the event and itself the history of salvation. Because these men are together in relation to God they are among one another in a very distinctive way. As the history of salvation takes place vertically as the act of God's love and the corresponding act of human love for God, it also takes place on the horizontal plane where these men are together reached by the divine act and together engaged in the corresponding act. It takes place unavoidably that there is a definite connexion of these men among themselves posited in and with their twofold passive and active relationship to

God. This connexion is their mutual love ; the love of each for his neighbour. It is their love for one another because they are those who together are loved by God and love Him in return. Since it is a matter of love on the vertical plane, how can it be anything else on the horizontal ? The two planes are distinct and must not be confused. But they are also inseparable. Liberation for God is one thing, and liberation for our fellow-men another. But if in the liberation for God we have the liberation of a people, it is followed at once by the liberation of the members of this people for one another. The awakening to mutual love succeeds instantaneously the awakening to love for God. The history of salvation is fundamentally this twofold history, and therefore side by side with that indicated by the first commandment, and inseparably from its fulfilment, it is also the history indicated by the second : " Thou shalt love thy neighbour as thyself." As the one who loves God you cannot do otherwise. As you love God, you will love your neighbour ; the one who with you is loved by God and loves Him in return.

It is to be noted that this is not stated quite so precisely by the Old Testament, but only by the New. It is the Jesus of the Synoptics who gathers together Deut. 6⁴ᶠ· and Lev. 19¹⁸ into the twofold commandment of love. We cannot deduce from Lev. 19¹⁸ that there is in this text the direct relationship between the two. Certainly it cannot be denied that in this text the command to love one's neighbour sheds a distinctive light in the true sense of the term. Yet it is also unmistakeable that it is prejudicially affected by the host of detailed provisions by which it is accompanied and which hardly seem to be of the same importance. And while the " I am Yahweh " is added as a solemn basis to many of these directions, it does not serve to distinguish the central character of the command to love, nor does it cause us to think specifically of what is commanded in Deut. 6⁴ᶠ·. The decisive demand of the prophets and the various strata of the Law in respect of the relationship between man and his fellows in Israel is not for love but honesty and justice. But these are, of course, very definitely demanded : so definitely that we cannot overlook the second and horizontal dimension resulting from the covenant with Yahweh, the significance of the fellow-countryman as the other to whom the Israelite owes respect side by side and together with Yahweh Himself ; and in such a way that there may be traced at least the indications of a line leading up from the Old Testament to the New.

All the same, the emphasis on love for the neighbour, and its express connexion with love for God, corresponds to the insight and witness of the New Testament rather than the Old. It is only now—obviously *post Christum natum* —that God and the fellow-man who is an associate in covenant with God are seen together in such a way that love for the latter as well as for God, and in consequence of love for God, becomes a second, strong and autonomous theme of proclamation, so that the command to love one's neighbour can even be called the βασιλικὸς νόμος (Jas. 2⁸), or its fulfilment the πλήρωμα νόμου (Rom. 13⁸, ¹⁰).

An apparent contradiction in the Johannine literature is explicable along these lines, and if the explanation attempted here is correct, fresh light is shed by it on the problem of the difference in accent as between the Old Testament witness and the New. That the disciples should love one another is described by Jesus Himself in Jn. 13³⁴ as an ἐντολὴ καινή. But in 2 Jn. 5 we read the direct opposite : It is not an ἐντολὴ καινή, but that which we had ἀπ' ἀρχῆς. And in 1 Jn. 3¹¹ the same commandment is described as " the ἀγγελία that ye heard ἀπ' ἀρχῆς." The two thoughts are brought together in 1 Jn. 2⁷ᶠ·. " Brethren,

I write no new commandment unto you, but an old commandment which ye had from the beginning. The old commandment is the word which ye have heard from the beginning. Again, a new commandment I write unto you, which thing is true in him and in you : because the darkness is past, and the true light now shineth." What is meant is disclosed by the remarkable " because " and by what follows : " He that saith he is in the light, and hateth his brother, is in darkness even until now. He that loveth his brother abideth in the light, and there is none occasion of stumbling in him. But he that hateth his brother is in darkness, and walketh in darkness, and knoweth not whither he goeth, because that darkness hath blinded his eyes." The content of 1 Jn. $3^{14f.}$ is to the same effect : " We know that we have passed from death unto life, because we love the brethren. He that loveth not his brother abideth in death. Whosoever hateth his brother is a murderer : and ye know that no murderer hath eternal life abiding in him." It may now be seen in what sense equal emphasis is laid upon the fact that the commandment is both old and new. It is obviously called old to remind us that we have here a decisive element of instruction handed down through the Old Testament and known from the very outset to every Christian. In this respect the writer may perhaps have in view Christians who tried to resist the urgency of this command by claiming that it was an innovation, or a special concern carried to excess by John or the Johannine circle. It is called new to draw attention to the fact that we have here a concretion of that which characterises the Gospel message as distinct from its Old Testament form, so that in the observance or non-observance of this commandment literally everything is at stake for the Christian, since the only alternative to love is hatred of one's brother, murder, the fratricide of Cain (1 Jn. 3^{12}), and it is concretely at this point that a decision is made between light and darkness, life and death. In this respect the author is perhaps thinking of Christians who know and accept the command to love as an Old Testament direction, but do not appreciate the new seriousness which it has acquired (" the darkness is past, and the true light now shineth "). Presented in this ultimate way, according to which the line between its observance and non-observance is the frontier between two worlds (and what worlds !), it is obviously like ($\delta\mu o\iota a$, Mt. 22^{39}) the first and great commandment. Presented in this way, and therefore as a strict and unconditional requirement, it is asserted in a form in which it is not yet asserted in the Old Testament but is necessarily so—obviously on the basis of its fundamental presupposition—in the New. As it is taken over in the New, it does not say verbally anything more than what was demanded of Israel in the Old. But as repeated in the New it has acquired a function which is perhaps latent but not yet patent in the Old. Now—and only now—it has become the second and no less significant and important element in the twofold commandment to love. If we think in New Testament terms, or in Old Testament terms as interpreted in the New, we cannot draw back from the view that the history of salvation has two dimensions, that it is therefore played out on two different but inseparable levels, and that Christian love has therefore a twofold object and direction. This view belongs to the very rudiments of Christian thought, because of the Christian life, at which we have always to start.

So far we have been concerned only to establish the fact that Christian love for God necessarily means Christian love for the neighbour. But having done this we are still confronted by the question why and to what extent this is the case, i.e., the problem of the knowledge of this rudimentary fact. For instance, who is my neighbour, my brother, the one who encounters me ? And who am I in relation to him on this second horizontal plane of the events of salvation ? In what quality is he one whom, in loving God as a Christian, I have also to love, and will love, with the same seriousness ? And in what quality do I for my part stand in relation to him as one who, in loving God, has to love and will love him too with the same seriousness ? What is the function which as those who together are loved by God and love Him in return we have to fulfil among ourselves, the one in relation to the other ? And to what extent is love the fulfilling of the function in which we have to be and are there the one for the other ?

In fact, these different questions all reduce themselves to one, and the all-embracing concept which suggests itself to answer them all is that of the witness. The neighbour is a witness to me, and I am a witness to him. It is in this quality that we mutually confront one another. It is this function that we have to fulfil in relation to one another. And we can fulfil this function only as we love one another.

A man is a witness to me when he gives me information which would otherwise be inaccessible, confirming it when otherwise I have no other means of confirmation. And I am a witness to him when I impart and confirm information in this way. The witness answers, therefore, for the information which he imparts and confirms. For the one to whom he imparts it, the truth and reality of what is told stand or fall with the human existence and activity of the man who imparts it. The more important and indispensable the information, the more important and indispensable is the existence and activity of the one who gives it, the witness. If it is the case, then, that what two men have to tell one another is absolutely important and indispensable to both, this means that its truth and reality stand or fall with their mutual existence and activity as its witnesses. The one is referred absolutely to the existence and activity of the other as a witness of that which is supremely important and indispensable. They are united absolutely by the mutual expectation that it will be imparted. They can thus have no more pressing concern than not to fail to pass it on, but to be to one another the mutual witnesses as which they confront one another.

The Israelite is a witness to the Israelite in this sense, and the Christian to the Christian. They have continually to proclaim to one another by their human activity the love of God which constitutes Israel, the community and the existence of each individual in Israel and the community, and this love as the basis of their freedom to love God in return. The love of God and these men need that this love should be continually proclaimed because God's love is a reality, not as a general truth about God, but in God's constant activity, and because the love of these men for God which is based upon it is not a state which can ever be presupposed, but finds realisation in constant human action. Thus this proclamation can never be rendered superfluous or unnecessary by earlier proclamation, but has continually to take place, to become an event. But the love of God and these men need that this love should be proclaimed, imparted and confirmed in

the form of human action because the love of God, and the corresponding human love for God which is based upon it, is also an event on the
level where man is confronted by man, so that the relationship between
the God who reveals Himself in His love and the man who is loved by
Him and loves Him in return must be reflected in a relationship of
man to man in which in the form of human action man answers to
man for the truth and reality of that which primarily and intrinsically
takes place on the other, vertical plane—the event of love between
God and man and man and God. Finally, the love of God and the
men who correspond to it with their love need that this love should
be proclaimed reciprocally because on the horizontal plane now under
consideration we have to do with a people loved by God and loving
Him in return, among whose adherents and members there is none to
whom the love of God is not addressed and who is not therefore free
to love Him in return, none who is not referred to the fact that this
is proclaimed to him by human action, and none who is not under
obligation to proclaim it to others by his action.

What, then, would I be, what would become of me, and how could
I become and be and remain what I am as a member of God's people
loved by Him and loving Him in return, if this being of mine, the being
of the whole people of God as such and in it my being, were not continually proclaimed to me by the human action of the one who is a
member with me, i.e., if he with his being did not guarantee the truth
and reality of mine ? What would I be if this other were not to me a
witness of God, of the history of salvation in which my life too has a
part, of the divine work which affects me too, of my liberation for the
love of God ? If this were the case, then on the level where man is
confronted by man I should be referred to myself even in respect of
the relationship between God and me and me and God, receiving
neither light nor strength from my fellow. Would the love of God
then be revealed ? Would I be able to perceive it and respond to it ?
Without the ministry of the people of God and its members, would I
be loved by God at all, or free to love Him in return ?

Conversely, what would I be, and how would it stand with my
being as one loved by God and loving Him in return, if even for a
moment I could cease to proclaim it to the other man who also has a
part in this being and needs this proclamation, i.e., if I for my part were
unwilling to answer for the truth and reality of his being as a member
of the people of God ? What would I be if I for my part were not to
this other a witness of God, of the history of salvation in which he
too has a part, of the work of God which is for him too, of his liberation
for the love of God ? This would mean that on the level on which I
confront him I would ignore the other in respect of his relationship to
God, leaving him to his own devices. But if I can do that, is the love
of God really revealed to me ? Am I really one who knows it and
loves God in return ? Holding aloof from the ministry of His people

as one of its members, do I not show that I am not really loved by God, and do not have the freedom to love Him in return ? Do I not automatically exclude myself from participation in the life of this people ?

No, the Israelite cannot be an Israelite, or the Christian a Christian, without having the other as a witness of what makes him such. And he cannot be an Israelite, or Christian, without being to the other a witness of what makes him such. The other whom he has as a witness is his neighbour, his brother. And as he for his part is a witness to the other ; he is his neighbour, his brother. Without this neighbour, this brother, and without being to him a neighbour, a brother, he would not be what he is.

We can call it the law of the common life of the people of God that none must be alone and that none can leave the other alone ; that each is set there as a witness to the other ; that each is ordained to accompany the other as a witness and continually to encounter him as such—a witness of the divine covenant which upholds and embraces them both, of the election from which they both derive as members of the people of God and by the authentication of which they both live, of the grace and mercy of God which are addressed to them both and without which they would instantaneously perish. The law of the people of God, the command which is continually given to each of its members, is to the effect that they are and may and should be to one another witnesses and therefore neighbours, brothers and sisters, in this way. As the members of this people are God's children loved by Him and loving Him in return, they are placed under this law and it is written on their hearts.

What the members of the people of God have mutually to attest and guarantee is simply that God loves them, and that they may love Him in return, as the first-fruits and precursors of the whole of the human race, typically and representatively for all men, as those who bear the message throughout the world and for the sake of their mission. The law particularly given to them is thus the law of their universal mission. They are to one another witnesses of that which as the people of God they have commonly to attest to every man. But to be this people and therefore God's witnesses to every man and to the whole world, it is indispensable that they should first and foremost be this to one another. As it is revealed and known among them that God loves them and that they may love Him in return, as this hidden thing is light in their midst, they are elected from among all human races and societies, and they of all men are gathered and built up as a community. They of all others are thus placed under this law and made witnesses to one another in order that together they should be witnesses to all men : not therefore for themselves but to be a sign of what God is and does for all and what all may be and do for God ; but from and among all others in order that they particularly should be this sign. To them first there has been vouchsafed that gracious inter-relating of man and man in virtue of which none can be his own neighbour in respect of the divine love which descends to man and the human love which ascends to God, but each may have a neighbour in the other who continually attests this love to him, and each may be to the other a witness of this love. Among them first there is a clear realisation that the event of reconciliation and salvation has also this dimension; that there is no revelation or knowledge of that great love apart from this inter-relating of man and man ; and that the freedom for life in that great love is identical with the freedom of the neighbour to be to me a witness and with my own freedom to be a witness to him. They first—the members of the people charged with the ministry of this witness to the world—are thankful for the fact that they have human witnesses of God, and willing to be themselves His human witnesses.

But how can and may and should and will the one be to the other a witness of God, i.e., of the fact that God loves us and that we may love Him in return ? The concept of the witness carries with it a restriction which we cannot ignore. When a man is a witness to another, he can only tell him about something, and answer for the truth and reality of what is told. He cannot produce the thing itself. None of us can reveal to the other that God loves him and that he may love God in return. This can be revealed to both only as it takes place that God evinces His love and in so doing gives the freedom to love Him. There can be no transmission of this event and freedom (e.g., by persuasion or suggestion) from one man to another. What can take place on this level, between man and man, as the one is witness to the other, can be only a reflection of what takes place on the vertical level, between God and both. It can be only a copy of it in a reciprocal human action. In the form of this human action, within the limits set to all human action and with the frailty and ambiguity characteristic of all human action, there is passed on from the one to the other, and *vice versa*, news of what God is and does for both, and of what both may be and do for God. But in the indirectness of this declaration the neighbour can and may and should and will guarantee to his neighbour, and the brother to his brother, the fact that God does really and truly love Him, and that he may really and truly love God. They and all the members of the people of God, each in relation to the other, need this declaration and are capable of it. And they are placed under this gracious law as mutual witnesses in order that they may by this means serve and help and uphold and comfort and admonish and therefore befriend one another—not as gods but as neighbours and brothers loved by God and loving Him in return.

This witness will be genuine and useful to the extent that between man and man, with all the imperfection of what one man can be and do for another, there is a true reflection and imitation of what takes place between God and man, so that while there is no replacement of the latter, or identity with it, there is a similarity, and what is done is calculated to give a necessary reminder of it. If even the best proclamation cannot take the place of what is proclaimed, there is no proclamation at all if what is proclaimed is not visible and perceptible in outline and may not be known even if only indirectly. But the similarity of the witness to God's love and to the freedom to love Him in return is to be found quite simply in the fact that the neighbour will love the neighbour, the brother the brother. He will do so in a human act of love. But within the limits and with all the frailty of human action he will do so in reality and truth. For he himself is loved by God and may love Him in return. He cannot conceal or deny this fact. He cannot place this light under a bushel. He cannot withhold it from the neighbour, the brother. On the level of what takes place between man and man he can proclaim it only in such a way that here too, in this encounter, there is love, the mutual love of these men. To be sure, there are other relationships between them as well. Apart from many that are unimportant, or only externally and technically important, there are those that involve a very inward and profound and significant and meaningful intercourse and exchange. These, too, may be a means of love. But in them they may withhold the witness which they owe to one another. In them they may still be isolated and left to their own devices. What counts in the inter-relating of the members of the people of God, and under the gracious law which obtains among them, is whether or not in the form of this or that relationship they love one another. If this is not the case, then even the most profound words which pass between them, the most effective works which they do for one another and the most devoted attitudes which they work up in their contact one with another, cannot alter in the very slightest the fact that they are transgressors of this law, that they are not fulfilling their reciprocal obligation and that they are seriously deluded in relation to their love for God and their experience of God's love. This great love must be declared in the inter-relationship of the children of God, and it can be declared only in love ; in the act of love for the neighbour and brother. If they fail to make this declaration they give the lie both to God who loves them and to themselves in their love for God. Their mutual love is the fulfilling of this law. Otherwise it is not fulfilled but broken. And where this is the case, it means that as far as they are concerned the life of the community is arrested and thrown into confusion, and its mission in the world is compromised.

For " by this shall all men know that ye are my disciples, if ye have love one to another " (Jn. 13³⁵). That is to say, what makes the community a distinctive and serious partner in discussion with the world is the fact that within it—but visible outwardly—it takes place that the men united in it do what is not done elsewhere : upholding (ἀνεχόμενοι, Eph. 4²) one another instead of causing one another to fall ; serving (δουλεύετε, Gal. 5¹³) one another by love instead of ruling over one another ; showing a φιλαδελφία which is inward (φιλόστοργοι, Rom. 12¹⁰), unfeigned, sincere, and constant (1 Pet. 1²², 4⁸), not stagnating or declining but increasing in each individual member (2 Thess. 1³) and confirming itself even to the one who has fallen (2 Cor. 2⁸). This action is so constitutive for the existence of the community and its members, and seems so self-evident in the New Testament, that Paul in 1 Thess. 4⁹ can say to his readers that he has no need to write about it explicitly. They are taught by God (θεοδίδακτοι), to love one another, as is proved by their obvious action in relation to their Macedonian brethren. Paul did not always find this self-evident thing quite so self-evident. Nor did the author of 1 John, whose writings are at once the sharpest and in every way the most illuminating in the exposition of this subject. We may refer to 4¹¹ : " Beloved, if God so loved us (namely, in the sending of His Son to be the propitiation for our sins), we ought (ὀφείλομεν) also to love one another " ; or 4¹⁹ : " We love him, because he first loved us " ; or 4¹⁶ : " He that dwelleth in love dwelleth in God, and God in him " ; or 4²⁰ : " If a man say, I love God, and hateth his brother, he is a liar : for he that loveth not his brother whom he hath seen, cannot love God whom he hath not seen " (οὐ δύναται, he cuts the root of his whole Christian existence) ; or finally 4²¹ : " This commandment have we from him, That he who loveth God love his brother also." It is to be noted that in this concluding verse we do not really have an imperative but an indicative : ὁ ἀγαπῶν (on the vertical plane, in direct answer to God's own love) ἀγαπᾷ (on the horizontal plane, in indirect but necessary repetition of this answer). There is thus a general inter-connexion, the one thing entailing the other. God's love evokes the love of the Christian for Him, and the two together the mutual love of Christians.

The function of the love for the neighbour and brother which corresponds to God's love and the love for God is thus to be the ministry of human witness in which the one guarantees to the other the turning of God's love to His people and the turning of His people to God, giving him a visible reflection and therefore reminder of the twofold movement of and in which this people and within it all its members live, and thus helping to maintain him in this twofold movement. What takes place in love is that the one calls the other to his true business as a Christian. No words or works or attitudes are able in themselves and as such to render this service. The rendering of this human, but on the human level indispensable, service takes place in love. It may well be said that what we have here is the ministry or service which continually renews and maintains the whole life of the community (as a common life of men), and therefore makes possible the life of the Christians united in it. It is, in fact, the *conditio sine qua non* of the life of this totality and its individual constituents. Nor may we play off against the decisive significance of love for the neighbour and brother either grace, or the Holy Spirit, or faith in the remission of sins. To do so is to overlook or forget or deny the second (and therefore the first !) dimension of the history of salvation, in which there must necessarily be, in the light and power of the first, an action of man not only in relation to God but also to the fellow-man who is also participant in it, to the one who is a neighbour and brother. Here, too, it is naturally a question of the free and sovereign grace of

God. But it is this grace which so vehemently demands brotherly love. It is this grace which neither God's people as a whole nor any individual member possesses in its own strength. It is this grace which has obviously to be mutually attested. It is in relation to this grace that it may be said that there is none that does not need its witness, but also none that can boast of it without becoming its witness to the other—which is the work of his brotherly love. Naturally, too, it is a question of the work and gift of the Holy Ghost. The members of the people of God should never imagine that they can and should help themselves and one another, exerting and forcing themselves to love one another. This kind of exertion is quite futile, since none can do it. Only by the Holy Spirit do they become free for this action. But by the Holy Spirit they do become free for it. By the Holy Spirit the individual becomes free for existence in an active relationship with the other in which he is loved and finds that he may love in return. The one who is most deeply filled with the Spirit is the one who is richest in love, and the one who is devoid of love necessarily betrays the fact that he is empty of the Spirit. Naturally, it is a matter of faith in the remission of sins, sins which will be present even where men stand in this active connexion as Christians filled with the Spirit and with love. There can be no question of their activity dispensing them from living by forgiveness. But it is a matter of practising faith in this forgiveness where one sinner (whose sins are taken away) may love as a neighbour and brother another sinner (of whom it may also be said that his sins are taken away). The one to whom much is forgiven (Lk. 7⁴⁷ᶠ·) can love much, whereas little is forgiven to the one who loves little.

No, it is not advisable to try to escape by appealing to the primacy and over-riding importance of what can take place only between God and man and not between man and man. There can be no limiting or contesting this primacy. The first commandment is always the first. But it is a matter of confirming this primacy in the fulfilment of the second commandment. As there can be no above without a below, no before without an after, so there can be no divine revelation without a human ministry of witness, no history of salvation between God and man without its reflection and repetition in a history between man and man. The one without the other would necessarily prove to be a mere mythology and illusion in the form of a " positivism of revelation." But its reflection and repetition can take place only as the men who are loved by God and love Him in return enjoy and make use of the freedom to love one another. If it is ever the case that they seem to be missing God's love and their own love for God, and no help is found by turning to the Bible and to prayer, the root of the trouble may be quite simply that they are not ready to make use of this freedom, and are not engaged in this confirmation of God's love and their own love for Him. There are no legitimate reasons for evading this confirmation. If we try to do so, we must not complain at the immediate consequences.

But what does it mean to *love* one's neighbour or brother ? More than once in our description of the ministry of witness which the one owes and for which he is indebted to the other we have spoken of the one guaranteeing to the other that God loves His people, that He therefore loves the two concerned, and that they may both love Him in return. We must take this thought quite seriously if we are to penetrate to a true understanding.

To guarantee something to another is to do more than offer something, or even to do or achieve something in his favour. We may do as much as this when we are well-disposed to someone, when we like him and wish him well, and desire that he should do the same to us. Many remarkable things, even the greatest, may be done simply to please him. But one thing we do not do—and that is to stand surety for him, to make ourselves responsible for him, to offer and give ourselves to him. On the contrary, in all that we do to please him we simply maintain and assert ourselves over against him. We do not want to be without this fellow-man who pleases us so much. We want to bind him to us, to make sure of him for ourselves. To take up the important biblical expression, we do not love him as ourselves, i.e., with the interposition of ourselves. On the contrary, we love ourselves and for this reason, for the sake of ourselves, we love this fellow-man. There are instances of this, of course, even among Christians and between Christians and others. The Christian does not like all his fellows, not even all his fellow-Christians. But he likes some of them and he is ready to do a good deal, perhaps the very greatest things, to please them. May he continue to do so, and may what he does on this presupposition be to the benefit of both parties ! But although Christian love for the neighbour and brother does not exclude this presupposition—it may indeed be realised on this presupposition —it is not in any way tied to it. It does not really depend upon the fact that the one likes another nor does it find realisation necessarily in what the one usually does for the other on this presupposition. It may also be realised in an action in which he does not earn his favour or win him to himself. Christian love for the neighbour and brother does not guarantee that the one will make himself " lovable " to the other in the shallower sense of the term. It begins as such at the very point where the pleasure which men have in one another, and the favours which they may show in consequence, do not necessarily cease, but may very well do so, or for various reasons find no place.

It consists in the fact that (whether he likes him and can earn his liking or not) the one interposes himself for the other, making himself his guarantor and desiring nothing else but to be this. It consists in the fact that he has no place for himself except as the guarantor of the other. It resembles God's love and love for God in the fact that it is self-giving ; the self-giving which reflects and therefore guarantees to the other the love of God and the freedom to love him. That it may be the pledge of this great love is the presupposition which marks it off from all the love which is based on liking and finds realisation in favours because its aim is to be liked in return. And the fact that it has to pledge this great love means that it cannot be less or other than self-giving. It means that the one has to love the other " as himself " : not as and because and in the same way as he loves himself (according to the well-established and frightful misinterpretation) ; but as he delivers himself to this other with the sole purpose of guaranteeing in his own person the fact that God loves him too, and that he too is free to love God. How can he bear witness to this fact except by imitating and reflecting it, by giving a representation of it in outline ? But how can he imitate it—this love of God and the love for God— except by interposing no less than himself for this other instead of asserting himself against him, by pledging himself in this service instead of seeking to win him to himself ?

Christian love for the neighbour and brother differs, of course, from that which it declares in the fact that it can be only a self-giving which pledges and guarantees. A man cannot be to another more than a witness even in the life of the people of God—a fact which is realised among this people, so that there no attempts are made to violate this frontier. Even Christian love for the neighbour and brother is a ministry of witness. What is to be attested in this self-giving which guarantees is itself more than witness or a pledge. It is the self-giving of God to man, and the event of man's liberation to give himself to God. In human love for the neighbour and brother we have only an imitation and reflection of this event ; its representation in outline. I cannot take the place of God and love another with the love with which God loves him. I cannot take the place of another and in his person use the freedom given him to love God in return. I can only answer for these two things in the representation of my person. And I can do so only as I love him, i.e., as I interpose and give myself as their pledge, unreservedly placing myself at his disposal as such. There is no point in trying to pretend to God, the other man or myself that I cannot do this. I can and may and must do it. If I am to be a Christian, this is the content of my life-act as such on the plane of dealings between man and man, just as on the plane of dealings between God and man it consists in the fact that I may and must respond to the self-giving of God to me with my self-giving to Him. I am not asked concerning the value of my self-giving, i.e., of my person as I give it to the other as a guarantee. Nor am I asked concerning the art or address with which I accomplish it. Nor am I asked concerning the success which I may or may not have with the other ; the impression which I may or may not make. Nor am I asked concerning the limits set to the perfection of my self-giving by my nature, by the fact that I am only a poor sinful man. I am asked only concerning my self-giving, my interposition as an only too human pledge, as the necessary and only possible form of my ministry of witness. I am asked only whether (however well or badly) I do this ; whether I love my neighbour as myself, i.e., in such a way that I place myself at his disposal just as I am, so that my heart is no longer my own but his. But I *am* asked concerning this. And I cannot find any way of evading this question. On this question depend my election and calling, my justification and sanctification, my eternal and temporal future. In this question I have to do with the Law and the prophets. And I have joy in the Gospel if I rejoice in the fact that I am asked concerning the pledge of my self-giving to the neighbour ; if the act of this self-giving is itself a cause of rejoicing to me. I do not really perform it if I do so joylessly and unwillingly and grudgingly and with a thousand " ifs " and " buts." And I will then find no joy in the Gospel, but prove only that so far I have not really heard the Gospel at all.

It is neither arbitrary nor accidental that the Gospel has to be described as the basis and meaning of Christian love for the neighbour. We have to do with the Gospel of Jesus Christ. The mystery of Christian love for the neighbour is finally and decisively, because originally, His mystery.

There can be no doubt that it is more clearly and emphatically attested in the New Testament than the Old. The Old Testament does, of course, know the neighbour and brother, and the importance of the relationship to him. But the fact that he and the relationship to him belong to the history of salvation, that an Israelite is ordained and called to be to the other a witness of the covenant, that the substance of this witness is to be to the other a guarantor of the covenant, that this action means mutual self-giving and therefore love—all this seems in the Old Testament to be still concealed in the settled order in which the shepherds and peasants and citizens of Israel are associated (within the framework of the order of their common relationship to their God). It all seems to be envisaged indirectly rather than directly, as promise but not yet as fulfilment. It does not yet seem to be expressly brought into relationship with the commandment of love for God in its twofold form. From this standpoint alone, in an abstract exposition of the Old Testament, we could not have said what we have said on this point.

But from the standpoint of the New Testament witness we could not help saying it. For this witness does not only look to the epiphany of Jesus Christ. It does do this. From first to last it declares His future, final and universal manifestation and revelation. But it looks to it in this second form only as it already derives from it in its first form, from the resurrection of Jesus Christ from the dead. The theological difference between the times *ante Christum* and *post Christum* may perhaps be perceived at other points too. But there can be no doubt that—in a very remarkable way—it is to be perceived here. It was only through the Gospel of Jesus Christ, which as the goal and meaning of the Law and the prophets could be proclaimed by the apostles not only to Israel but also to the Gentiles, that the neighbour and brother, and the love of brother for brother, necessarily took on this central significance. In the New Testament there is therefore a distinctive pattern (usually indicated by the adverb καθώς) of which Jesus Christ is the original and which the members of His community have to copy by mutual love. We can see this in Jn. 15¹², where Jesus says to

His disciples that it is His commandment that they should love one another as (καθώς) He loved them, or in Jn. 13³⁴ where this love is shown to be the aim of those who belong to Him : ἵνα καὶ ὑμεῖς. We may also refer to Rom. 15⁷ : " Receive ye one another, as (καθώς) Christ also received us " ; to Col. 3¹²f. where " the elect of God, holy and beloved " are summoned to " put on " (as the new clothes which suit them) a heartfelt mercy, kindness, humbleness of mind and longsuffering, " forbearing one another (ἀνεχόμενοι), and forgiving one another . . . as (καθώς) Christ forgave you, so also do ye (οὕτως καὶ ὑμεῖς). And above all these things put on charity, which is the bond of τελειότης (of the common goal set for and to be attained by you). And let the peace of God rule in your hearts, to the which also ye are called in one body (His) ; and be ye thankful " ; and finally to Eph. 5², ²⁵ where the demand of v. 1, that Christians should be followers or imitators of God, is explained by the further demand that they should " walk in love, as (καθώς) Christ also hath loved us (the ἐκκλησία in v. 25), and hath given himself for us " (the ἐκκλησία in v. 25). The secret of the brotherly love of Christians is to be found in this καθώς.

The man Jesus, whom we have particularly had in view in the whole of this second part of the doctrine of reconciliation, is both this secret and at the same time its revelation—He who is the new thing in the New Testament beside which all other things we can think of may only be called relatively new. Common to both Old and New Testaments is, of course, the proclamation of the covenant of grace as the promise of the lordship and salvation of God among men and for them ; and to that extent the proclamation of the love of God, and the freedom to love Him in return, as the promise of life for all men, of peace on earth to the men of His good-pleasure. But in the Old Testament this is only a promise. To be sure, there is there a people with whom this covenant is concluded and faithfully maintained on the part of God. But among all the men of this people there is none who corresponds on the human side to this faithfulness of God. It can be seen that Yahweh is the God of Israel. But it cannot be seen that Israel is the people of Yahweh. The promise given to it is not visibly fulfilled. The man Jesus is the fulfilment of this promise, the Messiah of Israel who in the place and name of all Israel does as man that which corresponds to what God does. Thus, although the New Testament still proclaims God and His covenant and will and lordship, it does so by proclaiming as His Word and work, not to be separated from Him, this man, the one man Jesus, elected and sent by God and exalted to His right hand. The new thing in the New Testament is the present and action of the invisible God in the existence, the words and deeds, the death and resurrection of this man, and therefore in the historical sphere in which there is a confrontation not only between God and man but also between man and man.

And now, as we look back on the " act of love " which has been our theme in this sub-section, we may ask : Who is the man who is loved by God and loves Him in return and who may be to His fellow-man as such the neighbour attesting and pledging that God loves him too and that he too may love God in return ? Who is the man who guarantees this to his fellow-man, sacrificing himself to render him this service ? Is there any such man ? If there is no such man, the fulfilment of the covenant of grace leads into the void as a mere promise which is not kept and fulfilled on the part of man. We have spoken all the time as if there is such a man and this service is rendered from man to man. But who is the man who renders this service ? Our answer has been that it is the Israelite, the Christian, the member of the people of God in the world in whom it takes place that the one may be to the other a neighbour and brother, a witness and pledge ; that the one may love the other. We have not spun this answer out of thin air. We have repeated it from the New Testament, and in the light of the New Testament from the Old. But even if we do meaningfully repeat it from Holy Scripture, and may thus boldly count on the fact that this does take place in the people of God, we have still to ask : Who is the Israelite ? And who is the Christian ? And our answer must be that in the true sense it is obviously not this or that, let alone every, Israelite, but the one Israelite, the Messiah of Israel who has come as promised, the man Jesus ; and that is the true sense it is obviously not this or that, let alone every, Christian, but, identical with the one Israelite, the one Christian from whom all others receive their name and in whom the community of Jews and Gentiles has its Lord. In the true sense this One who is the Head of the whole body is the man who is loved by God and loves Him in return and as such the One who loves His fellow-man. In the true sense He is the Samaritan who in Lk. 10[25f.] does not, like the priest and the Levite, pass by on the other side, when he comes on the man who had fallen among thieves and was left half-dead by the roadside, but shows mercy on him, thus acting as, and proving himself to be, the neighbour of the lawyer's question. In the true sense it is He who fulfils the commandments of Deut. 6[4] and Lev. 19[18]. In the true sense it is He who performs the act of love in both its dimensions.

If He did not perform it in the true sense, how could it be said that others perform it, that there may be and have been and are and will be other neighbours, brothers or Samaritans, and that we may count on mutual love not merely as an ideal concept and construct but as a plenitude of events which have actually taken place, and will take place, among the people of God in every age ? The love of the one for the other, by which there is evinced the love for God, has in fact a secret but very real history. The history of salvation would not itself be real if it did not find real reflection and repetition in this history in a varied series of human acts of neighbourly and brotherly love. We cannot say this, however, merely on the basis of an interpretation of the history of Israel and Church history as such, but only in the light of *the* history in which that of Israel has its goal and that of the Church its beginning—the history of the man Jesus. In relation to this history we may and can and must say it because in the uniqueness of His person and action He is not an isolated individual but the Head of His whole body and all its members ; because He constitutes an indissoluble whole with those who are His ; because what He is and does in the true sense is in their favour and determines their being and action. We may quietly admit that in relation to His action theirs will always be improper. But this action of theirs which imitates and reflects the love of God, the human response of love for God and the corresponding love for man as they are all actualised in Him, is as such a real action. Certainly the one will not be to the other—I prefer not to use Luther's expression—a " second Christ." But in the name and school of Christ he will represent what Christ is to them all. He will be a little witness, pledge, neighbour, brother and Samaritan who as such lives only by the fact that He is the great witness, who may live by this fact and who does not desire to live by anything else. The clearer the relation of discipleship in which " He is the Head and we His members " and not *vice versa*, the more forceful the reflection of the original in the copy, the greater the impress of similarity made by the action of the Master on that of the disciple, the more certain it will be that even among disciples there will be not merely a little love but much love, not merely little acts of love but great acts, and in any case a genuine actualisation of love.

The direction in which the one to whom the man Jesus has acted as a neighbour by showing mercy on him (ὁ ποιήσας τὸ ἔλεος μετ᾽ αὐτοῦ, Lk. 10³⁷) has himself not merely to look but to go is plainly indicated in the same verse : πορεύου καὶ σὺ ποίει ὁμοίως. In the ὁμοίωμα, or likeness, of Christ's act of love— and this is the aim of the καθώς which led us to this train of thought—he not only can perform acts of love and wants to perform acts of love but does actually perform them. Another Johannine passage may be recalled in conclusion. The story of the washing of the disciples' feet begins in Jn. 13¹ with some words of the Evangelist. He tells us that Jesus knew that the hour had come when He should leave the world and go to the Father, and that " having loved his own which were in the world (τοὺς ἰδίους τοὺς ἐν τῷ κόσμῳ), he loved them εἰς τὸ τέλος " (to the final point of love, as described in the story that follows). That is to say, He washed their feet the one after the other (Judas Iscariot was still with them) and then dried them with His own garments. The account closes with Jesus' own words (vv. 12–17) : " Know ye what I have done to you ? Ye call me Master and Lord : and ye say well ; for so I am. If I then, your Lord and Master, have washed your feet ; ye also ought (ὀφείλετε) to wash one another's feet. For I have given you an example (ὑπόδειγμα), that ye should do as (καθώς) I have done to you. Verily, verily, I say unto you, The servant is not greater than his lord ; neither is he that is sent (ἀπόστολος) greater than he that sent him. If ye know these things, happy are ye if ye do them." This benediction is the secret of the commandment : " Thou shalt love thy neighbour as thyself " —its promise and its fulfilment.

4. THE MANNER OF LOVE

In this section we have been treating of love as the life-act of the individual Christian as a member of the Christian community ; of its difference from the action of human self-love ; of its basis in the love of God in Jesus Christ ; and of its fulfilment as the act of self-giving to God and the brother. We will conclude with an attempt to describe the manner of this love. What we have in mind is (1) the manner in which love determines human life in the community as Christian life ; (2) the manner in which human life is lived in the Christian community as determined by love ; and (3) the manner of the promise which is peculiar to human life as determined by love and as such lived in the community. The answers to these three questions are as follows. It is (1) the manner of love that it alone decisively determines human life in the Christian community as Christian life. It is (2) the manner of love that human life in the community is lived victoriously only as determined by it. And it is (3) the manner of love that the promise which has eternal content is peculiar only to human life in the community as it is determined by it and lived as such. In short, it is love alone that counts, love alone that triumphs, and love alone that endures. This is the nature of love, and only of love. Hence these three statements can properly be made only of love when it is a question of describing the life-act of the Christian.

We have not spun these statements out of the void. To be sure, the New Testament also described the life-act of the Christian as the act of faith. But there is in the New Testament no hymn of praise to the manner of faith. Again, it describes it as the act of hope. But there is in the New Testament no hymn of praise to hope. Yet the New Testament does contain such a hymn (corresponding to the Song of Songs of the Old Testament with its magnifying of marital love) to Christian love and the manner of Christian love. This hymn is to be found in 1 Cor. 13, which is obviously built around the three statements that love alone counts, love alone conquers and love alone endures. Hence we cannot do better than give to our attempt to describe the manner of love the form of a paraphrase and exposition of the context and content of this chapter.

A recent work which is particularly stimulating for the study of this chapter is that of Götz Harbsmeier : *Das Hohelied der Liebe*, 1952—a book which will also be found helpful because of the references to other modern literature on the subject. For the rest, I have again found great profit in the observations of J. A. Bengel in his *Gnomon N.T.*

The Holy Spirit is the quickening power which underlies, capacitates and actualises the act of the individual in the Christian community in its totality, giving to it both its distinctive character and scope and also its distinctive direction. It is He who awakens man—each one in the form and to the task which He Himself allots to him. It is He who endows him with the corresponding abilities and freedoms and powers. It is He who enriches the whole Christian community with this endowment of the individual Christian, thus deepening and broadening its whole life, and extending its power for the fulfilment of its mission in the world. But those to and in whom the Holy Spirit is mightily at work in this way are men. Indeed, they are sinful men. And it is their human action which by His action He authorises and claims for service. This means that His gifts are jeopardised both in the person of each individual among them and also as they accrue to the Christian community as such. When the Holy Spirit bears witness with our spirit (Rom. 8[16]), it happens all too easily that in the hearts and heads of Christians the spiritual riches entrusted to them are unfortunately transformed into intellectual, moral and religious riches which each can begin to handle as if he had himself created them, as if they were at his disposal, as if he could claim them as his own possession and power and glory, playing them off against others and what seem to be their corresponding possessions without any regard for the fact that what is given him is not given him for himself but to equip him to serve the community, and that it is only relatively that what is entrusted to him is of greater or less importance. It always hangs by a hair's breadth whether this misfortune is avoided or whether, in consequence of the natural drag of human corruption, it takes place to a more or less dangerous degree, involving at once the external and certainly the internal dissolution of the community, the more or less radical transformation of its life into that of a religious society and finally the personal disqualification of those who succumb to the temptation. The more intensive the work of the Holy Spirit, the richer and more powerful His gifts, the greater obviously is the attraction and danger of this transformation and the more urgent the critical question, which no appeal to the power and plenitude of the life of the individual and the community must be allowed to suppress, concerning that which genuinely characterises as Christian the forms of their action (even as a human action) as awakened by the Holy Spirit. The more urgent it is indeed to call them back to this distinctive reality, which is love.

We have been describing the background and context of 1 Cor. 13. This short chapter interrupts the two sections of instruction given concerning the right way to deal with the different *charisma* in which the Corinthian community seems to have been particularly rich but in the expression and application of which it was correspondingly endangered. Paul does not question for a moment that they were genuine gifts. But in the light of the fact that they are genuine, and therefore that they derive from the Holy Spirit, the community is (1) admonished in chapter 12 to remember the unity of the derivation of that which is entrusted to it and therefore the fellowship of those who as members of the one body of Christ are counted worthy of one or other of these gifts ; and it is later (2) reminded in chapter 14 that their importance is only relative and therefore greater or less. This second note is sounded already in 12[31] : " But covet earnestly the best (μείζονα) gifts." In 14[1] and the whole of chapter 14 we learn that what Paul had particularly in mind was the precedence of prophecy over the speaking with tongues which was obviously so rampant and so greatly over-estimated in Corinth. Among the higher gifts he clearly counts the γνῶσις and πίστις of 13² and the readiness for poverty and martyrdom of 13³, while those of secondary importance seem to include (12²⁸ᶠ·) miracles (δυνάμεις), gifts of healing, helps, governments and the interpretation of tongues, which are not mentioned again. Bengel has described as *theologia comparativa* the process indicated in 12³¹ and carried through in 14. But before Paul goes on to the second part of his presentation with its clear differentiation, he cuts right across his own thinking and that of his readers with a threefold statement in which he brackets and leaves behind him for a moment the whole problem of *charisma* and questions concerning their distinction, their unity and their greater or less importance, and turns expressly to the factor which forms in some sense the key to the exposition which both precedes and follows : " And yet beyond this (beyond all spiritual gifts, beyond all that has to be said concerning the right way to handle them) I will shew you the way " (12³¹ᵇ). He refers to the way which Christians have always to tread whether or not they are endowed by the Holy Spirit or however they may be endowed. He refers to the human action which has as its basis, not a special liberation and endowment of the Spirit, but the one liberation and endowment which precedes every special liberation and endowment. He refers to the action whose occurrence is the criterion of a right handling of all the others. This way, this action, which is necessary " beyond all this " (κατ' ὑπερβολήν), which is the *unum necessarium*, is the distinctive reality concerning which the Christian is asked before and in and after the reception of all particular *charisma* if he is to use them as gifts of the grace of the Holy Spirit.

The way or action to which Paul refers is love. There can be no doubt that he is speaking of the love which is grounded in the love of God ; of the love whose primary human subject is Jesus Christ ; of the love which takes place in His fellowship with man and His discipleship ; of the ἀγάπη τοῦ πνεύματος (Rom. 15³⁰). There is this in common between love and the *charisma* to which it is opposed. The freedom for it too is the freedom of the children of God. It too is the freedom originally realised in Jesus Christ and then awakened in man by the Holy Spirit. It is no mere rhetoric that in the verses which follow Paul describes love almost hypostatically as a person coming and acting independently. If we read vv. 4–7 (and especially 7) we shall soon realise which person he has seriously and ultimately before him. And except with reference to this original, love could not be described in vv. 8–13 as the unceasing and never-failing element in Christian existence. To this extent it was quite in order that at an earlier point (*C.D.*, I, 2, p. 330) I stated that we best understand the concept of love in I Cor. 13 if we simply insert the name Jesus Christ in place of it. All the same, we must not allow this to obliterate the fact that Paul describes love as a way, obviously meaning that his readers must tread it, that they can and should do something for themselves, and that in the transition to chapter 14 (v. 1a) he could ask them to " follow after " love. Man does not merge at this point into God or Jesus Christ, but lives in and with Him as a new man in the human freedom given him by the Holy Spirit. It is to be noted that the word θεός, and even the name Jesus, does not occur in the whole chapter. The reference of the text is obviously to what is to be done by Christians in the freedom given them by God in Jesus Christ through the Holy Spirit. The idea of A. Nygren that love is to be understood only as an " effluence from God's own life " flowing through man (*op. cit.*, Vol. I, p. 120) is quite impossible in an exposition of I Cor. 13. How could Paul oppose love to the practical exercise of the *charisma* at Corinth if he was not thinking of it as itself a practice, as the true practice of the Christian, as the *via maxime vialis* (Bengel) ? On the other hand, it is certainly a matter of Christian love as grounded in the love of God. Thus in regard to the debate forty years ago between A. v. Harnack and R. Reitzenstein whether what is meant is love for the neighbour or love for (cf. Nygren, *op. cit.*, p. 114 f. and Harbsmeier, *op. cit.*, p. 33 f.), we must say q definitely that in relation to I Cor. 13 this is a false alternative. It is as well avoid both abstractions and look constantly at both the dimensions in which Christian love takes place. On the basis of God's self-giving to man, it is man's self-giving to God and therefore also his self-giving to his neighbour.

1. 1 Cor. 13^{1-3}. Because it is in virtue of the quickening power of the Holy Spirit that the Christian community, and in his own way each individual member, lives and works and acts and speaks, we cannot think too highly of the breadth and depth and height of the possibilities given to the community and to each Christian in his own way. God shows Himself to His people as a Lord who is not only kind but noble and generous, so that it is always better to expect great things—the very greatest—from Him than too little things. Accordingly, the Christian community can and must be the scene of many human activities which are new and supremely astonishing to many of its own members as well as to the world around because they rest on an endowment with extraordinary capacities. Where these are lacking, there is reason to ask whether in pride or sloth the community as such has perhaps evaded this endowment, thus falsifying its relationship to its Lord, making it a dead because a nominal and not a real relationship. Yet none of these activities decides the reality of this relationship as such, even though they may have their basis, not in illusions, but in a spiritual endowment of the community or its individual members ; even though their power may be ever so manifest in all kinds of successes and fruits ; and even though they may be activities which not only provoke surprise and astonishment but compel regard and admiration because as achievements of service they are supremely illuminating in their meaningfulness and purposefulness. Why not ? Why should there be no direct and unimpeachable perception by this means of the reality of the relationship of the community and its members to their living Lord ? Why cannot these acts be regarded directly as acts of God? The answer is that, notwithstanding the fact that they genuinely have their origin in the acts of God, the lordship of Jesus Christ and the gifts of the Holy Spirit, they are human acts which cannot be directly characterised by the fact that there takes place in and with them the true and proper thing which must take place if this relationship is to be a real one. What takes place in and with them is not as such the history of salvation. It may be done with great fulness, with the greatest extensive and intensive splendour, with supreme subjective and objective power and with every conceivable mark of being specifically Christian, and yet be lacking in that which really counts, so that there does not take place in it the history of salvation. Whether the true and proper thing takes place is decided exclusively by whether the life of the Christian and the community not only derives from the Spirit but is lived in the Spirit ; whether it is conducted not only in the name of Jesus Christ but in the discipleship of Jesus Christ ; whether it is offered not only with the appeal to God but to His glory and therefore

as a sacrifice which gives Him pleasure. And it may be that in spite of everything this does not take place. If it does not, this betrays itself in the fact that on the way from the divine endowment and equipment to the human acts there is a secret transformation of the freedom given by God into caprice exercised by man, of a spiritual dynamic into an intellectual and moral and religious which will very quickly cease to be dynamic and become static. No splendour or power of Christian activities as such is proof that in the course of the transition there has not taken place this transformation which makes impossible the fulfilment of the real relationship of the community and individual Christians to their living Lord, and therefore the enactment within it of the history of salvation. The true and proper thing which must take place within it may not take place for all the genuineness of the origin and glory of its activities. But if it does not take place then its activities lack no less than everything, for they lack the very thing which must characterise them as service in the cause of God in the world. And since there is no alternative they are then performed in the service of the cause of the world in conflict with that of God. They are then in truth secular activities, and as empty and futile and useless as the action of the world without God, the non-Christian world, always is. The whole strange world of the possibilities given where there is the community and Christians stands always, to the extent that it is actualised in human activities, in the crisis of the question whether in and with these activities there takes place or not the true and proper thing which must be actualised ; and if it does not take place it stands under the decision already taken that what the community or Christians do, in spite of everything that may commend them and suggest their sincerity and good intentions, is just as corrupt as any other human activity enterprised and executed without God and in opposition to Him. The true and proper thing which must take place, and the non-occurrence of which gives the lie to even the very best of anything else that may be done, is love. It is love alone that counts.

V. 1 : " Though I speak with the tongues of men and of angels, and have not love, I am become as sounding brass, or a tinkling cymbal." Paul begins by contrasting love with the exercise of one of the endowments which he will later describe quite clearly as of the second rank. In the eyes of his readers, however, it is of primary importance. He does not question that it is genuine, nor does he desire to suppress it : " I would that ye all spake with tongues " (14^5). Indeed, he knows and exercises it himself : " I thank my God, I speak with tongues more than ye all " (14^{18}). He has no wish to " quench " the Spirit in this respect (1 Thess. 5^{19}). Speaking with tongues lies on the extreme limit of Christian speaking as such. It is an attempt to express the inexpressible in which the tongue rushes past, as it were, the notions and concepts necessary to ordinary speech and utters what can be received only as a groan or sigh, thus needing at once interpretation or exposition ($14^{7f.}$). The fact that this is possible seems to show that we are not to think of it as a wholly inarticulate, inhuman and bizarre stuttering and stammering. Certainly there can be no question of purely " emotional eruptions " (Harbsmeier, *op. cit.*, p. 14), otherwise Paul could hardly have described the capacity for them as pneumatic. On the other hand, it is a speech which in its decisive utterances leaves any clear coherence behind, necessarily falling apart unexpectedly in its elements, or recombining in equally unexpected equations, and finally consisting only of hints or indications with very forcible marks of interrogation and exclamation. In the last resort, it may well be asked whether there is any Christian speech, any utterance of the evangelical *kerygma*, which does not finally become speaking with tongues, overleaping ordinary notions and concepts in its decisive statements, and then, of course, having to return by way of exposition to ordinary speech. In any case, however, this point cannot be reached artificially. It is not open to all and sundry to advance to it. Such advance presupposes a gift, a permission and a freedom, or it is simply a movement to absurdity. Human speech may reach here the limit in which it becomes the hymn, but even as Christian speech it is held within this limit. The Corinthian community enjoyed in its gatherings a superfluity in respect of the advance to this limit of Christian speech. Paul does not try to dissuade them from it. He knows that there are points where a choice has to be made between speaking with tongues—even at the risk that some will not understand—and illegitimate silence. He tries to curb their over-estimation of this advance, but not to dissuade them from it. He presupposes in 1 Cor. 13 that it may be lawful and right. He maintains, however, that it is possible to speak with tongues (as enabled to do so by the Holy Ghost) and yet not to have love but to omit all self-giving to God and one's neighbour. The capacity for the highly pregnant statement in which it is a matter of expressing the inexpressible, the *esprit* needed for it, cannot make good this lack. And where there is this lack, speaking with tongues—Paul takes his own case as an example—is an instrument which is not really a musical instrument because, although it is sound, it has only the one note and is therefore hollow and empty and inexpressive and wholly unmusical. The sound of a bell or a gong is not music. It is simply a noise. And so, too, is speaking with tongues without love—no matter how significant and arresting it may sound, or how seriously it may have God and Jesus Christ and the Holy Spirit in intention. If it is without love, its good intention is of no more value than the spiritual wealth which seeks expression in it. What sounds in it is only the exalted self-enjoyment and the forceful self-expression of the one who speaks with tongues, and it is something which is monotonous, tedious, uninspiriting and finally irksome and annoying. No *Kyrie* or *Gloria* can help a performance of this nature. Even if the one who speaks with tongues were miraculously placed already among the 144,000 of Rev. 14²f., and therefore able to learn and sing the new song of the angels before the throne of the Lamb—a song which is undoubtedly of an all-surpassing wealth—it would be of no avail if he is without love. Even in this exalted company he would still be " as sounding brass, or a tinkling cymbal." It is love alone that counts—and not speaking with tongues, not even statements which are full of content and spoken or sung enthusiastically in the best sense of the term.

V. 2 : " And though I have the gift of prophecy, and understand all mysteries, and all knowledge ; and though I have all faith, so that I could remove mountains, and have not love, I am nothing." It is now a matter of the gifts which according to 12³¹ and chapter 14 are higher and most to be desired. By προφητεία we have to understand a definite, important form of Christian speech, not given to all or to any in the same way, which differs from speaking with tongues—with which it is contrasted in 14³—in the fact that it makes use of distinct notions and concepts. In 12²⁹ (and Eph. 4¹¹) the Christian prophet ranks immediately after the apostle. The foretelling of the future is not the essential thing which constitutes the prophet. We are to think, perhaps, of the demonstration of the divine revelation in the *hic et nunc* as it takes place in consequence of the apostolic *kerygma*, of the " intelligible call to the obedience here and to-day " (Harbsmeier, *op. cit.*, p. 27), which may, of course, also and not least of all include the opening up of certain vistas into the future. Understanding of μυστήρια and γνῶσις is the not at all self-evident presupposition of all Christian speech : the apprehension of the message and its theoretical and practical implications ; the consideration of its different dimensions ; the reflection in the union and confrontation of God and man, in the context of the old and the new, which according to Mt. 13⁵² constitutes a " scribe instructed unto the kingdom of heaven." At its noblest this means " theology "—and we must remember that in current usage as heard and used by the Corinthians γνῶσις did not mean *intellectus* in a banal but in the highest sense of the word and therefore " an intelligent participation of the whole man in the redemptive deity " (Harbsmeier, *op. cit.*, p. 17). Finally, πίστις is used in the sense of the faith which works miracles. In this sphere, too, Paul does not raise any doubts or questions. He thinks of the extreme possibilities which may become realities—all mysteries, all knowledge, all faith, the faith which according to Mt. 17²⁰ moves mountains. And he again speaks in the first person and therefore of possibilities known to himself. But he again maintains that he may be enabled to do all these things, and actually do them, and yet be without love. And in this case, no matter how perfect they may be, his prophesying is only idle words, his knowledge a mystico-rational game and his wonder-working faith a higher magic or a massive but sterile orthodoxy. In spite of all his prophetic, theological or hierurgical brilliance, he is οὐθέν, nothing, a string of noughts before which there is unfortunately no " one." We are reminded of Mt. 7²²ᶠ· which tells us that we may speak as prophets, or cast out demons, or do many mighty works in the name of Jesus, and yet do that which is against God and therefore belong to those whom He has never known. It is love alone that counts—and not this brilliance, however great it may be within this limit.

V. 3 : " And though I bestow all my goods to feed the poor, and though I give my body to be burned, and have not love, it profiteth me nothing." Paul now works back to willingness for poverty on behalf of needy fellow-men, or for martyrdom at the specific awakening and in the particular enabling of the Holy Spirit, and he is again thinking of possibilities not unknown to himself. It is to be noted—and this verse is obviously the climax of this first section— how close he now comes to love itself in the description of Christian action— Is it not love for the neighbour when a man gives all that he has as alms ? Is it not love for God when he willingly offers himself up to death for the faith (Paul seems to have had in mind the LXX version of Dan. 3²⁵ᶠ·) ? Does he not expressly speak of a παραδοῦναι in the second part of the sentence ? But this is the whole point. There is in fact a love which is without love, a self-giving which is no self-giving, a paroxysm of self-love which has the form of a genuine and extreme love for God and one's brother and yet in which it is not really a question of God or one's brother at all, but only of the delight which can be found in oneself, in the unlimited nature of one's heroism, when all things, even life itself, are offered. And in these circumstances the action is of no avail. It does not in any sense qualify a man as a Christian. It has nothing whatever to do with the occurrence of the history of salvation in his life. It is love alone that counts —not acts of love as such, however great. The latter may be done without love, and if so they are without significance—indeed they are done in opposition to God and one's brother.

2. 1 Cor. 13⁴⁻⁷. It is of the nature of the true and proper thing which takes place in love alone as opposed to the realisation of all the possibilities of the Christian life (even those given by the Holy Spirit), thus making love the *conditio sine qua non* of the existence of the Christian community and the individual Christian, that love

conquers and triumphs and is victorious. To this extent it reflects the resurrection of Jesus Christ from the dead and prefigures the coming general resurrection. It is the revelation of the superiority of the divine Yes, the Yes of the free grace of God, over the dejected No of the man who is alienated from Him and his neighbour and therefore himself. It is the revelation of the superiority of life over death. What takes place in love is the transformation of the old creation or creature into the new ; the yielding of the old æon and the coming of the new. We have said already that the statements in this second part of the chapter about love as the life-act of the Christian are so strong that they are quite intolerable unless we refer them to the man Jesus as the original of all Christian action. But again we cannot fail to recognise that the reference is to what is done or not done by men—Christians, to be sure, but even as Christians men. It has to be said of this human action that in so far as it is love it triumphs over the forces which menacingly resist its fulfilment as self-giving to God and the brother, and therefore the fulfilment of the Christian existence as such (1) in the Christian himself as a sinful man, (2) in the brother who is also a sinner, and finally (3) its fulfilment as self-giving to God. Love triumphs over these forces, not in an idea of their inferiority or its own superiority, but by proving and demonstrating both in action, by actually overcoming and defeating these forces. The forces are not to be despised. They are powerful indeed. But love—the Christian in the act of love—has the longer wind, the light which outlasts and outshines, the more solid ground. When the Christian loves, he is their master and drives them from the field. Love is not a weak action but a strong. It is in this form and strength that it is the true reality concerning which the Christian is questioned in all his works, even the most spiritual. It is in virtue of this strength that love alone counts. What would the life-act of the Christian be if it did not attest and reflect the kingdom of God, the existence of the royal man Jesus ? And what would it accomplish if it were not a strong act and therefore itself a victory, an overcoming, a triumph ? As love, it is this, and in it the history of salvation takes place, the glory of God in Jesus Christ becomes an event in space and time, the Christian is qualified as such, and it serves to promote the edification of the community and its equipment for its mission in the world. Of no Christian activity can this be said unconditionally, not even of faith or hope. It is love alone that conquers. Of love it may and must be said unconditionally. It triumphs indeed.

V. 4a : " Love suffereth long, and is kind." This is a kind of heading for all that is to be considered in this section. If we were right to describe Christian love as free self-giving, we may now expound as follows. Just because it is self-giving it is longsuffering, it has that staying power, it is that bright and never-failing light, it stands on that solid ground. Where the wind is short, and the light necessary to the life of man flickers and fades, and the ground is uncertain under his feet, it is finally because he tries to live otherwise than in self-giving ; because he is not ready to be free for God and the brother and therefore himself ; because he wants always to be free for himself. In love he gives himself up. He has God and the brother always before him—and only in this way, in them, himself. And because love is self-giving it is also " kind " or friendly. The word is not to be understood in a weak sense. In the sense of the New Testament χρηστότης it is literally " fitness " and therefore the very opposite of anything weak or soft. A man is " kind " when he has the freedom, the ability, to be spontaneously good to another—a voluntary friend of God and therefore of men. As such he does not do anything alien or accidental. He is not " friendly " amongst other things—casually—when he gives himself to God and his brother. He does that which is most proper to him. He loves in doing it. It is this which makes him *a priori* superior. As, therefore, love is longsuffering and kind, it conquers and triumphs and is victorious, no power being able to match it.

VV. 4b–5b : " Love envieth not ; vaunteth not itself, is not puffed up, doth not behave itself unseemly, seeketh not her own." It is to be noted that its superiority is not easy ; that there is genuinely something to overcome. The many negations in this first list, which are increased in the second, have always demanded the attention of the exegete. In the light of these many negations it seems appropriate to regard the whole of this central part of the chapter from the standpoint of a conflict triumphantly waged by the Christian against hostile forces. The words quoted refer first to sinister powers which he encounters in himself—for he is only a man. All his other activities, even though they derive directly from the Holy Spirit, do not exclude the manifestations of these forces in his own thinking and volition. But love does. Even as one who speaks with tongues, or as a prophet, or as a theologian, or as a miracle-worker, or as an ascetic or martyr, he can still " envy," still covet rights and honour and the recognition he deserves and the clear-cut success of his action. But if he loves, there is no place for envy, and in the fact that this is so love conquers. Again, in all these activities he can " vaunt himself," displaying himself and his spirit-wrought accomplishments and achievements (perhaps set off against his weakness and cares and concern for the world) for the admiration of God and the world and himself. But if he loves, there is no place for boasting, and in the fact that this is so love conquers. Again, he can " puff himself up " like a bubble or a balloon. In defiance of the Holy Ghost to whom he owes it all, he can try to make of himself, perhaps as a pneumatic or gnostic (1 Cor. 8¹) or in an unnatural estimation of his particular interests and efforts, his particular " cause," a gigantic figure whose proportions bear no relationship to what he really is and has to offer and represent. If he loves, there is no place for this exaggeration. Again, in an obvious confusion of the freedom he is given with one arbitrarily fixed and extended by himself, he may think that he should ignore and transgress the bounds of what is proper, of decorum, of custom, of *civilitas* (Bengel), making himself of interest to himself and others as a kind of bohemian genius. If he loves, there is certainly no place for this. Love cannot in any way—the final phrase sums up all the rest—seek " her own " ; which means that the man who may love cannot seek " his own." The whole threat to his endowment which would at once poison its exercise at the root, the whole danger of a headlong fall from genuine spirituality into unspirituality, consists in the temptation to use the Holy Ghost for the self-assertion and self-preservation and self-embellishment of the man endowed by Him. If he loves, he gives himself (with the by-product that he is no longer of interest to himself), and thus overcomes this temptation. The fact that he is a man means that at any moment he may seek " his own." But the fact that he loves means that there is no place for the envy and boasting and exaggeration and affectation of genius in which he seeks " his own." For if he loves, then *per definitionem* he cannot seek " his own," himself. Thus far concerning the sinister forces which love has to conquer in the man who loves, and which in virtue of its power it does in fact easily conquer.

VV. 5c–6 : " It is not easily provoked, thinketh no evil, rejoiceth not in iniquity, but rejoiceth in the truth." In this second list we have to do with the sinister forces which the Christian encounters not only in himself but also very definitely in the being and action of his neighbour. It is to be noted that the list is shorter than the previous one, and that at the end there is for the first time a positive definition of love. The neighbour, the fellow-Christian (more perhaps than one's fellow-man generally, in whom much may be overlooked), is also a serious problem to the one who has noted that he is himself the most serious problem of all. It may be gathered from this passage that even those who were spiritually gifted in Corinth did not strike one another at once as pure angels. The neighbour can get dreadfully on my nerves even in the exercise of what he regards as, and what may well be, his particular gifts. And he can then provoke and embitter and in some degree enrage me. Love cannot alter the fact that he gets on my nerves, but as self-giving (and this perhaps with salutary counter-effects on my poor nerves) it can rule out *a limine* my allowing myself to be " provoked " by him, i.e., forced into the position and role of an antagonist. The Christian cannot become an antagonist of his neighbour. Love neither has nor cherishes nor tolerates any " anti "-complexes. This is one of the secrets of its superiority, its victory. But it may find itself even more seriously blocked by the neighbour. The fact cannot be altered that in his person, even if it is that of the most outstanding Christian brother, I will encounter at some point and in some form the " evil " in which he (like myself) unfortunately has a part. Shall I then reckon it to him (λογίζεσθαι) ? Shall I take it down in writing against him ? Shall I always hold it against him ? Shall I nail him to it so that in part at least I always interpret him in the light of it, shaping my attitude accordingly and always regarding him as in some degree a bad man ? I can do this, and there is no little inclination to do so. But love cannot and does not do it, not only because it is self-giving, but because as such it is a reflection of the love of God, which has to do with men who are wholly bad but according to 2 Cor. 5¹⁹ does not impute or reckon their trespasses to them. The man who loves does not compile a dossier about his neighbour. There is, however, a third possibility—the most dreadful of all. This consists in the blatant perversity of actually " rejoicing " that even the most upright of our neighbours continually put themselves in the wrong in relation to us and others, not to speak of God. There is a refined satisfaction which I can procure for myself by making perhaps a show of the deepest sympathy, by actually experiencing it in the guise and feeling of the greatest readiness to forgive, but by seeing that I am set by contrast in a much better light myself, that I am equipped and incited to a much more worthy representation of that which is good, and that I am thus confirmed and strengthened and exalted and assured in my own excellence. Is it not easy to come to the point of waiting expectantly for others continually to do something culpable, to put themselves in the wrong, in order that we may be nourished in this way ? How much of the impulse of private and common Christian action would fail at once if deprived of its basis and nourishment in this " rejoicing ! " But love finds no nourishment here. It does not live by this " rejoicing." How can it be self-giving·if it rejoices because it stands out against the dark background of the wickedness and folly and confusion of others ? It does indeed rejoice, but with a very different joy. And this leads us to the first positive definition—what we are to do in face of the wrong of others. We might have expected to be told that instead of rejoicing in the wrong of others love rejoices in the right that we always find in them as well. But this is not the case. The verse tells us rather (with the same antithesis to ἀδικία as is found in 2 Thess. 2¹⁰, ¹² and Rom. 2⁸) that it rejoices in the truth. It is worth noting perhaps that the verse uses the compound συγχαίρει, thus signifying that love rejoices together or in union with the truth which triumphs objectively over all human wrong. It is certainly a matter of the truth in whose service love itself may stand as an attestation of the divine covenant of grace, and therefore for the Christian of ἀληθεύειν ἐν ἀγάπῃ (Eph. 4¹⁵). As love for the neighbour, love is self-giving to the attestation of the truth that according to 1 Jn. 3²⁰ God is " greater than our heart " ; to the guaranteeing of that which is greater than all the corruption in which we may stand the one to the other. Love rejoices as it participates in this thing which is greater, and in its superiority. In this joy it will certainly not weaken in relation to the wrong of others. It will not call wrong right. For in and with the truth it undoubtedly has to bear witness to supreme right. But it will bear witness to this right with gladness, as the grace which avails for others too, and as the freedom for which they too are ordained. It will thus give them the desire to rejoice in this right as well, and in this rejoicing to recognise their wrong as wrong and cease to do it. This is its superiority in face of sinister forces in the being and action of others. In this superiority it is victorious from the very first in its encounter with them.

V. 7 : " It beareth all things, believeth all things, hopeth all things, endureth all things." On this aspect, too, it acts as love for the neighbour, overcoming the evil which we all meet in others and especially in ourselves. But the terms now used indicate that love for the neighbour, its conflict and conquest, and the most serious problem which the Christian meets in himself, are now seen as taken up into the love of God, and into the defeating of the forces deployed against this love. There are so many things between man and God : the many painful burdens of life which love has to bear ; the distressing invisibility of God in face of which love can only believe ; the darkness of the present world-order within which love can only hope ; the seemingly never-ending and purpose-less trials which love can only outlast and endure (ὑπομένειν). In all these respects we may waver in relation to God, tiring of our love for Him and therefore ceasing to love Him. And in all these respects there may be fellow-men and even Christian brothers in relation to whom we are tempted to this kind of doubt, weariness and suspension. On this wide and complicated front there is no certain victory apart from that to which Paul points—the victory which takes place in and with the fact that love cannot waver, tire or cease in relation either to God or the neighbour, because and as it does as such the only thing that there is left to do in face of all these perplexities, but the thing which certainly does not give way to these perplexities. It bears and believes and hopes and endures. It does do this. And note that in the two central phrases it is the subject of faith and hope : of the faith which according to 1 Jn. 5⁴ is the victory that overcomes the world ; and of the hope which according to Rom. 5⁵ does not make us ashamed. For this reason it is also the subject of a strong and victorious στέγειν and ὑπομένειν. And note especially the fourfold πάντα. At this point we catch an unmistakeable glimpse of the pattern of Christian existence. And this pattern, the royal man Jesus, is not only the pattern but also the living Head of His community and all its members, in whose life and therefore in whose victory they may participate as such, not just passively but actively, as active subjects. When they love, they become and are this. When they love, they withstand the whole world of hostile forces and defeat it. If in all activities wrought by the Spirit Christians are in undecided conflict with this world, when they love this world is already under and behind them. We may recall Rom. 8³⁷ : " In all these things we are more than conquerors." How ? " Through him that loved us." The cry " Jesus is Victor " (J. C. Blumhardt) is more than the applause of spectators. It is the cry of those who are his followers and triumph with Him. The final statement in the series—that love endures (ὑπομένει) all things—forms a transition to the third part of the chapter.

3. 1 Cor. 13⁸⁻¹³. The life-act of the Christian takes part in the strict and proper sense only to the extent that it takes place in the

form of love. It is again only in the form of love that it breaks the dominion of the sinister forces to which the man alienated from God, the neighbour and himself is subject. And we must now continue and conclude by saying that it is only in the form of love that it has an absolutely indestructible content and therefore an absolutely certain continuance ; that it is participation in the eternal life of God. Only as and to the extent that the Christian loves does he find himself already, in the temporal present of his existence, at the goal set for his and all existence and all the history enacted in time, and therefore in their eternal future. To be more precise, it is only as and to the extent that the Christian loves that the eternal future of his own and all existence becomes and is near even though it is distant, present even though it is future, at the heart of the temporal fulfilment of this existence. We have already called love the reflection of the resurrection of Jesus Christ from the dead ; the reflection of the first revelation of the exaltation and enthronement of this one man and therefore of the establishment of the lordship of God over all men and His whole creation. The second and final and universal and direct revelation of the royal dominion of God in Jesus Christ is the eternal future to which the whole world and each individual moves, and in the community each Christian as a witness of that first revelation. All the gifts of the Holy Spirit—deriving from Easter, from that first revelation—are designed to empower the people of God and its members for this movement, this pilgrimage. This is the greatness but also the limit of these gifts. They are exercised in works which have to take place between the times, in this time of the ministry of the community. But when the Resurrected, the living Christ, returns, i.e., when He is finally and universally and directly manifested as the One He is, they will reach their goal which is also their end in their present form, since the ministry of God's pilgrim people will then be completed and cannot continue. There is, however, one continuing form in which this ministry will outlast the present, the time between ; in which it will be rendered even when this goal is reached ; in which it is thus identical already with the eternal ministry of creation in the light of the final and conclusive revelation of the royal dominion of God in Jesus Christ. It is already an eternal ministry, taking place as a prefiguration of the return of Jesus Christ and therefore of the consummation, of redemption, as and to the extent that it is love. It is only in the form of love that the life-act of the Christian has this promise. To be sure, it also has it as faith and hope. But it has it as faith and hope only to the extent that love is the form of the Christian life-act accomplished in faith and hope. In the form of love, however, this act has the promise of a continuity reaching right into the goal and therefore beyond the end of the time between when the present ministry of the community and the gifts necessary for its discharge and the exercise of these gifts will all cease. Love—and all that was love in this exercise, in faith and hope—will never end, not even at this goal. Thus love is the indestructible element in the life-act of the Christian. It is, as we are forced to say, the promise fulfilled already in the present. Love alone abides. Everything else which may and must be done, even by Christians and on the basis of a supreme spiritual endowment, abides only to the extent that it is done in love and is thus itself the act of love.

V. 8a : " Love never faileth." There is a particular emphasis on the " never " (best brought out in German by Luther's rendering : *Die Liebe höret nimmer auf*). Οὐδέποτε πίπτει means that it is the one form of Christian action which does not require and is not subject to transformation or absorption into another, higher and future form, and to this extent to destruction. In virtue of love there is already in the temporal existence of the community and Christians a ὑπομένειν (v. 7) ; a persistence in face of hostile forces. In what follows there is no further reference to threats to Christian existence, but to a relativisation in the light of its glorious future, of the eternal light which is still hidden but will one day shine ; a relativisation to which it is already secretly but genuinely subject. But this relativisation will not overtake love, nor the whole life-act of the Christian to the extent that it is done in love. Love, therefore, is not subject to it. Love is the connecting link between now and then, between here and hereafter. In the famous sentence of Troeltsch, it is " the power of this world which already as such is the power of the world to come."

V. 8b : " But whether there be prophecies, they shall fail ; whether there be tongues, they shall cease ; whether there be knowledge, it shall vanish away." The futures are references to the goal and end of the time of the community. Prophecy, tongues and knowledge will then and there be subject to the relativisation to which they are already subject as determined and seen from this standpoint. Relativisation is the right word to use. To translate καταργηθήσονται by " set aside " (Harbsmeier) or even " destroyed " (Lietzmann) is a mistake. " We shall all be changed " (ἀλλαγησόμεθα, 1 Cor. 15⁵¹ᶠ·)—this and not destruction is what will there and then overtake our existence, even our existence and action as Christians. This is the future which already determines its present. We may begin by quoting a saying of J. C. Blumhardt : " The Saviour is not a destroyer." In the eternal light to which we move prophecy, tongues and knowledge will be taken up into a new and higher form. Their present form will certainly be destroyed. Prophets will have done their work, and those who speak with tongues will no longer need to deliver their ecstatic utterance because the extreme case will once and for all have become normal. And Paul definitely says of knowledge in v. 12 that it will not be set aside or abolished but will take place in a new and more perfect form : ἐπιγνώσομαι. It can certainly be said that it will " vanish away " (καταργηθήσεται), for there will be an end of the *theologia viatorum* as such and of its whole character, and its transformation and assumption wholly and utterly into the *theologia patriae*. Theological research and instruction will then be outmoded. Demythologisation will no longer be required. There will be no further scope for the investigation of a correct hermeneutics and debates concerning Law and Gospel, etc. No more volumes of *Church Dogmatics* will be written. There will be no further need for the *furor theologicus*. Not because all these things are vain and futile, not because they are ashes or wind, but because they will all be genuinely real only in their *telos* and perfection, which includes the fact that their worth and worthlessness will be weighed on the eternal balances, that the wheat will be separated from the chaff, that they will all pass through the refining fire of 1 Cor. 3¹²ᶠ· in which it will be shown whether the building is of gold, silver and precious stones or wood, hay and stubble, and there will be surprises in both respects for all theologians, both small and great, both regular and irregular, both orthodox and heterodox. This wholly salutary relativisation is the πίπτειν to which love is never, never exposed even there and then. And when the Christian loves, he already does something here and now which is not exposed to this relativisation but abides absolutely. Even in the best of cases the same cannot be said of his prophecy, tongues and theology in themselves and as such.

VV. 9–10 : " For we know in part, and prophesy in part. But when that which is perfect is come, then that which is in part shall be done away." The reason for the " ceasing " of v. 8 is not the fact that what Christians now do and should do in the power of the Holy Spirit is only " in part " (so Lietzmann). The reason for it is to be found in the coming of what is perfect, by which the time of the community and all that it contains is bounded. Measured by this great light the little lights by which we now live show themselves to be necessary and useful but in the last resort only a very feeble means of illumination. Their poverty, in which love does not share, is indicated by the ἐκ μέρους. The reference is no longer to tongues but to the endowments and activities which Paul obviously regards as of the first order. Tongues, too, are obviously shown to be impoverished in the light of the coming perfection. But the unmistakeable weakness even of prophecy and knowledge in this light consists in the fact that they are possible only " in part." Is this expression a reminder that the statements and arguments of Christian prophets and theologians are at best only approximations to their theme, or better perhaps the final remnants of its revelation as this has already taken place in the resurrection of Jesus Christ ? Or does it recall the discursive and therefore the disparate character of even their most learned and assured pronouncements ? Does it keep before us the fact that even the greatest prophet or the most cautious and penetrating theologian can speak only in the form of distinct loci, chapters and sections which have always to be completed the one by the other, and can never express the one whole truth as such in a single word or statement ? Are we referred to the distinctions and divisions and contradictions and antitheses which burden even genuinely Christian prophecy and theology because in the succession and conjunction of periods they are represented by so many different witnesses whose theses can never be reduced to a common denominator ? Are we to think of the differentiation of stages on life's way, i.e., of the aspects of the one truth which one and the same prophet or theologian may successively glimpse in the course of a lifetime ? Paul may well have had something of all this in mind. But at all events the partial character of prophecy and knowledge is their poverty. It is the form in which, although they do not become " worthless " (so Lietzmann), they cannot persist or continue when the perfect comes. It is the form in which they have to be taken seriously in gratitude and obedience, but also in their relativity, so that they cannot be confused with the true reality, but are asked only concerning their content as love (vv. 2–3).

V. 11 : " When I was a child, I spake as a child, I understood as a child, I thought as a child : but when I became a man, I put away childish things." This is a first comparison in elucidation of what is said in vv. 8b–10. As the comparison shows, Paul was not thinking of any suppression of the identity of the acting Christian in his transition from now to then, or of any extinction of his present being and activity in favour of the very different being and activity which will be his in the future. Even in the enjoyment and exercise of supreme gifts of the Spirit, the Christian is now a child from whom we can expect and require only childish thoughts and words. The same Christian will then be a man, and as such he will think and speak totaliter aliter. But even in this total transition he will not become another person, nor will he basically think and speak anything different. The statement in v. 11b is made rather too stark with the rendering of τὰ τοῦ νηπίου as " childish things " and of κατήργηκα as

" done away." It is a matter of the thinking and speaking which are appropriate to the child and do not disqualify it as such (i.e., the childlike rather than the childish). And it is a matter of the taking up of these things into a new and higher form rather than their abolition. Is not the child the father to the man ? And does not the child still persist in the man, even though he be seventy or eighty years old ? Man certainly goes through a radical change of form when he becomes an adult. And the same will be true of the prophecy and knowledge now living in the community with the coming of that which is perfect. And the fact that this will be so limits and determines its fulfilment in the present. In this connexion Bengel has made the acute observation that it does not say : *quum abolevi puerilia, factus sum vir*—which would mean that that which is perfect comes in and with the progress and maturity of the Christian and his activity. But as it is not winter that brings spring, but spring that banishes winter, so it is in and with the coming of that which is perfect that there comes about the transformation of the present form of childlike thought and speech, of Christian prophecy and knowledge in their present form, into the new form which awaits them, or rather which already comes to meet Christians, and with which they and their prophecy and knowledge have to let themselves be clothed upon (2 Cor. 5²ᶠ·) ; the form in which they will no longer take place in part, and therefore very differently from the way in which we see them now.

V. 12 : " For now we see through a glass, darkly ; but then face to face : now I know in part ; but then shall I know even as also I am known." A second comparison is offered in elucidation of vv. 8b–10. But first we must note the climax with which we have to do in this third section too. In v. 8 the reference was to prophecy, tongues and knowledge, in vv. 9–10 only to prophecy and knowledge and now in v. 12, corresponding to an obvious concentration of interest in Paul's own thinking, only to sight and knowledge as the presupposition of all that he wished to set against the true, the coming and eternal light as the epitome of " the best gifts " (12³¹). The continuity between now and then is, if possible, even clearer in this case than it was before, for both now and then it is a matter of sight and knowledge. Seeing in a mirror is already seeing, and seeing face to face is still seeing. Knowing in part is already knowing, and knowing " as also I am known " is still knowing. Nor can there be any material break because the present object of seeing and knowing is the same as the future, and the future will be the same as the present : God in His revelation, in His self-presentation ; and in the light of God man, the world, time and what takes place in time. To be sure, the change in the form of the same happening will be most radical between now and then. At the moment we see in a mirror. This has the general meaning that we see in an element and medium foreign to the object itself ; in the form of human perceptions and concepts ; in an earthly history visible in earthly terms ; in a consideration of the external aspect of the works of God, the life of the people Israel and even the life of the man Jesus. It also has the particular meaning that we see in a way which corresponds to the nature of a mirror : the interchanging of right and left ; God in His disclosure in which He conceals Himself and His concealment in which He discloses Himself. Thus even at best our life is an indirect seeing, a seeing *in contrario*, and to this extent an improper seeing. Even at best there is only a seeing ἐν αἰνίγματι ; a seeing which awaits its true fulfilment. Similarly there is only a knowing in part in the manifold sense of the expression already indicated in relation to vv. 9–10. This seeing and knowing is the presupposition of all Christian speech to-day both within the community and through the community to the world. But then there will be a seeing face to face. The revelation of God in Jesus Christ will mean that we " see him as he is " (1 Jn. 3²), directly, unparadoxically and undialectically. Paul was perhaps thinking of what was said of Moses in Num. 12⁸ : " With him will I speak mouth to mouth, even apparently, and not in dark speeches." And then there will be a knowing " as also I am known." As God understands me, I will understand Him, and through Him all things ; the whole context of providence. My present knowing in faith will then be taken out of its isolation and taken up into a knowing in sight (2 Cor. 5⁷). This is the change of form between now and then, and for all its continuity it is the most radical change. But in what does its continuity consist ? What is it that persists, that " abides ? " It is certainly not the present form of Christian activity, even though this derives from the quickening power of the Holy Spirit, and has thus to be rated very highly and is to be gratefully fulfilled with all zeal and fidelity. Its present form perishes in and with the perishing of the form (the σχῆμα) of this world. What does not perish, however, is the true reality in this activity, that which makes it Christian, that which counts in it, that in which it is already a triumphant activity. The true reality of Christian activity participates already in its future form which is still hidden from us but is carried toward it as its new clothing with the coming of that which is perfect.

V. 13 speaks of this true reality of the life-act of the Christian (in full agreement with v. 8a) : " And now abideth faith, hope, love, these three ; but the greatest of these is love." It is to be noted that faith also abides, even though in the coming great change it is taken up into sight. It is to be noted that hope abides, for how can it fail to do so when it is specifically the orientation of the life-act of the Christian on that which is perfect, whose coming will be its fulfilment ? But faith and hope abide only as and because love abides. It is in love that faith and hope are active, and that there takes place that which is specifically Christian in the life-act of the Christian. Thus love is the " greatest of these." It is the future eternal light shining in the present. It therefore needs no change of form. It is that which continues. For whatever else may be revealed in and with the coming of that which is perfect, in whatever new form Christian activity and the life of the community may attain its goal with everything that now is and happens, one thing is certain and that is that love will never cease, that even then the love which is self-giving to God and the brother, the same love for which the Christian is free already, will be the source of the future eternal life, its form unaltered. Already, then, love is the eternal activity of the Christian. This is the reason why love abides. This is the reason why to say this is to say the final and supreme thing about it. This is the reason why we had to say previously that it is love alone that counts and love alone that conquers. This is the reason why it is *the* way (12³¹).

INDEXES

I. SCRIPTURE REFERENCES

GENESIS

CHAP.					PAGE
$1-2$	.	.	.	.	588, 776
1^1	.	.	.	.	58
1^{27}	.	.	.	.	58
1^{28}	.	.	.	.	646
1^{31}	.	.	.	.	587
2^7	.	.	.	.	776
$2^{18f.}$	.	.	.	.	432
2^{24}	.	.	.	.	53
4^9	.	.	.	.	445
12 f.	.	.	.	.	768
12^1	.	.	.	.	578
$14^{18f.}$	.	.	.	.	808
17^3	.	.	.	.	429
24^{31}	.	.	.	.	301
46^{30}	.	.	.	.	160

EXODUS

1^7	.	.	.	.	646
3 f.	.	.	.	.	768
3^{14}	.	.	.	.	770
19^6	.	.	.	.	512
20^6	.	.	.	.	799
$20^{13f.}$	.	.	.	.	466
20^{17}	.	.	.	.	466
22^{31}	.	.	.	.	512
$23^{4f.}$	.	.	.	.	804
29^{43}	.	.	.	.	501
3^2	.	.	.	.	774
32 f.	.	.	.	.	768
33^{19}	.	.	.	.	770

LEVITICUS

10^3	.	.	.	.	501
11^{44}	.	.	.	.	501
19^2	.	.	.	.	501
19^{13-18}	.	.	.	.	804
19^{18}	.	.	.	804, 810, 823
19^{34}	.	.	.	.	804
$20^{7f.}$	.	.	.	.	501
$25^{8f.}$	.	.	.	.	205, 501

NUMBERS

CHAP.					PAGE
12^8	.	.	.	.	839
$13-14$	.	.	.	.	478 ff.

DEUTERONOMY

4^{37}	.	.	.	.	762
5^{10}	.	.	.	.	799
$6^{4f.}$	.	.	.	.	810, 823
6^5	.	.	.	.	780 ff.
7^6	.	.	.	.	512
$7^{6f.}$	.	.	.	.	768
7^8	.	.	.	.	762
7^9	.	.	.	.	799
$10^{12f.}$	.	.	.	.	799
$10^{14f.}$	.	.	.	.	768
10^{15}	.	.	.	.	762
11^1	.	.	.	.	799
11^{22}	.	.	.	.	799
14^2	.	.	.	.	768
18^{18}	.	.	.	.	160
19^9	.	.	.	.	799
$22^{1f.}$	.	.	.	.	804
23^3	.	.	.	.	804
23^5	.	.	.	.	762
23^7	.	.	.	.	804
28^9	.	.	.	.	512
$30^{1f.}$	.	.	.	.	781
30^6	.	.	.	.	780
$30^{11f.}$	.	.	.	.	780
30^{16}	.	.	.	.	799
$30^{19f.}$	.	.	.	.	781
33^3	.	.	.	.	512

JOSHUA

5^{14}	.	.	.	.	429
7^6	.	.	.	.	429
22^5	.	.	.	.	799
24^{15}	.	.	.	.	781

JUDGES

5^{31}	.	.	.	.	791 f.

II. NAMES

859

III. SUBJECTS